Voice of a City

The Edmonton Journal's First Century
1903 to 2003

EDMONTON JOURNAL.
3132

Edmonton Journal Group Inc.

Writers
Marc Horton
Bill Sass

Editor
Peter Collum

Designer
Rick Pape

Researcher
Patricia Beuerlein

Published by
Edmonton Journal Group Inc.
10006 - 101 Street
Edmonton, Alberta, Canada T5J 0S1

National Library of Canada Cataloguing in Publication

Horton, Marc, 1948-
Voice of a City: The Edmonton Journal's First Century 1903 to 2003 / writers, Marc Horton, Bill Sass; editor, Peter Collum; designer, Rick Pape; researcher, Patricia Beuerlein.

ISBN 0-9690184-3-6

1. Edmonton Journal. 2. Edmonton (Alta.)--History. I. Sass, Bill, 1947- II. Collum, Peter, 1947- III. Title. IV. Title: Edmonton Journal.

FC3696.4.H67 2003 971.23'34 C2003-905451-9

Printed and bound in Canada by Friesens Corporation
First edition, first printing, 2003
Second edition, first printing, 2003

Contents

v / *Introduction*

vii / *Acknowledgments*

O N E
1 / Mud, Manure & Ink — 1903 to 1910

T W O
45 / Boom, Bust & War — 1911 to 1919

T H R E E
87 / "Hullo, hullo, hullo!" — 1920 to 1929

F O U R
127 / Scrip, Sex & Scandal — 1930 to 1939

F I V E
167 / Guns & Gushers — 1940 to 1949

S I X
203 / Coming of Age — 1950 to 1959

S E V E N
241 / Prosperity & Change — 1960 to 1969

E I G H T
279 / Boundless Energy — 1970 to 1979

N I N E
319 / Rise, Fall & Recovery — 1980 to 1989

T E N
357 / Gloom & Boom — 1990 to 1999

E L E V E N
395 / Millennium Madness — 2000 to 2003

407 / *Epilogue*

409 / *Index*

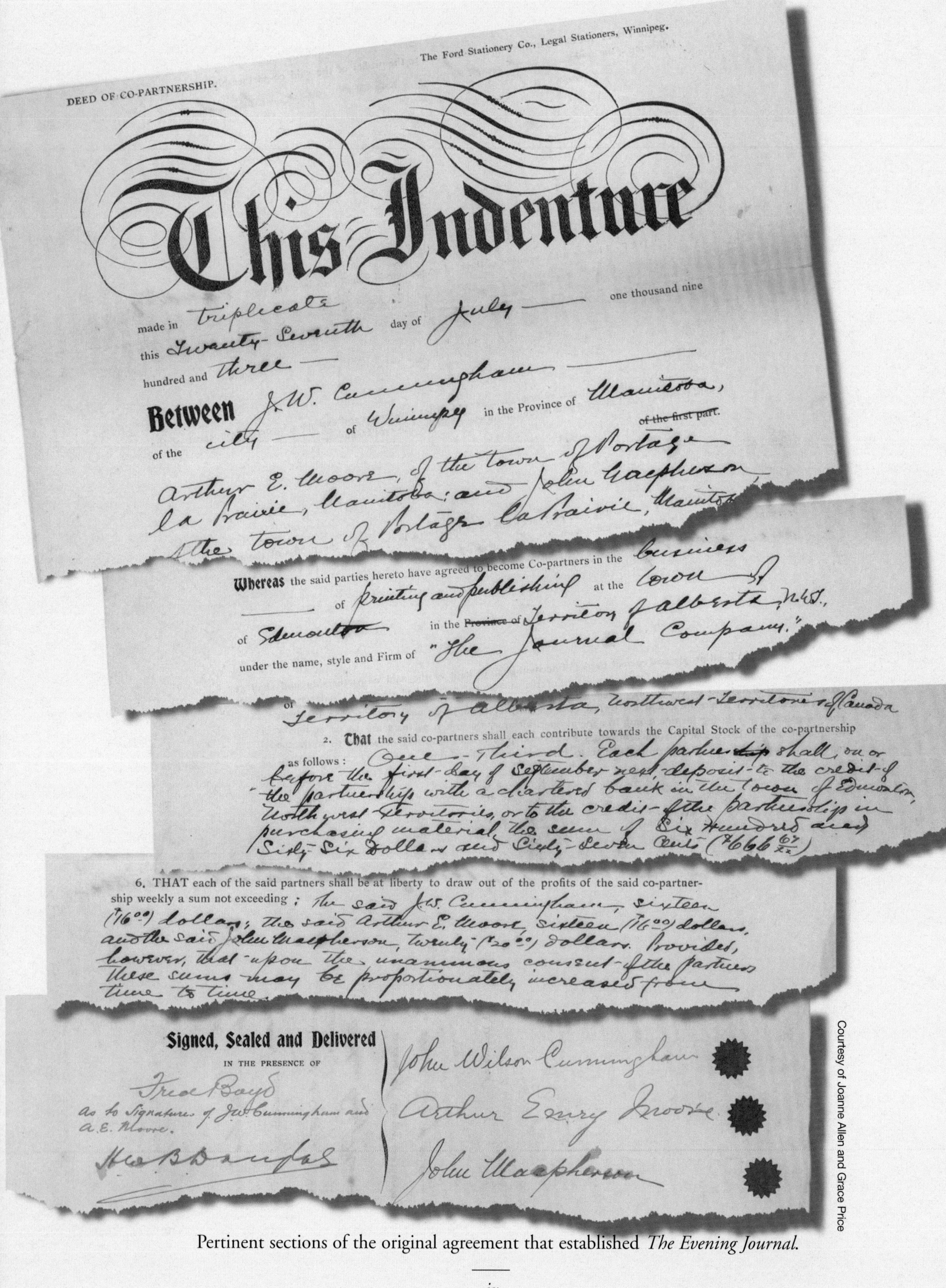

DEED OF CO-PARTNERSHIP.

The Ford Stationery Co., Legal Stationers, Winnipeg.

This Indenture

made in triplicate one thousand nine
this Twenty-Seventh day of July —
hundred and three —

Between J. W. Cunningham —
of the city — of Winnipeg in the Province of Manitoba, ~~of the first part.~~
Arthur E. Moore, of the town of Portage la Prairie, Manitoba; and John Macpherson, of the town of Portage La Prairie, Manitoba

Whereas the said parties hereto have agreed to become Co-partners in the business
— of printing and publishing at the town of
of Edmonton in the ~~Province of~~ Territory of Alberta, N.W.T.
under the name, style and Firm of "The Journal Company."

of Territory of Alberta, Northwest-Territories of Canada

2. That the said co-partners shall each contribute towards the Capital Stock of the co-partnership as follows: One-Third. Each partner shall, on or before the first day of September next, deposit to the credit of the partnership with a chartered bank in the town of Edmonton, North-west Territories, or to the credit of the partnership in purchasing material, the sum of Six Hundred and Sixty-Six Dollars and Sixty-Seven Cents ($666 67/xx)

6. THAT each of the said partners shall be at liberty to draw out of the profits of the said co-partnership weekly a sum not exceeding; the said J. W. Cunningham, sixteen ($16.00) dollars; the said Arthur E. Moore, sixteen ($16.00) dollars, and the said John Macpherson, twenty ($20.00) dollars. Provided, however, that upon the unanimous consent of the partners these sums may be proportionately increased from time to time.

Signed, Sealed and Delivered
IN THE PRESENCE OF
Fred Boyd
as to Signatures of J. W. Cunningham and A. E. Moore.
H. B. Douglas

John Wilson Cunningham
Arthur Emery Moore
John Macpherson

Courtesy of Joanne Allen and Grace Price

Pertinent sections of the original agreement that established *The Evening Journal.*

Introduction

Although there is a great deal of history in this book, it is not a history book in the traditional sense. It is neither a definitive account of the corporate history of the *Edmonton Journal* nor an exhaustive study of Edmonton's past. The latter is best left to trained historians and the former would interest only a small group of newspaper insiders.

Instead, this book is a celebration of 100 years in the life of Edmonton's oldest and largest newspaper and the building of the spirited city it serves.

If journalism is the first draft of history, this book is a re-reading of that first draft, with no attempt to rewrite or re-edit. We've pulled from our pages a scrapbook of memories from a century that saw more change than any other in human history.

Just as *The Journal* today bears little resemblance to the four-page broadsheet that heralded our birth in 1903, the same can be said for Greater Edmonton in 2003.

Now an important Canadian economic and cultural centre, with nearly one million residents and enviable prosperity, Alberta's capital is unrecognizable from the cluster of muddy streets and wooden buildings that constituted the hardscrabble frontier city a century earlier.

The story of the newspaper's growth and development runs parallel with the story of Edmonton. We began publishing just a year before Edmonton officially became a city and two years before Alberta was declared a province. And so, on a million or more published pages, we've had the privilege of reporting every day of the first century of Alberta's capital.

The way we recorded that history has changed dramatically through the years.

With each decade the writing became clearer, the reporting more rigorous and the design more accessible. There were few bylines in the early decades, despite a tendency to infuse opinion and hearsay into news coverage. It wasn't until the 1960s that reporters' names began to appear regularly on news stories and more emphasis was placed on writing technique and storytelling. At the same time, there developed a greater commitment to objectivity and balance in reporting.

In the past, newspapers had always been openly partisan and *The Journal* was no different, declaring itself a Conservative paper within the first few days of publication.

But even in those early days, the newspaper was never a mouthpiece for government, and through most of its history considered itself an independent voice, committed to keeping opinion out of its news coverage and providing a staunchly Western Canadian outlook on its editorial pages.

Looking back on more than 30,000 editions of *The Journal*, there are certainly headlines and commentary that make us cringe today, reflecting as they do the ignorance and prejudices of the times. Sometimes we were narrow-minded and many times we were simply wrong.

But there is much that makes us proud. More often than not, the paper was a progressive – if sometimes unpopular – voice fighting on the side of democracy, free speech and human rights. When powerful business interests attempted to ban black immigration into the province in the early part of the century, *The Journal* argued that all immigrants should be welcome, regardless of colour.

The paper stood up against the inroads of the Ku Klux Klan in the 1920s, was fearless in its defence of freedom of the press against the Social Credit government in the 1930s, recorded the evil in the rise of Nazism, warned against the tide of McCarthyism in the 1950s and demanded justice for First Nations peoples.

From the beginning we determined to be a voice for Western Canadians, but we were always, first and foremost, Edmonton's newspaper.

And this book is very much the remarkable story of Edmonton's growing up and coming of age, as told on our pages.

We were tempted to write more fully about the newspaper itself, particularly about the colourful characters, the talented and the not-so-talented journalists, the business leaders, the craftspeople and carriers. But we know very little about the early characters who populated the paper and we know perhaps a little too much about our more recent ones. More important, trite as it may sound, a newspaper is much more than the sum of its parts.

Thousands of people have worked at the paper over the years, hundreds of people put it together every night and every edition is the result of dozens of decisions made by many different people.

To focus on individuals would distract from the main story.

It's difficult to do justice to a century of history in one volume, and many important stories received only the briefest of mentions or were lost entirely in the editing process. The closer we came to the present day, the more difficult it became as we had more material to choose from, therefore making it harder to bring perspective to events and judge their historical significance.

In the end, like the daily newspaper, the book is best described as history on the run.

We dedicate this book to the people of Edmonton, with particular thanks to the many thousands who worked at *The Journal* — the writers, editors and photographers, the advertising sales people, the old linotype operators and compositors, the pressmen, the technicians, the marketers, the reader sales staff, the human resource and business office staff, the clerks and support staff, the truck drivers and the many thousands of carriers who have delivered the paper to city doorsteps for a century.

Their dedication and hardwork have allowed *The Journal* the privilege of being the "voice" of Edmonton.

Linda Hughes
Publisher, The *Edmonton Journal*

Acknowledgments

Because it is what we do for a living, publishing *The Journal* seems easy compared to producing a book, so first and foremost we must thank Linda Cameron and her University of Alberta Press staff members Alan Brownoff, Cathie Crooks and Mary Mahoney-Robson for the advice, encouragement and support they provided as we wended our way to completion of *Voice of a City.*

And although the vast majority of this book comes from the files of the *Edmonton Journal,* other sources were consulted as well.

Included among those are *Edmonton Stories, More Edmonton Stories* and *Edmonton: Stories from the River City,* all by Tony Cashman. All are written in Cashman's popular and chatty style and all celebrate the characters and their eccentricities that helped make Edmonton the city that it is.

Also useful was Cashman's *Gateway to the North,* an invaluable resource when it comes to the city's love affair with airplanes.

We are also grateful to Cashman for taking the time to read this book in manuscript form. His keen eye and profound understanding of Edmonton's past proved invaluable.

Another important look into the history of the city can be found in the pages of J.G. MacGregor's *Edmonton: A History,* a work that is crowded with the kind of detail that is often missing from the archives of a daily.

Both MacGregor's book and the series *Alberta in the 20th Century,* founded by Ted Byfield and edited by Paul Bunner, were useful in providing a roadmap, particularly when it came to the early years of the city and the province.

Much of the city's sports story is in the files of *The Journal,* but Brant Ducey's *The Rajah of Renfrew,* his loving biography of his father, John Ducey, also offered useful insights into an era of Edmonton's rich history of winners and losers.

For a unique political history of the province, Aritha van Herk's *Mavericks: An Incorrigible History of Alberta* offered not only an unconventional view of the men and women in the province's past, but was a delightful book to read as well.

For the war years, we also consulted *A City Goes to War* by G.R. Stevens, which offered a perspective of Edmonton's contribution to the defeat of Germany in the Second World War.

While Patricia Beuerlein was a tireless researcher and often worked long into the night poring over microfilm, *The Journal's* daytime librarians, Deb Dittrick and Caron Court, often stopped what they were doing to track down a stray fact or come up with a perfect quote. Research assistant Bev Boersma was also a volunteer whose contribution was willingly offered and gratefully accepted.

The assistance we received from Jennifer Parker, who worked at digging out many of the photographs and illustrations you see on these pages, cannot be overstated. Also not to be overlooked were the contributions of design desk stalwarts Calvin Caldwell, Jaime Cifuentes, Gail Echlin and Cecil Nickerson. Thanks also to Robert Flasha and Terry Elniski in image supply for their efforts.

And to eagle-eyed colleague Doug Swanson, copy editor Eva Radford and index ace Judy Dunlop, thanks for your patience.

Thanks also to Joanne Allen and Grace Price of Red Deer, respectively the granddaughter and daughter of Arthur Emery Moore, one of *The Journal's* three founders. Their family history gave insight into the first days of the paper.

In the end, this book was a team effort. Publisher Linda Hughes and editor-in-chief Giles Gherson offered guidance and advice throughout the project while other staff members were generous with their suggestions and contributions to the story of *The Journal* and its place in the history of the city and the province.

THE EVENING JOURNAL.

VOL. 1. NO. 1. EDMONTON, ALBERTA, WEDNESDAY, NOVEMBER 11, 1903. PRICE, FIVE CENTS

DECISION WAS FAIR

Premier Balfour Commends the Position Takey by Alverstone.

Canada got all was due Her in the Alaska Boundary Award

London, Nov. 10—Premier Balfour speaking at the Lord Mayor's luncheon said ample justice had been given Canada in the Alaska decision and he paid a tribute to Alverson for his course in the matter.

Portage Child took Poison.

Portage la Prairie, Man, Nov. 10—The three year old son of F. Thompson drank a bottle of eucaliptus oil. Prompt medical assistance saved the child's life.

Confessed the Murder.

Winnipeg, Nov. 10—At the assizes yesterday Lucas Kyrk was placed on trial for murdering a fellow-Galician at Brokenhead on July 5th last. Detective Seele read a confession of the crime signed by Kirk.

Winnipeggers Out of Work.

Montreal, Nov. 10—The Mechanical General Manager of the C.P.R., explaining the laying off of 200 men at Winnipeg by the Company, said it was due to the fact that crops did not come up to the company's expectations.

How to Spend a Million.

Winnipeg, Nov. 10—The City Council has decided to submit to rate payers at the municipal elections a bylaw totalling a million dollars to fund construction of a gas plant and Assinaboine water power plant.

Dog Patch's New Record.

Birmingham, Ala. Nov. 11—Dan Patch yesterday lowered the world mile pacing record to 2.03¼

A Husband's Conspiracy.

New York, Nov. 11—Mrs Roe Brand, formerly Miss Rosenblatt, of Winnipeg was acquitted yesterday on a charge of hiring thugs to maim or if possible kill her husband. The Judge says the charge was a conspiracy on the husband's part.

Not Afraid of the Americans.

London Nov. 11—Sir Gilbert Parker speaking at Gravesend combated Lord Roseberry's statement that the influx of American settlers would impair Canadian loyalty.
WW

Territorial Judge Retired.

Ottawa, Nov. 11—Judge Richardson, of the Supreme Court of the Territories, is superannuated, also Judge Caron of Quebec and Walkem of B.C.

A Regina Forgery.

Regina Nov. 11—John E. Foster, C.P.R. wiper, has been committed for trial for the forgery of 2 cheques The forgery was clumsily done and the banks refused to honor the cheques.

BRITISH OPINION CANADIAN DRESS

London Paper Says the Canadian Women Don't Dress Well.

London, Nov. 11—The Morning Leader discussing Canadian women says they are plain, hard featured and don't know how to dress.

Douks in Durance Vile.

Winnipeg, Nov. 11—Five fanatical Dukhobors passed through the city yesterday in charge of Mounted Police to serve a two years sentence in Stoney Mountain Penitentiary for burning a threshing machine belonging to the Doukhobor community at Swan River.
TT

GALWAY WILL BE THE FIRST PORT OF CALL.

The Fast Atlantic Line will Head Straight for the Irish Coast.

London, Nov. 10—The Canadian authorities have selected Galway as the first port of call for the fast Atlantic service.

WILL BUY THE OATS

An Opportunity for the Edmonton Farmers to market of Their Grain.

British Government Asking for Tenders for Supplies for Africa

Ottawa, Nov. 10—The Agricultural Department has received from the War Office a form of tender for supplies for troops in South Africa, including flours, oats and meats. Tenders must reach Pretoria by Jan. 11th.

About The Canadian Northern.

Winnipeg, Nov. 10—Dan Mann, vice-president of the C.N.R., said that they could not extend in the immediate future as the line was not yet a necessity.

THEY ARE COMING WEST

The new Opposition to the Bell Telephone is Becoming Active

Ottawa, Nov. 10—The Canadian Telephone and Telegraph Co., chartered at the recent session of Parliament, has completed organization. The company will compete with the Bell Co. and intends to go through to the Pacific coast.
S

RAT PORTAGE DOCTOR CHARGED WITH NEGLECT.

True Bill is Found in the Rat Portage Criminal Practice Case.

Rat Portage Nov. 11—The Grand Jury found a True Bill against Dr Sanson, on a charge of neglect, in connection with the death of Annie Johnson, the Winnipeg girl who died under sad circumstances at Rat Portage.

No Cattle to Export.

So much discussion is going on at the present time as to the low prices of western cattle, that a Free Press representative called on Mr. J. T. Gordon, M.P.P., of Gordon Ironside & Fares, and asked for information from him as one of the chief exporters, as to the present condition of western cattle trade.

In reply to the query, "How are shipments compared with last year?" Mr. Gordon said: "Up to the present time, including our own cattle, we have shipped just about one-third of the cattle that we had shipped at this date last year."

"How do you account for that?"

"Well, in the first place the cattle are not nearly so good as they were this time last year, and, indeed, in many previous years, owing in a measure to the big spring storm and also to the softness of the grass, due to unusually wet weather. Then there are a very large number of cattle on the ranges that have been shipped in from outside; and imported stockers usually require a year more to mature than cattle bred on the ranges; that is, a range bred steer is ready to go out at three years old, but an imported stocker is usually four and sometimes five years of age before being ready to ship; and the final reason is that we cannot buy cattle at their value. It is the first time, in the ten years we have been in the exporting business, that this has occurred. Commission men in Montreal have been sending out circulars to the ranchers advising them that Canadian cattle are worth 12c. in the British market. I saw one of these circulars this morning, quoting 12c. for Canadian cattle, when at the date of the circular, western range cattle were selling at 10c. The cattle that sell at 12c. are the Ontario domestic fed cattle. Ranchers naturally take the prices quoted them as applying to range cattle and are not willing to sell to us at 3½ lb., which is really the value of the animals at the present market prices. I fear that when the ranchers get the returns from the few thousand cattle that have been shipped through commission houses they will be both disappointed and dissatisfied. I venture to say that of the few thousands of these cattle that have gone through the yards here very few will net their owners more than they actually paid for them two years ago, say $31 to $32. We are in a position now to handle ten times the cattle we are shipping, but because we cannot buy them at their value is why we have shipped so few this season.

"A very good number of cattle offered this season are not even good butchers, let alone fit for export; and I fear the ranchers will more than realize this when they get their returns from their commission shipments."

"How about space?"

"Ranchers are paying far too high a price for space, for cattle selling at 9½c. per lb. Many of the ranchers, through the commission houses, have contracted for space at 50, 52 and even 55 shillings per animal, and, of course, every inch of this space must be filled at the price contracted for, no matter what the slump in the market. Let me give you an illustration. The average steer this year is running about 1,200 lbs.: such a steer would dress 60 lbs. to the cwt. here and 55 lbs. to the cwt. in the old country; that would 660 lbs. of beef, which at 9½ the present price of range steers, would be $62.70. Allowing 52 shillings for space, the carrying and other charges incident to selling that animal on the English market would be $32, which would leave $30.70 for the steer at the range, after two years keep. You can figure the profit on that deal for yourself."

"What are the prospects for the future?"

"We do not look for any improvement in the prices for two or three years, as the supply is evidently much greater than the demand, and as the laboring and trading classes are not doing so well in the old country as they have been doing for the past few years. Without a better demand we cannot hope for better prices."

"What do you think will be the outcome of the ranchers shipping on their own account?"

"Well, personally, I think when they get their returns, they will be willing to sell their later cattle for their value on the ranges, but you can never tell. If they are not, why we will not ship them, that is all."

The French and Old France.

Mr. Willard, the Canadian commissioner of immigration in France, who has lately been appointed to that position, is now in the west studying conditions of this country with a view to being able to describe methods of farming and give a correct outline of the life of new settlers here when he takes over his duties in the gay republic.

A reporter of the Free Press met Mr. Willard after his return from a visit to the French colony at Lourds about ten miles from Rathwell in southern Manitoba.

"I have often heard it said," Mr. Willard remarked, "that the French people do not know how to colonize, that while they love travelling here and there exploring, and looking for new fields they cannot resist the temptation, when the opportunity affords itself of returning to the fatherland. I had heard this so often that I had almost got to believe that to induce a Frenchman to migrate and live away from France for all time was impossible I knew, of course, that French peple can be found all over the world.but it was said that in these cases he people have not prospered well, and had not the means to return, but had still the inclination.

BETTER OFF HERE.

"Now take this colony at Lourds. I don't believe that large colonies here are good, but I must say that at Lourds there s an exception to the rule. There are eight hundred people living there, and on Sunday I stayed with them and attempted to get a truthful idea of what their feelings were regarding a return to France, I could not find one that wanted to go back. Why? Simply for the reason that they are ten times better off here than they were at home. Have you seen them—the French farmers, the poor, small farmer that cannot buy his land that he lives on—a miserable quarter or half an acre—if he wanted to? No. Then you can't understand the happiness that this class must feel here when they are owners of their own farms, and large farms, have good homes—homes, mind you, not mere huts that are more fit for animals. They had no complaint and I, who have seen such people smiling and bearing all kinds of poverty as their common lot in France, could not wonder they were well satisfied."

WILLARD AND HIS METHODS.

Mr. Willard is a man who has given French immigration to Canada careful study. He is a Frenchman himself and understands their feelings. A Frenchman who is once led to think that all in a new country is roses, and finds a few thistles among them, believes he has been thoroughly fooled and gets disgusted. The policy that Mr. Willard means to pursue is to let them know not only the rosy side, but also, if such there be, the darker side of life in this country. Then he means to induce them to find employment among those who know the country, live with them for a year till they have become thoroughly familiar with the methods of farming here, and then strike out for themselves. He firmly believes there will be an immense movement from France to Canada.

Wife—I dreamed last night that I was in a store that was filled with the loveliest bonnets, and—

Husband (hastily)—But that was only a dream, my dear.

Wife—I knew that before I woke up, because you bought me one.—Philadelphia Press.

"Mary, dear," said the newly married young man to his wife. "You can't bake bread like your mother does."

"No John," replied the newly married Mary, "and you don't raise 'dough' as father does."

HERE IS AN OPTIMIST

Tells What He Thinks of the Future Awaiting All Good Canucks.

They Will Be Healthy, and Wealthy and Perhaps be Wise.

Mr. Byron E. Walker, general manager of the Canadian Bank of Commerce speaks optimiscally of the future of Canada. He declares that this country will see the day when it will figure with any other manufacturing country in the world for the trade of either the British empire or Europe. Year after year it will see a greater output, greater skill, greater ability to obtain the raw material cheaply, until it reaches a point where it will be respected by every manufacturing country in the world.

Regarding agriculture, he considers that the development of the west has been retarded because Canadians cannot be induced to believe what a great country they have there. India and Australia seem to be out of the race as wheat-growing countries and Canada is coming nearer to the time when she will be able to take care of the empire in the matter of a food supply.

The tendancy of American firms to establish themselves in Canada he regards as an indication of the industrial development and commercial prosperity of this country. This is the one part of the Empire that is becoming a manufacturing country, and the large manufacturers in the United States appear to be recognizing this fact. They are establishing branches in Canada which turn out three or four times as much as the country can consume and are building up businesses here that will not only supply Canada, but will look after their foreign trade. They may, Mr. Walker says, be doing this because Canada has the raw material, possibly cheaper labor, and freedom from labor troubles, although it is a question whether this latter advantage will last long.

Cold Day for Georgia.

"Gentlemen," said the Georgia colonel, who was entertaining a group of amused listeners at one of the hotels in this city, the other night, "I suppose you have all heard what the Governor of North Carolina said to the Governor of South Carolina. Have you ever heard what the Governor of Georgia said to the Governor of Virginia? No? Well, the only difference in the two stories is that the Governor of Georgia was a blue nose temperance man.

"You remember what a blizzard Washington had the second time Cleveland was inaugurated? Well, the the wind blew sixty miles an hour. The snow cut the faces like a knife, and froze to the mustache of the soldiers as they waited in line in front of the capitol. The barrooms all along the line made big fortunes that day, and the doctors had their turn at the lucky wheel the next day with pneumonia cases.

"The governors of the different States were at the head of their troops with their staffs just behind them, on Capitol Hill, during the inauguration ceremonies. The Governor of Georgia had brought, even for the South, an unusually large staff with him to the inauguration. I was on his staff at the time, but as there were only about forty other Georgia colonels there I don't suppose you remember seeing me. Washington had never before had the honor of seeing so many Georgia colonels. There were so many of us that even with horses touching, as we marched abreast up Pennsylvania avenue, we stretched from curb to curb accross the widest avenue of the country. At times, however, there was barely a corporal's guard around the Governor of Georgia. Many and varied were our excuses for a few minutes' absence from our posts on the bleak and bitter hillside. None of us dared to tell our Governor openly what were our real reasons for our somewhat frequent absences, for the Governor of Georgia was a famous temperance man. He had never been known to take intoxicants in any form, and on all occasions had publicly advocated the temperance cause.

"He sat straight and stiff upon his horse in front of his troops, a dignified and silent figure, apparently completely unaware of the piercing icy blasts that swept over Capitol Hill. We began to think him more than mortal, for we felt as if we were rapidly freezing to death.

"Suddenly an aide from the staff of the Governor of Virginia dashed up to the Governor af Georgia and said with a salute-

"Governor, I am going to get something hot and strong for our Governor, and can I get some of it for you too?"

"The Georgia colonels were astounded by such rash ignorance, and we all settled down in our seats prepared to hear a temperance lecture from our Governor as a rebuke for such audacity. Imagine our surprise when our Governor thanked the Virginian colonel for his kind offer, and said he would be glad to take whatever he could get to drink.

"The Virginian aide dashed off on his quest, but a Georgia aide, not to be so out done, dashed off, too. In a very few minutes back came the Virginian colonel bearing a huge cup of hot punch. At the same time from another direction the Georgia colonel rode up with even a bigger cup of steaming liquor.

"The Governor of Virginia, who had also ridden up, intending to offer a toast to the new president, called to the Governor of Georgia'

" 'Now Governor, what drink you going to take?-

"The temperanre Governor of Georgia dropped the reins, held out his half frozen hands and said:

" 'Governor I shall drink both.

"And he did drain the cups, too while we all nearly fell off our seats in astonishment. The local instinct had triumphed over principle

HARDY ANNUAL STORY.

One of Depew's Good Anecdotes Riviled to a Botanicaly Repartee.

At a dinner given to a crowd of railroad men, Senator Chausey of Depew was the star speaker. In the course of his remarks, says the New York Times, he told wherein a certain manufacturer left practically all alone in his factory, through a lockout, was represented as pointing to the office clock over his desk and saying to his fiend

"There are only two hands in my office that never strike"

"Whereupon said the Senator said "the clock struck two."

After dinner one of Senator Depew's friends came up and congratulated him:

"Your speech was great," he said "That story about the clock is a daisy."

The Senator beamed. "I think it is pretty good," he said modestly

About five minutes later another friend came up who was not so eulogistic.

"Chauncy," he said, "I think that story about the clock better every time I hear it. I think to-night was the fiftieth time."

"Why, President Newell says that story is a daisy," epostulated Mr. Depew.

The other laughed. "You ought to study botany, Chauncy, and you will learn that the daisy is a hardy annual."

And thereupon the Senator subsided.

Don't forget to keep an eye on the man who flatters you.

Don't forget the fact that an honest man never has to proclaim the fact.

ONE

NA-1838-2 Glenbow Archives

A look east down Jasper Avenue in 1903. The three-storey McDougall and Secord store, left, was on the northwest corner of 101st Street.

Mud, Manure & Ink

1903 to 1910

Murder, Most Foul / 25

Hangman's Bluff / 29

The Little Tigers / 31

A Bold Undertaking / 35

Second-class Citizens / 37

Rutherford's Folly / 39

"There could be nowhere a more hopeful or buoyant people than the Edmontonese. They look upon themselves as being the makers of a city that will surpass Winnipeg in time."
— Edmonton became a city, Nov. 7, 1904

The Evening Journal was born on an old, hand-fed press in a makeshift office at the back of the Shamrock Fruit Store on Wednesday, Nov. 11, 1903. It was a modest beginning for the four-page broadsheet that sold for five cents and would evolve into the *Edmonton Journal*, one of the nation's most highly regarded papers.

Publisher John Macpherson's first editorial, simply headlined "Foreword," quietly stated the infant paper's goal.

"We're here to make a living."

His fellow citizens – the 4,000 merchants, farmers, trappers and their families – shared that plain spoken, simple sentiment. "The larger interests of Canada and the West will receive attention from time to time and the still wider movement of the world at large will not pass unnoticed," Macpherson promised, "but our efforts will be very largely restricted to the upbuilding of Edmonton and northern Alberta."

Truth be told, Macpherson's restrained editorial on page 2 was the most eloquent piece of prose in the inaugural edition. The rest of the paper was,

NA-477-1 Glenbow Archives

Settlers on Jasper Avenue in an ox cart, 1905.

NA-2544-3 Glenbow Archives

Hauling hay up McDougall Hill in 1904.

WE STAND CORRECTED

"It is regrettable in revision that a local calling attention to the advertisement of an Irish national concert to be held on St. Patrick's day should have been permitted to read for the benefit of the public hospital, when it should have read for the benefit of the public and the general hospital. The advertisement, however, states that the proceeds will be donated to the Edmonton hospitals. The friends of both of these deserving public institutions will kindly note the laudable object for which the Irish concert will be held."

— March 11, 1904,
An early correction

THE AUTOMOBILE

"J.H. Morris, accompanied by Mrs. Morris, yesterday traveled to Fort Saskatchewan and back in his automobile. The trip was made in record time. Mr. Morris left the city at 2:30 p.m. and was back at 5 p.m., nearly 40 miles in 2 1/2 hours."

— Nov. 9, 1905

LOVE AND MARRIAGE

"Mr. And Mrs. J.H. Picard returned from their bridal trip last night."

— Dec. 9, 1903

TARTE AND TURCET

"Hon. J. Israel Tarte surprised his friends when he announced Monday that he had been quietly married on Thursday to an employee of the Public Works department, Miss Emma Turcet, a popular French Canadian."

— March 2, 1905

EVEN THE LOWLY

"Edmonton paid a well deserved tribute to Madame Albani, one of the great singers of the world, an artist who has, by her wonderful art, won the hearts of the great and the lowly in many lands.

"Not less was the great audience that gathered in the immense Thistle Theatre a tribute to the intelligence and culture of our people."

— May 10, 1906

to today's eye, a typographical disaster as vertical cliffs of grey type tumbled into each other, making it a challenge to tell where one story began and another ended. It was also very difficult to read, with a typeface so small that most buyers probably had to squint, and the headlines were often longer than the stories. And many of those stories were rather random and not exactly hard news.

The Journal's first line, or main story, bore the following pithy headline: "Here Is an Optimist." It quoted Byron E. Walker of the Canadian Bank of Commerce predicting that Canada would become the industrial hub of the British Empire.

Many of the other stories were less than complete.

A strange one-line story from London read, "The Morning Leader, discussing Canadian women, was they are plain, hard figured and don't know how to dress." As grammatically awkward as that story might be, the headline "British Opinion Canadian Dress" was disastrous.

The front page also offered readers a rambling, unfocused tale about "the Georgia colonel who was entertaining a group of amused listeners at one of the hotels in the city the other night." The colonel wasn't identified and neither was the hotel nor the city where he kept listeners enthralled. Only one thing is certain: the city wasn't Edmonton and the listeners weren't Edmontonians.

Inside, an opinion piece from *Collier's Weekly* contended that the Golden Rule didn't work in politics. Another story revealed that some farmers had discovered that too much noise lowered milk production. And a fashion article suggested that certain dress colours could bring about mood changes in wearers. Parents were also advised to encourage erect postures in children, and women were admonished not to "prance" when they walked.

But as irrelevant as the stories about the Georgia colonel and impolite London perceptions of Canadian women might have been, these articles from around the globe separated *The Evening Journal* from its rival, the *Edmonton Bulletin*, the city's main newspaper since the 1880s.

Unlike its competitor, *The Journal* had access to stories from an early wire service from Winnipeg that allowed it to report national and international events sometimes days ahead of the competition.

News content aside, that first paper also met with a positive advertising response: 20 ads in its four pages, including a front page come-on from the Hudson's Bay, a company that has remained a loyal advertiser for 100 years.

Another advertisement offered for sale a book of photographs of Edmonton by C.M. Tait, while the paper's first classified ad, a lone entry under the title "Wants" on page 2, came from a person seeking "one or two rooms in a private dwelling west of Queen Street." Queen Street later became 99th Street.

Just like almost everyone else in Edmonton, the three exhausted and

***Nov. 11, 1903*:**
First 1,000 copies of *The Evening Journal*, comprising four pages, is printed in the back of the Shamrock Fruit Store and sells for 5 cents a day, 40 cents a month, $1 for three months and $4 per year.

SHAMROCK FRUIT STORE.
MILK

The Edmonton Journal

Shamrock Fruit Store and *The Evening Journal* office.

***Nov. 12, 1903*:**
***The Journal* publishes its first letter to the editor, signed Business Man, under the heading "A Suggestion to the Council.**
To The Journal.
The time has come when immediate action should be taken to number the business houses and also the private houses in our town..."

***Nov. 12, 1903*:**
***The Journal* starts the serialized novel, *The Awakening*, by "one of the best English novel writers." The true name of both the**

$550

For a Motor Carriage

Complete with Horn, Wheel Steer and 3 Lamps

—that has solid Rubber Puncture-proof Tires
—with Axles that run a year with one Oiling
—that runs 30 miles on ONE GALLON of Gasoline.

This $550 Tudhope-McIntyre Motor Carriage is just what most men have been waiting for

—a reliable, substantial, easy-riding carriage
—that will cover from 10 to 30 miles an hour
—that costs little to buy
—and next to nothing to maintain.

It is the Motor Carriage for every man—for Doctor, Lawyer, Merchant, Salesman, Real Estate Agent, Life Insurance Solicitor.

It is the carriage for every-day use. Goes everywhere that a horse can. Takes a lot of hills and roads that horses and big touring cars can't. Runs along in mud, sand, rock and snow—easier than a horse can pull the ordinary buggy.

Tudhope-McIntyre Model H H runs 30 miles on one gallon of gasoline. It has solid rubber tires—trouble-proof—no punctures, blowouts, delays or expense.

This $550 Motor Carriage has Chapman's Double Ball Bearing Axles which run for a year with one oiling.

12 horse power engine—Double Cylinder, 4 cycle, air cooled motor—two speeds forward and one reverse.

The whole carriage—body, engine, motor, axles, tires—*every part*—is fully guaranteed.

DEALERS

and others, who can handle a reasonable number of these cars should write us at once for terms and territory.

We make 15 models of motor vehicles from a Motor Buggy at $550 to a 9 passenger Pleasure Wagon at $1000. Our line excludes Stanhopes, Traps, 2 and 4 passenger Roadsters and Surreys.

The Tudhope-McIntyre Co., Dept. EJ Orillia, Ont.
3

NO ITEM TOO SMALL

"Hermann Paultz, a Dane, was fined $2 and $3 costs for being drunk and incapable today."

— March 10, 1905

RECOVERING

"Mrs. Thos. Cox is again able to move around with the aid of a crutch, after being laid up for a long spell from a broken leg."

— Feb. 18, 1905

"Captain McGregory dropped dead here yesterday.'

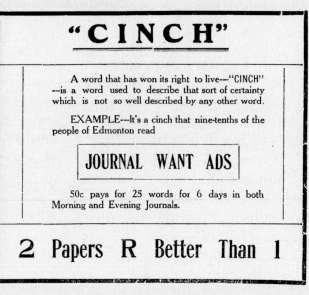

—Jan. 13, 1905

FRANTIC WOMEN

Organic disturbances of the feminine system act like a firebrand on the nerves of women, often driving them fairly frantic.

A nervous, irritable woman is a source of misery not only to herself, but to all those who come under her influence. That such conditions can be entirely overcome by taking

LYDIA E. PINKHAM'S VEGETABLE COMPOUND

Mme. Emma Chatel, Valleyfield, Belleriver, Quebec, writes to Mrs. Pinkham:

"I want to tell you that without Lydia E. Pinkham's Vegetable Compound I would not be alive. For months I suffered with painful and irregular periods and inflammation of the feminine organs. Doctors could do nothing for me, and said I must submit to an operation because I had a tumor.

"One of my cousins advised me to take Lydia E. Pinkham's Vegetable Compound as it had cured her.

"I did so and now I have no pain and am entirely cured. Your remedy is deserving of great praise."

FACTS FOR SICK WOMEN.

For thirty years Lydia E. Pinkham's Vegetable Compound, made from roots and herbs, has been the standard remedy for female ills, and has positively cured thousands of women who have been troubled with displacements, inflammation, ulceration, irregularities, periodic pains, backache. Why don't you try it?

Mrs. Pinkham invites all sick women to write her for advice. She has guided thousands to health. Address, Lynn, Mass.

LOCAL COVERAGE

"An accident occurred at Strathcona last evening which might have ended in more serious results. Mr. Jack Gurley of the Strathcona feed and livery stables was going to clean a revolver which he evidently did not know was loaded, the weapon exploded a cartridge. The bullet entered Mr. Gurley's hand below the third finger, coming out above the knuckle on the back of the hand. The accident was very painful but no other serious results are anticipated."

— Nov. 21, 1903

"Typewriter and stenographer wanted. Apply in own handwriting."

— Jan 18, 1906, classified ad

A NARROW ESCAPE

"Mrs. Powell, wife of Jas. A. Powell, manager of the Deering Implement Agency, had a narrow escape from fatal injuries as a result of a runaway accident yesterday afternoon. She now lies at her home, Namayo Avenue, suffering from a fractured limb, a severe concussion of the brain and dangerous internal injuries. Her son, George Powell, who was driving the cutter, had a miraculous escape, being dragged under the overturned cutter a hundred yards yet sustaining no injuries beyond a few bruises and a general shaking up."

— Dec. 24, 1903

"CINCH"

A word that has won its right to live—"CINCH" —is a word used to describe that sort of certainty which is not so well described by any other word.

EXAMPLE—It's a cinch that nine-tenths of the people of Edmonton read

JOURNAL WANT ADS

50c pays for 25 words for 6 days in both Morning and Evening Journals.

2 Papers R Better Than 1

ink-stained young men at the back of the Shamrock Fruit Store on first Street and 101A Avenue were rank newcomers.

Macpherson and Arthur Moore had arrived on the edge of Canada's western frontier two months earlier from Portage la Prairie, Manitoba, with a 19th century, hand-fed flat-bed press and a balky monoline typesetter. Their goal was first to set up a printing business, then to start their own newspaper. Reporter J.W. Cunningham had arrived on Oct. 31.

That Wednesday, Nov. 11, had been a good first day. But the trio – all of whom had been involved to one extent or another in the *Portage la Prairie Daily Graphic* – knew they had to do it again tomorrow and tomorrow and tomorrow. *The Journal* was here to stay.

John Macpherson.

"When we finally sat down in that room, cluttered with packing boxes and furniture, we were tired, but none of us could suppress a quiet sort of smile – we'd done it," an 83-year-old Macpherson recalled in a *Journal* story 50 years later. "All we needed was to know it was out and we could enjoy a good night's sleep."

Macpherson, who back in Manitoba had co-owned the *Daily Graphic* from 1897 to 1904, was the money man. In Edmonton, the 33-year-old was president, publisher and editor. Cunningham was the sole reporter, and Moore, 28, the 17th of a family of 19 children was the pressman who kept everything operating. And it was probably Moore who got a line on the trio's equipment from an older brother who worked at the *Winnipeg Free Press.* Moore and Cunningham worked for shares in the paper.

Macpherson's salary was $20 a month, the other two earned $16 – about $340 and $280 in today's money.

Job functions weren't hard and fast. Cunningham often ran the press and wrote headlines, pressman Moore delivered the freshly printed papers to the town's cigar stores and hotels, and publisher Macpherson took a hand in the typesetting. All three partners hand-folded the 1,000 copies of that first four-page broadsheet. Any one of them would have been happy to sell you an ad.

There is no record of why Macpherson selected Nov. 11, a Wednesday, to launch the new enterprise. Perhaps it was simply because that was when the enterprising trio was ready to go.

As the first paper came off the press, the real history of *The Journal* began.

It was an era when newspapers were the public's only source of information, comment and entertainment. And the

Courtesy of Joanne Allen and Grace Price

Arthur Moore was an avid curler.

novel and the author will eventually be revealed, promises the promo ad. The story runs regularly, then sporadically and, eventually, disappears without an ending or the revelation of either author or title.

***Nov. 14, 1903*: *The Journal* publishes its first correction. "A mix-up in the type is responsible for an error in the report of the judgment delivered by Judge Scott in the case of LeRose & Sterrit vs. Col. Sam Hughes."**

***Nov. 19, 1903*: *The Journal* purchases the semi-weekly *Edmonton Post*'s subscription list.**

***Dec. 3, 1903*: Alberta College opens on 101st Street.**

***Dec. 3, 1903*: *The Journal* announces its first contest. (1) Watch the ads, (2) Find a word of four or more letters spelled backwards, (3) Clip it out, bring it to The Journal, (4) Collect a numbered ticket. The draw is held Dec. 14 and was to be done by "some reputable citizen not on The Journal staff." Winner gets $5 worth of beauty products. Runner-up gets a year's subscription.**

NA-3471-27 Glenbow Archives

Billy Day, hotel bartender at Athabasca Landing, was a favourite at Edmonton parades and fairs with his pet moose in 1903.

NA-272-2 Glenbow Archives

Tent home at 105th Street and Jasper Avenue.

NO JOINTS

"Munvoro and Shanklin, the flexible Hottentots, were among the greatest attractions of the big fair. There appeared to be absolutely no joints in their bodies. They writhed and twisted like serpents and tied themselves into every manner of knot.

"The performance was a grotesque one, and was highly applauded by the onlookers."

— July 4, 1905

"The new coat of arms of Alberta shows a wheat field in the foreground, with snow-capped mountains in the background, surmounted by St. George's cross. They might at least have left off that snow."

— Editorial, May 28, 1907

SENTIMENT AND COMEDY IN FRENCH AND ENGLISH

"Mr. Perrichon on His Travels will be played in French on Friday next, the twenty-fourth, by the Cercle Dramatique of Edmonton. There will also be between each act a varied program of music and songs both sentimental and comic in French and English.

Mr. Perrichon on His Travels is one of the brightest, most truly pleasing and humorous comedies written by Labiche and his able companion, and has the rare merit of concealing under the sparkling and captivating surface, a profound knowledge of the human heart. A good program is promised. Go and see it tomorrow night."

— Feb. 23, 1905

You Can Spare Enough Money to Pay For a Journal Want Ad. Any Day

NOTICE.

Birth, Marriage and Death Notices may be inserted in The Journal (on condensed ad page at 50c per insertion.

Situations Vacant, For Sale, Lost, Found, etc., adsunder these headings:

25 words, 1day ...25c
25 words, 2 days ... 35c
25 words, 6 days ... 50c

No ad. accepted for less than 25c Cash must accompany the order.

LOST—A collie dog, answers to the name of Collie, black with white spot on breast, finder return to Geo. C. Laight. Hallier & Aldbridge, bakers.

COON-SKIN COAT— The person having in his possession a coon-skin coat taken from the Windsor Hotel on Monday or Tuesday is requested to return it at once or prosecution will follow.

FOR SALE—A good Milch Cow, fresh calvel, good milker and quiet. Apply to Ed Nagle, College Avenue, or at Calhoun & Ferguson's Stable, 1st street.

WANTED—Young man to wash bottles with the machine, no sleepy John. Apply "Wilson Limited," Chisholm block, 256 Jasper west, corner of Fourth.

TO RENT—A Shack suitable for a small family, situated near R.C. church; $6 a month. Apply H, Journal Office.

STRAYED—Into the premises of William Horricks, Gamayo Road, thirty hogs. Owner can have the same by paying damages and expenses.

— Examples of classified ads between 1903 and 1910

start of a new newspaper with a fresh point of view was a welcome event. Even at a nickel a copy – 87 cents in 2003 money – that first edition sold out. It was published every evening except Sunday and delivered to homes and offices.

The town the newspaper served had only a few dusty streets that turned to heavy, thick, prairie gumbo when it rained. Men on horseback shared the road with ox carts and horse-drawn carriages.

In winter, snow-covered streets froze as hard as iron, and cutters and sleighs whisked people from place to place. Winter or summer, runaways of panicked horses were frequent news events.

It was a frontier town of hitching posts, wooden sidewalks and stores that sold farm implements to immigrants clearing land and carving out their own futures. Clothing stores, displaying the latest fashions, stood next to trading outlets dealing in fox and muskrat pelts from the north. Old Fort Edmonton, located on what is now the south lawn of the present Legislature Building, was a ramshackle ruin, but the town's 120-year-old fur trading past was still close enough to touch.

The best hotels were the Windsor on the southwest corner of Jasper at 101st Street, which changed its name to the Selkirk in 1914, and the Jasper House. It's now the Hub Hotel at 9692 Jasper Avenue. When the paper began, the Alberta Hotel was under construction at Jasper Avenue and 98th Street and opened in June the following year.

"Once the stranger sojourns for a while within her gates amid such luxurious surroundings he will be sure to make his permanent home here," *The Journal* predicted in an article marking the Alberta Hotel's opening.

The birth of the new paper symbolized the promise of Edmonton's progress. One of the first local stories the newspaper covered was the ambitious proposal by Montreal businessman W.G. Tretheway to build a streetcar line down Jasper Avenue. His profit was to come from spur lines that would be built to the coal mines in Beverly and Jasper Place. The deal fell through when construction didn't start on the date promised and he forfeited his $10,000 performance bond.

With that seed money, the publicly owned Edmonton Radial Railway was started. It opened in 1908 at a cost $49,000. The track ran for 12 miles including the stretch on Jasper from 97th to 116th Street.

There were other changes, too. Merchant Joseph Morris brought the first automobile to town six months after *The Journal* began. The paper reported somewhat vaguely that it was a Ford "of the noiseless type with a gasoline motive power of neat construction." Two years later, when Morris and his wife were one of the first couples to drive from Edmonton to Fort Saskatchewan, the paper gave their excellent adventure extensive coverage. They had, after all, driven the 40 miles in the then rather breathtaking time of two and a half hours.

On Nov. 17, barely a week after *The*

***Dec. 12, 1903*:**
"Items Interesting to womankind" is *The Journal*'s first women's section. "A serious question is our social existence in that which appears to be year by year pressing more heavily on the household in the matter of the substitution for the old home-life for one and existence lived either out of doors, or by one in which the catering of the house is managed by some outside source." The writer is grousing about the growing trend to eat in restaurants.

***Dec. 14, 1903*:**
William Short is re-elected mayor.

***Dec. 30, 1903*:**
***The Journal* ends the year with daily circulation of 2,500.**

***March 25, 1904*:**
***The Journal*'s first "systems crash" occurs. The telegraph wires are down. "Journal readers may expect the day's happenings in the outer world chronicled in tomorrow evening's Journal."**

J.H Morris at the wheel of his Ford in 1904.

City of Edmonton Archives

YBUR, THE HANDCUFF QUEEN, the little lady with the mysteeious power, who opens a week's engagement at the Empire Theatre ton ight.

MR. THEODORE LORCH

In the great dual role of "Dr. Jekyle and Mr. Hyde," which he will give for one performance only at The Edmonton Opera House, Wednesday Evening, April 28

CIRCUS DAY at EDMONTON

WEDNESDAY, JULY 22

Performances at 2 and 8 p. m

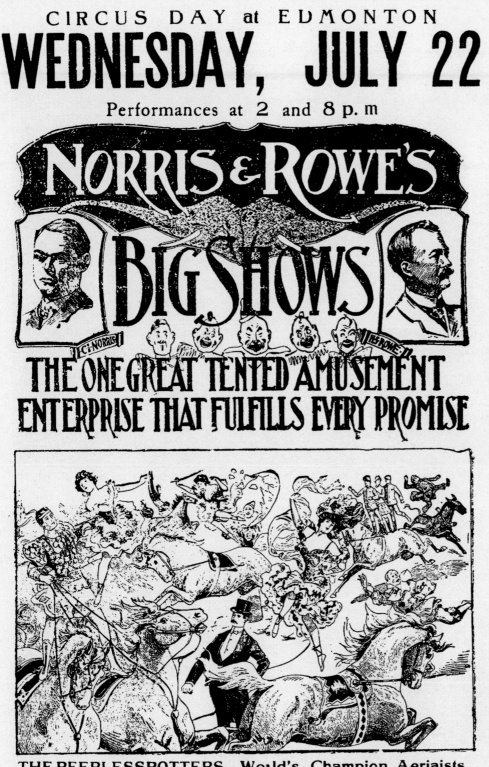

NORRIS & ROWE'S
BIG SHOWS
C.I. NORRIS
H.S. ROWE

THE ONE GREAT TENTED AMUSEMENT ENTERPRISE THAT FULFILLS EVERY PROMISE

THE PEERLESSPOTTERS, World's Champion Aerialists
THE HONEY MORA TROUPE, Germany's Premier Acrobats
THE ST. LEON FAMILY, Acrobats and Balancers
MISS ROSE DOCKERILL, Queen of Lady Riders
Grand Spectacular Street Parade at 10.30 a.m.

" Hogmany Social "

THE CALEDONIAN CLUB

will celebrate "Hogmanay Night," December 31st, Oddfellows' Hall, Norwood block, with a social con-consisting of Scottish songs, music, dancing, and refreshments. All members, Scotchmen and their friends invited.

Admission — Gentlemen 50 cents including ladies.

EDMONTON OPERA HOUSE

TONIGHT and MATINEE

The successful musical comedy.

"THE GIRL FROM CHILI"

Good comedy, fine dancing, and splendid singing.
Seats now on sale at Box Office.
PRICES—75c. 50c and 25cts.

PECK'S BAD BOY

MONOTONOUS

(No stars)

For the second time this season, Edmonton has been visited by a "Moving Picture Show." A small number of citizens visited the rink last night to witness a performance of Peck's Bad Boy, the posters throughout the city giving the impression that the ludicrous positions set forth in this famous book would be illustrated by "life-like moving pictures."

Instead, there appeared a common magic lantern show, not even dissolving views, accompanied by a monotonous reading instead of an interesting lecture.

True, there were some moving pictures, such as they were. Either the photos were a cheap lot or the operator was incapable of handling his machine, for the pictures were blurred and appeared to be pieces cut from a spoiled roll, for they were short and abrupt, and their appearance called forth exclamations of disappointment and such calls as "Turn on the light."

The whole performance lasted but an hour and a quarter, including moving the machine in the middle of the performance and wasting much time in the readjustment. At the close of the performance, a chorus of "Rotten" proceeded from the youthful audience who had dug into their slim purses for the necessary price to enable them to witness real "living pictures."

JIM BLACK,
The legless singing and dancing comedian at the Orpheum.

NC-6-519 Glenbow Archives

The steamer *City of Edmonton* heads downriver, past Fraser's Flats (now Rossdale) in 1904. D.R. Fraser's lumber mill is in the background.

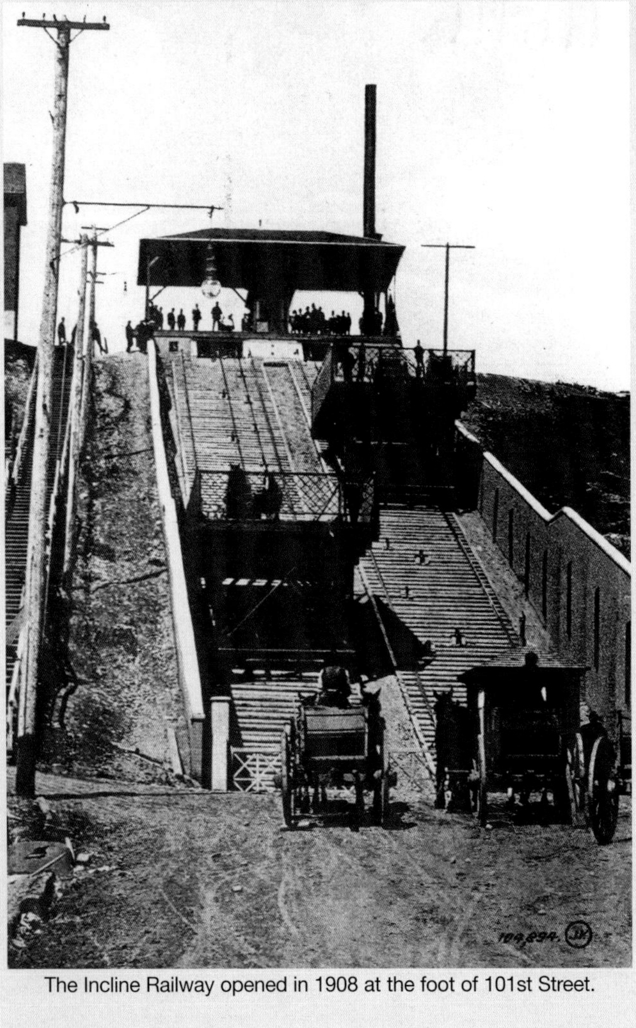

NA-1497-45 Glenbow Archives

The Incline Railway opened in 1908 at the foot of 101st Street.

NA-303-46 Glenbow Archives

A Cree camp in the river valley circa 1904.

CALGARY, ALWAYS A PROBLEM

"The Calgary Herald showed the small minds that control that newspaper in its Friday issue when to its telegraphic report of the inauguration ceremonies that reported the birth of the Province of which Calgary has been the chief city for years there was hitched on a contemptible statement to the effect that there was a rumour in Calgary of snow falling in Edmonton during the celebrations. There was not the slightest foundation for such a report which was doubtlessly a pure fabrication even as a rumour and was given a prominent position in the Herald's report with the object of doing all the harm possible to Edmonton and Northern Alberta."

— Sept. 5, 1905

Minnie Maddern Fisk billed as "America's greatest actress" in a *Journal* ad appears at the Thistle Rink in the play *The New York Idea.* She's accompanied by the "fine company from the Schubert Theatre" in New York. Admission is $3.00, $2.50 and $2.00.

— June 22, 1907

Marion Harland presents *The Journal's* first recipe column. Mince pie, chicken pie and baked beans are among the featured items.

— June 27, 1906

Journal's inaugural edition, Macpherson expanded his modest opening vision, telling readers that while the paper would continue to promote Edmonton and northern Alberta, it would also back the Conservative Party.

The decision meant the paper was swimming against a local political current that was stronger than the North Saskatchewan River in springtime. Edmonton was, after all, a die-hard Liberal town in a province-to-be that was staunchly Liberal, too. What's more, the Liberals already had a local trumpet in the 23-year-old *Bulletin*, owned by the popular Frank Oliver, an MP who eventually joined Wilfrid Laurier's cabinet.

The semi-weekly *Edmonton Post,* the previous Tory mouthpiece in town, had just folded. George Bradbury, a Conservative MP from Selkirk, Manitoba, approached Macpherson and company with a proposition that they take over the *Post's* circulation lists, advertising contracts and other assets, lock, stock and ink barrel.

The *Post* was owned by local Tory politician and businessman Richard Secord, a close friend of Bradbury's. It was a deal too good to pass up for the cash-strapped newcomers, even if the agreement called for them to compromise journalistic objectivity in matters political.

Macpherson did, however, lay the cards on the table for readers: "The Journal will advocate the interests of the country, and more especially, this western portion of it as set forth in the policy of the Conservative Party."

The paper supported provincial autonomy and opposed wide-open free trade with the United States, preferring a system of tariff barriers designed to protect Canadian manufacturers. Its readers may have agreed on the matter of autonomy, but not trade protection; many were farmers who wanted duties lowered on the more accessible American farm machinery.

Nevertheless, the paper persisted. Its view was straightforward. Business was good. Liberals were bad.

Concern about social issues such as poverty, disease and workplace safety were not to be found on the paper's pages.

Macpherson's Nov. 17 editorial contained another promise. "In its news columns The Journal will also endeavour to give its readers a fair and trustworthy view of such political events as may from time to time transpire."

"Fair and trustworthy," however, can be a matter of perception, particularly at a time when newspapers were unabashed supporters of political parties.

In the *Bulletin* Frank Oliver ran Hansard reports verbatim on debates between himself and the Conservative opposition in Ottawa, and *The Evening Journal* was really no better.

For example, when Secord, who sold the *Post* to Macpherson, was nominated as the Conservative candidate to run against Oliver in the federal election, *The Journal* offered its readers thousands of enthusiastic words in Secord's favour.

The "fair and trustworthy" report on the nomination meeting that appeared in the first edition was unrestrained and effusive, noting that the delegates were "inspired by confidence in the choice of the convention of a candidate to contest the riding in the forthcoming Dominion election – a candidate than whom no one is better fitted to carry the Conservative party in northern Alberta to victory."

***April 5, 1904*:**
Edmonton's first opera, put on in Robertson Hall, is Planquette's "famous romantic comedy" *The Chimes of Normandy*. Staged by the town's amateur artists. It gets a positive – and very long – review.

***May 5, 1904*:**
First six-page *Journal* hits the streets.

***May 26, 1904*:**
Jos. H. Morris brings the first car to Edmonton. It is a Ford "of the noiseless type with a gasoline motive power and of neat construction."

***June 8, 1904*:**
The Alberta Hotel opens.

***Nov. 7, 1904*:**
It's a Red Letter day for Edmonton as it officially becomes a city. To celebrate, *The Journal* prints the entire paper in red ink.

River Excursion
Steamboat Edmonton

Wednesday, Thursday and Friday -- Down the River--Leaves Bridge at 7 o'clock--50 cts

Saturday---Down the River. Leaves Bridge at 2 o'clock. $1.00.

***Nov. 18, 1904*:**
City council agrees to pay Alex Taylor $17,000 for the Edmonton District Telephone Service, and takes possession Jan. 1, 1905.

BUSTER BROWN AND HIS DOG TIGE

BUSTER BROWN
HE ASSISTS HIS MOTHER
BUSTER, COME HERE A MINUTE
HURRY BUSTER
JAM
I'M COMING MAMA DEAR
JAM
FASTEN MY DRESS
HER EASTER FROCK
BE CAREFUL TO GET IT STARTED RIGHT
OH HURRY UP YOU'RE AS SLOW AS YOUR FATHER
BE SURE TO GET THOSE BIG HOOKS ONTO THE SKIRT
WE MAY AS WELL PREPARE FOR THE WORST
DONE
THANK YOU BUSTER DEAR
I'LL TELL PAPA YOU ARE READY
WHY YOU'RE JUST COVERED WITH JAM
DONT SPANK HIM DEAR-I'LL BUY YOU A NEW DRESS
REMEMBER MA ITS SUNDAY
I'LL BET MA CAN LICK JEFFRIES
RESOLVED
THAT IT IS ALL POINT OF VIEW. MA DIDN'T SEE ANYTHING FUNNY ABOUT THAT INCIDENT, WHILE I DARE SAY SOME PEOPLE LAUGHED. POOR MA, I DONT BLAME HER. ITS HARD TO BE KEPT AWAY FROM CHURCH WHEN YOU'VE GOT A NEW DRESS AND HAT. I DONT BELIEVE MA APPRECIATES ME AS MUCH AS OTHER PEOPLE DO. THERE ARE LOTS OF PEOPLE WOULD GIVE ANY THING FOR A DEAR LITTLE BOY. THEN THERE ARE LOTS OF FOLKS WHO DONT KNOW WHY THEY ARE SO DISSATISFIED WHEN ALL THEY NEED IS JUST A BUSTER BROWN
R. F. Outcault

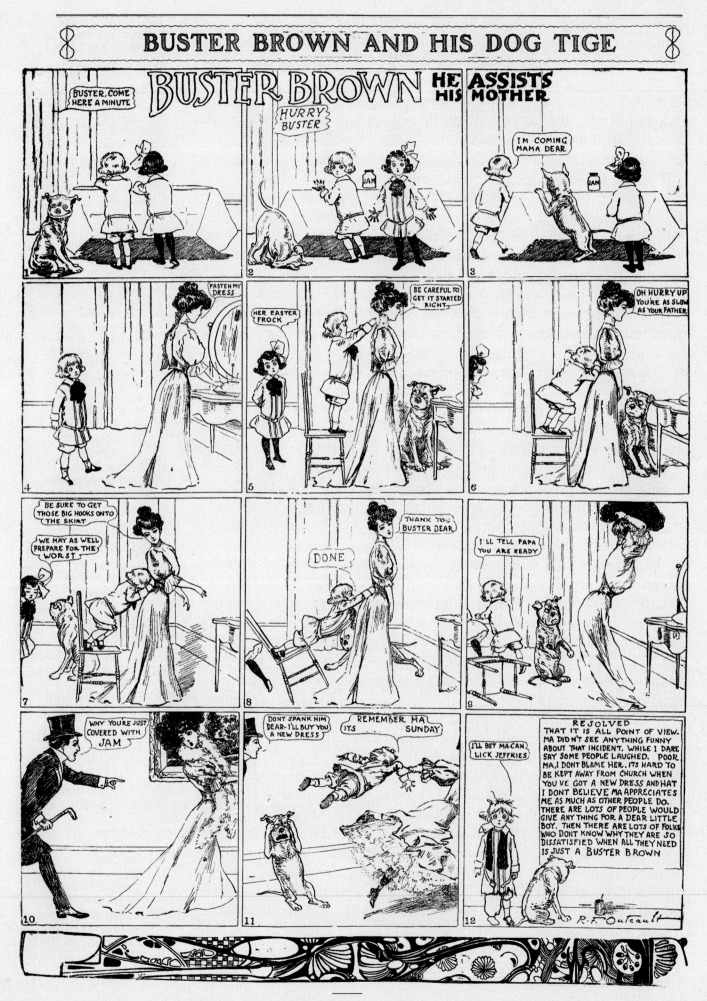

For the record, the *Bulletin* also reported the Secord nomination – in 19 words.

Secord lost the election, but his ties to the *The Journal* continued. In 1905, he and a group of like-minded Conservative investors bought shares in the newspaper and formed The Journal Company Limited.

Despite the fact that for the next two decades the paper continued to back Conservative candidates who didn't come close to being elected, readers were forgiving. Edmonton's population quadrupled from 4,000 in 1903 to 16,000 by 1910, and the newspaper's circulation mirrored that growth, rising from the initial 1,000 in 1903 to 8,000 by the end of the decade. Advertising increased from 20 ads a day to dozens, and the paper itself was often 12 or more pages, up from the original four.

However, the newspaper's financial health wasn't always robust.

In 1908, H.M.E. Evans, an Edmonton investment dealer, tipped off Wilson Southam, a member of the family that was building a newspaper empire in Eastern Canada, that *The Journal* might be for sale. The paper, Evans told the Southams, had been doing well until the real estate market slumped, and it was now in a tough spot. It was five weeks behind in its payroll, and was struggling to keep afloat a morning edition begun in 1906 to complement the evening edition. It was ripe for plucking.

The Southams were overextended and passed on the deal.

In 1909, Macpherson, Cunningham and W.S. Harris, the business manager who had bought out Moore in 1906, sold their controlling interest to John P. McConnell, the publisher of the *Saturday Sunset,* a Vancouver weekly. He, in turn, flipped his interest to J.H. Woods, who had ties to the Southams and who was a part-owner of the *Calgary Herald.*

By the next decade, the Southam family purchased both papers.

Even in its early days, *The Journal* offered a wide range of stories to entice readers. The writing style during the first years of the newspaper's life would today be considered overblown and wordy, but the objective then was the same as it is today: to inform and to entertain.

Many of the stories were funny, some were sad and others, by today's standards, downright illegal. The paper ran the names of hotel guests and published the individual test results of schoolchildren. Juveniles who committed crimes were identified by name, as were those subjected to abuse.

Getting stories first and getting them right has always been a tenet of the newspaper business, and barely into its third year of existence *The Journal* scooped one of the biggest stories in the province's history from under the nose of the politically connected Frank Oliver and his *Bulletin* staff.

On Monday, Feb. 13, 1905, readers learned their newly minted city would be named Alberta's capital when federal government legislation giving provincial autonomy was introduced later in the year.

The selection of a capital had been a horse race, and the issue was the subject of much front page and editorial speculation for most of a year.

While other cities and towns vied for the honour – Calgary was a strong contender, Banff sold itself on the basis of its location and Vegreville touted the cleanliness of its air which would make legislative deliberations easier – *The Journal* didn't waver. The capital belonged in Edmonton.

That Edmonton finally received the honour was largely due to Frank

***Feb. 5, 1905*:** **Partnership merges into a joint stock company and "local" Conservatives invited to buy shares in the new company to be known as the "*Journal* Company Limited." W. A. Griesbach and Dr. Harry R. Smith were early shareholders and later E. T. Bishop, the company's solicitor, Dr. Jamieson, J. D. Hyndman, later Mr. Justice Hyndman, Dr. Dunn, Richard Secord, A. Williamson Taylor, C. Hiebert, MLA, and A. J. Robertson, MLA, also joined the company by purchasing stock.**

***March 27, 1905*:** **Front page ad from the Hudson's Bay Company announces the opening of their new store on Jasper Avenue and 103rd Street and promises old and new customers "courteous treatment and fair play."**

***July 6, 1905*:** **The Alberta Autonomy Bill passes the House of Commons and goes to the Senate for approval.**

July 8, 1905*:** ***The Journal **increases in size to eight pages, and in the same month moves into its own, new one-storey building on 101st Street and 102nd Avenue where the Bank of**

Will You be Satisfied With $2,000 Next Year---A 5 Acre Fruit Farm in Peachvale Addition Will Pay it.

I wish to place before you three main reasons why you should buy a fruit farm in Peachvale Addition now. I wish to firmly fix in your mind that it is in your own interest to wire me to make a reservation for you.

1 The price I am asking for Peachvale Addition Fruit Farms is the first price, the original price. Peachvale Addition fruit farms will never be any cheaper.

2 Peachvale Addition is the last great area of rich fruit land in the Fraser Valley close to New Westminster city enjoying as it does excellent transportation facilities.

3 If you buy now or make a reservation by wire you have 90 days in which to inspect the property and if it is not exactly as represented and perfectly satisfactory in every way you need not take it; the $25 deposit which you will mail, the same day you wire, will be cheerfully refunded to you. If, after inspection, the farm is satisfactory and you wish to keep it, you will find that within the 90 days it will have advanced considerably in value. I say without fear of contradiction that 12 months from the date hereof every farm in Peachvale Addition will have advanced one hundred fold in value.

Peachvale Addition fronts right on the Fraser river. All the river boats call at the farms for freight and passengers. The S.S. "Kerland" makes regular trips between New Westminster City, Peachvale and Peachvale Addition. No charge is made whatsoever to actual settlers. All those who have purchased fruit land in Peachvale or Peachvale Addition have an annual pass.

Only a slight charge is made for freight. Of course those who don't wish to travel by water may take advantage of the Great Northern which has a station near the property or the new tram line between New Westminster, Vancouver and Chilliwack which is now under construction. This interurban road assures the farmers of rapid transportation.

Bear in mind that the fruit farms in Peachvale Addition are as good as any in all British Columbia. They need no irrigation and are well drained.

It is well to consider that a very small holding of say five acres, in Peachvale Addition is large enough and rich enough to keep a man and family comfortable and provide a neat sum for banking.

FIRST YEAR'S CROPS

Commencing with the first year's crop, potatoes will yield from $250 to $300 per acre. Such a crop could be planted between the rows of the young orchard which you can set out this spring. Other vegetables and small fruits would bring the first year's crop up to $2,000 from 5 acres. As the orchard advances toward maturity small crops of fruit from the same will materially increase the profit from the farm, while at the end of five years the young orchard is in full bearing and the crop from five acres will be from $2,500 to $4,000.

I am prepared to prove to the skeptical individual every detail pertaining to these statements. I won't ask you to take my word for it, but will produce unquestionable evidence that the soil of Peachvale Addition Fruit Farms is as good and as rich as any of the best farms in Western Canada.

Don't delay, wire me to reserve to-day. You have nothing to lose. If the property is not exactly as represented and in every way satisfactory your deposit of $25 will be cheerfully refunded.

Even now, while am preparing this advertisement, people are buying in Peachvale Addition. You must act promptly if you wish to get a farm close to the water front. The farms which front on the river in Peachvale Addition sell at $200 per acre, those farther back $100 per acre. When you send your message specify whether you want a farm at $200 per acre on the river or one at $100 per acre a little farther back. The terms are quarter cash and the balance in three years. The property is sub-divided into five, six, eight, ten and twelve acre plots. Remember there is no clearing, troublesome stumps or stones.

Don't waste time writing for information, because by the time we could exchange letters this property will in all probability, be off the market. At any rate there will only be a few farms left. You will make money if you wire me to reserve to-day. Send message "collect"

W. J. KERR, President, W. J. Kerr, Limited, New Westminster, B.C.

References; Any Bakn or Business House in New Westminster, B. C.

THE LONG AND SHORT OF IT.

TO START A BANK ACCOUNT

1st Take Jasper Avenue car and stop at "THE BOSTON" Clothing Store.

2nd Put $10.00 in the Bank and buy one of our $25 suits for 15 dollars. This is the first start in economy

3rd Remember the best is not always the cheapest, providing you don't pay too much for your judgment.

4th "THE BOSTON" grants privileges that no other firms do. That you are at liberty to return anything misrepresented and get your money back.

5th Our advice on correct attire for business or recreation Suits will not cost you a cent.

6th Bring your cheques to us. We will cash them cheerfully whether good or bad and not ask you "To take because you look or keep because you buy."

Last but Not Least "THE BOSTON" is the leading quarters for High-class Goods at a reasonable price.

HART & WAGAR, Fraser Block.

copyright

Dressed Meats

Now that the cold weather is here you may be contemplating buying your meats by the quarter. Before placing your order, get our prices on BEEF, PORK and MUTTON.

Stock of all kinds bought and sold by

WILLIAMSON BROS.

If you buy a quarter from us we cut it up.

Oliver's successful lobbying as a member of the Laurier cabinet. However, *The Journal*, consistent with everything else it had said about the man, neglected to give credit where it was due.

The language in the scoop was quaint, the Calgary bashing subtle and the three-deck headline a little awkward:

"Edmonton will
be the Capital of
Alberta Province."

But it didn't matter. *Journal* readers knew before anyone else that their frontier city would never again be the same.

And as befitted a new capital, politics swiftly became the unofficial sport of Edmontonians whether they were in their boardrooms or barrooms, and *The Journal* covered the players and the plays with the same unabashed enthusiasm it devoted to hockey and football.

Political meetings were standing-room-only events.

There were decisions to be made and the paper was there to report on them and attempt, often with marginal success, to sway public opinion.

During its first two years the biggest issue facing *The Journal* and its readers was achieving provincial status for Alberta, and the paper constantly jabbed at Laurier's Liberal government for what it saw as delaying tactics.

Editorials exhorted the federal government to move more quickly and allow the people of the territories to become "full citizens of Canada." Besides, the paper said, each year's delay cost the would-be province as much as $1.5 million in federal transfer payments. "It is up to the electors of the Territories to say whether or not they think themselves capable of managing their own affairs as the citizens of other parts of the Dominion."

And as always, there was Oliver's *Bulletin* to attack with unreserved passion: "The Bulletin, whose unenviable task it is to come to the rescue of every scandalous and unpleasant creeping thing that takes refuge beneath the ample skirts of the Grit party leaps to the defence of the system...," *The Journal* roared in an editorial decrying irregularities in voter enumeration for the 1904 Dominion election.

When provincial status was finally accorded Alberta, the newspaper was delighted, although it was quick to point out the province obtained fewer powers than the other, older provinces.

Revenue from natural resources continued to flow to Ottawa, and it was an issue that rankled for decades. It was wrong and, in no uncertain terms, the paper let its readers know.

Tory through and through, the paper paid unfailing if bumptious homage to R.B. Bennett, the Calgary lawyer and MLA who was also the provincial Conservative leader.

"With the persuasive eloquence of D'Arcy McGee, with the relentless logic of Edward Blake, with the statesmanlike and far-sighted appeal of Sir John A. Macdonald, Richard B. Bennett, the provincial Conservative leader, opened the campaign for provincial rights in Ross Hall, Strathcona, last night," *The Journal* wrote in one of is "fair and trustworthy" reports in 1905.

"His two-hour speech caused old-time Liberals to pause and think and inspired Conservatives to gird to the fight for the rights of the British people and the principles of the Canadian constitution."

Montreal building now stands.

***July 18, 1905*: After much debate and much name calling, city council decides unanimously that power should be provided all day, rather than simply from sundown to 1 a. m. The move is necessary because of the installation of elevators in both the Empire Block and the McDougall & Secord store.**

***Sept. 1, 1905*: Alberta becomes a province.**

***Sept. 6, 1905*: The *Times of London* reports on the new provinces, and gives them prominent page 1 display. Says the *Times*: "It seems by no means unlikely that the power of the Northwest, which must be one day the dominant political power in Canada, will one day be thrown into the scale against the Liberal party."**

***Nov. 9, 1905*: Alberta's first premier, Liberal Alexander Cameron Rutherford, is elected with a 22-seat majority in the legislature. Three Conservatives are elected.**

***Nov. 24, 1905*: "Edmonton Now a City on a Transcontinental Railway," trumpets the headline when the Canadian**

SECOND SECTION THE EDMONTON JOURNAL. PAGES 1 to 16

Vol. 5. No. 47. EDMONTON, ALBERTA, SATURDAY, OCTOBER 1, 1910 MORNING EDITION THIRTY-TWO PAGES.

FASHION EDITION
FALL and WINTER
1910-11
Paris and American Fashions

By contrast the Liberal government of Alexander Cameron Rutherford, the province's first premier, knew not to expect support from the paper.

When questions were raised in the legislature over a deal to build a rail link between Edmonton and Athabasca Landing, *The Journal*'s coverage of the province's first political scandal was timely and extensive. Railways were important to the future of both the city and northern Alberta, and coverage of the arrival of Canadian Northern Railway's first passenger car from Winnipeg in 1905 had been lavish.

This new line, however, was a different matter, and the paper pursued all of the details of the flawed agreement between the Rutherford government and the railroad men. The scandal – revolving around sloppy and naive business practices – ended Rutherford's political career in 1910. Yet *The Journal*'s reporting on the issue revealed a new level of journalistic maturity. While the editorials were still blindly partisan and many of the stories contained a clear bias, they were also more complete and credible.

As is the case today, newspapers in the first decade of the twentieth century were committed to local coverage, and *The Journal* understood the importance of covering Edmonton.

In 1907, the paper took an important editorial stance on development in the river valley and recommended action along the bank to prevent "the city front from sliding into the Saskatchewan."

"It would appear a big mistake were made when laying out the townsite of Edmonton in not reserving a boulevard a few hundred feet wide along the bank. There would have been lots of land between that and the North Pole for the city of Edmonton that is and that is to be."

But not every issue was as large.

And in a tradition that continues to this day, readers used the letters to the editor columns to debate everything from city hall's high-priced civil servants to the enactment of a dog bylaw, a matter of concern in a community where dogs ran free. "I have travelled considerably in my time," said a 1904 letter from Citizen, "but I must say I have never seen, anywhere, so many yelping curs permitted to annoy both drivers and wheelmen."

And little escaped the attention of the editorial page. The streetcar system could use some redesigning, pronounced a June 17, 1909, editorial: "The height from the ground of the entrance step of the Edmonton street cars appears necessarily great, and is an evident source of inconvenience, and sometimes of danger, particularly to women, to whom the height of the step is also, according to medical authorities, physically injurious."

But all good newspapers know their readers want more than politics, local or otherwise, and *The Evening Journal* quickly broadened its coverage.

Within its first month, the newspaper launched a new feature: "Items of Interest to Women." While women had not yet won the right to vote, and much of the coverage in the "women's" columns dealt with teas and social events, more important issues were not ignored.

Suffragettes received coverage with headlines like this from 1909: "Women Want Something More Substantial than Tea Cakes and Cigarettes – Typical Suffragette." Perhaps the worst example suffragette coverage occurred on Jan. 13, 1910, when *The Journal* reprinted a *Calgary Herald* story about nuns going to work with Indians north of Prince Albert.

Northern Railway arrives in the city. A return ticket on "the well-appointed" train to Winnipeg costs $45.

***Nov. 25, 1905*: *The Journal* publishes a Railway Edition in honour of the arrival of the Canadian Northern and calls it a "Day of Rejoicing."**

***Dec. 14, 1905*: The city's first electric passenger elevator, operating on a five-horse-power motor with electricity from the city power plant, begins running at the King Edward Hotel. Within months there were elevators in the Revillon Building and the Empire Block.**

***In 1906*: W.S. Harris takes "an interest" in *The Journal* and becomes advertising manager. Later in the year Arthur Moore sells his stock in the company.**

***Jan. 9, 1906*: *The Journal* reports that the Calgary and Edmonton CPR rail line, which ends at Strathcona, is to be carried through to Edmonton, on a bridge that is to be built across the river at a cost of $2 million.**

***Feb. 27, 1906*: Regular reporting of real estate news begins with an item saying real**

KLONDYKE
UNDERTAKER

City of Edmonton Archives

Strathcona residents attended the funeral service on 104th Street and Whyte Avenue for mine disaster hero George Lamb in 1907.

NA-2229-1 Glenbow Archives

Coal seams were abundant along the North Saskatchewan River.

COAL! COAL! COAL!

THE BEST CLOVER BAR COAL

Delivered same day as ordered.

THE COAL EXCHANGE LIMITED

36 JASPER EAST.

PHONE 1583

1909

RIGHT MIND, WRONG TONGUE

"I know that you sometimes feel a difficulty in expressing yourself in the English language, but I also know that behind that difficulty with a tongue which is not your mother tongue, there is a calm and judicial mind which weights and balances all things well…."

— Oct. 30, 1907, letter from Mayor W.A. Griesbach to Ald. J.H. Picard, urging him to run for mayor in the upcoming civic election.

Wanted at Once

50 miners to work at the City mines. Good wages.

Apply Edmonton Standard Coal Company, 40 Jasper Ave. East. Phone 1755.

1909

HIGH-CLASS DRAMA

"Taming of the Shrew, a rollicking comedy, is one where Shakespeare has shown how a super excellent dramatic talent can be allied with a keen sense of humour. The presentation of this play tonight by Harold Nelson will, it is safe to say, be one to be appreciated by every reader of Shakespeare and every admirer of this high class dramatic art."

— Dec. 26, 1903

"Mr. James McSweeney is building a house. The quilt he got at the ladies' social will soon be in use."

— May 20, 1904

"At a meeting of cabinet last night the Alberta University was given to Strathcona … Considerable disappointment will be caused to Calgary by this decision for the southern city considered that it had undoubted claims to the university."

— April 7, 1903

"Six noble women, not shrieking for the right to vote, but meekly gowned in the garb of Grey Nuns...," the story began.

Nevertheless, it was also on these pages that Mrs. Arthur Murphy's name first appeared. Emily Murphy was the convener of the province's standing committee on laws for better child protection, which also sought guarantees that a woman had a share in her husband's estate.

Crime and police news, including suicides, often made front page and were reported in great detail. Drinking carbolic acid or poison seemed to be the preferred choice of women while most suicidal men opted for the bullet. They were invariably described as "despondent" or "insane."

Workplace accidents were all too common as well, and the reporting of these was invariably highly descriptive and often downright grisly.

A 1906 accident in Strathcona's railyards that claimed the life of a brakeman identified only as "Thompson" left little to a reader's imagination.

"His head was badly smashed, the brains oozing from a great hollow on the right side while the left side of his face as also badly crushed."

Thompson was still alive at press time, but "the unfortunate victim of the catastrophe lies at the point from which the attending physicians have no hope of saving him," the story said.

Some misdemeanors were reported with a lighter touch. On Oct. 11, 1906, E.G. Fullerton, a "well-known chap in the city never known to be in a serious scrap before" was "gloriously drunk" when he entered the Dominion Express office "as large as life and just as natural."

Fullerton confronted the employees and "then drew a gun and gave them the merry ha-ha." No arrests were made.

Most of the time, however, crime meant punishment, and coverage was often surprisingly sensitive, if somewhat Dickensian.

The Oct. 1, 1907, sentencing of 12-year-old Charles Kurtz to two years hard labour for fraudulently obtaining goods worth more than $10, prompted an editorial calling for a reformatory to be built for young offenders.

"As The Journal representative passed down the line, he (Kurtz) lifted his tiny head in salute, his face beaming with an innocent smile. Next to him stood one in whose very countenance crime could be plainly discerned."

Serving as a counterpoint to the grim news of untimely deaths and criminals was the paper's coverage of sporting events, then as now a must-read element and source of pride for Edmontonians.

The Journal's very first sports story was preview of a hockey game on Nov. 14, 1903, between the Home Town team and the Strathconas, to be played the next day. Admission was 25 cents. The following day's report noted that the hometown team beat the Strathconas by a score of 8-7 before a crowd of 800 "men, women, youths and maidens."

Hockey was big, but curling was bigger, and bonspiels drawing as many as 2,000 spectators to the Thistle Rink on 102nd Street, north of Jasper, were reported on page 1. Professional sports were also closely covered, and stories about boxer Jack Johnson's fight with Jess Willard appeared months before the bout actually occurred.

Locally, Edmonton had a baseball team playing in the Western Canadian League and there was much passion expended editorially about its successes and failures.

estate men are of the opinion that west end property, situated between 1st Street and 9th Street and Jasper Avenue had peaked in value.

***March 15, 1906*: Edmonton is chosen as Alberta's capital by a vote of 16-8 at the first legislative assembly, held at the Thistle Rink. The ice was removed and a furnace installed, and *The Journal* predicts the "opening will, of course, be informal." Acting Mayor Bellamy declared a civic half-holiday in honour of the event.**

***April 6, 1906*: Prince Arthur of Connaught, nephew to King Edward, is the first royal visitor to Edmonton. "Edmontonians love a public function and it was not surprising that everybody in the city turned out and the Prince witnessed a great assemblage of the worthy citizens of Edmonton and its neighbouring town, Strathcona...But an undemonstrative crowd it was, for Edmontonians are as slow to cheer as Britishers. "They will turn out, young and old, they will applaud, but they cheer cautiously even when royalty drives past."**

THE EVENING JOURNAL.

VOL. 1 No. 100 EDMONTON, ALBERTA, MONDAY, MARCH 7, 1904 PRICE FIVE CENTS

A CLERK LIT OUT

But was Quickly Arrested at Carberry.

Was Fmployed in Neepawa Postoffice.

Neepawa, march 7.—John Scott, an assistant to the postmaster here, was arretted at Carberry yesterday, charged with stealing letters from the mails. Letters have been missed for some time, and Scott apparently taking his cue from the presence in town of the post office inspector, hired a livery rig and endeavored to escape by driving to Carberry and taking the train. He is a son of Wm. Scott, a wealthy farmer.

A FISHERY CASE.

Judgment Given in King vs. Courtepatte.

On a technicality, Norbert Courtepatte was acquitted by His Lordship Judge Scott on Friday of last week. The prisoner Courtepatte was charged with having on the 31st of last October, at Lac la Lanne, threatened with a gun and otherwise obstructing Guardian Fitzgerald while the ... the discharge of his duty ... net set in close season. ... given, but the pris ... judge holding ... convict, the

ATTACK ON VLADIVOSTOCK.

Japanese Fleet Appears Before The Great Naval Station of the North and Pours Some Big Shells Into It.

Used up $100,000 Worth of Ammunition on the Town, Whose Citizens Quietly Enjoyed the Exhibition. No One Was Hurt and Fleet Retreated.

Vladivostock, March 7.—A fleet of five Japanese ships and two cruisers appeared off this place at 1.25 o'clock yesterday afternoon and bombarded the town and shore batteries for 25 minutes. The fleet approached from the direction of Askold I... and about 32 mile... formed in line of... five and one-third... the shore batteries...

presence of the hostile fleet and of the prospects of an attack during the day, but it remained tranquil.

London, March 7.—Only Russian reports of the bombardment of Vladivostock have yet been received, and these

LUMBER FREIGHT

Canadian Pacific Makes a Reduction.

But Raises Rate on Foreign Lumber.

Vancouver, March 7.—Manitoba and the North-West are to get a reduction of $1 per thousand feet on all lumber. This is the result of a conference between T. W. Peterson, representing the C.P.R., and the coast lumbermen. The conference lasted all day and final arrangements were only arrived at after a lengthy discussion.

In return for this concession the C.P.R. has agreed to reduce the freight 10 cents per hundred pounds on all cedar and other lumbers except fir. The freight on fir is to remain 40 cents per hundred pounds. The new rate on lumber wil be forty cents instead of fifty cents, as formerly, which means a reduction of $2.50 per thousand feet. The C.P.R. further promises to protect the interests of the British Columbia mill men as against foreign trade.

COMPARING THE FIGHTERS

"The following comparison of the fighters in the far east is out of the ordinary...

"The Japs have a little country and are land hungry.

"The Russians have the greater half of all Europe and Asia and are land surfeited.

"The Japs are concentrated.

"The Russians are spread out.

"The Jap is an Islander and seafaring, a naval as well as a land fighter.

"The Russ is a landlubber, but a plodding fighter.

"The Jap is fighting in his own backyard.

"The Russ is fighting five thousand miles from home.

"The Jap is a teetotaler.

"The Russ is a hard drinker.

"The Jap has short legs.

"The Russ has long ones.

"The Jap has the sympathy of the Englishman, of the Yankee, or most of civilization.

"The Russ has few friends outside his country and has the incurred the just hatred of the world-wide Jew."

— March 2, 1904

READ WANT AD. COLUMNS

NA-1162-3 Glenbow Archives

The Edmonton-Calgary stagecoach was often mired in the mud.

A RELIEF FUND

"The Edmonton contribution to the Japanese Famine Relief Fund now amounts to $78.75. From Mr. Richard Secord, of the merchant firm McDougall and Secord, a contribution of ten dollars was yesterday received by The Journal."

— March 28, 1906

It's a Saturday and *The Journal* presents its first two-section newspaper, eight pages in the front, 10 pages in the back.

— March 10, 1906

NA-3190-1 Glenbow Archives

Gathering ice on the North Saskatchewan River.

NA-1334-2 Glenbow Archives

Homesteaders lined up at the Edmonton Land Titles Office on the southeast corner of 100th Avenue and 106th Street.

NA-989-2 Glenbow Archives

Trains, buses and wagons used the Low Level Bridge, shown here from the north end.

NA-303-33 Glenbow Archives

John Walter's ferry was replaced by the Walterdale Bridge.

Scavanger Work Done

Leave orders at the Fire Hall.

CAPITAL ENVY

"The city is in gala attire this afternoon to mark the opening of the first legislature of Alberta. Visitors from all parts of Alberta, members of the legislature and their wives, representatives of the press and professions, and politicians from neighbouring provinces are gathering in the city to be present at the opening ceremonies. The warmest controversy will range around the location of the provincial capital. Red Deer, Calgary and Edmonton will be strenuous rivals for the honour."

— March 15, 1906

ANNOYING BOYS

"Edmonton last night beat Wetaskiwin at baseball with a score of 6 runs to 5.

"An annoying feature of the game was the persistence with which a number of small boys continued to throw clods of grass at the players. This practice should be put a stop to, as it interferes with the play."

— July 22, 1905

NA-545-5 Glenbow Archives

THE GRANARY
OF THE EMPIRE

The archway at Jasper Avenue and 100th Street was nothing if not boastful. The Imperial Bank building is in the background.

Appleby & Armstrong,

Undertakers and Embalmers

Just received a shipment of the Latest Designs in Coffins and Caskets.

Calls. Day or Night promptly attended to. PHONE 223.

Hearse and Ambulance in Connection
Parlor over Larendeau Bros.' Store, Jasper Ave.

1909

How Does 16 p.c. On Your Money Strike You ?

We can sell you a dividend paying oil stock that will pay you the above. The company has just paid its 31st monthly dividend. See us.

Morris & Son
Stock and Share Dealers
619 First Street Edmonton

1909

ADVERTISING COPY

The ONLY specialist writer in Edmonton. Enquiries solicited.

H. Y. BURNETT
(Temporary Office.)
621 First Street.
Phone 2218.

STRESSFUL WEST NEEDS HOLIDAY

"The weekly half-holiday has been put into effect in a great number of important cities without causing appreciable inconvenience or loss of business, and a similar satisfactory result is to be expected in Edmonton. The holiday is, in the west, more essential than in other parts of the continent, for, in the west, life is at a higher pressure, the climate is more stimulating, business makes greater demands upon the nervous resources, and the need for a period of recuperation makes itself with unmistakable insistence."

— May 31, 1909,
editorial supporting Wednesday afternoon closings of retail outlets

"From a beauty standpoint the building formally dedicated last evening is an exact replica of the Alexandra school which was pressed into service last year with appropriate ceremonies."

— Feb. 27, 1909,
Norwood school opens

The subhead on a page 1 story on July 2, 1909, was typical, containing both comment and information: "Edmonton's Bunch of Back-Lot Ball Tossers Let Lethbridge Miners in for Three Runs on Costly Errors, While They Are Blanked – Game Uninteresting and Attendance Slim."

The paper also kept its readers abreast of more refined activities – lectures, the opera, vaudeville and early versions of movies.

The downtown Bijou Theatre on 100th Street and 101A Avenue took out an ad promising that "no pictures will be shown or anything said or done that can possibly offend the most refined taste."

Moving picture shows were still a novelty in 1903, although that didn't mean they were free of criticism.

A December 1903 review of *Peck's Bad Boy* was sharply critical. Instead of moving pictures, there was only a "common magic lantern show" accompanied "by a monotonous reading."

Touring companies brought the latest plays to town, and singers and lecturers added Edmonton to their circuits as well.

One early relationship nurtured by *The Evening Journal* was with Alberta College. The print shop business that helped finance the paper was proficient enough to get a contract to print the first catalogue for the newly built Alberta College.

This formed the foundation of a connection that lasted for years. And while there weren't many pictures in early papers – the technology was expensive and cumbersome – the first picture which appeared on Nov. 14, 1903, was that of Rev. Dr. J.H. Riddell, BA, principal of Alberta College. His words, usually in the form of sermons, often appeared in the paper.

And what of the three young men who started *The Evening Journal* in those hopeful, heady days in 1903?

The pipe-smoking Moore contracted what was called "printer's stomach," a slow form of lead poisoning. He reportedly sold his share in the paper back to the company in 1906 for $10,000.

He worked for a job printer in Edmonton until 1913, moved his family to Vancouver Island, working at the newspapers in Sydney and Victoria. He died of Spanish influenza in 1919 at the age of 43.

Cunningham stayed with the newspaper and remained as editor when it was sold to the Southams in 1912.

Macpherson was publisher until 1909 when the paper was sold to Vancouver's McConnell and moved to Montreal to work for the Canadian National Railway (CNR).

He served as an officer overseas in the First World War after which he returned to the CNR to work as purchasing agent.

In his spare time he wrote periodic stories for the *Montreal Gazette* on that's city's early history.

But regardless of their individual fates, what they started took root.

They gave Edmonton a newspaper that has endured.

***April 18, 1906*: *The Journal* reports as many as 10,000 people were killed in the great San Francisco earthquake. The City of Edmonton sends a $1,000 cheque to help with the relief efforts. Calgary sends $500.**

***April 24, 1906*: J. R. Boyle, MLA for Sturgeon, suggests an amendment to the Automobile Bill that would set a speed limit of five miles an hour when nearing a team of horses. "He had set the limit at five miles because he understood that an automobile could not be run at a less speed without considerable difficulty and a great deal more noise."**

***May 3, 1906*: Premier Alexander Rutherford's first budget calls for a total expenditure of $127,806.67.**

***May 21, 1906*: *The Journal* publishes a picture of the members of the first Alberta legislature on the steps of the McKay Avenue school. The caption reads: "The photograph is an excellent one and reflects the greatest credit on the photographer."**

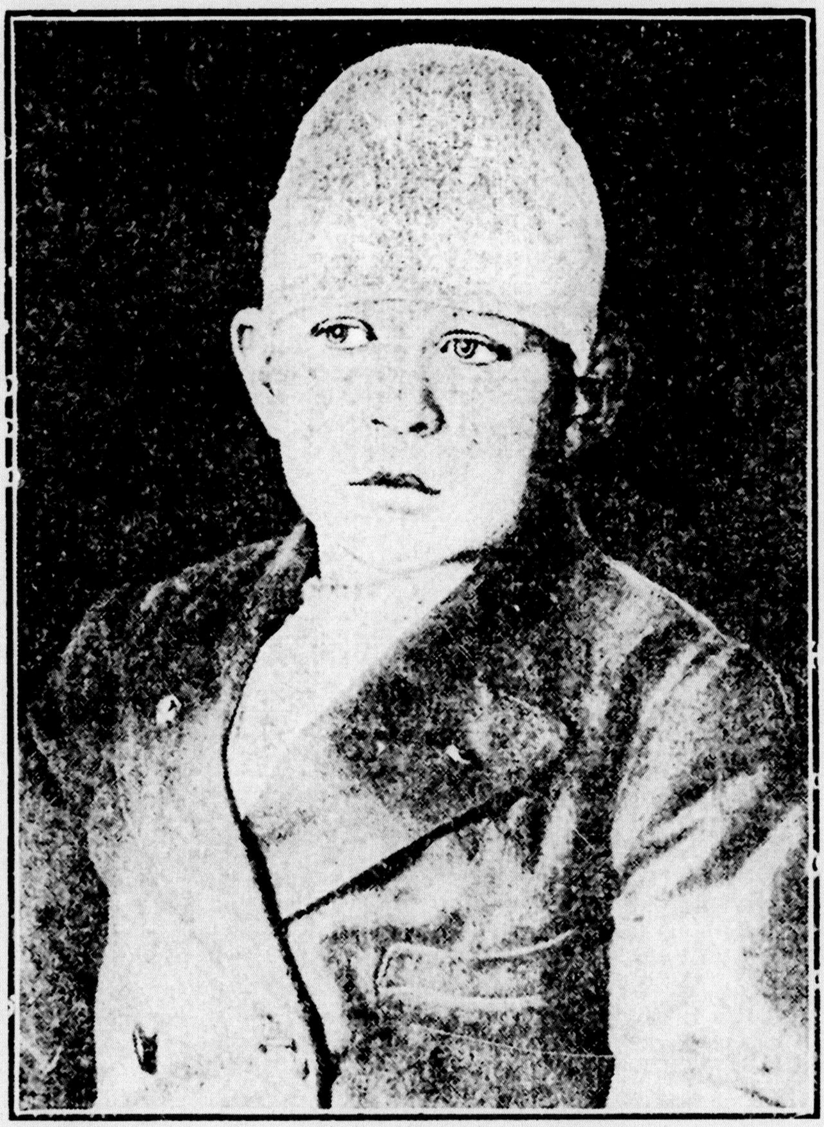

THIS BOY WAS SAVED FROM JAIL BY OPERATION

Christopher Halin, 12 years old, ha s been converted from "on of the worst boys in the city," to one of the best, b y means of surgery. .For nearly a year, he has been regarded as a terror, and af ter a number of offences he finally landed at the House of Detention, where h e was threatened with being sent to a reformatory.

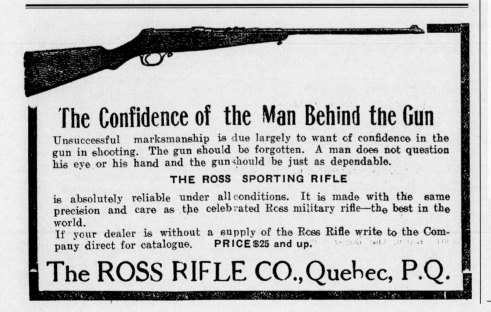

TERRIFIED INTO SILENCE

Black Hand, With Threats of Wholesale Assassination, Terrorize Community Into Suppressing Name of Murderer of Children—Surviving Victim Refuses to Divulge Assassin's Identity

UTICA, N.Y., Sept. 14.—Black Hand threats of wholesale assassination by dynamite, knives and pistols have apparently thrown the foreign colony of Utica into such a panic that it will never tell the names of the men who kidnapped the Infusino children and shot Freddie Infusino and Theresa Procopico to death. Tonight Fannie Infusino is lying at the point of death at the city hospital, and declares that she does not know the name of the assailant who kidnapped all three and shot them, on the outskirts of the city where they were found. Her father also declares that he cannot tell the name of the assassin. But it is known that the dying girl told the name to the woman who found her, and that she told it also to her father. The police believe that the girl and her father could give some clue to the crime but will not, for fear of further vengeance at the hands of the Camorra. Fanny Infusino, picked up half dead and brought to the house of Mrs. Gray 12 hours after the shooting, gave Mrs. Gray the name of the assailant. The woman, an American unfamiliar with Italian, failed either to put down or to remember it, and after young Freddie and the Procopico child were dead of their wounds the police were forced to go to Fanny for information.

Meanwhile the wounded girl had been visited by her father. After that visit she refused absolutely to speak, said she had been wrong in naming any man as her assailant, and did not know who it was that attacked the three. It did no good to promise her father the $4,000 that had been offered by the newspapers and the police for information leading to the arrest of the slayer-kidnapper. Infusino has been put under the third degree, but steadily insists neither his daughter or his son has divulged the slayer's name. His daughter, who will probably recover, has been put in a solitary ward in the hospital in the hope that she may give the police the clue that she tried to give Mrs. Gray before her lips were sealed.

Murder, Most Foul

"ON THE LONG TRAIL WITH DAWN OF DAY"

"Charles King, the Murderer of Hayward, Sees the Sun Rise for the Last Time as He Mounts the Scaffold at the Barracks of Fort Saskatchewan

Standing Beside the Fatal Drop at the Last Moment of His Life He Declares His Executioners are Hanging an Innocent Man. Officials and Reporters Only Witnesses of the Law's Penalty."

— Lengthy headline from Charles King's hanging, Sept. 10, 1905

***May 28, 1906*: There's a fire in *The Journal* building, but it doesn't burn down. Wesley Ingram, an employee of the Alberta Milling Company, spots smoke coming from a front window at noon. He breaks into the structure and throws a basin of water and pot of mixed lye on an electric motor that was overheating.**

The weather was unseasonably warm on March 9, 1905, when courtroom spectators, sitting shoulder-to-sweltering-shoulder, waited for the verdict in the biggest murder trial in the city's young history.

If the six-man jury returned with a guilty verdict, Charles King, the moustachioed, auburn-haired trapper/prospector who stood accused of murdering his partner, Edward Hayward, would most certainly hang.

The Journal had previously reported in great detail the evidence of the 71 witnesses at King's trial.

Twenty-four of those 71 were Indians from the Sucker Creek Reserve near Slave Lake where the murder occurred.

Readers learned that the Indians had become suspicious when they heard a gunshot ring out from the encampment shared by King and Hayward on the shores of Lesser Slave Lake.

They had fresh misgivings when they noticed that a dog owned by Hayward refused to obey, or even follow, King.

It was enough to cause them to send a 14-year-old boy, the son of Sucker Creek's Chief Moostoos, to the campsite where he sifted through the ashes of a large campfire with the rather sinister dimensions of six-by-three feet.

The boy's macabre discoveries included what might have been a tooth and possibly some skull bones. The grisly findings were given to the Royal North West Mounted Police (RNWMP) who arrested King and charged him with Hayward's murder.

The trial that followed was the sensation of the season.

Because of the number of witnesses and a defence suggestion that Hayward may simply have gone off by himself – there was no body, after all – the trial lasted almost two weeks.

Nevertheless, jury deliberations were swift, and the sentence was pronounced: Charles King would swing.

The trial was front-page news from the beginning. While there was great interest in the trial evidence, the newspaper was also fascinated by the Indians who had been brought to the city and were living in tents in the RNWMP compound on 96th Street and 101 Avenue.

On Feb. 25, the paper paid tribute to the Indian witnesses: "The chief points which were brought out by the evidence was the splendid work done by the RNWMP, who have already proved by their prompt and decisive actions

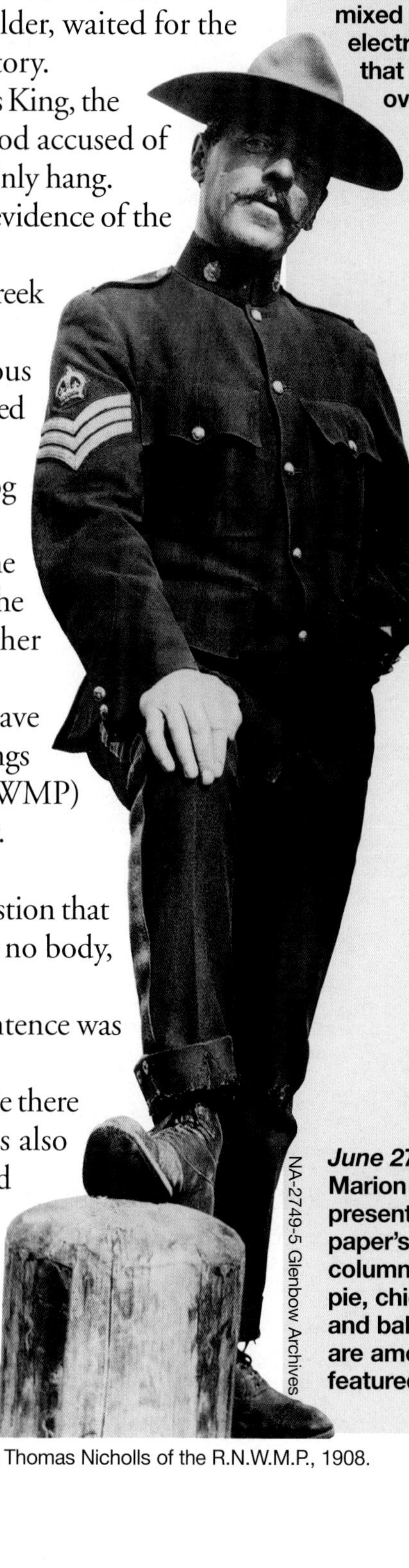

NA-2749-5 Glenbow Archives

Sgt. Thomas Nicholls of the R.N.W.M.P., 1908.

***June 27, 1906*: Marion Harland presents the paper's first recipe column. Mince pie, chicken pie and baked beans are among the featured items.**

NC-6-6898 Glenbow Archives

Commonwealth Stadium and Clarke Park now sit on land once occupied by the Edmonton Penitentiary.

CITY'S PROVINCIAL FAIR FREE FROM CALGARY'S DRUNKEN, SHAMEFUL WAYS

"Only three arrests were made this year inside the show grounds at the Provincial Fair. This is a showing of great credit and pride to the Association and particularly to Edmonton, and that our streets are notably free from the obnoxious and discreditable scenes seen so frequently in western towns. A Calgary gentleman who was up attending the fair was greatly astonished as the almost entire absence of signs of drunkenness or disorderly conduct. He said he saw only one intoxicated man during the four days.

"When informed that during the four days only three arrests had been made, he was more than visibly surprised.

"Why," he said, "in Calgary we would have had 30."

—July 7, 1906

THE BUCKEYE

Vol. I EDMONTON, ALBERTA, THURSDAY, OCTOBER 28, 1909. No. 8.

BUCKEYE

His Master's Choice

P.S.—Even the dog appreciates his Master's BUCKEYE. The dog knows, follow him.

1909

GRIM WALLS OF ATONEMENT

"While the city of Edmonton has been advancing by leaps and bounds in every line, and the citizens have going their several busy ways, there have been things doing at the penitentiary in the east end of the city that would surprise many because of their magnitude. Behind the grim walls that enclose the prison yard a band of men, some sixty-five in number, are atoning for their misdemeanours."

—**June 10, 1907**, feature story on the federal pen on the site where Clarke Stadium would be built.

SHE WAS TOO SENSITIVE

Winnipeg, Oct. 30.—Mrs. James Casemore, a boardinghouse keeper, on Martha Street, took carbolic acid and died soon after. Two burglars were discovered in her house as roomers recently and the stigma preyed on her mind

GOOD TIMES FOR LAWYERS IN OLD DAYS

Twenty-five Dollars For Drawing Mortgage—Hundred Dollar Fee For Police Court Case—Conditions Now Less Remunerative

MEMBERS OF OLD TIME BAR HAVE SCATTERED

Only Three Now in City—Death Has Laid Its Hand on Two—Others Have Removed Elsewhere

That the city of Edmonton has passed through a series of kaleidoscopic changes is well known to all who have been in the city for a few years, but it is more apparent to those who have had the fortune to live here for the past quarter of a century and watch its development from a mere trading point to one of the most important commercial centres in Western Canada....

BOATS FOR SALE

Clinker Built, 4x16

Suitable for lake resorts or rivers.

JOHN WALTER

Ferry crossing Strathcona.

P.O. Box 116, Strathcona Phone 3040

in this case that they are still the men who kept law and order in the days before the tide of civilization had set in through the northern portion of the Great West.

"Their work, however, might have been delayed for some time and rendered much more difficult had it not been for the able co-operation of the Indians of Sucker Creek Reserve, urged on by their chief Moostoos.

"The Indians are very superstitious and very curious. This latter trait, together with their wonderful intuition, quickness and accuracy of observation, combined to make them the finest of bush detectives. A broken branch, a strange track, an unexpected noise, immediately invites them to an investigation."

And there was no denying the paper regarded the Indians as quaint vestiges of a time fast disappearing.

"On their first occasion of hearing the train whistle as it came from Strathcona to Edmonton, they hurried to the riverbank eagerly watching for a view of the fiery monster and hailing its approach with a series of grunts and expressions of profound astonishment....

"After the trial, they might be observed stretched at full-length upon the sidewalk watching through the basement windows the game going on in the bowling alley below the courtroom, and evincing great pleasure whenever an extra fine shot was made."

But if *The Journal* found the Indians exotic, the unidentified reporter who covered King's hanging pulled out all the melodramatic stops.

The story on Sept. 30 painted a lurid, and somewhat sympathetic, portrait of the doomed man as he faced his end.

In his final statement he insisted he was guiltless. "I do not know what you are hanging me for. I am an innocent man, I have nothing to hang for. God knows I would not have that crime on my mind for killing him," he concluded, staring his executioner directly in the face.

The reporter went on: "It would seem that King had lived his boyhood an orphan waif, his youth amidst the scenes that never lifted up above the common earth, struggling daily for existence, buffeted by the storms of the world, thrown on his own resources with nothing to inspire him to a higher endeavour than the gain of barter and the trader's chance. No one to warm his soul with friendship's sympathy and communion, no one to teach him the sacredness of his own life and that of his brother.

"Where was his birth place, his parental home? Who was his mother, his father? Had he sisters or brothers, a sweetheart or friend of his heart?"

The Journal speculated that the murder might have been an act of self-defence that had simply gone too far. Perhaps Hayward was partly responsible.

"A partner with a hasty temper and perhaps a bullying manner as an impetuous aggressive Englishman such as Hayward, the sailor, the miner, the wanderer in many lands would likely be, a threatening act, and what then? A lifted gun by King, a hasty pull of the trigger, a shot in the dark and the deed was done, and then remained an ignorant man's only conception of self-defence, to hale the body of the victim of his hasty work on the camp fire, to pile high the poplar shrubs for a pyre in an endeavour to cover up all traces of the deed.

"Charles King was one of the earth's unfortunates. He seemed to have reached manhood's desire without coming in contact with religious thought, to have simply grown up without a good conception of a high life to guide or inspire him."

***Aug. 13, 1906*:**
First issue of *The Morning Journal*, four pages, six columns is published. It lasts until 1911.

***Sept. 11, 1906*:**
A new theatre is to be built on 3rd Street and Jasper Avenue. It will seat 1,000 people, according to a *Journal* story. It opens one month later as The New Edmonton Opera House making it, "probably the quickest constructed place of its kind," according a *Journal* review on Oct. 12.

***Sept. 17, 1906*:**
A weeklong strike of construction workers begins. The workers would win their demand of $2.50 a day in wages but, more importantly, The Journal notes a change in attitude among them. "A large number of the labouring class in the city are Galicians, and they are becoming conscious of their individuality and power, and active leaders are springing up among them...Pete Rotter, a young man of splendid physique and intelligent bearing, is one of their leaders and professes to be a strong union man."

***Oct. 12, 1906*:**
The location for the provincial legislature is chosen. It is to be built on the

Deputy-Warden Victim of Convicts Awful "Grouch"

No Motive But Moroseness Accountable For Lifer's Bloody Deed

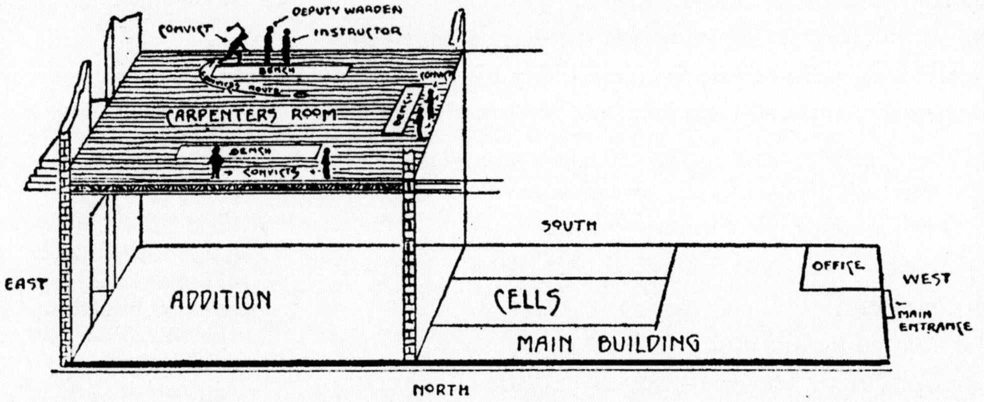

DEPUTY WARDEN
CONVICT
INSTRUCTOR
BENCH
CARPENTERS ROOM
BENCH
CONVICTS
SOUTH
EAST
ADDITION
CELLS
OFFICE
WEST
MAIN ENTRANCE
MAIN BUILDING
NORTH

Above is the sketch of the carpenter room in which the murder of Deputy Warden Stedman took place. There is a slight inaccuracy in the sketch, in that the instructor should be marked as on the opposite side of the bench of the

working, and leaning his arms on the bench, looked at the chain Pope showed him. "I have put a new link in this, Stedman," said Pope. "That's good," said the deputy." These were the last words he spoke. Even before the last word had left his lips, Pope

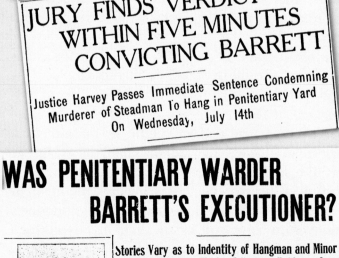

JURY FINDS VERDICT WITHIN FIVE MINUTES CONVICTING BARRETT

Justice Harvey Passes Immediate Sentence Condemning Murderer of Steadman To Hang in Penitentiary Yard On Wednesday, July 14th

WAS PENITENTIARY WARDER BARRETT'S EXECUTIONER?

Stories Vary as to Indentity of Hangman and Minor Details Point to Work of Novice---Evidence Connects Penitentiary, Guard With Execution of Laws Sentence---Belief That Barrett Was Insane--Ante-Mortem Statement Cut Short

Although the theory is neither admitted nor denied by the officials connected with the execution of Gary Barrett this

but the date nor place of interment has not yet been made known.

BARRETT EXECUTED

CLOSE SHAVE

Battleford, May 4.—John Barr, a well known resident, was shot at by Walter Salsbury of Hennietta, but a buckle saved his life. The trouble arose over a horse trade. Salsbury is connected with the Government telegraph service

"Alex. Johnson, an Edmonton youth, while riding horseback along the paved streets last evening, was thrown from his steed at the corner of Kinistino and Jasper when the animal took fright at a passing automobile, and was rendered unconscious. He was hurried to the public hospital, where his injuries were discovered not to be serious. He will be about again in a day or two."

—July 3, 1909

READ WANT AD. COLUMNS

NO CIGARETTES UNDER SIXTEEN

Senate Reduces the Age at Which It Is Lawful To Smoke

(Western Associated Press)

Ottawa, July 10.—The Senate on a vote of 33 to 13, adopted an amendment moved by Senator Power to a bill to restrain the use of tobacco by young persons, fixing the prohibitive limit at 16 instead of 18 years. The discussion on the point was quite animated.

Senator Lougheed declared that the best men Canada sent to South Africa were less than eighteen and one of them returned with the Victoria Cross.

BUTTING OUT

"The passing of the cigar machines in the city was of short duration. A few days ago the chief of police made the rounds of the cigar stores and informed the proprietors that they must remove these machines from the counters. To this they at first acquiesced, but after consultation with their lawyers they decided that the chief was exceeding his powers and that the merry hum of the machine is once more heard in the majority of cigar stores in the city."

—Jan. 25, 1909

"Mr. J.R. Boyle, member for Sturgeon, referred to the fact that nearly all were brought up in a free country where it was the custom of every free-born son of the soil, when he had reached a proper age, to go out and shoot game. This was one of the privileges that citizens of this country had long enjoyed, and that Europeans had been denied. He considered it a valued privilege, and he did not think it should be lightly taken away."

— March 1, 1907, story on a debate in the legislature of The Game Act and the licencing of hunters.

1906

Hangman's Bluff

"His action also in cutting up the rope and handing it to spectators in small sections also was unlike official executioners, who generally refuse to do so as they are generally anxious to get as far from the scene as possible."
— From coverage of Garry Barrett's hanging, July 15, 1909

There was absolutely no mystery to the April 15, 1909, axe murder of Richard A. Stedman, the popular deputy warden of the Edmonton Penitentiary, located at East Jasper Avenue and 92nd Street, near the present-day site of Clarke Park.

The deputy lay dead on the carpentry shop floor as Garry R. Barrett, an inmate already serving a life sentence for murder, calmly used his apron to clean the blood and gore from the heavy Hudson's Bay axe.

The trial was speedy and justice quick. Within three months Barrett mounted the gallows steps to be hanged. That, however, is where the mystery in The Case of the Carpentry Shop Murder began.

The date for the hanging was July 14 and Radcliffe, the well-known executioner, had arrived a few days earlier from Regina and was staying at the Strathcona Hotel.

The rather overweight Radcliffe had been here before, most notably for the hanging of Charles King in 1905, and was celebrated for his flawless gallows technique. He was, apparently, quick at his job and kept suffering to a minimum.

But when Barrett trudged up the gallows stairs it wasn't Radcliffe who waited to pull the trap.

RICHARD H. STEDMAN
The Murdered Deputy Warden of the Edmonton Penitentiary

Instead, there was a man wearing a false moustache who kept his back to the crowd that had gathered to watch Barrett die.

One of the witnesses interviewed following the execution pointed out that the hangman was wearing a standard prison guard suit and heavy prison guard boots. It certainly wasn't Radcliffe.

According to story, it was a clumsy job right from the beginning. The man posing as the executioner didn't appear to know what he was doing.

The paper, however, was generous in its reporting of the event. "Despite the fact that the execution was carried out in a very satisfactory manner, there were certain minor details which tend to show the executioner was an amateur at the work," readers were told on July 15.

"Among those was the fact that in adjusting the noose he did so before the doomed man was allowed to speak, and as a result the knot loosened. Also instead of drawing the noose tight under the left ear, according to Hoyle, it was placed a little to one side, with the result that instead of tightening under the ear when the drop was sprung it slipped on one side and caught over the mouth."

The question of who executed Barrett was never answered. Was it a prison guard seeking very personal revenge?

What happened to Radcliffe? Did he leave town *before* the execution? Was he ordered *not* to show up on that fateful morning?

Prison officials refused comment.

grounds north of the old Fort Edmonton. "Now that the site question is settled, preparation of the plans for the handsome architectural pile will be rushed and no doubt work on the excavation will begin immediately," the paper says.

***Nov. 13, 1906*: City council decides to experiment with paving the streets using two different methods to find out which one is best. Edmonton's annual Paving Festival begins in the spring of 1907 on Jasper Avenue.**

***April 7, 1907*: Strathcona is chosen as the site of the new University of Alberta.**

The J. Robert Black Collection, Edmonton

Edmonton's last Eskimo hockey club. Joe Simpson and Duke Keats, below, are Hall of Fame members.

Joe Simpson

"Duke" Keats

The J. Robert Black Collection, Edmonton

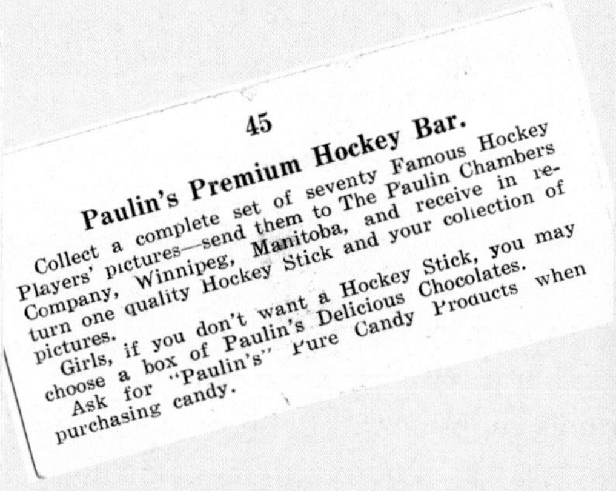

45

Paulin's Premium Hockey Bar.

Collect a complete set of seventy Famous Hockey Players' pictures—send them to The Paulin Chambers Company, Winnipeg, Manitoba, and receive in return one quality Hockey Stick and your collection of pictures.

Girls, if you don't want a Hockey Stick, you may choose a box of Paulin's Delicious Chocolates.

Ask for "Paulin's" Pure Candy Products when purchasing candy.

Win a hockey stick with the collection of all the player cards from the Paulin Company.
Girls had the option of winning chocolates rather than a hockey stick.

The Farmer's Underwear.
Ordinary underwear is not warm enough for a farmer. Working about the farm—out all day in the cold—he must be warmer than regular weight underwear can keep him.
Stanfield's Unshrinkable Underwear
is made in special weights for farmers. The finest Nova Scotia wool—knitted in a peculiar way—makes "Stanfield's" doubly warm, without any increase in weight or bulk.
The right size for every figure—and every garment guaranteed unshrinkable.

When The Servant "Gives Notice"---The Journal Want Ads. Are Important To You.

WANTED—A good general servant girl; no washing. Apply at Snow Flake Steam Laundry.

LESSONS given in French, German by a Parisian, Latin Greek, Mathematics, Shorthand. Drawing by an Englishman (Cambridge man.)
Box 108, Journal office.

GOOD BOARD—and room; $4.50 per week. Without room $3.50, Dominion Dining Hall, Queen's Avenue. E. Withinshaw, proprietor.

WANTED—A girl who will work for her board and go to school, in a family of two. Apply Box 93, Journal Office.

Japanese, young boy, desires to be employed for cook in family of the town or country. Hide, P.O. Box 109. Edmonton.

WANTED—Girl for general housework. One who can go home nights preferred. Apply Mrs. T. H. Greenway, corner Queens and Second St.

WANTED—A good general servant apply to Mrs. R. Secord.

WANTED—Boy so work for Journal. Apply at this office at once.

WANTED—Awidow, respectable, wishes work daily. Adress Box 134, Journal office.

The Little Tigers

"The Edmonton team are in splendid fighting trim for the first game in the Stanley Cup series tonight. As a last message to the Edmonton fans before the game, the boys state that they will gobble up the defenders of the old mug in a way that will surprise Montreal fans."

— From a story preceding game one of the two-game Stanley Cup final, Dec. 28, 1908

It began with a letter written in August 1908 by James A. MacKinnon, the president of the Edmonton Eskimos hockey club, a team from a city that was even then crazy about the game.

The Eskimos had been repeat winners of the Interprovincial Hockey League, made up of squads from Alberta and Saskatchewan, and felt they were ready for the big time.

What MacKinnon wanted was simple: the Stanley Cup, held by the Montreal Wanderers.

Back then it was a challenge cup, and any team that thought it had the moxie could step up to centre ice and take a shot. And if MacKinnon and the boys thought they were good enough, so did *The Journal*.

It was up to the Ottawa-based trustees of Lord Stanley's Cup to sort out the pretenders from the contenders. In their wisdom they decided the Edmonton Eskimos were a contender, and a two-game, total-goal series was arranged for the end of December.

All the team had to do was get itself to Montreal, prepared to play.

A story on Sept. 10, 1908, made this plea to readers:

"Any person interested in Edmonton, its advancement, glorification and extension, who has not already had this date, the importance thereof, scorched into his comprehension is hereby requisitioned to sit up and take notice."

A meeting was held that night in the Young Liberal clubrooms on Jasper Avenue where details such as financing were discussed.

The team needed $2,500 to get to Montreal, but that would be a bargain, *The Journal* promised.

At least a million dollars worth of good publicity would come from the team's appearance in the championship series.

"The man who stays away from this meeting is no patriot," the story concluded.

The money was raised and in mid-December the team boarded an eastbound Canadian Northern Railway train.

Player/coach Fred Whitcroft called his team "little tigers" but also had to counteract rumours that the Eskimos were made up of millionaire ringers, hired by rich Edmonton businessmen.

A *Journal* story backed the coach up. The Eskimos were, in fact, "cheap" despite the addition of future National Hockey League Hall of Famer Lester Patrick to the lineup. Patrick had left the Montreal Wanderers a year earlier and had gone to work in his father's lumber mill in Nelson, B.C.

The Journal's coverage was extensive. "Edmonton Will Battle To-Night for World's Hockey Championship," a headline screamed Dec. 26.

***June 1, 1907*: Home mail delivery comes to Edmonton – the only postmen between Winnipeg and Vancouver. *The Journal* offers this advice: "Don't forget to have your letter carefully addressed with the numbers. Don't forget to have your number clearly and prominently displayed on your house...."**

***June 7, 1907*: Construction begins on a "mammoth meat packing plant" in northeast Edmonton. A *Journal* story says the plant will mean 300 new jobs for the city.**

Bill Miner.

***June 8, 1907*: Five men die in a burning coal mine in Strathcona. Pit foreman, George Lamb, loses his life trying to save his co-workers.**

***July 11, 1907*: A bylaw is passed allowing for an incline railway to be built up the riverbank on the hill on 1st Street. It opens May 20, 1908.**

1906

Social Tragedy

Women Who Brave Death for Social Honors.

In the midst of one of the most brilliant social functions of the season, a noted society woman started suddenly from her chair with a scream of agony and fell insensible to the floor.

A few hours later the distinguished physician told her anxious husband that she was suffering from an acute case of nervous prostration brought on by female trouble, and hinted at an operation. Fortunately a friend advised her to try

Lydia E. Pinkham's Vegetable Compound

The result was that she escaped the surgeon's knife and to-day is a well woman.

The derangement of the delicate female organism sets every nerve in the body quivering with pain. Headaches, backaches, torturing bearing down pains and dragging sensations make women nervous and hysterical.

Mrs. T. E. Gillis, of Windsor, N. S., writes:

Dear Mrs. Pinkham:—When I commenced to take Lydia E. Pinkham's Vegetable Compound I was suffering with weakness and female trouble, headaches, backaches, and that worn-out, tired feeling. I have only taken the Vegetable Compound a few short weeks, and it has made me well, strong and robust. I believe that Lydia E. Pinkham's Vegetable Compound is without equal for female troubles.

Mrs. Laura Emmons, President Loyal Home Workers, Walkerville, Ont., writes:

Dear Mrs. Pinkham,—I am enjoying such good health that I feel it a duty to write and thank you for what Lydia E. Pinkham's Vegetable Compound has done for me. I suffered for more than five years with functional troubles, causing an unpleasant discharge and weakness which no amount of medicine, diet or exercise seemed to correct. Your Vegetable Compound, however, reached the root of my trouble, cured me and made me strong, healthy and well. I want to say to every suffering woman, don't dally with medicines you know nothing about, but take Lydia E. Pinkham's Vegetable Compound.

Mrs. Pinkham's advice is free to all. Her address is Lynn, Mass.

Lydia E. Pinkham's Vegetable Compound Cures Where Others Fail

SUSPICIOUS OF WOMAN WHO SMOKES

English Antiquarian Detained at Ellis Island Because She was Devotee of My Lady Nicotine—Doctor Thought She Must Be Insane — Has Smoked for Twenty-seven Years

NEW YORK, Aug. 30.—Mrs. Bessie Hill was detained at Ellis Island for examination by the immigration authorities because she smoked cigarettes on the steamship Philadelphia. She declared at the Hotel S. Denis that she was going to protest to England through the British consul here. Mrs. Bessie was taken to the Island Saturday and was not released until late on Monday. She reached the hotel at 6 p.m. and immediately cabled her friends in London.

"I came over to America for the first time to see two women of wealth and fashion. I am an antiquarian and have had a shop in the west end of London for years," she said. "I came across second class because I could not get a first-class berth. The whole trouble resulted from my habit of smoking cigarettes and cigars. I have been smoking them for 27 years.

"Coming over on the boat I could not smoke cigarettes on deck. There was nowhere else for me to go but the men's cabin. I smoked them there and once joined the men in a game of poker."

"Did you win?" she was asked.

"Yes one night I won $24."

"I was smoking a cigarette when I went for examination before the immigration doctor. That settled it. He evidently decided that I was not in my right mind. I was bundled into a barge, landed in a detention pen with rough men and women, and finally turned over to a nurse, who treated me as if I was insane. Finally my protests were listened to by Drs. Thornton and McMillan, and I was then handsomely treated and finally released."

PROOF ON THE DOORSTEP

"Two townsmen have within a week spoken to The Journal to the effect that they have on several afternoons had occasion to walk along various streets in the most thickly populated districts of the city. They have passed by shortly after the newsboys have gone their rounds with the evening papers and they have noted with interest the surprisingly large number of houses at which The Journal had been left.

"It means a lot to be The Paper on the Doorstep. It means being in touch with people. It means being the daily news supply of a large percentage of the population. It means being the accepted medium between the people and the business interests that want to reach the people."

— Sept. 30, 1907

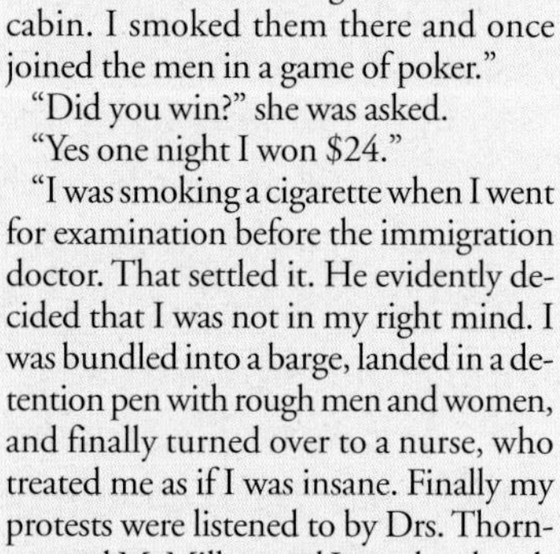

HAVE ONE YOURSELF

You will have no trouble securing the right girl, if we supply the livery turnout. Phone 1234.

HORNER'S LIVERY

"Line-up of Challengers Looks Like The Real Thing and Montreal Fans Entertain Feeling of Uneasiness," read the first subhead.

The second subhead should have put to rest any worries among those Edmontonians who were concerned about their collective $2,500: "Battalions of Eastern Dope Writers Camped at Montreal to Watch Progress of Events – Whole Broadsides of Advertising for Edmonton – Palace Car Loaded with Western Enthusiasts Arrives in Time to Witness the Big Struggle."

The story was puffed with pride.

"Not since hockey became a game in Canada has there ever been a team sent east which showed so many of the surface indications of greatness and the Montreal fans at once realized that the Wanderers' clutch on the Cup was as good as lost unless fortune favoured their idols."

Alas, fortune *did* favour their idols, much to the dismay of the hundreds of fans who crowded a half-dozen Edmonton cigar stores, the Orpheum Theatre, the Edmonton Opera House and the King Edward and Cecil hotels to follow the play-by-play via special wire direct from *The Journal*'s man in the press box.

Reports of the first game – the Eskimos lost 7-3 – consumed countless columns filled with meticulous detail.

Despite the score, The Journal Man, as the unidentified reporter was called, thought it quite wonderful.

"The struggle was a grand one, and the boys from the West met defeat fighting desperately and with courage undaunted even at the finish."

What's more, Lester Patrick told The Journal Man that it was the greatest game in which he had ever played.

Nevertheless, in order to claim hockey's hallowed chalice, the Eskimos needed to win the second game by four goals.

The Eskimos won the second game, but only by a single goal.

Regardless, a rather lengthy headline was unbowed:

"Only the Malevolent Machinations of the Goddess of Fortune Responsible for Failure to Bring Historic Mug to Capital of Alberta But Moorings of Trophy Have Been Badly Wrenched and Another Try Will Be Made to Move Canada's National Championship Westward."

Not so, said a somewhat bitter A.M. Stuart who had taken over as club president. There would be no more challenges. The team had fallen apart.

Bert Lindsay, the goalie, deserted the team after it stopped in Ottawa "and hasn't been seen since," Stuart told the paper.

He even missed the Ottawa banquet hosted by Frank Oliver and his wife.

Centreman Charlie Vair was called out of the banquet room and never returned, and defenceman Didier Petrie came in for some heavy criticism.

"We discharged Petrie because he persistently displayed a yellow streak," Stuart told *The Journal*.

"In the first game, in the first few minutes, he got a nasty knock on the face that cut open his nose, and after that he shirked his work."

Stuart was wrong about another challenge.

Two years later the Eskimos tried again.

And once again they lost to the Wanderers.

***July 18, 1907*:**
A reception is held as part of the opening ceremonies of the new Edmonton Club, an imposing brick structure that cost $22,000 to build and $8,000 to furnish. It is torn down in the 1970s to make way for McCauley Plaza.

***Aug. 10, 1907*:**
Bill Miner, who committed the first train robbery in Canada's history, escapes from jail and goes on the lam. His bold attacks on the unpopular CPR made him a hero to many Western Canadians and when he escaped from prison in Canada, *The Journal* devoted a half-page to his exploits. The movie *The Grey Fox* will be based on his life.

SPEEDY SKATERS.

Kenny Blatchford, wrestler and skater, has deposited $100 with the Sporting Editor of The Journal to meet any skater in the North West. He is willing to make this $300, but will not race for less than $100. Distance and date to be arranged.

O. B. Bush has deposited $50 as a side bet to meet R. Newmarch, distance ¼ mile, race to be held within five days.

***July 10, 1908*:**
George B. Cooper joins *The Journal*'s office staff. He retired in 1951 after 42 years as advertising manager.

THE EVENING JOURNAL.

VOL. 2, No 249. EDMONTON, ALBERTA, SATURDAY, SEPTEMBER 2, 1905. PRICE FIVE CENTS.

Alberta, a Province.

HISTORY IN THE MAKING IN ALBERTA'S NEW CAPITAL,

Inauguration of the Province Marked by Fine Weather, a Big Crowd, an Impressive Ceremony, Games, and Military Review.

Mayor Mackenzie then read the civic address of congratulation, to which His Honor replied in a speech that created a favorable impression.

The following is the civic address presented by Mayor Mackenzie to the Lieutenant-Governor.

To His Honor George Hedley Vicars Bulyea, Lieutenant-Governor of the Province of Alberta.

Your Honour:—

It is with the greatest pleasure that the Mayor and Corporation of the City of Edmonton welcome you to the city where, for a time at least, your duties will require you to reside. We congratulate your Honour upon your having been chosen to represent His Ma-

...Lord one thousand nine hundred and five.

Mayor K. W. Mackenzie.
Sec.—Treas. G. J. Kinnaird

LIEUT-GOVERNOR REPLIES.

The Lieutenant-Governor in acknowledging the congratulation of His Excellency Earl Grey, the Premier and Lady Laurier, the city and the other distinguished visitors who were seated near him on the platform, said in part'

This is a solemn day to a great many and to none does it appeal to more than to me. Grave responsibilities are laid upon the people of the province and grave responsibilities upon myself, upon whom the honor of representing His Majesty, the King, in the new province of Alberta ... conferred. But realizing ...

A. C. Rutherford, Premier of Alberta.

A. C. Rutherford, M.L.A., of Strathcona, was sworn in as Premier of Alberta this morning by His Honor Lieutenant-Governor Bulyea. The ceremony was held at Strathcona. C. K. Cross, who will run as Liberal member in the Edmonton constituency, is slated for the portfolio of the secretary and Attorney-Generalship and W. H. Cushing, who will be Liberal candidate for Calgary, for the Public Works. The portfolio of of education and agriculture is likely to be given to southern representa- education of education and agricultu

the delight of his compatriots in Alberta.

Hon. William Paterson, Minister of Customs, and Sir Gilbert Parker, the popular Canadian novelist and historian, delivered ringing patriotic speeches which evoked great applause Three cheers for the king closed the historic ceremony.

...the swearing-in ceremony

His Excellency did not leave until after supper and entered with evident pleasure into the evening's festivities.

The supper was served in the skating rink adjoining, which was fitted up tastefully for the occa... The home-going waltz wa... and the inaugural...

Earl Grey's
INAUGURAL ADDRESS

NA-919-48 Glenbow Archives

Earl Grey was one of many speakers on Sept. 1,1905, when Alberta became a province.

STRENUOUS BUT WARM RIVALRY

"The city is in gala attire this afternoon to mark the opening of the first legislature of Alberta. Visitors from all parts of Alberta, members of the legislature and their wives, representatives of the press and professions, and politicians from neighbouring provinces are gathering in the city to be present at the opening ceremonies. The warmest controversy will range around the location of the provincial capital. Red Deer, Calgary and Edmonton will be strenuous rivals for the honour."

— March 15, 1906

NEWS, IS NEWS

"Tom Groat, the well-known son of Malcolm Groat was stricken suddenly with paralysis at eight o'clock on Saturday evening in the rotunda of the Richelieu Hotel. He was reading the evening paper when he suddenly and without warning fell to the floor speechless and powerless.

"It is with relief that Mr. Groat's friends will learn that he is improving. This morning he is able to sit up in bed but wants not to speak much."

— Feb. 24, 1906

A Bold Undertaking

"Sir Wilfrid Laurier in eloquent terms, congratulated the people, on the new honour, and his pleasure at being present at the auspicious event."
— From coverage of Inauguration Day, Sept. 2, 1905

"Alberta, a Province" shouted the headline on the top of page 1 in the largest type size possible on Saturday, Sept. 5, 1905.

It was a bold headline for a bold undertaking.

By *Journal* reports, that first day as a province turned into a pretty fair party, too, as thousands of Albertans gathered at the present site of Telus Field to hear their new status proclaimed.

In the florid writing style of the day, the unidentified reporter didn't skimp on the use of superlatives as he covered the speeches of Governor General Earl Grey, Prime Minister Wilfrid Laurier, George Bulyea, the recently appointed lieutenant-governor of the province of Alberta, and Mayor K.W. Mackenzie.

With the boosterism expected of a loyal Edmonton newspaper reporter, he wrote: "With glorious Alberta sunshine, amid the cheers of thousands of the strong-armed, loyal and true-hearted citizens of the new province, before a sea of expectant faces of the fair daughters of a fair land, Alberta was proclaimed a province, a bright jewel in the constellation of the Empire."

Indeed, the city had never looked better. Merchants decorated their windows with displays predicting a bright, shiny future. Weeds in ditches, alleys and other public places had been cut. Readers were urged in daily front-page stories to decorate their houses with bunting.

Power, they read, would be free on Inauguration Day, and thousands of newly strung lights promised to turn Alberta night into day just as soon as all the speechifying was done and the sun set. In fact, power officials were a little concerned. With 1,000 new light bulbs installed at the Thistle Rink, the site of the evening ball, and thousands more around town, there was some question whether the generators could bear the load. They did, except for a single wobbly moment when all the lights dimmed.

No detail was too small. One letter to the editor wanted overhanging store signs removed before the big day because they made Edmonton look too much like a frontier town. Another letter writer informed his fellow citizens that punctuality was paramount both at the ball in the evening and at the public concert that preceded it.

An editorial, alert to the tiniest of particulars, demanded the nails be countersunk in the boardwalk leading down to the fairgrounds where the inauguration ceremony was to be held. Too many were sticking up, the editorial said, and could damage the fine footwear of the ladies.

And Ald. W.A. Griesbach insisted that his fellow city council members be measured for top hats – a news item that occasioned a 3,000-word story on the history of the stovepipe topper.

As for the ball itself, nothing could compare, at least according to the story the next day: "In the magnificent rink auditorium, ablaze with light, a riot of colour, there gathered an assemblage that would grace any similar affair ever held in the federal capital." It was simply splendid.

***Dec. 31, 1908*:**
The defending champion Montreal Wanderers retains the Stanley Cup, emblematic of world hockey supremacy, beating Edmonton by a two-game total of 13-10.

NA-3034-33 Glenbow Archives

Wilfrid Laurier.

***In 1909*:**
***Journal* partners Macpherson, Harris and Cunningham turn over their controlling interest to John P. McConnell of Vancouver, who immediately transfers his interest to J.H. Woods, of Calgary. M.R. Jennings becomes editor and general manager. John McLaren is appointed business manager.**

THE EDMONTON EVENING JOURNAL

VOL. 5. NO. 270 EDMONTON, ALBERTA, TUESDAY, OCTOBER 20, 1908 EIGHT PAGES

WHAT Have the Grafters Ever Done for YOU That You Should Vote to Give Them ANOTHER FIVE YEARS' Opportunity for PLUNDERING?

A POLITICAL SCANDAL THAT CONCERNS ALBERTA

Grit Conspiracy in Last Election to Defraud Alberta Voters Equals Famous Ontario Election Frauds.

(Special to The Journal.)

Moo... tended to several constituencies and ...

OCTOBER BUILDING EIGHTY THOUSAND

The building permits for the first twenty days of the month now total nearly $80,000 and there is no indication of a cessation in the number of permits being taken out daily. The following permits were taken out at the office of the building inspector this morning.

W. J. Richardson, Fourth street, residence $1,750.

W. J. Richardson, Fourth street, residence, $1,750.

... residence, $2,500.

THE ICE WIZARD TRAPS THE WISE

Multi-Millionaires Testify how They Were Lured by the Ice Trust Promoters

Department Issues Script

WAR CLOUDS IN EAST WELDING TIES IN WEST

CONSERVATIVES NOTICE

VOTERS NOT ON THE LIST

It is not necessary to be on the Voters' List to be entitled to vote. Every person having residence qualifications, i. e. at least one year in this province and the last three months in this constituency can vote at the polling station of the polling division in which he resides whether he is on the voters' list or not. Conservatives who are not on lists, be sure and demand a vote on Monday. If you do not know the proper polling station apply to the Conservative Committee Rooms, Howard St. If every Conservative votes, Hyndman will be elected

NA-2251-3 Glenbow Archives

Carriages lined up at Alberta College during inaugural festivities.

LAURIER INSULTS THE PEOPLE OF THE TERRITORIES

Ottawa, May 5 — Much comment is excited here by an article appearing in le Canada, evidently intended as a blow at the cause of provincial autonomy for the Territories. At least, as far as the Province of Quebec is concerned, le Canada is the confidential organ of Sir Wilfrid Laurier and Mr. Prefontaine, founded when La Patrie ceased, to support the Government. Haultain and Bulyea being in Ottawa in connection with the grant to the Territories and the question of provincial autonomy

Le Canada has seized this opportunity to misrepresent the situation through its Ottawa correspondent by declaring that the agitation for the provincial autonomy has originated, not in the West, but with the manager of the Montreal Star.

Le Canada declares that nobody takes any interest in the question and it cannot have any interest for any one, not even the people of the Territories.

— May 5, 1904

LOTS OF LOTS

On Friday next, there will be placed upon the market, a new suburban property, Westmount.

The lots are 50 foot frontages, by 110 feet in depth with a 20 foot lane in the back. The prices run from $100 and up.

Westmount will undoubtedly prove a splendid suburb. In a very short time the electric light, water, street car and telephone service will be extended to this section.

— Feb. 4, 1906

"Will the party who took the pair of gray persian lamb gauntlets out of the post office on Thursday last between 3 and 4 o'clock p.m., kindly return them to the Journal office or prosecution will follow."

— Jan, 11, 1904, classified advertisement

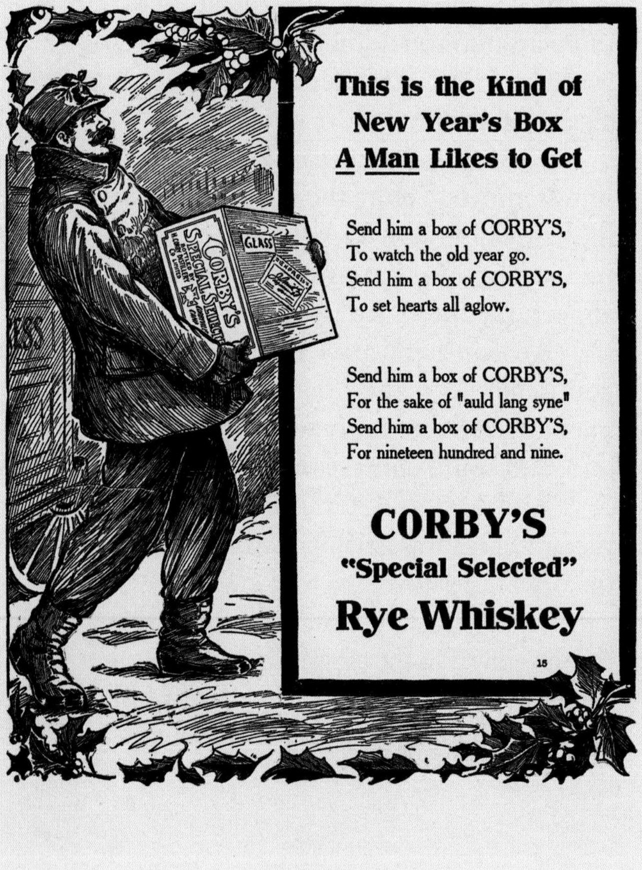
This is the Kind of New Year's Box A Man Likes to Get
Send him a box of CORBY'S, To watch the old year go. Send him a box of CORBY'S, To set hearts all aglow.
Send him a box of CORBY'S, For the sake of "auld lang syne" Send him a box of CORBY'S, For nineteen hundred and nine.
CORBY'S "Special Selected" Rye Whiskey
CORBY'S SPECIAL SELECTED
GLASS

1909

Second-class Citizens

"There was some objection to the name, Stony Plain. Frank Oliver explained that it was named after an Indian tribe which dwelt there and had no reference to the character of the land. He said it should be spelled 'Stoney.' "

— Story, June 27, 1905

Alberta was created one clause at a time in the spring and summer of 1905. Minutiae such as the names of constituencies were debated in exquisite and excruciating detail as the House of Commons considered the Alberta Autonomy Bill.

Perhaps that was the problem. Alberta was a made-in-Ottawa province – a fact that didn't escape *The Journal*'s editors even before the cork on the last bottle of Inauguration Day champagne hit the floor on Sept. 1, 1905.

Alberta was called a province, but it wasn't an equal province. While Quebec and Ontario really had full autonomy, Ottawa still reserved the right to control the two things Alberta had in abundance: land and natural resources. It was an issue that sparked a battle for equal rights that would last for decades and has echoes even today.

While the front-page story on Sept. 2, was over-written, it provided a subtle hint of what was to be a long and bitter battle over provincial power and autonomy. The unnamed reporter wrote: "The ceremony was pregnant with historic meaning and that was the note of the addresses of the distinguished sons of the Empire and of Canada who in felicitous, patriotic terms, extended their congratulations to the citizens who were on that occasion granted a fuller measure of governing powers and entrusted with greater responsibilities and wider opportunities to work out their destiny."

Perhaps so, but a "fuller measure" wasn't the fullest measure, and "greater responsibilities" weren't greatest responsibilities. This made Albertans famously resentful.

On the land and resources issue, *The Journal* was clear, almost from the day the bill that established Alberta was introduced in the Commons.

Corruption was suspected behind Ottawa's refusal to turn over full control to the province. The Liberal machine had its sinister reasons, said an editorial on Oct. 30, 1905: "It helps them to elect their nominees, both in provincial and Dominion elections, and for this reason in particular the hand and heel of Ottawa is to be kept upon the people of Alberta.

"There is another reason, also political, and that is by controlling these lands and natural resources they can be exploited for the benefit of the various friends of the party to the detriment of settlement, colonization and the true settlement of the West."

On Nov. 8, 1905, Western alienation is added to the mix: "Alberta is deprived of self-government in matters which come close to the welfare of every Albertan. It is to be subject in those matters to the government of men who have never been within a thousand miles of this province, who know nothing of conditions here, and who have no particular interest in our welfare."

Alberta wasn't getting a fair shake in Confederation.

***March 23, 1909*:** **The Journal publishes provincial election results: Six Conservative, one Socialist and 32 Liberals. It is a result not much to the paper's liking.**

***March 30, 1909*:** **The Grand Theatre burns to the ground after film in the projection room explodes. Twenty-five patrons manage to escape and only a quick-thinking fire department prevents the blaze from spreading to other businesses along Jasper.**

***June 5, 1909*:** **Results of the final term examinations at the University of Alberta are front page news. A.E. Ottewell receives passes in English, Greek, Latin, trigonometry and physics.**

***July 17, 1909*:** **The Grand Trunk Pacific arrives in Edmonton from Winnipeg, although it won't be ready to haul passengers until November. When it does begin operating, the trip to Winnipeg takes 26 hours, shaving nearly 10 hours off the running schedules of the Canadian Northern and the CPR.**

***Nov. 19, 1909*:** **The *Edmonton Weekly News* becomes the *Daily Capital*, edited by A. Balmer Watt, with publication to**

NA-1529-10 Glenbow Archives

The arrival of the passenger train from Winnipeg, whether the Canadian Northern in 1905 or the Grand Trunk in 1909, was always an event.

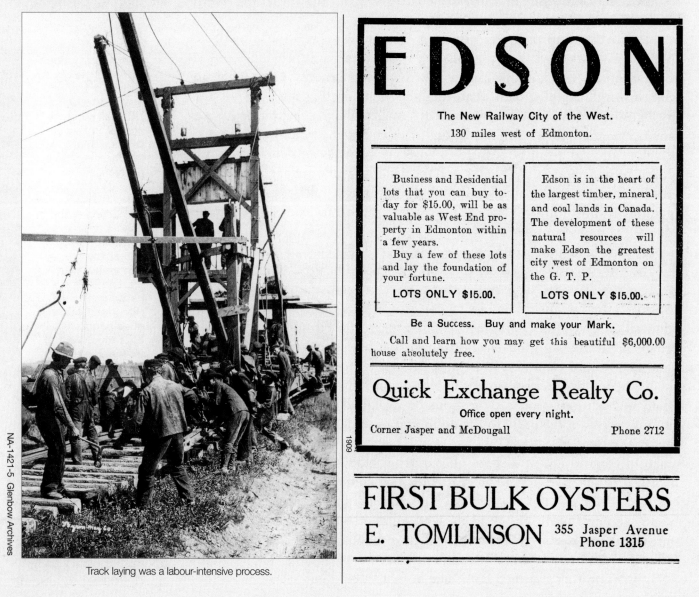

NA-1421-5 Glenbow Archives

Track laying was a labour-intensive process.

EDSON

The New Railway City of the West.

130 miles west of Edmonton.

Business and Residential lots that you can buy today for $15.00, will be as valuable as West End property in Edmonton within a few years.

Buy a few of these lots and lay the foundation of your fortune.

LOTS ONLY $15.00.

Edson is in the heart of the largest timber, mineral and coal lands in Canada. The development of these natural resources will make Edson the greatest city west of Edmonton on the G. T. P.

LOTS ONLY $15.00.

Be a Success. Buy and make your Mark.

Call and learn how you may get this beautiful $6,000.00 house absolutely free.

Quick Exchange Realty Co.

Office open every night.

Corner Jasper and McDougall Phone 2712

1909

FIRST BULK OYSTERS

E. TOMLINSON 355 Jasper Avenue
Phone 1315

Rutherford's Folly

"The newspapers are the eyes through which the entire population of the Province of Alberta is watching the developments in the legislature. The premier's efforts to blindfold those eyes, being futile, is absurd even from the point of view of his own interests."

— From a front-page story, March 1, 1910

If the first scandal of the province's young history could be compared to a freight train, then the story of the Alberta and Great Waterways Railway (A&GW) was an uncontrolled runaway.

It started slowly enough, but quickly built up such a head of steam that it wrecked the dreams of Alexander Cameron Rutherford, Alberta's first premier, and destroyed his political future.

Not surprisingly, *The Journal* covered it with the eagerness that newspapers everywhere display when a government is on the run. It became the story that simply would not stop.

The Alberta and Great Waterways Railway was to go from Edmonton to Waterways, just south of Fort McMurray. It was to provide a connection to the great river system that spills into the Arctic Ocean. By tapping the vast riches of the Mackenzie Valley, there was money to be made.

At first it seemed so easy.

It was Feb. 10, 1910, when the affable Rutherford, known as Uncle Sandy to his Strathcona constituents, took his seat as premier in the temporary quarters in the original Terrace Building located just south of where the legislature was being built.

He and his 35 fellow Liberals had trounced the Tories in the election of 1909 with the slogan Rutherford, Reliability and Railways. As Rutherford looked across at the opposition benches he saw only two Conservatives, an Independent, a single Independent Liberal and a lone Socialist.

But there was a strong voice in that tiny opposition from Calgary's articulate and dogged R.B. Bennett, one of the two Conservative members and the future prime minister of Canada. Bennett was a lawyer with a lucrative contract with the CPR, and there wasn't much he didn't know about financing a railway. More than most, he also knew that there was big money to be made in building a railroad, and very little in actually running one.

Within 12 weeks of the opening day of the 1910 session Rutherford would be out of office, his party in disarray and his actions subject to investigation by a royal commission.

Then as now, newspapers provided the wealth of detail demanded by the public. The A&GW Railway scandal was *the* topic under discussion, both in news stories and editorial coverage, although it was sometimes difficult to tell where one ended and the other began.

Even before the legislature opened, there were *Journal* stories reporting rumours that all was not what it should be with the A&GW Railway.

In early January, for example, Rutherford was quick to respond to a story that suggested the proposed route, guaranteed by the Rutherford government at $20,000 a mile, was wrong. Critics said too many settlements were missed along the way and the steel rails themselves were too light.

commence before the end of the year. Watt becomes assistant editor of *The Journal* on May 15, 1912.

NA-1514-5 Glenbow Archives

Alexander Cameron Rutherford, Alberta's first premier.

***Dec. 30, 1909*: *Journal* staff totals 33, with an annual payroll of $33,376. Over the year the paper uses 140 tons of newsprint for its daily circulation of 4,133 papers.**

***Jan. 20, 1910*: The champion Ottawa Senators beat the Edmonton Eskimos 8-4 in a challenge for the Stanley Cup.**

***March 5, 1910*: An avalanche in Rogers Pass in the Canadian Rockies kills 62 Canadian Pacific railway workers, who were clearing an earlier slide from the line.**

***March 14, 1910*: Lots in the Calder area of Edmonton sell for $175-$250.**

***May 26, 1910*: Arthur Sifton becomes premier of Alberta (and**

NA-1338-1 Glenbow Archives

REVILLON SPECIAL
THIS ENTIRE
TRAIN FOR
46448
44592
There was no mistaking which company's goods arrived on this train.

NA-1338-2 Glenbow Archives

REVILLON BROTHERS LIMITED.
The early Revillon Brothers store in Edmonton was a going concern.

FIRST PASSENGER TRAIN ARRIVES FROM WINNIPEG!

BREAKNECK SPEED PLEASES OFFICIALS

"The first Canadian Northern Passenger train on the CNR mainline arrived in the city this morning at three o'clock, making the run of 823 miles from Winnipeg in 27 hours.

"The railway officials are extremely well pleased with the run from Winnipeg over the new line at an average speed of 30 miles an hour."

— Nov. 24, 1905

NEVER ON A SUNDAY

"Sunday trains must stop. According to the Lord's Day Act no passenger trains must leave on a run between midnight on Saturday and midnight on Sunday. Those started before that time will be allowed to complete their run."

— March 13, 1907

FRANCS FOR ALBERTA

"Rene Lemarchand, one of Edmonton's most prominent financiers, returned yesterday from a three-months' trip to France, whither he had gone in an effort to induce French capitalists to come to this section of the north west.

"During his trip he met some of the most prominent capitalists of the old country and is assured that at least ten of these will visits Alberta about the first of June."

— March 20, 1909

BROS. LTD
EDMONTON

What's more, the roadbed itself wasn't up to the demands of a harsh prairie winter. Not to worry, Rutherford assured a *Journal* reporter. The contractors, Kansas City businessmen with Winnipeg connections, had promised to build spur and branch lines.

As for the rails and the roadbed, well, they had been tested and everything was fine.

According to the paper, there was something brewing as early as Feb. 11, the day after the session opened. J.R. Boyle, the Liberal member for Sturgeon, rose to ask for details in connection with the A&GW deal. He may have been sitting on the government side of the House, but his questions had a Tory ring to them.

"Why should J.R. Boyle become suddenly inquisitive about all the details in connection with the Alberta Waterways Railway?" asked a Feb. 12, editorial.

"The suspicion attached to the private relations of individuals and the generous application of provincial credit to the purpose, however, calls for an accounting which is now asked for."

Soon the embattled Rutherford faced a revolt in his own party. A group of disaffected Liberals who held caucus meetings in the King Edward Hotel on 101st Street and were dubbed the Insurgents by *The Journal*, were pressing for more and more details. Were there unseemly connections between the contractors and companies supplying material for the railway? At $20,000 a mile, was the route the right one or was it too long by as much as 80 miles? Were there some nasty doings between the Winnipeg contractors and members of the government? What did the premier know, and when did he know it?

When Rutherford finally agreed to table in the House all the relevant documents — many of them were apparently missing – *The Journal* and the Insurgents were certain they had what they needed.

Then on March 1, the paper reported that Rutherford restricted access to the papers. "Since the files were laid on the table two detectives from the attorney-general's department have been quietly on guard in the legislative hall, keeping a silent and almost unsuspected watch on the table on which the documents lie.

"Day after day, morning, afternoon and night, these detectives are to be found

leader of the provincial Liberals) after resigning as chief justice of the province's supreme court. He replaces Alexander Rutherford, who is forced to resign by a railway scandal.

***June 3, 1910*: Edmonton's first newsreel, the funeral of Edward VII, is shown at the Bijou, the city's first movie house.**

***May 9, 1910*: First log drive of the season, containing five million feet of trees, arrives in city to feed local lumber mills. The logs travelled 150 miles down the North Saskatchewan.**

***June 1910*: A second storey is added to *The Journal* building. It trebles the paper's floor space.**

NA-1337-9 Glenbow Archives

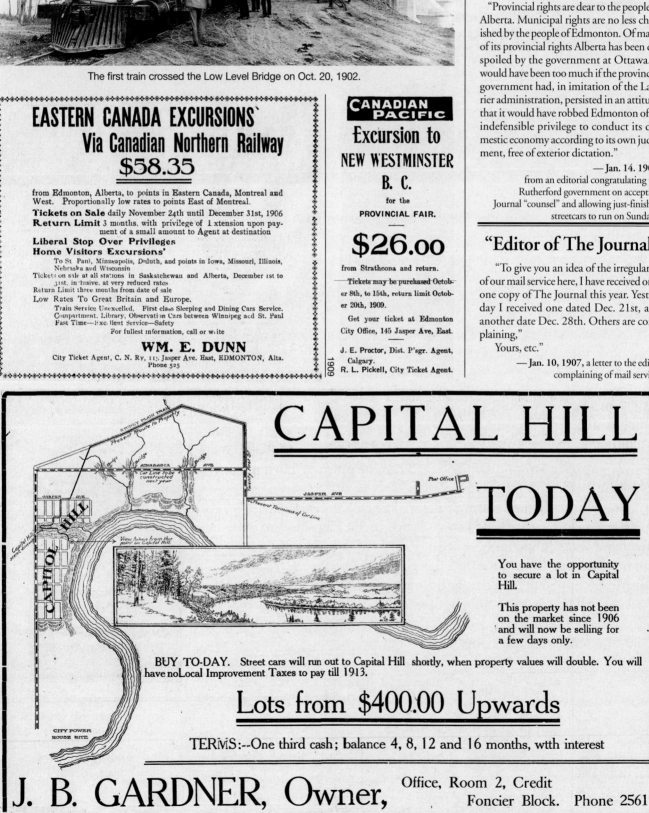

The first train crossed the Low Level Bridge on Oct. 20, 1902.

FULL AHEAD FOR SUNDAY STREETCARS

"Provincial rights are dear to the people of Alberta. Municipal rights are no less cherished by the people of Edmonton. Of many of its provincial rights Alberta has been despoiled by the government at Ottawa. It would have been too much if the provincial government had, in imitation of the Laurier administration, persisted in an attitude that it would have robbed Edmonton of its indefensible privilege to conduct its domestic economy according to its own judgment, free of exterior dictation."

—Jan. 14. 1909, from an editorial congratulating the Rutherford government on accepting Journal "counsel" and allowing just-finished streetcars to run on Sundays.

1906

1909

"Editor of The Journal:

"To give you an idea of the irregularity of our mail service here, I have received only one copy of The Journal this year. Yesterday I received one dated Dec. 21st, and another date Dec. 28th. Others are complaining,"

Yours, etc."

—Jan. 10, 1907, a letter to the editor complaining of mail service.

in the House, unknown to the throngs that crowd the hall. They mingle with the crowds, but keep near the table, and there is not a member or official who approaches the table or spends any time perusing the documents that does not come under the eagle eye of the legislative sleuths."

All of those precautions would be for naught the paper said in that day's editorial: "Alberta boasts some of the cleverest reporters in the Dominion of Canada, if not in America."

It also sounded a caution to the members of the legislature.

"The members can talk to only as many as they can get within the sound of their voices. The newspapers talk to the entire country at once, and do it in less time than a member takes to make a single speech."

The debate raged on, culminating in an eloquent speech from Bennett. It took five hours for him to deliver his address – "the greatest ever in the short history of the Alberta legislature" – and it ended Rutherford's hopes for seeing the railway built during his tenure.

In fact, Rutherford was cornered. Hammered by almost daily editorials and cartoons and with a crowded public gallery that watched as his members defected to the Insurgents, Rutherford's only solution was to establish a royal commission to investigate the A&GW deal.

Within six months the commission issued its report, but Rutherford didn't wait to see what they found out.

He resigned as premier on May 26 and sat as a private member until his defeat in the election of 1913.

When the royal commission released its findings in November, the results were anticlimactic.

There had been no corruption in the A&GW deal, the commission said, but Rutherford was sloppy and naïve.

The editorial the next day was strangely subdued.

There wasn't any crowing. "The report bears out what The Journal has contended from the commencement.

"To state the verdict in the briefest form, the judges find that there is no proof of dishonesty and less proof of business ability, i.e., that while there is nothing to show that the ministers criticized were crooked, they certainly showed a lack of ordinary sense.

"The commissioners say that there is nothing to show that the deal was corrupt, but it was almost childishly foolish."

Postscript: Construction on the A&GW Railway to Waterways began in 1914. The First World War intervened, but the railroad was completed in 1925.

It was operated by the J.D. McArthur Company until 1926 when the provincial government took over operation of the rail line.

In 1928, the CPR and the CNR jointly purchased the A&GW and it was renamed the Northern Alberta Railways (NAR) in 1929. In 1981, the NAR was sold to the CNR and ceased to exist as an independent company.

***June 22, 1910*:** **Construction of the Royal Alexandra Hospital begins. Estimated cost is $170,000.**

***June 27, 1910*:** **Ottawa says it will create a national park in Jasper. It will be the equal of Banff. *The Journal* notes: "The mountain scenery in the Yellowhead is even more beautiful than is the case in Banff."**

***June 29, 1910*:** **The Grand Trunk Pacific Railway announces Edmonton-to-Winnipeg service. The train runs three days a week and the express service of 30 hours cuts six hours off the trip offered by Canadian Northern.**

***July 7, 1910*:** **Construction starts on the original Union Bank Building on Jasper Avenue and what is now 100A Street. The building costs $60,000 and is "nearly fireproof."**

***Sept. 9, 1910*:** **The provincial government picks the site for Government House. It is built in Groat Estates on Athabasca Avenue (102nd Avenue) for about $33,000.**

***Also in 1910*:** **Local police call boxes are installed, Abe Cristall opens the Royal George Hotel and North Edmonton becomes a village.**

Back Up the Old Red, White and Blue and Buy Bonds

Last and Home Edition

Edmonton Journal

DAILY CIRCULATION FRIDAY, NOV. 8, 1918. 20,790 LISTS OPEN FOR INSPECTION

VOL. 15, No. 101 | EDMONTON, ALBERTA, MONDAY, NOVEMBER 11, 1918 | FOURTEEN PAGES

Will Keep Beyond The Rhine

Will Surrender the Entire Naval Force

HUN SUBMITS

Will Evacuate All Captured Territory

Will Hand Over All Engines of War

Teutonic Empire in Utter Collapse Agrees to Drastic Terms Demanded By the Victorious Allied Armies

Naval Terms Ask Surrender of All Submarines, Cruisers, Battleships and Ships—Luxemburg and Alsace-Lorraine Will be Evacuated Along With All Other Territory Captured in First Drive

WASHINGTON, Nov. 11.—President Wilson drove to the capitol at 12:45 o'clock through streets thronged with cheering people.

The terms of the armistice accepted by Germany were read to congress by him at 1 o'clock this afternoon. Assembled in the hall of the house, where nineteen months ago senators and representatives heard the president ask for the declaration of war, they today heard him speak the words which herald the coming of peace.

Th president spoke as follows:

"Gentlemen of the congress:

"In these times of rapid and stupendous changes it will in some degree lighten my sense of responsibility to perform in person the duty of communicating to you some of the larger circumstances of the situation with which it is necessary to deal.

"The German authorities, who have, at the invitation of the supreme war council, been in communication with Marhsal Foch have accepted and signed the terms of armistice, which he was authorized and instructed to communicate to them.

"The strictly military terms of the armistice are embraced in eleven specifications which include the evacuation of all invaded territories, the withdrawal of the German troops from the left bank of the Rhine and the surrender of all supplies of war.

"The terms also provide for the abandonment by Germany of the treaties of Bucharest and Brest-Litovsk.

"1.—Military clauses on western front: One—Cessation of operations by land and in the air, six hours after the signing of the armistice.

"2.—Immediate evacuation of invaded countries: Belgium, France, Alsace-Lorraine, Luxemburg, so ordered as to be completed within fourteen days from the signature of the armistice.

"German troops which have not left the above mentioned territories within the period fixed will become prisoners of war. Occupation by the Allies and United States forces jointly will keep pace with evacuation in these areas. All movements of evacuation and occupation will be regulated in accordance with a note annexed to the stated terms.

"3.—Repatriation beginning at once and to be completed within fourteen days of all inhabitants of the countries above mentioned, including hostages and persons under trial or convicted.

4—Surrender in good condition by the German armies of the following equipment: Five thousand guns (two thousand five hundred heavy, two thousand five hundred field) thirty thousand machine-guns; three thousand minenwerfers; two thousand aeroplanes (fighters, bombers—firstly D seventy-threes and night bombing machines) the above to be delivered in situ to the allies and the United States troops in acocrdance with the detailed conditions laid down in the annexed note.

Evacuated Land

5—Evacuation by the German armies of the countries on the left bank of the Rhine. These countries on the left bank of the Rhine shall be administered by the local authorities under the control of the allied and United States armies of occupation. The occupation of these territories will be determined by allied and United States garrisons holding the principal crossings of the Rhine, Mayence, Coblenz, Cologne, together with bridgeheads at these points in thirty kilometre radius on the right bank and by garrisons similarly holding the strategic points of the regions. A neutral zone shall be reserved on the right of the Rhine between the stream and a line drawn parallel to it forty kilometres to the east from the frontier of Holland to the parallel of Gernsheim and as far as practicable, a distance of thirty kilometres from the east of the stream from this parallel upon the Swiss frontier. Evacuation by the enemy of the Rhine lands shall be so ordered as to be completed within a further period of eleven days, in all nineteen days after the signature of the armistice.

All movements of evacuation and occupation will be regulated according to the note annexed.

Inhabitants Must Be Unmolested

6. In all territory evacuated by the enemy there shall be no evacuation of inhabitants; no damage or harm shall be done to the persons or property of the inhabitants. No destruction of any kind to be committed. Military establishments of all kinds shall be delivered intact as well as military stores of food, munitionsñ equipment not removed during the periods fixed for evacuation.

Must Pay Expenses In Rhine Land

The naval terms provide for the surrender of 160 submarines, fifty destroyers, six battle cruisers, ten battleships, eight light cruisers and other miscellaneous ships.

Prisoners to Be Repatriated

The immediate repatriation of all allied and American prisoners without reciprocal action by the Allies also included.

Washington, Nov. 11.—Stores of food of all kinds for the civil population, cattle, etc., shall be left in situ industrial establishments shall not be impaired in any way and their personnel shall not be moved. Roads and means of communication of every kind, railroad, waterways, main roads, bridges, telegraphs, telephones, shall be in no manner impaired.

7. All civil and military personnel at present employed on them shall remain. Five thousand locomotives, fifty thousand wagons and ten thousand motor lorries in good working order with all necessary spare parts and fittings shall be delivered to the associated powers within the period fixed for the evacuation of Belgium and Luxemburg. The railways. The railways of Alsace-Lorraine shall be handed over within the same period, together with all pre-war personnel and material. Further material necessary for the working of railways in the country on the left bank of the Rhine shall be left in situ. All stores of coal and material for the upkeep of permanent ways, signals and repair shops left entire in situ and kept in an efficient state by Germany during the whole period of armistice. All barges taken from the Allies shall be restored to them. A note appended regulates the details of these measures.

8.—The German command shall be responsible for revealing all mines or delay-acting fuse disposed on territory evacuated by the German troops and shall assist in their discovery and destruction. The German command shall also reveal destructive measures that may have been taken (such as poisoning or polluting of springs, wells, etc.) under penalty of reprisals.

9. The right of requisition shall be exercised by the Allies and the United States armies in all occupied territory. The upkeep of the troops of occupation in the Rhineland (excluding Alsace-Lorraine) shall be charged to the German government.

10. Immediate repatriation without reciprocity, according to detailed conditions, which shall be fixed, of all Allied and United States prisoners of war. The allied powers and the United States shall be able to dispose of these prisoners as they wish.

11. Sick and wounded, who cannot be removed from evacuated territory, will be cared for by German personnel who will be left on the spot with the medical material required.

1914 Frontiers To Be Preserved

11. Disposition relative to the eastern frontiers of Germany:

12. All German troops at present in any territory which before the war belonged to Russia, Roumania or Turkey, shall withdraw within the frontiers of Germany as they existed on August 1, 1914.

13. Evacuation by German troops to begin at once and all German instructors, prisoners and civilian as well as military agents now on the territory of Russia (as defined byfore 1914 to be recalled.

14. German troops to cease at once all requisitions and seizures and any other undertaking with a view to obtaining supplies intended for Germany in Roumania and Russia (as defined on August 1, 1914).

15. Abandonment of the treaties of Bucharest and Brest-Litovsk and of the supplementary treaties.

16. Allies shall have free access to the territories evacuated by the Germans on their eastern frontier either through Danzig or by the Vistula in order to convey supplies to the populations of those territories or for any other purpose.

African Forces Must Quit

17.—Unconditional capitulation of all German forces operating in East Africa within one month.

18.—Repatriation, without reciprocity, within a maximum period of one month, in accordance with detailed conditions hereafter to be fixed, of all civilians interned or deported who may be citizens of other allied or associated states than those mentioned in clause 3, paragraph 19, with the reservation that any future claims and demands of the allies and the United States of America remain unaffected.

Will Pay For Damage Done

19.—The following financial conditions are required: Reparation for damage done. While such armistice last no public securities shall be removed by the enemy which can serve as a pledge to the allies for the recovery or reparation for war losses. Immediate restitution of the cash deposit, in the National Bank of Belgium, and in general immediate return of all documents, specie, stocks, shares, paper money, together with plant for the issue thereof, touching public or private interests in the invaded countries.

Restitution of the Russian and Roumanian gold yielded to Germany or taken by that power. This gold to be delivered in trust to the allies until the signature of peace.

Naval Conditions Are Sweeping

V.—Naval Conditions.

20.—Immediate cessation of all hostilities at sea and definite information to be given as to the location and movements of all German ships. Notification to be given to neutrals that freedom of navigation in all territorial waters is given to the naval and mercantile marines of the allies and associated powers, all questions of neutrality being waived.

21.—All noval and mercantile marine prisoners of war of the allied and associated powers in German hands to be returned without reciprocity.

22.—Surrender to the allies and the United States of America of 160 German submarines (including all submarine cruisers and mine laying submarines) with their complete armament and equipment in ports which will be specified by the allies and the United States of America. All other submarines to be paid off and completely disarmed and placed under the supervision of the allied powers and the United States of America.

23.—The following German surface warships which shall be designated by the allies and the United States of America shall forthwith be disarmed and thereafter interned in neutral ports, or for want of them in allied ports, to be designated by the allies and the United States of America and placed under the surveillance of the allies and the United States of America, only caretakers being left on board, namely: Six battle cruisers, ten battleships, eight light cruisers, including two mine layers, fifty detroyers of the most modern type. All other surface warships (including river craft) are to be concentrated in German naval bases to be designated by the allies and the United States of America, and are to be paid off and completely disarmed and placed under the supervision of the allies and the United States of America. All vessels of the auxiliary fleet—trawlers motor vessels, etc.,—are to be disarmed.

24.—The allies and the United States of America shall have the right to sweep up all mine fields and obstructions laid by Germany outsid eGerman territorial waters and the positions of these are to be indicated.

25.—Freedom of access to and from the Baltic to be given to the naval and mercantile marines of the allied and associated powers; to secure this Allies and the United States of America shall be empowered to occupy all German forts, fortifications, batteries and defence works of all kinds in all the entrances from the Cattegat into the Baltic, and to sweep all mines and obstructions within and without German territorial waters without any question of neutrality being raised, and he positions of al lsuch mines and obstructions are to be indicated.

26.—The existing blockade conditions set up by the allied and associated powers are to remain unchanged and all German merchant ships found at sea are to remain liable to capture.

27.—All naval aircraft are to be concentrated and immobilized in German bases to be specified by the Allies and thet United States of America.

28.—In evacuating the Belgian coasts and ports, Germany shall abandon all merchant ships, tugs, lighters, cranes, and all other harbor materials and stores, all arms and armaments, and all stores and apparatus of all kinds.

29.—All Black Sea ports are to be evacuated by Germany; all Russian war vessels of all descriptions, seized by Germany in the Black Sea, are to be handed over to the Allies and the United States of America; all neutral merchant vessels seized are to be released; all warlike and war materials of all kinds seized in those ports are to be returned and German material as specified in clause 28 are to be abandoned.

30. All merchant vessels in German hands belonging to the Allies and associated powers are to be restored in ports to be specified by the Allies and the United States of America without reciprocity.

31. No destruction of ships or of materials to be permitted before evacuation, surrender or restoration.

32. The German government will notify the neutral governments of the world, and particularly the governments of Norway, Sweden, Denmark and Holland, that all restrictions placed on the trading of their vessels with the allies and associated countries, whether by the German government or by private German interests, and whether in return for specific concessions such as the export of shipbuilding materials or not, are immediately cancelled.

33. No transfers of German merchant shipping of any description to any neutral flag are to take place after signature of the armistice.

DURATION....... ... ...

34. The duration of the armistice is to be thirty days, with option to extend. During this period, on failure of execution of any of the above clauses, the armistice may be denounced by one of the contracting parties on forty-eight hours' notice.

35. This armistice to be accepted or refused by Germany within seventy-two hours of notification.

'NUFF SED

ANGLICAN BISHOP PUBLICLY GIVES THANKS FOR PEACE

Te Deum to be Sung When Epidemic Ban Is Lifted

To the Members of the Church of England:

Dear Brethren—By the grace of God, who has guided our counsels and sustained and helped our armies, we are permitted to see today the beginning of the dawn of peace.

Owing to the present epidemic, we are prohibited from joining together in a service of public thanksgiving. But while we cannot meet together, we can in our hearts and homes give God thanks for having crowned our efforts to maintain honor, liberty and justice. Not in vain has the blood of our men—aye, and of our women—been shed; to them God has given victory. Let us thank God for it!

I desire, as soon as the ban upon public worship has been removed, that at the first service held in any of our churches in the diocese a solemn Te Deum shall be sung not as fulfilling but as acknowledging our debt of gratitude which we can never pay. Then let us show forth our gratitude not only with our lips, but in our lives by planning and working that the fruits of victory may be preserved to us and succeeding generations. Canada has won great glory in this war. The world acknowledges her sturdy manhood. Let us see that she stands forth a champion of unselfishness and justice.

May the blessing of God be with you all.

Yours sincerely,

H. ALLEN EDMONTON.

SWIFTS CLOSE FOR DAY

On account of the news of peace the Swift Canadian company closed up this morning. No deliveries will be made during the day.

CORRECTION

At the foot of the five column advertisement for D'Allairds, which appeared in Saturday's issue, November 9, the following words were left out: "Winner of the first employes honor flag."

WORKERS ARE NEEDED

The peace news is causing the workers caring for "flu" patients much worry. It is earnestly requested that the sick be not neglected. The enthusiasm among convalescents may cause serious relapses and the exposures consequent upon celebration will develop new cases. Women attendants for the sick are absolutely necesary if lives are to be saved. Any woman who can assist in this important service is urgently requested to send her name to the central relief office. Noble service has been rendered and many nurses are much fatigued. Assistance is badly needed. Will you not phone 9251 and 9252 and help us out.

DOCTORS THINK INFLUENZA HAS REACHED A PEAK

Only Twenty-Seven Cases Were Reported Here Sunday

The influenza epidemic is rapidly subsiding in Edmonton, in the opinion of members of the health department. On Sunday there were but twenty-seven new cases reported, whcih was practically a drop of fifty per cent. Monday morning there was a similar absence of heavy reports.

The worst of the epidemic has clearly passed from Edmonton and a decided improvement is anticipated from now on. On Sunday, nursing centres reported a distinct falling off of new reports, but declare that there is still an imperative call for helpers.

Sunday's death list totalled thirteen. A good percentage of these were nonresidents. Mrs. J. W. Clarke, 9632 106A avenue, wife of the manager of the Lac La Biche Fish company died at the Isolation hospital on Sunday. The funeral arrangements are in the hands of the Wainwright and Jackson undertaking company.

Mrs. W. Neil, 12839 67th street, died at the Pembina Hall emergency hospital. She was thirty years old and leaves a husband and small family. Burial arrangements are in the hands of McCoppen undertakers, and the funeral takes ace from the family residence, 12839 7th street on Tuesday at 4 p.m.

Lewis Eric Hedlund died at the Isolation hospital. The funeral will be arranged by the McCoppen undertaking company.

Mrs. Lucella Earl died at Calmar. The funeral will take place at 2 o'clock Tuesday afternoon from McCoppen's.

Andrews, undertakers, report the following deaths: Edward Samis, Mabel Alexander ,Margaret Kinsella, Anastasia Teacher.

Carl Oberg died at the Pembina Hall emergency hospital on Sunday.

FOCH MEETS PREMIER

PARIS, Nov. 11. (11:10 a.m.)—Marshal Foch was received by Premier Clemenceau at ten o'clock this morning.

WILL HUNS KEEP FAITH AND HOLD TO PEACE TERMS?

Grave Anxiety Felt Over the Uncertain and Unstable Condition Government

LONDON, Nov. 11.—In view of the irregular and uncertain position of the new German government anxiety is expressed by some London newspapers lest difficulties arise to prevent acceptance and enforcement of the allied armistice terms.

The pleas of some German papers that the allies ought not to crowd Germany to the wall so hard that she would be unable to establish herself under a democratic government tend to confirm suspicious in some quarters here that the transfer of power to the Socialists really is a subtle device by which the former emperor and the military hope to obtain easier terms. It is contended that if such a scheme gained even partial success, it might easily lead to reaction in favor of the former autocrat.

The Times and the Daily Mail for instance recall that all Germany, including the Socialists, assented to the war, the failure of which alone leads them to abjure it now. They insist that the change in administration in no wise removes the necessity for reparation and restitution.

Allied with this view is doubt voiced by the Daily Express and elsewhere as to whether the armistice arrangement with the present government would provide the guarantees demanded as Chancellor Ebert's administration is conceived to be so fragile that it may fall at any moment.

MANY TOWNS IN DISTRICT EARN HONOR EMBLEMS

Wetaskiwin First in Alberta To Go Over Top in Loan Drive

F. B. Matthews is most enthusiastic over the way the various committees are working in his district from Strathcona to Lacombe. In spite of the epidemic the results being obtained are most gratifying as shown by the following brief report.

Wetaskiwin district — Full quota, \$100,000. Subscribed to November 9, \$91,250; number of subscribers 495; 1917 results \$102,000. This district has the highest percentage yet reported, namely 91.25 per cent, and Wetaskiwin was the first city in the province to win its flag. The district expects to exceed \$130,000.

Malmo canvassing unit 14 with a quota of \$8,000, has to date subscribed \$17,450 in fifty-two subscriptions and has a record hard to beat in as much as all but two in the district have applied for bonds and those who are thought to have subscribed through banks. They have won an honor flag with four British crowns.

Chairman Manley and his committee of Wetaskiwin are to be congratulated and special mention must be made of the untiring and efficient work of Organizer P. C. Peterson.

Lacombe district: Full quota \$300,000; results to November 9, \$205,650; 1917 results, \$267,000; subscribers, 719.

The results in this district are coming up to expectations and the committee headed by Chairman Jones are most enthusiastic and promise to exceed their quota. Honor flags have already been won as follows:

Lacombe, quota \$50,000, to date \$85,000.

Alix, quota \$12,000, to date \$30,000.
Clive, quota \$10,000, to date \$17,500.
Tees, quota \$5,000, to date \$5,500.
Rimbey, quota \$1,500, to date \$10,400.
Ponoka is doing well but returns are not all in and it is expected that 75,000 will be secured.

Strathcona District: Quota \$20,000; results to November 9, \$12,200, with 79 applications; 1917 results \$6200.

The district will likely exceed its quota under the able supervision of C. Ladue, whose team of twelve canvassers are hard at it.

Leduc District: Quota \$50,000; results to November 9, \$18,000, with 77 applications; 1917 results, \$42,000.

This district has suffered badly from the epidemic but the canvassers are now at work and the committee expect during the last week to reach their objective.

DRAFT CALLS OFF IN UNITED STATES

WASHINGTON, Nov. 11.—By order of President Wilson, Provost Marshal General Crowder today directed the cancellation of all outstanding draft calls, stopping the movement during the next five days of 252,000 men and setting aside all November calls for over 300,000 men.

HINDENBURG HAS GIVEN THE ARMY TO THE PEOPLE

LONDON, Nov. 11.—Field Marshal von Hindenburg has placed himself and the German army at the disposal of the new people's government at Berlin, says a dispatch from the German capital by way of Copenhagen.

HOUSE ADJOURNS

LONDON, Nov. 11. — When the house of commons met today Premier Lloyd-George, after the opening prayer was said, moved that the house adjourn immediately. He proposed that the members proceed to St. Margaret's church, on the western side of Westminster hall.

FORMER KAISER NOW IN HOLLAND

WASHINGTON, Nov. 10. —William Hohenzollern has arrived in Holland, and is proceeding to the town of Deisteeg, near Utrecht, according to a dispatch received by the American general staff today from The Hague.

The message said: "Press reports state that the kaiser arrived this morning in Maastricht, Holland, and is proceeding to Middachten castle, in the town of Deisteeg, near Utrecht."

KING OF SAXONY IS DETHRONED

COPENHAGEN, Nov. 11. — King Friedrich August of Saxony has been dethroned, according to an official telegram from Berlin.

CRUSHING NEWS PROVES TOO MUCH FOR HIGH HUNS

Three German Generals Are Said to Have Committed Suicide

PARIS, Nov. 11.—Many sensational rumors became current here as a result of the news of the signing of the armistice between the Allies and Germany. These reports were to the effect that Prince Eitel Friedrick, the second son of William II., was prevented from committing suicide and that the empress was dying.

Three German generals are said to have committed suicide.

EBERT PREDICTS A SPEEDY PEACE

COPENHAGEN, Nov 10 (8.30 a.m.) —Frederich Ebert, the Socialist leader, has been appointed imperial chancellor. He has issued a proclamation saying that he plans to form a people's government, which will endeavor to bring about a speedy peace.

COPENHAGEN, Nov. 10 (8.34 a.m.) —It is officially announced from Berlin that the war ministry has placed itself at the disposal of Friedrich Ebert, the Socialist leader, whose appointment as imperial chancellor was forecasted yesterday by the decree of Prince Maxmilian. This action was for the purpose of assuring the provisioning of the army and assisting in the solution of demobilization problems.

Ebert's election in June was taken to mean at the time that the Socialist minority in the reichstag had been either reclaimed by the military government or that the Socialists had gained the ascendancy. Later events have proved that the Socialists were in the saddle.

Ebert recently declared in the reichstag that the German people would no longer permit themselves to be without the right to decide their fate. It

OPEN AIR SERVICE

The acceptance of armsitice terms by the Germans will be celebrated by the ministerial association by an open air thanksgiving service at 4 o'clock this afternoon. The service will be held in front of the Y.M.C.A. building on 103rd avenue. Rev. Dr. McQueen, president of the ministerial association, will preside, and a short address will be given by Bishop Gray. A cordial invitation is extended to the clergy and the general public to attend.

FLAME OF REVOLT NOW BURNING UP HUNS AUTOCRACY

Revolution Is Now on a Firm Basis Throughout the Teutonic Empire

CROWDS DESTROY KAISER'S STATUE

Hun Soldiers Now Throwing Down Their Guns For Peace

COPENHAGEN, Nov. 11.—The revolution in Germany is today, to all intents and purposes, an accomplished fact.

The revolt has not yet spread throughout the whole empire, but fourteen of the twenty-six states, including all the four kingdoms and all other important states are reported securely in the hands of the revolutionists.

Wilhelm's Image Was Defaced

(Havas Agency)

PARIS, Nov. 11.—During revolutionary disorders at Cologne a crowd tried to demolish with machine-gun fire a statue of William II but finally contented itself by muffling up the statue and placing upon it a card inscribed: "A good journey." It is reported that Prince Henry of Prussia has fled to Denmark, taking with him his personal fortune.

Soldiers Throw Down Their Arms

AMSTERDAM, Nov. 11.—German garrisons along the Dutch frontier are reported in revolt. Officers are being disarmed and are being treated roughly in some instances. Many of the guardsmen threw down their arms and have gone home.

Thousands of Dutch workmen are streaming homeward from Krupps, at Essen.

Warsaw Bars Out Germans

AMSTERDAM, Nov. 11.—Street fighting is taking place in Warsaw the capital of Poland. The railway station there has been occupied by Polish forces who have refused the German troops in the city permission to pass through Polish territory.

Little Bloodshed; Revolt Is Orderly

BERLIN, Nov. 9 (German wireless to London, Nov. 10)—The text of the statement issued by the people's government reads:

"In the course of the forenoon of Saturday the formation of a new German people's government was initiated. The greater part of the Berlin garrison and other troops stationed there temporarily went over to the new government.

The leaders of the deputations of the Social-Democratic party declared that they would not shoot against the people. They said they would, in accord with the people's government, intercede in favor of the maintenance of order. Thereupon in the office and public buildings the guards which had been stationed there were withdrawn.

"The business of the imperial chancellor is being carried on by the Social-Democratic deputy, Herr Ebert.

"It is presumed that apart from the representatives of the recent majority group three independent Social Democrats will enter the future government.

"The first procession arrived from the Ackerstrasse and Brunnestrasse. As a preliminary the soldiers and officers were urged to remove their cockades and epaulets. In the majority of cases this took place voluntarily.

"There was a general fraternization of soldiers and workmen. The workmen penetrated the barracks, where they received an enthusiastic reception from the soldiers.

"The military occupants of factories mingled with the workers, left the works and treated with them in common.

"So far as known, the clash between the masses and armed forces took place on the occupation of the so-called 'cockshafer' barracks. In that was a guard of fusiliers, but only two officers fired.

"Three persons were killed and one was injured. This is to be regretted.

"The taking possession of a majority of the public buildings and establishments was completed without difficulty once it was clear that the military had gone over to the people."

TWO

McDERMID
385

NC-6-385 Glenbow Archives

By 1912, Jasper Avenue (looking east from 101st Street) was paved and packed with a mix of electric streetcars, horse-drawn wagons and automobiles. The four-storey building at the left is the first Empire Building, with the Bank of Nova Scotia as its tenant.

Boom, Bust & War

1911 to 1920

"... In Edmonton we have some thousands of men of the finest type to make good soldiers. Some are already trained. The majority are not. The trained men will, in the ordinary course, go first. When they are gone there must be others ready to take their places....
"Yours, E.B. Edwards."
— Letter to the editor, Aug. 8, 1914

A Temporary Measure / 71
Spanish Flu / 73
The Divine Sarah / 77
Visitors Extraordinaire / 79
Special Delivery / 81
Bombing Wetaskiwin / 83
Prohibition / 85

Vimy Ridge. Ypres. The Somme. Passchendaele.

As the second decade of the 20th century began, few *Journal* readers would have been able find many of those places on a map of Europe. In fact, few probably gave Europe and its political and economic tensions much thought at all. After all, they were too busy spinning money out of a local land boom that seemed endless. Wherever there was property to buy, there was an ample supply of Edmonton businessmen prepared to sign on the dotted line.

Whatever difficulties might lie ahead, the city, the province and *The*

LAST EDITION

Edmonton Journal

DAILY CIRCULATION
THURSDAY, AUGUST 27,
19,004
Lists open for Inspection.

Vol. 11, No. 39 — EDMONTON, ALBERTA FRIDAY, AUGUST 28, 1914 — SIXTEEN PAGES

20 GERMANS FALL FOR EVERY BRITISH SOLDIER

H.M.S. HIGHFLYER IS ENVY OF ALL BRITISH BOATS

Rid the Seas of a Dangerous Raider Harrassing Trade in East

VESSEL IS TRAINING SHIP FOR COLLEGIANS

Can Tell of How They Sunk Proud German Liner With Name of War Lord

(Special Cable to The Edmonton Journal and The Montreal Star)
[Registered according to copyright act]
(Windermere London Service)

LONDON, Aug. 28.—"Brave Highflyer!" Everywhere one goes today there are echoes of Churchill's message to Capt. Henry Buller and his merry men of the British light cruiser which has just sunk the German raider, Kaiser Wilhelm Der Grosse. They are envied by the whole British navy, not that their achievement is a great one, but that they were privileged to rid the seas of a raider which has been harrassing essential British trade to Cape Colony and South America before it was able to do further mischief on even more vital British food routes. Especial pride is shown this morning among British public school boys because the Highflyer is the training ship to which boys from Eton, Harrow, Rugby and other public schools enter as midshipmen, 40 having entered her last September. In these great historic English schools it will be long heard that their cruiser was the first to engage in a duel and sink a German opponent. Seventy years hence old men in the United Service clubs will tell the tale of how their ship sunk a proud German liner which bore the name of the great war lord.

—WINDERMERE.

KAISER IS FULL OF REGRETS FOR ...

:: THE BITER BITTEN ::

AHA, BEAR STEAK - DIE ALLE BESTE
RUSSIA
GERMANY

British Forces Attacked By Five of German Army Corps and Their Cavalry

Casualties are Reported to be Heavy—Field Marshal French Does Not Announce the ... the Battle But the ... royer Sunk

HOSPITAL MAY BE ERECTED FOR WOUNDED MEN

Canadian Associations Propose to Look After Overseas Contingent

MASONIC LODGE ORIGINATES IDEA

Question of Constructing Special Building Must be Settled

(Western Associated Press)

LONDON, Aug. 28.—Canadian associations here, dealing with philanthropic emergencies arising from the war, are discussing a proposal to erect a hospital for the use of the sick and wounded among the Canadian contingent. Yesterday considerable time was spent in attempting to reconcile the different suggestions.

The Canada Masonic lodge here, which originated the hospital idea, is anxious that the effort should proceed under the auspices of the order of the Knights of St. John of Jerusalem. Others interested think the proposed building of a hospital with 100 beds which would cost $100,000 to maintain only for one year is advisable. This has been turned down. The proposal now is for a fifty-bed hospital.

Some parties consider there is no necessity to incur the expense of building a special hospital considering that so many large houses have been offered for the purpose in dieffrent parts of the country. All these points have still to be considered. Certainly the number of houses in all sorts of places throughout the kingdom, either equipped or utterly impossible which have been offered is perfectly bewildering and warrants the belief that if all the offers were accepted every wounded British belligerent would almost have a ward to himself. The Canadian proposal in England as it now stands will, if proceeded with, involve an initial expenditure of 10,000 pounds, which may take some raising, considering the many calls upon all classes just now for national funds.

LONDON, Aug. 28.—The Morning Post today has an appreciative article upon Canada's military ... ent, in which complim...

Story of British Fighting Thrills Nation---Wounded Bring Back Description

Whitehall Lined With People Awaiting Further News—Injured, Who Have Arrived on English Soil, Are Anxiously Awaiting Chance to Return to the Front—Say Onslaught of Germans Was Terrific—Kaiser's Infantry Cannot Shoot, Say Soldiers, But Artillery is Deadly.

(Special Cable to The Edmonton Journal and The Montreal Star.—Registered according to Copyright Act.—Windermere London Service.)

LONDON, Aug. 28.—All England is thrilled with the stories of the first British fighting round Mons, brought back from the front by batches of wounded who have arrived at Rouen, Paris and Folkestone. No list of casualties has yet been received.

Whitehall was lined today with women and old men awaiting news with the deepest anxiety. Photographs of wounded Britishers as carried from trains and transchannel steamers show cheerful smiling Highlanders, Londoners, men from Middlesex, and other regiments with arms and heads in bandages, enjoying their first English cigarettes, all eager to be allowed by doctors to quickly return to the front. From survivors' stories, the German onslaught was terrific. Masses of Germans pushed forward over the dead bodies of their comrades in [illegible]. Some survivors declare that in some of the hottest engagements 20 Germans fell for every Britisher. "They can't shoot for nuts," one wounded Yorkshire man declared. "You can stand up in firing and they won't hit you. But it is quite different with their blasted artillery. Most of the wounded and killed in our regiment were knocked out by German sharpnel. The Zeppelins and German aircraft told them where we were lying, but they can't stand cold steel. That fairly knocks them out. The pity is that only one lot of our men, so far as I know, had a chance with bayonets.

WINDERMERE.

ITALIANS VERY ENTHUSIASTIC TO FRENCH NATION

Progress of Events Now Has Great Influence on Paris' Ultimate Fate

(Western Associated Press)

LONDON, Aug. 28.—No news reached ...

Ten million Russian soldiers have been enrolled under the standard of Emperor Nicholas, according to staff officers of the Russian army who have arrived here from St Petersburg. At sea also Rus...

NC-6-1210 Glenbow Archives

Family and friends bid farewell to the seven officers and 173 men of the 19th Alberta Dragoons as they left Strathcona station in 1914.

Journal exhibited the cocky confidence of a handsome adolescent. Clearly, all three were a little gawky, and probably somewhat unsophisticated, but completely certain that the future was theirs.

In 1911, the newspaper did not have wire services capable of providing instantaneous reports from around the globe, but that was coming.

By 1920, that gawkiness had vanished.

The guileless lack of sophistication was replaced by a weary worldliness forged in the bloody, muddy trenches of the First World War. Six thousand Albertans were among the almost 60,000 Canadians who gave up their lives between 1914 and 1918, and most of those names appeared in the daily casualty lists in the paper. Another 173,000 suffered from battle wounds or the aftereffects of German gas attacks.

As they read their *Journal* day after day, Edmontonians became haunted by those far-off places with the foreign names. Maps and descriptions printed in the paper provided the first acquaintance of Ypres and Vimy, the Somme and Passchendaele. The news itself may have been censored by military authorities, but readers had a desperate need to know all they could. The graveyards in Belgium and France were the final resting places of their sons and husbands, brothers and lovers.

But while the assassination of Archduke Francis Ferdinand, heir to the Austria-Hungarian throne, in the Serbian capital of Sarajevo did make the front page on June 29, 1914, its significance may not have been fully grasped. It wasn't the top story. That spot was reserved for a debate over whether the city's police chief or the magistrate had the right to set bail. After a few days, the assassination story disappeared from the news pages.

But by late July, events in Europe were heating up. Serbia (or "Servia," as it is spelled in the paper) became the catalyst for a major power grab in Europe. Mutual defence treaties going as far back as 1833 snapped into place like the bolt in a rifle.

This got *The Journal*'s attention: "Come What May England Will Stand By Her Friends," said the July 29, 1914, banner headline across the front page.

On Aug. 5, 1914, "What May" came, and the headline read: "Britain Sends 150,000 Troops To Belgium."

Where Britain went, the Dominion of Canada followed. The editorial that day was unequivocal: "The Overseas Dominions will leave nothing undone to ensure the successful carrying through of the great task to which the Motherland has set her hand."

On Aug. 8, 1914, the paper published a somewhat bizarre and less-than-reassuring front-page editor's message about its war coverage. "The best the newspaper can do is to make certain the sources from which its rumours are received are the most reliable available."

Like just about every other newspaper in North America, *The Journal* was a novice in the area of covering a global meltdown. It got better with practice.

The paper, first and foremost, supported the war.

***In 1911*:**
C.R. Morrison is appointed *Journal* news editor. He retires in 1929 as assistant editor. John Dixon Craig joins the news staff.

***Jan. 5, 1911*:**
***The Journal* reports the first cases of "infantile paralysis" in the city. The disease would become known in later years as polio.**

***Jan. 13, 1911*:**
"The growing boy's time should be employed, not in cramming knowledge into his head, but rather in training every power of mind and body in such a way as to develop them to their highest possible efficiency for the greater work in after life. This is what schools should be for. But when we add homework to our school work, we also add another letter to our object, 'mental training,' and thereby make it 'mental straining.' " Letter to the editor from A Constant Reader on the issue of too much homework.

***Jan. 16, 1911*:**
Alex Decoteau becomes Edmonton's and Canada's first treaty Indian police officer.

City of Edmonton Archives

Alex Decoteau.

Last Edition

Edmonton Journal

Daily Circulation
FRIDAY, JAN. 5, 1912.
8,185
Lists Open For Inspection

Vol. 3, No. 150. EDMONTON, ALBERTA, SATURDAY, JAN. 6, 1912. SIXTEEN PAGES

SUFFERING AND DEATH FOLLOWING IN WAKE OF COLD

All Middle States and Central and Eastern Canada Have Below Zero Weather

SEVERAL FROZEN TO DEATH IN STORM

Superior, Wisconsin, With 38 Below, Is Coldest Place in States —Wire Trouble Develops

(Western Associated Press.)

WINNIPEG, Jan. 6.—Fifty below zero at Whitemouth, Ont., and equally severe weather all along the north shore played havoc with wires last night, and early this morning Winnipeg was completely cut off from communication with the east. This would not have been serious were it not that similar conditions prevailed over the southern area of the Great Lakes, and totally affected the alternative routes of telegraph companies throughout American territory.

Wire trouble to the south usually develops around the international boundary, but on this occasion it is widespread, being most severe south of St. Paul, Chicago being completely cut off in the early forenoon today. Conditions nearly as severe have prevailed in the prairie section, temperatures running forty below being recorded pretty generally over the three wester nprovinces, with the result that wires are working slowly.

The intense cold makes train operation very difficult, and little freight is moving today. Several trains are reported frozen up as they stood.

Toronto's Poor Suffer.

TORONTO, Jan. 6.—The coldest snap of the season was experienced here last night and today. From 15 above yesterday morning the thermometer dropped to 15 below this morning. Many cases of suffering are reported in Toronto among the poor. All yesterday there was a continuous procession to the house of industry of applicants for relief. Many cases of tuberculosis have developed through the cold, and are being reported by the nurses of the medical health department. The observatory people see no signs of warmer weather.

Frozen to Death.

CALGARY, Jan. 6.—William R. Carleton, aged 36, was brought in from Gleichen this morning. Carleton, who was found frozen to death ...

The Tale of the Week as Told by the Journal's Cartoonist

SHOCKING!
J.B.
BRITAIN NOTIFIES TURKEY OUTRAGES MUST STOP IN THE BALKANS
OUR RIGHT LITTLE TIGHT LITTLE ISLAND
CONSERVATIVES MAKE BIG SWEEP OF PRINCE EDWARD ISLAND
HE LOOKS PRETTY STOUT
PRES. TAFT SAYS ONLY DEATH CAN KEEP HIM FROM THE PRESIDENCY
YLUCHEE FLIGHTEE NOW
GOLD CURE
CHINESE IMPERIALISTS GET BIG DONATIONS
IT'S A NICE PLACE BUT I DIDN'T LIKE THE GRUB
FRENCH OFFICER ESCAPES FROM GERMAN FORTRESS

GOVERNMENT TO BUILD A. & G.W.? AND SO CROSS ENTERS SIFTON FOLD

Reported In Winnipeg That Line to Fort McMurray Will Be Built Either By Government Itself Or Else Under Its Auspices—Stated Also That Conferences Have Been Held Between Premier Sifton and General Manager Chamberlain of the G. T. P.

(Western Associated Press.)

WINNIPEG, Jan. 6.—It is reported here that two conferences have taken place between Premier Sifton of Alberta and General Manager Chamberlain of the Grand Trunk Pacific railway, and as a consequence more cordial relations than previously existed between this railway company and the Sifton government are being established.

It is also said that when the premier makes his next announcement respecting his railroad policy, it will include a bond guarantee for the proposed G. T. P. Edson-Grande Prairie road, and for at least two other projected Alberta branches. There is also a rumor here that comes with some show of authority that the Great Waterways railway from Edmonton to Fort McMurray will be built by the government or under government auspices, and that this is the reason why Mr. Cross has entered the Sifton fold.

DUKE OF CONNAUGHT AVOIDS RED TAPE

Writes Direct to Deputy Minister of Education Regarding Awards For Scholars

His royal highness the governor-general ... Alberta in ...

TELLS VANCOUVER ALBERTA WILL TAP PEACE RIVER LAND

Frank Walker Assures Coast People "Edmonton Will Beat ...

FALLING TREE KILLS WOODMAN AT CLYDE

Out Chopping Trees With Two Brothers When One Falls On Him

A. Patrey, a woodsman living at Clyde, west of Morinville, was killed yesterday afternoon by a falling tree. With two of his ...

King George Stamps Make Appearance

New Issue, Now on Sale in This City, Are Being Used by Many.

During the week letters have changed in their appearance to those which arrived before the first of the year. The change lies in the fact that the stamps bearing King George's face have begun to supplant those bearing that of the late King Edward.

These stamps have been on sale at the local post office since the beginning of the year and will entirely supplant the older stamp as the supply of the latter runs out.

In many respects these new stamps are the most interesting ever issued by the Dominion, and the workmanship is very fine. The King's face is represented in profile and is very clear. The surrounding border is horseshoe in shape and bears the words "Canada Postage" at the top, and the ends of the shoe carry three maple leaves each. The denomination is to be found in the lower corners whilst the two upper are occupied by crowns.

The design was submitted to His Majesty previous to its adoption by the Canadian government and received his approval.

Electric Light Shows Big Gains

PRISONER TRIES TO COMMIT SUICIDE

John Barry Uses Belt In Effort to Slay Self In Cell of City Jail

When Constable Norman McRae of the city police force went into the cell department of the police station at 11:15 last night he found John Barry, who had been brought in by Constable Alex. Decoteau earlier in the evening on a charge of drunkenness, hanging to the top of his cell with a leather belt around his neck.

Barry had placed one end of the belt through the buckle, and put the loop around his neck after tying it securely to the top of the cell. McRae tried to untie the belt, but found it necessary to cut it to bring Barry down. Barry was badly choked, and it was only after hard work on the part of two constables who worked over him for several moments that Barry was revived. The police say that if he had hung at the end of the strap two minutes longer he would have been dead.

Investigation of the cell in which Barry had been placed showed that the man who attempted to commit suicide had torn his clothing to rags, destroyed the mattress in his cell ...

SEVEN LEADERS OF UNION LABOR ARE RE-INDICTED

True Bills Brought Against O. A. Tveitmoe, E. A. Clancey, J. E. Munsey, A. Johannsen and Dynamiters

CLANCEY IS ALLEGED TO HAVE CONFESSED

Under Dramatic Circumstances, Said to Have Told of Interview With McNamaras

(Special to The Journal.)

LOS ANGELES, Jan. 6.—The grand jury today in connection with the blowing up of the Los Angeles Times building reindicted seven labor leaders. They are: Olaf A. Tveitmoe, of San Francisco, secretary of the State Building Trades council; J. Munsey, of Salt Lake City, secretary of the Salt Lake Union of the International Association of Bridge and Structural Iron Workers; E. A. Clancey, formerly a member of the executive board of the Structural Iron Workers; Anton Johannsen, organizer of the State Building Trades council; J. B. and J. J. McNamara, the confessed dynamiters; and Ortie McManigal, who turned state's evidence.

Clancey is credited with a confession to Special United States Prosecutor Oscar Lawlor, which is said to have furnished the federal authorities with the most important evidence they have gained since their investigation began. This alleged confession is said to have been made in Lawler's office in San Francisco with Ortie McManigal sitting in an adjoining room with the door open. When Clancey left the place he was in a state of near collapse, attended by a nurse and a friend.

It has been learned from an official who was present at the ordeal that Clancey made the following alleged admissions:

That he (Clancey) met J. B. McNamara by appointment in Seattle in August, 1910.

That J. B. McNamara informed him that he would use the name of J. B. Bryce in California in jobs.

That J. B. McNamara had told him that he had been sent to California to spend six weeks in blowing up "scab jobs."

That he knew that J. B. ...

NC-6-530 Glenbow Archives

In 1912 *The Journal*'s second-floor newsroom overlooked 101st Street at 102nd Avenue, across from the King Edward Hotel.

Woe betide anyone who doubted the necessity of ridding continental Europe of the Hun scourge.

On Jan. 2, 1915, an editorial dismissed any second thoughts about the war: "It only serves to distract the attention from what is the plain duty of the moment. With so much depending on the result of the clash of arms in Europe, we only imperil this by moralizing on the evils of warfare."

"Making the supreme sacrifice for the Empire," was a dreadful, but necessary, part of war to the editors of the day.

However, there was a cost in men, which the paper acknowledged on Feb. 15, 1915: "We are proud to have them in the field and look for them to do themselves and their country the greatest credit. But we must also steel ourselves for the penalties which under no circumstances can be avoided."

The early editions of what became daily casualty lists contained names of those who died, not in action, but in hospital of pneumonia, meningitis and diphtheria. Many Canadian troops were first stockpiled in rain- and disease-soaked camps on the Salisbury Plain in England.

A Feb. 1, 1915, report showed how serious things were getting: "The latest order issued by the medical authorities requests Salisbury girls to refrain from kissing Canadian soldiers owing to the infectious diseases in camps and town."

But combat deaths came soon enough as one of the first major battles in which Canadians played a major role was Ypres, in April 1915.

On April 20, the paper reported 305 Canadians dead. The April 26 stories said there were 1,000 dead.

On April 29, it was "four or five thousand."

There was also an evolution of coverage. The news slant became more upbeat and less about Canadian or Allied casualties. While heroic Canadians overcame the odds in the trenches, Germans were vilified as sub-human beasts and cowards in stories and editorials.

For example, an April 26 story about one lieutenant's heroics at Vimy Ridge: "With seven of his men and an unknown sergeant of another command, he proceeded to bomb the enemy dugouts. In the first one he found over 150 Germans with seven officers, all of whom promptly surrendered to this little group of nine men."

The paper welcomed the United States' belated entry into the war April 6, 1917, but not without an editorial swipe at the reluctant U.S. President Woodrow Wilson: "History will never accuse the president of having acted without due caution. It will say that he continued to express confidence in Germany long after all warrant for that confidence had disappeared."

***April 28, 1911*:**
***The Journal* arranges the city's first airplane flight as an add-on attraction to the first horse show. For two days, pilot Hugh Armstrong Robinson flew a "Curtiss-type" biplane over the fair grounds.**

***June 13, 1911*:**
Fraser M. Gerrie joins *The Journal*'s staff as sports editor. After several promotions, he is appointed editor in 1953.

***July 21, 1911*:**
Mass communications guru Marshall McLuhan, best known for the phrase, "The medium is the message," is born in Edmonton.

***Aug. 1, 1911*:**
Canadian Newspapers Limited takes over the management and ownership of *The Journal* Company Limited, for consideration of 1,149 shares of common stock at $100 each.

EDMONTON JOURNAL.
3132
NC-6-682 Glenbow Archives
Getting the paper to market, 1913.

LAST EDITION

Edmonton Journal

DAILY CIRCULATION
FRIDAY, AUGUST 28, 1914
19,304
Lists open for Inspection.

Vol. 11, No. 40 | EDMONTON, ALBERTA SATURDAY, AUGUST 29, 1914 | TWENTY PAGES

BERLIN HAS BECOME PANIC STRICKEN

MUSCOVITE ADVANCE CONTINUES UNINTERRUPTED; GERMANS RETREAT; NET IS DRAWING AROUND LEMBERG

All Enthusiasm for War Has Disappeared From Capital of Kaiser's Empire, Says Official Dispatch—Scarcity of Food is Assuming Alarming Proportions—Socialist Movement Against Fight is Expected -- Travellers From East Prussia Increase Terror by Stating Russians Will Soon be in Berlin.

(Western Associated Press)

ROME, August 20.—"All enthusiasm has disappeared; Berlin is panic stricken," says an official dispatch received from the German capital today. Travelers arriving at Berlin from East Prussia have increased the terror with their declarations that the Russians will soon arrive there.

The scarcity of food in Germany, the dispatch adds, is assuming alarming proportions. A Socialist movement against the war is anticipated, though the leaders of that party thus far have been loyal to the government.

The last Landstrum is called to the colors to fill up the enormous gaps created in the western army by fighting with the allies, also to operate against the Russians, who may reach Berlin within a month.

PARIS, August ... ving official statement ...

GERMANS BREAK ALL THE RULES OF CIVILIZED WAR

Bombard Malines, an Open and Undefended Town—Infantry Occupy Place

ONLY OBJECT IS TO TERRORIZE CIVILIANS

Belgian Division Retires by Way of Sambre and the Meuse

(Western Associated Press)

LONDON, August 29.—The correspondent of the Reuter's Telegram company at Antwerp sends the following official statement which has oeen issued there:

"On Thursday the Germans, contrary to the laws of warfare, bombarded Malines, an open and undefended town.

"On Friday morning the town was partially occupied by German infantry, which withdrew toward the south in the afternoon, and the bombardment was renewed, shells falling about each quarter of an hour.

"The enemy also bombarded the region about Heyst-Opden-Berg, a town 17 miles southeast of Antwerp, an open ... not occupied by the military. ... operations had no less an ... rorize the civilian popu- ... systematically ... gaps at Namur ... suffered

CIVILIZED GERMANY

NOW THEN, TURN OUT YOUR POCKETS OR—
BELGIUM

RECKONING DAY WILL COME TO PAY FOR LOUVAIN

Oxford of Belgium Destroyed by Germans on Flimsiest Pretext

BEAUTIFUL CITY REDUCED TO ASHES

Abominable Act Shall be Expiated to Uttermost Says London Times

(Special Cable to The Edmonton Journal and The Montreal Star)
[Registered according to copyright act]
(Windermere London Service)

LONDON, Aug. 29.—The Times, which hitherto has been most restrained in its references to German barbarities, is aflame today at the destruction of the beautiful Belgian city of Louvain, which is the Oxford of Belgium, and has been the intellectual metropolis of the low countries since the fifteenth century. It is now a heap of ashes. The beautiful Hotel de Ville has been ruthlessly destroyed, also the stately church at Pierre, the famous university with its library of 70,000 volumes and priceless manuscripts. It has been completely wiped out on the most flimsy military pretext.

"This infamous crime," says the Times, "is without parallel even in the dark ages. Even Attila spared Milan. Our Attila of Berlin respects neither the laws of nations nor the laws of God. His evil deeds cry aloud to heaven and to the horror-struck watching nations. The wickedness of this abominable act shall be expiated to the uttermost when the ...

A Letter to Mother, or---

A remarkable photograph of a Belgian soldier writing a letter home after the battle of Haelen. He is writing on a carrier pigeon basket, the birds being used to send letters back from the front.

If there is a time when you feel a lump in your throat it is when the mail comes in. We stood outside a tent where a grey blanket lay on the ground. On it was dumped a huge sack of letters, packets and cards. Then there was such a scramble for mothers' letters, wives' letters, sisters' letters, letters from the only girl and letters from the other girls, fathers' letters, brothers' letters and letters from good friends. And as the boys eagerly tear them open you see some lips quiver as that feeling of home surges within them. Home is such a long way from Valcartier. But if the letters sadden some, no letters make others sadder. Was some one too busy to write? Was some one too tired and put it off for a day or two?

Not that those boys, who for us are sleeping out there in tents beneath the weeping skies of chilly Valcartier mind it much. We saw one gallant husband but laugh when the boys taunted him because her letter was not there.

"Oh," said he, "I got a good one yesterday. She asked me if I'd lost my pink slip yet, for if I had she was ready to send me another!"

And to see the boys answer their letters is another unforgettable sight of the camp. Some steal time when dead with sleep to write a few words by the light of their tent lantern. What shadows those very lanterns throw on those thousands of white tents. And to go through the lines after dusk is to see strange and wierd sights happening behind the canvas.

But to get back to those letters. To some of the lads they are the hardest task of their day. Some may write them in their tents, but when a fellow's bunking with nine others, a tent may not be just the easiest place for correspondence. So the Y. M. C. A. tent seems to be the most popular spot for this purpose on the grounds. There, after drill or Sundays, you can see a long table which is crowded man after man. Arms on table, heads almost on arms, there they sit writing like mad. What tales those sheets of paper could tell! What romances; what tragedies that whole camp could unfold!—Cornelia in Toronto Telegram.

NC-6-2394 Glenbow Archives

The barns at the Exhibition Grounds were used as barracks in both world wars. In 1916, a trench warfare demonstration took place at the Edmonton Exhibition.

Thousands of war and war-related stories kept anxious and worried readers as informed as the censors allowed. The use of pictures increased, but it was the hundreds of front-page editorial cartoons demonizing the Kaiser and the German people that helped to focus the purpose of the war in the reader's mind.

The paper also got to know its readers better as it dedicated one or two pages a week to stories of individual and family sacrifice. The concept of the "people feature" was new, but the tradition carries on in today's *Journal.*

As the war dragged on, men were more reluctant to head down to the recruiting office to replace the thousands killed or maimed in Europe. Editorially, *The Journal* called the less-than-enthusiastic patriots "slackers."

Serious talk about conscription began in 1915 and Prime Minister Robert Borden announced it would start in the summer of 1917.

Not all were pleased, and the issue came close to splitting the country, but on May 16, 1917, the paper was all for an involuntary army: "It has been apparent to everyone for many weeks past that, as the prime minister said 'the voluntary system will not yield further substantial results.' "

Not to meet personnel commitments to the war would "impair very seriously the glory it has brought us and to prove false not only to the cause of freedom and of civilization but to the men who have been representing us on the firing line."

While the paper supported the draft, it was dead set against recruiting children. More than a year earlier, on April 27, 1916, the paper scorned attempts by recruiters to induce boys as young as 15 to join their units.

An editorial writer had a better idea: "There would be no harm in lowering the age for the militia regiments in order to bring these up to strength and give the boys the chance to prepare themselves which otherwise would be denied them."

On Aug. 2, 1917, the war even found a place on the sports pages.

The paper took almost the entire sports page to print a letter from the trenches from Deacon White, who later remained prominent in Alberta sporting circles for decades. His 3,000-word letter to sports editor George Mackintosh reported on a baseball game played before 40,000 soldiers in the shadow of Vimy Ridge.

White had only recently recovered from serious wounds he received in the Battle of Vimy and was unable to play in the game. Instead, he served as manager of the team representing the 3rd Division of the Canadian Army Corps as it defeated a squad from the 1st Division, 11-9.

What was striking in Deacon's report wasn't the score or the painstaking details he gave of the game itself. What mattered most was that the few references to the war itself were almost unconsciously off-hand, as if Deacon, the players and the khaki-clad spectators wanted simply to put the horrors of it all behind them, if only for nine innings.

The story of the game ended with a near apology for sloppy play.

"The game was played in a sort of natural amphitheatre," Deacon wrote, "the ground behind the home plate rising at an angle of 30 degrees to a big height, and this hillside was packed tier on tier with soldiers, who hung breathlessly on the game until the last man was out, so close and exciting was it.

***Sept. 26, 1911*:**
Strathcona voters, on the south side of the North Saskatchewan River, approve amalgamation with Edmonton.

NB-16-173 GLENBOW ARCHIVES

Robert L. Borden.

***Oct. 25, 1911*:**
Return rail fare from Edmonton to Montreal is $64.90.

***Nov, 30, 1911*:**
The first Alberta legislature session in the newly built Legislative Building opens.

***Dec. 2, 1911*:**
Just in time for Christmas, *The Journal* announces it will give away a clock with every subscription. The "mission clock" has a retail value of $12 ($200 today). The clock is made of oak and brass and can run eight days with one winding.

***In 1912*:**
A printer at *The Journal* makes $1 an hour, while a

NA-1072-17 Glenbow Archives

The discovery of large gas fields started early in Alberta's history. Here the crew poses after Viking well No. 2 came in, 1916-17.
Pipelines connecting Edmonton to Viking soon followed.

IMPERIAL SHOE STORE
MASON & RISCH
PIANO Co.
TAILORING
PIANOS
MOIR'S
Chocolates
Soft Drinks

NC-6-1392 Glenbow Archives

In 1915 more than 1,000 infantrymen of the 51st Battalion crossed 102nd Street as they marched down Jasper Avenue
from their Exhibition Grounds barracks on the way to the CPR station at 109th Street.

"There was considerable betting on the game. In fact, I guess that everyone who had money got it down. In the box scores that follow, the errors and heavy hitting were due to the nature of the ground." His team registered eight hits and four errors on a field pocked with shell holes.

And if war news found a home on the sports pages, so did it too in other sections of the newspaper.

On Farmer Smith's Rainbow Children's Page, a regular Saturday feature, the following letter from a young reader appeared on Aug. 4, 1917:

"Dear Farmer Smith,

"You know I promised a picture of myself and the baby. I am sending you it in this letter. I am going to write a story also.

"The baby's daddy has never seen him. He is away in the fighting line.

"My daddy is away in the fighting lines also. I wish this war was over and the soldiers would come back safely.

"The baby is only six months old. He is awful fat. His name is Ronald Charles Neal.

"Why don't you put our picture in the paper Saturday?

"Our Sunday school at Calder had a picnic down in the east end park on Thursday and we all had a lovely time. The day was nice and warm.

"Your loving Rainbow, Alberta Martin."

The women's page also carried war news, including wrenching letters from the front lines sent by the husbands, sons and sweethearts, and regular reports on the production of socks, bed sheets and shirts from sewing and knitting circles.

Finally, the war was over. *The Journal*'s coverage of the Armistice on Nov. 11, 1918, reflected a maturity not present in the first confused days of the conflict: "It is not in the spirit of the ancient triumphal celebrations that we greet the new era that dawns today. The price that has been paid for victory is too great for that. The spirit of the day is rather one of profound thankfulness in which all must share, whether the war has brought them heavy personal loss or none at all."

That November it was hard to recall that the decade had began so well.

In 1911, the paper had no need to concern itself with German militarism, the fate of the Empire or the politics of the Old Country. It was too busy arguing whether reciprocity – a modest version of free trade with the U.S. – would lead to the country's salvation or its downfall.

According to a two-page exploration of the reciprocity issue on Feb. 22, 1911, free trade of any sort with the U.S. would only lead to annexation.

"Now what does Annexation imply?" the story asked.

"First, it implies absolute free trade between Canada and the United States.

"Down come our tall chimneys! Useless are our railways for the East-and-West haul! Abandoned are our ports! Empty are our canals!"

Western farmers supported free trade, mostly because they wanted the opportunity to buy cheaper American farm machinery, and they supported the government of Wilfrid Laurier, which backed reciprocity. The West wasn't able to swing the country and Laurier was defeated by Robert Borden's Tories, a result that the paper, always a supporter of the Conservative cause, hailed as the best possible outcome.

section editor makes $15 a week. The weekly *Rural North West* is started. It stops publication in August 1916, and its agricultural features are printed in the Saturday *Journal*.

***Jan. 23, 1912*: *The Journal* goes on the record against tipping. The anti-tipping movement in the U.S. had spread to Canada. The paper's editors were all in favour, calling tipping "the worst feature of travelling and the Bohemian life...The psychological moment has arrived. It's now or never. Stop tipping and they (waiters, porters, bellhops) will become earners of adequate wages instead of strong-arm beggars."**

***Jan. 31, 1912*: Strathcona Mayor Arthur Davies presides over the final council meeting before the south side city amalgamates with Edmonton.**

***Feb 1. 1912*: Edmonton and Strathcona amalgamate bringing Edmonton's population to more than 53,000.**

***Feb. 3, 1912*: *The Journal* publishes its first car page, "Motor news of Greater Edmonton." By the next week it will**

SNAPSHOT BILL
BY RUSS WESTOVER
BE MINE BETTY AND I'LL TAKE A PICTURE OF YOU EVERY DAY FOR NOTHING
YOU HAVE TO ASK DAD, BILL, YOU KNOW WHAT HE THINKS OF PHOTOGRAPHERS
I HAVE COME TO ASK YOU FOR YOUR DAUGHTER'S HAND, MR. BIRD
I SUPPOSE YOU WANT TO TAKE A PICTURE OF IT, HUH?
?
DAD MUST HAVE BEEN USING SOME GOOD HAIR TONIC
(COPYRIGHT, 1914, BY THE NEW YORK HERALD CO.) All Rights Reserved.
WHAT BILL GOT
WAIT TILL I GET THAT POSE
TAKE THAT CAT OFF MY HEAD!
MEW
I GOTCHA
CLICK!
I'M QUEERED
BONEHEAD
RUSS WESTOVER
IT'S A MISTAKE

There was also the burning issue of prohibition to debate, as well as getting the vote for women, and a new organization – the United Farmers of Alberta (UFA) – that believed in both. The UFA supported the Liberals provincially but played the reluctant coquette when it came to actually entering politics. It became bolder as the decade wore on, and elected its first MLA in a 1919 by-election. It took over the provincial government itself in the election of 1921.

In the pages of *The Journal* local issues prevailed during the early years of the decade as the paper and its readers worried about whether the streets in all the new subdivisions should be paved, and what to do about motor cars and traffic. It fretted over the problems that unfettered immigration might bring.

Newcomers flooded the province to take advantage of the homesteading opportunities. A story from the beginning of 1912 reported that the city had absorbed 3,632 immigrants in the preceding 12 months. Of those, some 762 were Americans – white Americans – and another 209 were "coloured" Americans.

Wherever settlers went, merchants followed. There were new towns with new schools. Implement dealers sold the latest in farm equipment and preachers sermonized from pulpits in churches where the smell of fresh-sawn lumber still hung in the air.

However, not all immigrants were favoured.

When black Americans from Oklahoma began searching out places where they could farm, there was a cool response from many.

In a story from April 19, 1911, reporting on an Edmonton board of trade meeting, Ald. J.D. Hyndman suggested that the federal government take away the homestead rights of black people to prevent more of them from coming to Canada.

Businessman W.H. Clark said black settlers would never be assimilated in rural Alberta, and that they would drive out white farmers. The paper quoted realtor George Fraser as saying "that he found the Negro to be an indigestible quantity in social circles everywhere."

A resolution asking that black immigration be curtailed received a negative response from a lone board member, identified only as T. Hindle, who called for "British fair play."

The paper agreed with Hindle. But it still referred to black immigrants as "darkies." In an editorial responding to the immigration of blacks, the newspaper said: "Provided the Negro immigrant measures up to other requirements, it is manifestly impossible to deny him admission on account of his colour.

"Under the circumstances we can but wish him well in his new home and express the hope that he may so conduct himself that he will live down the unfriendly and distrustful spirit which exists toward him."

The paper also suggested that those black immigrants who embraced the teachings of Dr. Booker T. Washington, the founder of the famous Tuskegee Institute in Alabama, were most welcome: "The gospel which Mr. Washington has preached is simply that of salvation by hard work. The newcomers will find lots of the latter in the districts into which they are going and if they set to it with a will and turn large tracts of wild land into

be simply called "Motoring" and contain news and ads about new cars, gadgets and experiments. The most expensive car on that first page is a 30-hp Mitchell, fully equipped with electric lights and full-floating gear axle that can be had for $1,800 from Taylor-Musson Auto Company, 649 Third St. That's more than $30,000 in today's money.

***Feb. 12, 1912*:**
***Journal* daily circulation is 9,233.**

***Feb. 13, 1912*:**
Southam Newspapers takes over the company that owns the *Edmonton Journal*.

***Feb. 16, 1912*:**
The newly amalgamated cities of Edmonton and Strathcona hold their first municipal election, voting in a new city council with George Armstrong as mayor. Bessie Nichols is the first woman elected to public office in Edmonton when she wins a two-year term as a city school trustee.

***Feb. 24, 1912*:**
J.H. McKinley of the undertaking firm of Connolly and McKinley brings the first auto ambulance to Edmonton. It's a Studebaker electric ambulance. "The

CHAMPION "JACK" JOHNSON, WITH ENGLISH STYLE AND MANNERS, IS HOME AGAIN; HAS NOT QUIT PRIZE RING, HE SAYS, AND WILL FIGHT ANY BODY FOR $30,000

OLD
DR. JOHNSON'S
LINIMENT

"DR." JOHNSON IN HIS LABORATORY.

G'MAWNING, KING. JACK JOHNSON.

"Jack" Johnson, the world's heavyweight champion, is home again after a long sojourn in England. When he landed in New York he denied emphatically that he had retired from the fighting game and said he would "fight anybody anywhere, any time, any distance, if I get my price. That's $30,000." "Lil' Arta" looked "real English, doncher know," as he tripped merrily down the gangplank. He saw the King during the coronation festivities, and "Jack" said he was greatly impressed.

As a side issue the champion has gone into the manufacturing of a liniment which he says is the greatest thing in the world for athletes. As a result he has been dubbed "Old Doctor Johnson" by his friends.

Here Lies
THE
Morning Journal
BORN
Aug. 13 - 1906
DIED
Sept. 30 - 1911
"Whom the Gods Love Die Young"
Rest In Peace

In 1911 *The Morning Journal* ceased publication and *The Journal* stayed with an evening-only edition until the 1980s.

well-cultivated farms, they will prove themselves much more desirable additions to our population than many of those who are now speaking so contemptuously of them and are loafing about the city streets."

Prejudice against foreigners ran deep, and at the inaugural meeting of the Women's Canadian Club on Jan. 21, 1912, club founder Emily Murphy spoke of her feelings about the presence of so many immigrants. Welcome them, she said, but she also sounded a note of caution in a speech that *The Journal* reported in full the next day.

"All great nations have come out of the north. With few exceptions, the tide of conquests has ever run from north to south.

"In the past five centuries the people of the heat belt have added nothing to civilization. The natives of the tropics have contributed nothing of first importance to literature, science, inventions, of the industrial arts…."

The Journal's Anne Merrill, one of the first writer/editors to receive a regular byline, was a co-founder of the club.

Merrill compiled the daily "Items Of Interest to Women" page, and covered the social scene of the young city's most important people.

But Merrill's page did more than record the teas and dances attended by the smart set. These pages ran the first photographs of Murphy and Bessie H. Nichols, who was elected school trustee of Greater Edmonton in 1912, and became the first woman to hold municipal office between Vancouver and Toronto. It took a special act of the legislature for Nichols to serve, and still four years passed before women were allowed to vote in provincial elections.

It was also on the women's pages that readers first encountered Louise McKinney, the prohibitionist Claresholm MLA who was elected in 1916 and was the first woman legislator in the British Empire. Other famous women appeared on Merrill's pages in those early days, such as Irene Parlby, destined to become a minister in the UFA government in 1921, and Nellie McClung, of whom much more was heard in the next decade.

When it came to First Nations people, the paper did not escape the racism of society, and often adopted a bemused, paternalistic attitude. In a story from the spring of 1911, there was a tone of begrudging respect for an Indian from Wabasca, identified only as Pete, who had successfully bilked white investors with phony stories of an oil well in northern Alberta. Although he used a shameful patois when quoting Pete, it's clear the reporter had been charmed by the story of oil riches.

"With the dramatic recital

City of Edmonton Archives

Emily Murphy.

principal advantage of the Studebaker car is the fact that there was no noise and jarring to disturb the patient."

Feb. 28, 1912*:** ***The Journal **masthead says the paper is published by "*The Journal* Co. Ltd."**

***March 1, 1912*:** **The masthead now says *The Journal* is published by "Canadian Newspapers Limited." Southam has taken over. By the next month, William Southam's name appears as "president." Editor and managing director M.R. Jennings becomes GM.**

March 1912*:** ***The Journal **becomes fully linked via a leased wire to Associated Press, Reuters and Canadian Press news services.**

***May 13, 1912*:** **Hundreds of Edmontonians line up to draw tickets setting the order for the Hudson's Bay Reserve land sale the next day. The Bay has decided to sell its large section of undeveloped land in central**

NA-200-34 Glenbow Archives

This photo of Bessie Nichols ran in *The Journal* in 1913.

A WANT SUGGESTION

You need extra money?

A little cheque coming in now and then gives a comfortable feeling.

How to find the ways and means of etxra cheque producing?

Read the Journal Want Columns carefully each day—your opportunity lies there.

The special chances are often times pretty evenly divided, and it takes but a reasonable amount of careful, painstaking attention to secure just the right opportunity. Maybe your chance is within your reach today.

Look carefully to the Journal Wants—consider their offerings and find the work you can do best.

— **TELEPHONE 1318 OR 4918** —

1836 **THE BANK OF** 1911

British North America

75 Years in Business. Capital and Reserve Over $7,300,000.

Two Members of a Family

particularly if they live far from town, frequently find it very convenient to take advantage of our **Joint Account** plan.

Either may make deposits or withdraw cash on his or her own signature alone. Thus either can do the banking when in town, as suits their convenience.

$1.00 opens a Savings Account, Joint or ordinary. Interest added half-yearly. Money may be withdrawn at any time.

Edmonton Branch . . . . . . A. K. Henderson, Manager

GIRLS

DON'T MISS THIS!

Free Embroidery Patterns

Greatest Offer Ever Made By a Newspaper

The Girl Who Can Do Hand Embroidery is the Envy Of All

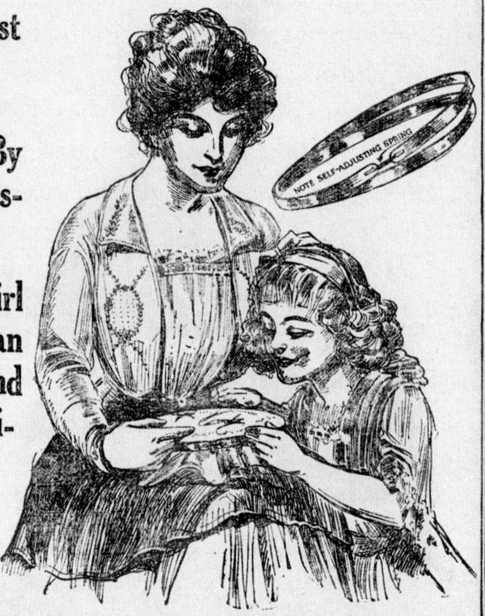
NOTE SELF-ADJUSTING SPRING

THE JOURNAL

will present to you a complete embroidery outfit consisting of 160 very latest designs — enough to last you for years — one all metal hoop, and booklet of instructions, which teaches you every stitch, all for

6 Coupons and 68c

you cannot buy one single pattern for less than 10c. Therefore, this outfit saves you over $10.00. You will be delighted with this, the greatest of all newspaper bargains, as it means prettier things to wear and prettier things for the home at a trifling expense.

For Our Readers Only

Please bear in mind the six coupons are to show you are a reader of this paper and are entitled to this bargain, and the 68c is to defray the expense from the factory, clerk hire, handling and other expenses of getting the outfit from the factory to you.

Coupon Printed on Another Page Daily

N.B.—Out of town readers will send 10 cents extra for postage

Taylor's Undertaking Parlors

Funeral Director and Embalmer.

Phone 3116. PRIVATE AMBULANCE. 14-16 Main St. N.

NIGHT AND DAY CALLS PROMPTLY ATTENDED TO.

of his tale told in the delightfully reassuring, aboriginally imperfect English, a swarthy Indian, with one of those splendingly noble countenances, with which nature gifts so many original North Americans, is said to be winning his way into the hearts and purses of many avaricious Edmonton pale faces; to be eating their food – not common eatables, but the best that local restaurateurs can dish up at the highest class prices."

The paper predicted that Pete would likely "dream in his lonely wigwam by the waters of the Wabasca of the great harvest of suckers in Edmonton."

Pete's scam reflected everyone's hope that oil would soon be discovered in northern Alberta. *Journal* advertisements offered shares in exploration companies in the tar sands decades before there was an economical method of extracting crude oil from the sands themselves. Until then, the oil-heavy sands were used for asphalt.

The Edmonton and Fort McMurray Oil and Asphalt Co., Ltd., promised big returns on the 50,000 shares they offered the public. With the shares at $1 apiece, it seemed like a good deal to many.

"The lowest price ever paid for asphalt on this market was $29.20 a ton and up to $40.00 which you will readily see makes an asphalt deposit such as ours equal to the best of silver mines," an awkwardly worded advertisement proclaimed to investors.

Typical was a front page story from the boom days of 1911. In an interview with prospectors who had just returned from the Athabasca River, readers were told that oil was positively seeping from the ground. In fact, one of the prospectors ventured, the presence of petroleum in water from the river and a nearby lake made it undrinkable. They were forced to melt snow.

Another still lucrative industry was fur trading – the business that a century before had created Fort Edmonton. It was page 1 news in March 1911 when Colin and Harry Fraser came down from Fort Chipewyan with seven silver fox pelts which sold at the McDougall and Secord fur rooms for $2,000. The two men also boasted that they would later bring down 20,000 muskrat pelts. It was also reported that other furs sold that day included 148 marten, 40 mink and 309 weasels.

Nevertheless, it wasn't all land deals and weasels. As always, there was entertainment in Edmonton.

A half-dozen theatres offered both moving pictures and live shows. The great Sarah Bernhardt performed her world famous Camille in a one-night stand, and in 1912 Forbes-Robertson, billed as the greatest actor of his day, brought Jerome K. Jerome's *The Passing of the Third Floor Back* to the Empire Theatre on 103rd Street, north of the Hudson's Bay store.

An editorial crowed that the arrival of such a personage in what was once a city-on-the-fringes proved just how far Edmonton had come.

John Philip Sousa brought his band in 1919, and countless thousands turned out to hear some of the greatest marches ever written.

In the early years of the decade, things looked to get even more entertaining. Alexander Pantages, known as the King of Vaudeville, who made his fortune in the Klondike, visited Edmonton in 1912 with plans to spend $200,000 on a new three-storey theatre that would be the finest between Toronto and Vancouver. He carried through on his promise and the

Edmonton. When the boom collapses not long afterwards, many of the new owners will lose their lots to the city for unpaid taxes.

NA-5395-4 Glenbow Archives

Louise McKinney.

***May 14, 1912*: Degrees are awarded to the first graduating class from the University of Alberta.**

***May 17, 1912*: City pioneer Malcolm Groat dies 51 years after coming to Fort Edmonton. Groat Bridge and Groat Road are named for him.**

***July 22, 1912*: Edmonton annexes Belmont in north Edmonton.**

***Aug. 2, 1912*: Edmonton takes over the books of North Edmonton after the village is annexed to the city.**

MOTORING

NA-6-2505 Glenbow Archives

A stylish, ornate 1916 hearse.

AUTO'S PLACE IN AMERICA.

Some idea of what the automobile means to a dozen or more industries in North America can be gained from the following figures. They are an estimate, conservative enough, of the consumption of supplies by the motor service or taxicab companies of North America. The motor service companies of America purchase annually 18,000,000 gallons of gasoline, 200,000 gallons of lubricating oil, 250,000 tires, 500,000 inner tubes, 25,000 weed chains, 1,000 motor cars, taxicabs, etc.; $1,000,000 in insurance premiums.

paper celebrated with the city as the splendid Pantages Theatre rose on the south side of Jasper Avenue on 102nd Street.

Over the years it played host to the likes of Buster Keaton, Jimmy Durante, Sophie Tucker and Will Rogers. It eventually became the Strand, a movie theatre, and sadly was torn down in the early '70s.

Edmontonians also crowded auditoriums and hotel ballrooms to hear the famous speak.

Buffalo Bill Cody drew big crowds to a luncheon on July 24, 1915, at the Empire Auditorium. It was his first trip to Western Canada, he said, and he was impressed.

Cody was here to judge a "Who is Buffalo Bill?" essay contest sponsored by the paper. There were 43 winners chosen from the hundreds of entries, although some of the losing essays were disappointing.

"Quite a number of entrants had copied verbatim biographies from encyclopedias," a story sniffed.

Regardless, the first prize of $12.50 went to J. Holtz of 114 Jasper Avenue East. All winners were urged to be on time to receive their prize and a handshake from Buffalo Bill.

And when Sir Arthur Conan Doyle, the author of the Sherlock Holmes mysteries, came to town in June 1917, the paper raved, somewhat awkwardly: "Sir Arthur's address was so unusual that it held the gathering spellbound until he finished.

"His hearers were impressed with several things. First of all, his loyalty to Great Britain; second, his confidence in Canada so far as he has seen it; third, his love for literary work and his advice to those inclined to became literary inclined and fourth, the author's knowledge of so many things at one time."

But whoever travelled to Edmonton in the second half of the decade had to do without liquor. Prohibition, which eventually proved unworkable, was approved by the voters in a plebiscite in 1915 and as of July 1, 1916, there was no legal drinking in Alberta.

The Journal opposed Prohibition and declared the law unenforceable. It took the high road and urged people to read the proposed legislation and come to the logical conclusion it would not work. Said a July 6, 1915, editorial: "If we are satisfied that it would lessen the amount of actual drunkenness, we should ask the further question if it would not introduce other evils that would make things generally worse than they were before."

Alberta went dry at midnight, June 30, 1916. Here is an excerpt from the story the morning after the night before written by an unnamed, but obviously not entirely objective reporter. "When 10 o'clock arrived last night most of the bars had sold their available stock … so they just closed.

"Some of the drinkers … sang and laughed hysterically and begged for bottled beer that was not to be had. Everything from Swanee River and Home Sweet Home to grand opera was chanted, sung or gurgled.

"There were one or two more or less pathetic sights in some Jasper Avenue bars. One man whose name is familiar to every uniformed officer in Edmonton because his name has adorned the police blotter times without number stood on the rail of one bar and begged the bar-keep to make him a present of a bottle of whiskey 'for old times sake.' He hadn't any money;

***Sept. 18, 1912*:**
***The Journal* reports Annie Jackson is to become the city's first female police officer.**

City of Edmonton Archives

Annie Jackson.

***Oct. 8, 1912*:**
The Dawson Bridge, then known as the East End Bridge, opens to traffic.

***Oct. 14, 1912*:**
Edmonton annexes Kennedale.

***March 13, 1913*:**
The Strathcona Library opens on the south side.

***March 13, 1913*:**
Elk Island National Park east of Edmonton is established.

***March 25, 1913*:**
Edmonton annexes land in the west, north and southeast regions, doubling the size of the city.

***March 27, 1913*:**
The Edmonton Public Library opens in temporary

Hearn Family Collection

Three Edmonton landmarks are featured in this 1912 photo, the High Level Bridge, foreground, the legislature in the centre background and Fort Edmonton at top right.

NC-6-1544 Glenbow Archives

Fort Edmonton was torn down in 1915. Officials said the city was too young to have buildings of historic significance.

he never did have any. The bar-keep recognized him, his whole shabby self – the seamed face, the burning eyes, the suit of clothes that has probably never known the feel of a pantorium iron – and gave him the bottle 'for old times sake,' whatever that means.

"Anyway, Edmonton today is more-or-less dry and headachy...."

As always, sports was big news. Curling coverage was prominent; heavyweight champion Tommy Burns operated a haberdashery in Calgary and promoted local boxing matches; and hockey, baseball and rugby, both professional and amateur, were popular.

A big story early in the decade was the construction of the High Level Bridge. *The Journal* followed its progress closely as it pushed its way across the North Saskatchewan River, bringing the day closer when Edmonton was amalgamated with Strathcona. Sure, there were growing pains involving streetcars, postal service and street names, but when annexation finally came it went smoothly enough. Initially Strathcona might have been coy, but Edmonton was an ardent suitor.

"It is not, as it might sound, a case of gobble," *The Journal* wrote on Amalgamation Day, Feb. 1, 1912, when 10,000 new citizens were added to Edmonton, raising its population to more than 53,000.

"Not a bit. It is what the name implies, Amalgamation – a union of two cities for mutual benefit and development. It is the occasion for wedding bells rather than the tolling of a dirge in the University settlement."

And, yes, the infant University of Alberta was doing just fine, too. In 1912, the paper proudly published the names of the first graduating class. Of the 18, five were women.

There was pride, too, in the new Legislature Building.

Finishing touches were put on the dome in 1912, and it looked magnificent, a seat of government that befitted a province where optimism was as bright as an Alberta summer day.

Premier Arthur Sifton replaced A.C. Rutherford. The latter, shamed by a railway financing scandal and a royal commission report that accused him of naivete´ and guilty of sloppy business practices, was still popular enough, but his political career was finished.

Sifton was a different sort altogether. While Rutherford was an affable, friendly bear of a man, Sifton was cool and aloof. Unsmiling and tight-lipped, he was called Little Arthur by some, although never to his face. The newspaper, ever true to the Conservative cause, often referred to the Liberal Sifton as The Sphinx, and made him the subject of dozens of bitter political cartoons.

On the national scene, readers were offered lengthy reports from special correspondent Fred Cook in Ottawa. While Cook didn't offer a great deal in the way of balanced journalism, he gave credit where due, including on rare occasions to *Bulletin* publisher Frank Oliver, the former minister of the interior, who sat on the opposition benches next to the tired and beaten Laurier.

The paper felt that Conservative Borden was just what the country needed. Indeed, in early 1912, the newspaper voiced agreement with a speech by Ald. W.A. Griesbach, the Boer War veteran, that the Borden government was, purely and simply, the best in history.

quarters over a meat shop and liquor store in the Chisholm Block at the corner of Jasper Avenue and 104th Street.

***April 17, 1913*:**
In the third provincial election, Andrew Shandro becomes Alberta's first MLA of Ukrainian descent.

***May 12, 1913*:**
The 1,600-seat Pantages Theatre opens in downtown Edmonton.

***May 15, 1913*:**
A civic census puts Edmonton's population at 67,243.

***June 2, 1913*:**
The first train crosses Edmonton's High Level Bridge. The bridge opens later to vehicle, pedestrian and streetcar traffic. The 105th Street Bridge also opens this year.

***Aug. 12, 1913*:**
Parimutuel betting is allowed on the Edmonton Exhibition's horse races — 8,500 attend.

***Sept. 30, 1913*:**
The short-lived Edmonton Interurban Railway opens, linking Edmonton and St. Albert.

***Oct. 7, 1913*:**
Government House, the official residence of Alberta's

SUFFRAGETTES SMASH THE WINDOWS OF THE C.P.R OFFICES
Charing Cross
PACIFIC SERVICES
Japan China AUSTRALIA
STEAMSHIP LINES
The Attack
The Consequences
The Result

ND-3-83 Glenbow Archives

The terrace of the Macdonald Hotel (circa 1916) was elegant place to dine.

In another story, it proclaimed that Borden did more in five months than Laurier had accomplished in years.

There were, of course, more mundane problems than war and peace, and the fate of provincial and national governments. City commissioners seemed always to be at loggerheads with city council, and there were troubles in the police department at the beginning of the decade, although they seem small stuff indeed.

R.W. Ensor was head of the police department in 1911, and had run afoul of city council because of his strict interpretation of the law.

When he requested the city provide him with a summer helmet on which the word "Chief" could be emblazoned, *The Journal* couldn't resist. "However, if the city feels it cannot stand the expense of luxuries the Chief might be induced to go without a hat – as there is a vacant spot on the top of his head where his title could be inscribed."

Mostly, though, Edmonton was a city where business was done and deals were made. In fact, in early 1912, the paper reported that the big draw at the recently opened Corona Hotel on Jasper Avenue and 107th Street were the telephones installed at each table in the dining room. It was an ideal lunch spot for those businessmen who had to be in constant contact with the office.

Even fancier was the Grand Trunk Pacific Hotel – later renamed the Macdonald Hotel – that overlooked the expansive North Saskatchewan River valley. The paper predicted that by the time it was completed the hotel would cost as much as a million dollars. An April 12, 1912, headline awkwardly proclaimed: "Magnificent New Structure at Brow of McDougall Avenue Hill Promises to Supply City's Need of High Class Caravansary and Add Much to Its Beauty."

The paper routinely carried a monthly report on the city's bank clearances, the total amount of money that had changed hands over the previous 30 days.

It was a cause for celebration whenever Edmonton's clearances were higher than those in Calgary.

But whenever there's a boom, there's a bust, and the one that hit the city in the early teens was terrible.

By the time it and the war were over, the city's population had contracted by a quarter and the bright lustre that had given the city its hope was dulled.

Like all busts, this one was born of the kind of exuberant hope that leads to overextended finances.

By 1913, land speculators had forced the city to grow too far, too fast.

Railroads that were to carry new settlers to homesteads in the rich new lands in the Peace Country were completed, so no rail crews crowded the city's hotels and bars.

The railroads themselves either went broke or were teetering on the brink of bankruptcy.

The coming war also meant that the flood of immigrants from Europe was choked off. From 1914 to 1918, there were virtually no new arrivals.

Not surprisingly, Edmonton's population tumbled, falling from more than the civic census figure of 72,000 in 1914 to 53,000 in 1918.

lieutenant-governor, is officially opened. The three-storey mansion and its furnishings cost about $350,000.

***December 1913*:**
The Journal **averages 24 pages a day with an average circulation of 16,020. Rotary presses installed in 1911 could roll out 12,000 editions every hour.**

NA-448-1 Glenbow Archives

Arthur Sifton.

***Dec. 25, 1913*:**
The first hockey game is played in the Edmonton Gardens, located on the exhibition grounds.

***Jan. 19, 1914*:**
Edmonton annexes Allendale.

***April 6, 1914*:**
Edmontonians vote in a plebiscite to designate streets and avenues by numbers instead of names. Exceptions will be made for major roads with long-established names, such as Jasper Avenue.

WHOLESALE BOOTS
McKENZIE & CO
H.B. DRAWING. EDMONTON. ALTA

NA-2413-2 Glenbow Archives

The Hudson's Bay land sale took place May 14, 1912, in the church, far left, on the east side of 103rd Street, near the corner of 102nd Avenue.

THE JOURNAL'S WANT AD. KID

I will present for your consideration a list of good jobs that promise steady, profitable employment.

WANTS
LIST OF
GOOD
JOBS

I AM A WANT AD.

(Copyright, 1914, by DeForest Porter.)

China Is At The Other End

When you buy a piece of real estate, you own the ground all the way down. Ever think of it? What other security is so substantial?

We know of no better investment than WHYTE AVENUE at the following prices.

Block 66, $5,000 cash $15,000
Block 65, Double corner, $12,000 cash handles this.
Block 132, $4,500 cash $9,000
Block 170, $2,500 cash $8,500
Block 142, $3,500 cash $6,500
Block 155, $2,000 cash $4,500

L. L. Fuller & Co.,

46 Whyte Avenue, South Side. Phone 3124

THE BRONX

We consider Bronx Property at current prices the best buying in Greater Edmonton today. We can deliver at from $325 up.

Geo. Kirby & Co.
Home Specialists
Room 123, Windsor Block. Phone 5847

Real Estate

HUDSON'S BAY LOTS ON MARKET MAY 14

Map on Exhibition in Company's Office in Tegler Block—To Pave Portage Avenue.

Lots out of every block in the Hudson's Bay reserve will be placed on the market May 14, and no matter what is told to the investors in Edmonton by the real estate merchants, the official announcement has been made of the intentions of the large company.

On May 14 the first lot will be sold, and in the meantime a large map of a portion of the reserve showing all lots on the market for sale will be on exhibition at the Hudson's Bay company land department, 405 Tegler block, and prices will be verbally given until the printed price lists and maps, now under preparation, are ready for distribution.

In connection with the coming sale the company intends to have Portage avenue paved and make other improvements thereon which will involve an expenditure of $500,000, contingent on the city. The city commissioners have already agreed to place a double track car line on this avenue.

The above information was given out this morning by the local land commissioner, G. P. Bellingham. He said that not one part of the reserve would be placed on the market, but that there would be lots in every block offered for sale. On the whole, there would be 50 per cent. of the reserve sold.

Some of the decline was due to men enlisting in the armed forces, but many other people left simply because they could no longer make a living in the city. There were no jobs and, worse, no prospect of jobs in Edmonton in the war years.

Not that the newspaper or anyone else saw the downturn was coming. Only a year before the collapse, hundreds waited overnight on May 13, 1912, for a chance to buy lots in the Hudson's Bay Reserve, land west of 101st Street, on both sides of what is now Kingsway Avenue.

Stories trumpeted success. Those who invested only a few hundred dollars in property on Jasper Avenue at the turn of the century were now cashing in for hundreds of thousands of dollars.

The newspaper was crammed with advertisements hawking real estate. At one point more than two dozen real estate agencies and hundreds of independent salesmen competed for advertising space.

It couldn't last. And it didn't.

In the six years between the outbreak of war in 1914 and 1920, the city found itself facing an acute problem of homeless men, many from laid-off railway crews, who crowded the city.

And the city faced a crushing debt load forced on it by building unneeded utilities. Stories and editorials insisted that Edmontonians support local business; those who didn't, were called "knockers." No one wanted to be a knocker, but few had any extra money to invest.

Just when things could look no worse, nature dealt a nasty blow. On June 28, 1915, the North Saskatchewan River crested at an astonishing 48 feet above normal levels. It was the worst natural disaster in the city's history, and it destroyed businesses in the Ross and Walter flats and left

***June 11, 1914*:**
The Edmonton Newsboys Band, made up of newspaper carriers, makes its first appearance. In 1924, they appear at the British Imperial Exhibition at Wembley, London.

***June 13, 1914*:**
A train chartered by the Edmonton Industrial Association leaves Edmonton on an excursion to promote Edmonton and the province of Alberta. The tour ends in Toronto at a conference of the Associated Advertising Clubs of America.

***Aug. 4, 1914*:**
Canada enters the First World War after Britain declares war on Germany.

***Aug. 22, 1914*:**
Some 900 men of Edmonton's 101st Regiment leave for duty in the First World War.

***Oct. 28, 1914*:**
Mayor W.J. McNamara is forced from office.

***Nov. 7, 1914*:**
The 49th Battalion of the Canadian Expeditionary Force, later the Loyal Edmonton Regiment, is authorized.

***In January 1915*:**
The Edmonton Commercial Graduates basketball team is formed with Percy Page as coach.

Last Edition

Edmonton Journal

Daily Circulation
MONDAY, APRIL 15, 1912.
10,227
Lists Open For Inspection.

Vol. 8, No. 237. EDMONTON, ALBERTA, TUESDAY, APRIL 16, 1912. TWENTY PAGES.

"S. O. S."---SAVE OUR SOULS WAIL THOUSANDS, AS GIANT TITANIC PLUNGES BENEATH WAVES

All World Mourns Over Worst Marine Disaster In History Of Atlantic

Many Canadians Unaccounted for—Flags are Flying at Half-mast in European and American Cities—Families Await All Night at Steamship Offices for News of Loved Ones.

NEW YORK, April 16.—Vice-President Franklin of the international mercantile marine said this morning that the company was holding back no information, and that the steamship Olympic was now standing off Cape Race relaying the names of passengers on the Carpathia to the wireless station at Cape Race.

Picks Up No Survivors.

HALIFAX, N.S., April 16.—The Allan liner Parisian reports via Sable Island that she has no passengers from the Titanic on board. The Pariian has just come into touch with the Sable Island wireless station.

Virginian Too Late.

MONTREAL, Que., April 16.—The Allan line has issued the following statement: "We are in teceipt of a marconi. via Cape Race, from Captain Gambell, of the Virginian, stating that he arrived on the scene of the disaster too late to be of service, and is proceeding on his voyage to Liverpool."

Winnipeg Buyer Aboard.

TORONTO, Ont., April 16.—On Sunday Mrs. Graham, who had come here from Winnipeg to meet her husband. received the following marconigram:

"S.S. Titanic. Cape Race, Nf., April 14.—New York Wednesday morning. Wire me Sandy Hook. Well.—George E. Graham."

Mr. Graham was buyer for the T. Eaton store in Winnipeg.

Mr. Graham's name did not appear in the list of the passengers, and the hope was held out that he had not sailed on the steamer, but this message removes the doubt. Of course, it is not known whether he is missing or among the passengers saved.

Throngs Await News.

LONDON, April 16.—The crowds gathered around the White Star offices increased in density every moment throughout the morning. Lines of automobiles and carriages containing inquiries are so extended that the late comers are unable to get within several blocks of the office.

Along the steamship offices and on many public buildings flags are flying at half-mast.

One of Builders on Ship.

BELFAST, Ireland April 16.—Thomas Andrews, jr., a director of the shipbuilding firm of Harlow and Firth, was aboard the Titanic. He was accompanied by mechanics, who were watching the working of the latest product of the company's yards.

Relatives of Crew Weep.

SOUTHAMPTON, ENGLAND, APRIL 16.—Distressing scenes have been witnessed throughout the morning. The White Star offices here are thronged by relatives of the crew ot the Titanic. The town is stunned by the news of the disaster, which is the greatest blow that Southampton has ever sustained. Every member of the crew had his home here, and a portion of them were natives of the town.

Germany Extends Sympathy.

BERLIN, April 16.—The speaker of the reichstag, Johannes Kaomp, at the opening of the session today after the Easter vacation, made a speach expressing sympathy and grief of the German empire over the loss of the Titanic with a large number of lives.

Flags at Half-Mast.

CHERBOURG, April 16.—The disaster to the Titanic has thrown Cherbourg into profound sorrow. The flags on the public buildings are fleating at half-mast. Thousands of citizens who had witnessed the liner's departure on her maiden voyage have waited all day at the steamship offices for details of the catastrophe.

Waited News All Night.

MONTREAL, April 16.—A number of prominent Montreal people were aboard the Titanic and to allay their anxiety the effort was made by the Allan line office here to obtain information from its steamers near the scene of the disaster. A succession of wireless messages from Halifax, however, brought no response up to 10:30 o'clock this morning. Thousands remained up all night waiting for news.

700,000 Letters Lost.

NEW YORK, April 16.—Postmaster Edward M. Morgan stated today that White Star Liner Titanic had on board 3,500 sacks of mail. It is not likely, he said, thta the mails were saved. As the standard mail bag holds about 2,000 letters, it is estimated that in all about 700,000 packages of mail matter have been lost.

PARTIAL LIST OF RESCUED FIRST AND SECOND CLASS PASSENGERS WHO ARE ON CARPATHIA

CAPE RACE, Nfld., April 16.—The follow[...] partial list of the first class passengers, w[...] Titanic :

The list was [...] ight from [...] ith the

The Unfortunate White Star Liner Titanic

Marine Horror That Has Set World Aghast Casts Blight on Edmonton Home

Rev. W. G. W. Fortune of 515 Seventh Street Had Brother and Latter's Wife and Family Abcard Sunken Steamboat Titanic—Three Women Are Reported Saved.

A great catastrophe like that which has just shocked the whole civilized world always has ramifications that stretch out their blighting arms far and wide, that griping in their clinging numbing folds quiet and hitherto happy homes, many thousands of miles away it may be from the actual scene of the horror itself.

Such has proved already the latest and greatest marine disaster that has ever fallen upon the modern world—the sinking of the Titanic off the east coast of the continent. From a peaceful Edmonton household out to the waste of tossing waters where the giant vessel fought out alone her last grim fight with the fate that was yet too powerful for her is a far cry, but it is one that has been bridged.

On the doomed ship that cast loose its moorings so blithely at Southampton, only to come to its last anchorage ground two miles beneath the surface of the ocean that it had ridden so proudly, set sail Mr. and Mrs. Mark Fortune and their family, of Winnipeg. The Fortunes have relatives in Edmonton. The Rev. W. C. W. Fortune of 515 Seventh street, city is a brother of the Mr. Fortune who registered as passenger on the ill-fated Titanic.

Mrs. Mark Fortune and her two daughters, Misses Alice and Mabel Fortune, were named among those whose saving was made possible by the sacrifice of men who proved themselves cast in the true heroic mould. The Rev. Mr. Fortune, of Edmonton, is at present away on a trip to Honolulu. His brother and family had been on a visit to Europe, and were returning to their western home when the disaster befell the noble barque upon which their lot of voyage had been cast.

Latest reports from the Atlantic seaboard indicate that Mark Fortune was one of the men who went down with the vessel, that the women and children might be sa[...]

CAPTAIN E. J. SMITH, COMMANDING OFFICER OF HAPLESS VESSEL

WINNIPEG LOSES SOME RESPECTED BUSINESS MEN

1341 Persons Are Lost; Storm Rages Along Coast; Steamers Abandon Search

Floating Wreckage Tells Last Sad Tale of Horror—Survivors Now Being Hurried to New York On the Allan Liner Carpathia, Where They Will Arrive On Thursday—Rescued Are Mostly Women and Children

PROMINENT CANADIANS NUMBERED WITH DEAD

NEW YORK, N. Y., April 16.—"Save Our Souls," was the last wireless message picked up from the Titanic early Monday morning. The faithful operator standing at his key, facing death until the last flashed out in frantic succession the urgent appeal for aid to those in danger at sea, "S. O. S."—"S. O. S."—and then the call ceased. The Titanic had plunged to her tomb, with her huge cargo of human souls, two miles below the surface.

ST. JOHN, APRIL, 16.—All hope of saving any of the passengers or members of th crew other than those on the Carpathia was abandoned this afternoon. All of the steamers which have been cruising in the vicinity of the disaster have continued on their voyages.

NUMBER THOUGHT SAVED

NEW YORK, April 16.—The White Star line has announced officially that they had received positive news that the number of survivors on board the liner Carpathia was 868. This dispatch was sent to the White Star offices from the Olympic, which is understood to be in wireless communication with the Carpathia, now proceeding to New York.

Of the 201 first cabin passengers thus far accounted for, 132 are women, 63 men and 6 children: of the 116 second cabin passengers reported surviving, 88 are women, 16 men and 12 children.

The fact that the names of only 315 of those saved sent in by wireless shows that there are 553 persons rescued from the Titanic whose names have not been received here.

STORM NOW RAGING

MONTREAL, QUE., April 16.—Weather signals on the St. Lawrence reported today that a heavy fog lay off Nova Scotia, and that a violent thunderstorm broke in that neighborhood last night, and is travelling eastward. It was said that such conditions left little hope for the rescue of any survivors of the Titanic that might still be drift in rafts or boats.

NO MORE ARE PICKED UP

HALIFAX, N.S., April 16.—The Sable Island cable ship Minia reported this afternoon through the wireless station here that she had sighted a great mass of wreckage, but no boats or rafts from the Titanic. This for the time being disposes of the hope that the Minia, which was anchored off Cape Race, when the Titanic first called for help, might have picked up some of the Titanic's passengers.

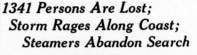

NA-2597-8 Glenbow Archives

Two men save a few possessions during the flood of 1915. The building with the three windows, left, was located at 9647 100th St.

2,000 homeless. Included in the report of the terrible devastation was a photograph of more than a dozen heavily loaded Canadian Northern Railway freight cars and locomotives on the Low Level Bridge. Only the weight of the train kept the bridge from being battered into rubble by the debris in the river.

It was a horrifying day in what was all too often a terrifying decade.

Through most of it, the newspaper kept its readers informed of international events. On April 1, 1912, it broadened its connections to the world by signing contracts with Associated Press and Reuters news services.

It was a timely arrangement, as two weeks later on April 15, 1912, the new wire services provided the paper's 10,227 subscribers with what would be one of the stories of the century – albeit with a falsely optimistic twist: "TITANIC REPORTED SINKING; PASSENGERS SAFE," shouted the page 1 headline.

The true horror of the sinking arrived with the next day's headline: "S.O.S. - SAVE OUR SOULS WAIL THOUSANDS AS GIANT TITANIC PLUNGES BENEATH THE WAVES."

As always, the paper found a local angle and reported that Mark Fortune, one of the male passengers who gave up a seat on a lifeboat and died in the freezing waters of the North Atlantic, was a brother to Rev. W.G.W. Fortune, an Edmonton clergyman who was secretary of the Alberta Moral and Temperance Association.

Within two days, *The Journal* started a fund for widows and orphans with a donation of $100.

By April 20, the fund stood at $1,129 and the money was cabled to Lord Strathcona, the Canadian High Commissioner in London.

"From this far-off corner of the Empire there will go forth tonight Edmonton's silent proof of her quick response to the calls made upon her by suffering and sorrow," the paper wrote.

In the end, it must be said that the years from 1911 to 1920 were cruel.

Readers had faced down the ravages of a depression, a flood and a war. With peace at hand in 1918, there came pestilence in the form of Spanish flu, a devastating disease which claimed more lives worldwide than the war. The paper not only printed death notices, but reported the number of people who had fallen ill.

There was no cure, and it abated just as mysteriously as it arrived.

There are hundreds of stories in *The Journal* files cataloguing the horror that it brought.

Schools and churches were closed, theatres were shut down, people wore masks on the street and in public places to avoid breathing in the pestilent air.

The next 10 years would let us catch our collective breath as a city, a province and a newspaper.

***Jan. 4, 1915*:**
Voluntary enlistments begin in Edmonton and northern Alberta for overseas duty in the new 49th Battalion. In eight days 1,000 men join up.

***March 8, 1915*:**
The Princess Theatre opens in the Strathcona area on Edmonton's south side.

***June 13, 1915*:**
Results of Edmonton's civic census show the city's population as 59,339.

***June 1915*:**
"Everyone Else Has One, Did You Get Yours," reads the ads for Canadian flags in *The Journal*. "What better way to show loyalty than to secure one?" You could pick your Union Jack and a staff to run it up at *The Journal* office for $4.

***June 28, 1915*:**
The North Saskatchewan River rises 12 metres above normal levels, flooding 700 houses and leaving 2,400 people homeless.

***July 5, 1915*:**
The Grand Trunk Pacific Hotel (later named the Macdonald Hotel) opens at a cost of more than $2 million. It is built by the Grand Trunk Pacific Railway.

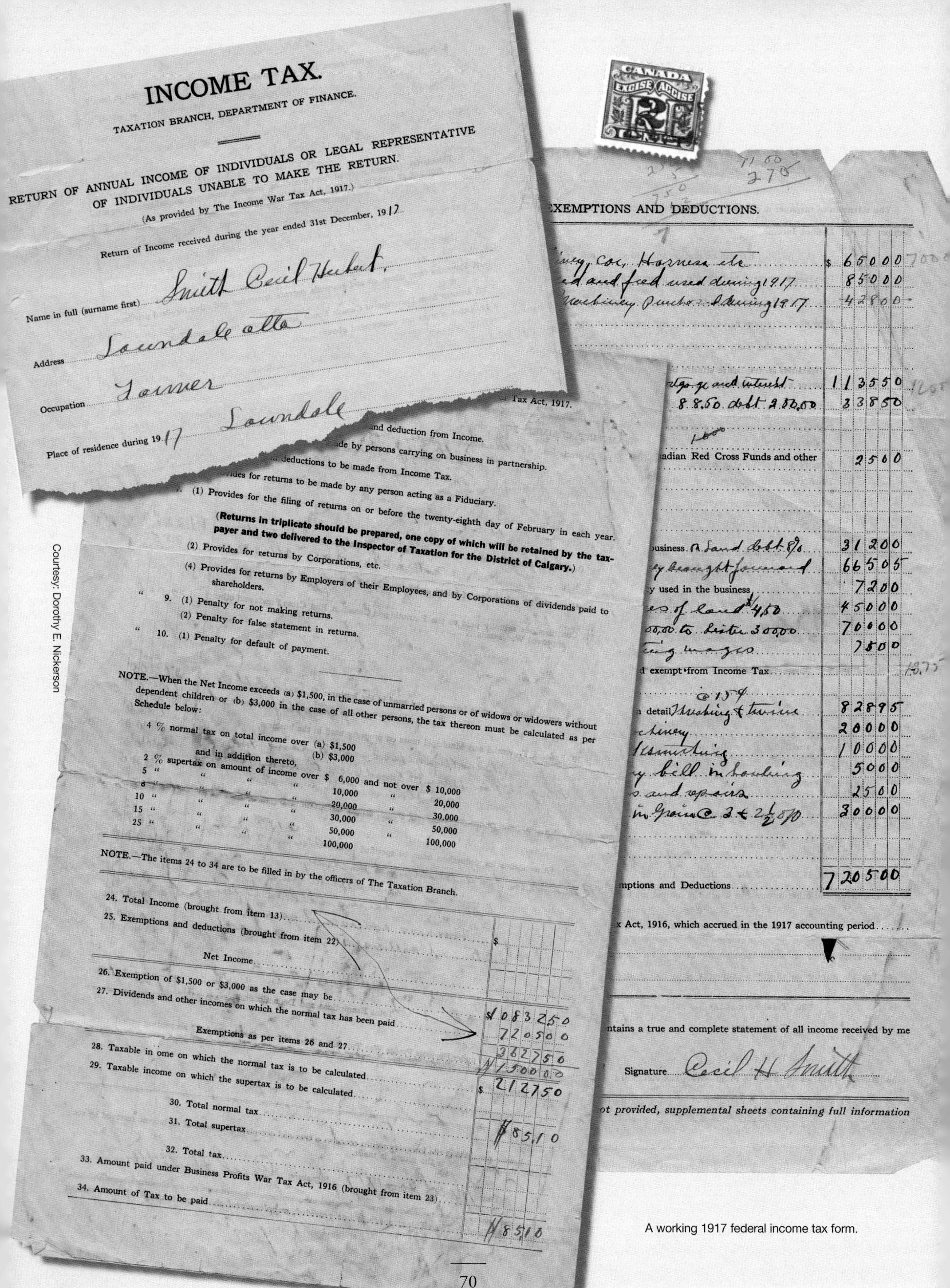

INCOME TAX.

TAXATION BRANCH, DEPARTMENT OF FINANCE.

RETURN OF ANNUAL INCOME OF INDIVIDUALS OR LEGAL REPRESENTATIVE OF INDIVIDUALS UNABLE TO MAKE THE RETURN.

(As provided by The Income War Tax Act, 1917.)

Return of Income received during the year ended 31st December, 1917

Name in full (surname first) Smith Cecil Herbert,

Address Lowndale Alta

Occupation Farmer

Place of residence during 1917 Lowndale

... Tax Act, 1917.

... and deduction from Income.

... made by persons carrying on business in partnership.

... deductions to be made from Income Tax.

... provides for returns to be made by any person acting as a Fiduciary.

" 7. (1) Provides for the filing of returns on or before the twenty-eighth day of February in each year.

(Returns in triplicate should be prepared, one copy of which will be retained by the tax-payer and two delivered to the Inspector of Taxation for the District of Calgary.)

(2) Provides for returns by Corporations, etc.

(4) Provides for returns by Employers of their Employees, and by Corporations of dividends paid to shareholders.

" 9. (1) Penalty for not making returns.

(2) Penalty for false statement in returns.

" 10. (1) Penalty for default of payment.

NOTE.—When the Net Income exceeds (a) $1,500, in the case of unmarried persons or of widows or widowers without dependent children or (b) $3,000 in the case of all other persons, the tax thereon must be calculated as per Schedule below:

4 % normal tax on total income over (a) $1,500 (b) $3,000

and in addition thereto,

2 % supertax on amount of income over	$ 6,000	and not over	$ 10,000
5 "	10,000	"	20,000
8 "	20,000	"	30,000
10 "	30,000	"	50,000
15 "	50,000	"	100,000
25 "	100,000		

NOTE.—The items 24 to 34 are to be filled in by the officers of The Taxation Branch.

24. Total Income (brought from item 13)	$10832.50
25. Exemptions and deductions (brought from item 22)	7205.00
Net Income	3627.50
26. Exemption of $1,500 or $3,000 as the case may be	1500.00
27. Dividends and other incomes on which the normal tax has been paid	
Exemptions as per items 26 and 27	
28. Taxable income on which the normal tax is to be calculated	$2127.50
29. Taxable income on which the supertax is to be calculated	
30. Total normal tax	$85.10
31. Total supertax	
32. Total tax	
33. Amount paid under Business Profits War Tax Act, 1916 (brought from item 23)	
34. Amount of Tax to be paid	$85.10

EXEMPTIONS AND DEDUCTIONS.

...inery, Cows, Horses etc	$650.00
...ed and feed used during 1917	850.00
Machinery purchased during 1917	428.00
...tgage and interest	1135.50
... 88.50 debt 250.00	338.50
...adian Red Cross Funds and other	25.00
...business. R Land debt 8%	312.00
...y brought forward	665.05
...y used in the business	72.00
...es of land $450	450.00
...00.00 to sister 300.00	700.00
...ting wages	75.00
...d exempt from Income Tax	
...in detail Threshing & twine	828.95
...chinery	200.00
...blacksmithing	100.00
...y bill in Lowndale	50.00
...s and repairs	25.00
...in Grain @ 2 & 2½ %	300.00
...mptions and Deductions	7205.00

...x Act, 1916, which accrued in the 1917 accounting period

...ntains a true and complete statement of all income received by me

Signature Cecil H Smith

...ot provided, supplemental sheets containing full information

Courtesy: Dorothy E. Nickerson

A working 1917 federal income tax form.

A Temporary Measure

"An income tax had also been suggested, but the sum which could be raised in this manner would not be large. He believed it undesirable to impose such a tax at a time when the cost of living is on the increase."
— Story on Finance Minister Sir Thomas White's federal budget, April 24, 1917

At first, Prime Minister Robert Borden's government resisted the idea of taxing income.

But wars are expensive, and by 1917 the dominion owed $1.3 billion in war debt. That year, it was projected Ottawa would collect $232,000,000 from its usual tax sources of customs and tariffs plus a newly imposed regimen of special war taxes on business profits and a "stamp tax" on financial transactions.

CANADA POSTAGE
THREE CENTS
3
3

Courtesy: Dorothy E. Nickerson

Banking transactions and a host of other activities required a war stamp tax.

While the special taxes raised a ruckus in some circles (for instance, every cheque written had to have a two-cent stamp affixed to it), *The Journal* solidly backed the extraordinary measures as shown on April 15: "The Canadian people are surely not the kind to demand large government expenditures on the war and on keeping the country's business going as usual and then object to paying additional imposts which all this involves."

Two months later, the federal government rethought the personal income tax and hinted it would impose more of a "wealth conscription," as it was called by politicians.

Once again, the paper rose to the aid of the (Conservative) party. This time, however, the July 14, 1917, editorial contained a caveat of sorts: "We must raise large sums of money by taxation to meet the expense of the war and in doing so we must impose it the most heavily upon those who are in the best position to bear it and in such a way as to cause the least harm to the country's economic position."

The tax was law by July and, while the paper still pragmatically supported its necessity, the July 26 editorial made two astute observations.

CANADA
WAR TAX
FOUR CENTS

"The machinery for its collection will have to be an elaborate and a somewhat expensive one.

"The minister stated that when the war is over the taxation should be reviewed … but there is no likelihood the principle, having once been adopted, it will ever be abandoned."

***Sept. 20, 1915*:** **Vegreville's Lillian Clements is the first woman admitted to the Alberta bar.**

***Oct. 11, 1915*:** **Workers begin demolishing the last Fort Edmonton, located south of the Alberta legislature building on the banks of the North Saskatchewan River. Since 1795 the fur-trading post had been built and re-built on five different locations along the river.**

***Dec. 13, 1915*:** **Edmonton voters defeat a proposal to pay city aldermen a salary of $1,000 a year.**

***In 1916*:** **A clerk in the phone room at *The Journal* makes $80 a month.**

***Feb. 12, 1916*:** **Pioneer Alex Taylor dies at age 62. The city's first telegraph operator, Taylor also launched the city's first telephone system and power utility. He chaired the public school board for 10 years.**

***March 1916*:** **Alberta women gain the right to vote, joining women in Saskatchewan and Manitoba.**

City of Edmonton Archives

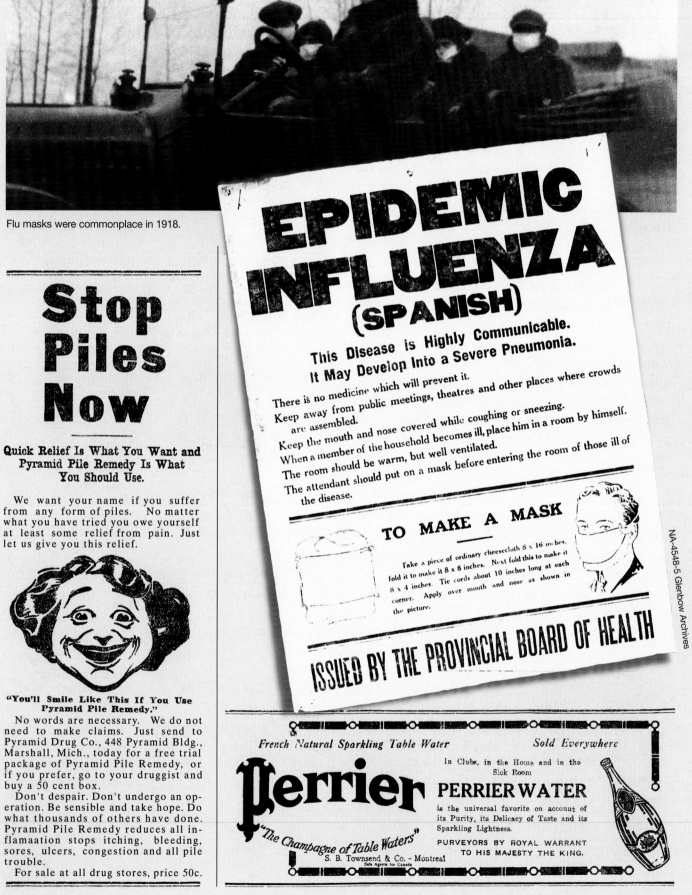

Flu masks were commonplace in 1918.

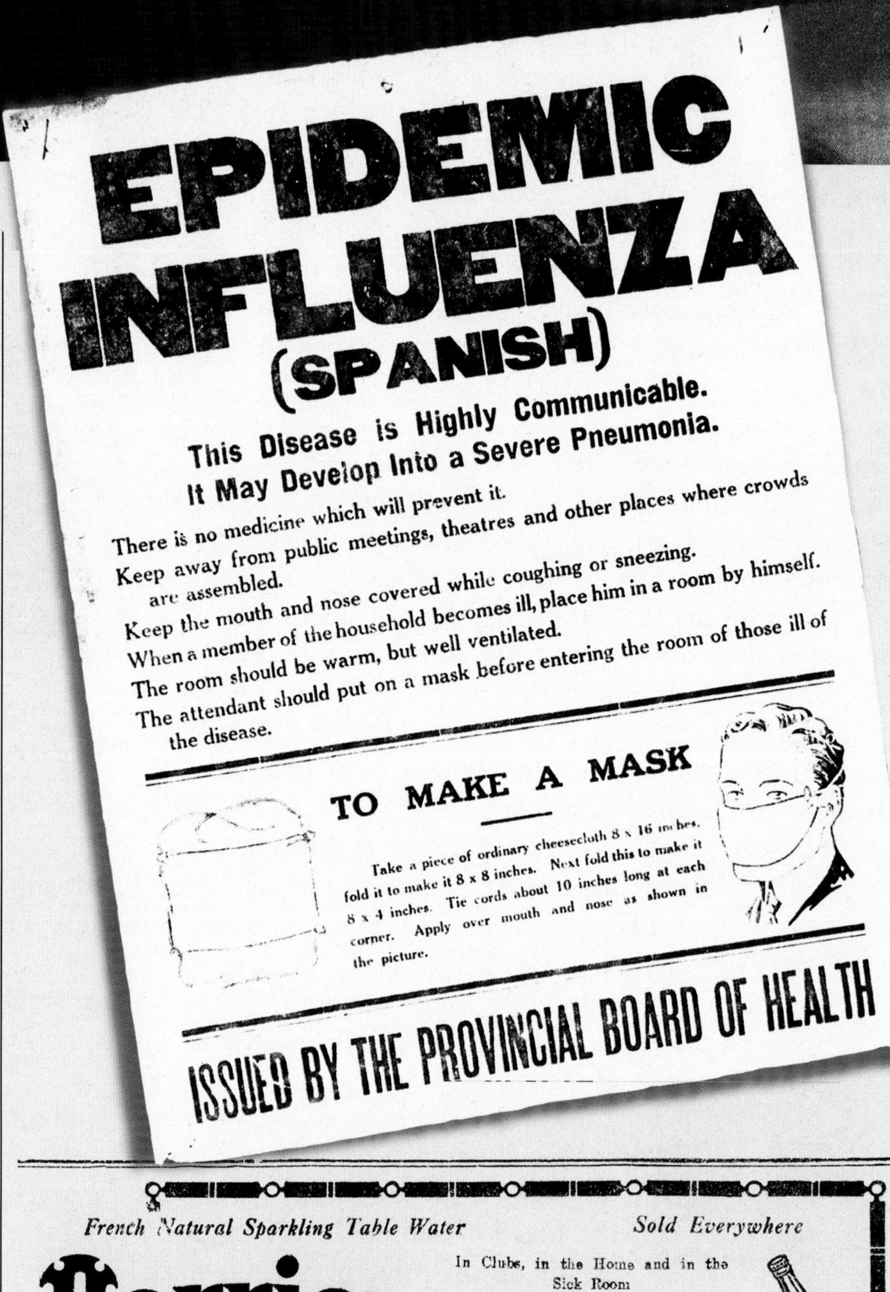

EPIDEMIC INFLUENZA (SPANISH)

This Disease is Highly Communicable.
It May Develop Into a Severe Pneumonia.

There is no medicine which will prevent it.
Keep away from public meetings, theatres and other places where crowds are assembled.
Keep the mouth and nose covered while coughing or sneezing.
When a member of the household becomes ill, place him in a room by himself.
The room should be warm, but well ventilated.
The attendant should put on a mask before entering the room of those ill of the disease.

TO MAKE A MASK

Take a piece of ordinary cheesecloth 8 x 16 inches. Next fold this to make it fold it to make it 8 x 8 inches. Tie cords about 10 inches long at each 8 x 4 inches. corner. Apply over mouth and nose as shown in the picture.

ISSUED BY THE PROVINCIAL BOARD OF HEALTH

NA-4548-5 Glenbow Archives

Stop Piles Now

Quick Relief Is What You Want and Pyramid Pile Remedy Is What You Should Use.

We want your name if you suffer from any form of piles. No matter what you have tried you owe yourself at least some relief from pain. Just let us give you this relief.

"You'll Smile Like This If You Use Pyramid Pile Remedy."

No words are necessary. We do not need to make claims. Just send to Pyramid Drug Co., 448 Pyramid Bldg., Marshall, Mich., today for a free trial package of Pyramid Pile Remedy, or if you prefer, go to your druggist and buy a 50 cent box.

Don't despair. Don't undergo an operation. Be sensible and take hope. Do what thousands of others have done. Pyramid Pile Remedy reduces all inflamaation stops itching, bleeding, sores, ulcers, congestion and all pile trouble.

For sale at all drug stores, price 50c.

French Natural Sparkling Table Water *Sold Everywhere*

Perrier

"The Champagne of Table Waters"

S. B. Townsend & Co. - Montreal
Sole Agents for Canada

In Clubs, in the Home and in the Sick Room

PERRIER WATER

is the universal favorite on account of its Purity, its Delicacy of Taste and its Sparkling Lightness.

PURVEYORS BY ROYAL WARRANT TO HIS MAJESTY THE KING.

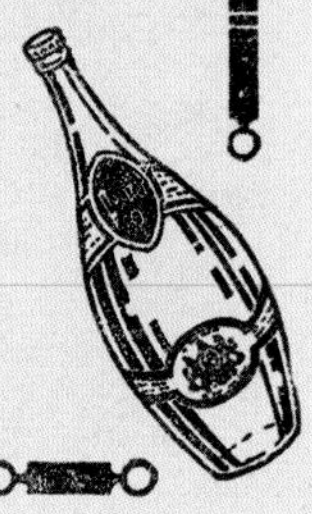

Spanish Flu

"There is no adequate explanation known for the amazing swiftness with which the epidemic sickness of this kind has swept across the globe."
— Comment on Spanish flu, Nov. 20, 1918

The disease was called Spanish flu, which was not exactly accurate. No one knew where it actually originated or precisely when it started.

In North America, the story began March 8, 1918, in Camp Funston, Kansas, when a soldier reported to the base hospital carrying a lethal variation of a bird or pig virus that jumped to humans.

A few weeks later, it wasn't confined to Kansas anymore. American soldiers who had trained at the camp took more "over there" to the battlefields of Europe than their allies bargained for.

In September, it arrived in Canada with the returning Canadian troops. Quebec was hard hit.

In less than two months it scythed a deadly path across the country.

Worldwide, 25 million died of the flu — more than were killed in four years of armed world conflict. In Canada, 50,000 died and of Alberta's 580,000 people, 3,300 were buried, twice the normal death rate.

The Journal's first headline about of the epidemic ran Sept. 24, 1918. "Spanish Influenza Taking Many Lives in the East. Epidemic Still Spreading."

The story was buried on an inside page. Few noticed the approaching disaster right away. There was a war on, after all.

The first Alberta cases appeared in Drumheller. An Oct. 4 report contained Alberta Health Minister A.G. MacKay's prediction the flu would likely hit epidemic proportions in the province.

"Probably from 30 to 40 per cent of the population will be attacked and each community may expect to have an influenzal epidemic of from four to six weeks."

As fate would have it, MacKay was one of the epidemic's victims.

The difference between this flu and "normal" flu was that it attacked the young and fit, mostly those between ages 15 and 35. Those who died, did so of hemorrhagic viral pneumonia within a day or two of being infected.

Exactly how the bug reached Edmonton isn't known, but an Oct. 8 story from Ottawa said a couple of dozen soldiers had returned from Europe and were scheduled to arrive in the city in "the course of a few days." Another report noted the epidemic had arrived in Winnipeg.

There were flu stories nearly every day as it raced toward the city. Officials did what they could to put plans into effect to lessen the impact of what they knew was coming. Student nurses were ready for deployment to small towns. People were told to avoid meetings and closed-in spaces.

But the medical community was largely helpless. On Oct. 16, a provincial health official said in *The Journal*: "No disinfectant has been found which would ward off the disease and no medicine will prevent it."

Anxiety built. City theatres combined to buy a full-page ad in an attempt to assure the public that "we are leaving no stone unturned to make our Theatres thoroughly safe and sanitary places for public attendance."

***March 30, 1916*:**
The Edmonton Rotary Club is founded at the Macdonald Hotel.

***June 12, 1916*:**
Emily Murphy is appointed a police magistrate for Edmonton, the first woman magistrate in the British Empire. Objections to her right to hold this office will lead to the Persons Case in which Canadian women are legally declared persons.

***July 1, 1916*:**
Prohibition comes into effect in Alberta as all beer houses and liquor parlours close.

July 10, 1916:
"The London Times History of the War – the second volume now ready for distribution by The Journal – will have an exceptional and unique value in future years as a vivid, fresh and accurate picture of the world's greatest war, made when the war was going on. It will carry to your children the hum and stir of this momentous period – the bugle call to arms – the rising of the Empire – the staunch loyalty of the colonies – the glorious achievement on land and sea."
- *Journal* ad.

***Sept. 16, 1916*:**
Private John Chipman Kerr of Canada's 49th Battalion (later the

NA-3452-2 Glenbow Archives

ALBERTA GOVERNMENT
TELEPHONES

The telephone company's offices were often the busiest in town, so High River workers wore masks during the flu epidemic of 1918.

ND-3-101 Glenbow Archives

EDMONTON CITY DAIRY, LTD JASPER AVENUE
100 39
SOME OF THE EX-EMPLOYEES OF EDMONTON CITY DAIRY LTD. WHO ARE SERVING KING AND COUNTRY
McDERMID A101

With patriotic fever running high, a group of Edmonton dairymen enlist for King and country.

Finally, on Oct. 17, *The Journal* entered the debate and recommended police enforce the $50 fine for one of the city's most-ignored bylaws – spitting on the sidewalk.

On Friday, Oct. 18, at midnight, the Edmonton Board of Health forbade all public gatherings – forcing the closure of schools, churches and theatres. An editorial called the response drastic since no cases of flu had yet been reported. "But if, as medical opinion seems to agree, it is inevitable that it should reach us, there is no use in waiting for it to do so before taking the measures which will prevent its spread throughout the community."

The first Edmonton flu report hit the paper on Oct. 19. There were 41 cases under quarantine, some of them soldiers taken off the train.

Today, this would be regarded as huge news, but oddly, despite the scale of the plague, no flu story ever attained billing as the main story on the front page. During the height of the crisis, flu stories were played on the front page, but the paper's main focus was on the final stages of war. The Hun was retreating. The Germans were surrendering. Then there was the post-war cleanup.

During the third week of October as the flu epidemic hit Edmonton, gauze masks became mandatory. The paper printed complete instructions – including a diagram – on making and wearing the masks.

But many people ignored them on the grounds that breathing through one all day seemed less sanitary than breathing fresh air.

On Oct. 23, four days after the flu hit the province, 1,035 cases were reported, 70 in Edmonton. "Few deaths are recorded."

The first stories of Edmonton deaths were published Oct. 24. Among them were May Ostlund, "a married woman," and library caretaker John Johns. By Oct. 26, hospitals were filled – schools and halls were opened to house the sick, who numbered more than 2,000. Doctors and nurses, stretched to the limit, were aided by volunteers. Hit with high absenteeism, businesses struggled to remain open.

By Nov. 2, the province reached its capacity to deal with more cases. A story reported that there were 8,000 people sick and the peak of the epidemic had yet to be reached. "The time has come when local boards of health and public men in the country towns and villages must do everything within their own reach to meet their own problems." The Edmonton death toll exceeded 140. Pembina Hall at the University of Alberta was turned into a hospital. Hotels in the city were also used to stockpile the sick.

There were 9,206 cases reported in the province on Nov. 5.

On Nov. 11, Armistice was declared and people gathered to celebrate. Amid the jubilation there was much hugging and kissing. Three days later *The Journal* reported the result of the indiscretions. "The abandonment of 'flu' masks by many persons Monday began to show on Wednesday when 58 new cases of influenza were reported…."

But the fever broke. As the epidemic peaked, cases totalled more than 15,000.

On Nov. 30, bans on meetings and gatherings were lifted. Pockets of plague reported were until May, but the worst was over.

In all, 7,914 people were treated for flu in Edmonton; 615 died.

The death toll and economic impact were counted over the months ahead, but the biggest question remained unanswered: "Why?"

Loyal Edmonton Regiment) earns the Victoria Cross by capturing 62 enemy prisoners in an attack on a German trench at Courcelette, during the Battle of the Somme.

***Oct. 9, 1916*:**
Rising flour prices force the cost of bread in Edmonton up to 12 loaves for one dollar.

***March 1, 1917*:**
The Alberta Provincial Police are established to take over law enforcement in the province from the RCMP.

***April 1917*:**
Arthur Yockney is named *The Journal's* business manager.

***April 26, 1917*:**
Edmonton annexes Calder, the railway village established in 1910 on the northwest edge of the city.

***June 7, 1917*:**
Alberta's general election is the first provincial election in Canada where women could vote and run for office. Louise McKinney and Roberta MacAdams become the first women in Canada elected to a legislature. Votes are not held in 11 ridings because of provincial legislation allowing MLAs on First World War active service to

STAGELAND

BARROW LE PAIGE
HEAVY MAN AND DIRECTOR, THE TRAVELING SALESMAN LYCEUM
MADAME BERNHARDT
IN THE EMPIRE JAN. 13
MUSICAL BEAR WITH APDALE'S ZOO CIRCUS ORPHEUM SHOWS EMPIRE JAN 14, 15, 16

Mme. Bernhardt's Art Moves Many of Audience To Tears

Famous Frenchwoman, Seen at Empire in Part of Marguerite Gautier in "La Dame Aux Camelias," Carries Her Hearers Out of Themselves by Splendid Acting of Death Chamber Scene

"My time in your city has been all too short, and I cannot help but open my heart to your people for the magnificent reception they have given to me."

Such was Madame Sarah Bernhardt's farewell greeting to Edmonton, given out last night through Louis Mercanter, her representative on tour. The Divine Sarah's engagement was only for a matinee and evening performance yesterday, and those who saw her at either will endorse to the full what she says about her stay being "all too short."

(By H. C. R.)

A darkened theatre thronged to the very doors, with the entire audience holding its breath in tense, almost painful quiescence; then throbbing, sobbing, stabbing through the gloom and the silence the low voice, like the tinkling of a silver bell, of her who is perhaps not only the greatest tragic actress of modern, but it may be of all times—that was how th...

the death bed. In the Pyrenees it was where Marguerite, who had repaired thither in the hope of restoring her shattered health, met young Armand Duval. That was the changing point in the lives of both; for her there was no more gilded sin; for him no more of peace; instead the beginning of a reciprocated "grand passion," which removed the shadow of shame from one life to cast a deeper shadow of woe on the other.

Reclaimed by Love.

Behold then the queen of the Parisian demi-monde, reclaimed by her love for Armand, all her old fripperies and gallantries cast aside forever. But Armand's father comes upon Marguerite while his son is absent; demands that she give him up; pleads that for her to persist in loving the boy will mean the shattering of his family's happiness. Her love is great enough to bear even this for its object; she leaves before Armand's return, sending him a ... the white and ...

regain a grip of themselves; that silence of moments is the greatest of all tributes to the spell which ... modern Circe of the board... about the hearts an... Ulysses, and she has ... cally every member ... Then like one the peo... up and down flies the ... ly yet can those who ... heard permit her to pa... sight. She stands swa... with reaction; those wo... shine half hid through her ... ed hair, like cornflowers t... ripe grain of an English har... then the last curtain and — ... but the memory. Once mo... atque vale"; not forever th... though, one must fain hope.

That the play was in an alien ... matterednot at all; the interpr... of genius makes an Esparan... Volopirk a universal language.

Madame Bernhardt was adequa... supported throughout, the Arm... Duval of M. Lou Tellegen being es... cially notable. The balance of t... cast was as follows: Gaston Riou... M. Deneubourg; Docteur, F. Favieres; Gustave, M. Terestri; Nanine, Mlle. Saylor; Prudence, Mme. Boulanger; Nichette, Mlle. Duo.

ORPHEUM BILL FAIR OFFERING.

The balance of the Orpheum vaudeville offering yesterday at the Empire, that which preceded and succeeded Madame Bernhardt's presentation, was of a very fair order. Though it had been the best or the worst that the ... stage has to offer, it would ... Before the ap... audi...

W. B. SHERMAN, MANAGER — BERT RUSSELL, RES. MANAGER

Empire Theatre — **Orpheum SHOWS** — THE STANDARD OF VAUDEVILLE

PHONE 2185

One Day Only—Monday Matinee and Night, January 13, 1913.
Most Stupendous Event in Vaudeville.

MARTIN BECK OFFERS

MADAME

SARAH BERNHARDT

And Her Company of French Players in Vaudeville.

ALSO A PERFECT VARIETY BILL

A Dramatic Novelty, "And They Lived Happy Ever After"
Chas. and Fanny Van and Company, In a New Laughalogue.
Josie Heather, The Winsome English Comedienne.
McMahon, Diamond and Clemence, "The Scare-Crow."

Matinee: $2.00, $1.50, $1.00 and 50c. Evening: $3.00, $2.50, $2.00 and $1.00.

Three Days Commencing Tuesday Matinee, January 14, 1913.
A Real Holiday Attraction—B. A. Rolfe's Extravaganza

"PUSS IN BOOTS"

... by Jean Bedini. American Book by Frank Kennedy. Music by B. A. Rolfe. A company of Twenty

The Divine Sarah

"Women weep and men are not ashamed to be seen with their eyes dewed with a moisture that has been a stranger to most of them for many a long day."
— Review of Sarah Bernhardt concert, Jan. 14, 1913

Sarah Bernhardt was almost 70 years old when her private four-coach train pulled into Edmonton from Winnipeg on Monday, Jan. 13, 1913.

Here was the greatest tragedian of all time – according to *The Journal* – and she was bringing high art to a city on the edge of the wilderness.

She was the Divine Sarah, maybe somewhat past her prime, but still celebrated for her controversial appearance as Hamlet and still remembered for her performance as Salome decades earlier in Oscar Wilde's banned play of the same name.

Bernhardt was big-time theatre magic in a place that was, even then, mad about theatre. Within five hours of her arrival, she was on stage for the matinee at the 400-seat Empire Theatre. She performed the dying courtesan, Marguerite, in the fifth act of *La dame aux camèlias* by Alexandre Dumas, a role she would repeat that evening at 8:30. Matinee tickets ranged from 50 cents to $2, and from $1 to $3 for the evening performance.

It was worth every penny, enthused the paper's theatre reviewer, identified as H.C.R, who on Jan. 14, heaped on the kind of praise and prose that make modern-day critics cringe: "A darkened theatre thronged to the very doors, with the entire audience holding its breath in tense, almost painful quiescence; then throbbing, sobbing, stabbing through the gloom and the silence the low voice, like the tinkling of a silver bell, of her who is perhaps not only the greatest tragic actress of modern, but it may be, of all times – that was how the revelation of art which is called Sarah Bernhardt stole its way into the hearts of those who were fortunate enough to be at the Empire yesterday, there to take its place for all the after-time with those other memories – so pitifully few – which are a joy forever.

"From the rising of the curtain till its fall, every movement of hand or body, every inclination of the head, every one of the few sweeping gestures that the famous French woman could make as the dying courtesan, every tone of voice – whether low and laboured, as is befitting one who is hovering on the threshold of that portal which opens and closes but the once for all mankind, or whether shrilling in husky, despairing cries, the toll of utter anguish taken from fast-failing strength – each and all of these had its meaning, its correct place in the artistic perfection of the whole; not a shade of tone or gesture that did not ring bitter true, or flash its message with an awesome realism." H.C.R. droned on for another 3,000 similar words.

Hardly a surprise, there was a standing ovation: "Then like one the people rise at her, up and down flies the curtain, scarcely yet can those who have seen and heard permit her to pass from their sight. She stands swaying slightly with reaction, those wonderful eyes shine half hid through her low-dressed hair, like cornflowers through the ripe grain of an English harvest field; then the last curtain and – nothing but the memory."

retain their seats. MacAdams was one of two elected at large in soldiers' vote; because of delays McKinney is technically the first woman elected.

***Aug. 27, 1917*:**
Canadian Northern's return train fare from Edmonton to the Vancouver exhibition is $29.15.

***Oct. 30, 1917*:**
Cecil Kinross of Canada's 49th Battalion is one of four Canadians to win the Victoria Cross for heroism in this day's fighting at Passchendaele.

***Dec. 10, 1917*:**
Harry M.E. Evans is elected mayor of Edmonton, in a city election that has a 70-per-cent voter turnout.

***In 1918*:**
A *Journal* compositor makes $1.06 per hour, while a mailer earns $10 per week.

***March 21, 1918*:**
Edmund de Wind earns a posthumous Victoria Cross for heroism fighting in France. De Wind was a clerk in Edmonton's Bank of Commerce when the war began.

***April 6, 1918*:**
More than 10,000 cheering Edmontonians welcome home

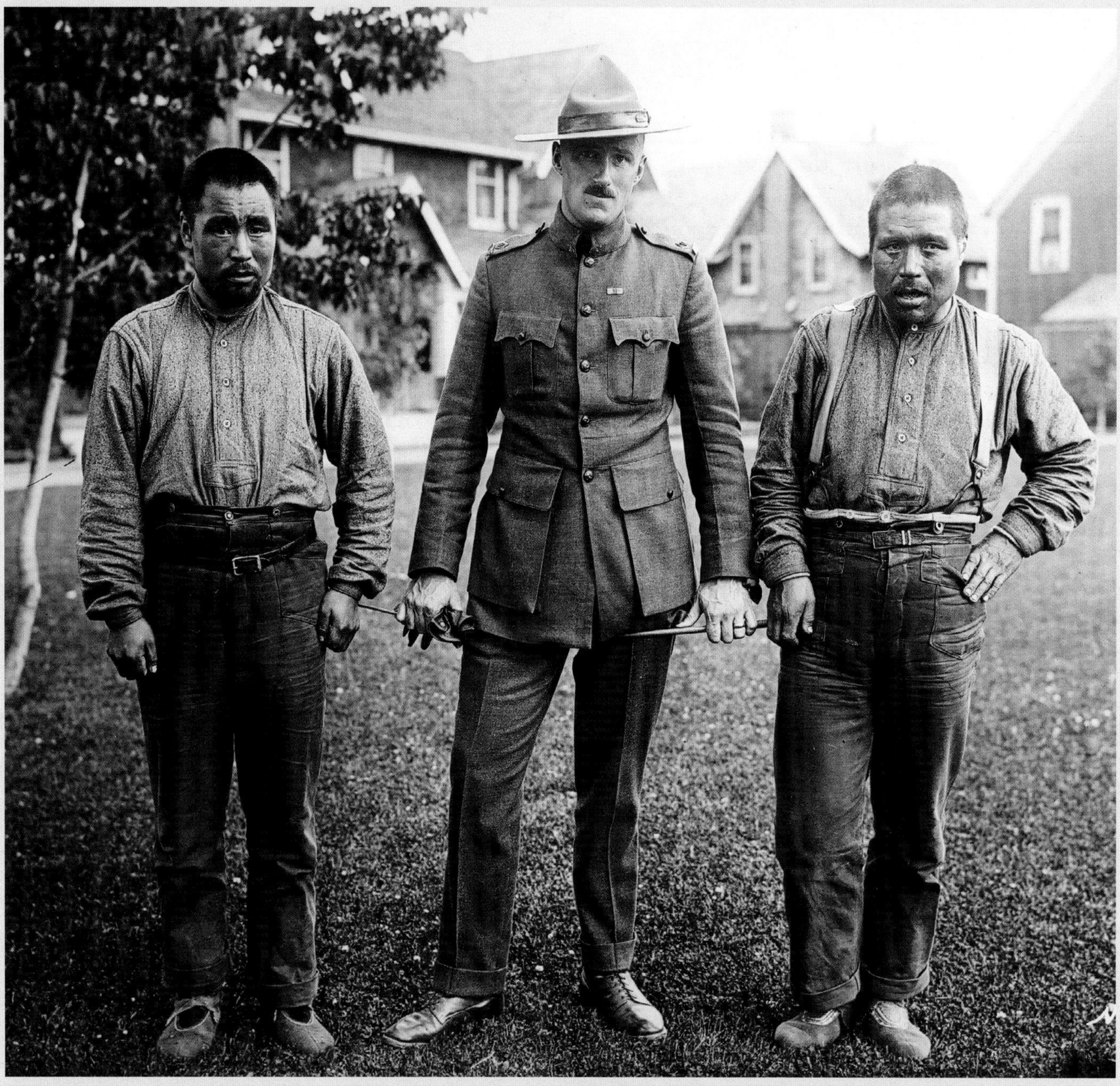

NC-6-534 Glenbow Archives

Prisoners Sinnisiak and Uluksuk with inspector Danny LeNeuze in Edmonton for their trial in August 1917.

DRAYS
FANNING MILLS
DRILLS
AGENTS FOR
1015
436

NC-6-444 Glenbow Archives

Edmonton's police force increased its capacity to control crime when it added two police cars, 1912.

Visitors Extraordinaire

"Though unenlightened, the Eskimos are a good kind. They have the disposition of children, and like children, they are sometimes sulky, breaking into fits of rage if too severely provoked, but as quickly are back again to their normal spirits."
— Column by "The Town Bellman," Aug. 11, 1917

The Aug. 10, 1917, headline, "LONG PATROL FOR ESKIMOS ENDS; ALLEGED MURDERERS REACH CITY," offered a diversion from the wartime casualty lists that were by now routinely the first focus of readers' attention.

Uluksuk and Sinnisiak, two Coppermine Inuit, were charged with the four-year-old murder of a pair of Oblate missionary priests named Jean-Baptiste Rouviere and Guillaume Le Roux. One of the priests had been shot, and the other bludgeoned to death at Bloody Falls, a cascade on the Coppermine River, south of Coronation Gulf on the Arctic coast.

In a blinding snowstorm, with the priests' dog team tangled in their traces, Sinnisiak slit open the bodies of the dead men and he and Uluksuk ate part of the victims' livers.

Their sensational trial was the first time that white man's law was brought to the Inuit and it was front-page news.

There were allegations that a fair trial in Edmonton would not be possible, given the coverage in the local newspapers, including *The Journal.*

Initially the pair were to be tried separately, and an Edmonton jury acquitted Uluksuk of the murder of Father Rouviere. The subsequent joint trial on the charge of murdering Father Le Roux was held in Calgary.

In that proceeding, both men were convicted and sentenced to hang. However at the urging of both the judge and the Calgary jury, the sentences were commuted to life imprisonment, to be served in the North.

But while they were here, the pair was the toast of the town, along with an Inuk special constable named Ivaninik, the witness Keoha and Patsy Klingenberg, a 17-year-old translator of Danish/Inuit extraction.

A *Journal* column, *The Town Bellman,* written by an unidentified writer about local events, set the tone the day after they arrived in Edmonton. Uluksuk and Sinnisiak were "visitors extraordinaire."

While the writer confessed that he didn't know much about the Inuit – Eskimos, they were called then – it didn't prevent him from writing 2,000 words on the culture of the Arctic people.

"In physique they are a little people, but are stockily built, and have great powers of endurance, their features are of a semi-Chinese cast, and their flesh colour is a dull copper. As a rule, despite their squatness, they are a rather pleasing people to look at because of their habitual cheerfulness."

John Chipman Kerr, who was awarded a Victoria Cross in 1916, and present him with a purse full of gold.

***April 27, 1918*: Edmonton's Lt. George McKean earns a Victoria Cross for his heroism during a night raid on a German trench in fighting on the Lys River in northern France.**

***May 25, 1918*: Canadian women age 21 or older gain the right to vote in federal elections.**

***June 15, 1918*: *The Journal* opens a fund-raising drive to send parcels to the 49th Battalion.**

***July 9, 1918*: Pilot Katherine Stinson completes delivery of the first airmail in Western Canada, flying from Calgary to Edmonton.**

***Aug. 5, 1918*: Canadian Northern charges $1 return fare on its civic holiday excursion train from Edmonton to Alberta Beach.**

***Oct. 17, 1918*: Frank Beevers is the first member of Edmonton's city police to be killed on duty while attempting to arrest a suspect in a murder-robbery.**

NC-6-3475 Glenbow Archives

On July 9, 1918, Katherine Stinson delivered the West's first air mail to Edmonton Exhibition's W.J. Stark and Postmaster George Armstrong.

BANK OF NOVA SCOTIA
CAPITAL $5,900,000
BANK OF NOVA SCOTIA
RESERVE $10,750,000
INCORPORATED 1832

NC-6-534 Glenbow Archives

Mike's News, with John Michaels, centre, got its start on the sidewalk at Jasper and 101st Street, beside the Empire Building.

Special Delivery

"She is such a slender bit of a girl, one can hardly realize that her hands have the strength to handle a biplane."
— Story about Katherine Stinson, from the Women's Page, July 10, 1916

The skies were quiet over Edmonton between 1911 and 1916 so *Journal* readers had to follow the rapid development in airplane technology vicariously in First World War stories about dogfights and daring aces.

The city proudly sent boys to battle above the trenches of France – boys like Roy Brown who saved his boyhood chum, Wop May, by shooting down the infamous Red Baron. Brown downed 13 enemy planes, May, seven, and fellow Edmontonian John Manuel, 10.

Still, reading about soaring in the clouds wasn't the same as actually seeing it, so in 1916 Edmonton Exhibition organizers staged an air show after they cancelled a fireworks display due to a lack of gunpowder.

Maybe a young, striking woman flyer would attract even more people to the fair than fireworks.

So on July 10, 1916, Edmonton made the acquaintance of Katherine Stinson. She was a remarkable 26-year-old poster girl for women's liberation in an era when women were usually free only to choose the schedule of their domestic chores.

Stinson hailed from San Antonio, Texas, where she ran a flying school. She had already taught 60 Canadians to fly – 59 of them had enlisted and were flying in the war. Stinson was known as The Flying Schoolmarm and her students as The Texas Escadrille.

She was also a barnstormer who travelled around North America putting on flying displays at fairgrounds. Her reputation as a skilled pilot preceded her.

Still, this was 1916 and the paper couldn't quite bring itself to treat her like one of the guys.

Stinson let her skill speak for her, and by July 12 the paper's editorial writers had changed their tune: "Miss Stinson's flying gave to many the first thrill they have had in years. We have heard and read a great deal about the advances that the science of aviation has made, especially under the stress of war conditions, but no one, until he sees a flyer of the calibre of this clever and fearless young Canadian girl, can have anything like an adequate idea of the marvelous mastery of the air that has been attained."

Of course, the paper apologized the next day for calling her a "Canadian," saying the writer was "misled by a paragraph in an outside newspaper."

"Let's hope some day she will be! Just at present the honor of possessing so plucky and clever a young woman must go to our southern neighbours."

Stinson returned to Alberta in both 1917 and 1918. She completed the first city-to-city flight in Alberta and first air mail service in Western Canada in 1918, when she flew from Calgary to Edmonton.

***Oct. 25, 1918*:**
Alberta's provincial board of health orders that gauze masks must be worn by every person outside of their own home to deal with the Spanish flu epidemic. Newspapers publish directions for making them; pharmacies sell them for 10 cents.

***Oct. 26, 1918*:**
Spanish flu epidemic has more than 800 cases in the city with at least 12 deaths. Pembina Hall at the University of Alberta opens as a temporary civic hospital as patients overflow existing facilities.

***Dec. 9, 1918*:**
Joseph Clarke is elected mayor of Edmonton.

***In 1919*:**
A stenographer at *The Journal* makes $20 a month.

***Feb. 20, 1919*:**
Edison phonographs and records, both disc and cylinder format, sell for $82 to $431 at Edmonton stores.

***March 22, 1919*:**
The City of Edmonton declares a public holiday and 30,000 people line the streets to welcome home Edmonton's 49th Battalion from the war. Of 4,050 men who served in the battalion, 977

NC-6-4329 Glenbow Archives

McDERMID 2114
4329

Journal publisher M.R. Jennings and pilot George Gorman load 75 pounds of newspapers bound for Wetaskiwin aboard The Edmonton in preparation for Alberta's first commercial flight in June 1919.

NC-6-4311 Glenbow Archives

Journal
10179
31
66
51
56
20
78
70

A bike race sponsored by *The Journal* in 1919 was a popular event.

Bombing Wetaskiwin

"The Journal will be the first to introduce to the citizens an Edmonton-owned airplane operated by an Edmonton pilot."
— Story, June 7, 1919

Every newspaper runs promotions. Sometimes they involve contests to win books or movie tickets.

But in 1919, *Journal* publisher M.R. Jennings wanted to do something really different. He wanted to promote aviation using *The Journal.*

Jennings, an American who fought in Cuba with Teddy Roosevelt, engaged war hero George Gorman of (Wop) May Airplanes, Ltd., to fly sacks full of newspapers, *The Journal* of course, to Wetaskiwin.

The articles about the feat, June 9, contained two novel elements. First, at the time when few stories accompanied by photos, there were several pictures of the plane, the pilots and Jennings shaking hands with Gorman. Second, the stories had bylines – the names of writers – another rarity.

Gorman wrote one article himself describing the experience from his vantage point aloft in the plane. He flew The Edmonton, a less-than-state-of-the-art biplane manufactured in Toronto and purchased on behalf of the city by realtor James Carruthers. May's company leased it for $25 a month. "The trip by air to Wetaskiwin and back was made without incident, except for a voluntary landing on the trip home to escape the heavy rainstorm," Gorman wrote with logbook conciseness.

The other story was written by H.W. Laughy, who suffered from an acute case of hyperbole.

"A dream of the ancients was realized Saturday when an aeroplane flew from Edmonton to Wetaskiwin with a load of Edmonton Journals.

"Circling the grounds at a dizzy height as a hawk sails floating on the wind, the swift machine swung easily to its helm, then dipped and dived like an eagle swooping on its prey, till fifty feet from earth it flattened out its course, rose gracefully to its circling flight and dropped its load in passing."

Yes. The good people of Wetaskiwin were bombed with 75 pounds of newspaper. This made Laughy nervous.

"Beautiful as the sight was, and graceful the swoopings of this swift (78 mph) bird a grim, cold tinge was added by the thought, 'Great God, if those were bombs,' for guiding that machine for our amusement was one of those who carried death across the German lines."

Jennings' interest in promoting aviation wasn't a passing fancy.

His wife Carolyn Louise, was the first woman passenger to fly from Edmonton to Calgary in 1920 in a demonstration of support for Jock McNeill's attempt to start an "air taxi service" between the cities.

never return. Another 2,282 were wounded.

***March 25, 1919*:**
A subscription to *The Journal* costs 15 cents per week.

***April 11, 1919*:**
Federal figures show 36,013 Albertans volunteered for military service in the First World War.

***May 13, 1919*:**
Edmonton city council endorses the formation of a city flying club. Also in 1919, the first flight out of what is now the City Centre Airport takes place. Edmonton Airplane Co., is organized and Edmonton Airforce Association is started.

***May 27, 1919*:**
A haircut at the Macdonald Hotel barber shop costs 35 cents, a shave 25 cents.

***June 7, 1919*:**
George Gorman pilots the first commercial flight from Edmonton, flying a cargo of *Journals* to Wetaskiwin.

***Aug. 30, 1919*:**
Constable William Nixon is the second Edmonton police officer to be killed in the line of duty. Shot while questioning a pedestrian about a recent robbery, he dies in hospital on Aug. 31.

"NATIONAL HERO'SERIES"
NO. 10

Kossuth—Greatest of Hungarians

THIS noble lover of Liberty was to his beloved Hungary what Patrick Henry was to American Independence. "Give me Liberty or give me death" meant to Kossuth all that made life worth the living. He lived for ninety-two years, and his long and honorable career was devoted solely to secure for Hungary National Independence. For it he suffered imprisonment and exile. For it he worked as few men have ever worked. His fiery soul was expressed in his writing, and his impassioned oratory thundered across the two continents. All the world read and listened to this high-souled Hungarian Patriot. When exiled our government sent the U. S. Steamer Mississippi to Turkey and brought him to our shores as the guest of the Nation. To-day we have millions of Hungarian citizens, each one a lover of Personal Liberty. To secure it they sought our shores, and to a man they will fight to the death to keep forever alive the spirit and letter of our immortal Declaration of Independence. They make good citizens, and like Kossuth detest prohibitory enactments which make the many suffer for the faults of the very few. For centuries Hungarians have as a nation been moderate users of barley brews and light wines. Their votes are always registered against any legislation which proposes to regulate human diet by law. "Thou shalt NOT eat this—thou shalt NOT drink that"—to those of brave Hungarian blood is insufferable tyranny. For 57 years Anheuser-Busch have been proud to serve their Hungarian patrons. They have helped to make the sales of their great brand Budweiser exceed those of any other beer by millions of bottles. Seven thousand, five hundred people are daily required to keep pace with the public demand for Budweiser.

ANHEUSER-BUSCH · ST. LOUIS, U.S.A.

Bottled only at the home plant.

BUDWEISER

The Hudson's Bay Co.
Distributors **Edmonton**

Budweiser
Means Moderation

Say Mr. Curler

Its great fun running up and down a rink, but doesn't it get cold once in a while? Besides its hard on a fellow's throat yelling, "Soop 'er up."

Try a wee drap o' H. B. Scotch, and don't forget to include a Tin of Imperial Tobacco.

Phone 1535. We'll send it doon tae the Rink.

Hudson's Bay Co.

WATSONS SCOTCH No 10

WHITE HORSE
Scotch

Rules the Waves
of Popular Opinion

Prohibition

"Alberta is dry, so very dry."
— Headline, July 1, 1916

The paper wasn't big on banning booze. It fought a long, acrimonious editorial battle against the forces of temperance and sobriety right up to last last-call on midnight Friday, June 30, 1916.

The story, however, started more than a decade earlier.

Edmonton – and Alberta, generally – had a hard time grappling with demon rum. The population was young, transient and there were more men than women. Hotels with bars went up at a furious rate.

There was a core of people who saw this as a problem. By 1910, the Women's Christian Temperance Union and the Alberta Moral and Temperance Association were well-organized and, literally, on the march.

A Jan. 10, 1910, story outlined the call of the Temperance advocates to close the bars on all holidays and shorten the hours of operation. Said Association secretary Rev. G.W.G. Fortune: "Alberta's wheat crop is insufficient to pay for the drink bill of the Dominion." The wheat crop, that year, was worth $97 million – $6 billion in today's money.

Bars and bootleggers flourished. On Feb. 15, *The Journal* reported that Ethel Williams was in court for the second time charged with selling illegal liquor from a tent set up at the top of the hill leading to Strathcona. She was fined $200.

But marching, sermons and fines didn't put much of a damper on liquor sales. That was accomplished by the Alberta Referendum Act of 1913, legislation foisted on Arthur Sifton's Liberal government by the United Farmers of Alberta, a powerful rural lobby group that wanted the right to bring legislation considered "unjust" to a public vote.

The temperance groups took advantage of the legislation and gathered names from 10 per cent of the electors in 1915 to bring prohibition to a vote. Sifton set the plebiscite for July 21.

The paper's stance wasn't popular with some readers. On July 14, Mrs. Wesley Howard said the paper "is a disgrace to be found in any Christian home ... there have been things in it during the last two weeks which have dragged down our Bible, our ministers and our Christian religion. Ladies, I cannot stand it."

In a final plea for a "no" vote, *The Journal* editorialized that the whole referendum was irrational. "Speaking and writing in the name of temperance they have been guilty of the grossest intemperance of utterance."

The province voted 50,037 to 29,259 to close the bars. Edmontonians passed the plebiscite by 3,500 votes. And it wasn't as if women like Mrs. Howard stuffed the ballot boxes – all the voters were men. Women didn't obtain the vote for another year.

In the day-after editorial, the paper bowed to the inevitable: "The dangers surrounding the legislation are very real, but if these can be overcome in its administration there will be no occasion for regretting its decision."

***Sept. 2, 1919*:**
Return fare from Edmonton to Vancouver on Canadian Northern Railway is advertised at $39.40.

***Sept. 12, 1919*:**
Thousands greet the Prince of Wales, the future King Edward VIII, as he arrives in Edmonton for a two-day visit. Activities on the first day include laying the cornerstone for the new veterans' Memorial Hall. The next day he is awarded an honorary degree at the University of Alberta.

***October 1919*:**
***The Journal* acquires land at the corner of 101 St. and Macdonald Drive and begins construction of a new 22,500-square-foot home. In May, an audit puts the paper's circulation at 19,269. It began the decade at 3,454.**

***Dec. 8, 1919*:**
Joseph Clarke is elected mayor of Edmonton.

MAGAZINE SECTION

Edmonton Journal

MAGAZINE SECTION

VOL. 21, NO. 239 EDMONTON, ALBERTA. SATURDAY, APRIL 25, 1925 SIX PAGES

'They Like It' is Verdict on CJCA

EXTENT OF JOURNAL RADIO SERVICE DURING THE PAST SEASON HAS BEEN WIDENED; THOUSANDS LISTENING IN

CJCA No Longer Most Northerly Station So More Suitable Title for Igloo Hut Planned; Work of Journal Radio During Past Season Reviewed

By J. REG. ASH

IT is the end of a cold and dismal day. The mantle of an Arctic night closes down all too rapidly upon the fur-clad, moccasined figure who, with aching bones and weary tread, is returning to the little hut of rough-hewn logs he calls his home. The bleak interior of that lonely domicile, with its fireless stove and air of emptiness, offers little enough respite from the haunting desolation of the daily round of the traps; the sight that greets him as he opens the creaking door is anything but inviting.

He steps within; the burden of furs is thrown aside, the parka and the big fur mittens doffed. There is a fumble for matches, a search for wood with which to start a fire, and soon the little cabin is undergoing a transformation. As the flames leap up, the spirits of the man rise with them. Soon he will have a hot meal ready, and nature and the wilderness will then seem less unkind.

But stay; another thought is passing through his mind. For a moment he hadn't remembered; years of monotonous routine and changeless existence had accustomed him to expecting naught but the same dull round. The cruel clutches of the Arctic winter, the icy blasts that go howling round the cabin are temporarily forgotten as the trapper his spirit of depression gone, prepares to realize a cherished dream.

Oh You Radio!

On a make-shift table near a corner stands an ebony-colored box—a strange-looking contraption, with wires, and dials and little knobs, that harmonizes not at all with the other crude furnishings of the cabin. The man moves across to it, eyes alight with pleasurable anticipation. A dial is turned, a knob adjusted, and suddenly, with an introductory howl or two from the little mystery-box, a voice from a far-away city is heard:

"Radio Station C-J-C-A, broadcastign from Edmonton, Alberta, Canada –the sunniest spot in sunny Alberta."

The Great White silence is forgotten; thoughts of the morrow, with its renewal of battle with the elements, are cast aside, as the trapper, in his lonely hut beyond the Arctic Circle, a thousand miles or more from Edmonton, prepares to "listen in."

Only those who have visited that frozen wilderness can realize what the radio has meant to the far northland. Where once the winter nights meant naught but loneliness and depression, the northman with his little radio set now is veritably set down in the midst of civilization, where cares can be forgotten and enjoyment reign supreme.

The Journal's Aim

CJCA, the Edmonton Journal station, has ever had this vision before it—of the day when the man at Resolution, or Aklavik, or Herschel Island, will just as surely be in touch with civilization as is the man in the town by the railway line; when the dull spectre of loneliness will be effaced from the life of the northerner. To a large extent the vision has been realized, though something more can be accomplished yet.

The "Igloo Hut", the Journal's station club, had this idea in mind when, eighteen months ago, its weekly programs were inaugurated. To give entertainment to Edmontonians doesn't so much matter; the important thing is that those in faraway districts, remote from all that civilization has to offer, may enjoy a little more of the pleasures of life.

Many letters are on record to show that the Igloo Hut concerts, like those given regularly from CJCA on other days of the week, have reached those for whom primarily intended. Fort Good Hope, Hay River and Fort Resolution on Great Slave Lake; Fort Smith, Fort Reliance, Fitzgerald, Chipewyan, Douglas City, Alaska, are some of the northern points from which letters have been received from grateful listeners in. Fort Good Hope, the most northerly post heard from, is within fifty miles of the Arctic circle, while practically all the other points mentioned are a thousand miles or more from the nearest centre of civilization.

The Farmers Also

There is another class of people, too, to whom the Igloo Hut concerts come as a boon. These are the farmers in outlying districts who, while less distantly removed from city attractions than are the trappers of the north, are none the less eager to enjoy the fund of amusement which radio provides. Throughout the entire Igloo Hut season just closed, groups of thirty and forty people congregated weekly at places where radio was installed, and collectively litsened in to the programs broadcast.

These concerts, as well as others given from the Journal station during the week, became, according to dozens of letters received by the radio operator and the "Big Chief" of the Hut, the feature attraction of social evenings, and farmers drove for miles to the home of a radio fan to enjoy the music and fun that came through the ether. Many a country dance, too, was made possible by the broadcasting of syncopated melodies from station CJCA.

And now the Igloo Hut has closed its second season; the final concert of the winter was given on April 16, at the conclusion of four and a half months of weekly programs with only one or two intermissions. The Hut with "Big Chief Polar Bear" (Dick Stevens) in charge, inauguarated its second annual term of fun-making on the night of November 6, and during the Thursday nights which followed, fans in every part of the North American continent came to watch for and appreciate the concerts given.

No More "Igloo Hut"

There will again be a station club in conjunction with CJCA next fall. It will not be known, however, as the "Igloo Hut." When this mirthful name was selected, two years ago, its suitability was based upon the fact that CJCA was the most northerly broadcasting station on the continent. Conditions since then, however, have changed a lot; governmental stations have been established in the Northwest Territories, many hundreds of miles north of the city of Edmonton. Before the summer has passed, there will be a radio plant either on Herschell Island or at Aklavik, both within the Arctic circle and two thousand miles beyond Edmnton.

Also, CJCA now numbers in its clientelo of listeners in. United States citizens from the Atlantic to the Pacific and from the Canadian border to the Gulf.

"Igloo Hut," with its suggestion of snow and ice, and "polar bears," is now scarcely a fitting designation of a radio station club in a metropolitan city of 60,000, in the centre of what has been proven the best wheat-growing and mixed-farming district on the continent, especially when that name conveys to some fans a total erroneous impression.

Brand New Name

When the Journal station club "opens up" in the fall again, therefore, it will have been completely reorganized and will bear a brand new name. Just what this name shall be has not yet been determined. There is a possibility that a contest may be staged, and prizes awarded for the best name submitted. In the meantime, however, fans may definitely count upon the reopening of the station club programs in the autumn months, on much the same basis of entertainment and fun-making as before.

There were many interesting features of the Igloo Hut last season; every concert was an outstanding one. Several innovations were introduced—"Gyro Night" for instance, when the Gyro club of Edmonton put on a special concert by its members; "Old-Time Melodies Night," on March 13, when fans had the time of their lives listening to songs and dances of "the good old days"; "Minstrel Night," when a real dyed-in-the-wool minstrel show was staged by the entertainers of the Hut, and various other similar occasions.

Two Contests

Two contests were staged during the year, also. The first of these, the "Old-Fashioned Song Titles" competition, in which entrants were reported to give correctly the titles of fifteen old-fashioned songs, played over the radio, brought responses from six hundred fans. The second, arranged to find a solution of the baffling problem of what had become of "Sally," the song heroine, evoked interest throughout Canada and in many states of the union, and replies to the puzzle were received from no fewer than 354 fans, scattered throughout the north American continent. Many ingenious solutions were given, and prizes duly awarded.

The important feature of this year's Igloo Hut, however, was the organization of the "Igloo Hut Eskimos," a group of singers and entertainers who every week were on hand to provide a program of merit for the Hut's extensive circle of listeners in. The group included Dick Stevens, ("Big Chief Polar Bear"); Dick Rice, station operator, ("Tiny"); Dennis Clayton, ("Piano Wrassler"); Frank Dallison, ("The Kandy Kid"); Bert Crockett, ("Stoney"); Hamish Gillespie, ("The Duke of Aklavik"); Alex. Huff, ("Wise-Owl, the Sage"); H. A. Mackie, Jr., ("Mickey Maguire"); Harry Brown, ("Hambone Artist"); Sandy MacPherson, ("Oatmeal Savage"); Joe Springer, ("Ye Olde Scribe"); Fred Doucet, ("The Hatitant").

Gave Generously

With the exception of the two first named—Dick Stevens and Dick Rice—none of these entertainers had any connection with the Edmonton Journal, but generously came up to the broadcasting station, week after week, to provide first-class programs for the fans. Many other singers, musicians and entertainers helped to make these concerts a success, of course, but the "Igloo Hut Eskimos" were always on hand, to fill in where needed. For their services, given entirely without remuneration, these chaps deserve great credit. The Journal also wishes to extend to all who contributed to the weekly program from the Hut its sincere thanks.

The Journal studio during the progress of the Hut concerts was a veritable mecca for country fans, and never a Thursday night went by that did not find its quota of from ten to twenty rural visitors on hand. On the final evening of the season's concerts, no fewer than forty radio fans came in from country districts, to enjoy first-hand the program that was broadcast. Always glad to see these visitors the Journal on each occasion extended to the country fans a hearty welcome.

Important Feature

Toward the end of the season, the Hut inauguarated a highly-important feature, involving the broadcasting of information concerning agricultural Alberta and its wonderful opportunities for the settler. By arrangement, Colin G. GGroff. provincial publicity commissioner, on the Thursday night of six successive weeks, gave during the progress of the Igloo Hut concert, a brief address, directed particularly to United States fans, telling something of the great natural resources of Alberta, the attractability of its climate, the owndertul fertility of its soil and the fine agricultural opportunities it offers. That these talks were effective in the interests of charity. The Edmonton Journal maintains a "Sunshine society" that all through the year dispenses cheer and aid to the needy, and at Christmas time is particularly active. Wishing to help in the work of this organization, the Igloo Hut decided to arrange a "Request Night," when the Hut entertainers would sing or play any selection chosen by an individual, the only condition being that a donation be sent in to the "Radio Sunshine Fund." Through the medium of this activity more than three hundred dollars was raised.

Souvenir Picture

A similar idea is now being put into effect. At the request of many fans, a souvenir picture of the Igloo Hut Eskimos has been prepared, and is being sent to any person who remits to the club twenty-five cents, the whole of the money thus collected to be donated to "Sunshine." Already some $70 has been received from the fans.

Toward the end of the season the Journal arranged to send to every United States fan from whom a letter was recived, a copy of the Alberta government's publicity booklet, telling of the opportunities in agriculture offered by this province. Some two hundred booklets have already been sent out.

Two banquets were given the Igloo Hut Eskimos during the season—one by C. Johnson, of Johnson's Cafe, the other by "Shorty" Martin, of the Shasta. Both were much appreciated. Every Thursday night, too, some fan or other sent up "eats" to the studio, and Johnson's Cafe supplied coffee. Entertaining for the Igloo Hut, therefore, was not without its reward.

4000 Letters

Nearly four thousand letters, expressing appreciation for the Igloo Hut programs, were received during the year, and a membership of more than a thousand was rolled up.

The Hut concluded the season of 1924-25 with a get-together dinner in Hepburn's on Thursday night, April 23, when the Hut entertainers, with their wives and friends enjoyed a social evening and made tentative plans for next season's activities.

If the Igloo Hut made progress during the season, so did the Journal radio department in general. Better concerts were put on, a wider circle of radio fans reached and a broader scope of usefulness entered upon than ever before.

Messages to North

Perhaps the most important feature of all was the development, during the winter, of the northern police and fraternal message broadcast. Growing out of the demand of other years, the Journal early in the season decided to set apart Saturday night for the broadcasting of personal messages to the far northland. By this arrangement, people in Edmonton and elsewhere, with relatives or friends in the north, were able to send them messages where the mail or telegraph could not reach. An average of ten such messages per week were sent, and many expressions of grateful appreciation of this service were received.

Police messages of various sorts were also common, and ranged from ordinary orders to detachments in the north to efforts to locate cars or round-up criminals. The messages were sent by both city and R. C. M. P. officers.

Many persons at far northern points are in constant touch with the ger at Fort Good Hope, for instance; or Canon Vale, at Hay River; Dr. Bourget, at Fort Resolution; Captain Bullock and Jack Hornsby, explorers, at Fort Reliance; J. A. McDougall, commissioner of the Northwest Territories, Fort Smith; C. S. Leggo and William Munro, Fort Fitzgerald; Mickey Ryan, trader, Fort Smith; Corporal Bryant, of the R. C. M. P. Chipewyan; Dan Patterson, at the mouth of the Embarass river; A. Tennant, at Keg River Post; Judge Bell and Inspector W. J. Moorhead, R. C. M. P., at Whitehorse, Yukon Territory; Dr. Smith, of Douglas City, Alaska, and many fans at Grouard, Wabisca, Fond du lac, McMurray, Waterways and other northern points.

Isolated Posts

For months on end such posts—or the majority of them, at least—are without connection with the outside world, except by radiophone. The last winter mail for the far north, for instance, left Edmonton on March 31, and all northern points will be cut off from communication except by radio, until the first river steamers make their voyages down the Mackenzie.

Not only has the radius of CJCA extended northward, however. Concerts from this station have been heard in practically every city in the United States and Canada, and have even reached Mexico City, from which point a post card, written in Spanish and addressed to "Estacion Difusers, Edmunt, Taylor Dominio de Can," was received, giving information to the effect that station CJCA had been heard even in Mexico. New York, Halifax, Los Angeles, Jacksonville (Florida), and similar faraway points "pick up" the Journal concerts at regular intervals.

Broadcasting of church services, of "Canadian National railways" (CNRE) concerts, of dinner programs from the Macdonald hotel, and, during the week of April 13, a light opera company from the Empire theatre, and a vaudeville show from the Pantages, were features of the Journal's broadcasts during the past winter.

In December, 1924, a considerable improvement was effected, when the broadcasting apparatus was moved to the roof of the Journal building, and the studio on the third floor enlarged.

As a result of this improvement, and of the arrangement of high class programs throughout the season 1924-25 may well be considered the most successful in the history to date of radio station CJCA.

ENTERTAINERS IN EDMONTON JOURNAL IGLOO HUT

C.J.C.A.
Edmonton Journal
"Igloo Hut Eskimos"
Edmonton - Alberta
CANADA
Season
1924-25
1
2
3
4
5
6
7
8
9
10
11
12

Above are shown the "Igloo Hut Eskimos" who dur ing the season just concluded gave so much enjoyment to radio fans. They are (1) Dick Stevens, "Big Chief Po lar Bear"; (2) Dick Rice, station operator, "Tiny"; (3) Dennis Clayton, "Piano Wrassler"; (4) Frank Dallison, "The Kandy Kid"; (5) Bert Crockett, "Stoney"; (6) Hamish Gillespie, "Duke of Aklavik"; (7) Alex. Huff, "W ise Owl, the Sage"; (8) H. A. Mackie, Jr., "Mickey Maguire"; (9) Harry Brown, "Hambone Artist"; (10) Sand y MacPherson, "Oatmeal Savage"; (11) Joe Springer, "Ye Olde Scribe"; (12) Fred Doucet, "The Habitant."

WITH PEN AND PENCIL

LITERATURE BY W. EVERARD EDMONDS ART

Building of the C. P. R.

By W. EVERARD EDMONDS

Building of the C.P.R.

The Canadian Pacific Railway company was incorporatd in 1880 with Sir Donald Smith and his cousin, Sir George Stephen, as its chief members. They were splendidly backed up by Sir John Macdonald and Sir Charles Tupper, and they were especially fortunate in having as their chief engineer such a man as Sir William Van Horne. Smith, Stephen, and their fellow directors of the Bank of Montreal embarked their last dollar in the enterprise, and even so, it looked for a time as if it must fail. A leading Canadian newspaper said it would never pay for its axle grease, and a prominent Canadian statesman laughed at the idea of building a railway through a "sea of mountains."

But the company triumphed over all obstacles. The line was pushed rapidly around the rugged shore of Lake Superior, over the tangled mass of rock and lake and wilderness between Lake Superior and Winnipeg, across a thousand miles of prairie where there was not an inhabitant save the buffalo and the Indian and a few hundreds of almost equally savage hunters, through the terrible Kicking Horse Pass, through Roger's Pass in the Selkirks, then down the valley of the Fraser, and so at last out to Burrard's Inlet where now stands the stately city of Vancouver.

At Headlong Speed

The line was built solidly but at headlong speed. On the prairie a record was established by the laying of six miles of rail in a day. A great army of men had to be fed a thousand miles from the base of supplies, but every difficulty yielded to the organizing ability of Van Horne. By the contract the company had been given ten years to complete the line, but so rapidly did the work proceed that it was completed in 1885.

The expense of the undertaking was enormous; the government had again and again to come to the relief of the company. Once, after the departure of Sir Charles Tupper to become Canadian high commissioner in London, Sir John Macdonald's resolution faltered. It is said that Sir George Stephen had packed his bag and was about to leave Canada a ruined man, when a friend persuaded the premier to call another cabinet meeting and to agree to give the last millions that were needed. On so narrow a chance hung the future of Canada's first transcontinental railway.

Sir William Van Horne

The story of the building of the line has been entertainingly told in "Canada's Great Highway," (Longman's, Green and Company), by J. H. E. Secretan who, as a civil engineer, was intimately connected with the undertaking from "the first stake to the last spike." In this little work of 250 pages, the author gives a vivid and racy account of his own personal adventures and experiences from 1871 to 1885. Mr. Secretan has a keen sense of humor and his thumbnail sketches of some of the great men connected with the project will be enjoyed by every reader.

Of Sir William Van Horne he says: "He was a lover of art and a great judge of ancient pottery, china, and all things beautiful. He could tell you their history, and how, when, and where they were made. And it goes without saying, if there was anything about a railroad that he did not know, it was not worth knowing. What always puzzled me was how in the world, in one lifetime, he had managed to accumulate so much information upon so many subjects. One way that I account for it was that he never seemed to require any sleep. He used to say to me, "Why do you want to go to bed? It's a waste of time; besides you don't know what's going on!"

"He knew every game of cards and played them all well. I can remember after an all-night session of poker, when the rest of us were dead to the world at 7 a.m., Van Horne simply rubbed his eyes and went down to the office to begin a long day's hard work."

The Southerly Route

In the original survey, the C. P. R. was to cross the mountains by the Yellowhead Pass. How the route was changed is described by the author in the following passage:

"The first year, under General Rosser (chief engineer), I had about four hundred miles of preliminary line run as far as Moose Jaw Creek, when Van Horne sent for me and announced in a most autocratic manner that he wanted 'the shortest possible commercial line' between Winnipeg and Vancouver; also that he intended to build five hundred miles that summer, lay the track, and have trains running over it. In discussing the projected location I pointed out that such a line would often run through an infertile country, and made many other objections; but he was adamant, and said he did not care what it ran through. He was evidently bound to get there.

Reason For Southerly Route

"This determination was no doubt the reason for the more southerly route being adopted, through the Kicking Horse Pass, which afterwards turned out to be so expensive, though no doubt of great scenic value. I doubted if he could possibly construct five hundred miles in a short summer (it was then about April), but he scowled at me fiercely, and before I left 'the presence' he informed me that 'nothing was impossible and if I could show him the road it was all he wanted, and if I couldn't he would have my scalp! thus ended a short but characteristic interview with the great magician. As a matter of fact he did lay about four hundred and eighty miles of track that summer."

Brandon and Calgary

"General Rosser, chief engineer, John MacTavish, land commissioner, and myself were driving west one starry spring night in search of a suitable place for the first divisional point west of Winnipeg. We were well ahead of the surveyed line and stopped that night at a farmhouse on the north side of the Assiniboine river. I forget the farmer's name, but he had been settled there for some years and had about 320 acres. It was an ideal site for a divisional point about 132 miles west of Winnipeg. The officials had a long talk with the farmer which lasted nearly all night until I understood an offer was made on behalf of the C.P.R. company of fifty thousand dollars son of the soil had never even read about so much money in books. The discussion proceeded, and some neighbors and relatives were called in and consulted, till at last towards dawn our genial host was egged on to demand sixty thousand dollars, no doubt thinking that if his farm was worth so much money he might as well get a lot more. The General thought otherwise.

"I think the farmer was astonished, and I hope disappointed, when the General ordered me to have the horses hitched up. We ferried across the Assiniboine River, and after driving a mile or two, came upon the future site of the City of Brandon on the south side of that placid stream. I received orders to return to the end of the track and continue the location of the main line, establishing the first divisional point at Brandon.

"Calgary" Suffered Similar Fate

"The proposed City of Calgary received a similar fate. Originally located on the east side of the Elbow River by a syndicate which had secured many acres, they failed to come to a satisfactory agreement with the railway company, and although the track was actually laid through their property, and many town lots were sold, the speculation was a failure as the railway people located the station on the other side of the little Elbow river, and started a town of their own which is now the City of Calgary."

The Last Spike

"I have often been asked," says the author in his closing chapter, "why the C.P.R. went through the Kicking Horse Pass instead of the Yellowhead, the latter being well known to have moderate gradients, and being far easier for construction. I can only say, as I have attempted to explain in this book, that the rumored reasons seem to have been because Van Horne put his finger on the map, and, czar-like, demanded the 'shortest possible commercial line'; then, Major Rogers reported favorably on the Kicking Horse; and finally, this euphonious name appealed to the sporting instinct of the London Stock Exchange and the English controllers of the money market who were handling the C. P. R. stock. Be this as it may, the prairie section was rushed to completion.

"The last act in the great drama of building a great continental railway was performed by Sir Donald Alexander Smith (afterwards Lord Strathcona). It occurred at a place now called Craigellachie in the Eagle Pass—Nov. 7th, 1885, at nine a.m.

"I once read in the work of some fiction monger that the golden spike used upon this occasion was afterwards withdrawn and presented to Mrs. Alexander Mackenzie, the wife of the Premier of Canada, and that he had often seen her wearing it in Ottawa as a pendant to her necklace. I regret to throw any doubt upon this romantic pipe dream, but in the first place I do not believe there ever was a 'golden' spike; secondly, I know that Mrs. Alexander Mackenzie was not the wife of the Premier of Canada in 1885, who happened to be the Right Hon. Sir John A. Macdonald; and thirdly, if there had been a golden spike, the weight of it, if worn on a pendant, would have broken the poor old lady's neck."

LITERARY NOTES

The Fifth Annual Convention of the Canadian Authors' association will be held in Winnipeg this year on June 25, 26, 27. Addresses will be given by prominent authors, and a larger delegation than usual is expected from the west.

"The History of Munitions Supply in Canada, 1914-1918," by David Carnegie, formerly member and ordnance advisor, Shell Committee, and Imperial Munitions Board, Ottawa, is the title of a useful and informative work published by Longman's, Green and Co., London. The story is one full of incident and accomplishment. From St. John's, Newfoundland, to Victoria, B.C., 675 factories in 150 different places, were engaged in the work of munitions making. For a nation of agriculturists to become expert in the manufacture of implements of war, requiring very considerable chemical, metallurgical and engineering skill was an accomplishment of no mean order. During her magnificent output, which was praised by the British cabinet in its report of 1917, Canada established new industries and new standards of skill, the results of which have been to add permanent value to her national assets.

THREE

"Hullo, hullo, hullo!"

1921 to 1930

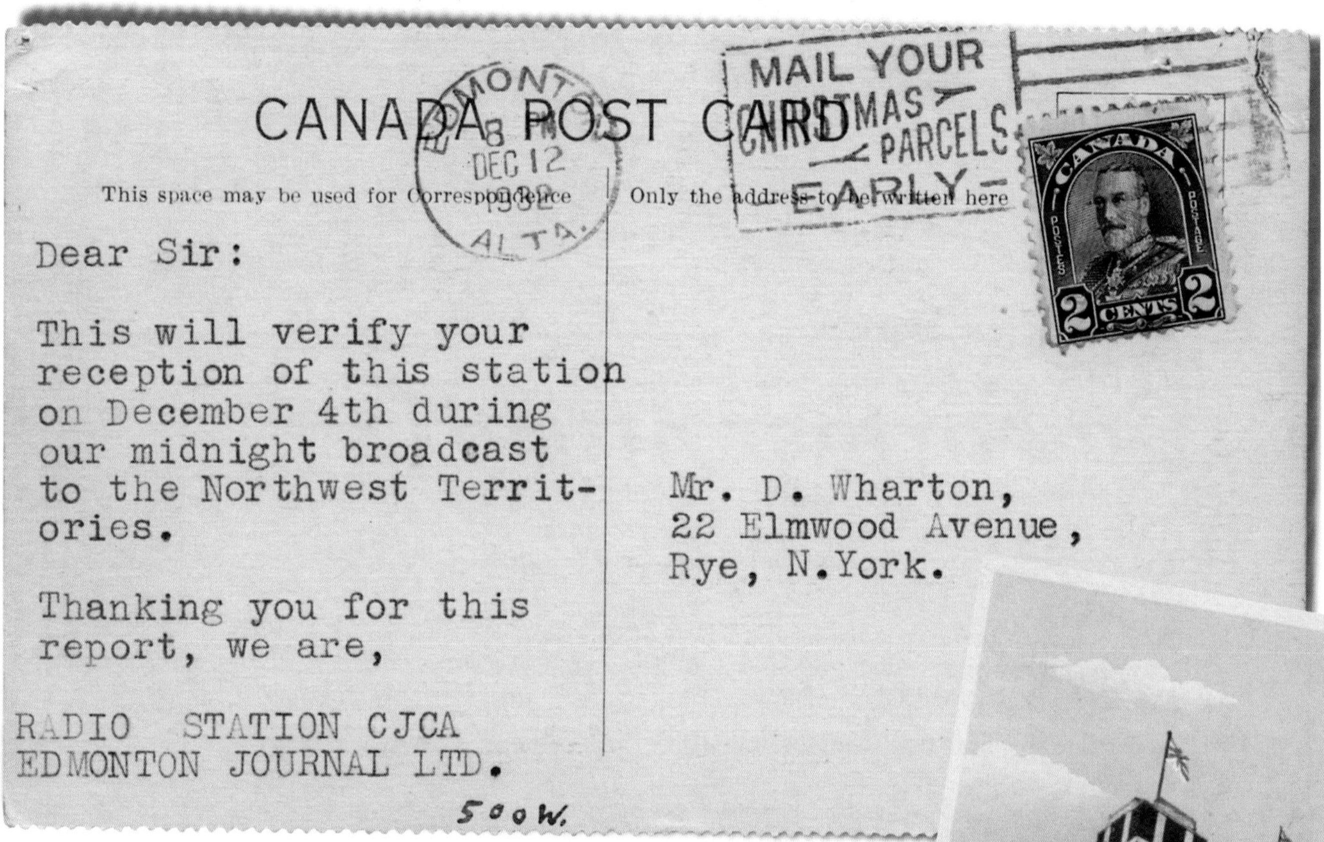
CANADA POST CARD

This space may be used for Correspondence | Only the address to be written here

MAIL YOUR CHRISTMAS PARCELS EARLY
CANADA
POSTES
POSTAGE
2 CENTS 2

Dear Sir:

This will verify your reception of this station on December 4th during our midnight broadcast to the Northwest Territories.

Thanking you for this report, we are,

RADIO STATION CJCA
EDMONTON JOURNAL LTD.

500 W.

Mr. D. Wharton,
22 Elmwood Avenue,
Rye, N.York.

Keith Spencer Collection

The Journal sent this confirmation postcard to a New York listener, confirming he had heard a CJCA broadcast.

Edmonton Journal

"Among a certain uncouth, uncultured class, insolence and ruthlessness are regarded as attributes of virile manhood and courteousness and consideration of others as effeminate. It happens that no other device ever made by men is so swift to reveal the character and temperament of its owner as an automobile."

— Commentary from "News and Views in Motordom," June 9, 1923

The Journal newsroom was more crowded than usual in the late evening of Monday, May 1, 1922. Copy editors were starting work on the next day's newspaper, but there was also a handful of curious reporters leaning back in their chairs, feet propped on desks, as they watched a half-dozen people tinker with a jumble of equipment crammed into the corner of the newsroom.

There was a microphone, three very up-to-date receiving sets, a Magnavox speaker and a transmitter. Wires snaked through the newsroom ceiling to the roof of the downtown *Journal* building and connected to a pair of 75-foot steel towers that had been erected only the week before.

A Woman's Right / 111

Tainted Legacy / 113

The Grads / 115

The Crash / 117

Booze is Back / 121

Movies that Talk! / 125

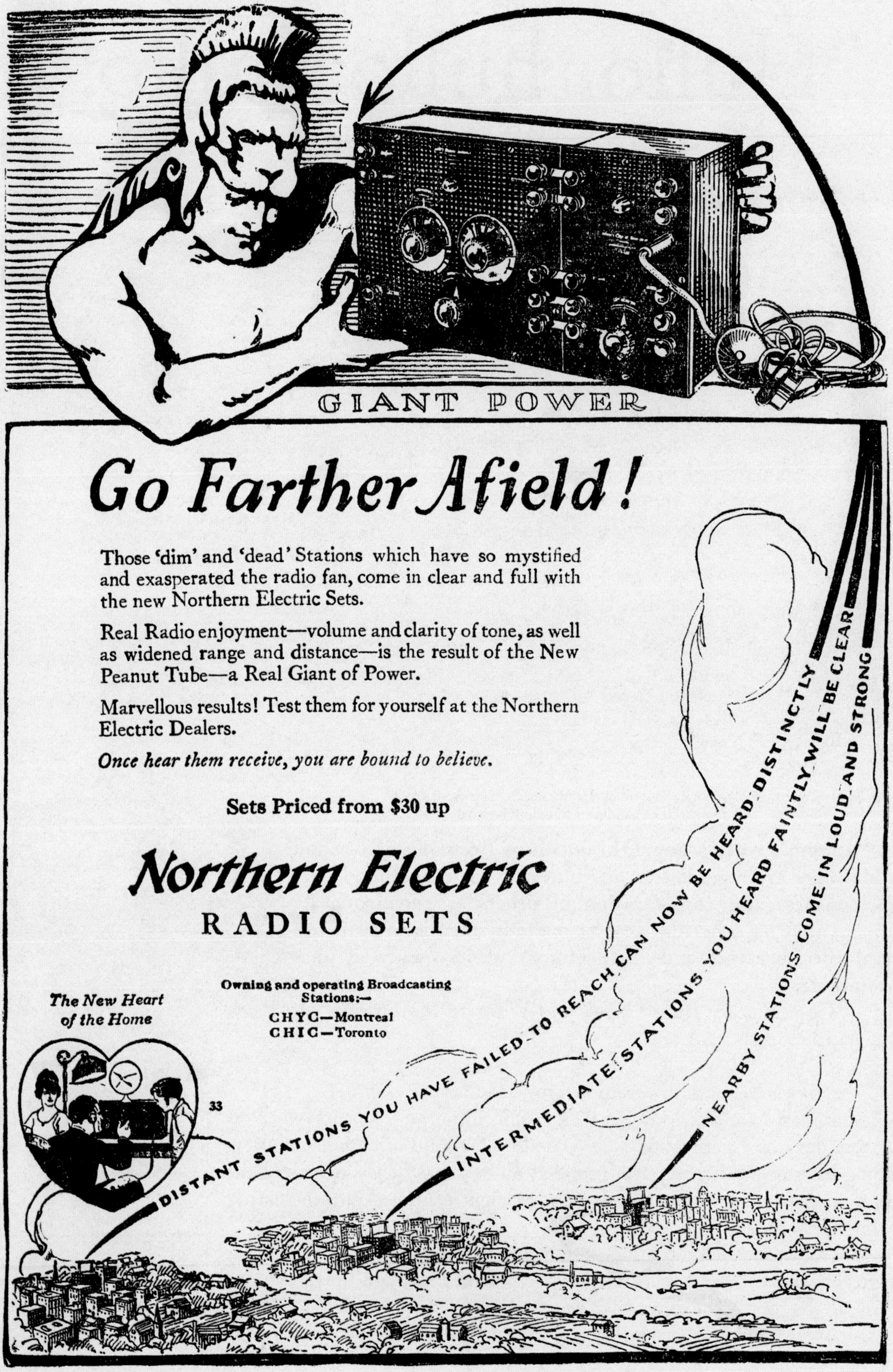
GIANT POWER
Go Farther Afield!
Those 'dim' and 'dead' Stations which have so mystified and exasperated the radio fan, come in clear and full with the new Northern Electric Sets.
Real Radio enjoyment—volume and clarity of tone, as well as widened range and distance—is the result of the New Peanut Tube—a Real Giant of Power.
Marvellous results! Test them for yourself at the Northern Electric Dealers.
Once hear them receive, you are bound to believe.
Sets Priced from $30 up
Northern Electric
RADIO SETS
Owning and operating Broadcasting Stations:—
CHYC—Montreal
CHIC—Toronto
The New Heart of the Home
DISTANT STATIONS YOU HAVE FAILED TO REACH CAN NOW BE HEARD DISTINCTLY
INTERMEDIATE STATIONS YOU HEARD FAINTLY WILL BE CLEAR
NEARBY STATIONS COME IN LOUD AND STRONG
33

At precisely 11 p.m., a switch was flipped, and 50 watts of power surged through the equipment. Mayor David Milwyn Duggan leaned into the microphone, cleared his throat and said, "Hullo, hullo, hullo!" the first words uttered on CJCA, the province's first radio station.

Journal management had decided just three weeks before to get into the radio business, and the federal government had quickly issued a commercial broadcasting licence.

Mayor Duggan was impressed. "No more election campaigns for me," he told his radio audience. "Edmonton is putting in radio broadcasting plants and you can sit at your firesides and hear my speeches.

"Edmonton leads the way in all Alberta. Calgary and others will follow.

"That is all. Good night."

Station manager Dick Rice then took the microphone and announced CJCA's first musical selection.

While he had a choice of hits from 1922 – everything from *Aggravatin' Papa (Don't You Try to Two-Time Me)* to *You Tell Her – I Stutter*, Rice opted for the Metropolitan Theatre Orchestra's rendition of the bouncy *Bla Bla Blues*.

"Please report on this selection," he asked listeners. And report they did. Impressed, they telephoned and wrote from as far away as Calgary and High River.

A day-after editorial predicted great things from this form of communication. "The Journal is proud of being the pioneer in this field and thinks that its pride is quite legitimate … as radio is expanded and comes into more general use there will be a veritable revolution in our lives."

The frequency, 580 kHz, was shared with several other provincial stations that came later, but *The Journal* was on the air with programs that included news, concerts, lectures, sports play-by-play and a kids' show that originated or were rebroadcast from that cramped corner for six years.

NC-6-10155 Glenbow Archives

CJCA staff member Frank Hollingworth, with a radio phone, circa 1922. Hollingworth's career at CJCA spanned 40 years.

***Jan. 20, 1920*:**
Anne Merrill, former editor of *The Journal*'s Women's Page, begins filing from England where she moved in 1919. In a dispatch in the newspaper of she reports that Newspaper World, a British publication commenting on journalism, had taken an unsparing look at Canadian journalism. *The Journal*, however, comes off much better than most of the competition, which is dismissed as rather bumpkin-like.

On the other hand, *The Journal* is discreet and dignified and covers "Edmonton and district like the dew."

***Feb. 1, 1920*:**
The Royal North-West Mounted Police become the Royal Canadian Mounted Police (RCMP), after merging with the Dominion Police.

***Feb. 4, 1920*:**
Census officials estimate Canada's population at 8,835,102 people; 587,770 of them live in Alberta.

***March 1, 1920*:**
The federal government orders the Alberta Penitentiary in Edmonton closed,

WHY DID

British Empire

GO TO WAR?

VISCOUNT GREY OF FALLODON

Answers Question in His Memoirs Which Commence in

THE EDMONTON JOURNAL ON SATURDAY

How Britain Switched from the Side of Germany and Austria-Hungary to that of France

Will be described by the statesman who guided British Foreign Policy up to the year 1916

While an important contribution to history, the series is also delightful as a very human autobiography.

Start It in Edmonton Journal Saturday

You tell 'em, Alberta

TRUDEL

makes the

BUFFALO COATS

The accompanying illustration shows Miss Alberta wearing one of our fur coats, clearly demonstrating the smart appearance of these beautiful coats.

Miss Alberta chose this particular coat from us, first because of its smartness, and secondly because of the fact that, with continued wearing, the Buffalo coat still retains its smart cut and line.

Not only that, the Buffalo Coat is an Alberta product and we can guarantee the long wearing qualities. Coats that have been worn for ten years in this city and district show no signs of wear. It is also a well known fact that there is no warmer Coat than the Buffalo Coat.

We have a number of Coats now in stock for both men and women.

The winter is now nearly over, but if you will take our advice you will come in immediately and order your Buffalo Coat for next winter. Our Fur Storage Plant is at your disposal.

Trudel Fur

Mfg. Co.

LIMITED

Phone 2213 10028 102nd Ave.

EASTER THOUGHTLETS

For You Poor Sinners

Saints Do Not Require 'Em

They Are All Dead

The station's transmitter moved in 1928 to the town of Oliver, 10 miles north of the city on the road to Fort Saskatchewan. In 1933 the studios were moved to the Magee Building at 10118-101A Street.

In 1934, *The Journal* turned management and operation of the station over to Taylor and Pearson Ltd., a local communications firm. *The Journal* retained ownership of CJCA until 1947.

It was life-changing, not only for listeners but for the news business as well because radio would become another primary source of information on current events.

It was more immediate than the daily newspaper, and in response *The Journal*, like dailies everywhere, began the slow evolution from providing the raw reporting of events to stories that put those events into context.

But back on that spring evening of 1922, the first radio broadcast was another indication that a city that had seen some tough times was now on the rebound.

Edmonton had begun the 1920s with a population of 61,000 people. That was a jump from the low of 51,000 only three years earlier and a sign that things were looking up. But it was still a far cry from the civic census figure of 72,000 residents in 1914 when there was money to be made in an overheated real estate market.

Journal daily circulation, once in the 30,000 range, dipped to 24,000 during the downturn, but climbed slowly and steadily as the population grew. By the end of the decade, with 65,000 people calling Edmonton home, the paper's circulation stood at more than 33,000.

The rising population aside, citizens took great pride in their city, and the paper and its new radio station became part of the Boost Edmonton campaign, a marketing thrust that began in mid-January 1920 when citizens packed the Empire Theatre on 103rd Street, north of Jasper Avenue, to organize a homegrown Edmonton First Club with the idea of encouraging residents to buy locally produced products.

The Boost Edmonton campaign was still going strong almost a half-decade later.

Readers were given a list of everything from boots and wool, to caskets and tin cans, all of which were made right here in Edmonton, and told that buying locally ensured your neighbour's job.

Even with the advent of radio, the paper remained the most important source of news for Edmontonians for the rest of the decade.

There was, however, no escaping the impact of the new medium, and the newspaper was crowded with advertisements for new and improved radios that promised to deliver a clear signal. A Radiola 111 with two tubes and a head set cost $45, while the premier Radiola X with tubes, head set and loudspeaker was priced at $325. In today's money the two-tube Radiola would cost $500 and the fancier Radiola X a whopping $3,600.

Buying a radio was a huge investment.

Skilled tradesmen worked 55-hour weeks at a little less than a dollar an hour. Nevertheless, radio was exciting, and if you couldn't afford one, your neighbours might invite you over to listen to theirs.

The paper's radio section – a page a week – offered tips on improved reception and *Journal* staffers read program listings over the telephone.

and the 147 prisoners moved to Prince Albert, Sask., or Stony Mountain, Man. A follow-up story March 3 says the move will cost the city $100,000 a year in payroll. Canada also loses some cheap labour. "Last year the dominion government opened up a valuable coal mine on the 'pen' site, which has been worked by the convicts."

***April 16, 1920*:**
Excavation starts for *The Journal*'s new building at corner 101st Street and Macdonald Drive. The same year, a *Journal* section editor earns $31 a week.

***July 22, 1920*:**
In Edmonton, Player's cigarettes cost 18 cents a package, ($1.66 today) or two packs for 35 cents. Wrigley's gum sells for five cents a pack.

***Oct. 17, 1920*:**
A monument to local men killed in the First World War is erected in Beverly. The northeast community was then separate from the city of Edmonton.

***Oct. 19, 1920*:**
Helen Barclay is the first Edmonton woman to be admitted to the Alberta bar.

-CAVB

NA-1821-2 Glenbow Archives

On Jan. 2, 1929, this 75 hp Avro Avian carried 600,000 units of diphtheria antitoxin to Fort Vermilion from Edmonton with Vic Horner and Wop May at the controls.

At top, from left, Mayor Ambrose Bury, Vic Horner, Wop May and Dr. Bow, deputy minister of health.

Right, Horner and May were cold and weary on their return from Fort Vermilion.

NC-6-12391a Glenbow Archives

CJCA also was the first to broadcast a live sporting event. On Sept. 30, 1924, it gave the play-by-play of a game between the Edmonton Commercial Graduates basketball team and the Warren Elks of Ohio. The game was part of a two-game series played at the Edmonton Gardens.

Two microphones were used. An announcer called the game through one and the other was directed toward the Edmonton Newsboys Band that provided musical numbers during the breaks.

Letters flooded into the paper praising CJCA for its undertaking. Wrote Alf Brown of South Cooking Lake: "I congratulate the man known as J.S. who did the announcing for his plain and accurate account. Every word was distinct and slow, yet had energy."

The most dramatic example of the co-operation between the radio station and the newspaper itself came during the now-famous mercy flight to Fort Vermilion in early January 1929.

Word came to Edmonton on Jan. 2 that diphtheria had broken out in Fort Vermilion and nearby Little Red River. Without antitoxin, the disease could devastate both small communities.

First World War hero Wop May and his partner Vic Horner came to the rescue. Despite warnings of an Arctic cold front threatening to push temperatures to 40-below Fahrenheit, the pilots headed north in their wood and fabric, open cockpit Avro Avian with the life-saving medicine.

"For more than an hour on Tuesday night, CJCA, the radio station of the Edmonton Journal, broadcast messages to the men of Vermilion and Little Red River, asking them to have a place prepared on which the machine could land," the paper reported on Wednesday, Jan. 2.

The radio station also broadcast pleas to trappers along the proposed route to keep a lookout for the intrepid flyers and report their progress.

An editorial said: "One can picture the scene. Some listener sitting in front of his loudspeaker, tuning in CJCA, hearing the arresting words: 'Hello, Fort Vermilion. CJCA speaking. Message for Dr. Hamman. The anti-toxin is being shipped in by plane....'

"Then the rush to tell Dr. Hamman. The rush to round up the men not stricken by the diphtheria, to get axes, to decide the best landing field, to clear it, and then the anxious scanning of the southern skies for the first glimpse of the moving dot that will mean life to the suffering."

The pilots returned on Sunday, Jan. 6, to a hero's welcome.

The Journal didn't publish on Sundays then, but had printed as many as three Extras the previous day. And publish or not, the paper was still heavily involved in the homecoming party: "The Journal, which will keep in close touch with the return flight on Sunday, will arrange for city sirens to be sounded, about half-an-hour

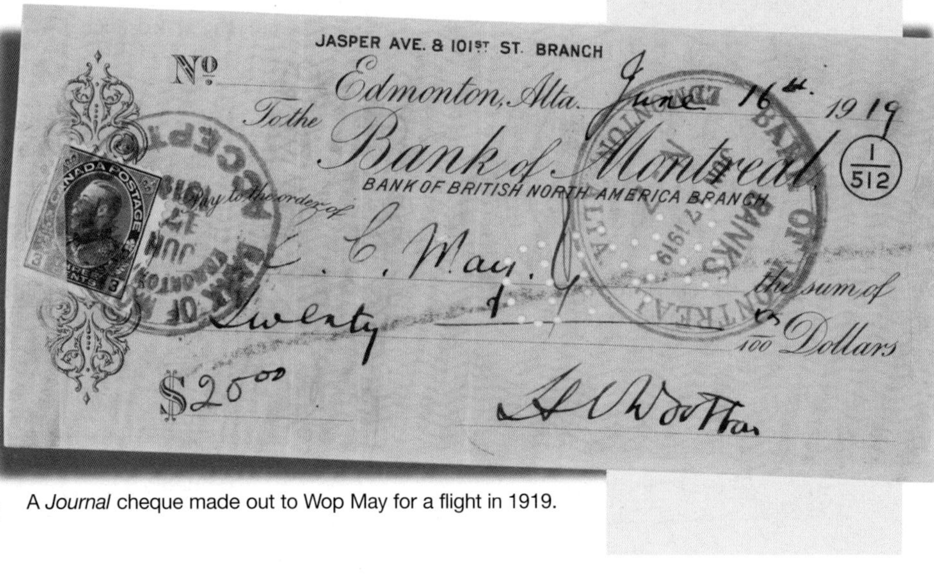
JASPER AVE. & 101ST ST. BRANCH
No
Edmonton, Alta.
To the
Bank of Montreal
BANK OF BRITISH NORTH AMERICA BRANCH
the sum of
Dollars

A *Journal* cheque made out to Wop May for a flight in 1919.

The Edmonton Journal

***Oct. 25, 1920*:**
In provincial plebiscites, voters in Saskatchewan, Manitoba and Nova Scotia favour prohibition of liquor.

***Dec. 1, 1920*:**
Edmonton's local bread price is 11 cents a loaf retail, nine cents wholesale.

***Dec. 8, 1920*:**
Henry J. O'Leary is installed as the Roman Catholic archbishop of Edmonton.

***Dec. 13, 1920*:**
D.M. Duggan is elected mayor of Edmonton for the first of three terms, defeating incumbent Joe Clarke.

***Dec. 26, 1920*:**
Pioneer city businessman John Walter dies 50 years after coming to Fort Edmonton as a Hudson's Bay boat builder. He established the city's first ferry across the North

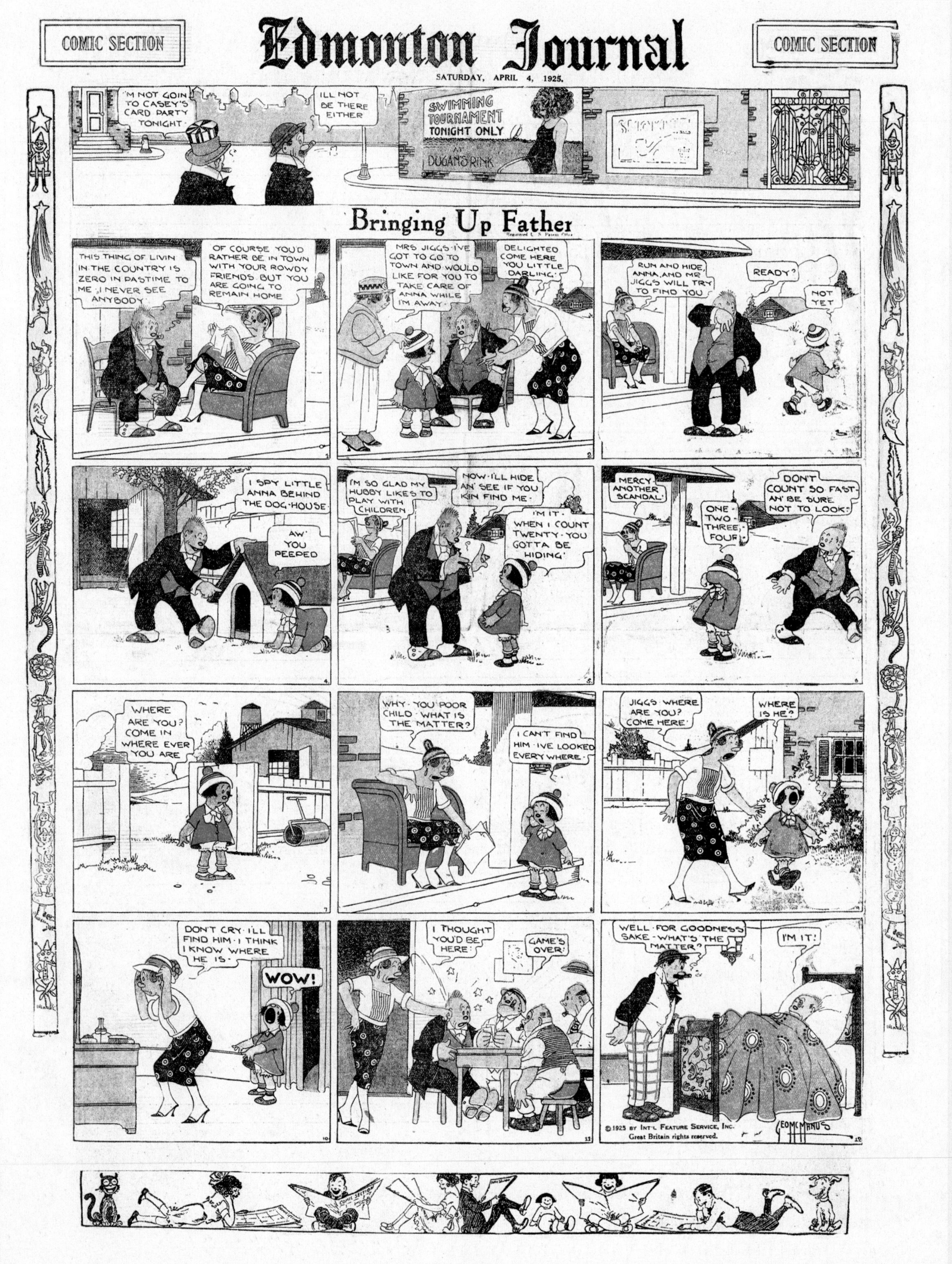
COMIC SECTION
Edmonton Journal
COMIC SECTION
SATURDAY, APRIL 4, 1925.
'M NOT GOIN TO CASEY'S CARD PARTY TONIGHT
ILL NOT BE THERE EITHER
SWIMMING TOURNAMENT TONIGHT ONLY AT DUGAN'S RINK
Bringing Up Father
Registered U. S. Patent Office
THIS THING OF LIVIN IN THE COUNTRY IS ZERO IN PASTIME TO ME ,I NEVER SEE ANYBODY
OF COURSE YOU'D RATHER BE IN TOWN WITH YOUR ROWDY FRIENDS BUT YOU ARE GOING TO REMAIN HOME
MRS JIGGS I'VE GOT TO GO TO TOWN AND WOULD LIKE FOR YOU TO TAKE CARE OF ANNA WHILE I'M AWAY
DELIGHTED COME HERE YOU LITTLE DARLING
RUN AND HIDE, ANNA, AND MR JIGGS WILL TRY TO FIND YOU
READY?
NOT YET
I SPY LITTLE ANNA BEHIND THE DOG-HOUSE
AW' YOU PEEPED
I'M SO GLAD MY HUBBY LIKES TO PLAY WITH CHILDREN
NOW I'LL HIDE AN' SEE IF YOU KIN FIND ME
I'M IT - WHEN I COUNT TWENTY - YOU GOTTA BE HIDING'
MERCY ANOTHER SCANDAL
ONE - TWO - THREE, FOUR
DON'T COUNT SO FAST - AN' BE SURE NOT TO LOOK!
WHERE ARE YOU? COME IN WHERE EVER YOU ARE
WHY - YOU POOR CHILD - WHAT IS THE MATTER?
I CAN'T FIND HIM - I'VE LOOKED EVERY WHERE
JIGGS WHERE ARE YOU? COME HERE
WHERE IS HE?
DON'T CRY - I'LL FIND HIM - I THINK I KNOW WHERE HE IS
WOW!
I THOUGHT YOU'D BE HERE!
GAME'S OVER!
WELL - FOR GOODNESS SAKE - WHAT'S THE MATTER?
I'M IT!
© 1925 by Int'l Feature Service, Inc.
Great Britain rights reserved.
GEO McMANUS

before the plane is due to land, and the shrieking sirens will be the warning for everyone to move toward the aerodrome."

"The Journal's switchboard will be held open all day Sunday, and calls of inquiry as to the progress of the flyers will be answered from 9271."

As befitted heroes, both May and Horner were humble. "We really didn't do much," said May. He told a service club at a luncheon held in his honour at the Macdonald Hotel that he would much sooner fly than talk.

"There was nothing in it as far as we were concerned.

"We just simply had to sit in the plane, turn it in the direction we wanted to go and keep going just as long as the engine didn't stop."

The paper would have none of it. They were heroes, and heroes should be celebrated: "Wop May and Vic Horner have taken chances aplenty in their lives before this, May when he rode the skies in France with Richthofen riding his tail, and Horner as an infantryman in the gallant Princess Pats.

"But this is the apogee of their career, to sail into the unknown in a small machine, to save lives and not take them."

Neither did it matter that only one man contracted the disease. The Hudson's Bay trader in Little Red River died, but his wife, a former nurse, had kept him quarantined when she suspected that he suffered from deadly diphtheria.

The paper's pride in the pair was obvious in a Jan. 5 editorial: "The courage of the two flyers and the hazards they ran in their flight over a winter wilderness should not be forgotten in the successful conclusion of their mission.

"Had any one of the dozen or more dangers through which they flew overwhelmed them, Edmonton would have poured out its tribute of praise. Our admiration for these two men is not diminished one whit simply because they are alive and safe and able to appreciate what we feel. Wop May and Vic Horner have entered Edmonton's hall of fame."

Two days later another editorial used the mercy flight to advocate for a better airport.

"How badly Edmonton needs a real airport was emphatically demonstrated to some 10,000 persons who gathered at and around the landing field yesterday afternoon to welcome Wop May and Vic Horner home."

The newspaper urged city council to immediately begin preparing a bylaw to have the airport improved. "Those who drove in motor cars across the field need no further demonstration of the necessity of leveling off that ground. Many a sturdy car spring was put to a severe test by unexpected jolts hidden in the long grass. What might happen to a plane that hit one of these bumps just as the wheels touched the ground and while it was still travelling at high speed, can be easily imagined."

Two days after they returned from their mercy flight, May and Horner were the subjects of a motion picture documentary. A film crew – the paper doesn't say where they were from or what happened to the footage that was shot – took pictures of the two in the airplane. The mayor and city officials were also part of the film.

But if the film had been shown in Edmonton, it probably would have been screened at the Capitol, the downtown theatre on Jasper Avenue that was the best in the city.

Saskatchewan Riverand ran several businesses in the river valley.

***In 1921*:**
Concordia College is founded by Lutheran Church-Missouri Synod.

***Jan. 24, 1921*:**
The Edmonton Federation of Community Leagues is founded.

***April 16, 1921*:**
***Journal* staff move into their new building.**

***June 23, 1921*:**
The fourth and last Alberta legislature governed by the Liberals is dissolved and a July election is called.

***June 20, 1921*:**
Pioneer Edmonton entrepreneur Robert Tegler, builder of the 1911 Tegler Building, the city's first skyscraper, dies. The fortune he leaves in his will establishes the first charitable trust in Alberta.

***July 6, 1921*:**
***The Journal* appoints John M. Imrie managing director. He resigns in 1941 due to ill health.**

***July 18, 1921*:**
Alberta's election is won by the United Farmers, sweeping the Liberals from power. All five Edmonton seats

BE PREPARED
Girl Guides' Motto

Girls' Own Journal

SERVE OTHERS
C. G. I. T. Motto

VOL. 2 — EDMONTON, ALBERTA, SATURDAY, APRIL 11, 1925 — NO. 36

BLUEBIRDS HELD FIRST BANQUET

Mothers and Daughters Will Get Together at Least Once a Year

The Beverly Bluebirds held their first annual Mother and Daughter banquet at Miss Kinghorn's home Thursday, March 26. It was a new departure in the social activities of this branch of the C.G.I.T., and proved an occasion of great enjoyment to those who were privileged to attend.

All did full justice to the good things which appeared upon the table on which the decorative scheme was prettily carried out in blue and gold.

Miss Jean Howie was an able and charming toastmistress and opened the after-dinner proceedings with a stirring speech and the proposal of a toast to "Our King and Country." Miss Katie Dawson welcomed the guests and Miss Peddle responded to the welcome on their behalf.

The toast to "Our Mothers" was proposed by Miss Marguerite Milburn and was responded to by Mrs. Charlie Milburn.

Mrs. J. Hunter answered Miss Lily Adams toast to "Alberta."

Miss Kinghorn gave a most interesting summary of the aims of the Institute.

A high note of endeavor in setting noble ideals was struck when Mrs. Errat responded to the C.G.I.T. toast proposed by Miss Alma Walters.

Interspersed with rousing choruses rendered with right good will by all those assembled at the festive board were vocal solos by Miss Maisie Weir and Floy Hill and a fine violin solo by Miss Vera Pike.

Four of the Bluebirds voiced the aims of the C.G.I.T., and then with many expressions of thanks to Miss Kinghorn, Mrs. Errat and Mrs. Pike the pleasant gathering broke up.

OWAIMA GROUP STARTS OFF WITH NEW OFFICERS

Each Girl Hammered Tack in Flags for Good Luck

The Owaima group, a division of the Robertson C.G.I.T. girls, held their second meeting Friday evening, April 3, under the leadership of Mrs. Morrison. First of all the girls hung up the Union Jack and the Christian flag, each girl taking a turn at hammering a tack in for good luck.

The meeting opened with a prayer by the girls, followed by one by the leader. All the officers were present and in their places. At a preceding meeting Margaret Morrison had been appointed president; Mary Alice Coffin, vice-president; Mary McDonald, secretary; Muriel Keeling, treasurer, and Marie Thompson, press reporter. Much business was discussed, and each girl chose a night to carry out her part of the program. Muriel Keeling read fourteen verses out of the Bible, as the devotional part of the meeting.

All the girls were called up in the church for a short time, but they soon returned, except Alice Coffin, who was so greatly charmed by the choir that it was about fifteen minutes before they saw her again, then to hear the exciting news that she had been locked up in the gallery. The meeting was closed with a prayer.

GIRLS PRESENT THEIR PLAY TO LARGE AUDIENCE

Orchestra Scored Hit With Their Various Musical Selections

HUGHENDEN, Alberta—On Wednesday, April 1, the C.G.I.T. girls held their play, with a large crowd present. An entertaining program was provided and all participants played their parts well. The musical numbers provided by the orchestra were very much enjoyed.

The program was as follows: Chorus, girls; recitation, Kathleen Ferries; selection, orchestra; duet, "A Girl That Men Forget," R. Webb and M. Teesdale; chorus by the girls, "Bridal Scene"; play, "Woogirls Under Difficulties"; duet, K. Ferries and E. Humphrey; serenade, A. Walker; selection, orchestra; song, Walker ladies' quartette; duet, K. Ferries and E. Humphreys; selection, orchestra; camp scene, by the girls.

It's a long road that has no motor

SWASTICA GIRLS KEPT BUSY ON THEIR SEWING

Members Are Anxious to Have Party During Easter Week

The mid-week meeting of the Swastica club was held at the home of Mrs. McLean, on Friday, April 3, at 7:30 o'clock, with seven members present.

The meeting was opened in the regular way, after which the girls got busy with their sewing. While this was being done Mrs. McLean played several records on the gramophone. Later on in the evening, the girls agreed to hold a party during Easter week.

The next meeting will be held at the home of Audrey McKinney.

Mrs. McLean then served delightful refreshments which brought the meeting to a close.

METROLITES AIM TO WIN CUP ANNUALLY

Sides Were Chosen for Debate to Be Held in Near Future

On Tuesday, March 31, the Metrolites C. G. I. T. group began their meeting with an enthusiastic singsong. The devotional period was taken by Florence Crawford. The final arrangements for the debate which is to be held at our intellectual meeting were made. ... ford and Dorothy Mor... to debate against Flo... and Hazel Burkholde... The council report ... Dorothy Morris in a ... manner. It was very ... helpful to the girls and ... ed it, especially the pa... our winning of the ... which was received wit... are planning on winning ... too, at least we are goin... hard, for, as Alice Lang... ed, it would be so muc... have "Metrolites" writt... way around the bottom, ... one place.

TOFIELD GRO... HAD SOCIAL ... JUNIOR C. G...

Dainty Refreshments Served After Games Contests Had Been ...

TOFIELD, Alta.—The Senio... I. T. group, held their regular ... ly meeting in the church ba... on March 25. The singing ... four-fold hymn opened the m... The roll call was answere... eight members and the minut... the previous meeting were rea... approved.

As this was the social meeting ... Junior C.G.I.T. group were ... tained. Games and contests ... the able leadership of Miss Hop... formed a greater part of the ... gram. The refreshment comm... served a dainty lunch to which ... did full justice.

After a rollicking sing-song ... girls left for their homes, well sat... fied with the evening's fun.

FIGURING EASTER

Thirty days hath September
Every person can remember.
But to know when Easter comes
Puzzles even scholars some.

When March the twenty-first is past
Just watch the silvery moon,
And when you see it full and round
Know Easter'll be here soon.

After the moon has reached its full
Then Easter will be here,
The very Sunday after
In each and every year.

And if it haps on Sunday
The moon should reach its height,
The Sunday following this event
Will be the Easter bright.

Too Realistic

"Dauber does very realistic work, doesn't he?" said one artist to another.

"So much so," replied the other, "that those apples he painted six weeks ago are now said by the critics to be rotten."

Not Cheating

"Stop! Stop!" cried the fussy old gentleman. "There's a lady just fallen off the bus!"

"It's all right," said the conductor, "she's paid her fare."

LITTLE EGYPTIAN PRINCE DRIVES OWN CAR

H.R.H. Prince Faruk, the heir to the throne of Egypt, driving his miniature automobile in the royal garden. This little vehicle is a real auto and the little prince has a wonderful time running around his own speedway. This picture was taken by his mother, Queen Nazli.

APRIL SHOWERS BRING MAY-LOU FLOWERS

May-Lou wrinkled her short nose at the sky. "Rain!" she moaned. "The first April shower, and just my luck to be caught in it!" She started running along the country road, though she realized she was far from home.

Then she became ...

"Oh, tell me some more," begged May-Lou. "Did you build a new hut?" And what was the hut made of?"

The rain continued to pour down steadily, but May-Lou ...

LIHTANIS INVITE MOTHERS TO PARTY

Mrs. Kerr Took Both Prizes in the April Fool Contests

The meeting of the Lihtani C. G. I. T. group of Norwood Methodist church on Friday, April 3, took the form of an April Fool party at which the girls entertained their mothers. Promptly at eight o'clock the girls and mothers met in the club rooms. The girls then staged an exhibition meeting to show the mothers just how they do business. During the meeting, the leader, Mrs. Kingsbury, presented the club with the banner which the girls won in the Sell-a-Star campaign. After the meeting a delightful program of vocal and instrumental solos and recitations was put over in fine style, every number being encored. Mary Snyder then led the games and contests for which the mothers and girls competed against each other. Mrs. Kerr, the mother of our worthy president won both contests and received two very weighty prizes. Light refreshments were then served and a merry time was had over the teacups. After a rollicking sing-song which nearly deafened every one the girls prepared to leave. Just before leaving Mrs. Powell moved a vote of thanks to the girls which was replied to by Peggy Kerr. Cheers were given for our leaders, our mothers and our president, after which everyone, (except, of course, the dishwashers) wended their way ...

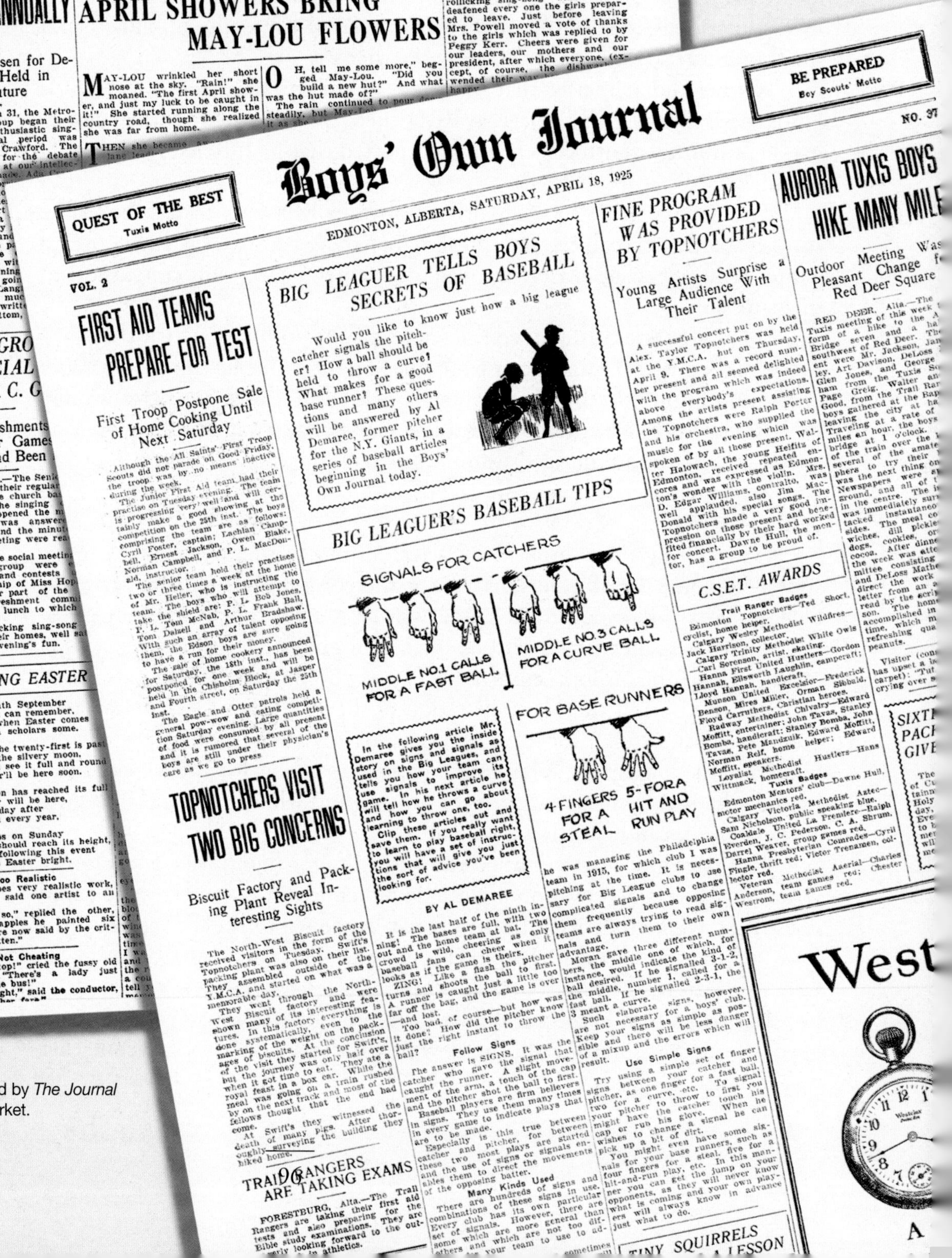

QUEST OF THE BEST
Tuxis Motto

Boys' Own Journal

BE PREPARED
Boy Scouts' Motto

VOL. 2 — EDMONTON, ALBERTA, SATURDAY, APRIL 18, 1925 — NO. 37

FIRST AID TEAMS PREPARE FOR TEST

First Troop Postpone Sale of Home Cooking Until Next Saturday

Although the All Saints' First Troop Scouts did not parade on Good Friday, the troop was by no means inactive during the week.

The Junior First Aid team had their practise on Tuesday evening. The team is progressing very well and will certainly make a good showing at the competition on the 25th inst. The boys comprising the team are as follows: Cyril Foster, captain; Lachlan Campbell, Ernest Jackson, Gwen Blake, Norman Campbell, and P. L. MacDonald, instructor.

The senior team hold their practises two or three times a week at the home of Mr. Heller, who is instructing the team. The boys who will attempt to take the shield are: P. L. Bob Jones, P. L. Tom McNab, P. L. Frank Ball, Tom Dalzell and Arthur Bradshaw. With such an array of talent opposing them, the Edson boys are sure going to have a run for their money.

The sale of home cookery announced for Saturday, the 18th inst., has been postponed for one week and will be held in the Chisholm Block, at Jasper and Fourth street, on Saturday the 25th inst.

The Eagle and Otter patrols held a general pow-wow and eating competition Saturday evening. Large quantities of food were consumed by all present and it is rumored that several of the boys are still under their physician's care as we go to press.

TOPNOTCHERS VISIT TWO BIG CONCERNS

Biscuit Factory and Packing Plant Reveal Interesting Sights

The North-West Biscuit factory received visitors in the form of the Topnotchers on Tuesday. Swift's packing plant was also on their list. They assembled outside of the Y.M.C.A. and started on what was a memorable day.

They went through the North-West Biscuit factory and were shown many of its interesting features. In this factory everything is done systematically, even to the marking of the weight on the packages of biscuits. At the conclusion of the visit they started for Swift's, but the journey was only half over when it got time to eat. While the royal feast in a box car was going on a train rushed by on the next track and most of the meal was gone. ... the fellows thought that the end had come.

Swift's they witnessed the death of many pigs. After thoroughly surveying the building they hiked home.

BIG LEAGUER TELLS BOYS SECRETS OF BASEBALL

Would you like to know just how a big league catcher signals the pitcher? How a ball should be held to throw a curve? What makes for a good base runner? These questions and many others will be answered by Al Demaree, former pitcher for the N.Y. Giants, in a series of baseball articles beginning in the Boys' Own Journal today.

BIG LEAGUER'S BASEBALL TIPS

SIGNALS FOR CATCHERS
MIDDLE NO.1 CALLS FOR A FAST BALL
MIDDLE NO.3 CALLS FOR A CURVE BALL
FOR BASE RUNNERS
4 FINGERS FOR A STEAL
5-FOR A HIT AND RUN PLAY

In the following article Mr. Demaree gives you the inside story on signs and signals as used in the Big Leagues, and tells you how your team can use signals to improve its game. In his next article he will tell how he throws a curve and how you can go about learning to throw one, too. Clip these articles out and save them. If you really want to learn to play baseball right, you will have a set of instructions that will give you just the sort of advice you've been looking for.

BY AL DEMAREE

It is the last half of the ninth inning! The bases are full, with two out and the home team at bat. The crowd is wild, cheering as only baseball fans can cheer when it looks as if the game is theirs. ZING! Like a flash the pitcher turns and shoots the ball to first. A runner is caught just a little too far off the bag, and the game is over —and lost.

Too bad, of course—but how was it done? How did the pitcher know just the right instant to throw the ball?

Follow Signs

The answer is SIGNS. It was the catcher who gave the signal that caught the runner. A slight movement of the arm, a touch of the cap and the pitcher shot the ball to first. Baseball players are firm believers in signs. They use them many times in every game to indicate plays that are to be made.

Especially is this true between catcher and pitcher, for between these two most plays are started and the use of signs or signals enables them to direct the movements of the opposing batter.

Many Kinds Used

There are hundreds of signs and combinations of these signs in use. Every club has its own particular set of signals. However, there are some which are more general than others and which are not too difficult for your team to ...

he was managing the Philadelphia team in 1915, for which club I was pitching at the time. It is necessary for Big League clubs to use complicated signals and to change them frequently because opposing teams are always trying to read the signals and turn them to their own advantage.

Moran gave three different numbers, the middle one of which, for instance, would indicate the kind of ball desired. If he signalled 3-1-2, the middle, number 1, called for a fast ball. If he signalled 2-3-1, the 3 meant a curve.

Such elaborate signs, however, are not necessary for a boys' club. Keep your signs as simple as possible and there will be less danger of a mixup and the errors which will result.

Use Simple Signs

Try using a simple set of finger signs between your catcher and pitcher, as one finger for a fast ball, two for a curve, etc. To signal your pitcher to throw to first you might have the catcher touch his cap or rub his glove. When he wishes to change a signal he can pick up a bit of dirt.

You might even have some signals for your base runners, such as four fingers for a steal, five for a hit-and-run play, etc. In this manner you can get the jump on your opponents, as they will never know what is coming and your own players will always know in advance just what to do.

FINE PROGRAM WAS PROVIDED BY TOPNOTCHERS

Young Artists Surprise a Large Audience With Their Talent

A successful concert put on by the Alex. Taylor Topnotchers was held at the Y.M.C.A. hut on Thursday, April 9. There was a record number present and all seemed delighted with the program which was indeed above everybody's expectations. Among the artists present assisting the Topnotchers were Ralph Porter and his orchestra, who supplied the music for the evening which was spoken of by all those present. Walter Halowach, the young Heifitz of Edmonton, received repeated encores and was expressed as Edmonton's wonder with the violin. D. Edgar Williams, contralto, was well applauded, also Jim MacDonald with his special songs. The Topnotchers made a very good impression on those present and were benefitted financially by their hard worked for concert. Dawne Hull, the mentor, has a group to be proud of.

C.S.E.T. AWARDS

Trail Ranger Badges

Edmonton Topnotchers—Ted Short, cyclist, home helper.

Calgary Wesley Methodist Wildfires—Jack Harrison, collector.

Calgary Trinity Methodist White Owls—Carl Sorenson, artist, skating.

Hanna First United Hustlers—Gordon Hannah, Ellsworth Laughlin, campcraft; Lloyd Hannah, handicraft.

Munson United Excelsior—Frederick Benson, Mires Miller, Orman Sibbald, Floyd Carruthers, Christian heroes.

Radway Methodist Chivalry—Edward Moffitt, entertainer; John Tavas, Stanley Bomba, handicraft; Stanley Bomba, John Tavas, Pete Mandzuik, Edward Moffitt, Norman Rolf, home helper; Edward Moffitt, speakers.

Loyalist Methodist Hustlers—Hans Wittmack, homecraft.

Tuxis Badges

Edmonton Mentors' club—Dawne Hull, mentor mechanics red.

Calgary Victoria Methodist Aztec—Sam Nicholson, public speaking blue.

Coaldale United La Premiere—Ralph Everden, J. C. Pederson, C. A. Shrum, Darrel Weaver, group games red.

Hanna Presbyterian Comrades—Cyril Fingle, thrift red; Victor Trenamen, colleader red.

Veteran Methodist Aerial—Charles Anderson, team games red; Chester Westrom, team games red.

AURORA TUXIS BOYS HIKE MANY MILE...

Outdoor Meeting Was ... Pleasant Change f... Red Deer Square

TRAIL RANGERS ARE TAKING EXAMS

FORESTBURG, Alta.—The Trail Rangers are taking their first aid tests and also preparing for the Bible study examinations. They are eagerly looking forward to the outdoor ... in athletics.

TINY SQUIRRELS ... A LESSON

Pages from a tabloid edition printed by *The Journal* aimed at the youth market.

It was, after all, the largest movie house between Vancouver and Winnipeg, the paper reported in early 1929. It had just been renovated and sat 1,500 moviegoers. "When the Capitol makes its bow for 1929 business, it will be offering sound and talking pictures, now creating widespread interest among all theatregoers."

Edmonton had always been a movie town.

Theatres went all out promoting their new films. Lobbies were decorated and bands hired.

In October 1924, moviegoers crowded the Empire on 103rd Street and Jasper Avenue to watch Douglas Fairbanks in *The Thief of Baghdad.* An advertisement promised that the Empire management would provide "atmospheric dialogue, a Mohammedan chanter and Arabian Musicians" to enhance the experience.

Clearly it worked. The paper's theatre critic, billed only as Marmaduke, was enthralled: "An eastern atmosphere pervades the whole theatre. There is an Arab musician at the door, and the foyer is elaborately furnished with oriental rugs, while the ushers are dressed in oriental costumes and coffee is served during the intermission."

Meanwhile, down the street at the Empress Theatre, *Plastigrams,* a sensational new film was playing. An early version of 3-D, it promised "A NEW THRILL! A REAL SENSATION!" There was no Marmaduke review, despite an advertisement that vowed: "The figures come off the screen and approach you so realistically you want to dodge them!"

And when Edmontonians wanted live theatre, the place to go was the Pantages on 102nd Street and Jasper Avenue.

The Gingham Girl, a Broadway hit of 1924, came directly to Edmonton from the Earl Carroll Theatre in New York and vowed to deliver an "enchanting chorus of dancing debutantes all in their teens." Tickets ranged from 50 cents to $2.50.

Edmonton was a readers' city, too. A four-page literary supplement from December 1923 had advertisements from four bookstores and contained dozens of tightly packed reviews.

The CanLit on offer was *Emily of New Moon* by Lucy Maud Montgomery and *Spirit of Iron* by Harwood Steele.

An advertisement from bookseller/stationer A.H. Esch and Co. offered the books at $2 apiece.

For the same price you could buy the just-released *Murder on the Links* by Agatha Christie and *Stella Dallas* by Olive Higgins Prouty.

With movies, bookstores and radio, the newspaper and its readers looked beyond Edmonton, the province and even the nation. Improved wire services brought the world to the doorsteps of *Journal* subscribers like never before.

Along with the complete coverage of local politics, sports and entertainment to which they had grown accustomed, readers demanded – and received – more national and international news.

The newspaper fretted over what was happening in Russia and was concerned about the emergence of Bolshevism there.

It was a pernicious ideology, the paper said, and the Communist vision of freedom was an illusory one.

are won by Liberals, among them women's rights leader Nellie McClung.

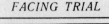

FACING TRIAL

ARCHIE KILLIPS

NICK HAWRYLUK

Nick Hawryluk and Archie Killips, Edmonton youths, are receiving their preliminary hearing in the police court on the charge of murdering Jacob Milner on Jan. 4.

***Aug. 12, 1921*:**
Charles Stewart, Alberta's last Liberal premier, delivers his resignation after losing an election to the UFA.

***Sept. 15, 1921*:**
Gen. William A. Griesbach of Edmonton, a former mayor of the city, is appointed to the Senate.

***Dec. 3, 1921*:**
The Edmonton Eskimos are the first western team to play in the Grey Cup, the Canadian

THE WEATHER
April 4, 1925
FORECAST—MILD; UNSETTLED.
Highest Today—40 Degrees.
Lowest Last Night—33 degrees.
Barometer, 27.65—Decreasing.
Sun Rises Sunday 6:00; Sets 7:14.
Sun Rises Monday 5:58; Sets 7:16.

Edmonton Journal

LAST EDITION

VOL. 21. NO. 221 — EDMONTON, ALBERTA, SATURDAY, APRIL 4, 1925 — FORTY-SIX PAGES

RUSSIA AGAIN ADMITS FAILURE OF COMMUNIST RULE

HERRIOT WILL PUSH PLAN OF CAPITAL LEVY

Government Doomed Is the General Feeling in French Political Circles

SENATE IS AGAINST PREMIER'S PROPOSAL

Capital Levy Scheme Provides for Collections Over Several Years

PARIS, April 4.—Premier Herriot this morning continued his consultations with political leaders regarding the proposed capital levy. It is generally understood that this proposition is the key to the plan of the radicals by which the government hopes to put French finances on a solid basis.

While details of the call to be made on fortunes in France should this scheme be carried through remain to be worked out, it is said by high authorities at the foreign office that it will be substantial enough to give relief for the existing difficulties and afford ample assurance against the recurrence of the present crisis.

The government's program on all questions now before the parliament will be presented to the chamber of deputies next Tuesday.

Foremost on this program will be the capital levy, the premier's collaborators say, adding that the intention is to push this measure through.

Capital Levy Doomed?

There is a lull in the political atmosphere pending resumption of parliamentary activities in the chamber Tuesday, but the prospects of Premier Herriot do not seem to improve as time goes on. His capital levy scheme, which he explained to a meeting of the radical group should be spread over a number of years and fall as much as possible on existing wealth, and not on wealth in the course of formation, does not appear to find much more favor with the senate than the idea of currency inflation, and it is even doubtful if the proposed scheme will succeed with the chamber.

While it is generally agreed that the end of M. Herriot's ministry cannot be far off, there are different views as to the manner of its passing and what will succeed it. Many observers maintain that the only way out is dissolution at a more or less early date, and new elections.

Would Use...

WONDER IF CANADA TO JOIN PACT

(Special to Edmonton Journal)

LONDON, April 4.—Germany is getting anxious to know if Canada is going to participate in the Anglo-German trade treaty now nearing completion or if the dominion plans to negotiate with Germany direct.

The trade department of the German government has been asking information along this line from the British government. It is known in Whitehall that New Zealand and Ireland do not intend to come in on the treaty which is due to be ratified by the home government shortly but no official intimation of Canada's policy has been received.

COW 'MOTHERS' PIGS; HEN LAYS BIG EGG, DIES

Dixie, Ontario, Crashes Into Front Page With Farmyard Freaks

DIXIE, Ont., April 4.—This district possesses a cow which had adopted a family of seven pigs, and also possesses the largest egg ever laid by a farmyard hen, but unfortunately "Biddy" gave her life in laying a three-yolker measuring 8½ inches by 6½ inches each way in circumference. Accomplishing feat was such a shock to the cackler that she died a few hours later.

The cow is owned by George Smith, and is having the time of her life looking after the litter of pigs, which prefer her to their own mother and joyfully partake of their nourishment in the old and direct method from the plant to the consumer.

PRINCE OF WALES LANDS IN AFRICA

Repulse Anchors Off Bathurst and the Governor's Yacht Meets Visitors

BATHURST, Gambia, West Africa, April 4.—The Prince of Wales has ... of his tour to ...

PRIVATE TRADE ONCE AGAIN TO BE PERMITTED

Far-Reaching Decision Affecting Future Economic Life of Russia

SOVIET GOES BACK TO LENINE'S POLICY

Thousands of Business Men, Forced to Close, Will Reopen

MOSCOW, April 4.—Far-reaching decisions affecting the future economic policy of Russia were taken yesterday by the council of labor and defense. Finding complete government control of trade and industry was a failure, the council meeting of which Leo Kameneff, acting premier, was chairman, decided to invite private capitalists to enter trade.

Remove Restrictions

Present restrictions regarding the sale of goods to private concerns by the state trusts and cooperative organizations will be removed and taxes on private traders greatly reduced. These reforms are considered the most important since the late Nikolai Lenine inaugurated the so-called new economic policy.

It is on the initiative of the supreme economic council that the new reforms are being introduced. It is now admitted that the drastic campaign which was waged against trade virtually ruined Russia's internal trade, bringing the country to the verge of an economic crisis.

Need Private Traders

M. Dzerjinsky, head of the supreme economic council, said Soviet Russia could not exist without the participation of private traders in the general trade of the country. He insisted the time had come for the adoption of new methods in the internal trade policy and declared that such a departure by the government from its present policy could not be regarded as "a retreat."

These reforms are being hailed with delight by private business men and firms who during last year were forced by thousands to suspend because of the government's decision to monopolize trade and industry.

ASKS LAW AGAINST DAYLIGHT SAVING

LATEST PICTURE OF THE KING AND QUEEN

For the first time since his recent illness, the King consented to be photographed at Calais, France, after his arrival from England and just before he boarded the royal train that carried him to Genoa, Italy. His Majesty, it was said, looked somewhat more pale and thin than he did before his attack of bronchial influenza which confined him to Buckingham Palace for several weeks. With his consort, he is now cruising in the Mediterranean.

MAY SUE PERSIAN BANK FOR LOSSES

CASEY, FAMOUS WARHORSE, IS DEAD IN EAST

CALGARY PIONEER TAKEN BY DEATH

$1,300,000 FOR PROBES IN 10 YEARS

OTTAWA, April 4.—A list of all the royal commissions appointed by the federal government was tabled in the house of commons yesterday. It showed that between 1911 and 1921, the two Conservative governments expended $755,035 for fifty-five inquiries, most of it in the war years. The Liberal regime since 1921 expended $568,462 on thirteen. The inquiry into British Columbia lands heads the list in the matter of cost, $316,782 having been expended.

Old Country Football Results

INTERNATIONAL

GLASGOW, April 4.—Scotland defeated England in an international soccer match today by two goals to nothing.

LEAGUE GAMES

LONDON, April 4.—Results of league soccer and rugby football games played in the Old Country today follow:

ENGLISH LEAGUE

First Division

Arsenal, 1; Cardiff City, 1.
Aston Villa, 1; Sunderland, 4.
Blackburn Rovers, 0; Notts C., 2.
Bury, 1; Burnley, 0.
Huddersfield Town, 2; Everton, 0.
Liverpool, 1; Birmingham, 1.
Manchester City, 2; Preston N.E., 1.
Newcastle U., 0; West Bromwich A., 1.
Nottingham F., 4; Leeds United, 0.
Sheffield U., 2; Tottenham Hotspurs, 0.
West Ham United, 1; Bolton Wanderers, 1.

Second Division

Barnsley, 1; Clapton Orient, 1.
Blackpool, 2; Leicester City, 1.
Bradford City, 2; Chelsea, 0.
Derby County 1; Manchester U. 0.
Fulham, 1; Oldham Athletic, 0.
Hull City, 0; Stoke, 0.
Middlesbrough, 0; Crystal Palace, 0.
Portsmouth, 1; Coventry City, 0.
Portvale, 0; Southampton, 1.
South Shields, 0; Stockport C., 1.
Wolverhampton, 1; Wednesday, 0.

Third Division—Northern Section

Barrow 2; Bradford 1.
Crewe Alexandra, 1; Halifax, 1.
Doncaster Rovers, 2; Grimsby Town, 2.
Durham City, 0; New...

NEAR 3,000,000 REFUGEES ROVE ABOUT EUROPE

Conditions in Greece, Macedonia, Bulgaria, Are Bad in Extreme

BRITISH M. P. HAS COMPLETED TRIP

Over Million Russians in Exile of Whom 200,000 Unemployed

By CLIFFORD L. DAY

LONDON, April 4. — Eastern Europe still has a seething mass of nearly 3,000,000 refugees, mostly destitute, surging to and fro over the national frontiers or within them as a result of the world war.

This at least, is the estimate brought back to London by Percy Alden, a prominent member of parliament, after an extended tour of Greece, Turkey, Bulgaria and Serbia.

There are more than 1,000,000 Russians in the non-Russian nations of Europe, he declares, 200,000 of them still being unemployed and unsettled. Germany has 500,000, France 400,000, Roumania 80,000 and Poland 70,000. The Russian refugee problem is at its worst, however, in China, according to Alden. There are 70,000 in Manchuria, nearly all of them in a destitute condition.

Greek Refugees

Greek refugees are not less than 1,450,000, of whom 80,000 are in the Athens and Piraeus area. In Macedonia and Thrace about 116,000 families are already established, comprising a population of approximately 350,000.

The Greek government and the settlement commission under the League of Nations are providing ploughs, draught animals, seed corn and forage for the cattle. About 40,000 families have been set up as tobacco growers. In many instances the carpet industry, a very important trade in Asia Minor, is being established near Athens and other large towns for the primary purpose of absorbing the new acquisitions to the populace.

Armenia's refugees still number 320,000, although about 1,000,000 of her people have been ... massac...

FAT EMMA ?

WE'RE GOING TO TELL YOU!

Why we say

"BOVRIL puts beef into you"

No food ever had higher voluntary praise than Bovril. Doctors and dietitians recommend Bovril. Chefs, cooks and housewives use it constantly. Explorers, travellers—and sailors have taken Bovril to the ends of the earth and have been loud in their praise of its sustaining and nutritive value.

But perhaps the most important tribute to Bovril comes from Science, because Science deals only with facts. Unknown to the Bovril Company, an independent scientific authority investigated the body-building power of Bovril. Extensive experiments were carried on and precise records taken. It was found that the nourishing value of Bovril to the human body is vastly greater than the amount taken.

The reason is this: Bovril is a scientific concentration of the vital principles of Beef—the albumen and fibrine with the extractives and flavours—which has remarkable powers of enabling the body to extract more nourishment from the other foods that are taken along with it. That is why Bovril sustains and builds, strengthens against sickness and disease and forms a perfect food for old and young, the strong and the delicate.

Because Bovril is not merely extract or essence of beef, but beef itself in concentrated and convenient form—we rightly say

"BOVRIL PUTS BEEF INTO YOU"

BOVRIL

BOVRIL

Sold only in Bottles. Made in Canada.

Sales Representatives for Canada:
HAROLD F. RITCHIE & CO. LIMITED
10-18 McCaul Street, Toronto

14

"They have freedom so free that it is tyranny," the newspaper said in a 1920 editorial. "It is a tyranny of fear of the consequence of freedom."

There was, as well, a chilling foreshadow of terrible things to come, on Friday, Nov. 9, 1923.

A front-page story, along with a picture of the two men, told readers that General Ludendorff and unknown house painter named Adolf Hitler had both been arrested following an attempted coup in Munich.

The Journal reprinted the statement issued by Hitler at the beginning of what became known as the Beer Hall Putsch. "Tomorrow will see the constitution of a nationalist government in Germany, or it will see us dead. There is no middle course," Hitler proclaimed.

And when an earthquake struck Japan on Sept. 3, 1923, and left a quarter-million dead, the newspaper remade the front page and put out an extra edition. The 'quake remained front-page news for days. A Sept. 4 editorial called for support for the Japanese.

"She has been taking a considerable proportion of the dairy and grain products of this province, so we have a very direct interest in her prosperity. But apart from this we should be profoundly moved by the news on broad humanitarian grounds, and show our active sympathy."

Not all wire service news told of disasters. Even then the mix of current events and entertainment was a staple.

When Sarah Bernhardt died on March 26, 1923, the paper ran three front-page pictures and thousands of words.

An editorial reminded readers of the Divine Sarah's visit to Edmonton a decade earlier when in two performances she appeared in the final act of *La dame aux camèlias.* "She was then approaching her seventieth year, but such was the perfection of her art that there did not appear to be anything incongruous in the assumption of the youthful role."

The First World War had whetted readers' appetites for more national and international news, and a decade later the battles in the trenches of Belgium and France still cast a long shadow over many lives.

In fact a regular feature called "Canada's V.C. Heroes," celebrated the wartime exploits of the country's 71 winners of the Victoria Cross. The stories invariably began with the cool, reasoned dispatches in which the hero's exploits were calmly outlined. Much more vivid accounts of the bravery that led to the award followed.

Returning soldiers, however, didn't always have an easy time of it.

The hard lives they and their wives led were obviously clear in entries to a *Journal* contest that offered a $10 first-prize to the soldier/farmer who wrote the best essay about life as a returned veteran. More than 5,000 had come to the Edmonton area to clear land and farm, and dozens wrote in.

Colin McKenzie, who was had taken advantage of a loan from the Soldier Settlement Board to buy land near Thorhild was the winner. Life was tough, according to McKenzie's story that ran on Jan. 17, 1920.

He had begun with the wrong kind of land-clearing equipment, and the work was slow and hard. His first home burned down shortly after his war bride arrived from England and, not surprisingly, she had trouble adjusting to her new life.

She didn't know how to milk a cow, and found life lonely at first,

football championship. The team is shut out by the Toronto Argonauts 23-0.

***Dec. 12, 1921*:**
Izena Ross is the first woman elected to Edmonton's city council, while D.M. Duggan is given a second term as mayor. When her term on council ends, Ross will go on to serve on the public school board.

***April 13, 1922*:**
The *Edmonton Journal* announces it will launch a radio broadcasting service within a month.

***May 1, 1922*:**
Alberta's first radio station, CJCA, goes on the air from a studio in a corner of *The Journal* newsroom. Mayor D.M. Duggan is heard as far away as Calgary and High River as he opens the broadcast.

***May 2, 1922*:**
The *Calgary Herald* launches radio station CHCQ, later CFAC, Alberta's second station.

***May 16, 1922*:**
The Edmonton Grads beat the London Shamrocks in a two-game series for the Canadian women's basketball title.

News and Views in Motordom

The First Rift, or Out of Gas

DRAWN BY
NELL BRINKLEY

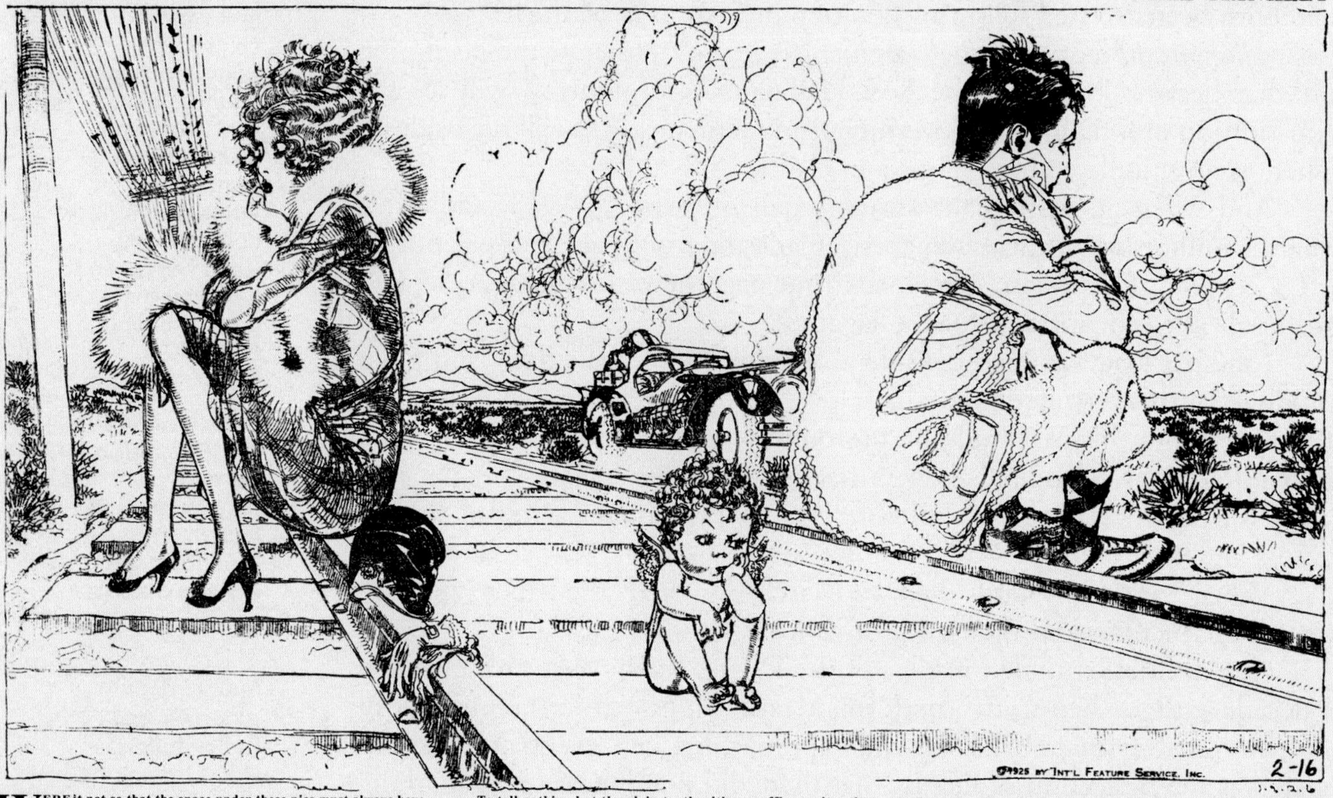
©1925 by Int'l Feature Service, Inc.
2-16

WERE it not so that the space under these pics must always have a bit of an essay, this one would have spoken for itself, and been called simply "A Story Without Words." However here's the diagram.

Never, in all the ten days of their married life had they even the faintest shadow of a cloud as big as your small girl's hand go over the radiance of their robin's-egg blue sky.

Her face beamed like a pink baby's every time she looked at him. His warmed and glowed like the kindly sun's every time he looked at her.

To tell nothing but the plain truth with no ruffles on it, they thought each other PERFECT—and said so—a hundred—nay, a thousand times a day. With plenty of frosting, and lace, and maple filling, and flowers!

And then—the sky suddenly filmed over, a big thunder-head lifted itself and looked over the horizon, and then mounted into the zenith and covered the sun!

For ten miles from the "Larkspur" gave out of gas.

And William was perfect no more! For no man even alive with flaws would have done such a thing!

And Williamette was perfect no more either. For the faultiest girl that was ever turned out, short of a shrew, would have known that nothing short of a temporary aphasia would have made a man forget GAS, would have guessed that the state of his heart had something to do with his loss of mentality, would have been gratified that SHE had blotted out even so important a thing from his mind—and forgiven him.

So there the were.

Love, disconsolate and highly surprised, and the two of them, camped on the railroad, too mad to begin the conference as to ways and means.

—*NELL BRINKLEY.*

TO CALGARY BY AIR ROUTE

Service Suggested for Summer

An aeroplane passenger service in Edmonton, similar to the one operating here two years ago with "Wop' May as pilot, may be instituted again during the coming summer. The machine that will be used, if Edmonton is decided upon as the centre for this aerial transportation scheme. is one that will carry two passengers and is fitted with the same kind of engine as that being used on the polar flight that is to take place from Alaska.

Last year the aeroplane was plying between points in southern Saskatchewan where there was no dearth of people willing to take flights. Similarly, all the way from Mexico north, over which distance the machine was flown, there was no difficulty experienced in procuring "fares" from any of the towns near which a landing was made.

Should the machine be brought to Edmonton it would probably run to Calgary and intermediate points in the south, as well as to some of the towns in the eastern part of the province. It is, however, not intended to take it out of its winter storage in Saskatchewan for some time yet.

McKenzie wrote. "But she is a dandy farmer now. She drives a team, holds a brush-breaker, gets the cows home, gets the mail and thinks the homestead is the place to be. I have had some bad luck, but I have been wanting to be a farmer since 1909 and, believe me, I am going to stick."

The Journal's editorial page was well pleased by the submissions. "Happiness is not always sitting in the lap of luxury, and the merit of hard work is never lost when one works as these chaps have done. They are building their own way, without fret or rivalry, and their example is a recrudescence of the great deeds that they did in France.

"The soldier pioneer is a very fine type indeed."

Neither could the influenza epidemic be forgotten.

As late as Nov. 23, 1923, a story warned readers that the flu could return. "The winter is at hand, and that demon flu may march through our midst again, leaving the victim whose life he spares weak, worn and devoid of all desire for work or play."

Rest, the story said, was probably the best prescription.

When polio struck in 1927, the city was much better prepared to handle the outbreak.

Schools were closed almost immediately on Sept. 6, to prevent the spread of the disease among youngsters who were most susceptible. They reopened on Sept. 26.

Being freed from attending class didn't mean that students could take a break. The paper published homework guides prepared by a committee of public school principals for students from grades 4 through 12. "Students should clip these outlines of study and keep them for reference."

While students and their parents may have stayed inside while the threat of polio stalked the city, everyone was car crazy and more than a dozen dealerships vied for business.

Classy indeed was the Oldsmobile convertible called the Thorobred. Ads said it was the "smartest new car of 1920" and was available only at Motordrome Limited on Jasper Avenue and 103rd Street. A Thorobred sold for $1,800, about $17,000 in today's money.

Somewhat less expensive was the Gray-Dort, sold by Capitol Motors. *Journal* ads could not have been plainer: "Own a Gray-Dort. You Will Like It." It came with a trouble light and a bull's eye flashlight. Electric cigar lighter. Rear-vision mirror. Plate glass windows. Oversize grooved-tread tires. Gypsy curtains. Real leather upholstery. Mahogany instrument board.

The price: $1,365 plus, of course, the War Tax that was still in effect. In 2003 dollars that's roughly $13,000.

Those who couldn't afford a new car turned to *Journal* classifieds. In the early days of 1920 you could buy a recently overhauled 1917 Ford Roadster, "complete with extra radius roads and an Atwater Kent ignition for $550 ($5,078.20 today) payable in 12 easy payments." and according to official estimates, by 1929 there were 97,000 cars registered in Alberta.

"You wouldn't think it so on a

***May 27, 1922*:**
The Mayfair Golf and Country Club in Edmonton's river valley has its official opening ceremonies.

***Aug. 2, 1922*:**
Queen Elizabeth Pool in Edmonton's river valley, the city's first public swimming pool, opens as Riverside Pool.

***Aug. 22, 1922*:**
Patricia Gyro Playground opens on 95th Street. It later becomes Giovanni Caboto Park.

***Sept. 14, 1922*:**
The University of Alberta presents an honourary degree to Canada's Governor General, Viscount Byng of Vimy.

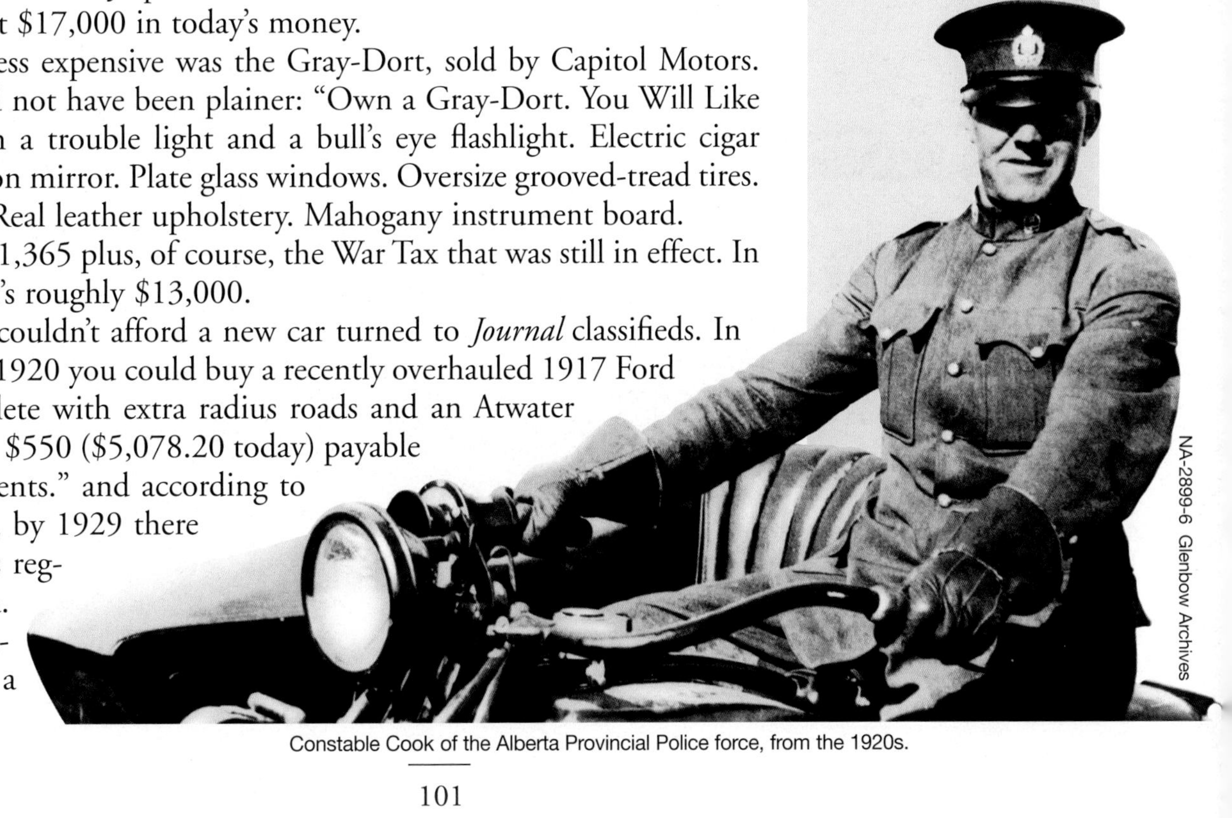

NA-2899-6 Glenbow Archives

Constable Cook of the Alberta Provincial Police force, from the 1920s.

DODGE BROTHERS
SPECIAL
TOURING CAR

The first cars bearing Dodge Brothers name were Touring Cars.

They were good and sturdy cars, so good and so sturdy that no radical change in basic design has been found necessary during these ten intervening years.

This fact has had far-reaching results. It has enabled Dodge Brothers to dedicate those ten years to the constant betterment of the original product.

More recently this endless process of improvement has manifested itself in various and impressive ways—in a new degree of riding comfort, a new smoothness of operation, a new and appealing beauty of line, and in those special details of appointment which distinguish the Special Touring Car.

MOTOR SALES, LTD.

10249 102nd ST., EDMONTON PHONE 6262

Calgary Edmonton Lethbridge

LIVE
EASTER
RABBITS

twenty-below day," the paper lamented during a particularly bitter cold snap in 1929 when the Grant Sixes, Thorobreds, Gray-Dorts and Ford Roadsters refused to start.

More than a few car engines, however, managed to turn over and make it to the CPR station on 109th Street and Jasper Avenue on a the bitterly cold evening of Dec. 19, 1929, one of the most important days in the political history of the province.

When Premier John Edward Brownlee, impeccably dressed as always, stepped down from the private rail car at 9:45 p.m., he had a special gold-plated fountain pen in his pocket and the biggest-ever Christmas present for Albertans in his briefcase.

He had used the special pen four days previously to sign an agreement with Prime Minister Mackenzie King's Liberal government in Ottawa that turned over control of natural resources to the province.

The deal, a quarter century in the making, seemingly ensured both Brownlee's political future and the economic well-being of the province.

And while the temperature was 20 below Fahrenheit and the wind threatened to send hats flying, the warmth of the reception from the 3,000 people awaiting his arrival took the chill off the night.

With the oil strike at Leduc still nearly two decades away, probably none of those present that wintry evening could possibly have guessed the ultimate value of the documents that Brownlee had in his possession.

What was understood was that the papers finally granted Alberta status as an equal member of Confederation. No longer was it denied the rights granted to more senior provinces in the Dominion.

"Citizens of Edmonton voiced in no uncertain manner their appreciation of the closing by Premier John E. Brownlee of the negotiations at Ottawa, whereby the dominion government returns the natural resources to the province," said a page 1 story on Brownlee's triumphant return.

The story reported that Brownlee was also met by the Edmonton Newsboys Band blaring their version of *Hail, Hail the Gang's All Here.* John Michaels, the former New Yorker who owned Mike's News and had started the band a half-dozen years before, signalled a friend holding a burning torch and a fuel-soaked pile of wood burst into a huge bonfire.

According to the newspaper, Michaels was also responsible for the "spectacular" fireworks.

"It is on special occasions as these that words fail the average man," Brownlee told the crowd.

"But I would not be human were I not able to say the warmth of your splendid reception has touched me deeply. I take it not as a personal tribute to myself so much as it is a tribute to those premiers and ministers of the government who over a period of 25 years, have striven to bring a successful conclusion to the negotiations which have at last terminated."

It was a generous speech from a gracious man.

Journal coverage of the resources rights issue had been almost non-stop since the day Alberta had become a province. Hundreds of thousands of words had been written, countless political cartoons printed and thousands of editorials had fulminated against Ottawa's reluctance to grant the province its due.

***Nov. 5, 1922*:**
Edmonton car dealership worker Paul Welch sets a record by driving the dirt roads to Calgary and back in just under nine-and-a-half hours.

NA-2784-9 Glenbow Archives

Premier John E. Brownlee.

***Dec. 2, 1922*:**
Queen's University beats the Edmonton Eskimos 13-2 in the Grey Cup. It will be 32 years before Edmonton again plays in the Cup championship.

***Dec. 11, 1922*:**
D.M. Duggan is re-elected mayor of Edmonton; future mayors Ken Blatchford and Dan Knott are elected to city council.

***Dec. 22, 1922*:**
A federal order-in-council creates Wood Buffalo National Park, straddling the border of Alberta and the Northwest Territories.

Courtesy Brownlee/Fryatt Law

Premier Brownlee, seated third from right, with dark-rim glasses, signs the energy accord.

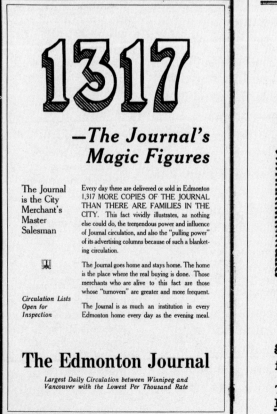

CHILDREN CRY FOR
Fletcher's
CASTORIA
MOTHER:– Fletcher's Castoria is a pleasant, harmless Substitute for Castor Oil, Paregoric, Teething Drops and Soothing Syrups, especially prepared for Infants in arms and Children all ages.
To avoid imitations, always look for the signature of Chas H. Fletcher.
Proven directions on each package. Physicians everywhere recommend it.

When the agreement was finally signed, the paper ran the full text so readers could have a complete understanding of the importance of the deal.

"The value is inestimable," wrote Charles Bishop, the paper's man in Ottawa on Dec. 16. "It runs to a billion or two."

While the paper's editorial writers did not always support Brownlee and his United Farmers of Alberta government, it showed a great deal of respect for the premier himself on Dec. 19: "Mr. Brownlee's modesty could not lead anyone to underestimate the value of the work that he himself has done.

"Alberta owes much to him for the ability, tact and patience that he brought to the handling of this vital and difficult problem and it was most fitting that the province's capital should honour him in so striking a way," *The Journal* said of the railway station welcome.

Brownlee, who paid tribute to both political friends and political foes, was a hard-working man who put all politics aside when trying to deal with the drought and the poor and unemployed. He brought old-age pensions of $20 a month to all Albertans over the age of 70 and understood the value of a fine education system. He also had deep concerns over the health of his fellow citizens. Brownlee looked unbeatable.

But it hadn't always been so, and the government of which Brownlee found himself the head had initially been reluctant to take power.

The United Farmers of Alberta elected their first member of the legislature in 1919 and formed the government in 1921. However, their path to becoming a political party, rather than simply a political force, was as sticky as prairie gumbo.

Indeed, Henry Wise Wood, the Missouri born-and-raised farmer from Carstairs, one of the founders of the UFA in 1909, argued long and hard against actively entering politics. He even wanted to restrict membership in the group.

It should, he said, be an organization of farmers. Allowing others to join would dilute the message.

Membership in the UFA itself and in the United Farm Women of Alberta was soaring, the paper reported. There was ambition in the air of the kind that sniffed at political power.

Still, the grass roots of the party held to their principles.

In a 1920 interview, outgoing UFWA president Irene Parlby expressed caution when it came to the group's participation in elections as a political party. Much more important, she said, was education, and she expressed the UFA's suspicions of cities. "Our schools have been educating the boys and girls away from

Journal carriers Roy Ashton Webb, left, and Harley Barnard Webb in Jasper, 1927.

ND-3-3700a Glenbow Archives

***Jan. 30, 1923*:**
The Canadian government takes over control of the Grand Trunk Railway, making it part of Canadian National.

***Jan. 31, 1923*:**
A *Journal* collections agent earns $50 a month and the paper starts the *Farm Weekly.* It ceases publication on Sept. 28, 1932.

***March 14, 1923*:**
CKCK radio in Regina broadcasts the first play-by-play broadcast of a pro hockey game. Reporter Pete Parker calls the Western Canada Hockey League match between the Regina Caps and the Edmonton Eskimos.

***March 31, 1923*:**
The Edmonton Eskimos of the Western Canada Hockey League lose the Stanley Cup to the Ottawa Senators, two games to none. In the second game Frank (King) Clancy becomes the only player to play all six positions in a single Cup game, when the Ottawa goalie is sent off for a penalty.

***May 2, 1923*:**
Prohibition rum runner Emilio Picariello

THE WEATHER
May 15, 1925
FORECAST—FAIR; WARMER.
Highest Today—62 Degrees.
Lowest last night—32 degrees.
Barometer, 29.00—Decreasing.
Sun Rises Saturday 4:35; Sets, 8:26.

Edmonton Journal

LAST EDITION

VOL. 21, NO. 256 — EDMONTON, ALBERTA, FRIDAY, MAY 15, 1925 — TWENTY-EIGHT PAGES

179 STUDENTS GIVEN DEGREES AT VARSITY TODAY

GRADUATES OF UNIVERSITY GET REWARDS

Degrees, Diplomas and Scholarships Presented at Seventeenth Convocation

SIR F. W. HAULTAIN IS DOCTOR OF LAWS

Registration of 1,354 for Past Year Set New Alberta Record

GOLD MEDALIST

Miss Joyce Petch of Edmonton, who won the gold medal for mezzo-sopranos at the festival today.

COMMANDER OF FIRST DIVISION AS 'BLACK ROD'

Appointment of Sir Archibald MacDonell to Post Is Urged

BUSH FIRE MENACE DIES DURING NIGHT

Fort William Reports Some Small Outbreaks Near to Settlements

EDMONTON GIRL MEZZO-SOPRANO GOLD MEDALIST

Miss Joyce Petch Wins in Competition at Festival Today

ALEX M'INTOSH IS JUNIOR MEDALIST

Bulyea Cup Goes to Knox Church, Calgary, This Year

By LILY MULLET

JANET SMITH'S DEATH AS YET DEEP MYSTERY

Crown Counsel Throws Doubts on Evidence of Police Officers

GIRL DID NOT DIE WHERE DISCOVERED

Magistrate Reserves Decision as to Committing Chinaman for Trial

WHITE GIRL CREE'S BRIDE

Miss Mae Hodgson, city stenographer, daughter of the late Frederick and Mrs. Mary Elizabeth Hodgson, now of Tullamore, Ontario, who is to become the bride of Mr. Joseph Charles Iserhoss, a full-blooded Cree Indian who is the factor of the Hudson's Bay company's post at Peterbell, Ontario, where the couple will establish their home after the marriage.

'UNINVITED' GUESTS HEAR ALL ABOUT ABBY'S WEDDING FROM LIPS OF PROUD DAD

John D. Rockefeller, Jr., Brings Startled Girls Watching House in to See Decorations; Special Bouquet for Old Negress Washerwoman Ends Reception

By FRANK GETTY

LOOKS LIKE CANNIBALISM AT CALGARY

CALGARY, May 15.—Seven steers will be roasted at the biggest barbecue ever held in America, along with five carvers and four waiters to serve the cuts when the Calgary exhibition and stampede is held on July 6-12. There will also be two hundred men to make sandwiches when the people gather here to celebrate Calgary's jubilee.

UNION DEPOT FOR 1926 NEW REPORT

Net Estimates Will Provide for Structure Claims Mayor Blatchford

DAWSON FLOODED BY YUKON RIVER

WILL NOT LIFT VEIL SHROUDING INCOME TAXES

Amounts Paid Must Remain Secret Is Decision of Committee

MR. GOOD RECEIVES ANOTHER LETTER

House Committee Decided They've Had Enough; Refuse to Listen

THE WEATHER
January 23, 1926
FORECAST—Colder; Some Snow.
Highest today 10 degrees.
Lowest Last Night—4 Above.
Barometer 27.89, increasing.
Sun rises Sunday 8:26; sets 5:06.
Sun rises Monday 8:25; sets 5:08.

Edmonton Journal

LAST EDITION

VOL. 22, NO. 161 — EDMONTON, ALBERTA, SATURDAY, JANUARY 23, 1926 — SINGLE COPY, 5 CENTS — THIRTY-EIGHT PAGES

SCIENCE MARKS BIG ADVANCE IN USE OF INSULIN

MINERS BURIED UNDER DEBRIS AS ROOF FALLS

Fatal Accident Shortly After Midnight at Chinook Mine

VICTIMS ENGAGED IN TIMBERING

Dead Man Was Buried Three Feet Deep in Collapse

Cardinal Mercier of Belgium Is Dead
Heroic Priest Passes Amid Relatives

MERCIER AND CITY HE LOVED

A glimpse of Louvain city hall and cathedral, for the rebuilding of whose university Cardinal Mercier (inset) labored long.

LION-HEARTED PRIMATE OF ALL BELGIUM BOWS AT LAST TO MAN'S GRIM CONQUEROR

Won Hearts of His People During War Years by Courageous Defiance of Germany and Denunciation of Despot...

FEAR FANATICS IN GENEVA SO DEFER PARLEY

Russians Afraid of Assassins' Bullets If Envoys Gather There

SO DISARMAMENT CONFERENCE WAITS

Special Police May Clear Swiss City of Notorious Spies

By CHARLES M. McCANN

SECOND HOP IS DEFERRED TILL MONDAY

Old Country Football

ENGLISH LEAGUE
First Division

Second Division

SOVIET ISSUES ULTIMATUM TO GENERAL CHANG

Chinese Warrior Imprisons Four Russian Officers of Eastern Railway

THREE DAYS GIVEN TO EFFECT RELEASE

Britain Watches New Crisis in Far East With Anxiety

DR. JOHN J. ABEL GETS PURE CRYSTAL INSULIN AFTER YEARS OF WORK

Dr. Collip, of Alberta University, Says It Marks Great Progress

CURE OF DIABETES MADE MORE CERTAIN

May Even Lead to Discovery of Preventatives, Scientists Hope

Canadian Honored

LIEUT. COM. W. J. S. TURNER
Who is the first Canadian officer of the Salvation Army to receive the rank of commissioner. He is en route to South America.

OUTLOOK TODAY BETTER THAN IN PAST 5 YEARS

View of Canada as Given by U. S. Trade Commissioner

GRADUAL CLIMB TO ...FACTORY LEVEL

Marks Big Advance, Dr. J. P. Collip

the farm," said Parlby, who later became a minister without portfolio in the first UFA government.

"The profession of farming has been one of such long laborious hours, with such incommensurable returns that naturally the farm children turned their eyes longingly towards easier lives in city offices and stores, and selling those things which their fellows toiled to produce."

Parlby herself would later join four other women – Emily Murphy, Nellie McClung, Louise McKinney and Henrietta Muir Edwards – to become the Famous Five in the Persons Case in 1928. In a landmark decision from the British Privy Council, women were declared "persons" under the British North America Act.

The Privy Council decision overturned an earlier ruling from the Supreme Court of Canada that had said women were not "persons" and thus not eligible to sit in the Senate.

The UFA and the UFWA also called for even more strict control of liquor in Prohibition-era Alberta.

The UFWA in particular was upset at the number of Albertans who managed to obtain the medical prescriptions in order to buy alcohol.

Louise McKinney, the MLA from Claresholm, elected to the legislature as a member of the Non-Partisan League but later allied herself with the UFA, was appalled by what she saw and heard.

According to a story from the 1920 convention, McKinney described those people who would squeeze liquor prescriptions out of doctors as "nothing more than Bolsheviks."

She admitted that Prohibition was not a complete success, but she urged her fellow believers to stay the course.

"When you hear people saying that there are far more women being made drunkards since prohibition went into effect than there was before, brand it a lie," she said.

"When they say that there are more minors drinking than there were three years ago, refuse to believe it.

"If the law can't be enforced," she said, "instead of repealing it, amend it. The public gets hysterical, we must keep sane."

By 1924, hysterical public or not, the government repealed Prohibition.

Nevertheless, the 1920 UFA convention hinted at the future.

The guest speaker was Liberal Premier Charles Stewart who said in an interview that he was not afraid of the UFA, whatever their ambitions.

Furthermore, he said, he was not "alarmed, worried or scared by their propaganda." Within 18 months, Stewart's government was swept from office, losers in the June 17, 1921, election in which the UFA won 39 seats in the 61-seat house.

Stewart was the last Liberal premier in Alberta's history.

The UFA was awkward when it came to power. They had only a single member with experience in the legislature, no leader prepared to be premier and it took them weeks to sort out the mess.

Even during the campaign itself, the new political party seemed baffled.

When the election was called, the UFA decided that – maybe – running in only 26 ridings was enough. Then halfway through the campaign

(Emperor Pick) from southern Alberta's Crowsnest Pass is hanged at Fort Saskatchewan, with associate Florence Lassandro, the only woman hanged in the province. The pair were convicted of the murder of an Alberta Provincial Police officer, who was fatally shot in a confrontation over the shooting of Picariello's son.

***June 12, 1923*:**
The Edmonton Grads get the first of two wins over the U.S. champion Cleveland Favorite Knits in a series that brings the Grads their first women's world basketball title.

***Aug. 30, 1923*:**
The Edmonton Public Library's new building opens on McDougall Drive overlooking the North Saskatchewan River valley. It remains in use until the Centennial Library opens in 1967.

***Oct. 24, 1923*:**
"No man could be in public life for so long a time without strong difference of opinion arising as to the policies that he has pursued. But it should be hard to forget these entirely on such an occasion as this and unite in doing honour to a fellow citizen to whose faith in Edmonton to

NC-6-6522 Glenbow Archives

A crowd gathers at *The Journal* office to catch elections results, July 18, 1921.

MOTHERS
AND THEIR CHILDREN
Going to Bed a Pleasure
I never punish my children by sending them to bed. For that reason I never have to coax or threaten to make them go. Sometimes they find a little surprise slipped under the pillow—a peppermint, a picture cut-out or some small toy.
"Tricks of the Trade in Raising Children"
Ideas for mothers, contributed by mothers. Ideas that really work—Ideals that will save hours of time and days of worry—Ideas that will prevent sickness and preserve health—Ideas that every wise mother is eager to get.
"MOTHERS AND THEIR CHILDREN"
Every Day in the
EDMONTON JOURNAL

What shall I do?
IT presented a real problem to her. Repeatedly he had urged her to marry him. He was attractive, of good family, and fortunate in a financial way.
Yet between them there was an invisible barrier that made her hold back: Something she couldn't bring herself to talk about.
* * *
You, yourself, rarely know when you have halitosis (unpleasant breath). That's the insidious thing about it. And even your closest friends won't tell you.
Sometimes, of course, halitosis comes from some deep-seated organic disorder that requires professional advice. But usually—and fortunately—halitosis is only a local condition that yields to the regular use of Listerine as a mouth wash and gargle. It is an interesting thing that this well-known antiseptic that has been in use for years for surgical dressings, possesses these unusual properties as a breath deodorant.
Test the remarkable deodorizing effects of Listerine this way: Rub a little onion on your fingers. Then apply Listerine and note how quickly the onion odor disappears.
This safe and long-trusted antiseptic has dozens of different uses; note the little circular that comes with every bottle. Your druggist sells Listerine in the original brown package only — never in bulk. There are three sizes: three ounce, seven ounce and fourteen ounce. Buy the large size for economy. — Lambert Pharmacal Company, Saint Louis, U. S. A.
For HALITOSIS use LISTERINE
LISTERINE Throat Tablets are now available. Please do not make the mistake of expecting them to correct bad breath. Rely on the liquid, Listerine. Containing all of the antiseptic essential oils of Listerine, however, they are very valuable as a relief for throat irritations — 25 cents.

leader Henry Wise Wood suggested that his association would be unable to take over the reins of government.

"If I had my way, we should put 20 of our best men in the legislature at this election and leave the responsibility of government on the shoulders of someone else," Wood said in a story on July 8, 1921.

As for *The Journal's* role in that election, which put an end to mainline party politics in Alberta for decades, it recommended to Edmonton voters that their best hope lay with electing a full slate of Conservatives. Voters chose five Liberals, including the redoubtable Nellie McClung.

It took the UFA almost a month before it finally settled on Westlock farmer Herbert Greenfield, as their premier.

Wood had appealed to lawyer Brownlee to become premier. According to a *Journal* story a week after the election, both men decided the first leader of a farmers' movement should, in fact, be a farmer. Greenfield stayed in office until Brownlee took over in 1925.

The paper, as usual had no shortage of advice for the government, but the tone it took toward Brownlee was always respectful of his abilities.

After all, the same year that he signed the all-important resources agreement, Brownlee also skilfully brokered a deal to sell the two provincially owned north country railway lines – the vexatious Alberta and Great Waterways Railway – to a joint venture made up of the CNR and the CPR. The province made $16 million on the sale, so the price seemed right, too.

Brownlee's party, long supporters of women's suffrage, had helped to bring the vote to the women of Alberta in 1916, and the difficulties of Prohibition, finally abandoned as a bad experiment, were behind him.

There had been a long-running dry spell, particularly in southern Alberta, but relief efforts seemed to be working.

Commodity prices remained generally high, making it easy to overlook the continuing drought and the increasing number of farm foreclosures.

There were some very unhappy days ahead, and there were hints of the Depression to come at that railway station celebration that had greeted the triumphant Brownlee on his return from Ottawa.

Only eight weeks before, the stock market had crashed, and while the minority of Edmontonians who owned stocks felt the greatest impact, the ripples of the price collapse soon became a tidal wave, sweeping everyone along with it.

As Brownlee stood amid the glow of well-wishers at the train station that Dec. 19, a very real glimpse of the future was there for him to see.

The Journal saw it and reported: "A large contingent of the unemployed attended the reception, massing under the red banner of the 'Edmonton Council of the Unemployed.'

"A cordon of Alberta provincial police under Superintendent Bryan maintained good order, however, and beyond some cries of 'When do we eat?' and the singing of choruses, the demonstrators behaved in an orderly manner."

Life in the next decade would be utterly unrecognizable to those who had heard Mayor Duggan's optimistic "Hullo, hullo, hullo!" only a few short years before.

whose zeal in its behalf all must recognize the city owes a great deal."
– Editorial on the occasion of long-time rival Frank Oliver, MP and *Bulletin* publisher, going to Ottawa to serve on the board of railway commissioners. Until *The Journal* ran his obituary on April 1, 1933, this would be the last kind thing the paper said about him.

NA-2204-3 Glenbow Archives

Herbert Greenfield in Denmark.

***Oct. 25, 1923*: Canadians Frederick Banting and J.J.R. Macleod win the Nobel Prize for Medicine for the discovery of insulin. Macleod shares his half of the $40,000 prize money with University of Alberta professor Dr. J.B. Collip, who also worked on the research, while Banting**

NC-6-1746 Glenbow Archives

Emmeline Pankhurst and Nellie McClung in front of the Alberta Legislature Building in 1916.

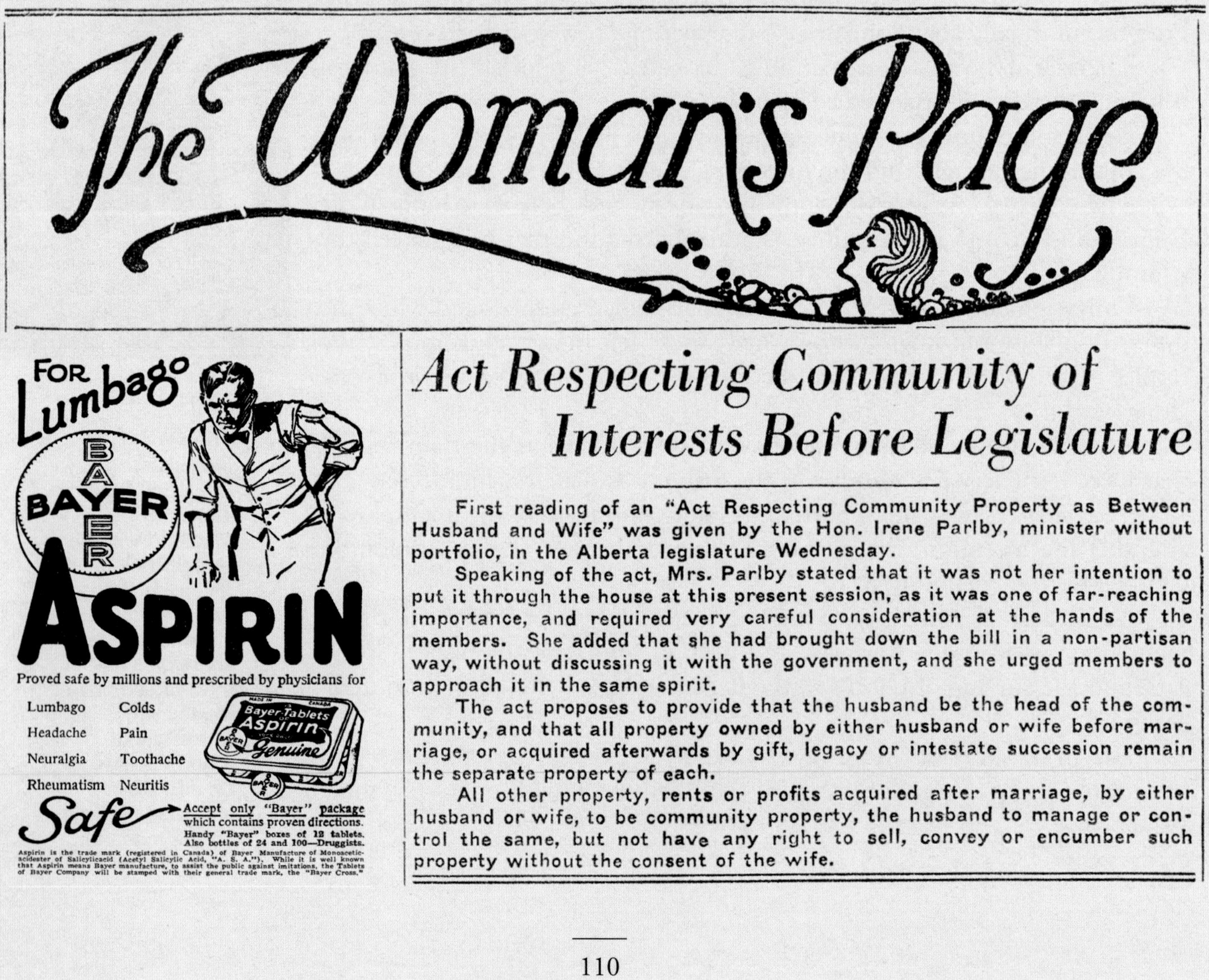

The Woman's Page

Act Respecting Community of Interests Before Legislature

First reading of an "Act Respecting Community Property as Between Husband and Wife" was given by the Hon. Irene Parlby, minister without portfolio, in the Alberta legislature Wednesday.

Speaking of the act, Mrs. Parlby stated that it was not her intention to put it through the house at this present session, as it was one of far-reaching importance, and required very careful consideration at the hands of the members. She added that she had brought down the bill in a non-partisan way, without discussing it with the government, and she urged members to approach it in the same spirit.

The act proposes to provide that the husband be the head of the community, and that all property owned by either husband or wife before marriage, or acquired afterwards by gift, legacy or intestate succession remain the separate property of each.

All other property, rents or profits acquired after marriage, by either husband or wife, to be community property, the husband to manage or control the same, but not have any right to sell, convey or encumber such property without the consent of the wife.

A Woman's Right

"Women exercise the franchise on the same terms as men and since 1921 they have had a representative in the House of Commons while others have been candidates for membership in that body. It would be absurd to deny them the right to a place in the other chamber."

— Editorial, April 25, 1928

The Journal championed the right of women to fully enjoy the country's biggest political perk – appointment to the Senate. The editorial was in response to the April 24, 1928, Supreme Court decision that women were not "persons" as defined by the British North America Act of 1867 and, therefore, could not be senators.

The paper was not a hotbed of gender equality in the 1920s. Advice columns such as "What Every Woman Wants to Know" by Mary Roberts Rinehardt on Jan. 2, 1924, told women to eschew careers, get married and raise children. "If she is born woman she is a born mate and child bearer."

A Nov. 14, 1929, article suggested: "For years now men have been printing articles that the short skirt was the sign and symbol of women's freedom. The burning question is not whether to wear long skirts, but what to wear with long skirts."

Still, *The Journal* recorded – and supported – women's struggles for political equality and coverage of the Persons Case reflected the paper's recognition that times and attitudes change. "The court interpreted the act in the light of the conditions existing in 1867. But these have since been radically altered," noted the post-decision editorial.

The decision was appealed to the British cabinet, the "highest court in the Empire" by the Famous Five, Irene Parlby, the first woman in Alberta to hold a cabinet post; Emily Murphy, the first woman magistrate in the Empire; former MLAs Nellie McClung and Louise McKinney; and Henrietta Muir Edwards, publisher and activist.

On Oct. 18, 1929, the British Privy Council ruled women were, indeed, persons. The Persons Case decision was given second billing in the double-barrelled banner head across the front page that day. The new president of the Edmonton Chamber of Commerce got top billing.

"J.F. McMullen New President of Chamber of Commerce"

"Privy Council Decides Women Are Eligible for Canadian Senate"

Nevertheless, the coverage was extensive. The paper ran a summary account of the Privy Council decision, including the line: "The exclusion of women from all public offices is a relic of days more barbarous than ours."

And in a rare move, the paper even quoted Parlby. "Women in Canada are not particularly desirous of entering the Senate, but they have felt if they desired to do so, the privilege should be theirs."

Another unusual element of the story was that the women – with the exception of Edwards – were referred to by their own Christian names.

Pictures of four of the Famous Five appeared on the front of the second section. The main page had photos of the new C of C executive, all men.

splits his money with fellow researcher Charles Best.

***Oct. 29, 1923*:**
The Alberta Wheat Pool begins operations, with about 25,000 farmer-members signed up to sell their grain through the marketing co-operative.

***Nov. 5, 1923*:**
Alberta voters in a provincial referendum opt for government control of liquor sales, ending seven years of Prohibition. Government liquor stores are set up in 1924.

***Nov. 9, 1923*:**
Northwestern Utilities brings natural gas to Edmonton homes.

***Dec. 7, 1923*:**
Edmonton experimented with proportional representation voting in the 1920s. For some reason, it never really caught on. Here's a *Journal* explanation of how it worked. "Let us assume that 14,000 electors will cast their votes for aldermen candidates securing one-seventh of the 14,000 and one more, that is 2,001 first choices are sure of election, because if six candidates get 2,001 each or 12,006, no other candidate can get more than 1,994, the total remainder of the

The Woman's Page

HAMILTON HAS A THOUSAND OF THEM

The above photograph of the officers of the Canadian order of the Women's Ku Klux Klan was taken at the home of one of the Hamilton officers on the occasion of the visit of high officials of the Canadian order. It will be seen that the robes are somewhat different from those in the States, masks being worn over the eyes only, instead of covering the whole face. A thousand women belong to the Klan in Hamilton.

MUTT AND JEFF—Poor Mutt. The Twins Are Driving Him Cuckoo. (Trade Mark Registered in Canada). Copyright, 1925, by H. C. Fisher. —**By Bud Fisher**

JEFF, HAVE YOU TOLD MUTT YET THAT I'M YOUR TWIN BROTHER AND THAT I'M THE STRONGEST LITTLE MAN IN THE WORLD?
NO, JULIUS! HE DOESN'T EVEN KNOW YOU'RE HERE! SMOKE UP WHILE I TAKE A BAWTH!
JULIUS
JEFF
I'M GONNA CHEAT THE BARBER OUT OF TWENTY CENTS!
PAPA
JEFF, I WANT TO SHAVE!
YOU CAN'T SHAVE NOW, MUTT! I'M TAKING A PLUNGE!
BATH
PAPA
JULIUS
PAPA
LIAR!
WHAT DO YOU MEAN, I'M A LIAR? ANSWER ME THAT!!
THE STRONGEST LITTLE MAN IN THE WORLD

Tainted Legacy

"Are we now going to turn the mental hospital into a manufacturing plant for the creation of eunuchs?"
— Letter to the editor, March 1, 1928

With the support of a number of doctors, the United Farm Women of Alberta of 1919 were all in favour of the latest developments in the field of eugenics (Greek for "well born"). The UFWA believed, as did others around the world, in social engineering and, backed by feminist superstars Irene Parlby, Emily Murphy and Premier John Brownlee, were determined to keep the insane and the immoral from breeding.

Eugenics was one of the pseudo-sciences created in the Victorian era.

While the idea of "culling" so-called "defectives" from the human herd had been kicking around for centuries, it was Charles Darwin's half-cousin Francis Galton who codified eugenic theory in 1865. In his words, the purpose of eugenics was "to give the more suitable races or strains of blood a better chance of prevailing speedily over the less suitable."

The UFWA reasoned that if farmers could breed better cows, there was no reason the government couldn't breed better people.

Unfortunately, for 2,832 Albertans over the next 34 years, the United Farmer of Alberta government was in a position to experiment with the theory. In 1928, the Sexual Sterilization Act was introduced, debated and passed in a mere three weeks.

But it didn't have an easy ride. *The Journal* reported strong opposition to the act "which proposes sterilization of the feeble-minded upon leaving a mental institution and after examination by a board."

On Feb. 28, *The Journal* opposed the bill in an editorial. "It is evident that there is wide differences of opinion among those who are competent to form conclusions on the subject and who have given it the thorough study that it requires. Alberta would not be at all justified in passing the proposed legislation in the face of so little support for the plan elsewhere."

That same day, Premier John Brownlee dismissed all arguments against the legislation and went as far to call it an economic necessity.

"Alberta cannot go on with this problem as at present, making extensions to its institutions year after year, without doing something about it."

The bill passed March 7 and *The Journal* editorial expressed an almost prophetic concern about the implications of eugenics.

"It has been made clear that the experiment has little scientific sanction. Pronouncements against it from bodies in older countries that have given the matter close study have been cited. They are convinced that greater evils are likely to result than those which it is sought to correct."

The Sexual Sterilization Act was repealed in 1972 by the Conservative government of Premier Peter Lougheed.

On Jan. 25, 1996, Court of Queen's Bench Justice Joanne Veit awarded Leilani Muir $740,000 for wrongful sterilization and being confined to an institution. Another 230 victims won settlements worth $325,000 each in 1999.

14,000 votes cast."

***Jan. 17, 1924*:**
The UFA opposes a conference resolution calling for the western provinces to separate from the rest of Canada.

NA-2204-12 Glenbow Archives

Irene Parlby, 1928.

***Feb. 5, 1924*:**
Edmonton's La Fleche Bros. Ltd. advertises men's suits at prices from $28 to $44.

***May 10, 1924*:**
After several years of Prohibition, Alberta's new Government Liquor Control Act gives the provincial government complete control of liquor sales.

***June 1, 1924*:**
Wop May and two *Journal* reporters answer the burning question: "Can a radio be heard by people flying in an airplane?" They pick up CJCA's broadcast of a

THURSDAY, APRIL 16, 1925 EDMONTON JOURNAL FIFTEEN

Sports Section

EDITED BY GEORGE MACKINTOSH

VICTORIA ALL-STARS NO MATCH FOR THE GRADS

COACH PAGE'S TOURISTS CHALK UP THIRD WIN OF COAST INVASION BY 30-6

World's Hoop Champions Had an Easy Win in the B. C. Capital Last Night—Connie Smith Again High Scorer—Last Game of the Tour at Kamloops on Saturday

VICTORIA, April 16.—The Grads experienced very little difficulty in winning the third consecutive game on their coast tour last night, taking the all star Victoria team which had been selected to play against them into camp by a score of 30-6. The local girls were never in the hunt and it was not until the last period had almost passed into history that they broke through the Grads' defence for the only baskets they scored—two in number. The prairie girls gave a masterful exhibition of basketball, and it is easy to understand why they have amassed such a brilliant record after seeing them in action.

As compared with the Victoria girls their passing, and particularly the speed with which they break away the moment they secure the ball, are things to marvel at. The chief difference in the play of the two teams was the method of passing the ball. The locals depended largely upon a long pass which the visitors were quick to intercept, and Victoria's inability to score can be laid largely to the case with which their well-intentioned passes were gobbled up. On the other hand, the Grads used a snappy, short passing game, in which one player acted as a sort of running interference very similar to the American style of rugby, and worked the ball down the floor time after time without encountering very much opposition. They also used an "exchange check" system by which their forwards dropped back and allowed their guards to pass through, an effective variation which enabled the visiting guards to pick up more points than the entire Victoria team.

Floor Was Slippery

Unfortunately the game was transferred at the last moment to the Armouries in order to accommodate the crowd and as the Armoury floor is used for dancing, it was extremely difficult for the girls to retain their balance. There was a great deal of slipping which marred the game to a considerable extent, yet the play was remarkably clean, only seven penalties being handed out.

During the first period the Grads rolled up a seven point lead thr... brilliant shooting on the part of ... Dunn and Dot Johns... was...

POSTPONE AMATEUR BOXING TOURNEY

Canada Will Be Forced to Withdraw from Boston Bouts

BOSTON, April 16.—The international amateur boxing tournament to determine the championships of the western hemisphere, between contenders of the United States, Canada and South America, which was scheduled to begin here on April 22, has been postponed until May 1, according to Chairman Cuddy, of the boxng committee of the Amateur Athletic union.

The South American boxers weighed in and were found to be over-weight, he said, so that the added time was given them to get in condition.

Will Withdraw

MONTREAL, April 16.—Dr. Lamb, head of the physical training faculty of McGill and general secretary of the Amateur Athletic Union of Canada, announced yesterday that if the report that the pan-American boxing championship for amateurs cannot be held until May 1 is true, the Canadian union will be reluctantly compelled to refrain from sending a team, as the dates for the Canadian championships have been set for April 27 to 29 inclusive, and are to be held at Winnipeg.

ANDY LYTTLE HANDS GRADS A NICE BOOST

Coast Scribe Liked Ability of Champs to Look After Themselves

In all of their appearances at the coast during their present tour of British Columbia, the Commercial Grads have won the respect of their opponents and the B.C. fans. Andy Lyttle, sporting editor of the Vancouver Sun, penned the article reproduced below following the first game the Edmonton girls played on the shores of Burrard Inlet. In view of the fact that the Grads had yet to show their best form in the following game the boost is especially pleasing. It runs as follows:

Ability to take care of themselves in strenuous action is a predominant feature of the successful play of the Edmonton Commercial graduate girls basketball team. It is a big factor in the success of any athletic endeavor which calls for vigor in execution.

In Saturday night's encounter at the arena, play was stopped more than once while a Vancouver girl recaptured suddenly-lost breath, nursed a protesting nose, or rubbed abrasions. During the entire course of the game not a sweet girl graduate paused for anything.

They dove furiously for the ball, checked with their weight, pushed, thrust, hurdled the opposition and generally gave a finished exhibition. Conspicuous, also, was their method of covering up at close quarters. Few boxers have this important feature of their art under better control. It was really the deciding point in a hard-fought match.

Somewhat after the manner of the All-Blacks, these girls from the wind-swept prairies opened their attack when the need arose. They know how to work the ball up along the sides, how to keep play from jamming up in mid-centre, and rarely indeed was there more than one black and gold figure under the basket in the completion of a raid.

All of them wore knee pads. The game of basketball as taught them by Coach Page, is no game for weaklings. Their style of play might well be taken to heart by officials of the Vancouver and District Basketball league, who seem inclined at times to criticize the rigor of play as adopted so long and so successfully by, for instance, the Vancouver Senior Y.M.C.A. five.

C.N.R. ELEVEN HAVE LITTLE DIFFICULTY IN DEFEATING SOUTH SIDE; SCORE IS 3-1

Winners Take Field With Reorganized Lineup That Works Smoothly—Forwards Played Weak Game for the Losers and Couldn't Get Going

First points to be chalked up to the credit of a first division soccer team this season were won by the C.N.R. eleven on Wednesday evening, when they scored an easy win over the South Side aggregation at Renfrew park. The score was 3-1 and it complimented the losers at that. The only tally registered by the boys from over the river was put in by a C.N.R. back, while only the good work of Candy in goal for the losers prevented the defeat from being much more decisive.

The railwaymen took the field with a reorganized lineup, and it worked like a well-oiled machine. Gregory took over the task of net custodian and Orchin moved up to the fullback line with Carlson, where he showed up to advantage. Gregory got little opportunity to show his real worth, as his team mates broke up the South Side attacks with great regularity, and he was not called upon to make many saves.

Forwards Were Weak

The back division of the South Siders was working fairly well, but the forwards couldn't get going at all. Their attempts at combination play were feeble and individual efforts were usually brought to a sudden conclusion when the C.N.R. defence was encountered. Tempers began to come to the surface towards the end of the game, and Hobbs was extended an invitation to cool his heels in the dressing room after a short but fierce battle had occurred.

The railwaymen won the toss and chose to play with the stiff breeze at their backs. During the first couple of minutes the South Siders looked dangerous, but their attack fell away and for the rest of the half the C.N.R. were on the offensive all the time.

The First Tally

The first score came twelve minutes from the start, when Hobbs drove the ball to Ray in an attempt to clear. The C. N. centre passed it over to Hesketh, who made no mistake about the shot, putting his team in the lead. Then followed a series of narrow escapes for the South Side aggregation, Candy turning aside what looked like certain tallies. Before the end of the half, however, the continued pressure bore results and Ray drove in a beautiful shot that had the goaler beaten all the way. The first period ended 2-0 for the C. N. R.

The second half had not been under way many minutes before the Nationals went even further in the lead, Ray again doing the deed. While the South Side resistance tightened up a bit their opponents continued to have the best part of the play. The lone South Side tally came when Pyper took the ball well up the side before he centred. Carlson, in attempting to clear, kicked the ball into his own citadel. The game grew somewhat rough towards the finish.

W. R. Davies refereed.

The teams lined up as follows:

Canadian Nationals—Gregory, Orchin and Carlson; Miller, Jones and Cozens; Patterson, Hesketh, Ray, Scott and Lynn.

South Side—Candy, Hobbs and Lumley; Hurman, Bryant and Graham; Porter, Phelan, Hamilton, Webster and Pyper.

Squabble Over Soccer Trophy

(Special to Edmonton Journal)

MONTREAL, Que., April 16.—Under a four column heading "discourteous and worse" the Montreal Star says:

"A remarkable situation has developed in dominion football circles. A serious movement is on foot to discard the Connaught cup, looked upon for years as representative of the dominion championship, and presented to the Canadian soccer players by His Royal Highness, the Duke of Connaught, uncle of King George and ...

Dominion Secretary Davidson made such a proposal last autumn and that according to information received from the west and Manitoba soccer section has passed a resolution favoring such a strange course. Fortunately the soccer men of Quebec will not hear of the proposal, though lately one or two local officials, evidently hypnotized by the gaudy glitter of the English association trophy have expressed themselves as leaning toward the royal cup's abandonment ...

CALGARY FANS HEAR LOTS OF HOCKEY RUMORS

And Like Most Spring Time Hockey Reports They're All Wrong

(Special to Edmonton Journal)

CALGARY, Alta., April 16.—Since the report of the probable departure of Lloyd Turner, manager of the Tiger hockey club, from Calgary, to take charge of the Portland team, rumors have gained currency that some members of the team will be taken out of this city next season. The report is flatly denied by Freddie Johnston, president of the Tiger club.

"No players are on the market and the team will be stronger than last winter," said Mr. Johnston.

"We are not doing any selling, but, on the other hand, we are doing some buying. The team will be better than ever before when the next race opens. We have no intention of letting any of our men go and these reports are just silly gossip."

It is known that many attractive offers have been made for Tiger players, and Tommy Gorman, now manager of the New York club, new entrant in the N.H.L., has bid for the entire team or any individual players that might be for sale. He has been advised that there is no Tiger material on the market.

HORSES TO JUMP

The big event at the horse show tonight will be the special jumping event between the old Calgary veteran, "Mademoiselle," owned by Welsh brothers, and "Bay Eagle," George Girvan's spectacular jumper.

There will be a purse of $400 at stake and the contest has aroused a great deal of interest amongst local horsemen.

In the event of the Edmonton entry winning, a match will be arranged with "Barra Lad," pride of the Welsh sta...

Alfie Welsh ...

TWO STRAIGHT WINS FOR BROOKLYN, CINCINNATI AND PHILADELPHIA AMERICANS

Senators and White Sox Get Their First Victories—Luque Pitches Grand Ball for the Reds—Heavy Hitting Won for the Athletics

NEW YORK, April 16.—East and west shared the major league peaks today after the second day's conflicts in both the National and American leagues.

Brooklyn divided the pinnacle in the senior loop with Cincinnati, each having two consecutive victores, while Boston hung at the edge by the thread of its triumph of Tuesday as the result of an incomplete game yesterday ending in the fourth under welcome rain drops with the Giants leading 2 to 0.

By another display of heavy batting artillery the Philadelphia Athletics stepped away to their second success of the campaign and a margin on the entire American league field, but Tris Speaker's Cleveland Indians, forced into idleness by showers, had their single victory of opening day by which to maintain a percentage tie at the pinnacle.

Although the champion run-makers of the inaugural games, the Cleveland and St. Louis teams, were given a vacation by the weather man, the American league continued to produce the most prolific hitting.

Free Hitting at Detroit

Chicago and Detroit collaborated in a carnival of clouting yesterday with 21 safeties, and the Tigers, with a majority of one, could not win because the six pitchers they called to the slab failed to check the base-hit fire of their foes. The Sox took the game nine to six.

The Athletics wasted most of their fifteen hits off Fullerton and Ruffing, leaving eleven base runners stranded, but the five men they brought home were enough to defeat the Red Sox 5 to 3.

The Washington Senators in an ... breviated game of ... their series with ... the curves of S... in the secon...

ZBYSZKO PINS MUNN TO MAT TO WIN TITLE

53-Year-Old Grappler Takes Crown in 14 Minutes of Wrestling

PHILADELPHIA, April 16.—Stanislaus Zybszko, 53-year-old veteran of the mat, again rules the world as champion of wrestlers. He regained the title he lost several years ago by conquering Wayne "Big" Munn, last night in two straight falls and in less than fourte... minutes of actual wrestling...

A clever forearm hold ... fall for the ... the second ... fore...

BRING ON YOUR EASTERN CHALLENGERS!

Daisy Johnson Guard
Elsie Bennie Guard
Dorothy Johnson Forward
Mary Dunn Guard
Hattie Hopkins Forward
Connie Smith Centre
Kate Macrae Guard

When the Grads trot out on the floor at the arena next Tuesday night for the first game of their series with the Toronto Young Women's Hebrew association for the Dominion championship the fans will probably have to rub their eyes in order to convince themselves of the identity of the home town representatives. Only four members of the 1924 team remain—Capt. Connie Smith, the Johnson sisters and Mary Dunn. The remaining members of this year's lineup are Elsie Bennie, Hattie Hopkins and Kate Macrae. It goes without saying that the fans will be highly skeptical as to the ability of this year's septet to maintain the wonderful record set by the Grads in years past, but close followers of the game are of the opinion that Tuesday night's spectators are in for an agreeable surprise.

Mayfair's New Pro

DAVE SPITTAL

Who takes up the position at the South Side golf course formerly held by Art Cruttenden, Alberta open champion. Spittal is a native of St. Andrews, Scotland, but came to Edmonton from Savannah, Georgia, where his brother holds forth as a pro. golfer.

The Grads

"A girls' team, the fabulous Edmonton Grads, was selected last night as Canada's greatest basketball team in the first half of the century. Voting in a Canadian Press poll, sports editors and sportscasters chose as the best the team Percy Page led to dozens of championships in the '20 and '30s."
— Story, Dec. 30, 1950

The Edmonton Grad's story began in 1915 at McDougall Commercial high school. Coach Percy Page was breaking ground by getting women involved in a relatively new sport. His first team was so successful, they decided to stay together after graduation, thus, Edmonton Grads.

By the time the 1920s rolled around they were THE team to beat in Canada and North America, although nobody could. They won national and international titles by the bushel with a couple of unofficial Olympic championships thrown in.

In 1922 the Grads were invited east to play the "world champion" London Shamrocks in a two-game series in which the first game was played under women's rules, the second with men's rules. London won the first game, but were routed by the Grads 41-8 in the second game.

Underwood, the typewriter manufacturer, established an international basketball competition for women, and the first series in 1923 pitted the Grads against the Cleveland Favorite Knits at the Edmonton Arena.

The Grads won the two-game series and, over the next 17 years, compiled a 114-6 record in Underwood competition.

A testimony to the Grads greatness came from none other than basketball inventor James Naismith, who told *The Journal* in 1929: "The magnificent playing of the Grads during past years is leaving an indelible mark upon the young people of Edmonton."

Page was the team's spokesman and was always good for a pre-game quote: "In practice, the girls have been showing a nice brand of basketball."

The Journal supported the Grads throughout their tenure on top of the world, reporting their games with great enthusiasm and detail until the team disbanded in 1940. Attendance was dropping because they had trouble finding good competition and the Royal Canadian Air Force had taken over the Edmonton Arena – their home gym – for the duration of the war.

In 1921 they lost their only provincial championship to the University of Alberta on a technicality when, after losing the game, the university squad protested a Grad player was still a student.

The Grads lost the rematch 29-23.

In all, 38 women played for the Grads. Their leading scorer was Noel MacDonald with 1,874 points, while Margaret MacBurney was the team's veteran, lasting 12 years.

The team won 502 games while losing only 20, at one point in the winning 147 games in a row. By decade's end the Grads were a familiar and important icon in national sporting circles.

ceremony at the legislature while flying 4,000 feet over the city.

***June 19, 1924*:**
The Edmonton Grads women's basketball team leaves on its first European tour, to include the Paris Olympics.

***July 2, 1924*:**
The temperature in Edmonton hits a city record high of 36.7 degrees Celsius.

***July 20, 1924*:**
The Edmonton Grads, in Europe to play in the unofficial Olympic tournament, defeat Strassburg to win the "undisputed championship of the world."

***Aug. 18, 1924*:**
The Edmonton Museum of Art, later the Edmonton Art Gallery, is incorporated.

***Oct. 8, 1924*:**
Edmonton's civic census shows a population of 63,160.

***Oct. 20, 1924*:**
Coal miners across Alberta are returning to work, ending a strike that began in March.

***Nov. 2, 1924*:**
Edmonton's Roman Catholic Archbishop O'Leary lays the cornerstone of St. Joseph's Cathedral (later Basilica).

THE WEATHER
April 3, 1925
FORECAST—Fair and Mild.
Highest Today—60 Degrees.
Lowest Last Night—32 Degrees.
Sun rises Saturday 5.04; sets 7:15.

Edmonton Journal

LAST EDITION

VOL. 21, NO. 220 — EDMONTON, ALBERTA, FRIDAY, APRIL 3, 1925 — TWENTY-FOUR PAGES

WHEAT AGAIN SLUMPS; MAY NOW QUOTED AT $1.38

FRENCH CAPITAL LEVY MOVE CAUSE OF SPLIT IN HERRIOT COALITION

Clementel, Minister of Finance, Resigns from Herriot's Cabinet

PREMIER HIT AT NEW NOTE ISSUE

Senator Anarole De Monzie is Named to Succeed Clementel

PARIS April 3.—A break in the coalition supporting Premier Herriot occurred this afternoon, to deputies comprising the radical left led by Louis Loucheur, deciding to withdraw their support.

The withdrawal which if permitted it will cut the government's chamber vote down to 300 out of a total of 584, is understood to be the cause of the cabinets reported tendency toward a capital levy.

By A. L. BRADFORD
(Special to Edmonton Journal by the British United Press)

PARIS, April 3.—Premier Herriot's cabinet has begun to crumble as the result of the greatest crisis of France's financial history.

M. Clementel minister of finance, already has resigned and the resignation of other members of the cabinet, including Herriot himself, is considered possible if not probable. President Doumergue today signed a decree appointing Senator Anatole DeMonzie to succeed Clementel.

Clementel's resignation came during an all night cabinet meeting predicated by his proposal of yesterday to increase the circulation of ban notes by two billion francs. The sudden resignation of the minister of finance was the outcome of a disagreement between the senate and chamber of deputies and also a disagreement with Premier Herriot.

Change Religious Policy

Premier Herriot and his colleagues in the cabinet after prolonged deliberation have changed their policy toward the Catholic church in France. They have determined to withdraw ...

QUITS CABINET

M. Clementel, who has resigned as minister of finance in France.

FLOOD DANGER IN MANITOBA PASSES

Assiniboine Drops at Portage and Brandon; Snow and Rain Fall

WINNIPEG, April 3.—Lower temperatures during the night brought about slight improvement in the flood situation along the Assiniboine valley today. Portage La Prairie ... the river was ...

JULY PRICE NOW ABOVE MAY FUTURE

WINNIPEG, April 3—Favorable reports from the United States winter wheat belt, lower cables and a lack of buying power resulted in wheat and coarse grains receding to new low levels today. May wheat led the decline dropping nine cents from the high for the day and closing 7½ below Thursday's close. It closed at $1.38¾.

Rye, with a drop of 9 cents from the previous close, led the coarse grains in the decline.

SUPPLEMENTARY ESTIMATES HAS VOTE FOR COAL

$50,000 Included for Moving of Alberta Fuel to the East

(Special to Edmonton Journal)

OTTAWA, April 3. — In the supplementary estimates a vote of $50,000 will be made to assist in the removal of Alberta coal to the central markets of Ontario.

One hundred thousand tons is the quantity proposed to be brought down, and Howard Stutchbury, Alberta fuel commissioner, who has been here in connection with the scheme has gone to Montreal to consult the Canadian National. Arrangements are being made to move it in train lots and to carefully check up the exact cost of transportation.

SUN YAT SEN'S RUSSIAN COFFIN PROVES SHODDY

Will Not Be Buried in Casket Like 'Friend Lenine's'

PEKING, April 2.—The last wish of Dr. Sun Yat Sen, first president of the Chinese republic, that he be buried in a bronze crystal coffin "like my friend Lenine," went unfulfilled yesterday. The bronze ...

MAKE TEST OF AIR SHIPS FOR EMPIRE LINES

Experiences of R-33 Will Form Basis for New Aircraft

GIANTS OF THE SKY NOW BEING BUILT

First Services Will Be to Egypt and British India

By CHARLES M. McCANN

LONDON, April 3.—Six weeks of experiments, from which is to grow a British empire air service, connecting South Africa, India, Australia, New Zealand and Canada with the mother country, have begun with the first flight of a dirigible over England since the fatal cruise of the ZR-2.

The army dirigible R-33 sailed from Cardington to Pullham yesterday and is resting at her mooring mast. She is covered with contrivances to test air pressure, gas pressure, wind resistance, torts and the other stresses and conditions that go to make up the equation of safety in the air.

Effect On New Ships

The results of six weeks of tests will be utilized on the construction of two 5,000,000,000 cubic feet airships which are now being built. Twice as large as the Los Angeles, these vessels probably will inaugurate an airship service to India in 1927. The R-36 is being reconditioned to inaugurate an experimental service to India by way of Egypt next year. If the flights of the R-36 and R-33 are successful, the two new ships, each able to carry 100 passengers at tremendous speed because they and the crews will be housed within the hull instead of in gondolas, will begin a regular service to India.

The first stop will be at Cairo, 36 hours from London. Four days will suffice to reach Karachi in India. Eventually the route will be extended to Singapore, which is to become a tremendous air base as well as a naval centre.

SUFFERS ANTI-CLIMAX

Mrs. Dorothy Muriel Dennistoun, central figure in the recent sensational London suit, who virtually lost her case when the judge reversed the verdict of the jury.

MRS. DENNISTOUN LOSES

Judge Reverses Verdict of Jury

LONDON, April 3.—Justice Sir Henry McCardie delivered his reserved judgment in the Dennistoun case this morning. He held that the alleged agreement for Mrs. Dorothy Muriel Dennistoun's support ... ruled that Mrs. Dennistoun's claim for damages for breach of contract had failed.

The judgment sets aside the verdict of the jury late last month awarding Mrs. Dennistoun £5,000, or nearly $25,000 for the alleged ...

FEARS SON IS STOWAWAY ON THE REPULSE

(Special to Edmonton Journal)

LONDON, April 3. — Mrs. Margaret Browning has reported to the Southsea police that her nine-year-old son Geoffrey disappeared last Saturday. She believes he is accompanying the Prince of Wales as a stowaway on the Repulse.

FINAL TESTS FOR FORT NORMAN OIL

Imperial Oil's Plans Will Depend on Results This Summer

CALGARY, April 3.—The Imperial Oil company will seek for a definite decision of the oil prospects in the Canadian Arctic this summer. The company, which has been drilling at Fort Norman since 1921, hopes this summer to establish the true worth of the field. It is known that a party under Angus Sutherland, who superintended the operations last summer, will leave here for Fort Norman as soon as it is possible to travel. Going in by way of Nelson they will avoid Great Slave Lake and will be able to reach their destination earlier than if they waited for the ice to clear from this body of water. With the best of luck, however, it is not likely that the party will reach Fort Norman before July 1.

When the party arrives at Fort Norman they will continue drilling the No. 2 well which is now down 800 feet. They will push the hole down another 500 feet, to the same depth at which oil was struck in No. 1 well. Great care has been exercised in drilling this hole in order not to freeze in the casing as happened in the No. 1 well.

The company's plans for the future in the far north will depend largely on the result of this summer's drilling.

STEWART WILL RUN IN WEST EDMONTON

Hon. Charles Stewart will be a candidate for nomination in the coming West Edmonton Liberal convention. It is semi-officially announced in the city today. It is said that a letter has been received by a prominent ... in the city from the ...

INDUSTRIES OF BRITAIN PROBE OWN FAILURES

Employers and Employes Study Why Other Nations Get Contracts

FIVE OF GREATEST INDUSTRIES CONFER

Railways to Join Cotton Coal, Ship and Engineering Trades

By HERBERT BAILEY
(Special to Edmonton Journal by British United Press)

LONDON, April 3.—A serious effort to find out what is wrong with British industry and why Britain is finding it increasingly difficult to compete in the markets of the world with other nations has been begun with the bringing together of employers and employes in the four leading industries in the country—cotton spinning, coal mining, ship building and engineering. It is expected that within a few days the railways will also come into this unique conference.

Seek Underlying Reason

The object of the gathering is to get down to the bed rock of the reasons why Britain is thus lagging behind and to discover some remedy.

It is the first time in the history of British industry that such a conference has been called and its meetings are being watched with the greatest interest not only by the trades concerned, by employers in allied industries and by labor generally, but also by a large number of professional men and men of small income whose living is affected by the present depression. Never before has an attempt been made to conduct such a thorough and searching investigation.

Use Strike Less

There is an evident tendency on the part of both employers and trades unions to reach some sure plan of understanding and the latter are showing less and less inclination to resort to the strike measures that are admittedly wasteful and costly. The aim of the delegates is that both employers and workers shall mutually prosper.

The recent speeches of the premier at Birmingham and in the house of commons have given a fillip to industry but the stark fact ... warranted ...

THE WEATHER
April 11, 1925
FORECAST—FAIR; COOLER.
Highest Today—53 Degrees.
Lowest last night—32 degrees.
Barometer, 27.70—Falling.
Sun Rises Sunday 5:45; Sets 7:26.
Sun Rises Monday 5:43; Sets 7:28.

Edmonton Journal

LAST EDITION

VOL. 21, NO. 227 — EDMONTON, ALBERTA, SATURDAY, APRIL 11, 1925 — FORTY-TWO PAGES

WHEAT JUMPS 12 CENTS IN WILD MARKET TODAY

BREAD CRUSTS, CUP OF TEA IS MINER'S RATION

Relief Committee at Sydney, N. S., Short $3,000 Per Day

15,000 STILL ARE NEAR STARVATION

Appeal Again Made for Help to Alleviate Deep Distress

By PAUL R. MALLON
(Copyright 1925 by United Press. Copyright in Canada)

SYDNEY, N.S., April 11.—On Easter eve this colony of misery—where a month's coal strike has thrown 3,000 people upon the threshold of starvation—relief chiefs announced they have about reached the end of their meagre charity resources.

More funds must be immediately forthcoming if the increasing number of destitute women and children who became public charges when their incomes ceased with the strike five weeks ago, are to be saved.

$3,000 Daily Shortage

The announcement was made by Father M. A. MacAdam, village priest in charge of the relief committee who said the organization now was nearly $3,000 a day short of necessary rations.

"If we get a cup of tea and a crust of bread to the 15,000 who depend upon us for Easter, we will do well," he said. "Our present slender resources and increasing task, while not affecting our resolution to stand by the needy, present a staggering difficulty, the end of which I cannot foresee."

The depths to which some residents of the Sydney district have sunk in this four-year-old struggle between the coal miners and operators was purported to be shown in a published affidavit by James Caine, caretaker of the Whitney Pier community house, who swore that he had seen between 100 and 200 persons picking over the city dump for food long before the strike began. The affidavit was printed by a labor newspaper. When confronted with it, Caine told me that "every word of it is true."

No Proof Evident

There are no miners living in that neighborhood and when I asked William Baxter, superintendent of the ... Mason Construction company ... leading resident of Sydney ... said, "You will find ... in most towns ... dump pickers ..." Upon ...

CHIEF FIGURES IN FRENCH CRISIS

Edouard Herriot, on the left, who resigned with his cabinet last night after eleven months as premier of France. Paul Painleve, mentioned as a probable successor, is shown on the right.

HERRIOT SUPPORTERS WILL DOMINATE NEW MINISTRY BELIEF IN PARIS TODAY

French Cabinet's Resignation Came Last Night After Adverse Vote in Senate; Painleve Talked of as Likely to Be the Next Premier

PARIS, April 11.—France, it appears, is to have another cabinet largely of Herriot persuasion.

As President Doumergue today pursued his conference in order to effect a quick solution of the parliamentary tangle growing out of Herriot's defeat and resignation yesterday, the conviction grew that the new government will be dominated by the left groups.

Leaders of both the right and left ... office where the letter of the ministry's resignation was drafted.

From the foreign office the defeated ministers, headed by M. Herriot, went to the Elysee palace, where they were immediately admitted to the office of the president. M. Herriot placed the resignation in ...

(Continued on Page Two)

GIRL DANCER SLAIN ON OWN DOORSTEP

London Shocked by Murder; Scotland Yard Hot on Trail

LONDON, April 11.—The Scotland Yard authorities are detaining an unnamed man in connection with the death yesterday of Grace Blakeley, a pretty 16-year-old dancing teacher, whose body was found with her throat cut Thursday night huddled on the steps of her mother's home in the fashionable West Kensington district.

The mystery of the case, which previously had been set down as one of assault, deepened when the police came into possession of a letter which reached the girl Thursday morning and which, they say, is of the greatest importance. Its contents are being closely guarded.

Prior to the detention of the man today, Scotland Yard had announced ...

Old Country ...

THINK VOTE ON BUDGET APT TO BE BAROMETER

Ottawa Correspondent of Montreal Gazette Does a Little Delving

PROGRESSIVES ARE IN UNHAPPY STATE

Effect of Split Within Ranks May Not Help Old Parties

MONTREAL, April 11.—A special despatch to the Montreal Gazette from its parliamentary correspondent at Ottawa says:

"The coming division on the budget will be awaited with eagerness for more reasons than one. Most of course, to the size of the government's majority, which is natural, for should it be defeated an early dissolution will naturally follow. But the nature of the lineup in the division will be important for the further fact that it will show the effect wrought by certain restless elements among the Progressives.

Attacks From Within

"There is a tendency in some quarters to dismiss these as unimportant, but this would be a mistake. Today Progressivism is being damaged much more by the attacks of some of its erstwhile members and allies than by members of the two old parties. This makes such attacks much more difficult to answer. A similar situation exists in the Ontario legislature where some of the worst thorns in the side of the Progressives are former members of their own group.

"In the discussion of the personnel of the ocean rates committee, J. T. Shaw was cutting in his references to the Progressives, and in his speech on the budget, W. Irvine criticized roundly their attitude on certain questions of policy. During the 1921 campaign, both of these members received a strong measure of Progressive support, and while nominally one has always been known as an Independent, still they have cooperated closely with the Progressives on most matters.

Rest Of Ginger Group

"Ten of the eleven other members of the ginger group were elected as ...

PLAGUE CAUSES CANCELLATION PRINCE'S VISIT

Trip to Nigeria Called Off; Crowds Might Spread the Disease

AT GRAND PALAVER BY NATIVE CHIEFS

Scene Was Perfect Riot of Gold on Notables' Dresses

NAKWA, Gold Coast, West Africa, April 11.—The Prince of Wales will remain in the Gold Coast colony until April 24 owing to an outbreak of the plague at Lagos, his next contemplated stopping place on the coast, it was announced today.

The prince may fill in the time by a visit to the northern territories of the Gold Coast, beyond Ashanti.

The journey to Nigeria, of which Lagos is a principal port, has not been cancelled because of anxiety for the royal party, it was stated, but in view of the possibility that the epidemic might spread among the great crowds which would gather to greet the prince at Lagos.

Taking advantage of the postponement of the prince's departure from the Gold Coast colony, 200 men from the battle cruiser Repulse, will go into the interior and visit the town of Kumassi for a few days.

KUMASSI, Ashanti, April 11.—The Prince of Wales yesterday met the chiefs of the Ashanti at a grand palaver, following his arrival here yesterday from Secondee. The chiefs presented the prince with an address of welcome and a gold duplicate of the Ashanti sword of state, made by local goldsmiths.

A noted figure among the chiefs who greeted the prince was former King Prempeh, who was exiled by the British in 1900 to Seychelles islands in the Indian ocean. He was released last year and yesterday was a member of the reception committee. Prempeh was the only native on the royal dais.

When the prince drove up to the gathering of the chiefs ...

WHEAT GAINS 12 CENTS IN WILD RUSH

WINNIPEG, April 11.—In one of the wildest markets of the year, both wheat and coarse grains recovered marked gains today. May wheat topping the list at an advance of 11⅞ to $1.66, the final figures for the day. The high for the day was $1.66½.

In coarse grains the advance ranged from 2⅝ to 5⅛, rye recording the high point. The bullish wheat report of the United States government released last Thursday, sent prices soaring. The United States official report indicated a large decrease in the estimated yield throughout the winter grain belt.

IN CLASH

E. M. Trowern — A. J. Banfield

INSURANCE COMPANY BOSSES RETAILERS?

Dominion Secretary Maintains Charge in Reply to A. J. Banfield

OTTAWA, April 11.—E. M. Trowern, who yesterday announced his resignation as secretary and general manager of the ... Association of ... August ...

SOVIET TO USE BRITISH LABOR IN PROPAGANDA

Agreement Between Trades Unionists Is Regarded With Deep Suspicion

IS THIN EDGE OF PROPAGANDA WEDGE

Labor Deplores Herriot's Fall; Tories Pleased at Senate's Action

By HERBERT BAILEY
(Special to Edmonton Journal by British United Press)

LONDON, April 11.—"Their bolshevist masters in Soviet Russia will in London extreme delight the report of the conference held between Russian and British trade unionists that has just been published."

So writes the London Daily Express this morning in a trenchant article in which it denounces the deliberations, of the conference and adversely criticizes the agreement reached by the delegates at their gathering. Several aspects of this agreement are arousing the gravest suspicion here not only in circles outside the great labor organization but among the more conservative of the rank and file of the trades unionists themselves.

Propaganda Wedge

The agreement provides for the free interchange of documents between the organized labor bodies of the two countries and is generally regarded and feared will result in opening wide the door for political propaganda which is exactly what the Soviet government is most anxious to accomplish, though it had previously agreed to refrain from distributing it further in British territory. It was propaganda in the form of the Zinovieff letter that brought about the downfall of the Labor government in Britain and revealed how strong was public opinion in Britain against such action. The possibility of renewing its circulation under the official cloak of the trades union ...

The Crash

"There is the most ample warrant for facing the new year with courage and confidence and to its readers The Journal extends its best wishes for their happiness and prosperity in the months that lie ahead."
— Editorial, Dec. 31, 1929

"New York and Toronto Stock Exchanges in State of Panic," screamed *The Journal*'s front-page headline on Oct. 29, 1929. "Many Edmonton Citizens Who have Been 'Dabbling in Market' See Profits Turned Into Heavy Loses as Prices Head Toward Basement," said the subhead.

It was Black Tuesday. Later, it became notorious as the catalyst of the Great Depression of the next decade.

In reality, however, the crash was merely a symptom of various economic weaknesses and excesses of the previous 10 years.

The Journal faithfully recorded the events of that day in a fairly dispassionate way. It was big news, but hardly anything that would single-handedly ruin one of the most prosperous years in the city's history.

Edmonton was not a corporate centre. It served the agricultural community. The high rollers who played the market paid their money and took their chances. A one-sentence editorial on Dec. 30 noted: "One consolation of those who lost money in Wall Street may lie in the fact they helped to make possible the $100,000,000 distributed as Christmas presents to brokers."

An economic analysis in the Dec. 31 edition noted: "Taking all the barometers, the forthcoming year should be a good one for the Dominion and there is no reason to look for a serious depression in trade in 1930."

In fairness to the editors of 1929, there were no legions of professional economists available to crunch numbers. There were no world computer links or think tanks to correlate and analyse data and offer dissenting or cautionary predictions.

All newspapers had upon which to rely were the reassurances of government, bank and business officials. Southam correspondent Charles Bishop quoted an unnamed government source reacting to the market crash. "Conditions are thoroughly sound. Business is exceptionally good and even if it only reverts to normal everything will be satisfactory. Banking conditions were never on a firmer basis."

The Journal believed the rhetoric and didn't even acknowledge the market crash editorially.

Still, that same day, on the same page, near the story announcing the Ku Klux Klan was setting up their district headquarters in Edmonton was another economic story foreshadowing the coming economic winter.

The wheat crop, for all intents, had failed.

The unusually dry summer cut Alberta grain production to half the 155 million bushels reaped in 1928.

"But it will be worth more money, both because of the smaller yield and the better quality," the reporter stated – incorrectly.

***Nov. 9, 1924*:**
CNR train fare from Edmonton to Vancouver is $45; it costs $92 to go east to Toronto.

***Dec. 8, 1924*:**
Ken Blatchford is returned for a second term as mayor in Edmonton's civic election.

***March 31, 1925*:**
The T. Eaton Company announces plans to set up shop in Edmonton and open a groceteria.

***May 16, 1925*:**
Sir Frederick Haultain, Chief Justice of Saskatchewan and former premier of the North-West Territories, is awarded an honourary degree at the University of Alberta.

***Sept. 1, 1925*:**
Horace Campbell joins *The Journal*'s circulation department. He becomes circulation manager in 1934.

***Dec. 14, 1925*:**
Ken Blatchford is elected to a third term as Edmonton's mayor.

***May 10, 1926*:**
Edmonton city council votes $400 to carve two runways on Hagmann farm for city's first "air harbour."

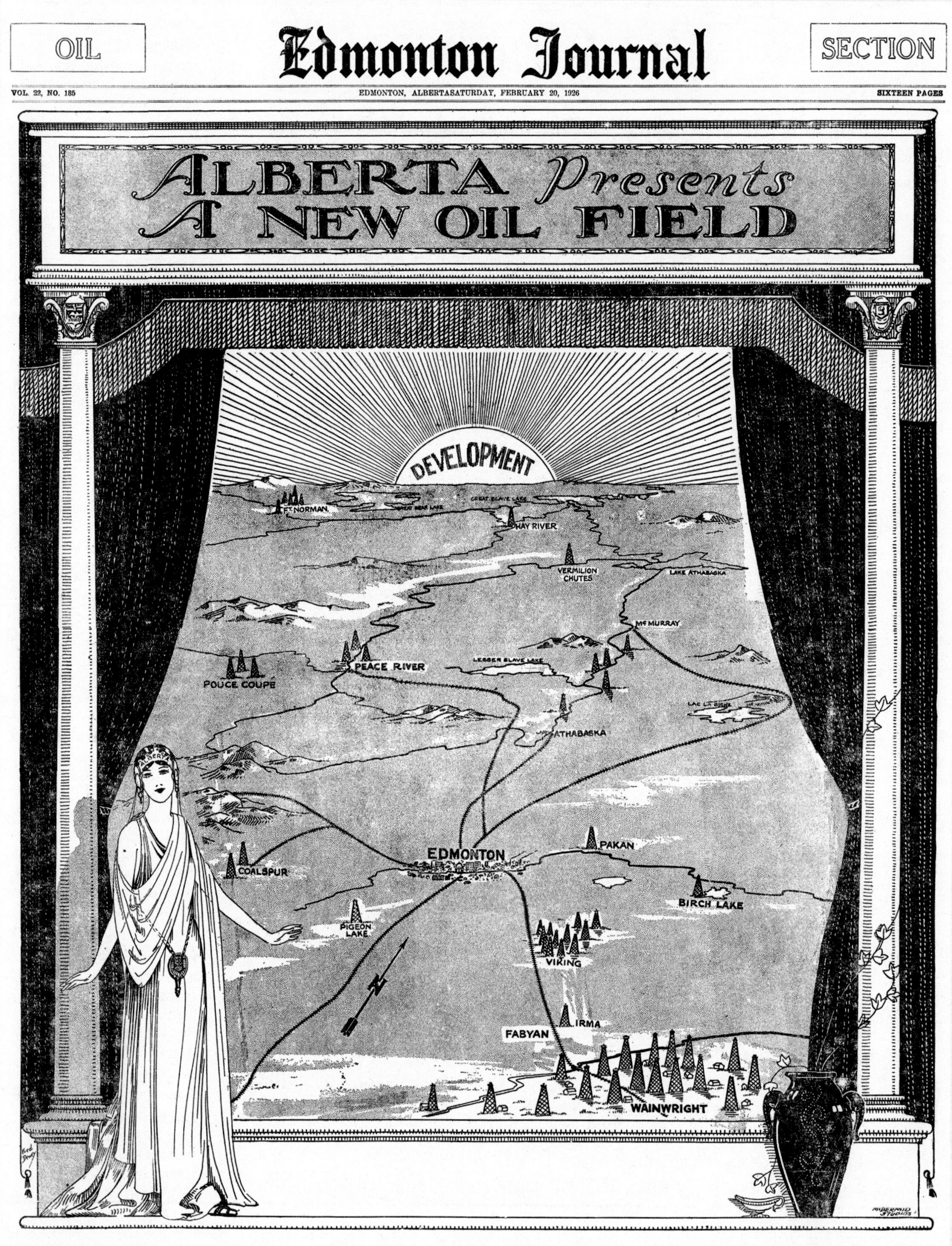

OIL — **Edmonton Journal** — SECTION

VOL. 22, NO. 185 — EDMONTON, ALBERTASATURDAY, FEBRUARY 20, 1926 — SIXTEEN PAGES

ALBERTA Presents A NEW OIL FIELD

DEVELOPMENT
FT. NORMAN
GREAT SLAVE LAKE
HAY RIVER
VERMILION CHUTES
LAKE ATHABASKA
McMURRAY
PEACE RIVER
POUCE COUPE
LESSER SLAVE LAKE
LAC LA BICHE
ATHABASKA
EDMONTON
PAKAN
COALSPUR
BIRCH LAKE
PIGEON LAKE
VIKING
IRMA
FABYAN
WAINWRIGHT

ND-3-3102 Glenbow Archives

Special 1926 "Oil Edition" *Journals* ready for shipment to New York to promote the province on the New York Stock Exchange.

Journal writers also didn't know the average wages in the city and province were dangerously low. The federal finance department had calculated it took an income of $1,200 to $1,500 for a "decent standard of living." The average per capita income in Alberta in 1929 was $548. Few people had any income safety nets.

There were also hints in the paper over the year's last two months that things were not as rosy as the experts were saying. The classified ad section of the Nov. 1 edition listed 43 jobs available in the city. On Dec. 30, there were fewer than 20 jobs advertised, most of them for maids and cooks.

Suddenly, *The Journal* discovered there was an unemployment problem in Edmonton. The first story was Dec. 20. "Premier Brownlee and Mayor Douglas are to have a conference on the unemployment situation at the weekend … Some 200 unemployed men paraded to the parliament buildings Thursday afternoon."

The next day, a municipal-city plan was announced to register jobless men and put them to work clearing underbrush in the city. "The work, Mayor Douglas stressed, is being done purely as a relief measure to obviate the necessity for a 'dole' or bread-line system."

By Dec. 27 the plan grew to clearing farmland in the district.

" 'By this scheme, unemployment should be virtually eliminated,' was the mayor's comment."

Then, on Dec. 28, a new fly augered into the ointment. Unemployed men outside the city heard of the program and started flocking here.

"The influx, according to prominent officials in the city relief department, may threaten the whole plan for giving work to unemployed here."

***June 16, 1926*:**
Ottawa issues first ever licence for a municipal airfield to Edmonton.

***In 1928*:**
A stenographer at *The Journal* earns $12 a week. The paper starts an oratorical contest.

***Aug. 15, 1928*:**
"Taking another forward step in the handling of traffic problems, the city is arranging for use of coloured concrete to mark pedestrian safety zones at important downtown intersections," says a *Journal* report from City Hall.

***Aug. 15, 1928*:**
"FORMER D.S.C.R. CHIEF BLOWN TO DEATH." A headline without a story.

***Dec. 4, 1928*:**
***The Journal* appoints Perry J. Giffen business manager.**

***Dec. 11, 1928*:**
Edmonton voters say "no" in a plebiscite to spend $23,000 for airport upgrades. The next year, on Dec. 9, voters OK $35,000 for improvements.

THE WEATHER
April 7, 1925
FORECAST—FAIR AND MILD.
Highest Today—52 Degrees.
Lowest last night—34 degrees.
Barometer—27.74, Steady.
Sun rises Wednesday 5:54; sets 7:19.

Edmonton Journal

LAST EDITION

VOL. 21, NO. 223 EDMONTON, ALBERTA, TUESDAY, APRIL 7, 1925 EIGHTEEN PAGES

MILLION DOLLAR LIQUOR RING RAIDED IN CHICAGO

PRISONERS GIVE NEW LIGHT ON ONTARIO BRIBE

Charles Matthews Tells of Cigar Box That Held Thousands

PETER SMITH GIVES COMMITTEE NEWS

Declares Never Got $15,000 He Pleaded Guilty to Receiving

TORONTO, April 7.—The most sensational evidence of Charles B. Matthews, former assistant provincial treasurer, taken by a sub-committee of the public accounts committee at Portsmouth penitentiary yesterday, and submitted to the full committee at its hearing this morning, dealt with rumors heard by Mr. Matthews that during the last says of the Hearst government there was a mysterious cigar box around the parliament buildings which contained a large sum of money.

Mr. Matthews, on advice of counsel, declined to state from whom he got the information concerning the cigar box.

Matthews also stated that he had heard Mr. McGarry, the provincial treasurer in the Hearst government, got money from somewhere.

Another sensational bit of testimony was the statement by Peter Smith, provincial treasurer in the Drury government, that he had been offered $15,000 by the late Colonel Cooper Mason, of the Home Bank.

He declared that he had refused the sum and had never received anything from the Home Bank.

Loan Was Made

Matthews said he remembered a little about a loan which went through in September, 1919, a few weeks before the defeat of the Hearst government. He had been told about the loan by Thomas McGarry, then treasurer. He said that Mr. Haney, of the Home Bank, had come several times to see Mr. McGarry before the loan was made. Mason met McGarry in his private office. He did not remember anyone else from the Home Bank ever being present.

Matthews said he did not know that anyone on behalf of the Home Bank gave any money to Mr. McGarry.

He declined to state who gave him the information about the cigar box. He was not told definitely how much money was in the box.

"What were you told?" he was asked.

"It was some thousands," he could not remember the amount but it was not ten thousand. He was told there was a sum of money "larger than would be accustomed to be lying around Mr. McGarry's office." It was a large sum, he said, but no definite sum was mentioned.

Was At Time of Loan

He did not know that it was left by anyone; he only heard of it being there. It was about the time of the Home Bank loan. Mr. Matthews said he had not told Peter Smith anything about the box.

W. E. N. Sinclair started the examination of Peter Smith, who, in reply to questions, said he had never had any dealings with the Home Bank. Mr. Sinclair said there was evidence that $15,000 had gone to Mr. Smith.

"Well, I have been tried for that," said Mr. Smith.

"You pleaded guilty?"

"Yes, but I am not on trial this morning."

"I am going to ask you on what occasion and at what place did you receive this $15,000?"

"I might say to the committee that I never received $15,000 and never heard of it until a year ago."

Never Got $15,000

"You pleaded guilty to the receipt of $15,000 which you never got?"

"Yes."

Mr. Smith explained that he was thinking of his wife and family.

"Were you offered the $15,000?"

"I was."

"Where?"

"In my office."

"Who offered it to you?"

"Colonel Mason. I thought it was offered as a rebate to the province and said I would call in the auditor. When I said I was going to put it to the credit of the province he refused to pay it and I refused to take it."

Witness did not know what form the money was in.

W. E. Raney asked about the "legals" alleged to have been paid to Mr. Smith.

On advice of counsel, Mr. Smith refused to answer any questions concerning them. However, he said he had legals and got them on the sale of his own and brother's bonds. He sold them for $7,000 and got seven one-thousand-dollar bills.

Smith said he had pleaded guilty to the charge, because "I had spent all my money in fighting and the cards were stacked against me." Smith, "that under the circum-

"It seemed to me," continued Mr. stances, being convicted, and the fact that I was playing a lone hand, and knowing that public opinion was against me, and the press against me, and as I had already been found guilty on one charge, there was no jury in the world, I thought, would ever acquit me on any other charge."

KURDISH REBELLION SPREADS TO PERSIA

LONDON, April 7.—An Exchange Telegraph despatch from Constantinople reports that the Kurdish insurrection movement has spread over the Turko-Persian frontier. The Teheran government has rushed troops to that locality.

RE-OPEN CONSULATE

VANCOUVER, April 7.—The French government has decided to reopen the consulate here which has been closed since 1907. P. Suzor will be in charge.

PRINCE NOW SAILING FOR GOLD COAST

FREETOWN, West Africa, April 7.—The Prince of Wales embarked this morning after farewell ceremonies ashore, and the Repulse sailed at 12:10 o'clock for Takaradi, on the Gold Coast. This port has been developed only recently, and the Repulse will be the first large vessel to enter the new harbor.

The British heir arrived in Freetown yesterday on his South African tour and was the guest of the governor last night.

GET GASOLINE FROM ALBERTA IS PREDICTION

Prospects Promising for Supply, Says Imperial Oil Vice-President

(Special to Edmonton Journal)

TORONTO, April 7.—Prospects for a supply of gasoline from oil fields in western Canada, particularly in the Calgary area, were promising, Victor Ross, vice-president of the Imperial Oil company and president of the Canadian club, told members of the Young Men's Canadian Club last night.

Future sources of gasoline supply were a real problem for Canada and it was essential, he said, that everything possible be done to develop Canadian fields.

In this connection several million dollars had been expended by his company, he said.

ONTARIO ESTIMATES TOTAL $43,822,302

TORONTO, April 7.—The main estimates tabled in the Ontario legislature last night total $43,822,302, all departments with the exceptions of agriculture and health showing decreases. Agriculture estimates total $2,368,095 as compared with $2,361,244 last year.

ST. CATHARINES TO VOTE AGAIN MAY 4

ST. CATHARINES, Ont., April 7.—Following the suggestion of Judge Campbell contained in his report on the conduct of the municipal elections last December in which he found irregularities, the city council yesterday decided to hold a complete civic election on May 4. All bylaws, including a daylight saving measure, will be voted upon again.

BILL THE BARBER IN FIFTH ESCAPE

WEYBURN, Sask., April 7.—Wasyl Mackenczuk, better known as "Bill the Barber" jumped through a window of the mental hospital last night and made good his getaway. This makes his fifth escape, and the third from the hospital at Weyburn.

He has succeded so far in evading a force of twenty-five from the hospital and a squad of provincial police.

PASSES BUCK BACK TO OTTAWA AGAIN

REGINA, April 7.—The Saskatchewan government has intimated to the federal minister of labor that the responsibility for the launching of a prosecution against an alleged fruit combine in western Canada should rest on the federal government, it was stated today from the office of the provincial attorney-general. That such a combine did exist, it was stated, was indicated in the Duncan Lewis report.

SEE BY RADIO WITH "PRISMATIC RING"

American Inventor Claims Transmission of Living Pictures Through Ether

BALTIMORE, Md., April 7.—Invention of a device known as "the prismatic ring" will enable radio fans to see the next Olympic games as well as hear their cheering, it is predicted in a report to the American Chemical society, in session here today by the inventor, C. F. Francis Jenkins, of Washington, D.C.

He also promises that the stay-at-homes may see football or baseball games, a regatta or baby parades while these things are actually happening.

POPE GRANTS AUDIENCE

ROME, April 7.—Pope Pius granted an audience to a California pilgrimage led by the Rev. Father Crowley.

SHIPPING LINES ASKED TO GIVE FULL DETAILS

Special Committee of the House Starts Probe of Ocean Rates

THROWING PRESTON REPORT IN DISCARD

Drayton Thinks Government Counsel Indicates He Has Weak Case

(By Canadian Press)

OTTAWA, April 7.—For an hour, the special committee of the house which is to investigate the contract with Sir William Petersen and the control of ocean freight rates discussed its procedure and then adjourned till Friday of next week when witnesses for the shipping men will first be heard.

At the outset, Andrew McMaster, of Brome, was appointed chairman of the committee.

H. J. Symington, K.C., counsel for the dominion government, asked for the production of a mass of documents relating to the workings of the North Atlantic shipping conference.

Sir Henry Drayton, while declaring that the fullest possible information should be available, added that the government was apparently throwing the Preston report into the discard. Evidently, he added, the government had no case to submit and Mr. Symington's request was a sad confession of weakness.

Counsel for the shipping companies pressed for the examination, in the first place, of W. T. R. Preston.

The chairman ruled that Mr. Symington should be given the information he asked for and that witnesses for the shipping companies should be heard first. He observed that ample opportunity would be given for the examination and cross-examination of Mr. Preston.

POSTMASTER'S LOT NOT A HAPPY ONE

Strange State of Affairs in Newfoundland Revealed in the Assembly

ST. JOHN'S, Nfld., April 7.—A tragedy of errors is the only name for the story related by Sir John Crosbie, minister of finance and customs, in the house of assembly yesterday in connection with the conditions found existing in the postal service following the election of the present government. An investigation was held as a result of which several officials were suspended. In eighty offices inspected a shortage was found of about $28,000, and the outgoing administration, it was reported, had left about $88,000 worth of bills in the postal telegraphs to be paid.

The minister vividly described two offices which he had personally inspected. He found that a clerk in the Humber area had handled as much as $282,000 in eight months, his only assistant being a boy. His daily issue of money orders was sometimes for an amount of $15,000 and frequently he had on hand $8,000 or $10,000 in cash. He had asked headquarters again and again for a safe, but his request was refused, and in order to guard the cash the distracted official concealed it in a disused stove, in a biscuit box under a heap of rubbish, in holes in the walls and floor, and some of it he buried in the ground. This man was receiving a salary of $75 a month. His shortage was $7,000. The minister expressed the belief that he was the most honest man in the service.

In another case in the same area, a postal clerk who never had been officially appointed handled, under similar conditions, $372,000 in about two years, and although his shortage appeared to be about $10,000, there was nothing to indicate that it was due to dishonesty. To this official, headquarters eventually gave a safe to which everyone in the office had a key. Until the safe arrived the best repository for the cash was a corner of the office where the money lay hidden under an accumulation of rubbish and mail bags. He too will probably receive a clean bill of health. In fact, the minister said himself that these officials deserved a Victoria Cross.

HAIG MAY COME WEST

CALGARY, April 7.—Art Wakelyn, provincial secretary of the Alberta G.W.V.A., received word Tuesday from Dominion Secretary C. Grant MacNeil there was a possibility that Earl Haig would be able to visit the west.

ROBINS ALREADY NESTING

Jack Miner Finds Four With Eggs

KINGSVILLE, Ont., April 7.—Jack Miner last week found four robins' nests on his bird sanctuary each with eggs. This according to the naturalist's statement was three weeks earlier than other records set in this way on the Miner game preserve. Besides the four nests which were found several other robins were seen making their nests. He says the robins starting to nest so early is a sure indication these "early birds" will raise three families this year. Several morning doves' nests were found but this is not unusual for this species of bird, as young doves were found last April 14.

Along the lake shore in front of Kingsville the flock of wild whistling swans are continually increased in number. During the week, the flock has increased to 2,000 by actual count. Several bird lovers and authorities from New York, Boston and Pittsburgh are visiting here these days to see the swans and geese which are in countless numbers on the bird sanctuary.

IS CHAIRMAN

A. R. McMaster, M.P. for Brome, elected chairman of the commons committee probing ocean freight rates.

ON WAY TO WORK WITHIN 5 HOURS

New Settlers Do Not Have to Wait Long for Jobs

(Special to Edmonton Journal)

WINNIPEG, April 7.—One of the finest bodies of new settlers to arrive in western Canada in many years reached Winnipeg this morning on a special Canadian National train from Halifax.

The party comprised the following nationalities: British, 147 (one Irish, three Scotch, 143 English); Hungarians, 82; Czecho-Slovaks, 42; Jugo-Slavs, 30; Roumanians, 5; Norwegians, 4; Swiss, 4; Russians, 3; Poles, 3; Greeks, 2; Danes, 2; Swedes, 1; Bulgarians, 1; Finn, 1.

By provinces the party will be distributed as follows: British Columbia, 20; Alberta, 48; Saskatchewan, 66; Manitoba, 198.

By noon today, less than five hours after their arrival in Winnipeg, the majority of the newcomers who were in search of farm work had been directed to farmers in the prairie provinces who had made applications for farm help to the Canadian National farm help service, several of the newcomers expressing themselves pleased with the prospect of work and wages awaiting them so soon after their arrival.

JAPANESE PREMIER TO RESIGN SHORTLY

(Special to Edmonton Journal)

TOKIO, April 7.—Viscount Taka Akira Kato, premier of Japan, is about to resign following the recent resignations of the ministers of commerce and railways.

N. Y. FIRM SECURES BIG TRUCK ORDER

(Special to Edmonton Journal)

BUENOS AIRES, April 7.—A New York firm has been awarded a contract to furnish Buenos Aires with $360,000 worth of motor trucks. The American firm won the contract in competition with German and British concerns.

WAS GOVERNMENT, NOT LEGISLATURE

Logan Corrects Statement in House on Coal Duty Approval

(Special to Edmonton Journal)

OTTAWA, April 7.—Before the budget was taken up this afternoon a small shower of questions were poured on the government. Mr. Campbell queried about a rural credits policy based on the report of Dr. Tory.

"Frankly," answered Hon. J. A. Robb, "I have not yet had time to read the report."

"When will an old age pension bill be ready?" queried Mr. Irvine.

"If you will look at the order paper you'll see that notice of it is given," Mr. Murdock replied.

H. J. Logan corrected a statement of his yesterday when, interrupted by Andrew MacMaster, he said that the "legislature" of Alberta had approved the increased duty on coal. It was the government not the legislature that did it.

"A premier is not necessarily a government," asserted E. J. Garland.

"When the premier speaks, the government speaks," responded Mr. Logan.

Mr. Meighen wanted to know when there is to be a report from the commissioners from parliament who went to Wembley.

Mr. Robb could not say.

Budget Debate

D. A. MacKinnon, Liberal member for Queens, P.E.I., spoke on the budget and held that according to the trade statistics business conditions throughout the country are not bad.

J. D. Chaplin, Conservative member for Lincoln, was severely critical of the budget and of the government. He was in favor of the added protection on slack coal. But, he asked, if protection was good for the miners of Nova Scotia and Alberta, why wasn't it good for the workers of Ontario and Quebec. The government had been clubbed into giving protection on coal.

NEW DIABETES "CURE"

BALTIMORE, Md., April 7.— new treatment for diabetes will be explained before the members of the American Chemical society here Thursday by Dr. Max Kahn of Beth Israel hospital, New York, and Dr. R. H. McKee of Columbia university.

GIVE WILLINGLY OR WAIT UNTIL FORCE IS USED

French Plan for Voluntary Capital Levy Explained to the Chamber

GIVE 3 PER CENT. INTEREST ON LOANS

Capitalists Dodging Levy Will Have Forced Assessment Made

LONDON, April 7.—The French financial crisis is reflected in the value of the franc here. Saturday the franc opened at 91.85 to the pound, while today it opened at 93.10.

PARIS, April 7—The government's new financial bill, embodying the provisions for the proposed capital levy, or forced loan was introduced in the chamber of deputies this afternoon by Finance Minister De Monzie. The measure was agreed to by the cabinet this morning. He asked its immediate reference to the finance committee and a report on it before the end of the day.

The government's financial plan also includes regularizing the currency situation by raising the limit of the bank bill issue by the Bank of France from 41,000,000,000 to a total of 45,000,000,000 francs and increasing the limit of advances by the bank to the state by four billion francs.

Debate on Wednesday

M. DeMonzie asked the chamber to set aside tomorrow afternoon's sitting for examination and discussion of the finance bill, and the chamber agreed to this.

"Owing to the extremely important nature of this bill and the public anxiety which must and will be reassured," said the finance minister, "the government will be at the chamber's disposition tomorrow."

It was announced that both Premier Herriot and Finance Minister DeMonzie will appear at once before the finance commission.

System Explained

The mechanism of the system as explained by the finance minister after adjournment of this morning's cabinet meeting, is intended to afford property owners and capitalists of France a chance to come forward and contribute proportionately to their wealth for the renovation of French finances.

It contains provisions obliging them to do so, if they refrain from voluntary subscription.

"It is a plebiscite on the question of free, voluntary contribution, each according to his means, or by constraint," was the way M. De Monzie put it. "If the French capitalists understand the system and patriotically respond to the call of the government, it will work without the slightest annoyance or interference in private affairs. On the contrary, if they make constraint necessary it will be resorted to."

Income Tax as Basis

Declarations for the income tax will be taken as a basis for obligatory subscriptions to the forced loan in cases where the capitalists fail to come forward voluntarily. Subsequently these declarations will be verified if there are reasons to suspect their exactitude.

Contributions to the forced loan may be spread over a period of five years and the contributors will receive three per cent. perpetual rentes.

"The principles at the bottom of the whole scheme," said M. De Monzie "are the maximum of option on the part of the capitalists and a minimum of constraint. If a capitalist so desires, he can, previous to his subscription, make a declaration of his fortune, which will make any intervention on the part of the government to ascertain his wealth unnecessary."

The minister gave it to be understood that pressure would be resorted to only in flagrant cases of dodging by a capitalist of his obligations under the new law.

Will Meet Opposition

Although the government has agreed on the measure and on the plan to raise the limit of the bank bill issue by the Bank of France to 45,000,000,000 francs and increasing the limit of the advances by the bank to the state by 4,000,000,000 francs its majority in the chamber is divided. Most of the radical group, presided over by M. Loucheur, will fight both measures, M. Loucheur announced this morning.

The Socialists will ask for consideration of a counter-proposition, providing for a straight capital levy of ten per cent.

MAY ASK NATIVES TO GO TO LONDON

C. R. Das and Mahatma Gandi May Join in Conference

LONDON, April 7.—The overtures recently made by C. R. Das, leader of the Swarajists, or home rulers of India, for reconciliation with the British government continues to occupy the press and parliament, both here and in India.

A suggestion has been telegraphed from India that Das and "Mahatma" Mohandas Gandhi, the Nationalist leader, should be invited to come to London at the same time as the Earl of Reading, the viceroy of India, to join in the discussion of Indian policy.

CLOSING STOCK SALES

NEW YORK, April 7.—Closing sale prices: C.P.R. 142; U.S. Steel 111¾; U.S. Steel Pfd. 123.

'BIG BUSINESS' METHODS USED BY BOOZE RING

Card Index and Ledgers Kept Track of Law Violations

HEADQUARTERS IS FOUND IN CHICAGO

Illicit Liquor Flowed Into City from Most U. S. Ports

(Special to Edmonton Journal)

CHICAGO, April 7.—Chicago police today turned over to federal prohibition authorities the books and accounts of one of Chicago's largest and most efficient industries—the distribution of booze and the management of disorderly resorts. The syndicate had been doing a business of many million dollars every year, police said.

Police raided the sumptuously furnished offices of the "gin syndicate" and found there, in neatly audited ledgers, filing cabinets, memoranda and other devices of modern bookkeeping, many accounts of law violation.

Many Hundred Names

Included in the information gathered from the data on the books, were the names of hundreds of wealthy liquor customers, saloon keepers with running accounts, the names of disorderly resorts and their inmates, as well as a list of police officers, government dry officials bribed, and carload booze deliveries.

In addition to the details of the liquor jobbing was an account of the operations of four of Chicago's great breweries.

At the head of the syndicate was Johnny Torrio, beer baron, Al Caponi, alias Scarface, and Al Brown, host at Chicago's most scarlet resorts, the raid revealed.

The offices of the trust were in an office bearing the name of a physician, a magnificently appointed place. On shelves about the room liquor of every description, from beer to champagne, was found. Telephone calls on record showed that liquor flowed into the offices of the Chicago bootleg trust from every known inlet in the United States, from New York city to Miami.

Bribe Offered, Says Officer

John Patton, former mayor of Burnham, a suburb, one of those arrested, was charged by Sergeant Edward Birmingham, of the raiders, with having offered him $5,000 "to forget the bookkeeping system."

The others arrested, the police said, were underworld leaders.

In the account books and loose-leaf ledgers detectives said, were listed names of more than 200 well-known Chicagoans and many large hotels here as patrons.

Search was made after the raid for the alleged heads of the syndicate, whose names were revealed through the records.

120 COLLIERIES IN BRITAIN CLOSE UP

Cheshire Miners Given a Chance to Operate Coal Pit Themselves

(Canadian Press Cable)

LONDON, April 7.—No fewer than 120 collieries in England and Wales have closed down since the beginning of the year, involving the acceptance of the unemployment dole by 20,000 workmen. The latest to cease operation is the Wyerly colliery in Staffordshire, employing 700 men.

William Davies of Liverpool, the owner of the Little Neston collieries in Cheshire, who lost £250 weekly and a total of £60,000 on the operations of his mines, has made an offer to his men to let them work the mine for themselves for nine months, the workers to keep any profit that might be made, while he would contribute £50 weekly toward any possible loss. The district miners' federation looked interestedly at the offer but apparently they intend to refuse.

JACK COOGAN GETS SIX CENTS DAMAGES

(Special to Edmonton Journal)

NEW YORK, April 7.—Jackie Coogan won the price of a lollypop in the New York supreme court today. He received judgment for six cents damages against the Adams-Balch Handkerchief Manufacturing company and Charles E. Weyan and company, who used the name and photo of the baby of the movies without Jackie's permission.

WHY U. S. COURTS FAIL?

Crowds Cheer Boy Eluding Police

BOSTON, Mass., April 7.—James Sheehan, 16-year-old automobile thief who played tag with Boston's force of motor cycle police for four days because he liked the "thrill" wearied of the sport yesterday and gave himself up to the authorities. In company with several newspapermen who had searched the youth out for an interview, Sheehan returned to the state school for boys at Shirley, from which he had escaped several months ago.

"I did it just for the fun of the thing" was the boy's explanation of his escapade. "I wanted to get a thrill."

Sheehan said that he began his recent career as a speedster March 24 when he stole an automobile in Clinton. From that time until last night he "borrowed" one car after another, his record on Saturday being four large automobiles. In a hide-and-seek game with the police in the Charlestown district Sunday crowds turned out to cheer the youth whose exploits had been widely heralded.

PRICE GAIN OF 5 CENTS FOR WHEAT

WINNIPEG, Man., April 7.—Stronger cables and an improved export demand imparted a firm tone to the local wheat market today and prices showed sharp advances. May reached a high of $1.53½ and closed at $1.51⅞, a gain of 5⅛ over Monday's final figures.

RAISE FUND IN MONTREAL FOR MADAME ALBANI

Aged French Canadian Prima Donna Finds Life Hard Today

MONTREAL, April 6.—La Presse, local French language newspaper, states that Premier Mackenzie King has invited that journal to organize a subscription on behalf of Madame Albani, the aged prima donna, whose musical successes in the latter part of the last century were world-wide. Madame Albani, who was Marie Emma Lajeunesse, born at Chambly, Que., in 1852, is living in straitened circumstances in London. The newspaper says: "His Majesty King George V has accorded his gracious patronage to the project of aiding the great artiste who was called by the masters of her time 'the spirit of the oratorio'."

Madame Albani

FIREWORKS PLANT WRECKED BY BLAST

At Least One Killed in Blaze at Hanover, Mass.

HANOVER, Mass., April 7.—One man is known to be dead and several other employes of the National Fireworks company plant here are believed to have lost their lives when a series of explosions followed by fire destroyed a large part of the plant this afternoon. The fire departments of seven towns were struggling to save the magazines and surrounding houses.

At two o'clock it was estimated that 100 of the 300 buildings had been destroyed. The number of dead will not be determined until a check-up has been made of the workers. At that hour the firemen believed that the powder magazine was safe. But in the path of the flames was the large shipping building in which hundreds of tons of finished products are stored.

SOON ELIMINATE SMALLPOX IN B. C.

VANCOUVER, April 7.—The outbreak of smallpox in Vancouver has taken a very decided turn for the better, according to city health officials and it is expected that the disease will be stamped out within a few weeks. On Monday 59 patients were undergoing treatment, all being of an extremely mild type, with no deaths reported since the epidemic started.

MOOSE JAW LEVY AT 48.72 MILLS

MOOSE JAW, April 7.—The tax rate for this city for 1925 was raised from 47.38 to 48.72 mills, an increase of 1.35 mills, when the city councillors adopted the tax roll for the year last night. The school levy was increased by over one mill, while the municipal levy was down .20 of a mill.

PROBE BI-LINGUAL AREAS IN ONTARIO

TORONTO, April 7.—The resolution of A. Belanger (Liberal), Russell, advocating the teaching of French and English, in accordance with principles and methods applied in the schools of bi-lingual countries, was withdrawn in the Ontario legislature last night after Premier Ferguson had stated that a survey of education conditions in bi-lingual areas in Ontario was being undertaken in the immediate future.

BALFOUR WEARIED AFTER BUSY DAYS

NAZARETH, Palestine, April 7.—The Earl of Balfour arrived here last night somewhat worn and fatigued after a strenuous day, in which he had visited the Jewish settlements of Nahalal and Balfouria, lying in the plains of Jehrael.

TWO SHOT DOWN IN DRUG STORE IN BELLEVILLE

Messenger for Bank Sends Bullets Into Two Unarmed Youths

POLICE SAY MOTIVE WILL BE REVEALED

Arthur Moon,, Held for Murder, Was Etranged from His Wife

BELLEVILLE, Ont., April 7.—The motive which prompted the shooting to death of Clayton McWilliams and John Cameron McGie in a local drug store last night, and in connection with which Arthur Moon, messenger for the Canadian Bank of Commerce is held by the police, is still somewhat of a mystery.

Moon was formally arraigned in police court this morning on two separate charges of murder and was remanded for a week. The inquest opened last evening before Coroner Boyce and was adjourned until next Monday. In court this morning Moon made no plea and the proceedings were of the briefest nature.

Police Learn Motive

Local police officials state that evidence will be brought out later which will make clear the reason for the shooting and events which preceded the tragedy. McWilliams and McGie are well known and respected residents of the city, the former being 26 years of age, while his companion is three years younger. Moon is 35 years of age. He is a married man with two children, but had recently been living apart from his wife.

It is believed that McGie was the innocent victim of the shooting. According to eyewitnesses, Moon walked into the store where McWilliams who was on duty, was conversing with his friend. With practically no hesitation he shot McWilliams through the heart, the bullet passing through his body and embedding itself in the wall. He staggered back into the dispensary while McGie at the same instant ran forward and attempted to disarm the assailant. He was shot and fell behind the counter. When the police arrived a few minutes later he was breathing, but died before a doctor reached the scene.

Following the tragedy Moon walked out of the store and into his apartment on the third floor of the Bank of Commerce. He made no resistance when the police appeared to place him under arrest.

About fifteen minutes previous to the two men being shot Moon fired his revolver twice from a window of his apartment, a short distance from the drug store. He was next seen to cross the road toward the store.

Three Eyewitnesses

At least three persons are believed to have been witnesses of the tragedy. They are Miss Eva Barlow, clerk at the soda fountain, and Miss Irene Woodley, who was making a purchase at the time. A girl named Cousins was in the act of entering the store. This morning she is suffering from the shock of witnessing the shooting and was unable to speak of it.

McGie was an accomplished musician and was employed as an accountant in the Carthage Machinery company. His father had been a member of the local board of education for thirty years.

It is stated that Moon had not shown any signs of mental derangement, although he was known to have brooded over his estrangement from his wife.

WILL USE AIRSHIP IN DASH FOR POLE

Algarsson Tells Plans for British Aerial Flight to Arctic

LONDON, April 7.—Giving details of the plans for the British North Pole aerial expedition on which he intends to start next month, Gretth Algarsson, a young Icelander, says in the Daily Express today that the final dash to the pole will be made in a small non-rigid airships, and not an aeroplane. The ship will be 150 feet long and similar to those used for patrolling the English channel during the war, but especially designed to withstand the exceptional polar conditions.

The airship will carry four passengers, a 30-day food supply, special cooking stoves, and spare gasoline as ballast.

It will also take a small light sled on which, in case of accident, enough food can be packed to last until the crew find their way back to the base ship or reach the Alaskan coast.

Algarsson is eager to beat Captain Amundsen, the Norwegian explorer who plans to make a similar expedition, also starting in May.

DIRECTOR OF FORESTRY

OTTAWA, April 7.—Acting Director H. Finlayson has been appointed director of forestry for Canada.

MARINE NEWS

Celtic	New York	Liverpool
Ausonia	New York	Southampton
Athenia	New York	Glasgow
Cleveland	New York	Hamburg
Martha Washington	New York	Naples
Leviathan	New York	Southampton
Minnetonka	London	New York
Cedric	Liverpool	New York
United States	Halifax	Denmark
Can. Volunteer	Halifax	West Indies
Veedam	Plymouth	New York
Ohio	Southampton	New York
Reliance	Southampton	New York
Cameronia	Glasgow	New York
Thuringia	Queenstown	New York

Booze is Back

"A woman was the first person to receive a permit and to depart with the first purchase under the new act, half a dozen bottles of Guinness stout being the sale recorded."
— Story on the day Prohibition ended, May 12, 1924

The Journal had the story, but – as was the custom of the day – the reporter didn't interview the Edmonton woman who, after all, made history of a sort.

Why only a half-sack?

Why Guinness?

Would this be her first taste of demon booze since July 1, 1916, when Alberta went dry?

The Journal was now 20 years old and seldom quoted real people doing real things at the scene of the action.

At any rate, Prohibition was over and the front-page story was a low-key, somewhat sarcastic account of the end of Alberta's eight-year, uneasy experiment of living without alcohol.

"Ten o'clock struck and Vendor Higinbotham swung open the door. The discreet window blinds lifted, showing a blaze of golden labels. The huge crowd, which had grown magically to a full dozen by reason of half a dozen who had been lurking coyly behind parked automobiles, surged quietly into the store, and the big rush was on."

Perhaps the paper can be forgiven its lack of enthusiasm for the day.

When Prohibition came in on July 1, 1916, it opposed shutting the bars. Now, it opposed opening them again.

A Nov. 1, 1923, editorial said there was too much uncertainty in the option of having the government control liquor sales, the most likely alternative to the status quo. "It is necessary to make an effort to find out what the legislature had in mind when it authorized the inclusion of the clause on the ballot."

The anti-Prohibition campaign had begun in earnest about 13 months before after a group called the Moderationists, lead by hotel owners, used the Alberta Referendum Act to gather enough names on a petition to force a province-wide vote on the Liquor Act of 1916 that ended Prohibition.

Ironically, it was the same act the prohibitionists used to force a vote to ban booze eight years before.

The Journal was never in favour of referendums because it felt politicians were elected to make decisions and laws, not voters checking ballots.

But the hotel owners fulfilled the referendum requirements and on March 12, 1923, *The Journal* gave in to the inevitable. "It is regrettable that such a step has to be authorized. But the direct legislation act having been allowed to remain on the statute books, there is no alternative."

Prohibition was not especially successful in Alberta. The province had remained more damp than dry because of loopholes in the legislation and the enthusiastic participation of bootleggers.

***In 1929*:**
Clifford S. Wallace joins *The Journal* as news editor. A *Journal* telephone operator earns $15 a week.

***Jan. 6, 1929*:**
A crowd of 10,000 greets aviators Wop May and Vic Horner on their return to Edmonton from a mercy flight to Fort Vermilion. They made the 1,000-kilometre flight in -40 F weather in an open cockpit plane to deliver diphtheria antitoxin.

***Feb. 18, 1929*:**
***The Journal* hires Thomas G. Brown as chief accountant. In 1952, he rises to business manager.**

***March 1, 1928*:**
"MOSCOW – Revival of the dead and extension of human life to its utmost potential duration, probably far beyond the century mark, are held possible by Prof. Feodor Andreieff. Prof. Andreieff told of starting life by chemicals in a finger cut off from a body that had been dead for more than a month. The 'revived' finger sweated, he said, and showed other symptoms of life." – *Journal* story.

THE WEATHER
MAY 7, 1925
Forecast—Fair and cool.
Highest Today—58 Degrees.
Lowest last night—38 degrees.
Barometer, 27.65; Decreasing.
Sun Rises Friday, 4:49; Sets, 8:12.

Edmonton Journal

LAST EDITION

VOL. 21, NO. 249 — EDMONTON, ALBERTA, THURSDAY, MAY 7, 1925 — TWENTY-TWO PAGES

U.S. GREAT LAKES RUM WAR MAY BREED TROUBLE

PRAIRIE GROUP LIKELY RESULT OF PARTY ROW

Ontario Wing Expected to Withdraw Active Support of Progressives

GINGERITES RETURN TO FOLD IS SEEN

Forke Retains Leadership But Whip and Chairman Are Ousted

LORD BYNG GOES NORTH NEXT JULY

OTTAWA, May 7.—It is announced here that Governor-General Lord Byng will leave Edmonton on Monday, July 13, for the long trip down the Mackenzie river to Herschel Island and Aklavik. The governor will be accompanied by Premier Greenfield, of Alberta. Lord Byng reaches Edmonton on July 12 at the conclusion of a trip to the Pacific coast. The northern trip will take about six weeks.

BIG CEREMONY WILL BE HELD BY UNIONISTS

First Meeting of United Church in June in Toronto

BLOOD PRESSURE EASILY CONQUERED

St. Catharines Doctor Tells Ontario Association of New Discovery

PRINCESS YOLANDA'S BABY SON IS DEAD

TROTZKY RETURNS

BRITAIN EYES RIFF ATTACKS WITH ANXIETY

Effect of Possible Victory by Abd El Krim Feared

CAUSE AGITATION IN MOSLEM WORLD

French Advance Against Tribesmen Meets With Stiff Resistance

Three French Columns Advance Against Riffs

CENTRAL SCHOOL AT DRUMHELLER BURNS

Frame Building of Nine Rooms Is Completely Destroyed

MEIGHEN SEES NO SUN BEAMS IN C. N. R. YET

Leader of Opposition Continues Debate on National Line Estimates

ROBERT FORKE IS AGAINST A MERGER

Wouldn't Trust C. N. to Take C. P.; Vice Versa Dangerous

GO STOCKINGLESS

BEATRICE LILLIE, who has called upon Englishwomen to start a stockingless vogue as a protest against Churchill's proposed tax on silk. Miss Lillie, who in private life is known as Lady Peel, has been seen on the stage in Canada many times.

LANCASHIRE HOWLS AGAINST SILK TAX

Manufacture of New Yarns and Fabrics to Be Affected

RETALIATION IF U.S. DRY BOATS FIRE ON LAKES

Windsor Lawyer Predicts Trouble Over "Unrestricted" Bootlegger Hunt

'OUTRAGE' DECLARES JOHN H. RODD, K.C.

22 Cruisers Carrying Cannon Sent Out on Lakes

FIGHT BITTER COLD IN EFFORT TO GET PLANE READY FOR POLE JUMP

Wireless from King's Bay Tells of Sudden Change in Weather—Oslo, Norway, Paper Learns Pathfinding Ship Has Reached Dane's Island

ALTERNATIVE VOTE BILL DUE AGAIN

OTTAWA, May 7.—Premier King announced in the house this afternoon that the government intends to re-introduce the alternative vote bill at an early date.

NEW CLASSIFICATION IN CIVIL SERVICE

Grading of Clerks and Others Is Announced at Ottawa

FAT EMMA

So Attractive and Pleasing!

Being Served at Teas and Social Functions.

Really, Folks, you have missed a treat if you haven't tried them.

NA-3217-2 Glenbow Archives / From This Fabulous Century

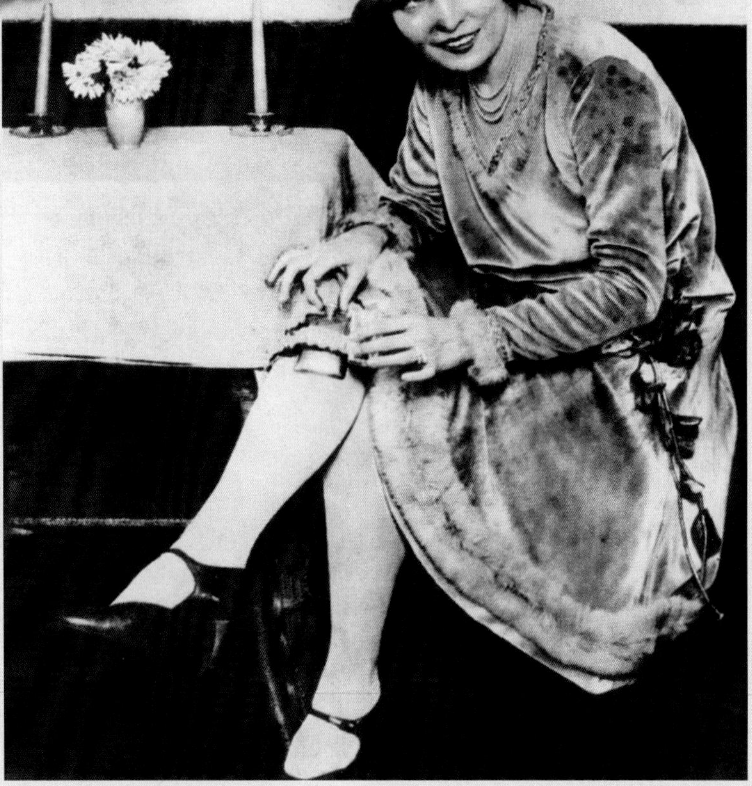

Liquor became legal again when Prohibition was repealed in 1924.

Doctors could write prescriptions for liquor for their patients and the "medicine" could be bought from local druggists.

On March 16, 1923, *The Journal* reported: "Alberta's profit from liquor sales to Dec. 31, 1922, are given as $2,606,616.60 ($29,099,319.86 today) in a report table by Attorney General J.E. Brownlee."

That was a lot of "medicine."

Despite its opposition to making laws by referendum and reluctance to change the status quo for a yet-to-be-defined alternative in dealing with booze, the paper displayed an even-handedness in covering the debate.

This was the one of the first times the paper discarded absolutes in covering a major issue – the Kaiser was bad, conscription was necessary – and let the participants tell their own side.

The paper allowed the Wets and Dries the occasional half-page each to make their case in the months leading up to the Nov. 5, 1923, referendum.

One example occurred March 3: "Rev. Hugh Dobson Declares Prohibition Lessens Crime; Quotes Figures As Proof."

"Law Useless Says Dr. Clark Unless True Sentiment Of People Stands At Its Back."

There were four options from which voters could pick – but "A," Prohibition, and "D," government sale of all liquors, were the only ones to which people paid attention.

A "D" vote would require government to establish some sort of a system to allow the sale of alcohol. How that would be accomplished was the question the paper was asking.

"Can anyone vote for 'D' in the belief that it will not lead to licensed sale? If he regards such sales as something to be avoided that clause cannot have his support," said the Nov. 1 editorial.

On Nov. 6 the paper reported the Wets prevailed over the Dries by more than 25,000 votes.

Editorial writers were a tad petulant about the outcome. "The people of the province had had enough of the liquor act … and were not disposed to listen to any advice to let it stand until they could be more certain that what was proposed in its place would be an improvement."

The Journal vaguely gave the address of that first government liquor store as being on 100A Avenue.

And vendor Higinbotham's past career was noted on a March 31, 1924: "E.N. Higinbotham of the department of the attorney general, formerly in charge of the branch of the administration of Lunatics' estates, will be the Edmonton vendor.

"The grim humor of this appointment is not likely to be lost upon seekers after liquor."

***May 7, 1928*:**
"MIAMI BEACH – After landing on the planet Venus by means of a huge projectile-like rocket he has invented, Robert Condit, Ohio inventor, plans to invent another rocket 'and bring back some natives…He will wear knickers on the flight…." - a story.

***June 14, 1929*:**
Northern Alberta Railways is incorporated. The NAR is made up of a number of financially troubled northern Alberta railways jointly purchased from the provincial government by Canadian Pacific and Canadian National.

***July 1, 1929*:**
Beginning this day the province of Alberta requires all operators of automobiles to hold a driver's licence, for a 50-cent fee. Licence No. 1 is issued to Premier John Brownlee.

***July 15, 1929*:**
50th Edmonton Exhibition opens.

***Oct. 18, 1929*:**
The British Imperial Privy Council rules that women are "persons" under the BNA Act and are eligible to sit in the Canadian Senate, reversing a decision of the Supreme Court of Canada.

At the Theatres

BY PRESS AGENTS

BEST SHOW OF YEAR

Coming to the Pantages theatre on Thursday afternoon is a vaudeville show that should suit the tastes of everybody. At least it has been a real delight to theatregoers in the eastern portion of the Pantages circuit, and there is no reason why the triumphs should not be repeated locally this week. A glance over the following list of attractions shows why this particular show has proved a knockout.

First and foremost is Jack Wilson, the most expensive individual performer who has ever played the Pantages time. The leading blackface performer in vaudeville today, he is bringing to Edmonton his nonsensical Revue in which he has the assistance of George Forsythe and Ruth Wheeler, accomplished singers and Willie Ward, a very clever midget. Wilson of course takes the lead in the funmaking and his methods are strictly original.

Dan Downing and Buddy have been here before. In June 1924, they appeared as added attractions. Playgoers will remember the "Cheerful Pessimist and His Pal." They provide a fast-moving program of music, song, and dance, blended with Dan's breezy line of talk. The other added attraction is a splendid dancing revue, presented by Al Calm and Charles Dale and entitled, "Stepping Around." No better dancers have ever been seen in Edmonton than Calm and Dale, while their three dainty feminine assistants also dance nicely and have good singing voices. Sumptuous costumes and stage setings add to the attractiveness of this act.

The Helen Bach trio, three athletic artists, will be seen in novel strength feats and out of the ordinary aerial stunts. They offer some very daring and thrilling tricks, with Miss Bach, a wonderful exponent of muscular development, doing the heavy work. The opening act is provided by Wanda's seals, clever animals who perform all the usual stunts and a lot more of their own.

Owing to the expensive nature of the bill and the fact that Friday afternoon it has been found necessary to dispense with the ladies' guest matinee for this week alone, in favor of a special holiday matinee. Reserved seats for the night shows are going quickly and seats should be secured at once to avoid disappointment.

BRANDON OPERA CO.

Edmonton is billed for a short festival of light and comic opera. The Brandon Opera company, heralded as "the best singing organization in America," is coming in revivals of the standard light and comic operas. The cast of principals is the same that has "made good" in more than two hundred cities and charmed more than a million music lovers throughout America during the past three years, and includes Theo Pennington, prima donna soprano; Jessie Evans, contralto; Harry Pfeil, tenor; Carl Bundschu, baritone; Jeanne Rae, soprano; Ed. Andrews and George Olson, comedians, and Delos Jewkes, basso. They have a remarkably good singing chorus of more than thirty voices under the capable direction of Clarence West.

The company comes to the Empire theatre on Tuesday, April 14, in Reginald DeKoven's comic opera masterpiece, "Robin Hood," and will offer this best loved of all American comic operas on Tuesday evening. On Wednesday afternoon the offering will be Gilbert and Sullivan's gem of gems, "The Mikado." Then comes Planquette's "The Chimes of Normandy" on Wednesday night, "The Bohemian Girl" by Balfe on Thursday evening, "The Spring Maid" on Friday evening, and "The Chocolate Soldier" on Saturday afternoon and evening.

That is a program interesting, romantic and colorful enough for anyone. The old favorites that have lived and will continue to live throughout the years are just as popular today as they were in the days of their first production. "Robin Hood," the vehicle in which the company appeared on their last visit, when they were under the management of Ralp Dunbar, will be interesting as long as music and scenic are are utilized to perpetuate beauty and as long as stage folk that can sing and act are ready to sing its lovely songs and enact the vicissitudes of its twelfth century characters. Sweet memories of its always changing, always beautiful harmonies, of its Sherwood forest in autumnal tints and shadows, of its tipsy tinkers and dimpled dairy maids, of its "Oh, Promise Me," "Brown October Ale" and "The Armorer's Song" which will live perpetually.

The seat sale for the entire engagement is now on at the Empire.

D'ALVAREZ'S CHILDHOOD

Wherever Marguerite D'Alvarez sings, the critics speak of her facility for painting with words and sounds, just as an artist does with brush and colors. Mme. D'Alvarez admits that she is quite aware of the power to do this, and says it is doubtless because of her colorful heritage.

"There lies in me," says Mme. D'Alvarez, "as the heritage, I think, of my strain of the blood of the Peruvian Inca people, a profound vein of mysticism. In my earliest years I was surrounded with an atmosphere of the marvelous and mysterious. I remember a tale my grandmother told me.

"In her youth she lived in a hacienda at the foot of the mountains. There she had Indian servants, people who were descendants of the glorious race of the ancient Peruvian empire. They were very proud and clannish. My grandmother, being in part the daughter of a princely, aboriginal house, was regarded by them, in spite of her mingling of Spanish blood, as one of their people. The time came when money misfortunes descended upon my family. My grandmother passed into an hour of pressing need. One of the servants, an old man, said to her, 'You are one of the inheritors. If you will come with us you can take what you like. But we cannot reveal our secret. We must blindfold you when we take you to the place!'

"They blindfolded her, placed her in a chair slung between two mules, and for two days they traveled through jungle and across mountain trail. Finally, they led her afoot along a steep trail, and then she felt her feet on grass. They unbound her eyes.

"Upon her vision came a wierd, marvelous gleaming from every side. She was in a small, mountain girt valley. This valley was garden, the most amazing of gardens. Its thickets of trees and flowery bushes were of purest gold and silver, with fruits and blossoms incrusted with emeralds and rubies.

Mme. D'Alvarez will be heard on Easter Monday, April 13, at the Empire theatre, where music lovers will have the opportunity of hearing this noted tone-painted, whose following is a large one on both sides of the world.

IN MOVIELAND

"THE TRAIL RIDER"

A cast of well known players will be seen in the supporting roles of Buck Jones' latest starring vehicle, "The Trail Rider," which opens a three-day engagement at the Empress theatre today.

The story calls for two leading ladies in the roles played by Nancy Deaver and Lucy Fox, both of whom are recognized as among the most beautiful girls now appearing in motion pictures. This is the first time Miss Deaver has been seen in a Western film, although she has played prominent parts in many big screen attractions.

Others in the cast are Jack MacDonald, well known screen villain; Carl Stockdale, who also plays a "heavy" in this production; George Berrell, and Jacques Rollens.

"EXCUSE ME"

Like all theatrical folk, Rupert Hughes, whose production of "Excuse Me" comes to the Capitol theatre today, has definite opinions on the subject of superstitions. He deliberately walks under ladders, claiming to find it much less crowded there. People who stop to pick up pins he considers very lucky —that they don't get run over and killed. And if he has any mascot (aside from the well-known walking stick he carries to no visible purpose, as it is too short to reach the ground) it is the notorious No. 13.

"Excuse Me," his most uproarious comedy, was completed in just thirteen days. In order to give a lucky start the play was given its out-of-town try-out on Friday the 13th of January, 1911, and made its Broadway debut on February 13. And now he has transferred the play to the screen thirteen years later, the release date being January 13, 1925.

"Excuse Me" is an epic of the Pullman car. The idea of the farce came to Hughes when meditating on the awful fate of an almost married couple imprisoned in a transcontinental Pullman for three days and condemned to spend "their first nights together apart." His father had been a railroad president, and in his comedy Hughes wrote feelingly of what he knew thoroughly. He wrote for an audience of several million Pullman travelers who also knew thoroughly and felt deeply on the subject, and his farce proved an almost instantaneous and universal riot. At one time four companies were playing it simultaneously; royalties soon ran into six figures; almost every town in the country got a chance to laugh at it, and he is still getting royalties from stock performances.

Also he made it into a book which had an enormous sale.

"THE TORNADO"

Crashing, hurtling logs tossed ahead of a resistless torrent make a terrifying spectacular background for some of the thrilling action in "The Tornado," Universal-Jewel starring House Peters, which will be shown in the Dreamland theatre commencing today.

"The Tornado" is the screen version of the famous Lincoln J. Carter melodrama of the same name and the part played by Peters is one of the most heroic in his long motion picture career.

The scene of the action is a logging camp, the great forests, and the turbulent waters of a river down which thousands of thousands of logs float to the mills, guided and controlled in their passage by the skill and daring of man.

"STORY WITHOUT A NAME"

"The Story Without a Name," a new Irvin Willat production for Paramount, with Agnes Ayres and Antonio Moreno featured in the principal roles is at the Princess theatre.

The story, by Arthur Stringer, first appeared as a Radio-Prize-Title story in Photoplay Magazine. Victor Irvin wrote the screen play.

It tells of a young inventor, working for the U. S. government, who had just perfected a "death ray" machine, an invention destined to revolutionize modern warfare. The instrument has been successfully tested, and the scientist is making preparations for his departure for Washington to turn over the machine to the proper officials when something absolutely unlooked for happens.

"THE SHEPHERD KING"

In reproducing the spectacular story of "The Shepherd King" at the Monarch for the last times today, every effort was made to obtain the right type for the character roles. William Fox sent Director J. Gordon Edwards with Violet Mersereau, who plays the leading feminine role, together with cameramen and assistants, to Italy and then to Egypt and Palestine where the rest of the cast were hired.

Scouts were sent out searching for a man of the right size for the part of Goliah, who was an important character in the play. At last one of the Fox representatives found an Italian-American, who seemed just suited for the role of the Philistine giant. He was seven feet tall, magnificently proportioned, broad shouldered, altogether a commanding figure. The man spoke good English but it meant a considerable loss of time to train him because he had never acted in a picture before. Even a good professional actor could not have done any better and there is no professional actor who could have rivaled this man's physical proportions.

"CHANGING HUSBANDS"

Two girls with but a single thought — how to find happiness. That just about sums up in a nutshell the theme of "Changing Husbands," the new Paramount picture featuring Leatrice Joy, which opened at the Rialto theatre last Monday. The story is an adaptation by Sada Cowan and Howard Higgin of the Saturday Evening Post serial, "Roles," by Elizabeth Alexander. Frank Urson and Paul Iribe directed the production under the personal supervision of Cecil B. De Mille. "Changing Husbands" is, incidentally, their first directorial achievement.

NOVEL APPEAL BY REV. BEN SPENCE

TORONTO, April 8.—Rev. Ben Spence, prohibition leader, has sent a small bottle, said to contain alcohol, to each member of the Ontario legislature along with a letter containing an appeal against the government's beer amendment.

The bottle is alleged to contain the equivalent in quantity of raw whiskey to one quart of 4.4 beer. "The amount of absolute alcohol in one quart of 4.4 beer and in 2 1-2 ounces of U. P. whiskey is practically the same," writes Mr. Spence.

GIANT STURGEON STUNNED BY BLAS[T]

NELSON, B. C., April 8.—Whe[n] thirteen cases of dynamite were ex[-]ploded in the river bed at Low[er] Bennington Falls yesterday in co[n]nection with the construction of t[he] new plant of the West Kootena[y] Power and Light company, a stu[r]geon eight feet, nine inches long an[d] weighing 171 1-2 pounds wa[s] brought to the surface stunned. Th[e] blasting was below the falls.

Movies that talk!

"When words were interpected into the action they fell with the force of a striking sword."
— Talking movies came to Edmonton on March 28, 1929

Maybe Edmonton was 18 months behind New York and, maybe, "interpected" isn't a real word, but the coming of "talkies" to the city fascinated and attracted thousands of moviegoers to the Capitol Theatre those first heady weeks.

Edmonton had an impressive selection of theatres on March 27, 1929. Among them the Pantages, which featured vaudeville acts such as Scrambled Legs, a dance review and Cardina, "The Suave Deceiver." At the Empire there was a live farewell performance of *Treasure Island*, starring Bransby Williams and at the Dreamland, Rex, King of Wild Horses galloped across the screen in silent splendor in *Guardians of the Wild*.

But at the Capitol, on Jasper Avenue, east of 101st Street, people were lining up to plunk down 45 cents (mezzanine loges 80 cents, children 15 cents) for the first matinee performance of *Mother Knows Best*, starring Madge Bellamy, Louise Dresser and Albert Gran.

An ad said it all: "The Dawn of a New Era in Entertainment."

And it was.

Talking pictures turned the entertainment world on its ear. It was so important that the paper published a 14-inch review on page 15 the next day by a reviewer identified as J.M.G. "No longer will the silver screen suffer by virtue of being a two-dimensional medium for the mimicry of human hopes and hates and loves and fears and tears."

Mother Knows Best was a "part talkie" featuring New York's 125-piece Roxy Theatre Orchestra playing the musical themes in the film.

The development had Edmonton house musicians playing their swan song. By December all the movie houses were sound-equipped and house orchestras took their last curtain calls.

Live theatre also took a hit as noted with little sympathy and a word of caution in a Dec. 20, 1929, editorial: "Of course, if the people who pay their money at the box office prefer the talkies to the real thing, then it's only a question of saying 'hard luck' to the (actors) and wishing them success in finding jobs in Hollywood. Probably the same public that is refusing to see these actors on the stage will go to see them in the talkies."

But by cutting legitimate theatre loose, the city lost a significant part of the entertainment workforce. "These people live here and spend their money here – But if the public has decided it prefers the talkies, there is nothing more to be said about it."

***Oct. 28, 1929*:**
The Edmonton Grads beat the visiting Cleveland Blepp Knits to win the Underwood Trophy emblematic of the ladies' international basketball championship.

***Nov. 14, 1929*:**
***The Journal* reports the Alberta village of Thorhild has been destroyed by fire, with damage amounting to $100,000.**

***Nov. 18, 1929*:**
A new Ford Roadster sells for $732 at Edmonton's Dominion Motors.

***Dec. 9, 1929*:**
James Douglas is elected mayor of Edmonton for 1930.

***Dec. 14, 1929*:**
Alberta Premier John Brownlee signs a landmark agreement with the federal government that awards control of Alberta's natural resources to the province.

Forecast—Continued mild, fair
Since Midnight—Highest, 59 at 2:00 p.m.
Lowest, 32 at 2:00 a.m.

Edmonton Journal

"ONE OF CANADA'S GREAT NEWSPAPERS"

THIRTY-FOURTH YEAR ** EDMONTON, ALBERTA, THURSDAY, APRIL 8, 1937 SINGLE COPY, 5 CENTS 22 PAGES

Hockey Coronations
In Preparation; Keep Informed
By THE JOURNAL

No Financial Aid For Alberta Recommended

Implement Price Rise Declared Unjustified; Probers Make Report

Implement Probe Findings In Brief

OTTAWA, April 8—Following are highlights of the report of the commons committee investigating farm implement prices tabled in the commons Thursday:

No justification for increase in prices of agricultural machinery in January, 1936. Any further increase unwarranted.

* * *

Farm implement companies compete in matter of sales but little competition in prices.

* * *

The companies can look forward to relative prosperity in the industry.

* * *

Increased freight rates have contributed to price boosts and consideration should be given to lowering rates.

* * *

Cream separators should be placed on the free list.

* * *

Companies should encourage standardization in replacement parts and reduce prices on parts.

* * *

Tariff duties on materials entering into farm implement manufacture should be removed.

* * *

Credit costs to farmers purchasing farm implements are excessive.

* * *

Distribution costs of implement companies are unnecessarily high.

Any Further Increase Now Would Be Unwarranted, Committee Declares

RAP CREDIT COSTS

Find Little Competition in Prices Prevails Among Companies

OTTAWA, April 8.—Farm implement companies pursue "little effective competition in the matter of prices," although they compete in the matter of sales, the report of the special house committee on farm implements presented to the commission Thursday declared.

The committee found no justification for increased prices of agricultural machinery "at the present time."

Tabled by Fred Johnston (Lib., Lake Centre) committee chairman, Thursday's report was the culmination of an investigation into the subject which has occupied the committee for two sessions. It is featured by 36 findings, all relating to prices, financial achievements of the companies concerned and effect of their operations upon Canadian farmers.

The committee estimated that during the depression a "back-log" of requirements approximating $200,000,000 had accumulated. (Back-log is the unsatisfied demand due in this case to lack of purchasing power).

"This will have to be satisfied by the implement companies during the next few years," said the report, "together with normal annual requirements of agriculture estimated at $51,000,000."

Profits made by the companies in invested capital had been "substan-

(Continued on Page 10, Col. 2)

Economic Parley Is Not Envisaged

LONDON, April 8.—Prime Minister Baldwin told the commons Thursday no international economic conference "is at present envisaged."

Questioned about economic proposals, Baldwin explained Britain had asked Premier Van Zeeland of Belgium to make an "informal investigation" of world economic conditions.

Van Zeeland's inquiry, he said would be made in "various countries as to the possibility of securing a general relaxation of quotas and other obstacles to world trade.

The prime minister added that "informal exchanges of views have taken place" regarding a world economic conference.

Won't O.K. Pact; M.P. Raps Reich

OTTAWA, April 8 — Declaring thousands of his constituents had been "insulted and humiliated beyond words" by action of the Nazi government, Sam Factor (Lib., Toronto-Spadina) announced in the commons Thursday he would oppose second reading of the bill ratifying a trade agreement with Germany.

"The German government," Mr. Factor who is a Jew, declared, "has seen fit to heap calmuny and abuse upon members of a historic race the world over."

Despite the protest, the house voted approval of the pact negotiated by Hon. W. D. Euler, trade minister, last autumn.

ERROR IS FOUND IN PRAYER BOOK

LONDON, April 8 — Collectors scoured bookshops Thursday for copies of the new book of common prayer when it became known a limited number of the cheap edition had reached the market with the omission of a complete line of five words from the prayer for His Majesty the King.

The error appears in the section of the prayer which should read: "Most heartily we beseech thee with the favor to behold Our Most Gracious Sovereign Lord, King George." The phrase omitted is "favor to behold our most."

Where To Find It

Amusements, Theatres . . 5
Bridge 12
Brain Twizzler 12
Crossword Puzzle 19
Comics 18, 19
District 12
Editorial 4
Financial and Markets . . 14
Off the Record 5
Radio 5
Ripley's Believe It or Not . 20
Stories 18, 19
Sport 8, 9
Uncle Ray's Corner . . . 18
Want Ads. 20, 21
Women's 16, 17

The Weather

Edmonton Weather

From 3:00 p.m. Wednesday:

3:00 p.m.	58	3:00 a.m.	32
4:00 p.m.	57	4:00 a.m.	34
5:00 p.m.	55	5:00 a.m.	36
6:00 p.m.	54	7:00 a.m.	36
7:00 p.m.	48	7:00 a.m.	38
8:00 p.m.	45	8:00 a.m.	42
9:00 p.m.	43	9:00 a.m.	47
10:00 p.m.	39	10:00 a.m.	51
11:00 p.m.	35	11:00 a.m.	55
12:00 mid.	33	12:00 noon	56
1:00 a.m.	33	1:00 p.m.	58
2:00 a.m.	32	2:00 p.m.	59

Average temperature April 7, 42.

Average temperature same date last year, 37.

At Edmonton, April 9: Sun rises, 5:48 a.m.; sun sets, 7:24 p.m.

Barometer reading 2:00 p.m., 27.70 down.

(Continued on Page 7, Col. 4)

May Search World For S.C. Advisers

Giving the proposed Social Credit board of five members the right to visit any part of the world to secure commissioners or technical experts or to study administration methods, a redrafted bill to amend the Social Credit Measures act was made available to members of the house Thursday.

The new printed copies of the bill contain the following names of those to be appointed to the board:

G. L. MacLachlan, S.C., Coronation.

F. M. Baker, S.C., Clover Bar.

Dr. J. L. McPherson, S.C., Vegreville.

W. E. Hayes, S.C., Stony Plain.

S. A. Berg, S.C., Alexandra.

Mr. MacLachlan is to be chairman of the board and Mr. Baker secretary.

Three of the names of those on the proposed board were on the suggested caucus "striking" committee, these being Mr. MacLachlan, Mr. Baker, and Mr. Berg. The two others on the committee were Dr. H. K. Brown, S.C., Pembina, and R. E. Ansley, S.C., Leduc.

One of the principal duties of the board will be to "procure suitable persons for appointment to the commission."

Three or Five Men

The commission, which would administer a Social Credit plan, is to consist of not less than three nor more than five men appointed by the board.

Other duties of the board are set out as follows: "To appoint suitable persons as Social Credit technical experts;

To examine Social Credit legislation and make recommendations for legislative action in respect thereof;

To co-operate with the commission in the performance of any of its duties and in the rendering of such assistance as may be requested by the commission;

To report their findings and negotiations and activities to the legislature of each session thereof;

To keep a record of all negotiations and transactions;

To Study Conditions

To study the economic conditions of the province of Alberta with a view to assisting the commission in every way possible;

To request the executive council for the advice and co-operation of any department of the government.

The bill proceeds: "With the approval of the lieutenant-governor in council, the board, or any member or members thereof selected by the board may visit any part of the world for the purpose of procuring prospective commissioners or technical experts; or for the purpose of studying administration methods which might be of value to Alberta."

Another section of the act provides that the board shall be deemed to be a committee appointed by the legislative assembly and "every member of the board shall be entitled to receive such sums for traveling expenses outside the province and subsistence while performing their duties" as may be paid to a committee so appointed.

TORNADO KILLS ONE

TROY, Alabama, April 8.—Tornado killed at least one person, injured numerous others and leveled houses in a lumber mill village at Brundige, Ala., early Thursday.

A. J. Hooke, Social Credit, Red Deer, who, on the floor of the house Wednesday, accused cabinet members of, in effect, breaking faith with private members on a vote to secure a three-months supply of money. Mr. Hooke's motion to debate the matter of "urgent public importance" was laid over for a ruling by the speaker, Hon. Peter Dawson, on procedure. It is expected to come up again Thursday.

Fortin Scheme Gets Blessing

Legislature Committee Approves "Ballot-less" Step by City

IN CHARTER CHANGE

Giving the city council power to refund the city's debt under the Fortin plan without any reference to the electors or burgesses, the legislature in committee Wednesday approved two enabling amendments to the city charter. These, it was explained, give the city authority to accept the Fortin plan or any other plan for refunding the city's $30,000,000 debt.

The first amendment permits the council and public and Separate school boards to fail to levy for sinking fund requirements this year and specified that no alderman or trustee may be disqualified for such failure.

The second amendment provides that regardless of any provision in the public utilities act, the city, public school board or Separate school board may enter into an arrangement to extend, consolidate or refund their bonded debts without the approval of the public utilities board. However, under an amendment added Wednesday on a motion of Hon. Lucien Maynard, minister of municipal affairs, should the city default under the Fotrin plan or any other plan of debt refunding, its fi-

(Continued on Page 10, Col. 1)

BUILDING REPAIRS WILL COST $15,000

Building permit for $15,000 was issued by the city building inspector's department Thursday to cover repairs to the Western Transfer building, 10249 104 st., recently badly damaged by fire. The one permit will cover all actual renovations to the building itself. Major part of the damage was to stock stored by various firms within the block.

Other permits listed on departmental records Thursday included the following: Mrs. J. Haines, 11343 69 st., $700 for frame dwelling; E. Foth, 12912 70 st., $500 for frame dwelling; Herman Freeman, 11907 81 st., $2,000 for frame and stucco dwelling; W. J. Bauldry, 11914 87 st., $900 for addition to dwelling.

To Ground Planes Within One Week

Rapidly crumbling ice on northern waterways threatened to close in on aerial activity from Edmonton within a week as aeroplanes continued to drone between supply bases and mining camps in a fever of activity Thursday.

Closing date for winter flying last year was April 17 and just a few days later the year before, but unless a sudden weather change aeroplanes will be grounded before next Thursday, according to estimates of company officials in Edmonton.

Flying activity to the Peace River area and Fort St. John will continue unhampered throughout the break-up season with aeroplanes using wheels for field landings, it was said by United Air transport officials.

After landing at the Cooking lake base late Wednesday from the far north, Pilot Marlowe Kennedy took off again Thursday in a Mackenzie Air Service aeroplane for Great Bear lake mining camps. E. J. Walli, manager of Eldorado at Cameron Bay was a passenger.

Northbound for their base camp at Yellowknife where they will take part in a five-year aerial survey of the North West Territories for mineral showings, Don McLaren and Harry Winnie, Territories Exploration Company pilots, took off in two Stinson cabin craft Thursday.

Pilot Con Farrell, Canadian Airways Limited, Alec Dame and Bob Randall in Mackenzie Air Service machines, were expected to land at Edmonton from the far north late Thursday.

125 Employes In 2 City Firms Out On Strike

New Method Laundry, Gainers, Ltd., Latest Concerns Hit

FOUR STRIKES NOW

Packing Plant Executives Declare Move by Workers Surprise

Two new sit-down strikes, which were converted later into picket demonstrations, broke out in Edmonton on Thursday, complicating the city's labor problems.

About 70 employes of the New Method Laundry and Dry Cleaners "sat down" at 7:30 a.m. on the firm's premises at 11060 Jasper ave.

Requested by police the laundry sit-downers vacated the plant at 9:30 a.m. and immediately established picket lines outside the premises.

Between 55 and 60 workers in the packing plant of Gainers Ltd. started a sit-down at 9:00 a.m.

Responding to a request by the management, they vacated the plant at 2:00 p.m. and started orderly picketing.

Thus 125 workers were added to the ranks of Edmonton sit-downers, begun Saturday when 300 employes of the Swift Canadian Co., Ltd., "squatted" in the plant and demanded union recognition and a Saturday half-holiday. Eight employes of the Champion Messenger Service continued on the sit-down strike they commenced Wednesday. Theats of other tie-ups to start Friday were heard.

At 2:00 p.m. Thursday H. T. Anderson, general manager of Burns and Co., Ltd., said he had answered "no" to a request for union recognition presented earlier in the day by union representatives. "We told them we will not negotiate with outside agencies," Mr. Anderson said.

Pickets continued to patrol entrances to the Swift plant in North Edmonton on Thursday. Sit-downers who evacuated the plant and grounds late Tuesday converted their ranks into picket lines, insisting they would maintain their vigil until their demands were granted.

Strike of 55 yorkers in Gainer's plant came as a surprise move to officials of the company, it was stated Thursday by C. E. Gainer, general manager. He said union representatives, dickering with the company Wednesday, had given the company until 4:30 p.m. Friday to accept or reject a formal request for union recognition.

Mr. Gainer declared his company "is not prepared to deal with outside interests. We are willing at any time to deal with any group of our workers, union members as well as non-unionsts; but we stand firmly

(Continued on Page 7, Col 1)

3,500 On Strike In Oshawa Plant

TORONTO, April 8.—Premier Hepburn will throw the force of the Ontario government behind General Motors of Canada to prevent domination of the automobile industry in Canada by the John L. Lewis labor forces of the U.S., it was learned authoritatively Thursday.

OSHAWA, Ont., April 8.—More than 3,000 General Motors of Canada workers answered a strike call by the Committee for Industrial Organization Wednesday, stopping production of automobiles here at starting time in the company's largest plants. Recognition of a C.I.O.-sponsored union was the issue.

"This is just an old-fashioned walkout," said C. H. Millard, chairman of a shop committee which negotiated with company officials. "Sit-down strikes have been recognized as legal in the United States but both federal and provincial governments in Canada hold them illegal."

About 400 non-union members were left in various departments.

Hugh Thompson, C.I.O. organizer, said General Motors would not build another car in Canada until an agreement was signed with the international union. If an attempt were made to import cars manufactured in General Motors plants in the United States, workers in U.S. plants would be called out.

Expecting the strike at any time, the company moved its newly-manufactured cars and trucks from Oshawa by the hundreds daily. More than 1,500 machines were driven to Toronto last week.

Refusal of General Motors to adopt an agreement similar to the "Detroit agreement" brought about the strike here, James B. Highfield, General Motors plant general manager, said.

"The present unfortunate turn of

(Continued on Page 7, Col. 4)

F. D. Sutcliffe, president-elect of the Optimist club, who will be installed along with the vice-presidents at the annual banquet in the Macdonald Thursday night.

Debt Act Gets First Reading

Private Obligations Entered Before July 1, 1932, Affected

MAYNARD SPONSORS

A 10-year instalment plan for payment of private debts created prior to July 1, 1932, after the original amount had been cut 50 per cent, is provided for in the Debt Reduction act given first reading in the legislature Wednesday. Hon. Lucien Maynard, minister of municipal affairs, is sponsor.

A bill to amend the Debt Adjustment act also was introduced Wednesday, sponsored by Hon. J. W. Hugill, attorney-general. This bill extends provisions for compromise in debts and protection allowed in restricting actions by permits to all debtors. Formerly this protection extended only to farmers and resident home owners.

The debt reduction bill is aimed to take the place of the Reduction and Settlement of Debts act, passed at the special session of the house last August and later declared by Mr. Justice Ewing to be ultra vires.

Under the terms of the new bill, which does not affect interest rates, the amount of principal recoverable shall be 50 per cent of the old debt as at July 1, 1932. Debts contracted since that date are not affected.

Under the old Reduction and Settlement of Debts act, interest due on old debts from July 1, 1932, was wiped out while the interest rate on debts contracted since that date was reduced to a maximum of five per cent.

The bill offers an option to creditors who are prepared to forego interest since 1932. They may give notice in writing to the debtor that the balance due at July 1, 1932, is to

(Continued on Page 6, Col. 1)

VICEROY IS WILLING TALK THINGS OVER

LONDON, April 8. — Viceroy of India, Lord Lithlingow, is prepared to talk things over with Mohandas K. Gandhi. If, R. A. Butler, undersecretary for India, told the commons Thursday, Gandhi or anyone representing the Congress party expressed a desire to see the viceroy, he had little doubt the King's representative would be willing to approach any such request with every desire to reach an understanding.

Birds' Feathers Cook His Goose

Four dark turkey feathers and one white goose feather found in a car which he had borrowed from a south side garage one evening last December were instrumental in convicting Joseph Wendell on a charge of bird theft at his trial by jury before Mr. Justice Ewing in supreme court Thursday.

Convicted of stealing 10 turkeys and one goose, the property of Emil Adam, Nisku farmer, accused was remanded for sentence. He is scheduled to answer a perjury charge in connection with a police court hearing of a related case when supreme court opens Friday.

SEVEN-HOUR BATTLE SAVES SICK CHILD

HAWKESBURY, Ont., April 8.—Seven-hour battle to carry a sick child through the flooded areas near Fournier, Ont., was described here Thursday.

Mr. and Mrs. Arthur Lalonde struggled through darkness and water for 10 miles to reach Alfred, Ont., carrying Rachael, five, who was seriously ill. Rachael's illness was diagnosed as acute appendicitis. She was recovering Thursday after an operation.

Interest Repudiation Rapped In Bank of Canada's Report; Waste of 1905-22 Condemned

Can Maintain Services Without Any Temporary Help, Is Finding

BUDGET SUFFICIENT

Scale of Taxation Equal to That of Manitoba, Saskatchewan

OTTAWA, April 8.—Alberta does not require temporary financial assistance from the dominion pending the findings of the royal commission on taxation, the federal government was advised Wednesday night in a report from the Bank of Canada, tabled in the commons by Finance Minister Dunning.

The bank found "that Alberta can maintain its government services on as favorable a basis as Manitoba or Saskatchewan without receipt of additional assistance and we therefore see no basis for recommending that temporary financial aid should be extended by the dominion government."

The bank investigated Alberta's financial position at the request of Premier Aberhart, following similar inquiries in Manitoba and Saskatchewan.

It recommended temporary assistance for both Manitoba and Saskatchewan because different conditions were found. It is expected the appropriations will be included in

(Continued on Page 2, Col. 1)

HON C. A. DUNNING

Premier Silent On Bank Report

Premier Aberhart said Thursday that while he had been advised of the recommendations of the Bank of Canada concerning its investigation of Alberta's financial position, he had no comment to make.

"After the government has considered the matter, I may have something to say," the premier remarked.

A summary of the report was received over the wire by the premier on Wednesday night, with the information that the text was being mailed immediately.

Conservative Leader Finds Statement True, Refreshing

INTERVIEWS HERE

Must Be Declared Legal First, Opinion of Some

Alleged inaction on part of the present provincial government toward devising new economies or establishing a sound business administration in Alberta was blamed by several Edmontonians Thursday for the Bank of Canada's report suggesting that this province was not in need of financial aid from the dominion. Interest-slashing actions of this government may have brought a temporary easement but only have aggravated the situation with regard to 'outside" attitudes toward this province, it was claimed.

Remark that "Alberta cannot have her cake and eat it," was made by one man, while another claimed the bank's report quite accurate in that the Alberta government had made no attempt to correct its own difficulties, but made them worse, resulting in a plea for outside assistance.

Other citizens took the view that interest-slashing actions of the Alberta government, not yet finally established as constitutional, are hardly justifiable grounds on which

(Continued on Page 7, Col. 2)

See Chance Yet For Alberta Aid

By Charles Bishop

(Special to Edmonton Journal and Associated Southam Newspapers)

OTTAWA, April 18.—Should Alberta agree to restore its recent bond interest slash and make payment in full, Ottawa aid might even yet be forthcoming.

Such is the interpretation placed by some officials here upon that section of the Bank of Canada's report, made public Wednesday, which deals with defaulted bonds.

It is jointed out in the report that, if Alberta had paid interest on its obligations "the province would, presumably, have had to borrow its full share of unemployment relief from the dominion." It is added that "a claim for assistance would no doubt be considered in the light of these facts." In other words, this is construed to mean that, if the province had paid up interest in full, it would have been aided and even that, if it still agrees to do so, aid may be forthcoming.

The expectation—and this goes for the Conservative side—was largely that $750,000 would be provided, as in Manitoba's case, but with a condition that interest would be met as a qualifying consideration.

In place, however, of Ottawa providing aid with such a restriction it is put up to the province to pay its obligations and, then, claim assistance with the idea, of the bank's experts, that it will be forthcoming.

The opinion expressed Thursday by a high authority in parliament, peculiarly familiar with Alberta was that "the reaction out there will be very bad."

The simple facts are that the dominion was put on the horns of

(Continued on Page 7, Col. 4)

Meighen Bitingly Raps Combine Bill

OTTAWA, April 8.—Liberty was being "thrown to the winds," Senator Meighen, Conservative leader, declared Thursday, as the senate banking committee began a study of the combines bill. At noon adjournment, the committee had approved only one section of the bill, that citing the name of the act.

Doubt was expressed that the bill could be finally dealt with this session.

Under the bill, a commissioner with wide powers of investigation is to be appointed and Combines act administration is returned to the department of labor. The commission would have wide powers to enter premises and seize documents without a search warrant. He would be able to impose penalties upon witnesses for contempt of court.

Senator Meighen thought it "unspeakable that we should be asked to consider a bill of this kind just as we are asked to prorogue."

Refunding Here 'Amateurish'

So Observes Member of Saskatchewan Legislature

REGINA, April 8.—Refunding of the provincial public debt must be done, declared J. A. Gregory (Lib. The Battlefords) speaking in the budget debate in the provincial legislature here Wednesday.

"But it must be done in an orderly manner, and not in the amateurish way it was done in Alberta," Mr. Gregory said.

"Too much taxation and too much sweat of the brow is going to the wages of money," the member said.

Orders Solloway Pay $3,296,591

TORONTO, April 8—Isaac W. C. Solloway, head of the former brokerage firm of Solloway, Mills & Co., Ltd., (dominion company) was ordered Thursday in a judgment by Mr. Justice J. A. Makins to pay $3,296,591 to G. T. Clarkson, liquidator of the company.

2 West Provinces To Get $2,250,000

OTTAWA, April 8.—Supplementary estimates for the fiscal year ending March 31, 1938, amounting to $11,339,955 were tabled by Finance Minister Dunning in the commons Thursday. Largest single item is $3,000,000 to take care of the restored five per cent salary cuts in the civil service.

Temporary grants to Manitoba and Saskatchewan account for $2,250,000. This is divided $1,500,000 to Saskatchewan and $750,000 to Manitoba.

Department of transport will receive $1,115,890 covering a variety of items. Monies for defence department total $875,500. Of that figure $840,500 is for engineer services and works.

EARMARK $915,000 FOR AIRWAY NEEDS

OTTAWA, April 8.—Construction of airways, airports and radio stations throughout Canada is scheduled for continuation on a big scale this year. In the supplementary estimates for the current fiscal year tabled Thursday, $915,000 is appropriated for that purpose.

In addition, the civil aviation branch is down for another vote of $500,000. This is to be applied as contributions to assist municipalities on the trans-Canada airway to improve existing airports, or provide new ones.

SEIZE EMPLOYES; GET $1,400 HAUL

WINNIPEG, April 8.—Forced into a taxicab by gunmen, two employes of Paulin Chambers Biscuit company were robbed of the company's $1,400 payroll here Thursday in a daring holdup. The two, H. G. Short and J. L. Turner, were driven by the taxi driver, whom the bandits directed at gun point, to another part of the city and then ejected from the cab.

Brigade Of Moors Said Slaughtered

BAYONNE, France, April 8.—Basque reports from the Bilbao front Thursday night told of the slaughter of a brigade of Moorish insurgent cavalrymen, mowed down by government machine guns in the Mount Urquiola sector south-east of Bilbao.

"Row upon row" of hard riding Moors were cut to pieces, the reports stated, when Basque militiamen rose to meet a cavalry charge with machine-gun bullets.

VITORIA, Spain, April 8 — Pine forest fires, set by insurgents to aid their advance in Bilbao, drove the last government defenders from Barazar Pass Thursday, opening the way to the Basque capital 18 miles northwest.

Eastern flank of Spanish government's southern army hammered at Villaharta Thursday, striving in the face of repeated counter-attacks to break the insurgent barrier around Cordoba.

Bullet Is Fatal To Edmontonian

(Special to The Journal)

WESTLOCK, April 8—Found shot through the head by a revolver bullet in his car on No. one highway near Nestow, 50 miles north of Edmonton, Frederick Belcher, aged about 45, died half an hour after at 9:30 a.m. Thursday.

He was office manager of the Independent Acceptance corporation of Edmonton and had recently come from the east. He was driving a car with an Ontario license.

He was attended by Dr. H. R. Mason of Clyde. R.C.M.P. who investigated considered it a case of suicide and said that no inquest would be held.

2 KILLED IN CRASH

PASCO, Wash., April 8.—Two unidentified persons were killed Wednesday night when their aeroplane crashed a mile from here. The machine was reported licensed to Earl Weller of Seattle. The bodies of the two victims were said to be a man and a woman.

Britain Buys War Machines From Germany, Over $1,000,000 In Orders Placed In Reich

LONDON, April 8.—Since Jan. 1 British defence departments have placed orders with German firms through British agents amounting to about $310,000.

In addition orders of approximately $840,000 have been placed in Germany for the so-called shadow factories.

It is explained that the machines ordered from Germany by the government are of a special class which could be delivered at an earlier date than from firms in United Kingdom.

British arms expenditure over a five-year period is estimated at $1,500,000 per annum.

FOUR

ONE
THE GOVERNMENT OF THE PROVINCE OF ALBERTA
PROSPERITY CERTIFICATE
DATE OF ISSUE
AUGUST 5, 1936
A 96158
THE PROVINCIAL TREASURER WILL PAY TO THE BEARER THE SUM OF ONE DOLLAR ON THE EXPIRATION OF TWO YEARS FROM DATE OF ISSUE HEREOF UPON PRESENTATION HEREOF PROVIDED THERE ARE THEN ATTACHED TO THE BACK HEREOF ONE HUNDRED AND FOUR ONE CENT CERTIFICATE STAMPS
GOVERNMENT OF THE PROVINCE OF ALBERTA CANADA
OFFICE OF THE PROVINCIAL TREASURER
DEPUTY PROVINCIAL TREASURER
ONE DOLLAR
PREMIER
PROVINCIAL TREASURER
WESTERN PRINTING & LITHOGRAPHING CO. LTD. CALGARY

NA-1170-4 Glenbow Archives

Alberta's Social Credit government issued its own currency, often referred to as funny money.

Scrip, Sex & Scandal

1930 to 1940

Brownlee's Blunder / 151

An Outstanding Day / 155

Wop May / 159

Freedom of the Press / 161

Canada's First Mosque / 163

Hitler / 165

"Blood flowed Tuesday afternoon on the city's market square when RCMP and city police broke up an attempted 'hunger march' allegedly organized by Communists in defiance of a government ban."

— Report on the hunger march that involved 3,000 out-of-work men and women at Edmonton's market square on Dec. 20, 1932

You did what you could to look good in the Depression.

Photographs in *The Journal* hinted that many people cut their own hair, and it often looked as if they had only dull scissors and a clouded mirror with which to work.

If you could afford tobacco at all, you smoked roll-your-owns. The prideful could buy a cigarette rolling machine for less than a buck that made a roll-your-own look pretty close to a tailor-made.

If a man was lucky, he might have one good suit. Chances were good that it was frayed at the collar and cuffs. A woman might have a couple of housedresses, usually made of printed cotton. Even in the black-and-white photographs, the colours appear as wan as the person wearing it.

Whether wearing a frayed suit or a faded dress, many people had empty pockets and empty stomachs. There were no *Journal* reports of anyone starving to death locally, but finding the next meal often wasn't easy.

Weather Forecast
Cloudy and Mild

Edmonton Journal

'One Of Canada's Great Newspapers'

THIRTY-SIXTH YEAR ** EDMONTON, ALBERTA, FRIDAY, NOVEMBER 18, 1938 SINGLE COPY, 5 CENTS 30 PAGES

Canada Loses British Preference On Wheat; Gains Freer Trade Entry Into United States

200 Unemployed Men Take Possession Lobby Jasper Avenue Hotel

Declare They Will Stay There Until Single Jobless Aided

GROUP IS ORDERLY

In a demonstration they said was planned to bring their plight to the attention of the authorities, 200 unemployed men took possession of the Corona hotel lobby Friday afternoon. They said they were representatives of the Single Men's Unemployed Protective association.

A squad of city police under Chief Shute was called to the scene immediately and up to :45 had made no attempt to eject the men. At that time over 100 men were seated or standing in the lobby and others were walking up and down outside the hotel.

H. Johnson, representative of the Single Men's association told THE JOURNAL the men were prepared to stay in the hotel until the authorities indicated they were ready to aid the single unemployed, for whom "no relief whatever is given at the present time."

The men were perfectly orderly. They indicated no plans yet had been made to secure food.

A committee of spokesmen was set up, consisting of Jack Nicholson, Harry Johnson, Gordon Wilson, Peter Evans and Leslie Robertson.

The unemployed said they had called a meeting at the Albion hall Thursday and invited relief officials and members of the legislature relief committee. No one showed up, the unemployed said.

The men assembled at the Market Square at 1:00 p.m. and marched to the hotel in a body. They arrived about 2:15 p.m.

Say Pact Benefits Argentine Wheat

By A. C. Cummings
(Special to Edmonton Journal and Associated Southam Newspapers)

LONDON, Nov. 18.—The London wheat market understands that in consequence of the operation of the most-favored-nation clause, Russian and Argentine wheat will enter the United Kingdom duty free under provisions of the Anglo-American trade pact signed Thursday.

Two TCA Pilots Killed As Plane Falls, Burns After Regina Take-off

Type of Trans-Canada Airlines Ship Which Crashed at Regina

Above is shown the type of Trans-Canada Airlines twin-engined ship which crashed two miles west of Regina airport early Friday after a night takeoff, killing two pilots. The liner was on the regular air mail run from Winnipeg to Vancouver. The pilots were the only occupants of the 14-passenger plane. A board of inquiry will be appointed by the dominion government to report to the department of transport.

Rumor Dominion To Take Refugees

Dominion May Do Its Part, Is General Opinion

By Charles Bishop
(Special to Edmonton Journal and Associated Southam Newspapers)

OTTAWA, Nov. 18.—Report from London that word reached there Thursday the Canadian government had agreed to the admission of several thousand Jewish refugees from Germany caused many inquiries Friday. It was impossible definitely to ascertain the background of this report.

Impression here is that if, as reported from London, other dominions are prepared to take a quota of German Jewish refugees, Canada will do its part, subject to certain understandings and the usual guarantee against any so admitted becoming a public charge.

Treaties Appro…
In British…

Premier Leaving At Once For Refund Talk in Ottawa

Will Leave for Federal Capital Immediately, He Announces

FOR WHOLE DEBT

Premier Aberhart plans to leave for Ottawa "immediately" for the purpose of discussing an Alberta public debt refunding scheme with the dominion government, he announced Friday.

The scheme involves the refunding of Alberta's total … $157,000,000, … savings …

Little Harm Seen In Wheat Change

CALGARY, Nov. 18.—Farmers of western Canada will suffer little as a result of the removal of the six-cent preference on Canadian wheat in the United Kingdom, in the opinion of Lew Hutchinson, chairman of the Alberta wheat pool board. Rather, an eventual increase … for Canadian … by Mr. Hu… sibility …

Ottawa Pledges Early Removal 3% Excise Tax on U.S. Goods

Lumber, Farm Products, Some Minerals Benefit By New Agreement

FISHERMEN TO GAIN

Livestock Quotas Increased; Washington Makes Concessions on 202 Items

By C. R. Blackburn
(Canadian Press Staff Writer)

OTTAWA, Nov. 18. — Broadened and smoother highway for Canadian products moving into the U.S. market was opened Thursday but at the cost of the dominion's wheat preference in the United Kingdom and a lessening of other preferences, including that on apples, in favor of the U.S.

This was revealed when details of the new Canada-U.S. trade agreement, signed in Washington, were made public in Ottawa, accompanied by an explanation of Canada's part in the Anglo-American trade agreement, signed at the same time.

Canadian concessions … U.S. also were … lowering or …

List Highlights Canada Position

OTTAWA, Nov. 18.—Highlights of Canada's new trading position as affected by the treaties signed in Washington Thursday between Canada and the U.S. and the United Kingdom and the U.S.:

The six-cent-a-bushel duty on foreign wheat entering the U.K. market is removed, putting U.S. and Canadian wheat on equal footing with respect to duty rates.

United Kingdom has made a seasonal reduction in the raw apple duty from four shillings, six pence a hundred-weight to three shillings. Canadian apples will continue to enjoy a substantial preference.

Entry is provided into the United Kingdom market of those kinds of lumber of which the U.S. is an important supplier of U.K. requirements on terms as favorable as those on which Canadian lumber is admitted into U.S. market.

There are 202 items and sub-items in the …

Britain Makes Large Concessions to U.S. on Farm Products

AFFECTS MUCH TRADE

Washington Gives United Kingdom Lower Duty On Textiles

By Andrue Berding
(Associated Press Staff Writer)

WASHINGTON, Nov. 18.—Three great merchant nations—Britain, Canada and the United States—offered one another far-reaching tariff reductions Friday in the expressed hope of increasing foreign

Additional stories on the trade pacts will be found on Pages 2, 5, 7, 10, 12 and 13.

Few could afford a car – registrations dropped to 86,041 in 1933 from a high of 102,652 in 1930 – and those who did, particularly in rural Alberta, often hitched it to a horse. They were called Bennett Buggies, after R.B. Bennett, the Tory prime minister blamed by many for failing to put an end to the crushing poverty of the times.

The Journal's regular automobile section, a paper staple in the '20s, disappeared in the mid-'30s.

No one knew what to do about the Depression. *The Journal* didn't, its readers didn't and the politicians didn't either. It came and it stayed.

Before it ended at the close of the decade, *The Journal* reported on the toll the economic hardship took on the city, including a riot of the unemployed in the city's market square that was crushed by police.

It also reported on one king's abdication, the visit of another king and his queen, a premier's scandalous departure from office, the emergence of a new political dynasty in Alberta, the rise of fascism in Europe and the first months of a war that lasted six long and bitter years.

The decade changed the face of the country, the province, the city and the newspaper.

Journal coverage retained an element of boosterism as it encouraged readers to stick with local merchants and manufacturers. But the newspaper itself matured in look and content, running more photographs and showing more sophistication in its coverage. It also became less partisan, although it still supported the Tories and was a fervent believer in the role of the Empire. Today's readers would begin to recognize the contemporary *Journal*, particularly in the latter half of the decade.

But despite the economic downturn, the thousands of homeless men on its streets and the hundreds of families on relief, Edmonton was a city that clung to a sense of optimism born of pioneer parents and grandparents.

Their newspaper shared that confidence, especially when the four-storey Birks Building on Jasper Avenue and 104th Street opened almost a year after the markets had crashed and the Depression had set in.

Montreal-based Birks, an upscale jewelry store, took up most of the main floor, with the three top floors rented to doctors and dentists. The building also housed the Commerce Drug Co., Ltd., which proudly proclaimed itself to be "Edmonton's finest drug store" in its first *Journal* ad on Sept. 8, 1930.

And *The Journal* knew a great building when it saw one. "With construction and style as near perfect as builders and architects can make it, the new Birks building at 104th Street and Jasper is the most modern building in Edmonton, and it is patterned after the latest in construction methods adopted in skyscrapers in the East."

It was eight years before the next major construction boom signalled the end of the Depression with The Bay's new building in 1938 on Jasper and 103rd Street and in 1939 with Eaton's at 101st Street and 102nd Avenue.

Despite the buoyant cheerfulness, there was no avoiding bad news.

A drought throughout Western Canada meant that the average yield per acre for wheat in 1931 was 11.6 bushels compared with 16.9 bushels in 1930. Other crops were worse. Barley production was cut in half; rye went

***Feb. 19, 1930*:**
The Alberta government reports issuing 136,355 driver's licences since July 1929, when it became a requirement for vehicle operators to have a personal licence.

***Feb. 22, 1930*:**
A new Ford Roadster sells for $540 ($5,974 today), the luxury Town Sedan car costs $835 ($9,237 today).

***March 27, 1930*:**
J.W. McDonald is elected leader of Alberta's Liberal Party.

***March 27, 1930*:**
The Edmonton Grads beat Seattle Ferry Lines by 59 points over two games to retain the Underwood Trophy and the women's international basketball title.

***May 24, 1930*:**
The airport at Red Deer, Alberta, is officially opened.

***June 19, 1930*:**
Led by Premier John Brownlee, the UFA is returned to power, taking 39 of 63 ridings in a provincial election.

***June 26, 1930*:**
Edmonton's civic census shows a population of 81,016.

AUTO WRECKAGE

ND-3-6742 Glenbow Archives

The Fehr family stops in Edmonton while making their way back to Saskatoon from Peace River, June 28, 1934.

VITAPHONE
DECEPTION
'DECEPTION'
CUT RATE SALE

ND-3-6265a Glenbow Archives

Volunteers with *The Journal*'s Sunshine Society prepare hampers for the needy in 1932.

from 22 million bushels to 5.3 million. Prices hit the skids because of low demand due to the world-wide depression, and what wheat there was sold for 38 cents a bushel.

Local merchants suffered, although jeweller H.B. Kline put topspin on the downturn. In a post-Christmas advertisement in 1932, Kline announced "owing to conditions, we were unable to dispose of our stock of quality jewelry at Christmas time. Literally, we are forced to stay in business and we have decided to carry on in the same location as we have in the past." Kline's store was located on the south side of Jasper Avenue, west of 100th Street.

The Western premiers met regularly and bandied ideas about, but grain prices remained low, not enough rain fell to water the crops, and unemployed men and women in the cities needed relief assistance.

Jobless rates climbed, and by early 1931 *The Journal* reported there were 5,171 unemployed men in the city, and their numbers were growing by as much as 300 a week.

In 1928, the average salary was $548 a year, less than half the amount needed for an adequate lifestyle.

Not great, but not too bad either when you could buy a very fancy dinner at the King Edward Hotel on 101st Street and 102nd Street for 35 cents. By 1933 the average yearly income had tumbled to $212.

"Like most other communities, Edmonton is a victim of a general condition whose chief characteristic is falling revenue and growing expenditure," said a Nov. 1, 1932, editorial.

"The annual reports to city council emphasize that Edmonton is still in the woods and must proceed with care, tightening its belt if necessary, but determined to win through."

It was a grim time all around. Figures reported in the newspaper pointed out that in 1931 the city had paid the rents for 331 families at a cost of $4,353 a month.

A year later the number was 1,065 and the cost had risen to $12,580. Homeless men found shelter where they could, sleeping under the High Level Bridge and in the river valley in summer, and in church basements and abandoned buildings in winter.

Some turned their hand to panning for gold in the North Saskatchewan. No one struck it rich.

In 1932, the United Farmers of Alberta government reduced provincial expenditures by more than $1.5 million.

"The government fully recognizes," Premier John Edward Brownlee said Jan. 4, "that every effort should be made to reduce expenditure before any additional taxation is imposed during the period of depression."

The city provided money to help the poor buy groceries. "We get five dollars a week for food and a dollar for milk. It's just enough to keep us alive," said a mother in a November 1932 story.

With her six dollars she was expected to feed herself, her husband, three sons, aged four, nine and 17, and two girls, aged five and seven. Her husband had been out of work for two years and their savings were gone.

Nevertheless, in 1932 a tweed suit with two pair of pants was worth $10 ($134.95 today) at Christie Grants department store on the west side of 101st Street just north of Jasper Avenue.

***July 1, 1930*:**
The wild rose becomes the official floral emblem of the Province of Alberta.

Sept. 13, 1930:
"Announcement that 207 barrels of commercially pure dry bitumen is being shipped from McMurry to be placed on the market marks another milestone in the development of the great tar sand deposits in northern Alberta. Experiments are still being carried out looking toward the use of these so-called tar sands as a surfacing material for highways. When these reach ultimate success, Alberta and the west generally will realize to the full just what a treasure-house lies in the northern part of this province." – editorial.

***Sept. 17, 1930*:**
Edmonton's first major air show opens at the Municipal Aerodrome, later renamed Blatchford Field.

***Oct. 1, 1930*:**
Alberta gains control of its natural resources from the federal government.

***Oct. 25, 1930*:**
Matt McCauley, in 1892 Edmonton's first town mayor, dies.

"Hangman" Ellis Passes in East

Executioner of Over 200 Passes in Montreal Hospital

WAS 73 YEARS OLD

MONTREAL, July 22.—Arthur Ellis, the methodical little executioner who seldom was known by his real name of Arthur Bartholomew Alexander English, died in hospital Thursday night after a brief illness of undisclosed nature.

The shuffling little man, of snowy-white hair, heavy spectacles and a flair for detailed ceremony when he stood on scaffolds at daybreak, was 73 years old.

Death came more slowly to the "five foot, three" man than to the 200 persons he was estimated to have dropped from the gallows during the quarter-century he served as unofficial executioner for Canada. He was stricken in his small rented room a couple of days ago, apparently, but the news leaked out only Wednesday when he was discovered in hospital.

Came From England

Hospital authorities and attending doctors declined to discuss the illness of English, who came to Canada from England about 25 years ago and became assistant to "Ratcliffe," the man who previously was the country's unofficial executioner.

For years he lived his private life, a far transition from that of a public hangman who took pride in relating to newspapermen the trouble he had experienced in perfecting details of a difficult execution. Away from the scaffold's shadow, he served as a political campaigner for the late Sir Lomer Gouin who learned of his agent's true identity only years later.

Coast to Coast

From coast to coast, Ellis used to travel, earning his $150 or $200 and expenses by pulling a lever that would drop a murderer to death. And in his craft he took the pride of a workman, accurate, methodical and fast. In his tall hat, frock coat, white carnation and gloves he would adjust the black cap, usually utter a word of assurance to the murderer

An imported steel-grey worsted suit that was woven "with hard service in view," was $33 ($445.32) was available at La Fleche Bros., on 102nd Street, north of Jasper Avenue.

To have that new suit dry-cleaned cost 40 cents ($5.40) at Dollar Cleaners. For 10 cents more ($1.35), there was home pickup and delivery.

And if you wanted to be a sport, you wore your new suit to the Shasta on Jasper Avenue and 102nd Street, where you had a choice of eating in three different dining rooms or at the counter.

A full-course, soup-to-dessert dinner in the Peacock Room, complete with a live orchestra for your entertainment, was a buck.

For 75 cents (about $10 today) the same menu was available in the Grotto, the Arcade or at the counter.

A haircut cost 35 cents ($4.72) for both men and women, and although men paid only 15 cents for a neck shave, women were charged a quarter for the same service.

Eight rolls of toilet paper sold for 29 cents at the Army and Navy on the east side of 101st Street, a half a block north of Jasper. The Hudson's Bay store on Jasper sold Rayon Uplift brassieres for 50 cents, and Windsor gas ranges for $59.

Rent for a suite in the Arlington on 106th Street and 100th Avenue started at $37.50 a month, ($796.18 today). With its high ceilings and steam heat, it was the most prestigious apartment building in the city.

Wants ads from 1933 told of cheaper places to live; if you were willing to share a furnished room in a house on 96th Street and 107th Avenue you could get by for as little as $5 a month in rent, including laundry service.

A shiny 1932 Pontiac Six with new syncro mesh transmission, a longer wheelbase and body by Fisher sold for $925 ($12,482.42) at Dayton Motors. Still, when a good job paid $400 a year, that Pontiac Six looked unattainable.

But even if they had no money, people loved cars. "Crowds of motor minded Edmontonians flocked to the array of modern engineering triumphs displayed at Edmonton's first motor show in the hall on 101st Street," *The Journal* reported on Feb. 26.

"Women showed particular interest in the smart new fashions in car lines and interior finishing with super simple control arrangement, but the more mechanically-minded males preferred poking their heads under hood covers to find out just what made the 1932 motors different from their outdated predecessors."

Dreaming of luxuries didn't make ends meet. Not when a job paying $15 a week was something to be coveted. These were hard years and many thought that political action was necessary.

A hunger march involving 3,000 out-of-work men and women descended on Edmonton's downtown market square on 99th Street and 102nd Avenue – the site of the current Stanley A. Milner Library – on Dec. 20, 1932, despite the refusal of both the city and the province to give approval for the demonstration.

"Blood flowed Tuesday afternoon on the city's market square when RCMP and city police broke up an attempted 'hunger march' allegedly organized by Communists in defiance of a government ban."

***Nov. 5, 1930*:**
Edmonton's Mayor J.M. Douglas is re-elected by acclamation when no other candidate files nomination papers. Civic elections move to November from December.

***Dec. 16, 1930*:**
Canadian National's return train fare from Edmonton to Toronto is $92.

***April 11, 1931*:**
Alberta Senator P.E. Lessard of Edmonton dies unexpectedly. Supporters of Emily Murphy hope the city woman who led the recent Persons Case fight to have women declared persons and eligible to sit in Canada's Senate will be appointed to the vacancy. Her supporters are disappointed as pioneer Alberta meatpacker and rancher Pat Burns is appointed to the Senate by fellow Calgarian, Prime Minister R.B. Bennett.

***June 11, 1931*:**
A federal act proclaims Armistice Day, Nov. 11, a holiday and renames it Remembrance Day.

***June 30, 1931*:**
Round-the-world flyers Wiley Post and Harold Gatty land at Edmonton's Blatchford Field.

Everybody . . .

WILL BE READING

JOURNAL WANT ADS

Next Week Is WANT AD WEEK

Prizes for Advertisers

A Printella Wash Frock
—From Emery Co., Ltd.

5-lb. Pail of Gainers' Lard
—Pure Kettle Rendered Lard.

4 lbs. Peanut Butter, Vanilla Extract
—Manufactured by Pioneer Mfg. Co.

10-lb. package of Soapone
A Laundry Soap from Soapone Products, Ltd.

1 lb. Coffee, ½ lb. Tea, Baking Powder
—From National Tea and Coffee.

Box of "Western Romance" Chocolates
—Manufactured by Pavey Candy Co.

Turn to the Want Ad pages for full details on how to win these prizes.

The Mighty Mite of Advertising Steps into the Limelight today inaugurating National Want Ad Week, April 17 to 24. This period is set aside for the purpose of focusing public attention upon one of the most economical and most effective of all forms of advertising.

Small in stature but tremendous in pulling power. A dwarf physically, but gigantic from the standpoint of results.

A JOURNAL WANT AD

Your decision to let Journal Want Ads help you is no experiment. Years of consistent and satisfactory results is your guide to a proven medium . . . Edmonton Journal Want Ads. For helpful suggestions to present your message in a clear and concise manner

Telephone 23481

April 17 National Want Ad Week April 24 Association of Newspaper Classified Advertising Managers

Edmonton Journal Want Ads

"If It's Fully Told—It's Quickly Sold"

Office Hours 8:00 a.m. to 10:00 p.m.

Want Ad Readers!

HERE'S HOW YOU CAN WIN

Cash Prizes and Theatre Tickets

During Want Ad Week

Turn to the Want Ad pages and read them over carefully then answer the five questions that are listed there. That is all you have to do to enter this contest. If your answers are correct and are written out neatly you have an excellent chance of winning.

1st Prize, $2 Cash

2nd Prize, $1 Cash

And the next 5 Prizes

Double Guest Tickets To RIALTO THEATRE

Turn to the Want Ad pages for full information on this new and interesting Contest.

NOW SHOWING
AT THE

RIALTO

"You Only Live Once"
Featuring SYLVIA SIDNEY and HENRY FONDA

ALSO

"Git Along Little Dogies"
Featuring the famous Singing Cowboy, GENE AUTRY

CAPT. HAWKS' Time Ray
BACK TO THE DAYS OF ATTILA THE HUN
TIME TURNS BACK 1504 YEARS
Capt. Frank Hawks has installed the Time Ray in his airplane—an invention that turns time backward and forward. Today Hawks with Tim and Patsy, charter members of the Sky Patrol, go back 1504 years to the Roman Province of Gaul—now France. Gaul is being invaded by Attila and the Huns. The Romans have sent General Aetius to drive them away. Capt. Hawks lands his plane near a Roman Army camp . . .
ARE WE REALLY BACK IN GAUL, CAPT. FRANK? GEE, I'M KIND OF SCARED!
DON'T WORRY, PATSY. THAT'S NO WAY FOR A SKY PATROL MEMBER TO TALK. WE'LL BE O.K.!
HA! WHAT STRANGE FOLK WE FIND IN THIS STRANGE LAND OF GAUL! TAKE THEM TO GENERAL AETIUS!
WHAT'LL THEY DO WITH US, CAPT. FRANK?
I DON'T KNOW. BUT THE SKY PATROL ALWAYS COMES THROUGH WITH FLYING COLORS!
GOOD! MORE CAPTIVES FOR MY TRIUMPH! THEY'LL LOOK WELL IN THE ARENA-FIGHTING LIONS! AWAY..
GENERAL! GENERAL! ATTILA THE HUN AND HIS HORDES ARE SWEEPING ON US!
ATTILA! WE HAVEN'T GOT A CHANCE! WE'RE DOOMED!
STOP! SET MY FRIENDS AND ME FREE! WE ARE A WHOLE LOT STRANGER PEOPLE THAN YOU THINK! WE CAN SAVE YOU!
GO, THEN-YOU DO ME NO GOOD NOW!
FLEE, MEN--ERE THIS STRANGE MONSTER DESTROYS US!
TERRORIZED BY THE GREAT PLANE'S THUNDEROUS ROAR, THEY FLEE IN PANIC AS HAWKS DIVES HIS SPEEDING PLANE DIRECTLY AT THEM.
IN THE NAME OF EMPEROR VALENTINIAN III, I GIVE YOU ROME'S THANKS. YOU AND YOUR THUNDER BIRD HAVE GIVEN ATTILA A FRIGHT HE WILL NOT SOON FORGET!
BACK AGAIN IN 1937
BOY! THAT WAS EXCITING, BUT-YOU CAN'T DOWN THE SKY PATROL!
YOU BET! NOW DIG INTO THOSE POST'S BRAN FLAKES! THEY SURE HELP TO KEEP YOU IN TIP-TOP SHAPE. I WANT ALL SKY PATROL MEMBERS TO EAT THEM EVERY DAY!
AND THEY TASTE BETTER THAN ANY CEREAL WE EVER ATE, TOO!
HOW YOU'LL "GO FOR" THIS DELICIOUS, NUT-LIKE FLAVOR
Post's Bran Flakes are really different from any other cereal you ever tasted . . . with a crunchy goodness and delicious, nut-like flavor you'll love. Ask Mother to get a package today. She'll be glad because she knows how good Post's Bran Flakes are for you.
Post's Bran Flakes
The Same Fine Cereal NOW IN NEW PACKAGE
REAL LIFE MOVIES
FOR GROWN-UPS
WHY POST'S BRAN FLAKES HELP KEEP YOU FIT
Often that dull, logy, tired feeling comes from sluggish intestines — result of too little bulk in your diet. Post's Bran Flakes help supply the needed bulk. Try this delicious cereal. It may do you a world of good.
MONTH LATER
Boys and Girls! JOIN MY SKY PATROL!
Get my swell new Sky Patrol Pin and big, new Sky Patrol Club Newspaper that tells the things expert pilots must know about planes, weather, "stunting", blind flying, etc. Also shows
MANY FREE PRIZES FOR SKY PATROL MEMBERS
SKY PATROL RING
Beautiful 24-carat gold finish. Adjustable to fit any finger. FREE for 3 box-tops.
HOW TO JOIN Capt. Hawks' Sky Patrol.
Fill in Coupon, send it with two Post's Bran Flakes box-tops to Capt. Frank Hawks. He will send your Sky Patrol Club Newspaper showing the wonderful free prizes.
Identification Bracelet with your initial on it. State which initial you want. FREE for box-tops.
Sky Patrol Official Badge
Two-tone bronze finish.
and Sky Patrol Club Newspaper
Lots of fascinating flying "dope". BOTH FREE FOR 2 BOX-TOPS.
Capt. Frank Hawks
Cobourg, Ont.
I enclose .... Post Bran Flakes box-tops. Please enroll me in your Sky Patrol and send me items checked.
☐ Official Badge and Newspaper (2 box-tops).
☐ Sky Patrol Pilot's Ring (3 box-tops).
Name
Address
City or Town
Prov.
B10-37
69

Farmers from outside the city, most of them single and unemployed and faced with foreclosures on their land, joined the marchers who demanded unemployment insurance paid for by their bosses, weekly cash payments to the unemployed, closure of the "slave" labour camps and the end of taxation until the economy improved.

More than two dozen people were arrested for unlawful assembly, though most were acquitted or had the charges dismissed. According to *Journal* coverage, 10,000 Edmontonians turned out to watch the demonstrators.

The newspaper had its own conspiracy theory about the Market Square riot: "The so-called 'hunger marchers' were not taken by surprise.

"Their leaders were told by the provincial government last month that any convergent march upon Edmonton could not be allowed. They evaded this order and brought in several hundred men, many of them farmers. They deliberately planned and provoked a test of strength.

"That may be in strict accord with Communist orders from Moscow but cannot be tolerated in Canada."

The newspaper, did however, show sympathy for the unemployed, encouraging readers to help the less fortunate, and published tips on how to get by on very little. There were recipes for how to cook cheaper cuts of meat such as beef heart and tripe, and advice on proper canning techniques so that produce could be put up for winter.

There was a willingness to try just about anything to find a way out of the Depression. Ald. J.W. Findlay proposed that a block of city-owned lots in the Hudson's Bay Reserve just north of downtown be sold for $1 apiece, as long as the purchaser agreed to build a home costing not less than $1,000 on the property.

"I say we should go the whole hog or none at all to get this land back on the tax roll," Findlay urged in the Jan. 6, 1932, story.

His fellow aldermen did not agree.

Three weeks later, another story reported that the city wanted the provincial government to set up a self-sustaining farm colony near the city that would provide food and lodging for up to 1,000 unemployed men. Nothing, however, came of it.

The newspaper grasped at hopeful signs. "Wheat Futures Up Full Limit, Stocks in Rise," said a front-page headline from Oct. 29, 1937, as commodity and stock prices showed a one-day rally.

"New York stock exchange, recovering from Tuesday's wild selling splurge, presented a cheery aspect as prices swept upward," said another story. "Canadian markets 'smiled' with it."

Farther down the page, there was gloomier news. The market was not on a permanent upswing at all. "President Roosevelt, officials said Tuesday, has no intention of exercising his authority to close the New York stock exchange. The president himself refused to discuss the falling market at a press conference."

In the midst all the gloom and hardship, the province was gripped by the juiciest political scandal in its history.

It was a down-and-dirty bit of business involving 51-year-old Premier Brownlee and Vivian MacMillan, the 18-year-old daughter of Edson's

They complete the last leg of their record eight-day, 15-hour flight the next day.

***July 21, 1931*:**
Alberta's record high temperature of 43.3 degrees Celsius is recorded at Bassano Dam.

***July 31, 1931*:**
The first Trans-Canada Air Pageant airshow is held at Edmonton's airport.

***Nov. 3, 1931*:**
Emily Murphy resigns as an Edmonton police magistrate.

***Nov. 11, 1931*:**
Labour candidate and *Journal* employee Daniel Knott defeats Mayor J.M. Douglas by more than 3,000 votes in Edmonton's civic election. More than 20,000 Edmontonians cast ballots, the largest municipal voter turnout then recorded, and printers are forced to produce additional ballots.

***Nov. 30, 1931*:**
The population of Alberta is 727,497, according to the Dominion Bureau of Statistics.

***Dec. 31, 1930*:**
"During the day a traffic count is being made at the corner of Jasper Avenue and 101 Street...It is stated that this is a preliminary to

Weather Forecast
Cloudy and Cool

Edmonton Journal

'One Of Canada's Great Newspapers'

THIRTY-FOURTH YEAR ** EDMONTON, ALBERTA, FRIDAY, APRIL 23, 1937 SINGLE COPY, 5 CENTS 24 PAGES

Cabinet Situation 'Intolerable' So Resigned, Says Cockroft Attacking Aberhart Principles

3 British Food Ships Smash Rebel Blockade; Warships, Guns Protect

Frantically Cheering Crowds of Basques Hail Arrival of Freighters at Bilbao With Much-Needed Supplies for City's Populace

BATTLE CRUISER HOOD STEAMS TO RESCUE WHEN SHELL CRASHES OVER BRITON'S BOWS

Government and Rebel Pilots Engage in Sky Fights as Vessels Dock—Over 6,000 Tons of Provisions Landed to Ease Famine

BILBAO, Spain, April 23.—Fleet of three British food ships, under the protection of British men-of-war and the barking guns of Basque shore batteries, ran a gauntlet of insurgent fire Friday to break through the blockade of Bilbao with desperately needed supplies.

Frantically cheering crowds of Basques lined the docks to greet the sturdy merchantmen as they came into view down the lower reaches of the broad Nervion river.

Crammed into their holds were 6,100 tons of foodstuffs for the starving population of the city, swollen to almost 400,000 by the steady influx of refugees from the surrounding country.

The three cargo vessels, the MacGregor, the Hamsterley and the Stanbrook, captained by veteran British seadogs, defied the shells of the insurgent fleet during the night and docked just after 8:00 a.m. (1:00 a.m. Edmonton time).

Government and insurgent pilots engaged in sky fights high over the capital while the cargo boats docked. Insurgent fliers dumped more than 50 bombs on Bilbao but made no attempt to damage the British ships. Government aviators, rising to battle the air raiders, lost one aeroplane.

Just before dawn, the ski[...] the Masterl[...] cessful br[...] th[...]

Thirty Injured In Strike Riot

Guns Blaze, Tear-Gas Used in Stockton, Calif., Melee

AT CAN[...]

Dr. J. S. Wright, well-known Edmonton physician, who is in Royal Alexandra hospital suffering concussion of the brain and other head and hand injuries as a result of an auto crash Thursday night in which two other men were hurt. Cars driven by Dr. Wright and Malcolm McCallum, 11216 Jasper ave., collided head-on at St. Albert trail and 118 ave. Both machines were wrecked.

Japan, Soviet Reach Accord

Report Agreement Reached in Principle on New Pact

PARLEYS SUCCEED

Oshawa Strike Comes To End; Work Monday

Agreements Provides No Affiliation With John L. Lewis Group

VOTE 2,205 TO 36

Five-Day, 44-Hour Week Provided for Employes

OSHAWA, Ont., April 23.—General Motors employes Friday voted 2,205 to 36 to return to work Monday, thus ending the 16-day strike which had tied up the vast automobile plant.

Charles Millard, president of the Oshawa Union, announced acceptance of settlement to a cheering crowd of strikers who had balloted in the armories here after terms were disclosed to them.

The agreement provides no affiliation with the John L. Lewis Committee for Industrial Organization, but "shall run concurrently with the agreement between the United Automobile Workers of America (C. I. O. affiliate) and General Motors corporation in the United States," J. L. Cohen, union counsel, stated.

The agreement provides a five-day, 44-hour week, employes to [...] nine hours a day for the first [...] of the week and eight [...]

Charles Cockroft, former provincial treasurer, who told his constituency executive at Stettler Thursday night the reasons for his split with Premier Aberhart. Mr. Cockroft levelled against the premier several specific charges of a serious nature.

Leaders Quit In City Strike

Thompson Announces Move, Denies Tie-up Is Ended

MEET AT WEEK-END

Victor Thompson, business agent of the Edmonton Meat Packing and Purveying union and central figure in the five industrial tie-ups which [...]rted in the city three weeks ago, [...]d at 1:30 p.m. Friday that [...] handed in his resigna-[...]

Ex-Minister Breaks Silence On His Split With Premier, Inviting Recall Proceedings

Grave Charges Levelled by Former Cabinet Member in Official Statement to Constituency Executive at Stettler

PROMISES RESIGN IF 40 PER CENT ELECTORS SIGN PETITION ASKING HIS RECALL AS M.L.A.

Specific Statements on Financial Policies, Relations of Alberta Government With Dominion Are Presented

(Special to The Journal)

STETTLER, April 23.—Breaking a silence he had maintained since January 1 when he resigned as provincial treasurer, Charles Cockroft, S. C., Stettler, Thursday night told his constituency executive why he had split with Premier Aberhart. Mr. Cockroft levelled grave charges against the premier relative to, in the ex-minister's words, "ethics," "principles" and "faith."

Serious and costly errors in governmental policy were laid at the premier's door by the man who had served the inner councils of the administration for 17 months.

"My position became intolerable," declared Mr. Cockroft, in outlining his complaints against the premier.

At the same time, Mr. Cockroft invited his constituency to institute recall proceedings against him, promising to resign if 40 per cent of the electors signed a recall petition, instead of the 66 per cent required in the recall act. Otherwise, said Mr. Cockroft, he would ask that his seat in the legislature be moved to the "independent" section of the house.

No action was taken by the executive on Mr. Cockroft[...] invitation for a recall petition. At the same time [...] by members of the executive, there was little li[...] action as Mr. Cockroft is believed to be su[...] majority of Stettler Social Credit-ers. [...] expected to leave [...]

Paralysis Aid In Cobra Venom

MEMPHIS, April 23—Cobra venom was reported as a new remedy in paralysis before the Federation of American Societies for Experimental Biology here Thursday. It reduces the tremors in "shaking palsy."

More than 1,000 scientists listened to reports of this and several other startling discoveries. One of them shows the hand receives orders from the brain 6-1000ths of a second quicker than the foot.

The cobra venom was used by David I. Macht of Baltimore on paralysis agitans, and found it is, in some cases, as good a pain killer as morphine without being habit forming.

Morris Baker Held At Coast

Ex-Mayoralty Candidate Sought Since Bail "Jumped"

more purchasing POWER
FOR YOU

NMA-2378-15 Glenbow Archives

Democracy Series
Pamphlet No. 4

WOULD A WORM STARVE BECAUSE— the APPLE was TOO BIG?

If It Is Physically Possible It Must Be Economically Feasible

MUST men and women and little children go **under-nourished** BECAUSE there is too much to eat?

MUST they live in **hovels** and **shacks** BECAUSE there is an **abundance** of home building materials?

MUST they go **cold** BECAUSE there is **so much** coal and wood and fuel?

MUST they be **ill-clad** BECAUSE we can make **all** the clothes **they need?**

MUST they go **ill-shod** BECAUSE we have **leather** in abundance, and BECAUSE we can make ALL the shoes we are able to wear?

NMA-2378-14 Glenbow Archives

Social Credit pamphlets, 1939.

mayor, A.D. MacMillan. Encouraged by Brownlee to come to the city to study and work, MacMillan alleged in a civil suit that the premier had seduced her.

Unwilling to offend its family readers *The Journal's* coverage was necessarily discreet, though it did run page after page of court testimony. The truly salacious coverage was left to *The Bulletin*, its longtime rival.

However, there was still plenty left to titillate readers.

Evidence suggested that Brownlee had urged MacMillan to engage in sex because the health of Mrs. Brownlee prevented her from doing so.

The Journal reported amorous car rides in the country, trysts in the Legislature Building itself, and heated couplings in the Brownlee home. Indeed, sex between the two took place in a bed next to the one where a Brownlee son lay sleeping.

It was almost enough to make readers forget the Depression.

The headline in *The Journal's* special Extra edition Sunday, July 1, "Brownlee Announces Plan Resign Premiership At Once," told readers of the premier's intentions after the jury found him guilty.

However it wasn't until the July 4 paper that readers found out Acting Justice W.C. Ives had reversed the verdict.

"Judge Dismisses Jury Finding, Orders MacMillans Pay Costs."

Mr. Justice Ives ruling was appealed to the Supreme Court of Canada which in 1937 overturned the decision in favour of the MacMillans. Brownlee appealed that to the Privy Council in England, then Canada's final court of appeal, but lost in 1940.

Brownlee sat as an MLA for Ponoka until the UFA was defeated in the Aug. 22, 1935, election.

It's interesting to note there were no letters published in the paper dealing with the case before or after the verdict and the only mention of public reaction was in the July 3 edition with a headline: "Orderlies clear court corridors when loud cheers greet verdict."

However, a one-paragraph item of interest appeared in the Friday, July 6, edition: "Ranks of the Canadian Civil Liberties Protective association are torn as a result of the action of its executive committee in sponsoring an appeal to the privy council for Vivian and A.D. MacMillan, whose award of $15,000 damages by a jury was recently reversed by Acting Justice Ives. Above are shown seven members of the association's executive." Those pictured were: vice-president, Miss Cox; president, Capt. C.D.C Koe; secretary, Mrs. Timbers; advisory, Norman Priestly; executive, S.A.G. Barnes; executive, Mrs. I. Ringwood; and solicitor J.A. Clarke.

Richard Gavin Reid, a bookish politician who served in a variety of portfolios from the time the first UFA government was elected in 1921, replaced Brownlee.

Emphasizing his happy family life, a *Journal* story warmly welcomed Reid on July 5. "The fact that her husband is premier of Alberta will interfere as little as possible with the even tenor of a happy family life, is the determination of Mrs. R.G. Reid.

"Sitting in her comfortable drawing room, fragrant with the scent of enormous bowls of peonies everywhere, with the morning sunshine streaming through the windows, and the odd teddy bear and kiddy car

determine if automatic electric traffic control signals would improve conditions...this is certainly not the time for the city to spend any money on such a project...To install and operate such a system would require the expenditure of several thousands of dollars. That sum would supply the chief with one or two extra men." – editorial.

Jan. 5, 1932:
Here's a sample of what was available on CKUA: 4 p.m. - Homemakers Hour.
4:10 p.m. - "The Importance of Keeping a Proper Degree of Humidity in the Home" by Dr. M.R. Bow.
7:30 p.m. - "Pictures of English Life in the 18th and 19th Centuries."
The broadcast day ended at 9:30 p.m. with the Farmers' Forum where Prof. L.H. Nichols and S.G. Carlyle, provincial livestock commissioner, discussed "Weather Lore" and "Livestock Problems."

Jan. 30, 1932:
RCMP Constable Edgar Millen is shot and killed by a man known as Albert Johnson, the Mad Trapper, since December the target of a police manhunt near Aklavik in the Northwest

The thrifty way to travel First-class
1937 Ford V-8 owners pay less for their cars in the long run, and travel first-class all the time!
Basic reason is the V-8 engine. Eight cylinders give smoother performance. V-type construction is the most advanced, and permits a much more compact power-plant. Space saved under the hood means more room in the body, and more comfort for you.
This year's V-8 engine is improved to give even greater fuel savings than previous economical Ford V-8 engines. The car itself is engineered throughout for the utmost economy. Long, trouble-free service is ensured by Ford soundness of design and simplicity of construction . . . by exacting Ford standards governing materials and parts built into the car. The number of features — seen and unseen — that makes the Ford V-8 thrifty to own is legion.
To Ford V-8 economy add the other Ford first-class features — Centre-Poise Ride, Easy-Action Safety Brakes, all-steel body, modern style — and you'll realize why the Ford V-8 is very definitely the quality car in the low-price field.
$30 A MONTH, with reasonable down-payment, buys any new Ford V-8 Car under Traders Finance National Plan.
TUNE IN Ford Sunday Evening Hour, 9 P. M., E. D. S. T., Columbia Broadcasting System.
Ford
Ford V·8
FOR 1937

BARGAIN
1¢ cent a mile
Trip to
Calgary
AND RETURN
From EDMONTON
$3.50
Correspondingly Low Fares from Intermediate Stations
GOOD GOING
Train 522 Apr. 22, and Trains 526-522 only, Apr. 23-24.
RETURN UNTIL
Train 523, Apr. 27
Good in Coaches only. No baggage checked. For additional information and train schedules, consult Canadian Pacific Ticket Agent.
Canadian Pacific

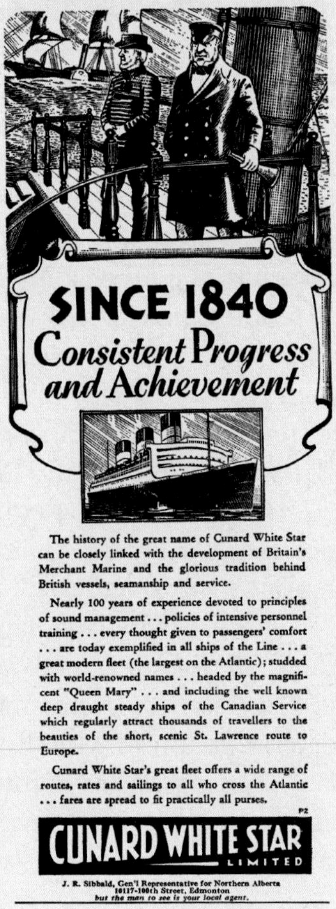

SINCE 1840
Consistent Progress and Achievement
The history of the great name of Cunard White Star can be closely linked with the development of Britain's Merchant Marine and the glorious tradition behind British vessels, seamanship and service.
Nearly 100 years of experience devoted to principles of sound management . . . policies of intensive personnel training . . . every thought given to passengers' comfort . . . are today exemplified in all ships of the Line . . . a great modern fleet (the largest on the Atlantic); studded with world-renowned names . . . headed by the magnificent "Queen Mary" . . . and including the well known deep draught steady ships of the Canadian Service which regularly attract thousands of travellers to the beauties of the short, scenic St. Lawrence route to Europe.
Cunard White Star's great fleet offers a wide range of routes, rates and sailings to all who cross the Atlantic . . . fares are spread to fit practically all purses.
P2
CUNARD WHITE STAR LIMITED
J. R. Sibbald, Gen'l Representative for Northern Alberta
10117-100th Street, Edmonton
but the man to see is your local agent.

SAY, THIS NEW INSTANT CUBE-RELEASE SURE BEATS MESSING UNDER A FAUCET! NO WASTING ICE, MELTING CUBES LOOSE.
RIGHT! AND ONLY FRIGIDAIRE HAS IT- IT'S IN EVERY TRAY IN EVERY "SUPER-DUTY" FRIGIDAIRE.
FRIGIDAIRE

Perfect Cleaning!
Perfect Confidence!
If you would be sure that you always look your best, have your clothes Sanitoned regularly. Exclusive in Edmonton with Capitol Cleaners. New Low Prices!
Dry Cleaned and Pressed
LADIES' DRESSES (Plain)
SPRING COATS (Men's and Women's) ....
MEN'S 3-piece SUITS .....
LADIES' SUITS ....
75c
Phone 24888 or 22508 for Fast Service
CAPITOL
CLEANERS AND DYERS, LTD.

giving evidence of the presence of children, Mrs. Reid told her visitor how she felt about being a premier's wife. In her dainty, flowered morning frock, she looked the ideal mother and homemaker."

Moral rectitude wasn't enough and Reid didn't last. Unable to withstand the populist appeal of Social Credit and William Aberhart, a Calgary schoolteacher and radio preacher, Reid's tenure as premier lasted a little more than a year, the shortest in the province's history.

For unemployed men who were paid 20 cents a day to work in camps or parents struggling to feed a family on less than $8 a week Social Credit held forth a beguiling promise. A $25 Prosperity Certificate, commonly called scrip, by the provincial government to every man, woman and child in the province would put everyone back on easy street. Even the provincial Liberals fell under the spell of the theories of Major Clifford Hugh Douglas, a British army officer and amateur economist who first devised the scheme, promising in their campaign that they, too, would study Social Credit in detail with a view to implementing it as soon as possible.

Aberhart proved unstoppable and on Aug. 22, 1935, he and his party trounced the Liberals, the Conservatives and the UFA.

The Journal's editorial writers consistently criticized the Social Credit platform as being too vague, too cumbersome and simply impossible to implement.

The newspaper warned that Social Credit fiscal policies, particularly those involving the payment of those bewitching dividends to the people of Alberta, were unworkable. Monetary reform, the paper correctly pointed out, was the constitutional responsibility of the federal government.

"For the province to adopt this scheme it would have to withdraw from the Dominion. What its plight then would be hardly needs to be pointed out," *The Journal* editorialized prior to the election.

In a page 1 editorial on Aug. 21, the day before the Aberhart landslide, *The Journal* urged its readers to reject Social Credit. "If Mr. Aberhart's proposals were put into force, they would mean a complete upsetting of the province's economic life. Instead of bringing about the improvement of living conditions within our borders, they would make things much worse."

The editorial following Aberhart's victory was grudgingly courteous. "It is hardly necessary for The Journal to say that it regrets the outcome of yesterday's election.

"But the people have spoken in an uncertain manner."

However, several weeks later *The Journal* did spot an up-and-comer in the ranks of the Social Credit Party.

On Sept. 9, when Aberhart was in Ottawa, the newspaper compared the acting premier, 26-year-old provincial secretary Ernest C. Manning, to William Pitt the Younger, who was only 24 when he served as British prime minister to George III in 1783.

It was the first of hundreds stories to be written about Manning, and it was one of the few flattering ones to appear in the newspaper in those early years of the Social Credit reign.

When asked for his thoughts on those who suggested that Social Credit was merely a form of inflation, Manning delivered the kind of unyielding

Territories. In response Edmonton bush pilot Wop May is commissioned to help locate the Johnson.

***Feb. 3, 1932*:**
A new weekly store closing bylaw goes into effect in Edmonton. All retail stores and shops are required to close at 1 p.m. on Wednesdays, except that restaurants may sell food and drugstores may sell medicine or medical supplies.

***Feb. 17, 1932*:**
The man known as Albert Johnson, the Mad Trapper of Rat River, is shot and killed by police after a 48-day Arctic manhunt.

***Feb. 21, 1932*:**
The Corona Hotel in downtown Edmonton is destroyed by an explosion and fire.

***March 31, 1932*:**
A new Ford Roadster sells for $515 ($8,663.29 today) in Edmonton. A more luxurious convertible sedan with the new V-8 engine costs $815 ($13,709.86 today).

***April 1, 1932*:**
The RCMP take over policing duties from the Alberta Provincial Police, the force that had replaced the Royal North West Mounted Police.

DINGLE-HOOFER UND HIS DOG.
BY H.H.KNERR.
Registered U. S. Patent Office
WATCHA GOT THERE, MR. DINGY?
DOT'S AN ELECTRIC SAFETY RAZOR!
TSK! TSK! TSK! ALWAYS CHASIN' MICE!
LOOKUT! HE'S GOT UNDER THUH BEAR RUG!
SCHNAPPS! COME OUDT FROM UNDER! STOP IT!
OOH! HE'S GOT MIXED UP WITH THUH CORD!
STOP IT, I SAID!
FOR HEFFIN'S SAKE!
GEE!
SOME RAZOR, MR. DINGY! IT SHAVED ALL THUH HAIR OFF'M THUH BEAR RUG AN' IT NEVER TOUCHED SCHNAPPSY!
DUMMOX!
11-27
Copr. 1938, King Features Syndicate, Inc., World rights reserved.

The Katzenjammer Kids

Registered U. S. Patent Office

GIFS PROMISE UF SOME FUN MIT DER CAPTAIN IF VE CAN GET HIM SORE ENOUGH!
DOT'S EASY STUFF!
CHUST VAIT! GIFS DER DUMB-BOOZLEDEST LICKING UF A LIFETIME! HOODLUMS!
AH-H, CAPTAIN! SITTING ON THE LID AS IT WERE?
CHASS! UND MIT A COUPLA DOD-ROTTED HYENAS INSIDE!
SO! GIFS PLENTY UF TIME!---
HM-M-M-M-M!
UND VEN I GET GOOD UND READY DER FIRE-VORKS BEGINS!
COME, HYNIE, OLD GROUCH!
STICK AROUND, ROLLO, UND I GIF YOU A EXHIBITION UF FENCY VALLOPPING VOT YOU NEFER SEEN BEFORE!
OH, CAPTAIN! PLEASE LET US OUDT! VE ISS SORRY!
VE VILL NEFER DO IT AGAIN!
HAR! HAR! LISTEN TO DER LIDDLE VEASELS BEGGING TO GET OUDT!
VOT DER-?
PULL DOWN, QVICK!
?
SAFED! CHUST IN DER KNICK UF TIME!
NOW! DO I GET THE FOUR BITS, YOU OWE ME OR DO I TIP THE CAGE OVER?
BETTER COME ACROSS, SHRIMPERS! DER HYENA LOOKS HUNGRY! HAW! HAW!
HEH-HEH-HEH-HEH-HEH!
11-27
Copr. 1938, King Features Syndicate, Inc., World rights reserved.
Knerr 38

COMIC SECTION

answer that *Journal* reporters heard over the subsequent years from the premier-to-be. According to the story, Manning slammed his swivel chair into an upright position and stared directly across the desk. "Those people are ignorant of the Just Price feature of our system," Manning snapped.

Manning became premier after Aberhart's death in 1943 and remained so until 1968.

The early days of the Social Credit regime set the tone for the sometimes bitter and always distant relationship between the newspaper and the provincial government.

The Socreds never much cared for *The Journal* or most other independent newspapers either, and that animosity led to the introduction of the Accurate News and Information Act on Sept. 30, 1937.

The law was intended to restrict press freedoms and require papers to publish government statements as directed and reveal information sources. Its intention was to suppress media criticism of the government and its unconventional economic and monetary policies.

On Oct. 1, the day after the act was given the second of three required readings, *The Journal* responded with a front-page editorial, the first of many defending the newspaper's right to publish what it deemed important.

"The press bill now before the legislature, if enacted, will sound the death knell of the liberty of the press in Alberta. It will mean establishment of censorship through control of news sources. It will mean a government dictatorship of the press.

"Are the people of Alberta prepared to accept a Social Credit dictatorship?"

The Journal's defence of freedom of the press earned it a special Pulitzer medal from the prestigious U.S. Pulitzer Prize committee, the first time a newspaper outside the U.S. was so honoured.

The issues faced by the government drew international attention, and not all of it was positive.

On Oct. 5, *The Journal* reprinted a story from the *London Times* that suggested the Social Credit government was losing its grip. "Premier Aberhart and his colleagues in the Social Credit government seem near to the end of the long gamble with the resources and credit of the province.

"The so-called Accurate News and Information bill is in itself a confession of failure and an admission that the measures in which they have committed themselves cannot stand the test of public discussion."

Confessions of failure or not, the Social Credit Party won widespread support throughout the province.

It couldn't, however, sweep away the problems of the Depression, all of which made life hardscrabble and arduous.

Adding to people's worries was the appearance of poliomyelitis, a disease that seemed to strike the young with particular ferocity in the city.

When on Sept. 10, 1935, *The Journal* reported a single case of the disease, city officials were quick to react, postponing school openings for a month.

Within a week of that first story, the paper reported 32 cases of poliomyelitis in the city, and 95 in the province.

Before the epidemic abated three weeks later, a dozen Albertans had

***Aug. 1, 1932*:**
Labour and Farmers party representatives meeting in Calgary form the Co-operative Commonwealth Federation, the forerunner of the NDP.

***Sept. 19, 1932*:**
Canada's Governor General, the Earl of Bessborough, is awarded an honourary degree by the University of Alberta during his first visit to Edmonton.

***Dec. 20, 1932*:**
Edmonton's Market Square riot occurs; dozens are arrested and several people are injured in a two-hour battle when RCMP and city police confront hunger marchers and unemployed workers attempting to parade from downtown Edmonton to the Alberta legislature.

***March 9, 1933*:**
Cliff Manahan skips the first Edmonton rink to win the Brier, the Canadian men's curling title.

***May 22, 1933*:**
***The Journal* starts its Learn-to-Swim campaign at city pools. By 1953 2,700 people had applied for the program.**

***May 25, 1933*:**
Edmonton's Renfrew Park

Grads, With Lighter Team, 'On Spot' Against Cleveland

But J. Percy Page's Girls Confident As Series Nears

This Year's Club Will Be Hard to Tag; Everyone of Girls Have Speed to Burn; Big International Series Opens at Arena on Tuesday; Cleveland Girls Here Monday; Ticket Sale Opens at Mike's

J. Percy Page and his famous Edmonton Grads are on the threshold of another international basketball series. No greater athletic organization ever represented any city than the Commercial Grads of Edmonton. And, for that reason alone, the fans here will certainly turn out in an effort to pay tribute to a wonder team.

This year, different than any previous season, the Grads are on the spot. They have a team that is smaller, but faster, than most of the previous Grad machines. But a tall girl in a basketball game has a great advantage. Thus the Grads this year must click with their plays, must avoid errors, must make certain of every shot if they hope to turn back the challenge of the "Fisher Foods" team of Cleveland.

This Cleveland team is big, strong and confident of success. They hope to accomplish what the Cleveland Favorite Knits failed to do in 1923—what the Newman-Sterns couldn't do a few years later.

Start On Tuesday

The series will be a three-out-of-five-game affair and opens at the arena on Tuesday with the next games Thursday and Saturday. The games will start at 8:30 each night.

The seat sale opens at Mike's News on Monday but reserved seat orders are now being taken.

Following is a sketch of a great team—some of the highlights in the career of the Grads.

The Grads were formed in the spring of 1915 from the graduating students of the McDougall Commercial High school. During their graduating year they played the first series of games for the championship of Alberta. They were successful, and with the single exception of 1920 they have won the Alberta title each season since that time—21 out of 22 possible championships.

Win Canadian Title

In 1922 the team went to London, Ontario, and took part in the first series ever staged for the Canadian championship. In a two-game series, the Grads (as they are now called) won the title, and have held it continuously since that time. (It should be noted that on three occasions the dominion playdowns have not been completed, because of financial and other difficulties.)

In 1923 the Grads challenged the Cleveland Favorite-Knits, champions of the United States, for the international title. The Edmonton girls were victorious in a remarkably fine series of games. Since that time the Grads have played from one to five American teams each year, and on only one occasion (1933) have they ever been defeated. On that occasion, the Cardinals of Oklahoma City won the series, but this single defeat was avenged in 1934, 1935 and again in 1936 when the Grads defeated the American champions in international contests. Teams from Chicago, Cleveland, Tulsa and El Dorado have won single contests from the Grads, but have never been successful in winning a series of games.

In 1924 the Grads made their first visit to Europe, and attended the Olympic games in Paris. In 1928, they attended the games in Amsterdam; in 1932 they went to Los Angeles, and in 1936 to Berlin. Basketball for girls was not an official event on any of these programs, but exhibition games were arranged on each occasion, all of which were won by the Grads with comparative ease.

Played 450 Games

From 1915 to the present, the Grads have taken part in 450 official contests, and have won 436. So far as is known, this record has never been approached. On one occasion, the Grads ran up a string of 78 consecutive wins. A former captain, Miss Margaret MacBurney, holds what is believed to be the free-throw record for girls—61 consecutive baskets! The same young lady played with the team for 10 years, and her all-time record is 13.3 points per game.

With the exception of two girls, who were educated in other schools, every member of every Grad team *is a graduate of Commercial high.* J. Percy Page, principal of the school, and who coaches merely as a hobby, has been in charge of the team since its inception, and expects to remain until 1940 when the girls hope to represent Canada in the next Olympic games in Tokio. A fairly accurate record shows that the Grads have traveled almost 100,000 miles in search of, or in defence of, their many titles.

Dr. James Naismith, the inventor of basketball, publicly declared that "the Grads have the finest team that ever stepped out on to a basketball floor."

1937 Edition of World Champion Grads

EDMONTON
GRADS

Edmonton's Commercial Grads will open their international women's basketball series with Cleveland Fisher Foods at the arena here Tuesday. The series will be decided on a three-game basis, the second and third fixtures being scheduled for Thursday and Saturday nights. When Coach J. Percy Page leads his world's champions on to the floor against the powerful American hoopsters, four new faces will appear on the Grad lineup for international competition. They are Betty Ross, Winnie Gallen, Jean Williamson and Frances Gordon. Shown in the above layout, reading from left to right, back row, are: Mabel Munton, Noel MacDonald, Coach J. Percy Page, Winnie Gallen and Betty Ross; front row: Etta Dann, Helen Northup, Babe Belanger and Sophie Brown. The latest Grad recruits, Jean Williamson and Frances Gordon, are missing from the picture.

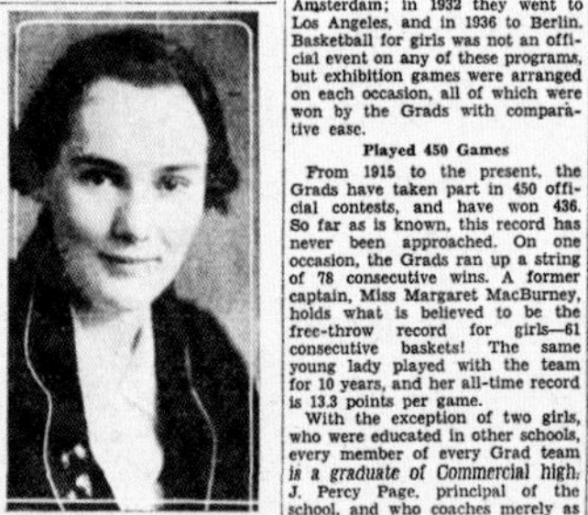

Jean Williamson, the latest addition to the Commercial Grads.

Exhibition Baseball

Detroit (A) 1, Cincinnati (N) 0.
Brooklyn (N) 8, New York (A) 1.
Chicago (N) 9, Chicago (A) 3.
Cleveland (A) 8, New York (N) 4.
Boston (A) 5, Holy Cross University 0.
Pittsburgh (N) 10, Hutchinson (WA) 2.
Baltimore (I) 7, Philadelphia (A) 6.
Washington (A) 7, Georgetown University 0.
St. Louis (N) 11, Portsmouth (CAL) 0.

FIGHTS LAST NIGHT

Chicago—Larry Greb, 134, Milwaukee, outpointed Frankie Terranova, 131, New York (10).

Detroit—Jimmy Adamick, 182, Midland, Mich., knocked out Johnny Miler, 180, Los Angeles (2).

San Francisco—Marty Simmons, 165, Saginaw, Mich., outpointed Angelo Puglisi, 164, New York City (10).

BLUE RIBBON
BAKING POWDER

died and all who had contracted the disease suffered varying degrees of debilitation for the rest of their lives.

In an attempt to ensure that students didn't fall too far behind in their studies, the newspaper published lessons until schools were reopened in mid-October.

It also pointed out in an advertisement on Sept. 11, that it had younger readers very much in mind.

"In these days when in the interests of health, the young folk of Edmonton are debarred from theatres, swimming pools and other gatherings, their interest in other things is accentuated."

The ad promised 14 comic strips every day, as well as a crossword puzzle, a daily "Good Night Story" and news of Scouts and Girl Guides. "The Journal is a family newspaper," insisted the ad.

But it wasn't all doom and Depression-era gloom. There was still plenty of fun to be had.

There were the Grads, of course, the world-vanquishing women's basketball team that drew thousands to their games.

British soccer scores and major league baseball standings were standard page 1 fare, as were bonspiels, sandwiched between the news coverage of politics, economics and a darkening international situation.

Despite its landlocked location, Albertans were caught up in the America's Cup races. In 1930, when Sir Thomas Lipton, the British skipper of the Shamrock V, challenged Harold Vanderbilt's Enterprise for the cup, the newspaper carried up-to-the-minute news of what was happening off Newport, Rhode Island.

"Model yachts ingeniously strung on wires stretching from The Journal's offices to the building opposite (McDougall Church) will graphically depict the headway the Shamrock and the Enterprise are making, and information will be broadcast by loudspeaker by Frank Barnhouse, commodore of the Edmonton Yacht Club," *The Journal* said on Sept. 12. If yachting fans found the going a little tedious, a choir was present to sing sea shanties.

And, in 1932, the same year that the first incarnation of the Edmonton Symphony died from lack of support, professional hockey returned.

It had been six years since Edmonton had a pro hockey team, and the city and its newspaper were joyous when local sports heroes Duke Keats and Art Gagne revived the Edmonton Eskimos. On Dec. 7, the Eskimos beat the Calgary Tigers 1-0 in a game attended by 2,500 fans.

"Medieval knight returning from the wars in olden times was never more royally welcomed at his castle than the sport received from its retinue of hardy fans here, who attended the opening game of the Western Canada Professional Hockey League," the paper reported.

Movie houses, such as the Rialto, the Capitol, the Strand and the Empress, all in downtown Edmonton, and the Princess Theatre on Whyte Avenue, did good business with first-run Hollywood movies.

However, with little money to spend on entertainment, many Edmontonians gathered around their radios.

The Journal not only ran listings for CJCA, the station it owned, but also listings for Edmonton's CFRN, CKJL from Red Deer, CJCJ from

baseball stadium, later named John Ducey Park, is officially opened. 3,500 people watch the South Side Arctics beat the Royals 3-0. Renfrew Park is considered the best sports facility west of Toronto. Local companies such as Army and Navy, Edmonton Motors, the Shasta Cafe and Union Buses sponsor teams to play at the converted soccer pitch, originally built in 1919 by Scottish soccer enthusiasts.

***Aug. 6, 1933*:**
Return fare on Canadian National's holiday excursion train from Edmonton to Jasper National Park is $4. Rooms at Jasper Park Lodge are $10.25.

***Aug. 7, 1933*:**
The Banff School of Fine Arts, later known as the Banff Centre for Continuing Education, (now the Banff Centre) begins as a special summer program in theatre arts sponsored by the University of Alberta's Department of Extension.

***March 9, 1934*:**
Golfer Marlene Stewart Streit, winner of multiple Canadian, American and British amateur titles, is born at Cereal, Alberta.

Weather Forecast
Somewhat Cooler

Edmonton Journal

"One of Canada's Great Newspapers"

THIRTY-FOURTH YEAR ** EDMONTON, ALBERTA, MONDAY, APRIL 12, 1937 SINGLE COPY, 5 CENTS 18 PAGES

Britain Limits Protection Of Own Shipping

Ottawa Ready To Give Alberta Financial Aid If Full Interest Is Paid

Darwin Theory Is 'Wet', Claim

TORONTO, April 12.—Dr. Arthur I. Brown, Vancouver surgeon, who arrived here Sunday to give a series of lectures on the origin of mankind, said the original man was not a baboon or a monkey and the Darwin theory of evolution "was all wet."

The surgeon who turned preacher received his medical training under Sir Arthur Keith, noted exponent of the Darwin theory. Dr. Brown said he became convinced man came from "the creative fire of God," and relinquished his medical work to become a preacher to further his ideas.

Pickets Posted At Week-End

Work Carried on at Five Plants Here Affected By Strikes

3 WOMEN CHARGED

Edmonton's second week of industrial tie-ups opened Monday with work in progress at all five plants where strikers are picketing. Partial operations were resumed early in the day at the New Method laundry, officials announced.

Other strikes were continuing at the Snowflake laundry and at the packing plants of the Swift Canadian Co., Ltd., ...

Has Treated Province "Fairly, Squarely," Says Dunning

HOUSE IS INFORMED

Bennett, Blackmore Unite In Protest Over Treatment

OTTAWA, April 12.—Federal government has treated Alberta fairly and squarely, Hon. C. A. Dunning, finance minister, told the commons Saturday night, replying to charges of financial discrimination against the foothills province.

The government stood ready, he said, to recommend next session to parliament that financial assistance be given Alberta, enabling it to maintain essential services, if it paid full interest rates on its bonds this year and thereby found itself with a scarcity of cash. The assistance would not be needed until late in its fiscal year, he said.

Conservative Leader Bennett and John Blackmore, leader of the Social Credit-ers, united in protest against financial treatment accorded Alberta. They agreed Alberta had fared badly, considering the money advanced to Saskatchewan and Manitoba.

Mr. Dunning stressed the report of the Bank of Canada on the finances of Alberta which recommended no assistance pending the findings of the royal commission on taxation. The bank found that by cutting $3,400,000 this year on bond interest Alberta could maintain all governmental services and save $1,200,000 for redemption of provincial ...

WORLD'S BIGGEST WARSHIP IS RUSHED TO SPAIN

H. M. S. Hood, largest warship in the world, has been rushed from Gibraltar to Bilbao, Spain, where an insurgent blockade has kept six British merchant ships from carrying food to the city's defenders, and thus creating a dangerous situation. In parliament Monday, Premier Baldwin said the government could not protect British shipping actually entering Bilbao port.

Uphold Validity Of Wagner Act

Applies to All Business Engaged In Interstate Commerce

HIGH COURT RULING

WASHINGTON, April 12.—United States supreme court gave the government a majority victory Monday by upholding constitutionality of the Wagner Labor Relations act as applied to all business engaged in interstate commerce.

Speculation was stirred immediately as to whether the tribunal's decisions in five cases would affect President Roosevelt's fight for reorganizing the tribunal.

William Green, president of the American Federation of Labor, had described the Wagner act as "the Magna Carta of Labor." ...

'Missing Million' Sought By Heirs

New Yorker Left Huge Sum Scattered In Banks

NEW YORK, April 12.—Heirs of John M. Phillips, New York sewer pipe manufacturer, sought Monday for the fortune of more than $1,000,000 he left scattered around in various unnamed banks and safety deposit boxes in Canada and the U.S.

For years before he died in 1928 Phillips made frequent secret trips away from New York, depositing huge sums of money under false names in banks whose location he revealed only to his son Francis, who carried the secret with him when he died in a plane crash.

Oshawa Strike ...

Four Farmers Oppose Pooling

Turgeon Commission Opens Sessions In Edmonton

FREEDOM IS DESIRED

Unanimous opposition to the wheat pool system was voiced by four farmers who testified Monday forenoon at the opening sitting in Edmonton of the Turgeon royal grain commission.

All condemned any method by which farmers would be compelled to market their grain through any agency, and all declared for perfect freedom in independent selling apart from any controlled or cooperative system.

The witnesses were Andrew Murchie, of Grande Prairie; ...

Food Ships Entering Bilbao Port Must Take Own Risks, Is Warning; H.M.S. Hood Sent To Trouble Zone

Six British Vessels Driven Off from Besieged Spanish Town

FRANCO IS DEFIANT

Starvation Conditions Prevail Among Refugees as Blockade Tightens

LONDON, April 12.—Prime Minister Baldwin told the commons Monday that Britain, while guarding her shipping "at sea" in the Bay of Biscay, could not protect British food ships actually entering the besieged port of Bilbao, Spain.

The prime minister outlined this stand, reached at a Sunday meeting of the cabinet, at a moment when H. M. S. Hood, the world's largest warship, had reached a position off Bilbao after a quick voyage from Gibraltar.

The cabinet had to consider a flat warning by Rebel General Franco that his fleet had been ordered to fire on British freighters if they attempted to enter Bilbao.

Baldwin, while insisting the British government was neither extending belligerent rights to the Spanish insurgent beseigers of Bilbao nor tolerating "any interference with British shipping at sea," explained:

"They (the government), are,

(Continued on Page 2, Col. 5)

Herridge Asks ...

3,000 Loyalists Slain, Say Rebels

WITH INSURGENTS OUTSIDE MADRID, April 12.—More than 3,000 government troops were estimated to have been slaughtered west of Madrid Monday in a surprise attack against the right flank of the government army.

Official insurgent communique described the rout of Gen. Jose Miaja's command as one of the greatest insurgent victories on the Madrid front. The government troops were caught in a cross fire from two strong insurgent positions.

The government artillery barrage opened in the early morning. As the curtain of shells rolled forward, 16,000 infantrymen advanced in staggered waves to attack the insurgent positions on the Aguila hill and Perdices hill.

As the Millicianos struggled up the slopes, filling the narrow valley between, General Saliquet, the area commander, gave the command to his troops to fire. Of the 16,000 men who charged the legionnaires' positions, 3,000 were reported officially to have been left dead on the field.

M. A. J. Pack, British commercial attache, will go to Burgos Tuesday to discuss with the insurgent authorities the question of British merchant ships proceeding to Bilbao.

ST. JEAN DE LUZ, France, April 12.—Spanish insurgents have entered Durango and Eibar, hoisting their flag over both key towns on the road to Bilbao, an insurgent broadcast from Vitoria claimed Monday.

No Bread Available to Populace for Two Weeks Past

300,000 ARE AFFECTED

Insurgent Fleet Lies Just Within Three-Mile Limit

HENDAYE, Franco-Spanish Frontier, April 12.—Starvation conditions among the civil population of besieged Bilbao were reported Monday to be spurring Insurgent General Franco to prevent the landing of food supplies for the Biscayan capital.

Refugees to Hendaye declared no bread had been available for two weeks for Bilbao's civil population, swollen to 300,000 by refugees.

EL FERROL, Spain, April 12.—Insurgent fleet, augmented by the new warship Neptuno, tightened its blockade of the Basque coast of northern Spain Monday in an effort to starve out the defenders of government-held Bilbao.

The fleet, half the size of the government navy, lay just within the three-mile limit, blasting holes in the seaboard highway ... Asturians from ...

MILLIONS CHEER IRIUM, NEW WAY TO END DULL LOOK ON TEETH!

PEPSODENT alone of tooth powders contains IRIUM, gift of science that safely wins new brilliance for enamel!

Pepsodent alone among Tooth Powders contains IRIUM

BECAUSE OF IRIUM . . . Pepsodent requires NO SOAP. Contains NO GRIT . . . NO PUMICE. *—Safe!*

BECAUSE OF IRIUM . . . Pepsodent gently softens film on teeth and floats it away like magic! *— Thorough!*

BECAUSE OF IRIUM . . . Pepsodent Powder leaves your mouth feeling clean and wholesome *— Refreshing!*

● Millions long denied the thrill of lovely, brilliant teeth are finding it again with IRIUM!

Once more they know the joy of gleaming enamel . . . of the sparkling smile that gives supreme confidence when heads come close together. All thanks to this amazing discovery contained in Pepsodent alone of tooth powders!

No wonder Pepsodent Powder has thrilled the whole country—has already won purchases to the tune of over 10,000,000 cans!

Once you change to this *modernized* tooth powder, you bid goodbye to dull, dingy, film-stained teeth. For IRIUM—being a totally new kind of foaming ingredient—first *loosens* the glue-like film. Then *floats it away* like magic . . . and safely restores thrilling radiance even to the dullest enamel!

That's why teeth look whiter, feel clean so much longer after using Pepsodent Powder containing IRIUM.

Teeth sparkle as they never did with old-fashioned, laborious methods.

Yet Pepsodent Powder is SAFE because it contains NO GRIT, NO PUMICE.

And it's so refreshing that a wholesome tingle rejuvenates your mouth, your sense of taste, with every brushing.

Try Pepsodent Powder containing IRIUM. You'll cheer it. And you'll agree it shows up any other tooth powder you ever used—BAR NONE!

All Pepsodent now on sale contains IRIUM

PEPSODENT
SUPER-SOFT

USE PEPSODENT POWDER! . . . it alone contains IRIUM—for thrilling luster on teeth!

IT MAKES ME MAD! MEN WON'T STAND "B.O." IN WOMEN . . . . YET THEY OFTEN OFFEND THEMSELVES! LET THEM USE THE SAME PROTECTION WE DO . . LIFEBUOY SOAP! ITS CREAMY LATHER KEEPS YOU SAFER, FRESHER LONGER. AND LIFEBUOY'S A JOY TO USE!

Calgary and the University of Alberta-owned CKUA. And while the radio brought the world into the living rooms of *Journal* readers, they still looked to the paper to fulfil their demands for more detailed reporting of the news.

The whole city held its breath on Friday, Dec. 11, 1936, when King Edward VIII renounced the throne in a speech heard around the world.

The British Empire still mattered and the abdication of the king touched the hearts of many.

"All Edmonton paused Friday in solemn silence to hear the farewell message of a king who renounced his throne because he could not carry on 'without the help and support of the woman I love,' " *The Journal* reported.

That woman was Wallis Simpson, a brittle, twice-divorced American.

"In every part of the city – in homes, offices, schools, stores, restaurants, theatres, and on crowded street corners – listeners who sensed they were in the presence of an historic moment gathered tensely about radio receivers."

On the day of the abdication *The Journal*'s coverage was extensive with dozen of photographs spread over 10 pages.

Readers had followed the abdication crisis for weeks, and local leaders urged that everyone remain loyal to the throne. Said First World War hero W.A. Griesbach: "To give up the throne of a mighty empire comprising one-quarter of the population of the globe for the love of a woman is to us a tragedy as well as it is the greatest love story of all time."

Not everyone agreed, Rt. Rev. A.E. Burgett, Edmonton's Anglican bishop, was less sympathetic. "It is much to be regretted that one who has so many outstanding and attractive qualifications for King should abdicate under circumstances that cannot meet with the approval from many of his loyal subjects."

Calling the abdication one of the "most distressing chapters in British history," *The Journal*'s editorial stand was even tougher. "This is no case of a 'world well lost for love'. It is, rather, even when viewed in the most charitable light, a desertion of the stern and lonely path of high duty at the call of personal desire.

"The King is more than a man. He is the visible symbol of British unity throughout the whole world – the straight path of duty would have been clearly marked to one who was a truly great British king."

Concerns that loyalty to King and Empire might weaken were dispelled when George VI and Queen Elizabeth came on a month-long tour of Canada in 1939, the public respect and the coverage were effusive.

On May 18, the day after the royal couple landed in Quebec City, *The Journal* published photographs of the event, no small feat given the level of technology.

"These pictures were taken soon after the landing of Their Majesties and were telephoned to Toronto, then placed on the transcontinental TCA mail plane," the caption informed readers.

If the coverage of the King and Queen was intense as they made their way across the country, it was nothing compared to what the newspaper did when they arrived in Edmonton for a six-and-a-half-hour visit on June 2.

Basil Dean and Homer Ramage, young reporters covering the royal tour who both later became *Journal* executives, wrote reams of copy on the

***May 25, 1934*:**
The first fatal plane crash occurs at Edmonton's municipal airport, during an Empire Day air show. Mechanic Fred Hodgins is killed, but Mackenzie Air Services pilot Matt Berry and airport manager Jimmy Bell survive the fiery wreck.

***May 26, 1934*:**
"Unless citizens take action voluntarily to curb the stray cat menace, city council may pass licencing or regulatory legislation, it was indicated at a meeting of the city bylaw committee Friday. The committee decided to seek information from Vancouver as to the success or otherwise of a cat-trapping scheme operated in that city."
— *Journal* news story.

***June 25, 1934*:**
Vivian MacMillan testifies that she had been seduced by Alberta Premier John Brownlee, in trial of civil suit filed under the Alberta Seduction Act.

***June 30, 1934*:**
Jury finds Premier Brownlee guilty. The next day, *The Journal* publishes a Sunday Extra edition telling of Brownlee decision to resign immediately.

Weather Forecast
Fair and Warm

Edmonton Journal

'One Of Canada's Great Newspapers'

THIRTY-FIFTH YEAR ** EDMONTON, ALBERTA, MONDAY, JULY 11, 1938 SINGLE COPY, 5 CENTS 16 PAGES

Hughes In Paris On World Hop Via Edmonton

Turner Valley Oil Production Record Broken

Frontier Royalties Well Produces 7,617 Barrels In 24 Hours

IN OFFICIAL TEST

Government Benefits by 10 Per Cent Royalty Provision

CALGARY, July 11.—Oil production records for Turner Valley, Canada's major field 45 miles southwest of here, were shattered during the week-end.

On a 24-hour government test, Frontier Royalties, located in the south crude section of the valley, produced 7,617 barrels, F. P. Byrne, president of Frontier Royalties Company Limited, an associate of Anglo-Canadian, announced. It is the first time a valley well has produced in excess of 7,000 barrels in a 24-hour period.

The record was established Sunday on the last day of an 11-day production test under provincial government supervision. The province will get 10 per cent royalty on production.

Frontier's potential has been determined at two-thirds its capacity or 5,078 barrels a day. The well is now produc... under the valley prora...

Death Took a Holiday in This Accident

Two women motorists escaped death or serious injury on the Cooking Lake highway Sunday afternoon when their automobile swerved sharply and crashed through the heavy guard rail of a bridge overlooking a ravine. Neither was injured. The fortunate motorists were Rita Cote and Irene Belanger, both of Chauvin. Scene of the accident was an intersection near Cooking Lake beach. Few minutes after the accident, Fred Eckhart, New Sarepta, plunged his automobile into the ditch nearby. Neither himself nor his passengers were hurt.

Japan Plans New Bombings; Urges Powers Move Citizens

Hankow...

... Activities

... Jews

His Majesty Ill With Flu; Is Mild Attack

Sudden Attack of Gastric Influenza Puts Monarch To Bed

REASSURANCE GIVEN

Is King's First Illness Since He Ascended Throne

WINDSOR, England, July 11.—Cheered by the fact His Majesty the King spent a quiet night, Her Majesty the Queen motored to Buckingham palace Monday from the royal lodge, Windsor Great Park, where the King is ill with gastric influenza.

Viscount Dawson of Penn and Sir John Weir, physicians attending the King, examined him during the morning.

The Queen packed her two daughters off to London Sunday and spent the day nursing her husband.

There was some concern in Britain over the King's illness, although reassuring reports came from the royal lodge.

It was His Majesty's first illness since be became King in December, 1936.

First signs of illness appeared Saturday night when he retired early with a slight temperature. He and the Queen had motored to Windsor Friday night.

Physicians were summoned f... London Sunday but...

His Majesty the King, who is suffering from a mild attack of gastric influenza. He remained in bed Monday, but reassuring reports were issued from the royal lodge at Windsor Great Park, where the King is resting.

Canadian Tied For Bisley Cup

Capt. T. E. Hayhurst, Windsor, Has Perfect Score of 50

WEATHER STILL BAD

Cuts Lindberg Time in Half; Bad Weather Delays Next Leg

Will Not Take Off on Hop To Moscow Until Tuesday

HOPES FOR RECORD

Makes Air Journey to Advertise New York World's Fair

NEW YORK, July 11. — Howard Hughes, millionaire airman, attempting a world-girdling flight, will decide when he reaches Alaska whether he will set his big silver monoplane down at Edmonton, on the last leg of his journey.

Hughes' flight headquarters here explained that Fairbanks, Alaska, one of the stopping points for Hughes and his four companions, is 3,312 miles from his New York goal. If Hughes thinks he can make it without a stop he will do so. Otherwise he will fly 1,375 miles to Edmonton and refuel before starting the last 2,060 miles lap to New York.

PARIS, July 11.—Howard Hughes, after spanning the Atlantic—New York to Paris non-stop—in less than half of Col. Charles Lindbergh's time, was delayed Monday night on his globe-girdling flight by bad weather and slight d...

Lindbergh, Hughes Times On Paris Hop Compared

(All Times are Mountain Standard)

Charles A. Lindbergh (33 hours, 29½ minutes)	Howard R. Hughes (16 hours, 35 minutes)
May 20, 1927	July 10, 1938
Left New York 4:51 a.m.	Left New York, 4:20 p.m.
Bryantsville, Mass., 6:40 a.m.	Boston, 5:26 p.m.
Milford, N.S., 11:30 a.m.	Margaretsville, N.S., 7:30 p.m.
Cape Breton Island, 12:05 p.m.	Cape Breton Island, 8:20 p.m.
May 21, 1927	July 11, 1938
500 miles off Ireland, 5:10 a.m.	600 miles off Ireland, 3:25 a.m.
Over Ireland, 9:20 a.m.	Over Ireland, 6:30 a.m.
Reached France, 12:45 p.m.	Reached France, 8 a.m.
Landed Le Bourget, 2:21 p.m.	Landed Le Bourget, 8:55 a.m.

Chamberlain Remains Vague Over Anglo-Italian Accord

Refuses to Be More Specific In Answering Opposition

"TOUCHY" PROBLEM

... July 11.—Confronted ... Monday with

British Warplanes Lead Paris Show

VILLACO BLAY, France, July 11.—Twelve British warplanes, putting on a breath-taking exhibition of aerial acrobatics, all but stole the show Sunday at the French ... tional air carnival here.

'One Of Canada's Great Newspapers'

THIRTY-FIFTH YEAR ** ...BERTA, THURSDAY, JULY 14, 1938 SINGLE COPY, 5 CENTS 18 PAGES

Record Halved As Hughes Ends World Hop

Alberta Loses Appeal On Bank Taxation

Privy Council Upholds Supreme Court Decision Ruling Act Ultra Vires

Reasons for Judgment Will Be Forwarded to Province

IS NO COST ORDER

Province Fails in Third and Final Appeal in London

LONDON, July 14.—Judicial committee of the privy council Thursday dismissed the appeal of the attorney general of Alberta from a judgment of the sureme court of Canada declaring ultra vires a measure to tax chartered banks, enacted by the Alberta legislature.

The decision, upholding the court ruling on the third and last of the appeals of the province from judgments invalidating legislation sponsored by the Alberta government, was announced by Lord Atkin, who said the privy council would not make a cost order and would communicate their lordships' reasons for the judgment to the parties concerned in due course.

A week ago the judicial committee discontinued the hearing of appe 's on the Alberta Press bill and a measure to regulate credit, allowing the judgments of the supreme court at Ottawa, which declared the bills unconstitutional, to stand.

Their lordships still ...

(Continued ...

Drag for Body; 'Victim' Is Safe

PRINCE ALBERT, July 14.—While his parents and neighbors dragged the South Saskatchewan river for his body in a search that claimed the life of 52-year-old Philip Bear, Arthur Dreaver, 16-year-old Indian was working on a farm south of Prince Albert.

Believed to have been drowned five days ago, Dreaver was found by an R.C.M.P. constable at the farm of L. Harvey, who reported the youth had come to his farm looking for work the day after he disappeared.

Canadians Win Kolapore Cup

Defeat Britain by Five Points in Great Bisley Competition

GREGORY IS HIGHEST

BISLEY CAMP, England, July 14.—Picked team of Canadian riflemen Thursday won the ...

Veteran Soldier, Seaman and Politician Meet in London

Sir Ian Hamilton, veteran British warrior, Winston Churchill, veteran politician, and Admiral Sir Roger Keyes, veteran navy man (left to right) are shown as they attend the Royal Naval Volunteer Reserve and Royal Naval Division reunion at Crystal palace, London, recently. The gathering was honored by the presence of the Duke of Kent, who took part in the memorial service on the terrace which was formerly known as the quarter-deck.

Shouting Woman Rows With Simon

Ejected From Commons Gallery After Creating Uproar

LONDON, July 14.—A shouting woman dressed in black was carried out of the commons gallery Thursday after she broke into a tilt between Sir John Simon, chancellor of the exchequer, and Labor questioner over a loan to China.

Struggling and kicking, she was ejected by attendants while screaming, "We want British justice. Why don't you look after England?"

Sir John told ... government ...

U.K. May Spend $100,000,000 For Canada-Made Bombers

Britain Endeavors to Keep Pace with Germany And Italy

FRANCE MAY FOLLOW

By A. C. Cummings

(Special to Edmonton Journal and Associated Southam Newspapers)

LONDON, July 14.—Provided Canada can quickly transform her ...

Plan 'Run Out' Cattle Rustlers

CALGARY, July 14.—Plans to "run out" cattle rustlers from the rangelands and farms of Alberta were discussed by directors of the Western Stock Growers' association meeting here Wednesday.

Rustling is on the increase, it was reported, and greater police aid will ... campaign against ...

4 Days Cut From Post's Time As Airmen Land in New York

Wildly Cheering Crowd of 25,000 Hails Fliers On Arrival

DAMAGE THREATENS

FLOYD BENNETT AIRPORT, New York, July 14.—The flying quintet, headed by Howard Hughes, ended their history-making round-the-world flight at 11:37 a.m. (Edmonton time) Thursday when they brought their silver monoplane down at this airport.

The monoplane circled the field twice before coming down to an easy landing before a wildly cheering crowd.

Total elapsed time for the 14,824-mile dash around the globe was set unofficially at 91 hours, 17 minutes, or three days, 19 hours and 17 minutes.

The multi-millionaire speedster whipped in from the west under a threatening overcast sky with a record that more than halves the seven day, 18 hour, 49 minute round-the-world time established in 1933 by the late Wiley Post, cutting about four days from the record.

Hughes drove the ship at full speed on the last lap of the flight from Minneapolis to Floyd Bennett airport, whence he took off at 4:20 p.m. Sunday. A spanking tail wind helped him along his last lap.

His speed for the elapsed time for the entire flight was approximately 161 miles an hour.

Hughes' and his companions' last stop before New York at Minneapolis, Minn., at 5:38 a.m. (Edmonton time), after a 2,441-mile flight ...

How Hughes-Post Times On World Hop Compared

Wiley Post—1933—Solo

	Distance	Flying Time (Cumulative) Hr. Min.	Time Elapsed (Cumulative) Hr. Min.
New York-Berlin	3,942	25:45	
Berlin-Koenigsberg	340	30:15	44:35
Koenigsberg-Moscow	651	35:50	53:12
Moscow-Novosibirsk	1,579	49:5	69:2
Novosibirsk-Irkutsk	1,055	53:38	91
Irkutsk-Rukhlovo	750	63:10	107:25
Rukhlovo-Khabarovsk	650	67:30	113:58
Khabarovsk-Flat	2,800	90:2	152:28
Flat-Fairbanks	375	93:16	162:45
Fairbanks-Edmonton	1,450	102:38	173:41
Edmonton-New York	2,004	115:54	186:49
Totals	15,596	115:54	186:49

Howard Hughes—1938—Crew of Four

	Distance	Flying Time (Cumulative) Hr. Min.	Time Elapsed (Cumulative) Hr. Min.
New York-Paris	3,641	16:35	25:4
Paris-Moscow	1,675	24:24	35:5
Moscow-Omsk	1,380	31:59	47:17
Omsk-Yakutsk	2,177	42:30	60:41
Yakutsk-Fairbanks	2,456	54:47	74:16
Fairbanks-Minneapolis	2,441	66:48	86:50
Minneapolis-New York	1,054	71:14	91:17
Totals	14,824	71:14	91:17

Strange Query Spurs Rumor Of Hore-Belisha Resignation

Member Says He Has In-...

BIG CHIEF WAHOO A Strange "Baby" By Saunders and Woggon

THE HOSPITAL STAFF IS BEGINNING TO GET ON CHIEF WAHOO'S NERVES— AND VICE VERSA!
FOR THE FORTIETH TIME—WE CAN NOT LET YOU OUT TILL WE ARE SURE YOU ARE QUITE WELL.
WAUGH! WAHOO LAY IN BED SO LONG HE WEAR OUT SEAT OF UM SHIRT!
UGH! TRAIL CLEAR! FIND UM PLACE TO HIDE NOW!
CHIEF WAHOO
506
Copyright, 1937, by Publishers Syndicate
CHIEF WAHOO IS GONE, DOCTOR I CAN'T FIND HIM ANYWHERE!
IS THAT SO! WELL GO ON ABOUT YOUR DUTIES IN THE NURSERY!
DOCTOR DOVE
HELP ME SET UP THIS BASKET. THAT PROUD PAPA WANTS TO SEE HIS DIMPLED DARLING!
WHY— HE'S FAINTED!
THESE NEW FATHERS!
KLUNK!
Indian SLANGO
TURTLE is "PANCAKE-WITH-UM-LEGS"
GENEVA RAWNSLEY ALGONAC, MICH.
PILLOW is "SOFT-ROCK-TO-LAY-UM-BLOCK-ON"
MARCIA JOHN PORTLAND, OREGON
MATCH is "RED-HEADED-FIRE-TWIG"
WAYNE GEIST VERDEN OKLA.
MAIL YOUR INDIAN SLANGOS TO CHIEF WAHOO % THIS PAPER

great day. It wasn't overkill, not with the newspaper reporting that 200,000 people crammed the city to cheer the royals. It was a great turnout for a city with a population of 85,000 that served a trading area of 410,000.

There was a parade down Portage Avenue, renamed Kingsway in honour of the visit, a tour of the south side along Whyte Avenue and a banquet at the Macdonald Hotel that night before the King and Queen boarded their special train. The visit was a source of civic pride for many years. It is also worth noting that the visit caused Edmonton's first traffic jam when cars clogged downtown streets.

"The wonderful manifestations of loyal affection that have been given elsewhere in the dominion will be repeated here. They cannot fail to impress Their Majesties deeply, coming as they do from those of the most varied racial and other antecedents," bragged a June 2 editorial.

"Alberta, like other western Canadian provinces, has a comparatively short history. It is still close to its pioneer days and its citizens have been drawn from all parts of the world. But nowhere in the Empire is there more intense devotion to the British throne and to what it represents or a more fervent admiration of the King and Queen whom we are greeting today."

Readers were clearly ecstatic about the royal visit, but the shadows cast from Europe were long and deep and dark.

Since the end of the First World War, readers were more cosmopolitan, demanding more international reporting from the newspaper. It responded by offering more complete coverage of an increasingly dangerous world.

Hitler's Germany was menacing Europe, Mussolini's Italy was looking to North Africa as the place to fulfil his imperialist dreams and the Japanese were marching through Manchuria. The portents were not good.

Photographs were finally becoming an important part of telling readers what was happening, and the paper struggled to get the most current pictures possible although it sometimes took weeks for photos to arrive from far-flung battle fronts.

Photographs from Manchuria and the devastation of Shanghai were the first examples in October 1937. They showed that in new conflicts not only were combatants at risk, so was the populace.

By 1935, there was little doubt about the wild excesses of the Nazis as Hitler mounted attacks on Germany's Jewish population.

A.C. Cummings of *The Journal*'s London Bureau wrote from Munich on Sept. 13 that Jews seen with "Aryan" women were taken into "preventative custody." "Preventative custody," he wrote, "is a police term for a beating up in the local equivalent of the 'Brown House' – probably with rubber truncheons or steel whips."

In the autumn of 1935, *The Journal* and the *Toronto Telegram* shared expenses and sent reporter Robinson MacLean to Ethiopia to cover the coming conflict between the Italian army and the ill-equipped soldiers of Haile Selassie, the Ethiopian emperor.

"Right in the heart of Ethiopia where war clouds hover as a clash with the mighty army of Premier Mussolini of Italy is momentarily expected is Robinson F. MacLean, 'Bobby' as he is known to a host of Albertans, 27-year-old reporter who pounded the beat for the Edmonton Journal in 1930-31," the newspaper said in a page 1 story on Aug. 1.

***July 4, 1934*:**
Acting Justice Ives throws out the jury's guilty verdict and orders the MacMillans to pay the $1,200 to $1,500 legal costs of Premier Brownlee.

***July 10, 1934*:**
Richard Gavin Reid of the United Farmers of Alberta is sworn in as the province's sixth premier. Reid leads the shortest government administration in provincial history, losing to a Social Credit landslide in August 1935.

***July 1934*:**
Four years after *The Journal* opposed them, the city installed traffic signals. A reporter is dispatched to see how things were going. "Sixty-two motorists sailed straight past the signal while it was either on red or yellow...Forty-five pedestrians started across when the signal light was either on yellow or red and of these five offended in addition by cutting 'kitty corners' or in a diagonal direction."
The tradition continues today.

***Nov. 1, 1934*:**
Dick Rice's newly formed Sunwapta Broadcasting takes over Edmonton radio station CFTP, changing the call letters to CFRN.

News of Central and Northern Alberta From Journal Correspondents

Lacombe-District Join For Hospital

New Community Project Will Be 20-Bed Capacity

TO BUILD IN TOWN

(Special to The Journal)

LACOMBE, April 9.—Erection of a 20-bed Lacombe and district community hospital, with maximum capacity of 34 patients, was recommended by the recently appointed joint committee reporting to a combined meeting of the town council and the council of Crown municipality. Contributions to the cost of the building are proposed on the basis of one-third by the town and two-thirds by the municipality, each to do its own financing.

A board of five members, two for the town and three for the municipality, will be appointed to manage the hospital.

Several localities were offered as building sites, but that most favorably considered was a property on York st., in a quiet part of the town, near the highway, surrounded on three sides by thoroughfares, and readily accessible to the utilities.

Question of the size of the building was laid over for further consideration, and another ... called for A... pected p... be sub...

CAUGHT HIS HAND, SAUSAGE MACHINE

(Special to The Journal)

TROCHU, April 9.—Gerald Seegar, employed at the Dubuc butcher shop, caught his right hand in a sausage machine which he was operating and cut the four fingers until they were hanging by the skin, with all the bones broken and tendons cut. One hundred stitches were necessary in sewing up the fingers, and it is not yet certain that they can be saved.

Bourcier's Action Pleases S.C. Group

(Special to The Journal)

GLENEVIS, April 9.—Approval of the action of A. V. Bourcier, M.L.A. for Lac Ste. Anne, in opposing the budget and demanding that Social Credit be implemented, was expressed in a resolution by the Social Credit group here, a copy of which will be sent each to Premier Aberhart and Mr. Bourcier. There was a general feeling of disappointment that the government had not yet moved more effectively toward Social Credit, while resentment was expressed against retaining and ever increasing the sales tax.

IRMA, April 9.—Social Credit group of Irma, at a recent meeting, registered continued support of Premier Aberhart and approved the co-operative movement, though taking no action regard...

Farmers On Land Usher In Spring

Peace River Has Early Season and Work Has Begun

MOISTURE IS SCANT

(Special to The Journal)

PEACE RIVER, April 9.—One of the earliest springs on record is being experienced by the north country. Snow has practically disappeared, and little danger of flooding is anticipated. Farmers have already commenced spring work on the higher areas, and around Peace River on the hills the middle of the week saw several farmers preparing soil for seed. With a continuance of almost summer-like weather each day of next week will see an increasing number of farmers on the land.

KELSEY, April 9.—Farmers are harrowing and preparing for spring seeding, George Baumle and Henry Potter being first reported on the land in this district. Moisture supply is scant, but wheat acreage is expected to equal that of last year.

LAVOY, April 9.—Many farmers in this district have begun spring work, and plowing and harrowing are well under way. The land is quite ...d farmers are not being de...

DESERTERS PROVE ITALIANS' AID

Pictured at the left is an Italian soldier, who deserted from the Spanish rebel forces to the defenders of Madrid with his machine-gun and gas mask. Note that he raised his clenched fist in the Leftist salute.

JUNIOR GRAIN CLUB MEMBERS SELECTED

(Special to The Journal)

RED DEER, April 9.—Thirty-five lads of the district, out of a large number of entries, have been decided upon by F. H. Newcombe, district agriculturist, for membership in the Red Deer Junior Grain club. The club, which is sponsored by the junior section of the board of trade, is expected to be the most successful yet conducted. Interest will be kept up by periodical visits to the plots throughout the summer by members of the board.

The boys chosen are: Harold Hueppleheuser, president, Blackfalds; Alfred Swanson, vice-president, Red Deer; Telford Kirkland, secretary, Red Deer; Charles Blackmore, Ralph Wadey, Elmer Wadey, Lawrence Landry, Donald Miller, Leslie Petry, Herbert Fackler, all of Blackfalds; Robert Woof, Robert DePauw, Louis Revesz, William Hazlett, jr., Frank Jarvis, Arnold Hillman, Ben Langton, George Braithwaite, Thomas Heywood, Floyd L. Heagle, Frederick Olynyk, Charles Eversole, Howard Henderson, Thomas Hoskin, John Currie, George Kirton, Robert Edgard, Glen Jones, Allen Smith, Donald Van Slyke, Thomas Brown, all of Red Deer; Allan Brock of Lacombe; Hugh Corrigan of Hillsdown; Joseph Allan and Arthur Newton of Penhold.

An advisory committee has been appointed, consisting of R. H. Edgar, Chester Miller and A. Hoskin, all well known farmers of the district.

STALLIONS ON CIRCUIT

(Special to The Journal)

ERSKINE, ...—Tw...

Second Election Arouses Feeling

Resignation of Councillor Followed Attempt to Unseat Him

VOTING ON APRIL 17

(Special to The Journal)

CASTOR, April 9—Progress municipal district will hold a new election in division No. 7 on April 17, arrangements for which were made at a recent meeting of council. The election was made necessary by resignation of Councillor J. Schnell when proceedings were begun to unseat him for alleged irregularities in the first election.

Owing to strong feeling throughout the division, election officers were appointed from other divisions. H. Knight will be returning officer, with J. A. Johnson and R. N. Byce as deputies. Nominations will be held one week before the election.

Estimates of $22,800 for the year were passed, and a seven-mill rate was struck. A vote of $100 was made to the Castor Coronation day committee.

PEOP... LEAGUE...

DRAMA FESTIVAL AT LLOYDMINSTER

(Special to The Journal)

LLOYDMINSTER, April 9. — Thirty-one pupils of the Lloydminster public school, ages 9 to 13, presented their first drama festival in the Alberta hall before a packed house. The program consisted of four short plays, under direction of Rev. M. Dobson, Mrs. F. Burling, Miss Joan Hydes, and Miss Clara Stevenson.

Ten prizes were awarded for individual excellence only, the winners being Nellie Tendeck, Joseph Cooke, Louise Moxley, Alan Miller, William Prince, Kay Hall, Muriel Westcombe, Betty Bush, Violet McLean, and Marion Rosen.

Proceeds of the festival were given to the Welfare league.

"Now he is on the biggest mission of his life, a job for which any reporter would give his typewriting two fingers."

MacLean was a wordy writer with a classical touch. "Do you remember the Lays of Ancient Rome – how Horatius held the bridge?" a MacLean dispatch from Sept. 9 asked readers.

And while most schoolchildren of the day knew the poem, MacLean reworked the Lord Macaulay verse with an Abyssinian twist. "This morning I sat in my hotel room while the rain lashed through the eucalyptus trees and thought about old Horatius and the perversity of fate," MacLean mused.

"Two interpreters had been my guests at breakfast. One was Ato Gululat, thin, bronzed, pure Amharic. The other was Bogalla Wallalu, interpreter and Number One boy for Dr. Ralph Hooper of the leper mission.

"We talked about war – and what would happen if it came.

"South and east and west and north the messengers road fast –" MacLean wrote, seemingly unable to leave the Lays of Ancient Rome behind.

Despite his style of reporting, MacLean exemplified the interest the newspaper and its readers took in affairs far from home.

From the start, *The Journal* took a hard line against Hitler and the Nazis. "Hitler's Head Executioner Takes Evening Off" read a 1934 headline above a picture showing Hermann Goering meeting with the queen of Siam at a reception in Berlin.

"Goering is wearing the full-dress uniform he designed himself," *The Journal* caption acidly noted.

At first Hitler's aggression was nearly bloodless. There would be peace in our time, British Prime Minister Neville Chamberlain promised as Hitler took Austria and then Czechoslovakia.

But then came Poland and it began.

"War. War involving Poland, France, and the whole British Commonwealth. War of savage destructiveness like no war ever before waged in human history," was the prophetic opening paragraph on the front-page story on Sept. 1, 1939. "Hitler in his madness started it. He has proclaimed to his army that his patience with Poland is at an end and ordered that army to march."

The Journal's editorial that day foresaw much suffering, but also argued that a declaration of war on the part of Canada was the only reasonable response. "It is a grave hour of history that has arrived.

"But there is no reason to doubt that the conflict precipitated by the one man who could have averted it, if he had been willing to abandon his reckless course, will result in complete victory for the forces on the ascendancy of which human progress depends."

Within two days, *The Journal* published photographs of Edmonton men lining up to join the army.

Eight days later Canada was at war.

***Feb. 28, 1935*:**
Prime Minister R.B. Bennett announces plans to establish a Canadian grain board to buy and sell wheat and other crops.

***In 1935*:**
***The Journal*'s staff of 147 turns out 50,000 daily papers on presses operating at speeds of 20,000 papers an hour. A total of 4,127,000 pounds of paper and 76,135 pounds of ink are used over the course of the year.**

***April 4, 1935*:**
The Alberta Social Credit party holds its first convention, in Calgary.

***April 15, 1935*:**
A baby is born in a taxi on the High Level Bridge. She is later christened Olive Marie Poncella (meaning "one from the bridge") Beauchamp, after a *Journal*-sponsored contest asks readers to come up with a name reflecting her unusual birthplace. Annette LaRiviere collects $5 for her winning entry.

***May 15, 1935*:**
Women's rights leader Irene Parlby receives an honourary degree from the University of Alberta.

ND-3-6750 Glenbow Archives

It ain't over 'til the premier speaks. A group of reporters sit outside Brownlee's office, waiting for a statement in 1934.

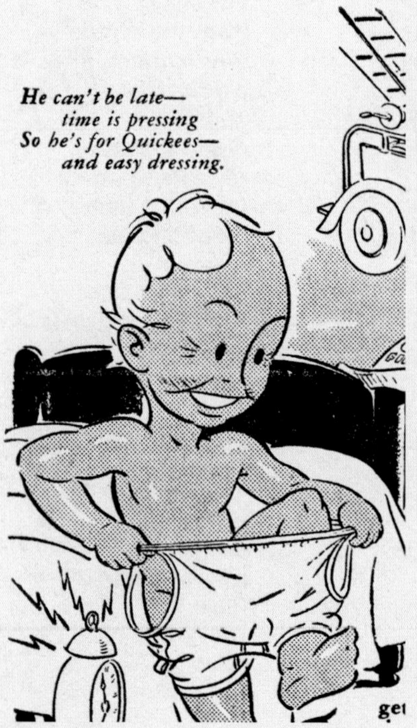
He can't be late—
time is pressing
So he's for Quickees—
and easy dressing.

SHIRLEY TEMPLE
Star of "WEE WILLIE WINKIE" A 20th Century-Fox Picture

Brownlee's Blunder

"He played me as a cat plays with a mouse."
— From Vivian MacMillan's testimony at Premier John Brownlee's seduction trial, June 26, 1934

How much sex was too much sex in a staunchly conservative paper that printed Bible verses on its editorial page?

As the June 25, 1934, trial date approached for the ultra-high-profile case of Alberta Premier John Brownlee versus vivacious Vivian MacMillan, a 22-year-old clerk in the attorney general's office, *Journal* editors had a decision to make.

MacMillan and her father, Edson mayor A.D. MacMillan, accused Brownlee of seducing her and had filed a civil suit under the Alberta Seduction Act. She was seeking $10,000 in damages and her father $5,000 ($139,000 and $69,500, respectively, in today's currency).

The Journal knew sex sold newspapers. After all, it sometimes printed stories about the romantic antics of Hollywood stars such as Charlie Chaplin and Clark Gable on the front page.

But this was different. The highest-profile man in Alberta, who had hired the most powerful Calgary lawyers he could find, was setting out to defend his reputation, his career and, ultimately, his government against accusations he seduced a girl young enough to be his daughter in the backseat of a Studebaker.

The editors decided to err on the side of caution. Rather than chancing the usual journalist practice of writing stories summarizing the daily court drama, they decided on the legally safer route of printing the testimony verbatim. They reduced the type size and, presumably sent shorthand experts to court to produce no less than 20 pages of most of the proceedings over the course of the four-day trial.

"Most," was the operative word. While actual court transcripts and a smattering of Alberta history books record MacMillan's chapter-and-verse descriptions of seduction scenes, *The Journal* stopped short of printing the naughty bits.

Here's an example from the first day of testimony, published June 26, related to what happened in the backseat of the infamous government Studebaker. Brownlee had offered MacMillan a ride and had driven to a deserted stretch of dark country road west of the city. He had just lured the young woman into the backseat.

Question to MacMillan: "Just tell us what happened on that occasion."

Journal story: "Witness said she had submitted to the defendant's advances."

Was this to protect the sensibilities of *Journal* readers?

Across town, the *Edmonton Bulletin* was having a field day with the scandal.

It didn't slough off the details with a vague sentence.

Here's what *The Bulletin* published: (MacMillan testifying) "He again forced me down onto the back seat of the car. I fought against him, but this

***Aug. 22, 1935*:**
William Aberhart leads the Social Credit party to election victory over the United Farmers of Alberta, to form the first Socred government in Canada. Aberhart, nicknamed Bible Bill for his religious radio broadcasts, did not run in the election and has to be elected to the legislature in a byelection.

***Sept. 24, 1935*:**
The Alberta government will sell "prosperity bonds" in an attempt to pay off the provincial public debt of $150 million.

***Nov. 16, 1935*:**
Joe Clarke is sworn in as mayor of Edmonton after being re-elected to his fourth one-year term in office.

***Dec. 19, 1935*:**
Boxing Day, Dec. 26, is declared a statutory holiday in Alberta under an order-in-council passed by the provincial cabinet.

***In 1936*:**
A reporter at *The Journal* earns $20 a week.

***April 1, 1936*:**
Alberta, under Premier William Aberhart, becomes the first province to default on a provincial bond. The dominion will

EXTRA **Edmonton Journal** EXTRA

"ONE OF CANADA'S GREAT NEWSPAPERS"

30TH YEAR. NO. 297 ★ EDMONTON, ALBERTA, WEDNESDAY, JULY 4, 1934 SINGLE COPY, 5 CENTS 20 PAGES

IVES DISMISSES JURY FINDING IN MacMILLAN DAMAGE CASE

Members Start Work Of Selecting Leader To Form Government

No Need for Stampede" Says Member—Won't Hurry in Selection of New Government Leader

HON. R. G. REID IS LIKELY CHOICE CLAIM OBSERVERS AT SESSION

All Members of Government Ranks in House Attend Opening Session of Caucus Tuesday

Resignations of Premier Brownlee and his cabinet were placed before the United Farmer members' caucus ... liament buildings at 10:00 a.m.

FARMER MEMBERS ARRIVE FOR CAUCUS

Overrules Jurors; Claims no Damage To Girl Or Parent

Judgment Is Entered in Seduction Action Brought By Edson Girl Against Alberta Premier

Mr. Justice Ives Wednesday entered judgment in the MacMillan-Brownlee case.

The judgment follows:

"In this action the father joins with his daughter in the action for seduction of the daughter by the defendant. The jury by a special verdict of questions and answers has found that the seduction took place on October 30, 1930, and has awarded damages to the parent plaintiff in the sum of $5,000 and to the daughter in the sum of $10,000.

"Upon the verdict being announced by the jury, counsel for the defendant moved for the dismissal of the action on the ground that there was no evidence of any interference with the daughter's services to the parent to which he was entitled and no evidence that the seduction in any way interfered with the daughter's ability to serve or at least interference with the woman's ability to serve.

"It is quite clear that the daughter left her home in Edson with the consent and approval of her parents and was accompanied to Edmonton by her mother.

"It is equally undoubted that no illness resulted from the seduction and there is no evidence that the ability of the daughter to render services was in any way interfered with.

"In my opinion the matter is well settled that damage is the gist of the action and I am also of opinion that the damage necessary to found the right of action in the woman must be of the same character as gave the master his right of action . . . that is loss of service.

I see nothing in our statutes to convey a con... ...tendment of the legislature. In my ... dismissed ... nd

MacMillans Plan Return to Edson

No Plans for Future Apart From That Says Mother

FATHER AT WORK

Planning to return to their home at Edson shortly, where, they say, they hope to be able to "forget about" the trial in which they participated last week, Mrs. Maude MacMillan and her daughter, Vivian MacMillan, to whom a jury awarded $10,000 damages against Premier Brownlee Saturday, were still in Edmonton Tuesday. Allan D. MacMillan, father of Vivian MacMillan, was back at work as assistant foreman in the Canadian National railways shops at Edson.

Speaking to a Journal reporter over the telephone Tuesday, Mrs. MacMillan said: "We have absolutely no plans for ... though we will ... home at Ed...

WHY DOES DADDY STAY AWAY SO MUCH?
Like a knife thrust, this innocent question! And then . . .
BUT, SIS, EVEN DOROTHY NOTICES HOW TOM NEGLECTS ME! I'M SO UNHAPPY
HONEY, I'VE WANTED TO HELP—BUT DON'T BE HURT. THERE'S AN AD IN THIS PAPER THAT WILL TELL YOU WHAT I MEAN
PERSPIRATION ODOUR IN UNDERTHINGS—I NEVER REALIZED THAT I WAS GUILTY—I KNOW LUX TAKES IT ALL AWAY—SAVES COLOURS TOO—I'LL NEVER OFFEND AGAIN!
Now Happiness Reigns
HURRY, DEAR, OR WE WON'T BE READY WHEN DADDY COMES. HE'S GOING TO TAKE US FOR A RIDE AFTER SUPPER
OH, MUMMY, DON'T WE HAVE GOOD TIMES NOW! DADDY GETS HOME EARLY NEARLY EVERY DAY
AVOID OFFENDING
Underthings absorb perspiration odour —protect daintiness this easy way:
Lonely, unhappy wives so seldom suspect that their own carelessness may be to blame. Perspiration odour in underthings kills romance! Luxing lingerie after every wearing whisks away perspiration odour, saves colours. Avoid cake-soap rubbing, and soaps with harmful alkali. Lux has no harmful alkali—safe in water, safe in Lux!
For Dishes, too!
So many soaps gradually dry the skin. Then red, rough "dishpan" hands result. Gentle Lux protects sensitive skin, for it has no harmful alkali. Soothing Lux suds are thrifty, too—cost less than 1¢ a day.
LUX
For all fine laundering
—for underthings
removes perspiration odour
—saves colours
Miss Claire Andree of the DeBoth Homemakers School used LUX in her demonstrations of correct washing methods here last week
MISS ANDREE says: "Anything that's safe in water is safe in LUX"
TUNE IN LUX RADIO THEATRE 7 P.M. every Monday COLUMBIA NETWORK

3 DIAMOND FEATURE
REGISTERED FOR YOUR PROTECTION
Beautiful New Style "BRIDAL WREATH"
This sparkler on her finger, will put a sparkle in her eye. 3 perfect Diamonds, 18 K. gold setting.
$62.50
EASY CREDIT TERMS
Other Diamond Rings Priced at
$15-$25-$35-$50
$2 DOWN—50c Week
Write for Self Measuring Ring Card
Beautiful Illustrated Jewelry Catalogue Free on Request
YOUR CR—IT IS FINE! WITH
IRVING KLINE
EDMONTON'S CREDIT JEWELLERS
10117 JASPER AVE. PHONE 25264
AT THE SIGN OF THE CLOCK
CANADIAN PACIFIC RAILWAY TIMEKEEPER

time he was too determined. He had one arm around me, holding me down on the seat of the car. He used his other hand to raise my clothes and undo his own. On that occasion we had complete sexual intercourse."

The jury found Brownlee guilty, but the judge, a stern-looking man named W.C. Ives, reversed the verdict, saying that while MacMillan might have been seduced, she wasn't incapacitated – a requirement for a guilty verdict under the law.

Adding insult to injury, he ordered MacMillan and her father to pay Brownlee's legal bill.

The Bulletin reacted with outrage, writing front-page editorials railing about the unfairness of the law and the contempt of court charge slapped on its publisher and reporter.

In its only response throughout the whole affair *The Journal* was slightly more subdued. In a tightly written editorial July 3, the paper offered up precisely 150 words on the case. "… Albertans as a whole must regret keenly the circumstances under which it has become necessary for Mr. Brownlee to vacate his post and at the same time they must recognize the ability and the zeal that he has brought to the discharge of his public duties."

Of the law, the judge or MacMillan, there was not a word.

On March 1, 1937, *The Journal* reported the Supreme Court of Canada's reversal of the Ives' decision.

"The settled rule is that the verdict of the jury must stand," Justice Lyman Duff."

The Journal had no editorial reaction to the decision.

Brownlee appealed, but in 1940 the Privy Council in England, then Canada's final court of appeal, found in favour of MacMillan.

The Privy Council's decision was recorded June 4, 1940, on page 16 under the headline, "Brownlee Loses London Appeal."

"Lord Russell of Killowen, giving judgment, said that if the language of the Alberta act were read in the natural and ordinary meaning, and apart from other considerations, an intention to give an unmarried female who had been seduced the right of action in her own name for damages plainly appeared.

"Seduction might well have been thought to be a wrong to her from whatever angle it was considered, Lord Russell continued, though no doubt, there were cogent reasons for great caution in giving her remedy for what might be said to be no more than voluntary loss of chastity," said The Canadian Press story from London.

Again, *The Journal* made no comment editorially.

MacMillan dropped out of the headlines. She remained in Alberta, married twice and died in Calgary Aug. 1, 1980, at the age of 68.

Brownlee resigned as premier July 10, 1934, and sat as an MLA for Ponoka until his government was defeated in the Aug. 22, 1935, election.

He went on to a stellar legal career and eventually became senior counsel for the United Grain Growers before assuming the office of president and chief executive officer in 1948.

Brownlee died in 1961, survived by Mrs. Brownlee who stood by her husband throughout. He is buried in Edmonton.

not supply aid until Alberta consents to a loan council, which Aberhart refuses to do.

***April 7, 1936*:**
The Alberta government gives assent to a law establishing a two-per-cent provincial sales tax called the Ultimate Purchasers Tax. It is abolished in 1937.

***June 4, 1936*:**
Cardinal Rodrique Villeneuve, archbishop of Quebec, is the first Catholic cardinal to visit Edmonton.

***Aug. 5, 1936*:**
Alberta's Social Credit government begins issuing Prosperity Certificates or "scrip," first in payment to highway workers. The "funny money" program fails because businesses, banks and even the province refuse to accept it as payment for goods or services.

***Aug. 13, 1936*:**
Edmonton's cenotaph, erected to the memory of the city's First World War dead, is unveiled by Gov. Gen. Lord Tweedsmuir. It's located on 102nd Street, southwest of *The Journal* building.

***Nov. 12, 1936*:**
Joseph Clarke is re-elected to a fifth one-year term as Edmonton's mayor.

Souvenir Edition

Edmonton Journal

Souvenir Edition

THIRTY-SIXTH YEAR | EDMONTON, ALBERTA, THURSDAY, JUNE 1, 1939 | SINGLE COPY, 5 CENTS

Greetings to Their Majesties

An Outstanding Day

"It was the most northerly point of Their Majesties' visit and, according to outside newspapermen – many of them distinguished journalists with an international reputation – provided the most spontaneous and stirring reception of the royal tour."

— Day-after report on the royal visit, June 3, 1939

When King George VI and Queen Elizabeth came to town on June 2, 1939, Edmontonians had never seen anything quite like it, and if you believed the newspaper's intense coverage, the entire world was enormously impressed, too.

The royal visit brought newspaper reporters from around the world to Edmonton, and if the King and Queen were only going to be here for a brief stop, the city was determined to show them the most memorable six-and-a-half hours of their entire cross-country tour.

For weeks leading up to their arrival, *The Journal* covered every detail of the planning. The royal visit appeared to be more important than Hitler in Berlin, Stalin in Moscow, Churchill in London or Franklin Delano Roosevelt in Washington. It was also a lot more important than Mackenzie King in Ottawa, unless King was saying something about the upcoming royal visit.

Pictures and biographies of the special CNR royal train crew – conductors Allan McGarrity and Arthur G. Webster and trainmen C.A. Gunter, Clifford A. Glover, George E. Welsh, Edward P. Otteson, Dennis J. O'Donnell, H.D. McColl and W. Waight – made page 1 on May 4.

The women who served as special switchboard operators to the King and Queen – Laura Watt, Elsie McCombs, Gladys Warnock and Sybil Hollingworth, misses all – were featured in a front-page picture on May 10.

Two weeks before the big day, the newspaper ran a photograph and a story on the proper way to curtsy and bow should you be one of the lucky women or men whom the royal couple might favour. A story reported that the public library was swamped with demands for information on etiquette.

Miss Evalyn Srigley, of the library's overtaxed reference department, suggested that Edmontonians might well copy the people in England when it came to cheering. Canadians were too boisterous, she felt. "We don't seem to get the throatiness of the English people," she said, "perhaps because we don't get the practice they do."

From the office of G.M. Little, the city's medical health officer, came the suggestion that people carry a half-dozen envelopes which, if folded properly, could serve as drinking cups. Cafes were urged to keep their menus simple so that they could feed the tens of thousands of expected visitors.

Hook Signs Ltd. was awarded the contract to decorate the city with 960 crowns, 215 coats of arms, 23,000 yards of bunting, 2,200 flags and 6,500 pennants.

The visit, in fact, changed the face of Edmonton. Starting with an editorial on May 9, *The Journal* led a successful campaign to change the

***Nov. 18, 1936*:**
"Registration and licensing of all barbershops in the province is required under the code for the barbershop trade which was proclaimed Tuesday...The price of a shave is set at 25 cents, while haircuts for men or women are fixed at 35 cents. For haircuts for children under 14, the price is 25 cents...A face massage will cost 50 cents, or swinging round to the neck, 35 cents. A neck shave is priced at 15 cents, but it costs 10 cents more for a woman's neck clip. Shampoos range from 35 to 75 cents. No service is to be less than 15 cents."
- *Journal* story.

***Dec. 15, 1936*:**
"But some parts of education must be learned. I look on the alphabet as necessary. I find very few women ever learn it any more than is necessary to use the telephone book. Then, you must learn the West Saxon kings and the branches of Amazon - and remember which is which..."
- Humourist Stephen Leacock, addressing University of Alberta graduates.

***March 5, 1937*:**
Cliff Manahan of Edmonton wins the Canadian men's curling title, the Brier, for the second time.

Weather Forecast
Possible Showers

Edmonton Journal

'One Of Canada's Great Newspapers'

THIRTY-FOURTH YEAR ** EDMONTON, ALBERTA, TUESDAY, MAY 11, 1937 SINGLE COPY, 5 CENTS 38 PAGES

Londoners Already Line Coronation Route

German-Made Planes Bomb Bilbao Outskirts, Convey Dire Warning

Order Surrender by Wednesday or No Mercy Shown

FRIGHT IS CAUSED

Successive Attacks Send Citizens Scurrying for Shelter

BILBAO, May 11.—Eleven insurgent air raids within less than five hours blasted the outskirts of Bilbao Tuesday.

The first armada of German-made bombers appeared over the city at 6:30 a.m. Successive fleets bombing the fringes of the city kept the refugee-swelled population of more than 300,000 in a steady scurry for shelter.

Although the most densely inhabited sections of Bilbao were unscathed, alarm spread that the air raids were General Mola's warning that insurgent forces would "bomb the city by land, sea and air without mercy unless Bibao surrenders by Wednesday (tomorrow)."

The threat was made in pamphlets dumped into the city by insurgent aeroplanes. Officials of the Basque autonomous government thus far have ignored it.

MADRID, May 11.—Night-long insurgent artillery bombardment left 40 persons dead and injured Tuesday and new ruins in the heart of the capital.

BILBAO, Spain, May 11.—Heavy artillery bombardment, covering operations of a defence army of about 65,000 Basques and Asturian allies

R. B. Bennett Brings $2,100

NEWMARKET, Suffolk, May 11.—Four horses, including "R. B. Bennett" of Lady Houston's stable have been sold for $8,715 here. The horse named after the former Canadian premier was purchased by the Epsom trainer, Walter Nightingall, for $2,100.

Calls Premier Prove Claims

Ansley Wants Details on Charge Finance Leads His Hand

CALGARY ADDRESS

CALGARY, May 11.—Challenging Premier Aberhart to show where finance "has payed any part in deciding my statements or actions, or those on the part of any of our colleagues who have opposed the policy of the government," R. E. Ansley, insurgent Social Credit member for Leduc, in an address here Monday night said he resents statements by Premier Aberhart which the premier knows full well are contrary to fact."

The member declared tha... because we refu... in deceiv... on th...

Long May They Reign!

First Enthusiasts Camp On Stools Along Curb, Await Glimpse of King

Allegiance of 400,000,000 Pledged by Empire Statesmen

PRESENT ADDRESSES

"I Stand on the Threshold of a New Life," Says Monarch

By George Hambleton
(Canadian Press Staff Writer)

LONDON, May 11.—"I stand on the threshold of a new life," His Majesty the King told the prime ministers of Canada, Australia, New Zealand and South Africa, and the representatives of India and the colonies Tuesday on the eve of his coronation.

These spokesmen from the empire's outposts came to Buckingham palace through a driving rain to pledge allegiance of the 400,000,000 British subjects they represent. Loyal addresses to the King were presented.

Weather forecast for Wednesday was: "Chilly; overcast skies." Yet the enthusiasm of the thousands milling through the streets, viewing notables and anticipating Wednesday's coronation and procession, remained undampened.

... than a full day be-

Diver Is Seeking Lost Railroad

BUFFALO, May 11.—A diver donned his underwater gear again Tuesday and descended 42 feet into an old rock quarry swimming hole, 20 miles across the Canadian border—looking for a lost railroad.

He hoped to find two locomotives, 100 dump cars, a big water pump and about 15 miles of railroad track, all covered by water for almost 20 years. The pump was shut off and water allowed to fill the quarry during the Great War.

H. P. Keith Said Ousted

Deputy Minister Public Works for Past Three Years

FALLOW IS SILENT

H. P. Keith, deputy minister of ... works for the past three

Edmonton Journal

EDMONTON, ALBERTA, TUESDAY, MAY 11, 1937

King George VI
Queen Elizabeth

Scenes From Lives of Their Majesties and Two Children

Princess Elizabeth, heir-presumptive to the throne. She recently celebrated her 11th birthday.

Her Majesty Queen Elizabeth with little Princess Margaret Rose and Princess Elizabeth are met by admiring throngs as they start on a shopping expedition. Husky London bobbies clear a path for them.

Princess Margaret Rose, baby sister of Elizabeth, and second in line to the throne.

The impressive north door of Westminster Abbey, the ancient and beautiful stone carvings cleaned for the coronation, is shown above. Note the "Virgin and Child" column in an almost perfect state of preservation.

A typical example of a happy family is this portrait of Their Majesties the King and Queen with little Princess Margaret Rose and her older sister Princess Elizabeth. The charming study was made by Marcus Adams, noted photographer.

Down this "middle aisle" in old Westminster Abbey the King and Queen will pass to receive the crowns of empire.

Their Majesties are here shown, dressed for the occasion, just before they descended down a Welsh coal mine on an inspection tour. The King is intensely interested in all industrial enterprises and frequently visits factories and mines throughout the United Kingdom.

The Monarch and his Queen with Princess Elizabeth, left, and Princess Margaret Rose, enjoying a romp with their dogs in Windsor Park grounds of the royal lodge. All the members of the royal family are great lovers of the outdoors and dogs receive special affection from the little princesses.

Their Majesties leaving 145 Piccadilly to attend the christening of the daughter of the Duke and Duchess of Kent at Buckingham Palace.

name of Portage Avenue to Kingsway. The broad thoroughfare bisected the old Hudson's Bay Reserve that had been part of the ill-fated land boom two decades previously. Council approved the change May 29.

The day before the arrival of the King and Queen, *The Journal* published a four-section, 48-page souvenir supplement. It sold for a nickel and included full-page reproductions of official portraits of the royal couple and marked the first time the newspaper used full-colour on its news pages.

The special section included a history of royalty from William the Conqueror up to George VI. Royal family life was depicted as happy and loving. There was a story on each country in the Empire.

The supplement was also crammed with advertisements welcoming the royal couple. Towns in northern Alberta vied for space, and retailers such as Johnstone Walker and the Hudson's Bay Company bought full-page ads proclaiming their loyalty to King and Empire.

The Edmonton Chinese Benevolent Association bought an ad as did the Edmonton Typographical Union. The two-column union ad was only slightly larger than the one that appeared directly below it from the Knights and Ladies of the Ku Klux Klan of Canada.

The royal couple spent most of their Edmonton visit in the "Royal car" as they made an extensive and tightly scheduled tour of the city.

The couple stopped several times, once to "gain a better view of the encampment of 1,200 Indians who had come into Edmonton from outside reservations" and listen to God Save the King sung in Cree.

Their second stop was a reception at the legislature chamber where they met, among others, Alberta's seven Victoria Cross Great War heroes.

And in what has now a staple of royal visits, "… a stop was made at the University hospital and a touching scene took place when the King and the Queen greeted war veterans and paralytic children patients in beds and chairs or supported by crutches on the lawn."

After a brief stop at the royal train to refresh themselves, the royal couple dined at the Macdonald Hotel with 175 invited guests.

Coverage in the next day's paper was massive. "Additional Royal visit pictures on pages 2, 3, 6, 7, 8, 9, 13, 14, 16, 17, 21 and 25 of this section," a subhead on page 1 told readers on June 3.

"The crowds that lined the streets and filled the stands must be regarded as of astounding proportions," a day-after editorial stated.

"That along each side of the two-mile stretch of Portage Ave., to be known henceforth as Kingsway, was a sight that, in all probability, could not be duplicated anywhere in the world. For its being possible we have to thank, of course, the over-optimism which led to the premature establishment of that thoroughfare a quarter century ago. But the long delay in turning it to ordinary purposes was compensated for by the use to which it was put yesterday."

It was, the editorial concluded, the most outstanding day ever in the history of Edmonton.

***April 25, 1937*:**
Ottawa announces a new agricultural research laboratory will be established at Lacombe.

***June 29, 1937*:**
Edmonton's record high temperature of 37.2 degrees Celsius is recorded, the same day as Quebec inventor J.-Armand Bombardier patents the Bombardier Snowmobile. The tracked vehicle will carry several passengers and costs $7,500 ($102,333.33 today).

***July 8, 1937*:**
Bush pilot Grant McConachie completes the first round trip of the newly established Edmonton-Yukon air mail and passenger service.

***July 15, 1937*:**
Edmonton's city assessor reports a population of 87,034 after the annual city census.

***Sept. 30, 1937*:**
The Socreds introduce the Accurate News and Information Act. The law would restrict press freedoms and require papers to publish government statements as directed and reveal sources, and is intended to suppress media criticism of the government and its unusual policies.

Weather Forecast
Fair and Warm

Edmonton Journal

'One Of Canada's Great Newspapers'

THIRTY-FIFTH YEAR ** EDMONTON, ALBERTA, MONDAY, JULY 18, 1938 SINGLE COPY, 5 CENTS 18 PAGES

Lone Flier Spans Atlantic In $900 Plane

Boy, 14, Woman Drown In Week-End Mishaps In Lloydminster Area

Mrs. H. Sutton Drowns on Farm, D. McCormick At Beach

RESCUE WORK FAILS

Bring Drownings to 15 In Edmonton Area This Year

Two more Alberta residents lost their lives during the week-end in drowning fatalities, one on a Lloydminster farm and one at Sandy Beach, 12 miles north of Lloydminster.

THE DEAD

Mrs. H. Sutton, Lloydminster.

Douglas McCormick, 14, Vermilion.

Mrs. H. Sutton was found late Saturday in a swimming pool, dammed up on a creek, 100 yards from her farm home. She was found by her husband shortly after he returned from visiting with neighbors.

The Suttons recently dammed the creek for the purpose of having a bathing pool. Mrs. Sutton apparently was overcome while swimming alone. One of Lloydminster's early settlers, she came here from England and leaves her widower and a sister, Mrs. A... of Kelowna.

Seeks Sell Eye To Pay His Bills

CALGARY, July 18.—Unemployed, William G. Whittit, 19, of Calgary, wants to sell his right eye—slightly injured.

"I am prepared to sacrifice my right eye to obtain money to pay off accumulated medical bills," Whittit said in an interview with newspapermen. "I am not a crank. I am serious about this offer."

He thinks $1,500 would be a reasonable sum for his eye—"just what I would receive if I obtained compensation for losing my eye in an accident. I am informed by doctors it can be put in good shape again."

Whittit expressed the wish to help some man or woman suffering from loss of sight.

70c Predicted As Wheat 'Peg'

Expect Ottawa to Name Guaranteed Price Shortly

SUB...

2 Die in Crazed Clubbing of 5 Victims

Manhunt for Harry Shire, 33, continued Monday in the Two Hills district, 70 miles east of here, following the alleged attack on his wife, baby son and three relatives at the Shire farm home early Friday. Shire allegedly fatally clubbed his seven-months-old son, Raymond, beat his wife into unconsciousness, and injured his wife's small cousins, James and Florence Wasyleski, and his brother-in-law, Peter Antoniuk, 17. Florence, seven, died Monday in the Vegreville hospital. The upper picture shows the alleged slayer and his wife photographed a year ago; below (left to right) are James, Florence and Peter.

Rumania Loses Great Figure As Queen Mother Marie Dies

Expect Crowds Jubilee Fair Break Records

Thousands Enter Grounds As Exhibition Gates Open

MIDWAY IS ACTIVE

Weather Perfect, Track Fast as Races Commence

Edmonton's diamond jubilee exhibition, biggest and most elaborate ever held here, got away to a memorable unofficial opening at noon Monday as thousands of excited young people stormed the fair grounds.

Monday was "Children's day," and although the fair's formal opening was not scheduled until 8:00 p.m., the big enterprise was well under way long before that hour, with children predominating in the eager first-day throng.

Last year 21,335 persons attended on opening day—a new all-time mark for Monday's crowd. With ideal weather prevailing Monday, fair officials predicted confidently an even higher peak would be reached during the day.

Free admission to the grounds and slashed prices to the grandstand and midway attractions were offered to young people Monday, and it was plain from noon on that they intended to take full advantage of the opportunity. By 1:30 p.m. fair officials estimated more than 10,000 youngsters, many of whom were...

Queen Mother Marie of Rumania, who died at Bucharest Monday after a prolonged illness. She was 62.

Second Victim Dies of Hurts

Posse Still Hunting in Bush Area for Slayer

Amazes Aviation World With Unauthorized Hop From N.Y. to Ireland

Said He Was Taking Off On Flight "To California"

ARE FLABBERGASTED

Air Journey Is Made Without Any Permit From Officials

DUBLIN, July 18.—Douglas P. Corrigan, the flier who took off from New York on a flight to "California," dropped unheralded from the skies Monday at Baldonnel, Ireland.

He made the flight in an antiquated 1929 model single-motored aeroplane of the vintage of Colonel Charles A. Lindbergh's "Spirit of St Louis" in 28 hours and 13 minutes. Corrigan himself valued the aeroplane at $900.

He took off from Floyd Bennett field Sunday at 2:17 a.m. (Edmonton time) and landed at Baldonnel, airport for Dublin, at 6:30 a.m.

Although a watch had been kept for the lone flier in Ireland after news of his "mystery flight" from New York, his landing here caused the greatest surprise.

Flabbergasted airport officials rushing to the machine saw a grinning pilot jump out.

"I'm Douglas Corrigan," he said. "Just got in from New York.

"It took me 28 hours and 13 minutes."

"By the way, where am I?" the flier asked the gathering Irish crowd.

The crowd looked at Corrigan, at his aeroplane and its...

Japan Shipping Specie Abroad

TOKIO, July 18. — Japanese finance ministry decided Monday to cut into the Bank of Japan's gold reserve to ship specie abroad for the purchase of badly-needed raw materials.

Only cabinet approval—expected Tuesday—is needed to free the Bank of Japan's 800,000,000 yen gold stocks for shipment abroad. This step was recommended last Friday by the price commission headed by Sotaro Ishiwatari, of the ministry of finance, for the stated purpose of bolstering Japan's sagging exports. The commission also recommended scaling down the prices of exported products 10 to 20 per cent.

In a world obsessed with aviation, Wilfred (Wop) May was a pioneer in this daring field. Photographed in England in 1917, May was an ace fighter pilot during the First World War.

NA-1258-2 Glenbow Archives

Wop May

"There are the thinkers and philosophers ... There are also men of action out on the frontiers doing the things that seem impossible."
— Rev. R. Douglas Smith, June 26, 1952

Wilfred (Wop) May's name was often found in the pages of *The Journal*.

It wasn't because he was powerful or rich. It was because he was a hero and *The Journal* always had space for heroes.

May lived in an era when daring pilots had names familiar to *Journal* readers and the simple fact of getting into the air was news.

"Making his first trip into Edmonton this season, the big all-metal Junkers with pilot Walter Gilbert, Canadian Airlines, at the controls landed at South Cooking Lake at 3 p.m.," reported a story June 18, 1934.

Geographically, Edmonton's air facilities truly did provide a Gateway to the North, and *The Journal* took licence to expand that definition in 1937 to Crossroads of the World when word came Soviet flyers were supposed to stop here. In fact, three times that summer expectant crowds gathered at Blatchford Field to see giant Soviet bombers land, only to be disappointed. Twice, planes diverted west and, in August, an ANT-41 (TB), the world's first four-engine bomber, crashed before it got here.

On April 1, 1939, *The Journal* took the start of Trans-Canada Airway's regular passenger service to the city rather matter-of-factly. "The inauguration of the TCA passenger service merely means to Edmonton an extension of this form of transport to the greater part of the Dominion."

Nine years later, on Feb. 15, 1948, a story noted that Edmonton's Municipal Airport led all of Canada in freight, commercial and military aircraft traffic.

And Wop May was in it from the start. By his death, June 21, 1952, Edmonton was on solid footing as the door to the North and beyond.

Word of May's death from a heart attack while on holiday in Provo, Utah, appeared in *The Journal* June 23.

The stories of his involvement in the demise of the Red Baron during the First World War, the mercy flight to bring diphtheria vaccine to Ft. Vermilion and his role in capturing the Mad Trapper were all well documented.

Less famous, but perhaps more important to the city, was his tenacity in pushing city council to approve the first $400 to clear two 300-yard runways at the Hagmann farm, just north of downtown at the end of Portage Avenue (later called Princess Elizabeth Avenue).

That was the beginnings of the Municipal Airport, later dubbed Blatchford Field in honour of Mayor Ken Blatchford who heeded May's advice in 1926 and joined May in badgering council.

May died at 57. In its editorial on June 24, *The Journal* said it was long enough to know his work was not wasted. "Fortunately, Captain May lived to see the solid edifice of northern commercial aviation built on the first fragile foundations he helped to lay a quarter of a century ago."

***Nov. 10, 1937*:**
John Fry is elected mayor of Edmonton for the first time, defeating incumbent Joseph Clarke. Fry will serve a record eight consecutive one-year terms.

***May 2, 1938*:**
The *Edmonton Journal* is awarded a special Pulitzer award for its "leadership in the defence of the freedom of the press." The paper led the battle against a Social Credit government Press Act that would have required papers to print statements under government order.

***May 9, 1938*:**
Alberta Lt.-Gov. John C. Bowen moves out of his Government House official residence and into temporary quarters at the Macdonald Hotel, after the Social Credit government passes an order closing the residence. Bowen and the government had clashed when Bowen refused to sign into law controversial legislation later ruled unconstitutional by the Supreme Court of Canada.

***Aug. 27, 1938*:**
Former mayor "Fighting" Joseph Clarke kicks the football to open the first game in Edmonton's new 3,000-seat Clarke

CFCN

NA-2771-2 Glenbow Archives

Bible Bill Aberhart broadcasting from his office on Calgary's CFCN radio, late 1930s.
Below, a special Pulitzer award given to *The Journal*.

"It is the essence of democracy that the people should have the opportunity to know and freedom to discuss the activities and policies of their government. That is essential to the formation of intelligent public opinion which in the final analysis is alike the motivating force and the effective safeguard of democracy."

From *Journal* publisher John Imrie's speech to Columbia University upon accepting a special Pulitzer award in 1938.

HONORIS
CAUSA
JOSEPH PULITZER MEDAL

Freedom of the Press

"His decision was a proper one, beyond any shadow of a doubt. It serves as an impressive reminder to the government of the province there are limits to what it can do in carrying out its policies."

— Editorial after Lt.-Gov. J.C. Bowen refused to give royal assent to the press bill Oct. 6, 1937

Relations were tense between *The Journal* and the newly formed Social Credit Party in 1935.

The paper, editorially, thought the populist, money-for-nothing party was founded on little more than half-baked, pseudo-economics.

Its challenge of Social Credit doctrine earned the animosity of the Socreds and, in a few years, a Pulitzer award for defending press freedom.

But Depression-struck Albertans seemed willing to try anything that promised them a regular meal.

The failing United Farmer of Alberta government called an election Aug. 22, 1935, and *The Journal* sensed, correctly, Social Credit would be the focal point.

William Aberhart promoted the economic theories of English engineer Clifford Hugh Douglas that fundamental changes in banking laws were necessary to get money and credit into the hands of people.

The Journal doubted the province had the power. "The only way in which the province could be placed in a position to adopt his (Aberhart's) scheme would be for it to withdraw from Confederation," cautioned an editorial July 25, 1935.

The Socreds won 56 of 63 seats and began attempts to pass laws to implement their theories.

But the federal government, backed by the Supreme Court and the British North America Act, held sway when it came to banking laws. The changes were declared unconstitutional.

A year later, Aberhart's popularity hit bottom.

Alberta had recall legislation and Aberhart was on track to be its first victim — until his government repealed it Sept. 30, 1937.

On the same day, the beleaguered Socreds also introduced the Accurate News and Information Act that would force newspapers to publish, unedited, government replies to any news story it deemed inaccurate. Failure to print the government response could result in the paper being shut down.

"The bill is Hitlerism rampant," sneered one of several heated editorials about the bill. "If enacted, it would place in the hands of a few men such power in this respect as no British monarch or government has presumed to assume for the past two centuries."

The paper's efforts came to the attention of the Pulitzer Prize committee in New York, which gave *Journal* publisher John Imrie and editor A. Balmer Watt a special public service award for the paper's tireless defence of press freedom.

It was the first time a newspaper outside the U.S. was so honoured.

Stadium, built at a cost of $50,000. The Eskimos lose 35-1 to Calgary.

***Sept. 28, 1938*:**
Canadian National charges $4.90 for a return trip on its Edmonton-Calgary excursion train; children under 12 travel at half fare.

***Oct. 12, 1938*:**
The first Edmonton branch of the Alberta government's new Treasury Branch "credit houses" opens in the city.

***Nov. 15, 1938*:**
Noel MacDonald, captain of the Edmonton Grads basketball team, is named Canada's outstanding woman athlete of the year.

***Nov. 22, 1938*:**
Alberta passes the Metis Betterment Act. Acting on recommendations of the Ewing Commission, it establishes Metis land colonies with a legal status unique in Canada.

***Dec. 11, 1938*:**
Edmonton's Al Rashid Mosque, the first mosque in Canada, is officially opened. The historic building is later moved to Fort Edmonton Park.

***In 1939*:**
An advertising copy chaser at *The Journal* earns $11 a week.

Shows
DICK POWELL-JOAN BLONDELL in "Gold Diggers of 1937" DREAMLAND
NELSON EDDY-JEANETTE MACDONALD in "Maytime" CAPITOL
MARLENE DIETRICH in "The Garden of Allah" EMPRESS
JEAN ARTHUR-GEORGE BRENT in "More Than a Secretary" STRAND
IRENE DUNNE MELVYN DOUGLAS in "Theodora Goes Wild" RIALTO
RANDOLPH SCOTT BINNIE BARNES in "The Last of the Mohicans" PRINCESS

Radio Listeners Thrown Into Panic By Play Depicting Attack From Mars

One Government Seen for Canada

MEDICINE HAT, Oct. 31.—Hope that there will be a united Canada under one government within 25 years was expressed by Col. Nelson Spencer of Vancouver, when he addressed veterans of the 175th battalion, Canadian expeditionary force, here Saturday night. Col. Spencer was commanding officer of the battalion during the Great War.

Speaking at the annual battalion reunion banquet, he said:

"The people of Canada will never make progress as long as we have 10 gods." He voiced opposition to "individual, provincial governments."

ONE WEEK STARTING SATURDAY
RIALTO
ONE WEEK STARTING SATURDAY
GAYEST OF ALL HER HITS!
You've Never Seen This Grace Moore Before!
She'll make you rub your eyes — and ears — with amazement — with her madcap rom-antics from Schubert to "Minnie the Moocher" . . . swinging and singing . . . loving and laughing . . . in a corking yarn of fun and frivolity from the writer of the smash stories "Mr. Deeds Goes to Town" and "It Happened One Night"! You'll say it's the hi-de-high-spot of a year's entertainment . . . . . .
Grace Moore
in
"WHEN YOU'RE IN LOVE"
with CARY GRANT
Aline MacMahon • Henry Stephenson • Thomas Mitchell
Written and Directed by ROBERT RISKIN
PASSED "U"
IMAGINE Glorious GRACE...
ADDED ENTERTAINMENT
"HOLD 'EM COWBOY" — Sport Reel
"PIGS IS PIGS"—Colored Cartoon
Saturday Morning and Afternoon Only
THE FOURTH CHAPTER OF "THE MYSTERY SQUADRON"
10 a.m. to 12:30 Noon, Children Admission 5c. Doors Open 9:30 a.m.
Hear the songs of JEROME KERN • VERDI SCHUBERT and "CAB" CALLOWAY
LAST TIMES TODAY
'Flying Down to Rio' With FRED ASTAIRE — GINGER ROGERS
'Bill Cracks Down' With GRANT WITHERS—BEATRICE ROBERTS

Alarms Flood Police as Attack on Earth Described

HOMES EVACUATED

WASHINGTON, Oct. 31.—United States communications commission began an investigation Monday of a dramatic radio broadcast which led some people to believe Sunday night that men from Mars had attacked the United States.

NEW YORK, Oct. 31.—A horrible broadcast fantasy of war waged on the United States by fearsome, space-conquering men from Mars brought near panic to thousands of radio listeners Sunday night.

In the double-quick tempo of the news broadcaster, the fiction of a Columbia program became so realistic that hysteria prevailed among listeners throughout the United States.

Demanding Probe

Demands for investigation and correction came apace Monday with the belated reports of almost fantastic panic.

It was purely a figment of H. G. Wells' imagination with some extra flourishes of dramatization by Orson Welles.

But the anxiety was immeasurable.

The broadcast was an adaptation of Wells' "War of the Worlds," in which meteors and gas from Mars menace the earth.

Sudden Bulletin

After an introductory explanation by Welles at 6:00 p.m. M.S.T., an announcer gave a commonplace weather forecast. Then after a few bars of dance music there came a "bulletin from the Intercontinental Radio News Bureau" saying there had been a gas explosion in New Jersey.

After that the bulletins came more and more rapidly with "Professor Pierson," played by Welles, explaining about the attack by Mars and the

(Continued on Page 3, Col. 1)

Manion Receives Bennett Cheques

By J. A. Hume

(Special to Edmonton Journal and Associated Southam Newspapers)

OTTAWA, Oct. 31.—Rt. Hon. R. Bennett, has not accep[illegible] August, any pa[illegible]

City Man Dazed By Radio Play

At least one Edmontonian reported Monday that he was still slightly dazed after hearing the Orson Welles radio drama that caused widespread panic throughout United tates Sunday night. He is Noel Iles, of 10292 92 st., who described to THE JOURNAL Monday his vivid impressions of the broadcast.

It is believed that few other Edmontonians heard the broadcast because of another popular program that is released in Edmonton Sunday night at the same time as the Orson Welles program.

"It was like a broadcast of a real great war or invasion. There were screams of dying men, clanking of war machines, cries of the horror-stricken women and children. I can easily understand the mass hysteria that the play caused. My father who was sitting in another room thought that the end of the world had come. A later news broadcast started with 'Trenton is still on the map.' (According to the radio play, the attack of Martians took place at a point near Trenton, N.J.)" Mr. Isles said.

Canada's First Mosque

"This couldn't happen in some lands which you are well aware of."
— Edmonton Mayor John Fry, Dec. 12, 1938

Edmonton's skyscraper – the McLeod Building, 25 feet taller than the Tegler Building – was only nine storeys tall and the city may have still been debating the necessity to pave all the roads, but on this day, Edmonton had something no other city in Canada had: a mosque.

There were about 40 families in Edmonton's Islamic community at the time, and a hundred people, not all Muslim, attended the opening ceremony over which Mayor John Fry presided.

The Journal had no comment about it editorially, but it did open space on the front of the second section for the event and even ran a rare (at the time) picture to highlight the story.

It was a photograph of celebrated Muslim scholar Abdulla Yusuf Ali, in the city for the ceremony, handing the keys to the building to D.M. Teha, president of the Arabian Moslem Association of Edmonton.

The $6,000 building at the northeast corner of 108th Avenue and 102nd Street looked like most other churches in the city, save for two concrete minarets at the front.

"First of its kind in Canada," proclaimed the story, "Edmonton's own Mohammedan mosque, dedicated to the faith of Allah and the teachings of the prophet Mahomet (as it was spelled in *The Journal*), was opened at a simple ceremony Sunday night."

Mayor Fry said he hoped the mosque would be a comfort to those of the Mohammedan faith.

"Briefly, he spoke of the significance it was for those of many faiths to be attending the ceremony and 'sitting friendly together.'"

Abdulla Ali, who set the standard for the English translation of the Koran, seemed to realize the people of his faith were a puzzle to the Christians who dominated the religious scene in town.

"There is nothing mysterious," he told the crowd, "nothing anyone cannot understand about a religion such as ours or this mosque."

He pointed to a niche in the southeast corner of the structure.

"All turn their faces toward Mecca so that all spiritual worship is one of unity. No matter where the followers of this faith are, they all turn toward Mecca, a symbol of unity among every brother."

The mosque, a historical resource, was moved to Fort Edmonton Park in 1990.

***March 8,1939*:**
Lynn Seymour, Canadian prima ballerina who starred with Britain's Royal Ballet, is born at Wainwright.

***April 17, 1939*:**
An Edmonton Athletic Club team loses the Memorial Cup Canadian junior hockey championship to the Oshawa Generals.

***June 2, 1939*:**
King George VI and Queen Elizabeth visit Edmonton during their tour of Canada, the first by a reigning monarch.

***June 24, 1939*:**
Edmonton's population is 90,419, according to the city census.

***Aug. 30, 1939*:**
***The Journal* says a provincial park has been established in the Red Deer River valley Badlands, to protect one of the world's richest dinosaur fossil deposits.**

***Sept. 1, 1939*:**
The Second World War begins when Nazi Germany invades Poland.

***Sept. 4, 1939*:**
Canadian pilots serving with Britain's Royal Air Force become the first Canadians in action in the Second World War. Among them is Flying Officer Robert Bisset of

Weather Forecast
Fair and Warm

Edmonton Journal

'One Of Canada's Great Newspapers'

THIRTY-FIFTH YEAR ** EDMONTON, ALBERTA, MONDAY, SEPTEMBER 12, 1938 SINGLE COPY, 5 CENTS 20 PAGES

Hitler Throws Gauntlet To Britain, France

Evasion, High Taxes, Public Extravagance Condemned by Beatty

Country Full of Money Kept Idle by Few, He Declares

AT MEETING HERE

Presages Railway Extensions as North Is Developed

Sounding a keynote of faith and confidence, Sir Edward Beatty, G.B.E., K.C., president and chairman of the C.P.R., expressed the conviction that "as development proceeds in the north, it will prove possible to increase and improve the railway transportation services of that area," when addressing a luncheon meeting of the Edmonton chamber of commerce and Kiwanis club at the Macdonald Monday.

"The Outlook for the North" was the subject of Sir Edward's address, during which he gave a summary of the early stages of western development and problems.

At the head table were Hon. J. C. Bowen, lieutenant-governor; Chief Justice Harvey, Mayor Fry, James A. MacKinnon, M.P., L. Y. Cairns, K.C., James A. Richardson, Col. James Ramsey, R. C. Marshall, W. A. Brown, John Callaghan, W. M. Neal, Charles Campbell, John M. Imrie, P. A. Woodward, J. M. MacArthur, J. Ivan MacKay, Ross J. McMaster, E. D. Cotterell, W. C. Owens, H. W. J. Maddison.

This country, said the speaker, was full of idle money, partly because of a general feeling of unrest and vague alarm "which always frightens capital into hiding; partly because of more definite fears of unjust treatment of those who venture to use capital for profit."

Making a passing reference to debt repudiation, the president said that sometimes he "heard the careless remark that repudiation is the road out of debt. I do not think that those who say this realize that the debts which they would repudiate are, in the last analysis, merely the stored labor of the past, the savings of the industrious," he observed.

Lower Taxation

Need of lower taxation also was discussed by Sir Edward who expressed the opinion that "if the people of this country realized to what extent the spread between what the producer sells and the consumer buys results from taxation, we should have a powerful movement for economy in public affairs."

He added that he had not the least hesitation in saying that "nothing is more important than this in influencing the development of the great north."

"It is my belief that when we emerge, as we are rapidly doing, from the period of doubt and hesitation which always succeeds a great economic crisis, enterprise and capital and labor will enter the north to develop, even more rapidly than has been the case, the great resources of that new empire to which Edmonton is the gateway," said Sir Edward.

Declaring that it was known that the mineral wealth of the north was enormous and had scarcely been touched, while it contained great stretches of rich arable land. Sir Edward added: "We know that if any country in the world seems to offer opportunities for development, it is northern Alberta and the north even beyond that."

After speaking of the development of air transport, the speaker expressed the hope that a genuine national policy would be adopted in regard to transportation.

"We have adopted unsound policies. We have provided surplus facilities of transportation in many parts of the country. We have followed what I believe to be unsound policies, not only in connection with the railways, but in dealing with our waterways and highways," Sir Edward declared.

Dealing with settlement questions, the speaker said that despite many erroneous statements on the point, he was not an advocate of unlimited immigration. He said that one of the most urgent problems before this country was to stimulate the occupation and development of the remaining agricultural lands not yet occupied. He thought there should be an increased effort "to attract to Canada those settlers who by type, by experience, and by possession of a reasonable amount of capital, are equipped to add to

(Continued on Page 2, Col. 1)

Sir Edward Beatty, G.B.E., K.C., president and chairman of the C.P.R., who announced on his arrival in Edmonton Sunday that survey of an extension of the N.A.R. in the Peace River country likely will be started next year.

Hitler Desires See Art Displays

NUREMBERG, Sept. 12.—Chancellor Hitler in an unusual burst of confidence disclosed Sunday he would like to get out of the limelight to visit foreign art galleries without being recognized.

The disclosure came as he was reminiscing with foreign correspondents about his trip to Italy last May.

"I know of but one other city that grips me as does Nuremberg," he said. "That city is Florence.

"There is an indescribable charm about it . . . I should have loved to have remained there another week—but, of course, incognito. Imagine going unrecognized into the Uffizi gallery! That, alas, is impossible."

Cobb Nears Speed Mark

Drives Auto at 342 M.P.H. On Utah Salt Flats

THREE MILES SHORT

BONNEVILLE SALT FLATS, Utah, Sept. 12.—John R. Cobb, London fur broker, attempted to shatter the world's automobile speed record Monday but fell short by less than three miles an hour. Piloting a 7,000-pound shark-shaped racer, he was clocked at 342.53 miles an hour but it was under Captain George E. T. Eyston's mark of 345.49 miles an hour, made here Aug. 29.

Cobb was timed officially at 343.8 on the south run and at 341.6 on the backward trip over the measured mile.

Aeroplane Carries 39½ Tons on Test

SEATTLE, Wash., Sept. 12.—Ballasted with lead and water to a gross load of 79,000 pounds, the big Boeing clipper cruised over Puget Sound Saturday night with a test crew of 10 engineering observers. She took off from Lake Washington with the heaviest gross poundage ever carried aloft by a heavier-than-air machine. Engineers reported she performed "admirably."

Rimbey Safes 'Blown' Cracksmen Get $35

Loot of $35 was obtained by cracksmen who "blew" two safes at Rimbey, 30 miles west of Ponoka, Sunday night, R.C.M.P. reported Monday.

Safe in the Beatty Bros. hardware store yielded all the money. Nothing was obtained from a strongbox forced in the White drug store.

Four Meet Death As Aeroplane Falls

DANVILLE, Ill., Sept. 12.—Four persons were killed Sunday when an aeroplane plummeted to earth near the municipal airport. The dead were Peter Britz, 41, owner and pilot; Charles Companion, 48; Harry Ice, 40, and James Kincade, 38, of Danville.

Escaped Monkeys Hold Wild Rampage

NEW YORK, Sept. 12.—Monkey business proved expensive to Henry Trefflich, animal dealer. A female monkey led three of her pals on a three-hour rampage after breaking out of their cage in his store. They broke a window, damaged a fruit stand and caused a pursuing policeman to tear his pants. Trefflick got a ticket for speeding while hurrying to the scene.

Where To Find It

Amusements, Theatres	5
Bridge	11
Crossword Puzzle	11
Comics	11
District	15
Editorial	4
Financial	8
Off the Record	5
Radio	18
Serial Story	11
Sports	12, 13
Uncle Ray's Corner	11
Wants Ads	16, 17, 18
Womens	14, 15

The Weather

Edmonton Weather

Sunday			
3:00 p.m.	78	2:00 a.m.	48
4:00 p.m.	76	3:00 a.m.	48
5:00 p.m.	73	4:00 a.m.	49
6:00 p.m.	71	5:00 a.m.	50
7:00 p.m.	68	6:00 a.m.	50
8:00 p.m.	65	7:00 a.m.	51
9:00 p.m.	61	8:00 a.m.	54
10:00 p.m.	55	9:00 a.m.	65
11:00 p.m.	50	10:00 a.m.	67
12:00 mid.	50	11:00 a.m.	72
Monday		12:00 noon	75
1:00 a.m.	50	1:00 p.m.	77
		2:00 p.m.	77

Maximum temperature Sept. 11, 78.
Minimum temperature Sept. 11, 50.
Barometer reading at 2:00 p.m., 27.70, steady.

(Continued on Page 6, Col. 7)

Spain Bombs Miss Small Freight Boat

MONTREAL, Sept. 12. — Red-headed Captain S. L. Spence says "they haven't got me yet" but keeps his fingers crossed when he says it.

Captain Spence and the tramp freighter Stancroft do business with loyalist Spain. They used to run cargoes in for the insurgents, but now they dodge insurgent bombs and insurgent gunfire in Spanish waters.

"Some bombs have come pretty close to us," Captain Spence recalled. "And those machine guns have come pretty close, too. But they've never hit us. I've had no casualties so far."

6 in Quebec Fire Victims

Husband, Wife, Daughter, Three Others Perish In Blaze

FOLLOWED DANCE

RIMOUSKI, Que., Sept. 12.—Six persons, including a husband and wife and daughter perished Sunday as flames raced through the Hotel des Vagues after a gay early-morning dance and reduced the year-old structure to a mass of charred wreckage.

Trapped in the blazing hotel, three members of Jean Roy's family and their little grand-nephew burned to death as the three-storey structure at Rimouski wharf was turned into a pyre. Two other men were killed as they leaped from upper windows.

The Dead

Jean Roy, 64; Mrs. Jean Roy, 67; Alfreda Roy, 40, their daughter, and 12 - year - old Mathieu Roy, their grand-nephew, all from Notre Dame du Lac, Que.; Andia Ripka, 33, Saint John, N.B., and a man named McNeil from Sydney, N.S.

The four Roys, caught in their beds or in corridors, died without getting out of the building.

The fire, its cause unknown, flared out just an hour after a dance had broken up at 3:00 a.m. All 17 persons in the hotel, most of whom had taken part in the dancing, were asleep.

When firemen arrived, the conflagration was beyond control. Running up ladders to the upper floors, they managed to bring out several of the trapped guests, but the building itself was destroyed.

NELSON, B.C., Sept. 12.—School at Shoreacres, 14 miles south of here, was burned early Sunday and B.C. police said incendiarists were responsible. The structure was used by English-speaking and Doukhobor children.

HOQUIAM, Wash., Sept. 12.—Hoquiam's worst fire in years swept through four frame buildings in the downtown area and damaged two others before it was controlled Sunday.

Two Killed, 6 Hurt When Car Crashes

WINNIPEG, Sept. 12.—Miss Clara Uderwood of St. Boniface, Man., and Walter Tymchyzn of Winnipeg were injured fatally two miles north of Winnipeg Saturday night when an automobile allegedly driven by James Duncan crashed into a stationary car.

There were four persons in each car and the other six were injured seriously although hospital authorities said they would recover. The injured are Duncan, Douglas Campbell, Tony Chambers, Frank Boyarski and Joseph Slobodian, all of Winnipeg, and Miss Mary Gibbs of St. Boniface.

Fascists Attacked By Aberdeen Crowd

ABERDEEN, Scotland, Sept. 12.—An angry crowd of more than 6,000 stoned a group of British Fascists attempting to speak from a sound truck here Sunday, injuring three of them.

Police rescued the Fascists. Among the injured was W. K. Chambers-Hunter, Fascist candidate for the house of commons, treated for cuts and bruises.

GRANDFATHER CHAMBERLAIN

LONDON, Sept. 12.—Prime Minister Chamberlain became a grandfather for the second time Monday with the birth of a daughter to Mrs. Stephen Lloyd of Birmingham, the premier's daughter. A son was born to Mrs. Lloyd in June, 1936.

Mighty Army In Readiness To Aid Czechs

Say France Offers 2,000,000 Men, 2,000 Planes, 200 Ships

PARIS CROWDS WAIT

France Completes Plans For General Mobilization

COPENHAGEN, Sept. 12.—Denmark was reported taking precautionary measures Monday along her Schleswing border with Germany. King Christian postponed his departure for his summer residence at Scaw because of the situation.

PARIS, Sept. 12.—French cabinet Monday completed plans for general mobilization in case it becomes necessary in the critical central European situation, informed sources asserted.

The ministers, who reviewed the nation's preparations in a meeting with Premier Edouard Daladier, were also said to have drawn up measures for evacuation and protection of the civil population if war should come.

An open telephone line connected the premier's office with 10 Downing st., London. Daladier and Prime Minister Chamberlain were said to have conversed frequently while their countries awaited Chancellor Hitler's pronouncement of German foreign policy.

In Paris and throughout France crowds gathered before news bulletin boards, anxiously watching latest reports from Nuremberg, Germany, where Hitler was addressing a Nazi party rally. Many Parisians abandoned work to gather on street corners and cafe terraces.

While the ministers were meeting in the war ministry office, French fighting forces were keyed to their highest pitch of efficiency. An estimater 2,000,000 men, 2,000 fighting aeroplanes and 200 ships were in readiness.

(A Havas news agency dispatch

(Continued on Page 6, Col. 8)

Ask Canada Labor Decide on C.I.O.

NIAGARA FALLS, Sept. 12.—Trades and Labor Congress of Canada was called upon Monday in the report of the executive council to decide on the policy to be pursued respecting the dispute between the American Federation of Labor and the Committee for Industrial Organization, and the Ontario government was asked to bring in legislation allowing workers to organize.

P. M. Draper, president of the congress, introduced the latter question by asking Hon. Peter Hecnan, Ontario minister of lands and forests, to press for such legislation.

Mr. Draper said he was pleased Nova Scotia and New Brunswick passed such bills, and Quebec passed enabling legislation. Manitoba, Saskatchewan, Alberta and British Columbia has similar legislation.

Major portion of the congress membership consists of international unions affiliated with the A.F. of L. There are five unions of international ramifications which joined the C.I.O. and had their charters revoked by the A.F. of L.

The executive's report said the decision to be faced by the convention was "not one of maintaining unity". Rather, it was to decide whether a policy would be adopted which would cause wholesale withdrawal of the international unions or one which, while maintaining these in affiliation, will necessitate dissociation of those organizations constituting the C.I.O.

The report also asked for repeal of Quebec's padlock law and reiterated labor's immigration policy—that present restrictions be maintained and no plan for government-assisted immigration should be made until the existing employment and agricultural depression has been overcome.

Question of relations between the American Federation of Labor and the Committee for Industrial Organization evoked the most resolutions. All asked for labor unity whereby C.I.O. unions remain in the congress although their corresponding international unions in the U.S. had their charters revoked by the American Federation of Labor.

Lethbridge Reports One New Polio Case

One new case of infantile paralysis was reported Monday in Alberta—a young man at Iron Springs, north of Lethbridge. Once midly sticken, he was receiving treatment in isolation hospital at Lethbridge.

No new cases were reported in Edmonton or anywhere in the north or central portions of the province.

Chancellor Hitler, who demanded in a speech Monday that the 3,500,000 Sudeten Germans be given "their rights" but did not indicate precisely what his intentions were toward Czecho-Slovakia. He said he was prepared to "take all risks" to settle certain national questions.

Crop Here Set $84,000,000

Alberta's Wheat Valuation $11,000,000 Over Last Year

MUCH BEST GRADE

Value of Alberta's wheat crop was placed at approximately $84,000,000 by an unofficial estimate on Monday. This figure exceeds last year's cash return by over $11,000,000, is 25 per cent greater than the 10-year average of $67,670,000.

Wheat yield for the province, estimated at 141,000,000 bushels by the dominion bureau of statistics, exceeds the 10-year average of 117,280,000 bushels by 20 per cent. It is the biggest crop since 1932.

Grading reports show a high quality for the bulk of the crop from southern Alberta with a great deal of No. 1 Northern. Little from central Alberta has yet moved to market, but much No. 2 and No. 3 Northern is expected. An average price of 60 cents net to farmers in Alberta is expected unofficially.

Record of Alberta's wheat crop of the past 10 years, with yields in round million bushels:

	Million bus.	Value.
1928	171	$117,008,000
1929	92	103,067,000
1930	147	51,831,000
1931	140	48,960,000
1932	167	53,554,000
1933	102	46,050,300
1934	112	62,250,000
1935	98	60,175,000
1936	67	58,290,000
1937	74	72,520,000
10-year average	117	67,670,000

Declares Canada Must Keep Unity

SAINT JOHN, N.B., Sept. 13.—Civil and religious liberty, with freedom of speech and thought, must be preserved in Canada, and to that end there must be development and growth of unity throughout the dominion, Col. W. W. Foster of Vancouver, president of the Canadian Legion, said here Saturday night at a dinner in his honor.

"There is need of unity, and we cannot serve as we should unless the people think in terms of country rather than in terms of self-endeavor," he said.

"Today we live in a world divided by thought, though united in destiny. We need to approach things in a broader spirit, not sectionally. We can clear up misunderstandings between nation and nation, but if Canada wants a voice in the world's destiny she needs to speak with a united voice."

ST. BONIFACE, Man., Sept. 12.—Creation of a greater Canada through greater unity of her peoples was urged by speakers attending celebrations marking the 200th anniversary of la Verendrye's landing at the forks of the Red and Assiniboine rivers.

Nine days of pageantry were climaxed Sunday with unveiling by Lieutenant-Governor Tupper of Manitoba of the monument sculptured by Emile Brunet of Montreal to perpetuate the memory of the French-Canadian fur trader. It is erected in Tache park here.

Hon. P. J. A. Cardin, dominion minister of public works, said at Saturday night's la Verendrye banquet he was "most happy" because the organizers had included in the celebrations the English-speaking people of Winnipeg.

Promises 'Unconditional Aid' To Win 'Rights' for Sudetens

Fuehrer Says He's Willing to "Take All Risks and Run All Dangers" But Fails to Disclose Exact Intentions

PRAGUE, Sept. 12.—Two Sudeten Germans were shot and injured, one seriously, in a political disturbance at Graslitz, Western Bohemia, Monday night after Chansellor Hitler's address at Nuremberg.

By A. C. Cummings
(Special to Edmonton Journal and Associated Southam Newspapers)

LONDON, Sept. 12.—Hitler's speech, while regarded in London as ominous and threatening, is nevertheless taken as meaning that a loophole may still be left for further brief negotiations between Sudeten Germans and the Prague government. The crisis is not over. However, breathing space for further peace efforts is seen.

NUREMBERG, Germany, Sept. 12.—Reichsfuehrer Hitler in one of the greatest oratorical efforts of his life, threw down the gauntlet to Great Britain and France Monday night, asserting that come what may Germany is determined to liberate the Sudeten Germans.

Hitler's promise of aid to the 3,500,000 Sudetens in Czecho-Slovakia was unconditional.

"I assure the democracies that the fate of the Sudetens is not a matter of indifference to us," he said. "If these harassed people feel they are without rights and aid they will get both from us."

"There are national questions for which I am ready to take all risks and to run all dangers," Hitler declared.

Hitler talked passionately for 78 minutes. It was the climactic event of the 10th annual Nazi party congress.

But he left unanswered the question the world had waited anxiously to hear him discuss—will Germany use force to achieve her ambitions for the Sudeten Germans?

Hitler made clear only that Germany was standing by to see that the Germanic minority obtained the "right of self-determination."

He ruled out the idea of a plebiscite because, he said, it "would only be conducted under brutal oppression."

The jammed congress hall cheered as Hitler attacked Czecho-Slovakia for "mistreating and oppressing" Sudeten Germans, whose demands for autonomy he supports.

He declared they were "being systematically ruined and doomed to slow extinction."

Hitler told his cheering followers that "we see democracy and Bolshevism arrayed in a solid front" against Nazi Germany.

The fuehrer, opening the speech for which the world was waiting, spoke at length of what he called "the sufferings" of Nazi adherents in Austria before the annexation.

The first portion of his pronouncement was devoted entirely to recalling the party's fight for supreme power in Germany.

Then he turned to his attack against the democracies and Bolshevism, asserting they were united against Nazilsm under "the slogan of 'liberty, equality, fraternity'."

"It is a bloody mockery of history," the fuehrer continued, "that the democracies are allied with the

(Continued on Page 6, Col. 1)

Sees Power Supply Adequate in East

NIAGARA FALLS, Sept. 12.—Ontario has provision for the power requirements of many years to come, Premier Mitchell Hepburn said on Saturday at the twenty-fifth anniversary dinner of the Ontario Paper company.

As far as the St. Lawrence waterways development was concerned, the premier said the cost of reconstructing all the piers and docks on the Great Lakes and their maintenance would be beyond the capacity of 10,000,000 people to pay. He foresaw future transportation development by trucks on superhighways, not by canals.

Youth Is Sought After Three Slain

DEER RIVER, Minn., Sept. 12.—Sheriff Elmer Adsen of Itasca county Monday had deputies beating through dense woods and patroling all roads in their search for a 16-year-old boy, missing since a farm couple and their adopted daughter were found slain.

Madsen said the youth, Harry Yern, had been reported seen near the blazing farm home at which the bodies of Mr. and Mrs. Matt Jama and Aila Jama, 23, were discovered Sunday. A light shotgun lay across the women's bodies, and two discharged rifle shells were found.

Chilean Cabinet Quits Over Putsch

SANTIAGO Chile, Sept. 12.—The Chilean cabinet resigned Monday as an aftermath of the unsuccessful Nazi putsch of Sept. 6.

Car Hits Tractor, Girl, 6, Is Killed

Mildred Calahoo, six, resident of the Calahoo district, 25 miles north west of Edmonton, received fatal injuries Saturday at 8:00 p.m., when an automobile in which she was riding collided with a tractor on a continuation of the Alberta ave. road, 11 miles west of the city.

R.C.M.P. said driver of the tractor was Douglas Vradvury, a farm worker employed by W. S. Walker, Winterburn district farmer. The automobile was being driven by the victim's father, Adolphus Calahoo, non-treaty Indian.

Vradvury was unhurt and none of the four other passengers in the automobile was injured, R.C.M.P. said.

Victim of a "freak" accident, Mildred Calahoo was thrown from her father's westbound car onto the eastbound tractor when a rear door in the automobile burst open under force of the impact. Her injuries were described as "internal."

It was believed brilliant rays of a setting sun may have obscured the automobile driver's vision. Hauling threshing equipment, the tractor was moving to Mr. Walker's farm, half a mile east of the accident scene.

Traveling in the automobile with the victim and her father were George Buck, Mrs. Morris of Calahoo and her two children. All reside near Calahoo. Mrs. Morris Calahoo is a daughter-in-law of Adolphus Calahoo. The six passengers were returning to their homes after visiting in the city.

Body of Mildred Calahoo was taken to Connelly and McKinley's funeral parlor. Burial will follow an inquest to be held at the funeral parlor Tuesday at 4:00 p.m.

Believe Mercury Seeks New Record

LONDON, Sept. 12.—Flying boat Mercury, which, it is reported, is being groomed for a hop to Cape Town, now is rumored as preparing to attack the world distance record held by Soviet Russia.

It is suggested the famous upper half of the pick-a-back aeroplane, which this summer flew to Montreal and New York, may be sent to Scotland for a take-off that would increase the airline distance record beyond the 6,306 miles Russian fliers covered when the established the record in a flight to the U.S. pacific coast.

De Valera Heads League Assembly

GENEVA, Sept. 12.—Eamon De Valera, prime minister of Eire, on Monday was elected president of the assembly of the League of Nations.

General Gloom

Briggs—You're looking blue, old boy. What's wrong?

Thompson—Oh, my wife has gone into hospital, my son lost his job yesterday, my daughter has mumps, cook has left us, and to crown it all Jenkins beat me five and four this afternoon.

Note Parallels 1914 Incidents

WASHINGTON, Sept. 12. — A striking parallel to the weeks preceding the Great War arises in the minds of informed observers here who watch the military movements in Europe.

Germany partly mobilizes for manoeuvres; then comes French and Czecho-Slovakia partial mobilization orders. As France pours men into the Maginot line along the German border, Germany sends men into her Siegfried line just opposite.

On the sea, Great Britain concentrates her fleet off North Scotland in a position to blockade Germany. France cancels leaves of naval men and places Marseilles under military law. Italy stands by ready for action.

Thus it was in 1914. The story of the military snowball is quickly told.

Austria mobilized against Serbia after the assassination June 28 of Archduke Franz Ferdinand, heir to the Austrian throne, and his wife, by a young Serb. After diplomatic exchanges and an ultimatum, Austria invaded Serbia.

Then, another parallel with the present occurred. Britain suggested as a compromise that Austria be content with the occupation of Belgrade until indemnification was paid for the assassination. The London Times, although disavowed by the British foreign office, has suggested that Germany be permitted to occupy the Sudeten portion of Czecho-Slovakia and be content with that.

On the ground that Austria also had mobilized troops in Galicia, facing Russia, Czar Nicholas issued pre-mobilization orders July 26 and later full mobilization decrees. Austria mobilized July 30.

Germany came into the military picture July 31 with an imperial order declaring "a state of threatening danger of war." She mobilized Aug. 1, following ultimata to Russia and France.

General mobilization had just been decreed in France. The five army corps which formed the frontier guard had taken their posts—the same sort of movement that has been effected recently on the Maginot line. On July 30, the French government ordered its troops to stay six miles back of the frontier to avoid incidents with German troops.

Belgium placed her army on a "reinforced peace footing" July 3 by calling out three classes of reservists. General mobilization followed the next day.

So diplomats gave way to generals and admirals when decisions had to be made. Germany's declarations of war against Russia and France came at 6:15 p.m., Aug. 3.

Soaring of Dollar Reflects Tension

LONDON, Sept. 12.—European tension was reflected in a further sharp rise in the dollar to $4.80½ Monday, supported by heavy continental buying.

Gold reached a new high since March, 1935, at 144 shillings 7½ pence ($34.76) an ounce, three pence dearer than Saturday.

Offerings of gold amounted to £1,298,000 ($6,238,577) at the time of price-fixing, when the dollar was $4.80⅜.

Some reports said continental investors were selling gold and investing in the dollar in fear gold might be taken by the government in emergency.

British government war loans were nearly one per cent lower at 100⅜ and European bonds were down small fractions. Transatlantics were around parity but there was scarcely enough business in other directions to test prices.

Two Japan Columns Advance on Hankow

SHANGHAI, Sept. 12.—Japanese troops continued Monday to concentrate their efforts on new overland drives toward the Peiping-Hankow railway, which would give them a direct approach to Hankow, provisional capital of China.

Two columns were moving westward about 125 miles apart, one aiming at Uschang, 40 miles south of the Lunghai railway junction, and the other at Siynang, 100 miles north of Hankow.

Free Food Sign Takes 55,000 to Political Meeting, Crowd Becomes Hungry, Raids, Wrecks Laden Tables

PITTSBURGH, Sept. 12.—Chanting "we want roast ox," several thousand hungry persons at a state Republican rally in a sururban park, Saturday, broke through police lines, invaded a dining hall, hurled several tons of food across the hall and trampled it underfoot.

Senator James J. Davis and Judge Arthur H. James, candidates for governor, and their party were surrounded in the hall while attempting to divert the crowd to a speaker's stand.

Tossed around in the melee, James shouted: "Ladies first," thrust his 23-year-old daughter, Dorothy, in front of him, and with Davis and others behind struggled 100 feet to the hall enarance.

Helpless park police, outnumbered and overpowered, estimated at least 55,000 persons were attracted by promises of free food. During the half-hour disorder they upset tables laden with 60,000 ears of corn, meat from four oxen, 50,000 buns, several bushels of tomatoes and gallons of olives.

Hitler

"These are days in which many people are disposed to take up new movements regardless of how unreasonable they may be or how contrary to the public interest. They flourish on attempts at suppression which are represented as persecution."
— Editorial about a pro-Nazi riot in Toronto, Aug. 18, 1933

The Journal's first mention of Hitler was in 1923 when it reported the attempted coup in Bavaria known as the Beer Hall Putsch. Hitler was one of the leaders and the paper covered his arrest and 14-month jail sentence.

He wasn't mentioned again in the paper until 1931 when, in a series of articles a year after Hitler's National Socialists won 109 seats in the Reichstag, University of Alberta professor Dr. John F. Coar analyzed the attraction Germans feel for extreme politics on Nov. 6. "Three thousand miles of Atlantic Ocean are no protection against the threat of political and social turmoil that hangs over Germany and Europe."

After the Nazis got 37.4 per cent of the vote in the 1932 German election, an Aug. 1 editorial stated: "As American writer Frank Simonds put it the other day 'Hitler heads not a political party with fixed principles but a mob united by an intricate mesh of passions and hatreds.' " The editorial called the Nazi showing a "most disturbing development."

On Aug. 8, 1933, international correspondent Karl Kitchen wrote in *The Journal* of the growing uneasiness in the Jewish community in Europe. He asked an unnamed Jewish banker if the Nazis worried him.

The response is chilling. "I have sent my sons out of Germany — one is in Paris, the other London. I do not want them to grow up in this unhealthy atmosphere."

The Journal had extensive coverage of the Night of the Long Knives, a June 30, 1934, army revolt, but a wry one-paragraph editorial July 3 showed an interesting perspective. "Were there not so much excitement, the European situation today would absorb the attention of Albertans."

The attempted coup occurred the same day Alberta Premier John Brownlee was found guilty of seducing Vivian MacMillan.

By 1935, there was little doubt even in Canada about the excesses of the Nazis. A.C. Cummings of the *The Journal*'s London Bureau wrote from Munich on Sept. 13, 1935, that Jews seen with "Aryan" women were taken into "preventative custody."

"Preventative custody," he wrote, "is a police term for a beating up in the local equivalent of the 'Brown House' – probably with rubber truncheons or steel whips."

On Sept. 1, 1939, a *Journal* extra edition headline screamed "War Engulfs Europe; Polish Cities Bombed."

Edmonton recruiting offices once again opened their doors.

Edmonton, part of a mission that drops propaganda leaflets over Germany.

***Sept. 10, 1939*:**
Canada officially joins the Second World War, declaring war on Germany with the near-unanimous approval of Parliament.

***Sept. 24, 1939*:**
Edmonton Transit System's first trolley buses go into service; each bus costs $17,000. Maximum speed is 30 m.p.h.

***Nov. 6, 1939*:**
Buffalo National Park at Wainwright in east-central Alberta is to be closed. The herd of buffalo will be killed or transferred to other parks, and the land turned over to Canada's military to use as a Second World War training site.

***Nov. 16, 1939*:**
Edmonton's first Zellers store opens in the downtown Tegler Building.

***Dec. 15, 1939*:**
About 1,000 troops of the Loyal Edmonton Regiment leave the city for overseas duty in Britain.

EXTRA **Edmonton Journal** EXTRA

THIRTY-SIXTH YEAR | EDMONTON, ALBERTA, FRIDAY, SEPTEMBER 1, 1939 | SINGLE COPY, 5 CENTS | 22 PAGES

WAR ENGULFS EUROPE; POLISH CITIES BOMBED

Hitler Accepts Danzig As Part of Germany; 'Reunion' Proclaimed

Lead Forces Against Poles

CHANCELLOR HITLER

HERMAN GOERING
Nazi Air Chief

JOSEPH GOEBBELS
Nazi Propaganda Minister

[illegible]IM VON [illegible]
Nazi Foreign Minister

Albert Forster, Nazi Leader Declared Head of Civic Government

LAW IS DECREED

Proclamation Suspends Constitution of Free City Immediately

NEW YORK, Sept. 1.—German Reichstag, after hearing an impassioned promise by Adolf Hitler to "meet bomb with bomb" and to be the "first soldier of the Reich," Friday unanimously confirmed the return of Danzig to Germany.

BERLIN, Sept. 1.—Hitler Friday "accepted" the Free City of Danzig into the Reich.

The fuehrer acted after Albert Forster, Nazi chief of state of the Free City and Nazi district leader there, had proclaimed the reunion of the Baltic city with Hitler's Germany, and begged the fuehrer to accept it.

Thanked for "Loyalty"

In a telegram to Forster, Hitler acknowledged the reception of Forster's proclamation and thanked him for "the loyalty of Danzig to Germans."

He proclaimed a newly-proclaimed law by Forster for the reunion of Danzig to Germany "immediately effective" and named Forster, already chosen by the Danzig senate as chief of state, to head the city government.

Article one of Forster's decree suspended the constitution of the free city immediatly.

(Under the city's League of Nations status its constitution was guaranteed by the league, and changes without its consent were declared illegal).

Article two of the decree placed all legal and administrative power exclusively in the hands of the chief of state, Forster.

Forster's telegram to Hitler read: "My fuehrer. I have just signed and then put into effect the following basic law, concerning the reunion of Danzig with the German Reich:

"The basic state law of the Free State of Danzig and the reunion of Danzig with the German Reich is effective Sept. 2, 1939."

"To lift the immediate distress of the people and state of the Free City of Danzig, I decree the following basic state law:

"Article one: The constitution of the Free City of Danzig has been suspended effective immediately.

"Article two: All legal and administrative power will be executed exclusively by the head of state (Forster)."

"Effective Immediately"

"Article three: The Free City of Danzig with its territory and its peoples forms a part of the German Reich, effective immediately.

"Article four: Until a final decision regarding the introduction of German Reich's laws by the fuehrer, the entire laws of the constitution remain in force as they apply at the moment.

"Signed at Danzig, Sept. 1, 1939, Albert Forster, Gauleiter (district leader)."

"I beg you, my fuehrer, in the name of Danzig and its population to consent to this basic state law and to carry out the reunion with the German Reich through federal law.

"Obediently, my fuehrer, Danzig pledges to you imperishable thankfulness and eternal loyalty. Hail my fuehrer.

"Signed, Albert Forster, Gauleiter."

Forster followed the act with a proclamation to Danzigers that "the hour for which you have longed for 20 years has come.

"Effective today, Danzig has returned to the great German Reich. Our fuehrer, Adolf Hitler, has freed us.

"The swastika flag, the flag of the German Reich, waves for the first time today on the public buildings in Danzig. It waves, however, also from former Polish buildings and everywhere in the harbor.

"Church bells peal forth and we thank the Lord for our liberation and also the fuehrer who has given us the opportunity to get rid of the evils of the Versailles treaty.

"Long live a free Danzig, now returned home, and long live our great fatherland.

"Wonderful Great Germany"

"We Danzigers are happy now also to be allowed to be citizens of the Reich. Danzig men and women, in this ceremonial hour, we want to stand together, clasp hands and give the fuehrer a holy promise to do everything within our power for our wonderful great Germany.

"Danzig is now returned home into the Reich. Long live our great fatherland. Long live our beloved fuehrer, Adolf Hitler."

Bombings Signal Europe's "Black Friday"

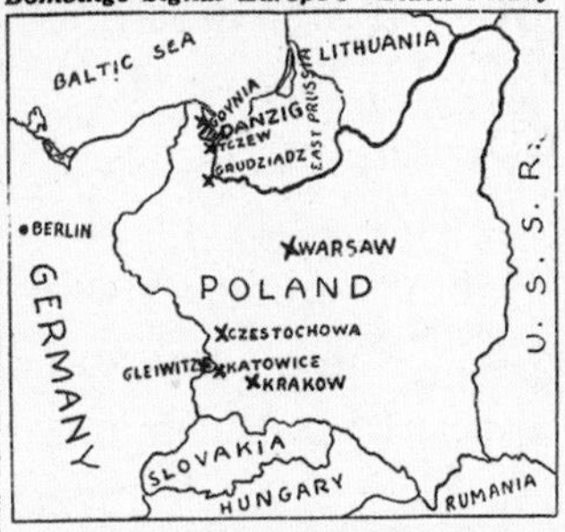
BALTIC SEA
LITHUANIA
DANZIG
GRUDZIADZ
EAST PRUSSIA
BERLIN
WARSAW
POLAND
GERMANY
U. S. S. R.
CZESTOCHOWA
GLEIWITZ
KATOWICE
KRAKOW
SLOVAKIA
HUNGARY
RUMANIA

This map shows graphically the crucial centres in the world's headlines Friday as Adolf Hitler's German troops and bombers launched a terrific attack on Poland, climaxing a protracted series of Nazi demands for the Free City of Danzig and the Polish corridor. Gleiwitz, in Germany near the Polish border, apparently is the base of Hitler's main army push. Fierce fighting was reported in and around Danzig itself, ancient commercial city which was placed under the protection of the League of Nations at the end of the Great War. German bombing attacks—the first since Hitler started building his mighty air force more than five years ago—were reported at Warsaw, capital of Poland, and at Tczew, Czestochowa, Grudziadz, Katowice, Krakow and other points. Grudziadz is at the bottom of the Polish corridor.

War Climaxes 12 Days Dramatic Developments, Realignment of Powers

Danzig's Nazi Chief Proclaimed Time Ripe Return to Reich

TENSION FOLLOWED

Latest Phase of Crisis Had Its Inception Aug. 20

Twelve days of lightning-like activities, including a dramatic realignment of central European powers and a tense exchange of diplomatic overtures, led up to Friday's open outbreak of Polish-German hostilities.

Between Sunday, Aug. 20, and Thursday, Aug. 31, the ominous events took swift shape and were followed Thursday night by an emergency meeting of the Reichstag, Hitler's command to the German forces ringing Poland to "meet force with force," and the reported German bombing of several Polish towns.

Here's how the war-clouds gathered in those last 12 days that shook the world:

Sunday, Aug. 20—Albert Forster, Nazi chief in Danzig, asserts hour is at hand for Free City's return to fatherland. Relations between Germany and Poland reaching crucial stage. German press in savage tirade demands Danzig and Polish Corridor, accuses Poles of anti-German "atrocities." Poles, preparing for the worst, move troops up to the 1,588-mile frontier with Germany. British cabinet leaders rushing back to London from vacations. In thunderbolt move, Reich and Soviet Union sign seven-year trade agreement providing for large-scale purchases by both countries of each other's goods:

Monday, Aug. 21—In further move shattering Anglo-French efforts to woo Russia, Soviet and Germany announce non-aggression treaty which presumably will keep Russia neutral in war. Traditional Hitler policy of hatred for Soviet is reversed. Peace from fear Germany

(Continued on Page 2, Col. 3)

Start Evacuation English Millions

LONDON, Aug. 31.—"Precautionary" evacuating of school children, mothers and invalids from London and other key cities Friday—a movement perhaps involving several million persons—was ordered Thursday by the ministry of health. The operation will require several days.

The government's announcement said:

"Evacuation, which will take several days to complete, is being undertaken as a precautionary measure in view of the prolongation of the period of tension. The government is fully assured that the attitude of quiet confidence which the public have been displaying will

(Continued on Page 8, Col. 1)

These Leaders Sought Peace

PREMIER CHAMBERLAIN

EDOUARD DALADIER
French Premier

IGNATIUS MOSCICKY
Poland's Premier

Call British House, France Mobilizes As Reich Planes, Troops Attack Poles

Hitler hurled his grey-clad hordes at Poland and German warplanes rained bombs on Polish cities early Friday and as Europe's "Black Friday" dawned, a general European war involving at least Germany, Poland, Britain and France appeared under way.

No word came immediately from Germany's axis partner, Italy, as His Majesty the King summoned a meeting of the British privy council and parliament was called into session Friday.

General mobilization was ordered in Paris after a meeting of the French cabinet and in London it was stated on highest authority that if developments mean, as it appears, that Germany has declared war on Poland, Britain and France will fulfill to the uttermost their obligations to the Polish government.

As German troops launched a full scale attack all along the Polish border and Nazi bombers raided Warsaw, Gydnia, Krakow, Katowice and other Polish cities, Hitler addressed an emergency meeting of the reichstag, making it clear that war was in progress but failing actually to declare war on Poland. There were no immediate reports as to early casualties.

In the midst of rapid-fire developments, Hitler announced that the Free City of Danzig, Poland's entrance to the sea, had been reincorporated into the reich.

In his reichstag speech Hitler said Germany did not count on Italian support, but added that Russia was now the reich's "friend."

LONDON, Sept. 1—(Passed by British Censor)—Text of an authoritative statement:

It is pointed out in official circles that if the proclamation to the German people by Herr Hitler which has already been announced should mean as it would seem to mean that Germany has declared war on Poland, it can be stated on the highest authority that Great Britain and France are inflexibly determined to fulfil to the uttermost their obligations to the Polish government.

The German account of the course of the negotiations is of course wholly misleading.

On Aug. 29 the German chancellor informed the British ambassador that he expected a Polish plenipotentiary to appear in Berlain by the following day with full powers to negotiate a settlement.

He added that in the meantime he hoped to elaborate the proposals. In other words the Polish government was expected to submit to the procedure imposed on the president of Czecho-Slovakia and to dispatch an emissary to Berlin who was to accept terms, the character of which was wholly unknown to the Polish government.

LONDON, Sept. 1.—His Majesty the King summoned the privy council to a meeting Friday and parliament was called to meet Friday afternoon as reports were received of a German offensive against Poland.

The cabinet met at 11:30 a.m. and the privy council was to meet at noon.

Parliament was called to meet at 5:00 p.m. (10:00 a.m., Edmonton time).

The Polish ambassador conferred with Prime Minister Chamberlain before the cabinet meeting.

PARIS, Sept. 1.—France today ordered general mobilization. Martial law was proclaimed in Paris.

The orders were issued after an emergency meeting of the French cabinet at the Elysee palace under President Albert Lebrun.

Parliament was called to meet Saturday.

Here is the dramatic story of developments in the European crisis as told in press dispatches pouring into the Journal during the night:

BERLIN, Sept. 1.—Fuehrer Hitler, in his order of the day to the army, Friday ordered the German military to meet force with force.

The order of the day to the army read:

"The Polish state has rejected my efforts to establish neighborly relations, and instead has appealed to weapons.

"Germans in Poland are victims of a bloody terror, driven from house to home.

"A series of border violations unbearable for a great power show that the Poles no longer are willing to respect the German border.

"To put an end to these insane incitations, nothing remains but for me to meet force with force from now on.

"The German army will conduct a fight for honor and the right to the life of the resurrected German people with firm determination. I expect that every soldier, mindful of the great traditions of the eternal German military, will do his duty to the last.

"Remember always that you are representatives of the National Socialist great Germany. Long live our people and our reich!"

GLEIWITZ, Germany, Sept. 1.—Gleiwitz residents reported artillery fire was heard "in the distance" at 5:30 a.m. Friday (9:30 p.m. Thursday Edmonton time). Gleiwitz is but a few miles from the Polish-Silesian border.

Between Buethen and Gleiwitz on the border an almost unbroken line of pack wagons, artillery, cavalry, motorized machine guns and military lorries and infantry was to be seen earlier Friday.

Military traffic between the two cities was the heaviest noted here in almost a week.

Thursday it was noticed that several officers were called away from their afternoon coffee by helmeted messengers coming on motorcycles from company headquarters. The hotel

(Continued on Page 2, Col. 1)

Command Armies of Allied Nations

Commanding the armies of Britain and France are Lord Gort, chief of the British imperial general staff (above left), and General Gamelin of the French army, shown above as they recently conferred in Paris. Under an agreement between the two nations, British land forces in Europe are placed under the control of General Gamelin while French naval forces are directed by the British admiralty.

Hitler Says Hostilities Launched by Germany To Back Up Demands

Will Die Fighting If Necessary, He Tells Reichstag

SUCCESSOR IS NAMED

BERLIN, Sept. 1.—Fuehrer Hitler told a momentous gathering of the reichstag Friday that Field Marshal Hermann Goering would be his successor if he should meet death in war.

Hitler spoke throughout as if war already were well under way, but he did not officially declare war and said he intended to be "the first soldier of the German reich."

"I am putting on the uniform and I shall take it off only in victory or death," he said.

The reichstag passed a law annexing Danzig.

Hitler said that "it is a lie that we do all by force."

Hitler, greeted by a great ovation by the reichstag that had been summoned at 3:00 a.m. for a special 10:00 a.m. meeting, plunged directly into the subject of Poland and Danzig by declaring:

"We meet to solve the problems raised by the Versailles treaty."

Contradicts Self

Denying the reich is not peaceably inclined—the fuehrer less than five hours before had announced his army was meeting "force with force" because of alleged border violations by the Poles—declared that we "tried to solve many problems peacefully."

"Fifteen years of peaceful effort to meet this issue were of no avail," he added.

"Danzig is German. The corridor (The Polish province of Pomorze) was and is German.

"More than 1,000,000 Germans who

(Continued on Page 2, Col. 4)

Order Blackout Nightly in Paris

PARIS, Aug. 31.—French government drove swiftly ahead Thursday with its preparations for war, if it must come, by decreeing that Paris henceforth must be blacked out.

The government moved 16,313 children out of Paris on Wednesday

(Continued on Page 9, Col. 1)

See Early Ending U.S. Neutrality

NEW YORK, Aug. 31.—The U. S. Neutrality act seems certain to receive a quick death-blow in event that war breaks out in Europe.

In talk of possible revision of the

(Continued on Page 9, Col. 2)

Turn to Pages 2, 3 Stories, Pictures

FIVE

CANADIAN
SOCIETY
Edmonton Red Cross Auxiliaries
NA-2903-54 Glenbow Archives

Edmontonians were quick to jump into the war effort. A Canadian Red Cross Society van in England, a gift of Edmonton Red Cross Auxiliaries, 1939.

Guns & Gushers

1940 to 1949

"Edmonton and its citizens will, it is to be hoped, keep their feet planted firmly on the ground, however rosy may be their dreams of a rich future floating on black gold."

— Editorial after the discovery of oil near Leduc, Feb. 14, 1947

Dieppe Disaster / 185

Battle for Ortona / 189

Batter Up! / 191

Death Camp Horror / 193

On Strike / 195

Meter Matters / 197

Promise of Prosperity / 199

The Bomb / 201

They wore silly hats and danced until 2 a.m. at the Macdonald Hotel on New Year's Eve in 1939.

Others gathered at the Masonic Temple on 100th Avenue near 103rd Street where *The Journal* reported that the tables, decorated in a motif of silver and blue, provided a colourful backdrop to the fun.

The RCMP held a dance in their barracks at 95th Street and Jasper Avenue, and the officers of the 19th Alberta Dragoons ate a midnight supper of roast turkey following their formal ball in the Connaught Armoury at 103rd Street and 85th Avenue.

"To some 1939 may have been a red banner year, while to others it may have been just another 365 days, but almost everyone, young and old, rich and poor, is planning to see it out in true carnival style," *The Journal* reported on Dec. 28, 1939.

"Though Canada is at war, social activities do not seem to have been curtailed to much extent."

There were private parties, too. At Hazlefield, their Glenora home, Mr. and Mrs. Robert Dingwall entertained a party of 40. *The Journal* reported

SAMPSON
How about you?
Buy
VICTORY BONDS

NA-3338-1 Glenbow Archives

that the Dingwall billiard room had been cleared for dancing, and holly and cedar boughs decorated the walls.

Mrs. Dingwall was "very smart," according the newspaper, in a mauve formal evening gown set off by an amethyst necklace. She danced the '30s away in a pair of silver slippers.

The provincial legislature was under militia guard since the start of the war, but it was more for show than real threat. It certainly didn't prevent 1,000 people from crowding the legislature building's ground floor for presentation to Lt.-Gov. J.C. Bowen at the New Year's Day levee in 1940. More than 600 citizens also drove through the snow to visit the Garneau-area home of Mayor John Fry where he and Mrs. Fry offered New Year's wishes. She wore a "charming model of apricot-lace, styled on formal lines. Her flowers were talisman roses, worn en corsage," reported the paper.

However, the war was never far from people's thoughts. It was page 1 news and would remain so, almost every single day, for the next half-decade, as reports from The Canadian Press and other news services brought the war to the doorsteps of *Journal* readers.

New Year's messages from Bowen, Fry and acting premier Ernest Manning on the front page Saturday, Dec. 30, 1939, all made reference to the events in Europe.

Bowen urged people to keep their spirits up and Manning called for prayers that peace be restored.

For his part, Fry pointed out that imperial unity had never been more important. There was a silver lining, he said.

"While dark clouds float all over the world, there is a bit of blue to be seen as far as Canada is concerned.

"The selection of Canada as the empire's training ground for her Royal Air Force is bound to have favourable economic effects on Canadian industry, and in this expansion of business along innumerable lines, Edmonton and district will benefit."

Fry was right. Even as Edmontonians grieved the loss of loved ones in battle, the war meant that the airport at Blatchford Field was the busiest in Canada, with a one-day record 860 in-and-out flights. A new airport, with the longest runway in North America, was constructed at Namao in 1943, and thousands of American and Canadian troops crowded the city, as it became the jumping-off point for the defence of the northwest.

The city over which Mayor Fry presided in 1940 had a population of just a little over 90,000. By the end of the decade almost 150,000 people called Edmonton home. Many were drawn here by the boom that followed the discovery of oil near Leduc in 1947.

No one, of course, knew exactly what the discovery meant, although the newspaper bragged that the oil gushing from Leduc No. 1 was "so clean you could put it in your transmission."

In an editorial following the oil strike, the newspaper was cautious. "Edmonton and its citizens will, it is to be hoped, keep their feet planted firmly on the ground, however rosy may be their dreams of a rich future floating in black gold."

But before the discovery of oil could put a strut in the air and a bounce in the civic step, there was a war to be won.

***In 1940*:**
Edmontonians could buy a beaver lamb coat for $45 from Eaton's. It wasn't beaver, but rather lamb dyed to look like beaver. Silk stockings sold on special for 54 cents a pair and sheer hose, on sale, cost 59 cents a pair.

***Jan. 25, 1940*:**
Members of the University of Alberta graduating class this spring will wear mortar board hats for the first time in the history of the university.

***March 13,1940*:**
The first singing telegram delivered in Edmonton is sung by CN telegraph messengers.

***June 5, 1940*:**
More than 6,000 Edmontonians watch the Edmonton Grads basketball team play its final game. "You won't see their like again," wrote *Journal* sports editor George Mackintosh.

***June 13, 1940*:**
The new General Hospital on Jasper Avenue between 111th and 112th Streets opens with 100 beds. It cost $300,000.

***July 4, 1940*:**
Edmonton's civic census shows a population of 91,723.

Air Raid Precautions Supplement

Edmonton Journal

Full Directions in Case of Attack

THIRTY-NINTH YEAR — EDMONTON, ALBERTA, THURSDAY, JUNE 18, 1942 — 12 PAGES

Three sightless tots in a British home for the blind huddle in a shelter during a Nazi air attack.

As the new decade began, *The Journal* surveyed its readers, asking for predictions on what the '40s might bring.

"We should experience good times in the 1940s, as the Liberal government in Ottawa will be returned to office and the Social Credit government in Alberta will be defeated at the next general election," predicted lawyer Gerald O'Connor, a Liberal MLA for the city.

He was half-right.

The Liberals held office throughout the war and beyond, although the Social Credit party remained in power for three more decades.

For his forecast, Const. William Lamb, the turnkey in the lock-up at the city police station, took a more international view. "Adolf Hitler, the rodent of the Rhine, will be dead by September," he said.

And Jack Clark, a messenger boy for the Canadian Pacific Railway, wasn't interested in world affairs or politics.

"The New York Yankees will lose the world championship in 1940. They can't keep winning all the time."

Of all the predictions, Jack's was the most accurate.

The Tigers won the pennant in 1940, although the Yankees won again in 1941, 1942 and 1943.

But no soothsayer, no matter how prescient, could have foretold the desperate days to come in the approaching spring, and the long, hard battles in North Africa the following year.

No one foresaw the Japanese sneak attack on Pearl Harbor in Hawaii that drew America into the war in 1941 nor could they predict the 1944 D-Day landings in Normandy. Still ahead was the dreary, deadly fighting in Sicily and Italy where the Loyal Edmonton Regiment – christened the Red Patch Devils by the Germans – fought with valour in places such as Ortona, Regalbuto and the Liri Valley.

Certainly no one contemplated the lengthy casualty lists that would take up column after column of space in *The Journal.* Those lists carried the names of sons and fathers, husbands and lovers, nephews and cousins. On those lists would be neighbourhood teenagers who only a few months previously had borrowed dad's car to take their favourite girl to the movies at the Rialto downtown, or delivered *The Journal* to the front door.

Neither could anyone have envisaged the horrors uncovered in the German concentration camps and their six million dead. Far ahead, too, was the incomprehensible power that was unleashed when an atomic bomb was dropped, first on the Japanese city of Hiroshima on Aug. 6, 1945, and then three days later when another destroyed Nagasaki.

No one imagined that it would take until the spring and summer of 1945 before *The Journal's* compositors at last dusted off their largest possible type font to compose the three headlines that meant the war had finally ended.

On May 1, the headline was HITLER DEAD, followed a week later by GERMANY QUITS. Finally on Wednesday, Aug. 15, 1945, readers had the simple, concise headline for which they had longed: WAR ENDS.

Neither was anyone clairvoyant when it came to the troubled peace that saw former allies, both now armed with atomic weapons, facing off against each other over a troubled world. The Soviets had been allies, but

***July 6, 1940*:**
The Varscona movie theatre opens on Edmonton's south side.

***Nov. 13,* 1940:**
Edmonton Mayor John Fry is elected to the fourth of eight consecutive one-year terms.

***In 1941*:**
A *Journal* collections agent makes $15 a week.

June 3, 1941:
Edmonton elects first Liberal woman to serve in the Canadian parliament. Cora T. Casselman beats Socred Orvis Kennedy in an Edmonton East byelection.

***Sept. 10, 1941*:**
Alberta schools are ordered to remain closed until later in the fall due to the epidemics of polio (infantile paralysis) and encephalitis (sleeping sickness).

***Oct. 1, 1941*:**
***The Journal* appoints W.A. MacDonald managing director. He becomes publisher on Jan. 1, 1942.**

***Oct. 10, 1941*:**
Edmonton Public Library introduces mobile library service — in a streetcar.

***Dec. 7, 1941*:**
Canada becomes the first western nation to declare war on Japan

Weather Forecast
Snowflurries

Edmonton Journal

'One of Canada's
Great Newspapers'

FORTY-SECOND YEAR ** EDMONTON, ALBERTA, MONDAY, NOVEMBER 17, 1941 SINGLE COPY 5 CENTS 18 PAGES

Fiendish Slayer Stabs Girl, 15, To Death

J.L. Lewis Defies F.D.R., Orders Work Stopped In Captive Coal Mines

From The Times—

The War Today

Canucks at Hong Kong
Russian Front is Stable
Nazis Grow Desperate

(Copyright by The Southam Co.)

LONDON, Nov. 17.—Describing the arrival at Hong Kong of "substantial reinforcements of Canadians," the Times' correspondent said the population was astonished by the early morning entry of large ships adequately escorted while planes roared overhead and motorboats fussed protectively. A large crowd, mostly Chinese, quickly gathered and thousands lined the route six deep from the wharf to the camp as the newcomers marched off, headed by a band. It is understood the majority of the Canadians already have seen service elsewhere. Welcoming them, Maj.-Gen. Maltby, general officer commanding at Hong Kong, said the arrival was an historic occasion as this was the first time dominion troops have served in Hong Kong.

The Far East situation hasn't deteriorated in the past week but the present crisis is certain to come to a head before the end of the month, well-informed observers in Singapore believe, according to the Times' correspondent there. Not much military importance is attached to reports the Japanese are

(Continued on Page 5, Col. 6)

Union Head Refuses Bid Of President to Call At White House

UNION SHOP ISSUE

Believe Roosevelt May Order Army to Take Over Coal Mines

WASHINGTON, Nov. 17.—In open defiance of President Roosevelt's injunction that "the coal must be mined," United Mine Workers union members, on orders of their president, John L. Lewis, Monday halted nearly all production in the captive coal mines that supply the big steel companies engaged on defence contracts.

In a letter to the president, Lewis asserted the U.M.W. refused to accept an open shop agreement in the captive mines because it would "invalidate" other agreements in operation throughout the soft coal industry.

Meanwhile Speaker Sam Rayburn said flatly the house of representatives would be given an opportunity to pass on defence strike legislation "at the earliest date consistent with proper consideration." Members have demanded legislation to outlaw strikes in defence industries.

The union shop was the sole issue in the dispute which culminated in a work stoppage Monday.

Lewis did not call at the White House, as he had been requested to do when Mr. Roosevelt asked last Friday that negotiations be extended over the week-end in an 11th-hour attempt to halt the threatened shutdown.

At the time the letter to the presi-

(Continued on Page 2, Col. 4)

Where City Girl Brutally Slain as Vicious Killer Plunged Knife Into Body Ten Times

SECOND BLOOD STAINED GLOVE FOUND NEAR GRANDIN SCHOOL
5
FIRST LEATHER GLOVE FOUND IN GARBAGE CAN
4
SPOT AT WHICH FLEEING MURDERER THREW BLOOD STAINED HUNTING KNIFE
3
DARKENED KITCHEN WINDOW FROM WHICH A. J. LAJOIE WITNESSED COUPLE STRUGGLING AND AT FIRST BELIEVED THEM TO BE INTOXICATED
WHERE TAXI DRIVER FOUND GIRL, FACE DOWN, BLEEDING FREELY FROM SEVERAL KNIFE WOUNDS —AS SHE WAS TURNED SHE MUTTERED "MAN-MAN"
MAN RAN 12 YDS. TO LANE CORNER THEN NORTH UP LANE
2
6
110 ST
98th AVE
1
WHERE BRUTAL MURDERER CAUGHT UP TO GIRL FROM BEHIND AND WHILST ATTACKING HER BOTH FELL TO SIDEWALK
GIRL STAGGERED 100 FT. TO TREE
7
CAR CONTAINING JOS. NADEAU & WIFE STOPS, TAKES GIRL TO MISERICORDIA HOSPITAL ½ BLOCK ← NORTH WEST
8
TAXI IN WHICH CONTI AND FAMILY WERE RETURNING FROM PICTURE SHOW, STOPS UPON SEEING GIRL LYING AT CURB. CONTI SAID SHE LOOKED LIKE THE VICTIM OF A HIT AND RUN DRIVER.

Dorothy Hammond Dies With 10 Knife Wounds; Dragnet Out for Man

Victim's Hands Badly Cut as She Tried to Avoid Ghastly Death—Slaying Was Work of Maniac, Says Chief Constable Shute

LETHAL KNIFE, KILLER'S GLOVES FOUND; CITY EXITS ARE GUARDED BY R.C.M.P.

Her chest and throat pierced deeply 10 times by a hunting knife with a four-inch blade, Dorothy Hammond, 15, blonde, grade seven schoolgirl, choir singer and speed skater, died in hospital Saturday at 10:00 p.m., 61 minutes after she had been set upon by a fiendish slayer.

Her mother was with her as the child murmured "Mama" and died. (On Sunday, relatives gave the girl's age as 14. On Monday, the father said she was 15.)

Chief Constable Shute, after a week-end of fruitless search by his men, described the slayer as a maniac. The knife blows were struck with such savage ferocity that the knife sank nearly to the hilt every time. Two of the wounds, close to the heart, were thought to have caused death. The girl's hands were cut badly as she tried to keep the knife away from her.

Dorothy, youngest of three children in the family of Mr. and Mrs. R. M. Hammond, 9725 111 st., was returning from a theatre and was within a block of her home when the murderer caught up to her at 98 ave., between 110 and 111 sts., stabbed her and fled. He dropped the blood-stained knife and a pair of gloves as he ran up a nearby lane.

Struggle Witnessed From Window

The fatal struggle was witnessed from a window in his home by A. J. Lajoie, 9802 110 st., who thought it was a row between "two intoxicated persons." He saw the girl struggle to her feet after the fatal wounds were suffered, stagger a short distance, clutch a tree, and then sag to the ground.

The police dragnet at the week-end was out for a man described as "five feet, six or seven inches; young and slight." He was believed to be dressed in dark clothing and was wearing no hat.

At 2:00 p.m. Monday, with no apparent progress in the hunt, Chief Constable Shute issued this statement:

> **"I think this is the most atrocious crime ever committed in the city. It is imperative that this man be apprehended, and we hope for the best co-operation from the citizens."**

R.C.M.P. were co-operating with city police in the hunt for the brutal murderer and were checking all city exits as a search went on within the city itself. Directing the search with the chief were Detective Inspector John Leslie, city police, and Detective Sgt. F. A. Broadribb, R.C.M.P.

Mr. Hammond, father of the slain child, was in Grande Prairie Saturday. He came back to Edmonton by Yukon Southern Air Transport airplane on Sunday in response to a message that his daughter had been injured seriously. He did not know until he arrived that she had been slain.

Knife Used by Murderer Found

The gloves and the knife used by the murderer were found by police in an inch-by-inch examination of the area around the scene of the slaying. The gloves, badly worn, are of doeskin. The blood-stained knife was found lying beside a fence on the east side of the lane, between 110 and 111 sts., north of 98 ave., about 65 yards from the avenue. One glove was discovered in a garbage can 10 yards further. The second glove was lying close to the back of a school further north in the lane.

Mr. Lajoie told police he saw a girl walking west on 98 ave. He saw a man catch up to her, struggle with her, and they both fell to the ground. He heard a scream. The man got up and ran away. The girl pulled herself to her feet, staggered about 100 feet, clutched a tree, then fell forward to the ground. This was about 9:00 p.m.

Mr. Lajoie recently was invalided home from Britain where he was serving with an Alberta regiment.

"I thought it was either a family quarrel or two intoxicated persons," Mr. Lajoie said. He was sitting at the window having a smoke, clad only in his trousers and stockings. "I turned to a friend and said, 'I think there are a couple of intoxicated persons outside'."

A few seconds later, a taxi driven by Peter Cron, of Jack Hays Ltd., and occupied by Mr. and Mrs. Micky Conti, of 11114 99 ave., and their two children came east on 98 ave.

Almost simultaneously, the driver and Mr. Conti saw the girl lying on the north side of the avenue, a few yards west of the lane. The driver stopped the car and he and Mr. Conti jumped out.

"I could see her lying across the curb, partly in the gutter, with her head resting on her arm. She seemed to be half kneeling. She was moaning," Mr. Cron related. "I walked over and turned her over on her back. She was bleeding from the mouth, nose, chest and hands.

"I thought she had been struck by a car or was suffering a hemorrhage. Mr. Conti stayed with the girl and I went and telephoned police," he said.

Mr. Cron said he usually drives Mr. Conti home by a different route. "I don't know what in the world made me go this different way on Saturday night," he said. He was sorry he wasn't there "10 minutes earlier. There would have been a hell of a fight with that devil."

Cron went to the home of D. A. Petrie, 9747 111 st., and telephoned Sgt. George Edwards at the police station that he had found a girl, apparently struck by a hit-and-run driver, lying beside the roadway.

Sgt. Edwards immediately dispatched Constables Art Hamelin and Harry Nelson. On their arrival, they telephoned back to police headquarters that the girl had been stabbed.

Donald Mortimer, 17, University of Alberta student living in the Petrie home, was reading in the den. The Petrie home is on the southeast intersection of 98 ave. and 111 st. The den is next to the avenue.

Mortimer said he heard a scream but thought it was "children playing in the street." When Cron telephoned for police from the Petrie home, Mortimer told Cron of the scream, then the student dashed over to where the girl was lying. A few

(Continued on Page 3, Col. 1)

Restiveness Among British Embarrassing to Cabinet

Plan New Alberta Recruiting Tour

CALGARY, Nov. 17.—Another province-wide recruiting tour will be undertaken by 12 recruiting missions, commencing Dec. 1, Maj. J. H. Gainor, M.C. district recruiting officer, announced Monday.

Practically every town to Peace River in the north and the border towns to the south will be visited. One of the purposes is to contact men who were engaged in harvesting operations during the last drive and to recontact men who had expressed a willingness to join up when approached during the last drive and who have not yet reported for duty.

Icebreaker Sails Over World's Roof

SEATTLE, Nov. 17.—Blunt-nosed and bow-sided, the big Soviet icebreaker Krassin lay at a Seattle pier Monday, behind her a 10,000-mile trip through ice-bound seas north of Siberia.

The vessel came here for overhaul and for repairs to her pilot house, smashed in a Bering sea storm; but in so doing she also demonstrated that the fantastic roof of the world ocean route actually is available for movement of U.S. supplies to Russian armies fighting Germany on the shores of the White sea.

Her master, Capt. N. Markov, indicated the Krassin, when overhaul is completed, would return to Vladivostok to keep open a narrow lane through the ice from the Pacific to the beleaguered ports of Murmansk and Archangel. This route, he said, could be used in the spring and summer although now the the ice re-freezes so fast that any ship less sturdy than the Krassin would be crushed by the floes.

Where To Find It

Amusements, Theatres	11
Bridge	7
Casualty List	18
Comics	6, 15, 16, 17
Crossword Puzzle	17
District	7
Editorial	4
Financial	16
Off the Record	11
Radio	11
Serial Story	17
Sport	6, 7
They'll Do It Every Time	10
Uncle Ray's Corner	17
Want Ads.	15, 16
Women's	12, 13

The Weather

Edmonton Weather

Sunday		Monday	
2:30 p.m.	35	1:30 a.m.	31
3:30 p.m.	32	2:30 a.m.	31
4:30 p.m.	32	3:30 a.m.	31
5:30 p.m.	31	4:30 a.m.	31
6:30 p.m.	31	5:30 a.m.	30
7:30 p.m.	32	6:30 a.m.	30
8:30 p.m.	31	7:30 a.m.	27
9:30 p.m.	31	8:30 a.m.	28
10:30 p.m.	31	9:30 a.m.	30
11:30 p.m.	31	10:30 a.m.	30
Monday		11:30 a.m.	31
12:30 a.m.	31	12:30 p.m.	33
		1:30 p.m.	35

Maximum temperature Nov. 16, 35.
Minimum temperature Nov. 16, 31.
Barometer reading at 1:30 p.m., 27:56, steady.

(Continued on Page 2, Col 3)

Writer Says Pent-Up Energy Represents Tremendous Force

HATRED OF GERMANS

In this article, a continuation of his series on Britain, Ralph Ingersoll, publisher of the New York newspaper PM, describes how he found the British people in their attitude to the war. In a trip around the world, Mr. Ingersoll recently visited all fronts in the world war against Fascism.

By Ralph Ingersoll

NEW YORK, Nov. 17.—No one in the aid-to-Russia movement in England knows quite what he is talking about. That is, no one has a clearly defined and publicly expressed plan of how to aid Russia — where, with what, when. It is not as well worked out as was last year's aid-to-Britain movement in America. Americans had the lend-lease bill to campaign for, convoys to urge and everyone would pull together for the 50 destroyers. The problem of how to get help to Russia is infinitely more complicated.

Ralph Ingersoll

To begin with there are only three ways into Russia.

One requires Arctic convoys to an Arctic port. There is not even agreement among authorities as to whether this port can be kept ice-free. Until it is known whether Hitler can and will drive an army between Moscow and Leningrad, no one can tell whether supplies from Archangel can be gotten to where the Russian armies are fighting.

The second way into Russia is even more difficult. It is the long and very arduous mountain-desert route through Iran and the Caspian sea. There is no through railway.

(Continued on Page 11, Col. 1)

Nippon Envoy Talks With Roosevelt About Explosive Far East Situation

WASHINGTON, Nov. 17. — A formal conference brought President Roosevelt and Japan's special envoy, Saburo Kurusu, together for more than an hour Monday to talk of "many things" centring around the explosive Far Eastern situation.

But there was no indication immediately whether any satisfactory progress had been made toward achieving a better understanding on Pacific problems between the U.S. and Japan or whether any decisions were approached which might lead to assurance of continued peace in the Pacific.

Kurusu was accompanied to the White House by Japanese Ambassador Nomura, and Secretary of State Hull, with whom the Japanese had conferred earlier.

Both Kurusu and Nomura showed reluctance to discuss with newspapermen any aspect of the situation. Kurusu parried a question as to whether Japan would be willing to make some concession in the direction of withdrawal of her troops from China by gesturing toward Nomura with the smiling remark:

"Here is the Japanese ambassador. Ask him. I am only the ambassador's assistant."

Nomura indicated he and Kurusu

(Continued on Page 2, Col. 4)

Canuck Troops In Hong Kong

King Says Move as Defence Against Aggression Part of Policy

FAR EAST CRISIS

HONG KONG, Nov. 17.—Unexpected arrival of a large contingent of Canadian infantry troops to reinforce this strategic naval fortress was greeted jubilantly Sunday, especially among the Chinese population, as news of the landing spread through the city.

Disembarked, the contingent formed on a nearby field and, led by two military bands, including bagpipers, marched with full war equipment and fixed bayonets to specially outfitted barracks, while hundreds of Chinese and Europeans gathered to watch.

The Hong Kong colony's population of nearly 2,000,000 was taken completely by surprise as the Canadians' transport, a former liner, steamed into the harbor, strongly convoyed.

The reinforcements, who include some U.S. volunteers, reached here within a week of Prime Minister Churchill's announcement Britain would declare war on Japan immediately in event of hostilities between Japan and the U.S., and their landing coincided with arrival in Washington of a special Japanese envoy, Saburo Kurusu, for conference to avert a Pacific clash.

(Prime Minister King, announcing in Ottawa Saturday night the arrival of the Canadians at Hong Kong said "defence against aggression, actual or threatened, in any

(Continued on Page 3, Col. 5)

Charges U.S. Navy "Wars" in Pacific

WASHINGTON, Nov. 17.—Senator Burton Wheeler (Dem., Montana) said Monday he had "definite information that the United States navy is engaged in aggressive warfare in the Pacific as well as the Atlantic."

In support of his contention, he made public a letter which he said was sent from a seaman on the U.S. cruiser St. Louis to his mother in Tennessee. The letter, dated at Honolulu Oct. 25, said the cruiser's mission had been to take a convoy of oil tankers to Vladivostok, Russia's Siberian port.

The communication added that the vessel then was ordered "to look for a German raider operating in the South Pacific."

It continued: "We left immediately for Singapore . . . where we were joined by two British destroyers . . . From there on the cruise was a nightmare. We sailed around and reached every rock sticking out of the Pacific from Bombay to Byrdstown . . . We stopped several ships but didn't find the raider."

This drawing shows the scene between 110 and 111 sts. on 98 ave. where Dorothy Hammond, 15, was viciously slain Saturday night as she walked home from a movie. Inset is a picture of the girl. Police Monday still were hunting for the slayer. The drawing is self-explanatory. Below is A. J. Lajoie, 9802 110 st., who witnessed the fatal struggle but believed it was a row between "two intoxicated persons." The lower picture is the knife used in the murder, along with one of the two gloves found near the scene. Chief Constable Shute said Monday the slaying "was the work of a maniac," and declared it was one of the "most brutal slayings I ever have heard of in Canada." The girl's hands were badly cut, apparently in an effort to hold the knife away from her body.

American Warship Captures Nazi Ship Flying U.S. Flag

Vessel Said Loaded With Rubber, Metals From Japan

REACHES SAN JUAN

SAN JUAN, Puerto Rico, Nov. 17.—The German motorship Odenwald, seized in the South Atlantic by the United States navy, arrived here Monday under American escort.

She was traveling under her own power.

It was understood prompt action would be brought in United States court to forfeit the ship, a 5,098-tonner listed as owned by the Hamburg-American Line, for disguising herself as a United States merchantman.

She was en route to Germany from Japan when she was seized. Much of her cargo was understood

(Continued on Page 2, Col. 3)

Litvinov's Plane Safe at Teheran

TEHERAN, Iran, Nov. 17.—A plane bearing Maxim Litvinov, Soviet ambassador to the United States, and U.S. Ambassador Laurence Steinhardt landed here safely at noon Monday, five days after departing from Kuibyshev, Russia, in a snowstorm.

The plane also carried Sir Walter Monckton, British information service officer, and two United States journalists, Quentin Reynolds and Alice Moats.

Aid From Canada Goes to Russia

OTTAWA, Nov. 17.—Canadian aid to Russia has gone forward to the extent of $1,035,000 during October, it was shown Monday in a trade report from the dominion bureau of statistics.

Berlin Claims Kerch Capture

Russians Report Enemy Thrown Back at Kalinin, Tikhvin

TELL OF MUCH SNOW

MOSCOW, Nov. 18. (Tuesday)—Soviet counter-attacks on the outskirts of Tula, Russian munitions centre, 110 miles south of Moscow, have put German units "into a panic-stricken rout," the Moscow radio announced Tuesday.

(Soviet troops have dislodged the Germans from positions before Leningrad which they had held for two months, said a Reuter's dispatch to London Monday night which gave Tass news agency as its authority.)

(By Canadian Press)

Germany claimed Monday her forces, with Rumanians, had captured Kerch, the eastern Crimean stepping stone to the oil-rich Caucasus.

Seizure of Kerch, after a long and bitter contest, if true left the Germans separated from the side entrance into the mineral-rich Caucasus only by a narrow strait and more than ever the area loomed as the next theatre of major action.

The Russians reported counter-attacks forced back Nazi troops in the zones of Kalinin and Tikhvin.

With soldiers floundering through snow and icy winds, Kuibyshev reports said a determined Russian counter-attack, in what was called the most important battle of the war, threw back a German drive into Tikhvin, a junction on the railway linking Leningrad, Archangel and Moscow and a possible route of British and American war supplies.

Reuter's correspondent declared 4,000 Germans were killed in vain attacks on the Russian positions in a general offensive in Karelia, launched two weeks ago.

Tanks from Britain and planes

(Continued on Page 2, Col. 5)

All-Out Effort In War Demanded

(Special to The Journal)

RED DEER, Nov. 17.—Annual meeting of the Alberta board of trade and agriculture opened here Monday, President J. B. Holden of Vegreville in the chair. The chairman gave his presidential address to about 60 delegates representing chambers of commerce and boards of trade from many parts of the province, including Edmonton, Lethbridge, Calgary, Red Deer, Lacombe, Bentley, Rocky Mountain House, Castor, Vegreville, and other points.

"One year ago we were assembled here from all parts of the province

(Continued on Page 16, Col. 2)

Sees Unlikelihood Girl Knew Attacker

It is possible 15-year-old Dorothy Hammond did not recognize the killer who stabbed her to death with 10 blows of a hunting knife on an Edmonton street Saturday night, according to Dr. A. Ralph Schrag, psychiatrist in charge of the "guidance clinic" of the Alberta health department's mental hygiene division.

Questioned by THE JOURNAL Monday and asked for an opinion, the behavior expert said the fact that the dying girl muttered only "A man, a man," when rescuers first reached her, though later she was able to state plainly her own name, might indicate she did not know who dealt her the fatal wounds.

But Dr. Schrag warned it is almost impossible to build up a sound psy-

(Continued on Page 3, Col. 7)

More Patrolling, Better Lighting Asked by Women After Girl Slain

Roused by the tragedy which struck an Edmonton home Saturday night when 15-year-old Dorothy Hammond was stabbed to death by an unknown assailant, city women are protesting against what they say is inadequate lighting and inadequate police patrol of lonely parts of Edmonton.

Principal of Grandin school, Sister Augustin, said Monday it would be "a very, very wise move to provide better lighting facilities around our school. It is so dark about this place, and we have had to call the police a number of times in the past two years on account of little vagrancies and incidents we could not cope with ourselves. It would be such a help to have proper police protection and lighting.

"Dorothy was an exceptionally fine girl. She was a most desirable pupil in every way, showing a keen interest in sports in which she was quite successful. She was popular among the pupils. Her grading at school does not give a clear picture of her intelligence for though she was only in grade seven it must be remembered that she did not start

(Continued on Page 2, Col. 5)

were now enemies. There were Reds everywhere, at least potentially, and the paper warned its readers to be on guard.

It wasn't long, however, following those predictions and all those New Year's Eve parties that rang in 1940, that the war was brought home.

The new decade was only two days old when a full page of pictures in *The Journal* underlined just how close, and how personal, it had all become.

The photographs on the page had been taken two weeks previously, and showed 800 members of the Loyal Edmonton Regiment marching to the Canadian National Railway Station in Toronto at the present site of the CN Tower to board eastbound trains destined for Halifax. It was there that the Loyal Eddies would board a ship that would carry them to England.

Military censors, worried about reports of troop movements falling into enemy hands, had demanded that news of the start of the regiment's trans-Atlantic journey be withheld until it was well under way. Although upwards of 10,000 people had watched the troops in full battle dress parade to the train station, *The Journal* didn't run the story for two weeks.

Nevertheless, when it was finally published, *Journal* subscribers read a story that was written with both sensitivity and pride. "As each of the long trains began to pull away from the station, a great cheer went up from the crowd," an unnamed reporter observed.

"At the same time, some of the wives, daughters or sweethearts – and even some of the men relatives of the departing soldiers – had eyes glistening with tears or shoulders shaking with sobs."

The regiment arrived in England in time to face the darkest days of the war. The only thing that saved that nation was an under-gunned Royal Air Force which beat back Germany's Luftwaffe in the Battle of Britain.

That and, of course, British Prime Minister Winston Churchill's stirring, unforgettable speeches, said to be worth a half-dozen regiments on their own. *Journal* readers thrilled to the memorable phrases broadcast by BBC Radio that were invariably front-page news.

"I have nothing to offer but blood, toil, tears and sweat," he told a hushed British House of Commons on May 13, 1940. "Our policy is to wage war by sea, land and air with all our might and with the strength that God can give us and to wage war against a monstrous tyranny never surpassed in the dark and lamentable catalogue of human crime."

Things looked bad then, but five weeks later they were even worse.

The British Expeditionary Force on the continent huddled on the beaches of Dunkirk as a flotilla of boats of all descriptions – pleasure craft, fishing trawlers, tugboats – ferried as many troops as it could back to England and safety. More than 40,000 men were left behind.

France would fall in days; the Germans had already overrun Holland; and Belgium had also capitulated.

Under a headline on June 4, 1940, that read "335,000 Troops taken from Dunkerque Region, Churchill Tells House," *The Journal* quoted the redoubtable British prime minister speaking some of the most famous and memorable phrases of the war: "We shall defend our island. We shall fight on the beaches, we shall fight on the landing grounds, we shall fight in the fields and streets and in the hills.

"We shall never surrender and even if, which I do not for a moment

following the Japanese attack on America's Pacific fleet ships and military bases at Pearl Harbor in Hawaii.

***In 1941*:**
Community Chest of Greater Edmonton (now the United Way of the Alberta Capital Region) is formed. It's a federation of 28 social service agencies that band together to establish a single fundraising campaign dedicated to "taking care of our own." Harvey Harrison chairs the first campaign, which raises $102,905.

***In 1942*:**
A *Journal* ad salesman makes $16.50 a week, while a stenographer earns $14 a week.

***March 7, 1942*:**
The first train of American army troops passes through Edmonton heading north to begin construction of the Alaska Highway.

***Nov. 12, 1942*:**
Voter turnout in Edmonton's municipal election is only 15 per cent and city council remains the same.

***Nov. 15, 1942*:**
The biggest snowfall in Edmonton history begins, dumping nearly 50 centimetres of heavy snow on the city by the next

Edmonton Weather
24-hour forecast: Fair Sunday morning, scattered showers during afternoon, continuing cool.

Edmonton Journal

'One of Canada's Great newspapers'

FORTY-SECOND YEAR ** EDMONTON, ALBERTA, SATURDAY, JULY 28, 1945 SATURDAY, 10 CENTS

Plane Crashes Into N.Y. Skyscraper

Report Jap Battleship Sunk in Bombing Raid

GUAM.—A Japanese battleship was reported sunk Saturday as nearly 1,500 British and American carrier planes battled through heavy flak and fighter screens and dealt the third heavy blow of the week to the broken and bleeding enemy fleet in the Inland sea.

Pilots reported that the 29,990-ton battleship Hyuga, a converted warship with a flight deck for catapulting planes, had been sunk at the great Japanese naval base of Kure, where the remnants of the Mikado's fleet took futile refuge under extensive camouflage.

In order to bore into their targets along the Inland sea, the swarms of Allied carrier planes knocked down scores of Japanese planes which came out of hiding and tried to ward off the pre-invasion blows.

The Hyuga had been reported damaged in strikes earlier this week. An Associated Press dispatch from the fleet did not make clear whether it had been sunk Saturday or in the previous raids.

Three of the first four naval planes which roared in through a heavy curtain of flak landed their half-ton bombs squarely on warships already hard hit by raids Tuesday and Wednesday, Associated Press Corespondent Richard O'Malley reported.

After the third attack within a week, Japan was left without a single heavy warship fit for action. Admiral Halsey's hard-hitting carrier planes knocked out 26 warships, including three battleships, six aircraft carriers and four cruisers in strikes Tuesday and Wednesday alone.

Fires raged through the harbor at Kure, O'Malley reported, and flames spurted skyward from the ships of what once was the third mightiest fleet in the world.

Weary Japanese anti-aircraft gunners, who had opened up when the first planes heaved into view in the raids earlier in the week, held their fire Saturday until the planes began whining down on the warships.

Despite the accuracy of the flak, the attackers pressed home the attack, bent on carrying out orders to erase the enemy's fleet as a factor to be counted upon when invasion comes.

The Japanese said the planes came over in waves of from 80 to 300, beginning at 5:40 a.m., Japanese time, and that the attacks still were in progress at noon.

The enemy declared the raiders not only struck the Inland sea and

(Continued on Page 2, Col. 1)

Five Albertans Decorated at All-Canadian Investiture

Five Albertans were among those who were decorated at the all-Canadian investiture at Buckingham palace on July 13. The top picture shows left to right, Regimental Sgt.-Maj. G. A. Trottier, Montreal; Sgt.-Maj. J. J. Quinn, Toronto; QMS. O. Hanson, Edmonton; Sgt.-Maj. H. R. Cotton, Cape Breton Island; QMS. J. M. McRae, Regina; RSM. D. McGowan, Toronto. In the lower picture, left to right, Lt.-Col. F. T. Jenner, Olds; Maj. L. G. Alexander, Calgary; Maj. K. A. C. Clarke, Calgary; Maj. D. F. Cameron, Edmonton. All received the M.B.E.—(Canadian Army Overseas photograph).

15 Die When Explosion Sets Afire 102-Storey Empire State Building

NEW YORK.—An army bomber crashed into the fog-shrouded Empire State building at 9:45 a.m. Saturday, killed at least 15 persons, set the tower of the 102-storey building—tallest in the world—afire and scattered debris over a wide area.

Nine dead were civilian occupants of the building. Six were soldiers thought to be crew members of the plane. At least two other persons were badly burned, and about 25 more were injured.

The fire was brought under control 40 minutes later, Mayor La Guardia said.

The southbound plane shortly after 10:00 a.m. crashed into the 34th street side of the building between the 82nd and 86th floors, tearing a huge hole and littering Fifth avenue with plane wreckage, glass and masonry. One motor of the twin-engined B-25 apparently passed through the building to fall into 33rd street.

All elevators above the 66th floor were out of order and hundreds of office workers walked to safety after what police described as a "terrific explosion" after the plane crashed.

Unknown was the fate of passengers in two elevators which fell to the bottom of their shafts and were seen burning.

Four of those killed were on the 78th floor when the plane struck the building. Another was on the 79th. At least six of the injured were reported in critical condition.

Eleven floors of the building above and below the 86th floor of the towering structure were in flames and the spire of the building soon was enveloped in a vast smoky, foggy screen.

Flaming gasoline and fumes poured into the building through a huge scar on the 34th street side and a soldier who saw it said "it looked like a flamethrower in action."

Broken glass splattered into Fifth avenue as far south as 29th street.

More than an hour after the crash smoke still poured from the upper structure of the building—top of which remained invisible from the street in the rain and mist—but firemen were bringing the blaze under control and had extinguished flames which sprang up in adjacent buildings.

One of the injured, Mary Schinnell, 26, operator of the "observation" elevator which carries passengers up the building's tower, originally designed as a dirigible mooring post, suffered severe burns and bruises and probable fractures.

Others reported injured were Elevator Operator Kay Oliver, and a John Mate. Both were on the 79th floor and were reported badly burned.

Firemen, summoned by a "full" alarm signal, brought flames spreading to adjacent buildings under control.

Top of the Empire State could not be seen from the street as dense fog and smoke swirled about it.

Police said a "terrific" explosion followed the crash and an eyewitness, Edward Hughes of Louisville, Ky., said smoke poured from three or four storeys at a time.

Sirens screaming, ambulances and police cars converged through rainy mid-town New York to the scene. Other nearby buildings already were aflame minutes after the crash, witnesses said.

James W. Irwin, management consultant and former managing

(Continued on Page 5, Col. 2)

EMPIRE STATE BUILDING

Japanese Comment Is Vague On Ultimatum for Surrender

SAN FRANCISCO.—Japan's semi-official Domei agency said Premier Suzuki would broadcast Saturday "his determination for the decisive battle in the streets," but a series of Tokyo broadcasts failed to report an official rejection of the Allied ultimatum to surrender.

Japanese propaganda agencies went through successive stages of professed fury and vague "double-talk" in connection with the declaration in which Britain, the U.S. and China bluntly told Japan to quit now or be destroyed.

Domei started with an angry statement that the ultimatum would be ignored and that Japan would "fight to the bitter end."

The Tokyo radio soon toned this down by saying that Nippon would "adopt a policy to strive toward completion of the Greater East Asia war in conformity to the hitherto-established basic principles."

This broadcast was vague enough to mean anything that its unidentified authors intended it to mean.

Domei then returned to the air, and while omitting any further reference about fighting "to the bitter end," it announced Premier Suzuki would broadcast to the people Saturday, and would express "his determination for the decisive battle in the streets for sure victory and firm and unshakable measures to

(Continued on Page 5, Col. 4)

The Times Says—

Churchill Stands Firm
Huge Task for Bevin
Potsdam Decisions Near

LONDON.—Former Prime Minister Churchill is not likely to return to Potsdam with Prime Minister Attlee and Ernest Bevin, the new foreign secretary, according to the Times' parliamentary correspondent. During the election campaign Mr. Churchill said plainly and repeatedly he could not continue to serve the nation unless his government was returned with a good majority. That majority has been denied him and given to the Labor party and Mr. Churchill is not likely to seek to play any part in affairs which would appear to diminish the full authority of the new prime minister.

Dealing with Mr. Bevin's task as the new foreign secretary the Times editorially says he is a forceful personality. The main lines of the foreign policy are already agreed between all parties and no spectacular break is in any way contemplated. As so many countries in Europe look to Britain now for leadership the new government and the new foreign secretary, in particular, will bear a heavy responsibility.

(Continued on Page 2, Col. 4)

Four City Golfers To Play in East

Four Edmonton golfers are on their way to Toronto to play in the Canadian open golf tournament when it opens at the Thornhill Golf and Country club, Toronto, next Thursday.

Glen Gray, of the Mayfair Golf and Country club, left Friday night for Toronto. Also in the national tournament from the Mayfair club will be Pete Olynyk, Henry Martell and Pat Fletcher, of the Highlands club, are the other two Edmontonians entered in the tournament.

Where To Find It

Amusements, Theatres	8
Bridge	12
Church Page	7
Comics	12, 16, 17
Crossword Puzzle	12
District	4
Editorial	4
Financial	10
Gallup Poll	4
Herman N. Bundesen, M.D.	13
Music	14
Off the Record	12
Paul Reynaud	20
Radio	20
Ramblings from Home	6
Sport	8, 9
They'll Do It Every Time	12
Uncle Ray's Corner	12
Want Ads	16, 17, 18, 19
War Veteran's Guide	7
Women's	14, 15
Young People's	20

The Weather

Estimated low tonight, 50. Estimated high tomorrow, 70. At Edmonton Sunday, sun rises 5:43; sets 9:37. Monday, sun rises 5:44; sets 9:35.

Overnight low 60.

Hourly readings since 12:30 p.m. Friday:

12:30	81	8:30	82	4:30	62
1:30	82	9:30	73	5:30	62
2:30	84	10:30	75	6:30	60
3:30	86	11:30	70	7:30	61
4:30	86	12:30	67	8:30	61
5:30	87	1:30	67	9:30	60
6:30	86	2:30	67	10:30	60
7:30	84	3:30	64	11:30	60

Montreal	82	60	Calgary	85	54
Toronto	83	60	Kamloops	99	60
Winnipeg	76	54	Vancouver	77	55
Saskatoon	87	60	Victoria	77	56

8:30 a.m. readings:

Fort St. John	58		Peace River	48	
Dawson Creek	58		Ft. Vermilion	50	
Grande Prairie	55		Athabaska	60	
Fairview	55		McMurray	55	

Far north readings:

	H.	L.		H.	L.
Aklavik	75	49	Wat. Lake	64	47
Whitehorse	61	45	Ft. Simpson	78	47
Dawson	70	51	Yellowknife	78	55
Ft. Nelson	74	48	Norman Wells	72	50

Canadians Counter Suicide Aircraft

SAN FRANCISCO.—Sixty Canadian warships proceeding soon to the Pacific to battle Japan will be equipped with a new "disintegrator" weapon against suicide-plane attacks, the Melbourne radio said Friday.

The Australian broadcast said the new weapon was invented by an Australian, passed on to the British admiralty, tested by Canadians within a week, and installed in a Canadian ship within a month.

Nature of the new weapon was not disclosed.

Abasand Winner In $100,000 Suit

Payment of a $100,000 claim under a boiler insurance policy to Abasand Oils Ltd. by the Boiler Inspection and Insurance Co. of Canada was ordered Saturday in a supreme court judgment by Mr. Justice Shepherd.

The insurance company, it was claimed insured the Abasand Co. against loss from accidents to a boiler in the oil company's plant at Waterways. The company agreed to pay, under the terms of the policy, the sum of $1,000 for each day of ...

17 British Seats Remain Unfilled

LONDON.—The commons, with 17 of its 640 seats still unfilled, now has 388 Labor party members, 193 Conservative, 14 Liberal National, 11 Liberal, 10 Independent, three Independent Labor Party, two Communist, one Common Wealth and one National.

Three of the vacancies were caused by death of candidates since polling day, and one by cabinet appointment. Results of the election in 12 university districts and one "deferred" will be announced within the next two weeks.

Byelections are necessary ... Smithwick where Alfred J. Dobbs, newly-elected Labor member, was killed in an auto accident Friday ... in Bromley and Monmouth where Conservatives Sir Edward Campbell and L. R. Pym have ... since polling day, and in Ashton-Under-Lyne where another Labor member, Sir William Jowitt, has been named lord chancellor in Prime Minister Attlee's cabinet.

Murder of Mandel Enters Petain Trial

PARIS.—The murder of ... Colonial Minister Georges Mandel, most celebrated martyr to French resistance to the Nazis, was brought into the testimony as the trial of Marshal Petain for "intelligence with the enemy" and plotting against the security of France entered its sixth day.

Michel Clemenceau, son of France's "Tiger" of the ... war, told from the witness stand of a visit he made to a ... where M. Mandel was held before his slaying last year.

"His murderers have ... cuted." M. Clemenceau ... the question is, who is ... crime?"

M. Clemenceau half ... looked squarely at Marshal Petain as he spoke.

M. Mandel, who was minister of colonies under former Premier Daladier, was taken from his cell in the Sante prison to be killed on July 7, 1944. Two men already have been executed for his murder. M. Mandel had defied Marshal Petain and refused to agree to the armistice with the Germans.

M. Mandel had told his captors, "I will show you a Frenchman who knows how to die."

Bevin as Foreign Secretary Heads Attlee's New Ministers

LONDON.—Prime Minister Attlee Friday night chose husky Ernest Bevin, a two-fisted, bespectacled, ... pound trade union leader, as foreign secretary of his new Labor government and his right-hand man in guiding British foreign policy through the Pacific war and a host of thorny post-war problems.

Attlee announced selection of six Labor party stalwarts as the nebulus of his cabinet, and on Saturday the new ministers took the oath of office.

They include Hugh Dalton as chancellor of the exchequer, third most important post, and Herbert Morrison as lord president of the council and leader in the commons.

Mr. Bevin, who succeeds the suave Anthony Eden, told a Labor audience less than 24 hours before his appointment that he thought "blunt Lancashire" better than "political diplomatic phrases" in the new world of international relations. had declared the new Labor government intended to speak "as common men to common men of other nations."

Prime Minister Attlee went to Potsdam Saturday as the freshman member of the Big Three. Herbert Morrison, Mr. Attlee's ...

Electrical Storm Makes Goering Ill

MANDORF-LES-BAINS, Luxembourg. — Reichsmarshal Hermann Goering suffered a heart attack during an electrical storm Thursday night and there now is a question whether he can figure in a war crimes trial.

Capt. Clint L. Miller, army surgeon at the interrogation centre where Goering is interned, said no one could prophesy how a man under such high tension would react under the stress and excitement of a war crime trial and added "Goering is so emotionally unstable you never can tell about his type."

Capt. Miller attributed Goering's attack to his fear of thunder and lightning.

Mr. Attlee to Potsdam, along with Sir Edward Bridges, secretary to the cabinet, and Gen. Sir Hastings Ismay, chief of staff to the ministry of defence.

The partial list of cabinet appointments included:

Mr. Attlee as minister of defence,

(Continued on Page 2, Col. 2)

Potsdam Parley May Conclude Next Week, Observers Believe

POTSDAM.—Prime Minister Attlee and his foreign secretary, Ernest Bevin, have arrived in Berlin and the Big Three conference with Marshal Stalin and President Truman will be resumed Saturday evening.

POTSDAM.—The Big Three conference neared its climactic stage Saturday, and the conviction persisted that the final conclusions may be signed within the next few days.

Clement R. Attlee, Britain's new prime minister, was due back, accompanied by Ernest Bevin, his newly-appointed foreign secretary. Mr. Attlee's decision to return to the meeting promptly cleared away misgivings over possible undue prolongation ... in which the ...

Striking Packers Ask Vacation Pay

TORONTO.—Some striking members of the United Packinghouse Workers of America are seeking vacation pay from the strikebound Canada Packers plant here, it was announced Saturday.

Sam Hughes, district organizer for the union, said the workers are those who were to go on vacation at this time. He spoke of the cheese department, saying it was to be closed for vacation in the two weeks beginning next Monday.

"The company said workers they would have to return to work to get vacation pay," said Mr. Hughes.

Morrison Wanted As Prime Minister?

LONDON.—The younger, left-wing element predominates in Labor's representation in Britain's new parliament and there were signs Friday night this section would prefer to see Herbert Morrison replace Clement R. Attlee as prime minister.

Of 390 Labor candidates returned to the commons, 290 of them were drawn from the political section of the Labor movement. The remainder are old-time trade unionists, supporters of Mr. Attlee and usually automatic supporters of party parliamentary policy.

The temper of the revitalized Labor movement will be tested when Mr. Attlee is to be formally re-elected party chairman.

Bush Fire Menace Extremely Serious

Bush fire situation throughout northern and northwestern Alberta is extremely serious with at least three new outbreaks reported Saturday, according to T. F. Bielgen, director of forestry, provincial government.

In addition to fires reported earlier this week from Edson and north of White Court, new outbreaks have occurred near Kinuso on the south shore of Lesser Slave lake.

One is about 40 miles southeast of ...

believe, this island, or even part of it, is subjugated and starving, then our empire across the sea, armed and guarded by the British fleet, will carry on the struggle until, in God's name, the new world, in all its strength and might, sets forth to the rescue and liberation of the old."

The Journal knew where it stood, and sounded a bellicose note of its own in responding to Churchill's speech. "Mr. Churchill, in suggesting as a remote possibility the part that 'our empire across the seas', guarded by the British fleet, might be called upon to play, gives the King's overseas subjects something to think about most seriously.

"They are bound to heed his words closely. No doubt he had Canada particularly in mind and, if such a responsibility should devolve upon her people, it is safe to predict they would not be found unworthy in any way."

Judging by the number of young Edmonton men and women who rushed to join the army, navy and air force, they were ready to accept whatever duty was thrust upon them by war.

Journal files are filled with stories of young people – peacetime grocery clerks, car mechanics, postmen, university students – who volunteered and were all were transformed into fighting men during the war. Many were interviewed when they returned to the city on leave.

Flight Lieut. F.A. Wilkins, on leave in 1945, explained that he was part of a bombing run that blasted open the walls of a prison camp at Amiens, France, setting free thousands of French POWs held there.

"It was something to see," said the laconic Wilkins who worked as an installer for Hook Signs before the war.

Don Laubman, a 23-year-old flight lieutenant in the RCAF, was a Spitfire pilot who shot down 15 enemy aircraft and had been part of a dive-bombing squadron that destroyed a dozen German trains.

"I was extremely lucky," Laubman told the paper in a 1944 interview.

"I was in the right place at the right time and we were flying a superior type of aircraft and that means a great deal."

Before the war, Laubman worked behind the counter in Gordon's Groceteria on 100A Street and 100A Avenue.

Seaman Gunner Lorne Roberts was just out of his teens and worked at a service station on 118th Street and Jasper Avenue prior to the outbreak of war. He served on HMS Achilles, part of the five-cruiser group that attacked the German ship the Graf Spee just outside the port of Montevideo, Uruguay. Crippled by the shelling at the hands of the cruiser group, the Graf Spee commander scuttled his ship.

Scotty Munro, a bugler with the Edmonton Regiment and a peacetime *Journal* staffer, corresponded regularly with the newspaper in the early days of the war. He wrote of the little things that affected a citizen-soldier's way of life away from home, and told of the food they were served and what a thrill it was to play for the King when he toured the training facility at Aldershot in Britain.

It wasn't long before the war began to tell in ways both large and small on the home front.

In 1940 new cars were subjected to a $700 tax ($9,144.68 today), although new automobile production was soon completely curtailed in order to free up factories to make tanks, airplanes and the heavy equipment

day. The city's shortage of snow removal equipment forces it to call on American air force and Alaska Highway crews to help clear the snow.

***Nov. 20, 1942*:**
The Alaska Highway opens in a ceremony at Soldiers Summit near Kluane in the Yukon.

***In 1943*:**
A cashier/clerk typist at *The Journal* makes $16 a month.

***Jan. 8, 1943*:**
The population of Edmonton and its suburbs Jasper Place and Beverly reaches 103,000.

***July 7, 1943*:**
The Edmonton Regiment is designated the Loyal Edmonton Regiment.

***July 10, 1943*:**
The 1st Canadian Division, including members of the Loyal Edmonton Regiment, joins the British and American troops in the invasion of Sicily during the Second World War.

***July 12, 1943*:**
New York Mayor Fiorello La Guardia visits Edmonton while returning from a trip to Alaska and the new Alaska Highway.

STALE SMOKES?
NOT NOW-A-DAYS!
Veterans of the last war will recall how often they opened a package of precious smokes only to find cigarettes dry as dust ... mouldy with damp ... or tabacco without flavour. Buut not in this war! Using the remarkable protective qualities of "Cellophane", manufacturers are able today to keep their products fresh and stisfying at all times and in all places—on the battlefield, in camp or in the corner store at home.
Smoking provides a solace and comfort in these trying times. That's why the "Cellophane" overwrap on smokes is more important now than ever—it is your assurance of a *better* product and greater smoking enjoyment.
Cellophane
C-I-L CELLULOSE FILM

BEGINNING AT ONCE
TEA AND COFFEE
ARE RATIONED
TEA
COFFEE
Ships and lives must be conserved
To bring tea from Ceylon and India, to bring coffee from South America, ships must cross oceans infested with sub-
ose ships and their
ired for more essen-
, every foot of cargo
rry war materials,
goods to Canada.
reduce their con-
offee. You must
umption of tea by
st reduce your
offee by at least
ions are abso-
TEA CONSUMPTION
MUST BE CUT AT LEAST IN HALF
COFFEE CONSUMPTION
MUST BE CUT AT LEAST ONE FOURTH
THIS IS THE LAW
You must not buy more than 2 weeks' supply of tea or coffee for yourself and household in any one week.
You must not make further purchases of tea of coffee at any time when you have two weeks supply on hand at the reduced ration. (Exception: those in areas remote from supply.)
Retailers have the right to limit or refuse customers orders if they suspect the law is not being kept.
Retailers must not have on hand more than one month's supply of tea and coffee, wether packeged of bulk.
There are heavy penalties for violations of this law.
RTIME PRICES AND TRADE BOARD

Ottawa, May 22nd, 1943
MEAT
RATIONING BECOMES EFFECTIVE
THURSDAY, MAY 27TH
After midnight May 26th, it is unlawful for a consumer to buy rationed neats and for anyone to sell rationed meats to a consumer exept on surrender of valid ration coupons.
WHAT MEATS ARE RATIONED?
Beef, Veal, Pork, Mutton and Lamb.
WHAT MEATS ARE NOT RATIONED?
Poultry and Fish are not rationed. "Fancy" meats such as Heart, Tongue, Liver, Kidneys, Brains, Sweetbreads, and cooked sausages such as Weiners and Bologna are not rationed. Meat cuts containing 50% more of bone such as spare-ribs, oxtails, and pigs' feet are not rationed.
HOW MUCH RATIONED MEAT AM I PERMITTED TO BUY?
An average of two pounds per person per week. You get less of meats containing no bone and more of meats containing considerable bone. See the chart of coupon values below.
WHAT COUPONS DO I USE WHEN BUYING MEAT?
The brown Spare "A" coupons from your No. 2 ration book—the book you are now using to buy tea, coffee, sugar, and butter.
HOW OFTEN CAN I BUY MEAT?
Two coupons become good each Thursday. The first pair of No. 1 coupons become good May 27th. Each coupon is good for 1/2 of one week's ration.
HOW LONG DO COUPONS REMAIN GOOD?
Coupons becoming good before the 15th of a month are good until the end of that month. Coupons becoming good on or before the 15th of a month are good until the following month.
DO I HAVE TO USE THE TWO COUPONS AT THE SAME TIME OR IN THE SAME STORE?
No. you can use a coupon at any time during the period in which it is valid, and in any store you wish.
CAN I BUY ONLY ONE KIND OF RATIONED MEAT WITH A COUPON?
No. You can buy whatever rationed meat is available and as many kinds as you want providing the coupon value is not exceeded.
MEAT COUPON VALUE CHART
GROUP A - ½ LB. PER COUPON
SMOKED MEATS
Back Bacon (Sliced and Rindless)
Side Bacon (Sliced and Rindless)
Side Bacon (Sliced Rind on)
PORK CURED
Boneless Back (Sliced Not Smoked or Cooked)
COOKED MEATS
Butt (Boneless)
Ham (Boneles)
Any Uncooked Group "B" Cuts — when Cooked
GROUP B - ¾ LB. PER COUPON
BEEF - FRESH or CURED
Chuck Roast or Steak (Boneless)
Flank Steak (Boneless)
Hind Shank Meat (Boneless)
Minute Steaks and Cube Steaks
LAMB or MUTTON-FRESH
Frontquarter (Boneless)
VEAL - FRESH
Cutlets and Fillets (Bone in)
Front Roll (Caul Wrapped, Boneless)
PORK - FRESH
Back (Boneless)
Belly (Boneless)
Butt (Bone in)
Ham (Boneless)
Ham, Centre Cuts (Bone in)
Picnic (Boneless)
Picnic Skinless (Boneless)
Tenderloin
PORK - CURED
(Not Smoked or Cooked)
Back (Boneless)
Belly (Boneless)
PORK - SMOKED
Back Bacon (In the piece, Boneless)
Cottage Roll (Boneless)
Ham (except Shank End, Bone in)
Ham, Skinless (Boneless)
Picnic (Boneless)
Pork roll (Bonelss)
Side Bacon (in the piece)
COOKED MEATS

needed to fight a war. Tires were impossible to get without a permit, and staples such as meat, sugar, eggs, coffee, booze and flour were rationed.

Early in the war, provincial bakers decided to hold the cost of a loaf down but to reduce the luxuries. No longer was it possible to buy sliced bread. An unsliced Polly Ann loaf cost eight cents ($1.05 today) when the war began, and remained under 10 cents for the duration. In 1940, in the Bay Groceteria, sirloin steaks sold for 13 cents a pound and two pounds of wieners cost a dime. A dollar in 1940 is worth $13.06 in today's money.

At a time when members of Canada's armed forces earned a $1.10 a day, *Journal* wartime advertisements also showed that a man could buy a made-to-measure suit at the Hudson's Bay for $25.95, a pair of socks for 60 cents, and top-brand shoes for $7 a pair. Woodward's sold women's casual coats for $18.88 and "smart" shoes for a clearance price of $1.87 a pair. The finest of one-piece bathing suits for women could be had for $1.98.

Canadians were also called upon to support the war effort through the purchase of a series of government bonds required to finance the war. All of the issues were oversubscribed, and 8,000 Edmontonians brought Jasper Avenue traffic to a standstill when Hollywood stars Claire Trevor and George Murphy made a 1945 appearance on the balcony of the Selkirk Hotel at the corner of 101st Street selling the eighth bond issue.

The Salvation Army made its pleas, too, most notably in an appeal to raise money to fund such things as entertainment and recreational programs for the men serving in the armed forces, alcohol-free canteens for servicemen, and a chaplain service for troops seeking spiritual guidance.

Other, more prosaic, requests were made of the public. Advertisements regularly exhorted readers to send tax-free Sweet Caporal cigarettes to soldiers in Europe. For a $1 donation, a member of the armed forces would receive 300 cigarettes or one pound of Old Virginia pipe tobacco.

Then, as now, politics was never far from people's thoughts, nor from *The Journal*'s front page.

The Liberal government of Mackenzie King confronted a conscription issue that divided the country along linguistic lines. In an April 1942 national plebiscite, almost three million Canadians went to the polls and by a 68-per-cent majority agreed to allow the government to conscript able-bodied men for service overseas.

In Quebec the vote went three-to-one against. In Alberta, which voted for conscription by a more-than 70-per-cent majority, only the riding of Vegreville voted against it.

Provincially, the Social Credit government was confronted with the death of party founder, Premier William Aberhart, who died of a liver ailment on May 23, 1943, while on holiday in Vancouver.

The Journal had opposed Aberhart from the beginning, and its posthumous editorial did not hide the fact that the newspaper had viewed the Social Credit government with considerable skepticism.

Not surprisingly, the newspaper's tone was a grudging acknowledgment of what the 64-year-old Aberhart had meant to the province.

"The political movement that the late premier initiated in Alberta was responsible for controversies of great intensity," the editorial said.

***Aug. 13, 1943*:**
The rent of new wartime housing being built in Edmonton is set at $32, $36 or $40 a month for four-, five- or six-room dwellings.

***September 1943*:**
The Juniorat Saint-Jean becomes the College Saint-Jean (now Faculte Saint-Jean), a private Catholic school offering education in French.

***Sept. 23, 1943*:**
A record 860 aircraft pass through Blatchford Field, Edmonton's municipal airport, at the height of the Second World War. During the war it was the busiest airport in Canada. Many of the planes were en route to Russia as part of a wartime lend-lease plan.

***Nov. 13, 1943*:**
Edmonton coal miners agree to return to work, ending a two-week-long strike that defied a government order banning all coal strikes for the duration of the Second World War.

***Dec. 21, 1943*:**
The Loyal Edmonton Regiment and other Canadian troops attack the City of Ortona in Italy.

Cream of Comics Every Day

Edmonton Journal

'One of Canada's Great Newspapers'

FORECAST: CLOUDY, MILDER. * * EDMONTON, ALBERTA, WEDNESDAY, FEBRUARY 12, 1947 SINGLE COPY, 5 CENTS

Delay Execution of Jewish Terrorist

Cut Electricity For All Britain

LONDON, (Reuters)—Domestic electricity cuts will be extended to all Britain Thursday, the ministry of fuel and power announced Wednesday.

Britain also will go back to the blackout, it was announced, with drastic cuts in street lighting to be enforced.

Between 5,000,000 and 6,000,000 are idle from direct and indirect effects of the industrial power stoppage in 16 English counties, a board of trade spokesman estimated. He forecast even greater unemployment next week.

"This is going to affect rations, clothing, household appliances, shoes—everything," he said. "Most people don't yet realize the most serious personal effects this will have."

The spokesman predicted exports probably will drop one-third from December's £82,900,000 but warned the "real effect" will not be felt before March either in exports or home consumption.

Home supplies already are disappearing. Carreras, Limited, advised tobacconists no further cigarettes would be delivered until further notice because all production has stopped. Bottled beer is scarce and production of draught beer halted. North sea gales have wiped out fishing operations.

In manufactured consumer goods the effect is cumulative. When stores sell out they will be unable to replenish present supplies for weeks, and perhaps months, the board official said.

"For Britain today the disease is the rapid wasting away of all industrial production, everywhere," the official added.

Miners, railmen, merchant sailors, servicemen and government officials struggled to move life-giving coal to generators from which power could be provided to maintain vital services.

For winter-weary Britons, who could not take a direct part in what newspapers dubbed the second "Battle of Britain," there was one more unhappy aspect to the fuel crisis—the Sunday dinner in millions of British homes may be cold.

The fuel crisis also is hard on the British sweet tooth. Bakeries are forbidden to make anything but bread and that means no pies, no tarts, no cookies, and no cakes.

Lehman Proposes U.S. Send Coal to Britain

NEW YORK, (AP)—Herbert H. Lehman, former governor of New York and first director-general of UNRRA, urged President Truman in a telegram Wednesday that "this country dispatch immediately to England as many shiploads of coal as possible."

"While I am bitterly disappointed at the attitude of the British government toward Palestine," Lehman said, "I cannot permit this to blind me to the urgent needs and suffering of men, women and children.

Oilmen At Leduc Live In Turner Valley And Provost Huts

With living accommodation at Leduc at a premium, Imperial Oil company and its employes working in the new Leduc oil field are trucking portable huts to the town from Turner Valley and Provost to provide housing for themselves and their wives and families. The huts vary in size and are loaded on the back of a large truck for transportation. The cost of moving each is about $125 and this is paid by the hut owner. The top photograph shows some of the small dwellings set up in the Leduc baseball park which has been turned into an oil settlement. In the lower picture, Lew Glendenning, a driller on No. 2 rig, is shown in his comfortable home-made hut with his wife and five-year-old daughter, Paddy. The homes are exceptionally clean and tidy and are heated by oil stoves. They have electric light supplied by the Calgary Power company. Mr. Glendenning's hut was taken to Leduc from Provost where he was drilling several months ago.

Report Barker Resigns Command in Palestine

JERUSALEM, (AP)—The government announced Wednesday that the execution of Dov Bela Gruner, condemned terrorist, was being delayed because of legal complexities which authorities said might "take months or possibly a year" to untangle.

Gruner's impending execution had stirred the underground Jewish organization of which he was a member, Irgun Zvai Leumi, to vow reprisals, and had hung threateningly for weeks over the troubled Holy Land while he lived on the basis of a day-to-day reprieve.

In another development, Lt.-Gen. Sir Evelyn Barker, general officer commanding British troops in Palestine, was reported reliably to have relinquished his command and to have left by air for Cairo on his way to Britain.

His successor, Maj.-Gen. G. H. A. Macmillan, is expected to reach Palestine by air Thursday. Both generals were reported to be dining Wednesday night in Cairo with Gen. Sir Miles Dempsey, commander-in-chief Middle East forces.

Palestine remained quiet Wednesday after Tuesday night's outbreak of rioting between Jewish extremists and Jewish anti-terrorists in the all-Jewish city of Tel Aviv. However, a new security measure was adopted. Lt.-Gen. Sir Alan Cunningham, high commissioner, now is convoyed by a jeep-load of soldiers and an armored car on his visits to the secretariat. Previously he had driven alone in an armor-plated car.

The technicality in Gruner's case revolves about a claim that the high commissioner had not confirmed the sentence imposed on Gruner last May for taking part in a raid on a police station in which two policeman were killed.

Meanwhile, R.A.F. spotter planes roved the skies above the eastern Mediterranean amid unofficial reports that a Jewish refugee ship, with 600 uncertified immigrants aboard, had left Algiers Sunday for Palestine.

A Reuters dispatch from Haifa said the ship had been intercepted by British naval units. There was no immediate amplification of the report.

Reliable sources said at least 12 persons were injured when Jewish extremists clashed Tuesday night with anti-terrorist Jews in Tel Aviv in the first struggle of Jew-against-Jew in Palestine since the British army began its drive to stamp out underground violence.

The fight was said to have begun when youths "presumed to be adherents of Irgun Zvai Leumi," Jewish underground group, attempted to storm the clubrooms of Hashomir Matzair, Jewish political party openly opposed to terrorism.

Allow 300 Jews To Go to Palestine

HERFORD, Germany, (Reuters)—Three hundred Jewish displaced persons from the British zone of Germany are to be allowed immediate and direct entry into Palestine, it was announced officially here Wednesday.

The Jews, all skilled tradesmen, will travel through Belgium and France to a port near Marseilles. From there they will embark for Haifa.

The announcement said the scheme would be financed jointly by UNRRA and Jewish relief societies.

Adjourn Hearing Robbery Charges

The largest crowd since preliminary hearing of the Dorothy Hammond murder charge against Chester Johnston in 1940 jammed city police court and adjacent hallways Wednesday when alleged robbers of the Imperial Bank of Canada were scheduled to appear.

Those of the 300 persons who crowded the city police station Wednesday who were able to get seats in the courtroom saw Ernest Amato, William G. Capstick and Donna Lee McKay, three Vancouverites arrested 11 hours after the Feb. 3 daylight downtown $3,543 bank robbery, for only four minutes. Charges against the trio were remanded to Friday.

They heard a new charge of operating a car without consent of the owner read against Amato and Capstick, and a charge of illegal possession of drugs read against Capstick. A week earlier the pair were charged with armed robbery of the bank, while the McKay woman was charged with possession of stolen property, $3,033 in currency, and illegal possession of liquor.

The new adjournment was granted by Magistrate Millar when Crown Prosecutor Donald Masson stated police investigation was con-

(Continued on Page 2, Col. 5)

Opposition Hits Chinese Bill Demands Immigration Policy

By Richard Sanburn

OTTAWA. — The hottest debate of the current session was touched off Tuesday by a government move to repeal the 24-year-old Chinese Immigration act, sometimes called the Chinese exclusion act.

Heated talk on this bill and immigration in general took up most of the day, and at 11:00 p.m. the government measure had not passed second reading. These points stood out:

1. The government had promised to repeal an old and almost forgotten order-in-council which makes it difficult or impossible for most Chinese in Canada to become Canadian citizens.

2. Several speakers declared the proposed bill, instead of abolishing discrimination against Chinese, actually "perpetuated it." Under it, only Chinese who are Canadian citizens will be allowed to bring in their families.

3. Members of all parties demanded the government announce an over-all, long-range immigration policy.

4. All British Columbia members, with the exception of the C.C.F. came out flatly against Oriental immigration, said they feared it

(Continued on Page 2, Col. 6)

Planes Rush Food To English Villages

LONDON, (AP)— Emergency food supplies were rushed by plane Tuesday to English villagers isolated by month-long winter storms.

The cold wave—worst in Britain in more than 50 years—showed no sign of abating. Similar conditions existed in Germany, the Low Countries and in Scandinavia. France, after three days of slightly warmer weather, faced the prospect of more snow and sub-freezing temperatures.

Flying squads of police in Germany broke up crowds—sometimes as many as 600—who sought to loot coal cars on rail sidings. Coal and grain shortages threatened Finland. Frozen reserviors endangered Norway's power supplies.

Say 50,000 May Come to Canada

QUEBEC, (CP) — L'Action Catholique said Tuesday if shipping lines can get vessels, between 50,000 and 60,000 European immigrants to Canada are expected to land next summer at Quebec.

The story said the Canadian immigration service has organized "flying squads" to visit camps of displaced persons to examine potential immigrants.

Where the immigrants would go after reaching Quebec was not known.

Ottawa dispatches reported it is known that top labor and immigration officials are conferring to iron out details under which immigrants from Europe might be brought to Canada to relieve shortages in agriculture, mining and logging.

These conferences followed an announcement by Resources Minister Glen last week, relaxing immigration regulations to admit men experienced in various basic industries.

Suggests Moving Hutterites North

LETHBRIDGE, (CP) — Suggestion that a large block of land suitable for farming and ranching be set out, perhaps in northern Alberta, to eliminate the concentration of Hutterites in the southern part of the province was made here Tuesday to the provincial legislative committee probing Alberta's "Hutterite problem."

Coming from the Cardston irrigation and development committee, the suggestion was presented to the committee shortly before it concluded its investigation here with an inspection of a Hutterite colony near Chin lake.

Two other briefs protested vigorously against the operation of private schools by Hutterites.

The committee sits in Calgary Thursday and Friday and reconvenes in Edmonton Feb. 24-25.

In the Cardston brief, J. S. Smith of Cardston, offered these three suggestions:

Restrict Hutterites to their present holdings where they are located, set out a block of unoccupied land for farming and ranching; the department of education could insist that the Hutterian pupils be sent to nearby centralized schools.

A royal commission investigation into the Hutterite question was urged by J. Prowse, representing 20 southern Alberta organizations.

2 Escape Injury As Plane Crashes

CALGARY, (CP)— Alfred Gates and Richard Pike of Banff escaped injury when their plane crashed into a mountain near Sunshine ski lodge Tuesday while attempting a forced landing.

The plane was badly damaged, possibly beyond repair. Officials of the aviation company will investigate the cause of the engine trouble which forced the plane down.

Passenger and pilot made their way by skis over to the ski lodge.

The Weather

Forecast: Cloudy today and Thursday, milder, light winds.

Temperatures have risen rapidly in southern Saskatchewan and thawing is now reported from Moose Jaw west to the mountains. Fairly cold air remains over the northern district with the boundary line between it and the warm chinook air lying from Red Deer to Regina. Slowly rising temperatures are expected to the north of this line but thawing is unlikely. Over the southern regions the temperature will average between 40 and 50 above accompanied by strong southwest winds.

Estimated low tonight, zero.

Estimated high tomorrow, 20 above.

At Edmonton Thursday, sun rises 1.59; sets 5.39.

Yesterday's maximum, 8 above.

Overnight low, 1 below.

Snowfall, .3 of an inch.

Heffernan Hangs For Girl's Murder

SAINT JOHN, N.B., (CP)—Thomas Henry Heffernan, 28, was hanged in Saint John county jail early Wednesday for the murder last September of Miss Leversey Powers, 25.

Heffernan surrendered voluntarily Oct. 1, led police to nearby Ashburn lake and indicated the spot where Miss Powers body was found.

At his trial, Heffernan admitted luring the young woman to the lake the previous night, striking her with a mallet and throwing the body into the water. He maintained he was insane but psychiatrists testified they found no evidence of insanity.

Belgium to Admit 20,000 Homeless

FRANKFURT, Germany, (AP)—Gen. Joseph T. McNarney, United States army commander in Europe, announced Tuesday his approval of an agreement under which Belgium will become the first country in Europe to open its doors to mass resettlement of displaced persons from the American zone of Germany.

At least 20,000 volunteer displaced persons and their families will be admitted to work in Belgium coal mines with the prospect of becoming Belgian citizens.

Rules Talmadge Is Legal Governor

McDONOUGH, Ga., (AP)—Judge Hendrix ruled Wednesday that Herman Talmadge is the legal governor of Georgia.

Judge Hendrix said the state legislature was within its constitutional rights when it elected Talmadge Jan. 15 to the four-year term of the late Eugene Talmadge, his father.

The court dismissed a suit of Lieut. Gov. M. E. Thompson which had asked a declaratory judgment ousting Talmadge from the governorship.

Judge Hendrix's decision was in direct opposition to the finding of another superior (circuit) judge last Friday at Rome, Ga. There, Judge Porter took the view that the legislature had exceeded its authority and ruled Talmadge's election was invalid.

Counsel for Thompson said judge Hendrix's decision would be appealed "at once" to the Georgia supreme court.

Small Nations Get More Active Role

LONDON, (AP) — Eighteen small Allied countries were assured Wednesday of a more active part in drafting the peace treaty with Germany after Russia agreed to take a "wider view" in consulting small nations.

Russia's retreat from its previous view that the Big Four should have the major task of dictating peace to Germany was made clear Tuesday night by Moscow's deputy foreign minister, Feodor Gousev during discussion of United States proposals to set up consultative committees of the small Allies.

The action came after protests from Canada, Brazil, Australia and other small nations.

FILM ACTOR DIES

HOLLYWOOD, (AP) — Sidney Toler, veteran stage and screen actor best known in recent years for his characterization of Charlie Chan, the Chinese detective, died Wednesday.

Test of Oil Well Near Leduc Is Arranged for Thursday

Great search for oil in central Alberta may be climaxed Thursday when an attempt will be made to bring the Imperial Oil company's Leduc No. 1 well into production.

The cement plug holding the precious liquid in the 5,066-foot hole was being drilled away Wednesday in preparation for the production test. If the flow occurs and the grading of the oil lives up to advance reports, Edmonton for the first time will be linked closely with an oil-producing area.

The discovery of oil in the Edmonton district—long a thriving agricultural and distribution centre and "gateway to the north"—will assure more than ever before the city's destiny as one of the big urban areas of the west, it was pointed out by businessmen.

As the crews of Leduc No. 1 worked day and night to prepare the well for the final production test, excitement was running high in the town of Leduc, whose population already has swelled by the influx of oil workers and their families.

When the test is made and the expected flow reaches the surface, it will be piped through a separator—a machine that separates the oil from the gas—into tanks. The fluid that goes into the tanks then will be tested and the results made public immediately.

Previous reports indicated the type of oil found was green in color, with a gravity rating of 38 degrees or 38 percent naptha. In the Turner Valley field, the oil from some wells has a gravity of 48 degrees.

It was not known at exactly what time the test would be carried out Thursday, but it was expected it would be around noon.

A second well, located one mile south of No. 1, was being drilled Wednesday by the same company.

The land on which No. 1 is located was owned by Mike Turta, who

(Continued on Page 2, Col. 4)

Oil Strike Means Cash to Students

The oil strike in the Leduc area is paying off to University of Alberta law students who are making $10 to $30 a day searching titles to land in the Leduc district for at least four oil companies.

Four legal firms in Edmonton, with clients interested in "freehold" land in the vicinity where Imperial Oil Ltd., has struck oil, have hired university law students to search titles in the land titles office.

In the case of land titles granted many years ago oil rights were given with surface rights and at least four rival oil companies are having the titles searched to find the owners of these "freehold" lands.

The companies then would be in a position to approach the owners and negotiate for the land. It is understood Imperial Oil Ltd., already has searched the titles but others believe there still is a large amount of "freehold" land available.

U.K. Coal Crisis Drains U.S. Loan

LONDON, (Reuters) — On the third day of Britain's fuel catastrophe it becomes clear the most serious effects will be the indirect and external ones, including an increased drain on the United States loan to Britain.

Consumption, partly because of payments to unemployed workers, has been well maintained while production is down.

The brunt of the stoppage therefore falls on exports, and the dollar loan will be used all the faster. This is serious, since already there were doubts whether the United States loan would last half as long as necessary and whether Britain could repay her war debts during this century.

Discover 40-Mile Snowless Oasis In Frozen South Pole Continent

ABOARD THE U.S.S. MOUNT OLYMPUS, (AP) — The discovery on the frozen South Polar continent of a remarkable inland "oasis" of muddy pea green lakes dotted with tall dark brown mounds of apparently bare earth was announced Tuesday. The discovery may be one of the most important made by the navy expedition.

A 40-mile-wide land of lakes region with conical mounds rising 500 feet above the surface in an area completely devoid of ice was located inland in the vicinity of the Knox coast by fliers of the expedition's western task group reconnoitering in navy planes Monday, Capt. Robert S. Quackenbush, Jr., chief of the expeditionary staff, said.

Discovery of the lakes and mounds, which resembled chocolate drops from the air, raised the question as to whether the area might be warm enough to support year-round human settlements comfortably. Expeditionary leaders said they considered the discovery of greatest significance from the standpoints of geology and geography.

'Imposed' Peace Plan Set Aside

LONDON, (AP) — An American informant said Wednesday the United States had put aside, temporarily at least, Robert Murphy's idea of imposing an international "peace statute" on Germany rather than a formal peace treaty.

Murphy broached the idea in the conference of deputy foreign ministers preparing peace pacts for Germany and Austria. The American deputy said his goal was to save a future democractic government in Germany from criticism at home for signing a treaty.

Canada and Australia formally proposed the same plan.

A source close to Murphy said he referred the suggestion to the United States state department some time ago and had received neither approval nor disapproval. The informant said Murphy thus was proceeding on the theory that a conventional treaty would be signed.

Pioneer of Banff, J. Brewster Dies

CALGARY, (CP) — James Irvine Brewster, president of the Brewster Transport Co. Ltd., and pioneer Rocky mountain guide and outfitter, died suddenly at his home in Banff at midnight Tuesday, one day after his 65th birthday anniversary.

He was an interested spectator at the Banff winter sports over the week-end.

"Jim" Brewster grew up with Banff and no single individual played a more important part in transforming the village into a world-famous tourist resort. Starting in 1895, at the age of 13, with a modest pack outfit, he built up his interests until, at the time of his death, he was operating the biggest tourist concern in the Rockies.

Asks Soviet Intent On Atomic Secrets

LAKE SUCCESS, (AP) — Great Britain intends to ask assurances that the Soviet Union has no intention of trying to use proposed United Nations arms reduction machinery to obtain atomic secrets, the British U.N. delegate said Wednesday.

Warren R. Austin, United States representative on the U.N. security council, intimated Tuesday he believed Russian opposition to an American proposal to prohibit invasion of the atomic energy field by an arms commission resulted at least in part from such an intent.

Sir Alexander Cadogan, British delegate, told The Associated Press he would ask Russian delegate Gromyko for a specific statement Wednesday.

Falls 3 Storeys From Fire Escape

CALGARY, (CP)—James Langvie, Milo truck driver, suffered spinal injuries and possible internal hurts when he fell three storeys from a fire escape ladder at the rear of the Queen's hotel Tuesday. He landed on the paved lane.

Telephone wires broke Langvie's fall and may have saved him from more serious injury.

Towers Sees Economic Peril In Export Sales on Credit

OTTAWA, (CP) — Graham F. Towers, governor of the Bank of Canada, warned Wednesday "Canada cannot continue indefinitely to sell on credit in overseas markets while she is incurring a substantial cash deficit in her balance of payments with the United States."

Mr. Towers issued the warning in his annual report to Finance Minister Abbott on operations of the government-owned bank and in statements made prior to tabling the report in the commons.

Mr. Towers stressed the extent to which Canadian prosperity depended on foreign trade. He said he was not trying to paint a gloomy picture but rather a realistic one.

One of the principal factors in Canada's present prosperity was the high level of exports, one-third of which were financed in 1946 on credit.

Mr. Towers said it was in Canada's own interest to assist in the re-establishment of war-disrupted countries, because Canada's employment standard and living "so greatly depended" on export trade.

(Continued on Page 2, Col. 3)

Manahan Defeats Olsen Rink, 10-5

Twice winner of dominion premier curling honors, Cliff Manahan Wednesday took one step toward the curling crown won by Sedgewick's Billy Rose last year. He defeated E. B. Olsen 10-5 in the first game of a best-of-three series in the northern Alberta British Consols playdowns at the Royal rink.

The game was tied when the ninth end was completed. In the 10th end, Olsen lost both his rocks and Manahan counted three. He added two more in the 11th. As the house was kept clear in the 12th, play was suspended when Olsen saw it was impossible to overcome Manahan's lead.

Score by ends:

Manahan	001 101 110 32	10
Olsen	110 020 001 00	5

$60,000 Blaze Hits Westlock

WESTLOCK. — Fire discovered at midnight Tuesday destroyed a Main st. garage and did damage estimated at $60,000. Fourteen automobiles stored in the garage were saved by quick action of volunteers.

The garage, built in 1945 on Westlock's main street, was owned by Ray Hide. The building was valued at $30,000 and stocks of parts and accessories for cars and farm machinery, valued at $22,000, were wiped out. Cause of the fire was unknown early Wednesday.

Offices of the Westlock town council on second floor of the structure were destroyed, along with many of the town records. Also listed as total loss were premises of a photograph studio and a law office, which occupied space in the building.

Absence of wind aided volunteer fire-fighters in saving other buildings in the main business section.

Canada, U.S. Keep Full Defence Link

OTTAWA, (CP) — Prime Minister King disclosed in the commons Wednesday Canada and the United States have decided their national defence establishments shall, "to the extent authorized by law," continue to collaborate for peacetime joint security purposes.

25 Greeks Killed In Village Attack

ATHENS, (AP)— Heavily-armed leftist guerrillas, striking at a Greek village 10 miles from the Yugoslav border, killed 25 inhabitants, wounded 50 and seized 10, a press dispatch from Salonika said Tuesday night.

The leftists struck at Constantia, north of Mount Paikon, the dispatch said. Mortars were used by the attacking force. The wife of Starvros Euthimiades, a Populist party M.P., was among those seized, the dispatch said.

The attack was made while a United Nations commission was in Greece investigating Balkan disturbances.

Fly Food to 500 At Sanitarium

REGINA, (CP)— Ambulance planes rushed food to Fort San tuberculosis sanitarium about 40 miles northeast of Regina Tuesday when officials there reported they were almost out of necessities, also in short supply in hundreds of southern Saskatchewan communities.

Two aircraft of the provincial government service took meat, bread, flour, yeast and other articles to the 500 patients and staff at the hospital.

Elsewhere in the blizzard-bound region, commercial planes were moving supplies to small communities reporting serious shortages.

Regina's coal shortage eased somewhat with arrival of trains from Alberta, but only a few days' supply was contained in the shipment.

Public and separate schools in Regina will remain closed until next Monday. Schools have been open only one day since Feb. 3.

Milk was beginning to flow into the city again as some branch lines opened, but packers reported no deliveries of cattle.

Little progress in opening roads was reported. The 50-mile section between Regina and Moose Jaw was the longest stretch cleared.

TORONTO, (CP)— Improvement in snowbound southern Ontario's road situation is being reported hourly to headquarters of the department of highways here.

"But they are all stilled by the sudden ending of the career of such an outstanding public figure."

In an editorial June 1, 1943, welcoming Ernest Manning to the premiership, *The Journal* issued a warning. "The strong personality of the late premier only adds to the initial difficulties of his task, for as Today and Tomorrow, the Social Credit weekly, put it in a special editorial article paying tribute to Mr. Aberhart 'no one can take his place.' "

Aberhart had been premier for eight years. Despite *The Journal*'s suggestion, Manning had no trouble assuming the office and remained premier for the next quarter century.

While the Edmonton home front may have been thousands of miles from any real threat, there was still concern that the city might be vulnerable to an air raid.

On Thursday, June 18, 1942, *The Journal* published a 12-page supplement on an air raid drill that was planned for the following Sunday.

The supplement warned readers to take the drill very seriously, and was crammed with ads for everything from house paint – Protect Your Home with Sherwin-Williams – to a warning from Campbell's Furniture that Edmonton was closer than Vancouver to Tokyo, the Japanese capital.

"Even now our enemies may be studying maps of Edmonton, our airport, our bridges, the surrounding country. WE URGE YOU TO BE PREPARED," the furniture store cautioned.

The T. Eaton Co. offered wallboard suitable for quickly cutting into window-fitting sizes should a blackout be ordered. A 10-foot sheet sold for $1.70 and was buff-coloured, although it could be "painted if you wish for inside good looks."

When mock paratroopers threatened the airport and landed in Clarke Stadium, no detail was too small for *The Journal* to report. "Capt. Huff spent some minutes looking for an ARP (Air Raid Precaution) sticker to attach to someone's windshield. He found it stuck to the seat of his pants."

The war ignited fundamental social change as not only were women actively recruited into the armed forces, but by 1945 a million women were also working in offices and factories around the country. They were filling in for the men serving overseas, and while many would quit their jobs at war's end, many thousands continied to work outside the home.

Even as the war drew to a close, Mrs. Rex Eaton, the associate director of National Selective Service, told a Women's Canadian Club luncheon on Jan. 12, 1945, that there was a continuing shortage of women in the workplace. The shortage would likely continue into peacetime.

The war also brought with it the arrival of thousands of war brides, women who had fallen in love with Canadian troops and who now found themselves facing a new life in a strange new country.

One wonders whether they truly understood what awaited them.

When Christine Bourassa, a young British woman who met her husband, Robert, while he was at the training depot in Aldershot, arrived in Edmonton on Feb. 19, 1945, she was met by a *Journal* reporter because her husband Robert was unable to meet her train as he had resumed his career as a trapper north of Peace River.

Christine, accompanied by the Bourassa children, 18-month-old

***In 1944*:**
An ad copy chaser at *The Journal* makes $15 a week.

***Jan. 3, 1944*:**
Fifty male students and 28 female students failed in their Christmas examination at the University of Alberta and "are expected to seek other employment in which they can make a more successful contribution to the war effort," Dr. Robert Newton, university president, announced Monday.

***Jan. 4, 1945*:**
Edmonton's street railway system reports it served 32,100,255 fares in 1944.

***Feb. 22, 1945*:**
The Colonel Mewburn Pavilion veterans' hospital opens at the University Hospital.

***April 10, 1945*:**
The speed limit for trucks on Alberta highways is raised to 40 miles an hour.

June 16, 1945:
A. Balmer Watt retires after 33 years as associate editor and editor of *The Journal*. He becomes editor emeritus.

***July 14, 1945*:**
The Hudson's Bay store sells men's suits to returning war veterans for $29-55. Men returning to civilian

Edmonton Weather
24-hour forecast. Clear today and Tuesday, light winds, little change in temperature.

Edmonton Journal

'One of Canada's Great Newspapers'

FORTY-FIFTH YEAR * * TELEPHONE 25171 EDMONTON, ALBERTA, MONDAY, AUGUST 16, 1948 SINGLE COPY, 5 CENTS 22 PAGES

City To Ban Children's Gatherings

New Meeting With Molotov

Berliners Fear Red Vengeance

MOSCOW, (AP) — Envoys of Britain, the United States and France conferred again late Monday with Foreign Minister Molotov in the Kremlin.

The series of conferences started July 31.

The western diplomats are seeking a basis for talks to end the east-west differences and to solve the problem of blockaded Berlin.

Ambassador Walter Bedell Smith of the United States, Frank Roberts, special British envoy, and French Ambassador Yves Chataigneau left the British embassy and drove in a heavy rain to the Kremlin.

BERLIN, (AP) — Berlin's liberal democratic press declared Monday the Communists have prepared a purge list of hundreds of thousands of anti-Communists upon whom revenge would be taken if the Western Allies left the city.

The newspaper Montags Echo, said a Communist fifth column is working in the blockaded western sectors of Berlin, occupied by Britain, the United States and France.

"The Communist spy system has wormed its way into industrial workers' councils, into commerce, into postal and telegraph systems of Western Berlin and there makes systematic preparation for 'X-Day' —the day the Communists hope the Western Allies will leave Berlin," the liberal democratic newspaper said.

Berlin's anti-Communists urged the West to take a firm stand in the Big Four negotiations in Moscow, while German Communists prodded the elected city government of Berlin to quit.

The Montags Echo reported it had learned from Soviet sources here that Russian administrative policies in Germany — even on relatively minor questions — are now dictated directly from Moscow. It declared the Russian commander-in-chief here, Marshal Vassily D. Sokolovsky, had fallen into disfavor with the Kremlin because of his administration.

Ernst Reuter, whose election as lord mayor of Berlin was vetoed by the Russians in June, 1947, declared "there cannot and must not

(Continued on Page 3, Col. 1)

Pair Rescue Man As Canoe Capsizes

An unidentified man whose canoe tipped in the middle of the Saskatchewan River between the city and White Mud Creek Sunday afternoon was rescued by Charles B. Atkins, 10049 114 st., and Miss Evelyn Allen, 7918 Riverside drive.

Mr. Atkins reported to police Monday that he and Miss Allen were attracted by shouts and saw the man struggling in mid-stream. They paddled out in a canoe from the shore and found the man afloat in an inner tube, holding on to his submerged power-canoe.

Mr. Atkins said they brought the man to shore, and the canoe was carried downstream. The rescuers did not obtain the man's name, and a later attempt by a power boat to catch up to the drifting craft was unsuccessful.

American Officer Accused

U.S. Sees Red Spy Charge As Attempt 'To Cover Up'

WASHINGTON, (AP) — Russia's belated spy blast at a United States naval officer is viewed by officials here Monday as an attempt to cover up waning Moscow interest in the Kosenkina-Samarine school teacher cases.

Moreover, the state department insists that the espionage charge against Lieut. Robert Dreher is a deliberate Soviet frame-up.

The department disclosed that American Ambassador Walter Bedell Smith bluntly told Andre Vishinsky, Soviet deputy foreign minister, last April, that he considered the evidence against Dreher had been "arranged" with the connivance of the M.V.D. — Russia's famous secret police.

The Moscow press and radio made a tremendous fuss Sunday about the apprehension of the alleged American spy last April 23 at the very moment when he was receiving secret and "unauthorized" information from a Soviet customs official identified only by the mysterious designation "E."

Officials here immediately raised two questions:

Why had the Russians waited almost four months to break the case and then chosen a moment of great excitement here and abroad over the Kosenkina and Samarine incidents?

Also why should the customs official be designated only with the letter "E" in the public release if the Soviets considered the charges legitimate and were bringing legal action against him?

The Russian government considers any unauthorized dealings between a Soviet citizen and a foreigner to be an offence, and the release of official information in that way is an extremely grave crime in Soviet eyes.

State department officials tentatively concluded that the Soviet government is recognizing that it badly over-played its charges of

(Continued on Page 2, Col. 2)

Russian Teacher Remains 'Critical'

NEW YORK, (AP)—Mrs. Oksana Stepanovna Kosenkina, the 52-year-old Russian school teacher who leaped from a third-floor window of the Soviet consulate where she said she was being held a prisoner, was reported still in critical condition Monday at Roosevelt Hospital.

Mrs. Kosenkina has been technically under the protection of the United States government since she accepted a subpoena Saturday to testify before the house of representatives committee on un-American activities in its probe of alleged Communist spying in the United States.

It may be three months before she can appear before the committee.

Violent Storm Strikes Coast

VANCOUVER, (CP) — A freak lightning and windstorm caused extensive damage to British Columbia fruit crops during the week-end.

The storm swept the Okanagan Valley and the Kootenays late Sunday, disrupting telegraph and telephone communications with the east. Some communication channels were disrupted for five hours.

Hailstones the size of golf balls fell in the Nelson district where the storm lasted only eight minutes.

Where To Find It

Amusements, Theatres	10
Angelo Patri	13
Bridge	20
Comics	8, 16, 17, 18, 19, 20
Crossword Puzzle	20
District	5
Editorial	4
Financial	21
Off the Record	12
Radio	2?
Sydney Harris Article	7
Sport	8, 9, 10
They'll Do It Every Time	20
Uncle Ray" Corner	20
Want Ads	16, 17.18, 19
Women's	13, 14, 15

The Weather

(Issued by the Dominion Public) Weather Office at Edmonton)

Cool air pushing eastward across the mountains from British Columbia set off a large number of thunderstorms on the western prairies overnight. In most localities the rainfall was less than a 10th of an inch, but Jasper reported .83, Coronation .35, Calgary .29 and Saskatoon .26. However, skies have cleared again in Alberta and the clearing will spread into Saskatchewan Monday night. Bright sunny weather will be general in all regions on Tuesday with afternoon temperatures near the mid-August normal of 75. Overnight minimums in the high 40's or low 50's are forecast.

Estimated low tonight, 48 above.

Estimated high tomorrow, 76 above.

At Edmonton Tuesday, sun rises 6:16; sets 8:00.

Yesterday's maximum, 78 above.

Overnight low, 53 above.

Rainfall, .06 of an inch.

Other Readings

Vancouver	6? 54	Regina	84 63
Pr. Rupert	71 47	Winnipeg	80 53
Gr. Prairie	76 51	Toronto	79 57
Calgary	77 47	Ottawa	81 53
Lethbridge	85 42	Montreal	84 58
Med. Hat	89 60	Halifax	76 61

Transport Minister Chevrier And Family Spend Holiday At Jasper National Park

Hon. Lionel Chevrier, federal minister of transport, and his family are at Jasper Park Lodge, following the minister's tour of northland air and weather stations in connection with landing system devices which will make landings and takeoffs of aircraft safe under virtually any weather conditions. He is enjoying relaxation, the scenic beauty of Jasper Park, and bicycling with his children. Left to right are Mrs. Chevrier, Adele, Robert, Marie, the minister, Bernard, Lucie and John. Mrs. Chevrier, with the children will visit the Pacific Coast before returning home.

Eight Athletes Will Not Return To Red Homes

LONDON, (CP)—At least eight Olympic athletes have decided against returning to their Communist-ruled homelands. Two of them, Czech swimmers, have indicated they want ultimately to go to Canada.

Jiri Kovar, 23-year-old architectural student from Jicin, Bohemia, and Jiri Linhart, 24-year-old Prague electro-mechanical engineer, have asked through Czech relief organizations about going to the dominion.

However, the Czech committee for political refugees told the Canadian Press they will be remaining in England for the time being. Their decision not to go home was taken on political grounds.

The two Czechs and three Hungarians disclosed Sunday that they intended to stay in England, but finally one of the Hungarians later went back to Hungary. Monday four more Czech athletes decided against returning home.

Except in the case of Kovar and Linhart, the Czech committee withheld the names for fear of retribution against relatives still in Czechoslovakia.

"But six Czech athletes who came here for the Olympic games definitely have decided against returning," a committee spokesman said. "Two of the athletes are swimmers. The other four were on the rowing team."

The Hungarian Olympic committee admitted that two Hungarian swimmers, Oszkar Csuvik, 23, and Elmer Szatmari, 22, are staying in England with British permission. The Hungarian committee insisted the Csuvik and Szatmari were not political refugees, but only "two adventurous young men" who want to make their living as professional swimmers.

Army Exercise Begins In North

ENROUTE TO DAWSON CREEK, B.C.—A troop train carrying servicemen from active and reserve force army units from Alberta and British Columbia left Edmonton late Sunday afternoon for Dawson Creek and the start of exercise North II, which will take the troops 1,000 miles up the Alaska Highway.

Designed as a tactical exercise to familiarize officers of the two western provinces with problems dealing with defence of the north country, the scheme will last for two weeks. Whitehorse, Yukon, is the goal.

Maj.-Gen. M. H. H. Penhale, G.O.C. Western Command, is in charge of the exercise, assisted by Brig.

(Continued on Page 3. Col. 3)

Fighting Grows Heavier

Claim Arabs Fire On Jews

JERUSALEM, (AP)—The Israeli army said Arab snipers fired on Jewish traffic Monday on the Judean mountain road two miles west of Jerusalem.

The report followed a day in which Jerusalem resounded to the heaviest fighting since the second United Nations truce started four weeks ago.

The army announcement said there was skirmishing in four areas of Jerusalem and asserted that "Arab military activity continued steadily in the last 24 hours."

Mortar and heavy machinegun fire resounded throughout the Jerusalem area Sunday only 48 hours after the deadline for a new truce. Count Folke Bernadotte, the United Nations mediator, had asked both sides not to fire after the early morning hours of Friday.

The Jews, listing five casualties, said the Arabs were responsible.

(A spokesman for the Trans-Jordan Arab Legion said in Amman that the Jews attacked Legion forward posts.)

Montreal-born Dr. Bernard Joseph, Israeli military governor of Jerusalem, said the Jews reserve the right to self-defence. But he said his command had re-issued instructions not to open fire and not to reply to enemy sniping in order that U. N. observers might establish responsibility for violations.

In other developments:

1. Brig. John Glubb Pasha, British commander of the Arab Legion, said in Paris that nearly 500,000 Arabs "driven from their homes in Palestine will die from starvation" unless something is done before winter.

2. A group of 355 Jews, identified by the French press agency as Exodus 1947 refugees, arrived at Bandol, France, in special trains. The agency said the Jews are part of those who sailed without immigration visas for the Holy Land in the Exodus 1947 from southern France 13 months ago. Royal Naval warships intercepted the vessel and the refugees were sent back to France.

Fireman Injured In Train Wreck

Floods in the Rocky Mountains caused further heavy damage early Monday when a C.N.R. freight train plunged into a washout at Hinton, about 40 miles east of Jasper. One crewman was injured and the engine and seven boxcars badly damaged.

The injured man is J. Donnelly, Jasper, a fireman on the engine, whose leg was crushed as the train broke through weakened rails. He was reported to be under treatment in hospital at Jasper.

Officials in Edmonton said a "flash" flood had caused the washout, which will delay main line traffic at least until midnight Monday. Crews were dispatched to the scene immediately, to clear the wreckage and repair the damageed track.

It is the second accident on C.N.R. tracks west of Edmonton within a week. Officials here said traffic between Edmonton and Vancouver has been disrupted by floods and high water since the spring breakup. The said in loss of time and damage to property, the cost would be "tremendous."

Westbound transcontinental trains arriving here will continue to Hinton where passengers will be transferred across the washout in cars and buses. No. 1 transcontinental left Edmonton on time but the No. 3 section was held about two hours.

1,058 Vote Here At Advance Poll

Voting at the advance poll in Edmonton for the provincial general election Tuesday resulted in 1,058 votes being cast, officials reported Monday. In the 1944 general election, the advance vote here totalled 1,161.

Saturday afternoon and evening, the poll was crowded with persons desiring to vote because they will be out of the city election day. Votes cast during the afternoon totalled 287, with an additional 192 at night. The poll also was open Thursday and Friday.

Mrs. A. V. Carter was the deputy returning officer in charge of the poll.

At Calgary, 1,130 votes were cast at the advance poll during the three-day period.

Inquest Continued In Traffic Death

MEDICINE HAT, (CP) — Inquest into the traffic death of Albert Olsen, 16, will be continued Monday night. The inquest into the death, which occurred Friday when a truck in which Olsen was riding, overturned, pinning the boy to the ground, opened Saturday with formal identification of the body. Earlier it was reported that Wilbert Knodel, 17, driver of the truck, had been killed and Olsen injured.

Mystery Surrounds Grim Discovery

KETCHIKAN, Alaska, (AP) — A coast guard party reported Sunday it has found the scattered remains of what appear to be six bodies in an airplane wreckage on Cape Chacon at the southern tip of Prince Wales Island.

Searchers identified the plane as a Royal Canadian Air Force Hudson bomber. They said it appeared the wreckage had been there for several years.

An Ellis Airlines plane spotted the wreckage Saturday. The coast guard group, headed by Cmdr. John Glatz hiked in Sunday.

Glatz reported the wreckage was strewn over a large area. He said the remains of the passengers also were widely scattered, but it appeared that six died in the crash.

The R.C.A.F. stopped using Hudsons late in the war, indicating the plane may have gone down as early as 1939 or 1940. R.C.A.F. officers in Vancouver and Northwest Air Command at Edmonton were checking the list of missing Hudsons.

ATTLEE IS GRANDFATHER

BRISTOL, England, (Reuters) — Clement Attlee, Britain's 65-year-old prime minister became a grandfather Sunday when his eldest daughter, Janet, gave birth to a girl here. The former Miss Attlee married Harold Shipton, a local engineer, last November.

Thugs Invade Lake Vessel, Abduct Four

HAMILTON, (CP)—A boarding party of about 15 men captured four crew members of the freighter Westmount early Sunday and, police said, forced them to dog-trot ahead of a jeep for several miles through city streets before releasing them. If they stopped, they were beaten, the seamen said.

The Westmount is owned by the Canada Steamship Lines, one of four companies against which the Canadian Seamen's Union called a strike some time ago to force them to sign new bargaining agreements. The ship was lying at the Steel Company of Canada docks here.

The four seized seamen, one of whom was injured in the scuffle, identified themselves as members of Pat Sullivan's rival Canadian Lake Seamen's Union.

Police said the raiders, some carrying clubs and one hooded boarded the ship about 6:00 a.m. The freighter's captain, W. H. Montgomery, said the affair was over "in two or three minutes" and it all took place at the aft-end of the ship.

"The boarding party carried clubs but they did not come forward as the steam hose was manned at that end," he said.

Briton Accused In Bomb Outrage

JERUSALEM, (AP)—The Israeli government Monday accused Frederick Sylvester, a British utility engineer already facing espionage charges, of helping plan the Ben Yehuda st. bombing here last Feb. 22. More than 50 persons died in the blast.

Formal charges against Sylvester and William Hawkins, also a former Jerusalem electric corporation official, were read in court at the opening of their hearing. Both were charged on nine counts of obtaining and broadcasting military information to the Arabs.

Sylvester, in addition, was charged with artillery spotting, having an unlicensed transmitter and with "conspiracy to deposit explosives in Ben Yehuda st. calculated to cause death to persons therein." The hearing is expected to continue all week.

Three other Britons arrested with Sylvester and Hawkins were released after a hearing in Tel Aviv a week ago. They have been warned by Irgun Zvai Leumi to leave Israel. Irgun seized all five July 6 during what was called a spy hunt.

ENTRIES AND SELECTIONS FOR TUESDAY'S HORSE RACES AND SELECTIONS FOR MONDAY'S RACES ON PAGE 6.

Fought British Five Years

Sheik's Band Of Arabs With Jewish Stern Gang

JERUSALEM, (CP)—Sheik Yussuf Abu Gosh, 27-year-old Arab village chieftain, Sunday said he has commanded a group of 70 Arab fighters with the Jewish "fighters for the freedom of Israel," the so-called Stern Gang.

At a press conference, the sheik disclosed he was the first Arab to fight with the Jewish underground against both the British troops and Arabs in Palestine

The sheik said his group "fought the British actively for the last five years in co-operation with the Jewish members of the Stern group."

The sheik gave as his reason for joining the Stern group his conviction that "the British were in Palestine for their own ends and not to promote peace among the people or to do constructive work."

(In Tel Aviv, it was announced that a group of Circassians, a tribe originating in the Caucasus area, who are longtime residents of the Galilee area of Palestine, will join the Jewish army tomorrow. The Circassians, who are mostly Mohammedans, will take an oath of allegiance to the Jewish army. A Bedouin tribe in Galilee has been fighting with the Jewish army since the beginning of Palestine hostilities.)

Polio Still Increasing

May Delay School Opening

All Edmonton children under 16 years of age will be forbidden to attend swimming pools, theatres, schools and all public gatherings while the threat of poliomyelitis hangs heavy over the city, if a recommendation by Dr. G. M. Little, medical office of health, is accepted at Tuesday's special meeting of the Edmonton Board of Health.

Such action already has been taken in Mayerthorpe and Claresholm. A recommendation that such bans be enforced was sent to local boards of health in Alberta Friday by the provincial health department.

Monday, when Edmonton's 22nd polio case this year and the 105th case for the province was reported, it seemed certain the Edmonton Health Board would accept Dr. Little's recommendation without argument in view of possibilities in Alberta of an epidemic of infantile paralysis.

If the recommendation is adopted at Tuesday afternoon's meeting it will become effective immediately in Edmonton, under powers given to the local board of health by the Provincial Health Act.

Procedure, however, probably would be for the board to make an official announcement of the ban, effective Wednesday.

The announcement would bar children under 16 from theatres, swimming pools, Sunday schools and any other types of schools in operation during the ban, picnics and parties of all sorts. It would include all types of public gatherings, even band concerts and the like.

School Question

If city health officials still feel that the polio threat exists in Edmonton when the time comes to open public and separate schools here in the first week of September, the ban would keep all children affected out of school until officially lifted.

Some hope was expressed Monday by Dr. Little that such a ban might be necessary only for a short period, if evidence corroborates an opinion that possibly the peak for the disease has arrived in Edmonton at an early date this summer.

"The upward curve of the disease seems to have arrived earlier than usual this season," said Dr. Little. "It is possible with 22 cases already reported, the peak for polio may already have been reached here. But this a promise that cannot be taken for granted at this time, making the ban still necessary in my opinion."

Forecasting Difficult

He stated that in 20 years, epidemic behavior of polio in Edmonton had been so erratic that "it is difficult to forecast" the start and the end of a peak polio period for any one year. Usually the peak period is during the last three weeks of August for Edmonton.

Three new cases were reported to provincial health authorities on Monday. Two of them are in Edmonton and district, a girl of five years and a man of 25 years. The other is a boy of four years at Hondu, near Smith.

Dr. Little said banning public gatherings of children under 16 years probably would be worth while, as medical authorities had reason to believe that the polio disease spreads through personal contact. "It would not disorganize any community to any great extent," he stated.

Ald. Gariepy is chairman of the Edmonton board of health.

Forrestal Talks Said 'Profitable'

By H. R. Hardy
(From The Journal's Ottawa Bureau)

OTTAWA. — "We had a very profitable, interesting and useful exchange of views on common defence problems," said James Forrestal, United States secretary of defence, at a brief press conference at noon Monday, following a two-hour meeting with the defence committee of the cabinet.

Mr. Forrestal said that he hoped for a continuation of close co-operation on defence in the future.

Hon. Brooke Claxton, minister of national defence, said that he felt the defence committee meeting Monday morning was one of the most satisfactory conferences of its kind ever held between representatives of the two governments concerned.

He "foresaw no difficulty whatever" in the United States and Canada ironing out the problem on military bases in Newfoundland which the United States has operated under lease for sometime past. "It is still too early to be precise about the future arrangements as to Newfoundland bases because the status of Newfoundland is in the process of change," he added.

Mr. Forrestal wanted to know if Canada had any official secrets act, and Mr. Claxton explained that it was part of the criminal code, and that the Russian spy inquiry had been handled under the act.

Mr. Forrestal and Mr. Claxton indicated that problems of "standardization" of military weapons as between the United States and Canada are being studied constantly. Mr. Claxton added that it is too early as yet to say whether Canadian weapons will follow the British or American patterns.

Any Spies Here? Queries Forrestal

By H. R. Hardy
(From The Journal's Ottawa Bureau)

OTTAWA. — When James Forrestal, United States secretary of defence, met Canadian newspapermen at an informal press conference Monday, he looked over the crowd and then quipped, "any spies here?"

In the group was Simeon Shcherbatykh, correspondent for the Tass News Agency who looked a bit embarrassed.

However, Brooke Claxton, Canada's defence minister, who was present at the conference, proved himself an able diplomat.

"There are some Russians here," he said, "but they are all friends."

Went For Visit

Object Of Week-End Search, Child Found With Uncle

A 10-year-old girl who had been the object of an intensive week-end search by R.C.M.P., city police and family after she was missed from an incoming bus Saturday, was located Monday.

Vera Lindbeck, formerly of Viking, was brought to Edmonton by her uncle who had taken her to his farm at Rollyview when he saw her walking in the city Saturday. Police said the girl's uncle was told late Sunday than an alarm was out for the girl.

He had understood that the girl's mother was coming to the city Monday from Viking and intended to meet her in the city with the girl.

The girl was put on a bus at Viking Saturday morning by her father, and was to have been met in Edmonton by Robert Herbert, 10356 107 st., a friend of the family. Mr Herbert told police that he was a few minutes late for the bus arrival and did not see the girl in the bus depot.

The bus driver R. W. Pickard, 10831 112 st., said he remembered the girl getting off the bus here. Det. Inspt. Bert Petheram, head of the city detective department, who is working closely with Chief Constable Jennings on the case, on Monday appealed to any person who rode on the Viking-Edmonton bus to the city Saturday to report to his department. He said there was a chance that someone might have noticed which way the girl walked or left the bus depot.

Another 10-year-old girl of the Thorhild district was reported missing Monday morning according to R.C.M.P.

She is Norma Schryver, who left her parents' farm at 8.30 p.m. Saturday and was not located Sunday. She is described as being fair small for her age and was wearing a sleeveless yellow dress pink coat, brown oxfords and yellow ankle socks.

Thanksgiving Day Expected Oct. 11

By H. R. Hardy
(From The Journal's Ottawa Bureau)

OTTAWA. — Officials of the department of the secretary of state said Monday that while no proclamation had yet been issued, it is expected that Thanksgiving will be observed on the second Monday in October, namely Oct. 11.

Thanksgiving Day is set by proclamation each year.

LABOR PIONEER DIES

CALGARY, (CP)—One of the first presidents of the Calgary Trades and Labor Council, 83-year-old James E. Worsley, died Sunday. He had been prominent in labor movements since 1890.

Sunday Harvesting Saves Rain-Soaked British Crop

Worst Storm In Years

LONDON, (CP) — It was Pitchfork Sunday on countless English farms.

At Sutton Scotney, in Hampshire, floodlights burned all night while horse carts and trucks brought in storm-damaged crops from miles around. The grain was placed on layers of trays and hot air from oil-fired furnaces fanned over it.

Elsewhere, thousands of workers toiled until dark repairing some of the damage done by the wettest August on record. Where the sun and dry weather permitted, harvesters turned out and restacked the sodden sheaves and reaped flattened oat and barley fields by hand.

Harvest combines and mowing machines operated in some districts for the first time in two weeks.

Only in Lincolnshire, with 200,000 acres of wheat still to be brought in was there no Sunday harvesting.

Meanwhile, army reconnaissance teams toured the desolate flood areas of southeast Scotland planning to restore communications and services to the stricken border county of Berwickshire. Bailey bridges and other engineering equipment were moved up and troops were expected to begin work Monday.

In the Berwickshire and East Lothian areas eight important spans were swept away by the swirling floods that followed the heavy rains Thursday night, said to be the worst in 70 years.

Rivers in the English-Scottish border country returned to normal after rampaging through many miles of lowland, drowning hundreds of head of livestock and washing thousands of tons of stacked food grains and fodder into the North Sea.

Yvonne and seven-month-old Tina, certainly seemed confident in her interview. "Mrs. Bourassa feels quite equal to any demands life in Canada may make upon her.

"I'm quite prepared to set traps and catch animals, too, if my husband needs my help," said the plucky Mrs. Bourassa.

Edmonton faced an acute housing shortage which began during the war and continued after. Everyone who came to the city, war brides, returning veterans, troops stationed here and even post-war oil workers, faced the same dilemma. There was simply no place to live.

The paper offered up opinions on the subject starting with an editorial from the summer of 1942. "Edmonton must remember that some other centres in Canada are in a worse position with regard to housing. Halifax, for example, is trying to house about twice as many people as it can accommodate decently. So it is certain Edmonton must wait its turn."

By the spring of 1943, there were almost 2,000 people on a waiting list at the Edmonton emergency accommodation bureau, and *The Journal* called on their readers' loyalty to country.

"Anyone with a spare or empty room in their homes would be doing a patriotic service if they rented them," the newspaper said.

By the following year, the newspaper's patience had run out. Part of the problem, the paper said, was that families of men serving overseas were crowding into the city. "It was last November that the federal prices board announced that 'families of service men and civilian workers are continuing to move into these areas,' and that 'all unnecessary moving about of families should stop.' Unfortunately, 'should' is little heeded; 'must' is the required verb, and even then enforcement is necessary."

And classified ads had a desperate tone: "American pilot, wife and year-old infant desire suitable 2-bedroom suite or house in good neighbourhood. Will pay well. Please phone 81916."

And though *The Journal* wrote dozens of editorials on the housing shortage, the problem remained insoluble until the city turned its post-war attention to providing basic services to the suburbs that had been part of the land boom almost a generation before.

It was in this decade that *The Journal* started using bylines on stories to identify writers who became more familiar to the paper's readers over the coming years. Longtime sports reporter Don Fleming made his debut; Hal Pawson, who eventually became sports editor, arrived after seeing wartime service in the Royal Canadian Air Force; and Art Evans began writing the whimsical columns that entertained readers for the next 30 years.

As always, sports mattered. Sports editor George Mackintosh wrote a daily column called "The Sporting Periscope," commenting on everything from the success of the Waterloo Mercurys in their bid for the 1950 World Hockey Championship to the agreement baseball promoter John Ducey signed with the city at the close of the '40s.

The paper also hired Pat Hollingsworth, one of the first women sportswriters in the country, who wrote a regular column entitled "Feminine Flashes."

And it was at the start of the decade that the sports department lamented the passing of one of the city's sporting institutions.

life have priority certificates for clothing.

***July 17, 1945*:**
Edmonton's civic census shows a population of 111,745.

***Aug. 12, 1945*:**
The Loyal Edmonton Regiment holds a memorial service in Holland for more than 350 unit members killed in the Second World War.

***Aug. 16, 1945*:**
Bread costs eight cents a loaf in Edmonton Safeway stores.

***Aug. 28, 1945*:**
Alberta's monthly hard liquor allowance is increased to 52 ounces from a wartime limit of 13 ounces. The wine and beer rations remain at 26 ounces and 24 pints each.

***Oct. 6, 1945*:**
Thousands of Edmontonians line the city's streets to welcome the troop train bringing the Loyal Edmonton Regiment home from the Second World War.

***Nov. 7, 1945*:**
Harry Ainlay of the Civic Democratic Alliance is elected mayor of Edmonton.

***In 1946*:**
A *Journal* compositor makes $35 a month.

UNTIL HE COMES BACK!
BUY
VICTORY BONDS

NA-1623-2 Glenbow Archives

"It's curtain time for the Grads," read the opening paragraph of a story on April 11, 1940.

Percy Page, the school principal and the Grads' only coach, had been elected as an Independent member of the provincial legislature and simply didn't have the time necessary to be an effective coach, he said.

Sportswriter Joseph Dwyer wrote a tribute to the team and its coach: "There's many a city below the border that greatly would have enjoyed being home to Coach Page. But he turned down tempting offers to stay where he likes to be. Edmonton is grateful for it and so are the girls who came under his teaching. The names of Page and the Grads will be green when Aklavik is a city."

The Grads played their last game against a squad from Chicago in June 1940, and more than 6,000 Edmontonians came out to watch and cheer and bid them farewell. To no one's surprise, the Grads won.

As for Page, he was appointed lieutenant governor in 1959, serving six years in that office. Page died on March 2, 1973.

The passing of the Grads was sad to be sure, but it had been a decade marked by much sadder stories by far: war, the Bomb, the continuing threat of a Cold War between former allies becoming a hot one. The end of the decade brought with it the terrible knowledge that, for the first time in history, humanity had the power to obliterate itself.

That sobering fact, however, didn't stop revellers in 1949 from ringing in the new decade much like the parties that greeted the 1940s.

More than 300 couples wore silly hats again as they danced the night away at the Macdonald Hotel before being served a midnight supper. Others gathered at the popular Trocadero Ballroom downtown on 103rd Street, a half-block north of Jasper Avenue, to hear bandleader Bob Lyon bring in the New Year. The Mounties again had a full-dress affair at their barracks and the Edmonton Garrison Officers' Mess hosted 125 couples at the Prince of Wales Armouries on 104th Street and 108th Avenue.

Many of them made it to the legislature the next day as well, after all, the lieutenant-governor's levee was a long-standing tradition.

While the decade just ending had been tragic for millions and tumultuous for millions more around the world, a page 1 story on New Year's Eve in 1949 fairly glowed with optimism.

It was the best-ever year in Edmonton's history, the paper said. The population had grown to 150,000, up more than 10 per cent from 1948.

City Hall had issued a record-setting $40 million in building permits, and more than 30 miles of new sanitary sewers, eight miles of storm sewers and 45 miles of newly paved streets were being built to help solve the housing shortage. It was enough to make a businessman's buttons pop.

Nevertheless, the world outside Canada's borders was a dangerous place. Premier Manning's front-page New Year's message made his feelings clear. "The peoples of many countries have suffered cruel hardships and oppression during the past year and face the new with little hope of early deliverance from the ruthless tyranny of Godless totalitarianism.

"To be realists we must recognize that the one and only hope for lasting security, peace and individual freedom is inseparably bound up with individual and national acceptance of the true Christian way of life."

***Jan. 13, 1946*:**
A shortage of hockey sticks across Canada threatens to postpone league play in some Western Canada cities. The equipment shortfall is blamed on labour shortages in the last year of the Second World War that led to reduced wood cuts and lumber production.

***May 30, 1946*:**
***Journal* printers go on strike in sympathy for colleagues in Winnipeg. Publication of the paper continues without interruption.**

***June 25, 1946*:**
Edmontonians pay $1.65 to see Duke Ellington and his orchestra at the Arena.

***July 8, 1946*:**
Edmonton's civic census shows a population of 114,976. Later in the year, the Dominion Bureau of Statistics reports Edmonton's population is 109,997 compared with Calgary's 98,101.

***Sept. 4, 1946*:**
Edmonton's Clarence Campbell becomes president of the NHL, a post he holds until 1977.

Weather Forecast
Partly Cloudy, Warm

Edmonton Journal

'One of Canada's Great Newspapers'

THIRTY-NINTH YEAR ** EDMONTON, ALBERTA, THURSDAY, AUGUST 20, 1942 SINGLE COPY, 5 CENTS 20 PAGES

Canucks Carried Attack Right Into Dieppe

King Announces Manpower Control Plans

Use Services Where Needed, Said Intention

Says Government Plans to Make Full Use Womanpower Also

NEED JOB PERMITS

By C. R. Blackburn
(Canadian Press Staff Writer)

OTTAWA, Aug. 20.—Prime Minister King Wednesday night announced proposed new measures of control over manpower and womanpower designed to place "all but the very old, the very young and the disabled" behind the war effort.

Mr. King, speaking over the C.B.C., declared the government's policy was that "every man and woman capable of performing some form of war service should undertake the service for which he or she may be best qualified and which the demands of war require."

To this end he said controls would be exercised so that, "after a fixed period," unemployed persons may be required to accept any work for which there is special need.

Mr. King said use of manpower

(Partial Text of Prime Minister King's speech on Page 3.)

for non-war purposes was essential up to a point, but beyond the necessity of meeting minimum requirements it was non-essential.

"The government, accordingly, has decided that non-essential civilian activities should be curtailed or eliminated," he said, and added that the Wartime Prices and Trade board had been directed to take the steps necessary to this end.

Mr. King opened his broadcast with a reference to the part played by Canadians in Wednesday's raid on Dieppe, and said "we were proud to hear that our troops had a foremost place" in that action.

But, he said news of the raid should not destroy "our sense of perspective" and declared that "we

(Continued on Page 3, Col. 1)

Confident Canada Will Meet Demand

Confidence that the national War Finance committee will reach its goal of two billion dollars in voluntary savings was expressed Thursday by Dr. M. M. McOrdum of Ottawa, member of the committee, who spoke at the luncheon meeting of the Rotary club in the Macdonald.

Introduced by R. E. Staples, Dr. McOrdum said announcement of the new budget had at first acted against the committee's efforts, but now every worker on the committee feels that whatever amount is named by the government, will be achieved.

"Canada is really in this war, despite the talk of apathy. There is no easy way to win a war or to pay for a war," the speaker declared. "To finance this war, we are prepared to be hurt in our pockets, but what he give is peanuts in comparison to what our boys and girls in active service are giving.

"I ask each man and woman in Canada to feel a member of the National War Finance committee. We are faced with an unprecedented demand for money and one-half must come by voluntary loans.

"We are already on a campaign to conserve present holdings for it is vitally necessary that people hold on to the investments they have made.

"There will be another war loan drive in the fall, probably in October, but my present tour of western cities is primarily earmarked for organization.

"We are not prepared in this fight

(Continued on Page 14, Col. 5)

Where To Find It

Amusements, Theatres	7
Bridge	13
Logan Clendening, M.D.	13
Comics	8, 16, 17
Crossword Puzzle	19
District	18
Editorial	4
Financial	8
Off the Record	3
Radio	11
Serial Story	19
Sport	8, 7
They'll Do It Every Time	10
Uncle Ray's Corner	19
Want Ads	16, 17, 18
Women's	12, 12

The Weather

Edmonton Temperatures

Yesterday's maximum, 81.

Overnight low, 52.

At Edmonton Friday sun rises 6:22, sets 8:49.

Rainfall at airport, :08; rainfall in Highlands: .10.

Temperatures Elsewhere

Highest temperatures from 6:30 p.m. Tuesday to 6:30 p.m. Wednesday; lowest temperatures from 6:30 p.m. Wednesday to 6:30 a.m. Thursday:

	H.	L.		H.	L.
Kenora	81	57	Pr. Albert	81	56
Winnipeg	81	55	Battleford	83	60
Brandon	82	53	S. Current	86	60
Dauphin	80	48	Med. Hat	[illegible]	62
Regina	85	54	Lethbridge	92	65
M. Jaw	88	56	Calgary	85	55
Saskatoon	86	59	Edmonton	81	52

Forecasts

Alberta—Partly cloudy and somewhat cooler Thursday with scattered showers, Friday fair.

Peace River district—Partly cloudy and moderately warm Thursday and Friday.

Gave Protection to Commando Troops

FLT. LT. WHITHAM

FLT. SGT. MATHESON

Taking part in the attack on Dieppe Wednesday were at least three Edmonton airmen—Flt. Lt. James Whitham, son of Mr. and Mrs. C. H. Whitham, 11121 125 st.; Flt. Sgt. Douglas Matheson, son of Mrs. Eva Matheson, 10125 125 st., and Flt. Sgt. Sydney Mills. Flt. Sgt. Mills is a brother of J. Mills, now of Onoway.

City Airmen Help Provide Cover During Dieppe Attack

Aid in Bagging 91 German Planes; Many More "Probables"

ACTION IS DESCRIBED

By Alan Randal
(Canadian Press Staff Writer)

LONDON, Aug. 20.—Canadian airmen protecting their own troops from enemy air assault for the first time gave the dominion's attack force in the Battle of Dieppe the greatest aerial cover ever provided, it was indicated Thursday.

Flt.-Sgt. Mills

(Among the pilots taking part in the action were Flt. Lt. James Witham, and Flt. Sgt. Sydney Mills and Flt. Sgt. Douglas Matheson, all of Edmonton.)

Flying with the R.A.F., Spitfire and army co-operation squadrons of the R.C.A.F. formed a big proportion of the trans-channel shuttle service during the operations Wednesday.

Some made two or three trips, pausing only long enough at their home base to refuel and reload.

While Canadian losses were not announced—it is known Allied losses were 98 planes while the Nazis lost 91—the Canadian victory score stood at nine German aircraft destroyed and many "probables."

But these were just early figures on the Canadians' part in this amazing triumph over the German air force in French skies—amazing from the Canadian and Allied point of view because the losses were so nearly equal, whereas the Germans lost four and five to one in the Battle of Britain.

It is expected the Canadians' tally will rise as reports are checked and double-checked. It is likely that

(Continued on Page 2, Col. 5)

Hollander Captured In Dieppe Attack

NEW YORK, Aug. 20.—B.B.C. said Thursday that one prisoner captured in the Dieppe commando raid was a Hollander who had been sent with a draft of reinforcements to the Dieppe area. The broadcast was heard here.

The prisoner said he had been forced into the German army, but gave himself up as soon as he had a chance.

Brazil Seizes Nazi Hostages

Sixth Brazilian Steamer Sunk by U-Boat Off Coast

SPIES SAID ACTIVE

RIO DE JANEIRO, Aug. 20.—All Germans except diplomats who had embarked on the exchange ships Bage and Cyaba were ordered held as hostages Thursday by President Getulio Vargas shortly after the sinking of the sixth Brazilian ship in recent days was announced.

The ships already were filled with German nationals, ready to sail for Lisbon in exchange for Brazilian nationals. The voyages had been postponed earlier in the week when a crisis arose over the sinking of five Brazilian ships by Axis submarines, claiming the lives of perhaps 600 persons including Brazilian troops.

The sixth U-boat victim, announced Thursday, was the coastal steamer Jecy.

It was sent to the bottom a few miles off the northeast coast after all aboard were ordered off in lifeboats.

One high official of the government navigation line declared Thursday that the sinkings, which brought Brazil into undeclared conflict with the Axis, were the result of "brazen operation of Nazi spies who informed on planned troop movements."

Ex-Envoys to U.S. Arrive in Japan

TOKIO, Aug. 20.—The liners Asama Maru and Conto Verde reached Yokahama Thursday with 1,421 Japanese repatriates, mainly from the United States, exchanged from Americans taken from the Orient to Portuguese East Africa by the same liners.

Admiral Nomura, who was Japan's ambassador to Washington, and Saburo Kurusu, special envoy to Washington when the Pacific war broke out, were among the passengers.

Greek Steamship Sunk by Jap "Sub"

NEW YORK, Aug. 20.—The Australian radio said Thursday a 10,000-ton Greek steamship which one day earlier had sighted a blazing United States vessel, was sunk by a Japanese submarine 40 miles from Noumea, in New Caledonia. The broadcast was heard here.

An Australian submarine chaser picked up the Greek vessel's crew eight hours after they had taken to the boats.

Downed 100 Nazis In Convoy Attack

CAIRO, Aug. 20.—The R.A.F. announced Wednesday night that about 100 Axis planes were known to have been shot down or were listed as probably destroyed during attacks on the recent British convoy moving through the Mediterranean to Malta.

BANK CLEARINGS

Edmonton bank clearings for the week ending Thursday were $6,202,826, an increase of $704,492 over the $5,498,434 cleared in same week of last year.

Say Initiative Taken by Russ On Four Fronts

Heavy Losses Inflicted on Nazis in Central Sectors

KRASNODAR IS LOST

By Henry C. Cassidy
(Associated Press Staff Writer)

MOSCOW, Aug. 20.—The Red army has taken the initiative in battles developing on four key central Russian fronts along the 400 miles from Bryansk to Lake Ilmen while holding doggedly before Stalingrad and in the Caucasus, battlefront dispatches reported Thursday.

Centres of the Russian attack were listed as the Bryansk front, 210 miles southwest of Moscow; the salient 130 miles west of Moscow in the Vyazma area; the Kalinin-Rzhev salient, 130 miles northwest of the capital; and the Lake Ilmen front south of Leningrad.

(This was the first specific mention of Red army offensives on these fronts in Russian dispatches, although German communiques for days have told of desperate resistance there by Nazi forces hurled onto the defensive by strong Soviet attacks.)

No details of the central campaigns were given, but the Russians said they had taken a heavy toll of garrison forces left to man the central and northern battleline while the Nazis massed their greatest strength for the Don bend and Caucasus offensive.

"Great losses were suffered by the Germans on the Bryansk, western, Kalinin and northwestern fronts where the initiative in active military operations belongs to our troops," said Red Star, army newspaper.

In the south, where the Germans concentrated newly-reinforced troop and air strength, the Russians said some Axis troops had forced a crossing in the elbow of the Don in their

(Continued on Page 2, Col. 3)

See Decision Soon On Alaska Railway

VANCOUVER, Aug. 20.—Decision by the United States government regarding the building of a railway to Alaska is expected within a month, Premier Hart of British Columbia said here Thursday after his return from Edmonton where he took part in a conference discussing possible routes for such a project.

Mr. Hart said he and public works and engineering officials attended the Edmonton meeting "to explain advantages of the British Columbia route" to United States army officers now making an investigation. Representatives of the Canadian National Railways and the Alberta government attended, the latter to advocate construction of a route that would link up with Northern Alberta Railway facilities.

Announce Identity Of Crash Victims

LETHBRIDGE, Aug. 20.—Names of the three airmen from No. 8 bombing and gunnery school here killed Wednesday in a Fairey Battle crash during training operations were released Thursday.

The crash victims were Sgt. Pilot L. R. Low, Foxwarren, Man., whose wife resides in Lethbridge; LAC. G. G. Morin, whose mother lives at St. Boniface, Man.; LAC. R. B. Sandman, whose father resides at Jarvie, Alberta.

ICELAND RAIDED AGAIN

REYKJAVIK, Iceland, Aug. 20.—German planes bombed and machinegunned a British trawler off the Iceland coast and also machinegunned two Icelandic lighthouses Tuesday, U.S. army headquarters announced Wednesday. The communique said, however, there were no casualties and only superficial damage.

New Policy May Transform Economic Life of Dominion

Object Is to Eliminate or Curtail Non-Essential Industry

WIDE POWERS GIVEN

By Charles Bishop
(From Edmonton Journal's Ottawa Bureau. Copyright, 1942, by the Southam Co.)

OTTAWA, Aug. 20.—What is construed as capable of bringing about a large transformation in the economic life of the country is the policy outlined by Prime Minister King Wednesday night whereby the Wartime Prices and Trade board becomes the arbiter as to what is essential and what is non-essential industry. The announced objective is to "curtail or eliminate" the latter. Combined with this is the purpose to save for, and divert to, war industry the manpower, womanpower, materials, machinery, electric power and steam power now employed in such industries. It may be done partially or it may be done wholly.

That really was the new thing in Wednesday night's pronouncement. Nearly everything which was said about selective service, the principle and purpose of it, and the method of procedure to be followed, had been said before. A great deal, however, remains to be outlined in the way of regulations by which the scheme will be applied in detail. Director E. M. Little is to supply such details before the month ends.

The prices board has already begun preparation for its widened responsibility. A committee of its experts has been at work on it for some time and extensive study is indicated. The board is unlikely to be enlarged for the purpose.

It was stated Thursday that the new program will call for considerable study before there is an outline of what is to be done and how it is to be gone about.

Generally it will call for new classifications, the delimitation of dividing lines between essential and non-essential production, or the relative degree of each, and to what lines each of the affected industries would switch. There is no intention of putting any industry out of business without proposing an alternative outlet.

Co-operation will be established with the division of displaced industry in the department of munitions and supply. This prescribes three courses of action—substitution of non-essential materials, conversion from one line of civilian goods to another not requiring critical material and conversion, in whole or in part, to the production of war stores. At the department, there is a showroom of samples of things which a "displaced" industry may manufacture.

Depends on Need

To what extent, and with what rigor, the new regulations will be applied will depend upon the need which is disclosed. That, in turn, will be learned by study and survey and the degree of demand for manpower, materials and equipment.

But the board was impressed Thursday with the magnitude of its new responsibility and the measure of dislocation which may result from the exercise of such powers.

Otherwise, the principle of selective service which is to be applied is the same, and the procedure the same, as has been outlined. It is not a new statute in any sense. The National Mobilization act was passed in parliament in June, 1940. Then, and until a few weeks ago, it had a limitation to its compulsory features. Each compulsion could not be applied for service overseas. Now it can be.

Inasmuch as the full enforcement of an enactment of June, 1940, is to be in September, 1942, no speed record will have been broken. At all events, what could have been done before is now to be done in and throughout Canada.

There is a reminder of the fact that conscription has long been the law in this country. Whether, with the complete freedom of the act as amended, this will be extended overseas is still problematical, "depending on circumstances."

The only suggestion of it—if it can be so construed—is the solemnity of Mr. King's emphasis upon the present gravities and menacing implications of the war as it stands just now on a dozen fronts.

News About War As Seen at Glance

(By Canadian Press)

Commandos—Dieppe raid will permit Allies to assess prospects of opening second front; real strength of German defences now probably known.

Russia—Red army in offensive action in four key central fronts; holding in Caucasus and west of Stalingrad.

Pacific—Allied bombers blast Japanese fleet off Solomons; loss of Australian cruiser Canberra announced.

Casualty List In Raid 'Severe'

Ralston Says Canada Must Be Prepared to Pay Cost of War

CANADIANS HEROIC

OTTAWA, Aug. 20.—Defence Minister Ralston said Wednesday night that "casualties were severe" in Wednesday's monster combined operations raid on the channel port of Dieppe.

"For that we must be prepared, for war is a grim business," the minister said in a statement on the raid in which Canadian troops commanded by Maj.-Gen. J. H. Roberts had a big part and numbered one-third of the attacking force.

(Col. Ralston could not be reached immediately for clarification of his reference to "casualties" but sources close to him said it was not a specific reference to casualties among the Canadians involved—that it was based on the general expectation that casualties would necessarily be heavy among the whole force involved in such a major operation.)

The real test of whether the price of the Dieppe raid—in which he said Canadian troops who spearheaded the invaders "bore themselves with stout-hearted resolution and matchless courage"—was great or small lay

(Continued on Page 5, Col. 6)

U.S. Army Seizes Defiant War Plant

WASHINGTON, Aug. 20.—President Roosevelt ordered War Secretary Henry Stimson Wednesday to take possession of and operate the plant of the S. A. Woods Machine company at South Boston, Mass., where a management-labor dispute has impeded war production.

The company management had refused to comply with a War Labor board order that it grant arbitration and maintenance of union membership privileges to the C.I.O.'s United Electrical Radio and Machine Workers.

Asks Farmers Aid Break Prices Jam

WASHINGTON, Aug. 20.—Agriculture Secretary Claude Wickard called upon U.S. farmers Wednesday night to take the lead in breaking a price control "log-jam" by giving up a provision of the price control law prohibiting ceilings on farm prices at less than 110 per cent of parity.

"Today the 110 per cent provision is being pointed to by other groups to prove that farmers are asking for more than their fair share," he said. "It is being used as a argument to slow down economic controls in other fields. I believe it would be wise to repeal this provision."

Wickard also advocated the payment of government subsidies in cases where parity prices provided an insufficient incentive.

Calgary Tank Unit Included In Daring Commando Force

Canadians Battled Germans In Streets, Captured Part of Town

LEFT PALL OF SMOKE

By Ross Munro
(Canadian Press War Correspondent)

LONDON, Aug. 20.—Units of two infantry regiments—the Royal Hamilton Light Infantry and the Essex Scottish of Windsor, Ont., with the Calgary Tank Regiment carried the main attack on the Dieppe raid Wednesday right into the town itself and battled the Germans in the streets to capture the main portions of the town.

Maj.-Gen. J. H. Roberts, senior ranking officer of the expedition, commanded the Canadians.

(Another London dispatch revealed two other high Canadian officers took part in the Dieppe operations. They were Brig. Sherwood Lett, Vancouver, and Brig. W. S. Southam, Toronto.)

After a tremendous naval bombardment and aerial bombing of the promenade area by the sea, these units landed on the beach in front of the town and stormed Nazi - held buildings, barricades and strong points.

On the flank, units of the South Saskatchewan regiment and the Cameron Highlanders of Winnipeg landed at Pourville, two miles west of Dieppe, and the Royal Regiment of Toronto went in at Puits, one mile east of the port.

Units of the Fusiliers Mont Royal, a French-Canadian battalion, were floating reserves and finally were sent into Dieppe.

By this operation, the Canadians carried out the underlying objective of the raid, which was to test German defences on the coast and obtain information about them.

Dieppe was left with many parts of the town wrecked and burning and, as the raid-fleet sailed for England, I could see from the boat I occupied with an attack force a pall of smoke hanging over the port.

Several strong gun positions and batteries of coastal artillery were destroyed and a radio direction-finding station was smashed. Hundreds of Germans were killed. The Nazis themselves admitted 400 killed and wounded.

The Canadians brought back a number of German prisoners.

British commandos operated with the force and at Varengeville, five miles west of Dieppe, a force led by Lord Lovat captured and destroyed a battery of six-inch howitzers.

Eight miles west of the big target, another commando unit took out other coastal guns and a Royal Marine commando unit landed at Dieppe as reserves.

Defences at the channel port were strong. At vulnerable points there was evidence they had been bolstered recently.

Canadian shock troops had a rough time of it at several points and losses probably will not be small.

This is really just the story of the Canadian assault operations, but there was more to it than that.

Great Air Combat

Throughout the eight- to nine-hour smash at Dieppe and surrounding strong points behind a spearhead of tanks, Canadian and British pilots battled overhead in one of the greatest air combats since the 1940 Battle of Britain.

Two commando units assigned to destroy coastal guns which, if they had been firing, could have blocked the landing at Dieppe, stole over the English channel and attacked in the early hours of Wednesday.

Lord Lovat's commando unit killed the gun-crew with bayonets and destroyed the howitzers.

While the preliminary attacks were being made, the main raid force under Gen. Roberts was crossing the channel in a flotilla that included a large number of ships of all types, including giant tank-laden craft that looked like Great Lakes oil freighters. These craft were being used for the first time to transport tanks at sea on combined operations.

Trained for Five Weeks

Destroyers, motor launches and motor gunboats screened the assault craft during the whole voyage. This force was trained for five weeks last

(Continued on Page 14, Col. 1)

Tells How Canucks Stormed Through Defence Inferno

(Ross Munro, 28-year-old Canadian Press war correspondent, landed in France with the Canadian-led commando forces Wednesday, the first Canadian newspaperman to step on European soil with a commando. Munro was the only newspaperman with the Canadian forces raiding Spitsbergen a year ago; on the recent manoeuvre-workout for this assault on Dieppe he was along. His full-time job is "covering" the Canadian troops in Britain.)

By Ross Munro
(Copyright, 1942, by Canadian Press)

WITH THE CANADIAN RAIDING FORCE AT DIEPPE, Aug. 19—(Delayed)—For eight raging hours, under intense Nazi fire from dawn into a sweltering afternoon, I watched Canadian troops fight the blazing, bloody battle of Dieppe.

Ross Munro

I saw them go through this biggest of the war's raiding operations in wild scenes that crowded helter skelter one upon another in crazy sequence.

There was a furious attack by German E-boats while the Canadians moved in on Dieppe's beaches, landing by dawn's half-light.

When the Canadian battalions stormed through the flashing inferno of Nazi defences, belching guns of huge tanks rolling into the fight, I spent the grimmest 20 minutes of my life with one unit when a rain of German machinegun fire wounded half the men in our boat and only a miracle saved us from annihilation.

A few hours later there was the spine-chilling experience of a dive-bombing attack by seven Stukas, the dreaded Nazi aircraft that spotted out the small assault landing craft waiting off-shore to re-embark the fighting men.

Our boat was thrown about like a toy by their seven screeching bombs that plunged into the water around us and exploded in gigantic cascades.

There was the lashing fire of machinegunning from other Nazi aircraft and the thunder of anti-aircraft fire that sent them hustling off.

Over our heads in the blue, cloud-flecked French sky were fought the greatest air engagements since the Battle of Britain, dogfights carried on to the dizzy accompaniment of planes exploding in the air, diving down flaming, some plummeting into the sea from thousands of feet.

Hour after hour guns of the supporting warships growled salvoes at

(Continued on Page 18, Col. 5)

Sees Nazi Air Force Smashed In Dramatic Air-Sea Battle

Result Was Decisive Allied Victory, Says Associated Press Writer

WATCHED FIGHTING

(Drew Middleton of the Associated Press, one of the American newsmen selected to represent the United States press on the Dieppe raid, observed Wednesday's operation from one of the vessels that lay offshore. He was not permitted to land. Middleton, 28, was accredited to the original British expeditionary force of this war and spent considerable time with it in France in the early months. He was withdrawn to England just ahead of the troops in the 1940 retreat through Dunkerque.)

By Drew Middleton

ABOARD A MOTOR LAUNCH OF the ROYAL NAVY RETURNING FROM OFF DIEPPE, Aug. 19.—(Delayed)—I have just watched the R.A.F. and the Royal Navy smash the German air force in the fiercest and most dramatic air and sea battle of the war in the west.

For seven hours in the blue skies over Dieppe and on the glassy waters of the channel, Briton and German, airman and seaman, fought for the lives of thousands of Canadian, American, French and British soldiers who scrambled ashore this morning to storm the ancient port of Dieppe.

The result was a decisive Allied victory.

Its full measure is not 91 aircraft shot down by British pilots and gunners but a long line of landing craft full of weary but triumphant men now passing our ship.

They are homeward-bound because of the magnificent job done

(Continued on Page 14, Col. 6)

Build Big Plant For Aviation 'Gas'

CALGARY, Aug. 20.—Construction of an aviation gasoline plant at a cost of $1,000,000 on Imperial Oil property in Alberta now is under way, it was announced officially Thursday.

The Allied War Supply corporation, backed by the British, United States and Canadian governments, is undertaking the project which may be completed this winter.

The plant will produce alkylate. This fluid when blended with ordinary gasoline yields a high octane product essential in the operation of powerful modern warplanes.

While aviation gasoline has been manufactured in Alberta by the Imperial and British American companies, it has been necessary to import the alkylate from the United States. The new plant will be entirely self-sufficient.

Union's Director Gets Strike Power

SAULT STE. MARIE, Ont., Aug. 20.—C. H. Millard, national director of the United Steel Workers of America (C.I.O.), has been given complete authority to take any further action he sees fit regarding the Algoma Steel Workers' union's demand for a basic labor rate of 55 cents hourly for employes in the Algoma Steel corporation plant here.

This decision was taken Wednesday night at a meeting of the committee of the steward's council which met to consider the result of the vote favoring a strike if necessary to enforce the union's demand for boosting the basic hourly wage, now 45½ cents.

From The Times—

The War Today

Allies Gain Experience
Attack Said Success
Reds Retreat Further

(Copyright by The Southam Co.)

LONDON, Aug. 20.—Canadians, British, United States and Fighting French troops spent nine hours in their memorable raid on Dieppe, smashing German targets with tanks, artillery and aircraft and gaining important experience in combined operations.

The air fighting was intense and 91 Nazi aircraft were shot down.

The operations, says the Times' aeronautical correspondent, were notable for the fact that ground troops were provided with air support on an unprecedented scale. All day long the sky over France was filled with British fighters and bombers and the Luftwaffe was forced into battle on a scale unknown since it was defeated in the Battle of Britain.

During the tremendous struggle of 1940 over southern England, Nazi losses were several times as big as those of the Royal Air Force. But this time over France the losses on both sides were about equal. Most of the Allied machines were lost in low-flying attacks on strongly-defended positions. Many of the 100 Nazi aircraft claimed as probables

(Continued on Page 2, Col. 2)

Dieppe Disaster

"Because of the price paid by the men of Dieppe, Allied landings in Africa, Sicily, Italy and, most important of all, on the beaches of Normandy and those of southern France, were carried through with astonishingly small losses."

— Editorial, eight months after the D-Day landings, Dec. 14, 1944

In the summer of 1942, the war was going badly on all fronts. Josef Stalin, the Soviet leader, was demanding a second front in Europe to distract the German army from Russia and relieve the pressure on his beleaguered, under-equipped and desperate troops.

The result was the event known to Canadian history simply as Dieppe, and Aug. 19, 1942, would be the single most costly, most bloody day in Canadian military history.

A page 1 story that ran the day of the raid on Dieppe, a small Normandy town, was full of optimism. "The Canadians were said to have fought with their traditional courage and initiative in their first brush with the Nazis.

"There was nothing to indicate the extent of either Allied or enemy losses, though it was understood the operation went off with clockwork precision."

Military planners called for a 16-kilometre front along the Normandy beaches. What they hadn't expected was that platoons of soldiers from Hamilton's Royal Regiment, the Black Watch, the South Saskatchewan Regiment and Cameron Highlanders would be subjected to deadly machine gun and mortar fire.

When the Calgary Tank Regiment made it to shore, it faced not only unrelenting fire, but also a shale beach and a seawall that prevented many of the tanks from making their way into Dieppe itself.

Those that negotiated the seawall were confronted with concrete obstacles that brought them to a halt.

It was a disaster.

Ross Munro, at age 28 one of the country's best war correspondents and the man who later became *Journal* publisher in the '60s, wrote a 5,000-word first-person account of what he saw that day.

He was, as ever, moving, balanced, dramatic and direct.

It was a report that was crammed with the kind of detail that would be a hallmark of Munro's wartime journalism.

"Over our heads in the blue, cloud-flecked French sky were fought the greatest air engagements since the Battle of Britain, dogfights carried on to the dizzy accompaniment of planes exploding in the air, diving down, flaming, some plummeting into the sea from thousands of feet," he wrote.

"There was heroism at sea and in the skies in those hours, but the hell-spot was ashore, where the Canadians fought at close quarters with the Nazis. They fought to the end, where they had to, and showed courage and daring."

***Oct. 3, 1946*:**
Montreal jazz pianist Oscar Peterson, 22, plays in Edmonton during his first cross-country tour.

***Nov. 1, 1946*:**
The federal government returns control of Edmonton's municipal airport to the city. The airport had been under federal control since the start of the Second World War.

***Nov. 6, 1946*:**
Harry Ainlay is re-elected mayor of Edmonton.

***Nov. 20, 1946*:**
Imperial Oil begins drilling for oil south of Edmonton at Leduc.

***Nov. 23, 1946*:**
Greyhound bus fare from Edmonton to Toronto is $38.75, one way. It costs $19.15 to go to Winnipeg and $7.85 to travel to Saskatoon.

***Dec. 23, 1946*:**
John Fry, elected to eight one-year terms as mayor of Edmonton from 1937 to 1945, dies at age 69.

***Dec. 24, 1946*:**
Joe Krol of the Toronto Argonauts is named Canada's outstanding athlete of 1946; Edmonton's Henry Martell finishes second in the voting.

Journal Files

Canadian wounded and dead on the beach at Dieppe, above and below right.
Below left, correspondent Ross Munro, witness to the bravery and carnage of Canadian troops in this historic battle.

While casualty figures on the Dieppe raid would not be known for some time, Munro predicted they would not be light.

He was right.

Five thousand Canadian troops had sailed from Portsmouth and Southampton to Dieppe. Of those, 907 were killed on the beaches or died later of wounds, 2,460 were wounded and 1,874 were taken prisoner by the Germans. Of the 2,210 who returned to England, only 236 were unhurt, and 200 of those were men who had failed to land on the beaches at all.

Munro, the first newspaperman to land with a commando unit in Europe during the war, was one of the unhurt. The scene he recorded on the landing craft that carried him away from the beach is chilling.

"I will forever remember the scene in that craft: wounded lying about being attended by medical orderlies oblivious to the fire; the heroism of the Royals as they fought back and strove as desperately as any men could to get on the beach and relieve their comrades still fighting ashore; the contempt of these men for danger and their fortitude when they were hit.

"I never heard one man even cry out."

Over the next weeks, the newspaper ran column after column of tightly packed names. The casualty lists would be as detailed as possible. Categories would include "killed in action," "dangerously wounded," "missing, believed killed," "wounded," "missing, believed wounded," "wounded" and, finally, "missing."

Two days after the raid, *The Journal* reprinted Shakespeare's stirring St. Crispin's Day speech from *Henry V*:

"We few, we happy few, we band of brothers;
For he today that sheds his blood with me
Shall be my brother; be he ne'er so vile,
This day shall gentle his condition:
And gentlemen in England now abed
Shall think themselves accursed they were not here
And hold their manhoods cheap while any speaks
That fought with us on St. Crispin's Day."

The editorial pointed out that Henry V's speech stirred the souls of his men before they routed the enemy at the Battle of Agincourt on Oct. 25, 1415.

"It is worth noting, that the distance between Dieppe and Agincourt is only about 50 miles."

Controversy would surround the Dieppe raid for years. Many would question whether it was really necessary at all. Others would ask if their British commanders regarded Canadian troops as simply expendable.

For its part, *The Journal* stood firm on the necessity of the raid.

In an editorial on Dec. 14, 1944, eight months after the D-Day landings, the newspaper made its position clear.

"Dieppe's purpose was to probe German coastal defences and to test men and equipment trained and designed for amphibious operations by combined sea, land and air forces."

***Dec. 31, 1946*:**
Edmonton's Trocadero Ballroom opens.

***Jan. 3, 1947*:**
Wasyl Eleniak of Chipman, who in 1891 was one of the first Ukrainians to officially settle in Canada, receives one of the first Canadian citizenship certificates in an Ottawa ceremony celebrating Canada's new Citizenship Act.

***Jan. 8, 1947*:**
"We cannot help but view with concern the provincial government's intention to establish a rigid censorship over all motion pictures, commercial and non-commercial alike. Last February, Mr. Hooke said that provincial government censorship will 'eliminate Communist thought from Alberta-shown movies.' As we said last winter, we had an idea that in a democracy, adults were entitled to learn by any and every means all that they may, or care to, about political doctrines of every hue – and any other subject under the sun." – editorial.

***Jan. 22, 1947*:**
Edmonton movie-goers experience yet another first. The Empress announces that it has installed the

Journal Files

After the city was was captured, Canadian troops shared Christmas dinner in the square at Ortona, above.
Below, Canadian troops work to free a soldier from the rubble of a collapsed wall.

Battle for Ortona

"Some of the bitterest fighting of the Italian campaign has been compressed into the narrow limits of this small Adriatic port during a period of ten days."
— Editorial, Dec. 29, 1943

A reporter from The Associated Press dubbed the Battle of Ortona "Canada's Stalingrad," because the bloody hand-to-hand combat with elite German paratroopers was reminiscent of what went on in the Russian city the year before.

Canadian troops in Italy spearheaded the British 8th Army's efforts to secure the Adriatic coastline and delay German attempts to reinforce its army to the south. The Canadian 1st Division, which included the Loyal Edmonton Regiment, crossed the Moro River earlier in December.

Ortona's fall would clear the way for an advance 18 kilometres up the coast to Pescara, the eastern terminus of a highway running across the peninsula to Rome.

The enemy made Ortona, a town of 9,000 people, a killing ground, barricading and boobytrapping side streets to force Canadian troops into the town square to face battle-hardened troops.

The Journal's first report, Dec. 21, 1943, said: "The Canadians established themselves in the southern side of the town before dark and brought up supporting weapons."

Post-battle body counts showed casualties on both sides were horrendous, but *The Journal* story took a one-sided approach.

"Although the Canadians are not yet in possession of Ortona or the crossroads, they have administered a terrific beating to the Germans."

The stories of the few days leading up to Christmas described a painful, metre-by-metre advance of the Loyal Eddies and Seaforth Highlanders.

Reports on Dec. 23 indicated the Canadians had taken the south-eastern section of the town. "With this encounter, the Ortona battle drew to a bloody climax." The report was premature.

Dec. 24 was a Friday. *The Journal* didn't publish again until Monday, but G.R. Stevens, in his book *A City Goes to War*, said the fighting continued.

On Monday, Dec. 28, *The Journal* reported tanks were added to the repertoire of Canadian weapons. The desperate Germans, for the first time, turned flame-throwers on the Canadians, luckily with little strategic success. The main headline that day declared "Canadian Troops Drive Nazis Out of Ortona." This time, the battle for the town was over and by the next day the Allied troops began the push toward Pescara.

About 1,400 Canadians died at Ortona. The Loyal Edmonton Regiment lost a third of its strength, with 61 killed and 109 wounded.

The Canadians, during the battle, rewrote the book on urban warfare and their strategy of using directionally-controlled explosives to blast between buildings was used by the Allies for the remainder of the war.

first popcorn machine in the province.

***Feb. 13, 1947*:**
Imperial Oil's Leduc No. 1 well goes into production, launching Alberta's modern oil boom.

***June 13, 1947*:**
Edmonton Mayor Harry Ainlay reports Imperial Oil plans to run a pipeline from its newly discovered oil wells at Leduc to Nisku, and possibly to build a refinery east of Edmonton in the Clover Bar area.

***June 20, 1947*:**
The new speed limit on Alberta highways is 50 miles an hour for cars, 40 for trucks.

***July 7, 1947*:**
The Alberta government announces hard surfacing of the highway between Edmonton and Leduc has been completed.

***July 12, 1947*:**
Provincial old age and blind pensions are increased to $35 per month.

***July 31, 1947*:**
A city census puts Edmonton's population at 118,541.

***Aug. 8, 1947*:**
An Edmonton-to-London flight on Trans-Canada Air Lines is $441.75.

Edmonton Weather
24-hour forecast: Clear and cool tonight, bright and warmer Wednesday.

Edmonton Journal

Victory Loan Standing
Canada ---- $500,002,150 *(Objective* $1,350,000,000*)*
Alberta ---- $22,528,400 *(Objective* $47,300,000*)*
Edmonton -- $2,348,450 *(Objective* $6,350,000*)*

FORTY-SECOND YEAR ** EDMONTON, ALBERTA, TUESDAY, MAY 1, 1945 SINGLE COPY, 5 CENTS

HITLER DEAD

New Zealanders Link With Tito's Partisans

ROME.—New Zealand troops striking through northeast Italy linked Tuesday with Yugoslav Partisans at the head of the Adriatic sea.

This historic link-up came just 24 hours after Gen. Mark Clark, 15th Army Group commander, announced that German armies in Italy have been virtually eliminated as a military force.

Headquarters also announced Tuesday that Marshal Graziani on Sunday, after his capture by the Allies, ordered unconditional surrender of the Fascist Ligurian army in Italy.

He ordered troops of this Italian army holding the Ligurian coast in northwest Italy to lay down their arms.

In northeastern Italy, the British 6th Armored Division entered Udine, 60 miles northeast of Venice, and 29 and 33 miles from the Yugoslav and Austrian borders. Udine is 42 miles northwest of Trieste, which the Yugoslavs declared they had entered.

Americans advancing along the Gulf of Geno meanwhile occupied Savona, Spotorno, and Noli.

New Zealand troops of the British 8th Army, driving toward a junction with Marshal Tito's Partisans in Trieste, were reported more than 15 miles northeast of the Piave river.

The only fighting reported officially in northern Italy Tuesday was in the area north of Lake Garda, where the enemy was attempting to hold back an American drive toward the Brenner pass, gateway to Austria.

A headquarters spokesman said the enemy apparently was attempting to "reassemble his disjointed force at a point on this route in order to attempt the long and tortueus march up into the Alps."

These reports underscored Monday night's statement by Gen. Clark, commander of the 15th Army Group, that the German armies in Italy have been "virtually eliminated as a military force" by the shattering Allied drives.

The 8th Army took about 10,000 prisoners Monday alone.

Alberta Near Half-Way Mark In Victory Loan Campaign

Recording a gain of $213,000 over the same period of the last loan, Edmonton sales in the Eighth Victory Loan campaign had climbed Monday night to a total of $2,348,450. This was 37 percent of the city's quota of 6,350,000.

Meantime, Alberta's sales total was $22,528,400, representing 45.7 percent of the province's over-all objective of $47,300,000.

Brisk sales with the advent of fine weather showed that on Monday, seventh day of the campaign, Edmonton had 1,927 applications for subscriptions amounting to $296,800.

So far, Edmonton unit shows a total of 9,953 applications. The same period of the Seventh Loan gave Edmonton 9,011 applications and a subscription total of $2,130,450, which was 38.7 percent of the quota. In that loan, however, the quota was lower than the present.

Throughout the province, there was a general report of improved weather conditions, resulting in sales amounting to approximately $3,000,000 for the day.

A summary of the first seven days of the loan disclosed that 66,845 Albertans have purchased bonds. In the same period of the Seventh Loan, the total was 65,510.

In the civilian section, 53,636 applications have been received in the province for sales totalling $18,434,100, compared with 53,141 for sales aggregating $14,788,500 in the same period of the previous loan.

OTTAWA. — Victory Loan sales Monday totalled $67,894,150, bringing the cumulative total for the first seven days of the three-week campaign to $500,002,150, national loan headquarters announced Tuesday.

The total for the corresponding Monday of the Seventh Loan last fall was $72,583,500 while the cumulative total at the same stage of the last campaign was $501,109,750.

Canvassers reported sales to individuals, target for at least half the national minimum objective of $1,350,000,000, at $253,432,650 up to Monday night, compared to $231,746,000 on the corresponding day of the seventh campaign.

Canadian National Railways employes passed the $6,000,050 mark by the end of the first week. Total of employes buying $6,085,850 worth of bonds was 51,129, of whom 2,426 were Trans-Canada Airlines employes who subscribed $318,400 and 649 were National Railways Munitions Ltd. workers who subscribed $112,000.

With 48 percent of its objective attained, the C.N.R.'s western region leads, headed by Prince Rupert Dry dock at 82.3 percent of quota.

Loan headquarters said purchase by the Canadian Pacific Railway Company of $17,500,000 in bonds sparked the opening of the second week. The C.P.R. purchase included $3,500,000 for the employes' pension fund. Toronto head office of the Imperial Life Assurance company announced purchase of $5,000,000 in bonds.

Rumor Plan for Surrender Of Nazis in Denmark, Norway

STOCKHOLM — Count Folke Bernadotte flew to Stockholm from Copenhagen Tuesday and a well-informed American said he might be bearing a German-Swedish agreement for peaceful surrender of German troops in both Denmark and Norway.

The Swedish nobleman refused to say, upon arriving here, whether he had brought from Denmark a new communication from Heinrich Himmler, chief of the German gestapo. He went into conference with Erik Boheman, undersecretary of state in the Swedish foreign office.

(However, the Stockholm radio said the Swedish foreign office announced he "did not bring any message to be handed to the Allies through the ministry.")

Danish underground sources in Sweden reported German troops already were moving out of Sjaelland, the island on which Copenhagen is situated, toward South Jutland.

A Danish radio broadcast from Malmo recorded in Stockholm said the Germans had evacuated the Sjaelland towns of Slagelse, Nastved and Hileroed and that German Red Cross workers were en route to Copenhagen to care for German refugees. It urged Danes to be calm.

The American informant said that whether a final agreement on procedure in Norway had been reached was still uncertain, but he expressed belief the Swedes had proposed or that the Germans had requested transportation for their Norwegian forces to Sweden for disarming.

The Times Says--

Himmler Said in Command
Italian Campaign Ending
Mussolini Was Arch-Traitor

LONDON.—If Himmler agrees to surrender to Britain, the United States and the Soviet Union, says the Times' diplomatic correspondent, it is probable the greater part of the wehrmacht will obey his orders and lay down arms. The generals who do not belong to the Nazi party are in favor of surrender because they know the war is utterly lost. No leader in the Nazi party can challenge Himmler's authority.

Hitler is no longer in control and it is possible Himmler will see that he dies at the proper time. What remains of the German radio has dropped all reference to Hitler's presence in Berlin.

The Times advises caution in accepting reports that Himmler is willing to surrender to Russia as well as to the other Allies. Marshal Stalin has made it clear in his May Day pronouncement that Himmler's tricks and attempts to cause dissension among the Allies will fail.

The end of the Italian campaign is in sight, says the Times' special correspondent on the Italian front. Twenty-five German divisions have been torn to pieces by men under Field Marshal Alexander's com-

(Continued on Page 5, Col. 6)

Thousands of Captured Nazi Soldiers Jammed Into Enclosure

Here are a few thousand of Hitler's "supermen" who terrorized and tortured Europe for four years. Captured by the U.S. 7th Army, they are herded in a former Nazi military academy where young thugs were taught fine points in the art of murder and pillage. From D-Day to April 29, the western Allies captured 2,628,529 of these specimens.

V-E Day Is Likely To End Call-ups

OTTAWA. — Labor Minister Mitchell said Tuesday it was "probable" that call-ups for compulsory military service would end with the proclamation of VE-Day.

"The National Selective Service advisory board now is considering the techniques which will have to be adopted when the call-up is ended," Mr. Mitchell said.

Demand Growing For Tax Relief

By Charles Bishop
(From Edmonton Journal's Ottawa Bureau)

OTTAWA.—The war won't long be over before organized representations are made to Ottawa about the heavy taxes now imposed and the system of taxation. Advance intimation of this are said to be impressive.

The general attitude indicated all through has been that a war is on, that it is costly as well as ghastly and that, having regard to this fact, there has been little to do but "grin and bear it"—that is while the war with Germany lasts.

When this war is over, Ottawa has been advised to look out for demands for some changes in taxation in the nature of relief and as well, and about as important, changes in the whole system.

The complaint has been persistent that little but rigidity is ever shown in the taxation laws and regulations and their administration. It will be recalled how the government strongly resisted the pay-as-you-go principle before it was finally adopted.

Monday was the day when personal income tax returns were due and it furnished an impressive reminder to many people of the extent of the burden that war imposes.

The recognized fact that the money has to be raised by taxation and borrowing does not submerge the widely prevalent idea that the pressure in Canada is needlessly heavy.

Governor-General Arrives Wednesday

The Earl of Athlone, governor-general of Canada, and Her Royal Highness Princess Alice will arrive in Edmonton at 8:10 a.m. Wednesday over the C.N.R. for a three-day visit.

Among those who will greet the vice-regal party will be Hon. J. C. Bowen, lieutenant-governor, Premier Manning and Acting Mayor Winslow Hamilton.

During their visit, the governor-general and Princess Alice will make a number of public inspections and attend receptions. They will be guests of the provincial government at a dinner at the Macdonald Thursday night.

This is regarded as a farewell tour of the west for the governor-general and Princess Alice as plans provide for them returning to England this summer.

Windsors to Visit Ranch in Alberta

NASSAU, Bahamas.—The Duke and Duchess of Windsor will leave the latter part of this week for the United States and will go immediately to Palm Beach, Fla., to visit friends.

The duke is leaving Nassau after serving more than four years as governor of the Bahamas.

Afterwards, they will go to New York for a stay and then to the duke's ranch at High River, Alta.

Foe Supplies Running Low In Last Fortress in Berlin

LONDON.—Russian troops have captured Brandenburg, 22 miles west of Berlin, Marshal Stalin announced Tuesday night in a second order of the day.

MOSCOW.—The German air force made a last-gasp attempt to parachute supplies to the besieged defenders of Berlin Tuesday as the final chapter of the battle for the German capital unfolded.

Soviet troops were closing in on the Tiergarten, core of the last-ditch German defence, and that fortress was getting low on water, food and ammunition.

(The Hamburg radio said efforts of the German 9th Army to relieve Berlin had been abandoned because of strong Russian attacks, and that the German 4th Army west of Berlin "also has had to endure strong Soviet flank attacks.")

Nine thousand more German troops surrendered in Berlin, raising to 65,500 the toll of enemy dead and captured in four days.

Soviet units which captured the reichstag and the interior ministry hammered south through the Platz der Publik and down the Sieges Alle which runs into the Charlottenburger Chaussee, the avenue which bisects the Tiergarten. A junction of Marshal Konev's 1st Ukraine Army and Marshal Zhukov's 1st White Russian Army in this sector seemed imminent.

"The fighting has been transferred to the immediate centre of Berlin," said a front dispatch to Red Star, Soviet army newspaper. "The Nazis are adopting the most desperate efforts to hold the last prepared lines of defence."

Sharp resistance and concentrated fire came from the Tiergarten, apparently being supplied from a great fortress underground. Special squadrons of Soviet soldiers stormed German positions frequently in gory encounters in the subways, which evidently have some connection with the fortress beneath the Tiergarten.

Dozens of suicides were reported. German officers draped themselves over their machineguns after wrapping themselves in Nazi banners

(Continued on Page 2, Col. 1)

U.S. 3rd Crashes Southward 58 Miles From Berchtesgaden

LONDON.—The Hamburg radio Tuesday night said American airborne troops and gliders landed in the British sector in the north German plain.

PARIS.—U.S. 3rd Army crashed southward to within 58 miles of Berchtesgaden Tuesday as the U.S. 7th Army advanced south from captured Munich against Innsbruck and the Brenner pass.

The 3rd Army entered Griesbach in its closest approach to Hitler's roost in the Alpine redoubt. The town near the Austrian border is 16 miles northeast of Hitler's birthplace at Braunau and 47 north of Salzburg, eastern rampart of the final Nazi hideaway.

Seventh Army infantry crossed the Austrian frontier and captured Scharnitz, 10 miles northwest of Innsbruck and 15 north of the Brenner pass.

The 13th Armored Division of the U.S. 3rd Army drove 25 miles out of its Isar bridgehead today and reached the Inn river near Braunau, Hitler's birthplace on the Austrian-Bavarian border.

The 11th Armored Division of the 3rd Army crossed the Austrian border in force at Oberkappel, 27 miles

(Continued on Page 2, Col. 4)

BANK CLEARINGS

Edmonton bank clearings reported Tuesday: April, $42,219,611; same month last year, $39,464,696; increase, $2,754,915.

City Hockey Star Loses 65 Pounds While Held in Nazi Prison Camp

Weighing only 125 pounds, R. "Bobby" Carse, 24, well-known Edmonton hockey player, has been released from a German prison camp and is recuperating in an old country hospital.

A member of the Winnipeg Rifles regiment, Carse weighed only 115 pounds—65 pounds less than his weight when he went overseas—when he was released from the camp about April 8. He has gained 10 pounds in the British hospital. He was taken prisoner last October after being wounded in the shoulder while advancing with a Bren gun.

In a letter received recently by Harold Boyle and Dan Carrigan, his former employers, Rfn. Carse stated: "At present I am recovering from dysentry and malnutrition as a result of being a prisoner of those Germans."

The letter went on: "I don't think you would recognize me right now as I only weigh 125 pounds. However, I put on 10 pounds since I arrived back here a week ago. So at that rate I'll be back to normal soon."

His wife and two young daughters are in Winnipeg with their grandparents. Rfn. Carse's parents, Mr. and Mrs. William Carse live at 9321 93 ave. His brother, William, is overseas with the Canadian army.

RFN. BOBBY CARSE

Rfn. Carse played with the Edmonton Athletic Club junior team in the Memorial cup finals in 1939 and later went to the Chicago Black Hawks of the National hockey league. He also was an outstanding golfer and captured the Edmonton Golf and country club championship several years ago.

Churchill Hints to Commons V-E Day Is Possible Soon

LONDON.—The German radio announced Tuesday night that Hitler is dead. The Hamburg radio broadcast the announcement.

The broadcast said Grand Admiral Karl Doenitz, commander of the German fleet, was Hitler's successor.

The Hamburg radio said Hitler died Tuesday afternoon.

"At the fuehrer's headquarters it is reported that our fuehrer Adolf Hitler has fallen this afternoon in his command post at the reichs chancellery, fighting up to his last breath against Bolshevism," said the announcement.

The radio broadcast a statement from Doenitz in which he said:

"My first task will be to save Germany from the advancing Bolsheviks. Only for this do we continue the fight."

"Give me your confidence," Doenitz appealed to the German people. "Keep calm and be disciplined. Only i nthat way will we be able to save off defeat."

The announcement said Hitler had appointed Doenitz April 30 (Monday) as sis successor.

No mention was made of Heinrich Himmler, gestapo chief who had been dickering in an attempt to surrender what remained of Germany to Britain and the United States but was turned down because he did not include Russia in his offer.

"German men and women, soldiers of the German army, our fuehrer Adolf Hitler has fallen," Doenitz announced dramatically.

"With deepest sorrow and reverence the German people bows.

"He had recognized the horrible danger of Bolshevism very early and consecrated his existence to the fight against it. At the end of this his struggle and his straight and unerring road he dies a hero's death in the capital of the German reich.

"His life was entirely given to the service of Germany. His struggle against the Bolshevist storm floods was, furthermore, not only for Europe, but for the entire civilized world. The fuehrer has appointed me to be his successor. Fully conscious of the responsibility, I take over the leadership of the German people in the fateful hour."

LONDON.—Prime Minister Churchill hinted Tuesday that announcement of peace in Europe might come before Saturday, but told a packed house of commons that he had no statement at this time.

He answered questions in the house as Count Folke Bernadotte conferred in Stockholm with Erik Boheman, undersecretary of state in the Swedish foreign office, after flying from Copenhagen.

The Swedish count refused to tell reporters whether he had brought a new message from Heinrich Himmler. There were no signs that he had made contact with Allied representatives in Stockholm, but such contact most likely would be established through the Swedish foreign office.

(A Reuters news agency Stockholm dispatch said the Swedish radio reported that Count Bernadotte brought with him a new capitulation offer from Himmler. Reuters said later, however, that the Swedish foreign office denied that the count had brought such an offer.)

Replying to a member's question, Mr. Churchill declared "I have no special statement to make on the war position in Europe except that it is definitely more satisfactory than it was at this time five years ago."

Mr. Churchill said that if information of exceptional impo..ance "reaches the government during the sittings of the house this week—as it might do," he would make a brief announcement.

"With regard to the condition and requisition which would occur if an announcement on decisive consequence justifying celebration were to be made this week or at any time in the future, and V-E Day were announced, a number of arrangements have been prepared, and will be issued tonight in a home office circular," he said.

The implication that peace might come before the house rises for the week on Friday evening was the nearest to a prediction that Mr. Churchill permitted himself.

"Of course," he said, "I shall make no statement here that is not in accord with statements which will be made by our Allies," explaining such announcements would be made only after consulting military commanders in different theatres.

The prime minister said he did not consider that the information in "a major message" reaching the government should be withheld "until the exact occupation of all the particular zones was achieved. The movement of troops and the surrender of enemy troops may both take an appreciable period of time."

"Good news will not be delayed," he said in answer to Lady Astor's question whether, if peace news came while the house was adjourned he would hold it until the commons again sat, or would release it through the B.B.C.

The prime minister indicated a peace announcement not only might precede final surrenders, but that such surrenders might not be worth an additional announcement.

"It is by no means certain at this time that complete surrender of all the enemy's forces will make the subject of a future announcement," he said.

The fact that he made no mention

(Continued on Page 2, Col. 8)

Bag of Prisoners Totals 2,628,529

WASHINGTON.—The Allied bag of prisoners from D-Day in Normandy through last Wednesday totalled 2,628,529.

The war department Monday said more than 317,000 were taken in the Ruhr pocket alone In the last seven weeks more than 1,500,000 were captured.

Borneo Invaded, Japanese Report

CANBERRA. — Treasury Minister Joseph B. Chifley told the house of representatives Tuesday night that a famous division of Australian troops which had fought in the Middle East now was participating in an action against the Japanese in Borneo.

SAN FRANCISCO.—Tokyo radio Tuesday claimed Allied assault forces had landed on Borneo.

The broadcast said invaders hit the east coast in the Tarakan area Monday night and were engaged by defending garrisons in "fierce combat."

As usual in reporting such landings the Japanese broadcaster claimed that the invaders were repulsed.

American planes have bombed the oil-rich island every day of April. Tarakan is a small island off the northeast coast of Borneo, an easy jump from American-held Tawi-tawi in the Sulu archipelago.

Borneo, rich in oil, is the most sparsely-settled island of the southwest Pacific, averaging two persons to a square mile of the mountainous, jungle-covered area.

Parley Votes 31-4 Admit Argentina

SAN FRANCISCO. — The United Nations security conference Monday voted 31-4 to invite immediate Argentine representation at the conference after a spirited debate in which Foreign Commissar Molotov of Russia said he questioned whether the South American country was free of Fascism.

Pleading for admission of the Warsaw Polish government, Molotov suggested a few days' delay before the full session voted on Argentine representation.

The world cannot forget, he said, that Argentine "helped the enemy throughout the war," but the Poles fought from the first for the Allies and thus were entitled to a part in the security conference.

Canada lined up with the nations approving Argentine acceptance. Prime Minister King took no part in the debate but stood with the majority when the vote was taken.

The four opposing Argentine admission were Russia, Czecho-Slovakia, Yugoslavia and Greece. Eleven nations did not vote.

Alberto Lleras Camargo, Colombian minister of foreign affairs, pleaded Argentine's cause. No one should forget, he said, that Argentine declared war on the Axis in hostilities not yet ended.

The conference steering committee earlier voted to extend an in-

(Continued on Page 5, Col. 1)

Army Groups Set New Loan Quota

Rolling up total subscriptions of $6,095,600, northern Alberta units had reached 41.8 percent of their quota at the end of the seventh day in the Eighth Victory Loan campaign. For the same period of the Seventh loan, the total was $4,886,700 or 38.9 percent of the quota.

Having passed the original objective of $760,000 with sales amounting to $800,300, army groups in Military District No. 13 and the C.W.A.C. are aiming for the $1,000,000 mark. The district stands in fourth place among Canada's 13 military districts.

Two pennants in the army campaign were awarded to No. 13 district company, R.C.O.C., at Calgary, and to Northwest Territories and Yukon Signals, in the north.

These were the Chief of the General Staff pennants, awarded to the two groups with the highest percentage of quota obtained in the first week of the Victory Loan campaign.

Victory Loan authorities at Northwest Air Command said the unit continues to lead all other air commands in Canada in the race for the

(Continued on Page 2, Col. 7)

Batter Up!

"We didn't expect the girls would be taught to chew tobacco ... It reads like baseball, but that make-up gag. Wow!"
— Toronto writer Charles Edwards in *The Journal*, May 29, 1943

Women, in two world wars, had stepped without hesitation into "traditional" male occupations to keep the country's economy going.

But there was a new twist in 1943. Women were being drafted into professional baseball. Among their numbers were two Edmonton fastball pitchers, Helen Nicol and Annabelle Thompson, who had already gained respect in local play.

On May 12, *The Journal* reported that Nicol and Thompson had been recruited to the All-American Girl's Baseball League to play a hybrid game of baseball and softball. The young Edmontonians were two of the athletes who, a half century later, were the subject of the Hollywood movie, *A League of Their Own.*

The league was the brainchild of Philip K. Wrigley Jr., chewing gum magnate and owner of the Chicago Cubs.

The Second World War was sucking dry the male talent pool and Wrigley was desperate to find a way to keep up fan interest in the sport until the Boys of Summer came marching home. He put up $100,000 ($1.1 million today) as seed money for the new league.

By June 1, 12 Canadian women had signed on and were dispersed among teams in Wisconsin, Illinois and Indiana. Nicol went to the Kenosha (Wis.) Comets and Thompson to the Racine (Wis.) Belles.

Edmonton's Mille Warwick McAuley, sister of Billy Warwick, and her friend Lucella McLean Ross, who now lives in Lloydminister, both from Saskatchewan, played in the league. McAuley played for the Rockford Peaches, and Ross for the South Bend Blue Sox.

While *The Journal* had always been big on baseball coverage, its interest in the women's league was sporadic and ranged from straight sport reporting to condescending digs.

On June 4, it published a column by Toronto sports writer Charles Edwards, based on a letter Nicol sent home describing the personal rules under which the women live. "The girls are being given lectures on beauty treatments, make up, how to walk properly, etc. How awful! There's no mention of the correct words of apology when a player bumps the catcher when sliding home.... There's no mention of caps."

Actually, they did wear caps, but suffered the indignities and leg scrapes by having to play in crowd-pleasing skirts.

Their schedule was grueling. Between June 1 and June 29 the teams played more than 30 games.

As of June 29, when the league expanded to 10 teams, reports said Nicol had a 7-4 record and Thompson was at 6-6.

The league drew more than a million spectators before its demise in 1954, but readers knew little of it. After the first month, *Journal* coverage dwindled from sporadic to non-existent for the rest of the decade.

***Aug. 9, 1947*:**
Imperial Oil announces it has purchased a Whitehorse oil refinery which it plans to dismantle and move to Edmonton to process oil from its Leduc discovery. The refinery had been built for the wartime Canol project.

***Aug. 9, 1947*:**
The quirky Edmonton streetcar nicknamed the Toonerville Trolley makes its final run on the McKernan Lake line. The shallow south side lake was a popular winter recreation site until it was drained.

***Nov. 5, 1947*:**
Harry Ainlay is elected mayor of Edmonton for the third time. Voters pass a plebiscite increasing the mayoral term of office to two years.

***Jan. 16, 1948*:**
Wildcat walkouts by 11,000 union coal miners in Alberta and B.C. shut down all six union mines in the Edmonton district.

***Jan. 28, 1948*:**
Edmonton's first small animal hospital opens.

***March 3, 1948*:**
The city engineer's department announces that four more sets of traffic lights will be added to the three sets operating downtown.

Edmonton Weather
24-hour forecast: Bright and warm.

Edmonton Journal

'One of Canada's Great Newspapers'

FORTY-SECOND YEAR ** EDMONTON, ALBERTA, WEDNESDAY, AUGUST 15, 1945 SINGLE COPY, 5 CENTS

WAR ENDS

Historic Date Blazed As Japan Surrenders

WASHINGTON.—A new date was blazed on the historic calendar of the world Tuesday night—Aug. 14, 1945—as Japan accepted Allied surrender terms and brought to an end the Second Great War.

President Truman made the announcement at 7:00 p.m. E.D.T. (5:00 p.m. Edmonton time) at a press conference in the White House even as Prime Minister Attlee broadcast a similar message over the B.B.C. from London. Moscow radio also carried the news for which the world had waited breathlessly for days.

Orders went out immediately to silence the guns in the far-flung Pacific theatre.

Thus was ended a world conflict which began when Hitler invaded Poland Sept. 1, 1939, and which spread to the Orient with Japan's sneak attack on Pearl Harbor Dec. 7, 1941.

Washington, like every city in the Allied world, went wild with the news. Days of strained waiting ended in a tumult of cheers, horn-blowing and bell-ringing.

In a brief press conference which sent reporters racing to spread the gladdest tidings they perhaps ever will make known, the president read a historic document in the form of a message from the Tokyo government, which was transmitted to him through Swiss government agencies.

Emperor Accepts Surrender Terms

It said in brief that the emperor accepted the surrender terms outlined in the Potsdam declaration and would issue the necessary orders to all armed forces under his control to cease operations and place themselves and their arms at the disposal of the Supreme Allied Commander.

The president announced that Gen. Douglas MacArthur has been named supreme Allied commander to receive the surrender. He will have high British, Russian and Chinese officers with him when the surrender terms are signed.

Arrangements still must be completed for the signing of formal surrender terms. Then V-J Day will be officially proclaimed.

"Meantime," the president announced, "the Allied armed forces have been ordered to suspend offensive action."

While the world celebrated with unrestrained joy, the

(Continued on Page 5, Col. 1)

Gasoline Rationing Ends In Canada, United States

OTTAWA. — Effective immediately, gasoline rationing and all restrictions on the use of fuel oil in Canada are removed, Munitions Minister Howe announced Wednesday.

The action followed an announcement from Washington that gasoline rationing in the United States would be terminated immediately.

A munitions spokesman said lifting of the ration was effective "right now—this minute if you can convince a service station operator that the order has been issued."

WASHINGTON.—The Office of Price Administration Wednesday announced immediate termination of the rationing of gasoline, canned fruits and vegetables, fuel oil and oil stoves.

Price Administrator Bowles said meats, fats and oils, butter, sugar, shoes and tires will stay on the ration list "until military cutbacks and increased production bring civilian supplies more nearly in balance with civilian demand."

The Times Says--

Cruel Aggression Ends
Prisoners Huge Problem
Radar Greatest Story

LONDON.—Victory, final and unqualified, brings to an end the half century of selfish expansion and cruel aggression by the rulers of Japan, says the Times editorially. The news came at the end of a series of untrustworthy rumors. Apparently the delays in Japan's acceptance of surrender was due to an attempt to bargain over the continuance of the emperor's prerogatives. But these will now pass under the control of the supreme commander of the Allied forces and the emperor will be compelled to see that surrender terms are fully observed.

Thus, to bring the emperor into the arena of politics, says the Times, is probably the best way to ensure that the reality of defeat is brought home to the Japanese people. The imperial throne can no longer be divorced from the disaster which overwhelming ambition has brought upon the governing classes. When Allied plans for governing Japan have been completed the emperor will

(Continued on Page 5, Col. 6)

Edmonton Races

WEDNESDAY'S SCRATCHES

2—Sweet Wind.
4—Kelley Somers
5—Skip the News.
7—Hazelgreen, Red Chalk, Beaming Son.
Track fast.

Where To Find It

Amusements, Theatres	11
Bridge	14
Comics	14, 22, 23
Crossword Puzzle	14
District	15
Editorial	4
Financial	20
Garry Myers	14
Off the Record	14
Radio	15
Sport	10, 11
They'll Do It Every Time	14
Uncle Ray's Corner	14
Want Ads	22, 23, 24
Women's	16, 17

The Weather

Estimated low tonight, 50.
Estimated high tomorrow, 80.
Yesterday's maximum 82.
Overnight low 52.
Hourly readings since 12:30 p.m. Tuesday:

12:30	72	8:30	75	4:30	55
1:30	77	9:30	71	5:30	54
2:30	79	10:30	66	6:30	52
3:30	81	11:30	63	7:30	58
4:30	81	12:30	61	8:30	61
5:30	82	1:30	59	9:30	65
6:30	80	2:30	58	10:30	73
7:30	79	3:30	54	11:30	72

Combat Continues Until Last Minute

NEW YORK. — Peace was declared officially throughout the world Wednesday, but in the broad expanses of the Pacific war theatres, armies or their components faced each other in a score of places and in most instances sharp combat continued right up to the official declaration.

In the greatest land movements of the war's closing week, the Soviet armies of the east drove fiercely against Japanese on broad fronts in Manchuria and Korea and on the island of Sakhalin, just north of Japan.

Southward, in southern and central China, the final day of hostilities found Chinese armies battering against retreating enemy columns in half a dozen provinces.

Far to the west, British and Indian forces continued mopping up against defeated and bottled up Japanese in Burma, meeting scattered stubborn resistance.

In the islands of the Pacific, American, Australian and Dutch formations faced similar situations.

Explosions Rock East Coast Village

ST. MARTINS, N.B.—Explosions shook houses in this village on the Bay of Fundy coast 30 miles northwest of Saint John after a scow loaded with gasoline and ammunition caught fire from a flare thrown up late Tuesday night in celebration of the Japanese surrender.

Several explosions occurred but no injuries or damage were reported, aside from the fire on the scow.

Edmontonians Celebrate End of Second Great War in "Most Orderly Fashion"

Within minutes after the official announcement of Japan's surrender was made, downtown streets were jammed with thousands of citizens, young and old, who cheered the good news, threw paper streamers to the street and patted members of the armed forces on the back for a good job "well done." The top picture shows a large group of citizens at 101 st. and Jasper ave. early Tuesday evening. The crowd increased later. The bottom photograph shows some wounded veterans at the Col. Mewburn hospital as they heard the "welcome news" of the surrender. Story on page 13.

Aldershot People Still Like Canucks

ALDERSHOT, England. — The town council of this garrison town Tuesday decided to invite every member of the Canadian army who has served overseas in this war to become a freeman of the borough.

The decision came at a special meeting a little more than a month after Canadian troops did thousands of dollars' damage during two nights of window-smashing demonstrations. Tuesday in an interview with a London Daily Express reporter, Mayor Jack White said no ill-feeling had been created against the Canadians by that "liveliness."

State Ownership Promised Britons

LONDON. — Britain's new Labor government called formally for state ownership of the Bank of England and nationalization of the coal mining industry Wednesday as His Majesty the King opened the new parliament.

Outlining the Labor government's program, the speech from the throne said peacetime legislative powers would be sought "to insure the right use of our commercial and industrial resources and the distribution and fair prices of essential supplies and services."

The new government promised:

1. Orderly release of those in the armed services "with the greatest speed consistent with our military commitments and fair treatment to serving men and women."
2. Aid—expanded where necessary—for war disabled.
3. Use of national resources in

(Continued on Page 5, Col. 3)

Special stories and pictures reviewing the war in the Pacific will be found on pages 6, 7, 8 and 9.

Thousands Cheer V-J Parade As City Celebrates Victory

Thousands of Edmonton and district residents—many of them carrying flags and banners—lined paper-littered, downtown streets Wednesday for the city's victory parade, in which more than 5,000 members of the navy, army, air force, veterans of the First Great War, civilian organizations and provincial and civic officals took part.

Headed by a motor cycle escort and a color party, the parade, one of the largest held in Edmonton in more than 10 years, left the market square at 11:00 a.m., proceeded south to Jasper ave., west along Jasper ave., to 108 st., south on 108 st. to 100 ave., east on 100 ave. to 101 st., and north on 101 st. to the Canadian National Railways station after passing the reviewing stand at 102 ave. Stirred by the rousing music of eight bands, including one of 29 pieces from Wetaskiwin, the crowd cheered loudly all along the route, giving an exceptionally loud cheer for wounded veterans from the Col. Mewburn hospital who were taken along the route in 75 cars donated by members of Edmonton service clubs.

The salute was taken by Hon. J. C. Bowen, lieutenant-governor of Alberta. He was accompanied on the reviewing platform by Premier Manning and several members of his government, Mayor Fry and high-ranking civic officials, Wing Cmdr. L. H. Phinney, special commissioner for northwest defence projects, and members of the 6th Service Command of the U.S.A.A.F.

Forty-two outfits took part in the V-J Day parade. Included was the U.S.A.A.F., Royal Canadian Navy, Canadian Army (Active), R.C.A.F., Canadian Army (reserve), veterans' organizations, navy, army and air-

(Continued on Page 19, Col. 3)

Jap War-Minister Commits Suicide

NEW YORK. — Japanese War Minister Korechika Anami has committed suicide, the Japanese Domei agency reported Wednesday.

The broadcast Domei dispatch, directed to the North American zone, said Anami had taken his life at his "official residence" to "atone for his failure in accomplishing his duties as his majesty's minister."

World's Statesmen To Meet Thursday

LONDON.—Statesmen of 14 United Nations will meet Thursday within the shadows of ancient Westminster Abbey to prepare for the birth of a new international peace-keeping organization.

These statesmen — representing Australia, Brazil, Canada, Chile, China, Czecho-Slovakia, France, Iran, Mexico, the Netherlands, Russia, the United Kingdom, and United States and Yugoslavia—form the executive committee of the United Nations' preparatory commission. They will set in motion machinery which they hope will guide the world into paths of permanent peace.

When the commission is not in session, the 14-man executive committee will exercise its functions and powers. Meeting Thursday, the committee will make provisional arrangements for the first sessions of the United Nations' general assembly, the security council, the economic and social council, and the trusteeship council.

The King to Speak To Empire Today

LONDON.—His Majesty the King will broadcast to Great Britain at 9:00 p.m. (2:00 p.m. Edmonton) Wednesday, it was announced.

Speech of His Majesty will be heard in Canada over the C.B.C. network.

Fighting Continued Since July 7, 1937

(By The Canadian Press)

Japan's surrender will bring world peace for the first time since July 7, 1937, when Japanese and Chinese soldiers clashed at Marco Polo bridge near Peiping.

Just three months and five days after the unconditional surrender of Germany, Japan yielded to the might of Allied arms.

Actually, sporadic fighting had been under way in Asia since Sept. 18, 1931, when the Japanese invaded Manchuria.

Great Britain had been at war since Sept. 3, 1939.

For the United States, Wednesday was the first full day of peace since Dec. 7, 1941.

Russia had fought from June 22, 1941, when she was attacked by Germany, but was at peace for three months between May 9, when Berlin capitulated, and Aug. 9, when she declared war on Japan.

The First Great War started on July 28, 1914 and ended Nov. 11, 1918.

More than 8,500,000 men died in the 1914-18 conflict and casualties totalled 37,494,186.

In the war just ended the European phase alone cost the lives of more than 8,000,000 men in battle, with a total estimate as high as 40,000,000 casualties. The cost was close to $1,000,000,000,000.

Japs Are Ordered Cease Hostilities

(By the Associated Press)

The Second Great War has ended. Japan has surrendered unconditionally and formal arrangements for the cessation of hostilities are moving rapidly toward completion.

A Reuters dispatch from Manila reported that Gen. MacArthur had radioed Tokyo directing the Japanese to cease hostilities immediately and send a representative to Manila to receive instructions.

Earlier it was announced Gen. MacArthur had notified the Japanese emperor that he (MacArthur) has been designated supreme commander of Allied powers and empowered "to arrange directly with Japanese authorities for cessation of hostilities at the earliest practicable date."

Tokyo radio said Wednesday that "the imperial order to cease fire is expected soon," but warned enemy warships away from Japanese home waters until then "so as to avoid any untoward incident."

In his instructions to the Japanese, MacArthur ordered the designation of a station in the Tokyo area for continuous use in the handling of radio communications between the two headquarters.

The Japanese cabinet Wednesday issued a "proclamation to the nation" calling on the Japanese people to obey Emperor Hirohito's imperial rescript announcing Japan's surrender to the Allied powers and pledging itself to do likewise, the Japanese Domei agency reported. The proclamation was signed by Premier Suzuki, who has since resigned.

"Imperial judgment has already been passed," the proclamation said, as transmitted textually by Domei in an English-language wireless dispatch to the North American zone. "The way for his majesty's subjects to follow is self-evident."

Allied armed forces have been ordered to suspend offensive action.

There were no conditions to the Japanese surrender, although the foe had sought last Friday to win guarantees that the emperor would remain a sovereign ruler.

The empire which set out in 1937 to conquer the Pacific and lands beyond caved in completely.

The war has ended, but no steps taken anywhere could make up for the losses of life and treasure already lost in mankind's most frightful conflict.

The countries of the world altogether suffered incalculable casualties; some persons put the total at more than 23,000,000 killed and wounded exclusive of air raid and starvation losses that never can be known.

Fleet Downs Five Jap Planes After Surrender Announced

GUAM. — Five Japanese planes have been shot down around the 3rd Fleet since noon Wednesday Japanese time, or four hours after Hirohito's surrender announcement.

There was no report of damage to the Allied warships.

Admiral Nimitz did not indicate whether the enemy planes were attempting to attack or welcome the units of Admiral Halsey's great fleet. Nor did he say whether they were shot down by ship gunfire or combat air patrol.

The admiral said Gen. MacArthur has been asked to inform Japanese authorities that 3rd Fleet defence measures require naval forces to destroy any aircraft approaching them.

The commander-in-chief of Pacific naval forces carefully avoided the use of the word "attack." He reported merely that units of the 3rd Fleet in the vicinity of Honshu, main island of Japan, were being "approached" by Nipponese planes.

Admiral Nimitz announced earlier that the cease fire order was issued at approximately 9:00 a.m. Wednes-

(Continued on Page 5, Col. 5)

Japan Explains Attack on Fleet

NEW YORK.—A Domei dispatch broadcast by the Tokyo radio on Wednesday said Japanese imperial headquarters is endeavoring to transmit the imperial surrender order to every branch of the forces, but before it took full effect a part of the Japanese air force is reported to have made an attack on the Allied bases and fleet in the south.

"While the imperial headquarters is trying its best to prevent the recurrence of such incidents, the Allied fleets and convoys are again requested not to approach Japanese home waters until cease-fire arrangements are made," Domei said.

Issues His Final War Communique

MANILA. — Gen. MacArthur, designated as supreme commander for Allied forces in Japan, has issued his final communique of the war and his first instructions to Japanese Emperor Hirohito

In closing out his formal series of communiques, Gen. MacArthur disclosed that American planes had damaged 20 Japanese ships in sweeps over Japanese empire home waters Tuesday and had shot down 17 enemy planes.

Japan's surrender envoy will fly in all white plane, decorated with green crosses, when he comes to learn the Allied terms for surrender, Gen. MacArthur disclosed in a note to the Japanese.

Petain Is Given Death Sentence

PARIS. — Marshal Petain was convicted and sentenced to death early Wednesday by three judges and a 24-man jury who deliberated almost seven hours.

The high court of justice added it "hoped the sentence would not be executed."

(This recommendation for clemency presumably will be considered by Gen. de Gaulle, president of the French provisional government.)

Persons in the courtroom close to Gen. de Gaulle, a former protege of Petain, said the general was almost certain to commute the sentence to life imprisonment. Petain was once de Gaulle's regimental commander.

Besides condemning the 89-year-old former chief of the Vichy state to death for "plotting against the internal safety of France," the court also sentenced him to national in-

(Continued on Page 19, Col. 2)

EDMONTON RACE ENTRIES FOR THURSDAY WILL BE FOUND ON PAGE 19.

Death Camp Horror

"The story of the 'horror camps' in Germany began more than 12 years ago. Its first bloody chapters were written in 1933 within a few days of the seizure of power by Hitler and his Nazi thugs."
— Editorial, May 16, 1945

The world, in 1933, was at least aware of the potential for evil in the hearts of the Nazis.

The Journal published stories about German pre-war ethnic and political "policies" that foreshadowed the gruesome orgy of death to come.

War news in the 1940s was a mix of reports from on-the-scene reporters and official communiques. Generally, the stories told the tales of brave Canadian and Allied fighting men beating the Nazi menace. The real cost of victory was in the daily casualty lists that ran on the inside pages.

Stories of German brutality were common throughout the war.

"As British forces move into Greece, new chapters are being added to the old story of German barbarism ... the long tale of inhuman cruelty deliberately practiced by German armies of occupation must be retold again and again," said an Oct. 16, 1944, editorial.

The spine of the German army bent, then broke after the main Allied push in Normandy, June 6, 1944. As its army retreated on the Western and Eastern fronts, Germany's darker secrets began to be exposed.

By 1945, *Journal* readers recoiled in revulsion at the stories that went far beyond the general horror of war, stories written by hardened war reporters, overwhelmed by the magnitude of the scenes they encountered.

William Frye wrote April 21, 1945, from the Belsen, Germany, concentration camp. "No coffins or flowers at this funeral. No tears or well-bred sympathy. No music. These naked corpses were hauled in trucks and dumped into a pit. Their pallbearers were SS men and women, now Allied prisoners.

"Their litany was the hoarse shouts of British soldiers, sick with disgust and fury, ordering these marked members of Hitler's chosen legion about their horrible task.

"I saw Belsen – its piles of lifeless dead and its aimless swarms of living dead, their great eyes were just animal lights in skin-covered skulls of famine."

Journal editorials screamed for justice, but feared it would never come. "The broken and tortured bodies of millions of our fellow human beings, deliberately done to death in the most fiendish manner, cry out for justice.

"How shall justice be assured? Already here and there voices are raised to protest that nations cannot be judged by the actions of individuals.

"We have been assured by our leaders that the men who ordered these crimes against humanity, and the men and women who carried them out, will be punished. But leaders change, governments change, people not directly hurt forget so soon."

***May 8, 1948*:**
The Edmonton Flyers beat the Ottawa Senators 5-3 to win the Allan Cup, the dominion senior amateur hockey championship, for the first time.

***May 18, 1948*:**
The University of Alberta graduates its largest class to date, forcing convocation ceremonies to be held over two days for the first time. An honourary degree is awarded to Premier Ernest Manning.

***July 11, 1948*:**
Greyhound bus fare from Edmonton to Vancouver and return is $37.35, plus tax.

***July 17, 1948*:**
Imperial Oil opens the first oil refinery in Edmonton's Clover Bar area.

***July 20, 1948*:**
City officials report 28,168 telephones are in operation in Edmonton.

***July 23, 1948*:**
Sod is turned for the Aberhart Memorial Hospital for tuberculosis patients, on the University of Alberta campus.

***July 26, 1948*:**
Parking meters go into operation on the streets of Edmonton on a year's trial.

Edmonton Bulletin Edmonton Journal

SIXTY-SIXTH YEAR EDMONTON, ALBERTA—FRIDAY, MAY 31, 1946 Telephone 26121 PRICE 5 CENTS

Printers of Three Southam Papers on Strike

Strike Statement Issued By Publisher of Journal

Mr. W. A. MacDonald, publisher of The Edmonton Journal, makes the following announcement:

Journal printers failed to report for work on the Thursday night and Friday morning shifts. The strike thus commenced, without notification to the management, appears to be a sympathy movement designed to aid Winnipeg printers who struck work on the Winnipeg Free Press and the Winnipeg Tribune last November.

THE JOURNAL has no dispute with its printers. Relations with the union have been cordial for many years. Contracts with the union were renewed only last November, and the strike now begun is in complete violation of the terms of those contracts.

In the November contracts, which would be effective in toto until May 15, 1947, and thereafter unless then re-opened by either party on sixty days notice, The Journal agreed, subject to approval of the Regional War Labor Board, to an increase of the hourly wage scale to one dollar six and two-thirds cents for the day shift; one dollar thirteen and one-third cents for the night shift; two weeks vacation with pay; a forty-hour week for the day shift and a thirty-seven and one-half hour work week for the night shift to become effective as soon as the union could supply sufficient men to produce the required type in such hours.

WITHIN TEN DAYS of signing the above mentioned contracts, the local printers' union, under strong pressure from its international officers in the United States, repudiated their signatures on the very day their representatives and The Journal were to have made joint application to the Regional War Labor Board for approval of the above mentioned terms.

There is no disagreement between The Journal and its printers. If the union members will withdraw its letters of repudiation, return to work and give assurance that they will respect their contracts now and in the future, Journal management will be glad to make joint application with the union to the Regional War Labor board for approval of the contract terms.

THE PRINTERS' strike here is based on no local issue; it is obviously intended as a method of assisting striking printers in Winnipeg whose action in striking there was found to be quite illegal and in defiance of Dominion regulations.

The Journal has always been proud of its happy labor relations and regrets the present occurrence, but it will continue to publish, with or without its striking printers. The situation in Winnipeg will in no way influence the course of The Edmonton Journal.

Anglican-United Union Is Mooted

TORONTO, May 31.—(CP)—The question of union between the Church of England in Canada and the United Church has progressed to the point where reports will be presented to the Dominion meetings of both churches next September, it was reported last night.

UNION WAS DISCUSSED here last week by representatives of the two great Protestant denominations, meeting as a joint committee. The joint chairmen are Rt. Rev. John Lyons, of Kingston, bishop of the Ontario diocese of the Anglican Church, and very Rev. J. R. P. Schlater, Toronto, former moderator of the United Church.

Talk of union has cropped up for several years but the meetings here were the first concrete action. The United Church at latest official figures had 2,204,807 adherents in Canada, while membership of the Anglican church in the same estimate was given as 1,751,188.

The last great union of Protestant denominations in Canada was the formation of the United Church in 1925, consisting of the Methodist, Congregationalist and Presbyterian Churches, although a considerable body of Presbyterians

(Continued on Page Three)
See CHURCH UNION

Hard Coal Miners Strike in States

NEW YORK, May 31. — (AP) — Pennsylvania's 75,000 hard coal miners struck today at 12:01 a.m. after union and operator negotiators failed to agree on a new contract, shutting down the state's anthracite fields.

AN AFL UNITED Mine Workers representative at the Lehigh Valley Coal Company in Hazelton, Pa., declared that reports from the hard coal districts showed that "the whole region is idle."

"There are no collieries in the anthracite fields working," said Jack Reno, chairman of the grievance committee, Hazelton shaft, of the Lehigh company.

Meanwhile a high government official in Washington who could not be quoted directly said President Truman had been counselled by his advisers against seizing the mines.

THE OFFICIAL said the advice was based on the hope that the anthracite industry would shortly agree to terms similar to those in the government contract which ended the soft coal shutdown.

Eight-Storey Fall Kills City Woman

VANCOUVER, May 31—(CP)—Mrs. H. R. Plommer, 44, wife of the general manager of Canadian Collieries at Nanaimo, B.C., was instantly killed late yesterday when she fell from the window of her eighth floor suite of a Vancouver hotel, police said last night. Mr. Plommer told police he was in the suite at the time but in another room. He said his wife had just returned from the lobby after buying a magazine. He heard her enter the suite, but a few minutes later, when he called to her he received no answer.

60-Year Romance to End in Marriage

MOUNT PLEASANT, Ont., May 31.—(CP)—Romance which started 60 years ago when Bill Atkin carried Florence Walls' school books in Lincoln, England, has led to marriage plans for the two, who have not seen each other since Atkin came to Canada in 1907. Atkin, now 68, is on his way to Lincoln to marry his childhood sweetheart after a three-year exchange of yetters which began when his son Brant, a Canadian soldier, visited Lincoln. Miss Walls heard of the visit, wrote Mr. Atkin, and their romance was rekindled.

ARGENTINE STRIKE

BUENOS AIRES, May 31.—(Reuters) — Workmen of the Buenos Aires Southern Railway last night declared a general strike as the Buenos Aires Pacific Railway ordered complete suspension of suburban services in the Argentine capital for an indefinite period.

Blame For Strike Placed on Printers

MONTREAL, May 31—(CP)—Blame for the spread of labor difficulties from Winnipeg to other cities where Southam newspapers are published "must rest completely upon the shoulders of the International Typographical Union and the several local unions which have submitted to its instructions," P. S Fisher, president of the Southam Company, Ltd., said today in a statement.

MR. FISHER'S statement, issued in connection with a strike of linotype operators at the Ottawa Citizen, Hamilton Spectator and Edmonton Journal, follows:

The position of the head office of the Southam, Company in connection with these strikes can be quite simply stated. It is our conviction that daily newspapers must be administered in the cities in which they are published, and authority to deal with labor relations in the different cities in which we operate has been traditionally vested in the local publisher.

THIS METHOD of negotiation on a local basis has been traditional practice for many years throughout Canada and the United States. It has been accepted by all the printing trades unions, and the position of the Southam Company was further justified when on May 23 the National Wartime Labour Relations Board rejected an application of the International Typographical Union to have the company ordered to negotiate on a group basis.

The present strikes at Ottawa, Hamilton and Edmonton do not result from differences of opinion between the publishers in those cities and the local unions concerning local wages or conditions. They are sympathetic strikes, embarked upon by those local unions under instruction from the international officers of the ITU, in an effort to force the company into action favorable to the union in Winnipeg.

DIFFICULTIES between the Winnipeg Typographical Union and the Winnipeg newspapers, both the Winnipeg Tribune owned by the Southam Company, and the Winnipeg Free Press, arose last November when, during the course of negotiations for a renewal of contract, the union absolutely refused to accept impartial arbitration, to be binding on both parties, which was offered by the publishers, and engaged in an illegal strike while a government-appointed conciliator was endeavouring to assist in the completion of a contract.

Neither the company as a whole, nor any of the publishers of Southam newspapers are against trade unionism. Their relations with the other printing trades unions have traditionally been and are still completely cordial. Their relations with the ITU were cordial until the unjustifiable strike in Winnipeg forced the Winnipeg Tribune, in common with the Winnipeg Free Press, to hire other printers to preserve its very existence.

EVEN SINCE the Winnipeg strike, the publishers of other Southam newspapers have been quite prepared to continue amicable relations with their respective local typographical unions, and if the difficulties which originated in Winnipeg have spread to other cities, the blame must rest completely upon the shoulders of the International Typographical Union and the several local unions which have submitted to its instructions.

Transport Sailing Given Long Delay

OTTAWA, May 31. — (CP) — The sailing of the transport Ile de France, originally scheduled to dock at Halifax June 9 with 8,000 Canadian servicemen and 100 dependents, has been delayed until June 21, because of engine trouble, army officials said yesterday. Some 5,000 of the servicemen will be transferred to the Aquitania, docking at Halifax about June 8, and the 1,100 dependents who were to have sailed on the Aquitania and the remaining 3,000 servicemen would be accommodated as soon as possible, officials said.

Ask Appeal Body For Tax Disputes

OTTAWA, May 31. — (CP)—The Senate yesterday called for appointment of an independent board of appeal for income tax payers after hearing a Nova Scotian Senator bespeak objections which were interpreted by a colleague to mean he felt his fellow Nova Scotian, Finance Minister Ilsley, had been slighted.

The upper chamber approved the report of a special committee to enable its recommendation for such a board to be placed before the government in final consideration of its approaching budget.

The only objections came from Senators J. J. Kinley (L-Nova Scotia) and G. G. McGeer (L-British Columbia).

SAID THE FORMER: "I haven't much faith in such a board doing much for the common man. . . . If we had regional inspectors to aid the taxpayer with advice perhaps it would do some good."

Senator McGeer contended the decision of the appeal board should be final rather than, as proposed, the first step in litigation which could reach the Privy Council. He was heartily in accord with the general recommendation but held that it "would have more power if it weren't rushed through too hurriedly."

If the board was one of final appeal, it would contribute to speed, finality and uniformity.

Say Stettinius Is Retiring From UN

WASHINGTON, May 31—(AP)—Government officials who would not permit use of their names last night reported Edward R. Stettinius, Jr., has sent to President Truman his resignation as United States representative on the United Nations Security Council.

The White House and Mr. Stettinius declined comment.

THE INFORMANTS said they were not fully acquainted with Mr. Stettinius' reasons for his reported wish to withdraw, but he was believed to feel his organizing task in the international organization has been completed.

The 45-year-old Stettinius is the only representative the United States has had on the Security Council.

Edmonton Firm Options Property

Gateway Gold Limited announced Friday that a new property has been acquired by option. This group of six claims adjoins Sparta group recently sold by "Spud" Arrenault to Beaulieu Yellowknife for $100,000 cash.

Development of this new group of claims is scheduled to begin within the next two or three weeks.

D. A. Campbell, manager director, who returned recently from Red Lake, Ont., has announced the appointment of Jack Bergman, formerly of Edmonton, as consulting engineer in charge of development program on the Red Lake property of Gateway Gold Limited.

Boys' "Tree-House" Is Found by Police

A complaint laid with city police by Mrs. E. J. Barrett, 12236 133 street, that a group of boys were shooting .22 rifles in a large growth of trees near her home, resulted in the discovery of a "tree-house" that had been erected by the boys in the midst of a large stand of poplars between 130 and 132 streets south of the Calder elevator.

The youths had built the house and suspended it in mid-air from some of the largest trees in the group and it is believed that they were shooting from their unique home. About 100 trees in the stand are said to have been cut down by the lads.

New Site For Hall

A new site for the community hall and skating rink was decided upon by members of the McKernan Community League at a meeting held in the community hall Thursday night. It was decided to accept the city's offer of the property between 115 and 116 streets on Bennett avenue. The community hall and skating rink will now be moved to this new location.

HEART ATTACK FATAL

Charles M. Dupee of the Saddy apartments, 95 street, suffered a heart seizure in Drummond's grocery store, 10334 95 street, and died while being rushed to the Royal Alexandra hospital by Jack Hays' ambulance. Funeral arrangements, which are in charge of Connelly and McKinley, will be announced later.

TWIN WAR BRIDES ARRIVE: Twin war brides of boyhood Canadian friends, Mrs. Tom Harvey, left, and Mrs. Charles Gray, arrived in Canada aboard the liner Queen Mary to join their Peterboro, Ont., husbands. The men, L-Cpl. Tom Harvey and Cpl. Charles Gray, enlisted together in the RCE, went overseas together, met the twin sisters together at Croydon, Eng., and were married together. Each has a small daughter.

Correspondence Between City Papers, Typographical Union

Reproduction of the correspondence below, which passed between the Edmonton Typographical Union and Edmonton daily newspapers in recent months, will supply the public with the background of the printers' strike at The Edmonton Journal which began Thursday night when the night shift failed to appear for work.

Union Repudiates Contracts

On November 27, 1945, the union repudiated its contracts with both Edmonton newspapers, in the following terms, addressed to both publishers:

COPY
Edmonton Typographical Union No. 604
Edmonton, Alberta, Canada.
November 27, 1945.

Mr. W. A. MacDonald,
Vice.-Pres. and Managing Director,
The Edmonton Journal,
A Division of the Southam Co. Ltd.,
Edmonton, Alta.

Dear Sir:

With regard to the contract and supplemental agreement with this union signed on Nov. 13 and 22 respectively, and to which our officers affixed their signatures, with the understanding that such signatures were provisional pending approval by our International President.

Since we have been notified that the contract in its present form cannot be approved by our International president, Edmonton Typographical Union No. 604 in regular meeting assembled has unanimously instructed its officers to repudiate their signatures to said documents pending consummation of an agreement which can be approved.

The scale committee of the union is prepared to meet with the publisher in an effort to negotiate such a contract at your convenience.

Yours truly,
JOHN T. KELLEY, President.
DANIEL K. KNOTT, Secretary.

Copy to Mr. Campbell.

Publishers' Joint Reply

To this the publishers of The Journal and Bulletin replied jointly as follows:

COPY

Mr. D. K. Knott,
Secretary,
Edmonton Typographical Union, No. 604,
c/o Journal Composing Room,
Edmonton, Alberta.

Dear Mr. Knott:

This is to acknowledge receipt of your letter dated November 27,

(Continued on Page Two)
See CORRESPONDENCE

Pulp Mill Workers Continue Parley on "Hot Log" Question

POWELL RIVER, B.C., May 31—(CP)—A meeting of some 1,800 American Federation of Labor Workers at the British Empire's largest newsprint mill to consider their attitude toward handling logs which striking CIO woodworkers labelled as "hot" ended late Thursday afternoon and will be resumed Friday morning.

The AFL paper and pulp workers claimed the logs are "fair" as they were cut and shipped to the mill before the walkout of some 35,000 British Columbia loggers and millworkers began May 15. The latter demand wage increases of 25 cents an hour, a 40-hour week and union security.

THE NEWSPRINT workers have to decide whether to cross CIO picket lines to handle the logs or to honor the picket line and break their new agreement with the Powell River Paper and Pulp

(Continued on Page Three)
See B.C. STRIKE

Pope to Broadcast Important Address

ROME, May 31.—(AP)—A Vatican City source said yesterday that an address by Pope Pius Saturday probably would be 25 to 30 minutes long and his text probably would be about 4,000 to 5,000 words. It will be broadcast by the Vatican radio at 9:45 a.m. (2:45 a.m., MDT). There was no indication of his topic, but the source said it will be an important speech. The pontiff will speak in Italian. The address will be to the Sacred College of Cardinals in reply to their greetings on the occasion of the Pope's name day, the birthday of St. Eugen.

TO USE JET PLANES

LONDON, May 31.—(Reuters)—Britain's military and civil aviation will from now on be powered by jet or gas-turbine engines, Supply Minister John Wilmot announced yesterday.

SOLDIERS TO HANG

HEIDELBERG, Germany, May 31. — (AP) — Three United States Negro soldiers have been sentenced to be hanged and two other Negroes were given life imprisonment for killing a white American soldier and wounding three others, United States 3rd Army headquarters said yesterday.

Variable Skies Forecast Here

Rain clouds which have been hanging over Edmonton and district for the last 48 hours are passing, and a promise of warmer and clear weather is foreseen by the weather bureau. The forecast for Friday reads "variable sky and warmer." Estimated high temperature is 65. Reading at 8:30 a.m. was 52.

High temperature Thursday was 58 recorded at 3:30 p.m. Low was 47 at 8:30 a.m. Overnight low was 43 at 1:30 a.m. Friday. Sun rises Saturday at 4:12 a.m. and sets at 8:50 p.m.

New Airliner Passes Tests

LONDON, May 31.—(CP)—The Avro Tudor I, Britain's first high-altitude airliner with pressure cabin, has completed flight tests up to 30,000 feet and probably will be in service by the year-end on the North Atlantic run.

No matter how high the plane must fly to reach smooth air, pressure inside the roomy cabin will be the same as at 8,000 feet. Need for oxygen masks, bugbear of North Atlantic flights so far, is eliminated.

Twenty of these 77,000-pound planes, built to carry 24 passengers in seats and 12 on sleeper service, have been ordered for Britain's government-owned airlines.

The Tudor I has been criticized on grounds of uneconomic operation, since 12-passenger trans-Atlantic capacity is only half that of similar four-engined American aircraft. But the benefits of successful pressurization have received nothing but praise.

U.S. Coal Price Expected to Rise

WASHINGTON, May 31. — (AP) —Government officials predicted last night that the strike gains of John L. Lewis' miners will hike the price of soft coal 30 to 35 cents a ton for consumers. Mine owners indicated they would wait for the ceiling price decision before making a new try for a contract with Mr. Lewis and for recovery of their government-held workings. They decided against making any public statement on the agreement signed Wednesday between Mr. Lewis and the United States government, which includes a $25,000,000 employer-financed welfare fund.

No Solution Near In Seamen Strike

By The Canadian Press

The lake shipping strike was no nearer solution today—government efforts to achieve a settlement apparently had reached a deadlock—and flare-ups along the docks of the great inland seas were multiplying.

AT MONTREAL, Conrad Sauras, business agent there for the Canadian Seamen's Union, said today he has received a telegram from J. A. (Pat) Sullivan, union president, "advising all ports and members to continue their legitimate battle to keep scabs off ships."

The telegram said these instructions were issued because "Canada Steamship Lines and Sarnia and Colonial Steamships, Limited, have issued public statements in contravention to the requests of Labor Minister Humphrey Mitchell."

(Mr. Mitchell announced in the House of Commons yesterday that the union had agreed its members still on ships would continue operating them provided shipping companies would cease efforts to man strike-bound ships with non-union crews.

(THE LABOR MINISTER also said that operators of the larger lake shipping companies would be invited to a conference, tentatively

(Continued on Page Three)
See SAILOR STRIKE

River Now 11 Feet Over Normal Level

The North Saskatchewan river during Thursday and Friday morning rose six feet six inches to a level of 11 feet above normal, W. I. McFarland, power superintendent, stated Friday.

HE SAID THAT observations Friday morning would indicate that the peak of the rise occasioned by the recent rains has been reached, and that a decline in the river levels was indicated.

Mr. McFarland stated also that the regular run-off from the mountain regions at the source of the river could be expected about June 20 or a little later than that date.

Invitation to U.S. Declined by Stalin

WASHINGTON, May 31.—(BUP)—President Truman disclosed today that within the last 30 days he had invited Generalissimo Josef Stalin to visit Washington, but that Stalin declined because of poor health. Truman told his news conference that he had not proposed a formal Big Three meeting but had simply invited Stalin here for what he described as a social visit.

KING DINES PREMIERS

LONDON, May 31. — (Reuters) — Three Commonwealth prime ministers and a deputy prime minister were the guests of the King and Queen last night at an Empire dinner party at Buckingham Palace. The prime ministers were Clement Attlee of Britain, William Lyon Mackenzie King of Canada, and Field Marshal Smuts of South Africa. The deputy was Walter Nash of New Zealand.

Edmonton, Ottawa, Hamilton Plants Affected by Walkout

OTTAWA, May 31—Composing room employees of the Ottawa Citizen, Hamilton Spectator and the Edmonton Journal, all three members of the Southam Company Ltd., chain, went on strike Thursday night.

The Citizen, which publishes both morning and afternoon papers, did not issue a morning edition today. Publication would be resumed as soon as possible, with or without the assistance of the union, officials said.

A STATEMENT issued by H. S. Southam, publisher of the Citizen, said the strike was in sympathy with the Winnipeg members of the union and was not called because of anything the Citizen has neglected or declined to do in fulfilment of its contractual obligations.

Printers, linotype operators and other composing room employees who were on strike were numbered by the company at 45.

THE UNION issued a statement in which it indicated the dispute stemmed back to the strike of members of the union at the Winnipeg Tribune, a Southam paper, Nov. 8, 1945, in disagreement over the terms of a new contract. Printers at the Winnipeg Free Press went out at the same time and both papers subsequently hired new composing room staffs.

The Typographical Union said the strike which started last night had as its main issue the "open shop" which the Southam Company was seeking to institute. There had been persistent refusal to negotiate a settlement or to negotiate "with respect to basic conditions of employment traditional to the industry." Provincial and national labor

(Continued on Page Two)
See PRINTERS

Man and Woman Traffic Victims

A man and a woman suffered injuries as the result of traffic accidents on city streets Thursday evening.

Mrs. Emma Welton, 10120 156 street, suffered bruises and possible chest injuries when the taxi in which she was riding was hit by a car driven by Harry McDermott, 14215 101 avenue. Mrs. Patricia E. Hay, 10120 156 street, driver of the taxi, stated that she stopped to pick up a member of the Corps of Commissionaires after passing McDermott's auto and that her car was struck at the rear.

MRS. WELTON, who was riding in the back seat, was injured when she was thrown against the front seat. She was taken to the General hospital for medical attention.

D. N. Overton, 12025 87 street, suffered minor bruises when he was knocked to the pavement at 102 avenue and 100 street by a youth riding a cycle. The cyclist, who also fell, got up and ran off leaving his bicycle behind, which was taken to the city police station.

Scientist Dies After Atom Blast

LOS ALAMOS, N.M., May 31.—(AP)—Dr. Louis Slotin, 35-year-old scientist from Winnipeg, died yesterday from the effects of exposure to radiation, the United States army announced.

Dr. Slotin and seven other physicists and technicians of the Los Alamos atomic bomb laboratory were injured May 21 in an accident while working with fissionable material. All were exposed to radiation, but the other seven are reported recovering.

DR. N. E. BRADBURY, project director, credited Dr. Slotin with dispersing the material "at the moment of the accident to prevent greater injury to fellow scientists."

A native of Winnipeg, Dr. Slotin was unmarried. He was granted his Ph.D. by the University of London and came to the atomic bomb laboratory from Oak Ridge, Tenn., in December, 1944. He had been associated with the Manhattan engineer district since 1943.

Western Crops Need More Rain

WINNIPEG, May 31.—Continuing dry weather is a matter of concern at many points in western Canada, as seeding of the current crop nears completion. Small percentages of coarse grains and some flax remain to be sown, the latter being delayed by farmers pending arrival of additional rainfall. Weed growth, particularly wild oats, is heavy in some northern sections, which has necessitated ploughing down and reseeding, according to the weekly crop report of the department of agriculture of the Canadian National Railways.

LIGHT SCATTERED showers are reported from many districts in the Edmonton territory but are insufficient for requirements. The topsoil is very dry with subsoil moisture still fairly good. Wheat seeding is completed and rapid progress has been made with coarse grains. Growth is very slow due to cool weather but early sown grains are up four inches. Pastures are generally poor and need rain.

Heavy rains have fallen in many areas north of Edmonton and crop conditions are considered good in this territory. Seeding of all grains is practically completed with early sown crops up four inches.

Awaiting Elevator, Woman Bears Baby

VANCOUVER, May 31—(CP)—It's not often the stork gets a chance to race with an elevator, but inexperience was no drawback here yesterday. A baby girl was born while her mother and father stood waiting for an elevator on the fourth floor of old Hotel Vancouver. The parents, Mr. and Mrs. Bill Scanlon, were on their way to a nursing home where Mrs. Scanlon expected to give birth to her child. Both mother and daughter are doing well.

PAINLESS DENTIST

TORONTO, May 31. — (CP) — Dentistry can be painless, claims Dr. Roger E. McMahon, Montreal extraction specialist, and he proved it yesterday before the national convention of Canadian Dentists by pulling the tooth of a Toronto dentist who didn't even flick an eyelash during the extraction.

Britain Prepares To Ration Bread

LONDON, May 31—(CP)—Herbert Morrison, Lord President of the council, told the House of Commons today that Britain is preparing a system of bread rationing for emergency use. He compared the world food situation to the black days of Dunkerque "when all the news was bad".

"THE VERY BLACKNESS" of the situation", he said during debate on Britain's food administration, "is calling forth forces which might make this the turning point in human history".

Mr. Morrison spoke after Winston Churchill, opening debate, criticized the food administration as short-sighted and pressed for an explanation of last week's resignation of Sir Ben Smith as food minister.

MR. CHURCHILL said he would not attack Herbert Morrison, Lord President of the council, for the recent Anglo-American misunderstanding over United States food commitments arising from Mr.

(Continued on Page Three)
See BREAD RATIONING

Urge Alteration Of Pension Rules

OTTAWA, May 31.—(CP)—The Veterans' Committee of the Commons voted yesterday, in effect, to eliminate the long-standing deadline principle in award of pensions to widows and children of disabled veterans of the First Great War.

Spurred by a motion by Maj.-Gen. G. R. Pearkes, V.C. (PC-Nanaimo), the members voted 12-10 to abolish the law that no woman who married a First Great War pensioner after May 1, 1944, could be pensioned after his death. Elimination of a similar deadline covering children born to such a veteran after the same date was recommended previously.

THE RECOMMENDATIONS will go before the commons.

Committee Chairman Walter Tucker warned that such action could mean that a young girl who in the future married a veteran of the first war could get a pension for 50 years after his death.

Mr. Mackenzie warned "we've gone further in this than any country. . . . Let's be careful we don't go too far."

On another principle rooted in the depression of the thirties, the committee agreed that pensions for veterans of the Second Great War could be made retroactive for as long as 36 months where there has been an unjust delay in award through administrative difficulties.

Arab League Bans Entrance of Jews

CAIRO, May 31—(AP)—The rulers of the seven states in the Arab League formally rejected yesterday any proposals for admitting more Jews into Palestine, and one delegate to the meeting here said attempts to resettle 100,000 Jews in the Holy Land "will result in a hundred thousand corpses." The delegate, who could not be quoted by name, said that any efforts to implement the recommendations of the British-American inquiry committee that 100,000 Jews be admitted into Palestine would result in guerilla warfare. The delegate said "the beaches of Palestine must be defended if necessary. If you want to use the atomic bomb against us, very well. We will die."

Elect Officers

CALGARY, May 31.—(CP)—A T. Kloeper, Calgary, was elected state deputy of the Knights of Columbus at the Alberta state convention. Other officers elected were: W. B. Cranley, Lethbridge, treasurer; J. D. Pilon, Edmonton secretary; J. C. Hart, Edmonton, warden; W. Lambert, St. Paul, advocate, and J. J. Branniff, Pincher Creek, is past state deputy for the 1946-1947 term.

On Strike

"You know of the long-standing agreement between The Journal and The Bulletin, under which either paper will co-operate with the other to publish, for any reason beyond the control of either. The Journal published the Bulletin on one occasion and the Bulletin published the Journal on two occasions during the past 20 years."
— Chas. E. Campbell, *Edmonton Bulletin* publisher, in *The Journal*, May 31, 1946

The printers' strike really had nothing to do with *The Journal* or *Bulletin*. Printers in Edmonton, Hamilton and Ottawa walked off the job May 30, 1946, in support of the International Typographical Union in dispute with the *Winnipeg Tribune*.

Printers, also called compositors, were the people who put the type, pictures and ads together for the press run.

Both local papers had negotiated identical contracts with the union the previous November without incident.

But the ITU made a tactical move to pressure Southam Inc., owner of the *Tribune*, *The Journal*, *Hamilton Spectator* and *Ottawa Citizen* to settle the contract in Winnipeg. *The Bulletin* simply got caught in the fight.

Southam wasn't bending and *The Journal* and *Bulletin*, archrivals for nearly 43 years, on May 31, 1946, started a marriage of convenience that continued for 19 months.

The first *Edmonton Bulletin-Edmonton Journal* nameplate appeared in the city. Page 1 was full of published correspondence between the union and the papers and more-in-sorrow-than-in-anger statements from the publishers about the situation.

"The Journal has always been proud of its happy labor relations and regrets the present occurrence, but it will continue to publish with or without its striking printers," wrote publisher W.A. MacDonald.

The next day, the paper editorial staffs used the larger *Journal* presses to produce a four-page photo engraved edition that looked like someone had written the words on the page with a cheap typewriter.

Beyond first-day coverage, however, the papers dropped the topic of their own labour troubles. Ironically, there was full coverage of other postwar labour problems around the nation.

For three weeks in June, the pressmen were also on the picket line, leaving circulation, advertising and newsroom workers to put out the paper.

Gradually, replacement printers arrived from weeklies and the pressmen returned to work on June 27. The paper began to look like its old self again. By fall, the papers were publishing separate front and editorial pages, although they ran identical advertising and shared the revenue.

On Jan. 2, 1948, *The Journal* announced it and *The Bulletin* had resumed separate lives. It also reported *The Bulletin* had been sold to a Calgary consortium headed by G. Max Bell for $600,000.

The new *Bulletin* owners made peace with the ITU.

The Journal never settled.

***Aug. 3, 1948*:**
"A new era has opened for the ancient trade of piracy. The attempt by Chinese pirates to seize a Hong Kong airliner two weeks ago was, so far as we know, the world's first venture in airborne buccaneering. One of the charms of piracy in the old days was that it required no technical or professional qualifications whatever...But to practice the gentle art in the air, a great deal of specialized training will be required. The better class gangs may not accept a recruit unless he is a properly trained pilot, radio operator or flight engineer. The time may come indeed, when all pirates will need a licence from the department of transport."
- editorial.

***Aug. 29, 1948*:**
An Imperial Oil crew begins drilling the well on which they make the massive Redwater field discovery northeast of Edmonton.

***Sept. 8, 1948*:**
CBC radio station CBX goes on the air in Edmonton.

***Nov. 25, 1948*:**
The cornerstone is laid for the University of Alberta's new Rutherford Memorial Library.

Edmonton Bulletin — Edmonton Journal

Forecast - CLEAR, WARM | EDMONTON, ALBERTA, WEDNESDAY, JUNE 5, 1946 | SINGLE COPY, 5 CENTS

Bevin Gives Soviet 'Last Chance' Warning

Chicago Hotel Fire Kills 52, Hurts 200

CHICAGO, (AP) -- Fifty-two persons perished and about 200 others suffered injuries, many believed serious, early Wednesday when fire swept through the lower floors of the 20-storey LaSalle hotel in Chicago's financial district. The district was thrown into wild, tragic, screaming confusion.

No Canadians were among the first identified dead.

Many screaming guests, trapped on upper floors, leaned out of windows, waving bed blothes and apparently trying to decide whether to jump or stay in their rooms.

On the streets below, firemen and bystanders shouted:

"Sit tight -- we will get you all out."

Streams of nightgown and pajama-clad guests clogged fire escapes.

Bodies of more than a score of victims had been removed from the 838 room hotel. Hours after the fire had broken out in the lobby of the 25-year old hostelry, firemen hunted bodies.

See Danger of Ship Strike Spreading to West Coast

TORONTO, (CP) -- The Welland canal, vital artery between Lake Ontario and Lake Erie, was blocked temporarily Tuesday when strike pickets of the Canadian Seamen's union succeeded in persuading non-union crews to leave four vessels in the waterway.

But the passage was cleared by removal of the collier Osler.

Elsewhere on the Great Lakes Tuesday the strike scene mostly was peaceful. Pickets patrolled the other Great Lakes artificial waterway, the Cornwall canal, but there was no repetition of Monday's disorder when gangs of men boarded two ships, smashed doors and windows, and took off 40 non-union members

At Vancouver, James Thompson, vice-president of the Canadian Seamen's union, told the A.F.L. labor council there is a danger the Great Lakes seamen's strike may spread to the Pacific coast, unless the government takes some action to stop strike-breaking activities.

Wednesday at Ottawa, Labor Minister Mitchell is scheduled to meet separately with ship owners and with union representatives who called a strike of the some 5,000 membership to enforce demands for a straight eight-hour day seven days a week.

C.S.U. crew members of the coastal freighter Seven Oaks Park boarded the collier Keybar at her dock in North Sydney, N.S., and forced nine of her crew ashore.

Wild Pitch Brings City Man's Arrest

George Hodgson, city resident, faces a charge of wilful damage following the breaking of the front window of the Puritan Cafe, 10369 97 street, Tuesday night. A mustard pot was hurled through the glass.

According to data gathered by Const. R. McNichol, Hodgson had an argument with a girl in the cafe.

She started to leave, and Hodgson allegedly hurled the mustart pot after her. It missed her, but not the plate glass window.

Petrillo Defies Congress Threat

ST. PETERSBURG, FLA. (AP) -- "Oh, that bum," defiant James C. Petrillo, president of the American Federation of Musicians, shouted Tuesday when told that rep. George Dondero (Rep.-Mich) had voiced a threat of new congressional action against him. Petrillo has threatened to halt all radio network broadcasting if the Lea bill designed to curb his power is upheld by the supreme court.

Referring to the strike control bill, Petrillo said:

"The bill is no good. You can't shackle the working man. They won't stand for it. Abe Lincoln freed the slaves. Now they are going to make us all slaves."

Say Way Opened For China Peace

NANKING, (AP) - A high government source said Wednesday that Generalissimo Chiang Kai-shek had agreed in a conversation with Gen. George C. Marshall, special U. S. envoy to China to halt the central government offensive in Manchuria and leave the way open for peace negotiations with Chinese Communists.

Gen. Marshall was understood to have laid the proposals before Gen. Chou En-lai, chief negotiator for the Communists.

What's On At the Movies?

See the joint theatres' advertisement on page 8 for particulars.

Coast Radial Men Will Vote June 7

VANCOUVER, (CP) -- The 2,800 members of the Street Railwaymen's Union (AFL) will vote June 7 on the British Columbia Railway Company's counter-proposals to workers' demands for higher wages and a shorter work-week.

It is understood union members in Vancouver, Victoria and New Westminster are asking a 16-cent an hour wage boost, a 40-hour week and five cents differential pay for night shift workers. Details of the counter-proposals have not been made public.

Bread Shortage On Wane in U. S

CHICAGO, (AP) - The U.S. has "struck bottom" in the current domestic flour shortage, the Millers National federation said Tuesday, and a gradual easing of the critical bread shortage may start soon.

Garrison Commandant Quits After 35 Years Army Service

As he retired from the army Tuesday, Lt.-Col. R. Walter Hale, M. C., E. D., right in above picture, is shown as he received commendations and thanks from Col. T. E. Snow, district officer commanding M. D. 13, for his efficiency during service as Edmonton area commandant. After serving overseas with the Princess Patricia's Canadian Light Infantry and the 49th Battalion in the First Great War, Col. Hale was active in militia circles. In civilian life, he was a postal inspector. Shortly after the outbreak of the Second Great War, he rejoined active service. He will be succeeded as garrison commandant by Maj. J. R. C. Carter.

Sloan Proposals Rejected By 3 B.C. Logger Locals

VANCOUVER, (CP) -- Possibility of new moves in the 22-day-old strike of 35,000 British Columbia loggers and mill workers, members of the International Woodworkers of America (C.I.O.-C.C.L.), was seen Wednesday following a meeting in Victoria of Labor Minister Pearson and Harold Pritchett, union president.

The surprise meeting came after Mr. Pritchett had advised Chief Justice Sloan, government-appointed arbitrator, that the union no longer desired him to act in efforts to reach settlement in the wages dispute.

Spokesmen for the union said the rejection of Chief Justice Sloan as arbitrator did not mean his recommendations for settlement had been rejected.

The recommendations included proposals for a 15-cents-an-hour wage increase, a 44-hour week and voluntary check-off.

There was no comment from either Mr. Pritchett or Labor Minister Pearson following the Victoria conference but labor circles believed the meeting indicated new moves.

Meanwhile, union locals in Vancouver, Victoria and New Westminster rejected the Sloan recommendations at meetings Tuesday night.

The Victoria local instructed the district council of the I.W.A. to stand firm on its original demands of 25-cents an-hour wage increase and the 40-hour week.

World Television Said Possibility

LONDON, (CP) -- Empire newspapermen Tuesday heard the prediction the day will come -- though it is still far of -- when "most spot news and nearly all entertainment" will be transmitted by television.

Sir Ernest Fisk, governing director of Electrical and Musical Industries, Limited, said there now is "a technical possibility" the entire world could be covered with sound and vision services.

Radke Is Named School Principal

Appointment of E. E. Radke as principal of King Edward Park school was approved at a meeting of the public school board Tuesday night. Forty-one further appointments to the teaching staff were passed.

Resignations were accepted from Dr. R.A. McCormack, school dentists; E. H. Carson and Jean Robertson. Leaves of absence were granted to Agnes Fleming and Frances McConnell.

The board approved the purchase city lots in Westmount for playground purposes for Westmount school.

Choir Conductor Gives Up Post

Herbert G. Turner, 10255 114 st., one of Edmonton's best known musicians, has resigned as conductor of Christ Church (Anglican) choir in order to devote him self to other activities. He will continue to live here. Appointed as his successor is Leonard Betts.

For many years Mr. Turner has been secretary of the Edmonton Musicians' Protective association. For several years he has been secretary of the Alberta Musical Festival association

Thomas Cross Heads Liberals

Thomas L. Cross, Edmonton barrister, will head the Edmonton Provincial Liberal association for another term, it was decided at a meeting of the association Tuesday night. He was re-elected by acclamation.

Other officers named were: C.H. Grant, K.C., vice-president; Ranald D. White, secretary, and Mrs. Paul Ragan, treasurer.

City regional officials elected were: south side, vice-president, George Perring; secretary, Duncan Innes; west end, vice-president, E. R. Horton; secretary, R. V. Bellamy; east end, vice-president, J. C. Marshall; secretary, Mrs. A. L. Rodwell.

The meeting passed a resolution urging the government to explore further the feasibility of assisting veterans who want to enter a small business.

Speaker Eases Dignity of House; Allows Hatless Women in Galleries

By Richard Sanburn

OTTAWA, -- An unwritten law was repealed in the commons Tuesday, and from this day forward women may enter the galleries without hats.

It was a victory for Gladys Strum, C.C.F. member for Qu'-Appelle and only woman member of the house.

On behalf of her arbitrarily be-hatted sisters she complained about the situation the other day. Women visitors shouldn't be forced to cram handkerchiefs, flowers, gloves or borrowed fedoras onto their heads before being allowed in the chamber

Speaker Gaspard Fauteux with great gravity gave his ruling Tuesday that women didn't have to wear hats any more if they didn't want to.

Provost Man Dies Of Heart Seizure

Victim of a heart seizure, a man identified through a registration card as Henry Reinhardt of Provost, collapsed and died in front of 11835 95 street at 7:35 p.m. Tuesday.

W. Robertson, at that address heard the man fall. He called medical assistance and city police.

Chief Coroner Dr. E.A. Braithwaite said there would be no inquest

Total Peace or Total War Said Only Alternative For Europe

LONDON, (CP) - Foreign Secretary Bevin declared Tuesday that permanent peace in Europe can be assured "only if Russia enters freely into the European settlement," and told the Russians bluntly:

"If you value peace above all, do not miss this opportunity. It may never come again."

"If we don't want to have total war we must have total peace," Mr. Bevin asserted.

Replying to Foreign Minister Molotov of Russia, Mr. Bevin said a "great obstacle to peace" was the Soviet idea that the Russian method alone represented democracy, and that Russia can have security "only when every other country in the world has adopted the Soviet system."

Opening two days of debate in the commons on foreign policy, Mr. Bevin implored the United States to disregard Soviet rebuffs and continue seeking a four-power, 25-year pact to ensure German demilitarization. He urged Russia to accept this proposal as "giving the greatest possible hope for the removal of misunderstanding and the creation of confidence".

Meantime, he said, Britain would continue trying to extend her 20-year friendship pact with the Soviet Union to 50 years.

Of Trieste he said: "I cannot bring myself to hand over Trieste to Yugoslavia. Trieste must be an international port and not an international pawn."

On the Balkan question, Britain had "met with obstacles everywhere in trying to reach trade agreements with Romania, Hungary and other countries."

He said that if the foreign ministers failed to agree at their next conference, scheduled for June 15, on Europe's treaties, he would insist on submitting the disputed treaties to a peace conference of the 21 powers involved.

"We cannot go on in a state of war forever," he declared.

Mr. Bevin always had regarded it a tragedy that Russia did not participate in the making of Europe's peace after the First Great War.

On the question of the Dardanelles, Mr. Bevin said:

"We have been willing, equally with our predecessors, to consider revision of the Montreux Convention (governing status of Dardanelles straits). What we are anxious to avoid -- and I emphasize this -- is to do or agree to anything which will undermine the real independence of Turkey or convert her into a mere satellite state..."

He said Britain would welcome Russia's merchant ships on all the seas of the world.

Advance Act To Provide Government-Owned Firms

By Torchy Anderson

OTTAWA - An unprecendented appeal, in that it was direct to parliament rather than to the government, for support of the "Hellenic Parliament", and the second reading of Hon. C. D. Howe's government-owned companies act highlighted Tuesday's commons sitting.

The Greek appeal was read by Speaker Fauteaux. It is not likely to appear in Hansard. There was some surprise in government benches when the speaker read the appeal. He had not informed the government he received the message.

C. C. F. applauded, but Progressive Conservative and Social Credit members criticized, when Mr. Howe, minister of reconstruction, moved the government-owned companies act through second reading. On a division, the vote was 107 to 47.

Maj. Carter Named Commandant Here

CALGARY, (CP) - Appointment of Maj. J.R.C. Carter as garrison commandant of the Edmonton sub-area of M.D. 13 was announced here Tuesday. Maj. Carter will fill the vacancy created by the retirement of Lt.-Col. Walter Hale.

Rare White Rat Captured Here

Temporarily, Mr. and Mrs. Donald F. Olson, 10214 106 ave., have become possessors of a white rat. Their cat made the capture behind their house and they relieved puss of his prey before he had a chance to liquidate it.

Mr. Olson believes rats of any kind are unusual in Edmonton and this is the first white rodent he has ever seen in the city

Ex-Coast Mayor L. D. Taylor Dies

VANCOUVER, (CP) - A colorful pioneer, L.D. Taylor, 88, former mayor of Vancouver and for many years a newspaper publisher here, died in hospital Tuesday night.

Five-term mayor, Mr. Taylor retired from public life in 1934 when he was defeated in the civic election by senator G. C. McGeer.

Holdup-Man Robs City Resident Of $125 at Point of Revolver

Held up at the point of a revolver by a bandit who later eluded a police dragnet, Marcel Meleshko, 11432 69 Avenue, was robbed of about $125 at 12:20 a.m. Wednesday.

The holdup took place at the victim's home.

Meleshko was able to give only a sketchy description of the robber. He is believed to be in his early twenties, about 5 feet eight inches, weighing about 125 pounds.

Several city police department squad cars under the direction of Inspector Mike Kelly raced to the hold-up scene.

An intensive search was carried out but no immediate arrest was made.

It was the second holdup on successive nights.

Cost-of-Living Index Increases

OTTAWA, (CP) -- The cost-of-living index calculated by the dominion bureau of statistics jumped 1.2 points during April, the bureau reported Tuesday.

Calculated on the basis 1935 - 1939 equals 100, the index was 122 on May 1 compared with 120.8 April 1, when for the first time the index had reached a higher level than at any period in the war.

Order Secret Army Disband

WUPPERTAL, GERMANY, (REUTERS) -- British military quarters Monday disclosed that the military authorities had broken up a semi-secret royal Yugoslav army which had been drilling, and in some cases, arming itself in the British occupation zone.

The authorities have ordered the army to be disbanded, its soldiers stripped of their uniforms and its general and officers segregated from the men.

Hope to Avert U.S. Sea Strike

WASHINGTON, (AP) -- All discharges from the Coast Guard were suspended Tuesday -- an apparent move to conserve manpower for the running of merchant ships if there is a maritime strike in the United States.

Negotiations to avert the threatened June 15 walkout on all coasts for higher wages and shorter hours took a brighter turn. Two unions indicated willingness to make further concessions.

Other government sources have said privately the navy might halt demobilization of officers and men who have merchant-ship training, as a strike-preparedness measure.

Meyer Is Elected World Bank Head

WASHINGTON, (AP) - The world band Tuesday elected its first president Eugene Meyer, 70 - year-old publisher-editor of the Washington Post, one-time private banker and first board chairman of the Reconstruction Finance corporation.

A strong advocate of loans to war-torn countries as a key to reconstruction abroad and business expansion at home, Mr. Meyer declared in a statement:

"The world is well aware today of the food famine. At the same time we must become equally aware that the world is starving for the products of industry.

"The bank was organized to promote reconstruction and development in both these essential activities."

The bank presidency pays $30,000 a year tax-free, more than any U.S. official receives except President Truman.

Cyprus Seen Base

MALTA, (CP) - High-ranking officers here gave the opinion Tuesday that Cyprus, lying off the Syrian coast within striking distance of Suez Canal, would become Britain's chief Mediterranean base.

Meter Matters

"Those little round holes punched in the sidewalks on 101 Street south of Jasper are a reminder that we shall soon have our downtown streets decorated with parking meters. Most of us, we are sure, will not regard them as improving the appearance of the city."
— Editorial, July 5, 1948

The Journal wasn't quite sure what to make of parking meters. There was a parking problem downtown and meters were a proposed solution. Besides, as the editorial pointed out, "They seem to be all the rage in American cities. We can only hope that they will prove beneficial here."

The writer probably didn't know meters were invented by journalist Carl C. Magee, or that they were first installed in Oklahoma City in 1935.

But he did know news when he saw it and parking meters represented a fundamental change in the heart of the ever-growing city. They were also a novelty item and an endless source of amusement to a city full of people who had never been to Oklahoma City.

Veteran *Journal* reporter Art Evans was on the story July 10, 1948: "Some naive experimenters in this field of science thought this contraption vended lucky prizes, not being aware of the fact that Harpo Marx is the only man in history to have hit the jackpot on a parking meter.

"For better or worse the parking meter is with us and barring calamities visited upon it by gum-chewing youngsters with no place to deposit the wad, should operate with reasonable efficiency and public satisfaction."

The meters officially became a part of the bylaw landscape at 9 a.m. on July 26, causing *Journal* editors to order pictures taken to go with the story.

To this point in the paper's history, readers either got a picture or a story. Rarely both.

The first photo showed a metered curbside occupied by one car and the second a non-metered street a block over, crammed with the cars of people unwilling to cough up a nickel for an hour's parking.

The story of the first parking fines appeared four days later, on July 30.

"If complaints were hammers there would have been well over 100 badly battered parking meters in Edmonton Thursday night."

About that many people showed up at the police station to pay their first $1 fine.

The even-more-inevitable story appeared on Aug. 5. Another page 1 picture showed city treasurer Charles M. Small with a collection of washers and slugs that scofflaws used to plug the meters.

The counterfeit treasure, however, paled in comparison to the actual first-week's take of $598.98.

The page 13 story said the amount was actually half of what officials expected because of soon-to-be-rectified technical glitches in the machines and misunderstandings by motorists who thought five cents would buy them a day's worth of parking.

Estimates put the first year's parking take at $50,000 to $60,000.

***Feb. 21, 1949*:**
A special meeting of Edmonton city council raises transit fares from 17 tickets for $1 to 14 tickets for $1 in reaction to a $330,000 deficit.

***March 30, 1949*:**
The Alberta government bans the sale of coloured margarine in the province.

***April 27, 1949*:**
The University of Alberta's extension branch announces it will open the first "mud school" to train oil well drillers and contractors.

***May 23, 1949*:**
The newly twinned Low Level Bridge opens to traffic.

***June 6, 1949*:**
Edmonton's first drive-in movie theatre, the Starlite, opens in the west end.

***June 14, 1949*:**
***The Journal* announces support for the Liberals in the federal election campaign. An addressograph and telephone operator at *The Journal* each earn $20 a week.**

***July 5, 1949*:**
Civic census puts the city population at 137,469.

***July 6, 1949*:**
"Sir: In a recent issue of your valued paper a correspondent, styling himself

Cream of Comics Every Day

Edmonton Journal

'One of Canada's Great newspapers'

FORECAST: CLOUDY. MILD — EDMONTON, ALBERTA, FRIDAY, FEBRUARY 14, 1947 — SINGLE COPY, 5 CENTS

Rate Leduc Well 500 Barrels Day

Coal Bed Fire Castor Menace

CASTOR,—Many thousands of dollars worth of buildings in the business section of this town, 83 miles southeast of Edmonton, are menaced by a fire smouldering in a coal bed under the town. The firewas considered under coltrol Friday but authorities feared it might flare again, bringing fresh menace to the community.

Because of the costant danger, an emergency meeting of the Castor town council was being held Friday afternoon to discuss the situation.

Since resesidents found themselves above a burning mass of coal, that spreads over an entire district, two Edmonton officials were rushed to assist town firemen, giving advice and helping direct the fight against the burning coal bed are Austin Bridges, inspector from the fire marhsal's office and J. A. Dating of the department of lands and mines.

Bridges, Dating and Harry Cousineau, chief of the Castor volunteer fire fighting brigade and owner of one building damaged, agreed Friday that the situation was serious. While the fire is considered under control at one point they said that the blaze may creep along deep cracks in the coal seam and may break out again under any building in the town.

Since the fire was first noticed by Raymond J. Wiart, proprietor of one of the main store businesses here, the entire cement floor of the basement of the store has been broken up. Thousands of gallons of water from the C. P. R. water tank have been poured into the burning coal seam. Pouring of water is continuing while a large amount of the burning coal is being dug up and removed.

The fire is believed to have started about 10 days ago. Cause is said to have been spontaneous combustion when heat form a coal pit in the store basement overheated the "slag" coal about 10 feet below ground level.

Town officials reported the coal bed covers the entire townsite and is from half a foot to six feet thick and lies under the ground from three to 14 feet.

Actual burning of the seam was notived by Mr. Wiart when he was in the basement checking the furnace. He saw smoke issusing from the cracks in the cement floor. The cement was very hot

Ask Separate Freight Act To Govern Rates in West

OTTAWA, (CP) — Counsel for western provinces Friday told the board of transpoert commissioners they were paying higher freight rates than in the east and claimed the disparity would be accentuated through the granting of 30-percent increases sought by the railways.

A "western freight rate rates act" to "correct disparities" was proposed by M. A. MacPherson, counsel for Saskatchewan, while C. H. Locke, representing British Columbia, announced that province intended to bring a separate application for removal of the "mountain differential" charged for haulage over the Rockies.

Argument continued over the scope of the board inquiry being held into the railway's application for increases. Railway representatives urged the hearings should be narrowed to the question of the carriers' financial needs, with regional disabilities taken up later, while the provincial lawyers claimed the investigation should be in more general terms.

Opposing forces fought the case before the board of transport com-

(Continued on Page 2, Col. 6)

Britain Declines U.S. Coal Offer

WASHINGTON, (AP)—President Truman made public Friday a message from Prime Minister Attlee declining an American offer of aid in the British coal crisis.

Attlee's message said the need for coal in Europe is "no less pressing" than that of the British Isles and added "we could not ask that cargoes should be diverted from Europe to the United Kingdom."

Attlee's message followed a statement by Truman Tursday offering whatever aid the United States could muster and proposing to divert coal shipments to continental Europe to meet the British fuel emergency.

Possible Easing Fuel Crisis Seen

LONDON, (CP) — Prime Minister Attlee and his "coal cabinet" sought Friday to fix an approximate data for ending the industrial shutdown in Britain.

The conference was the first indication to the island's 49,000,000 browned-out and shivering inhabitants that the end of the fuel crisis might be in sight.

As drastic electricity restrictions were maintained into the fifth day, government sources said the return to normal might be gradual.

However, with only slight gains registered in coal stocks at power stations, the British Gas council warned the country's 1,100 gas plants to be ready to shut off gas supplies to non-essential industries.

Here are some sidelights on the fuel crisis:

Britain's fuel ministry is jammed with letters containing suggestions.

One proposed that electricity be "pumped" from Norway or Eire. An official said it would take 10 years to get the necessary cable laid from Norway. As for Eire—she depends on British supplies. In the Evening Standard another writer urged the "upper classes" to cut out

(Continued on Page 2, Col. 2)

Parley to Discuss Mine Wage Plan

GLACE BAY, N.S., (CP)—Maritime miners Friday looked to Ottawa for the next development in their wide dispute with Dominion Steel and Coal corporation as company and United Mine Workers (C.C.L.) leaders headed for the capital in a last-hour attempt to avert a major colliery shutdown.

At a conference to be held in Ottawa Saturday, before a midnight strike deadline, the disputants expected to hear discussed a federal formula providing the $1.40 a day wage increase asked by the miners but partly contingent on increased production.

That formula was enunciated Thursday by Labor Minister Mitchell when he suggested that 40 cents of the proposed wage increase be provided through an increase in the ceiling price of coal and the other $1 be paid by the company on a graduated basis dependent on increased per-man production.

The union, however, already had rejected a somewhat similar formula recommended by Mr. Justice Carroll of the Nova Scotia supreme court, government-appointed conciliator, who had described the union's wage demand as "justified."

The Weather

Forecast: Clear becoming cloudy Saturday morning, light winds increasing to west 20 tomorrow. Temperature tonight at Edmonton steady near 20 above, increasing early Saturday morning to 30.

Fine weather continues on the western prairies with temperatures about 20 degrees above normal in the Calgary-Lethbridge area, and close to normal elsewhere.

The cool air that has covered Saskatchewan and northern Alberta for the past few days will retreat slowly northeastward Friday and westerly winds will carry the mild Pacific air into all regions by noon Saturday. Temperatures are expected to remain steady during the night and then climb rapidly Saturday to give thawing over the entire district except in the Prince Albert region.

Prospects for Sunday are for continued mild weather.

Estimated low tonight, 20 above.

Estimated high tomorrow, 45 above.

At Edmonton Saturday, sun rises 7:55; sets 5:43.

Yesterday's maximum, 20 above.

Overnight low, 8 above.

Trace of freezing rain.

Report Russians 'Seized' B-29's

NEW YORK, (AP)—The New York Times said Friday "at least three B-29's (Superfortresses) in operational condition vanished after having made emergency landings near Vladivostok," in extreme eastern Russia, before the Soviet declared war on Japan.

"In at least two instances," the Times said, "Russian fighter planes opened fire on the obviously friendly American planes and, in at least one instance, Russian anti-aircraft batteries opened up, in daylight, on a stricken Superfortress."

The crews, the Times said, were intern[illegible] with other army and navy aviat[illegible] Tashkent in south-central [illegible] in a camp that at one time [illegible] Americans.

Canadian Leads In Figure Skating

STOCKHOLM, (CP)— Displaying all the grace and skill which won her the European title earlier this month, lovely Barbara Ann Scott of Ottawa Friday won the first half of the women's compulsory figures in the world figure skating championships here.

Miss Scott, 18, scored 873.4 points. Gretchen Merrill, United States champion, was second with 842.6 points and England's Daphne Walker was third with 834.1.

Scenes 20 Miles Southwest of Edmonton As Leduc Oil Well Starts Producing

Excitement ran high among 500 persons Thursday who watched the Imperial Oil company's Leduc No. 1 well, 20 miles southwest of Edmonton, come into production. In (1) the 156-foot derrick is seen in the background, with a separator tank in the forground. Two 500-barrel tanks are on the right. In (2) a giant smoke ring, measuring about 20 feet in diameter, floats in the sky. The ring was formed by smoke which belched from a fire at the end of a flare-pipe. In (3) the flame and mushroom-like smoke roars upward from the flare-pipe, darkening the sky. Interested spectators are shown in (4) watching activities by the derrick. They include Mayor Ainlay and acquaintances, Mike Turta, owner of the quarter-section of land on which the well is located, is shown in (5). Valve which diverted the flow of oil and gas in a separator and then into huge tanks is shown being turned in (6) by Hon. N. E. Tanner, minister of lands and mines. In the centre is Vernon Taylor, assistant production manager for Imperial Oil in western Canada, and Walker Taylor, right, production manager.

British Laborite Is 'Lost' in Greece

ATHENS, (Reuters) — T. G. Thomas, Labor member of the British commons, has been unreported since he was believed to have entered guerilla-held territory in Thessaly four days ago, a British embassy spokesman said.

Thomas came to Greece last month primarily to give evidence for the defence at the trial of members of the Greek left-wing youth organization Epon.

Air Crash Kills 4 In South Alberta

LETHBRIDGE, (CP) — Four men were killed in the crash of an aircraft west of Coleman Friday morning. Coleman is in the Crowsnest Pass area, 75 miles west of Lethbridge.

The men were believed to be construction officials from Calgary.

U.S. Envoy Won't Return to Poland

WARSAW, (Reuters) — Artaur Bliss Lane, United States ambassador to Poland, will not return to Poland after his recall to Washington for consultations about future United States policy regarding Poland, it was authoritatively learned Thursday night. Lane informed the Polish foreign office Thursday night he would leave for Washington Feb, 24.

Palestine Issue Will Go to U.N.

LONDON, (AP) — Foreign Secretary Bevin said Friday Britain would take the Palestine issue to the United Nations.

Bevin made the announcement to Arab delegates in the final session of the British-Arab conference which attempted unsuccessfully to solve the Holy Land problem by agreement.

Say Prospects "Best In West"

The giant, billowing flame and dense, black smoke that spiralled skyward with a roar Thursday was enough evidence for 500 persons that the Imperial Oil company's Leduc No. 1 well, 20 miles southwest of Edmonton was producing oil—oil at the rate of an estimated 500 barrels a day.

Unoffical Edmonton observers who saw the well come into production said they would estimate the initial flow to be about 500 barrels per day flash production, although they pointed out this flow might increase or fall off sharply at any time.

Imperial Oil officials refused to comment on the flow, but declared it will take many production tests before the actual amount taken off in barrels per day can be estimated. Some wells in the Turner Valley field ran 1,000 barrels or better flush production. Now, few prodduce more than 300 barrels per day, under the government's conservation regulations.

Linking this city for the first time with an oil development that has the possibilities of being the biggest field in Canada next to Turner Valley, the wildcat well "kicked in" with a flow of oil and gas at 3:50 p.m., shooting flames and smoke into the sky from a relief pipe.

For a moment, it seemed as though a miniature atomic bomb had been dropped as the smoke formed a mushroom-like cloud and beat its way upward with a roar.

The full impact of the possibility of oil being discovered in the Edmonton area was felt by many as the flame from the dark, brown oil lit the darkening sky.

The magic word — oil — was formed on the lips of men, women and children as the gusher finally shot its way through tons of water and mud in the hole — nearly a mile below the earth's surface — to daylight and the use of man.

Registering a grade of 38 degree gravity, the oil is worth in the neighborhood of $2 per barrel, but no one, not even company experts, could predict on the spot what the flow will be.

"It's producing . . . That's oil," was the way Walker Taylor, western production manager for the oil com-

(Continued on Page 2, Col. 1)

Rescue Vessels Remove 150 From Ship Stranded Off B.C.

VANCOUVER, (CP) — Rescue ships, after battling through a southeasterly gale, early Friday removed 150 passengers and crew members from the SS. North Sea, aground on Middle Reef near Bella Bella, B.C., 300 miles north of Vancouver.

In a pounding sea, the 3,133 ton ship struck the reef in Seaforth channel on the inside route to Alaska, late Thursday night.

The rescued were taken to the fishing village of Bella Bella where some were housed in the hopital for the night and others given shelter in private homes. Two stretcher cases, sick passengers en route to hospital at Seattle, were among the rescued.

The North Sea, bound for Seattle from Ketchikan, Aladka, was reported resting easily, but her hull was damaged and the No. 2 hold full of water.

The Canadian National Steamships' Prince Rupert is due at Bella Bella during the morning and will pick up the rescued for transportation to Vancouver.

150 FLEE FIRE

OGDENSBURG, (AP)— About 150 persons fled to safety when a general alarm fire gutted the new Ogdensburg hotel Thursday night, causing damage estimated unofficially at $150,000.

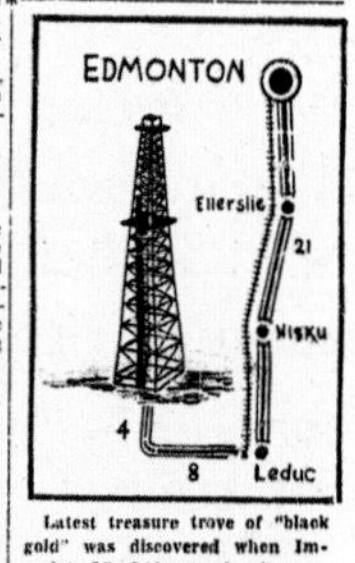
EDMONTON
Ellerslie
21
Nisku
4
8
Leduc

Latest treasure trove of "black gold" was discovered when Imperial Oil Ltd. struck oil near Leduc. The above map shows how to get there, the numbers representing miles. From Edmonton, go 21 miles south to Leduc, eight miles west and four miles north. You will then be standing by Alberta's newest oil well.

2 Coast Men Plead Guilty To Edmonton Bank Holdup

Two Vancouver men pleaded guilty in Edmonton police court Friday to the armed daylight robbery of the Imperial Bank main branch Feb. 3, when $3,543 was stolen.

Magistrate Millar remanded Ernest Amato, 25, and William George Capstick, 39 to 2:00 p.m. Friday for sentence. The pair, both tight-lipped during an impassioned plea on their behalf by H. L. Spankie, defence counsel, shuddered in the prisoner's box when the magistrate delayed sentence on an offence which carries a maximum of life imprisonment and lashes.

Charges of possession of stolen property, $3,033, and illegal possession of liquor against Donna Lee McKay, 26, of Vancouver, were set aside to 2:00 p.m. with no pleas entered. Magistrate Millar ordered restitution to the Imperial Bank of Canada of $552 found on Amato and Capstick, when they were arrested

(Continued on Page 2, Col. 6)

Woman Faces Trial For Officer's Death

ROME, (Reuters) — Maria Pasquinelli, 33-year-old Italian teacher who is alleged to have shot Brig. R. W. de Winton, commander of the 13th Infantry Division at Pola, will be tried by a British court martial, it was learned Friday. She is no longer believed to be a member of a gang or involved in an anti-British conspiracy.

After her arrest the woman produced a letter in which she said she intended to shoot a senior army officer as a protest against the former Italian port of Pola being transferred to Yugoslavia under the peace treaty.

There was a tense atmosphere in Pola Friday. Furniture of families going to other parts of Italy before the Yugoslavs took over was lined on the quayside of the port. Officials said 29,000 people were leaving the city.

Find Trio Guilty War Frauds Case

VANCOUVER, (CP)— J. L. Northey, pioneer 65 year-old Vancouver builder, and his two sons, Paul and Archibald, late Thursday were remanded for sentence after being found guilty in county court of conspiracy to defraud the federal government on war contracts during 1942 to 1944.

Conviction was entered by Judge C. J Lennox after a five-day trial. Sentence will be pronounced Feb. 20.

The crown presented more than 100 exhibits of allegedly fictitious invoices and cheques of Northeys wartime company, Millwork Industries Limited, which supplied furnishings for ships built here during the war.

Individual invoices mentioned in testimony involved such sums as $340 and $700 but there was no indication of the total amount involved.

Crown Prosecutor G. L. Fraser told the court that the accused reduced the profits of Millwork Industries on war contracts by charging personal and housing supplies against the company.

Promise of Prosperity

"The giant billowing flame and dense black smoke that spiraled skyward with a roar Thursday was enough evidence for 500 persons that the Imperial Oil company's Leduc No. 1 well, 20 miles southwest of Edmonton, was producing oil – oil at the rate of an estimated 500 barrels a day."

— Story, Feb. 14, 1947

There are certain days in history that can change the direction of a society forever. The day Leduc No. 1 gushed out its payload was such a day for Edmonton and Alberta.

The Journal editorial writers sensed this when they wrote, Feb. 15: "The hope of the company and all of us is that the preliminary work under way near Leduc will be but the prelude to the opening and full utilization of a large and productive oil field in the Edmonton district.

"All of this is good news indeed, but it does not mean Edmonton is to become a great oil refining centre over-night. If development does reach that point, it will be only after years of the hardest kind of work and the expenditure of vast sums of money by oil companies."

The editorial also carried a caution.

"In the meantime, Edmonton and its citizens will, it is to be hoped, keep their feet planted firmly on the ground, however rosy may be their dreams of a rich future floating in 'black gold.' "

New strikes were being reported almost daily.

Some of the farmers and landowners in the Leduc-Calmar area were cashing in on the windfall as well. At the time, many still owned mineral rights on their property. On July 28, reporter Ian MacDonald turned in a rare "people" story.

"This unceasing search for black gold is bringing unexpected riches to tillers of the soil." Farmer John Praystow, for instance, got his first royalty cheque that July – $980.05. It was just in the nick of time.

"Farm is no good," he was quoted. "Dry years – no crop." But Praystow wasn't satisfied. "Income tax heavy," he told MacDonald.

The Leduc discovery alone created 22,000 jobs by 1956. In 1948, Imperial Oil dismantled a refinery in Whitehorse , trucked it south and set it up south of Edmonton, just east of the river. Pipelines to the rail terminus at Nisku were built. By 1950, there were three refineries in the area with more on the drawing board.

British reporter Don Iddon of the *London Daily Mail* visited the city and *The Journal* reprinted his article July 28, 1951.

"The city and the people believe that they are merely on the brink of their development; that one day they will make Texas look like a pup … the province is happy about almost everything.

"Whatever happens in Persia there will always be oil for the lamps of the empire in Alberta."

De La Pole, boasts about getting by in refusing to tell a census taker anything about his religion. As an old census taker I have encountered many De La Poles, male and female, in my rounds. As a rule the C.T. knows the party's religious affiliation anyway, so it's my practice, when refused, to fill in the space on my own. If the party is entirely unknown, I have – like other C.T.s with whom I have compared notes – written in possibly 'undecided' or 'very little, if any,' if you know what I mean. Should the government, at this late date, review my reports and place me in court for accepting payment under false pretenses, my only plea to the judge would be that on certain occasions, to speed up the reports, a certain amount of lying is necessary."

– letter to the editor.

***Sept. 5, 1949*: The revived Edmonton Eskimos play their first game after a 10-year break, losing 20-6 to the Stampeders. They win for the first time, beating Winnipeg 14-11, on Sept. 10.**

***Sept. 15, 1949*: The minimum wage for women in Alberta is raised from $18 to $20 a week.**

Edmonton Weather
24-hour forecast: Fair and warm

Edmonton Journal

'One of Canada's Great Newspapers'

FORTY-SECOND YEAR * * EDMONTON, ALBERTA, MONDAY, AUGUST 6, 1945 SINGLE COPY, 5 CENTS

Atomic Bomb, Equal to 20,000 Tons of TNT, Raining 'Utter Destruction' on Jap Homeland

Ottawa Offers Pay $30 Monthly To All Persons 70 Years or Over

FO. Douglas Stewart, son of Mrs. M. G. Stewart, 10605 79 ave., who returned home over the week-end after being a prisoner of war in Germany for a year. Well-known baseball player and employe of Trans-Canada Airlines, FO. Stewart was reported missing, then prisoner of war in May, 1944. He had been on operations over Berlin, Essen and Le Mons. He enlisted in 1941.

By Frank Flaherty

OTTAWA.—The dominion government Monday offered the nine provincial governments new and stable sources of finance and at the same time asked them to withdraw completely from the fields of personal income, corporation and estate taxation.

The government also proposed greatly to increase financial assistance to health services and bear the full cost of paying old age pensions of $30 monthly to all persons 70 years or over, regardless of their incomes.

These offers were made as the dominion-provincial conference on reconstruction opened in the green-carpeted chamber of the house of commons and were contained in a 52-page 35,000-word brief.

While the general purport of the federal proposals was not new—it was foreshadowed in the recommendations of the pre-war royal commission on dominion-provincial relations which were the subject of an unsuccessful conference in 1941—there was a completely new approach to the problem.

The provinces were asked to surrender no constitutional rights, to make no binding irrevocable commitments. They were asked to do the things proposed by agreement and, if agreement is made, not to withdraw from the pact for three years. At the same time no provision was suggested which would make it impossible for a province to withdraw at any time.

Proposes Increase in Subsidies

To compensate the provinces for leaving the dominion a clear field in the three spheres of taxation the dominion proposed a substantial increase in subsidies payable to the provinces. They are to be on the basis of $12 per head of population as at the 1941 census. That is to be the irreducible minimum but they are adjustable upward as population increases and upward as the total value of national production increases.

Under wartime tax agreements the provinces withdrew from the personal income and corporation tax fields to enable the dominion to levy uniform, higher rates. In return they were compensated by extra subsidies on the basis of their pre-war revenues from those tax sources. They still levy estate or succession duty taxes and the dominion also taxes the same source.

Under the new proposed subsidy arrangement the irreducible minimum payments to all provinces will be $138,000,000. The province's present receipts from federal subsidy and their own estate taxes total $125,000,000.

Would Have Received $207,000,000

If the arrangement proposed had been in effect in 1944 on the basis of the population and gross national production, the provinces would have received $207,000,000. Their estimated receipts in 1948, if national production holds to the present scale of $12,500,000,000 or $1,000 per capita, would be $215,000,000. If it drops to $10,000,000,000 or $800 per capita they would get $172,300,000.

In addition the dominion proposes to assume new commitments in the field of social security, particularly old age pensions, support of employable unemployed and health insurance, to

(Continued on Page 2, Col. 1)

Set $600,000,000 For Social Plans

By Torchy Anderson
(From Edmonton Journal's Ottawa Bureau)

OTTAWA.—The federal government proposes to spend on its new social program about $600,000,000 annually. That is a lot more than average pre-war annual over-all budget for Canada.

In being and proposed, the tally in costs is:

Family allowances (net)	$200,000,000
Unemployment insurance	20,000,000
Health insurance and grants	163,000,000
Old age pensions	217,000,000
	$600,000,000

In the case of family allowances the figures represent estimated net cost after income tax reductions are offset. In old age pensions a certain amount, not estimated, will be recovered in the case of persons receiving the pension who are within income tax brackets.

Roughly three-fifths of the cost of health insurance and grants comes from the federal treasury, the rest from the provinces. The federal government wants to make both health insurance and old age pensions contributory.

The figure for unemployment insurance represents the federal contribution and cost of administration. Employes and employers also contribute.

Early Vote Light, Glengarry Riding

ALEXANDRIA, Ont.—A "very light" vote during the morning, with expectations of an increase Monday afternoon, was reported in Monday's federal byelection for Glengarry riding, being contested by Prime Minister King and Dr. Richard Monahan, Independent Liberal.

A combination of fine weather and Civic holiday served to restrict the vote as town residents went into the country for the holiday and farmers took advantage of the good weather to tend their crops. Town shops were closed.

Polls opened at 8:00 a.m. and will close at 6.00 p.m. (4:00 p.m. Edmonton time) with the early returns expected to become available shortly afterward.

Where To Find It

Amusements, Theatres	7
Bridge	15
Comics	12, 13, 15
Crossword Puzzle	15
District	3
Editorial	4
Financial	8
Garry Myers	15
Off the Record	15
Paul Reynaud	2
Radio	16
Sport	6, 7
They'll Do It Every Time	15
Uncle Ray's Corner	15
Want Ads	12, 13, 14
War Map	2
Women's	11

The Weather

Estimated low tonight, 55.
Estimated high tomorrow, 85.
At Edmonton Tuesday, sun rises 5:58; sets 9:20.
Yesterday's maximum 78.
Overnight low 54.
Rainfall Saturday, .26 of an inch.
Hourly readings since 12:30 p.m. Sunday:

12:30	72	8:30	74	4:30	56
1:30	75	9:30	71	5:30	56
2:30	76	10:30	67	6:30	54
3:30	76	11:30	64	7:30	57
4:30	77	12:30	63	8:30	61
5:30	78	1:30	60	9:30	65
6:30	77	2:30	58	10:30	70
7:30	77	3:30	57	11:30	74

	H.	L.		H.	L.
Montreal	80	60	Calgary	78	48
Toronto	76	60	Lethbridge	79	48
Winnipeg	73	59	Jasper	81	43
Saskatoon	72	51	Kamloops	83	54
Regina	67	46	Vancouver	75	55
Med. Hat	81	62	Victoria	83	56

8:30 a.m. readings:

Fort St. John	56	Ft. Vermilion	60
Dawson Creek	58	Grouard	48
Keg River	59	Slave Lake	63
Grande Prairie	55	Athabaska	62
Peace River	48	McMurray	62

Far north readings:

	H.	L.		H.	L.
Aklavik	45	38	Wat. Lake	75	51
Whitehorse	61	53	Ft. Simpson	81	51
Dawson	64	51	Yellowknife	79	50
Ft. Nelson	64	55	Norman W.	58	49

Big Three Say Smiling Farewell as Potsdam Parley Ends

Interrupting their final session of the Potsdam conferences, the Big Three smilingly posed a moment for the cameraman. As pictured, they are, left to right, Prime Minister Clement Attlee of Great Britain, President Harry S. Truman of the United States and Generalissimo Josef Stalin, of Soviet Russia.

New Discovery Promises Greatest Ruin Ever Seen

WASHINGTON.—An atomic bomb which looses pent-up forces of the universe equivalent to more than 20,000 tons of TNT and represents one of the greatest scientific advances of history has been dropped on Japan.

President Truman told Monday of the terrific destructive power packed into the missile which was dropped 16 hours ago on Hiro Shima, an important Japanese army base. His statement, released by the White House, said the bomb "added a new and revolutionary increase in destruction" on the Japanese homeland.

This awful bomb is the answer, President Truman's statement said, to Japan's failure to heed the Potsdam demand that she surrender unconditionally at once or face utter destruction.

The new bomb produces more than 2,000 times the blast of the largest bomb ever used before.

The product of $2,000,000,000 spent in research and production—"the greatest scientific gamble in history," Mr. Truman said—the atomic bomb has been one of the most closely-guarded secrets of the war.

The late President Roosevelt and Winston Churchill, former British prime minister, gave the signal to start work on harnessing the forces of the atom. Mr. Truman said the Germans worked feverishly, but failed to solve the problem.

Of the new bomb, Mr. Truman said:

"It is an atomic bomb. It is a harnessing of the basic power of the universe. The force from which the sun draws its power has been loosed against those who brought war to the Far East."

The base that was hit is a major quartermaster depot and has large ordnance, machine tool and aircraft plants.

The city of 318,000 also contains a principal port.

The president disclosed that the Germans "worked feverishly" in search of a way to use atomic energy in their war effort but failed. Meantime, American and British scientists studied the problem and developed two principal plants and some lesser factories for the production of atomic power.

The president disclosed that more than 65,000 persons now are working in great secrecy in these plants, adding: "We have spent $2,000,000,000 on the greatest scientific gamble in history—and won.

"We are now prepared to obliterate more rapidly and completely every productive enterprise the Japs have above ground in any city. We shall completely destroy Japan's power to make war."

The president noted that the Big Three ultimatum issued July 26 at Potsdam was intended "to spare the Japanese people from utter destruction" and the Japanese leaders rejected it. The atomic bomb now is the answer to that rejection and the president said "they may expect a rain of ruin from the air, the like of which has never been seen on this earth."

Mr. Truman forecast that sea and land forces will follow up this air attack in such numbers and power as the Japanese never have witnessed.

The president said this discovery may open the way for an entirely new concept of force and power. The actual harnessing of atomic energy may in the future supplement the power that now comes from coal, oil and the great dams, he said.

Ottawa Lifts Restrictions Imposed on Sale of Liquor

OTTAWA.—Repeal of the wartime alcoholic beverages order, which imposed restrictions on the sale of liquor, was announced Sunday night from the office of Prime Minister King. Liquor advertising still is prohibited.

"In view of the termination of hostilities in Europe, the principal reasons for the imposition of the restrictions on supply contained in the wartime alcoholic beverages order, 1942, no longer exist," a statement said.

"The government accordingly has decided to remove these restrictions to the extent that they were operative in the field of jurisdiction normally exercised by the provinces.

The order was passed in December, 1942, aimed at a reduction in consumption of liquor. Its effect was to reduce the amount of liquor which would be sold and the alcoholic content of distilled liquor.

It directed that in the year beginning Nov. 1, 1942, and from then on, the amounts to be released from bond as compared with the previous 12 months should be reduced by 10 percent in the case of beer, 20 percent in the case of wine and 30 percent in the case of spirits. Alcoholic content of distilled spirits was to be reduced to not more than 30 percent under-proof. All liquor advertising was prohibited and this ban remains.

Subsequently the restrictions on beer were removed but although there were protests from provincial

(Continued on Page 2, Col. 3)

Here Are Highlights Of Dominion Brief

OTTAWA.—Following are highlights of government proposals to the dominion-provincial conference on reconstruction:

Inter-governmental co-operation and reallocation of functions and powers to be achieved by agreement and not be constitutional change.

* * *

Dominion to pay higher subsidies to the provinces on the basis of a minimum of $12 per head of population as of 1941 census.

* * *

Provinces to withdraw completely from imposition of taxes on personal incomes, corporations and estates.

* * *

Minimum total dominion subsidies to be $138,000,000 compared with

(Continued on Page 2, Col. 6)

See Big Saving In Pension Offer

Alberta would save an estimated $465,000 over its present costs of old age pensions under the scheme outlined at Ottawa whereby the dominion would bear the whole cost for those over 70 years, it was unofficially estimated here Monday.

The dominion's announced plan is to pay $30 per month to all persons 70 years or over, regardless of their incomes.

A report from Ottawa says that this will mean, so far as Alberta is concerned, that the dominion will pay $12,500,000 per year and the province $1,000,000 which would be its 50-50 share of old age pensioners between 65 and 70.

Under the provincial government estimates for the 1945-46 fiscal year, total old age pension costs were put at $4,365,200, while reimbursements were estimated at $2,900,000, leaving a net cost to the province of $1,465,000.

Hitherto, the dominion has provided 75 percent of old age pension costs, with the province providing 15 percent and municipalities 10 percent.

The federal plan should mean that Edmonton and other cities, towns and municipalities in the province which have been contributing to the costs of old age pensioners will be saved this outlay each year.

Old age pensioners have been entitled to receive a federal pension of $25 per month while Alberta has supplemented this with a $5 cost of living bonus, making the amount $30 per month. The cost to the province of this bonus has been $730,000 a year.

E. C. Fisher, president of the Alberta Pensioners' society, said Monday that the dominion plan was a step in the right direction. One advantage was that it meant the $30 pension plan would be on a permanent basis. When the federal pension was increased from $20 to $25 per month, it was stated at the time to be a war measure.

Mr. Fisher also stated that the new plan would mean the elimination of the "means" test.

3 Are Drowned In Westlock Area

Three persons were drowned in the Westlock district during the week-end, R.C.M.P. said Monday. They were Sydney Keen, 14, and Edmund Pail, 15, both of Barrhead, and Thomas Bateman, 21.

Sydney Keen and Edmund Pail were accidentally drowned when the boat in which they were crossing a small lake six miles south of Barrhead overturned. Edwin Keen, 15, brother of the drowned boy saved himself by swimming to shallow water. It is believed the Pail boy was unable to swim and dragged his companion to the bottom when he attempted to save him. No inquest will be held, R.C.M.P. said.

Bateman was accidentally drowned at a bend of the river about 11 miles west of Westlock. He was with a party and had returned to shore earlier suffering from a cramp. When the cramp had gone he returned to the water and it is thought the cramp seized him again.

Take Polish Force Out of Czech Area

PRAGUE.—The defence ministry said Saturday that the United States 3rd Army, at its request, had withdrawn units of a Polish occupation brigade from Czecho-Slovakian territory. The announcement said there had been friction between the Polish troops and the residents because Czechs had charged some Polish elements with collaborating with German werewolves.

Huge Flying Boat Sinks on Landing

ROCK HALL, Md.—The navy's Hawaii Mars, world's largest flying boat, sank in Chesapeake bay Sunday after a rough landing.

A navy announcement said the force of the landing opened the giant craft's hull. Only one member of the 10-man crew was injured.

Schedule Listed For Work Return

Eight of 23 departments at Canada Packers' plant here will go into operation Tuesday and it is expected that by Thursday night nearly all of the 600 workers who went out on strike a week ago, will be back at work, according to an announcement by plant officials Monday.

"Operations will be resumed as soon as possible starting Tuesday morning but owing to the nature of the business and the necessity of having products available for processing, it will be impossible to start all the employes at once," it was stated.

Complete departments returning to work Tuesday will be the cattle killing, hog killing, smoke house, freezer, feed division, stores, plant services and repair staff.

All employes but graders and packers will start Tuesday in the casings department, with graders and packers returning to their jobs Wednesday morning. There will be regular shifts in the rendering department Tuesday morning.

In the coolers, workers will start back Wednesday with the calf skinners reporting to that department Thursday morning. Complete department of pork trimming will get back into operation Wednesday morning, and the pork cutting department will start at the same time.

Pulling gang in the export cellars will start Tuesday night, and the complete department and packing gang will begin work Wednesday morning. Beef boners will get to work Wednesday morning with the balance of the department starting Thursday morning. Canning shifts will start Thursday morning.

Regular shifts in the edible rendering department will start Tuesday morning with the runoff Wednesday. Complete department at the loading dock and city delivery will start work Wednesday morning.

Workers in the smoked meats, sausage kitchen, central shipping and stockyards are asked to report to their foreman Tuesday afternoon.

Edmonton Driver Wins $500 Race

LETHBRIDGE.—Cy Pyke, of Edmonton, whirled home to victory in his speedy racing car Saturday in the headline event of the Junior Chamber of Commerce Model T race meet. Four thousand saw the races.

Pyke won handily over the runner-up, Tommy Fraser, of Standard. The Edmonton driver won a cash prize of $500 and the Jaycees silver cup emblematic of the Southwestern Alberta Model T racing title.

First of 30,000 Canadians In Advanced Pacific Areas

GUAM.—Canadian troops, the vanguard of 30,000 men of the Canadian Army Pacific Force, have arrived in advanced Pacific areas.

They will be followed by R.C.A.F. squadrons and 60 ships of the Royal Canadian Navy, including two aircraft carriers, two cruisers, destroyers and frigates.

(The reference to Canadian troops no doubt is to a number of observers and technicians who have been in the Pacific for some months. The vanguard of the main Canadian army for the Pacific is due to leave Canada almost immediately for training in the United States.)

Col. Richard S. Malone, director of the Canadian Army public relations, said the Canadians will fight alongside the Americans in the Pacific, using American weapons, organization, tactics and terms.

The Canadians, Col. Malone said, will be an integral part of the American army, but did not disclose the number already in advanced areas.

Among the units which will be in the Pacific are the Seaforth Highlanders of Canada, of Vancouver; the 48th Highlanders, of Toronto, the Royal 22nd Regiment, of Quebec and the Princess Patricia's Canadian Light Infantry—all famous old Canadian army units.

The Highlanders, despite their use of the American rifles in place of the traditional Enfields, will not forsake their bagpipes, Col. Malone said.

Troops of the first contingent are all battle-hardened in Europe and have been trained in Kentucky in American tactics and weapons. Extensive training for the Canadians for Pacific fighting is not indicated, however, Col. Malone added, as the mountainous terrain of Sicily and

(Continued on Page 10, Col. 5)

The Times Says—

Japan's Plight Grave
Franco Bargaining Off
Canada Talks Problems

LONDON.—That the Japanese navy is now little more than a ghost of its former self—an assertion made by United States officials and observers—the Times thinks is extremely probable. So many crippling blows have been inflicted on warships taking refuge in enemy ports that few fighting units can now be left, especially since the battle off the Philippines last October undoubtedly cost Japan one-quarter of her battle fleet. The toll taken by British and other submarines is also formidable.

In addition, Japanese air power has declined until it can no longer prevent tons of bombs from crashing down on ports and cities, nor British and United States warships from bombarding harbors from the sea. While there may be secret weapons to come, the Times thinks this unlikely. On the whole Japan's plight is becoming grave and if the war continues it can only be assumed that the addiction to suicide is not confined to the military caste.

* * *

Franco's protests against the Potsdam conference decisions, ruling his regime out of association with other

(Continued on Page 5, Col. 8)

Plan to Continue Control of Wages

OTTAWA—War emergency powers held by the federal government in industrial disputes and conciliation should be continued in the period of transition to a peacetime economy, the dominion government said Monday in a brief to the dominion-provincial conference.

Wage control would have to be carried into the transition period as part of the anti-inflation program but relaxation was proposed as soon as conditions warranted it.

The government proposed an amendment to the British North America act leaving the way open for provinces to delegate to the dominion, if they desired, jurisdiction over certain industries in industrial disputes.

Agreement Reached by Conference On Procedure of War Guilt Trials

LONDON.—The four-power war crimes conference approached agreement Sunday night upon an historic document indicting aggressive war as an international crime.

The document will blueprint procedure for an unprecedented mass trial of Germans listed as arch criminals — men who formulated Nazi policy, high military chiefs who executed it, ranking diplomats who intrigued for it, industrialists and financiers who gave it substance.

The trial itself will be held in Nuernberg before an international military tribunal Sept. 1, with representatives of Britain, France, Russia and the United States prosecuting.

The prospective list of defendants was reported by a responsible American source to include Hermann Goering, Joachim Ribbentrop, Franz von Papen, Alfred Rosenberg and members of the German general staff such as Grand Admiral Karl Doenitz and Field Marshals Gerd von Rundstedt and Wilhelm Keitel.

Simultaneously, the high tribunal will be asked to convict the Nazi terror-atrocity organizations. If a guilty verdict is returned, it will

(Continued on Page 2, Col. 3)

Seven Fliers Killed In Eastern Crash

HAMILTON.—Four airmen died Sunday in a mid-air collision between two planes from No. one wireless school, R.C.A.F., at nearby Mount Hope. Aircraft were believed to be on a routine flight in connection with wireless training.

WINNIPEG.—Three members of the R.A.F. in training at No. 18 S.F.T.S., of the R.C.A.F. at Souris, Man., were killed last Thursday when two aircraft collided, No. 2 Air Command announced Sunday.

Six Japanese War Centres Set Ablaze by Super-Forts

GUAM. — Striking savagely for the second time in five days, 680 Super-Fortresses and fighters spread fire and destruction through six Japanese war centres stretching almost from the imperial palace in Tokyo to the southern home island of Kyushu Sunday and Monday.

Once again an all but helpless Japan forewarned that the big bombers were coming on a mission of death, was unable to offer effective resistance while the industrial areas of Nishinomya, Imabari, Maebashi and Saga burned and fell apart from 3,850 tons of incendiary and high explosive bombs dropped by a fleet of 580 Super-Forts.

Sunday air raid sirens screamed throughout Tokyo in a warning that 100 fighters had returned to strike terror with rockets and machine-guns against anything they could find in the Tokyo area.

Radio Tokyo said 150 fighters carried the assaults into the daylight Monday with an attack on the Tokyo area.

A single Japanese fighter watched them come Sunday and then fled.

The B-29s in two raids Aug. 2 and Monday have sown 10,500 tons

(Continued on Page 5, Col. 7)

Enlarged Militia Foreseen in U.S.

WASHINGTON.—President Truman may propose an enlarged and modernized national guard as an alternative to peacetime military conscription, it was reported Sunday.

Warner Electors Casting Ballots

WARNER.—First test of Premier Manning's Social Credit government since the Alberta general election a year ago, was taking place Monday when citizens of Warner constituency went to the polls in a provincial byelection.

The election was caused by the resignation of Solon Low, national leader of the Social Credit party, who resigned his Warner seat to contest successfully the Peace River seat in the June 11 federal general election.

Two candidates are running in Warner, L. C. Halmrast, Social Credit, and H. J. Hierath, Single Tax nominee.

Seven thousand ballots and 36 ballot boxes were sent to Walter Jones, returning officer.

In the 1944 voting, 4,273 ballots were cast in the riding.

Present standing in the legislature is: Social Credit 50; Independent three; C.C.F. two; Veterans 1; Armed Forces 3; vacant 1; total 60.

Results are expected to be known shortly after the 28 polls close at 6:00 p.m.

Want Industries In Small Centres

OTTAWA.—Government policy in the sale of government-owned war plants and industrial equipment is to encourage industry in the smaller centres, the dominion said Monday in a brief presented to the dominion-provincial conference.

List Returnees On Ile de France

Total of 33 officers and 354 other ranks of the Canadian army who arrived in Halifax Sunday aboard the liner Ile de France from overseas, are expected to arrive in Calgary via C.P.R. Wednesday.

It was explained by officials of headquarters, M.D. 13 that it is possible a number of men included in the following list of names may be granted leave en route from Halifax and will not be arriving in Calgary with the main group on Wednesday's special train.

Following is the list of Edmonton district soldiers who have returned to Canada:

L/Sgt. Ainsworth, J. E., Red Deer; Gnr. Adzich, M. P., 10553 108 st., Edmonton; Gnr. Ahern, K. L., Halcourt; Dvr. Ames, W. J., Wabamun; Bdr. Astley, R. C., Minburn; Pte. Anderson, A., Grimshaw; Pte. Auger, C., High Prairie; Pte. Arnold, L. E., 13507 67 st., Edmonton.

L/Cpl. Allen, W. M., 9610 102A ave., Edmonton; Lt. (N/S) Clara C. Albers, Wetaskiwin; L/Sgt. Brown, A. L., Red Deer; Sgt. Brown, T. C., Red Deer; Bdr. Barnett, R., Vermilion; Bdr. Birse, W. E., Shaunessey; Pte. Boitnott, F. E., Didsbury; Pte. Borle, E. M., Gunn.

Rfn. Bliss, M. H., Grande Prairie; Cfn. Bradley, E. A., 9319 94 st., Edmonton; Pte. Briete, A., Cold Lake; Tpr. Banderob, W. H., Cremona; A/Cpl. Bates, M., Langdon; Pte. Brown, R. T., 11119 101 st., Edmonton; L/Cpl. Barnes, H., Suffield; Pte. Basarab, A., High Prairie; Lieut. Prairie; Lieut. Beaton, F. L., Sylvan Lake; Sgt. Cheshire, C. J. A., Ashmount; Sgt. Chiles, S. T., Rimbey; Pte. Callas, J., Wainwright; S/Sgt. Campbell, G. W., Camrose.

Gnr. Coombes, J. R., 9948 104 st., Edmonton; Cpl. Cameron, H. P., 9807 106 st., Edmonton; Pte. Chapin, W. R., Caroline; Pte. Collins, J., 9838 104

(Continued on Page 5, Col. 4)

Urges Western Hemisphere Defence Be Left to "American Republics"

By R. T. Bowman
(From the Journal's Washington Bureau)

WASHINGTON.—The state department has received a proposal from Senator Arthur Vandenberg that "American republics" alone be responsible for policing the western hemisphere under the new world security organization.

In a letter to James F. Byrnes, the ranking Republican said the United States might well accept, in connection with her inter-American Allies, the exclusive responsibility for any armed forces required to maintain peace and security in the western hemisphere.

"I doubt," he said, "whether she shall ever want any other armed forces to enter this area."

This bureau is now trying to get the senator to explain his statement with respect to Canada which cannot be included under the heading "American republics." It is possible that he may include Canada in "inter-American Allies" and suggest the creation of a military alliance with Canada and the Pan-American nations including the U.S.

The state department is not believed to be warmly disposed toward Senator Vandenburg's plan. It might lead to other nations excluding U.S. forces from their spheres of influence.

Nevertheless suggestions put forward by the ranking Republican must be given careful consideration. He played a leading part in the American delegation at San Francisco, and his support is needed in the senate during the next few months when other important international measures will be considered.

The Bomb

"What was written in the history of the 'forties?' Mostly, it was the story of a war, of many dying, of a bomb and of a new bloodless but menacing kind of conflict between two ideologies."
— Story, Dec. 31, 1949

The Journal greeted the destruction of Hiroshima and dawn of the atomic age on Aug. 7, 1945, with a mixture of relief and trepidation.

"An atomic bomb which looses pent-up forces of the universe equivalent to more than 20,000 tons of TNT and represents one of the greatest scientific advancements of history has been dropped on Japan."

The next day the paper's editorial writers saw the lead lining in the mushroom cloud.

"The vistas which this development opens up are terrifying.

"And this is only the beginning. There is no reason to doubt that the present atomic bomb bears the same relation to the bomb of the future that World War I aeroplanes bear to the Superfortress. Soon we may have devised missiles capable of obliterating a city like London or New York.

"In the presence of this new terror, the current efforts to establish a lasting peace take on a new significance. The human race will either eliminate war, or war will eliminate it."

After the U.S. dropped another A-bomb on Nagasaki three days later, reports of the appalling death and destruction in the two Japanese cities flowed onto the news pages.

Editorially, on Aug. 12, the paper took a pragmatic view of it all. "We doubt whether any action was more dramatically and completely justified than was the use of the atomic bomb by the United States Air Force. There is every reason to hope that they ended a great and terrible war, or that a few more of them will do so.

"The atomic bomb can be justified because it is ending a war. It will be justified still more if history can record that it ended all war."

It was an odd sort of optimism.

On Friday, Sept. 23, 1949, U.S. President Harry Truman announced that the U.S.S.R. had exploded its first atomic bomb on Aug. 29, over the volcano-ruined wilderness of Kamchatka, but downplayed its significance.

The Saturday editorial was insightful and more than a little paranoid.

"It goes without saying that this development will affect profoundly the whole international situation.

"The one saving feature in the situation is that American atomic development has not stood still since the end of the war, so that the Soviets are still two or three years behind.

"The balance is still far enough against the Russians – we may hope – to discourage them from doing anything really irrevocable, though how long this situation will last no one can say."

***Sept. 20, 1949*:**
The Alberta government reports record revenue of $70.45 million for 1948-49.

***Oct. 9, 1949*:**
Safeway sells Thanksgiving turkeys for 55 cents a pound; in 1959 the price is down to 35 cents.

***Oct. 17, 1949*:**
Imperial Oil reports discovering its first producing well in Alberta's Peace River district.

***Nov. 6, 1949*:**
A cenotaph is unveiled in honour of the community's war dead in Calder neighbourhood .

***Nov. 15, 1949*:**
A record wind speed of 132 km/h is recorded in Edmonton.

***Nov. 20, 1949*:**
CHFA, the first French language radio station, opens in Edmonton.

***Dec. 3, 1949*:**
The Canadian National Institute for the Blind opens a new Edmonton service centre and residence on Jasper Avenue.

***Dec. 31, 1949*:**
The Alberta oil-boom villages of Devon and Redwater are incorporated.

The Edmonton Journal

FIFTIETH YEAR | EDMONTON, ALBERTA, MONDAY, JUNE 1, 1953 | PRICE: NOT OVER 5 CENTS

Long May She Reign . . .

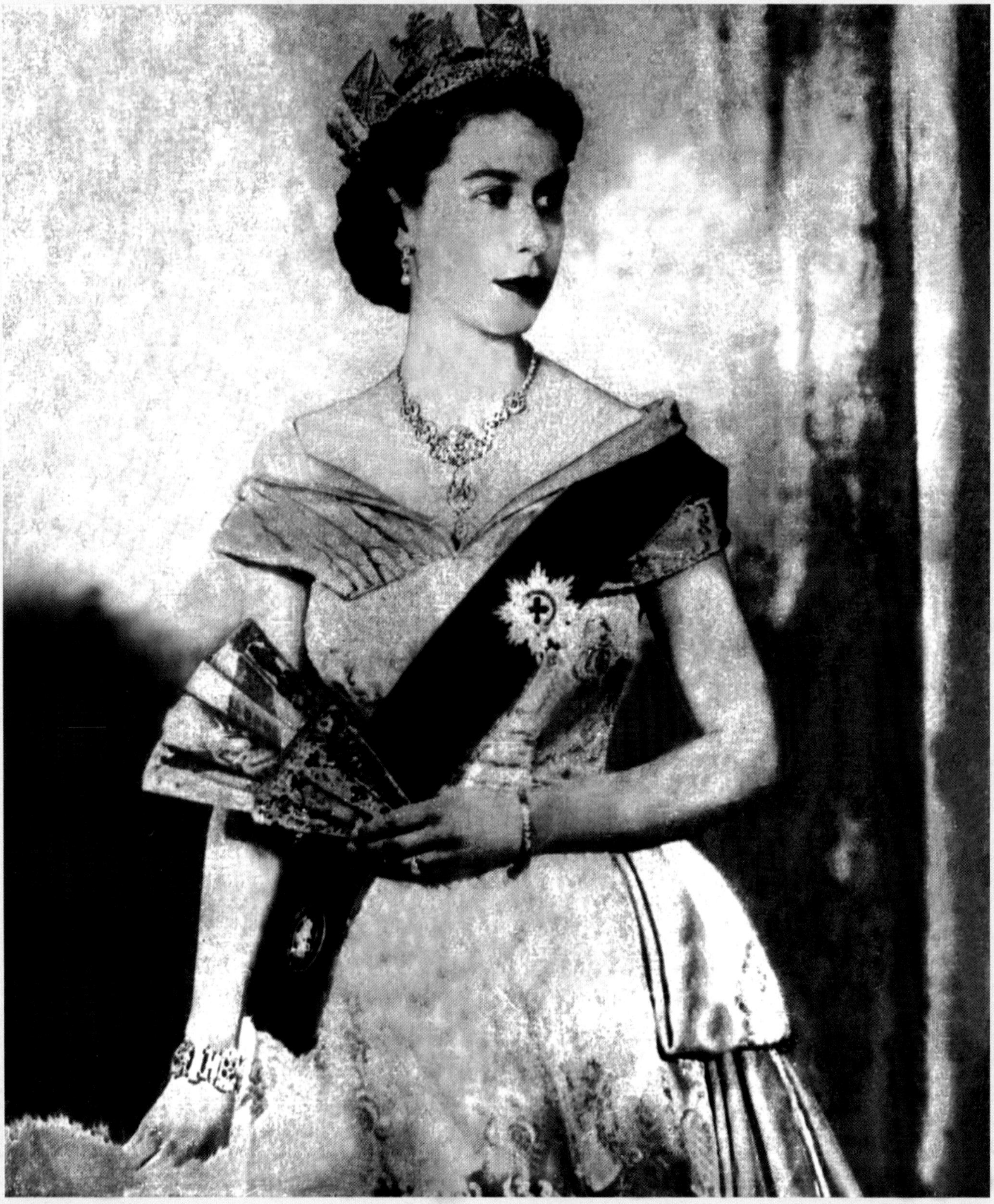

—Copyright, Dororthy Wilding.

Elizabeth the Second, by the grace of God, of the United Kingdom, Canada and her other Realms and Territories, Queen, Head of the Commonwealth, Defender of the Faith

S I X

Final Reminder!
EXPIRED
YOUR SUBSCRIPTION IS OVERDUE
DAILY MAIL RATES
In Alberta, N.W.T., Y.T., Peace River Block
One Year $10.00 | 6 Months $6.00 | 3 Months $4.00 | 1 Month $1.50
Elsewhere in Canada, British Isles
$12.00 | $7.00 | $5.00 | $2.00
IN UNITED STATES
$15.00 | $9.00 | $5.00 | $2.00
SERVICE TO YOU MUST BE STOPPED
UNLESS YOUR RENEWAL IS MAILED...
5 CENTS
NOW
CANADA 1954
The Edmonton Journal
ONE OF CANADA'S GREAT NEWSPAPERS

Coming of Age

1950 to 1959

First Nations / 223
William Hawrelak / 225
Olympic Gold / 231
Only in Westmount / 233
Everlovin' Esks / 235
The Boob Tube / 239

"Edmonton may not yet realize it, but perhaps the greatest boom in Canadian history is well under way here."
— An unnamed Edmonton builder on the building boom in 1950

Edmonton's pride at being the most northerly big city on the continent was clear when representatives of more than two dozen civic organizations met in City Hall in the spring of 1950. They had gathered to come up with a smart, new, up-to-date slogan that would capture the essence of their city.

Possibilities included Edmonton – Gateway to the North, Oil Capital of Canada, and Edmonton – Gateway to the North with a Flying Future. Finally, they settled on something more simple and direct: Edmonton – Gateway to the North.

It was fitting, and it defined Edmonton, a bustling city with all-important connections to the fertile farmland of the Peace River Country and the mineral wealth beyond in the Northwest Territories.

"Edmonton's position as the doorway to Canada's vast, rich northland, the feature that literally put Edmonton on the map 150 years ago, should be revived to put this city on the publicity map of the world now, it was decided by a meeting of 55 representatives of 31 organizations Wednesday night," a March 12, 1950, *Journal* story recounted.

Edmonton may have been on the frontier, but it was rapidly shedding

Edmonton Weather

24-hour forecast: Cloudy today and Wednesday, continuing mild, light winds.

The Edmonton Journal

'One of Canada's Great Newspapers'

FORTY-SEVENTH YEAR * * TELEPHONE 25171 EDMONTON, ALBERTA, TUESDAY, FEBRUARY 7, 1950 SINGLE COPY, 5 CENTS 26 PAGES

$90,000,000 Building Program Seen

U.S. Miners Ignore Order

PITTSBURGH, (AP) Coal production in the United States plummeted Tuesday in the wake of the soft-coal miners' country-wide strike. All signs point to rising unemployment in coal-using industries.

About 372,800 diggers are on strike in 14 states. They insist they won't be "blackjacked" into heeding the federal Taft-Hartley Labor Act. The strikers can produce about 2,220,000 tons of coal a day.

Nearly 20,000 workers in steel mills and on railroads were laid off the last few months because of the three-day work week ordered July 1 by President John L. Lewis of the United Mine Workers (Ind.). Now railroads say more thousands of lay-offs are in the cards.

Throughout the country, less than two weeks' coal reserves remain stored above ground. The coal industry said the supply is poorly distributed.

Through the coalfields, the miners are out for a showdown in their struggle for a new contract and the five day week.

The sporadic walkouts that made idle 100,000 soft-coal diggers last week in the United States spread to nearly all of the 400,000 United Mine Workers members Monday.

The embittered miners have termed this a show-down fight in their battle with the coal operators for more pay, and an increase in welfare fund payments.

In invoking the Taft-Hartley Act, the president's first action was the naming of a fact-finding panel to investigate the drawn-out contract dispute.

His next step under the act would be to ask Attorney-General J. Howard McGrath to go to federal court and obtain a court order directing the union to get its miners back on the job for 70 or 80 days. If the union should refuse it would face heavy fines.

Lewis and the union were fined $1,420,000 in 1948 for disobeying a back-to-work order.

Mercurys Down Swiss Team 4-2

AROSA, Switzerland, (CP) — Edmonton Mercurys Tuesday showed all-round hockey mastery to down a Swiss team 4-2, maintaining the winning streak of their current continental tour. Al Purvis paced the Mercs with a hat-trick.

In a heavy snowfall, 2,000 fans crowded Arosa's outdoor rink to watch the Canadian entry for the world amateur hockey championships at London next month. The Mercs kept the Swiss goalie dancing in the nets, despite injuries that sent Billie Dawe and Marsh Darling off in the second period for the rest of the game.

Purvis and Leo Luchinni gave the Canadians a two-goal lead in the opening period and Purvis followed with two more in the second period before Ueli Polterra was able to put Arosa on the scoreboard. Oldrich Zabrodsky, ace exiled Czechoslovakian player, notched the other Swiss goal in the final period.

Pair Missing Since Sunday Found Near Disabled Plane

Two men, over

on a flight

been f

dis

Frozen Evidence Wins Man's Appeal

SCRANTON, Pa., (AP)—Judge T. Linus Hoban appeared startled as attaches dragged a k

into county court.

"What have we h

"It's a bear

corpus d

Alberta Dairymen Here For Annual Three-Day Convention

Annual convention of the Alberta Dairymen's Association opened at the Macdonald Tuesday with 250 of the expected 450 delegates in attendance. After official welcome addresses by Mayor Parsons and Oliver McIntyre, president of the Edmonton Chamber of Commerce, business sessions were started. Shown here at the registration desk, are Lloyd Cook and John Nixon, both of Edmonton, seated, as A. F. Bennett, of the provincial dairy branch, department of agriculture, rings the cow bell signalling the commencement of sessions.—(Story on Page 13.)

Kremlin Leaders Bent On War With West Once World Power Shifts, Says Writer

What are the calculations of the Soviet leadership of war or peace? How is the great monolithic state being geared for the eventuality of conflict? Edmund Stevens, staff correspondent of the Christian Science Monitor, recently left Moscow after more than 10 years of close observation of Russian affairs from both sides of the Iron Curtain. He has tried to answer the most anxious questions of Westerners concerning the enigma that is the Soviet Union today.

NEW YORK, (AP)—The leaders of the Kremlin are bent on eventual war with the West, if they ... away with it, say ...

three-year assignment as correspondent for the Christian Science Monitor in Russia, says Soviet aims and policies have, since the war, become plain for all to see—expansion through superimposing the Communist system.

Do the Soviet leaders, who have an atom bomb now, want war?

For the immediate future, he said, the answer is no. In the long view, with the shifting of world power in the Kremlin's favor, the ans... The Communist ...

of hope for peace in the realization by the Kremlin that it would be difficult to sell the Soviet people on a war of aggression.

To beat Soviet propaganda, Stevens writes, the West should miss no opportunity to go over the heads of the Soviet leaders, directly to the Rusian people.

The West must remember, Stevens says, that "despite doctrinaire aims and ...

Soviet ...

Expect Expansion Here Set Pace For Continent

Edmonton this year may expect a construction program totalling at least $90,000,000, a survey revealed Tuesday. The survey indicated that the greatest per capita construction pace on the North American continent will be established here in 1950. In 1949, Edmonton's construction rate equalled that of any city on the continent on a per capita-dollar basis.

With $65,000,000 in building projects already under way or definitely planned for 1950, officials predict the year's construction total in Edmonton and immediate district may be expected to reach nearly $100,000,000.

In prospect are 1950 Edmonton building permits valued at between $45,000,000 and $50,000,000. Taking the smaller of these two figures, plus a $28,000,000 refinery and pulp mill construction program immediately east of the city, along with a $20,000,000 carry-over from Edmonton's record 1949 construction program, the prospective 1950 total exceeds $90,000,000.

The construction industry probably will employ some 20,000 persons directly and indirectly to tackle the huge 1950 program which threatens to more than double last year's construction boom when city building permits totalled $40,050,063. When oil was discovered in this area in 1947, building permits totalled $13,000,000 for the year. The total rose to $27,000,000 in 1948.

"Edmonton may not realize it, but perhaps the greatest boom in Canadian history is just well under way here," declares one Edmonton building authority.

All categories of the ... tion boom promise ... 1950. ...

B.C. Supports Gas Pipeline From Alberta

By T. A. Mansell
(Journal Staff Writer)

CALGARY. — The B.C. government took a hand in Alberta's gas export hearings here Tuesday.

Attorney-General Gordon Wismer, representing the coast government is prepared to facilitate the building of a pipeline system.

In the northeast area of B.C. comprising the Peace River block, there is an estimated area of more than 50,000,000 acres of potential oil and gas lands, on which some exploratory work has been done, said the B.C. minister.

At the opening of Tuesday's hearing on the West Coast Transmission Co.'s application for a gas export permit, Chairman I. N. McKinnon announced the board's decision on the point raised Monday by S. Bruce Smith of Edmonton concerning the scope of evidence. Counsel had urged that testimony be restricted to first hand evidence.

"The board has decided to hear all evidence we consider relevant," said the chairman.

He added that the board realized that hearsay evidence was almost unavoidable. It will give consideration to the weight of such evidence when objection is taken to its admissibility.

Hon. Lucien Maynard, attorney-general, welcomed Mr. Wismer at the opening of Tuesday's sitting.

(Continued on Page 12, Col

Weather Cle... For North...

May Ask Industry To Slow Lay-Offs

By Ross Munro
(From The Journal's Ottawa Bureau)

OTTAWA.—The government is considering sending a letter to employers across the country soliciting their assistance in dealing with the current unem... situation.

It is ...

GOOD LUCK IS SO GOOD, I JUST CAN'T BELIEVE IT'S MARGARINE!

says Mrs. GEORGE SPENCER of Halifax

IT'S DELICIOUS! WE ALL LOVE ITS SWEET-CHURNED FLAVOUR!
Mr. GEORGE SPENCER
WILLIAM SPENCER
MARGARET SPENCER

No wonder Mrs. Spencer can't tell the difference! Good Luck's sweet-churned flavour is so delicate, so country-fresh!

As a spread it's tops! And wait till you taste the wonders it works in your cooking and baking! Good Luck adds such richness and lusciousness, people can't believe it's margarine!

Try Good Luck yourself — today!

Get SWEET-CHURNED

GOOD LUCK

CANADA'S LARGEST-SELLING MARGARINE!

GOOD LUCK IS GOOD FOR GROWING YOUNGSTERS. NO OTHER SPREAD GIVES THEM MORE VITAMIN A AND REAL NOURISHMENT!

GOOD LUCK
MARGARINE

Foil-wrapped in twin bars for extra freshness, each with its own handy colour wafer.

Only

SERVEL

THE NATURAL GAS

Refrigerator

GIVES YOU

10 YEAR GUARANTEE

CHECK THESE FEATURES

- No Noise
- No Moving Parts
- Low Operating Cost
- Frozen Food Locker

(LIMITED QUANTITIES)

Priced at 369.50 and up (Installed)

TRADE-INS ACCEPTED EASY TERMS

SOUTH SIDE ELECTRIC

10550 82 Ave. Ph. 31313

THE SMART LOOK IS

WELL GROOMED HAIR instantly!

THE BRYLCREEM LOOK

A DISTINCTLY DIFFERENT HAIR DRESSING! Here's Why:

- *Super-concentrated* to give more for your money — goes further than any other hair dressing.
- Grooms *perfectly;* hair *stays* well-groomed *all day!*
- Not greasy, not sticky — contains no alcohol.
- Neutralizes perspiration acids — helps keep your hair and scalp clean and fresh.
- Removes loose dandruff, relieves dryness.
- Liquifies *speedily* — quickly spreads throughout hair — keeps it soft, lustrous, haelthy-looking.
- Over 45,000,000 sold yearly! Try it — *see why!*

BRYLCREEM

Buy at all drug counters — and ask your barber for a Brykreem application!

Convenient tube or handy jar

More Men Buy BRYLCREEM Than ANY OTHER HAIR DRESSING in the World!

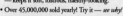

the hair dressing that Conditions as it Grooms

the trappings of a frontier town. The population influx of the Second World War and the subsequent postwar boom was partly responsible for the city's new attitude. With 159,631 residents in 1950, Edmonton was one of the fastest growing cities in the country.

By the end of the decade, the population had almost doubled again to 303,000, and with $100,000,000 in building permits issued by city hall in 1950, the city set the pace for North America, boasting the greatest per-capita construction rate on the continent. Calculated today, that would mean almost $800 million in new construction.

There was little that could puncture the buoyancy of a young city on the move. New oil fields added to the discoveries at Leduc, Redwater and Golden Spike enhanced the spirit of optimism.

And Edmontonians had only to take a short Sunday drive past the city's eastern boundaries to see a bright, hopeful future. Oil refineries signalled a turning point in the economy of the city and the province.

When the British American refinery opened in 1950 – the second after the Imperial Oil plant that had opened a year before – *The Journal* editorial was effusive. "All this refinery construction reflects the ever-growing confidence in the future of the productive oil pools with which the city is now virtually surrounded.

"This reflects the shift in Alberta from a mainly agricultural economy toward one also grounded in industrial development of mineral resources."

It certainly did. For the first time in the province's history, Alberta's urban population outstripped the number of people living on farms. By 1952, 488,188 people – 51.96 per cent of the population – lived in cities and towns.

The Journal's pages reflected that increased urbanization and refinement of manner with increased coverage of the arts and entertainment.

And when the Paramount Theatre opened on Jasper Avenue across from The Bay in the summer of 1952, the paper told its readers that the city now boasted the largest theatre between Toronto and Vancouver that was also "the last word in motion picture entertainment." The opening film was *Jumping Jacks*, starring Dean Martin and Jerry Lewis.

With Edmonton teams enjoying success, most notably the Edmonton Eskimos and their string of Grey Cup victories, the paper also devoted more space to sports coverage.

Jeanette MacDonald, the star of the hit movie *Rose Marie*, noted that fact after she performed to two sold-out shows in the cavernous Sales Pavilion in the fall of 1952.

It was also a smelly venue – cattle auctions were regularly held there – but that didn't seem to deter MacDonald, whose concert included her signature tune *Indian Love Call*.

"In places this size," the tactful soprano said in a *Journal* interview, "I think people provide for sport before art."

As always, a good newspaper is one that covers its city well, and *The Journal* continued to report on recent weddings and meetings of social clubs. The reincarnation of the Edmonton Symphony Orchestra, defunct since the Depression, was taken as another example of a city being on the

***In 1950*:**
A compositor at *The Journal* makes $29.25 a week, while an advertising copy chaser earns $17 a week. In February installation of new, high-speed, state-of-the-art press begins. The press begins operation on July 17. In December 1950 excavations start on an addition to the paper's building. The four-storey structure has a full basement which houses the new presses.

***Jan. 2, 1950*:**
A retail tradition begins with Henry Singer's Dirty Shirt Sale. Dress and sports shirts could be had for as little as $1.65, knocked down from a high of almost $7.50. Singer followed that up a week later with his famous Cat and Dog Sale.

***Jan. 12, 1950*:**
Two RCAF officers are killed when their light aircraft crashes on an Edmonton street (105th Street between 112th and 113th Avenue) near the Royal Alexandra Hospital.

***Feb. 1950*:**
The Detwiler Plan, a privately financed scheme for city centre redevelopment, is presented to council but fails to win public support.

HELP KILL POLIO

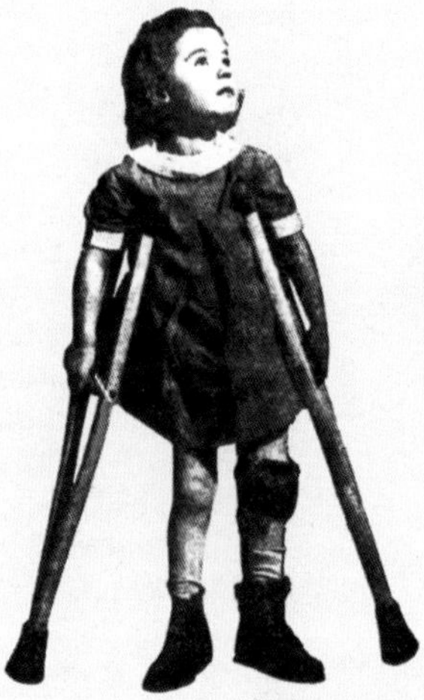

THE CRIPPLER

KEEP THIS HORRIBLE CRIPPLER AWAY FROM YOUR CHILDREN, YOUR NEIGHBOR'S CHILDREN AND ALL THE CHILDREN IN THE COMMUNITY! LET OUR CHILDREN GROW HAPPILY WITHOUT THE FEAR OF CRUTCHES, BRACES, THE LIMP AND THE MADDENING PAIN OF INFANTILE PARALYSIS. CHILDREN ARE THE HELPLESS ONES. WE AS GROWNUPS, MUST FIGHT FOR THEM. OURS IS THE PRIVILEGE OF GIVING TO THE CANADIAN MARCH OF DIMES. OURS IS THE DUTY TO PROTECT THE CHILDREN . . . TO HELP THOSE STRUCK DOWN BY AN AGONIZING, LIMB-TWISTING CRIPPLER!

GIVE TO THE CANADIAN

MARCH OF DIMES

Send Contributions with Name and Address To

ANY CHARTERED BANK IN CANADA

THIS PAGE MADE POSSIBLE THROUGH CO-OPERATION OF THE FOLLOWING FIRMS:

Adby Construction Co., Ltd.
Calgary Ginger Ale
H. G. Macdonald
Poole Construction Co., Ltd.
Government of the Province of Alberta
Bakery Employers' Association of Alberta
H. Kelly & Co., Ltd.
Northwestern Utilities Limited
Northern Alberta Dairy Pool Ltd.
Woodland Dairy Company Limited
Edmonton City Dairy Company
Murray & Farrah
City of Edmonton
Prudham Building Supplies Ltd.
Allen McBain Lumber Co., Ltd.
Magid Upholstering Ltd.
Taylor & Pearson Ltd.
General Tinning Co., Ltd.
Sparling-Davis Company Ltd.
Sunley Electric Co.
Hancock Lumber Co., Ltd.
W. H. Clark Lumber Co., Ltd.
Wanless Home & Building Supplies Ltd.
Barrigan Woodwares
A. V. Carlson Ltd.
Electric Motor Sales Ltd.
Murray's Upholstering & Draperies Co. Ltd.
The Douglas Printing Co. Ltd.
Recreation Bowling Academy Ltd.
Corona Hotel
Wood, Buchanan & Campbell
Seven Seas Restaurant
Independent Insurance Exchange Ltd.
Edmonton Supply Co.
MacKillop Electric Ltd.
Lockerbie & Hole Ltd.
Upright Bros. Ltd.
Kenn's Service Garage Ltd.
Rule, Wynn & Rule
Precision Machine & Foundry Ltd.

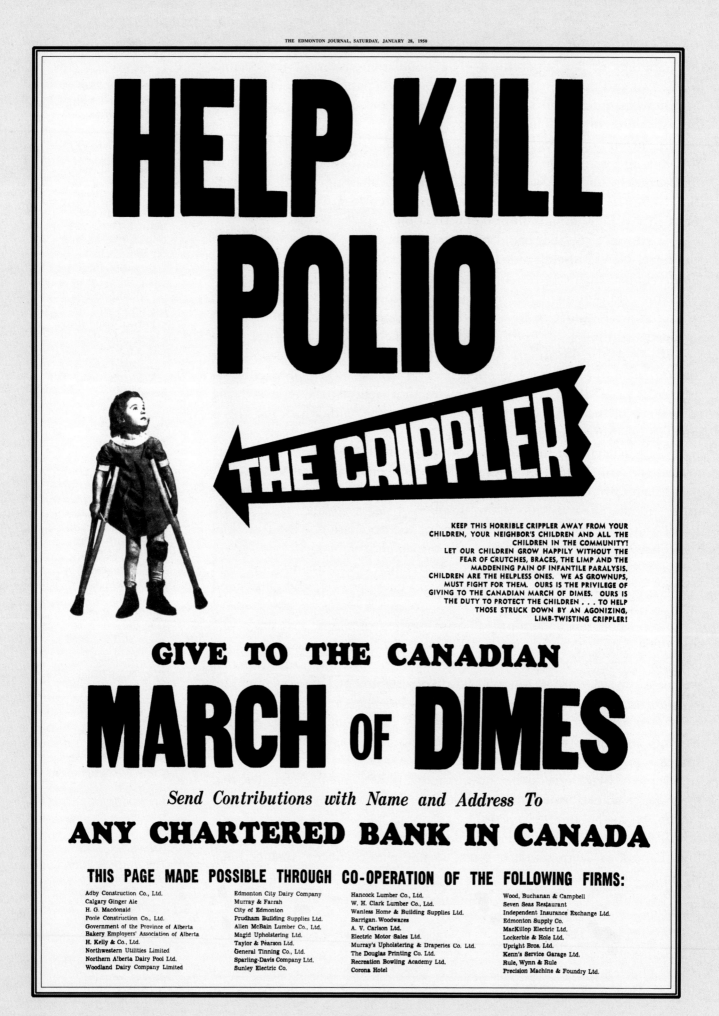

move. When the new symphony, some 60 musicians under the direction of Lee Hepner, made its debut at the Capitol Theatre on Nov. 30, 1952, the unnamed *Journal* critic was full of praise. He lauded the orchestra for its musicianship, cohesion and "sincere attention to vital shadings of colour and expression."

The soloist was Soulima Stravinsky, son of Igor Stravinsky, who predicted the new orchestra would be the envy of the music world.

In providing service to its readers, the paper continued to publish lists of names of students at the University of Alberta who had successfully completed their courses and earned their degrees. For many, *The Journal* list was the first indication they had passed.

And then in 1951, the *Edmonton Bulletin*, part of the city for more than 70 years and *The Journal's* long time rival, ceased publication.

A brief front-page story in *The Journal* on Jan. 20, 1951, announced the closure. "H.L. Straight, publisher of the Edmonton Bulletin, announced Saturday that the paper will suspend publication with the issue of one final edition Saturday.

"The decision was announced to an employees' meeting Saturday morning as the last issue of the paper, founded here in 1880 by Frank Oliver, was going to press. Mr. Straight said the 179 employees would be given two weeks' pay. All would finish work Saturday with the exception of a few being kept on to wind up accounts.

"Mr. Straight said the decision to close the paper had resulted from being 'too successful.'

"He said it was now confronted with the problem of building a new plant and buying a new press at an outlay of $1 million. In addition, the paper had been unable to obtain adequate newsprint supplies."

Editorially, *The Journal* lamented the death of its adversary. "The Journal will miss the energetic competition of the Bulletin.

"That competition was always helpful to both papers, so much so that the Journal has always declined offers to buy the Bulletin or take it in amalgamation. Many opportunities to buy the Bulletin have occurred in the past 30 years, and the last of many offers was declined only last week."

The editorial also revealed that *The Journal* had often assisted *The Bulletin* when it failed to pay its debts.

"Indeed, there have been occasions in the long history of the Bulletin when it could not have published had not The Journal paid its paper bill or supplied it with paper," the editorial said. "We regret its passing and the circumstances which brought about its death."

Almost immediately, *The Journal* picked up more than 20,000 subscribers, pushing its circulation in the spring of 1951 to 77,000. By the end of the decade, circulation stood at 105,000 daily.

To help produce the papers for the new readership, *The Journal* bought up $852,000 ($6,715,625 today) worth of *The Bulletin's* assets in January 1951. The purchase included the defunct paper's circulation lists, office furniture, bus benches, carrier depots, type metal, ink and 10 linotype machines.

Those readers were given a full diet of news about the oil and gas boom in the province.

***Feb. 7, 1950*:**
Bread sells for 10 cents a loaf at Edmonton Safeway stores.

***Feb. 24, 1950*:**
Voters in West Jasper Place approve the name Jasper Place for the newly incorporated village at the western edge of Edmonton.

***March 3, 1950*:**
The Edmonton Petroleum Club is incorporated, with six original members – P.D. Bowlen, D.J. Avison, O.W. Wall, S.G. Coultis, A.D. Foulds and J.L. Wilson – signing the application.

***March 12, 1950*:**
***The Journal* reports that, "Edmonton's position as the doorway to Canada's vast, rich northland, the feature that literally put Edmonton on the map 150 years ago, should be revived to put this city on the publicity map of the world now, it was decided by a meeting of 55 representatives of 31 organizations Wednesday night."**

***March 22, 1950*:**
The Edmonton Waterloo Mercurys win the World Hockey Championship in London.

***March 29, 1950*:**
"A former Edmonton girl is pirouetting her

Edmonton Weather
Forecast: Cloudy and much colder with light snow, light winds. Low tonight 15 below, high tomorrow 10 below.

The Edmonton Journal

One of Canada's Great Newspapers

FIFTIETH YEAR | TELEPHONE 25171 | EDMONTON, ALBERTA, MONDAY, JANUARY 26, 1953 | PRICE: NOT O... R 5 CENTS | 30 PAGES

Luxury Liner "Total Loss" In Fire

Reds Hurl Back Allied Attack

SEOUL, (AP)—Allied fighter-bombers ripped into Communist battlefront positions today after United Nations troops took a licking on the western Korean front in an elaborately-planned "program" raid.

The 4½-hour raid was the heaviest ground action of the new year. Allied infantry, tanks, flame-throwers, artillery and planes were thrown into the unsuccessful assault on Spud Hill.

High "brass" and correspondents provided in advance with a pamphlet describing each phase of the attack—watched from nearby bunkers. Called "Operation Smack," it had been planned since Jan. 19.

But the Chinese Communists were ready. They caught the charging UN infantrymen in a deadly crossfire.

Then the Allied troops tried to burn out the Reds with flame-throwers. However, in many instances, the flame-throwers ran out of fuel. AP correspondent Forest Edwards reported from the scene — at the southern end of T-Bone hill — that a hail of artillery shells and napalm (jellied gasoline) also failed to dislodge the Communists.

One of the Allied wounded told Edwards:

"If we could only have had more flame-throwers we could have burned right through them. We were doing a good job but suddenly there weren't any more flame-throwers."

Another wounded man told AP photographer Fred Waters that the flame-throwers ran out of fuel and added grimly:

"And so did the guy who was shooting it."

An 8th Army spokesman declined to report Allied casualties but estimated 95 Chinese were killed.

After the raid, 5th Air Force and navy carrier planes swarmed over the entire front.

Fourteen Okinawa-based B-29s Sunday night blasted a 30-acre military staff installation at Yangdok and the lateral rail line to Pyongyang.

The United States cruisers Los Angeles and Rochester pounded the northeast port of Songjin and Communist supply lines.

In continuing air battles, U.S. Sabre jets destroyed one MiG-15 and damaged another Sunday. The air force said that brought the January total to 39 Red jets destroyed, six probably destroyed and 39 damaged.

2,000 Refugees Flee German Reds

BERLIN (AP)—The week-end brought another 2,000 frightened refugees into West Berlin from the purge-ridden Soviet zone. Refugee facilities were taxed to the limit.

An estimated 20,000 have crossed the Red frontier this month in a flight covering all walks of East Germany's Communist-dominated life. They include:

1. Jews, who are the latest target of Moscow's wrath.
2. Farmers being squeezed out of their chances of making a living through rigged crop quotas which the Communists know in advance they cannot fill.
3. Little business men bowing to the inevitable in a land where everything is rapidly being nationalized into "peoples' owned" enterprises.
4. Borderline officials who had Communist blessing for a time and now either have lost it or fear they are about to lose it.
5. Poor families unable to get enough to eat because they lack political influence to get special rations and also lack extra money to buy in the high-priced "state stores."
6. Germans living on the fringe of West Berlin in a 70-mile perimeter the Communists are clearing to create a "death zone" between Red Germany and West Berlin.

Allied intelligence agencies have assigned their top men to the refugee centres to spot Eastern officials who may have valuable information and also to help West Berlin authorities in their "screening" of suspected planted agents.

Those who get swept into the Allied net are swallowed up by a tight security veil.

Candy Vending Machines Seized By Police In City Stores

Det. Sgt. Bill Smith, chief of the city police morality section, inspects 11 candy vending machines which were seized in Edmonton stores as illegal under the Alberta Slot Machine Act. Sgt. Smith said "upwards of 700 of the machines had been in operation in the city, and that all but the 11 shown were taken out by store owners after police warnings. The ones seized probably will be smashed, police said.

Flaming Gas Well Melts Derrick, Menaces Others In Gulf Of Mexico

MORGAN CITY, La., (AP) — An offshore gas well burned uncontrolled today in the Gulf of Mexico and firefighters battled to prevent explosions of four other wells only 14 feet away.

After the well exploded and burst into flames Sunday, pumps were set up on barges in an attempt to keep the four surrounding wells cool until the arrival of a fire-fighting specialist.

Forty-nine men were working on the platform, located 36 miles south of here, when the explosion occurred. Officials of the Pure Oil Company, which operates the well, said they escaped injury only by a "miracle."

A firefighter who specializes in extinguishing this type of blaze was expected by chartered plane from California.

Oilmen at the scene called it a multi-million-dollar blaze, but company officials said no accurate estimate of the loss could be made.

Intense heat from the blast and fire melted a 150-foot derrick on the well platform within 30 minutes and it toppled into the gulf.

Candy Machines Seized By Police

Eleven candy-vending machines, classed as illegal under the Alberta Slot Machine Act, have been seized by police, in connection with the province-wide crack-down on gambling and lotteries.

Acting under the morality section chief, Det. Sgt. Bill Smith, Dets. Douglas Ellis and Bill Fedoruk made the seizure after the machine-owners failed to withdraw them from operation.

"Upwards of 700 of these machines were in operation in the city," Det. Sgt. Smith said. He added that most of them were installed in small confectionery and grocery stores, and that all but 11 were taken out of operation by owners acting on police warnings.

The machines, standing about 15 inches high, are brightly colored and topped with a large glass container displaying the candy. Mixed with the candy are numerous small metal and plastic knicknacks such as rings, "good luck charms" and fobs for watch and key chains.

"It's the presence of the trinkets which makes the machines illegal," Det. Sgt. Smith said. "They act as inducement for children to squander pennies in the hope of coming up with one of them," he said, adding that with-

(Continued on Page 14 Col. 4)

Lamont Woman Killed In Car Crash

Mrs. Mabel Poloway, 70, of Lamont, was killed about 4:00 p.m. Sunday, as the car in which she was riding was in collision with another vehicle three miles east and one mile north of Chipman, at a municipal road intersection.

RCMP reported a car driven by John Romaniuk was proceeding south along the highway, and the other car, driven by Peter Poloway of Lamont was proceeding east.

The driver and other passengers in the Poloway car, John Poloway, 72, and Paul Poloway, were not badly hurt, suffering bruises and cuts. Romaniuk's car went out of control, and he was thrown out and pinned between his car and the ditch at the side of the road.

Visibility on the road at the time of the accident was reported as poor, as it was snowing heavily.

Coroner Dr. M. A. R. Young of Lamont has ordered an inquest to open Monday.

Britain May Build Atom Power Plant

LONDON, (Reuters)—The British government is thinking of building an experimental atomic power station and considers that before long atomic energy will provide a useful source of industrial power, Supply Minister Duncan Sandys told the House of Commons today.

Answering members' questions about the use of atomic energy in industry, he disclosed for the first time the progress British scientists are making in national research stations.

WASHINGTON, (AP) — The U.S. atomic energy commission announced today it will test "new and improved nuclear devices" at the Las Vagas, Nev., proving grounds beginning in March.

The announcement did not go into detail about the nature of the new series of tests. It said only:

"The new series of tests is designed to advance development of new and improved nuclear devices and will provide additional weapons performance data essential to military and civil defence effects studies."

'FLU HITS EGYPT

CAIRO, (AP) — A spokesman for the ministry of health estimated today that more than 100,000 Egyptians have been stricken with influenza during January. The spokesman said there were no serious cases and that the death rate had not increased as a consequence.

Charge Cab Driver Assaulted Woman

Stanley P. Aspeslet, Edmonton taxi driver, was arrested early Sunday by city police and booked on a charge of criminal assault.

In police court Monday he was remanded without plea for a preliminery hearing on Feb. 3.

The charge was laid after a married woman reported to police she had been criminally assaulted by a taxi driver. She said she had hired a cab about 2 a.m. Sunday to return home, after a visit with friends.

The woman said that instead of driving her home the taxi driver went to Fraser Flats, near the west end of the Dawson bridge, where the alleged attack is said to have occurred.

Destroyer Blast Fatal To Stoker

PORTLAND, Eng., (Reuters)—A stoker was killed and three other crew members injured today in an explosion in the boiler room of the Royal Navy destroyer Duchess.

The Duchess is one of the modern Daring class destroyers, the largest and most expensive ever built by the Royal Navy. She was launched two years ago.

Railways, Trainmen Meeting In Effort To Avoid Strike

MONTREAL (CP) — Canada's railways and the Brotherhood of Railway Trainmen meet again today in an effort to settle a country-wide wage strike set for Feb. 2.

It was the third meeting between the carriers and the BRT which represents 25,000 trainmen. The brotherhood set the strike date more than a week ago, pending "no reasonable settlement" of their demands.

The brotherhood originally sought a 35-per-cent wage increase. The majority report of a conciliation board recommended 12 per cent and a minority report 20 per cent.

The union wanted discussions to centre around the minority report while the railways held out for the majority report as the basis of negotiations. This brought about cessation of talks at the first two meetings.

The railways proposed today's meeting last Friday in a joint telegram to A. J. Kelly, BRT vice-president. At the time, Mr. Kelly said "we will respect their notice" but expressed concern at the "additional delay."

The railways' telegram expressed unwillingness "to conclude that the position is as hopeless as the meeting yesterday (last Thursday) with our negotiating committees indicated and that a com-

(Continued on Page 14, Col. 6)

Man Is Injured As Shoes Explode

BOISE, Idaho, (AP)—A Boise ditchmaster is in hospital because his shoes exploded.

Clarence Martin said he put sodium chlorate in some ditches about three weeks ago. The weather was wet and his shoes apparently soaked up some of the explosive chemical.

Last Friday, as he was installing a headgate, he set a grass fire to clear a ditch. He kicked some burning trash into the fire and his shoes exploded, leaving the uppers in shreds.

He ran across the street and jumped into a puddle of water. Shortly afterward, he entered hospital with burns.

Where To Find It

Amusements, Theatres	16
Angelo Patri	18
Baby Care	18
Births, Deaths, Marriages	20
Bridge	28
Comics	25, 28, 29
Crossword Puzzle	28
District	8
Dorothy Dix	18
Editorial	4
Financial	27
Gregory Clark's Packsack	28
Off the Record	29
Our Boarding House	22
Out Our Way	22
Radio	29
Sport	10, 11, 12, 13
Sydney Harris Article	29
There Oughta Be A Law	23
They'll Do It Every Time	21
Uncle Ray's Corner	28
Wants Ads	21, 22, 23, 24, 25
Women's	17, 18, 19

The Weather

(Issued by the Dominion Public Weather Office at Edmonton)

The second marked outbreak of Arctic air this winter Monday became firmly established over the prairies. The cold air, which had been stalled by a series of Pacific disturbances, now has pushed southward over the entire forecast district. Sub-zero temperatures are expected for all regions Tuesday.

Estimated low tonight, 15 below.

Estimated high tomorrow, 10 below.

At Edmonton Tuesday, sun rises 8:24; sets 5:04.

Snowfall, 4.4 inches.

Temperatures

Maximum temperatures yesterday and overnight lows are:

Edmonton	18	-1	Vermilion	21	2
Keg River	-8	-23	Saskatoon	22	14
Fairview	3	-13	Pr. Albert	20	14
Gr Prairie	-2	-10	Pr. Rupert	34	28
White Ct.	24	-8	Victoria	46	38
McMurray	-3	-12	Vancouver	44	37
L. La Biche	18	-6	Penticton	45	37
Penhold	[illegible]	-1	Kamloops	35	26
Calgary	26	4	Regina	26	19
Lethbridge	[illegible]	17	Winnipeg	17	13
Med Hat	[illegible]	20	Ft. William	11	17
Banff	31	12	Toronto	22	8
Jasper	18	1	Ottawa	34	5
Coronation	22	3	Montreal	38	11

City Will Have New Radio Station

OTTAWA, (CP) — The CBC board of governors today recommended licenses for new radio stations in Edmonton, New Glasgow, N.S., and Kingston and Eastview in Ontario.

Applications for the new stations were considered by the 11-member board at public meetings last week. The board's recommendations are forwarded to the transport department and invariably are accepted.

The new Edmonton station will be operated by Hugh M. Sibbald, Edmonton business man. It will broadcast on a wavelength of 1080 kilocycles.

"It is the opinion of the board that there is a place for an additional privately-owned station serving the Edmonton area," said the board. "It is understood that this station will be operated entirely independently from any other station."

At the public hearings, the Edmonton application was opposed by station CFRN of Edmonton and by the Alberta government which finances operation of station CKUA, by the telephone department.

Strike Ties Up Railway In U.S.

CHICAGO, (AP) — A strike by the men who run the trains has halted operations on the Chicago Great Western Railway, mainly a freight carrier serving five Mid-west states.

Edward Reidy, general manager of the railroad, said traffic was being shifted to connecting lines, and perishable freight had been cleared before the strike.

But the Great Western is the only rail line into the St. Paul stockyards, and Anton Olson, president of the yards, said the strike will seriously affect meat shipments there and at South St. Paul.

Some 800 members of five unions went on strike Sunday over an accumulation of 600 claims and grievances, some said to have been pending six years. The disputes ranged from pay rates to sanitary conditions on cabooses.

The line operates in Illinois, Iowa, Minnesota, Missouri and Nebraska, from Chicago to Omaha and from Kansas City to the Twin Cities.

Empress Of Canada Burns To Gutted Hulk

LIVERPOOL, (CP)—A charred and gutted hulk was all that remained today of the Empress of Canada, proud trans-Atlantic luxury liner swept by almost 24 hours of raging flames.

The 20,235-ton Canadian Pacific ship, a regular traveller between Liverpool and eastern Canadian ports, was declared a total loss today as firefighters finally won their long battle to control the blaze.

The $5,000,000 ship had been berthed in a floating dock here for her annual overhaul as she prepared to return to service for the heavy pre-Coronation trade.

Pockets of fire, mostly below decks, still burned during the morning but the blaze was under control and largely out. Five firemen suffered minor injuries.

A fire officer emerging from the dense smoke in the forward end nearly 24 hours after the fire first was reported said the ship is "very hot right along the hull."

"She is still burning furiously," he added.

Dense clouds of smoke still rose in the sky after the 25-year-old ship, her life at an end, lay on her port side, propellers out of the water.

Canadian Pacific Steamships announced that arrangements were being made to provide other bookings for persons who had planned to sail from Canada on the Empress for the Coronation June 2. Canadian Pacific said passengers would be informed individually of arrangements.

Police Superintendent Hubert Balmer made a preliminary investigation and asked the home office for the assistance of scientists. He said: "The possibility of sabotage cannot be ruled out."

The ship had been due to leave for Saint John, N.B., Feb. 11 under command of Capt. J. P. Dobson, on leave at his Liverpool home at the time of the fire.

Hundreds of tons of water were poured into her and speeded a sharp list to port. Her superstructure and funnels crashed

(Continued on Page 14, Col. 1)

Victim Of Fire Was Familiar To Canadians

MONTREAL, (CP)—A ship familiar to thousands of Canadians went up in flames as the Empress of Russia in similar circumstances in 1945.

Loss of the Empress of Canada was a blow to hundreds who had planned to sail in the 20,235-ton veteran of the Atlantic to the Coronation. With most liners and air lines booked to capacity, it was feared that many persons might be unable to book other transportation.

Flagship of Canadian Pacific Steamships, the Empress for 25 years plowed her stately way down the St. Lawrence from Montreal, calling at Quebec City, then at Saint John, N. B. before entering the open Atlantic or her run to Liverpool.

She wasn't always the Empress of Canada. She was best known, perhaps, as the Duchess of Richmond — one of a line of ships known affectionately to Canadians as the "drunken duchesses" because of a reputation for rolling.

She was renamed after the war, in which she carried 187,000 Allied troops 436,000 miles, in honor of the first Empress of Canada, a victim of enemy action off Freetown, West Africa, in 1943, with a loss of 400 lives.

The first Empress of Canada was one of 14 ships lost by the Canadian Pacific in war service. Another was the pride of the line, the Empress of Britain, whose role of flagship was taken over by the Duchess of Richmond when the Duchess was raised to the Empress class and refitted after the war.

The fire at Liverpool, which

(Continued on Page 14, Col. 3)

100 Albertans Booked On Liner

About 100 Alberta residents had booked passage on the Empress of Canada, which was gutted by fire at its moorings in Liverpool Sunday night.

Edmonton officials of Canadian Pacific Steamships said Monday that the Albertans were to have sailed from Canada on March 25, April 17 and May 8—considered the coronation sailings of the flagship.

The Edmonton agents said no word had been received as to what steps will be taken to accommodate the 2,000 passengers that would have made the trip to England on the three pre-coronation voyages. It is believed an emergency meeting was called Monday at Montreal, to decide a course of action.

The firm's other two liners, the Empress of France and the Empress of Scotland, are booked "almost solid" between now and July.

Officials said the Coronation had meant no significant increase in passenger traffic from Alberta. The average number of Albertans that sail with the Empress of Canada is about 35 or 40, they said, and bookings for March, April and May crossings stood at about this level.

Norwegian Ship Runs Aground

ST. JOHN'S, Nfld., (CP)—The Norwegian freighter Kent County remained hard aground on Little Bell Island Sunday night as another craft, the British-owned Saint Edmund, limped toward port with her topside split.

The 7,233-ton Kent County clipped her moorings off the iron ore centre of Wabana during a winter storm Thursday.

The salvage tug Foundation Lillian out of Halifax made several attempts to free her. Other attempts possibly will be delayed until Thursday when higher tides are due.

The Saint Edmund, meanwhile, came toward port under her own power with a United States Coast Guard cutter as an escort.

The same storm which drove the Kent County aground gave the 7,174-ton Saint Edmund a split across her starboard deck plates.

Size of the rip was not known but she was not believed in any immediate danger.

NEW YORK, (AP)—The tiny Icelandic freighter Foldin, battered by 45-foot waves, called for help Sunday from a little-travelled lane in northern seas.

Her steering gear broken, the Foldin sent an SOS from 100 miles off the southern tip of Greenland.

The message said the 621-ton ship and crew of 15 were at the mercy of gale winds.

Two U.S. Coast Guard cutters left weather stations to help.

Queen And Duke To Visit Ceylon

COLOMBO, (Reuters) — The Queen and the Duke of Edinburgh will make an 11-day visit to Ceylon on their way back to Britain after the Australian tour, it was announced today. The royal couple, who begin their tour in New Zealand Dec. 23, 1953, will arrive in Ceylon April 10 and stay until April 21.

Communists Propose To End East German Free Enterprise

By Tom Reedy

BERLIN, (AP) — The Communists have proposed that the entire supply network in East Germany be nationalized into a vast state corporation, thus spelling the end of private enterprise in the Soviet zone.

The proposal, made by the Socialist Unity Communist party's central committee, was published prominently Sunday in Taegliche Rundschu, the Soviet Army newspaper. That makes it appear the idea has Russian blessing and is thus practically an actuality.

The resolution calls for complete communizing the entire system of wholesaling and retailing food, coal and other daily necessities, about the only private enterprise left in the east zone.

"Capitalistic" methods used by the ministry of supply were blamed by the central committee for tremendous shortages plaguing the East German state. Families have been doing without

(Continued on Page 14, Col. 1)

5 U.S. Marines Win Air-To-Ground Duel

SEOUL, (AP) — Five United States Marines in a helicopter killed a Communist guerilla Saturday in one of the oddest duels of the Korean war.

The guerilla opened fire first and hit the helicopter three times with an American .45-calibre pistol—rated notoriously hard to shoot straight without long practice.

The Marines, 50 feet above the ground and travelling nearly 60 miles an hour, were even better marksmen. Firing carbines and pistols, they shot the guerilla in the head and chest.

The guerilla had put one slug into the instrument panel of the helicopter. The Marines were not hit.

Pope's Condition Said Improved

VATICAN CITY (AP)—The Pope, suffering from bronchial pneumonia, was reported slightly improved today. Vatican sources already had said there was no cause for concern.

No official bulletin was issued today on the condition of the 76-year-old Pontiff, who has been in bed since last Thursday. His ailment at first was described as influenza, but Vatican sources confirmed Sunday it was bronchial pneumonia.

No official information has been released on the treatment given the Pope. Sources at the Vatican said, however, it could be assumed that such modern medicines as penicillin were being administered.

The Pontiff's persistent fever late Sunday night hovered around the 101-degree mark. His doctor, Prof. Riccardo Galezazi-Lisi, has been staying at the Vatican since last Friday.

The Pontiff's attention to church duties continued despite his illness. He has been receiving his pro-secretaries of state regularly for discussion of church affairs. Sunday he listened to mass celebrated by a member of the Vatican household in a small studio adjoining the Pope's bedroom. He also recited the rosary for the return to Italy of war prisoners reported still held in Russia.

The only reference to the Pope's ailment in the Vatican newspaper l'Osservatore Romano was published last Saturday. It said his illness was accompanied by "irritations of the respiratory tract."

OIL OUTPUT DOUBLED

BAGHDAD, (AP) — Iraq produced a record 18,000,000 tons of oil last year compared with 9,000,000 in 1951, the Iraq Petroleum Co. said Sunday.

British Family Slain In Kenya

NAIROBI, Kenya (Reuters)—About 1,500 white settlers marched to Government House today and demanded to talk to Governor Sir Evelyn Baring about the brutal slaying of a British family Saturday night.

Farmer Roger E. Ruck, his wife Esme, a doctor, and their six-year-old son Michael were found hacked to death at their North Kinangop farm in the Aberdare mountains north of Nairobi.

Thirty Africans, including some women, have been arrested in connection with the crime, the most brutal against Europeans since the Mau Mau terror sect emergency began last September.

Baring declined to speak to the settlers, but Michael Blundell, leader of the European elected members of the legislature, said the governor had promised to improve Kenya's military organization and consult more closely with the white population on executive decisions.

Canadian Pacific Flagship Declared Total Loss After Fire

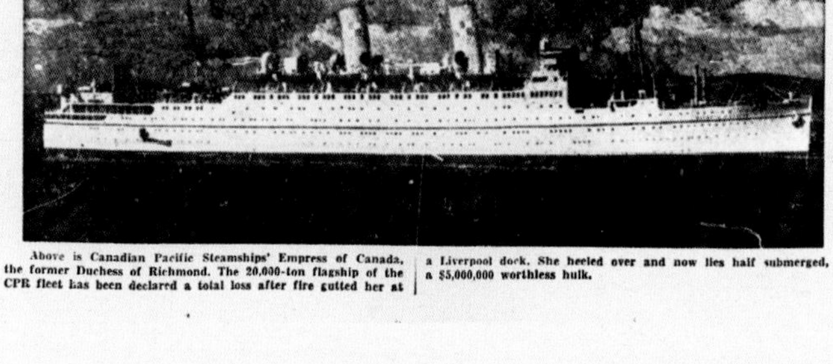

Above is Canadian Pacific Steamships' Empress of Canada, the former Duchess of Richmond. The 20,000-ton flagship of the CPR fleet has been declared a total loss after fire gutted her at a Liverpool dock. She heeled over and now lies half submerged, a $5,000,000 worthless hulk.

"Record-breaking $1,611,711 was paid for a quarter section in the Redwater oilfield Thursday as the Alberta government collected $6,607,184 for oil leases," read a typical page 1 story from the early '50s.

"The Alberta government in the past 14 months has collected about $36,000,000 in oil leases." A dollar in 1952 was worth $7.27 today.

Oil lease sales led to oil pipelines, and the paper celebrated their construction that resulted in thousands of barrels of Alberta crude being sent east each day for refining. Oil sold for $2.88 a barrel in 1950.

Canada's first oil pipeline – a 20-incher that ran 439 miles from Edmonton to Regina – cost $93 million and opened in the fall of 1950. When the pipeline began operating, there were already 500,000 barrels of Redwater crude stored in tanks.

An Oct. 5, 1950, editorial noted its significance. "The construction of the pipeline has been a notable achievement.

"No less striking has been the development of the Alberta oil fields in the three-and-a-half years since Imperial Oil Limited, the sponsor of the pipeline, made its historic Leduc discovery.

"The whole achievement is, indeed, concrete evidence of the worth of free enterprise."

The Journal followed intensely the progress of pipeline construction.

"An army of 1,000 men, whose weapons range from double-bitted axes to giant 'Big Inch' ditchers, this week are settling down to a back-breaking, machine-shattering assault on the Canadian Rockies," reported Hal Pawson in June 1952.

"They are pipeliners, a strange, carefree breed of 'cats' who in two years literally will claw out a five-foot-deep trench from Edmonton to Vancouver, and tenderly bury in it the $82,000,000 Trans-Mountain oil pipeline."

Never before in world history had a project of such magnitude and such difficulty been attempted, Pawson said.

The city and the newspaper swelled with satisfaction at the money that petroleum brought.

"Edmontonians have become accustomed to the fact that they are surrounded by oilfields," stated an editorial in spring 1953.

"What is perhaps less widely appreciated is the extent and significance of the distribution centre.

"This year will see trunk-line construction not only between Edmonton and Vancouver, but also from the Lake Superior terminus of the interprovincial pipeline to Sarnia, and between eastern Canadian cities. The total investment involved is around $183,500,000."

Pipelines, the megaprojects of their day, were big business – and a political quagmire as well.

The Journal approved the exporting of oil but was somewhat less eager to see natural gas sold to the United States, unless the needs of the province and the country were first guaranteed.

When in 1951 the province turned down a proposal to build a natural gas pipeline south, *The Journal* applauded its decision in a Jan. 25 editorial. "It would have been easy for them to have done otherwise, for the pressure of companies ready to spend scores of millions of dollars on pipelines to the United States markets was intense."

way to fame in New York City...She is Ruth Carse, daughter of Mr. and Mrs. William Carse, who joined the Radio City Music Hall Ballet in March." Two years after this story appeared, Carse returned to Edmonton and founded the Alberta Ballet Company.

***April 26, 1950*:**
***The Journal* and six other Southam papers share the honour of being accorded a place on the walls of the front-page corridor in Washington's famed National Press Club – the first Canadian papers to receive the honour.**

***June 22, 1950*:**
Edmonton's civic census puts the population at 148,861.

***Aug. 5, 1950*:**
Land in the Whitemud area is annexed.

***Aug. 18, 1950*:**
Fire destroys the grandstands at Renfrew Park baseball stadium.

***Oct. 4, 1950*:**
Canada's first major oil pipeline opens. The $95-million pipeline connects Alberta's oil fields to refineries in Ontario.

***Nov. 1, 1950*:**
Edmonton voters fail to approve the Detwiler Plan for

We've Come a Long Way TOGETHER

Let's Carry On Together!

Mrs. Stella M. Baker

Harry D. Carrigan

Edgar Gerhart

Williston Haszard

Ambrose Holowach

Dr. J. Donovan Ross

From the verge of bankruptcy to her present enviable position ... Alberta's record of progress under SOCIAL CREDIT Government stands unequalled in Canada -- AND THE BEST IS YET TO COME!

ERNEST C. MANNING

Premier of Alberta

Here Are The Highlights

Of What Your Social Credit Government HAS Done, IS Doing and WILL Do In The Interests Of Alberta and Her People!

1 A comprehensive program of practical co-operation with those engaged in Alberta's First Industry with particular attention to the needs and problems of farm people.

2 Substantial additional government assistance to bring the cost of rural electrification in settled areas within the financial reach of more Alberta farmers.

3 The continued orderly development of Alberta's vast natural resources, through individual and competitive enterprise and in the best interests of all citizens.

4 The progressive extension of Alberta's "Share the Wealth Program of Municipal Assistance" under which all municipalities and school districts will be guaranteed a generous measure of provincial aid in meeting both operating and capital expenditures. The Government will continue to share jointly with municipalities the gasoline tax revenues.

5 Continued improvement in our overall educational program and facilities with the Province assuming a larger share of the costs.

6 The progressive introduction of new features into Alberta's comprehensive public health and welfare program to further improve and extend the services provided and bring their benefits within the financial reach of all our people.

7 The most extensive program of highway construction and road improvement in Alberta's history is planned for the next five years. An expenditure of over $100,000,000 on main highway construction.

8 Sympathetic government attention to the problems of both management and labour with due regard at all times for the rights and interests of the public as a whole.

9 A comprehensive program of practical measures designed to assist and encourage industrial, economic and cultural development on a province-wide scale.

10 A constant and uncompromising stand for a free democratic way of life in which the rights and responsibilities of each individual citizen are recognized and respected.

You Have Put Alberta In The Lead.
Let's Keep On Working Together
And Keep It There!

VOTE SOCIAL CREDIT

BAKER, Mrs. Stella M. SOCIAL CREDIT
CARRIGAN, Harry D. SOCIAL CREDIT
GERHART, Edgar SOCIAL CREDIT
HASZARD, Williston SOCIAL CREDIT
HOLOWACH, Ambrose SOCIAL CREDIT
MANNING, Ernest C. SOCIAL CREDIT
ROSS, Dr. J. Donovan SOCIAL CREDIT

Vote the Straight SOCIAL CREDIT Slate

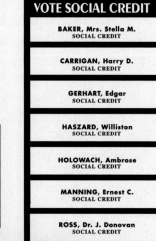

A year later, the approving tone of *The Journal's* editorials changed.

As Social Credit Premier Ernest Manning sought another mandate from the people in August, 1952, the newspaper warned that he might be planning the early export of natural gas before Canada's needs were met.

"The evident determination of Mr. Manning to push the premature export of Alberta's natural gas is in keeping with the government's 'I-Know-Best' attitude on many things," an editorial said just before the election.

Even if electors wanted to vote for Social Credit again, *The Journal* urged them to at least consider electing a strong opposition so that government policies could be fully examined in the legislature.

Readers paid little attention and 52 Social Creditors were elected to the 61-seat house, an increase of one seat for Manning. Three of the seven Edmonton seats remained in Social Credit hands.

And when in early 1951 Celanese Corporation announced the creation of the city's petrochemical industry with the building of its $40-million plant in the city's east end using the province's supplies of natural gas, the paper was elated.

It would be as "big as the oil discovery," an editorial said. "The announcement should immediately dispel all doubt as to the value of retaining our gas resources within the province."

The Journal drew parallels between the significance of the new plant and the province's agricultural past. It was, after all, being built on the old Ottewell farm, which 70 years previously had given the northern half of the province its first wheat crop.

"The chemical plant is expected to give the Edmonton area its real industrial birth, just as 70 years ago the farm gave the district its agricultural birth."

Fred and Frank Ottewell, two of the surviving members of the Ottewell family agreed to sell the homestead, including a 50-year-old, 15-room house built from 90,000 bricks.

Their price was $340,000, the equivalent of $2.6 million in 2003 dollars.

The region's oil economy spawned a major building boom that in many ways created modern Edmonton. Old buildings that were part of the city's history were torn down and replaced by new ones.

In 1955, the provincial government gave the city its Jubilee Auditorium to celebrate the 50th anniversary of Alberta becoming a province, and the Federal Building, a massive stone structure on 107th Street and 99th Avenue, was also opened the same year.

By 1951, the Royal Alexandra Hospital had added a maternity wing and the General and Misericordia hospitals doubled in size.

Construction of single-family homes, hotels, new apartments, such as the multi-unit Bel-Air development north of Westmount, continued throughout the decade.

In the early 1950s, the city voted down a proposal called the Detwiler Plan that would have seen a major, multi-million-dollar facelift for downtown. When a plebiscite failed to receive the necessary two-thirds vote, Clarence Paylitz, the New York financier behind the scheme, built the Westmount Shopping Centre instead, the city's first.

downtown, city centre redevelopment. It is rejected as only 60.78 per cent voted for the project, and the approval of 66 per cent was needed for it to go ahead.

***Nov. 11, 1950*:**
The province's worst hotel disaster occurred when a natural gas explosion ripped through the Leduc Hotel, killing 10 and injuring 16 others.

***In 1951*:**
A package of 20 cigarettes costs 35 cents.

***Jan. 6, 1951*:**
"Petroleum engineer Sidney Blair has just reported to the Alberta government, after careful and thorough study, that oil products from this province's vast northern sand beds can be feasibly and economically marketed in direct competition with oil from normal underground fields...This is Big News and no mistake...The sands contain one of the greatest single reserves of oil known. At the lowest estimate, it greatly exceeds the total oil production of the world in the last 100 years."
– editorial.

***Feb. 27, 1951*:**
Victoria Composite high school

Edmonton Weather
Forecast: A few clouds tonight and Saturday. Continuing mild with light winds.

The Edmonton Journal

'One of Canada's Great Newspapers'

FORTY-SEVENTH YEAR * * TELEPHONE 25171 EDMONTON, ALBERTA, FRIDAY, MARCH 24, 1950 SINGLE COPY, 5 CENTS 40 PAGES

Dynamite Blast Kills Gas Well Blaze

Crisis Grows Deeper In Row Over Leopold

BRUSSELS, (CP) — Former Premier Count Henri Carton de Wiart Friday abandoned his attempt to form a government after bitter rioting in which parading Brussels demonstrators wrecked 200 street cars during a 24-hour "warning strike" against the return of exiled King Leopold.

The 80-year-old politician had been striving to break the deadlock which followed the indecisive 57.6 percent vote for the king's return in the referendum March 12.

Angry crowds battled armed police in the heart of the capital as more than 300,000 workers in the city and the French-speaking Walloon provinces staged the protest strike, called by the Socialist-dominated General Federation of Labor.

University students defying 200 gendarmes with rifles, gas masks and tear gas bombs burned effigies of priests, chanting "down with the clergy" and "abdication."

About 5,000 workers joined the parade at the start near the Socialist party headquarters. They carried slogans saying "abdication." It was good humored at the outset but as the number of marchers increased their mood turned surly and violence flared.

The street cars were running in defiance of the Socialist call for a general transport walkout. The parade, held despite a police ban, tied up traffic for almost two hours in the busy Brussels shopping district.

Paul-Henri Spaak, Socialist leader, told the paraders before they began to march that return of Leopold would lead to "grave trouble for our country."

The Socialists and other anti-Leopold forces say the advisory referendum which showed 57.68 percent of the Belgians favoring his return has split the country. In some areas — particularly in areas dominated by the Walloons—Leopold won only 40 percent of the vote.

Leopold's foes have been unwilling to forgive his surrender of the armed forces to the Germans in the Second Great War and his marriage to a Flemish commoner.

Aerial Search Fails To Find Distress Signal

A two-hour aerial search by a flying doctor in the area 20 miles south of Fort St. John in northern British Columbia Friday failed to reveal any trace of a distress signal reported made by spreading branches in the snow there, R.C.A.F. officials here reported.

The signal was reported to have been seen Thursday by the crew of a United States Air Force plane and was considered a possible clue to the whereabouts of a C-54 transport lost two months ago with 44 aboard.

Dr. George M. Cormack of the pioneer settlement at Fort St. John flew over the area in his light plane in an attempt to trace the signal. Flying weather was "very good," the air force said, but he was unable to find any signal.

Air force officials said no further planes will be sent over the area unless further reports are received. They said the doctor is well acquainted with the region and would likely notice any signal.

Farms are scattered throughout the area, and officials said land clearing operations might have been mistaken for a distress message.

The airplane crew reported seeing the word "If" outlined with tree branches. This is the international code word for "serious injuries, doctor required, food and water needed." The sighting was reported on the airway used by planes flying to and from the Arctic.

The plane was flying at 9,000 feet and immediately circled low over the spot when the apparent message was spotted. Air force officials said it was 7:00 p.m. and fading light would have impaired visibility of ground objects. The aircraft reported by radio to the air traffic control centre at Fort St. John before continuing to Fairbanks.

The C-54 was en route from Anchorage, Alaska, to Great Falls, Montana when it disappeared after reporting to the weather station at Snag, Yukon, 1,300 miles northwest of here.

Well Blows Wild Only 150 Yards From Excelsior Farm Buildings

This air view of the blazing Pacific-Excelsior "gasser", 12 miles north of Edmonton, taken by Peter Minchuk, shows proximity of wild well to buildings on the Beatrice Hall farm. In the foreground is a pile of drilling pipe and a big storage tank also is prominent in the glare of the blaze. The well derrick, an all-steel structure, melted and toppled into the flames. (Other pictures appear on Pages 15, 20 and 21.)

Two Men Carry Charge Few Feet From Inferno

By Eric Young

Thirty pounds of dynamite blasted out the fire at Pacific Petroleums Excelsior No. 2 well Friday morning. The fire had been burning since the well burst out of control before noon, Thursday. The well is located 12 miles north of Edmonton.

Casey Ball, colorful oil well shooter from Lloydminster, performed the hazardous part of the operation. Using a slow-burning fuse set for about four minutes, Mr. Ball and Garnet Edwards, driller for Commonwealth Drilling Company, carried the charge to within a few feet of the burning well head.

Because the terrific draft would have made it difficult to ignite the fuse near the well head, Mr. Ball lit the fuse before carrying it in. The two then carefully took it in and placed it near the well, packing dirt around the charge.

Both men walked quickly to a spot about 100 yards from the well. Several minutes later the terrific blast snuffed out the flame.

Mr. Ball said, "It was a comparatively easy operation since the gas was rising straight into the air. In some cases the first charge doesn't always do the job. He said he had little fear of a failure on this one.

A "failure" as far as oil is concerned, the well became a gigantic natural blowtorch Thursday when a cementing job gave way in the Viking sands, about 2,730 feet below the earth's surface.

Tha drilling crew of seven men saw water suddenly spew into the air and took to their heels knowing something had gone wrong. Four of the crew couldn't get away fast enough and were burned as a spark ignited the escaping gas with a deafening roar.

The Pacific well still is running wild, but now that the flames are out it is expected to be a fairly easy job to bring it under control.

Lyle Caspell, production manager for Pacific Pete, said control valves would be forced down the well head Friday afternoon.

Mr. Ball remained calm throughout the operation. Asked if he ever had been injured while bringing a well under control, he said he had been burned sometimes, but never seriously. "I've often lost my eyebrows and some of my hair," he said, smiling. "But that's generally from the heat of

(Continued on Page 20, Col. 3)

Chrysler Workers Refuse Offer

DETROIT, (AP)—Chrysler Corporation Friday offered the striking United Automobile Workers (C.I.O.) a $30,000,000 pension fund. The union immediately rejected the proposal as inadequate.

It was the second proposal made this week by Chrysler in an effort to end the strike that has made 89,000 Chrysler workers and 50,000 others idle. The strike started 59 days ago.

Three days ago the company agreed in principle to a funding plan. It went further Friday with an offer to set up a $30,000,000 fund to back its promise to pay pensions. The proposal would provide $100 a month pensions, including federal social security. The company called for a five-year contract.

U.A.W. President Walter Reuther, said it "still falls short of the pattern established by Chrysler competitors." He said it "does not provide Chrysler workers with pensions and medical benefits which other companies have granted their workers."

In addition, Reuther said, the company "still insists on freezing unsatisfactory contract provisions for five years."

The main issue in the long strike has been the method of providing pensions. The union has insisted that they be paid out of a trust fund. Chrysler previously had insisted on backing pensions by its "promise to pay."

Council Approves Estimates In City's Record 1950 Plans

Faced with a 1950 departmental spending bill that bids to reach almost $9,000,000 before the Edmonton mill rate is struck next Wednesday, a special session of city council Thursday night gave tentative approval to current budgets for 19 departments. Score at the end of the night was that operation of these 19 departments will cost $468,250 more this year than in 1949, as expenditure totalled $2,764,037 or $339,209 more than in 1949, while revenues totalled $936,810 or $129,041 less than last year.

Again starting in the afternoon and continuing through the evening, council will meet in second special session Friday to consider tentative expenditures and revenues of 12 other departments and the five civic utilities. Requested departmental current expendi-

(Continued on Page 2, Col. 1)

Where To Find It

Amusements, Theatres	22
Angelo Patri	24
Births, Deaths, Marriages	28
Bridge	35
Canasta	6
Comics 16, 29, 30, 31, 32, 33,	35
Crossword Puzzle	35
District	10
Editorial	4
Financial	36, 37
Gregory Clark's Packsack	22
Off the Record	8
Radio	8
Sport	16, 17, 18, 19
Sydney Harris Article	22
They'll Do It Every Time	35
Uncle Ray's Corner	35
Want Ads 29, 30, 31, 32, 33,	34
Women's	23, 24, 25, 26, 27

The Weather

(Issued by the Dominion Public Weather Office at Edmonton.)

All prairie districts are enjoying mild spring weather today, although skies are cloudy over most of Alberta and southern Saskatchewan.

Skies will be cloudy tomorrow in southeastern Alberta and southern Saskatchewan. All regions will continue mild with afternoon temperatures near 40.

Estimated low tonight, 25 above.
Estimated high tomorrow, 40 above.

At Edmonton Saturday sun rises at 6:36 a.m.; sets at 6:53 p.m.

Overnight low 23.
High yesterday 41.

Other Readings

G. Prairie	35	18	Penticton	45	34
Fairview	38	23	Banff	37	17
Penhold	39	20	Jasper	42	19
Lethbridge	43	28	Regina	33	27
Calgary	45	25	Winnipeg	37	21
Vermilion	40	13	Toronto	38	35
Coronat'n	34	11	Ottawa	35	31
Med. Hat	46	28	Montreal	38	33
Saskatoon	36	23	Halifax	36	34
P. Albert	39	12	Aklavik	18	2
Victoria	46	42	Yel'knife	14	-7
Vancouver	47	40	Whiteh'se	38	15
P. Rupert	46	33	Snag	13	-4

Maybe The Dress Didn't Suit Her

NEW WESTMINSTER, B.C., (CP)—Why keep a dress you don't like—even if you got it free?

A woman snatched a dress from a clothing store here, evaded police, then returned later and tossed the garment back into the store.

2 Escape Death As Load Tumbles

Two workmen had a close brush with death Friday morning when a load of telephone poles tumbled from a flat car at the Canada Creosoting Co. Ltd. plant in North Edmonton.

In the Royal Alexandra Hospital, suffering undetermined injuries, are August Dyksley, 11951 52 st., and Nick Chopek, 12208 57 st., who were on top of the load when it broke loose.

According to plant officials, the men were cutting wires stretched over the poles when retaining stakes broke and released the load.

The two men were taken to hospital in Smith's ambulance. Their injuries are not believed to be serious.

FACE SECOND STRIKE

BUENOS AIRES, (Reuters)—Buenos Aires port, paralyzed up to Wednesday by a dock strike, was back to normal Thursday but will be tied up again Friday by a 24-hour strike of seamen. The dockers were out three days for higher wages.

Manitoba To Start Highway This Year

WINNIPEG, (CP)—Manitoba's minister of public works said Thursday his government expects to start construction of its portion of the Trans-Canada Highway this year. He told the legislature the government is willing to build either on the northern or southern route.

Hon. Errick F. Willis, who is also deputy premier, said copies of the dominion-provincial agreement now are in the hands of the government. It provides that the dominion pay 50 percent of the costs for seven years.

"The prospect is that the agreement . . . will be completed and construction started this year," he said.

Choice of the north or south route rested largely with Alberta and British Columbia. Manitoba and Saskatchewan would "probably fall into line."

Chinese Famine Said Widespread

HONG KONG, (AP)—Reports indicated Friday Communist China's famine has hit possibly 50,000,000 persons. For one-fifth that number, the food situation is reported desperate.

There is no way of learning the true situation behind the bamboo curtain.

This is what reports reaching here say:

The famine, which broke out in the east provinces, has spread west and south. The Reds' Peiping radio said the famine has hit six provinces.

Where famine strikes, disease thrives. Plague, smallpox and diphtheria are rampant in Anhwei, Shantung and Kiangsu provinces. Animals are dying fast in the food-short land. March floods have washed out spring plantings.

A Canton report said, "Nine out of 10 farmers in the region 18 miles northeast of Canton are moving south in search of food as all rice stocks are exhausted."

Chinese Communists say the famine is not their fault. Critics assert bitterly that the Reds shipped foodstuffs to Russia when they knew China would need it.

Moreover, they blame the Reds for affronting the West from which help has come in the past.

Recall's Protest On Supplying Cheap Bread For Unemployed

CALGARY, (CP) — Evidence that the larger Calgary bakeries all submitted the same agreed price when making bids for institutional contracts was given Friday at the preliminary hearing of bread combine charges.

Lt.-Col. George Weir of Edmonton, former secretary of the Alberta Master Bakers' Association, told the court the association then awarded the business in rotation to the bakeries.

Col. Weir also stated that in December, 1937, he had written to W. D. King, provincial deputy minister of trade and industry, protesting against Edmonton bakers delivering bread to the Calgary relief soup kitchen. The Edmonton bakers supplied bread at 11 cents a loaf while the Calgary bakers had submitted a tender of 13 cents for a 40-ounce loaf.

Magistrate G. H. Rose is presiding over the preliminary hearing, now in its fifth day, where the Bakery Employers Association of Alberta (formerly the Alberta Master Bakers' Association) and six western Canada bakeries are jointly charged with combining to prevent or lessen competition in the baking industry.

Story on Thursday's sitting on Page 15.

The bakeries being prosecuted by the federal justice department are Canadian Bakeries Ltd., Calgary, Edmonton City Baking Ltd., Weston's Bread and Cake (Canada) Ltd., Winnipeg, and three McGavin bakery companies at Winnipeg, Edmonton and Vancouver.

Col. Weir said it was the prac-

(Continued on Page 20, Col. 3)

Wife Spoils Story; Hubby Must Pay

BRISTOL, England, (AP) — A man who wanted a new set of free false teeth under Britain's national health scheme told the Bristol health committee: "I lost them during illness."

His wife interrupted: "Don't believe him. He left them in a dressing gown at a girl friend's home."

The husband got his new teeth—and paid for them.

Mother Reluctant To Give Up Quads

SAULT STE. MARIE, Ont., (CP)—Mrs. C. O. Hargreaves was quoted Friday as having said she loves her quadruplets too much to part with them, but "if the worst comes to the worst, we'll board them out, two by two, with friends here."

Meanwhile, Mrs. Charlotte Barclay of Stratford, Ont., who has raised 11 children, Thursday offered to take the quadruplets and care for them for two years. She told Mrs. Hargreaves in a telephone conversation that there still is room for more children in the Barclays' 11-roomed house.

The father of the 5½-month-old babies said last week that financial difficulties over caring for the children had led him to consider offering the quads for adoption.

In Toronto, City Treasurer G. A. Lascelles was prepared to handle donations to assist the Hargreaves—but so far no money has come in.

In Hamilton Friday Mayor Lloyd Jackson declined to support a campaign initiated there to supply clothing for the quads.

Describing Sault Ste. Marie as a "wealthy town," the mayor said: "People there should look after them. We have many of our own children who probably need help."

CRIPPS REPORTED ILL

LONDON, (AP)—The treasury announced Thursday that Sir Stafford Cripps, chancellor of the exchequer, has contracted bronchial infection following influenza and will be confined to his home for a few days.

Airlines Sued For $250,000

NEW YORK, (AP)—Mrs. Agnes S. Knickerbocker, widow of H. R. Knickerbocker, war correspondent and radio commentator who was killed, with 44 others aboard a K.L.M. Royal Dutch Airlines plane at Bombay last July, has filed a $250,000 damage suit against K.L.M. She complained that the death of her husband, a Pulitzer Prize winner, was due to "wilful misconduct in the operation" of the air liner. Thirteen other reporters died in the crash.

Expected To Live Despite 5 Shots

MONTREAL, (CP)—Police reported Friday that a 43-year-old night watchman is in hospital with five self-inflicted bullet wounds in his body.

Hospital authorities said the case was "remarkable" and gave the victim an "even chance" of pulling through. Four of the wounds are in the chest and the other in the head.

Police identified the man as Alphonse Beaulieu.

Sixteen-year-old Claude Morin, a messenger employed by the same firm as Beaulieu, told police what happened.

The youth said he stood and watched in terror as Beaulieu shot a bullet into his head, then three into his chest.

Beaulieu then called his wife at home on the phone and told her:

"I'm tired of it all. I'm killing myself."

Morin then grabbed the phone and called police.

As two constables arrived, Beaulieu said:

"I'm trying to kill myself but it's hard." Then he raised the revolver again and fired another bullet into his chest.

Deputy Premier In Prague Is Reported Assassinated

OTTAWA, (CP)—The Ottawa Evening Citizen Friday quoted Frantisec Nemec, former Czech minister to Canada, as saying he has received "definite word" from behind the Iron Curtain of the assassination of Zdenek Fierlinger, deputy prime minister of Czechoslovakia.

Mr. Nemec, who left his post at the Czech embassy in Ottawa to remain in this country, also said that Gen. Rudolf Slansky, Communist party secretary in Czechoslovakia, had been seriously wounded.

He told the Citizen he was satisfied his information was authentic, but that he had no details except that the two men were both shot at the same time.

Fierlinger, who was known as a quisling because he delivered over to the Communists after their coup the support of the Social Democratic party which he led, served as Czech ambassador to Russia during the war, Mr. Nemec said.

"He knows everything," the former ambassador added. "Perhaps he knew too much."

Had it not been for Fierlinger, it would have been difficult for the Communists to carry on in

(Continued on Page 20, Col. 1)

Contest To Decide Best Woman Driver

VANCOUVER, (CP)—Scoffers at women drivers will do well to keep the date in mind when a dozen women take part in a contest here soon.

The city's first "off-street" parking lot will open with a women's parking competition. Prizes will be awarded to all entrants and the winner gets a special award.

The date? April Fool's Day.

U.K. Health Bill $1,218,098,500

LONDON, (AP)—Health Minister Aneurin Bevan handed parliament a bill for £392,935,000 ($1,218,098,500) Friday to run the national health service for the year starting April 1.

This is £34,425,450 more than the estimate for last year, which was £358,509,550.

Sir Stafford Cripps, the chancellor of the exchequer, already has warned Bevan publicly that the figure in 1950-51 is the ceiling. Sir Stafford told the house of commons no further expansion of the service can be permitted.

Loss Is $20,000 In Alliance Fire

ALLIANCE.—Fire which broke out at 11:15 a.m. Friday in the Alliance Sales Service garage here caused loss estimated at $20,000.

The fire started after an explosion in the garage. Two cars, a tractor and other equipment were lost in the blaze. The garage is owned by Orville Fallis.

Oil Well Explosion Victims Recovering In Hospital

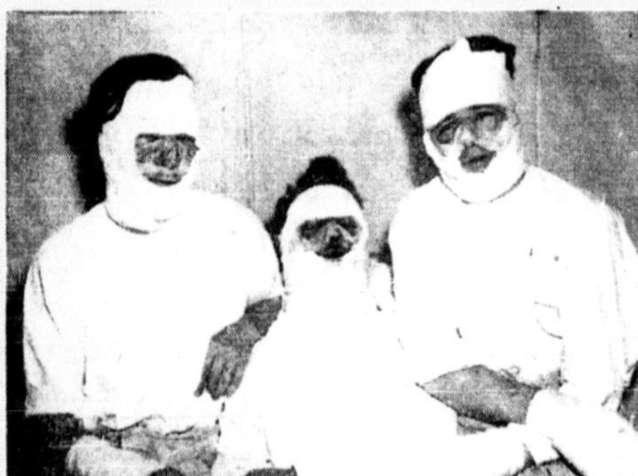

Three victims of the fire at Pacific-Excelsior No. 2 gas well 12 miles north of Edmonton are shown here. Recovering at the Royal Alexandra Hospital are Norman Dease at left, John Allen, most seriously injured, and Allan Holt. The three men, working on the drilling platform when the gas ignited, had to run through flames to escape. (Story on Page 15.)

Speedy Tito Defeat By Red Army Before Summer Forecast By Exile

By Leonard J. Schweitzer
(North American Newspaper Alliance)

WASHINGTON.—The Red army will attack Yugoslavia before summer, most likely in May when roads will be open for tanks and mechanized equipment. Marshal Tito's resistance will be smashed in even less time than the 12 days it took Hitler to beat the Yugoslavs in 1941.

This estimate of the situation is made by Lt. Col. Zivan L. Knezevich, Yugoslav military attache here during the Second Great War. Col. Knezevich, now connected with the United States war department in a civilian capacity, is a former member of the Yugoslav general staff.

As commander of the Yugoslav royal guard in April 1941, he led a coup d'etat against the government which had signed a treaty with Italy and Germany, designed to bring his homeland within Hitler's orbit. Following the coup d'etat, the new Yugoslav government repudiated the pact. A few days later Hitler, enraged by the setback to his plans, ordered his forces to invade Yugoslavia.

Col Knezevich's appraisal is based on his belief that the Soviet Union is openly preparing for a Third Great War and considers it necessary to occupy strategic Yugoslavia to protect its left flank, "just at Hitler in 1941 had to secure Finland's co-operation and occupy the Balkans, in order to safeguard his flanks before he moved against Russia."

The Russians must seize the Scandinavian peninsula and hold the Balkans before attacking the West.

Knezevich believes the Soviet Union gladly would postpone a general war until they're better prepared to meet the United States. Nevertheless, he holds it

(Continued on Page 20, Col. 1)

Massive water and sewer construction tore up city streets, and hundreds of miles of paved streets and concrete sidewalks were put down.

The opening of St. Joseph's, Ross Sheppard, Eastglen, Bonnie Doon Composite and Victoria Composite marked the biggest high school construction splurge the city had ever seen. Vic Comp was billed as the "best teaching establishment in the world."

Not yet 50 years old when the decade began, the University of Alberta also added to the city's sense of pride with a campus building boom that included the completion of the Rutherford Library, designed to hold 265,000 volumes, the Students' Union Building, a major addition to the University Hospital that provided state-of-the-art obstetric and pediatric care, and the construction of the Aberhart Sanitarium, which provided 400 southern-exposure beds for victims of tuberculosis.

There was also a new $800,000 agriculture building and a million-dollar engineering building.

But Edmonton's most controversial new building was City Hall.

On April 2, 1954, *The Journal* ran an artist's conception of the new $2.5-million building.

An accompanying story suggested that some citizens might not like it. "Architect Max Dewar said he expected the public, although it will be shocked at first, will grow to like the modern-style building....

"The architect added that the building was designed to be as dignified and functional as possible in a modern style but not to be bizarre or modern merely for the sake of being modern."

Editorially, *The Journal* was appalled.

"The glassy-eyed stares seen on the faces of many Edmontonians during the week-end suggested a dazed condition.

"Most of the serious cases, we suspect, were due, not to an overdose of snake-bite remedy, but to the picture of the proposed new City Hall that was published on the front page of Saturday's *Journal*."

Calling the proposed structure "horrifying," *The Journal* said it could rival any for the title of "ugliest" building in the world, including the United Nations building in New York.

And when the building opened in 1956, readers didn't hesitate to express their feelings about their new city hall. Then, as always, they expressed their opinions in letters to the editor.

This time they focused on the 12-foot-high stylized sculpture of Canada geese by B.C. architect and artist Lionel Thomas.

The work of art stood in a small reflecting pool to the left of the main entrance of city hall.

To many, it looked like twisted and welded rebar.

In one of hundreds of letters received by the paper, Edith Mills called for the city to scrap the $16,000 sculpture, known as *The Spaghetti Tree*, and replace it with something more appropriate.

"Right now, it is an eyesore."

Another writer, identified only as J.P., called the bronze sculpture a "monstrosity."

"I thought it was a plumber's nightmare and I resent my tax money being spent on such rubbish," he said.

officially opens. *The Journal* says it is regarded as the best "complete teaching establishment" in the world.

***March 7, 1951*: "The dubious distinction of being the only city in Canada in which horse meat is sold for human consumption is one that Edmonton can well do without. More than that, we'd venture a guess that 99 out of every 100 persons here want no part of the horse served on the dinner table – at home, in a boarding house or lunch counter." – editorial.**

***Jan. 29, 1952*: Ground beef sells for 65 cents a pound at Safeway.**

***Feb. 20, 1952*: The Aberhart Memorial Sanatorium for tuberculosis patients officially opens on the University of Alberta campus.**

***Feb. 24, 1952*: Edmonton's Waterloo Mercurys capture the gold medal in men's hockey at the sixth Winter Olympic Games at Oslo, Norway.**

***April 10, 1952*: A new Alberta law permits fluoridation of public water in the province. Edmonton voters wait until 1966 to approve it.**

THE EDMONTON JOURNAL, WEDNESDAY, JANUARY 11, 1950

HENRY SINGER LTD.

CAT AND DOG SALE

MONSTROSITIES, BUYERS' MISTAKES, WHITE ELEPHANTS

STATION WAGON COATS

These are sheep-lined, ¾ length, belted models. If the dumb manufacturer had used the oil in his machine instead of getting it onto the linings, we'd sell these for $47.50. So if you don't intend to wear 'em inside out they'll be plenty smart at ---------- CRAZY PRICE **$29.95**

Also a few full length quilt lined numbers included.

TOP BRASS TUXEDOS

In the 60 and 70 dollar bracket. 12 only, suitable for an undertaker, a Cabinet member, or a music critic—or say, it just occurred to us, maybe your butler could use one. Until they start going formal to hockey matches and football games, you can take one away for ---------- CRAZY PRICE **$42.50**

WINTER OVERCOATS

20 Coats on one rack. Make a dandy cover for your car these cold nights. ---------- CRAZY PRICE **$18.50**

28 coats on another rack. If these weren't double-breasted, we'd be getting $45.00 for 'em. CRAZY PRICE ---------- **$28.50**

The Better Business Bureau Advocates

TRUTH IN ADVERTISING

. . . Boy, Will They Love This Ad!

If you have to miss breakfast to make this sale, don't worry—

We serve hot coffee and doughnuts to anyone crazy enough to stand in line until our store opens at 9:30.

It's an old Henry Singer Custom

Two Ways To Pay:

C.O.D. and CASH

No Phone Calls – No Returns

A DOLLAR A HANDFUL

TIES -- TIES

A barrel full. All you can grab for One Dollar. Here's how to get even with a bunch of friends next Xmas for a buck. The only stipulation we make is that if these ties are unsatisfactory,

we will refund the dollar

But, You Must Keep The Merchandise

ONE RACK OF TIES

Monograms—Silks—Foulards

Reg. $2.50. Crazy Price ---------- 95c

2 for $1.90, 3 for $2.85 or 100 for $95.00

LADIES' SKI SLACKS We cut these down once from $23.50 to $11.75—HOW LOW CAN WE GO. Not a darn thing wrong with these except that we bought too many. No alterations at ---------- **Crazy Price $10.00**

MEN'S SKI SLACKS Same sad story as above—Reg. $26.50 ---------- **Crazy Price $12.00**

The "War's Over" KHAKI SHIRTS Not many, but enough. Reg. $4.95 ---------- **Crazy Price $2.65**

LADIES' RIDING HABITS By Irving. Jackets and jodhpurs. Tally-Ho and all that stuff, but it's apparent that not enough ladies have the habit. Broken sizes. They should canter out at ---------- **Crazy Price Jackets $22.50; Jodphurs $14.50**

25 prs. FLUORESCENT SLACKS They're draped—they're pleated—they're zippered—they're AWFUL (the color we mean) ---------- **Crazy Price $8.00**

DIRTIER SHIRTS These were the balance of shirts we had left from our Dirty Shirt Sale—all we can say for 'em now: they're even dirtier!!! Reg. $7.95, $5.95, $5.50, $4.95, $3.95, all grouped together ---------- **Crazy Price $2.65**

BOXER SHORTS Very small size, very poorly made. Make good dish rags. ---------- **Crazy Price 10c pr.**

STRIPED T-SHIRTS Same story as above. Sold for $1.75. Make good cat blankets ---------- **Crazy Price 65c**

PYJAMAS Slightly—and we honestly mean SLIGHTLY, soiled. Reg. $6.50 and $7.50 ---------- **Crazy Price $5.00**

COAT SWEATERS in 7 BILIOUS SHADES We saw some of these in our competitor's window. We liked them so much that we ordered them—better we shouldn't be spying on our competition ---------- **Crazy Price $3.75**

5 MONTAGNAC OVERCOATS Genuine French Montagnac Sedan Overcoats. It's supposed to be the world's best overcoat at $135.00. THE ONLY THING WRONG WAS WE DIDN'T HAVE 5 CUSTOMERS LEFT WITH $135.00. But we should be able to scare up 5 fellas willing to pay ---------- **Crazy Price $67.50**

LOUD BLANKET CLOTH COATS Reg. 23.95 and 29.95. These were originally bought for our Calgary store. After selling the Calgary store, we didn't have the nerve to sell 'em here—after all, we live here. However, if you're planning on visiting Calgary, get one at ---------- **Calgary Special $12.00 and $15.00**

LADIES' CASHMERE SWEATERS Beautiful Indian Cashmere sweaters. Only one thing wrong, we ran out of Indians. Reg. to $20.00 ---------- **Crazy Price $9.00**

TECHNICOLOR SPORTS COATS A rare group—if you can stand a ribbing get one at ---------- **Crazy Price $15.00**

PLASTIC RAIN JACKETS You can fold these up into a neat package, throw them in the car and forget you every bought one. In 1946 we got $2.95—now we'll take **Crazy Price 25c**

TOO COLORED JAC SHIRTS Loud and itchy all-wool jac shirts. Wear 'em hunting—you will make a terrific target. Make good wearing Hallowe'en. Reg. $7.95 **Crazy Price $5.95**

OPTIMISTIC RAINCOATS If you have faith that there will be another summer and can back it up with a few bucks, here's some terrific values in raincoats. Reg. to $35.00 ---------- **Crazy Price $15.00**

HENRY SINGER LTD.

200 ONLY SUITS

200 ONLY SUITS

These ARE From Our Regular Stock This IS The Best Suit Value In The Dominion Of Canada

Worsteds—Gabardines—Flannels—Glen Plaids—Coverts

$39.95

HENRY SINGER LTD.

10158-101st ST.

The opinion of reader G.S.D. Wright was a little less vitriolic, although a lot more ironic in tone.

"As a fountain it is a miserable failure. It fails in the first purpose of a fountain, which is to fount. Where are the great jets of a great fountain?"

The paper received so many letters that it finally called a halt to publishing any more of them.

The sculpture remained, regardless of what the critics said. And when a new city hall was built in the '90s, the piece of art was moved to an outdoor alcove on the east side of the building where it remains to this day.

Through the decade of go-go growth *The Journal* bragged that things in Edmonton were, almost invariably, bigger and better. No city was as up-to-date, and every new business had something to celebrate.

New refineries, new schools, a burgeoning campus, a controversial city hall and even slick new pool halls were important, but Edmonton also found itself more and more connected to the outside world.

And the city's proud aviation history received a boost on April 31, 1950, when two American airlines established service to Edmonton.

"Sunday was an important aviation day for Edmonton as the city strengthened its hold on the title 'Crossroads of the World,' by welcoming the official entry into the city of two large U.S. airlines," said the paper.

"The two new services by Northwest and Western Airlines provide Edmonton with a direct air link between St. Paul, Minneapolis, Denver and Los Angeles in the U.S. and Alaska and the Orient to the north and west."

It didn't take Northwest long to offer three flights weekly to New York and Washington with a stopover in Detroit.

A daily Convair flight on Western promised to whisk Edmontonians to Los Angeles in seven hours. In 2003, flying to L.A. from Edmonton with a stopover takes eight hours.

The paper was pleased with the extra flights, but not with the state of the airport, and as early as 1951, *The Journal* began campaigning for an international airport located on the outskirts, and soon.

With more than 137,000 flights per year by mid-decade, the paper was convinced that a downtown airport was too dangerous.

A May 9, 1952, editorial made it clear.

"The federal government's new bill to restrict construction near airports will butter no parsnips in Edmonton. The essence of the situation here is that the airport is located near the centre of the city, surrounded by built-up areas, and thus creates a danger to residents.

"The only way to eliminate the danger is to remove the airport outside the city."

There was a sense of relief, therefore, when the federal government announced in the fall of 1955 that a 16-square-mile area near Nisku had been set aside for a new airport.

Mayor Bill Hawrelak told *The Journal* that Department of Transport officials were impressed with the site, "but it is quite a distance away."

In fact, Hawrelak said, the officials called the land "marvelous."

No matter was too small for the paper to draw positive comparisons between Edmonton and other places. Edmontonians seemed to be constantly trying to reaffirm their place in the world.

***May 26, 1952*:**
The city census puts Edmonton's population at 158,912.

***July 3, 1952*:**
The Paramount Theatre opens in downtown Edmonton.

***July 15, 1952*:**
Fire destroys Jasper Park Lodge's main lodge, one of the world's largest log buildings.

***Nov. 15, 1952*:**
***The Journal*'s newsroom receives a new teletype-setter and reperforating unit.**

***Nov. 29, 1952*:**
The Edmonton Eskimos play in the Grey Cup for the first time since 1922, but lose 21-11 to the Toronto Argonauts. It's the first Grey Cup game to be televised by the CBC.

***Nov. 30, 1952*:**
The Edmonton Symphony, defunct since the Depression, makes its debut with 60 musicians under the direction of Lee Hepner at the Capitol Theatre.

***In 1953*:**
***The Journal*'s circulation is 84,000 and a reporter earns $40 a week. The number of oil wells producing in the spring of 1953 is 3,973. They produce 297,625 barrels daily.**

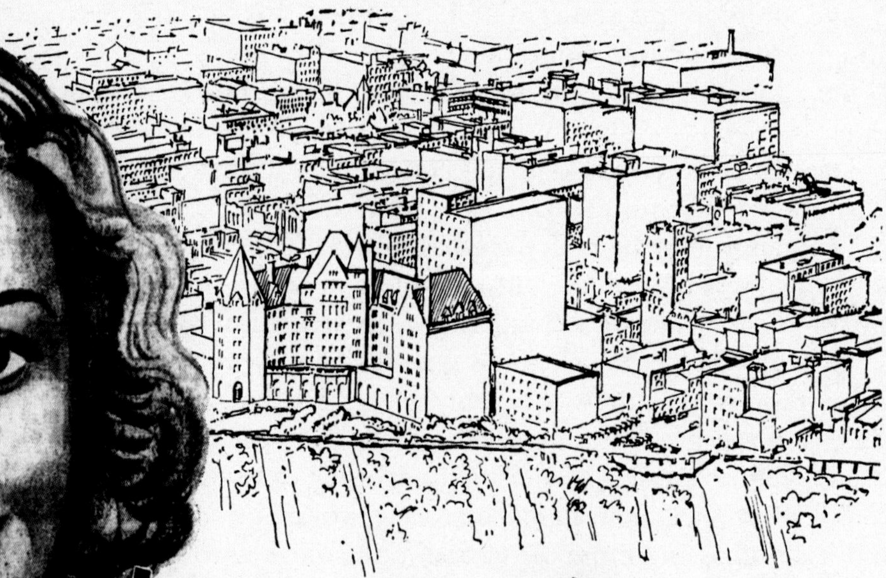

Gas is Cheap* in Edmonton

40,000 cubic feet — the average householder's consumption for a cold winter month — costs Edmonton customers **$11.65.** This same 40,000 cubic feet costs in Canada's seven largest cities anything from **$28.00** to **$55.39** — an average of **$39.20.**

* Winnipeg	**$28.00**	Quebec	**$55.39**	Hamilton	**$30.30**
Montreal	**$42.12**	Toronto	**$42.12**	Ottawa	**$40.50**
Vancouver	**$42.04**				

And another thing — gas in these cities has less than half the heating value of Edmonton gas! The facts speak for themselves — gas IS cheap in Edmonton.

YOUR GAS COMPANY

NORTHWESTERN UTILITIES, LIMITED

A brief story trumpeting the city's paving program in the spring of 1950, one of thousands of similar ones printed before decade's end, proved the point. "Faced with a $2,000,000 paving program this year, one of the largest in Canada for cities under 500,000 population and even larger than in some of the bigger centres, Edmonton paving crews are working nine hours daily, it was reported Friday."

The suburbs were pushing beyond the city limits. The towns of Beverly and Jasper Place were filled to near capacity, and both amalgamated with the city. Sherwood Park was attracting builders and homebuyers, and venerable St. Albert was on the cusp of adding population and neighbourhoods. But Edmonton was no mere boomtown, *The Journal* insisted in a Sept. 28, 1953, editorial. "The publicity surrounding Northern Alberta's oil discoveries seems to have given many Americans, and even some Canadians, the idea that Edmonton is a new settlement which mushroomed out of the prairie in the wake of Imperial Leduc No. 1."

That was simply not so. There was a solid foundation for a city long before the discovery of oil, the newspaper said. "These facts need to be better known. The stereotype of Edmonton as a fly-by-night boom town, dependent on the fluctuations of a single industry, has probably done some harm, making the city seem a risky place in which to live – or invest."

And unlocking the oil in the tar sands was seen as a key to removing any of the perceived risks of investing in Edmonton.

Thus, as the decade drew to a close, the paper was crowded with stories about a proposal to use a 10-kiloton nuclear bomb in a test blast to "melt" the oil in the tar sands.

Richfield Oil Corporation, a Los Angeles petroleum company, was behind the idea that managed to receive cautious approval from the federal Department of Mines.

A technical committee of the provincial Energy Resources Conservation Board said that the explosion could take place without "any danger to the public health, plant or animal life," a story from Sept. 16, 1959, said.

Two weeks later, *Journal* readers learned the blast was off. "The reason given is a warming of the Cold War following Russian Premier Khrushchev's United States visit. Resumption of nuclear tests, even for peaceful purposes, now is considered unlikely."

By the half-century mark, however, the Cold War had become part of the fabric of our lives. There were daily stories of Soviet spies stalking our streets, and ever larger and more lethal bombs being built and tested.

While there wasn't another world war, Canadian soldiers once again were sent to do battle in Korea. The conflict, fought under the auspices of the United Nations, was first listed as a police action but rapidly escalated into a war against Communist aggression.

The Journal was fervidly anti-Communist but drew the line at excesses.

In fact, an editorial called the McCarthy-era goings-on in Washington "very disturbing."

It found the logic used by Senator Joseph McCarthy and his congressional committee to prove or disprove membership in the Communist party to be impossible to understand.

***Jan. 12, 1953*:**
The Edmonton Stock Exchange, the sixth in Canada at that time, opens for business under president Eric Duggan.

***Jan. 16, 1953*:**
"More than 5,000 hockey fans watched the junior Oil Kings thrash the Moose Jaw Canucks 11-2 on Sunday, the first Sunday hockey game in more than a decade...Rookie centre Len Lunde scored a hat trick, while Ron Tookey, George Congreve each counted two. Lionel Repka, Eddie Johnson, Dave Joyal each scored a single." On Feb. 15, Lunde set a league record against the Canucks when he scored seven goals in a 13-3 win.

***Jan. 26, 1953*:**
"Eleven candy-vending machines, classed as illegal under the Alberta Slot Machine Act, have been seized by police in connection with the province-wide crackdown on gambling and lotteries."

***June 6, 1953*:**
A *Journal* story announces that the city's first brick building, the manse of the McDougall United Church on 101st Street and Macdonald Drive, will be torn down.

EDMONTON NEEDS TWO AIRPORTS!

- An International Airport
- A Secondary Airport Of At Least The Same Standard As The Present Municipal Airport.

If Edmonton is to maintain its leadership in the aviation industry, it must provide adequate airport facilities. "Business" flying, or the use of airplanes in the executive and sales branches of industry, is increasing, and will continue to increase by some 50% in the next five years. Fortune Magazine states in the January issue: "The growth of general aviation can be largely conditioned by the availability of airports."

Every major city has the same problems as those facing Edmonton. Toronto is enlarging its secondary airport within the city and Vancouver is doing the same. Chicago's Skymotive Terminal is spending 4 million dollars for additional facilities. Boston prides itself on having an airport that is within 5 minutes of the industrial centre of the city.

The Edmonton Municipal Airport Association wishes to congratulate the Civic Administration of the City of Edmonton and the Federal Government on their decision to establish an International Airport in the Edmonton region, and on their further decision to maintain a Secondary Airport in Edmonton.

THE EDMONTON MUNICIPAL AIRPORT ASSOCIATION *

"B" HANGAR — MUNICIPAL AIRPORT

* *ORGANIZED IN THE INTERESTS OF DEVELOPING EDMONTON'S AVIATION INDUSTRY.*

Marilyn MONROE

JOSEPH COTTEN
JEAN PETERS

All its excitement filmed on location at Niagara Falls Ontario.

20 Century-Fox presents
Niagara
...a new high water mark in suspense!
TECHNICOLOR
ADULT ENTERTAINMENT

OPENS TODAY

Come to the MATINEE! Up to 1 p.m. 40c

PLUS
Cartoon - News
Special "Breath of Disaster"
Novelty "Grid Iron Goliath"
First Full Show 12:40
Feature 1:20, 3:27, 5:34
7:40 and 9:56

PARAMOUNT
A FAMOUS PLAYERS THEATRE

IN NATURAL VISION
3 DIMENSION
IT'S LIKE NOTHING YOU'VE EVER SEEN BEFORE!

Half-man half-monster—he stalks a panic-swept city craving the show world's beauties for his Wax Museum Chamber of Horrors!

WARNER BROS. BRING YOU THE FIRST FEATURE PRODUCED BY A MAJOR STUDIO IN 3D!

EVERY THRILL OF ITS ASTOUNDING STORY COMES OFF THE SCREEN RIGHT AT YOU!

HOUSE OF WAX
COLOR BY WARNERCOLOR

STARRING
VINCENT PRICE · FRANK LOVEJOY · PHYLLIS KIRK
CAROLYN JONES · PAUL PICERNI · SCREEN PLAY BY CRANE WILBUR PRODUCED BY BRYAN FOY DIRECTED BY ANDRE deTOTH

● DEFINITELY ADULT! ●

CAPITOL — STARTS TODAY!

PLUS ● UPSWEPT HARE ● BRITAIN'S SKY BLAZERS ● NEWS

ADMISSION PRICES — Opening to 1:00 p.m. 60, 1:00 to 6:00 75c, 6:00 to Close $1.00 — Children 35c to 6:00 Then Till Close 50c — All Tax Included
DOORS 12:15 — COMPLETE SHOWS 12:30, 2:38, 4:47, 6:56, 9:10

PALACE — 9621 - 82 Ave.
Adult
TODAY
Drama in Color
John Payne, Rhonda Fleming in "CROSSWINDS"
Mark Stevens, Arlene Whelan in "TARGET UNKNOWN"

DREAMLAND — 1 - 2 p.m., 25c, Tax. Inc.
Today and Wed. — *Adult*
BERT LANCASTER in "Brute Force"
Added GINGER FOGERS in "Roxy Hart"

Princess
TONIGHT AND WEDNESDAY
Family
Color by Technicolor
"Nancy Goes To Rio"
With Jane Powell—Ann Sothern
Plus
"PLEASE BELIEVE ME"
With Deborah Kerr—Robert Walker

Gem Theatre
TODAY WED. AND THURS. Adult
WHIP WILSON in "OUTLAWS OF TEXAS"
"CITY ACROSS THE RIVER"
Plus Short

Under McCarthy's ground rules, "it is difficult to see how anyone could ever prove that he is not a Communist – short of sneaking into the Kremlin some dark night and pushing Stalin off the battlements," an editorial said.

Regardless, some members of the provincial legislature saw Communists at every turn. Social Credit member William Tomyn from Willingdon was particularly incensed at teachers. In a legislature debate in spring 1951, Tomyn wondered whether the Alberta Teachers' Association was attempting to "form an international union to put us over a barrel."

Too many teachers, he said in a March story, were "exalting to the skies conditions in Russia and flouting Canadian institutions."

His request that every teacher in Alberta take an oath to show loyalty to "our British and Christian way of life" came to nothing.

The Journal dismissed Tomyn's claims in an editorial and condemned him for defaming thousands of loyal teachers. "The RCMP, we feel sure, knows better than anyone just who are Communists, who are fellow-travellers and who are potential traitors and spies. They can be relied on with confidence to get their man."

There were other major social and cultural changes afoot as well. In 1951, the city's significant Ukrainian population flexed its political muscle and helped elect William Hawrelak, an ambitious 37-year-old businessman, to the mayor's chair. He was the first mayor of Eastern European stock in the city's history, and one of its most colourful politicians.

He may not have been universally admired or respected, but his supporters never let him down.

The Hawrelak political machine and the Hawrelak shadow had an impact on civic politics until the '70s and beyond.

Edmontonians were busy folks back in the '50s, apparently, sometimes even too busy to cook. A cornucopia of convenience foods – tea bags to canned spaghetti that required only a can opener and a pot in which to heat it – arrived early in the decade.

French's Mustard offered Instant Potatoes. In a June 7, 1950, ad, readers were told that Instant Potatoes provided a hungry family with mashed spuds in one minute. Recipe suggestions included splitting open a wiener, stuffing it with instant potatoes and baking it golden brown in only 10 minutes. And nothing, the ad promised, beat Instant Potatoes as a topping for shepherd's pie.

And, for the first time, people who were too harried to cook could order food delivered hot to their door. Chi-Del, a typical delivery service, charged $3 for southern fried chicken and French fries brought to the door in a red plastic basket.

Mixed drinking in Edmonton beer parlours wasn't allowed until the end of the '50s, and it took a province-wide plebiscite to liberalize the liquor laws even that far.

The Journal strongly supported the changes.

Journal readers showed more sophistication in the arts. Classical entertainers such as pianist Artur Rubinstein and conductors Antal Dorati and Sir Ernest McMillan played to sold-out audiences.

A Celebrity Concerts circuit brought famous classical artists to the city.

***June 27, 1953*:**
Official sod-turning ceremonies launch the building of the Kinsmen Sports Centre in the river valley.

***July 6, 1953*:**
The provincial government begins testing all new drivers living within a 15-mile radius of Edmonton and Calgary.

***July 25, 1953*:**
The $3-million addition to the Hudson's Bay store downtown opens.

***Aug. 1, 1953*:**
Edmonton's worst rain storm ends after dumping 144.8 mm of water since beginning the previous day.

***Aug. 18, 1953*:**
The Clover Bar Bridge opens, connecting North Edmonton and Beverly to the Refinery Row area and the highway heading east.

***June 19, 1953*:**
Inuit will now have the right to vote in federal elections.

***Nov. 10, 1953*:**
***The Journal* publishes a 120-page 50th anniversary section.**

***In 1954*:**
A collections agent at *The Journal* makes $18 a week.

Edmonton Weather
Forecast: Cloudy, little change in temperature. Estimated low tonight 40 above, high tomorrow 65 above.

The Edmonton Journal

'One of Canada's Great Newspapers'

FORTY-SEVENTH YEAR * * TELEPHONE 25171 EDMONTON, ALBERTA, TUESDAY, MAY 16, 1950 SINGLE COPY, 5 CENTS 28 PAGES

Red Flood Level Held For 40 Hours

Rail Strike In U.S. Ends

CHICAGO, (AP) The worst railroad strike in the United States in four years was settled Tuesday and striking firemen on five major rail systems were ordered back to their jobs immediately.

The affected carriers, their passenger and freight service disrupted by the six-day walkout, planned to resume normal service "as rapidly as possible."

The striking Brotherhood of Locomotive Firemen and Enginemen recalled picket lines and ordered the strikers to return to work.

Both sides expressed satisfaction over settlement terms.

The carriers said they won the fight on the principal issue, not to hire a second fireman on multiple-unit diesel locomotives. They said the union withdrew its demand on the issue, which has been in dispute between the brotherhood and carriers for more than 10 years.

Union President David B. Robertson, in a statement, termed as "satisfactory," the settlement "of all issues involved."

The union said it did not withdraw "entirely" its request for assignment of a third man on big diesel locomotives. A spokesman said the brotherhood "modified" its demand.

The union said the agreement eliminated wage differentials which it said existed in pay of firemen on oil burning steam locomotives and straight electric locomotives. They had lower rates than those on coal burning or diesels, the union said. The new agreement, it said, brings all rates at the same level. No figures were given.

The strike, originally set for April 26, started May 10 against parts of the Pennsylvania, New York Central, the Southern Rail-

(Continued on Page 12, Col. 1)

Lie, Stalin Talk For 90 Minutes

MOSCOW, (AP) Prime Minister Stalin and United Nations Secretary-General Trygve Lie talked for 90 minutes at the Kremlin Monday night.

The conference climaxed the "save the U.N." mission which had brought Lie halfway round the world to see the Russian leader.

Diplomats speculated that China's representation in the U.N. was a major topic at the discussions. No details of the talks were disclosed but it is not thought here that the Russians showed any signs of modifying their refusal to participate in any U.N. organization in which Chiang Kai-shek's government is represented.

Russia has demanded that the Peiping government of Mao Tze-tung be recognized as China's representative in the United Nations.

Present with Lie and Stalin at the meeting were Vice-Premier V. M. Molotov and Foreign Minister Andrei Y. Vishinsky. The interview came after Lie, seeking to ease East-West tension, had conferred with President Truman in Wash-

(Continued on Page 12, Col. 6)

... Earlier Accident ... Crash

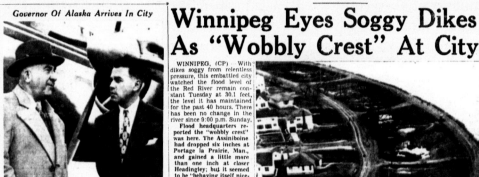

Governor Of Alaska Arrives In City

Dr. Ernest Gruening, governor of Alaska since 1939, was met at the airport Monday by Dr. Walter Johns, executive assistant to the president of the University of Alberta, and Paul Seddicum, U.S. consul in Edmonton. Dr Gruening addressed graduates at convocation Tuesday and received an honorary degree of doctor of laws. In the picture he is seen at the left with Dr. Johns, just after he stepped from a T.C.A. plane.

Award 628 Degrees At First Convocation Ceremony Here

Graduates are stepping out into a world divided between two basic philosophies, Dr. Ernest Gruening, governor of Alaska, declared in delivering the University of Alberta Convocation address in McDougall Church Tuesday. Entitling his addre... "A Mid-Century Challenge," he called for democracy to mobilize its full force to meet the menace of Communism.

Dr. Gruening himself was awarded an honorary degree of doctor of law by Hon. J. J. Bowlen, lieutenant-governor. A similar d...

Winnipeg Raises $102,000 So Far For Own Relief

By The Canadian Press

In Winnipeg local contributions to the Manitoba flood relief fund amount to $102,000, officials announced Tuesday. The fund was bolstered by a $50,000 donation from the T. Eaton Company Limited and $33,000 from ... division employees ... ment store.

Winnipeg Eyes Soggy Dikes As "Wobbly Crest" At City

WINNIPEG, (CP) — With dikes soggy from relentless pressure, this embattled city watched the flood level of the Red River remain constant Tuesday at 30.1 feet, the level it has maintained for the past 40 hours. There has been no change in the river since 9:00 p.m. Sunday.

Flood headquarters reported the "wobbly crest" was here. The Assiniboine had dropped six inches at Portage la Prairie, Man., and gained a little more than one inch at closer Headingley; but it seemed to be "behaving itself nicely . . . but bears watching."

At noon the forecast was for light rain Tuesday night and Wednesday morning, with unsettled conditions for two or three days.

Meanwhile pace of voluntary evacuation from flood-battered Greater Winnipeg has tapered off gradually, flood-control headquarters said.

The eyes of two flood-weary, crippled cities focussed on a precarious, 14-foot-high dike and the hundreds of empty homes it protects from the bloated Red River.

For three weeks the river, higher than anytime since 1832, has eaten at the huge earth-and-sandbag barrier which skirts St. Boniface and its Norwood suburb, oposite the Winnipeg business district.

Other whole suburbs in the metropolitan area have been inundated by the Red. The Winnipeg business section has been threatened. Even most of S... has been evacuated...

In 1950 alone, soprano Eileen Farrell, contralto Marian Anderson, tenor Jan Peerce and pianist Jose Iturbi visited Edmonton.

The Journal took notice of them with preview stories and reviews. Pop artists fared somewhat less well when it came to coverage.

In 1951, the Mills Brothers, a popular singing quartet, visited the downtown Trocadero Club, the former Empire Theatre on 103rd Street and Jasper Avenue, and were granted a two-paragraph story the following day.

"Featuring a program of barbershop harmonies," a reviewer said somewhat dismissively, "the Mills Brothers, popular entertainers, entertained two capacity audiences at the Trocadero on Tuesday evening.

"Although their portion of the program was brief, it was representative of the songs for which they are famed, including such favourites as Paper Doll, Across the Alley from the Alamo and Nevertheless."

Fats Domino visited in 1957, Marty Robbins and Paul Anka in 1958, but *The Journal* paid little attention. The paper accepted the ads for the rock shows, but didn't review them.

And until the Jubilee Auditorium was finished in 1957, many entertainers performed in the Gardens, the Sales Pavilion on the Exhibition grounds, McDougall Church or Victoria Composite high school.

The Gardens had a rustic flavour with the acoustics of a barn, and a railway spur line in regular use just outside the Pavilion's rear doors made that particular venue difficult.

A letter, signed Pro-Edmonton, protested the fact that the Leslie Bell Singers, an all-woman 21-voice choir from Toronto, had to contend with the odiferous environment of the Pavilion when they visited in 1950. Only hours before they appeared, it had been used for a cattle auction.

"The Leslie Bell Singers performed beautifully – one momentarily became oblivious of the familiar aroma of the sales pavilion.

"In the intervals, however, it was very distinct. We also had the 'trimmings' in the form of hungry flies which shared our space, and of course, the inevitable train which 'brought the house down' following the rendition of Gounod's Ave Maria."

For those who wanted recorded music, the '50s brought 45 rpm records. A November 1950 ad urged readers to get into the "swing to 45" by spending $19.95 on RCA Victor's fully automatic changer that could attach easily to any radio or record player.

For those with more money to spend, Heintzman and Co. on Jasper Avenue sold walnut-veneer RCA Victor 3-speed radio/phonographs for $299.50 ($2,519.08 today). The price was slightly higher for mahogany, but what was important was that they played 45s, 78s and the relatively new 33⅓ records.

Furthermore, by the end of the decade in which television became a cultural force, *Journal* ads urged people to become a two-set family.

If readers wanted all-new, of course, Philco offered The Safari, at $399.95 ($2,713.47 today), the world's first cordless television. It was "15 lbs. of portable fun!", and worked anywhere.

The decade of plenty ended with the re-election of the Socreds but the '60s were coming, and with them, political and social upheaval that would present Edmonton and *The Journal* with a new set of challenges.

***Jan. 8, 1954*:**
An extension to Interprovincial's pipeline allows the first oil from Edmonton to reach Sarnia, Ont.

***Feb. 13, 1954*:**
The giant $5-million, 25-building Bel-Air apartment complex in Westmount opens to customers.

***March 2, 1954*:**
Edmonton annexes about 800 acres to the city's southeast (Hardisty area) from the M.D. of Strathcona.

***March 3, 1954*:**
CHED radio begins broadcasting.

***March 4, 1954*:**
The province announces the first divided highway for Alberta, a four-lane expressway on a 30-mile stretch north of Calgary on Highway 2. Estimates put the cost to be $200,000 per mile.

***March 5, 1954*:**
Hometown favourite Matt Baldwin wins the 25th Brier, hosted in Edmonton for the first time.

***March 10, 1954*:**
Reserves of Alberta's new giant oil discovery at Pembina, west of the city, are estimated at 760 to 950 million barrels.

***March 15, 1954*:**
Students attend Eastglen Composite HS.

THUGS GET $45,000

CHICAGO, (AP) — Three men held 17 persons at gunpoint Friday in the bank in Lyons, Ill., southwest of Chicago, scooped up an estimated $45,000 in cash and escaped in a car driven by an accomplice.

Judge Orders Giant Firms To Get Rid Of Affiliates

NEW YORK, (CP) — Imperial Chemical Industries Ltd., of Britain and E. I. Du Pont Nemours Inc., of the United States have been ordered to present a plan within 60 days for ending their joint ownership of Du Pont affiliates in Canada, Argentina and Brazil.

The decree is the final judgment in the United States government's anti-trust suit against the two giant industries.

Du Pont and I.C.I. hold approximately 42 percent of the stock of Canadian Industries Limited. Du Pont has a fraction of one percent more than I.C.I. The remainder is held by employees and the public.

Judge Sylvester Ryan's decree says the plan should provide for sale of the companies' stock in the affiliates to independent interests or segregation of the physical properties of the affiliates. He directed that the plan be consummated within a year.

Du Pont is responsible for the development of nylon. An agreement between Du Pont and I.C.I. covering nylon has been cancelled, the judgment says.

A U.S. government suit, filed in 1944 and tried in 1950, charged the firms used a patent agreement as a screen to divide world markets and stifle competition.

Judge Ryan ordered that I.C.I. reassign to Du Pont within 90 days all of the foreign patents previously assigned to I.C.I. The judge ruled that if the firms cannot agree upon reasonable royalties within two months, applications should be made to the court to fix royalties.

POPE SENDS BEST WISHES

CASTEL GANDOLFO, Italy, (AP)—The Pope Friday sent best wishes to the British people and the Royal Family while receiving the Duke and Duchess of Windsor in private audience.

See Oil Shortage At Pacific Coast

SEATTLE, (AP) — Petroleum industry spokesmen said in Seattle Friday that Pacific northwest fuel oil supplies had been "tight" for 60 to 90 days and there may be a shortage in the winter months.

They blamed an increased demand and the Korean war.

Official sources said they did not expect the situation to become critical, however, unless there is an unusually hard winter.

Their comment came after Lawrence W. Lee, director of the marketing and distribution division of the Petroleum Defence Administration, said in a speech at Traverse City, Mich., that the Pacific northwest might have shortages of petroleum products this winter.

Lee spoke at a meeting of the National Oil Jobbers Council.

PLAN ICELANDIC FETE

GIMLI, Man., (CP) — About 4,000 Canadians and Americans of Icelandic origin are expected to attend the 63rd annual Icelandic festival of Islendingadargurinn here Monday.

Sea Gull Scourge Hits In Manitoba

WINNIPEG, (CP)—A mysterious disease which wiped out thousands of sea gulls in the Round Lake district, 140 miles northwest of here, has died out.

Investigating biologists of the provincial game and fisheries branch said Friday the epidemic is over. But the nature of the disease still remains a mystery.

Department officials said it is not botulism as first believed. Botulism is a toxic poison generated by polluted waters.

An area of 200 square miles near Hanover, Germany, is laid out in settlers' farms in a move to reduce Germany's grain food requirements.

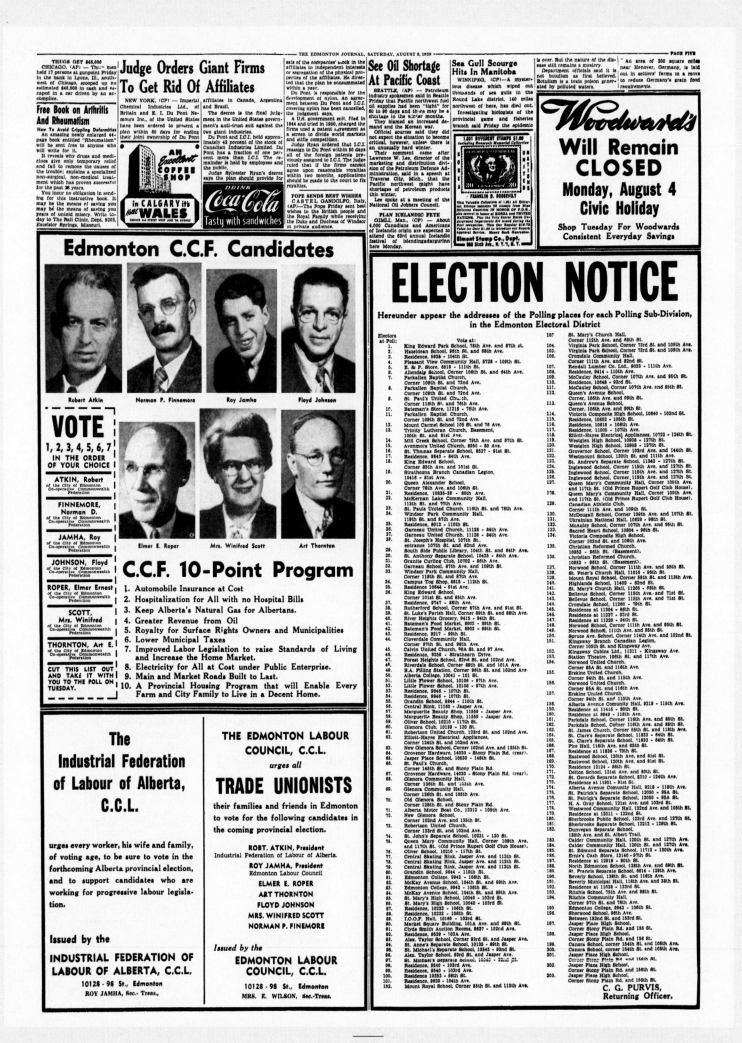

Edmonton C.C.F. Candidates

Robert Atkin

Norman P. Finnemore

Roy Jamha

Floyd Johnson

Elmer E. Roper

Mrs. Winifred Scott

Art Thornton

VOTE

1, 2, 3, 4, 5, 6, 7 IN THE ORDER OF YOUR CHOICE

ATKIN, Robert
of the City of Edmonton Co-operative Commonwealth Federation

FINNEMORE, Norman D.
of the City of Edmonton Co-operative Commonwealth Federation

JAMHA, Roy
of the City of Edmonton Co-operative Commonwealth Federation

JOHNSON, Floyd
of the City of Edmonton Co-operative Commonwealth Federation

ROPER, Elmer Ernest
of the City of Edmonton Co-operative Commonwealth Federation

SCOTT, Mrs. Winifred
of the City of Edmonton Co-operative Commonwealth Federation

THORNTON, Art E.
of the City of Edmonton Co-operative Commonwealth Federation

CUT THIS LIST OUT AND TAKE IT WITH YOU TO THE POLL ON TUESDAY.

C.C.F. 10-Point Program

1. Automobile Insurance at Cost
2. Hospitalization for All with no Hospital Bills
3. Keep Alberta's Natural Gas for Albertans.
4. Greater Revenue from Oil
5. Royalty for Surface Rights Owners and Municipalities
6. Lower Municipal Taxes
7. Improved Labor Legislation to raise Standards of Living and Increase the Home Market.
8. Electricity for All at Cost under Public Enterprise.
9. Main and Market Roads Built to Last.
10. A Provincial Housing Program that will Enable Every Farm and City Family to Live in a Decent Home.

The Industrial Federation of Labour of Alberta, C.C.L.

urges every worker, his wife and family, of voting age, to be sure to vote in the forthcoming Alberta provincial election, and to support candidates who are working for progressive labour legislation.

Issued by the

INDUSTRIAL FEDERATION OF LABOUR OF ALBERTA, C.C.L.
10128 - 98 St., Edmonton
ROY JAMHA, Sec.- Treas.,

THE EDMONTON LABOUR COUNCIL, C.C.L.

urges all

TRADE UNIONISTS

their families and friends in Edmonton to vote for the following candidates in the coming provincial election.

ROBT. ATKIN, President
Industrial Federation of Labour of Alberta.
ROY JAMHA, President
Edmonton Labour Council
ELMER E. ROPER
ART THORNTON
FLOYD JOHNSON
MRS. WINIFRED SCOTT
NORMAN P. FINEMORE

Issued by the

EDMONTON LABOUR COUNCIL, C.C.L.
10128 - 98 St., Edmonton
MRS. E. WILSON, Sec.-Treas.

ELECTION NOTICE

Hereunder appear the addresses of the Polling places for each Polling Sub-Division, in the Edmonton Electoral District

Electors at Poll:	Vote at:
1.	King Edward Park School, 78th Ave. and 87th st.
2.	Hazeldean School, 96th St. and 68th Ave.
3.	Residence, 5926 - 104th St.
4.	Pleasant View Community Hall, 5728 - 109th St.
5.	E. & P. Store, 6519 - 111th St.
6.	Allendale School, Corner 106th St. and 64th Ave.
7.	Parkallen Baptist Church, Corner 109th St. and 72nd Ave.
8.	Parkallen Baptist Church, Corner 109th St. and 72nd Ave.
9.	St. Paul's United Church, Corner 116th St. and 76th Ave.
10.	Bateman's Store, 11218 - 76th Ave.
11.	Parkallen Baptist Church, Corner 109th St. and 72nd Ave.
12.	Mount Carmel School 105 St. and 76 Ave.
13.	Trinity Lutheran Church, Basement, 100th St. and 81st Ave.
14.	Mill Creek School, Corner 79th Ave. and 97th St.
15.	Avonmore United Church, 8950 - 80 Ave.
16.	St. Thomas Separate School, 8527 - 91st St.
17.	Residence, 9843 - 84th Ave.
18.	King Edward School, Corner 85th Ave. and 101st St.
19.	Strathcona Branch Canadian Legion, 10416 - 81st Ave.
20.	Queen Alexander School, Corner 78th Ave. and 106th St.
21.	Residence, 10835-39 - 80th Ave.
22.	McKernan Lake Community Hall, 113th St. and 77th Ave.
23.	St. Pauls United Church, 116th St. and 76th Ave.
24.	Windsor Park Community Hall, 119th St. and 87th Ave.
25.	Residence, 8012 - 110th St.
26.	Garneau United Church, 11128 - 84th Ave.
27.	Garneau United Church, 11128 - 84th Ave.
28.	St. Joseph's Hospital, 107th St., entrance 107th St. and 82nd Ave.
29.	South Side Public Library, 104th St. and 84th Ave.
30.	St. Anthony Separate School, 10425 - 84th Ave.
31.	Granite Curling Club, 10702 - 86th Ave.
32.	Garneau School, 87th Ave. and 109th St.
33.	Windsor Park Community Hall, Corner 119th St. and 87th Ave.
34.	Campus Tog Shop, 8815 - 112th St.
35.	Residence 10644 - 91st Ave.
36.	King Edward School, Corner 101st St. and 85th Ave.
37.	Residence, 9747 - 88th Ave.
38.	Rutherford School, Corner 87th Ave. and 91st St.
39.	St. Luke's Parish Hall, Corner 89th St. and 88th Ave.
40.	River Heights Grocery, 9415 - 94th St.
41.	Bateman's Food Market, 8902 - 99th St.
42.	Bateman's Food Market, 8902 - 99th St.
43.	Residence, 9217 - 99th St.
44.	Cloverdale Community Hall, Corner 97th St. and 98th Ave.
45.	Calvin United Church, 96A St. and 97 Ave.
46.	Residence, 9259 - Strathearn Drive.
47.	Forest Heights School, 82nd St. and 102nd Ave.
48.	Riverdale School, Corner 89th St. and 101A Ave.
49.	B.A. Filling Station, Corner 96th St. and 102nd Ave.
50.	Alberta College, 10041 - 101 St.
51.	Little Flower School, 10106 - 97th Ave.
52.	Little Flower School, 10106 - 97th Ave.
53.	Residence, 9846 - 107th St.
54.	Residence, 9846 - 107th St.
55.	Grandin School, 9844 - 110th St.
56.	Central Rink, 11160 - Jasper Ave.
57.	Marguerite Beauty Shop, 11559 - Jasper Ave.
58.	Marguerite Beauty Shop, 11559 - Jasper Ave.
59.	Oliver School, 10210 - 117th St.
60.	Glenora Club, 10139 - 120 St.
61.	Robertson United Church, 123rd St. and 102nd Ave.
62.	Elliott-Hayes Electrical Appliances, Corner 124th St. and 102nd Ave.
63.	New Glenora School, Corner 102nd Ave. and 135th St.
64.	Grovenor Hardware, 14030 - Stony Plain Rd. (rear).
65.	Jasper Place School, 10030 - 148th St.
66.	St. Paul's Church, Corner 145th St. and Stony Plain Rd.
67.	Grovenor Hardware, 14030 - Stony Plain Rd. (rear).
68.	Glenora Community Hall, Corner 136th St. and 105th Ave.
69.	Glenora Community Hall, Corner 136th St. and 105th Ave.
70.	Old Glenora School, Corner 128th St. and Stony Plain Rd.
71.	Alberta Motor Boat Co., 12312 - 105th Ave.
72.	New Glenora School, Corner 102nd Ave. and 135th St.
73.	Robertson United Church, Corner 123rd St. and 102nd Ave.
74.	St. John's Separate School, 10231 - 120 St.
75.	Queen Mary Community Hall, Corner 109th Ave. and 117th St. (Old Prince Rupert Golf Club House).
76.	Oliver School, 10210 - 117th St.
77.	Central Skating Rink, Jasper Ave. and 112th St.
78.	Central Skating Rink, Jasper Ave. and 112th St.
79.	Central Skating Rink, Jasper Ave. and 112th St.
80.	Grandin School, 9844 - 110th St.
81.	Edmonton College, 9942 - 106th St.
82.	McKay Avenue School, 104th St. and 99th Ave.
83.	Edmonton College, 9942 - 106th St.
84.	McKay Avenue School, 104th St. and 99th Ave.
85.	St. Mary's High School, 10040 - 103rd St.
86.	St. Mary's High School, 10040 - 103rd St.
87.	Residence, 10232 - 106th St.
88.	Residence, 10232 - 106th St.
89.	I.O.O.F. Hall, 10169 - 103rd St.
90.	Market Square Building, 101A Ave. and 99th St.
91.	Clyde Smith Auction Rooms, 9637 - 102nd Ave.
92.	Residence, 9529 - 102A Ave.
93.	Alex. Taylor School, Corner 93rd St. and Jasper Ave.
94.	St. Anne's Separate School, 10135 - 89th St.
95.	St. Michael's Separate School, 10545 - 92nd St.
96.	Alex. Taylor School, 93rd St. and Jasper Ave.
97.	St. Michael's Separate School, 10545 - 92nd St.
98.	Residence, 9540 - 103rd Ave.
99.	Residence, 9540 - 103rd Ave.
100.	Residence 10352 - 98th St.
101.	Residence, 9629 - 104th Ave.
102.	Mount Royal School, Corner 55th St. and 113th Ave.
10?	St. Mary's Church Hall, Corner 112th Ave. and 68th St.
104.	Virginia Park School, Corner 73rd St. and 109th Ave.
103.	Virginia Park School, Corner 73rd St. and 109th Ave.
106.	Cromdale Community Hall, Corner 111th Ave. and 82nd St.
107.	Rendall Lumber Co. Ltd., 9023 - 111th Ave.
108.	Residence, 9414 - 110th Ave.
109.	McCauley School, Corner 107th Ave. and 95th St.
110.	Residence, 10648 - 93rd St.
111.	McCauley School, Corner 107th Ave. and 95th St.
112.	Queen's Avenue School, Corner, 106th Ave. and 99th St.
113.	Queen's Avenue School, Corner, 106th Ave. and 99th St.
114.	Victoria Composite High School, 10840 - 102nd St.
115.	Residence, 10652 - 105th St.
116.	Residence, 10618 - 106th Ave.
117.	Residence, 11005 - 107th Ave.
118.	Elliott-Hayes Electrical Appliances, 10722 - 124th St.
119.	Westglen High School, 10908 - 127th St.
120.	Westglen High School, 10908 - 127th St.
121.	Grovernor School, Corner 103rd Ave. and 144th St.
122.	Westmount School, 130th St. and 111th Ave.
123.	St. Andrew's Separate School, 11342 - 127th St.
124.	Inglewood School, Corner 115th Ave. and 127th St.
125.	Inglewood School, Corner 115th Ave. and 127th St.
126.	Inglewood School, Corner, 115th Ave. and 127th St.
127.	Queen Mary's Community Hall, Corner 109th Ave. and 117th St. (Old Prince Rupert Golf Club House),
128.	Queen Mary's Community Hall, Corner 109th Ave. and 117th St. (Old Prince Rupert Golf Club House),
129.	Canadian Athletic Club, Corner 111th Ave. and 109th St.
130.	McDougall School, Corner 109th Ave. and 107th St.
131.	Ukrainian National Hall, 10629 - 98th St.
132.	McAuley School, Corner 107th Ave. and 95th St.
133.	Sacred Heart School, 10804 - 96th St.
134.	Victoria Composite High School, Corner 102nd St. and 108th Ave.
135.	Christian Reformed Church, 10952 - 96th St. (Basement).
136.	Christian Reformed Church, 10952 - 96th St. (Basement).
137.	Norwood School, Corner 111th Ave. and 95th St.
138.	St. Peter's Church Hall, 11010 - 96th St.
139.	Mount Royal School, Corner 55th St. and 113th Ave.
140.	Highlands School, 11409 - 62nd St.
141.	St. Mary's Church Hall, 11205 - 68th St.
142.	Bellevue School, Corner 115th Ave. and 71st St.
143.	Bellevue School, Corner 115th Ave. and 71st St.
144.	Cromdale School, 11260 - 79th St.
145.	Residence at 11304 - 86th St.
146.	Residence at 11227 - 93rd St.
147.	Residence at 11220 - 94th St.
148.	Norwood School, Corner 111th Ave. and 95th St.
149.	Norwood School, 111th Ave. and 95th St.
150.	Spruce Ave. School, Corner 114th Ave. and 102nd St.
151.	Kingsway Branch Canadian Legion, Corner 105th St. and Kingsway Ave.
152.	Kingsway Cabins Ltd., 11311 - Kingsway Ave.
153.	Station Theatre, 106th St. and 117th Ave.
154.	Norwood United Church, Corner 95A St. and 116th Ave.
155.	Erskine United Church, Corner 94th St. and 115th Ave.
156.	Norwood United Church, Corner 95A St. and 116th Ave.
157.	Erskine United Church, Corner 94th St. and 115th Ave.
158.	Alberta Avenue Comunity Hall, 9218 - 118th Ave.
159.	Residence at 11416 - 90th St.
160.	Residence at 8949 - 118th Ave.
161.	Parkdale School, Corner 116th Ave. and 85th St.
162.	Parkdale School, Corner 116th Ave. and 85th St.
163.	St. James Church, Corner 55th St. and 118th Ave.
164.	St. Clare's Separate School, 11833 - 64th St.
165.	St. Clare's Separate School, 11833 - 64th St.
166.	Fire Hall, 118th Ave. and 65th St.
167.	Residence at 11836 - 79th St.
168.	Eastwood School, 120th Ave. and 81st St.
169.	Eastwood School, 120th Ave. and 81st St.
170.	Residence 12124 - 86th St.
171.	Delton School, 121st Ave. and 89th St.
172.	St. Gerards Separate School, 8310 - 124th Ave.
173.	Residence at 11951 - 91st St.
174.	Alberta Avenue Comunity Hall, 9218 - 118th Ave.
175.	St. Patrick's Separate School, 12050 - 95A St.
176.	St. Patrick's Separate School, 12050 - 95A St.
177.	H. A. Gray School, 121st Ave. and 103rd St.
178.	Westwood Community Hall, 122nd Ave. and 105th St.
179.	Residence at 12011 - 122nd St.
180.	Sherbrooke Public School, 123rd Ave. and 127th St.
181.	Sherbrooke Separate School, 12212 - 128th St.
182.	Dunvegan Separate School, 130th Ave. and St. Albert Trail.
183.	Calder Community Hall, 120th St. and 127th Ave.
184.	Calder Community Hall, 120th St. and 127th Ave.
185.	St. Edmund Separate School, 11712 - 130th Ave.
186.	Ernie's Cash Store, 13140 - 97th St.
187.	Residence at 12919 - 90th St.
188.	North Edmonton School, 128th Ave. and 69th St.
189.	St. Francis Separate School, 6614 - 129th Ave.
190.	Beverly School, 138th St. and 116th Ave.
191.	Beverly Municipal Hall, 118th Ave. and 38th St.
192.	Residence at 11038 - 123rd St.
193.	Ritchie School, 75th Ave. and 98th St.
194.	Ritchie Community Hall, Corner 97th St. and 78th Ave.
195.	Edmonton College, 9942 - 106th St.
196.	Sherwood School, 98th Ave. Between 152nd St. and 153rd St.
197.	Jasper Place High School, Corner Stony Plain Rd. and 156 St.
198.	Jasper Place High School, Corner Stony Plain Rd. and 156 St.
199.	Canora School, corner 154th St. and 105th Ave.
200.	Canora School, corner 154th St. and 105th Ave.
201.	Jasper Place High School, Corner Stony Plain Rd. and 156th St.
202.	Jasper Place High School, Corner Stony Plain Rd. and 156th St.
203.	Jasper Place High School, Corner Stony Plain Rd. and 156th St.

C. G. PURVIS,
Returning Officer.

First Nations

"Chronic poverty, virtual starvation, disease and squalor, these are the lot of the northern Alberta Indian. For many, death is a merciful release from the misery of life."

— The opening paragraph in the first of a series of articles on the plight of northern natives by Jack Deakin, May, 16, 1950

The Journal began serious coverage of First Nations interests in the '50s when reporter Jack Deakin was assigned to what was then called the "Indian" beat.

A sign of the times was that many of the stories and the editorials had a tone of racial superiority. And Deakin's work reflected that; it was sympathetic but also paternalistic. "More than 100 years of wandering has ended for the last of Canada's nomadic Indians – a wandering band of Chippewas of the Rocky Mountain House district," Deakin wrote on May 16, 1950.

"At last the wandering of the Chippewas in the Rocky area has ended. They will be provided a reservation from which, it is hoped, they will provide themselves with a greatly improved existence."

The headline on the story read: "Last Nomadic Indians Sign Treaty Accepting Rule of Whiteman."

Deakin may have borrowed the tone of his stories from *The Journal's* editorial page. The texture of the language in one typical editorial seemed borrowed, in turn, from Kipling's poem *The White Man's Burden.*

Titled "Indians and the Vote," a March 23, 1950, editorial was typical of the time: "Most of Canada's racial minorities have always been most anxious to secure the vote and all the privileges of full citizenship. But the Indians – or at least some of them – are proving an exception. They have shown a marked lack of enthusiasm about proposals recently made in parliament to give them the right to vote and generally enfranchise them.

"Why this is so was explained recently by John Laurie of Calgary, secretary of the Indian Association of Alberta.

"He says that the Alberta Indians realize they are not ready for the franchise. The lack of proper schooling – few Indians, for example, can speak English adequately – and the paternalistic reserve system under which all the Indian's important decisions are made for him by the agent, have left them unprepared to face political responsibility.

"What the Indians need now is not formal political rights, but a real effort to lift them out of their present poverty and ignorance. This means better schools – as near as possible to the standard for white children – better medical care and a chance to earn a decent living through the conservation and development of whatever resources the reserves possess. This is the Dominion's primary responsibility towards its wards. Only when the treaty Indian has been enabled to look after himself in the modern world will political emancipation have meaning."

Indians had to wait until 1960 before they were fully enfranchised, although Canada's Inuit received the vote in 1953.

***March 17, 1954*:**
Announcement that Alberta highways will be patrolled by police "ghost cars" is made in the legislature.

***April 30, 1954*:**
Lt.-Gov. J.J. Bowlen pulls the first spike to herald the removal of 9.2 miles of track of the Edmonton, Yukon and Pacific railroad. The railroad served as a link between the north and south sides of the city, but hasn't carried passengers for almost three decades.

***July 3, 1954*:**
Second World War food rationing in Britain ends as meat is taken off the restricted list. Rump steak immediately goes from 35 cents to 84 cents a pound.

***July 11, 1954*:**
A city bylaw passes that allows shops to stay open until 9 p.m. Thursdays, while community groceries are allowed to remain open until 11 p.m. six nights a week.

***Sept. 29, 1954*:**
RCMP announces it will use a radar gun to catch speeders.

***Oct. 17, 1954*:**
CFRN, Edmonton's first TV station, goes on the air.

Edmonton Weather
Forecast: Partly cloudy with afternoon showers, little change in temperature, winds west 15. High tomorrow 60.

The Edmonton Journal

One of Canada's Great Newspapers

56th YEAR, NO. 251 | TELEPHONE GA 4-0271 | EDMONTON, ALBERTA, WEDNESDAY, SEPTEMBER 9, 1959 | PRICE NOT OVER FIVE CENTS | FOUR SECTIONS

MAYOR HAWRELAK RESIGNS

5713
UP
NAVY 42

DRONE RECOVERY — This helicopter is recovering a USAF drone which ended up in the sea after a flight designed to give information on supersonic conditions. The information was recorded by instruments carried by the drone. — Fednews photograph.

Model Capsule Fired

CAPE CANAVERAL, Fla. (AP) — A space capsule like the one an astronaut will ride in orbit was fired hundreds of miles across the Atlantic today and quickly recovered intact. Space experts said main research objectives were met despite a mechanical mishap that shortened the flight.

The bottle-shaped steel chamber was hoisted aloft from this missile test centre by an Atlas rocket, the vehicle chosen for the first manned flights. Instead of a man, however, it carried only instruments.

All went well on the launching itself but when the powerful first stage burned out after two minutes and 40 seconds it failed to disengage and fall away as planned.

Mayor Topped Polls

Forty-five-year-old William Hawrelak has topped the polls consistently since 1951 when he ran for his first term as mayor and won by the largest vote ever accorded a mayoralty candidate in Edmonton to that time.

In the following two mayoralty elections he set a modern record by winning two terms by acclamation, then racked up a record majority again in 1957.

Mr. Hawrelak was born at Wasel, 60 miles northeast of Edmonton, the son of a pioneer farm family, but received most of his education in Edmonton. He operated the family farm at Wasel for a few years before moving to Edmonton permanently 12 years ago.

Since then he's become one of the best-known municipal figures in Canada, a persistent crusader for more municipal aid from senior governments and a past president of the Canadian Federation of Mayors and Municipalities.

DEFEATED IN 1948

Mr. Hawrelak's first bid for municipal office was in 1948 when he ran for an aldermanic seat. He came seventh and lost. The following year he was back again as a Citizens' Committee candidate and won a seat on council.

From there he never looked back until 1957 when he ran unsuccessfully for the Liberals in Edmonton East in the federal election. The Conservatives won that election, and it was the first real setback in Mr. Hawrelak's political career.

Had the Liberals been returned to power in 1957, Edmonton's mayor might now be a federal cabinet minister. It was widely rumored that Prime Minister St. Laurent had promised him an Alberta cabinet vacancy.

The following year there was a movement to draft him as the new provincial leader of the Liberal party, but he turned it down.

SERVED IN AFU

Mr. Hawrelak was active in community affairs long before he held public office. He served as vice-president of the Alberta Farmers' Union in the 1940s, and later when he moved to Edmonton took an interest in the Federation of Home and School Association and Community leagues.

In private life he is president of the Prairie Rose Manufacturing Co. and has been president of the Alberta Bottlers' Association.

He has served on the council of the Edmonton Chamber of Commerce, the executive of the South Edmonton Businessmen's Association, and as chairman of the business section of the Community Chest.

He also has been an officer

(Continued on Page 15, Section 1)

Porter Report Charges "Misconduct" In Office

* * * * * *

Suggests City Consider Recovering Mayor's "Gains"

WILLIAM HAWRELAK

Mayor Hawrelak Wednesday submitted his resignation to a special session of city council, in the wake of the Porter Royal Commission report which charges him with "gross misconduct" on a land deal. The report suggests that council consider obtaining legal advice "upon the city's right to recover the mayor's gains" in certain property transactions.

The 100-page report, prepared by Mr. Justice M. M. Porter of Calgary, after 21 days of hearings this spring into charges of civic maladministration, suggests that evidence on two land deals should be turned over to the attorney-general "for such action, if any, as he may deem it his duty to take."

On three other property transactions the report says there was no improper policy or administration on the part of the city. At one point it says

Full text of Mr. Justice Porter's report will be found on Pages 12 to 15 of this section.

the accomplishments in the city during a period of remarkable growth and progress "are an outstanding tribute to the talent and effort of the mayor and commissioners."

After submitting his resignation, Mr. Hawrelak left the mayor's chair, which was taken by Ald. Reg. Easton, deputy mayor. The resignation was accepted unanimously. Ald. Laurette Douglas was not present. During a brief recess, Mr. Hawrelak left the council chamber, tears in his eyes.

Following the recess, the special session was adjourned to 4:30 p.m., when an acting *mayor was to be elected. The acting mayor would hold office until the civic election* Oct. 14.

The report charges planning director W. R. Brown with "complete abandonment of responsibility" in connection with property in Boulevard Heights—now part of the Ottewell subdivision—when he wrote a letter "which may be described as a declaration of intent by the city that it would not permit in the zoning of Boulevard Heights provision for a site for a shopping centre."

The investigation was ordered in January by Premier Manning, attorney-general, at the request of city council. It arose out of a petition submitted to council last fall by 568 persons. A select council committee consisting of five aldermen and the mayor, originally attempted to investigate the charges of civic maladministration levelled by the petitioners, but decided to turn the matter over to the attorney-general after four formal hearings.

Mr. Justice Porter writes that it "would not be proper (for the commission) to make any direction about the wisdom of council complying with the petitioners' request" (that the city pay the fee of Frank Dunne, counsel for the petitioners). However, he adds: "There can be no doubt that the work of the commission could not have proceeded, let alone have been accomplished, without the very excellent assistance received from Mr. Dunne and from numbers of his clients."

The report deals with each land transaction in the order in which it was heard at the inquiry, then turns to charges of improper handling and administration of town planning and excessive cost and improper purchasing, and leasing and renting of equipment by the city.

The first charge concerns the sale of city land at the southeast end of the airport, now occu-

(Continued on Page 15, This Section)

Mayor's Statement In Resigning Office

Here is Mayor Hawrelak's statement of resignation, given to the Edmonton City Council at noon:

Prior to this meeting I have read the report of the Hon. Mr. Justice Porter. Mr. Justice Porter has come to certain conclusions which make it impossible for me to continue to act as mayor of this city. I have, therefore, prior to this meeting, furnished written notice to the city clerk, pursuant to Section 40 of the City Act, of my resignation. The city clerk will be placing the same before you at this meeting. It is for this council to set the date upon which the resignation is to become effective, but I would respectfully ask that you make the same effective immediately.

In reaching his conclusion, the Hon. Mr. Justice Porter expressed his opinion that certain reputable people who appeared before the inquiry voluntarily and who are not compellable as witnesses, were untruthful under oath in their evidence relating to my part in certain matters under investigation. It appears that he is also of the opinion that my explanations in regard to these matters were unsatisfactory. Contrary to the implications inherent in the report, any private transactions that I had were not with the City and did not involve any City funds or land. The principle which has apparently been applied and which seems to flow from this report, is that a person, upon accepting public office, must relinquish and avoid all private business ties. I believe in electing me to the office of mayor, the citizens of Edmonton expressed a desire to entrust this position to a business man and that there was no need for me to divest myself of this status as long as my business dealings were not transacted at the expense of the City of Edmonton. I categorically deny that there was any improper conduct on my part in regard to any of the matters under investigation or that I violated my oath of office.

I have served the city as alderman and mayor for ten years and I regret that I feel obliged to sever my connection. Although it is my opinion that there is no legal requirement for my resignation, I feel that I must resign because the statements made in the report make it impossible for me to do justice to the office of Mayor of the City of Edmonton, a position which I hold in high regard and respect.

Report Highlights

Evidence on two city land deals should be turned over to the attorney-general for such action as deemed necessary, says the commission.

* * *

No improper policy or administration on part of city in three property transactions.

* * *

The report finds no foundations for any implications of impropriety in the mayor's conduct in visiting manufacturing plants in Europe when the firms paid his expenses.

* * *

No evidence of wrongdoing was found on the part of any city officer or employee in the purchasing, leasing or rental of equipment or material.

* * *

Mayor Hawrelak charged by report with "gross misconduct" in a land transaction.

* * *

Planning director W. R. Brown criticized for "complete abandonment of responsibility" in connection with Boulevard Heights property.

* * *

Improper handling and administration of town planning is claimed by the commission which refers to "piecemeal control of development."

* * *

ALD. REG EASTON, deputy mayor of the City of Edmonton, who Wednesday took the mayor's chair after William Hawrelak submitted his resignation at a special noon council meeting.

SUCCESSFUL FIRING

VANDERBERG AIR FORCE BASE, Calif. (AP) — U.S. air force troops today successfully fired their first Atlas intercontinental missile, having triple the range of previous combat missiles.

Where To Find It

Angelo Patri	2	8
Births, Deaths, Mar.	4	4
Bridge	4	6
Comics	4	7, 13
Crossword Puzzle	4	8
Dennis The Menace	4	9
District	4	14
Dorothy Dix	2	4
Dorothy Kilgallen	2	11
Editorial	1	4
Financial	1	12, 13
Off The Record	4	10
Our Boarding House	4	5
Out Our Way	4	5
Packsack	4	13
Sport	3	1-5
Theatres, Entertain.	3	12
They'll Do It Every	4	5
Tizzy	4	8
T.V.	4	7
Uncle Ray's Corner	4	13
Want Ads	4	5-12
Women's	2	1-16

Chou En-Lai Asks Border Negotiations

* * *

At Same Time Charges India Started Trouble

TOYKO (AP) — Red China pledged today that she will respect the territories of Bhutan and Sikkim as Indian protectorates, and offered to settle her border disputes with India through friendly negotiations.

At the same time the Peking regime declared all the border trouble was "caused by trespassing and provocations by Indian troops."

The pledge and the offer were made by Premier Chou En-lai to India's Prime Minister Nehru in a letter dated Sept. 8. It was broadcast today by the New China News Agency, which said the letter was in reply to a letter from Nehru of March 22. That was before the border incidents began.

Chou offered to settle all China's border disputes with India "through friendly negotiations conducted in a well-prepared way, step by step."

Chou said "China is willing to live together in friendship with Sikkim and Bhutan, without committing aggression against each other." She would also respect "the proper relations between them (Bhutan and Sikkim) and India."

CRITICIZES RECEPTION

The letter expressed displeasure at the way some Indians are handling the map dispute between India and Red China.

"Some people in India . . . are raising a big uproar about the maps published in Communist China, attempting to create a pressure of public opinion to force China to accept India's unilateral claims concerning the Sino-Indian boundary. Needless to say, this is neither wise nor worthy."

BLAMES INDIA

At the same time Chou blamed the Indians for starting the trouble.

"The tense situation recently arising on the Chinese-Indian border was all caused by trespassing and provocations by Indian troops," he wrote.

The premier named Longju, an outpost in the northeast frontier agency, as one spot invaded and occupied by the Indians. This is the same outpost the Indians accuse the Chinese of holding illegally.

MAP CONTROVERSY

Turning to the controversy about Communist Chinese maps showing as Chinese large sectors of territory claimed by India, Chou said it was not his country's maps "but British and Indian maps that unilaterally al-

(Continued on Page 2, Col. 1)

Outpost Held Reds At Bay

NEW DELHI (Reuters)—Outnumbered defenders at lonely Longju outpost on India's northeastern frontier held off an attacking force of about 500 Communist Chinese for a night, but finally fell back when they ran out of ammunition, it was reported today.

Official sources confirmed a story in The Times of India which for the first time gave details of the incursion by Chinese forces last month from Tibet.

The Times of India says an attack on Aug. 25 was described by the Assam riflemen who vacated Longju outpost and reached Limeking, another garrison in the Subansiri division.

That night the Chinese besieged Longju outpost, but were held at bay by steady fire until the defenders ran out of ammunition the following morning.

The Weather

(Issued by the Dominion Public Weather Office at Edmonton)

A new disturbance from the Pacific will bring cloud and a few showers to north-central Alberta this evening and overnight. Unsettled weather will continue Thursday with shower activity in most northern and central regions.

Low tonight, 45.
High tomorrow, 60.
Rainfall, .66 of an inch.

Sunset today	7:07 p.m.
Sunrise tomorrow	5:58 a.m.
Moonset tonight	10:58 p.m.
First Quarter today	3:07 p.m.
PROMINENT STARS	
Altair, high in south	9:06 p.m.
Arcturus, sets	10:51 p.m.
VISIBLE PLANETS	
Jupiter, sets	8:33 p.m.
Saturn, low in southwest	10:17 p.m.
Venus, low in east	5:40 a.m.

Temperatures

Maximum temperatures yesterday and overnight lows are:

Edmonton	51	30	Vermilion	52	28
Fairview	51	36	Saskatoon	50	35
Gr. Prairie	53	37	Pr. Albert	48	36
Whitect.	52	26	Pr. Rupert	55	46
Wagner	52	30	Victoria	62	47
McMurray	48	23	Vancouver	63	46
Lac La B.	49	31	Penticton	68	36
Penhold	47	30	Kamloops	67	44
Rk. Mt. H.	46	30	Regina	66	37
Calgary	45	30	Winnipeg	76	49
Lethbridge	55	30	Toronto	95	69
Jasper	48	34	Ottawa	85	66
Coronat'n	46	31	Montreal	85	60
Whitehse.	49	38	Nor. Wells	43	27
Snag	53	30	Yellowkn.	40	31
Aklavik	37	32	Ft. Smith	44	31

Laotians Retake Post

VIENTIANE, Laos (Reuters)—The Laotian Army has recaptured the key military post of Muongson, in the heart of the Communist-infiltrated Muongson Valley, it was officially annouced today.

This is the fourth time the post has changed hands since the jungle war flared up in mid-July.

Muongson, standing in an inaccessible valley in Sam Neua province about 30 miles from the border with Communist North Viet Nam, was the scene of a heroic defence during the first rebel attacks July 24.

The garrison lost 15 of its 40 men but was reported to have killed or wounded 80 attackers.

The communique said guerrilla groups were once again moving against Muongson.

Rebel attacks were also continuing around Sam Teu fort, in southeastern Sam Neua province, where a major assault is believed to be imminent. It was reported Tuesday that the garrison had been ordered to evacuate Sam Teu.

Vegreville Boy, 8, Is Missing

Mounted police, a tracking dog, and civilian searchers are trekking through dense bush country east of Vegreville in an attempt to find an eight-year-old boy missing since 5 p.m. Monday.

The boy, George Ferlayko, did not return home after going out to bring in the cattle Monday night. The farm is in heavy bush country eight miles north of Lavoy. The boy's parents searched for him and when they were unable to locate their son they reported to RCMP.

RCMP say the boy is blond, with a thin build and light complexion. He is lightly dressed.

MR. JUSTICE M. M. PORTER, of the Supreme Court of Alberta, whose report on Edmonton's civic administration led to Mayor Hawrelak's resignation Wednesday.

William Hawrelak

"In this huge vote, which shows keen public interest in the management of city business, Mayor-elect William Hawrelak deserves congratulation on his clear-cut victory."
— Editorial Nov. 8, 1951

"Clear-cut" was certainly an understatement. Bill Hawrelak crushed his opposition by nearly 20,000 votes, beginning a remarkable love-hate relationship with Edmonton that would span the next 34 years.

In 1951, Edmonton had embarked on its greatest boom ever. Wells in the Leduc area were being spudded daily. Money flowed like the oil from whence it came.

It was time to elect the person who would lead the city to greatness, and on Nov. 7, 1951, the people spoke. Hawrelak was a 37-year-old native-born Albertan of Ukrainian descent who came to Edmonton in 1945 to establish a soft drink company, Prairie Rose Manufacturing Co. He was a populist, a Liberal and he had run twice in federal elections without success. He lost his first aldermanic race in 1948. He ran again in 1949 and won. Win or lose, Hawrelak would always run again.

Politics was his passion.

And people were passionate about him. It was a rare Edmontonian who didn't have an opinion about Hawrelak.

The Journal, however, managed to keep its passions in check. Its relationship with Hawrelak over the years could fairly be described as tepid.

Hawrelak won the next two elections after 1951 by acclamation.

But by 1957, some members of the community were becoming uneasy with the mayor and his administration. Lots of money was changing hands.

Thirty new subdivisions had been created in six years and there was a perception Hawrelak was running a one-man show.

In this election, he was challenged by trucking company owner Ed Clarke. But rather than attack him on his style, the over-riding criticism by his opponents was Hawrelak's decision the previous June to run in the federal election in Edmonton East. Prime Minister Louis St. Laurent had offered him a cabinet seat.

Hawrelak lost that election and St. Laurent lost his government.

The Journal, in a rare show of enthusiasm for the mayor, came to his defence, Oct. 10, 1957.

"The voters should ask themselves whether the flimsy criticism of Mr. Hawrelak's candidature in the last federal election is any reason why the city should deprive itself of the experience and ability he has acquired and demonstrated in six years as mayor."

This was the first and only time *The Journal* actively backed Hawrelak in a pre-election editorial.

He won back his mayor's seat by 23,000 votes.

But the magic carpet upon which he rode into office was about to be pulled out from under him.

In December 1958, city businessman Ed Leger presented a 588-name

***Nov. 27, 1954*:**
The Eskimos win the Grey Cup for the first time, defeating the Montreal Alouettes 26-25.

***Dec. 30, 1954*:**
The Petroleum and Gas Conservation Board reports that Alberta's oil production is 301,471 barrels a day.

***In 1955*:**
A cashier/clerk typist at *The Journal* makes $25 a week, while a mailroom worker earns $32.50.

***Jan. 1, 1955*:**
The village (now city) of Spruce Grove west of Edmonton is incorporated. Camrose gains city status.

***Feb. 12, 1955*:**
The first underground parking garage in Canada opens east of the Macdonald Hotel.

***July 5, 1955*:**
The Mayfair, Canada's first drive-in hotel, with underground parking for 50 cars, opens.

***Aug. 18, 1955*:**
Edmonton's first shopping centre, Westmount Shoppers' Park, opens.

***Oct. 19, 1955*:**
Mayor Hawrelak wins a third two-year term.

Check the difference and you'll

JOIN THE SWING

to '53 FORD

CRESTLINE VICTORIA

GOLDEN ANNIVERSARY OF THE GREATEST NAME IN MOTORING

*Fordomatic Drive, Overdrive and white side-wall tires optional at extra cost.

Go over the Ford of your choice carefully . . . compare all the features of Ford—the safety of Full-Circle Visibility . . . the convenience of Centre-Fill Fueling . . . the comfort of foam rubber seats—the unmistakable quality in every detail of workmanship and style. You'll be convinced that this is your year to change to Ford.

When you try Ford's "Wonder Ride" . . . you'll see how it smooths out the roughest road—how efficiently it handles in traffic—how easy it is to park. Check the ride before you decide and you'll buy a Ford!

Test-Drive its V-8 smoothness—for Ford has the high-compression Strato-Star 110-Hp. V-8—the type of engine that powers the finest cars. And Ford gives you a choice of three drives—Fordomatic*, Overdrive* or Synchro-Silent Shift. Yes! Check the difference and you'll join the swing to Ford! When Ford offers you *so much* more . . .

WHY TAKE LESS THAN THE BEST?

V-8

POWERED with the finest
PRICED with the lowest

Ford MONARCH YOUR FORD DEALER WILL GLADLY ARRANGE FOR YOU TO... *TEST-DRIVE* **FORD**

DOMINION MOTORS LTD.

YOUR FORD AND MONARCH DEALERS FOR 30 YEARS

West End Br. — Corner 120 St. and 107 Ave. TELEPHONE 29421 Downtown — Corner 107th St. and Jasper Ave.

LOOK FOR THE A-1 SIGN OF VALUE WHEN YOU BUY A USED CAR — SEE YOUR FORD DEALER petition to council calling for a provincial government probe into charges of "maladministration" on the part of yet-to-be-named civic officials.

In the public meeting, Leger refused to name either of the officials, the specific charges or the other petition organizers. But instead of ignoring Leger's bare-bones petition as unfounded, council ordered a city committee be established to look into the matter.

The Journal's journalistic excitement over the prospect of a headline-grabbing witch-hunt at City Hall was tempered.

On Dec. 10, 1958, the paper seemed more reasonable than rabid when it wrote: "For many months rumours of wrongdoing at city hall have been in circulation. The city council now has a duty to find out whether there is any ground for the serious charges that have been made."

By Jan. 16, 1959, the province ordered a judicial inquiry led by Justice Marshall Porter of the Alberta Court of Appeal, into the administration's business dealings.

Over 21 days of testimony between March and May of that year, the commission started hearing names and Hawrelak's was at the top of the list.

In its report Sept. 9, the commission determined Hawrelak had indeed made money off a city land deal.

Other questionable city transactions included participation by Hawrelak's brother-in-law and a handful of city administrators who took kickbacks for performing favours for land speculators.

While criminal-level corruption was not alleged, Hawrelak resigned anyway on the day the report was released and printed verbatim in *The Journal*.

"Although it is my opinion that there is no legal requirement for my resignation, I feel I must resign because the statements made in the report make it impossible for me to do justice to the office of the Mayor of the City of Edmonton," Hawrelak told the city.

Once again, the paper offered a curious response to the events. "The report of the commissioner, Mr. Justice Porter, relating to certain actions of Mr. Hawrelak, was such as to convince the latter that he had no alternative but to resign as mayor, an office he has held with distinction and discharged with energy and great ability for nearly eight years."

To Hawrelak, the unfavourable commission report was a setback, not an obituary. He put his name forward as mayor for the 1963 election.

The Journal endorsed political newcomer Stanley Milner in its pre-election editorial Oct. 12. No mention was made of Hawrelak.

The voters, however, had their own ideas, and gave him 53,340 votes to Milner's 44,950.

In the obligatory post-election editorial, *The Journal* reservedly wished Hawrelak well, making only an oblique reference to the 1959 scandal. "In a democracy the majority rules and everyone will now expect that Mr. Hawrelak will live up to the letter and spirit of his campaign promises of efficiency and integrity."

A year later, Hawrelak faced another election. Mayors had been elected for two-year terms since 1947, but as the result of a 1962 plebiscite the whole council faced election every two years.

In its pre-election editorial, Oct. 6, 1964, the paper conceded

***Nov. 2, 1955*:**
Pupils begin attending classes at Alberta's School for the Deaf.

***Nov. 19, 1955*:**
Groat Bridge, the first bridge over the North Saskatchewan River in the city's west end, opens.

***Nov. 26, 1955*:**
The Edmonton Eskimos defeat the Montreal Alouettes 34-19 to become the first western team to win two consecutive Canadian football championships. *The Journal* publishes a special eight-page Grey Cup edition distributed free of charge at newsstands that evening.

***Jan. 6, 1956*:**
***The Journal* begins including *Weekend* as a Saturday full-colour magazine feature with the paper. An ad taker at the paper makes $230 a month.**

***Jan. 26, 1956*:**
Strathcona Composite high school opens.

***Feb. 25, 1956*:**
University of Alberta's Wilfred Watson and Red Deer nature writer Kerry Wood win Governor General's Awards for literature in poetry and juvenile writing.

THE EDMONTON JOURNAL, WDNESDAY, SEPTEMBER 1, 1954 — PAGE THIRTEEN

Your SAFEWAY suggests

A Backyard Picnic

for a carefree and easy Labor Day

No heavy road-traffic in this picture! Just backyard comfort and perfect picnic foods from Safeway. Plan *your* picnic today...plan it around these appetizing and money-saving values. You'll find everything you need—from pickles to watermelons. Work-saving items, too—like paper plates, napkins, forks. And, *of course*, wonderful meats for barbecuing!

Hot Dog Buns Fresh, delicious .... 12's pkg. **27c**

Sandwich Bread Skylark. Sliced .... 20 oz. loaf **17c**

Beans with Pork Taste Tells. In tangy tomato sauce. 15 oz. .... 3 tins **35c**

Blended Juice Blend O'Gold Fancy .... 48 oz. tin **34c**

Peanut Butter Beverly Homogenized. Tastes like fresh roasted peanuts. .. 24 oz. jar **53c**

Salad Dressing Cascade. Smooth delicious .... 16 oz jar **39c**

Picnic Suggestions

"A" Large Eggs — Breakfast Gems. In cartons ... doz.	57c	Paper Plates — Lily colored or white ... pkg.	19c
Strawberry Jam — Empress Pure. New 1954 Pack . 4 lb. tin	1.09	Paper Napkins — Nook Nap White ... 70's pkg.	18c
Boneless Chicken — Chicken Licken .. 7 oz. tin	49c	Wax Paper — Hand-E-Wrap. Refill ... 100 ft. roll	27c
Hot Dog Relish — Heinz ..... 12 oz. jar	41c	Orange Base — Real Gold. Make one quart ... 6 oz. tin	21c
Prepared Mustard — Libby's . 6 oz. jar	12c	Sandwich Spread — Kraft's Miracle . 8 oz. jar	30c
Ripe Olives — Ebony Brand. Standard size ... 1's tin	30c	Fruit Cocktail — Libby's Fancy ... 15 oz. tin	27c
Potato Chips — Hunter's ..... large pkg.	23c	Cheez Whiz — Kraft's ... 16 oz. jar	66c
Marshmallows — Lowney's Angelus. Plain or colored .... 16 oz. pkg.	41c	Paper Cups — Lily. Hot drinking. 5's ..... pkg.	13c

Thursday Night Family Shopping

For the convenience of our customers all Safeway stores in Edmonton will remain open until 9:00 o'clock every Thursday evening.

Safeway will remain closed Labor Day. Monday, September 6th. Please shop early and avoid the rush.

Breakfast Foods

Rolled Oats — Quaker. Non Premium ... 3 lb. pkg.	33c
Sunny Boy Cereal ..... 4 lb. pkg.	44c
Corn Flakes — Kellogg's ..... 12 oz. pkg.	23c
Rice Flakes — Nabisco ... 9 oz. pkg.	28c

Canning & Pickling Needs

Gem Fruit Jars — Medium size (Reputed quarts) ... 12's case	1.79
Gem Rubber Rings — 12's .. 2 pkgs.	19c
White Sugar — Alberta Granulated .. 10 lb. pkg.	1.05
White Vinegar — Heinz ..... gal. jug	1.19

Coffee — Tea

Nob Hill Coffee — Rich, aromatic. Fresh ground when purchased .. 1 lb. pkg.	1.25
Airway Coffee — Mild and mellow. Fresh ground when purchased ... 1 lb. pkg.	1.23
Instant Coffee — Edwards. 100% Pure ... 2 oz. jar	79c
Tea Bags — Canterbury. Finest Orange Pekoe Quality ... 60's pkg.	70c
Canterbury Tea — Fragrant, full bodied flavor ..... 1 lb. pkg.	92c

Canned Foods

Fancy Peas — Sugar Belle Blended. Sieves 2, 3 and 4 ..... 15 oz. tin	19c
Fancy Corn — Whole Kernel. Vacuum pack. Country Home ... 14 oz. tin	18c
Green Beans — Briargate. Fancy Cut. 15 oz. ... 2 tins	37c
Fancy Peaches — Castle Crest. Halves ... 15 oz. tin	20c
Fruit Cocktail — Dole's Fancy ... 20 oz. tin	34c

Everyday Needs

Frozen Orange Juice — Old South. 6 oz. ... 2 tins	37c
Frozen Peas — Fancy ... 12 oz. mastex bag	25c
Evaporated Milk — Cherub. 16 oz. ... 2 tins	33c
Kitchen Craft Flour — 10 lb. pkg.	67c

PILLSBURY CAKE MIXES

Redeem your Pillsbury 8c coupons at Safeway.

White Cake Mix — Pillsbury ... with coupon pkg. only **29c**

Chocolate Cake Mix — Pillsbury ... with coupon pkg. only **29c**

EDWARDS COFFEE

EDWARDS
COFFEE
REGULAR GRIND

A blend of the world's richest coffees. Vacuum packed . . . yet costs no more than other quality coffees packed in paper bags. Regular or drip grind, 1 lb. tin **1.29**

SANDWICH IDEA

Delicious Empress Strawberry Jam on fresh Skylark White Bread.

Skylark White Bread — 20 oz. loaf ... **17¢**

Strawberry Jam EMPRESS — 2 lb. tin ... **59¢**

Soaps—Cleaners

Rinso Detergent — Redeem your 15c coupon at Safeway ... With coupon lge. pkg. only	26c
Surf — Redeem your 10c coupon at Safeway ... With coupon lge. pkg. only	31c
Lux Soap Deal — Regular size ..... 3 bars	25c
Javex — Special offer . 32 oz. bottle	21c
Old Dutch Cleanser — tin	14c

Juicy-ripe *Fresh Peaches*

Beautiful, luscious 3V peaches. Wonderful flavor for canning. Get enough for tasty desserts, with cream or ice cream, for peach shortcake .... 17 lb. lug **2.55**

Bartlett Pears B.C. 80's and larger. For canning and tempting desserts ..... Junior Box **2.55**

Malaga Grapes Crisp and sweet .... lb. **17c**

Seedless Grapes Thompson. Crisp and sweet .. lb. **18c**

Peach Plums B.C. Plump and sweet .... lb. **12c**

Bananas Golden ripe. Delicious .... lb. **22c**

Apricots B.C. .... 14 lb. lug **2.59**

Tomatoes California Field. Red ripe .... 14 oz. ctn. **21c**

Cucumbers — B.C. Field. For pickling or slicing ..... 17 lb. case	1.79	Sunkist Oranges — Sweet and juicy .... lb.	17c
Celery Hearts — Crisp and tender .... lb.	18c	Wealthy Apples — For delicious pies or sauce ..... lb.	12c
Corn On Cub — Sweet, milky kernels .... lb.	10c	Crabapples — Transcendents . 2 lbs.	19c

Plump, juicy *Frankfurters*

Serve these picnic favorites over the long weekend . . . fresh, delicious hot dogs. Swift's .... 1 lb. cello pkg. **37c**

Boneless Loin Roasts Or chops, Pork .... lb. **65c**

Standing Rib Roasts Red or Blue Brand Beef. Well trimmed .... lb. **67c**

Round Steak or Roasts Red or Blue Brand Beef .... lb. **71c**

Fully Cooked Hams Swift's Ready-to-Serve .... lb. **65c**

Midget Cottage Rolls Gainers, Ready-to-serve .... lb. **72c**

Boneless Veal Roasts Swift's Boned and rolled .... lb. **45c**

Red or Blue Brand Beef

Shoulder Roasts — Chuck, Round Bone and Blade Rib ..... lb.	45c
Boneless Pot Roasts — Boned and Rolled. Plate or brisket ..... lb.	45c
Short Ribs — For braising ..... lb.	29c

Veal

Fillet Roasts ..... lb.	67c
Shoulder Roasts ..... lb.	39c
Breast And Neck — For stewing lb.	21c

Safeway Guaranteed Meats

Ground Beef — Extra Lean. Freshly ground ..... lb.	41c
Cooked Picnics — Swift's Ready-to-serve ..... lb.	47c
Cottage Rolls — Boneless. In visking casing. Half or whole ..... lb.	65c
Side Bacon — By the piece. Swift Oriole. End cuts ..... lb.	61c
Pork Shoulder Roasts — Well trimmed Montreal style ..... lb.	38c
Lamb Legs — Half or whole ..... lb.	75c
Pickle & Pimento Loaf — Swift's ..... 6 oz. pkg.	21c
Bologna — Sliced or by the piece ..... lb.	25c

Roasting Chicken	Frying Chicken	Boiling Fowl
Grade A. 3½ to 4½ lbs. (Equivalent to chicken with head and feet on at 41c lb.) lb. 46c	Swift's Tendergrown. Cut up. On tray. Pan ready. lb. 73c	Grade A. 3½ lbs. and under. (Equivalent to fowl with head and feet on at 26c lb.). lb. 29c

We reserve the right to limit quantities. Prices effective September 2, 3 and 4.

SAFEWAY

CANADA SAFEWAY LIMITED

Hawrelak had behaved himself, but noted, "In the manner of politicians, Mr. Hawrelak during the current campaign has claimed considerably more credit than is due him." *The Journal* backed businessman George Prudham as a "team builder."

Voters again disagreed with *The Journal's* political assessment and gave Hawrelak 60.1 per cent of the vote on Oct. 14. The next day, the paper once again put on a brave face. "It is not often that one man is given such repeated opportunity to serve his city."

But two months later, the mayor once again felt the ground shaking. A company in which Hawrelak owned 40 per cent of the stock, Sun-Alta Builders Ltd., had done $9,350 worth of business with the city.

Three months later, Chief Justice C.C. McLaurin declared Hawrelak disqualified as mayor for conflict of interest. Ald. Vincent Dantzer sat in the mayor's chair for the rest of the term.

Bent but unbroken, Hawrelak gave it another shot in the October 1966 election, facing Dantzer who, by all accounts, did an efficient job for the 18 months he pinch-hit as mayor.

The Journal endorsed Dantzer and this time it was entitled to go to the victory party. Dantzer got 64,233 votes to Hawrelak's 54,544. Sixty per cent of the city's eligible voters turned out. The headline, Oct. 20, proclaimed "The Answer Is Dantzer."

An election-day story by *Journal* reporter Lynne Cove talked about the "end of an era" and quoted Hawrelak as saying he won't run again for mayor.

And he didn't. At least not until Oct. 17, 1974, when he played the political phoenix once again and won the hearts and votes of 67,741 Edmontonians, defeating his nearest rival, Cec Purves, by 35,000 votes.

Reporter Steve Hume wrote: "It was clear Wednesday that the past had little impact on the outcome of Mr. Hawrelak's fierce grassroots campaign.

"He shattered his opposition at the polls and later played conquering hero at a victory celebration worthy of Caesar."

A higher authority than any removed Hawrelak from office for a third time only 13 months later. This time, it was for keeps. He died Nov. 7, 1975, of a massive heart attack.

In an editorial that day, *The Journal* seemed to gain some insight into the perennial question that lingers even today: "Why would anyone keep voting for him?"

"Public figures are, in the final analysis, judged by the people and the people of this city judged Bill Hawrelak as their leader and friend."

***April 19, 1956*:**
Goalie Glenn Hall from Spruce Grove is named the NHL's rookie of the year.

***May 7, 1956*:**
Civic census population is 223,549 in the city proper, and 245,599 in greater Edmonton including Jasper Place, Beverly and military base housing.

***May 10, 1956*:**
Edmonton's new $450,000 All Saints Anglican Cathedral is dedicated.

***Sept. 4, 1956*:**
"Rudy H. Wiebe of Coaldale, Alta., has won top honours in a national short story contest sponsored by the National Federation of Canadian University Students."
The University of Alberta grad would go on to win two Governor General's Awards as well as the Order of Canada.

***Sept. 27, 1956*:**
The cornerstone is laid for *The Journal's* new press building at the corner of 102nd Street and Macdonald Drive, across the alley from the existing building.

***Oct. 4, 1956*:**
Mel Hurtig opens his bookstore at 10116 103rd St.

Back home after a 3½-month hockey tour of Europe, Edmonton's world champion Mercurys received a tumultuous reception at the city airport when they arrived by plane shortly before 11:00 a.m. Thursday. Left to right: Ab Newsome rejoins his wife and daughter who waited anxiously amid the huge airport crowd for his return; receiving a champion's welcome on the airport runway is Bob Watt, greeted by a friend; another warm reception awaited Netminder Jack Manson, once again with his wife, Joan, after his long cross-Atlantic jaunt; Wilbert Delaney is greeted by his sister, Jean Christie and her daughter, his wife and mother, and his two children, Lynn, five, and Jimmy, two. Bad weather delayed the champions' return by almost an hour.

Edmonton Weather

Forecast: Cloudy, continuing cold Friday. Estimated low tonight 5 above, high tomorrow 20 above.

The Edmonton Journal

'One of Canada's Great Newspapers'

FORTY-SEVENTH YEAR * * TELEPHONE 25171 EDMONTON, ALBERTA, THURSDAY, APRIL 6, 1950 SINGLE COPY, 5 CENTS 38 PAGES

60,000 Welcome Champion Mercurys

Session Ends After Passing Of 84 Bills

Alberta legislature prorogued at 8:13 p.m. Wednesday, 30 working days after the 57 members from all parts of the province gathered to consider some of the most important legislation in many years.

Hon. J. J. Bowlen, lieutenant-governor, entered the assembly shortly after 8:00 p.m., accompanied by Premier Manning and other government officials, and gave royal assent to 62 bills which had been given third reading at the Wednesday session.

Altogether 84 bills went through the legislature during the session, and 22 of these had been given royal assent previously. It was the first time Lieutenant-Governor Bowlen had performed his official duty of proroguing the house. He took office in February.

The official prorogation came after Hon. Peter Dawson, Speaker and member from Little Bow, had read the bills given third reading.

During the third session of the 11th Alberta legislature which opened Feb 23, Premier Manning announced a record budget of $74,676,781. The premier, for the first time since he took office, announced the province had budgeted for a surplus. The surplus set by the province was $2,000,000.

Lively Debate

Wednesday afternoon the members entered into their most lively debates of the session. These occurred during the third readings of the bill to incorporate the Northern Alberta Jockey Club and the one dealing with establishment of county system. The County Act

(Continued on Page 2, Col 3)

ESCAPE IS COSTLY

PENTICTON, B.C., (CP) — Lorne Lee Ames, 20-year-old ranch hand, traded two days' freedom from Penticton jail for six months' hard labor when he appeared in police court Wednesday. He was convicted of escaping Monday from Penticton jail after serving 13 days of a 15-day sentence for theft.

The Weather

(Issued by the Dominion Public Weather Office at Edmonton.)

Fresh northerly winds have brought a return of winter to the western prairies. Temperatures today and Friday will be some 20 to 30 degrees lower than Wednesday's and snow will cover the ground in many regions. The cold air being lifted against the mountains and foothills is giving heavier falls than previously expected in western Alberta. In Saskatchewan and eastern Alberta the snow will be quite light.

Although the temperature trend in most regions will be upward on Friday no marked moderation is expected before Saturday at the earliest.

Estimated low tonight, 5 above.

Estimated high tomorrow, 20 above.

At Edmonton Friday, sun rises 5:58; sets 7:17; Saturday sun rises 5:55; sets 7:19.

Yesterday's maximum, 46 above.

Overnight low, 14 above.

Snowfall, .1 of an inch.

Other Readings

G. Prairie	34	5	Banff	55	31
Fairview	30	2	Penticton	53	41
Penhold	40	20	Jasper	50	17
Lethbridge	54	34	Regina	33	25
Calgary	49	25	Winnipeg	32	22
Vermilion	41	24	Toronto	39	17
Coronat'n	37	24	Ottawa	46	10
Med. Hat	57	34	Montreal	44	17
Saskatoon	42	29	Halifax	50	38
P. Albert	41	26	Snag	24	-11
Victoria	57	31	Whiteh'se	32	2
Vancouver	64	40	Yel'knife	3	-20
Kamloops	65	40	Aklavik	34	11

Hockey Champions Step From Plane At Edmonton's Airport After Long Journey Home

A warm welcome offset cold winds and blowing snow at the airport Thursday as the world champion Mercurys returned home after a 3½-month hockey tour through Europe. The team, happy to have won the coveted championship were happier still to be home with their families and friends. "It's great to be back," said one, as the players stepped from the big T.C.A. airliner which brought them from England, where they won the final game and the championship crown.

Canada To Get German Consulate

DUSSELDORF, (Reuters) — West German consuls for Britain, the United States and France will leave at the end of this month—first of 43 to be sent abroad by the spring of 1951, the West German government announced Thursday. The next consulates will be set up in Canada, Australia, the Benelux countries, Denmark, Norway, Italy, Greece and Turkey. Consular service is the only form of diplomatic representation permitted by the Allies.

Hitch-Hiker Dies After Car Crash

Eugene Planz, of Regina, hitch-hiker, died in University Hospital about 11:15 a.m. Thursday, from severe head injuries suffered in a highway accident in Red Deer at 9:30 p.m. Wednesday.

Planz was injured while a passenger in a car being driven south on the highway by George Roth, well-known Red Deer farmer and councillor for Red Deer municipal district.

Roth and Oscar Beutel, a second hitch-hiker from Regina, escaped with only a shaking up. Roth told police he had reached the top of the north hill in Red Deer when he was momentarily blinded by headlights. His car ran into the rear of a truck driven by Chester Black, 19, of Red Deer.

Protruding from the truck were several planks and one of these pierced the windshield and struck Planz on the head. Planz was taken to Red Deer hospital and attended by Dr. Mack Parsons. Later he was transferred to the University Hospital here by ambulance.

Shortly after his arrival here, Planz underwent a head operation. According to reports, Planz is married, and his widow is believed to be en route to Edmonton.

Dr. M. M. Cantor, provincial chief coroner, says an inquest will be held into the fatality.

6 Children Perish In Fire As Toronto Home Destroyed

TORONTO, (CP)—Six children died in their beds early Thursday when fire blamed on hot coals in a bucket on a back porch roared through a stucco cottage in suburban Scarboro Junction.

Mr. and Mrs. Roy Harding, the parents, who slept on the ground floor, escaped with two other children. The mother carried the youngest child, Harold, three, to safety from his downstairs crib. Paul, 14, jumped from the only upstairs window.

Harding, 43, a coal delivery man, said the fire apparently started in a bucket of red embers he set out in the back porch and forgot to empty. He had cleaned out a stove because it was smoking.

"Just before I fell asleep, I thought I should get up and put the pail of coals outside," he said. "But I didn't do it. I thought there were only a few coals in the pail and, because it was the heavy kind like a lot of people use for garbage, figured everything would be all right."

Plans are under way for a mass funeral for the six victims, Ruth, 16; Davie, 15; John, 13; Tim, 11; Earl, 10; and Edith, eight.

Firemen said they had not ascertained the cause of the blaze which destroyed the house in less than an hour. Eye-witnesses said, "It went up like a torch."

Harding awoke shortly after 1:00 a.m. to find the rear of the house afire. He roused his wife and they tried to awaken the children by shouting while Mrs. Harding struggled through flames to the doorway with the youngest child.

Both parents collapsed as they reached saftey and are under a doctor's care.

Neighbors were forced to stand by helplessly.

One of the first on the scene,

(Continued on Page 18, Col. 4)

Ice Breaks Up At Medicine Hat

MEDICINE HAT, (CP) — The South Saskatchewan River in Medicine Hat shed its wintery coat of ice Wednesday. The break-up was one of the fastest in years and only a small amount of ice was thrown along river banks.

W. E. Hole of Medicine Hat won the $100 first prize in the ice derby sponsored by the Medicine Hat Fish and Game Association. An electric clock timed the break-up at 1.29:45 p.m. M.S.T. Mr. Hole's guess was 6½ minutes earlier.

Predict Easter Will Be Chilly

Snow was falling steadily over central and northern Alberta Thursday. Forecasters said chilly weather is in store for Good Friday and there is no sign of a change over the Easter week-end. Snowfall is expected to stop in Edmonton Thursday night.

Throughout Alberta strong north-northeast winds have been blowing and temperatures overnight ranged from four above at Grouard to 33 above at Medicine Hat. Maximum in Edmonton of 46 Wednesday at 2:15 p.m. dropped off to an overnight low of 14 at 8:30 a.m. Thursday. Estimated high for Thursday is 20 above.

The snow here began at 2:22 a.m. and by 5:30 one-tenth of an inch had fallen. Temperatures were lower and more snow fell in the Peace River district. Fort St. John had 3.1 inches. Fairview two inches and Grande Prairie 1.3 inches. There was a trace of snow at Rocky Mountain House, Penhold and Calgary.

Total Of Refugees Said 60,000,000

GENEVA, (AP)—Paul Ruegger, president of the International Red Cross committee, said Wednesday the world contains more refugees now than at any time in human history. He estimated the world's refugee total exceeds 60,000,000 persons.

100 Brazilians Die In Bridge Collapse

RIO DE JANEIRO, Brazil, (CP)—More than 100 persons were killed when a crowded train early Thursday plunged into the flooded Indian River near Tangua, the Brazilian news agency reported.

The train, loaded with Easter holidayers, was said to have tumbled into the river from a collapsing bridge. Tangua is in Rio de Janeiro state about 100 miles from here.

Earlier reports said 40 persons were killed and 200 injured.

Collapse of a bridge near Rio prevented another train carrying medical aid from reaching the disaster scene.

Two sleepers and one coach fell directly into the turbulent river. Three other coaches telescoped and sagged from the bank into the waters.

Will Prosecute Glass Companies

TORONTO, (CP) — A grand jury decided Thursday there is enough evidence to warrant prosecution of nine Ontario and Quebec glass companies for alleged operation of a price-fixing combine.

The jury made the decision after a study of a report by F. A. McGregor, former combines investigator, Justice Minister Garson announced Feb. 7 the federal government would proceed with prosecution if a grand jury returned true bills of indictment against the nine firms.

Cheering Crowds Line Mile-Long Parade Route

Sixty thousand Edmontonians—the number was anybody's fuess, with estimates ranging from 50,000 to 70,000—made it plain at noon Thursday that the Edmonton Mercurys had arrived home, and more than welcome, with the world's amateur hockey championship.

Disregarding cold, snow, normal business and everything else but cheering the Mercurys, most of Edmonton took two hours off to stage the greatest public homecoming reception this city has known. Lining both sides of the mile-long parade route, as many as 25-persons deep, hilarious Edmontonians were in an unprecedented carnival mood as they whooped, hollered and cheered the returning hockey heroes.

It was one of the greatest parades the city has seen. The Mercurys were just moving out of the parade marshalling point at the C.P.R. station when the front end of the procession reached the reception stand at the Recreation Building a mile away.

Aftermath of the parade was the greatest traffic jam Edmonton has known. It took motorists more than an hour after the parade to untangle the jam of cars on streets and avenues two blocks on each side of Jasper ave., and around 100 st., between Jasper and 103 aves.

Better organization, plus a half-holiday for 20,000 school children, resulted in the Mercurys homecoming overshadowing the reception given the Edmonton Flyers when they brought the Allan Cup here two years earlier. For sheer numbers on the streets, and on roof tops and at windows of buildings along the route, the reception even outdid those first giant

(Continued on Page 18, Col. 1)

Jockey Club Bill Rejected By 26-23 Vote

Bill to incorporate the Northern Alberta Jockey Club was rejected by the Alberta legislature Wednesday. When it came up for third reading 26 members voted against the measure and 23 for it.

The day before, members had voted out one section which would have allowed the proposed club to carry on horse racing.

It had been proposed the club would be incorporated and would conduct a race meet on a new track to be built within or just outside the city limits. The proposed club which named as directors H. P. Milner, George H. Steer, George E. Gleave, Murray Montague, Walter Sprague, John A. McMullen and Lee Williams, had plans to build a clubhouse, grandstand, track and barns to complete its project.

Stiff opposition to the bill was received from the Edmonton Exhibition Association and the city. Both stated that additional racing in the city or close to the city would injure the close relationship existing between the racing association and city businessmen. The Exhibition Association pointed out they had an additional eight days racing franchise available which they had not used because they considered it would

(Continued on Page 13, Col. 1)

Mercury Parade Has Highlights

A touch of New York came to Edmonton at the McLeod building where employees threw balloons, streamers, and confetti from the front office windows. The effect was spoiled somewhat by the fact that a north wind was blowing and the majority of the streamers skidded south along the building and into the alley.

The balloons provided excitement for the school youngsters who scrambled to grasp them as they floated down. By the time the Mercurys began arriving in twos and threes on the floats, most of the balloons and streamers had been thrown.

* * *

Every wife, mother or girl friend of the champion hockeyists found a little surprise in store when they arrived at the airport. The parade committee had a stack of corsages ready to hand out. There was an extra one too. It was for Mrs. Parsons, wife of Edmonton's mayor.

* * *

One of the proudest and happiest mothers in Edmonton was Mrs. Agnes Macauley whose son, Doug, is the youthful centre forward of the Mercurys' starting line. She was almost lost in the milling crowd but somehow, "my boy Doug" spotted her as he stepped down the ramp from the air-

(Continued on Page 9, Col. 2)

Mercurys Happy To Be Home After Absence From Families

By Johnny Hopkins
(Journal Staff Writer)

Conquest of the world's amateur hockey championship behind them, a jubilant band of Edmonton Mercurys flew home Thursday — uppermost in their minds a happy reunion with their families.

As the hockey club changed aircraft at Calgary and were denied their 55 minute stopover, because of late arrival, I found them quietly but sincerely happy that they had brought honor to Canada and especially to Edmonton.

The enthusiasm which gripped the club when they won the world championship was tempered by something much more personal—they were only minutes away from home. Long minutes to be sure but only a fraction of the time that the trip had taken them away from loved ones.

Several players, adamant in their assertions that they would hang up their skates for good, were grateful that they had been given the chance to end their hockey careers in this manner. Instead of gradually slipping into obscurity as is the fate of so many, they can call it quits while still champions, a privilege denied all but a very few.

The team was one hour late arriving in Calgary and instead of a 55-minute stopover, they just had time to change planes. But nothing could have mattered less.

Once they were in the air again for the last lap of their journey home, they were jubilant. With

(Continued on Page 9, Col. 4)

Journal To Mark Holiday Friday

Good Friday, April 7, will be observed as a holiday by The Journal. Complete coverage of holiday news and sport events will be carried in Saturday's editions.

H-Bomb Research Said Underway

SANTA FE, N.M., (AP) — The Santa Fe New Mexican Wednesday said a high-ranking nuclear physicist has made the first official indication that research on the hydrogen bomb is underway at Los Alamos.

The newspaper quoted Dr. Alvin C. Graves, University of California scientist, as saying he had often thought of United States preparedness in "my work in Los Alamos on the atom and hydrogen bombs."

The statement was attributed to Graves during a public forum at the restricted atomic centre on "Must We Prepare For the Third Great War?"

60 Are Missing As Boat Founders

OPORTO, Portugal, (CP) — Sixty persons were missing Thursday from a crowded ferry boat, reported to have more than 80 on board, which sank in the Douro River Wednesday night after it struck a rock.

Lt.-Col. Moura Bessa, commander of the Oporto police, said that only 20 persons, including the crew of three and the operator of the ferry, were known to be safe.

The ferry was reported to have had its full load of 80 on board, but more passengers may have embarked after it left Oporto.

The ferry left Oporto in the evening packed with people from riverside villages near Oporto, many of whom worked in the city during the day.

Officials ordered a door-to-door search in river villages in an attempt to fix the number of missing.

Where To Find It

Amusements, Theatres 11, 12, 13
Angelo Patri ... 21
Births, Deaths, Marriages ... 26
Bridge ... 33
Canasta ... 13
Church Page ... 26
Comics 14, 27, 28, 29, 30, 31, 33
Crossword Puzzle ... 33
District ... 35
Editorial ... 4
Financial ... 34
Gregory Clark's Packsack ... 13
Know Your Alberta Birds ... 13
Off the Record ... 35
Radio ... 8
Sport ... 14, 15, 16, 17
Sydney Harris Article ... 13
They'll Do It Every Time ... 33
Uncle Ray's Corner ... 33
Want Ads 27, 28, 29, 30, 31, 32
Women's ... 21, 22, 23, 24, 25

Olympic Gold

"Sixty thousand Edmontonians – the number was anybody's guess, with estimates ranging from 50,000 to 70,000 – made it plain at noon Thursday that the Edmonton Mercurys had arrived home, and more than welcome, with the world's amateur hockey championship."
— Front page story, April 6, 1950

When the world hockey champion Waterloo Mercurys arrived back in Edmonton on a cold and snowy Thursday, April 6, 1950, the city did what it always seemed to do whenever there was something to celebrate.

It let 20,000 kids out of school and had a parade downtown.

"Disregarding cold, snow, normal business and everything else but cheering the Mercurys, most of Edmonton took two hours off to stage the greatest public homecoming reception this city has known. Lining both sides of the mile-long parade route, as many as 25 persons deep, hilarious Edmontonians were in an unprecedented carnival mood as they whooped, hollered and cheered the returning hockey heroes," said the page 1 story.

The Mercurys, a team that played in the intermediate league, were often overlooked in a city where the minor league Flyers and the junior Oil Kings drew good crowds.

But on that day in 1950, everyone knew the Mercurys. Jack Manson, Doug Macauley, Wilbert Delaney, Jim Graham, Al Purvis, Lee Lucchini, Jim Kilburn, Jack Davies, Marsh Darling, Harry Allen, Harrison Young, Billy Dawe, Peter Wright, Ab Newsome, Don Gauf, Bob Watt, Rob Davie and Don Stanley all became part of Edmonton's rich sporting history.

It really had been no contest. In the round robin leading up to the final, they allowed only two goals against. In one memorable game against Belgium, the score was 33-0, with every Mercury getting his name on the scoring summary. The Mercurys defeated Sweden 3-1 in the final.

Jim Christiansen, sports enthusiast and the owner of the sponsoring car dealership, was "puffed with pride," *The Journal* reported. "There's just one word – wonderful – to express our feelings."

The Mercurys did it all again two years later at the Olympic Games in Oslo; however, coverage of the gold medal triumph was strangely muted.

Reporting on the Flyers and Oil Kings often overshadowed coverage of the games in which the Mercurys played. Many of the Olympic stories were less than a half-dozen paragraphs and the gold medal game ran on the second sports page. In fact, the main headline trumpeted the fact that the Oil Kings had taken over second place.

No *Journal* columnist commented that day on the win, and the paper's next-day editorial was oddly subdued, combining congratulations to the Mercurys along with a celebration of Edmonton's Doreen McLeod's tie with Detroit's Barbara Marchettie for the North American senior speed skating title.

It would be 50 years before Canada won its next Olympic gold medal.

***Nov. 6, 1956*:**
New federal census figures rank Edmonton as Canada's sixth largest city, passing Ottawa and Quebec to rise from eighth on the list.

***Nov. 24, 1956*:**
The Edmonton Eskimos win their third consecutive Grey Cup, defeating the Montreal Alouettes 50-27.

***Dec. 10, 1956*:**
Saskatoon becomes the first Prairie city to use the "drunkometer." Scientists had discovered a direct correlation between booze breath and blood booze.

***In 1957*:**
A *Journal* proofreader earns $55 a week ($388.16 today).

***Feb. 10, 1957*:**
The first motorists to drive from Fort McMurray to Edmonton begin their 18-hour expedition.

***March 8, 1957*:**
Matt Baldwin of Edmonton goes undefeated as he wins his second Brier title.

***March 19, 1957*:**
The public gets its first look at the inside of Edmonton's new City Hall.

***April 28, 1957*:**
Edmonton's Jubilee Auditorium officially opens.

SATURDAY VALUES AT WOODWARD'S

DAY - LONG DENIMS

FOR AFTERNOON OR SPORTSWEAR

Denim is vying for a top place in the fashion world this season . . . with the most delectable styles you've seen. Denim pops up in the crispest dresses for afternoon . . . or for the sunniest sportswear styles ever!

DENIM DRESSES

Denim goes highbrow . . . steps out of overalls . . . and takes the limelight in smartly styled dresses . . . some even have their own stole.

- Plain shades of brown, blue and grey.
- Novelty striped patterns.
- Sizes 11 to 15 and 14 to 16.

AT WOODWARD'S, each **$13.95**

Ready-to-Wear, Second Floor

FADED BLUE DENIMS

Slick denims in a dashing collection of match-mates for your sportswear wardrobe. Each item is spiced with sporty details . . . styled with a flare for comfort and smartness. Rough-n-tough denim . . . the fabric that wears and wears . . . and washes so well. Sizes 12 to 20. Check these. AT WOODWARD'S.

ZIPPER CLUB JACKETS, each,	PEDAL PUSHERS each,	JAC-SHIRTS each,	SKIRTS, each
$5.95	$3.50	$4.95	$5.95

Sportswear, Second Floor

LADIES' SLACKS

Sleekly Tailored of "Tyconda"

The fit is most important to have slacks looking trim and neat . . . so hie to Woodward's where there are styles for the petite miss . . . and the Tall Gal!

- Distinctively made from "Tyconda" a nylon blend.
- Belted models with pleats and side zipper closure.
- Sizes 12 to 20.

AT WOODWARD'S, pair **$8.95**

Sportswear, Second Floor

LADIES' CORDUROY JAC-SHIRTS

A soft touch for your casual wardrobe . . . bright corduroys for clever combining with your skirts and pedal pushers. You'll love the way this corduroy whisks through the suds and needs nary a touch of the iron.

- Three-quarter length sleeves and zipper front.
- Colors of red, yellow, rust, wine, mauve and green.
- Sizes 12 to 20.

AT WOODWARD'S, each **$8.95**

Sportswear, Second Floor

WOODSONIA CASUALS

Gay playshoes that forecast a bright summer . . . are here again in many delightful styles and colors. For a real treat . . . step into a pair of cool, light, comfortable Woodsonia casuals from Woodward's.

- Medium or low wedge heels with Elk uppers
- Cross straps . . . halter straps . . . sabot straps.
- Black, blue, natural, beige, grey, green, red and white.
- Sizes 4 to 10 in widths AA and B.

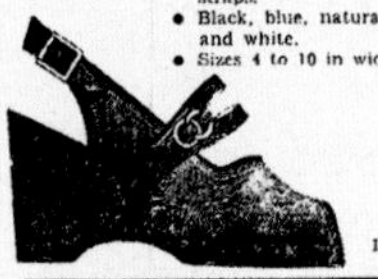

AT WOODWARD'S **$5.95** pair

Ladies' Footwear, Main Floor

MEN'S FINE FOOTWEAR

Better grade footwear that offers the best in styling . . . with attention to careful workmanship and fine leathers. Choose a new pair now . . . step into Spring with your best foot forward.

- Black, brown or oxblood colors
- Brogue, moccasin toe and toe cap styles.
- Choice of leather or Neolite soles.
- One-strap, gore, loafer and lace styles.
- Sizes 6 to 11.

AT WOODWARD'S, pair **$9.95, $10.95** and **$12.95**

Men's Footwear, Main Floor

Special Purchase

Men's Gabardine

TRENCH COATS

Come in Saturday . . . choose your trench coat now . . . be ready for Spring weather. Check the low price . . . check these features:

- Medium weight rayon gabardine.
- Trench coat style with gun patch and all around belt.
- Fully lined with rayon satin.
- Wind and water repellent.
- Colors of grey, taupe, blue.
- Sizes 34 to 46 . . . regular, tall and short fittings.

WOODWARD SPECIAL, Each **$19.95**

Men's Clothing, Main Floor

VEST-O-JAC SPORTS SHIRTS by "Philmac"

These set the record for casual comfort . . . and smart good looks! Novel styling that men will like.

- Check cord front with gabardine back.
- Neat-fitting knit-grip waist.
- One breast pocket.
- Two-button neck, sports collar.
- Colors of red, navy, brown and green.
- Sizes small, medium and large.

AT WOODWARD'S, each **$8.95**

MEN'S TEE SHIRTS

- Fine quality cotton with crew neck.
- Fancy self pattern.
- Short sleeves and breast pocket.
- Colors of blue, yellow, grey and white.
- Sizes small, medium and large.

AT WOODWARD'S, each **$2.95**

MEN'S "MUNSINGWEAR" SHORTS AND VESTS

- Nationally advertised . . . fine combed cotton.
- High resilient quality . . . will not stretch out of shape.
- New comfortable support, elastic waistband.
- Athletic style vest without sleeves.
- Shorts sizes 30 to 42, vests in sizes small, medium and large.

AT WOODWARD'S, each **$1.00**

Men's Furnishings, Main Floor

FOR A COMPLETE SELECTION OF *Rubber Footwear* FOR ALL THE FAMILY VISIT *Woodward's*

LADIES AND CHILDREN'S SHOE DEPT — MENS AND BOYS SHOE DEPT

JUNIOR BOYS' BLAZERS

- All wool flannel blazers in single breasted style.
- Two button front, white braid trim and two patch pockets.
- Colors of wine, green and navy.
- Sizes 2 to 6X.

WOODWARD SPECIAL, Each **$2.69**

JUNIOR BOYS' FLANNELS

- Heavy all wool flannel slacks to wear with his blazer.
- All around shirred elastic waist.
- Zipper closure.
- Grey only in sizes 4 to 6X.

WOODWARD SPECIAL, Pair **$2.69**

BOYS' SEERSUCKER SPORT SHIRTS

- Long sleeve style with one heart pocket.
- Washable . . . requires no ironing.
- May be worn in or out of trousers.
- Assorted shades and patterns.
- Sizes 6 to 14 years.

WOODWARD SPECIAL, Each **$1.79**

BOYS' PANTS

- SPECIAL PURCHASE! 500 pairs of trousers.
- Assorted materials and styles in the group.
- Made with belt loops, suspender buttons and zipper closure.
- Various shades in sizes 6 to 14 years.

WOODWARD SPECIAL, Pair **$3.99**

Boys' Wear, Third Floor

Attention **KNOT-HOLE GANG MEMBERS!**

ATTEND THE RALLY

At The Capitol Theatre

Saturday, April 11th at 10:00 a.m.

- Special Films.
- Talks By Your Favorite Athletes.

ADMISSION BY MEMBERSHIP ONLY

TAILORED CLOTHING

For Lads . . . Just Like Dad's

Sure 'nuff fellas . . . you'll look mighty sharp in a new outfit from Woodward's. Here are all the latest styles designed with a fellow's outlook and tailored with an eye to lasting wear . . . tailored along grown-up lines "just like Dad's."

Plan a visit soon to the

Woodward's Boys' Wear Department, 3rd Floor

Your Knot-Hole Gang Headquarters

BOYS' FROM 6 to 60 . . . CHOOSE

MECCANO

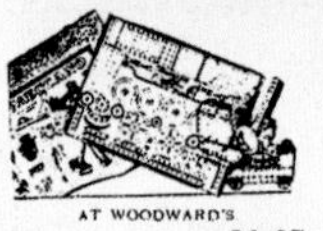

Fun for young and old alike . . . so visit the Toy department tomorrow . . . and see our large selection of Meccano Sets.

AT WOODWARD'S — MECCANO OUTFIT

No. 0	$1.65	No. 4	$6.95
No. 1	$2.50	No. 5	$9.50
No. 2	$3.50	No. 6	$12.25
No. 3	$4.95	No. 7	$18.00

To Complete Your Sets . . . we Carry A Large Supply of Accessory Outfits . . . and Be Sure to See the Assortment of DINKY TOYS.

GOOD NEWS FOR THE

YOUNG RAILROADER!

Woodward's has an American Flyer Section where you'll find a complete line of tracks, bulbs, smoke tablets and other accessories.

AMERICAN FLYER FREIGHT SETS, each **$22.25** and **$31.50**

Toys, Fourth Floor

WHEEL GOODS EVENT CONTINUES SATURDAY

BEAUTY BARROW

The Streamlined Wheelbarrow

- Well constructed, lightweight barrow designed with many uses around the yard.
- Tubular steel frame with beautifully enamelled tray.
- Puncture-proof tire that will not mar the lawn.
- Rubber hand grips.

AT WOODWARD'S, each **$17.95**

With each purchase you receive a toy wheelbarrow.

PHONE AND MAIL ORDERS PROMPTLY FILLED

Hardware, Fourth Floor

Store Hours 9:30 a.m. to 6:00 p.m.
Telephone 913 — 101 St. - 102 Ave.

Woodward's ALBERTA'S FOREMOST FOOD FLOOR

Selling Saturday, April 11th.
Mail Orders Accepted April 11th to April 18th
WE RESERVE THE RIGHT TO LIMIT QUANTITIES

PRIZE WINNING SHOW BEEF

Purchased by Woodward's
At Edmonton's Futurity Calf Show
Now on Sale at Regular Prices

- **Rump Roast** Lean. Tender. Lb. — **65c**
- **Prime Rib Roll** (Boneless.) Lb. — **67c**
- **Boneless Pot Roast** Lb. — **57c**
- **Minced Beef** Lb. — **35c**

- SAUSAGE—Breakfast Style — 2 lbs. 45¢
- PORK ROAST—Shoulder, lb. — 39¢
- LOIN OF PORK—As cut, lb. — 49¢
- FOWL—For casserole Grade "A", lb. — 49¢
- CHICKEN—Young, tender Grade "B", lb. — 49¢

Meat Dept., Lower Main Floor

WOODWARD'S GROCETERIA VALUES

- **Sweet Mixed Pickles** Libby's, 16 oz. jar — **40c**
- **Dill Pickles** Raymore, 24 oz. jar — **48c**
- **Invincible Olives** Stuffed Manzanilla, McLarens. 6 oz. ice box jar — **38c**; 8 oz. ice box jar — **49c**

- FANCY PEACHES—Aylmer Sliced. 15 oz. tin — 24¢
- FRUIT COCKTAIL—Dole. Serve as a dessert or in salads. 20 oz. tin — 32¢
- SALAD DRESSING—Wonder Whip, Marrs. 16 oz. jar — 45¢; 32 oz. jar — 72c
- JELLY POWDERS—Nabob. 7 delicious flavors, pkg. — 3 for 25c
- MARMALADE — Shirriff's. Good Morning. Start the day right. 12 oz. jar — 31c; 24 oz. jar — 53c
- ALTA SWEET HONEY—1 lb. mono cup — 25c
- CORN SYRUP—Karo, 2 lb. tin — 36c; 5 lb. tin — 86c
- FROSTEE DESSERT MIXES—Lipton's, Vanilla or Chocolate, pkg. — 2 for 29c
- SUNDAE OR ICE CREAM TOPPINGS—Stafford's, Caramel, Butterscotch, marshmallow or chocolate, 6 oz. tin — 2 for 29¢
- EVAPORATED MILK—Pacific, talls — 2 for 33¢
- MEXICORN—Niblets, 14 oz. tin — 21¢
- PORK AND BEANS—Clark's, in Chili sauce, 15 oz. tin — 2 for 37¢
- TEA BISK—A prepared baking mix. Directions on box. 2½ lb. box — 49¢
- SAUERKRAUT—Libby's. Fancy quality, 15 oz. tin — 15¢
- WOODWARD'S, NO. 4 PEAS—Fancy, 15 oz. tin — 21¢
- GRAPENUTS FLAKES—Post's, small pkg. — 16¢; Large pkg. — 23¢
- SCOTCH BROTH SOUP— Campbell's, 10 oz. tin — 2 for 37¢
- TOMATO SOUP—Aylmer, 10 oz. tin — 3 for 29¢
- TOILET TISSUE—Perkin's. Colored. Downy-soft — 2 rolls 29¢
- HEAVY WAXED PAPER—Woodward's. Refill roll, 100' — 28¢

Groceteria, Lower Main Floor

WOODWARD'S FINEST PROVISIONS

- **Woodward's Rindless Sliced Side Bacon** Mild cure. All centre slices. 1 lb. pkg. — **75c**
- **Woodward's Fresh Eggs "A" Large** 1 doz. Carton — **54c**
- **Woodward's Creamery Butter** First Grade. Lb. — **64c**
- **Woodward's Supreme Margarine** The Tasty Spread for any bread. Lb. — **35c**

- MILD CHEDDAR CHEESE—Lb. — 47c
- OLD ONTARIO CHEESE—Lb. — 65c
- GORGONZOLA CHEESE—Lb. — $1.50
- DANISH BLUE CHEESE—Lb. — 89c
- CLOVER VALLEY HI-LOW CHEESE 2 lb. loaf. High in food value—low in calories — 99¢
- KRAFT IMPERIAL CHEESE—¼ lb. tub — 42c; 1 lb. tub — 75¢
- KRAFT VELVEETA CHEESE—½ lb. pkg. — 33¢
- SMOKED HAM—Mild, sugar cure, tender, lb. — 65¢
- Smoked Picnic Shoulders, lb. — 37¢
- COTTAGE ROLLS—All meat, no waste, lb. — 61¢
- LEAN BONELESS PICNICS—Cooked, ready to serve, Pineapple decorated, easy to slice, lb. — 69¢

Provisions, Lower Main Floor

FRUITS & VEGETABLES

BUNCH CARROTS
California Sweet, crisp.
3 bunches 29c

LETTUCE
California large crisp green heads. Each — 15c

TOMATOES
Mexican Field. Firm ripe. In 14 oz. cartons
2 for 49c

Vegetables Selling Saturday, Lower Main Floor

PASTRY

Weekly Feature!

BURNT SUGAR LAYER CAKE
45¢, 59¢ each.

- MAPLE ICED DO-NUTS—Dozen — 45¢
- ICED ANGEL FOOD CAKE—Each — 39¢
- CHERRY TARTS TOPPED WITH WHIPPING CREAM—Each — 6¢
- CRUSTY DINNER ROLLS—Dozen — 25¢

Pastry Counter, Lower Main Floor

CANDY

- COCOANUT MARSHMALLOWS—Pavey's. Fresh-toasted, lb. — 49¢
- ASSORTED FRUIT JELLIES—Pavey's, lb. — 59¢
- SUGARED COATED PEANUTS—Pavey's, lb. — 59¢

Candy, Main Floor

DAFFODILS

- King Alfreds
- Large Yellow Trumpets
- Long Stems

2 dozen 49c

RUSHED BY T.C.A. FROM VANCOUVER

Flowers Selling Saturday, Lower Main Floor

NYLON BLOUSES

It's News for Spring—

Here's a blouse equally sophisticated with suit or skirt. A brand new blouse trend to give a spring fresh lift to a tired winter wardrobe.

- Rows and rows of tucking, back and front, double collar.
- Tailored in 15 denier Nylon Tricot.
- Spring Fresh Shades—white, red, lime, mauve, lemon, purple, pink and aqua.

AT WOODWARD'S, each **$6.95**

Blouses, Second Floor

Only in Westmount

"There's nothing in eastern Canada to compare with this."
— Retailer W.C. Woodward, Aug. 18, 1955

W.C. Woodward could have mouthed no truer words. There was nothing like Westmount Shoppers' Park in Eastern Canada. In fact, there was only one other thing like it in North America, Highland Park Village in Dallas, Texas, built in 1931.

However, *The Journal* didn't seem to realize the significance of the edifice to retailing to the city. It was treated as just another business story.

The first story about an anonymous group of American financiers' proposal to city council made the paper on Oct. 20, 1952. "U.S. financial interests are proposing to construct a $3-million shopping centre in Westmount district between 111 and 114 avenues and 133 and 135 streets."

Council was asked to re-zone six city blocks from agricultural to business. Lanes and streets would have to be closed or moved. The first phase would be 87,000 square feet.

It took council one day to jump at the deal, approving it in principle Oct. 21, and an editorial the next day offered low-key praise to the civic leaders. "This has every appearance of being a business-like proceeding."

One of the attractions of the mall was it would offer some 3,000 free parking spaces.

At the time, the city centre was truly the heart of the city. The Bay, Woodward's and Eaton's dominated the shopping district that was also populated by dozens of smaller shops selling anything from furs to hardware. Downtown was also the entertainment destination for city dwellers who attended the movie houses, restaurants and bars radiating out from Jasper Avenue and 101st Street, and parking was a real problem.

"The persistence of a downtown parking problem in Edmonton is not open to question," said an editorial Aug. 11, 1955. "It is attested by the many motorists who repeatedly have to spend 15 minutes or more circling the block in a vain search for an open spot."

Seven days later, on Aug. 18, Westmount Shoppers' Park opened.

The Journal noted the event on page 7, when thousands of happy shoppers and gawkers filled the free parking lot for the ribbon cutting.

Mayor William Hawrelak praised the U.S. investors for their foresight. "The building of the centre speaks well for their faith in the future of Edmonton."

Also present were W.C. Woodward and Stanley Kresge whose stores would anchor the 40-shop facility.

"Following the ceremony, many stores offered favours and door prizes, ranging from yardsticks and colouring books to flowers. Two clowns beat a drum and passed out nuts outside the Nut House."

It was surely an affair to remember.

The main investor turned out to be Clarence Y. Paylitz, director of the First New Amsterdam Bank.

***May 8, 1956*:**
Civic census puts 238,353 in the city, and more than 262,000 in the greater Edmonton area. The total includes Jasper Place, Beverly and housing at Namao.

***June 15, 1957*:**
"Two recent inquests and a court case touching on accidents in the Edmonton district in which eight persons lost their lives serve to emphasize how great is the menace of the drinking driver on our highways." - editorial.

***June 15, 1957*:**
"Live surgery will be seen by a non-medical audience for the first time in Canada Monday night on special closed-circuit colour television programs originating in the University Hospital. Eight hundred persons will attend two public forums in the banquet room of the Macdonald and witness appendix operations on a 4½ by 6½ foot colour TV screen. Dr. S.S. Parlee said that the programs are designed to demonstrate to the public how they are protected against unnecessary surgery."

***July 2, 1957*:**
The last of the wooden paving blocks that once covered Edmonton

Edmonton Weather
Forecast: Cloudy with Tuesday afternoon bringing snow, colder weather and north winds.

The Edmonton Journal

One Of Canada's Great Newspapers

FIFTY-SECOND YEAR | TELEPHONE 25171 | EDMONTON, ALBERTA, MONDAY, NOVEMBER 29, 1954 | PRICE: NOT OVER 5 CENTS | 42 PAGES

EVERY ESKIMO A HERO

U.S. Studies Retaliation Against Reds

WASHINGTON (AP) — Red China Sunday rejected as "unacceptable" a United States protest against imprisonment of 13 Americans on spy charges. The British government notified the state department of the Red Chinese action.

State department officials, it was learned, already had under consideration further measures for action against Communist China and indications were that a naval blockade is among the possibilities being considered.

Officially informants would say only that "all appropriate measures are being considered."

They said this answer covered inquiries about state department reaction to the suggestion of Senate Leader William Knowland (Rep. Calif.) for a naval blockade. Knowland spoke out at a press conference Saturday.

Privately diplomatic experts saw little evidence of favor for a blockade policy, which they thought would involve new U.S. military commitments in the Far East. The Eisenhower administration has for several months been following a policy of trying to minimize incidents and get peace as widely established as possible in that area.

One of the arguments apparently in favor of a blockade is that it is one of the forcible actions which could be taken by the U.S.

Other possible forceful measures would appear to involve some kind of direct military action such as was considered at the time of the Korean war stalemate, including bombing of Red Chinese military targets, but there has been no suggestion to date that any such course would be considered now as "appropriate measures."

The Chinese regime at Peiping announced last Tuesday that 11 American airmen and two civilian employees of the U.S. Army had been tried on spy charges and sentenced to prison terms.

Friday the state department denounced the charges as "baseless" and demanded release of the 13 forthwith.

Meanwhile, the United States and Nationalist China have substantially agreed on terms of a defence treaty by which Ameri-

(Continued on Page 20, Col. 1)

Scenes Of Joy Centre Around Grey Cup After Big Game

The coveted Grey Cup passed from hand to hand among the victorious Edmonton Eskimos after Saturday's game. In the top picture, Frank "Pop" Ivy, the coach who masterminded the conquerors throughout the season, and Mayor Hawrelak, show the reaction of officialdom to the Eskimos' win. Below, Jackie Parker, who scored the winning touchdown after a thrilling 95-yard dash in the last minutes of the game, is tired and happy as he clasps the prized trophy.

16 Feared Dead In Avalanche

MT. FUJI, Japan (AP) — A two-pronged avalanche swept 38 university students off the slopes of Mt. Fuji Sunday.

At least one of the young mountaineers was killed. Fifteen others are missing and feared lost under the tons of snow. Several of the 22 who escaped were injured.

The avalanche, starting only a short distance below the 12,425 foot crest, split as it roared down the mountainside. One prong caught a party of 14 students climbing up, the other a group of 24 coming down from the peak.

Two Men Die, Third Injured In Camrose Car-Truck Crash

Two men were killed and a third seriously injured in a car-truck collision near Camrose shortly before 1 p.m. Saturday.

DEAD

William P. Bradshaw, 46, of Alhambra.

E. L. Fowler, 62, of Westerose.

INJURED

Kenneth Martin, of Alhambra.

RCMP in Edmonton reported Monday the accident occurred on Highway 13, three miles east of Camrose. The three men were passengers in a car which police state was driven by Lorne Batke, 50, of Edberg.

Hugh Sheets, of Ohaton, the truck driver, was uninjured. Police did not give any details of how the accident happened. Dr. C. H. Smith, of Camrose, stated he had ordered an inquest.

PHILANTHROPIST DIES

CASSILIS, Australia (Reuters) — Sir Frederick Duncan McMaster, 81, prominent Australian philanthropist, died at his Dalkeith sheep ranch here today. He was widely known for his gifts toward scientific research and sheep-breeding.

Where To Find It

Amusements, Theatres	22
Angelo Patri	27
Baby Care	26
Births, Deaths, Marriages	28
Bridge	36
Burgess Bedtime Story	37
Comics	32, 33, 36, 37
Crossword Puzzle	36
District	34
Dorothy Dix	26
Editorial	4
Financial	35
Gallup Poll	40
Gregory Clark's Packsack	36
Off the Record	37
Our Boarding House	30
Out Our Way	30
Radio	9
Sport	10 to 17
Sydney Harris Article	37
There Oughta Be A Law	31
They'll Do It Every Time	29
Uncle Ray's Corner	36
Want Ads	29, 30, 31, 32, 33
Women's	25, 26, 27

The Weather

(Issued by the Dominion Public Weather Office at Edmonton)

As a deepening storm centre in the Gulf of Alaska moves southeastward along the British Columbia coast Tuesday afternoon, cold air will move down the eastern side of the mountains. North winds and snow will mark the advent of this fresh outbreak of winter weather.

Estimated low tonight, 15.

Estimated high tomorrow, 30.

At Edmonton Tuesday, sun rises 8:25; sets 4:19.

Temperatures

Maximum temperatures yesterday and overnight lows are:

Edmonton	16	12	Vermilion	25	13
Fairview	25	12	Saskatoon	29	15
Grande Pr.	31	10	Pr. Albert	21	13
White Ct.	30	22	Pr. Rupert	41	38
Wagner	20	14	Victoria	46	37
McMurray	17	-1	Vancouver	44	26
Penhold	30	18	Penticton	44	30
Rky. Mt. H.	32	24	Kamloops	40	33
Calgary	31	20	Regina	25	16
Lethbridge	38	20	Winnipeg	24	16
Med. Hat	28	15	Ft. William	30	25
Banff	30	16	Toronto	51	39
Jasper	31	23	Ottawa	46	33
Coronation	25	10	Montreal	43	33

Italy Appoints Envoy To Canada

ROME (Reuters) — The Italian government today announced the appointment of new ambassadors to Canada and the United States.

Segio Fenoaltea, attached to the North Atlantic Treaty Organization in Paris, will be the new Italian envoy in Ottawa.

Manlio Brosio, former Italian ambassador to Russia and now ambassador to Britain, will be transferred to Washington.

22
SHOPPING DAYS TILL CHRISTMAS

Head-On Collision Kills Japanese, 70

LETHBRIDGE, (CP)—A head-on collision here Saturday night claimed the life of an elderly Japanese, Togi Kana, 70, of Iron Springs, and sent another man Borroku Majasota, Coaldale, to hospital with serious injuries.

Kana was driver of the car which collided with one driven by Jack Graves. Graves was not injured in the crash.

New Light Thrown On Age Barrier

MIAMI, Fla. (AP)—You have a good chance of living to be 100—if you first hurdle a curious invisible barrier at ages 60 to 75, a medical team reported today.

This barrier is a period in which certain chemical and physical processes of the body begin to re-

(Continued on Page 20, Col. 1)

Block In Chicago Blasted By Bomb

CHICAGO (AP) — A bomb shattered 200 windows and caused damage estimated at $10,000 in a one-block area of the Loop early Sunday.

The bomb was placed near a factory where punch-boards are manufactured but the owners could give no reason for the bombing.

Victory Over Montreal Is Saga Of Courage

BY HAL PAWSON
(Sports Editor, The Journal)

TORONTO — Edmonton Eskimos, "the team that couldn't win," won the Grey Cup, 26-25.

Courage, the will to win, desire, spirit, team effort—these words were given new meaning athletically Saturday in Canada's football classic when the Edmonton Eskimos rose painfully off the scarred turf of Varsity Stadium to defeat the gallant and great Montreal Alouettes by a single point and give the Alberta capital its first Grey Cup. Eskimos inaugurated the east-west play in 1921 but lost out that year and in subsequent trips east.

Jackie Parker, blond, curly-headed Mississippi State halfback who runs like the ambulance case he is but always manages to outrace the ambulance, was the instrument of victory. His knee wrenched, his broken foot throbbing with pain, Parker scooped up Chuck Hunsinger's fumble and out-distanced Sam Etcheverry, Canada's fastest quarterback, 95 yards for the winning touchdown, which was converted by nerveless Bob Dean who hasn't missed once in 51 tries for Edmonton.

But the story was the team, which finished the contest with four men playing with broken bones, another with stove-in ribs, and most with bruises, sprains, cuts and pain. All 27,321 fans at the game cheered these hurt heroes to the echo.

Less than three minutes after that electrifying run the final gun boomed to end the "greatest Grey Cup ever," and launch the greatest post-game celebration Toronto has known in 63 years of Grey Cup play. One thousand Edmonton fans, and at least 2,000 other westerners, owned Toronto. And 4,000 disappointed but gracious Montreal fans stood by to make certain the victors received their share of the spoils, which for the western fans was a night-long jamboree.

The final gun, heard and seen from coast to coast by radio listeners and by 55,000,000 Canadian and American televiewers,

(Continued on Page 23, Col. 2)

Fans' Voices Down To Whisper On Way Home

WINNIPEG (CP) — Edmonton football fans, their voices down to a whisper, are homeward bound today, a mighty happy crew.

They saw their fondest wishes fulfilled. Their Eskimos were returning home with the Grey Cup after a 26-25 victory over Montreal Alouettes in Toronto Saturday.

"Everyone made money," said Thomas Visser, one of the fans who passed through Winnipeg today aboard the CPR special that arrives in Edmonton Tuesday.

Mr. Visser claimed one Edmonton fan, whom he did not identify, made $50,000 in bets. Another made $5,000 and yet another $4,500, he said.

Most fans had partially regained their voices after a week-end of merry-making. Mrs Mamie McNabb, vice-president of the Eskimos' Ladies Quarterback Club, said the Toronto reception was "terrific" and Saturday's game "the most exciting and drama-packed" she had ever seen.

The scene at the CPR station—where fans swirled along the concourse singing and snake-dancing—was duplicated at the CNR station where a second spe-

(Continued on Page 20, Col. 2)

Eskimos Prepare To Fly Home

BY JIM BROOKE
(Sports Writer, Edmonton Journal)

TORONTO — Amid a flood of rumors while still riding the crest of their fabulous Grey Cup triumph over the Montreal Alouettes at Varsity Stadium Saturday, the Edmonton Eskimos football champions of Canada, prepared for tonight's flight home to Edmonton via a TCA chartered aircraft.

The team was scheduled to leave Toronto at midnight and reach Edmonton around 7:00 o'clock Tuesday morning. However, it was possible that the flight departure time might be scheduled a little later so that the team won't arrive in Edmonton at an inconveniently early hour.

Rumors circulating through

(Continued on Page 20, Col. 1)

Russian Protest Is Brushed Aside

WASHINGTON (AP)—The U. S. Monday brushed aside a Russian protest filed nearly four months ago and said U. S. planes will continue to check all ships plying the waters around the Nationalist Chinese stronghold of Formosa.

The state department released the text of a brief note delivered to the Soviet foreign ministry at Moscow in response to a Russian protest of last Aug. 4.

The Soviet note had objected to U. S. aircraft buzzing five Soviet ships, one of them the tanker Tuapse which was seized by the Nationalist Chinese June 23.

The American reply made no gesture of denial. It said, however, that the incidents were neither illegal nor in violation of international law governing freedom of the high seas.

Parade At 2:30 Wednesday To Welcome Victorious Esks

The new football capital of Canada is preparing a tumultuous welcome to the Grey Cup and those "ever lovin' Esks" who are bringing it to Edmonton for the first time.

The waves of joy that followed the Edmonton Eskimos 26-25 triumph against the Montreal Alouettes in Toronto Saturday are expected to hit their peak of enthusiasm when the cup and the team parade through downtown Edmonton Wednesday afternoon in a delayed-action welcome. The TCA North Star will bring the team home at 6 a.m. Tuesday but the players will be given a day's rest.

The Grey Cup, symbolic of Canadian football championship, will be carried through the streets on a fire engine. Twenty-three convertibles will carry members of the team.

The parade, including 500 marching athletes and at least six bands, will start at 116 St. and Jasper Ave. at 2:30 p.m. Wednesday. It will move down Jasper Ave. to 98 St. and then turn north to 103 Ave.

Officials of the civic welcoming committee headed by Arthur Potter, expect stores along the route will be decorated with flags and bunting, to welcome the heroes of the west.

The public and separate school boards declared a half-holiday for Wednesday afternoon so students can attend the parade and

(Continued on Page 20, Col. 2)

Schools To Close For Esks' Parade

Edmonton school children will be given a half-holiday Wednesday, to attend the 2:30 parade of the Grey Cup champion Eskimos, it was announced Monday.

A proclamation urging Edmontonians to give the Eskimos a vociferous welcome Wednesday afternoon and to make merry at a public dance in the evening was issued by Acting Mayor Ald. Roy Monday.

Both the public and separate school boards announced Wednesday afternoon will be a school holiday to permit students to take part in the welcome for the Eskimos. In his proclamation, the acting mayor urged all employers and employees to attend the parade.

All the Eskimo players are expected to appear at the free public dance which is to start at 8:30 p.m. in the Prince of Wales Armories.

Fort Man Killed In Plane Crash

A native of Fort Saskatchewan, FO B. P. Whitson, 37, died Friday in the crash of an RCAF Harvard training plane in a farm field near Broadview, Sask., 100 miles east of Regina. Also killed was FO. J. N. Hultnam, 31, of Vancouver.

An RCAF board of inquiry from Moose Jaw has begun an investigation into the crash, which occurred while the plane was en route from its base at Claresholm to Portage La Prairie, Man., on a training flight.

FO Whitson was flying control officer at the Claresholm station, where his widow and one child, Susan, are living. FO Hultman was an instructor.

Born and educated at Fort Saskatchewan, FO Whitson enlisted in the air force in 1940. Discharged following the war, he rejoined in 1950.

Survivors at Fort Saskatchewan include two brothers, Harry and Arnold, and a sister, Mrs. Harry Stepson. FO Whitson was the son of Mr. and Mrs. Thomas Whitson, both of whom died some time ago.

British Farmers Hard Hit By Storm

LONDON (AP) — The continuing heavy rains flooded roads and fields in 17 counties of England and Wales Monday and in some areas farmers reported disastrous losses of crops.

Coastal towns meanwhile went to work clearing away the debris left by five days of gales which smashed beach huts and boats, knocked holes in sea walls, blew down hundreds of telephone poles and trees and caused at least 10 deaths at sea.

Farmers in many parts of England and Wales were in despair, with their fields so saturated they neither could harvest root, wheat, pea and hay crops nor sow their winter wheat.

More than 20,000 acres of wheat remained uncut and on a still greater acreage wheat which was cut lay rotting in the mud. Tractors and harvesting combines were mired by the hundreds. Hay and wheat losses in Cornwall alone

(Continued on Page 20, Col. 4)

Firm Fined $1,000 On Prices Charge

TORONTO (CP) — Parsons-Steiner Ltd., Toronto chinaware importer, has been fined $1,000 for infractions of resale price maintenance regulations.

The company pleaded guilty to two charges of attempting to induce certain merchants in Ontario and Quebec to resell china and porcelain at prices not less than minimums specified by the company.

Special Pictures, Stories Depict Eskimos' Triumph

Complete coverage of the Grey Cup classic is recorded in The Journal today with three special pages of pictures, other photographic highlights elsewhere in today's editions, and by stories by several writers, including Journal staff men.

Pictures will be found on pages 10, 11 and 12 with stories by Hal Pawson, Journal sports editor; Jim Brooke, Journal football writer; George Mackintosh, former sports editor of The Journal; Jim Coleman, of Toronto, and Fred Parker, brother of Eskimo star Jackie Parker. Other special stories are reported by The Canadian Press.

Everlovin' Esks

"Western football is king. The vanquished legions of the East have limped sullenly back to their lairs to lick the gaping wounds of defeat."
— Sportswriter Jim Brooke after the Edmonton Eskimos defeated the Montreal Alouettes 50-27 in the 1956 Grey Cup game

Throughout its history, Edmonton has been blessed by the best of sports teams. There was the remarkable Grads, the women's basketball team whose victories became so commonplace that fans grew blasé. Then there was the Edmonton Mercurys, a team that won both the world amateur hockey championship and Olympic gold in the '50s. The Oil Kings and Flyers packed the Edmonton Gardens.

However, the football Eskimos of the '50s was the gold standard. The names of the players on those teams from the '50s – Normie Kwong, Johnny Bright, Rollie Miles, Jackie Parker and dozens of others – are woven into the fabric of the city's proud sports history.

The nickname Eskimos had been used for baseball, hockey and football teams throughout Edmonton's history.

The first Eskimo team to vie for the Grey Cup was put together by Deacon White and made its first trip East in a losing cause in 1921. The Eskimos lost to Toronto 23-0.

The name itself, however, was given to Edmonton teams by, gasp, Calgary sportswriters in the late 1800s, when upset that Edmonton scribes dismissed their city as a "cow camp," the Calgary writers struck back by calling Edmonton teams "Esquimaux," in reference to our sometimes awful weather. The name stuck. The spelling didn't.

And on Saturday, Nov. 27, 1954, *Journal* sports editor Hal Pawson had to spell it correctly many times as he filed his stories from Toronto.

The Eskimos had defied the odds and won their first-ever Grey Cup, beating the highly favoured Montreal Alouettes 26-25.

A last-minute fumble – maybe it was a lateral pass gone awry – was snatched off the turf by halfback Jackie Parker who ran 95 yards for a touchdown. Kicker Bob Dean won the game with the single-point convert.

Pawson knew sporting history had been made and did a masterful job talking to dozens of people to get it just right: winners, losers, officials from both the Eskimos and the Alouettes, league executives and fans.

"Courage, the will to win, desire, spirit, team effort – these words were given new meaning athletically Saturday in Canada's football classic when the Edmonton Eskimos rose painfully off the scarred turf of Varsity Stadium to defeat the gallant Montreal Alouettes by a single point and give the Alberta capital its first Grey Cup," Pawson enthused.

"Jackie Parker, blond, curly-headed Mississippi State halfback who runs like the ambulance case he is but always manages to outrace the ambulance, was the instrument of victory. His knee wrenched, his broken foot throbbing with pain, Parker scooped up Chuck Hunsinger's fumble and outdistanced Sam Etcheverry, Canada's fastest quarterback, 95 yards for the winning touchdown.

streets are removed, along with unused street railway tracks along Kingsway.

***Aug. 2, 1957*:**
Soldiers of the first battalion of the Princess Patricia's Canadian Light Infantry move into Edmonton's Griesbach Barracks from their previous post at Calgary.

***Aug. 11, 1957*:**
The Edmonton Eskimos beat the B.C. Lions 9-6 in a Canadian football exhibition game in San Francisco.

***Sept. 30, 1957*:**
The price of a weekly *Journal* carrier-delivered subscription rises five cents, to 35 cents a week.

***Oct. 1, 1957*:**
***The Journal* reports that the University of Alberta gets its first computer.**

***Feb. 10, 1958*:**
Mixed drinking in Edmonton and Calgary beer parlours starts.

***March 7, 1958*:**
Edmonton's Matt Baldwin becomes the second three-time winner of the Brier.

***March 8, 1958*:**
The $6.5-million Federal Building on 109th Street opens.

***March 22, 1858*:**
"Cocktail lounges, liquor in better-

Edmonton Weather
Forecast: Mostly clear, continuing very cold, winds northwest at 10, low tonight, 20 below, high tomorrow, five below.

The Edmonton Journal

One Of Canada's Great Newspapers

FIFTY-THIRD YEAR | TELEPHONE 25171 | EDMONTON, ALBERTA, SATURDAY, NOVEMBER 26, 1955 | PRICE: NOT OVER 10 CENTS | 58 PAGES

Miss Eskimo Wins Grey Cup Contest

U.S. Authorizes Import Of Gas From Canada

BY GEORGE KITCHEN
(Canadian Press Staff Writer)

WASHINGTON (CP) — The Federal Power Commission Friday authorized a U.S. pipeline company to import Canadian natural gas at a rate of approximately 300,000,000 cubic feet daily in a decision which could favorably affect future proposals to bring gas from Canada.

The commission approved plans by Pacific Northwest Pipeline Corporation to import 303,462,000 cubic feet a day at a point on the British Columbia-Washington state border. The gas will be supplied by Westcoast Transmission Company Limited from gas fields in the Peace River area of Alberta and British Columbia.

The proposal also provides for Pacific Northwest Corporation to export 120,000,000 cubic feet a day to the Vancouver area in the fall of 1957. Pacific Northwest will sell the remainder of the Canadian imports to its customers in California and other U.S. west coast markets.

Legal sources said Friday's decision was regarded as important because it confirms the U.S. need for Canadian natural gas supplies and sets a pattern for other proposals to import the Canadian product.

Another U.S. pipeline firm, Tennessee Gas Transmission Company, has an application before the commission to import gas at Emerson, Man., from the projected trans-Canada pipeline. Completion of the trans-Canada line, in which the U.S. firm will participate on a partnership basis, hinges on the Tennessee Company case. Hearings are expected to start after the new year.

Under Friday's decision, Pacific Northwest Corporation also will export back to Canada 12,600,000 cubic feet of gas daily to the Trail area of British Columbia, with a delivery point near Boundary, Wash. This export, primarily for industrial use, will continue for a 20-year period.

In Ottawa Trade Minister Howe said he was delighted to hear the Federal Power Commission's decision.

"Westcoast's construction now will be able to proceed at full speed," he said.

In Vancouver, a statement issued on behalf of Westcoast president Frank M. McMahon said the auth

(Continued on Page 2, Col. 4)

Expect Decision To Spur Drilling

VANCOUVER (CP)—An extensive drilling program in northern Canadian fields was seen by a spokesman Friday as a result of the authority granted a United States pipeline firm to import natural gas from Canada.

The statement was issued here Friday on behalf of Frank M. McMahon, president of Westcoast Transmission Company Limited and chairman of the board of Pacific Petroleums, Ltd. Mr. McMahon is in New York.

"The authorization granted to Pacific Northwest Pipeline Corporation to import 300,000,000 cubic feet a day of gas means the Westcoast Transmission Company will be able to complete its $150,000,000 pipeline through British Columbia by early 1957," the statement said.

"This will be the first major natural gas line in Canada and will mark one of the most important steps in the forward advance of the Canadian oil and natural gas industry."

The statement, issued through Mr. McMahon's office here, said: "Construction of the Westcoast line will mean the immediate start of the most extensive drilling pro-

(Continued on Page 2, Col. 2)

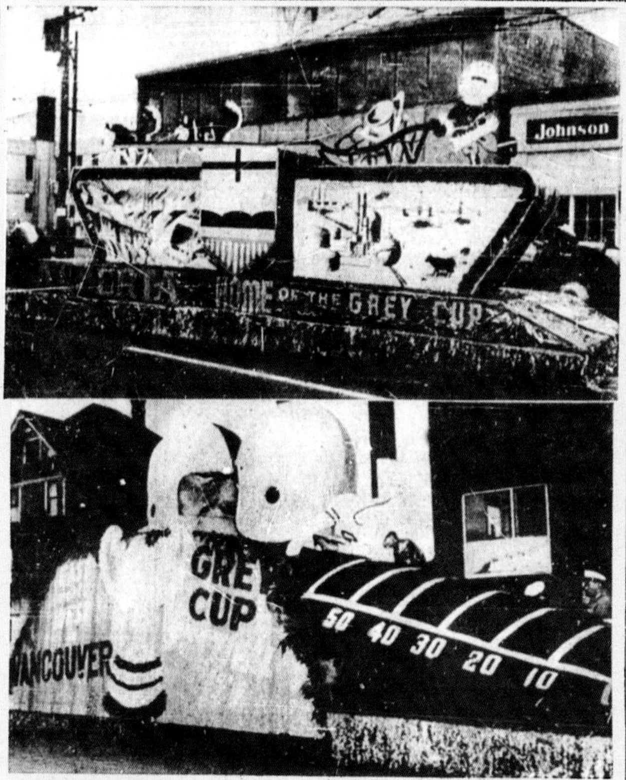
Johnson
HOME OF THE GREY CUP
GREY CUP
VANCOUVER
50 40 30 20 10

GREY CUP PARADE — An estimated 250,000 persons lined 10-deep along Vancouver's streets Saturday, to watch the Grey Cup parade which preceded the game between Edmonton Eskimos and Montreal Alouettes for Canada's football championship. The Alberta float in the big parade is shown at the top, and the Vancouver float is shown below. Streets in the coast city were packed to capacity. The photographs, taken Saturday as the parade started, were received over The Journal's wirephoto equipment.

Edmonton Girl Rules Over Coast Festivities

BY RUTH BOWEN
Women's Editor, Edmonton Journal

VANCOUVER—Barbara Beddome, "Miss Edmonton Eskimo" is "Miss Grey Cup."

More than 5,000 guests of the Junior Chamber of Commerce at Exhibition Park Friday night danced, saw the stage performance, but really waited for just one show, the parade of the 10 lovely charmers representing 10 football clubs in Eastern and Western Canada and competing for the all-Canadian title, "Miss Grey Cup."

Barbara, choice of the judges and the crowd, proudly wor her colors, the stipulated cheer leaders' uniform in gold lame, the short pleated skirt faced with green, the green and gold banner of "Miss Eskimo" over her shoulder.

The green and the gold offset the vivid brunette, five feet, six, dark-eyed, lissome. The contest was among seven brunettes and three blondes. Barbara's arms were filled with flowers, mauve and yellow chrysanthemums, as she held the Miss Grey Cup trophy, the gold-winged statuette, shield mountings noting that twice the trophy had been won by "Miss Saskatchewan Rough Rider," once by "Miss Winnipeg Blue Bomber" and last year by Joan Hunter, "Miss Toronto Argonaut."

"I'm thrilled . . . I'm thrilled . . . I'm thrilled," she told reporters who swarmed back stage when the trophy had been awarded.

"Are you going to drive your new car back to Edmonton?" asked a reporter.

"I can't think. . . . It's so wonderful." She was shown the

(Continued on Page 20, Col. 7)

Friday Night Shenanigans Set New High In Exuberance

BY HAL PAWSON
(Sports Editor, The Journal)

VANCOUVER — The West's first Grey Cup week last night and today became the maddest, craziest, wildest and most hilarious this west coast metropolis, Canadian football or, for that matter, the whole of Canada has known.

Last night 100,000 Vancouverites and their 10,000 visiting football fans cut loose in the downtown hotels and on the streets with an abandon never before matched in the East, where the Grey Cup game had always been held since it came into existence in 1909, until this city wheedled the event for the West this year.

Curious Vancouverites, long blamed for not knowing that Canada also stretches eastward beyond the Fraser River several thousand miles, discovered the rest of the world thanks to the

(Continued on Page 20, Col. 1)

Good Weather Game Prospect

(Special to The Journal)

VANCOUVER—The weatherman indicated early Saturday the Edmonton Eskimos and the Montreal Alouettes will fight it out for the Grey Cup under good football weather conditions.

He forecast temperatures will be between 35 and 40 degrees at kick-off time, and there will be a slight wind of five to ten miles an hour blowing into the stadium from the northeast. Skies will be overcast, and there is a slight chance some rain mixed with snow may fall before the contest ends. Early Saturday it was raining heavily south of Vancouver, but the forecaster is hopeful the present system will stay fairly stationary for most of the day.

On one thing he is definite: "You can quote me as saying there will definitely be no fog. Visibility will be good."

Low Substantiates Articles On Life Of North Indians

Conditions among northern Indians are "bad" and were correctly described in the series of articles by Jack Deakin, Journal staff writer, Solon E. Low, national leader of the Social Credit party, said in an interview here Friday.

Mr. Low arrived from a visit to the Peace River district, for which he is member of Parliament. He addressed a group meeting in the SC hall Friday night when he gave an illustrated lecture on his visit to Palestine.

On Saturday night, the SC leader was scheduled to speak at Salmon Arm, B.C. He will return to Calgary for the party's provincial convention which opens Wednesday.

"I read the Deakin articles and am more or less familiar with the situation described," said Mr. Low. "Part of the reports deal with conditions, among Indians in the Fort Vermilion area, which is part of my constituency.

"What Mr. Deakin says about conditions is absolutely correct. Hon. J. W. Pickersgill, (minister of citizenship and immigration) would be well advised to make a personal visit to that area to see for himself.

"When Mr. Pickersgill makes this trip, he should also visit some of the Metis colonies set up

(Continued on Page 2, Col. 1)

Farm Couple Die Of Heater Fumes

A Wetaskiwin district couple, Mr. and Mrs. Charles Parker, 81 and 75 years old, were found dead Friday evening in their Buck Lake area farm home, apparently overcome by fumes from a stove, RCMP in Edmonton reported Saturday.

Police said they were found about 7 p.m. Friday, by a son, Norman, who went to the farm to visit his parents.

Investigation indicated they had been overcome by fumes from a propane heater which was being installed. The installation was not complete, and the vent pipe did not reach the ceiling outlet, police said.

Police said a wood stove was being used to heat the home but that apparently the couple also lighted the propane heater, not realizing the danger from the incomplete installation.

District coroner Dr. D. Adamson of Wetaskiwin is investigating to decide if an inquest will be held.

Weston Buys Firm For $22,000,000

CHICAGO (AP)—Garfield Weston, leading Canadian and British food merchant, Friday purchased controlling interest in the National Tea Co.

Announcement of Weston's move was made by John F. Cuneo, who said he had sold his control of the firm to Weston and associates for $22,000,000.

National Tea, the fifth largest food chain in the United States, operates in 13 states, mostly in the midwest and has sales of about $575,000,000 a year.

Weston and associates also bought about 200,000 shares of National held by the company's founding family, the Rasmussens. R .V. Rasmussen will resign as a director, Cuneo is retaining a small number of shares and will continue as a director.

Where To Find It

Angelo Patri	25
Births, Deaths, Marriages	32
Book Reviews	8
Bridge	26
Builders	14, 15
Church Pages	6, 7
Comics	26, 27
Crossword Puzzle	26
District	30, 31
Dorothy Dix	24
Editorial	4
Financial	29, 30
Gallup Poll	30
Music	9
Our Boarding House	34
Out Our Way	34
Radio-T.V.	10
Sport	16, 17, 18, 19
Theatres, Entertainment	30, 31
There Oughta Be A Law	35
They'll Do It Every Time	33
Want Ads	33 to 39
Women's	25, 24, 25
Young People's	62

Sound And Color Blend In Bedlam Of Pre-Game Fun

VANCOUVER (CP) — This football-crazy town, rocking as it never rocked before, was up early Friday to the blare of bands and the hootin' and tootin' of merrymakers, few of whom saw more than a few hours of their beds the night before, as the festivities preceding the Grey Cup football final moved into high gear.

Ribbons of the green and gold of Edmonton's defending champion Eskimos, of the red and white of the challenging Montreal Alouettes and the colors of every other major football team in the country fluttered from coat lapels and hats.

Mammoth badges displaying team slogans, hats in red, green, blue, white, hats of every shape and style, jackets, coats, shirts—nearly every item of wearing apparel identified the individuals who crowded in huge throngs with their cities and teams.

At the Hotel Vancouver, starting point for most of the activities, a band blared so loud at 10 a.m. that the 1,000 or more persons milling about the lobby

(Continued on Page 20, Col. 6)

Crowd Of 250,000 Sees Big Grey Cup Parade

BY HAL PAWSON
(Sports Editor, The Journal)

VANCOUVER — The greatest crowd to watch a parade in Vancouver's history—and this west coast seaport has seen some big ones over the years—assembled along miles of downtown streets Saturday morning to join the Grey Cup fun and frolic.

About 250,000 strong, according to early police estimates, the crowd made the 1955 Grey Cup parade the greatest event of its kind since the cup was put up for competition. The parade, too, was the biggest and most colorful to be staged by football boosters in Canada. It boasted more than 80 units.

The crowds ignored overcast skies and a light but chilly breeze and began taking their places three hours before the mid-morning parade was due to start moving along Georgia St., from Stanley Park eastward half the way to Empire Stadium. Visiting fans for the most part watched it from their hotel windows, although most cities' floats were jammed with beribboned supporters.

The best outside fan representation at the Grey Cup, the Edmonton delegation, also put up the strongest fan delegation in the parade.

Edmonton rooters almost despaired of an Eskimo touch in the parade, as the home floats were smack in the middle of the 84-unit affair. The Albertans mainly watched from the main hotels and the streets in that area and their cheers of relief were obvious when the 40th item appeared, the Government of Alberta float.

It was worth the cheers, featuring an Eskimo driving a sled team, carrying the Grey Cup back home to sunny Alberta.

Behind it came the Edmonton Schoolboys' Band, proud and loud in their wine-colored uniforms. I. made a fitting guard of honor for Barbara Beddome, Miss Eskimo of 1955, and Miss Grey Cup, who rode along in a convertible with her white fur robes. Behind her came the Grey Cup, in its own car, and the City of Edmonton float which was one of the prettiest, featuring the Cinderella City theme. The city float was convoyed by four convertibles and Eskimo fans on the float and in the cars tossed 10,000 Eskimo ice cream pies to the crowd as they rolled by.

All in all, they gave Edmonton fine representation and provided the key to public sentiment. The west coast is pulling for Edmonton.

Another highlight of the parade was the Toronto portion, made up of eight comical floats, all of which poked fun at the Ontario capital and the fact it lost the Grey Cup game to Vancouver this year. The floats have been criticized for "being

(Continued on Page 20, Col. 8)

This Wouldn't Be Alouette Strategy?

VANCOUVER (CP) — Edmonton Eskimos nearly lost half its Grey Cup team before Montreal Alouettes could even get a crack at them, it was disclosed here Friday.

Sixteen members of the team, displaying fleetness of foot, scampered to safety as a fishing pier collapsed beneath them Thursday at Brentwood Bay near Victoria.

The 16 had gone fishing with Andy Anderson, president of the Victoria and Saanich Inlet Anglers Association. They fished him out of the bay.

The team caught 20 grilse and ate them for supper.

Grey Cup Special Edition Free At Newsstands On Saturday Evening

Grey Cup fever in Canada will culminate at Empire Stadium, Vancouver, between 3 and 5 p.m., (Edmonton time) today with the playing of the game between the Edmonton Eskimos and the Montreal Alouettes.

Thousands of Edmontonians are making the trip to Vancouver, Many thousands more, equally interested, but unable to attend are remaining at home. Every one of these will want to read the story of the game as speedily as it can be made available. Recognizing this fact, The Journal will publish a special eight-page Grey Cup edition this evening. This special edition will be available, free of charge, at city and district newsstands ONLY. It is expected that copies will be available at downtown newsstands by 8 o'clock, and somewhat later in outlying areas.

This special edition will contain, in addition to the play-by-play story of the game, reports by Hal Pawson, Journal sports editor, and Jim Brooke, Journal football writer, as well as by other experts. It will also contain wirephoto pictures flashed to The Journal from Empire Stadium, (providing coastal fog does not "block" our cameraman) over The Journal's telephoto equipment. Monday's Journal, in addition to complete Canadian Press coverage, will also contain several pages of pictures of the game, extensive coverage by Hal Pawson and Jim Brooke, stories by Ted Reeve, noted Toronto football writer, Vern DeGeer, of Montreal, and Ken McConnell, of Vancouver. The last is a widely-known former Journal sports writer.

Miss Esk

MISS GREY CUP, 1955 — Barbara Beddome, Miss Edmonton Eskimo, was named Miss Grey Cup, 1955, at Vancouver last night. The Canadian Press picture shows her with the trophy awarded at the annual Grey Cup dinner. This picture, taken just after the award was made, was received at The Journal by wirephoto from Vancouver.

Burris Will Dress For Game; Andrews, Glantz To Watch

BY JIM BROOKE
(Sports Writer, Edmonton Journal)

VANCOUVER—When the Edmonton Eskimos take the field in the 1955 Grey Cup game against the Montreal Alouettes here today, a perfectly healthy all-Western selection will be riding the bench. No other football club can make that statement—and none could be unhappier about it.

Edmonton's all-Western centre and linebacker Kurt Burris will definitely be a starter. But Rupe Andrews, all-Western at safety, and guard Don Glantz, both of them fit and ready, won't be dressed. They are the two imports Coach Frank Ivy had to bench in order to make the CRU limit of 10 American players for this Grey Cup game.

Eskimo coach Ivy mulled over the problem from the moment the Eskimos defeated the Winnipeg Blue Bombers to win the western title. This was his only feasible solution and he was stuck with it. Glantz and Andrews are fine ball-players but they have to sit it out.

"I just have to have Burris in there on offence," Ivy said in an exclusive interview with this reporter during the annual individual players awards presentation at the Terminal Club last night. "We have plenty of solid reserves at line-backer on defence. But we need Kurt at offensive centre."

Burris suffered a torn ligament in his knee 10 days ago against Winnipeg but has recuperated remarkably. The leg isn't 100 per cent but the club physicians think it's good enough to stand the strain.

The player cut created, some

(Continued on Page 20, Col. 3)

All Alberta Fans Sure To Arrive

BY DAVE ADAMS
(Journal Staff Writer)

VANCOUVER — Rail officials declared definitely Saturday that all football fans from Alberta points will arrive here in time for the Grey Cup classic.

The greatest worry centred around more than 300 fans from Edmonton aboard a CNR special which left the Alberta capital late Friday afternoon, and was running up to three hours late early Saturday.

However, a CNR spokesman said the train would arrive here at least 2½ hours before the 1:30 p.m. kickoff.

Meanwhile, the four CPR trains carrying the football faithful are running on time and will be in Vancouver well before game time.

The Eskimo ticket office in the Hotel Vancouver will stay open until it is assured the last possible fan has picked up his pasteboards.

Late arriving trains Friday night threw the office into an uproar and the staff worked until well after 2 a.m. passing out tickets.

They were back at work early Saturday and fans were forming long lines in second-floor corridors.

"But the story was the team, which finished the contest with four men playing with broken bones, another with stove-in ribs, and most with bruises, cuts and pain."

Pawson went on for another 3,000 words, praising the team's grit and determination and marvelling at centre Eagle Keys being able to continue play despite a broken leg.

He wasn't finished then, either. Pawson had another 2,000-word story to write, this time taking on all those disbelieving eastern sportswriters who had called the five-to-one underdog Eskimos a "two-buck football team." Pawson served out a helping of western crow on which they could dine.

No wonder, then, that Pawson was written out. However, he still had his daily column to write, and he did. It was the shortest column in the history of the newspaper, but it also reflected how the city and the province felt on that Grey Cup weekend.

"TORONTO – Eeeeeeeeeeeeeeeeeeee-yyyyyyyyyyyyowwwwwwwwww-eeeeeeeeeeeee."

It was enough.

It may have been boosterism, but it was only a reflection of how important sports were, and are, to a city that has often defined itself by the championships its teams have won.

When the newspaper and the fans referred to them as the "Ever lovin' Esks," they meant it.

And if Easterners didn't understand the faith the city and the paper had in the team, so be it. We would simply have to show them again.

In 1955, in fact, the Eskimos were once more discounted by the eastern media who crowded the press box in Vancouver's Empire Stadium for the first Cup game to be played in the West in 46 years.

It was a rematch with the Alouettes, but this time there was no one-point margin of victory. The Eskimos trounced the Als 34-19. It was the first time a team from the West had won back-to-back Cups.

Said Pawson in his game story to 93,000 subscribers: "The Edmontons' savage second half ground attack literally tore apart an eastern champion that came west with the name of being the best second-half club this nation has known. Those cotton-picking Eskies stripped the Als, who roared out of the East, of every possible alibi."

It would be even better in 1956, as one more time they faced the Alouettes, and again, few had picked the Eskimos as favourites. They lost 33-0 to the Als in an exhibition game. The Esks had barely squeaked by the Saskatchewan Roughriders in the best-of-three Western semi-final series.

At half time, Montreal led 19-14. But Parker told *The Journal* after the game that he noticed the Alouettes were slower to get up. They had been bashed and bruised and were losing heart.

Battered by the Eskimo running game, the Als collapsed in the second half. The final score was 50-27. With so much scoring and so many footballs kicked into the stands in Toronto's Varsity Stadium that there simply weren't any left. With 12 seconds left on the clock, the game ended.

Future Eskimo teams would enjoy similar seasons of excellence. But those first wins were the best. Beating the East gave the city confidence in itself.

class dining rooms and drinking in nightclubs would be permitted in Alberta under new liquor laws given first reading in the Legislature Friday night."
The legislation also allowed liquor on trains, but there would be no liquor on airplanes over Alberta airspace.

***March 26, 1858*:**
"An Edmonton doctor Tuesday suggested high school students should be taught not to become fat men or women." Dr. J.A. Gilbert, clinical professor of medicine at the University of Alberta, describes obesity as the No. 1 enemy of public health and one of the chief causes of shortened life.

***Oct. 15, 1958*:**
Jasper Place ratepayers vote almost four to one in favour of amalgamation with Edmonton.

***In 1959*:**
A stenographer at *The Journal* makes $65 a week.

***Feb. 25, 1959*:**
Five months after students arrived for classes, Bonnie Doon Composite high school officially opens.

***March 8, 1959*:**
The ESO sells out for the first time in the Jubilee Auditorium. The next day the ESO holds its first out-of-town concert, in Camrose.

Television Edition

The Edmonton Journal

THE EDMONTON JOURNAL, EDMONTON, ALBERTA, SATURDAY, OCTOBER 16, 1954

Section Three Page One

T-V IS HERE ON CHANNEL 3

MILTON BERLE
WINSTON CHURCHILL
OUR MISS BROOKS
DINAH SHORE
ROY ROGERS
EISENHOWER

FIRST PROGRAM BEGINS 3 P.M. SUNDAY

CFRN-TV--Another Chapter In Edmonton's History

Another important milestone in the development of northern Alberta will be marked Sunday at 3 p.m. From Canada's most northerly capital city, the signal of CFRN-TV will carry the first regular telecast to thousands of central and northern Alberta homes.

From that moment on, television will be a daily habit in the lives of central and northern Alberta citizens.

On the western outskirts of Edmonton a 488-foot tower and antenna marks the location of this newest addition in Edmonton's amazing expansion. On the site of the CFRN Radio transmitter, a modern one-storey grey cement building, measuring 91 by 84½ feet, houses the CFRN-TV studios, offices and transmitter.

Rising high above the building is the 488-foot "tower" on top of which rests the 10-ton, six-bay antenna. From this antenna, one of few six-bay units in use across Canada, will be telecast the programs to be seen by Edmonton district viewers on "Channel three."

Unlike the early development of television's older sister, radio, this new electronic medium requires hundreds of man-hours and vast sums of money before operation of the station can begin. Before viewers in northern Alberta received their first programs, close to half a million dollars had been spent, or committed, for construction and equipping of station CFRN-TV.

Opening of CFRN-TV brings to G. R. A. "Dick" Rice another "first" in the broadcasting field. One of Canada's first radio pioneers and manager of Edmonton's first, Journal-owned radio station, Mr. Rice is the owner-manager of the Sunwapta Broadcasting Co., operators for both CFRN-Radio and CFRN-TV.

Every consideration has been given to the future expansion and development of CFRN-TV. From transmitter, through the telecine room, studios and control facilities, ample space for additional equipment and power has been allowed so that CFRN will develop into one of Canada's most powerful television stations.

CFRN-TV transmits a power of 27,600 watts video and 13,800 watts audio. For the past two and a half weeks, during telecasting of test-patterns, reports have been received from towns 20 and 30 miles outside the projected fringe area of 90 miles. In the "A" and "B" coverage areas, which are the most favorable receiving areas, more than 100,000 northern Alberta homes can be covered by CFRN-TV. Of these, about 40,000 are estimated to be within the city limits.

For the beginning of telecasting the station will schedule 40 hours of programs a week. On week days from Monday to Saturday telecasting will begin at 6 p.m. and continue to 11:15 p.m. or midnight. On Sunday, programming will commence at 3:30 p.m. and extend through to the regular sign-off time.

Although the Edmonton station will not, for a time, be connected by micro-wave link for the direct reception of programs, it will receive major programs from four networks—CBC, National Broadcasting Company, Columbia Broadcasting System and the American Broadcasting Company.

Programs will be kinescoped in eastern Canada by the CBC from the micro-wave link to the

(Continued on Page 18)

G. R. A. RICE . . . First Radio, Now Television

PROGRAMMING FOR CFRN-TV

Sunday — 3:00 p.m. — Introducing CFRN-TV (Sun., Oct. 17th only)

SUNDAY

3:30—Burns And Allen
4:00—Gruen Playhouse
4:30—W.I.F.U. FOOTBALL
6:30—My Favorite Husband
7:00—Small Fry Frolics
7:45—News
8:00—Toast Of The Town
9:00—Four Star Playhouse
9:30—C.G.E. Showtime
10:00—News
10:30—Tzigane
11:00—News
11:15—Channel 3 Playhouse

MONDAY

6:00—Hobby Workshop
6:30—News
7:00—Living
7:30—On The Spot
8:00—Syd Caesar Show
9:00—Dragnet
10:00—Studio One
11:00—News
11:15—Sign Off

TUESDAY

6:00—Let's Go To The Museum
6:30—News
7:00—Let's Make Music
7:30—Dinah Shore
8:00—Martha Raye (Alternating with Bob Hope and Milton Berle)
9:00—Pick The Star
9:30—General Motors Theatre
10:30—Press Conference
11:00—News
11:15—Sign Off

WEDNESDAY

6:00—Folk Songs
6:30—News
7:00—Living
8:30—Liberace
9:00—Ford Dramas
9:30—On Stage
11:00—News
11:15—Sign Off

THURSDAY

6:00—Range Riders
6:30—News
7:30—Dinah Shore
8:00—The Plouffe Family
'8:30—Amos 'N' Andy
9:00—Duffy's Tavern
9:30—The Concert Hour
11:00—News
11:15—Sign Off

FRIDAY

6:00—Hidden Pages
6:30—News
7:00—Living
7:30—Art Linklatter And The Kids
8:30—Window On Canada
9:00—Frigidaire Entertains
9:30—Dear Phoebe
11:00—News
11:15—Sign Off

SATURDAY

5:00—Wild Bill Hickok
5:30—Disneyland
6:30—Mickey Rooney
7:30—Holiday Ranch
8:00—The Jackie Gleason Show
9:00—On Camera
9:30—At Home With John Newmark
10:00—Tzigane
11:00—News

This is the schedule for the first week. Other name stars will be featured in programs beginning in the next few weeks.

G.R.A. Rice, Radio Pioneer, Heads First TV Station

G. R. A. "Dick" Rice, president and general manager of the Sunwapta Broadcasting Company Ltd., adds another "first" to his career in the broadcasting industry with the beginning of the regular schedule of telecasts on CFRN-TV.

Born in Teddington, Middlesex, England, Mr. Rice has been in radio his entire business life, starting at the age of 15 with the Marconi Co. in England. He attended the National Physical Laboratories of Great Britain and London College. Prior to the First Great War he joined the Marconi British Admiralty Wireless Service and served throughout the war with this organization.

He first came to Canada in 1919 for a visit and liked the country well enough to return the following year and start in radio broadcasting in his adopted land. At that time the only broadcasting stations were at Montreal and Toronto. These were operated by the Canadian Marconi Company. He set out for western Canada and in 1922 opened CJCA for the Edmonton Journal, one of the first stations to go on the air in Canada. For 12 years he operated the station and pioneered, along with the other early broadcasters, much of the growth of radio technique. In 1934 he applied for a license for CFRN and opened a 100-watt station. Since that time CFRN has grown and kept pace with the development of Edmonton and northern Alberta until today, with modern studios in the CPR Bldg. and latest equipment it operates 24 hours a day on 5,000 watts.

The name of Dick Rice is well-known throughout the broadcasting industry. With a number of other western Canadian Broadcasters, he formed in 1941 a co-operative representative organization with offices in Montreal and Toronto, Radio Representatives Ltd. He is past president of the Western Association of Broadcasters and served as president and chairman of the board of the Canadian Association of Broadcasters.

The firm name, Sunwapta, is known to vacationists in the mountains as a Stoney Indian word. Students of Indian lore, who number Mr. Rice as an associate, recall a translation of the word as "rippling or radiating waves."

Some say it must have been the poet in Mr. Rice when he chose such an apt name for CFRN in 1934.

The call letters CFRN incorporate the initials of the owners—R for Rice and F for H. F. Nielson, a partner in the venture at its inception.

Besides managing a radio and television station, Mr. Rice is active in the Canadian Cancer Society. He was president of the Alberta branch of the society for three years—from 1951 to 1954. He is also an honorary member of the Edmonton branch of the Associated Canadian Travellers. This honor was bestowed on him in 1951 in appreciation of CFRN's support of the ACT crippled children's project.

Looking back over the early days of radio, Mr. Rice admits there were many complicated difficulties, such as temperamental microphones. "Microphones were our major headache," he recalls. "When they failed we never had a replacement handy. We simply made another one."

That "simply" is typical of Mr. Rice. He tackles complicated problems with simplicity. Here's a job. Here are the ways to do it. This is the best way. Let's do it. Just like that.

The Boob Tube

"Television is one of the most fascinating miracles of our day."
— "Television Edition," Oct. 16, 1954

Editorially, *The Journal* had nothing to say about the advent of television, the most fascinating miracle to hit the city since a radio station was set up in the paper's newsroom 32 years earlier.

At that moment, its entertainment focus was on a raging controversy of the contents of "horror" comic books that portrayed scantily clad women in moral-bending situations. *The Journal*'s editorialists held no truck with the scantily clad women, but were even less happy at the prospect of censorship of any form of book, comic or otherwise.

But its lack of attention to the coming of television didn't mean it didn't reap the whirlwind of paid ads during the half-month before CFRN opened a 21-inch window on the world, 3 p.m., Sunday, Oct. 17, 1954.

The paper produced two 16-page sections on Saturday, Oct. 14, dedicated to CFRN, its upcoming programs, pages of ads hawking TV sets and accessories and the how-tos of television care and viewing. Under the headline, "5 Good Rules For TV Care," was this helpful hint: "1. Protect your set from dampness. If you use it on an open porch or on a patio in summer, take it indoors at night."

Another story told readers: "A dark room is to be strictly avoided. If the room is dark, the pupils of the eyes try to adjust in size for the darkness of the room, and the brightness of the screen. This can't be done, so the result is eye-strain."

For the record, after a 30-minute station introduction, Edmonton viewers were treated to the likes of the *Gruen* (later *Chevron*) *Playhouse*, a Western Interprovincial Football Union game, a couple of comedies, news and the music show *Tzigane*.

The next day the paper had a four-paragraph story on page 21, the first page of the second section. "... While many Edmontonians viewed the first CFRN-TV telecasts in the comfort of their living rooms Sunday, thousands more saw the programs from city sidewalks.

"In scores of electrical and appliance store windows, television sets had been turned on. Crowds of viewers were grouped around the windows from the time the first telecast began at 3 p.m."

Canadian content had not been invented and network television didn't become a reality until 1957. CFRN's line-up featured a constellation of high-profile American stars and shows. Variety shows hosted by the likes of Sid Caesar and Dinah Shore, westerns and cop shows such as *Wild Bill Hickok* and *Dragnet* and the music of Liberace were shown the first week in what later became known as "prime time" on Channel 3.

CFRN was owned and managed by Dick Rice, the same gentleman who put CJCA Radio on the air for *The Journal* some 32 years before.

As for the impact of television, the story heralding the event predicted: "Television will be a daily habit in the lives of central and northern Alberta citizens."

***March 16, 1959*:**
One student is shot dead and five others injured in the halls of Ross Sheppard high school, which opened in October 1958.

***April 25, 1959*:**
The ESO presents the first-ever symphony orchestra concert at Yellowknife, in Canada's Arctic.

***May 6, 1959*:**
Civic census accounts for 303,000 people in the greater Edmonton area, including Jasper Place, Beverly and the housing at Namao and Griesbach.

***July 1, 1959*:**
The children's zoo, subsequently called the Valley Zoo, opens in Laurier Park.

***July 28, 1959*:**
Charles W. Willis, *The Journal*'s first subscriber, dies at age 87.

***Oct. 14, 1959*:**
Elmer Roper is elected mayor of Edmonton for a two-year term. A proposal to fluoridate the city water supply fails to gain enough support.

***Dec. 30, 1959*:**
The city annexes 6,950 acres of land in southwest Edmonton.

The Edmonton Journal

FORECAST: COLD | EDMONTON, ALBERTA, FRIDAY, NOVEMBER 22, 1963 | FIVE CENTS

PRESIDENT KENNEDY KILLED IN AMBUSH

STRICKEN PRESIDENT FALLS TO SEAT OF LIMOUSINE
. . . Mrs. Kennedy and unidentified security guard aid president

Assassin Suspect Arrested

A man has been arrested in Dallas, Texas, in connection with the fatal shooting today of President Kennedy.

Deputy chief Edward Krews of the Dallas sheriff's office said in a long distance telephone interview with The Journal. "The man's name cannot be released."

"The sheriff's office and Dallas police are working with the Federal Bureau of Investigation on the case."

"There are more than 1,000 men working on the case," he added.

FLASH

WASHINGTON — Government sources said Friday that President Kennedy is dead.

BULLETIN

DALLAS, Tex. (AP)—Two priests stepped out of Parkland Hospital's emergency ward Friday and said President Kennedy died of his bullet wounds.

DALLAS, Tex. (AP) — President Kennedy and Governor John Connally were shot today just as their motorcade left downtown Dallas.

Mrs. Kennedy jumped up and grabbed Mr. Kennedy. She cried, "Oh, no!" The motorcade sped on.

Associated Press photographer James W. Altgens said he saw blood on the president's head.

Altgens said he heard two shots but thought someone was shooting fireworks until he saw the blood on the president.

Altgens said he saw no one with a gun.

U.S. Representative Albert Thomas of Texas said both were still alive in a hospital emergency room.

Connally, remained half-seated, slumped to the left. There was blood on his face and forehead.

Reporters saw Kennedy lying flat on his face on the seat of his car.

Bell said a man and a woman were scrambling on the upper level of the walkway overlooking the underpass.

Lawrence O'Brien, presidential aide, said he had no information on whether the president still was alive.

Mrs. Kennedy was weeping and trying to hold up her husband's head when reporters reached the car.

The secret service said the president remained in the emergency room and the governor was moved to the general operating room of Parkland Hospital.

One secret service man was overheard telling another that there was no need to move the president because emergency facilities were entirely adequate in the emergency room.

Two Roman Catholic priests were summoned to the emergency room where the president lay.

One priest was identified as a Father Huber.

Malcolm Kilduff, acting White House press secretary, said that the two priests had been "asked for."

It was not immediately known who made the request for the priests.

At 12:10 MST, Mrs. Lyndon Johnson was escorted by secret service agents into the emergency room where the president lay.

Police said they did not know whether Vice-President Johnson was in the room.

The last attempt on the life of a United States president was in Nov. 1950 when two Puerto Ricans rushed into the presidential residence with pistols blazing.

Security guards cut the men down before they could get inside temporary presidential residence, Blair House.

In the gun battle one guard was killed and two others wounded.

One of the Puerto Ricans was shot dead, the other Oscar Collazo, 37, stood trial and was sentenced to death only to have the sentence commuted to life imprisonment.

Other United States presidents to die at the hands of assassins were Abraham Lincoln in 1865, James Abram Garfield in 1881, and William McKinley in 1901.

Last Victim Of Assassin President McKinley, 1901

The last United States president to die at the hands of an assassin was William McKinley who was shot while attending the Pan-American Exposition at Buffalo, NY, on Sept. 6, 1901.

Leon Czolgosz, an anarchist terrorist, was the man who pulled the trigger while concealing his gun beneath a bandaged hand.

President McKinley died Sept. 14.

His last words were: "It is God's way. His will, not ours, be done."

MOMENTS BEFORE ASSASSINATION
. . . a smiling president and wife greet Dallas residents

Art EVANS

National Funnybone

AN AMERICAN WRITER taking a week-long look at Canadian television (shows produced in Canada by Canadians) was struck by the absence of humor.

Richard Gehman (writing in Maclean's magazine) reports, "At straight forward, honest communication Canadian television has it all over television in the States." However he socks us pretty good on drama shows ("posturing silliness") and on variety shows ("awful").

Then he goes on to say something about the absence of humor on Canadian TV:

"Finally, I saw practically no humor and little evidence that there would be some to come. Humorlessness seems to be a national condition — but why? If there is more freedom in Canada, as there seems to be, isn't there bound to be more wit? . . . It seems a shame, with Canada's great resources in lively brightness and humor, that most of the brightness seen on its television should have to come from the U.S."

★ ★ ★

MR. GEHMAN'S REMARKS could touch off a solemn-faced debate: Resolved that Mr. Gehman is all wet and that Canadian television is loaded with laughs. End of debate.

Well, outside of the infrequent appearances of gentlemen like Wayne and Schuster and Dave Broadfoot, what have we got? I like to think that somewhere Canada has a Jack Paar, Groucho Marx, Bob Hope, Shelley Berman or Mort Sahl, hiding his light under a bushel of wheat or behind a Douglas fir. But if this guy does exist will he get a chance to come out of hiding and audition for a national show? Somehow I doubt it.

This is not surprising. There is no national craving that I have been able to discern for made-in-Canada humor. We publish books and magazines and newspapers but their humorous content compared to the total package is a thin slice indeed. It would be strange if our television shows were any different.

★ ★ ★

HUMORLESSNESS IS NOT a national condition as Mr. Gehman understandably concluded after his TV sampling. Humorlessness is only the outward image of Canadians and one we seem determined to preserve. Privately we're gassers and laugh uproariously on private occasions. Publicly we stand on our dignity.

We insist on the right not to laugh unless the joke is on the Americans, or the British, or the Russians, or what-have you. We may demand that the CBC's Max Ferguson (a genuine Canadian humorist in my view) be removed from the airwaves or deplore an innocent joke dropped by a politician in an unguarded moment of levity. Publicly we take ourselves very seriously and it must be some kind of sin to do otherwise. I accept the fact without professing to know the reason or reasons. The "why" can be left to unfunny experts.

Canada does have a national funnybone. I'm convinced of it. Leacock found it but it was more exposed in his day. Since his time the national funnybone has been hidden under layers of solemnity, a burial process still going on.

The search goes on. Writer Eric Nicol has done valiant exploratory work and digging at the site continues, supported by a handful of hopeful spades.

I expect to get a very serious letter about all this.

John Kennedy Was First Roman Catholic President

John Fitzgerald Kennedy was the 35th president of the United States.

He was inaugurated president at the age of 43 in 1961.

Born May 29, 1917, in Brookline, Mass., President Kennedy was the second of nine children of Joseph P. Kennedy, wealthy financier and Ambassador to the Court of St. James's, London, England.

The president graduated from Harvard in 1940 and later served in the United States navy commanding a PT boat in the Pacific.

During his naval service the president won the Navy and Marine Cross and was awarded the Purple Heart.

FORMER REPORTER

A former reporter for International News Service, the president covered the Potsdam Conference and the start of the U.N. at San Francisco.

He served as a Representative in Congress from Massachusetts from 1947 to 1953, and defeated Henry Cabot Lodge for the Senate in 1952. He was reelected in 1958.

In 1956 he came close to winning the vice-presidential nomination.

He won the Democratic nomination for president in Los Angeles on July 14, 1960 on the first ballot over Lyndon Johnson and Adlai Stevenson and went on to defeat Richard Nixon in the presidential election.

ROMAN CATHOLIC

President Kennedy was the first Roman Catholic to be elected president.

Where To Find It

Ann Landers	20
Births, Deaths, Marriages	32
Book Reviews	27
Bridge	34
Classified Ads	33-44
Comics, Features	54
Financial	12, 13
Horoscope	35
Letters To The Editor	4, 43
Patterns	36
Radio	24
Sport	49-52
Theatres, Entertainment	55-57
TV	24, 25
Women's	19-23
Youth Page	6

Total Pages 60

Weather

Snow tonight, cloudy and cold tomorrow, winds east 15, low tonight 10 below, high tomorrow zero. Details on Page 2.

SECURITY GUARDS SEARCH CROWD FOR ASSASSIN
. . . a suspect was arrested and is being held by Dallas police

S E V E N

VOICE
STOP THE BOMBING RIGHT NOW
SCHOOL
ERADICATE POVERTY NOT PEOPLE

A '60s protest march down Jasper Avenue.

Prosperity & Change

1960 to 1969

Northern Adventure / 263

Women & The Pill / 267

The Citadel / 269

The Oil Kings / 273

Hair Down to Here... / 277

"It was a time of prosperity and change. Edmonton lost its prairie town image and mushroomed into a metropolitan centre."
— Civic affairs reporter Olive Elliott in a decade-ending story in Dec. 23, 1969

The Journal's first editorial of the 1960s, titled "The Sensible 'Sixties?" exuded confidence in the future that was as solid as the Rocky Mountains.

And why not? It was a time when there was a place for everything and everything was in its place.

Journal editorial writers had every reason to think that any changes to come would all be to the good. "Viewing the larger picture, of the world as a whole, the beginning of the new decade poses the pertinent question of whether, in another ten years, we shall be able to look back and label this decade as the 'sensible 'sixties.' The prospects are dazzling in every area of man's activities in the world and the space beyond. The question is whether he will so conduct himself as to achieve them."

Edmonton Weather
Forecast: Snowflurries tonight. Cloudy, cooler Thursday, winds north 15. Low tonight 25, high tomorrow 35.

The Edmonton Journal

One of Canada's Great Newspapers

58th YEAR, NO. 127 | TELEPHONE GA 4-0271 | EDMONTON, ALBERTA, WEDNESDAY, APRIL 12, 1961 | PRICE NOT OVER FIVE CENTS | FOUR SECTIONS

MAJ. YURI GAGARIN

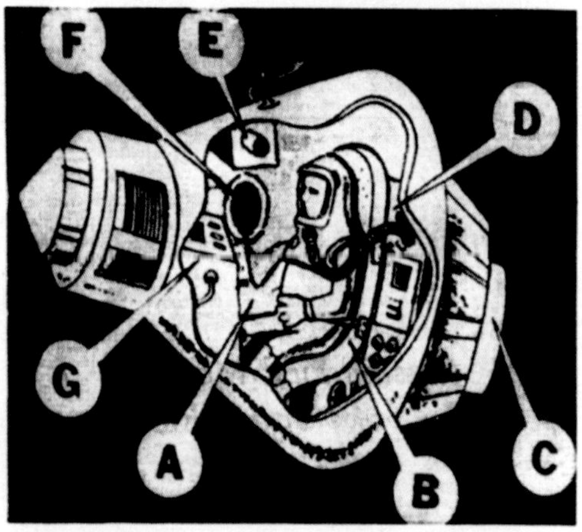
F
E
D
G
A
B
C

ARTIST'S IMPRESSION — The Communist London Daily Worker carried this drawing today of the Soviet space capsule. A—pressurized cabin; B—foam-padded seat; C—parachutes to slow speed on descent; D—air supply; E—television cameras and microphone; F—porthole; G—instrument panel.
AP Wirephotos to The Journal

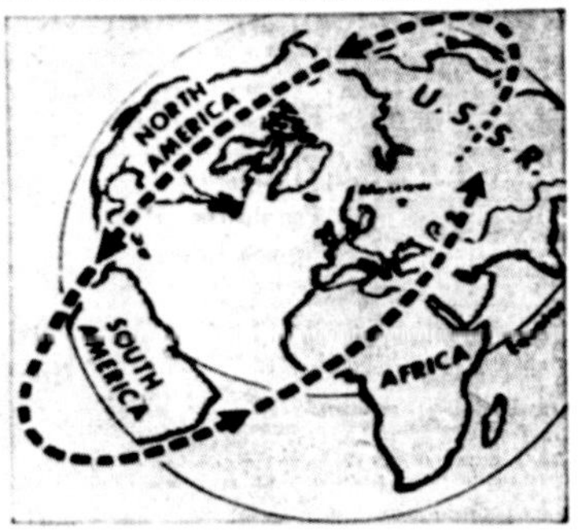
NORTH AMERICA
U.S.S.R.
SOUTH AMERICA
AFRICA

Words Came From 200 Miles Out

MOSCOW — As he whistled around the globe at more than 17,000 miles an hour — six times faster than man ever travelled before — Gagarin reported he was withstanding his state of weightlessness well.

"I am watching the earth," he said. "The visibility is good. I hear you well."

A little later:

"The flight is proceeding well. I am watching the earth. The visibility is good. I can see everything. Some places are shrouded by clouds."

Then another message:

"I am continuing my flight. Everything is normal. Everything is functioning well. I am proceeding on my way."

The last message:

"I feel well and cheerful. The flight continues. Everything is going well. The machine is functioning normally."

Dogs Led Way

IT WAS JOKE FOR BELKA

LONDON (AP) — The first living thing projected into orbit by human scientists was the dog Laika, which went aloft in Russia's Sputnik No. 2 Nov. 3, 1957.

Laika, a martyr to progress, whizzed around the earth for a week and then died.

The first living higher animals to be orbited and brought back alive were the dogs Strelka and Belka. They went up and returned safely Aug. 19, 1960, in what Russia called Spacecraft No. 2.

March 9 the dog Chernushka (Blackie) orbited and came back with a guinea pig and a black mouse in Spacecraft No. 4.

Spacecraft No. 1, sent up May 15, 1960, was without living passengers. Spacecraft No. 3, with two dogs aboard, orbited Dec. 1, 1960. The recovery system failed and it burned up in the atmosphere.

The first artificial satellite of all, the Soviet Union's Sputnik 1, went into orbit Oct. 4, 1957.

Since then Russia and the United States have put more than 50 satellites into space.

They included the American Pioneer V, sent up March 11, 1960, and placed in orbit around the sun, and Russia's Venus probe, launched Feb. 12, 1961, and still bound in the general direction of earth's sister planet.

* * *

Red Astronaut Given Honor

LONDON (Reuters) — The city council of Kishinev, capital of Soviet Moldavia, Wednesday decided to rename one of its busiest streets, the Muchchestsky Boulevard, after spaceman Yuri Gagarin, the official Soviet news agency Tass reported.

RED SPACE MAN ORBITS EARTH IN 89 MINUTES

CP FROM AP—REUTERS

MOSCOW—Russia fired a man into orbit around the earth today and brought him back unharmed after 108 minutes in space.

Maj. Yuri Alekseyevich Gagarin made a little more than one complete orbit of the globe in a five-ton spaceship and then was brought down to a safe landing at a pre-arranged spot in the Soviet Union.

"I feel well," he said as he emerged from the spaceship after landing. "I have no injuries or bruises."

Gagarin, a 27-year-old father of two young children, one of them born just a month ago, told the

Moscow took on a May Day air to celebrate. Reports on Pages 2 and 36.

official Soviet news agency Tass that everything went as planned both during the flight and on the landing.

He asked Tass to report this "to the party and government and personally to Nikita Khrushchev."

The astronaut was put into an orbit that took him around the earth in 89.1 minutes. He reported by radio during the flight that he was "feeling well" and "withstanding the state of weightlessness well."

A statement from the Soviet government and the Communist party said the satellite space ship Vostok (East), with Gagarin aboard, rose into outer space at 9:07 a.m. Moscow time "and, having rounded the globe, safety returned to the sacred soil of our homeland, the land of the Soviets."

Vostok landed at 10:55 a.m. Moscow time, 108 minutes after the launching, the Russians said. Neither the point of the takeoff nor the location of the landing was announced.

Soviet scientists watched Gagarin during his flight by television and he was in constant radio communication with a Russian control station, the Russians said. Messages from him while in flight saying that he was well were broadcast to the breathless public.

Moscow Radio said the orbit took him within about 110 miles of earth at its nearest point and about 188 miles away from earth at its farthest point.

The launching and successful return of a human to earth gave Russia victory in the gruelling race with the United States to put the first man into space and made space flight — long the province of science fiction — an actuality.

The spaceship weighed 10,640 pounds with the astronaut aboard but not including the weight of the final stage of the carrier-rocket.

(Continued on Page 2, Col. 4)

* * * * * *

Warning Given To Eichmann

JERUSALEM (AP) — Israeli Attorney-General Gideon Hausner, pointing his finger directly at Adolf Eichmann, exclaimed in court today that the Jewish people will never forget Eichmann "succeeded in part" in carrying out the Nazi plan to exterminate Europe's 11,000,000 Jews.

Hausner's outburst came in the second morning of Eichmann's trial on Israeli charges of "crimes against the Jewish people and crimes against humanity." One of these is the crime of genocide—mass murder. The state alleges that Eichmann, as chief of the Jewish affairs section of the Nazi Gestapo, bears direct responsibility for the slaughter of an estimated 6,000,000 Jews.

OTHER ATTEMPTS MADE

Hausner reminded the three-judge court that in 2,000 years of Jewish history there had been previous attempts to wipe the Jewish people off the face of the earth.

Then, suddenly raising his voice and stabbing the air with his left hand, he said:

"There is no pardon and there can be no forgetting."

Eichmann looked a little haggard when he came into court on this second day.

Through most of the morning session, he sat still, cupping his chin on his right hand.

SHOWED ANIMATION

The only time he showed any animation was in the moment before the judges came into the courtroom. Then, speaking through the private microphone in the glass-enclosed prisoner's dock, he exchanged a few words with his chief defence lawyer, Dr. Robert Servatius.

Hausner spent the whole

(Continued on Page 8, Col. 1)

50 Years Make Big Difference

LONDON (AP) — Fifty years ago Wednesday, a Frenchman, Pierre Prier, flew from London to Paris in four hours and eight minutes. This morning, a Soviet foundry worker, Yuri Gagarin, orbited the earth in a space ship in 89 minutes.

SUBSIDIES "STAGGERING" —Premier Manning Tuesday described as "staggering" the $97,300,000 in subsidies recommended by a transportation inquiry report to lift Canada's major railways out of the red during 1961-62. Varied reactions met the recommendation. (Reports on Pages 14 and 35.)

SPY ACCUSED — Montreal engineer, Tomasz Biernacki, who came from Poland last year, will plead not guilty to charges of spying. (Report on Page 36.)

The Legislature

Legislature May Wind Up This Afternoon

The second session of the 11th Alberta Legislature is expected to prorogue today. (Report on Page 14.)

A request is made for repeal of the 1912 Edmonton-Strathcona amalgamation agreement because it is outdated. (Report on Page 44.)

Members defeat a move by an Opposition member to set up an insurance fund to compensate farmers for livestock killed by hunters. (Report on Page 47.)

GOVERNOR "UNFIT" — CCF Leader Hazen Argue, above, Tuesday demanded the resignation of Hon. Frank Bastedo, lieutenant-governor of Saskatchewan, who withheld royal assent to a mineral lease bill passed by the provincial legislature. Mr. Argue described the lieutenant-governor as "unfit" to hold office. (Report on Page 50.)

Israel Defies U.N. Edict

JERUSALEM (AP) — Israel says it will defy the U.N. Security Council and hold an Independence Day military parade as planned April 20 in Jerusalem.

The Security Council in New York Monday ordered the parade cancelled because of Jordan's complaint that such a show could provoke a rival demonstration in Jordan-ruled old Jerusalem. (Report of U.N. demand on Page 7.)

Where To Find It

Angelo Patri	18
Births, Deaths, Marriages	50
Bridge	52
Comics	40, 53
Crossword Puzzle	55
Dennis The Menace	54
District	10, 37, 59
Dorothy Dix	[illegible]
Dorothy Kilgallen	21
Editorial	4
Financial	12, 13
Out Our Way	51
Packsack	40
Sport	31 to 34
Theatres, Entertainment	44, 45
T.V.	53
Uncle Ray's Corner	40
Want Ads	51 to 57
Women's	17 to 30

The Weather

(Issued by the Dominion Public Weather Office at Edmonton)

Cold Arctic air will plunge southward to cover all of the central and northern regions by noon Thursday, holding temperatures below freezing all day Thursday north of a line through Edmonton and Saskatoon. Winds of 15 to 30 m.p.h. will accompany the cold outbreak.

Low tonight, 25.
High tomorrow, 35.
Snowfall, .4 of an inch.

Sunset today .... 7:29 p.m.
Sunrise tomorrow ... 5:40 a.m.
Moonrise tomorrow ... 5:25 a.m.
New Moon ... Friday night

VISIBLE PLANETS

Mars, in the west ... 11:14 p.m.
Jupiter and Saturn, low in southeast ... 4:11 a.m.
(Pollux is the star right above Mars; Altair is the star well above Jupiter and Saturn.

Temperatures

Maximum temperatures yesterday and overnight lows are:

Edmonton	48	35	Coronat'n	50	28
Peace R.	41	29	Vermilion	44	30
Fairview	40	27	Saskatoon	45	32
Gr. Prairie	52	30	Pr. Albert	30	26
Whitect.	48	32	Pr. Rupert	46	41
Wagner	37	31	Victoria	51	42
McMurray	30	27	Vancouver	54	44
Lac La B.	31	28	Penticton	53	42
Penhold	51	29	Kamloops	61	41
Rk. Mt. H.	51	31	Regina	49	34
Calgary	57	34	Winnipeg	25	19
Lethbridge	57	37	Ft. Will'm	49	30
Med. Hat	59	36	Toronto	51	30
Banff	51	36	Ottawa	46	33
Jasper	56	37	Montreal	42	31
Whitehse	28	6	Nor. Wells	1	-18
Snag	27	9	Yellowkn.	9	-19
Inuvik	-7	-24	Ft. Smith	28	14

VOTE SPLITS CABINET, SOCRED CAUCUS

Denturists' Bill Survives

Alberta dental mechanics Wednesday appeared to have won their fight for the right to deal directly with the public in making and fitting false teeth.

A bitterly-contested bill, which will incorporate the Alberta Cer-

Detailed reports Pages 3, 11.

tified Dental Mechanics Society survived a critical test in the Legislature Tuesday on a 36 - 25 count. The legislation is expected to receive third and final reading Wednesday.

However, controversy continues to swirl around the legislation, which is strongly opposed by the province's dentists.

Two cabinet ministers Tuesday attacked a statement made earlier this week by Alberta Dental Association president Dr. Gordon C. Swann of Calgary. Dr. Swann is reported to have said the private bills committee which studied the bill could have been compared with a "kangaroo court."

"IGNORANT STATEMENTS"

Minister Without Portfolio Fred Colborne accused Dr. Swann of "ignorant and irresponsible statements." Highways Minister Gordon Taylor said the dentist's attack is "ridiculous, unfair and untrue."

Liberal Michael Maccagno of Lac La Biche said the dentists' stand during committee hearings last week was so offensive they lost his support.

Before the bill left the private bills committee Tuesday, Health Minister Donovan Ross delivered a warning.

"I still think we are doing the wrong thing (in proceeding with it) and we'll later regret what we have done," he said. Dr. Ross was one of the strongest critics of the dental mechanics' bid for the right to work in clients' mouths when the battle raged for two days in private bills committee.

Meanwhile Dr. Swann continued to fire away at the bill.

He said approval of the measure would "reduce the science of dentistry in this province into a quackery that will be the laughing-stock of all North America."

MAY WITHDRAW

Dr. Swann also said Alberta dentists may withdraw their support of a health department program to cover the province with dental service if the denturists should win their bid.

"If this happens, the plan will be doomed to failure," he stated.

The plan announced by the provincial department of health is aimed at filling the need for dental attention in outlying areas. It would employ volunteer dentists from other communities, full-time dental officers, specially trained auxiliaries and students who have completed their third year of dentistry at the University of Alberta.

Dr. Swann claimed that soon after their activities have been legalized, the dental mechanics would begin violating their charter and begin repairing and extracting teeth.

CABINET DIVIDED

Tuesday's crucial vote brought the measure back to the Legislature from the private bills committee. It divided the cabinet, with such members as Premier Manning and Health Minister Dr. J. Donovan Ross voting against the measure.

The bill then was referred back to the committee of the whole Assembly, where it was passed again.

Space Timetable

MOSCOW (Reuters) — Following is the timetable of main developments and announcements in the launching by Russia of a man into space:

11:07 p.m. MST: Soviet spaceship with man on board launched.

11:58 p.m.: The Soviet news agency Tass announces that the first man had been put into space. Moscow Radio interrupts its programs to give the historic news.

12:41 a.m.: Tass quotes spaceman Yuri Gagarin, then over South America, as reporting by radio at 11:22 p.m.: "Flight is proceeding normally. I feel well."

12:49 a.m.: Moscow Radio quotes Gagarin, over Africa, as reporting at 12:15 a.m.: "I am withstanding state of weightlessness well."

1:12 a.m.: Moscow Radio reports that at 12:25 a.m. the spaceship's braking system was put into operation and Gagarin began his descent to a predetermined spot in the Soviet Union.

2:07 a.m.: Moscow Radio announces that spaceship landed safely at 12:55 a.m. and that Gagarin said on landing: "Please report to the party and government and personally to Nikita Khrushchev: The landing was normal, I feel well. I have no injuries or bruises."

3:47 a.m.: Khrushchev sent Gagarin a personal telegram saying: "With my whole heart I congratulate you on your happy return to the homeland from your space journey. I embrace you. Until our meeting in Moscow soon."

How wrong the editorial writers were. To many of our readers, and often to the paper, the '60s were anything but sensible.

By the time the decade ended, fundamental changes turned Edmonton's cozy contentment on its head. Nothing – not music, movies, theatre, health care, television, religion, youth nor sex – would ever be quite the same again.

Nevertheless, our editorial writers could be forgiven the complacency that insisted life would continue on at its comfortable pace.

After all, only six months before that New Year's Day in 1960, Social Credit under Premier Ernest Manning had routed its opponents in a provincial election. Albertans clearly liked the kind of conservative government they were getting, and when Manning looked across the floor of the legislature, he saw a lone Tory, a single Liberal, an MLA who described himself as a Coalition member and another who was listed as Independent Social Credit.

Three years into the decade, Albertans once again went to the polls, and this time they almost fulfilled the Socred election slogan that called for a clean sweep.

"It was almost 63 in '63'," wrote *Journal* political affairs reporter Ben Tierney on June 18, the day after Manning crushed his opponents. "Instead it was 60 to 3 – just 2,592 votes short of the clean sweep predicted in the Social Credit pre-election slogan."

Veteran *Journal* columnist Art Evans reflected on the victory and particularly on what Social Credit had meant to Albertans back in 1935 when the party came to power in the depths of the Depression.

"Social Credit did not draw its support from a rabble," Evans recalled. "In East Calgary where I lived the Social Credit vote was solid and so were the people. They were honest and law-abiding and respectable and they had dignity and pride when times were toughest.

"They weren't after something for nothing, the handout. They were used to working and working hard for what they got."

In 1963, Manning had only one more election in him. The 1967 provincial vote, in which six Tories under Peter Lougheed were elected to the legislature, was the beginning of the erosion of Socred popularity.

And on Sept. 27, 1968, *The Journal* ran one of its bigger headlines in the size of type reserved for bombshells: "MANNING RESIGNS."

The Journal's editorial was balanced in its assessment of Manning and gracious in its appreciation for the sacrifices that 33 years of public life demands. "However, it can be argued that he is not really fully in tune with modern Canada and the bilingual problem we face today.

"Yet no one can doubt that Mr. Manning has been an able leader who has done much for Alberta. He has served it well, and outside of the most partisan opponents who would like his mettle, there will be none who do not regret that he is stepping down. We are pleased to salute a distinguished career."

And Eaton Howitt, the newspaper's political affairs writer, looked into the future of the Manning family on that day: "Whatever the future of Ernest Charles Manning might be, that of Ernest Preston Manning will be of interest and importance to Albertans."

***In 1960*:**
The salary of a teacher with six years of training and 11 years of experience is $8,700. A "mailer" at *The Journal* makes $34.50 a week.

***Jan. 7, 1960*:**
"The city would have nothing to gain and much to lose by selling its telephone system. Long ago the city disposed of its natural gas franchise to a private company but we have resisted numerous efforts in the past by others to gain control of our remaining utilities. Let us always continue to do so."
— An editorial following a suggestion that the city sell EdTel to a private concern.

***Jan. 13, 1960*:**
"A building which housed the first civic offices when Edmonton became a city in 1904 is to be razed soon by demolition crews...Historic Old. No. 1 Fire Hall at 98th Street and 101A Avenue was home for the city's first fire hall and police department as well as civic offices. Built in 1893, the old brick structure is now beyond repair, according to city officials."

***March 8, 1960*:**
The Edmonton Public School Board imposes dress restrictions on students. In a

Edmonton Weather
Forecast: Sunny and a little warmer Friday, light winds. Low tonight 35, high tomorrow 55.

The Edmonton Journal

One of Canada's Great Newspapers

58th YEAR, NO. 134 | TELEPHONE GA 4-0271 | EDMONTON, ALBERTA, THURSDAY, APRIL 20, 1961 | PRICE NOT OVER FIVE CENTS | THREE SECTIONS

FIDEL CLAIMS VICTORY OVER INVADING REBELS

School Bill Bars Setting '61 Mill Rate

City council began its scrutiny of the 1961 capital and current estimates Wednesday in a unique position: It has no hope of setting a final, overall mill rate for some time.

Finance Commissioner Malcolm Tweddle said, however, that if the 32 mills the city is required to pay for education is adequate for Edmonton's schools, a mill rate of 63 could be struck.

Council will not be able to arrive at a definite levy until details of the province's new school foundation program are known. Under it, all municipalities will contribute 32 mills on an equalized assessment, but at the moment there is no way of knowing just how much Edmontonians will have to pay for education.

The yield from 32 mills falls short of the public school board's tentative budget, and it is not known how the gap will be bridged.

Mayor Roper said council had three alternatives before it:

1. It could approve city department estimates and nothing more. These are estimated at 27.38 mills.

2. It could approve the estimates and tack on 35.62 mills for schools—the city mill equivalent of 32 provincial mills. This would give the 63-mill figure.

3. It could decline to approve anything at this stage.

No Definite Stand

Aldermen took no definite stand on the school issue. Instead they tackled the city's own $28,780,970 current and $29,743,009 capital budgets. In a four-hour session they disposed of eight department budgets, including the utilities.

These are all expected to earn surpluses. The electric light and power department estimates a surplus of $1,454,374; the power plant $755,527; the telephones department $800,978 and the water work department $630,000.

Commenting on the surpluses, Commissioner D. B. Menzies said he is growing increasingly uneasy over using utility surpluses to keep the mill rate down.

He pointed out that in 1959, $1,028,958 had been put in the electric light department's reserve. Last year $661,845 was set aside, while this year only $351,351 was earmarked as reserve.

The Edmonton Transit System will be dealt with today. It is expected to chalk up a deficit of $230,735.

Revenue Also Up

Civic spending this year is estimated to total $28,780,970, up $1,809,868 from last year's $26,971,102. Revenues are also up, but far less sharply. This year they are set at $18,845,667 compared to $18,574,243 in 1960 for an increase of $271,424.

The amount to be raised from taxes this year is $9,935,303. Last year it was $8,396,859. This represents an increase of $1,538,444.

Aldermen could trim these figures tonight. Departmental estimates dealt with Wednesday went through unscathed.

One big change in the current estimate picture is the municipal airport. Last year it earned a surplus of $160,891. This year it is expected to return a deficit of $44,623. Transfer of airline operations to the Edmonton International Airport at Nisku is responsible for the reversal, said Commissioner Malcolm Tweddle.

Tentative approval also was given the library board spending of $595,107. Much of it will be taken up with increased repairs and the purchase of a $20,000 bookmobile to replace the present 20-year-old Italian vehicle that has come to the end of the road.

Morton Colborn, library superintendent, said in reference to the repairs that maintenance and overhaul of buildings have been delayed for several years because of lack of money, but since they now come under the building maintenance depart-

(Continued on Page 16, Col. 1)

Portugal Bolstering Forces In Colony

LISBON (Reuters) — Two ships laden with troops and weapons Thursday were reported bound for the revolt-hit Portuguese West Africa territory of Angola.

Portuguese press reports said the ships left here Wednesday for Angola and Portuguese Guinea in Africa, but their names and the number of troops aboard were not disclosed.

Two other ships bound for the same destinations will leave "very soon" and at least three other vessels will sail before the end of the month, newspapers say.

Meanwhile, reports from Angola said an uneasy calm settled today over the northern area where rebel attacks first erupted more than two months ago.

The Portuguese news agency Lusitania said several Africans were killed Wednesday in a clash with a group of whites on the road between the village of Macuba and Carmona in northern Angola.

NEW YORK (AP) — Eight Methodist pastors have been reported killed in Angola, the Methodist board of missions said Thursday.

The mission said the pastors, all Africans, "were killed by either Portuguese civilians or military forces after hurried trials."

At least half the denomination's 150 African pastors in Angola "are reported either in prison, have fled with their wives, or have been killed," the board said.

The reports were received by the board's division of world missions.

The Weather

(Issued by the Dominion Public Weather Office at Edmonton)

Fine dry weather will prevail over most of Alberta today and Friday. Temperatures Friday will be a little higher than today's, reaching the mid-50s in most places.

Low tonight, 35.
High tomorrow, 55.

Sunset today .... 7:44 p.m.
Sunrise tomorrow ... 5:21 a.m.
The Moon rides high tonight and will set at .... 1:25 a.m.
First Quarter .... April 22

PROMINENT STAR
Arcturus, high in southeast .... 10:51 p.m.

VISIBLE PLANETS
Mars, sets .... 2:01 a.m.
Jupiter and Saturn, in the southeast .... 3:42 a.m.

Temperatures

Maximum temperatures yesterday and overnight lows are:

Edmonton	42	29	Vermilion	39	28
Gr. Prairie	51	29	Pr. Albert	60	33
Whitect.	54	22	Yorkton	65	38
Wagner	50	26	Pr. Rupert	45	33
McMurray	52	26	Victoria	51	40
Lac La B.	53	30	Vancouver	50	36
Penhold	42	29	Kamloops	44	29
Rk. Mt. H.	40	30	Penticton	51	30
Calgary	38	30	Swift Cur.	55	27
Lethbridge	47	29	Moose Jaw	60	36
Pincher C.	45	30	Regina	61	34
Med. Hat	52	26	Winnipeg	65	47
Edson	53	21	Ft. Will'm	46	37
Banff	36	24	Toronto	47	28
Jasper	50	24	Ottawa	50	30
Coronat'n	41	32	Montreal	48	32
Whitehse.	39	26	Nor. Wells	14	-4
Snag	30	16	Yellowkn.	31	10
Inuvik	-3	-6	Ft. Smith	48	22

23 Lives Lost In Rail Crash

CALCUTTA, India (AP) — A passenger train hurtled over a bridge near Siliguri, on the border with Bhutan, Wednesday night, killing 23 persons and injuring 81.

Police said sabotage was suspected.

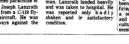

WEARY BUT TRIUMPHANT—Four members of the Edmonton Oil Kings appear a little battle-worn but happy as they hold the Abbott Cup, symbol of Western Canada junior hockey supremacy. The Kings shown here, after their 7-5 victory over the Winnipeg Rangers in Brandon Wednesday night, are, from the left: Wayne Muloin, Tom Burgess, Don Chiz and goalie Paul Sexsmith. The Oil Kings defeated the Rangers 4-1 in games to advance to the Canadian final for the Memorial Cup.—CP wirephoto to The Journal.

Hockey Fever Hits City

Memorial Cup fever, a disease almost as catching as that autumn malady, Grey Cup fever, gripped Edmonton last night—and the epidemic has just barely begun.

It broke out in many places in the city about 10 p.m. when the Oil Kings rallied in Brandon to defeat Winnipeg Rangers 7-5 and bring Edmonton its second straight western Canada junior hockey title.

It was certain to break out again on the city's streets this afternoon, with the Kinglets scheduled to arrive home, at the Canadian National Railways depot, at 2:45 p.m., to be paraded through the downtown area.

Additional reports and pictures on Page 8.

FIRST CHANGE

The fever won't die down until the Memorial Cup is decided, two or three weeks from now. For in winning the West this time, the Oil Kings gave Edmonton its first opportunity to watch a Canadian junior hockey final. On all four previous years that an Edmonton club has won its way into the final, the Memorial Cup has been played in the East.

This time it is to be played in Edmonton, a city which has taken the Kings to its heart in a fashion not known since Flyers won the Allan Cup in 1948.

POSTPONE RODEO?

Edmonton Exhibition officials Thursday said the Rodeo of Champions, scheduled for the Gardens May 1 to 6, may be postponed to make way for a full Memorial Cup series in Edmonton. Otherwise the key games would have to be transferred to Calgary.

Junior hockey fans in several parts of the city spent last night and this morning in hurried preparation for the Oil King homecoming. The young players were to be serenaded at the railway station by bands, cheer leaders and placard-carrying rooters.

U.S. Tax Plan Hits Investing Abroad

WASHINGTON (AP)—President Kennedy today sent a tax plan to Congress which he said would help modernize American business and create 500,000 jobs.

The president said his proposal would attack "expense account living," discourage tax cheating and reduce the worrisome flow of U.S. dollars abroad without cutting into federal revenues.

Kennedy described his program as "a first though urgent step" toward broad tax reform in 1962—reform which he said could combine elimination of loopholes and discriminatory provisions with a lowering of basic tax rates.

NOTABLE ITEMS

These were among the most notable items in the first-step package:

A special tax incentive for business to modernize and expand, withholding of taxes on dividends and interest, repeal of the special tax treatment given dividends and discouragement of corporate investment in competing industrial countries.

To help reduce the flow of dollars abroad and the resulting balance of payments deficit, Kennedy advanced several recommendations. The most important would tend to discourage American corporations from investing in subsidiaries in other industrial countries—Western Europe plus Canada, Japan, Australia, New Zealand and South Africa.

TAXES AVOIDED

Under present law, an American company doesn't have to to pay U.S. taxes on the profits of overseas subsidiaries unless it brings these profits home. As a result, it is common practice to keep reinvesting such profit abroad.

Kennedy asked Congress to "tax each year American corporations on their current share of the undistributed profits realized in that year by subsidiary corporations or-

(Continued on Page 2, Col. 1)

Britain, Russia Near Accord On Laos Truce

LONDON (AP) — The foreign office announced today that Britain and Russia "now seem very near" agreement on a cease-fire in strife-torn Laos.

The British government intends to dispatch fresh instructions to Ambassador Sir Frank Roberts in Moscow.

With luck, the foreign office believes, Roberts will be able to get Soviet agreement to a cease-fire after one more consultation with Soviet Foreign Minister Andrei Gromyko.

ITALY SHOOTS ROCKET

ROME (Reuters)—An Italian Nike-Asp rocket Wednesday night was shot 155 miles into space from a base in Sardinia to probe atmospheric conditions, the defence ministry announced.

Colored Influx Alarms U.K.

LONDON (Reuters)—A member of Parliament said Thursday Britons are "frightened and alarmed" at the immigration of colored Commonwealth citizens into Britain.

Conservative MP Cyril Osborne made the statement in the House of Commons during a debate on immigration.

Osborne said immigration into Britain, much of it from the West Indies, in the first two months of this year was five times the number recorded during the same period in 1960.

Home Secretary R. A. Butler said the government is considering legislation to enable deportation of "undesirable characters" from Commonwealth countries.

He added that such legislation would be used only for convicted criminals and would not be on "a color basis."

PARATROOPER MAKES RESCUE IN MID-AIR

LONDON, Ont. (AP) — A paratrooper Wednesday grabbed the snarled parachute of another in mid-air and carried the other man 1,200 feet to the ground during an exercise of the Royal Canadian Regiment.

A freak updraught collapsed the partly-opened parachute of Drum Major Joseph Lanzrath as he leaped from a C-119 flying boxcar aircraft. He was thrown sideways against the risers of Pte. K. A. Barrett's 'chute.

Barrett, realizing that Lanzrath's parachute would probably stay collapsed, caught the silk as it passed by him, and held on.

Both men floated to earth on Barrett's parachute, with the drum major dangling about 15 feet below the other man. Lanzrath landed heavily and was taken to hospital. He was reported only badly shaken and in satisfactory condition.

Casualties Said High

MIAMI (AP)—Prime Minister Castro said today he has wiped out rebel invaders on Cuba's southern beaches and captured large stores of U.S. arms, including Sherman tanks. He conceded his forces have suffered heavy losses.

The rebel leaders insisted the main invading force has fought through to guerrillas waiting in the Escambray Mountains of central Cuba to carry on the civil war.

Echoing Castro's claims, Moscow radio charged U.S. marines are poised to strike and repeated Soviet government warnings that the use of American forces would have dire consequences.

Moscow said Castro had "dealt a colossal blow to the forces of aggression" but "this does not mean that the threat to the independence of Cuba has been removed and that the interventionists have relinquished their criminal schemes."

CLAIMS NEW LANDING

An anti-Castro leader in Puerto Rico reported Wednesday night that a new landing had been made in Cuba. He did not give the location of the beachhead.

There were rumors — entirely unconfirmed — that more landings were imminent.

The Cuban government communique claiming total victory over the invasion force that hit the swampy beaches of Cochinos Bay Monday said "Giron Beach, which was the last stronghold of the mercenaries, fell at 5:30 p.m. Wednesday."

HEAVY CASUALTIES

Signed by Castro as prime minister and commander-in-chief, the communique claimed the invaders "suffered heavy casualties, dispersing in a swamp area from which no escape is possible." Castro conceded his forces paid a "high toll in courageous lives."

The prime minister said a "large quantity of arms of U.S. manufacture were captured, including various Sherman heavy tanks."

The Cuban revolutionary council in New York, which organized the striking force of Cuban exiles, had said earlier that the "landings" were only a phase of its campaign to overthrow Castro. It disclaimed them as "an invasion."

SUPPORTS CASTRO

Red China again proclaimed its support of the Castro regime and said: "The Chinese people are fully determined to take all necessary measures in all spheres to help the Cuban people in their just and patriotic struggle."

Prime Minister Nehru told the Indian Parliament today that the anti-Castro invasion of Cuba could only have been

(Continued on Page 2, Col. 3)

* * *

Rebels Admit Losses

NEW YORK (AP) — The Cuban revolutionary council said Wednesday night: "Regretfully, we admit tragic losses in Wednesday's action by a small holding force."

The force, a communique issued by the council said, "courageously fought Soviet tanks and artillery while being attacked by Russian MIG aircraft — a gallantry which allowed the major portion of our landing party to reach the Escambray Mountains."

The communique — issued prior to the Cuban government's claim of victory — continued in part:

"We did not expect to topple Castro immediately or without setbacks and it is certainly true that we did not expect to face, unscathed, Soviet armaments, directed by Communist 'advisers.' We did and survived!

"The struggle for freedom of Cuba continues."

* * *

Moscow Repeats Warning

MOSCOW (AP)—The Communist party newspaper Pravda said today that United States policies on Cuba might bring war to the soil of the United States itself. The grave threat was made in a special article signed by Observer, the signature which is reserved for important Soviet policy declarations.

* * *

MIAMI, Fla. (AP)—Thousands of exiled Cubans gathered in Miami's Bayfront Park to pray for the success of the counter-revolutionary invasion of their homeland.

* * *

MIAMI, Fla. (AP)—The Cuban radio said today seven more alleged terrorists—including Humberto Sori Marin—have been executed by Fidel Castro's firing squads. Sori Marin was a one-time Castro lieutenant and a former minister of agriculture in the Castro government.

Where To Find It

Angelo Patri	19
Births, Deaths, Marriages	26
Bridge	28
Comics	6, 28
Crossword Puzzle	31
Dennis The Menace	30
District	15, 34, 36
Dorothy Dix	18
Dorothy Kilgallen	20
Editorial	4
Financial	12, 13
Off The Record	32
Our Boarding House	27
Out Our Way	27
Packsack	6
Sport	8, 9, 10
Theatres, Entertainment	22, 23
They'll Do It Every Time	27
Tizzy	33
T.V.	28
Want Ads	27 to 33
Women's	17 to 20

INDIAN SHOT AT OFFICE DESK

Lay Murder Charge In Diplomat's Death

BY CHRISTOPHER YOUNG
The Journal's Ottawa Bureau

OTTAWA — A senior Indian diplomat was fatally shot in his office here Wednesday, and a Canadian citizen was charged with murder.

K. Sankara Pillai, number two man at the Indian high commissioner's office, was working at his office desk about 2.15 p.m. when a man burst through the door and shot him twice in the chest with a rifle.

Mr. Pillai died almost instantly.

The killing stunned the quiet world of Ottawa diplomacy, where violent death is dealt with only in dispatches. It happened on a sleepy residential street in the central part of the city.

The Indian high commission occupies a Victorian three-storey red-brick house, and Mr. Pillai's office was at the head of the stairs on the second floor.

The killer slipped downstairs and out the front door of the building before any member of the high commission's staff was aware of what happened. A receptionist caught an oblique glimpse of his reflection in a hallway mirror.

About an hour later a man carrying a gun walked into the downtown headquarters of the RCMP and reported the incident.

CHARGE LAID

Ottawa city police have charged Shana Ferizi with murder. Ferizi immigrated to Canada from Yugoslavia in 1951 and is a naturalized Canadian. He came to Ottawa only a few days ago.

In magistrate's court today he was remanded without plea to April 27.

Mr. Pillai, 38, was a graduate of India's Kerala University and Cambridge University, England. He had achieved swift promotion in the Indian external affairs department since he joined its staff in 1948. He was posted to Ottawa as first secretary and charge d'affaires last August after three years as deputy secretary of his ministry in New Delhi.

He lived with his wife and two school-age children in the Ottawa suburb of Alta Vista.

B. N. Bose, press attache at the high commission, said Mr. Pillai had been called out of a meeting Tuesday afternoon by a man who wanted to see him on urgent business. When he returned to the meeting, Mr. Pillai said the caller had asked for help in getting a job in India. Mr. Pillai spoke to him briefly and told him to return on Wednesday.

JOB INQUIRY

It is rare for a Canadian to inquire about jobs in India, and the high commission staff regarded the incident as rather curious. They reported that the man was very rude.

The caller returned on Wednesday morning, but Mr. Pillai was busy and unable to see him. It was the same man, the receptionist reported, who returned early Wednesday afternoon. By this time he knew where Mr. Pillai's office was and he did not stop to ask for an appointment.

The high commissioner, B. N. Chakraverti, and Mr. Bose, the press attache, were both in their offices on the same floor. About 30 members of the high commission staff were in the building. Several heard shots but did not attach any significance to the reports. Two or three minutes later someone looked through Mr. Pillai's office door and saw his body.

The Journal's editorial response to the selection of Harry Strom, the awkward, evangelical southern Alberta farmer who replaced Manning, was cool following the Socred leadership convention in the fall of 1968.

"The future is cloudier at the moment than it has been for some time.

"Revenues are declining in relation to expanding costs. There are great needs in almost every field of government operation. Mr. Strom will not be long in office before he finds himself sternly tested."

It wasn't long at all.

Provinces were redefining their relationship with the federal government, partly because of increased nationalism in Quebec and partly as a result of a changing view of Confederation.

All of which meant that Strom had to confront an activist federal government intent on promoting such policies as bilingualism and biculturalism, medicare, a national pension plan and new divorce legislation. Society itself was demanding changes, too, and Strom found himself pressured into liberalizing the kinds of conservative policies that he and his party held dear. Furthermore, the more urban, younger Lougheed and his team regularly outflanked him and his ministers.

Strom continued to serve into the early years of the '70s, but he was the province's last Social Credit premier.

If the provinces were attempting to come to terms with Ottawa on what this country could become, individual citizens also found themselves pondering the meaning of being Canadian.

Many of those concerns were expressed in the paper, particularly following the arrival of Basil Dean, a former foreign correspondent and *Calgary Herald* editor, who became *The Journal*'s publisher late in 1961.

With his arrival, the newspaper took on a certain intellectual heft, and acquired a *gravitas* that had previously been missing from its pages.

Dean liked the clash of ideas, and in the spring of 1963 he initiated "A Journal for DISSENT," a full page of essay-length submissions from experts and the public on a variety of issues.

"If it succeeds, and we think it will, it may in future be increased in frequency, since we can see no theoretical limit to the amount of discussion that is desirable in a society like ours," he wrote.

The Dissent page sometimes appeared twice weekly, and continued throughout most of the '60s.

The Journal also took on a decidedly different look as well. Shortly after Dean arrived, he lured Dave Colville, the chief photographer at the Calgary Herald, to *The Journal*.

The paper would now have its own photo department with four full-time photographers, a darkroom and a darkroom technician.

Previously, the paper had relied on photographers from Goertz Studios to shoot pictures on a contract basis, but now, with its own staff the number of local pictures in the paper increased dramatically.

The paper also became part of The Associated Press wire photo service out of Seattle, Wash. While a majority of international pictures were from the U.S., the new service meant that readers started seeing a lot more photographs from around the world.

And it was under Dean's watch, and that of editor-in-chief Andrew

***Journal* story, the W.P. Wagner, superintendent said dress for high school males should be slacks or trousers, shirt properly closed and worn inside the trousers, jacket or sweater suitable for indoor wear, shoes without cleats or studs and hair should be properly trimmed and neatly combed. Female students should wear dresses or skirts with blouses or sweaters, neat hairstyle and inconspicuous makeup.**

***March 26, 1960*: The ESO makes the first live symphony performance at Whitehorse, in the Yukon.**

***April 14, 1960*: "To be able to live in a modern new home, in a quiet residential district, free from the noise and bustle of the city, is the dream of many a householder. Two such ideal districts lie within 15 minutes' drive of Edmonton in the professionally planned new satellite town of St. Albert." Feature on Grandin and Sturgeon Heights in St. Albert. A fully serviced 60-ft. frontage lot costs $2,580 says an ad.**

***May 11, 1960*: Population of greater Edmonton is 327,151. *Journal* circulation stands at 110,000.**

The Edmonton Journal

FORECAST: SUNNY — EDMONTON, ALBERTA, FRIDAY, AUGUST 9, 1963 — FIVE CENTS

WHO IS 'BRAIN'?

By FLORA LEWIS
The Washington Post

LONDON — All the top and many of the less elevated brains of Scotland Yard were poring through the annals of British crime today in a search for clues to the identity of The Mastermind.

That is the only name so far for the leader of the gang which carried out the biggest mail train robbery the country has ever known early Thursday.

Estimates of the loss—in used banknotes which can never be traced, diamonds, and registered parcels — have ranged from $3 million to $9 million.

Dubbed Fantastic

The Cheddington ambush robbery has already been christened the Million-Pound Fantastic.

Its closest rival for loot and effrontery in police records is the $1 million Eastcastle Street affair 11 years ago when a gang of seven looted a post office truck full of used banknotes on their way to be pulped.

British papers speculated that it was the same mastermind who had struck again, but they could not guess his name. Any movie film could have helped. It is obvious the double or the scriptwriter for Sir Alec Guinness, because the plot — which has the press and police agog at its extraordinary and surprising cunning — is lifted straight from two Guinness' films.

Compared To Films

Anyone who saw The Lavender Hill Mob and The Ladykillers can easily imagine the precise planning details of the big gang of 30 which so startle and mystify the authorities.

In each successful robbery, the thieves have relied on cunning and meticulous planning rather than upon violence.

But the police can remember the movies as well as the robbers. The Evening News quoted a senior Scotland Yard detective as saying that the very size of the Cheddington gang might be their undoing.

Furthermore, the detective confessed to being worried about the way the gang appeared to have pierced the security barrier of the bank, the post office and the railways. In Lavender Hill Mob, Guinness could accomplish it because he had worked in the vaults of the Bank of England all his life.

Somebody besides the police and the gang knew what belonged in the script. Another special post office train was four hours late with engine trouble and so passed the train marked for robbery in the opposite direction just as though it was braking for the cleverly changed signals.

Another few seconds and the crew of the Birmingham train would have seen the gang pouncing, said The Evening News. The timing was perfect for the extra twist of suspense.

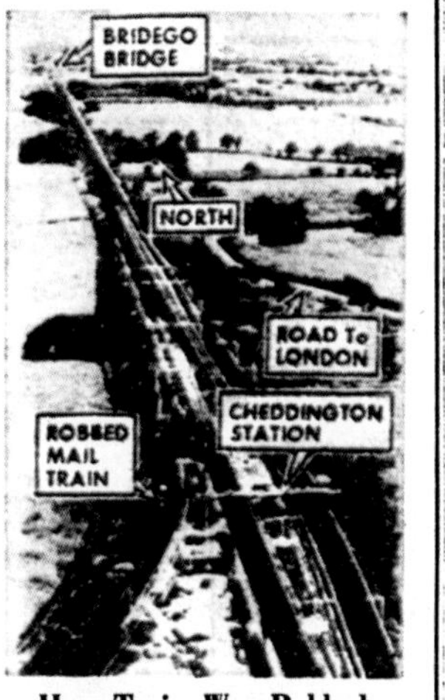

BRIDEGO BRIDGE
NORTH
ROAD To LONDON
CHEDDINGTON STATION
ROBBED MAIL TRAIN

How Train Was Robbed

A fake red signal halted the London-bound train at lonely Sears Crossing (not shown), north of Bridego Bridge. After two coaches were uncoupled the train was taken onto the bridge, where some of the bandits unloaded mail sacks. The train then was shunted to siding.

25-Storey Tower $8 Million Project

Construction Set For Spring

Construction will begin next spring on the new $8,000,000 Canadian National Railways office building.

Plans for the 25-storey building were announced this morning by G. R. Graham, vice-president of the CNR.

Described by the CNR as the "largest office complex west of Toronto," the new building will contain a new CNR passenger station, a large shopping arcade, and a three-storey parking structure.

> Mayor Roper said today he is "thoroughly gratified" by the CNR announcement.
>
> He praised the railway for its foresight and expressed the hope the project would lead to redevelopment of the entire area north of city hall.

The CNR estimates that it will take approximately eight months to complete detailed work drawings of the building and let contracts for its construction. The construction period is estimated at between 18 and 20 months.

An Alberta company, Cal-Mor Management Ltd., will finance and construct the building. The CNR will be the main tenant.

OLD STATION DOOMED

The building is to be located on 104th Ave. near 100th St., on the site of the present CNR station. The old station is to be torn down and replaced by a temporary structure while the new building is under construction.

The CN Telecommunications and CN Express wings of the present CNR building will be left standing, but will be refaced to harmonize with the design of the new building.

The three-storey parking structure will be capable of accommodating 300 cars, but will be planned so that it can be extended over the top of the CNR tracks in the future to link with a second parking structure capable of holding up to 5,000 cars.

OFFICE SPACE

Each of the floors in the 25-storey tower will contain 11,700 square feet of office space for a total office area of close to 300,000 square feet.

The shopping centre area is to be immediately above the passenger station area in what is described as a "twin-level" ground floor.

The station will be slightly below ground level. Passengers will reach trains by up-bound escalators.

LANDSCAPING

The inside and outside of the building are to be landscaped with shrubs and small pools.

Reinforced concrete, with reinforced steel, will be used in the construction of the new building.

OFFICE BUILDING SOARS 25 FLOORS
. . . "largest office complex west of Toronto"

Council To Vote On Costs

City council will be asked Monday to take its first concrete step towards construction of the proposed coliseum complex.

The aldermen will be asked to approve two bylaws authorizing the borrowing of close to $15,000,000 for land purchases and actual construction of the coliseum buildings.

One bylaw, authorizing the borrowing of about $4,000,000, will cover the cost of land purchases. The second bylaw will cover the actual construction costs.

If approved in principle by city council, the bylaws will be advertised by city commissioners to determine whether there is any opposition to the proposed project.

A petition signed by five per cent of the voters in protest against the project could force a plebiscite.

Approval of the two money bylaws, in the event that the city decides to finance the project on its own, is necessary now in order to allow enough time for any protest petition to be filed with the city and the project legally placed before the public in a plebiscite at the same time as the civic elections in October.

If put to a plebiscite, approval of the coliseum complex would require a two-thirds majority.

CITY POLICE NOW ADMIT BONES-IN-FIELD INCIDENT

Edmonton city police did an about-face this morning regarding reports of bones discovered in a farmer's field near Beaumont.

When questioned on reports that farm workers had brought in remnants of bones discovered in a shallow grave in a hayfield, Insp. Ken Shaw said: "There has never been any such incident. This is the first I've heard of it."

Shortly before press time today Insp. Shaw admitted that a jar of bones had been brought to the police station on June 24. He added that in the opinion of

Pictures on Page 3

the police the bones were between 40 and 50 years old and the matter had not been pursued.

Insp. Shaw said the bones were powdery and yellow and officers dismissed the possibility that they might have been those of murdered golf pro Frank Willey.

Willey disappeared in April, 1962. His body has never been found though two men, William Huculak and Raymond Workman were found guilty of his murder and sentenced to death. The death penalty later was commuted to life imprisonment.

SEARCH AREA

At the time of Willey's disappearance the search for his remains was centred in the Camrose-Beaumont area.

Farmer Remi Berube, on whose farm the bones were found, agrees with city police that the bones could not be those of Willey.

But he doesn't agree that they had been in his field for 40 or 50 years.

"I sowed the land last sum-

See POLICE Page 2

Art EVANS

Shattered Career

INDEED FAME IS FLEETING as the pocketbook of Rudy Roo (stage name) knows to its sorrow.

One short year ago Rudy Roo was firmly established in television. His future seemed secure. The money was rolling in. He had a racing car, a five-year subscription (paid up) to Playboy and monogrammed initials on the shower curtain of his very own apartment.

Today he is broke, his career shattered, his hopes extinguished.

Never heard of Rudy Roo, you say? Naturally. The real stars of television commercials are anonymous. But you've seen Rudy scores of time, his ruggedly-handsome young features lighting up the living room as he urged the youth of the nation to enjoy the good things in life. He was one of the biggest and busiest in the business.

Rudy's specialty was the cigarette commercial pitched to young moderns. He was a young modern himself, brimming with vim, vigor and vitality, the white-capped teeth perennially parted in a winning smile.

★ ★ ★

IT WAS FUNNY HOW HE got his first break. He had started out to be a dramatic actor but only one thing stood in his way — he couldn't act. One day he tried out for a bit part playing the role of a minor nut in 'Psychiatric Playhouse,' a Freudian horse opera you may have been lucky enough to miss. Rudy didn't get the part but he did catch the eagle eye of a cigarette commercial scout who had been out front at rehearsal.

"I liked the way you smoked that cigarette in the last scene," the scout told him. "You project deep-down satisfaction."

"But that was only the part," Rudy protested. "Off-camera I don't smoke at all. Long ago I promised my grandmother that . . . "

"Your grandmother's elderberry wine!" the scout snapped peevishly. "The clean-lunged way you smoke a cigarette can make you a fortune".

"Do you really think so?" asked Rudy, impressed by now.

"You've got what Bogart and Bette Davis had in the movies — nicotine know-how," the scout assured him. "In the field of TV cigarette commercials you can be king-size."

"Will I have to inhale?" the neophyte asked anxiously.

"If it bothers you fake it," he was told.

★ ★ ★

RUDY WENT ON TO MAKE A lot of commercials and a lot of money. He puffed contentedly on mountain tops and in coal mines, on skis and in submarines, on trains and in aeroplanes, at the opera and at summer camp, in the shower and at the races. In a hundred pictured situations smoke rings hovered over his youthful crown.

And then, just when Rudy's career was going so well, the pressure of the anti-cigarette forces grew so great that the tobacco industry announced sweeping changes in advertising techniques. As the Saturday Review put it, "Youthful-looking heroes would disappear from cigarette ads and industry spokesmen proclaimed a new era of 'good judgment and good taste.' "

Today Rudy Roo is an unemployed non-smoker. He can't afford the habit.

Municipal Airport Protest To Be Heard By Aldermen

Another episode in the struggle over the Municipal Airport is likely to unfold at city council Monday.

The Journal learned Thursday that a private citizen will protest continued operation of the airport in a letter to be placed before council. The protest will be based on the safety factor at the airport.

In reply, city commissioners are prepared to supply council with statistics prepared by the Federal Aviation Agency between 1950 and 1960. These statistics indicate that danger from overhead aircraft is much less than the danger to pedestrians from cars, taxis, buses and trains.

The statistics show that during the 10-year period, more than 90,000 people died in the United States after being struck by a car or taxi, more than 11,000 died when struck by a train and more than 4,000 died in pedestrian accidents involving buses.

During the same period, 46 people died as a result of being struck by falling aircraft.

City's Capital Budget To Total $30,000,000

By BEN TIERNEY
City Hall Bureau

A record capital budget of close to $30,000,000 is to be made public at city hall today.

It will contain expenditures amounting to $5,000,000 more than last year's budget and just slightly more than the previous record budget of $29,946,000 brought down in 1957.

Allowances of $2,500,000 for land acquisition for the proposed coliseum complex, farmers' market and other civic centre developments are contained in the budget.

Also likely to be included is a $875,000 appropriation for the city's share of construction costs of the proposed pediatrics wing of the Royal Alexandra Hospital.

The largest single expenditure in the budget is expected to go to utilities development. Last year the transit system, power plant, electrical distribution system, telephones and waterworks took $9,498,000. This year the total is expected to be slightly lower.

MOST FOR ENGINEERS

The biggest single departmental expenditure will be for engineering. Its total this year is expected to extend over the $6,000,000 mark, with approximately half going to public works and half to sewer construction.

Local improvements, to be borne by revenue from property, are expected to exceed $7,000,000. Last year they totalled $6,242,000.

Last year's engineering total was more than $5,500,000 of which $2,180,000 went to public works and $3,063,000 to sewer construction.

Also included in the budget will be allowances for a covered skating rink and a YMCA Swimming Pool in the City's west end.

No provision has been made for possible amalgamation with Jasper Place.

Pledge On Price To Be Reviewed

OTTAWA (CP)—The Liberal government's promise to maintain a minimum wheat price of $2 a bushel is being reviewed, it was learned today.

It may be superseded by some other proposals to be put before the resumed parliamentary session in the autumn.

The whole of the government's agriculture policy is under review by Prime Minister Pearson and government officials.

Symbol

The checkered flag is a symbol of stock car racing, and Thursday it went down in Edmonton's Gold Cup race to mark the victory of Billy Foster of Victoria, B.C. The win brought him $6,500. Story on Page 7.

Where To Find It

Ann Landers	17
Births, Deaths, Marriages	38
Bridge	30
Classified Ads	29 - 41
Comics, Features	24
Financial	22, 23
Horoscope	31
Letters To The Editor	4
Patterns	32
Radio	21
Sport	7 - 13
Theatres, Entertainment	18, 19
TV	20, 21
Women's	15 - 17

WEATHER

Sunny and very warm with light winds. Low tonight 60, and a high of 85 tomorrow. Details on Page 2.

Kennedy Baby Loses Battle

BOSTON (AP)—The White House announced early today that the newly-born son of President and Mrs. Kennedy died early this morning from a lung ailment.

White House press secretary Pierre Salinger said: "The struggle of the baby boy to keep breathing was too much for his heart."

The president spent the night at the medical centre here. With him when the baby died was his brother, Attorney General Robert F. Kennedy.

The baby was christened Patrick Bouvier Kennedy shortly after birth by caesarean section early Wednesday afternoon. The baby, 5½ weeks premature, weighed four pounds, 10 ounces at birth.

Respiratory distress due to his lungs not being fully developed was apparent to physicians immediately.

His ailment was diagnosed as hyalane membrane disease. It is not considered uncommon in premature births.

Because of his breathing difficulty, the baby was placed in an isolette, a device which attempts to create an environment as in a mother's womb.

Shortly after his birth at the Otis Air Force Base Hospital, the baby was taken to Children's Medical Centre by ambulance, because of the Boston hospital's extraordinarily-fine equipment.

The baby took a turn for the worse early Thursday afternoon, and it was placed in a submarine-like high pressure

See KENNEDY Page 2

DISEASE CUTS OXYGEN

Hyalane membrane disease is a condition in which a thin membrane forms over the microscopic air sacs of the lungs and keeps oxygen from entering the blood. It was responsible for 31 of 163 newborn babies' deaths in Edmonton in 1961, the last year for which figures are available.

Snaddon, that the sports and entertainment sections took on more bulk. Both men liked an argument, and with writers such as Barry Westgate in entertainment and Wayne Overland in sports, they got what they wanted.

Dean was also the first publisher to regularly write a column under his own byline, and his weekly "Publisher's Notebook" dealt with everything from politics to the Eskimos to the Beatles to his love of fine French wines.

Mostly, though, he encouraged debate.

"The purpose of newspaper opinion is to stimulate discussion and nothing more. Like many other publishers in Canada, I have a sense of mission about my job, but I do not envisage that mission as using the power of the newspaper which I manage to reshape my community or my country to suit my own preferences.

"My mission is to generate public discussion because, like John Milton and Thomas Jefferson, I believe that if a free people, given all the facts, discuss a subject for long enough they will eventually come up with something very close to the correct answer."

Certainly Centennial celebrations in 1967 caused many to think about their own personal relationship with their country.

In the hundreds of stories and letters to the editor that *The Journal* published on the country's 100th birthday, it was clear that most felt confident about the strength of the nation and its future.

Thousands of Edmontonians took part in Centennial events, including musical concerts, art and historical exhibits and an arts festival in which Laurence Olivier and Britain's National Theatre put on William Congreve's restoration comedy *Love for Love* at the Jubilee Auditorium.

The city built a new downtown library in honour of the Centennial – the newspaper said it was as comfortable as your living room – and the Provincial Museum was opened that year as well. *The Journal* dismissed the latter and its contents as only vaguely interesting and said that the building design itself was merely utilitarian.

And anyone familiar with Molson's I AM CANADIAN rant will find something similar, although much more sober-sided, in a June 3, 1967, full-page advertisement from Rothman's Tobacco. It concluded with: "I am a Canadian, and I am deeply myself. For this privilege I give thanks to my country. May she never falter, and may she never swagger. May she realize her potential without losing her character. May she have peace, and may she give it. May it always be a proud thing to say: I am a Canadian."

Centennial also meant Expo 67, the world's fair in Montreal, and for many Westerners, their first trip to Quebec. *The Journal* sent assistant editor Stan Williams, his wife Margaret and their seven-year-old daughter Patricia to Montreal for two weeks.

The family dressed in Klondike Days attire for the duration of their stay. And their costumes were decidedly in keeping with Edmonton's own pavilion at the fair, which featured a K-Days saloon, complete with dancing girls. According to Williams, the pavilion wowed Expo-goers.

But flying above the heads of all those celebrants and on poles in front of all those shiny new Centennial buildings was Canada's new flag.

It was only two years old, and some of the wounds over its replacement of the Red Ensign were still raw.

***May 17, 1960*:**
The $3.5-million Physical Education Building on the University of Alberta campus opens and is billed as one of Canada's best.

***May 26. 1960*:**
The CBC receives the necessary approval to operate a television station in Edmonton that would begin broadcasting in the spring of 1961. CFRN, the local station that had been a CBC affiliate, will operate as an independent.

***June 1, 1960*:**
Edmonton Public Library's Idylwylde branch opens in the Bonnie Doon area.

***June 16, 1960*:**
Edmonton city council votes to raise residential phone rates to $3.75 a month. Business telephone rates will rise to $10 monthly.

***Sept. 19, 1960*:**
The first buildings of the University of Alberta at Calgary open. The campus becomes the separate University of Calgary in 1966.

***Sept. 22, 1960*:**
Queen Elizabeth Planetarium in Coronation Park opens. It's the first municipal planetarium in Canada.

The Edmonton Journal

FORECAST: COOL — EDMONTON, ALBERTA, WEDNESDAY, MAY 24, 1967 — TEN CENTS

Manning Again

Lougheed To Lead Opposition As PCs Get 6 Seats; Liberals Keep 3 MLAs And NDP Is Wiped Out

PETER LOUGHEED
. . . new opposition leader

MIKE MACCAGNO
. . . Liberal votes slump

By EATON HOWITT
Of The Journal

The Social Credit ship of state goes sailing on.

The boat was gently rocked by the Progressive Conservatives in Tuesday's provincial election, but E. C. Manning is still the skipper and master of all he surveys.

The Socreds captured 55 of the 65 seats.

The election among other things, saw:

- The Progressive Conservatives, under Peter Lougheed, claim six seats after having no representation since 1963.
- The obliteration of the New Democratic Party which lost the first and only Alberta seat it had ever had. The old CCF party held two seats at one time.
- Mike Maccagno, retain his seat as Liberal leader with his two mates, Bill Switzer of Edson and Bill Dickie of Calgary, but lose his post as opposition leader to Mr. Lougheed.
- The defeat of daylight saving time.
- The defeat of Education Minister R. H. McKinnon.
- The Socreds pick up 45 per cent of the vote, the Conservatives 26, NDP 16, Liberals 11, Independent one and others one.

Although there is no doubt it was a victory at the polls for Ernest Charles Manning who now commands a 55-10 majority in the house, it was a moral victory of great proportions for Conservative Peter Lougheed. At dissolution the Socreds held a 58-5 edge.

Hand-Picked

Mr. Lougheed, a 38-year-old Calgary lawyer, had fought a tremendous campaign and surrounded himself with hand-picked youthful candidates.

Don Getty, former Edmonton Eskimo quarterback and Lou Hyndman Jr., Edmonton lawyer, picked up city seats for the Tories.

Like their leader, neither has any political experience. Mr. Hyndman won Edmonton West in a tough three-way fight with Socred Bill Johnson and Liberal Bernard Feehan while it was Mr. Getty who toppled Mr. McKinnon in Strathcona West.

In Calgary, Mr. Lougheed picked up his own seat in Calgary West with a lop-sided victory over veteran Socred Donald Fleming and added the new seat of Victoria Park where alderman Dave Russell won a squeaker and in Calgary Bowness where Len Werry, a 39-year-old accountant, ousted Socred Charles Johnston.

Action Sure

The other Tory seat goes to an experienced politician who is bound to stir up action on the opposition side of the house, Dr. Hugh Horner of Lac Ste Anne.

Dr. Horner, a former Conservative MP for Jasper-Edson, and a former contender for the leadership of the PC party at Ottawa, kicked over Socred Bill Patterson.

A. J. Hooke, minister of municipal affairs, who was supposed to be in trouble in his Rocky Mountain House riding, was returned without too much trouble.

Two other Socred cabinet ministers came through unbeaten but most certainly bloodied.

Toughest Fight

Ambrose Holowach, provincial secretary, had the toughest fight of his career in Edmonton Centre where he finally came through over a youthful Conservative Hal Veale. And in Calgary Centre, Public Works Minister F. C. Colborne, fought to the wire with radio personality Chuck Cooke, also running for the Lougheed team.

If there was any politician in the province unhappier than NDP Leader Neil Reimer it must have been Mike Maccagno, leader of the Liberals.

Mr. Maccagno captured his own seat and retained his status quo with three in the house. But the percentage vote for his party dropped from 20 to 11.

Turcott Out

Garth Turcott, who was the first New Democrat ever to sit in the house, went down to inglorious defeat to newcomer Socred Charles Drain in Pincher Creek-Crowsnest.

Mr. Turcott, who won the seat in a byelection last fall, in his brief few months of glory, forced the Manning government into calling a judicial inquiry into his charges of impropriety on the part of Mr. Hooke and former provincial treasurer E. W. Hinman.

He charged that the minister and former minister had used their public offices for private gain. Mr. Turcott sat in the house for a two-day special session last November and again for one full session.

Close Second

In riding after riding the Conservatives, since 1963 a "nothing" on the Alberta political scene, ran a close second. In Okotoks-High River, Cardston, Edmonton Northwest, Edmonton Centre, Calgary East, and many others they were just votes away from toppling incumbent Socreds.

In Banff-Cochrane, Independent Clarence Copithorne, a well-known rancher, took over the reins laid down by coalition member Frank Gainer who has retired. Mr. Copithorne is known to have Tory leanings.

Mrs. Ethel Wilson, who had no trouble what-so-ever in Edmonton North, will be the only woman member in the 16th Alberta Legislature.

Although this was the first time Alberta Indians had the vote, two Indians, running under the NDP banner lost out. Stan Daniels lost to Roy Ells in Grouard while Phil Thompson lost to another Socred, Ernie Lee, in Dunvegan.

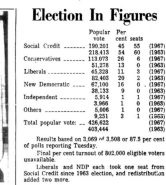

PREMIER MANNING
. . . victory old hat

Other election stories and pictures, Edmonton poll-by-poll and constituency results on pages 3, 14, 15, 16, 17, 18, 21, 22, and 23.

Art EVANS

Any Old Suits?

HAVING PRIVATE means enables a politician to make contributions beyond what is normally expected.

For example, Senator Robert Kennedy has donated six of his old (or less than new) suits for a charity auction. A sampling of the Senator's summer shorts and striped trousers is also included.

While there are no statistics available, one would be willing to bet that most politicians don't own six suits. They might be able to donate one suit to charity, and in some cases, two, but any larger bequest would prove embarrassing. It wouldn't be the taxpayer that cartoonists portrayed naked in a barrel.

Some politicians choose to appear, year in and year out, in the same suit. At least it looks like the same suit. This could be a matter of strategy rather than necessity. In the absence of private means, continually popping up in a new outfit could arouse suspicion, however ill-founded.

★ ★ ★

THE SUIT that inspires voters' confidence should be neither too old nor too new. People won't vote for a threadbare candidate or a clothes-horse. They like a nice, middle-of-the road, pepper-and-salt job. There may even be some politicians who are so afraid of appearing in a new suit that they have a friend break it in for them.

One imagines that Senator Kennedy's old suits will be snapped up at that charity auction.

Whether they will be worn by the purchasers is something else again. The announcement, "I'm wearing one of Senator Kennedy's old suits," could promote heckling, particularly if made at a Republican rally.

It seems more likely that such acquisitions will be retired to a closet and perhaps searched periodically in the vain hope that the lining will yield a misplaced bill of large denomination. And if the Senator one day makes the White House, his old suits could bring more at a second auction.

★ ★ ★

HOME-ON-WHEELS

A LADY MOTORIST in England was tootling along when she noticed that the driver of a car that overtook and passed her, was shaving with an electric razor.

She phoned the police and when they asked for a description of car and "shaver," it was their turn to be surprised. The lady reported the vehicle was a police car and the chap wielding the razor was in police uniform.

Shaving while driving is only the beginning. The car is becoming a home-away-from-home and in a few years' time domestic scenes of all kinds may be commonplace on the freeway. We can look for drivers to be reading, watching television, doing crossword puzzles, filling out income tax forms, helping children with homework, and so on.

★ ★ ★

THERE IS nothing new about using an electric razor in a car. I knew a fellow who was doing it as long ago as 1949. I didn't approve but as a passenger I was only thankful that he didn't use an old-fashioned shaving mug and straight razor.

Then there was a cab driver I remember who was never without his pocketbook, generally a murder mystery. Granted, he only read at red lights, and provided he hadn't reached a particularly thrilling part, he did move on the green signal.

The car radio gives some drivers the impression that they are listening at home and not on the highway. Waltzes aren't so bad but jam sessions are dynamite.

I once rode with a Gene Krupa fan who kept beating the wheel in a frenzy, and once was enough. I thought he was going to get up and dance, all at high speed. At such moments there is lot to be said for Guy Lombardo's music which has long observed the speed limit.

Egyptians Mine Gulf Of Aqaba

UN To Take Up Tense Middle East Situation

From Journal News Services

Egypt has mined the entrance to the Gulf of Aqaba as part of a large-scale land, sea and air operations to block Israeli-bound shipping.

And in the United Nations, the Security Council decided without a vote today to take up the critical situation in the Middle East.

In other developments, UN Secretary-General U Thant began talks in Cairo with Egyptian leaders in an effort to avert war between the United Arab Republic and Israel.

NO FORMAL OBJECTION

Despite strong statements by the Soviet Union and India opposing a council meeting at this time and expressions of reservations by France, no formal objection was raised.

The meeting was called at the request of Canada and Denmark.

Canadian Ambassador George Ignatieff said Canada is asking "that the Security Council and in particular all of its permanent members, who bear special responsibilities, add the weight of its influence collectively by asking that no member of the United Nations take any action which would worsen the situation or jeopardize the efforts of the secretary-general to preserve peace."

COURSE OF ACTION

Ignatieff said the Security Council had the responsibility to agree on some course of action that would help Secretary-General U Thant in his efforts to preserve peace in the Middle East.

Soviet Ambassador Nicoli Fedorenko said the Canadian ambassador did not take into account "the simple fact" that Thant now is in Cairo to gather "the necessary information" about the Middle East situation.

He said the council should await his report.

The Soviet ambassador said Ignatieff, together with certain other Western representatives, is "artificially dramatizing" the situation.

Arthur Goldberg, U.S. ambassador, said:

"This council would have to be burying its head in the sand if it refused to recognize the threat to peace implicit in the events that have occurred since the secretary-general left two days ago."

The United States has backed Israel and Russia the Arabs in the dispute.

SEA PATROLLED

Cairo's semi-official newspaper Al Ahram said blockade operations were launched Tuesday on orders of President Nasser. It said Egyptian planes and torpedo boats are patrolling the Red Sea at the mouth of the gulf.

"War with Israel might break out any moment," the paper said in banner headlines above a four-column picture of a big

More CRISIS Page 2

Other Stories Page 55

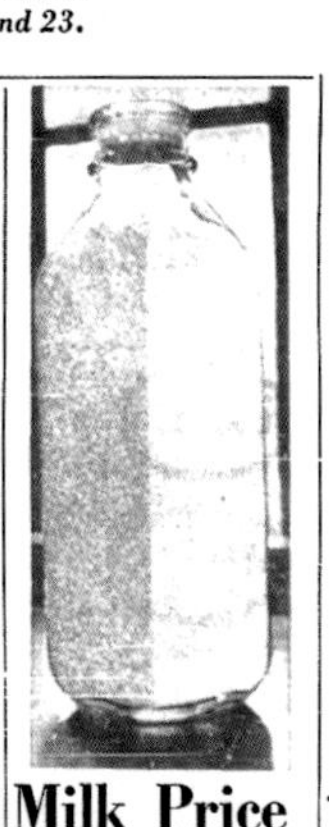

Milk Price Goes Up Two Cents

Edmonton housewives will be faced with a two-cent a quart increase in the retail price of milk June 1.

The Public Utilities Board announced today the price of standard and homogenized milk will increase to 28 cents a quart, with similar increases for other lines of fluid milk products.

At the same time, a 40-cent per hundredweight increase was set in the price paid to producers for whole milk. Details Page 3.

Election In Figures

	Popular vote	Per cent	seats	
Social Credit	190,201	45	55	(1967)
	218,413	54	60	(1963)
Conservatives	113,073	26	6	(1967)
	51,278	13	0	(1963)
Liberals	45,328	11	3	(1967)
	82,403	20	2	(1963)
New Democratic	67,100	16	0	(1967)
	38,133	9	0	(1963)
Independent	5,914	1	1	(1967)
	3,966	1	0	(1963)
Others	5,006	1	0	(1967)
	9,251	3	1	(1963)
Total popular vote:	426,622			(1967)
	403,444			(1963)

Results based on 3,069 of 3,508 or 87.5 per cent of polls reporting Tuesday.

Final per cent turnout of 802,000 eligible voters unavailable.

Liberals and NDP each took one seat from Social Credit since 1963 election, and redistribution added two more.

Where To Find It

The National Energy Board has given Trans-Canada Pipe Lines and its major distributors one week to seek agreement on a new proposal for increased natural gas capacity. Story Page 46.

Ann Landers 24
Births, Deaths, Marriages 62
Bridge 64
Business, Stocks 45-47
Classified Ads 63-73
Comics, Features 48
Comment 4
Crossword Puzzle 67
Horoscope 65
Journal for the Family 21-30
News Digest 33
Sport 39-42
Theatres, Entertainment 60-61
TV 35
Wayne Overland 39

Totol Pages 76

Weather

Cloudy tonight and Thursday morning. A few sunny periods Thursday afternoon. Scattered thundershowers tonight. Low tonight 40, high Thursday 60. Details on Page 2.

When Prime Minister Lester Pearson announced in May 1964 that the country was due for a new flag, and he had one in mind, *The Journal* accused him on May 20 of stirring up unnecessary trouble.

"The personal courage of Mr. Lester B. Pearson on the national flag issue cannot be questioned.

"Unfortunately, the same cannot be said for his judgment."

His timing was terrible, editorial added, particularly at a period "when calm judgment is needed if Canada is to be preserved as a viable nation.

"The Pearson government has already appointed a commission on biculturalism and bilingualism, a commission which may find the means to preserve a united Canada. So far, the first visible effect of the body has been that of stirring emotions. Now the prime minister has taken a course which will excite them even further."

It certainly did, as witnessed by the thousands of letters received by the paper. One writer, identified as Legionnaire, insisted that Pearson's action was the kind of dictatorial high-handedness that he and his fellow soldiers had fought against in two world wars. "He has the unmitigated gall and intolerable shortsightedness to present his idea of a Canadian flag which appears to be an obsession with him."

Another, under the pen name Canadian Veteran, took the opposite view and supported the concept of a new flag. "Now we will have a flag of our own. The foreign emblems, the Quebec 'Drapeau des-fleur-de-lys' and the British 'Union Jack' will be regarded with respect, but certainly not as any part of our national emblem."

Canadians had sent hundreds of suggested designs to Ottawa, and *The Journal* conducted a straw vote of its more than 110,000 subscribers.

Almost 6,000 cast ballots, and the old Red Ensign won by more than 1,000 votes.

By December 1964, the wrangling was over. The flag bill passed through the House of Commons and the Senate, and while it wasn't the three-leaf design favoured by Pearson, the arguing was over at last.

"Almost incredibly in this House of Minorities," *The Journal* said in reference to Pearson's minority government, "a design eventually was found which was acceptable to a substantial majority."

The new flag would speak for Canada to the rest of the world, the editorial said. "Mr. Pearson has invited the country to rally around it.

"If some feel reluctant now, future generations probably will not."

But if the flag stirred emotions, Pierre Elliott Trudeau's arrival on the federal scene brought a new kind of excitement to politics.

From the beginning, when he received his first senior cabinet post in the Pearson government, *The Journal* saw something special in Trudeau.

"His mind and his manners are bound to startle a good many grey Canadians. But it is also refreshing to have a senior minister who admits to strong liberal views on laws governing divorce, birth control and abortion; who sees a need for administrative tribunals, who sees needs for reform in the area of contempt of court; who has been deeply involved with constitutional reform and strong federal government, and who has a wide base of support and rapport with activist Quebec."

When Pearson resigned following Canada's Centennial year – *The*

***Oct. 15, 1960*:**
Demolition begins on the last house on downtown Jasper Avenue, torn down to make way for an expansion of the Corona Hotel on 107th Street.

***Nov. 29, 1960*:**
A freight train crashes into a school bus at Lamont, northeast of Edmonton, causing the deaths of 17 high school students.

***Dec. 3, 1960*:**
The new Edmonton International Airport officially opens.

***In 1960*:**
The Community Chest of Greater Edmonton becomes the United Community Fund and raises $1,012,337 under chair E. M. (Joe) Blanchard.

***Feb. 4, 1961*:**
A *Journal* editorial complains of the inconvenient airline schedule that sees eastbound flights leave the city at 12:35 a.m., and arrive in Toronto at 5:45 a.m.... "The gratification felt by Edmonton citizens over the inclusion of their city on the fast, pure jet service of Trans-Canada Air Lines will be dashed for those who use the service and experience the schedule...Once again, in accordance with its long neglect of

Party Lines Eliminated In Commons Debate On Execution

BY CHARLES KING
The Journal's Ottawa Bureau

OTTAWA—A bill to substitute life imprisonment for hanging as a murder penalty appears headed for certain defeat in the House of Commons.

Ten members of Parliament, dividing across party lines, spoke in favor of the abolition measure, introduced by Conservative Frank McGee, in a day-long debate Thursday. Seven MPs spoke firmly against it.

While the abolitionists held the lead, at least temporarily, the mood of the Commons appeared strongly in favor of the minority who opposed the bill.

The signs were so evident that a leading abolitionist forecast privately that no more than 85 MPs will line up in support of the bill when the test comes, probably next Thursday night.

"It will be badly beaten," he predicted. "It will really be snowed under."

Two hundred and sixty-three MPs will be eligible to vote. There is one vacancy in the 265-seat Commons, and the Speaker, Roland Michener, votes only in case of a tie.

RARE SIGHT

The division cut right across party lines, a rare sight in a Parliament that normally follows the leader unquestioningly. This time there was no leader to call the tune.

Prime Minister Diefenbaker, Liberal Leader Lester Pearson and CCF House Leader Hazen Argue sat through most of the debate, listening intently. They gave no sign, however, of their personal feelings, and refrained from the customary desk-thumping that signals approval of a Speaker's comments.

The pro-and-con score, to Thursday's 10 p.m. closing:

For abolition of the death penalty: five Conservatives, three Liberals and two CCF-ers.

For retaining it: Five Conservatives and two Liberals.

There was no discernible bloc of opinion along religious lines, or any other.

The bill was introduced by Conservative backbencher Frank McGee, a Roman Catholic and a descendant of Confederation's D'Arcy McGee. It won strong support from another Roman Catholic, experienced criminal lawyer Arthur Maloney.

It was sharply opposed, however, by three members of the same faith, two Liberals and one Conservative, from the province of Quebec.

Two other Conservatives, both Roman Catholic, one from Quebec and one from Manitoba, supported it strongly.

Arthur Smith of Calgary, Conservative and an Anglican, opposed it. Alan MacNaughton of Montreal, Liberal and an Anglican, supported it.

This same division appeared all the way through the long debate. The only sign of unanimity showed in the ranks of the CCF, all of whose eight members are understood to support abolition.

Abolitionist McGee opened the crucial, emotional and highly personal debate with a quiet, reasoned but lack-lustre analysis of the case for throwing out the death penalty.

CLEAR ISSUE

Ignoring a crudely-worded threat on his life, received a few hours before the debate opened, the 33-year-old Conservative declared the "clear, single issue" is the substitution of life imprisonment for hanging as a penalty for murder.

"I have read everything I could find on both sides of the subject," he said ernestly. "I have been accused of showing sympathy for murderers, at the expense of their victims.

"My main concern is for society. I would like to make my contribution and change the law."

He cited Britain's experience in the abolition field. In the 18 months before hangings were suspended a few years ago, there were 256 murders. In the 18 months of suspension, there were 246. In 17 months after hanging was restored, there were 310.

"I contend that capital punishment is not an effective deterrent," he said, "and not a unique deterrent, either. I feel it is morally wrong for the state to take a human life."

Capital punishment, he argued, is based on "revenge and retribution," rather than reform and rehabilitation of the criminal.

Society should respect the sanctity of human life, he added. With the death penalty, there is always the risk of error. The present law is illogical and contradictory.

How could the public be protected without the death penalty as a deterrent?

"By ensuring that no person is released so long as his imprisonment is necessary to protect society. Surely our laws can be written to assure that."

Harold Winch (CCF, Vancouver East), a 25-year opponent of capital punishment, spoke next.

"Don't worry about threatening letters," he counselled Mr. McGee.

"I received five myself in the last two weeks. There is only one place for them and that is the wastepaper basket."

Mr. Winch reviewed events of the quarter-century he has fought for abolition, a hanging he witnessed—of a 21-year-old man convicted of driving a getaway car in a bank robbery where a teller was shot.

"I have never found one logical statement or position that could be taken in support of retaining capital punishment," he declared.

"Emotionally, yes," he admitted, "but not one logical, reasonable, Christian basis for retention."

He cited the classic ar[...] reasons under analysis," he declared.

"For every biblical quotation 'Thou Shalt Kill,' I can produce three 'thou shalt not kills'."

STATISTICS PRODUCED

He also produced some interesting statistics: capital punishment was abolished in 1863 in Belgium, 1892 in Denmark, 1826 in Finland, 1860 in Holland, 1822 in Luxembourg, 1876 in Norway, 1867 in Portugal, 1838 in Romania, and 1919 in Sweden.

European homicide rates today, compared with Canada's 1.2 per 100,000: Holland, 0.4; Norway, 0.5; Sweden, 0.8; Switzerland, 1.0; Denmark, 1.0; West Germany, 1.2, the same as Canada.

"No matter how you look at it," he argued, "emotionally, as a Christian, statistically and factually — any thinking person can come to only one conclusion — capital punishment is inhuman, out of date, and should be outlawed."

The two convinced abolitionists failed to make any impression on Conservative Fergie Browne, Mr. Winch's next-door neighbor from Vancouver Kingsway.

"I completely reject their arguments," he said simply.

"I don't believe that their opinions in any way reflect public opinion. It surprises me that anyone so far removed from public opinion could get into the House of Commons."

Canada's national defence, he declared, is based on the principle of deterrence.

"Surely, if it works on that principle — and it has worked successfully for many years now since the formation of NATO — we have contained the enemy in that regard and it has been proven to have worked. I suggest that in the case of criminals it will work to the same extent.

"The public wants. . . a change in the Criminal Code. However, the only course we are now able to follow is to see that this bill is disposed of, that it be voted down, because I am absolutely certain that it will be — and I am also absolutely certain that will be in accordance with the wishes of the public."

Perhaps, Mr. Browne suggested, the gas chamber or electric chair could be substituted for hanging. Certain crimes could be exempted, and circumstantial evidence ruled out as a proof for conviction.

The principal of abolition is "absolutely wrong." The death penalty "does act as a deterrent, and we should retain it, but in a different form." he said.

Liberal Hubert Badanai (Fort William) saw the issue as a choice between "thirsting after justice in a mood of vengeance" and "the practice of Christian charity and the rehabilitation of criminals."

There is no valid [...] said the MP, that [...] study and personal experience in too many depressing cases.

"To me the sole question is: is the penalty of death the only effective deterrent? or is there another?"

He found a "wealth of incontrovertible evidence" that the death penalty is not the only effective deterrent. Life imprisonment, he said, is equally effective.

The "inescapable conclusion" is that the incidence of homicide bears no relationship whatsoever to the presence of the death penalty in the law of the land.

He urged MPs to read the testimony of witnesses before a joint parliamentary committee which studied capital punishment in 1956 (and recommended that it be retained).

"Watch for the witnesses who testified as to facts, and those who testified as to beliefs," he said. "The facts are that the death penalty is not the only effective deterrent."

Mr. Maloney referred to the "mental torment" of the condemned murderer.

"They suffer more," he said. "than any torture meted out by the murderer to his victim."

Experience had taught him that crime was caused by slums, broken homes, poverty, drunkenness, divorce and the lack of opportunity.

"We should ponder less," he said, "on the need for the death penalty, and ponder more on eradicating the roots of crime.

"The death penalty is out of date — it's not the answer. We should be ready here and now to vote in favor of its abolitions."

SECOND LAWYER AGREES

Quebec Conservative Martial Asselin, a lawyer, supported the abolitionist side.

"Must we always follow the commandment 'an eye for an eye'?" he asked, "or rather the other commandment 'Thou Shalt Not Kill'? Our Lord's life was one long work for those who were against him."

His law experience had taught him that much crime resulted from the negligence of parents, and unhappy childhood.

"A large number of criminals are unbalanced people, unable to act of their own free will; and it's often hard to convince a jury of an insanity defence."

The present law, he suggested, has made perjury "a very common crime—and it often escapes the attention of a judge and jury."

If a trial of abolition should show it to be a failure, Parliament could always reverse itself later, he argued.

The same set of facts didn't appeal to another Quebec lawyer, Liberal Guy Rouleau [...] the danger of sentimentality. The bill is mature, but opinion is divided in this house and among the Canadian people.

"If we couldn't select a Canadian flag because opinion in the country was divided, we should be even more cautious when it's a matter of life and death.

"I believe every member of this House should be called on to express his view, and that is why I am expressing mine, to the best of my knowledge and according to my conscience. I express the opinion of the majority of my electors and the majority of the Canadian people. My vote will be against the bill."

To another French-speaking Roman Catholic, Conservative Laurier Regnier (St. Boniface), the issue was simple. He couldn't understand how Mr. Rouleau had not been convinced by the abolition argument.

"There are no valid reasons why we should retain capital punishment. To those who say that capital punishment serves as a protection to society I state that capital punishment has the reverse effect.

"In the first 49 years of this century there were 2,346 persons charged with murder in Canada. Only 895 of that total were sentenced and only 480 received a sentence of capital punishment.

"In other words, out of a total 2,346 persons charged with murder 1,451 went scot free. They are free to walk our streets and enter our homes.

WHAT PROTECTION?

"If you ask the judges, policemen and Crown attorneys who have attended murder trials where the accused has been acquitted, they will tell you that these people are murderers, in the large majority who escaped punishment. What protection is that to society?"

Liberal Alan MacNaughton of Montreal supported the abolition side, with reservations.

Punitive justice, said this lawyer, is now outmoded, and even under the best conditions, men make mistakes.

"Frequently the cards seem to be stacked against a fair trial for the accused, where prejudice has already been created. Once executed, he is dead, and there is no appeal."

The state, he argued, has no right to take what it cannot give. It could not give life, and should not take it.

He found the McGee bill "very inadequate," and promised to listen carefully to the argument before making a firm decision.

He cited an Anglican church summary as best representing his views:

"It may well be that public [...] penalty in the Canadian law.

"3. Following this, that the use of the power to respite murderers be more commonly used in those cases where the murderer was not previously an offender.

"4. Before any abolition of capital punishment is possible there must be a more or less lengthy period during which the law that allows it is an abeyance."

Conservative Robert Stewart of New Brunswick ran into trouble with the abolitionist side when he argued—in opposition to the bill—that "anyone with a reasonably good standing" gets a fair trial today.

"That's not British justice as I know it," bellowed Mr. Winch, and Mr. McGee protested:

"The Hon. member is attaching qualifications to the person who will get a fair trial."

NO CASE

Mr. Stewart pressed on with his attack, declaring that no case had been made out for abolition.

"We want liberty and freedom —but liberty does not mean licence. When we have raised the moral and educational standards of our people we shall be in the position to abolish capital punishment.

"Let us not abolish one of the protections that we have. Let us rather go to the (Criminal) Code and make those changes which we consider necessary so that as a Canadian people we may grow and prosper."

Another powerful attack against the abolitionists was delivered by Calgary Conservative Arthur Smith. Said he:

"It is a long established fact that before an act is changed the opposition to it must substantiate the claim that it should be altered. They (the abolitionists) have failed to make their case."

Parliament would be doing a "disservice to the public," he argued, in passing the bill.

"It is well established that the churches are as divided as are many of our citizens as to the right or wrong of capital punishment.

"Capital punishment has been with us for a long time. It has proven to be a deterrent."

He capped his argument by quoting the words of his father, the late Arthur L. Smith, who represented the same Calgary riding until his death:

"I speak . . . as a firm believer in capital punishment for murder . . . and a firm believer in hanging as the method."

The younger Smith added:

"So long as this deterrent exists, so long as there is in the mind of the individual who pulls the trigger that he may lose his life in the event that he takes another man's life, so long will the public have a feeling of safety."

CCF-er Erhart Regier (Burnaby-Coquitlam) spoke with equal force for the other side.

"I have waited since 1953 for the opportunity to express myself." He said.

LAW SUBVERTED

"Parliament is behind the opinion of men and women who are asked to serve on juries. Jurors are subverting the law because of the result of a finding of guilty.

"I don't like to think that we may be voting against the bill, and then getting out from under by hiring a hangman. We escape our responsibilities when we do that."

Conservative Remi Paul, another Quebecker, argued for "reason" and declared that God delegates his authority to those chosen to govern. The death penalty should be retained.

Sentences are pronounced now because of "the love of good," he declared. It was "regrettable" that the pity of abolitionists did not extend to the families of murder victims.

More of the same from Liberal Lucien Cardin, a lawyer from Sorel:

The government, he charged, was shirking its responsibility by allowing a private member to introduce the abolition bill. It was "playing by ear."

Abolition might make criminals "more trigger-happy, and I for one am not willing to take that risk."

Outright opposition again from Conservative Frank Lennard, the veteran MP from Wentworth, Ont.

Capital punishment, he said, is deterrent. If it were done away with, Canada would become "a battleground for thugs from the U.S."

Police forces would have no protection, he argued.

Finally, two more for the abolition side:

Conservative Margaret Aitken of Toronto, who voted to retain capital punishment in 1956, but since has changed her mind, argued that Parliament "must give leadership."

LAST WORD

The last word came from Liberal Chesley Carter, a Newfoundlander and supporter of moral rearmament.

He was in favor of the bill "on balance," although other capital punishment bills on the Commons' order paper were "more suited to this discussion."

There had been cases where innocent men had been hanged, he said, and he suspected that under present law, rich men had a "much better chance" of receiving justice than the poor.

While there was a "fifty-fifty chance" that his decision would be wrong, he was prepared to vote for abolition.

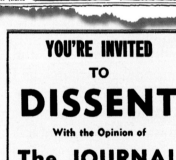

A Journal For DISSENT

"A democracy is a society in which honorable men may honorably disagree." — Adlai Stevenson

DR. A. G. McCALLA ARGUES THERE IS . . . *"Distortion By Truth"*

FREQUENTLY, after reading a short newspaper account of a speech given by a prominent person, I find myself thinking, "How can anyone in his position make such a stupid remark?"

But then I think, "Wait a minute, is that really what he said and, if it is, does this report give a true idea of what he meant?"

Many speakers and many people who hear speeches know that published reports are all too often very misleading.

Quite frequently this is because the reporter has picked out one statement and made it appear as the most important thing in the address whereas both the speaker and all who heard him know that it was only a casual remark.

What follows sets out, in some detail, an example of such reporting and some of its consequences. I am assured that it is by no means an isolated case.

On March 3, 1962, I took part in a conference sponsored by the World University Service Committee at the University of British Columbia. The conference dealt with the problems faced by foreign students at Canadian universities. I had been asked to speak on academic problems while other speakers dealt with the foreign student in relation to student activities, employment, immigration, and personal problems.

How It Went

My talk was to lay the groundwork for group discussions. I spoke for about 40 minutes; there was general discussion for over an hour; the small study groups each took one of the main items for detailed consideration; and finally, these groups reported to a general session.

The following Monday morning I received a phone call from a reporter at The Edmonton Journal saying that the paper had received a Canadian Press report of the talk and he would like my [...]

This was followed by: "Dr. A. G McCalla, Dean of the Faculty of Graduate Studies, University of Alberta, suggested that overseas students should be given a 'sensitivity test' before coming to Canada." The editor then referred to some of the other statements made at the conference, commented on the achievements of some foreigners and added, "It is difficult to see that a sensitivity test, as proposed by Dr. McCalla, would accomplish anything that an intelligence test would not. . ."

Ridiculous

I HOPE that you will see, as I proceed, that the very distorted report received from Canadian Press put the editorial writer in the ridiculous position of taking seriously something that was said as a joke at the very end of a lengthy discussion.

This is what actually happened.

I had dealt with the problems faced by a Canadian university in selecting foreign students and in arranging suitable programs for them; and with the problems that the foreign students themselves have in relation to our educational methods, language difficulties, achieving satisfactory records and in dealing with staff and other students.

In the discussion that followed the talk, there were many comments about the problems the students faced, with most of the time being spent on basic academic problems.

Toward the end of the discussion, a participant referred to the possible difficulties that [...]

Because short quotations in the press are often wholly inadequate to give a true picture, says Dr. A. G. McCalla, they may, in fact, result in distortion by truth. Dr. McCalla is dean of the Faculty of Graduate Studies at the University of Alberta.

is so out of context that it is a gross distortion of the truth-by-the-truth.

At Their Mercy?

No paper can be expected to give the whole text of the many speeches that are reported, and many speeches aren't worth more than a few lines—if that.

BUT — and this is my main point — surely a speaker is entitled to expect that the report will give the reader a fair idea of what the speech was about. If it does not, then, although every quotation is accurate, the report is a distortion. [...]

For four weeks in the summer of 1961, I was one of five Canadian staff members at the World University Service International Seminar held in Sweden. We found the Swedish press meticulous in reporting on the speeches and discussions. When a speaker was quoted in a report, the quotation was as near a literal translation as the language permitted. We were repeatedly astonished to note the precise phraseology used in the news reports.

I wish I could say the same regarding reports of comparable meetings published by the Canadian press in general.

Dean's View

ments that had been made, in The Gateway, about the address he had given at the university. In this letter he said: ". . . I made rather a point, as I recall, of observing that a newspaper has a duty to print the news and to report opinion of all varieties. ." and while I have taken this out of the context of the letter, it is not distorted by quoting it in this way.

NOW I ask — how can my opinions, my deep concern for our responsibilities to foreign students and my genuine appreciation of the great contribution being made by such students, be conveyed to the reading public if a newspaper takes one incidental remark made at the end of a discussion and reports it as if it were the meat of the address?

I DID make the remark that was quoted but, if the newspaper report conveyed the correct impression, then I should not have been speaking at all.

No one questions the right of an editor to comment on, discuss and attempt to interpret the news but this belongs in the editorial, and not the news columns. Surely news is news and the newspaper "has a duty," to use Mr. Basil Dean's phrase, to report it accurately.

The fact that a speaker is correctly quoted is not enough — because short quotations are often wholly inadequate to give a true picture and may, in fact, result in distortion by truth.

In a letter to The Manchester Guardian, an 18-year-old student says it isn't safe to dissent in South Africa.

SIR:—There is only one purpose in writing this letter: I wish it to be known that there still exists in South Africa a number of people who believe in the freedom of thought, the freedom of ideas, and the freedom of movement.

In the no-trial bill, Mr. J. Vorster, the minister of justice, is given the most tremendous powers. Indeed, the measure is described as one containing the most drastic power ever given to a government in peacetime. It will not be long before the rule of law is wholly non-existent in this country. The official Parliamentary Opposition, the United Party, has once again betrayed the civilized world.

In the near future it is likely that we will not even have the right to voice a mass protest publicly.

[...] al obligation. Those of us who still wish to uphold the democratic way of life are frightened for our country's future. We want it to be known and recorded in all the civilized countries of the world that there is still a core of civilization in existence in South Africa. We will regard it as our duty always to respect the rights and dignities of the individual, regardless of creed or motto.

My country's motto is "Unity is Strength," yet all I see around me is disunity combined with racial hatred and discrimination. The country is being divided up and the wounds of these incisions will leave deep and irremovable scars. I believe in my country's motto. I wish I could live to see the day when the ideal could be transformed into action.

This is not an unbiased account of South Africa's present situation and I am glad of it. With thousands of other [...]

YOU'RE INVITED TO DISSENT

With the Opinion of **The JOURNAL**

or with any widely-accepted viewpoint . . .

"The Journal for Dissent"

A new weekly Page 5 feature offers an opportunity for the expression of the dissenting view on current issues — whether that opinion be contrary to the opinion expressed by this or another newspaper, or contrary to the common opinion of the day.

Opinions should be presented in the form of an article (The Journal for Dissent is not to be confused with the Letters to the Editor column) and forwarded to The Journal for Dissent, Edmonton Journal. This "open forum" will be available to everyone and material will be governed only by the customary limits of libel, blasphemy, obscenity and a very liberal interpretation of good taste. When articles are edited for length or other good reason, the author will be consulted.

The Journal is looking for genuine controversy and lively dissenting views. Watch The Journal for Dissent and consider contributing your own views.

A New Feature Page . . .

EACH TUESDAY

'The JOURNAL for DISSENT"

Journal gave him faint praise and suggested it would take the long view of history to judge his success as prime minister – the paper didn't pick Trudeau as a front-runner to replace Pearson.

However, when Trudeau did succeed Pearson and lead the Liberals to a landslide win in 1968, the paper clearly liked what it saw, and so did many of its readers.

His May 1968 campaign stop here was typical. Greeted by enthusiastic crowds everywhere he went, he gamely donned a Klondike Days hat and twirled a Klondike Days cane before the thousands who came to cheer him at the square in front of City Hall. For the moment he embodied the future: young, self-assured, smart, bilingual.

It was a time when young men grew much longer hair, and young women wore much shorter skirts, and many schools sent them home to don more appropriate attire.

J.F. Hollinshead had one of the earliest missives on rebellious youths on Jan. 2, 1960. "The action of the St. Albert Protestant Separate School Board in passing a resolution which will empower them to regulate clothing worn by the students might well be the start of a new era in youth training.

"It will be a pleasure to drive out to St. Albert and observe the absence of the flop-haired, duck-tailed, oil-pated, black-coated, hairy-chested, tight-jeaned, insolently swaggering 'hep cats' and their 'swerpy-swerp' feminine counterparts…."

If the hep cats and the swerpy swerps annoyed Hollinshead in 1960, it's hard to imagine his chagrin at what hit town in the late '60s after San Francisco's famous Summer of Love.

Hippies were young people who rejected traditional societal norms, and Edmontonians were fascinated by the phenomenon and other cultural changes in the '60s.

So fascinated, in fact, that *The Journal* sent Jaron Summers to San Francisco in July 1967 to hang out in the Haight-Ashbury district, the heartland of hippiedom, and report back on what he saw.

While a popular song of the day urged people to go to San Francisco and wear flowers in their hair, it was clear from Summers' copy that he kept his own hair flower-free.

"Most hippies are dropouts but it is more of a 'wishin' than a 'mission.'

"Hippies are wishin' they could do something to bring happiness to the world. Unfortunately, that's as far as they go."

He admitted that some hippies might be spotted on Jasper Avenue, but a lack of money and cold weather would temper the invasion.

"The largest of employers of hippies in California is the United States Post Office who hire them for temporary work.

"Certainly the provincial and dominion governments would not hire part-time office workers or part-time anything from the bearded ranks of hippies," he said.

"Their long hair and smell would probably deter most other employers, too."

By the autumn of 1967, "wandering hippies" were spotted in the city. What's more, they were luring young girls into their free and easy lifestyle, according to a *Journal* story in early September.

this city's best interests, TCA has shown secondary consideration for its Edmonton patrons."

***Feb. 4, 1961*:** **Contracts signed to complete St. Joseph's Cathedral on Jasper Avenue and 113th Street. Construction of the cathedral had begun in 1924 but was abandoned during the Depression. When completed, it will be one of the largest cathedrals in the country.**

***March 10, 1961*:** **Hec Gervais wins the Brier. His team included lead Wally Ursuliak, second Ray Werner and Ron Anton at third. Journal curling writer Don Fleming reports that the 26-year-old Gervais is the youngest-ever to win the Brier and, at 256 pounds, also the heaviest. Later that month Gervais would win the world championship in Edinburgh.**

***April 23, 1961*:** **The $2-million Royal Glenora Club opens in the river valley.**

***Aug. 3, 1961*:** **A Journal story reports that crews begin filling the gravel pit south of the Mayfair Golf and Country Club. "It marks the first step in the rehabilitation of the gravel pit which will eventually become**

SPEED LIMIT CHANGE SOUGHT ON HIGHWAY

A request to step up the 30 miles per hour speed limit on Highway 16 along the western boundary of Jasper Place came before town council Monday.

Joe Check, mayor of the resort town of Alberta Beach, appeared before council and asked that the speed limit be increased to 40 mph.

Mr. Check said motorists entering the town from the west are usually travelling about 65 mph. They are notified of a reduced speed zone ahead then pass under the underpass and are confronted with a 30 mph sign, he said.

This causes congestion in the heavy weekend traffic, he continued, and creates a traffic hazard when the automobiles back up for some distance.

Mayor Kenneth Newman suggested the town might erect signs indicating a progressive traffic slow-up from 60 to 50 to 40 to 30 miles per hour along the highway. The matter was referred to the traffic committee for study.

City Police Seek Motive For Deaths

"They're dead . . . they're all dead."

With this near-hysterical cry, a neighbor ran from the two-storey frame house at 9739 81st Ave. where the bodies of a family of four lay, Tuesday.

And today, police are still searching for a motive for what they have termed the murder-suicide slayings of Gunther Wilke, a 43-year-old plasterer, his wife and two young children.

The pyjama-clad bodies of the Wilke family were discovered Tuesday morning when a neighbor, who had noticed the curtains drawn for three days, walked into the house to check.

SPEAK TO NEIGHBORS

Half a dozen detectives and members of the identification branch spent Tuesday afternoon at the house investigating the deaths and interviewing neighbors.

Wilke was found shot to death on the floor of the master bedroom. A few feet away the body of his wife lay on the bed. She had been shot in the head.

The bodies of Hartmut Wilke, 10, and Marion, 8, were found in their beds across the hall, both shot in the head. Police said both children had been shot three times.

SEEK RELATIVE

Neighbors said they had not seen the Wilke family since the previous Sunday. A distant cousin of the dead woman lives in Edmonton and a sister lives at Wainwright.

Wilke, described by neighbors as a short stout man, was said to be suffering from an ulcer. His wife, believed to be in her 40s, had recently recovered from a stroke.

A .22 calibre rifle was used in the shootings although police would neither confirm or deny this. Heading the investigation are Insp. Ernest Roberts and Det. S/Sgt. Sid Laverty.

Wilke's employer, Eric Weidman of 96391 85th St., described him as a "good plasterer."

Weidman said the man had been acting strangely for several months and had asked to be put back to laborer's work because he felt he was unable to do his job properly.

3 Candidates Nominated In Calgary

Two Liberals and a Communist candidate Tuesday entered the political race in Calgary.

Howard G. Cook, a lawyer, was named candidate in Calgary South. William Miller, a company manager, will contest the seat of Calgary Centre.

Dave Raichman, member of the Calgary committee of the Communist Party, was chosen to contest the Calgary centre riding.

NDP Wants CS Union

New Democratic Party leader Neil Reimer Tuesday night called for bargaining rights for Alberta's 11,000 civil servants.

Speaking at a party meeting in Edmonton East, where he is candidate, Mr. Reimer said civil servants have been treated as "second-class citizens."

If the civil service is to be keen on job training, promotions, improving qualifications, and is to be free of patronage and favoritism, it must have the right of appeal, he added.

Mr. Reimer said he has accepted an invitation from the Calgary Chamber of Commerce to meet other party leaders in a debate in the Southern Alberta Jubilee Auditorium June 11.

Journal Photo by Dave Clark

ELECTRIC STARTERS ARE OUT WHEN A STEWARDESS IS NEAR
. . . Diane Jamieson of Vancouver provided service and scenery of first flight

Edmonton Sugar Price May Increase — Again

Another sugar price increase is looming.

The retail price in Edmonton Wednesday was $1.83 for 10 pounds, but by Saturday or Monday, it is expected to go up at least another three cents a pound.

There have been 41 price boosts since Oct. 1 and within the past 10 days it has increased $3.45 per 100-pound bag at wholesale level: 45 cents on Monday, 60 cents Wednesday.

... erts crossings was probably purchased originally by wholesalers who were smart enough to "see ahead."

"Sugar across the line costs more than $1.15 a bag and that is in the raw state. You have to add refining, packing and selling costs. This is my personal opinion, but I feel sugar, brought into this country by travellers is a loss-leader, or a come-on for the grocer selling it. This is not a realistic price."

The Canadian Press report said Canadian visitors to the United States, on returning to this country were bringing sugar in lots from 10 to 50 pounds. Custom officials said the Canadians didn't seem to mind paying the two cents-a-pound duty, because they are still saving money.

MONTREAL (CP) — Increases today brought the wholesale price of sugar for a 100-pound bag to $17 for two Montreal sugar refineries and to $17.10 for a third.

It was the 34th increase since Jan. 1, when the wholesale price was $9.10.

TREE PLANTIN...

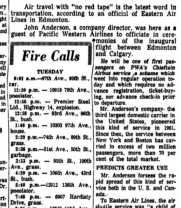

'Calgary Closer' As Air-Bus Run Gets Under Way

Now Calgary is one hour closer.

Pacific Western Airlines new Chieftain Airbus service—the first of its kind in Canada—starts regular Edmonton to Calgary flights today.

Some 60 Calgary and Edmonton business and civic leaders along with PWA officials sampled the new service Tuesday when PWA held its inaugural flight between the two centres.

An hour is cut in travel time by eliminating time-consuming procedures such as advance ticket-processing, check-ins and baggage disposal, and by using facilities of the Edmonton Municipal Airport.

FARE REDUCED

Passengers using the new service will also discover a saving in ticket rates as well as transportation time. The one-way fare of $11 compares to a $13 competitive fare in flights from the International Airport at Nisku. Payable by cash, cheque, or credit card, the fare is collected once passengers are inside the plane.

Tuesday's flight was part of a day long series of inaugural activities.

The 64-passenger DC-4 left at 1 p.m. In Calgary the inaugural party was swiftly transported downtown for a reception at the Calgary Petroleum Club.

Here, the Edmonton group met Calgary business and civic officials who joined the entourage for a return flight to Edmonton and a banquet and reception at the Mayfair Hotel. Calgary officials were returned home a few hours later, again aboard the Chieftain Airbus with its specially planned Indian interior decor.

FLIGHT TIMES

Three daily flights to Calgary leave Edmonton at 7 a.m., 1 p.m. and 7 p.m. Return flight will arrive in Edmonton at 9:30 a.m., 3:30 p.m. and 9:30 p.m.

It will be a single class service.

Should an unexpected overload of passengers occur on any day, a PWA DC-6 aircraft will be available to accommodate the extra passengers.

Officials at PWA have adopted a "wait and see" attitude in regard to the new service and will adjust their future plans in direct relation to customer response.

* * *

STRIKERS PICKET CITY TERMINALS

Striking employees of Pacific Western Airlines turned out in full force to picket air terminals in both Edmonton and Calgary Tuesday.

Some 30 employees and strike sympathizers were stationed at both centres to protest PWA's inaugural flight of its new Chieftain Airbus service between the two cities.

At both terminals they carried placards and distributed literature explaining their side in the three-month-old strike between the company and members of the Stewardesses Union.

They were joined in Calgary by members of the Calgary Labor Council.

The demonstrators at Calgary had mostly driven from Edmonton earlier in the day to be on hand for the landing of the inaugural flight which, in addition to guests, carried most of the major company officials from both the Edmonton and Vancouver offices as well as four stewardesses, three of whom were long-term staffers from Vancouver who quit their union rather than honor the strike.

A union spokesman said the Calgary demonstrators would probably remain to picket incoming flights for the balance of the week but, "we're going to wait and see what happens."

* * * *

'No Red Tape' In PWA Service

Air travel with "no red tape" is the latest word in transportation, according to an official of Eastern Air Lines in Edmonton.

John Anderson, a company director, was here as a guest of Pacific Western Airlines to officiate in ceremonies of the inaugural flight between Edmonton and Calgary.

He will be one of first passengers on *PWA's Chieftain Airbus service ,a scheme which* went into regular operation today and which requires no advance registration, ticket-buying, nor advance check-in prior to departure.

Mr. Anderson's company, the third largest domestic carrier in the United States, pioneered this kind of service in 1961. Since then, the service between New York and Boston has carried in excess of two million passengers, more than 70 per cent of the total market.

PREDICTS GREATER USE

Mr. Anderson forsees the rapid spread of this kind of service both in the U. S. and Canada.

To Eastern Air Lines, the air shuttle service was "a child of necessity."

It established an hourly service between New York and Buffalo, and eliminated "built-in costs and causes of delay."

Town Approves Construction Worth $214,500

LAC LA BICHE—Town Council has authorized building permits worth $214,500.

The largest single permit was for $160,000 extension to the Dr. Swift High School.

Two officials from the department of transport in Edmonton and A. Ambly, caretaker of the local airport, discussed the future of the Lac La Biche airport with ...

Fire Calls

TUESDAY

9:01 a.m.—97th Ave., 95th St., car.

12:20 p.m. — 10918 79th Ave., pneolator.

12:56 p.m. — Premier Steel Ltd., Highway 14, explosion.

12:58 p.m. — 93rd Ave., 96th St., bush.

1:46 p.m. — 10303 97th Ave., house.

2:29 p.m.—74th Ave., 89th St., grass.

2:36 p.m.—51st Ave., 50th St., garbage.

3:53 p.m. — 95th St., 100th Ave., grass.

4:20 p.m. — 106th Ave., 43rd St., bush.

5:40 p.m.—12912 136th Ave., pneolator.

7:48 p.m. — 6907 Hardisty Drive, grass.

8:34 p.m. — 13847 110A Ave., pneolator.

9:45 p.m. — 9918 112th St., ...

CHARMING AIR HOSTESSES—Ready for a summer of travel and fun are these pretty University of Alberta students. They will spend their holidays both in Europe and Canada, acting as air hostesses for Wardair Canada Ltd. Pictured from left are Margaret-Ann Maddison, Brenda Mallen, Carolyn Arnold, Nancy Duggan, Marilyn Smith and Kathy Oborne.

Varsity Students Find Employment In The Air

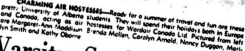

Seven pretty University of Alberta co-eds will be literally "walking on air" from ...

"They are relatively new in Edmonton," city police Insp. S.G. Hooper told *The Journal*, "but the first frost should discourage them."

"Reports tell of girls, under the age of 18, leaving home to follow mop-haired idols and hippie bands from one city to another."

That first hippie winter did send them packing apparently, but they were back the following summer. Many were teenagers who hung out in front of the Hudson's Bay store at Jasper Avenue. For its part, the store regarded them as pests and refused them service in its cafeteria.

Summer reporter Bob Ramsay was dispatched to The Bay corner in an attempt to find out why it was such a popular spot. He didn't come back with the complete answer, but his story offered some insight into a lifestyle that many found either intriguing or appalling, or possibly both.

"I don't care what the straights think," one young man told Ramsay. "I just want to be myself."

That meant smoking marijuana.

"The straights think dope is bad," the young man said. "But if they gave it a chance, they'd be liking it too."

The police occasionally moved them along, but the young people slowly drifted back to their favourite corner.

And in a quote that could only have come from an Edmonton hippie – clearly more conservative than his California counterpart – readers learned that many of the long-haired young people found the police to be all right.

"After all, they have a job to do," one told the paper. "And if they don't do it, they won't have a job any longer."

For those who didn't like the street corner, there was Middle Earth, a drop-in centre operating out of the basement of All Saints' Cathedral on 103rd Street, south of Jasper Avenue in downtown Edmonton.

When the church needed the basement for other purposes and had to close Middle Earth, a group of young people went to city council to seek help in finding a new place that would, according to an Aug. 20, 1968, story cost about $10,000 a year to operate.

That was too rich for the blood of Ald. Julia Kiniski, the only city council member to vote against city support for a new centre. "Why have a centre for the dirty devils we see around here?" she harrumphed at council.

"They're not like me, at least I wash myself."

Rev. David Crawley, who supervised the centre at the cathedral, was quick to defend the young people, and his stirring call for assistance, he pleaded for an "attractive human city centre, rather than a concrete canyon during the day and an empty echo at night." *The Journal* story also quoted Rev. Crawley as saying that everyone who went to Middle Earth felt a personal responsibility to the place and was eager to supervise the goings-on and to maintain the property.

Ten days later police raided Middle Earth. Nine young people, all between 16 and 20 were convicted of dealing in LSD and marijuana. They were sentenced to jail terms ranging from nine months to two years.

Other young people sought to make themselves heard in other, more constructive ways. While it was generally quiet on campus at the University of Alberta, there were occasional protests over issues such as tuition fees and representation on the governing bodies of the institution.

Edmonton's first year-round park." Originally named Mayfair Park, the site is renamed Hawrelak Park in the 1980s.

***Oct. 1, 1961*:**
Edmonton's second TV station, CBC's CBXT, goes on the air.

***Oct. 6, 1961*:**
Federal census figures move Edmonton from sixth to fourth place on the list of Canada's largest cities.

***Oct. 18, 1961*:**
Elmer Roper, 68, wins re-election as the city's mayor by polling more than 37,000 votes.

***Dec. 30, 1961*:**
The town of Beverly is annexed.

***In 1962*:**
An advertising copy chaser at *The Journal* makes $37.50 a week.

***Jan. 26, 1962*:**
Jasper Place Composite high school opens. It's the largest school between Vancouver and the Great Lakes.

***Feb. 1, 1962*:**
***Journal* circulation is 119,066 when Basil Dean succeeds Walter A. Macdonald, publisher since September 1941.**

***May 7, 1962*:**
The population according to the civic census is 294,967.

GENERAL PLAN REVISION COMING

Edmonton's chief planner William Hardcastle said a "sophisticated version" of Edmonton's general plan will be presented to city council by mid-September.

The new plan, a condensation and revision of the 13 chapters of the general plan so far released, will include policy recommendations for future development.

City planners have spent two years on the general plan, which charts the city's future development needs to 1980.

To date they have produced detailed statistical data on the city's industrial, land use, residential and commercial development and utility needs.

The city studies are being aligned with the Metropolitan Edmonton Transportation Study, chapter one of which (policies and recommendations) has been released. The study was prepared by the Edmonton District Planning Commission in co-operation with the provincial government.

City Firms' Support Seen For Coliseum

City businessmen will support the coliseum project, Mayor Roper believes.

Businessmen are "the people who will pay most" for the project in taxes.

The $14,250,000 project will go to a plebiscite Oct. 16.

Mayor Roper said the 10 or 12 cities in the U.S. which have adequate convention centres have benefitted immensely.

AVERAGE LENGTH

"How much money do 10 or 12 thousand people spend in a city?" he asked.

Statistics show the average conventioner spends $30 a day. The average length of a convention where delegates stay in hotels is 3.2 days.

Stanford Research Institute, which prepared the city's coliseum report, conducted a survey of major groups which hold conventions (over 180 inquiries were sent out) and concluded that Edmonton would realize $3,000,000 a year from the coliseum in business which would not otherwise come to the city.

$6 EACH

It is estimated that the citizens will pay $6 each per year for the complex.

The city is trying to interest private developers in the project — who would pay the shot for the project and lease it to the city (for adequate remuneration) on a yearly basis. Two local investors have expressed interest.

A cultural galvanization in the city would follow the development of the coliseum complex, the mayor believes.

He believes the coliseum question "shouldn't be just a financial question."

WHAT WORTH?

"What is it worth to the people of Edmonton (say people of European extraction who have a great yen for grand opera) to have a coliseum here?"

Attractions which would come to Edmonton because of the coliseum which were cited by Mayor Roper include the Bolshoi Ballet (which will be presented at the Jubilee Auditorium this fall).

The cost is too high for "the average person" to see such an attraction at the Jubilee Auditorium, said the mayor.

But since the coliseum would seat about 12,000, the price of tickets could be reduced from $6 to $3 or even $2.

American cities have benefited immensely from having convention facilities, the mayor said.

Coliseum Expense Recorded

Edmonton's proposed coliseum complex may eventually cost more than $37,000,000.

But the experts predict the project will bring $120,000,000 to the city in 40 years.

The $37 million plus figure is the amount required to retire $14,250,000 over a 40-year-period at six per cent interest.

But the Stanford Research Institute, after an extensive survey, estimated that the coliseum would attract $3,000,000 worth of business annually to the city — business which would not come here without the coliseum's facilities for conventions.

The Stanford group prepared the city's coliseum report.

YEARLY PAYMENTS

Retiring the debt at six per cent would require about $930,000 a year—which after a 40-year period would amount over $37,000,000.

Mayor Roper has suggested that the city could get the coliseum, convention centre and parking garage built by a private developer on a lease-back arrangement if the Oct. 16 coliseum plebiscite fails to get the necessary two-thirds majority.

Considering that the developer would have to pay at least $855,000 yearly for his investment in Edmonton's coliseum, the city's lease-back payment would probably amount to at least $1,000,000 a year.

The city has another alternative — paying for the project from capital on hand.

UNLIKELY MOVE

This is an unlikely possibility, since the city could hardly justify a $14,250,000 expenditure out of hand.

But if this were done, the project would still cost the city in the neighborhood of $37,000,000 — in the long run — since the interest revenue from this money would be lost to the city.

So however the $14 million plus for the coliseum is raised, the eventual cost to the city will be in excess of $37,000,000.

Bits of News FROM TODAY'S Classified Section

Numbers before items denote classification heading

(39)—We buy items you no longer need, furniture or miscellaneous items of any value

(42)—Baby Tenda, blue Gendron carriage. Good condition.

(43)—As new, excellent quality. 120 bass accordion with case. Hardly used. Cost $275. Sacrifice $150.

(46)—Lovely Sealpoint Siamese kittens. Trained. Reasonable.

(66)—2 new 9x7 Berry garage doors. $52.

(125)—1955 Dodge V-8. 4 door. Good condition.

For the complete story on these and other "Wants" of Journal readers turn to the classified section.

Medical Plan Results Disappointing Say Government, Insurance Firms

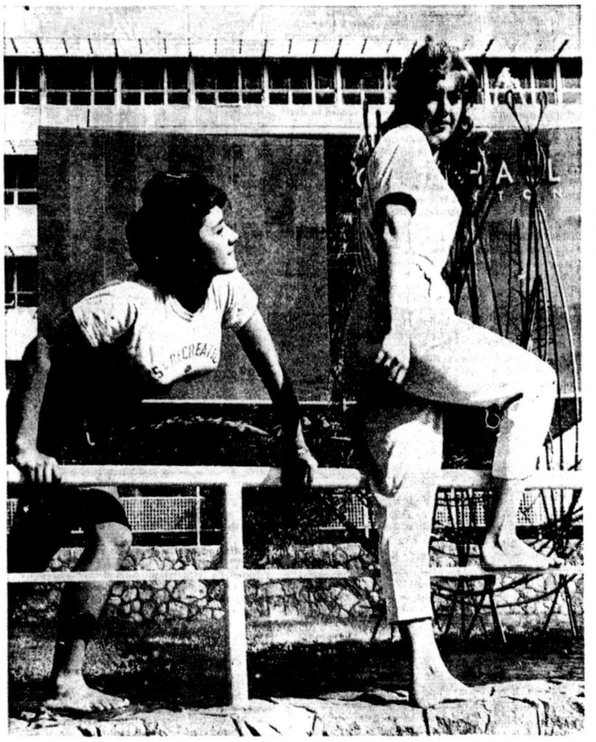

BETTY ZIELINSKI AND JOAN PENDLETON
. . . don't like their sweater issue

Playground Directors Shun T-Shirts; Say They Make Them Look 'Too Sexy'

By DAVE LAUNDY
Journal Staff Writer

Sweater girls?

Nosiree.

And 10 pretty playground directors assembled in front of city hall last night at midnight to prove it.

They said they were fed up with the parks department T-shirts they'd had to wear all summer.

So they gave them to the geese — the abstract metal geese outside city hall.

Two and a half feet of cold water separated the girls from the geese. But off came the shoes and socks and on went the T-shirts—on the geese.

"They look better on the geese than they did on us," said Joan Pendleton, 20, 6706 112A Ave. "They made us look sexy and that's a bad influence on the children."

SAME SHIRTS

The girls complained they had to wear the same shirts all summer and that they were hot and sticky.

"And they didn't allow us much of a tan," added Betty Zielinski, 17.

The directors didn't object to distinctive identification but said they would prefer white blouses and navy blue shorts.

A park official said the T-shirts had been an experiment to make the directors easily identified to the public.

He said a request had been made for a change and the department was considering something new, "perhaps head gear or armbands."

Fire Beats Extinguisher

A $2,000 aircraft burned today while a service man was installing a fire extinguisher.

The Tiger Moth aircraft, being serviced by Falconer Aircraft Maintenance at the east end of the Municipal Airport, was extensively damaged when flames flared from the edge of one wing.

Service man Bill Attewell was inside the aircraft installing an engine fire extingisher when he noticed the flames.

"It is absolutely, completely freakish," said Chris Falconer, owner of the company.

"I've never heard of anything like it before."

The only reason he could give as the cause of the fire, was a concentration of sunlight through the aircraft's plexiglass top.

Rush Anticipated Before Deadline

Albertans apparently have adopted a wait-until-the-last-minute attitude concerning the government's medical plan.

Either this is the case, or the plan has not caught fire as was intended.

Despite the claims of the politicians that the plan has caught the imagination of Albertans and is sweeping the province, both government and insurance company officials involved say things are slow—in fact slightly disappointing.

But they still anticipate a final rush just before the program goes into operation Oct. 1. Registration began July 1.

Medical Services Incorporated with 600,000 policy-holders does about 80 per cent of the province's medical health insurance business. So far, it has had only 7,000 applications for subsidies under the government's program. And few of these are new policy holders. The majority of cases involve persons who now have policies seeking subsidies to cut the costs of their premiums.

NO RUSH

A. G. Hamilton, assistant general manager of the doctor-sponsored non-profit organization, says people have not been rushing to participate in the government's plan.

But he feels that many are waiting until the plan begins operation before enrolling.

"They aren't rushing to pay their money now for a policy which dosen't take effect until October."

MSI has been busy in the plan chiefly transferring the accounts of policy holders from regular membership to the subsidy-qualifying category. This is done only when an application for a subsidy is made by a policy holder.

Government officials say that about 100,000 policies will have to be issued to cover the 3 to 400,000 people eligible for the government subsidy of part of the cost of the premiums.

MSI INDICATIVE

MSI will obtain the largest amount of business under the government's plan and so officials feel that its activity is an indication of public reaction.

Insurance company officials report that they have received many inquiries concerning the plan, but actual writing of new policies is not great.

One local manager said his firm intends to do its biggest business in rural areas once the holiday season and harvest operations are over.

The government's computing centre still is making preparations to process the subsidy application cards, none of which have yet been turned in by insurance companies.

Unwed Mothers' Home Set

Construction of a new building to replace the Beulah Home will begin this year, Hon. L. C. Halmrast, minister of public welfare, announced Thursday.

The minister was speaking at the official opening of Pineview Home for unwed mothers. The $325,000 facility in Jasper Place was built by the provincial government and will be operated by the Sisters of the Misericordia.

"Another home very similar to this will be built by the government to replace the Beulah Home," Mr. Halmrast said. "Construction should begin very soon and it should be completed early in 1964."

The new home will be built in north Edmonton on the same site as the old one.

CALGARY HOME

The government is planning to build another home for unwed mothers in Calgary to be operated by the Salvation Army, the minister added.

He said the government is concerned about the increase in the number of illegitimate births in the province. A steady month by month increase has occurred in 1963.

Through May of 1963 there have been 1,144 births out of wedlock, he said. This involved 692 unmarried mothers and 452 mothers living common law.

For comparison, he said, there were 968 illegitimate births in the province during the first six months of 1962 and during the whole year there were 2,430.

Pineview Home will accommodate 38 girls. There are 28 pre-natal beds and 10 post natal beds. The girls will be taken to a hospital for delivery.

It is built at 8770 165th St., near the site where the Misericordia Hospital proposes to build a $13,000,000 hospital.

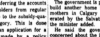

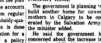

There was no violence at any of the demonstrations, but that didn't mean the U of A sidestepped the phenomenon of protests and marches. In fact, its first protest of the '60s occurred on March 11, 1960, over the relatively mundane issue of student housing.

More than 300 marchers peacefully made their way from the campus to the provincial legislature to express their concerns over a government decision by Social Credit Provincial Treasurer E.W. Hinman to expand training facilities at the expense of new housing projects.

"Spokesmen for the students at the building were identified as Joseph Clark, James Coutts and Dan deVleiger. They were identified as the leaders of the Progressive Conservative, Liberal and CCF student groups, respectively."

While Hinman said he appreciated the students' interest in the issue, he regretted that they used a method "which is usually associated with countries other than ours."

Clark went on to lead the federal Progressive Conservative Party and was elected Canada's 16th prime minister in 1979. Coutts served as a high-ranking adviser to Prime Minister Pierre Trudeau.

Other young people chose to express themselves through rock music, which went through a profound change during the '60s.

By 1960, Elvis Presley was acceptable to just about everyone, and Edmonton teenagers crowded the downtown Melody Lane music store at 104th Street and 100th Avenue to listen to the top 10 tunes as reported by *The Journal* in its weekly polls.

In 1960, The King sang comfortable songs like *It's Now or Never, Are You Lonesome Tonight* and the mild rocker *Stuck on You.*

Then came The Beatles, the band that led the British rock invasion and dismayed so many parents.

But by the end of the decade, the early '60s Beatles seemed positively benign compared to the drug-inspired psychedelic music that shouldered bubblegum tunes from the record charts.

By the end of 1967, *The Journal* list of hit songs put *White Rabbit* by Jefferson Airplane at the top of the charts. If parents weren't too sure what singer Grace Slick meant when she sang "one pill makes you larger and one pill makes you small," their kids understood.

Movies, too, were more realistic, and risque after the provincial government eased the classification categories in 1964. Albertans, at last, saw once-banned movies such as the switchblade drama *Blackboard Jungle* and the sexy historical romp *Tom Jones.*

Sex itself became sexier as the nation debated just how readily available birth control pills such as Enovid should be.

A bill to ease Canada's birth control laws foundered in the fall of 1964 when members of the Creditiste Party – Quebec's federal party based on Social Credit principles – refused to support it. The bill, they said, was a "diabolical" work that came "straight from hell."

Although Enovid had been available in the U.S. since 1960, it was illegal in Canada. In fact, everything about contraception was illegal. People who so much as distributed information about it committed a Criminal Code offence, and could face a two-year prison term.

***July 15, 1962*:**
Rain falls on the first-ever Klondike Days parade, although more than 100,000 Edmontonians line Jasper Avenue to watch.

***Sept. 28, 1962*:**
The provincial government gives the go-ahead to limited development of the Athabasca oilsands, the world's largest known oil reserve.

***Oct. 17, 1962*:**
In a municipal plebiscite Edmonton voters support holding city elections every two years instead of annually.

***Nov. 2, 1962*:**
The results of a *Journal* survey on teenage drinking habits published show that 69 per cent of male high school students drink alcohol regularly while 34 per cent of the "co-eds" described themselves as regular drinkers. Only nine per cent of the males and six per cent of the females described themselves as total abstainers.

***Nov. 25, 1962*:**
The Edmonton Huskies beat Montreal 7-2 to win the Little Grey Cup.

***Dec. 8, 1962*:**
***The Journal* stages its first long-service awards banquet at the Macdonald Hotel.**

The Edmonton Journal

FORECAST: WARMER — EDMONTON, ALBERTA, TUESDAY, MAY 17, 1966 — TEN CENTS

Ottawa Signals 'Go' On Medicare Plans

Gemini 9 Flight Delayed

CAPE KENNEDY (AP) — An Agena satellite failed to achieve orbit today and ruined the Gemini 9 mission.

The launching of astronauts Thomas P. Stafford and Eugene A. Cernan, who were to have chased and caught the Agena, will be postponed at least two weeks.

Last Oct. 25, the Gemini 6 shot was ruined when another Agena failed to go into orbit after a perfect Atlas launch

"We have lost the Agena," said William Schneider, Gemini mission director. "We do not know exactly what happened to it.

"The Gemini will not fly today."

The Atlas had boosted the Agena skyward at 8:15 a.m. Edmonton time.

Gemini 9 pilots Stafford and Cernan, were to have spent three days in space practising manoeuvres essential to Apollo man-to-the-moon trips.

"Oh, shucks," was the reaction of Stafford on hearing of the failure.

"Oh, no! Oh, no!" said Cernan.

Stafford said: "You can't get your hopes up until that Agena gets across the states." He referred to the fact that the Gemini would be launched after the Agena had gone around the globe once and was again over Cape Kennedy.

For Stafford, it was the second similar disappointment. He and U.S. Navy Capt. Walter M. Schirra were in the Gemini 5 spacecraft Oct. 25 last and had their mission postponed when their Agena target satellite exploded six minutes after lift-off.

The Atlas launch appeared to be normal

About two minutes into the flight, mission control at Houston, Tex., reported it had temporary loss of radio contact with Agena and then had regained it.

A minute later, the control centre reported all contact lost.

Where To Find It

Climate control for downtown areas is quite practical, an urban renewal seminar has been told. Story on Page 8.

Ann Landers	20
Births, Deaths, Marriages	28
Bridge	30
Business, Stocks	15-17
Classified Ads	29-38
Comics, Features	25
Comment	4
Crossword Puzzle	25
Horoscope	31
Journal for the Family	19-21
Journal For Dissent	6
Letters To The Journal	4
News Digest	2
Patterns	32
Radio	9
Sport	11-14
Theatres	22, 23
TV	9

Total Pages 42

Weather

Clearing tonight, winds dropping to northwest 15 Wednesday. Low tonight 40, high Wednesday 60. Details on Page 2.

Art EVANS

Vampire For Hire

ORDINARILY THE "heavy" in a cowboy picture does not attract audience sympathy.

Whether he is ventilated by the hero's six-guns or stretched from a cottonwood by Judge Lynch, the general feeling is "good riddance." The polecat had it coming.

But one could not help feeling sorry for a villain on television's late movie the other night who had the misfortune to pull a gun on a vampire in cowboy clothing. He beat the ghoul to the draw but the poor dope didn't know who he was up against.

A vampire doesn't have to be the fastest gun in the west. He (or it) can be as slow as molasses and still win a shoot-out, as the other guy's slugs have less effect than a water-pistol. Unless a bullet is notched in the shape of a cross it won't prove fatal to a vampire. (It would be wise to remember this should the need ever arise.)

For movie fans familiar with Count Dracula's film career, it was a strange experience to see a vampire riding the range. It is doubtful if the late Bela Lugosi, Hollywood's chief vampire for years, would have approved of the script. Sticking to legend, Mr. Lugosi terrorized European communities and left the American west to flesh-and-blood varmints.

He was a vampire of the old school, owning castles and always dressing for dinner. He would have frowned on a vampire who brawled in frontier town saloons. Bad for the image.

★ ★ ★

HOWEVER, VAMPIRES are where you find them and no one in the cattle town even suspected that Drake Robey, professional gunfighter, was a member of the club. Certainly, pretty ranch-owner Dolores Carter didn't suspect anything was amiss. She had her troubles — father and brother killed, water cut off, cattle stolen — but these inconveniences were ordinary for the times. Her big worry was badman Buffer, a land-hungry crook, who was trying to force her to sell her ranch at bargain prices.

The sheriff was no help. Once bitten by the vampire he was never quite the same again. In fact he was dead.

Preacher Dan was sweet on Dolores but he was a man of peace and hardly Buffer's match in an unfair fight which, as you know, is the only kind of fight in which movie villains are interested.

It was understandable therefore that Dolores should accept vampire Robey's offer to knock off Buffer. "You can sleep in the cottage near the old cemetery," she told him, not knowing that Robey was already sleeping in the cemetery.

And then Dolores said a very funny thing to say to any vampire. She told Robey not to be afraid of the dead, and Robey (obviously a vampire with a sense of humor) replied deadpan, "I don't mind the dead. It's the living who give me trouble." So true, so true.

Preacher Dan didn't like the idea of Dolores hiring Robey and told her so. She couldn't have been madder if he said her seams were crooked. Preacher Dan was advised to save his sermons for church.

★ ★ ★

UP TO A POINT killer Robey was a handy vampire to have around. He gunned Buffer and he produced an old Spanish land grant which proved that Dolores owned the controversial water-rights. Tiring of being a vampire, Robey was actually thinking of marrying Dolores and settling down when preacher Dan, the snoop, upset the hearse.

The preacher found an old book (planted by the film's producer) which proved that Robey was a vampire. He blabbed the truth to Dolores but she was one of those girls who don't believe everything a fellow tells them. "It's real crazy," she said, updating the dialogue by one century.

But Dolores changed her tune when preacher Dan used a specially-notched bullet to blast Robey and the vampire dissolved, leaving only his cowboy clothing lying in the middle of main street. You've just got to believe something like THAT.

OIL KINGS AT CITY HALL FOR WORDS OF PRAISE
. . . cheers, crowds, and Klondike lighters

600 Greet Oil Kings

A crowd of 600 people, including civic officials, greeted Canada's junior hockey champions, Edmonton Oil Kings, when they flew home from Toronto Monday night. Later the Oil Kings were congratulated at City Hall by Mayor Vince Dantzer and Jack Reilly of the recreation department. Pictures and story Page 11.

FALKENBERG (CENTRE), HIS FATHER (LEFT), COACH KINASEWICH
. . . the airport crowd caused a traffic jam

MP Says Farm Drug May Harm Humans

From Canadian Press

OTTAWA — A synthetic hormone known as stilbestrol could be having adverse effects on humans.

So says Percy Noble, a mink rancher and member of Parliament for Grey North.

Mr. Noble said the hormone, which is used in livestock and poultry feeds, has been known to sterilize mink.

He suggested the effects of the hormone could be reaching humans consuming the livestock and poultry and proposed a ban on its use.

Mr. Noble made the banning proposal before the Commons agriculture committee today.

NO RESEARCH

Dr. S. C. Barry, deputy minister of the federal agriculture department, said the hormone promotes rapid development of poultry and livestock, out the department has done no research on the possible effects on humans. That is a question for the food and drugs division of the federal health department, he added.

Members of the committee expressed concern about the story told by Mr. Noble.

NO PROOF

Investigations have not proved conclusively whether the hormone had been fed to the animals improperly or whether they were just unusually susceptible to its effects, Mr. Noble said.

"What effect does stilbestrol have on people when it is fed to cattle and poultry?" he asked. "It sterilized the mink. What's it doing to humans?"

"The minister of agriculture about a year ago (Harry Hays, now a senator) told me that it is used out west on the ranches to make cattle abort before they are sent to market. I've even been told by a druggist that it is used by humans for the same purpose."

Minister To Ignore Provinces

OTTAWA (CP) — The federal government plans to enter the medical insurance field July 1, 1967, regardless of the number of provinces willing to go along.

Health Minister MacEachen said this in the Commons today.

Legislation would be introduced in Parliament to authorize Ottawa to extend aid to any province that sets up a medical care plan meeting federal standards.

The minister said "several" provinces have given indications in recent public statements that they are ready to proceed with the federal - provincial medical insurance program.

The federal government would not await the approval of all provinces before entering the picture.

Federal payments would start July 1, 1967, to any provincial medical care plan meeting four fundamental requirements set down by the federal government last year.

U.S. Acts In Viet Crisis

Journal News Services

WASHINGTON — U.S. ambassador Henry Cabot Lodge is on his way back to Saigon today.

His instructions are to put the heat on South Viet Nam's ruling generals not to block elections.

Lodge left after a series of conferences with a worried group of top officials here, including the president, over the growing possibility of more civil strife in South Viet Nam.

A division of South Vietnamese troops have been moved from the Mekong Delta to the Saigon area following a series of savage Viet Cong attacks on the capital's outskirts Monday.

Viet Cong agents struck five times during the night in and around Saigon and a South Vietnamese defence spokesman said the movement of troops was "to ensure the security of the capital."

SHOWDOWN THREAT

Buddhist leaders, meanwhile, have threatened a showdown with Premier Nguyen Cao Ky's regime, pledging to give their lives if necessary to force the government to end its crackdown in the northern part of the country.

At the end of the top-level

More VIET NAM Page 2

Firecracker Warning Given

With a holiday weekend approaching city legal officials warn of dangers involving fireworks.

They point out the maximum fine for selling fireworks in Edmonton to any person under 21 years of age is $500.

Safety officials also advise having adults supervise any use of fireworks.

Escape That (Legally) Never Was

BY GERRY BALL
Of The Journal

Two city men who escaped from Saskatchewan Penitentiary in 1961, have had the charge of escaping lawful custody dismissed on a legal technicality.

Roy Holland, 40, and Donald Kolot, 34, were serving 10-year terms for conspiracy at the time of their escape.

The dismissed charge means that they will now be released from the penitentiary at Prince Albert next year instead of in 1975 which would have been their release date had they been convicted.

This decision came about because a judge in magistrate's court in Prince Albert lost jurisdiction in the case.

Due to the technicality which favors Holland and Kolot, they now legally have served nearly two-thirds of their 10-year sentences, And inmates of federal penitentiaries are eligible for release at that point with time off for "good behavior."

The two men were physically missing from the penitentiary for almost three years, but legally they never did escape, so penitentiary officials cannot penalize them by taking their good behavior remission away.

The monumental legal headache for police, court officials and penitentiary authorities started in May, 1961, when Holland and Kolot were sentenced in Edmonton to 10-year terms along with three other men after they were convicted of conspiracy in an attempted armed robbery of a Spruce Grove farm family.

Six months later they escaped in what prison officials described as an ingenious and clever method. After fashioning dummies in their cells who appeared to be reading newspapers, and make them "present" for the all-important prison count, they hid in the exercise yard and scaled the 25-foot wall by climbing up a piece of pipe that had footholds attached to it.

The fugitives travelled undetected into the United States. Once in the U.S. they embarked on a crime spree which covered many states until they were finally caught in Texas in April, 1962. Sentenced to five years in Huntsville Prison in Texas, the pair were released after serving 26 months, and were turned over to RCMP who brought them to Prince Albert in May, 1964.

At the time of their deportation to Canada, it was assumed by police authorities that Holland and Kolot would have to serve nine and one-half years "solid time" of their 10-year sentence.

In addition it was expected that they might be sentenced to the maximum two-year term for escaping lawful custody, this sentence to run consecutive to their initial sentence.

This could have meant that from 1964, with a total sentence of 11½ years, without time off for good behavior, they would have been released in 1975.

However, when they appeared before Judge E. Z. Anderson in Prince Albert Magistrate's Court, they elected to be tried by judge alone. But as Judge Anderson had said prison escapees would receive the maximum two years for escaping custody, Holland and Kolot asked to be waived to district court where their case could be heard by Judge Walter Nelson.

Judge Nelson did sentence the pair to a maximum of two years but by this time a legal error had been made. The sentenced men did not have a preliminary hearing into the charge against them in Judge Anderson's court.

Canadian doctors could, by the mid-'60s prescribe Enovid to "regulate menstrual cycles" of their patients. Under this "wink-and-a-nudge" system, Canadians were buying 50 million contraceptive devices a year by 1963.

Even doctors were unsure of the pill's effect if taken over a number of years. A Sept. 12, 1964, *Journal* story quoted Dr. T.R. Clarke, a University of Alberta obstetrics professor as saying that he feared the long-term consequences of taking the pill.

"If a woman has a sane form of contraception why put her in a pre-menstrual condition day in and day out?

"God knows they're hard enough to live with just for a few days a month in that condition."

Homosexual acts between consenting adults were no longer criminal offences when Justice Minister Pierre Elliott Trudeau rather famously pronounced in 1967 "the state has no place in the bedrooms of the nation."

In fact, in an end-of-decade survey on the biggest stories of the '60s, one reader foresaw doom in the Trudeau pronouncement.

A gloomy Edward Sweeny of Peers, Alta., predicted that the new lax morality would lead to society's downfall. "God only knows what will happen in the next decade."

Other readers found much to celebrate in humanity's accomplishments in the '60s. The biggest story, according to many, was the moon landing of July 21, 1969, as thousands of Edmontonians joined 500 million television viewers world-wide watch as Neil Armstrong and Buzz Aldrin left their footprints on the dusty lunar surface.

It's likely that many *Journal* readers dined off TV trays that day – four "king-sized" trays were available at Eaton's for $7.49 – as they sat glued to their $800 ($4,271.30 today) colour sets.

The next day they read all about it in a special 12-page *Journal* souvenir section, the front page of which showed a blurry Armstrong taking the first step onto the moon's surface.

While many readers marvelled at the accomplishment and made it their most memorable '60s story, *Journal* reader Bill Steele made a different choice for the most significant story of the '60s: violence.

For Steele, the darkest phenomenon were the assassinations, and called the violence he found in North America to be incomprehensible." Doubtless the list of assassinations to which Steele referred was a grim one.

It was page 1 news on June 12, 1963, when civil rights activist Medgar Evers was assassinated on his doorstep in Jackson, Miss.

Southam News Services' Bruce Phillips reported from Jackson the next day on the violence that followed Evers' death.

"It was a never-to-be-forgotten scene. It would last barely 10 minutes, but it will last me a lifetime. In that 10 minutes I saw:

"A white man clubbed to the ground for the great crime of shouting 'We want freedom.'

"A brother and sister, both teenagers, pursued into their own home, one of them clubbed, both of them arrested.

"Newsmen and photographers threatened with clubbing, shoved and jostled….

"And, of course, 80 Negroes, some of them as young as 10 and few

Basil Dean, the newspaper's publisher, presented Ollie Macdonald with a ring containing five diamonds in honour her 49 years of service.

***Dec. 18, 1962*:**
Fire destroys the Selkirk Hotel at 101st Street and Jasper Avenue.

***In 1963*:**
A *Journal* reporter makes $140 a week.

***Feb. 2, 1963*:**
From Don Fleming's column: "WELCOME BACK – Making it back onto the airwaves is Bryan Hall, who shows up with CJCA starting tomorrow…It's great news that this audio outlet has chosen to improve on that outlandish sound of the last few years…"

***Feb. 18, 1963*:**
The Edmonton Eskimos trade star Jackie Parker to the Toronto Argonauts for five players and $15,000 cash, one of the biggest trades in CFL history.

***May 11, 1963*:**
The Edmonton Oil Kings win their first Memorial Cup, beating the Niagara Falls Flyers in six games.

***May 15, 1963*:**
The Royal Alexandra Hospital opens.

Ulster's night of death heightens war fears

From AP-Reuters

BELFAST (AP) — More than 50 persons were injured today as gunfire and rock-throwing broke out again between rival religious factions in Belfast.

The fighting came after a night of violence in Northern Ireland that left at least six persons dead.

At least two men were wounded by gunfire and were taken to hospital, with others injured by flaming gasoline bombs and flying paving stones.

The rioting broke out along barricades erected by the residents of the mainly-Roman Catholic Falls Road community.

The new outbreak was restricted to rival gangs and police were not called immediately to the area.

Residents of the Falls Road area toppled lamp posts and telegraph poles, set fire to trucks and appeared ready for a new night of violence.

Britain flew fresh troops to Northern Ireland and recalled others from leave today for possible use in helping to quell the warfare.

A vacationing Irish-Canadian was the first person killed in the latest round of clashes. He was shot to death in Armagh by an unknown gunman. The other deaths were in Belfast.

The RAF flew 600 more troops into Ulster, and they headed for Belfast, where the rattle of automatic weapons echoed the threat of outright civil war.

In the wild rioting Thursday night, gunmen had taken control of entire sections of the city, lit by flames from burning factories, stores and homes.

The British troops were sent to Belfast to back up civil authority and all began moving into the capital. One company stayed at Lisburn, about six miles south.

Another 600 men of the Royal Green Jackets were being recalled from leave and put on standby "because of the seriousness of the situation" in Ulster, the British defence ministry announced.

Observers feared that the night of deaths, in which at least 42 persons were treated for gunshot wounds, may add new fuel to the rioting throughout Ulster cities.

Although the police gave six dead and 192 injured as the official toll, Catholic sources contended the dead might number as many as 10 and the injured "several hundred."

Fifty-eight of the injured were policemen.

At the same time the government announced that 13 persons —eight in Belfast and five elsewhere—were being held on suspicion of being members of the illegal Irish Republican Army.

Fires were still burning in embattled Falls Road at midday. Catholic children were evacuated from the area.

Falls Road was an ugly, gnarled scar running through the centre of the battlefield.

Not one building in its two miles was unscathed. In two places, large terraced buildings had been reduced to heaps of bricks.

The religious factions battled through the night Thursday, and their war spread through all six counties that make up Northern Ireland.

John Gallagher, 29-year-old father of three, was gunned down in Armagh by a man who leaped from a car. Two others were wounded.

Gallagher, born in Ireland, had emigrated to Canada and was vacationing in the town of 10,000.

The five other deaths—all by gunshot—were in Belfast. One of them was a nine-year-old boy, and observers feared the killings would intensify the fury of the armed Catholic and Protestant mobs.

The bloody violence of Bog-

More IRISH Page 2

Dublin prepares for peacekeeping

DUBLIN (Reuters)—The government of the Irish Republic today announced it is mobilizing army reserves to be ready for a peacekeeping operation in riot-torn Northern Ireland.

The announcement said the first line of reserves—about 2,000 men—was being called up. At present, it is unofficially estimated the republic has only 2,500 combat troops in the country. Another 500 are with UN peacekeeping forces in Cyprus.

Two days ago Irish Prime Minister Jack Lynch called for a UN peacekeeping force to be sent to Northern Ireland, saying the situation there was out of control.

The government information bureau today said the republic's external affairs minister, Patrick Hillery, who flew to London overnight, would press the British government to agree to a peacekeeping force.

This could be either a UN force or a joint British-Irish force, the announcement said. The reserves were being called up ready to join a British-Irish force, it added.

The Edmonton Journal

FORECAST: HOT — EDMONTON, ALBERTA, FRIDAY, AUGUST 15, 1969 — 64 PAGES — 10c

IT'S STILL BETTER THAN WALKING

. . . ETS Superintendent Donald MacDonald, who always rides the bus, rides to work on a bicycle

ETS strikers block non-union workers

Members of the Amalgamated Transit Union today were refusing to allow some non-union personnel to cross picket lines at four ETS offices and garages.

While 50,000 bus commuters tried to thumb, walk or cycle their way home from work, the union was to meet with city officials to try to settle the picket line problem.

The city contends it is vital that 61 non-striking employees—including security and maintenance personnel—be allowed to cross the picket lines.

The ETS building could be without heat, for example, if steam engineers are not allowed across the picket lines.

Ironically, among the personnel not allowed to get to their are payroll clerks for the bus drivers.

The drivers have yet to be paid for their four days' work this week before the strike began.

They are due to get their cheques two weeks from Tuesday, but if clerks aren't allowed into their offices, the cheques could be delayed.

City officials said today they had no emergency plan to get people home tonight in their first day of the bus strike.

But they do have some advice:

Workers without autos are asked to solicit rides from passing motorists—as most of them did this morning.

However, instead of standing at their nearest bus stop, as they did this morning, the city is advising downtown workers to first walk to the fringes of the downtown area tonight before waiting at a bus stop.

Filtering process

Transit Superintendent Donald MacDonald said the filtering process is the only way of overcoming the confusion that will exist if everyone awaits rides downtown.

If they do that, none of the passing motorists will know whether the downtown people are going their way.

It's simple in the morning, said Mr. MacDonald, for everyone is generally heading the same way—towards the downtown area. But at night, they'll be going to all points of the outer city.

The city commission board said it may come up with concrete plans for pickup and drop points and for emergency parking if the strike extends—as expected—into next week.

"It's a nothing strike," said W. L. Mack, president of the Amalgamated Transit Union Local 569. "There are no money values at stake.

"I am saddened that the system had to be tied up over a very, very insignificant issue—a four-month shortening of the term of agreement."

With the red and cream buses off the road, morning traffic moved fairly smoothly, apart from slightly longer than normal delays for South Side motorists.

Drivers "are co-operating well" with the city's appeal to pick up people at bus stops, Commissioner Stan Hampton said this morning.

"It looks good."

The irritation to many transit members, say union officials, is that they no longer have wage parity with police and firemen. They began dropping in the 1940s and have continued losing ground.

"The membership feel they're being treated as second-class citizens by city hall," Mr. Mack said.

Mr. Hampton said at the meeting planned for this afternoon he would repeat the city's demand that its latest offer of a 16.2 per cent increase over two years be presented to the membership.

Asked if this meant the city

More STRIKE Page 12

DENTIST'S APPOINTMENT KEPT DESPITE STRIKE

. . . Mrs. Oliver Robertson, of 13317 89A St., and children Karen, 8, and Brian, 10, thumb a lift

Spirit of co-operation gets workers there on time

Thousand of Edmontonians used any means of transportation available to get to work today—and the vast majority made it on time.

Hundreds, in fact, were on the job up to a half-hour before their normal starting times as the traffic flow was smoother than expected.

They travelled in cars and trucks, on motor scooters and bicycles, and by thumb and foot.

Staff Inspector George Mitchell, in charge of police traffic, said there were more cars than expected—but no congestion developed. Police directed traffic at all major intersections.

Business and government offices, stores and factories reported that almost all employees were on time. A few were late, others were early. It appeared most people made arrangements well ahead of time.

Insp. Mitchell said vehicles such as light trucks with camper units—which are normally not seen during the morning rush—were everywhere. Many two-car families brought both cars downtown.

Insp. Mitchell warned that many people were parking unlawfully in bus zones and would be tagged. The zones are being kept open as pickup spots for hitch-hikers.

Most suburban bus stops were empty, except where people were waiting for arranged rides. A spirit of camaraderie seemed to be in evidence as citizens got together to help each other out.

Thousand of bicycles, "dune buggy" vehicles and motor cycles were pressed into service. One driver, just to be sure, tied a motor cycle to the back of his car—just in case the congestion got to be too much for the larger vehicle.

Taxi firms were surprised to find less demand than expected Yellow Cab and City Cab both said this morning was like any other, although both were prepared for a rush.

The strikers themselves were

More WALKERS Page 12

China accuses Russia of border buildup

From AP-Reuters

China accused the Soviet Union today of stepping up military deployment along their central Asian border.

The Chinese said the Russians have created a "no man's land" 12 miles wide from which inhabitants have been driven out to intensify "its threat of war against China."

Peking's official radio said Soviet authorities were pouring in "heavy reinforcements" and staging "military exercises."

It also claimed the Russians were "hastily building strategic highways and railways in areas adjoining the Chinese border."

The Soviet Union said today two of its soldiers were killed in Wednesday's clash and warned that Russian frontier guards were ready to repel any new incursion by Chinese troops.

The labor union newspaper Trud said they were killed in an assault on a Chinese cliff-top machine-gun nest.

An official Soviet Army report on the fighting, which both sides have accused the other of starting, was published in the defence ministry newspaper Red Star and the Communist party newspaper Pravda. But it made no mention of Soviet dead.

The Red Star report said one Chinese soldier was killed when a Soviet bullet hit his grenade thrower and blew him up.

After the battle, which took place six miles east of the Soviet settlement of Zhalanaskhol in the Semipalatinsk region, Russian troops found discarded machine-guns, rifles, pistols, grenades, a camera and a radio transmitter and receiver, Trud said.

In Hong Kong local newspapers today reported travellers arriving from Canton said military training in China was being intensified.

Alta. views ignored on incentives—Strom

The federal government has ignored Alberta recommendations on which areas should qualify for the new department of economic expansion incentives program, Premier Harry Strom said today.

In a letter to Prime Minister Trudeau, released by the premier's office today, Mr. Strom said the areas designated in Alberta as eligible for assistance "are most restrictive." "It is regrettable that when the area was designated, it was not in mutual agreement between the two levels of government."

The federal government designated areas in Southern Alberta as eligible for the economic incentives but Northern Alberta was excluded.

Without stating in the let-

More STROM Page 12

Where to find it

Ann Landers	16
Births, Deaths, Marriages	22
Book Review	59
Bridge	24
Business, Stocks	47-52
Charles Lynch	13
Classified ads	23-37
Comics, Features	63
Comment	4
Crossword Puzzle	27
Family Section	14-19
Focus on People	11
Health Column	51
Horoscope	25
Letters To The Journal	4
Music	54, 55
News Digest	12
Sport	8-10
Theatres, Entert'nment	60-62
TV, Radio	56-58
Youth News	46
Wayne Overland	8

Weather

Sunny and warm, thunder tonight, with a risk of hail early this evening. Mainly sunny Saturday with scattered showers. Winds northwest 20. L v tonight 55, high Saturday 70.

Canada bans U.S. killer gas train

WINDSOR, Ont. (CP)—Hartley Purvis, district collector of customs, today issued an order prohibiting the shipment of First World War killer gas through southern Ontario.

It is being moved on the Chesapeake and Ohio Railroad.

Mr. Purvis said:

"I notified the railway officials and our officers shortly after I received a call from Robert Elley, in charge of our rail, air, marine customs division."

The shipment, bound for Lockport, N.Y., from Colorado, was to enter Canada at Windsor at 5:30 p.m. MST, travel through St. Thomas and Welland and return to the U.S. through Niagara Falls at 3 a.m. Saturday.

Mr. Purvis said the shipment is banned under the Customs Tariff Act.

Picture of train on Page 13

over 20, loaded into police vans and city sanitation trucks and driven off to a makeshift jail…."

It was page 1 news, too, when Martin Luther King was shot to death on the balcony of a Memphis motel on April 4, 1968. King was in the city in support of striking garbage workers.

A *Journal* editorial called the killing an "unspeakable crime," and Art Evans, the page 1 columnist, said the kind of violence seen in Memphis "has become a world-wide sickness at the growing expense of what is best in man's heritage. It is the spreading cancer of our time."

But it was the assassination of U.S. President John F. Kennedy in Dallas, Tex., on Nov. 22, 1963, that had the most impact.

Kennedy was driving through Dealey Plaza when a bullet fired from the Texas Book Depository, overlooking the square, shattered his skull.

The Journal's special edition that day showed a four-column picture of a smiling Kennedy waving to the crowd. He looks relaxed and happy, as does First Lady Jackie Kennedy. She was wearing a pillbox hat and the Chanel suit that was soon splattered with her husband's blood.

When 23-year-old Sirhan Sirhan in Los Angeles killed presidential hopeful Robert Kennedy, brother of the slain president, on June 5, 1968, *The Journal's* editorial had a tone of despair.

The shooting itself was a "national disgrace," but it also led "to a feeling that the structure of the United States society is weak, and there is something sick about the outlook of a great many people in that country."

Oddly missing from the readers' list of most significant stories of the '60s was the war in Vietnam. There was ambivalence in letters to the editor and in *Journal* editorials about American involvement in Southeast Asia, but that was accompanied by willingness on the part of most Canadians, although by no means all, to accept U.S. draft dodgers into the country.

Still, Vietnam was front-page news throughout much of the decade, most notably after the Americans increased their bombing runs following the Gulf of Tonkin Resolution, passed by the U.S. Congress in 1965. The resolution was the closest America came to a formal declaration of war and followed attacks on U.S. destroyers that were patrolling the Gulf of Tonkin in the South China Sea.

Much of what was published from Vietnam made grim, even haunting reading. When the famous picture of the Saigon chief of police executing a suspected member of the Communist Viet Cong moved on the wire, it received front-page prominence on Feb. 1, 1968.

There were significant local news events too, many of which would begin to change the city's downtown core. Indeed, hardly a year passed in the '60s without an architect or a developer proposing a dream of a unified, grandiose facelift for the city centre. All were debated by the public, the newspaper and city council. None were ever fully adopted.

Probably one of the most exciting came in 1963 from the New York firm of Webb and Knapp that called for the overall development of 86 acres in the downtown area, centred on the present city hall.

It included a 20-acre civic centre site and would take 15 years to build at a cost of more than $100 million, an amount that would have made it the largest downtown revitalization scheme in the country. What's more,

***May 22, 1963*:**
Pacific Western Airlines' new Chieftain Airbus service linking Edmonton and Calgary makes its inaugural flight. Tickets on the no-frills service cost $11, one way.

***May 27, 1963*:**
The new $16-million Northern Alberta Institute of Technology (NAIT) opens in Edmonton. It's the first institution of its kind in the country.

***May 28, 1963*:**
The first "Journal for DISSENT" appears.

***June 15, 1963*:**
"Cecil 'Tiger' Goldstick and wife Hazel, leave today on a brief coast trip…The Tiger, jobless since professional hockey folded here, will scout Vancouver's employment prospects. Cec would like to stay in Edmonton (certainly he belongs here) but so far no job has materialized on the local scene. I hope one does. The Tiger's life has been wrapped up in Edmonton sport, he's done more than his share in helping the youngsters, and in my book he doesn't rate the closed-door treatment. Let's hope something turns up for Cecil right here in Edmonton. As I said, he belongs." – Art Evans.

The Edmonton Journal

FORECAST: COLDER — EDMONTON, ALBERTA, TUESDAY, DECEMBER 18, 1962 — FIVE CENTS

Journal Photo by Ken Orr

FIREMEN BATTLE SELKIRK HOTEL BLAZE FROM JASPER AVE.
. . . loss estimated at $1,000,000

Loss $1 Million As Blaze Hits Selkirk Hotel

- The clock on the Selkirk Hotel at 101st St. and Jasper Ave. said midnight when the fire was spotted Monday night.
- Four hours later the masonry building housing nine business firms was in ruins. Fifty hotel guests fled the smoke-filled building and only one suffered injury.
- Damage has been estimated at more than $1,000,000.

See Pages 15 and 35 For Additional Reports, Photos

FIRE SCENE FROM NEW BANK OF MONTREAL
. . . 50 guests fled in night

Journal Photo By Colin Price

'Smoke...Panic Everywhere' Then Hectic Rush To Safety

By BARRY WESTGATE
Journal Staff Writer

Ever had a moment of silent, yet screaming, panic?

Ever awake from comfortable, untroubled sleep, with someone yelling "fire," alarm bells ringing, and the acrid, frightening smell of smoke everywhere?

Well I did, Monday night in the Selkirk.

It was dark, and I stood for a moment, a half-understood fear crowding in.

I reached for the light switch, couldn't find it, groped for the wall, and the room came to life.

Panic!

There was smoke everywhere. It was gushing through the floor of the building, through the door too, filling the small room.

★ ★ ★ ★

I HAD to do something.

Get out! I screamed to myself.

But I needed clothes, my typewriter, my radio.

Which first?

Hurry!

The smoke was eddying in, thicker, and there was an ominous, muffled drumming on the floor below. Doors were crashing in, people were crying out, running, pounding on doors, and I was packing — frantically throwing everything into open suitcases.

"Get out!" someone screamed through the smoke.

"Get out," my mind screamed through the hustling panic.

How long, how long did I have?

And then I was running along the hallway.

Which way, which way was the exit? Where the hell was the . . . ah, there.

Relief, flooding in.

★ ★ ★ ★

My suitcases clattered down three storeys, and I started after them — eager to escape. Someone rushed past me, going back in, calling for his brother, his shirt in tatters. A woman followed, clutching after him, and knocked me off the landing.

But I was out in the glorious fresh air. It was dark, and cold, and confusion everywhere.

A hose knocked me down — but I was laughing.

I was safe.

450 Battle Flames, Smoke At Major City Intersection

By AL DAHL and BOB DONAHUE
Journal Staff Writers

Four hundred and fifty firemen fought the Selkirk Hotel blaze at its height about 3 a.m. today. Thirty-two rooms were occupied.

At noon today the hotel looked reasonably normal—from the outside. Inside it was a different story. In the lobby two inches of water sloshed beneath the feet of dejected workers. Upstairs water-soaked rugs squelched to each step. In bedrooms, hastily left beds were tilted at crazy angles and the heavy stench of smoke filled the air.

At the rear, firemen doused still-smouldering ruins.

150 AFFECTED

About 150 persons were employed in premises occupying the Selkirk Hotel block.

insurance on the hotel totalled approximately $700,000. Assessors from the insurance company were checking the building this morning.

Businesses affected by the fire in the half-block-long building were: The Selkirk Hotel, United Cigar Store, The Shaver Shop, Johnson's Restaurant and Dining Lounge, Bata Shoe Store, The Nut House, L. F. Bewley, optometrist, Olympic Billiards and two unoccupied offices.

Fifty-six of the hotel's 97 rooms were destroyed and many of the remaining rooms were heavily damaged by smoke and water.

GUESTS TRANSFERRED

Guests were taken to another hotel owned by Sam Hoffman, part owner of the Selkirk.

It was a general alarm fire which pressed into service firemen from seven fire stations. More than 15 fire rigs, including two aerial ladder trucks, were at the scene. Forty off-duty firemen were hurried to

See FIRE Page 2

Art EVANS

Family Report

AT PRECISELY 2.56 A.M. MONDAY my wife Una happily disqualified me as a childless child expert by giving birth to our first-born, a son.

This report is not, as critics may claim, a pretty sneaky way of getting a birth announcement in the paper without paying. I shall only say that the baby, like all babies, is remarkable in every way and let it go at that. There will be no daily or weekly or monthly progress report for which the average reader will be moderately thankful if not eternally grateful.

However I should like to take this opportunity to warn all males approaching parenthood for the first time to disregard the experience as portrayed in the movies or on television. Over-exposure to the standard script can mislead the prospective father to entertain some rather fanciful notions about the arrival of babies.

★ ★ ★

I'VE SEEN LITERALLY hundreds of films in which no baby was born before at least three people had turned to the camera and shouted, "Boil some water! Lots of it!" It was a hard, fast Hollywood rule.

If an actor really knew his stuff, say a fellow like Raymond Massey or the late Lionel Barrymore, half the audience jumped up and ran out for hot water before they realized it was only a movie they were watching. This scene might have been called, "The Return of the Sheepish."

It would not surprise me in the least if, one day, the movie industry offers a special Academy Award for the actor or actress who boils the most water with the most feeling. Boulder Dam wouldn't hold all of it.

★ ★ ★

ALSO, PROSPECTIVE FATHERS sitting in the waiting room should not be too disappointed when certain stock characters they have seen at silver screen accouchements fail to put in an appearance. I kept a sharp eye peeled but not once did a sturdy midwife stop and solemnly intone those rustic lines conceived by sophisticated bachelor scriptwriters, "Her time has come, Zeke," or again, "Git out of y'ar Jeb. This izz wuman's work."

Finally I must report that there is little chance in this modern day and age that the faithful family doctor, aged 97, who brought the whole kit and caboodle of your clan into the world, will arrive on horseback waving a black bag and a buggywhip. I listened intently but didn't hear a hoofbeat all night.

It is not pleasant to shatter popular myths but it is time men learned the truth. This will save them from boiling 500 gallons of water and keeping a fast horse saddled in the city like I did. These precautions are not really necessary.

★ ★ ★

FINAL WORD — When one has been helped it is customary to say thank you and I do to Dr. H. A. Lloyd and the nursing staff of the Royal Alexandra Hospital maternity wing.

TCA To Operate Prairie 'Milk Runs'

By BRUCE PHILLIPS
Southam News Services

OTTAWA — Trans-Canada Air Lines will continue to operate the southern prairies "milk run" for the time being, a company spokesman said today.

At the same time, the publicly-owned airline decided to take over the Regina-Saskatoon-Prince Albert run from Pacific Western Airlines, which had operated the route for the last five years. These decisions were taken at a weekend meeting of TCA directors in Montreal.

TCA is continuing with the milk run, pending a report on the service from the federal Air Transport Board. The milk run serves the smaller cities such as Medicine Hat, Swift Current and Brandon which lie between Calgary and Winnipeg.

Trans-Canada has complained of recurring losses on the milk run and is willing to turn over the route to another carrier.

See TCA Page 2

5

Shopping Days Until Christmas

NOT A DANCE—She's not demonstrating a new ballroom step. For the answer to what she and many like her are doing, see The Journal For Women, Page 17.

Police, Firemen Cool, Courageous

By Journal Staff Writers

Edmonton can be proud of its police, firemen and citizens. They came up calm and courageous when it counted most at the Selkirk fire this morning.

There were heroes everywhere.

Policemen carried suitcases, jewelry, papers, furniture and a jukebox out of burning buildings. One constable forcibly restrained an overwrought man from rushing into the inferno to search for documents.

There were the 500 spectators who cheered the drenched firemen as they went into action time and time again.

There was the restaurant owner who ordered coffee be brought to the scene for the 450 firemen.

And the little old lady who placidly stepped out of the smoke long after the Selkirk tenants were believed evacuated. Fully-dressed and carrying two suitcases, she walked up to the amazed firemen and asked "where do I go now?"

And the pyjama-clad woman who calmly carried her two sleeping children to safety, wrapped in her fur coat.

Twenty spectators spontaneously rushed into the United Cigar Store, not to plunder but to form a salvage line. Thanks largely to their efforts, most of the store's contents were saved.

There was Selkirk bar manager Rocky Wagner, who, surrounded by smoke, water and sirens, turned to a reporter and commented "there must be a fire somewhere."

Pair Held In Robbery Attempt

Two men were arrested and one is being sought in connection with an attempted armed robbery Monday at 108th St. and Jasper Ave.

Nicholas Toma, 24, and Harold Desmond, 48, were arrested following an attempt to rob Frank Galarneau, a messenger for Acme Novelty. He was carrying money to the Canadian Imperial Bank of Commerce. The money, reported at several thousand dollars, was carried in two cloth cash bags.

Police said three men, dressed as workmen were sweeping in the lane behind the bank when Mr. Galarneau drove up.

Two of the men jumped in the car and one of them threatened the messenger with a gun.

One man had driven the car a short distance when police moved in.

Toma has been charged with armed robbery and Desmond will face a charge of conspiracy.

Both men were remanded to Friday without election and plea by Magistrate S. V. Legg in city police court.

Magistrate Legg set bail at $5,000 property and when Desmond heard the bail, he said: "A little high, isn't it?"

Magistrate Legg answered: "This is a serious charge you're up against, hence the bail."

East, West Abandon Efforts For Nuclear Test Ban By Jan. 1

GENEVA (AP)—The United States, Britain and the Soviet Union abandoned their efforts today to negotiate an end to nuclear testing by Jan. 1.

The three-power test-ban subcommittee of the 17-nation disarmament conference held its last meeting before the conference goes into a Christmas recess.

Soviet delegate Semyon Tsarapkin told the last three-power meeting that all the nuclear powers should stop testing by Jan. 1, "regardless of whether we can reach agreement by that date or not."

Another Hint

Western officials said they regarded this as another hint that Russia is planning to declare a one-sided test suspension before the end of the year.

The Western powers refuse to accept a ban on underground tests unless the Russians allow a certain number of on-site inspections a year to prevent cheating. The Russians have consistently rejected any on-site inspection, but have proposed the erection of three "black box" detectors in the Soviet Union to help keep check of suspicious earth tremors.

Resumes Jan. 15

The disarmament conference resumes here on Jan. 15. At the closing meeting of the test-ban subcommittee the U.S. called on the Soviet Union to take part in a detailed scientific review of the black box proposal.

U.S. Ambassador Arthur H. Dean told the test-ban subcommittee the black box proposal failed to resolve the test ban deadlock because it is intended to bypass the Western demand for on-site inspection of suspicious earth tremors.

Soviet delegate Tsarapkin has proposed that three black boxes—robot seismographs—be installed in the Soviet Union and serviced by foreign inspectors.

What Council Did

At its meeting Monday Edmonton City Council:

- Approved in principle a civic centre tower construction program by Webb and Knapp.
- Authorized commissioners to go ahead with plans for an urban renewal study.

Reports On Page 3

Frantic Effort Ends In Fine

A man who claimed he was searching for his brother believed to be inside the burning Selkirk hotel was charged in police court this morning.

Malcolm Stewart, about 25, pleaded guilty before Magistrate S. V. Legg to causing a disturbance during the height of the fire.

Police told the court that Stewart would not stay out of the way during fire fighting operations.

He was fined $25 or 15 days jail term.

WHEAT SALE ANNOUNCED

OTTAWA (CP)—A new contract for the sale of 34,000,000 bushels of wheat to Communist China, valued at $65,000,000, was announced in the Commons today by Agriculture Minister Hamilton.

WEATHER

Cloudy with light snow, colder, winds east 15, low tonight 10, high tomorrow 20. Details on Page 2.

Where To Find It

Ann Landers	20
Births, Deaths, Marriages	28
Bridge	30
Classified Ads	29 to 34
Comics, Features	22
District	24
Financial	12, 13
Patterns	32
Radio	28
Sport	8 to 10
Theatres, Entertainment	27
T.V.	31
Women's	17 to 20

Journal readers learned, it would partly be designed by I.M. Pei, the world-famous architect who eventually designed such landmarks as Pyramide du Louvre in Paris, the Jacob Javits Centre in New York and the National Gallery in Washington, D.C.

The plan called for a $100-million subway system and a series of freeways that would skirt a downtown of sparkling new highrise office and apartment towers. The proposal called for a downtown that would be packed with retailers and restaurants, and pedestrians would move along elevated sidewalks that linked the new buildings.

"The downtown plan to be submitted to the city council tonight is so big that it cannot be taken at a gulp," a July 22, 1963, editorial said. "It will give aldermen plenty to chew on during the next few months...."

After public meetings, and hours of city council debate, the plan was rejected as being too rich to swallow.

But in 1967, the same year in which Ivor Dent was elected the mayor, voters approved a study that could have led to the construction of an omniplex, a structure that would serve as a sports arena and convention complex. Suggested locations for the omniplex were the river valley and downtown, including one where Canada Place was built in the '80s.

"The majority of 73 per cent in support of the principle of the omniplex trade, convention and sports centre clearly indicates that Edmontonians realize that to make progress, investments must be made. And if the price is high, it's because this is no small town project."

The omniplex was never built, as again, city council, backed by voters in a plebiscite, decided that at $30 million, it was too expensive.

But if none of the big plans came to pass, there were still substantive changes. Grand old buildings such as the public library and the Edmonton Club were torn down to make way for buildings like Telus Tower, which changed the city's skyline. More would fall in the upcoming decade.

Certainly, the population had boomed, growing from 209,324 in 1960 to 410,105 in 1969, partly as a result of the annexation of the towns of Jasper Place in the west and Beverly in the northeast.

Nevertheless, the pressure for more land remained intense, wrote civic affairs reporter Olive Elliott in a decade-ending story. And, she said, the need for more affordable housing would mean a fresh concept of urban life.

With the passage of the Alberta Condominium Act of 1965, a new word entered the vocabulary of the newspaper and its readers.

With some condominium units going for as much as $42,000, it was clear, Elliott suggested, that "condominium living has become a preference rather than a necessity." Living arrangements aside, Elliott said that the entire surprising decade had meant the city and its people had changed in fundamental ways. It was a big city now, she said.

What she didn't know was that even bigger changes were coming. The province would ride a wave of soaring energy prices in the '70s that would mean conflict between the province and Ottawa as well as crushingly high interest rates and inflation.

Despite those problems, Alberta would grow unexpectedly rich and, in many ways, become the envy of the country.

***June 24, 1963*:**
The first "Astrological Forecast" by Sydney Omar runs in *The Journal*.

***Aug. 6, 1963*:**
The first Edmonton Folk Festival is held at the Edmonton Gardens. Acts included Peter, Paul and Mary, a trio who sold out the Gardens a year previously, Bud and Travis and Odetta. "Seldom does a Gardens audience sit for so long in such mannerly, well-disciplined appreciation or go home with such satisfaction," reports *Journal* staffer Pat Johnson.

***Aug. 30, 1963*:**
Women playground directors with the city's parks and recreation department protest the T-shirts they are forced to wear. In a protest in front of city hall, the demonstrators put the T-shirts on the controversial metal geese. "They look better on the geese than they did on us," says 20-year-old Joan Pendleton. "They made us look sexy and that's a bad influence on the children."

***Sept. 16, 1963*:**
"Les Canadiens," a comic strip that was designed to turn readers bilingual, runs for the first time in the page of *The Journal*. The first

APOLLO 11
A SOUVENIR SECTION

The Edmonton Journal

FORECAST: CLOUDY | EDMONTON, ALBERTA, MONDAY, JULY 21, 1969 | 52 PAGES | 10c

Moonmen head home after perfect link-up

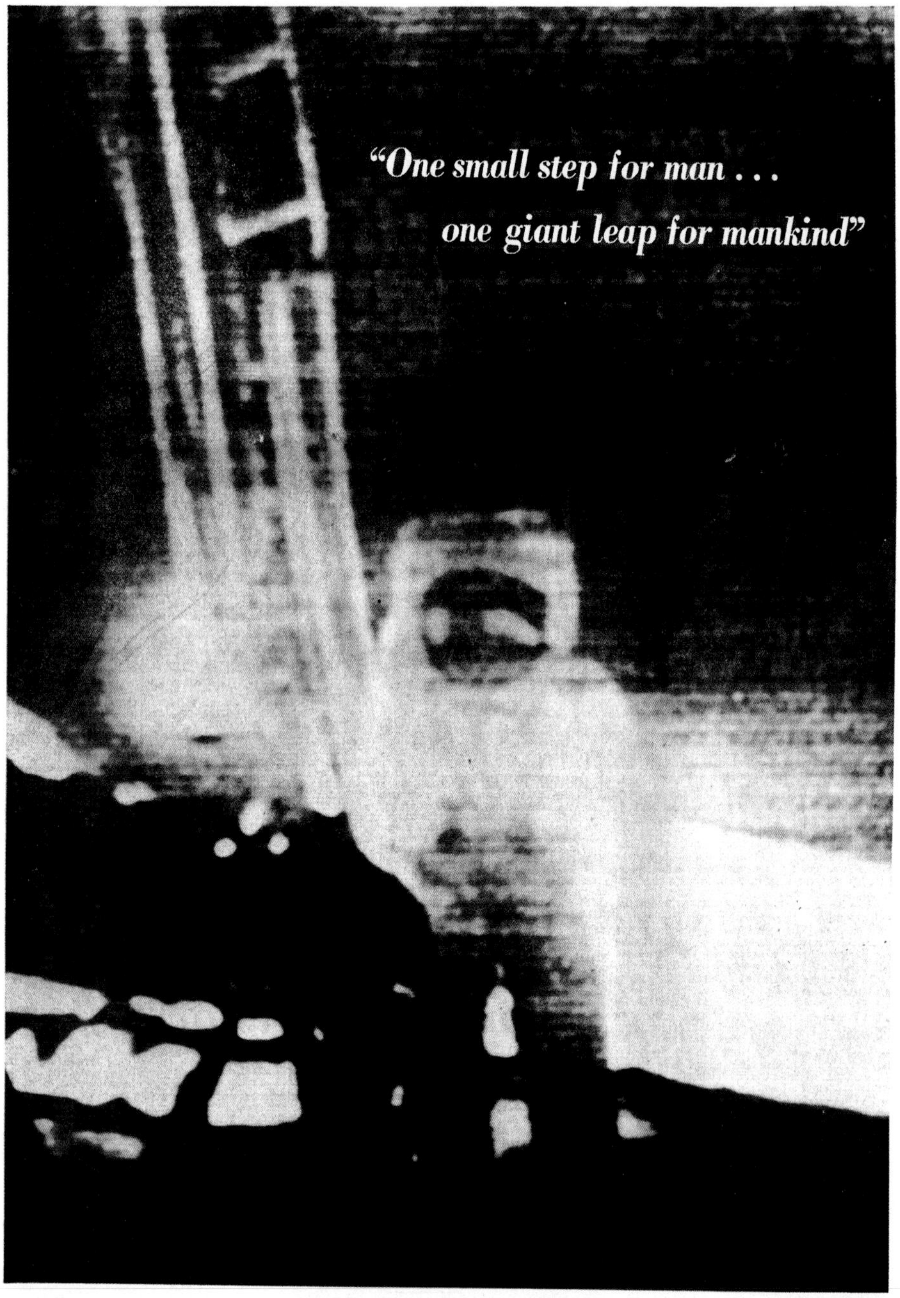
"One small step for man . . .
one giant leap for mankind"

MAN ON THE MOON
– AN HISTORIC MOMENT

Red craft on moon but its fate a mystery

HOUSTON (AP) — The moonmen blasted off the bleak lunar surface today, chased their mother ship for 3½ hours and then linked up safely for the voyage home.

Neil A. Armstrong and Edwin E. Aldrin Jr., of Apollo 11, the first humans on the moon, put their truncated spaceship through a series of four complex rocket firings to catch up with Michael Collins in the command ship circling the moon for the 27th time.

The lunar ship Eagle, using its descent stage as a launching pad, lifted off with a burst of fire at 10:54 a.m. and caught the mother ship, Columbia shortly after 2:30 p.m. Edmonton time.

In the final minute, when they were in sight of each other, Collins steered his capsule straight toward Eagle, gently nudging the two ships together until mechanical latches engaged and locked the two ships together.

Meanwhile, the Soviet Union's puzzling satellite, Luna 15, touched down on the moon today after a highspeed descent that raised doubts that it landed intact.

The craft swooped down from orbit at a velocity of about 300 miles an hour, scientists at the British Jodrell Bank Observatory said, and halted in the area known as the Sea of Crises — a mere 500 miles from the Eagle.

Observatory director Sir Bernard Lovell said that nothing is likely to survive such a high-speed landing intact, but added that does not necessarily mean the robot machine crashed.

Lovell also clung to his theory that the Russians are aiming to have the probe collect rock samples and bring them back to earth ahead of Apollo 11.

The Luna 15 landed as the astronauts of the Eagle were preparing to blast off from the moon.

The liftoff was the only aspect of the Apollo 11 mission that had never before been tested — and it had to work, just right, just as it did . . . or Armstrong and Aldrin, those two giants of the 20th Century, would almost certainly have been doomed

"Beautiful, very smooth," Aldrin commented as Eagle took off from the moon.

"A very quiet ride. There's that one crater down there.

"We've a little bit of slow wallowing here," he said later.

"Shutdown," he called out as the engine stopped.

"Great," mission control said and reported Eagle in a near-perfect orbit ranging from about 11 to 54 miles high.

And now, all the critical phases of the mission behind them, the moonmen can prepare for a relatively easy coast back to earth, with splash-down in the Pacific late Thursday morning.

Just before take-off, the astronauts dumped out all their space "junk" so they had as little weight as possible to lift.

Left behind, along with the U.S. flag, the two-ton descent stage of the lunar module, scientific gear, their overshoes, the portable lift support systems that enabled them to walk outside the space ship, cameras, gloves, and old fod containers.

Mission control awakened the moonmen shortly after 8 a.m. following a six-hour rest period. Instruments which monitored Armstrong during the night indicated he slept fitfully. There is only one set of biomedical instruments in the cabin so Aldrin was not monitored.

Armstrong, the first man to set foot on moondust, and Aldrin had treated the earth to a spectacular televised showing of their moon walk hours before.

The climactic moment in history came at 7.56

More APOLLO Page 2A

SOUVENIR SECTION

Today's Journal includes a souvenir pullout section on the U.S. astronauts' historic landing on the moon.

It comprises this page, Page 2A and the back two pages of this section.

Northern Adventure

"The San Bruno, Calif., electrical worker, and the self-styled adventuress from Brooklyn have written an incredible chapter in the annals of human endurance and fortitude."
— Reporter Bob Hill, March 25, 1963

"Cold, Starvation, Pain Fill Fifty Tortured Days" read the main front page headline in *The Journal* on March 26, 1963.

The story beneath the headline, by *Journal* northern correspondent Bob Hill, was an incredible one.

Helen Klaben, a brash 21-year-old New Yorker who described herself as an adventuress, and Ralph Flores, 42, a Mexican-American former DEW line electrician from San Bruno, Calif., had survived the crash of his single-engine aircraft.

For 50 bitterly cold days on a mountainside a few miles south of the B.C.-Yukon border, they had huddled together for warmth.

He had broken ribs and a broken jaw. She had a crushed right foot and a broken arm. Gangrene had set in on her toes.

Their food – four tins of sardines, two cans of tuna, two tins of fruit salad and a box of crackers – had been eaten in the first four days of their ordeal. For the remaining 46 days, the pair had survived on melted snow water. Temperatures had plummeted to the –40 F range.

For Hill, it was the story of a lifetime, and he won *The Journal*'s first-ever National Newspaper Award. Media around the world were fascinated by the story and looked to the paper for photos and coverage.

Hill, who went on to become both a national and international correspondent for Southam News Services and eventually served as associate editor at *The Journal*, was the right man in almost the right place when news of the missing couple's discovery first broke.

Appointed a year earlier as the newspaper's first full-time northern reporter, Hill had just finished covering a resources conference in Whitehorse and had decided to spend the weekend in the Yukon capital.

On Sunday night, word arrived that Klaben and Flores had been spotted, and aircraft from Watson Lake, some 265 miles down the Alaska Highway, would be going to the crash scene the following morning.

Along with the manager of a local Whitehorse radio station, Hill drove all night down the icy highway but arrived after the rescue planes had taken off. He was there, however, when Klaben and Flores were flown in shortly before noon.

His first story on the rescue quoted Chuck Hamilton, the pilot who had spotted the downed airplane when flying supplies to a big-game guide in the Rocky Mountain Trench in B.C.

"Hamilton said the wing was all he could see of the plane because smoke from a nearby campfire obscured everything but the marking 'N588'," Hill wrote.

"An SOS, he said, was tramped in the snow of a meadow about a mile from the crash scene."

strip introduces English readers to 22 different verbs and nouns.

***Oct. 11, 1963*:**
The Edmonton Professional Opera Company, later Edmonton Opera, presents its first production, *Madame Butterfly*. The company began as the Edmonton Capital Choral Society in 1955.

***Nov. 18, 1963*:**
The Edmonton Huskies win the Canadian junior football championship.

***In 1964*:**
A *Journal* phone room employee makes $37.50 a week.

***Jan. 6, 1964*:**
Following the opening of the city's new Royal Alexandra Hospital, the old Royal Alex, reopens as the Glenrose Provincial General Hospital, dedicated to convalescent patients, rehabilitation services and medical care and education of handicapped children.

***Feb. 15, 1964*:**
The $10-million terminal at the Edmonton International Airport opens, bringing the total cost of the airport to $20 million.

The Edmonton Journal

FORECAST: SHOWERS — EDMONTON, ALBERTA, WEDNESDAY, JUNE 5, 1968 — TEN CENTS

Kennedy chances slim

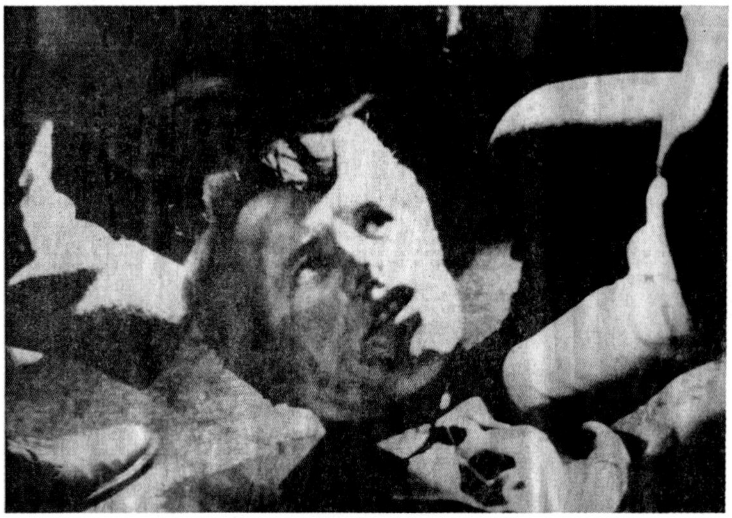

KENNEDY MOMENTS AFTER SHOOTING
. . . gravely wounded on floor of Ambassador Hotel

'He may not make it' says one of surgeons

From Journal News Services

LOS ANGELES — Senator Robert F. Kennedy was in "extremely critical condition" today following an assassination bid by a gunman.

One of the three surgeons who assisted in the nearly four-hour operation to recover a bullet from Kennedy's brain said the senator "might not make it."

Dr. Henry Cuneo said several major arteries were severed and the senator's brain suffered extensive loss of blood and oxygen as well as several blood clots. It was unlikely the senator will be able to recover fully, and, in fact, it was "doubtful that he could live."

As Kennedy fought for his life, police identified the man arrested as the shooting suspect. They said he is Sirhan Sirhan, 23, who has a brother in nearby Pasadena.

SIRHAN SIRHAN
. . . shooting suspect

Four $100 bills found

For hours the man had stubbornly refused to say who he was. Mayor Samuel Yorty said police found four $100 bills on him "with which he was planning on leaving if he could get away" and a newspaper clip not favorable to Kennedy.

In New York, neurosurgeon Dr. Lawrence Poole quoted Dr. Cuneo as telling him in a phone conversation that he feared the outcome of the shooting "may be extremely tragic".

Dr. Cuneo, a former pupil of Dr. Poole, who is professor of neurology at Columbia-Presbyterian Medical Centre, was quoted as saying:

"There was evidently serious damage to the cerebellum, the part of the brain on the extreme back of the head on the right side; to part of the right cerebral hemisphere . . . and to the mid-brain, which is the main cable connecting the brain itself with the rest of the body.

"This mid-brain deals with not only the function of motion in the arms and legs and sensation to the body but also with eye movements and even the life function itself, such as blood pressure, breathing, heart rate.

"So it's a very critical area, and this was injured, and this is why I fear—as Dr. Cuneo indicated—the outcome may be extremely tragic."

Kennedy is breathing without the use of special oxygen equipment following the operation but he is in a resuscitator.

He was taken to an intensive care unit of Good-Samaritan Hospital following the operation.

The medical bulletin said the next 12 tc 36 hours would be the "very critical period."

With the senator at the hospital were his wife, Ethel, and his brother, Senator Edward Kennedy of Massachusetts.

Police held Sirhan and the .22-calibre pistol he is alleged to have emptied at Sen. Kennedy and five other persons minutes after the senator had delivered a victory speech hailing the results of the California primary election Tuesday.

The assassination attempt rocked the capital and horrified the world. President Johnson ordered Secret Service protection for all presidential candidates and members of their families.

Kennedy was hit by two of eight shots fired into the crowded victory celebration scene in the Ambassador Hotel at 12:29 a.m., Edmonton time. Five others near him were also wounded, but none as critically.

One bullet hit Kennedy's shoulder and a second entered his ear, lodging in his brain. Kennedy was conscious for some time after the shooting, but lost consciousness en route to hospital.

Sen. Eugene McCarthy, who lost out to Kennedy in the vital California primary, called on his supporters to pray for Kennedy's recovery. He cancelled all his campaign plans and prepared to fly to Washington.

President Johnson, who followed the tragedy through the night via television, issued this statement today:

'No words equal to horror'

"There are no words equal to the horror of this tragedy. Our thoughts and our prayers are with Senator Kennedy, his family and the other victims. All Americans pray for his recovery.

"We also pray that divisiveness and violence be driven from the hearts of men everywhere."

A graphic eyewitness to the shooting was Martin Petruski, a waiter at the Ambassador Hotel ballroom.

"I had just shaken hands with him . . . All of a sudden, this man, not too tall, rushed out . . . He started to fire.

"Someone yelled, 'grab him, grab him,' and the senator started to slide to his knees.

"I started to move out . . . the gun was still firing . . . Then another guy, about two feet from Sen. Kennedy, fell down . . . There were five or six shots. I saw just one man with a gun."

The man was quickly overpowered by Kennedy aides, with Los Angeles Rams football star Roosevelt Grier jumping him first. Grier handed the gun, a light hand-gun, to decathlon champion Rafer Johnson, another member of the Kennedy entourage.

Witnesses said that after the man was seized, he cried: "I did it for my country . . . I love my country."

More KENNEDY Page 2

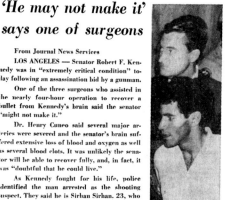

Other stories, pictures Pages 2, 10, 63

Terror in dark corridor

By ROBERT HEALY
Copyright Boston Globe Newspaper Co.

LOS ANGELES (AP) — In that narrow, darkened corridor, there was terror, profanity, tears, blood and the violence of a nation.

Senator Robert Kennedy of New York had walked down the same back corridor in the kitchen of the Ambassador Hotel just 15 minutes before. He had won California. And he came over to shake my hand, I congratulated him and we talked about his big win.

Now, I was standing on a steel serving table directly over the same place where we had shaken hands. He lay there, struck down by bullets. His right hand held a bleeding side. His face was white. His eyes were open. His lips moved just slightly.

But he did not cry.

Against the steel serving table, Roosevelt Grier, the huge Negro lineman for Los Angeles Rams, had the assailant pinned. He held tight to the man's right wrist and he smashed it against the side of the serving table. He tried to free the gun from his hand.

There was this great man, towering over the small man and with all his strength it took him more than a minute to take that gun.

Another man, atop the table, was trying to kick the gunman in the face.

"Bastard . . . kill him," he shouted. And he would have.

Kennedy waited until his victory was secure in the California primary before he came down to talk to his workers. There was a huge crowd in the ballroom. They had waited for several hours.

Then the senator came. There were few people in the corridor — some kitchen workers and some television cameramen forewarned of his arrival.

I listened to him speak for a few minutes, then walked into the press room. The reception was better on the television in the press room.

A few seconds before he ended his speech. I left the television and went to the door that led to a corridor behind the ballroom stage and off the kitchen, Kennedy would come off the stage and walk down this corridor.

I was only a few feet inside the corridor, walking toward Kennedy, when I saw his head bobbing in the crowd. We were 25 or 30 feet

More TERROR Page 2

California voters gave him a win

By GEORGE BRIMMELL
Southam News Services

WASHINGTON — Bobby Kennedy had just won the big one when he was shot.

Senator Kennedy had only minutes before issued his victory statement, with a pledge to go on to the Democratic national convention in Chicago to continue his fight for his party's presidential nomination.

He had come back from the brink of political oblivion after losing the Oregon primary the week before, with a narrow but important victory Tuesday in California over Senator Eugene McCarthy. The win gives Kennedy the state's 172-man delegation.

RFK AHEAD

Late returns showed Senator Kennedy with 46 per cent of the Democratic vote. Senator McCarthy, his main opponent in the primary, received 42 per cent. An uncommitted delegation headed by State Attorney General Thomas Lynch received the remainder — 12 per cent.

Running unopposed on the Republican ballot, Gov. Ronald Reagan, the "favorite son," thus received all GOP ballots.

Early returns from California, mainly from the northern portion of the state, had given Senator McCarthy a lead of up to five per cent. But as the results from populous Los Angeles County began to come in, the trend was reversed.

Los Angeles County contains nearly 40 per cent of the eligible

More PRIMARY Page 2

PM promises cities probe, urban planning support bill

By GUY DEMARINO
Of The Journal

Prime Minister Pierre Trudeau announced here Tuesday the federal government will conduct a comprehensive study of urbanization problems.

"God willing," he said, the study will start right after June 25 and will be undertaken by Transport Minister Paul Hellyer, who is also responsible for housing.

Mr. Trudeau told the annual b a n q u e t of the Canadian Federation of Mayors and Municipalities, at the Macdonald Hotel, that provincial and municipal governments, as well as interested citizens, will be asked to collaborate in the project.

He added the government will discuss with the provinces the development of urban research centres at Canadian universities, to study the problems of urbanization and train the men who will deal with them.

PLANNING ASSISTANCE

Mr. Trudeau also announced to the 900 assembled civic officials from across Canada that his government plans to introduce legislation to provide new federal financial assistance for the planning and the development of urban regions.

He also announced plans to introduce, in the next session of Parliament, a Canada Water Act to provide for federal-provincial planning for water resource development and management, including pollution control.

NHA AMENDMENTS

He mentioned the possibility of developing new cities in congested areas such as Montreal and Calgary and promised amendments to the National Housing Act to provide more effective assistance to smaller communities.

Mr. Trudeau said his government plans special legislation to provide new financial aid for the planning and development of urban regions.

Many of the CFMM delegates didn't seemed too impressed by Mr. Trudeau's speech, including Federation President and Edmonton Mayor Vince Dantzer.

Asked what he thought of the speech, Mr. Dantzer replied: "Nothing, absolutely nothing."

And he added: "Who's kidding whom? We know the problems, we just need the solutions."

Other stories, pictures Pages 3, 61.

Where to find it

The University of Alberta annual spring convocation was held Tuesday. Stories and pictures on Page 16.

★ ★ ★

Viet Nam peace talks resumed in Paris today. Story on Page 2.

Ann Landers 22
Births, Deaths, Marriages 46
Bridge 48
Business, Stocks 77-79
Classified Ads 47-58
Comics, Features 64
Comment 4
Crossword Puzzle 51
Horoscope 49
Journal for the Family 21-38
Letters To The Journal .. 4
News Digest 2
Patterns 50
Sport 71-76
Theatres, Entertainment .. 80
TV, Radio 65
Stamps 36
Learning And You 31
Camera Column 45
Counter Points 26
Car Talk 34
See Here You Men 23

Total Pages 84

Weather

Continuing cloudy with showers tonight and Thursday. Chance of thundershowers tonight. Winds light. Low tonight 45, high Thursday 70. Details on Page 2.

Art EVANS

Dorset Dogies

AN ASSOCIATED Press story about a dud British naval shell landing on a Dorset farm and causing "a cattle stampede," brought a speedy beef from a Journal reader.

"Whoever heard of a cattle stampede in England?" the caller scoffed, pointing out that dressed cold-storage beef from the Argentine is past spooking.

Granted, the Great North road out of London isn't exactly the Old Chisholm Trail. One can drive from Land's End to John O' Groat's without hearing a single trailhand singing, "Git Along Little Dogie."

On the other hand, there is no set formula specifying how many critters it takes to make a stampede. A stampede is in the eye of the beholder. It's all a matter of degree, of time and place.

★ ★ ★

YOU HAVE TO remember that Dorset is a lot smaller than Texas. Two head running wild in Dorset may be the equivalent of 2,000 head running wild in Texas. As for movie and television cowboys, they wouldn't climb out of their bedrolls to turn any herd numbering less than 5,000.

Those movie herds are really something. Trailing up from Texas, the hero loses stock to rustlers, Indians, drought, cloudbursts, blizzards, stampedes, and quicksand, and still arrives at Dodge or Abilene with enough longhorns to plug the Chicago stockyards.

If describing the Dorset incident as a "cattle stampede," was an exaggeration, it should be remembered that overstatement is not unknown in North America. A holding described as a "ranch," may be small enough to give a Shetland pony claustrophobia.

★ ★ ★

BUS BYRON

ARE THERE any practising poets among Edmonton bus drivers?

The query is prompted by an item in yesterday's paper about a bus driver in Sussex who, "thinks out the rhymes while he drives and scribbles them down when he stops."

The driver was quoted as saying, "I've lost a lot of good poems through not being able to stop when a good theme strikes me." Possibly, but if the muse suddenly slammed on the brakes without warning, the bus might be struck in the rear by something more substantial than a good theme.

Bus drivers who sing, whistle, hum or just tell jokes, are not uncommon. But a bus driver who writes poetry on the job has to be a rare find.

I've never encountered one, not even on Calgary's famed Burns Avenue bus which, in its artistic heyday, symbolized culture in motion. On Saturday nights the performance of the homeward-bound Stockyards Symphonette and Glee Club was always exquisitely sensitive.

But if the bus driver was a budding Byron, he worked under a handicap. One cannot compose passable poetry and at the same time shout, "Stop that racket or get off this bus!"

★ ★ ★

UNTAMED

AN ADVERTISEMENT for colored bathroom tissue warns dramatically: Not for the tame!

This should work wonders for shy folks who have always yearned to have others think of them as daring and untamed. Once visitors cast their awed optics on that colored bathroom tissue, they'll get the message.

They'll know they are in the house of a party capable of derring-do that "The Avengers" on television wouldn't dare tackle.

The next day, Flores and Klaben were flown to hospital in Whitehorse, with Hill along for the ride.

Their spirits, Hill reported, were good, despite all that they had lived through.

"On the flight here, Miss Klaben cracked: 'The next time I go camping I'll take supplies.'

"When the two were found, doctors agreed that they had little time left to live."

An unnamed physician in the Yukon said that Flores would likely have died within four days and Klaben might have lasted another week.

It was a tale that took on a life of its own.

Hill recalled the rescue in a story written in 1975, 12 years after their discovery in the wilds of northern B.C., and shortly before *Hey, I'm Alive*, a made-for-television movie on the rescue, was broadcast.

The main reason the story hadn't slipped from public memory was the two central characters themselves, Hill wrote.

"Everybody appreciates a story of courage and endurance but this one had special appeal because Klaben and Flores (despite his DEW-line job) were both northern innocents. They were scandalously ill-equipped and unprepared for their ordeal but they took it all – the plane crash, the injuries, the hunger and the cold – and survived."

Nevertheless, Hill said, there were still nagging doubts.

"There were those, northerners among them, who refused to believe the story. Most of them were convinced Klaben and Flores had far more supplies with them than they claimed. Others even suspected they took off from the crash scene and stayed for six weeks in a comfortable cabin and then returned to be rescued.

"The second question, invariably asked with a wink or knowing smile: Did Klaben and Flores have an affair during their long stretch of enforced companionship?

"For the answer to that one, you'll have to ask them. In the far-off, almost puritanical days of 1963, reporters did not question people about such matters."

As for the movie, *Hey, I'm Alive*, which was based on a book by Klaben and starred Sally Struthers as Klaben and Ed Asner as Flores, Hill gave it a mixed review in a *Journal* critique.

The dialogue, Hill said, would embarrass the worst Hollywood hack, although "the characters emerge pretty much as I remember them from Watson Lake and Whitehorse."

One person, however, wasn't quite right.

"The strangest character in the story, though, is the reporter.

"He's a dazed looking non-entity who goes around asking dumb questions and making even dumber observations."

***March 28, 1964*:**
***The Journal*'s northern reporter, Bob Hill, wins a National Newspaper Award, the paper's first, for the best spot Canadian news story of 1963 for his coverage of the discovery of two northern plane crash survivors seven weeks after their light plane went down in the B.C. wilderness.**

***April 27, 1964*:**
Edmonton's city council votes to expand to 12 aldermen.

***April 29, 1964*:**
The marigold is nominated as Edmonton's official flower.

***Aug. 17, 1964*:**
Jasper Place, Alberta's biggest town with about 38,000 people, amalgamates with its eastern neighbour, Edmonton. The city's population nears 350,000.

***Oct. 14, 1964*:**
William Hawrelak is re-elected mayor of Edmonton, until he is forced from office for the second time. A water fluoridation plebiscite again fails to pass.

***Dec. 18, 1964*:**
Syncrude Canada is incorporated to exploit the massive oilsand deposits at Fort McMurray.

Humphrey calls for probe on violence at convention

NEW YORK (CP) — Vice-President Hubert Humphrey called Monday for a committee to study the violence that occurred at last week's Democratic national convention in Chicago.

Humphrey, who received the presidential nomination at that convention, opened his campaign for the Nov. 5 election by marching in brilliant sunshine up Fifth Avenue in New York's first Labor Day parade in five years.

He suggested the investigating committee during a television interview. He said the committee, which might include lawyers, professors, police and journalists, could examine "the actions of the demonstrators, the conduct of the police and the role of the media."

'OVER-REACTED'

During the interview, Humphrey said four times that Chicago police "over-reacted" in dealing with last week's disorders. And he added that he is sure that Mayor Richard J. Daley of Chicago "didn't want to condone the beating of these people with clubs."

"I didn't condone it," he said.

Last Saturday, Humphrey had said on TV that "we ought to quit pretending that Mayor Daley did something that was wrong."

"He didn't condone a thing that was wrong. He tried to protect lives."

Mr. Humphrey said he had been "targeted by an assassination team" at the convention.

The mayor did not want another assassination in Chicago," he said.

Humphrey said it was unfortunate "people were led to believe the police waded in without provocation."

'FILTH ON RUG'

Humphrey spoke of a policeman stabbed with a broken beer bottle, "filth and manure" spread on the rugs of the Conrad Hilton Hotel and "many things that were incredibly bad and shameful."

Before heading back to Minnesota Monday night for a week of rest and planning, the vice-president marched 25 blocks in the Fifth Avenue parade here.

Heavy security, including policemen perched on top of buildings, was in force all along the parade route.

Humphrey was in good spirits, waving to the estimated 100,000 marchers from a reviewing stand for 90 minutes and engaging in small talk with well-wishers and labor officials.

IN SECLUSION

Richard Nixon, the Republican presidential candidate, also was in the city, but remained in seclusion in his 62nd St. apartment. Mayor John Lindsay also stayed away from the parade.

Meanwhile, the Republicans announced they are setting up party branches in Europe to raise money from expatriate Americans.

Party Chairman Ray C. Bliss said the European group will have committees in France, West Germany, Belgium, Britain and Italy.

He said about 2,000,000 Americans reside in Europe, including military personnel.

WALLACE ENCOURAQED

In Darlington, S.C., George Wallace, the third-party presidential candidate said the troubles at the Democratic convention in Chicago helped his chances of being elected.

Wallace, former Alabama governor, said he felt the Chicago police "used the tactics they ought to have used" against demonstrators during the Democratic convention.

Of 583, all but one freed

CHICAGO (AP) — Of the 583 persons arrested last week in demonstrations accompanying the Democratic national convention, "everyone but Dick Gregory" has been released on bail.

A spokesman for the Chicago Legal Defence Committee made the comment Monday.

Most were charged with disorderly conduct and some with resisting arrest. Perhaps 75 per cent of the bail bonds set were for $25, the legal defence committee spokesman said.

However, bonds ranged as high as $25 000 in a few cases.

Gregory, a Negro comedian and writer who submitted voluntarily to arrest Thursday night when he tried to pass through a police blockade at the head of a line of marchers, has refused bail.

Commonwealth ministers meet

LONDON (CP) — Commonwealth finance ministers meeting here Sept. 25-26 are expected to discuss world economic trends and the international monetary situation, with special reference to their own countries.

The office of Canadian-born Arnold Smith, Commonwealth secretary-general, said Thursday the ministers will receive from him a report on aid matters. Governors of central banks are also expected to attend the meeting.

Presented to

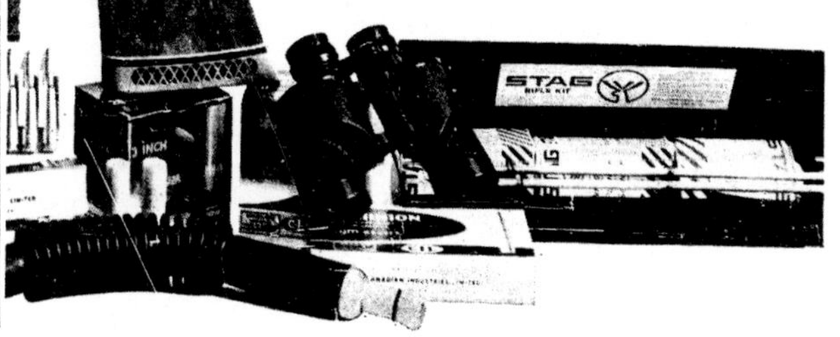
STAG

Women & The Pill

"Mr. Henry Latulippe (Creditiste Compton): 'A pregnant person is perhaps not in a position, on account of her condition to judge matters adequately by herself.' "

— Report on abortion debate, May 7, 1969

At the dawn of the 1960s, Canada remained a fairly repressive nation in terms of women's rights. This changed by the end of the decade.

One of the main engines of that shift appeared in the United States at the start of the decade in the form of a little white pill called Enovid.

The Pill, was a form of emancipation for American women. The inexpensive, effective birth control method gave them more command over their reproductive cycles and their lives. But it was illegal in Canada.

In fact, everything about contraception was illegal. People who so much as distributed information about it faced a Criminal Code offence and a two-year prison term. People did, however, find a way around the law.

Doctors prescribed Enovid to "regulate menstrual cycles" of their patients. Under this "wink-and-a-nudge" system, Canadians were buying 50 million contraceptive devices of one sort or another a year by 1963.

On May 25, 1963, *The Journal* published an editorial backing a private member's bill that would remove contraceptive sales from the Criminal Code. "It is time, as Mr. Robert Prittie's bill (NDP MP, Vancouver) has told Parliament, for public discussion of birth control laws in Canada.

"Whether to have children would be a personal matter between husband and wife and, perhaps, between them and their church. The only difference would be that freedom of choice would be entirely lawful."

Likely, this liberal attitude placed the paper at odds with many of its conservative readers.

Prittie's bill failed. Prime Minister Lester Pearson's minority government couldn't sway Quebec's Creditiste MPs who were dead set against it, but *The Journal* was undetered, and on Nov. 24, 1965, stated: "Canada's present birth control laws, in their palpable fossilization, do a grave disservice to the poor.

"As the law stands, the department cannot provide these families with the information or birth-control devices they need to keep their families within manageable proportions."

Pierre Trudeau became prime minister April 20, 1968, and that June he won a majority government and a free hand to act. As justice minister in 1967, he said "the government has no place in the bedrooms of the nation," and in 1969 the Liberals began reforming the Criminal Code. Abortion and birth control were made legal by the end of that year.

And on Sept. 21, 1970, the newspaper embraced the new liberalism of the new decade. "With family planning, Canada's over-all high infant mortality rate of 20.8 deaths for every 1,000 live births in 1968 – will hopefully be corrected."

In 1997, the infant mortality rate in Canada was 5.2 deaths for every 1,000 live births. In Alberta, it was 4.8.

***In 1965*:**
An *Journal* ad salesman makes $105 a week, while a front counter clerk earns $40 a week.

Feb. 4, 1965:
***The Journal* reports tuition fees at the U of A: Arts, Music, Education and Phys Ed: $300; Science, Law and Nursing: $350; Engineering: $400; Dentistry: $500.**

***Feb. 10, 1965*:**
"Kidnapping comely co-eds is legal at the University of Alberta this week...Provided, of course, it has been cleared by the dean of women...It's part of the battle of pranks between engineers and students from other faculties marking Engineers Week on the campus... So far, the engineering students have won in the early skirmishes....'

***In 1966*:**
***The Journal* pays its cashier/clerk typists $40 a week.**

***Feb. 4, 1966*:**
Irving Guttman becomes the artistic director of the Edmonton Professional Opera Association.

***Feb. 10, 1966*:**
"... Alberta should be ashamed of what it pays to the man who may well be the best provincial premier in Canada...But there should be no

The Journal of Leisure

It's exciting, perceptive, frank and loud; it's today's music

IT'S ROCK

THE WHO'S FLAMBOYANT DRUMMER
... demonstrates theatrics are as important as volume in rock

MEMBERS OF LED ZEPPELIN MAY HAVE LONG HAIR
... but they play emphatically masculine-aggressive rock

By BOB HARVEY

Are you one of those who remember Deep Purple only as a song Bing Crosby sang in the 1940s?

Or do you think Canned Heat is just another name for the canned fuel you use in campstoves?

And so what if you think Led Zeppelin is a metal blimp or that Grapefruit is something you eat for breakfast?

Who cares that these unpretentious words are just weird names for freaky-looking groups who play rock music? You're not missing anything. Rock is too loud and not fit for any but juvenile ears.

Considering the drugs, sex and violence that creep into the songs, perhaps it's not fit even for the kids.

10 million fans

The big beat and electronics disguise the musicians' poor playing and lack of training. And the fans — they don't know clarinet from an alto saxophone.

That's what I used to think three years ago.

Rock's practically the only music anyone under 25 listens to, and half the population is currently under 25. Servicing their demands for music is a billion-dollar industry.

Rock accounts for about half of the album and 80 per cent of the single record sales. In Alberta alone, distributors made $2,329,817 on records and $1,258,645 on tapes in the first eight months of this year.

Then there's the profits record stores make when they re-sell the tapes and records at a 30-40 per cent markup. And the sales of musical instruments, music lessons, and the money paid out to the hundreds of local amateurs and professionals who play at dances.

Nobody knows exactly how big a business rock is in Edmonton. But on rock records alone, city stores will make about $500,000 this year.

Good rock concerts in the city currently draw about 3,500 people, who together pay $10,000 or more to see a show.

The economics behind the scenes at such concerts are also surprising. Two weeks ago, The Collectors, with the help of another Vancouver group, Django, attracted the biggest crowd ever to attend an all-Canadian rock concert anywhere in the country. The 3,500 people who jammed the Edmonton Gardens had the benefit of a sound system worth at least $50,000.

On stage, The Collectors played with at least $10,000 worth of equipment.

Clearly rock is a powerful factor in our economy.

The hip capitalists who run the rock business across the country may have long hair, and may never wear suits, but they've paid their dues to society by making money.

Many of the musicians proved years ago their right to make a living with their instruments. The four Collectors range in age from 25 to 29, two have degrees in music, and all have been playing professionally for several years.

Other top groups, like Britain's Deep Purple and Procul Harum were trained in music academies and use their knowledge to weave classical themes and melodies into rock structures.

Alejandro Planchard, an arranger for Elvis Presley, is a professor of music theory at Yale University and specializes in baroque string quartets and Renaissance music when he's not working on a rock album.

Rock has not only borrowed from classical music, it's also enriching it. Leonard Bernstein, who recently resigned as conductor of the New York Philharmonic, often sits in at rock concerts and is currently writing a serious work with contemporary overtones.

In Vancouver, in New York and London, symphony orchestras have invited groups like The Collectors, Guess Who and Procul Harum to compose pieces and play with the orchestras.

Jazz has also enriched and been enriched by rock. Many rock groups are moving closer to jazz in their techniques and improvisations and many top jazz musicians back up rock groups in the studio.

Rock musicians are dedicated as well as trained. It's the rock musicians, not the painters, who are starving in garrets today.

Gaye Delorme, lead guitarist with Django, started out playing flamenco guitar and was good enough to accompany master Carlos Montoya on tours. Delorme played briefly with a Toronto rock group but then came back to Edmonton and gave up playing professionally until he found the right people to form a rock group.

Django now plays in a small Vancouver club for just enough money to keep them eating. Three of the group's five members gave up lucrative jobs to work together.

Poor music doomed

As in any profession, there are rock musicians, some with top groups, who don't care about their work or aren't really very good at it. Generally, they don't last very long.

The generation listening to rock is too perceptive to tolerate poor musicianship.

They've grown up with transistor radios growing out of their ears and because of the way rock has reached out to include music of all types and from all times and places, they're as interested in Ravi Shankar's sitar music as they are in the music of the big band era.

Bob Smith, a middle-aged music critic for the Vancouver Sun, recently wrote about the quizzes he uses to test the musical ears of the school students.

"How many of you adults ... can detect the differences in tonal sound between alto, tenor and baritone saxophones? Or (between) ... a coronet, trumpet, trombone or fluegelhorn from the brass section? And to really test your ears, the differing yet similar roles of the string bass versus its fender cousin.

"Well, the young people I have been meeting get a very high rating on these simple tests and for me as an older listener it is amazing.

"Because only recently have some of the reed and brass instruments been employed in today's major groups, hence heard on the younger generation's radio stations or bought for their personal record collections."

Drugs, as in Steppenwolf's song The Pusher, often come into rock lyrics. So do sex in the Rolling Stones' hit Let's Spend the Night Together; violence in the Beatles' tune Maxwell's Silver Hammer, a tale of a homicidal youngster who bashes in heads with his hammer.

But not all the tunes push sex, drugs and violence. Anyway, they're a part of reality and subjects of great concern to today's young people.

It's increasingly impossible to live in a saccharine world and rock lyrics are an improvement, both in subject and quality, over those of the "moon, June, spoon" variety.

Part of the attraction of rock admittedly is in its rebelliousness. The "straight" older generation freezes at the sight of long hair, at the mention of drugs, and is so deafened by the volume of amplified rock that it doesn't really listen to the music or lyrics.

Rock is like any other music; you have to approach it with an open mind and listen to it until you can get over any dislikes you may have for the way it is being played or the instruments being used. Only then can you appreciate the music for itself.

Young people write rock for other young people, and it reflects their thoughts, feelings, problems and responses to life, but the music is strong and vital enough to have something to say to anyone who cares to listen, whether he's over 30 or under 15.

Rock is the only music that really reflects the chaotic pressured life we lead.

What finally turned me on to rock was the number of hours I spent listening to local groups while I was preparing an article on the half-million dollars earned by city rock groups every year.

Surprising originality

The emotion and originality they put into their music surprised me. In the last year I've listened to literally hundreds of rock albums and attended at least 20 rock concerts. I've learned a lot.

Much of today's rock isn't really written or performed for 13- or 14-year-olds, and audiences at concerts reflect that fact: they're getting older every year.

When The Collectors played here for the first time a year ago, they left their agonizing What Love suite to the end of the concert. After listening to the suite for more than 20 minutes, the audience was wrung dry of emotion. The music died out, the audience sat stunned and absolutely silent for long seconds, then rose crying and clapping in one spontaneous wave.

For this kind of experience it's worth going to 50 concerts that are merely ordinary, just so that you won't miss the occasional supreme experience.

Rock is serious music, and it has important things to say. Young people today may not be more creative than young people of previous generations, but because of rock they're unafraid to create, and more of them than ever before are writing music or poetry, or making films.

Although this city's apparently one of the most creative in Canada, we don't recognize it yet. Rock musicians from Edmonton are to be found everywhere in the country.

Hans Stamer says his group, Django, left Edmonton to live in Vancouver because it is impossible to work in Edmonton.

"Promoters, managers, booking agents are just killing anything that comes out of here.

"If you come up with anything honest, it's smothered by a money trip."

The Edmonton Symphony Orchestra has shown some progress in its way. Arthur Fiedler of the Boston Pops has conducted the orchestra in rousing Beatles tunes and the orchestra will present a jazz concert with Tommy Banks Dec. 9. It should shuck any fears it might have and invite a rock group to perform with it.

As Bob Dylan wrote in 1962: "You know that something's happening, but you don't know what it is, do you, Mr. Jones?"

PRIVILEGE, ONE OF THE TOP LOCAL ROCK GROUPS
... earned about $100,000 a year at dances, concerts

CREAM HAS OVER 30 YEARS EXPERIENCE
... between three members of 1968's top group

The Citadel

"At the end, when this cast of four was taking deserved acclaim, one knew, heavily, that this had been an extraordinarily fine theatre experience."

— Drama critic Barry Westgate following *Who's Afraid of Virginia Woolf?*, the Citadel Theatre's first-ever play on Nov. 11, 1965

There was certainly no indication in that first season in 1965 that the Citadel would become a major force in Canadian theatre.

But Joe Shoctor, the lawyer/impresario/producer/football fan, was confident enough to buy the rundown former Salvation Army mission on 102nd Street, south of Jasper Avenue, and convince a handful of partners to contribute to its quarter-million dollar renovation.

By early October, the theatre, with its 286 seats, was still in chaos. The final program was still up in the air, the actors hadn't been hired, the seats weren't in, the carpet wasn't down and the stage wasn't finished.

Shoctor and John Hulburt, the Citadel's first artistic director, had just a little over a month to convince Edmonton that it was ready for professional theatre.

They did. Their first play, a searing production of Edward Albee's *Who's Afraid of Virginia Woolf?* put nearly all doubts to rest.

Barry Westgate wrote that the Albee play had, "lacerated the nerves of audiences everywhere. To attempt it needs a combination of brute courage and child-like faith. I hope people honour that faith. Because here is a work that deserves it."

Subsequent productions in that first year would not go quite as smoothly. *Under the Yum Yum Tree* had a "little naughtiness but too few laughs," *The Journal* reported. The next play, *Bell, Book and Candle* by John van Druten, was worse.

The play limped on, playing to houses where the attendance was at less than 50 per cent.

Hulburt, a man with significant experience in regional theatre throughout the West and midwestern America, was fired in January, six months after he arrived.

From the beginning, his replacement, Robert Glenn, seemed to hit the right notes. His first play, Sumner Arthur Long's *Never Too Late*, was "delightful," Westgate said, and showed a masterful touch at comic theatre.

"Robert Glenn is coming up aces at The Citadel where his first project, the hilarious comedy Never Too Late, has drawn the best attendance to date to the fledgling professional theatre."

"And here an even happier message to take away … New Yorker Glenn, whose last play here was to be Arthur Miller's Death of a Salesman opening next Wednesday, will stay on to do the comedy Come Blow Your Horn in April."

Before he left two years later, Glenn was responsible for some daring productions such as Albee's *Tiny Alice*, which raised the ire of a clutch of Edmonton churchmen who were offered free passes to the play.

delay in raising Mr. Manning's pay to at least $30,000 a year. The raise is long overdue."
– editorial

***March 28, 1966*:**
"Edmonton Symphony Orchestra conductor Brian Priestman today called Edmonton a big city with a small town atmosphere. Edmonton audiences are snob audiences," he said. "They are not prepared to accept local talent."

***April 11, 1966*:**
"Earl Mountbatten of Burma is astounded with the size of Edmonton, which he had believed was a frontier city…I'm absolutely staggered…I always had a picture of it as a sort of frontier city, with perhaps a few thousand people and buildings perhaps four storeys high."

***June 1966*:**
"Gone are the days when Edmonton was known by irreverent visitors as a sneakers-and-sweatshirt town…The city has been growing and remaking itself in recent years, and in appearance, it's turning into a veritable Baghdad-on-the-North Saskatchewan."
– Southam News Service Chief Charles Lynch.

The Edmonton Journal

FORECAST: COOL | EDMONTON, ALBERTA, MONDAY, MAY 13, 1968 | TEN CENTS

Peace Role For Canada?

Trudeau, Thant Discuss Possibility Of UN Police Force In Vietnam

Canada may play a role in re-establishing peace in Vietnam, Prime Minister Trudeau said today.

He and United Nations Secretary General U Thant met this morning to discuss ways in which Canada could take part in Vietnam peacekeeping operations.

The prime minister said at a press conference later that while Canada is not making any specific overall agreement now, "the Canadian government will do all it can to play a role in re-establishing peace in that area."

However, Mr. Trudeau suggested that Canada may have to become "a bit more realistic and not automatically get involved in every conflict."

His discussions with Mr. Thant were inconclusive because it is not known now whether the United Nations will be asked to police a peace agreement and if so, what type of force would be sent.

Mr. Trudeau said Canada has no reservations about the idea of peacekeeping, but it has about the peacekeeping operations proper.

He made a renewed plea for an immediate and complete halt of U.S. bombing of North Vietnam.

"That is a precondition to fruitful peace talks," he said. "I don't think the talks will get very far until the bombing stops."

Prime Minister Trudeau also said Canada is considering bilateral discussions with Red China which may lead to diplomatic recognition.

But, he said, it would not be "useful at this stage to line up a series of conditions and see if Peking would recognize them."

"We would be concerned with such things as the freedom our diplomats would have, what freedom of the press would exist, what trade and tourism would be acceptable to both parties.

"These must be negotiated bilaterally."

On Vietnam, the prime minister said the situation must reach a stage where South Vietnam is not relying so heavily on U.S. military might, "but it would be a mistake to ask the U.S. to pull out without sending in some international force to make sure there would be no invasion of South Vietnam.

"What kind of international force it might be, I can't say particularly."

He said U.S. bombing of North Vietnam must halt because "you can't psychologically bomb a people to the negotiating table."

The prime minister, in reply to a question, said he was aware of Canada's native population, "but I supposed like so many Canadians I'm not aware enough."

He visited Yellowknife and Whitehorse before coming to Edmonton to discuss with officials the problems of Canada's native people. He said he is coming to the conclusion that the native people outside reservations should not be dealt with under one specific act, but should be treated "fully as Canadians."

"But I have no solution to the problems of reservations."

Asked about the Canadian Liberal Multicultural Council, Mr. Trudeau said it was "only briefly mentioned" to him Sunday, and added he's not "quite sure what the council is."

Former mayor William Hawrelak is the chairman of the council, an organization set up three weeks ago to advise the Liberal party executive about views of multicultural groups.

The prime minister said he doesn't know who belongs to the council nor who set it up; so he could not comment further. However, he favored multicultural organizations.

Asked about private meetings with provincial Liberal officials Sunday, Mr. Trudeau said he attended only as a matter of courtesy but that no specific election campaign plans for Alberta were laid.

He added his visit to Edmonton is non-political and that is why no public meeting has been scheduled.

Trudeau promises increased autonomy for the Northwest Territories but shatters Yukon Territory's hopes of having the Alaska Highway paved in the near future. Stories on Page 17.

PRIME MINISTER TRUDEAU AND UN SECRETARY-GENERAL U THANT
. . . together for a brief meeting in Edmonton

Hanoi, U.S. Promise To Scale Down War

PARIS (AP) — The United States and North Vietnam challenged each other today to take new steps to scale down the war in Southeast Asia.

Both pledged serious efforts to find some basis for a peaceful settlement.

Ambassador Xuan Thuy (pronounced Swan Twee) of North Vietnam, who spoke first at the opening round of substantive talks, called on the United States to end the rest of the bombing and "all other acts of war" against his country, but did so in words softer than expected.

He made no threat of breaking off the talks if the demand is not quickly granted.

President Johnson's spokesman, Ambassador W. Averell Harriman, asked for some sign of military restraint by North Vietnam that would meet the president's request for a de-escalation response to his March 31 ban of part of the bombing.

What actually has happened, Harriman charged, is that North Vietnam has moved substantial and increasing numbers of troops and supplies from the North to the South."

Thuy made the opening statement, a U.S. spokesman said, after Harriman suggested that he lead off. It was Harriman's second initiative in courtesy.

SHAKE HANDS

When the two delegations assembled in the International Conference Centre, Thuy and his group entered the glittering, grey and gold rand salon a few seconds ahead of Harriman.

When the American diplomatic troubleshooter caught sight of the slight, smiling Vietnamese Communist official he quickly turned, walked to him with extended hand and said "Mr. Thuy." Thuy smiled and they shook hands.

That was how the talks began after years of violence and long, frustrating months of efforts to bring the two governments into direct ambassadorial discussions. After three hours 15 minutes, they adjourned to meet again Wednesday.

U.S. officials expected a blast from Thuy and they were not surprised when they got it. He accused the United States of aggression in South Vietnam and said the more it was defeated the more cruelly it responded—increasing attacks and sending in troops. But when he put the often-stated demand that all attacks on North Vietnam must stop before any other subjects can be discussed, he avoided threats and warnings and said his government is "hoping that the problem . . . will be resolved."

EXPRESSES GOOD WILL

At the same time, he said he and his delegation had "come here with an attitude which is serious and full of good will."

U.S. officials said they found the start, on the whole, serious and businesslike.

Harriman opened his statement by saying the United States rejected many points Thuy had made but that the U.S. statement today would not be a reply but "an affirmative statement."

He proposed that restoration of the demilitarized zone between North and South Vietnam as a buffer free of military forces be made "an important test of faith on each side."

He accused the North Vietnamese of "aggression" and of taking an increasing military role in South Vietnam alongside the Viet Cong guerrillas. He called the introduction of regular North Vietnamese army units "a blatant violation of the Geneva accords."

Harriman called for Hanoi to

More PEACE TALKS Page 2

Giggling Youngsters Mob PM

If giggles, squeals and screams can be translated into votes Pierre Trudeau is a shoo-in here in Edmonton.

Almost 3,000 persons pressed around city hall Sunday afternoon when the new prime minister made his first visit to the city and became the first prime minister ever to sign the city's guest book.

Young people made up most of the audience and accounted for most of the vocal enthusiasm, but there were many adults in the crowd.

He signed dozens of autographs and kissed at least one young lady. She was 18-year-old Pat Manning and she thought it was great.

Liberal candidates and officials thought the whole thing was great too.

Mr. Trudeau spoke at the Chateau Lacombe with party people and granted private interviews to a few, including Mike Maccagno and H. A. (Bud) Olson.

Mr. Maccagno, provincial leader who is running federally in Athabasca said his twenty minutes with the prime minister were ones he won't forget.

NORTHERN ALBERTA

He said that Mr. Trudeau expressed tremendous interest in northern Alberta and agreed that he (Mr. Maccagno) could well act as a go-between in feredal-provincial matters.

The prime minister arrived at the International Airport about an hour after U Thant, secretary general of the United Nations. Both were to receive honorary degrees at the University of Alberta today.

After a brief speech at the airport he was hustled to city hall where the official welcoming took place.

Mayor Vince Dantzer presented him with a Klondike hat and cane and escorted him up stairs to sign the guest book.

After signing, he tilted his hat, twirled the cane, asked: "Does it look all right for the kids?" and walked down into the mass of people waiting for a glimpse of Pierre Elliott Trudeau.

"SIGN THIS"

The car carrying the prime minister could just inch its way through the crowd.

Everywhere he went, Mr. Trudeau had bits of paper shoved under his nose and a young voice cried "sign this please."

He signed . . . and signed

More TRUDEAU on Page 2

Where To Find It

The Journal's battle for press freedom during the hectic thirties is recounted in Charles Bruce's book on the Southam publishing family. It begins on Page 10.

Ann Landers 20
Births, Deaths, Marriages 28
Bridge 30
Business, Stocks 12-15
Classified Ads 29-42
Comics, Features 25
Comment 4
Crossword Puzzle 33
Horoscope 31
Journal for the Family 15-21
Letters To The Journal 4, 43
News Digest 5
Patterns 32
Sport .... 6 - 9
Theatres, Entertainment 23
TV, Radio 22

Total Pages 44

Weather

Continuing cloudy tonight and Tuesday with few sunny periods. Cool; winds light. Low tonight 32, high Tuesday 50. Details on Page 2.

TRUDEAU MOBBED DURING BRIEF CITY HALL VISIT
. . . teenie-boppers press forward for sought-after autograph

Manning Hands Over A-G Post To Gerhart

Edgar Gerhart, 44, today became Alberta's attorney-general.

Mr. Gerhart took over the portfolio held for 13 years by Premier Manning.

Mr. Gerhart will continue as minister of municipal affairs although the premier said after the swearing-in ceremonies that there would be another change soon and that the minister would hold both jobs only temporarily.

The new attorney-general said there were a number of things he wanted to do in the new job but would not elaborate.

Mr. Gerhart, Social Credit member for Edmonton Northwest, was first elected to the Alberta legislature in 1952.

A lawyer, one of only two on the government side of the House, he was named to the cabinet just last June, taking over municipal affairs from A. J. Hooke. Mr. Hooke is now minister of public welfare.

The other Social Credit lawyer member of the legislature is Albert Ludwig of Calgary.

The new attorney-general also has a degree in pharmacy. Both his pharmacy and law degrees were obtained at the University of Alberta.

Ray Speaker, minister without portfolio, may be the next cabinet minister elevated. He could become minister of agriculture with the present agriculture minister Harry Strom miving into municipal affairs.

Both Mr. Speaker and Mr. Strom attended the brief swearing-in ceremony this morning. The ceremony was conducted by Lt.-Gov. Grant MacEwan.

Premier Manning said this morning he had contemplated for some time giving up the attorney-general's portfolio. He said he did not make the move earlier because of the heavy workload carried by Mr. Gerhart, both before and during the session of the legislature.

Both the Liberal and Conservative opposition have been urging the premier to relinquish the job and turn it over to a lawyer.

John Hart is the deputy attorney-general. Both the premier and Mr. Gerhart met Mr. Hart this morning.

Mr. Gerhart is married with five children.

Conservative MLA Lou Hyndman, the opposition critic of the attorney-general's department, said the only disappointment connected with Mr. Gerhart's appointment is that the new attorney-general is "being forced" to retain the municipal affairs portfolio.

"A full-time attorney general is the goal the premier should set for this province," he said.

Mr. Hyndman said Mr. Gerhart's appointment means the minister will be able "to start to deal effectively with some of the problems and policies in the administration of justice."

He suggested the new attorney-general must consider modernization of Alberta's prison system, a new emphasis on combatting juvenile crime and a revision of court procedures so the average man will have easier access to and a quicker hearing by the courts.

Mr. Hyndman also said Mr. Gerhart should review the law which prohibits Sunday movies in Alberta.

A charcoal sketch of Premier Manning is the first in a series of portraits to be done by Canadian artist George Lonn. The series, to be included in Lonn's book, Canadian Profiles, Volume III, starts today on Page 26.

He also lured some of the most distinguished names in theatre to Edmonton, including Canadians Kate Reid and Peter Donat, and Donat's wife, Michael Learned, who went on to fame as Olivia Walton in the hit '70s television show *The Waltons.*

His successor, Sean Mulcahy, a Toronto director and actor, brought a certain buoyant self-assurance to the place, and would ultimately fulfil his own stated ambition when he first arrived in town.

He promised to make the theatre a national force.

Mulcahy's arrival marked the beginning of a three-year joust between the director and the newspaper.

His first three productions – *The Odd Couple, Philadelphia, Here I Come* and the musical *Irma La Douce* – translated into 80-per-cent houses, despite some wicked January weather in 1968, Mulcahy's first year running the theatre.

"When I came here I promised not an empty seat by the second season," Mulcahy told the paper. "And now I want the theatre completely sold out before that season opens. All I need is 2,000 more subscribers. The way things are going, I'll get them. And they'll be glad."

It worked. By 1969, the combination of Shoctor and Mulcahy meant 5,500 season ticket holders, despite occasional carping from the paper that the theatre was offering fare that was too lightweight.

The chain-smoking Mulcahy would have none of it. He defended his choices when he took up an entire front-page of *The Journal's* entertainment section. It was a funny, feisty piece of writing where Mulcahy pitted "20 years of hard-won experience against Mr. Westgate's extraordinary critical perception any day."

Mulcahy and Shoctor also had a sometimes-feisty relationship, and in 1972, five years after arriving in Edmonton, Mulcahy left the theatre. It was not the most graceful of exits.

"The theatre's progression doesn't coincide with where I would like to see it go," the outspoken 42-year-old told *The Journal* when he announced that he was quitting.

"I don't think the theatre's growth is being handled in the right way by the administration."

Three weeks later, Shoctor and the board of directors issued their own statement. Mulcahy hadn't quit they said, he'd been canned.

"I consider myself a personal friend of Mr. Mulcahy," Shoctor told *The Journal.* "We've come a long way together in theatre. I hope the personal relationship will continue, and that he will be able to help the theatre in some capacity in the future."

He never did.

Mulcahy's final official comment was terse: "They didn't like the things I said about the theatre … that's their prerogative. They run the place."

And he was gone, leaving behind a city that he and Shoctor had turned into the best theatre town in the country.

***Nov. 4, 1966*:**
The 25-storey CN Tower and Terminal officially opened in downtown Edmonton.

***Dec. 20, 1966*:**
"The only major development needed to complete Edmonton's civic centre is the downtown coliseum," Mayor Vincent Dantzer said Monday. "And the coliseum is not as far away as some people think."
– story on the announcement of the AGT tower project, the 30-storey tower was the tallest west of Toronto at the time.

***Dec. 30, 1966*:**
"I came back from a Christmas trip to the coast convinced that what we get on our two channels are the best programs television has to offer…"
– item in a column by Dave Laundy, *The Journal's* television critic, in which he predicted that cable television would destroy Canadian networks.

***Jan. 19, 1967*:**
Edmonton's population is listed as 381,230, a *Journal* proofreader makes $135 a week and Edmonton gets the first touch-tone phone in Western Canada.

Ever-Lovin' Oil Kings Bag Memorial Cup

Hal PAWSON
Sports Editor

What's A Minute, A Measly Minute?

What's a minute, any minute, in this too-busy, too-sombre vale of tears?

Particularly a minute with the audacity to crash its way out of a sports event and try to intrude on history by capturing the minds of men?

Such a minute is nothing—nothing, unless you were an Edmonton Oil King or a Niagara Falls Flyer, or one of about 6,800 fans for whom time was almost stopped by excitement Saturday night at the Gardens.

A mere minute, it is already lost in the immensity of the trillions of minutes ahead of it and the trillions to follow in the greater scheme of things.

But it may be etched forever in some of the memories of persons who experienced this raucous, searing sixty seconds, ripped raw from its sports setting to inflame its witnesses and knarl their every nerve end.

It was the final minute of the 1963 Memorial Cup championships.

It was the minute that made Oil Kings the first of seven Edmonton teams to realize junior hockey's greatest dream.

It was the minute that robbed Niagara Falls Flyers of one of the greatest comeback stories Canadian sport has known.

Yet it still was the minute that branded them as the most valiant of runners-up for this elusive junior hockey honor.

It was the minute which proved that, no matter what men such as Hap Emms might try to do in misguided selfishness to tarnish it, that the Memorial Cup still remains one of the shiniest jewels in this nation's sports crown—a championship too great to be spoiled.

It was a minute of which all Edmonton, and all Alberta can be forever proud, a minute that most of western Canada's hockey faithful will cherish for years to come.

It was the epitome of everything that is wonderful about true sport and sportsmanship.

Sixty Suspended Seconds

How was that frantic, awesome fraction of time spent by some of the men—a junior final it may have been but these players were men—to whom it mattered most.

Russ Kirk, Oil King goalie who played his finest game: "It wouldn't end. Every second was a year. I thought I was going to die, and I think I played on instinct. I don't remember much of the stops, or shots. Suddenly the puck was in the corner and people started jumping over the boards and I knew we had won."

Don Awrey, Niagara Falls defenceman-forward who was one-two the series star with anyone: "I thought we had enough time to do it. I was sure we could tie it—and then there was no more time, and the world seemed to end for a couple of minutes."

Terry Crisp, Flyer captain and spark: "I hit the post. I can't believe it, to be that close."

Ron Hergott, Flyers' assistant captain: "It wasn't your fault, Terry. I hit the post at the end, too.

Roger Bourbonnais, *Oil King captain and leader: "It was about the most frightening minute I've ever known. I kept saying don't let them tie it, and then it ended and it was a happy minute. But it was a sad one, too, for me — for it ended junior hockey, the time of my life, for me."*

Buster Brayshaw, Oil King coach: "I stood there trying to think what I could do to help. A hundred things went through my mind. Had I told them not to ice the puck if possible, unless they could score? Did I have the best, coolest checkers on the ice. Was there anything I had forgotten to teach them about such a minute?

"And I couldn't help feeling sorry for the Flyers when it ended, they were that great when they had to be."

Leo LeClerc, Oil King manager who has wooed such a Saturday night with every talent he could bring to bear for years: "I was in the dressing room. I can't watch such times. Somebody yelled for me that it was 'Four-Two,' and I ran out in time to see it go 'Four-Three.'

"I jumped into the players' box and began yelling, 'Fight, fight, guys, fight,' and I almost got carried out onto the ice by a line change, and the bell went and it was the most glorious minute I've known in hockey."

There were 6,800 such final minutes, all as poignant, all as gripping.

ROGER BOURBONNAIS
. . . the king of Kings

The Journal Of SPORTS

THE SWEET WINE OF VICTORY
. . . Glen Sather and Max Mestinsek lap it up

Plucky Niagara Comeback Held Off By Brayshaw's Boys

By **DWAYNE ERICKSON**
Journal Sports Writer

Champions are the Edmonton Oil Kings.

They reached and they wrapped their sweaty arms around the Memorial Cup Saturday night.

It was the climax to a sometimes wonderful, sometimes tearful and always thrilling struggle that began in the spring of 1959.

Hours, days, weeks, and years of sweat, blood, honest labor, and yes, even luck, all finally seemed worthwhile on this night of jubilation.

It was precisely 10:51 p.m., May 11, 1963 when the final buzzer sounded to make it official.

The scoreboard read:

Edmonton 4, Niagara Falls 3.

The Oil Kings of coach Buster Brayshaw had won the Memorial Cup in six games. They came off the floor as only this club has done so many times before.

When the opening gun was fired the night of May 2, a seemingly all-too-powerful band of Flyers from Niagara Falls laced these same Oil Kings by a lop-sided 8-0 score.

But the Kingly crew came back with 7-3, 5-2, and 3-2 victories, lost the fifth game 5-2, then capped the series with a stirring effort Saturday night.

The gritty Flyers bowed out as champions only can, coming off a 4-0 deficit in the third period to force the issue to the last dying second.

It was a valiant comeback and made those who knew these young men from the east wish that maybe there should be two Memorial Cups . . . two winners . . . and never a loser.

Etched Hectic Climax

Saturday night the men who run the game gave the series back to the players. And the players made it the spectacle the Memorial Cup has come to be known.

For two hours and 30 minutes the players entertained 6,800 Gardens faithful as they have never been entertained before.

And then, in one minute, the last minute, they etched a climax that could never be recreated in words.

Maybe the fact that six Edmonton clubs before them had tried and six Edmonton clubs before them had failed made this Oil King chapter the most stirring of them all.

Never before had Edmonton put its stamp on the Memorial Cup. This night marked the first time since 1926 — Calgary Canadians defeated Kingston — that the time-worn trophy had found a resting place in Alberta.

And it was the first time since 1930 when Regina Pats won it all, that the coveted mug had come west of the Manitoba border.

This was Edmonton's fourth consecutive crack at the Memorial Cup, long regarded as hockey's "Grail" for Canadian boys.

Oil Kings took a 1-0 lead in the first period. And they scored twice in the second period to make it 3-0. Another, early in the third, made it 4-0 to set the stage for Niagara's desperate and almost successful bid.

Penalty Started Rally

A penalty, the game's only penalty, to Max Mastinsek for interference at 9:01, launched the rally.

In seven seconds Bill Glashan put Flyers on the board. Three minutes and one second later Ron Schock shaved the deficit to two goals.

Then, at 18:21, Terry Crisp, the "guts" of the eastern champions, poked the puck through Russ Kirk's pads at the corner of the net to make it 4-3.

With a minute remaining, the same Terry Crisp slid a screened 30-footer by the open corner.

A face-off resulted seconds later and Niagara goaltender George Gardner left his cage in favor of a sixth attacker.

Roger Bourbonnais slid the puck back to defenceman Butch Barber. He let a rink-long drive go.

It skidded down the ice and it blew past the open net by scant inches.

Another face-off.

The puck dribbled into the corner, two players fought for it. Then the puck sprung free and Glashan dropped it back to defenceman Ron Hergott.

He, the man with the shot that terriorized the Ontario Hockey Association through the winter, drilled a hard one along the ice.

The puck caught a piece of Barber, deflected to the right, and grazed the goal post.

Harmlessly it skidded into the corner as the crowd's roar became deafening.

In a fleeting moment, the crowd, players, officials photographers and all were spilling onto the ice.

An inspired Doug Fox started the victory march with the first period's only goal. Glen Sather and Butch Paul found the mark in the second.

Gregg Pilling picked off what proved to be the winner, snapping up a free puck from Harold Fleming's drop pass. The big fella moved in two strides and drilled a back-hander in the short side.

The young Kirk deserved a large hand and he got it as the players hoisted him onto their shoulders. He saved his best for the last in stopping 29 well-placed shots.

Gardner turned aside 32 Oil King thrusts but had to take a back seat to his adversary on this night.

Victory Parade Tuesday

The Edmonton Oil Kings, first Canadian junior hockey champions in Edmonton's history, will be publicly feted with a parade Tuesday.

The Oil Kings won the Memorial Cup at the Gardens Saturday night by withstanding a tremendous last-minute drive and defeating the Niagara Falls Flyers 4-3.

The downtown parade will honor the Oil Kings. Starting at 4 p.m. Tuesday, the parade will form at City Hall, move south on 100 St., to Jasper Ave., then west to 109 St., and south to the Legislative Buildings.

The young team's sponsors, the Edmonton Exhibition Association, will honor the team with a victory dinner Wednesday night at the Macdonald Hotel.

An Alberta Government-City luncheon for the Kings Tuesday at noon also was announced. The Calgary Canadiens won Alberta's only other Memorial Cup, in 1926.

Meanwhile tributes in the form of gifts, such as were made for the Allan Cup hockey Flyers in 1949 and the football Eskimos in their Grey Cup years of 1954, 1955 and 1956, were being offered the Oil Kings by various organizations. Watches, slacks, coats were included in the congratulatory offers for Canada's junior hockey monarchs.

Edmonton Booters Score Victory, Tie

Edmonton Shamrock Rovers tied Calgary Royals 2-2 while Edmonton Scottish edged Calgary Callies 1-0 in Alberta Soccer League action over the weekend.

John McGrandle, Scottish outside left whipped in a blistering cross shot at 40-minutes to give Edmonton their victory in the first games of the inter-city 10-team league in play Saturday night at Calgary. A goal by Chris Bakaard at the 12th minute of the second half gave Royals their tie with Rovers before 850 fans yesterday afternoon at Clarke Stadium.

Pat Nolan scored the first Edmonton goal at the 10-minute mark from close range after a clever pass from Chris Braiden. Seven minutes later Nolan scored his second goal with a well directed shot from a brilliant combined movement in which all Rover forwards took part.

* * *

Just three minutes before the 45-minute first half was completed, Rinus Cramer, put the visitors on the scoreboard with a sizzling shot from 36-yards out that crept under the top crossbar, just over the outstretched fingertips of goalie Brian Bundred.

Despite gallant defensive work by Pat Kennedy and Braiden, Bakaard triggered Calgary's second goal into the twine after a great solo effort.

Next action in the league goes tonight at Clarke Stadium when First D.F.C. take on Italia Canadians at 8 p.m., this is a rescheduled game which was put off from last week. Tuesday night's action will see Victoria meet Scottish at 8 o'clock at the Stadium turf.

MEMORIAL CUP SCORING

Niagara Falls 3, Edmonton 4

First period: 1. Edmonton, Fox (Bourbonnais, Falkenburg) 11:42. Penalties: None.

Second period: 2. Edmonton, Sather (Mestinsek, Paul) 7:55; 3. Edmonton, Paul (Sather, Mestinsek) 17:01. Penalties: None.

Third period: 4. Edmonton, Pilling (Fleming, Rochefort) 4:11; 5. Niagara Falls, Glashan (Hergott, Schock) 9:08; 6. Niagara Falls, Schock (Maxner, Crisp) 12:09; 7. Niagara Falls, Crisp (Maxner) 18:21. Penalty: Mestinsek 9:01.

Stops				
Gardner	11	12	7	30
Kirk	11	8	8	27

The Oil Kings

"Robust hockey? The Oil Kings? They're just plain dirty."
— Niagara Falls Flyer coach Hap Emms in a page 1 story on the Memorial Cup series played in Edmonton, May 11, 1963

Hap Emms, the decidedly unhappy coach of the Ontario Hockey Association Niagara Falls Flyers, had just seen his team beat the Edmonton Oil Kings 5-2 in the fifth game of the 1963 Memorial Cup, but it wasn't enough to put a smile on his face.

No sir.

It had been a tough, hard-fought series in the Edmonton Gardens as the two clubs battled for junior hockey supremacy in a town that was – and is – nuts about the game.

But game 5 had been the bloodiest.

"In my book, they should cancel the whole thing," wrote columnist Hal Pawson. "It's gone beyond a joke. Grown men have turned hypocrites, hockey players are bashing each other over the head, and visiting fans have flipped their lids."

Oil King Greg Pilling had whacked defenceman Rich Morin over the head with a hockey stick, sending the Flyer into the dressing room with a concussion and a wound that required a dozen stitches to close.

Calling the Edmonton Gardens "a stinking barn," coach Emms was livid.

"That Pilling," he fumed at sportswriter Al Dahl, "should be barred from hockey. We believe in throwing checks all right, but when it comes to waving sticks like swords....

"Say, if he's ever traded to Hamilton (a then-current rumour) it will be a pleasure to meet him again.... "

Edmonton led the series three games to two on that night in early spring 1963, but clearly no quarter was asked nor given as the Oil Kings tried for the fifth time in their 12-year history to win the Cup.

The casualty list published on May 10, 1963, provided a handy wrap-up of the wounded on the Flyers' team. In fact, the list of broken, battered and bruised was longer than the game 5 scoring summary.

"If they want the cup that bad they can have it," Emms growled at sportswriter Wally Cross. "My players can't go on the way things are going right now and risk the chance of being crippled for life. They shouldn't be expected to do that."

Since the series began, the Flyers had suffered a total of two broken legs, one to winger Gary Dornhoefer and another to forward Gary Harmer. Morin, Bill Glashen and Ron Hergott shared 32 stitches. There were three black eyes and two concussions spread between Don Awrey and George Gardner. Bill Goldsworthy had torn muscles in the solar plexus, Terry Crisp was nursing a bad charley horse and Wayne Maxner was suffering from badly stretched rib muscles.

For their part, the Oil Kings had only one player injured: defenceman Pat Quinn who was sporting four stitches closing a gash on his face. Quinn

***Feb. 18, 1967*:**
The Chateau Lacombe opens. According to *The Journal*, La Ronde, the restaurant atop the hotel, is the largest of its kind in the world.

***June 15, 1967*:**
The Centennial Library on Churchill Square opens. *The Journal* declares it as "magnificent" with "living room comfort."

***Oct. 30, 1967*:**
Andrew Snaddon is appointed editor of *The Journal*. Don Smith is appointed managing editor.

***Dec. 30, 1967*:**
Cartoonist Yardley Jones heads off to Toronto as his final cartoon appears in *The Journal*. It includes, of course, a mention of New Sarepta and, naturally, a statue of a naked lady titled Mother.

***In 1968*:**
A *Journal* ad taker makes $50.50 a week, while a stenographer makes $85. The minimum wage is now $1.25 an hour. It had been $1 since 1966.

***Feb. 29, 1968*:**
Ross Munro is appointed *Journal* publisher.

***June 1, 1968*:**
Ruth Bowen, *The Journal*'s longtime women's editor and columnist, retires.

Exit the 60s... a decade of global violence

Charles' investiture

Queen Elizabeth led her son, Prince Charles, from Eleanor's Gate at Caernarvon Castle, Wales, in July, 1969, after his investiture as Prince of Wales. The future British monarch's father Prince Philip is to the right.

Man on moon

In July, 1969, man first flew to the moon, walked on it and returned safely to earth. While on the lunar surface, Edwin Aldrin, standing by an experiment, and Neil Armstrong, deployed instrument packages near the moonship Eagle.

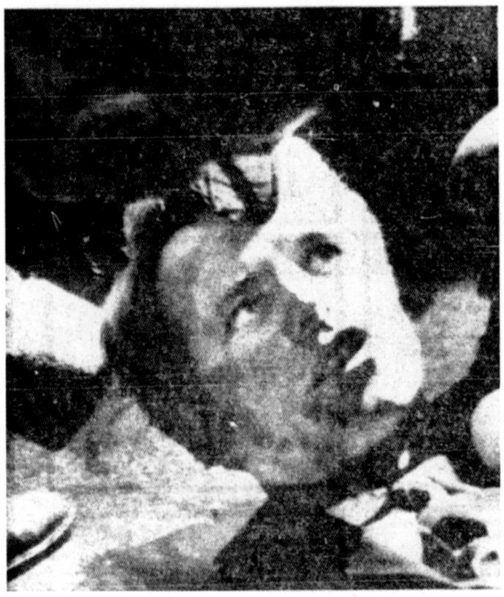

RFK assassinated

Three assassinations in the U.S. shocked the world in the 1960s. Robert Kennedy (above) was fatally shot in June, 1968, after a victorious Los Angeles rally in his bid for the Democratic presidential nomination. His brother John was slain while U.S. president, in November, 1963, while visiting Dallas, Tex., where anti-administration feeling ran high. Civil rights leader Martin Luther King was shot down in Memphis, Tenn. in April 1968.

Transplant hero

Dentist Dr. Phillip Blaiberg lived almost 20 months after receiving the world's second human heart transplant, in Cape Town, South Africa. Here he was in high spirits as he strolled in Cape Town in July, 1969. After the Blaiberg transplant, surgeons around the world took heart and dozens more such operations were performed.

Khrushchev embraces Castro

A jovial meeting of Soviet Premier Nikita Khrushchev and Cuba's Fidel Castro occurred at the United Nations in September, 1960. The association of these Communist nations would create a world crisis when Soviet missiles would be deployed on Cuban soil, spotted by high-flying U.S. photo aircraft, and under pressure from the U.S., removed from Cuba.

Violence in streets

The United States was shaken in the '60s by violence in the streets of many of its major cities. Here a National Guardsman stands at the ready in a Detroit intersection during the July, 1967, riots.

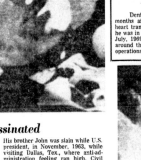

Clay floors Liston

The name's Cassius Clay, but he prefers to be called Muhammed Ali. In May, 1965, as world heavyweight boxing champion he flattened challenger Sonny Liston in a return title bout in Maine, then stood over the boxing giant and screamed at him.

Moment of death

South Vietnam's national police chief shocked the world when he executed a Viet Cong officer in February, 1968, on a Saigon street, and a photographer instinctively pressed his camera shutter to catch the moment of death.

had been directly responsible for one of the broken legs when he put a crushing game 3 check on Flyer Dornhoefer.

While the standing room only crowd of 7,000 was pleased that the Oil Kings had won that game 5-2 to take a two-game-to-one lead in the series, it was Quinn's check that was the talk of the town.

"Quinn finds little humour in a man who delights in cross-checking and butt-ending smaller rivals and, generally, committing the kind of sins no 219-pounder could let go," wrote sportswriter Ron Glover.

"So he picked his spot – charged across the ice and ended the season for Dornhoefer in one pain-filled explosive second.

"Gary's knee went. And all of a sudden Hap Emms finds himself without one third of what could be the nation's top junior line."

It may have been the turning point in the series.

"I don't want to say anything about refereeing at this point," Emms told Pawson, "but I don't want to come back to Edmonton ever. There was our star, Gary Dornhoefer, stretched out in agony, and the Edmonton people were cheering."

It wasn't only Edmonton fans that were happy with Quinn.

"If ever a guy deserved it, Dornhoefer did," pronounced Scotty Bowman, then a scout with the Montreal Canadiens. "He's made a career out of bullying little fellows … and he got it good."

Punch Imlach, the Maple Leaf coach who was also watching the games at the Gardens, agreed. "If you live by the sword, you die by it," he said.

In 1963, the Oil Kings were making their third consecutive appearance in the Memorial Cup series, but they had never managed to win it.

But under head coach Buster Brayshaw, and with players such as Quinn, Pilling, Glen Sather, Bob Falkenberg, Butch Paul, Roger Bourbonnais, Max Mastinsek and Doug Fox all playing "robust" hockey, this was their year.

Mind you, the Flyers had their muscle and speed too. Players such as Awrey, Crisp, Goldsworthy and Butch Barber all were headed for the NHL.

Regardless, it was all over for the Flyers in game 6.

"Champions are the Edmonton Oil Kings," was Dwayne Erickson's rather awkward first paragraph on the May 13, 1963, game story that reported their 4-3 victory.

"When the opening gun was fired on the night of May 2, a seemingly all-too-powerful band of Flyers from Niagara Falls laced these same Oil Kings by a lopsided 8-0 score.

"But the Kingly crew came back with 7-3, 5-2, and 3-2 victories, lost the fifth game 5-2, then capped the series with a stirring effort Saturday night."

As for Pawson, who had called for cancellation of the series, all was forgiven, particularly when he reflected on the hectic final minute of the final game as the Flyers buzzed the Oil King net.

"It was a minute of which all Edmonton, and all Alberta, can be forever proud. It was the epitome of everything that is wonderful about true sport and sportsmanship."

***August 1968*:**
***The Journal* hires cartoonist Edd Uluschak.**

***In 1969*:**
An addressograph operator at *The Journal* makes $65 a week, while a copy editor earns $125.

***Feb. 4, 1969*:**
The city has been locked in a cold snap that began on Jan. 7 and *The Journal* offers its readers an "I Was There Certificate" drawn by Edd Uluschak. More than 75,000 certificates were printed and distributed.

***March 9, 1969*:**
Canada's first 911 system goes into operation in Edmonton.

***July 29, 1969*:**
"There is a movement under way now to promote the preservation and restoration of the two-and-a-half blocks concerned. The Edmonton historical board would like to see a 'clean-up, paint-up' campaign begin the plan. The entire program could take a few years according to Mr. Cam Finlay of the city's historical department.... Something must be done before redevelopers move in."
– On restoring Old Strathcona.

***Aug. 15, 1969*:**
A transit strike forces 50,000

22 THE EDMONTON JOURNAL, Wednesday, July 12, 1967

SAN FRANCISCO HIPPIE PLAYS IT COOL
. . . he's bathing in publicity

Hippies

Edmonton Is Unlikely To Lure Converts To The Growing 'New Generation' Movement

Third of series

By JARON SUMMERS
Of The Journal

Hippies are happy with the way things are going for them.

Said one: "Life is a game and we're going to play it until the cars stop. Then we'll play it in the streets. . ."

He smiled and ran his fingers through a two-year growth of shaggy hair.

It will be a long time before the hippies take over the streets but they are gaining converts to their "new generation."

Newsweek bills the hippies as "Dropouts with a mission." Most hippies are dropouts but it is more of a "wishin' " than a "mission." Hippies are wishin' they could do something to bring happiness to the world.

Unfortunately, that is as far as they go—wishin'.

A writer in San Francisco magazine says: "The future of the hippies can only be described as dynamic, outlined with random, action words."

NOT CONSTRUCTIVE

They admittedly do some things -- such as starting a campaign to change Haight Street's name to Love Street. But none of the "dynamic" action is put into anything much more constructive.

Bathing in publicity and an "I'm-right" philosophy, hippies think it is just a matter of time before the rest of the world joins them. Tom, a hippie who lives in the Sunset area of San Francisco, said: "Man, you can see it everywhere. The movement is coming out all over. Where do you think the paisley designs come from? We started them. They're worldwide already. Look at pop art. That's us. Can't you see it, Man? F a s h i o n s—that's us. Everyone who is hip is starting to come alive."

NOT IN EDMONTON

With a hippie promise of 100,000 flower children in San Francisco this summer and colonies of the new generation budding from Vancouver to Winnipeg — how long before a Haight - Ashbury develops in Edmonton?

A long time.

There is a possibility Edmontonians may see a few hippies on Jasper Avenue, but that's about it.

In the first place, money—even hippies need some — is harder to get here than in San Francisco. The largest employer of the hippies in California is the United States Post Office who hire them for temporary work.

Certainly the provincial and dominion government would not hire a part-time office worker or part-time anything from the bearded ranks of the hippies. Their long hair and smell would probably deter most other employers too.

Edmonton's climate is not conducive to a hippie atmosphere. Except for a few days, the weather is just too cold for habitual park sleepers.

Numbers are against hippies in Ca ada, especially in Edmonton. There are not enough would-be hippies to start anything like another Hashberry in Edmonton. Canadians may feel the urge to drop out but they certainly don't have to start a counter - civilization to "get away from it all."

It is easier to walk a few miles to get back to nature.

One reason for becoming a hippie is to revolt against war and the "plastic" or material world. Canada is not involved in the military action the United States is—so Canadians probably do not feel strongly about starting a counter-civilization which espouses love, love and more love.

NOT SO POWERFUL

Madison Avenue has turned America into a country which worships the material. True, Canadians have this tendency of "I want to possess everything" but the drive is not nearly as powerful here as it is south of the border. If a Canadian wants to be a hippie—it is much easier to join the movement in the USA. And a true hippie does everything with the least effort.

Some hippies come from the elite of college students — the so-called cream of the crop. Is it possible this group is contributing anything good toward society?

Yes.

Hippie-ism has the possibility of producing one or two beneficial side-effects.

Some, who become hippies, will "find" themselves. And once discovering their potential, they may become a productive party of society. They will no doubt stress the importance of non-material things.

Diggers lost their good name when they started to use extortion m e t h o d s to collect scraps for their communal soup pots—but many achieved a feeling of helping. There will certainly be a need for diggers this summer as naive high school students drift to the Haight in search of an experience with the new generation.

REMOTE CHANCE

There is always the chance, the remote chance, hippies will produce a race who freely give of themselves for the pure joy of satisfying the desires of their partners.

This philosophy may have a certain nobility to it but in practice is dangerous. Squalor plus free sex produces an alarming rate of VD.

"We've had 4,295 cases of gonorrhea this year. That's up 40 per cent over last year. We'll probably have over 11,000 cases by the end of the year," said one health employee.

Yesterday, it was the Mods of England and before that the Bohemians of New York.

Tomorrow? Who knows?

How large the hippie movement will become, is impossible to forecast. But it will increase until something else comes along. As Canada continues to copy much of what America does, the s a m e conditions which spawned the hippies south of the border may produce them here.

As you walk down Haight Street, you cannot help but feel sorry for p e o p l e who are searching for a way past the plastic world. They cannot be chided for expressing empathy for the napalm-bombed villages of Vietnam. You cannot criticize their disillusionment with America and the world.

In many cases the disillusionment is good but the manner they register displeasure is sad.

EASY WAY OUT

They have taken the easy way out. Drugs and idleness.

And it won't work, for the hippies are trying to replace the reward of serious introspection w i t h the hallucination caused by a pill.

Man has always struggled with the questions of why he is here and where he is going. LSD isn't solving it for the hippies. One has only to look into their glazed eyes to realize this.

"That back to nature scene is okay when you're 20," said one hippie, "but when you're looking at 35 you want to know something's happening to you."

100% CANADIAN OWNED 100% CANADIAN OWNED

Faith Clash On Law

Two religious groups clashed politely on provincial adoption laws this morning.

The Salvation Army asked the government to take a second look at the adoption law which forbids children to be placed in a home where the parents are of a different religious faith to the natural mother.

The Council of Catholic Charities and the Catholic Family and Child Service Committee asked the government to stand fast with present adoption laws.

SAME FAITH

Salvation Army officials said in a brief submitted to the public expenditure and revenue s t u d y committee that they agreed that it was better if a child could be placed in a home of the same religious faith as its mother.

But, they stressed, "a child should not be deprived of a good home merely because the prospective adoptive parents are of a different faith."

Catholic officials argued that if the adoption law was changed, Catholic unmarried mothers, who intend their children to be brought up in that faith, would not surrender their children for adoption.

This could result, the brief stated, in an increase in illegal abortions and "shotgun marriages."

DISCRIMINATION

Any change in the law could lead to charges of religious discrimination against the Alberta government from inside and outside the province, the Catholic brief suggests.

Salvation Army officials also asked for a tightening of welfare payments to employable men.

Sometimes payments reached proportions where the incentive to work is taken away.

The brief added that some men on welfare did seek work in order to pay their way weekly but stressed there were many who "drink" their w e l f a r e cheques and adopt the attitude "why should I work while I'm on provincial welfare."

The Council of Catholic Charities' brief called on the government to increase efforts to help Indians and Metis adjust to city life. The suggested examples were, giving Indians the right to buy liquor and to vote in the provincial election.

It pointed out that the average Indian-Metis has a grade seven education and as a result experiences difficulty in getting employment. Most of them who move to the city find themselves either on welfare or in trouble with the law.

THE NEW TEEN-AGE LOOK
. . . Bev Muzka, Dale Letourneau, Valerie Hartfeil and Bethy Wright admire the new hairstyle of Dave Manning

It's The Beatle Cut — A New Teen-Age Craze

By PAT JOHNSON
Of The Journal

It's a bird! It's a plane! — No! It's a beatle.

And if that sounds mixed up, it's small wonder. So is the beatle.

To the uninitiated, the beatle is a hairstyle — and a weird one. To teenage boys, it's the latest rage.

And it's contagious.

It started in England with the British musical team, The Beatles — four young lads who wear their hair combed straight down over their foreheads, almost covering their eyes.

Now it's here.

One of the first city lads to give it a try was David Manning, 18-year-old Grade 12 student of Victoria Composite High School. He thinks it's great, although "mine isn't long enough yet."

His school principal thinks it is quite long enough.

"Get a haircut," he wrote on David's last report. So far, however, there's been no critical issue made of David's coiffure.

This isn't the case in Ottawa. There, four lads seen w e a r i n g the controversial haircut at Lisgar Collegiate were ordered to comb their hair differently or stay home from school. The boys complied.

IT'S SPREADING

In Edmonton, the beatle has not yet reached epidemic proportions requiring such ultimatums.

It is, however, spreading.

Last week at Scona Composite School there were none of the new hair style. This week, there's half a dozen.

And at St. Joe's and Austin O'Brien and others, the hair is starting to grow — down, down, towards the eyes.

Will it last?

Who's to say. Or what's more to the point perhaps when the beatle gets long enough, who's to see?

Study Will Urge Transport Web, Seven Freeways

A ring-road skirting downtown Edmonton, at least two more bridges and seven freeway systems are among recommendations of the Metropolitan Edmonton Transportation Study.

This word came Tuesday from Edmonton town planner William Hardcastle who said the METS reports hold the solution to Edmonton's traffic problems over the next 20 years.

Mr. Hardcastle told the Edmonton Civic Protective Association a preview of METS proposals indicated "a substantial amount of money" would be involved.

Specifically he mentioned:

- A ring road to ease increasing cross river and downtown traffic congestion problems.
- Freeway systems serving the road from seven different directions.
- More bridges over the North Saskatchewan River, possibly two.

EARLY FEBRUARY

Latest date for publication of volume two of the METS study is early February, according to the Edmonton Regional Planning Commission. The second volume will contain specific proposals about city traffic conditions.

Mr. Hardcastle said at least one third of the present downtown traffic would not be there with improved roadways systems.

"We do not have a really serious traffic problem now," he said, "but in 10 years things will be a lot different."

Commissioner D. B. Menzies said two weeks ago that the METS study would show a need for increased provincial and federal financial assistance in major traffic development projects.

Big Program Slated For '64 Mardi Gras

If you can call a moose, you're in demand.

Just phone 429-1962.

That's Polar Park, where the Junior Chamber of Commerce is looking for entrants to Muk-Luk Mardi G r a s' moose-calling competition.

Duck callers and geese callers are not forgotten either. There are competitions for both these skills, too.

Snowshoeing? Cross-country skiing? Motor cycle ice racing? Motorized toboggan racing?

Hopefuls in these pursuits still have three weeks to get in shape.

Muk-Luk Mardi Gras will be held this year, Feb. 7 to 9.

And the Junior Chamber is looking for as many participants as possible.

Among other competitive events: junior and regular dog team races, flour-packing, s q u a w wrestling, dancing canoe portaging, ladies nail-driving, ice statue building.

All these activities will centre in the winter festival's new Polar Park—located this year in Laurier Park next to Storyland Valley Zoo Here. Junior Chamber officials promise, plenty of supervised parking, lighting and rest room facilities.

On the just for fun side, Muk-Luk officials have provided many Polar Park facilities as well.

Price tag to this winter wonderland will be $1 per car, and 25 cents for adult pedestrians. Children are free.

The park will open 4:30 p.m. Feb. 7, with official opening ceremonies 7 p.m. that evening.

Events will continue through the three days until Feb. 9 at 6 p.m.

Boldness In Planning Supported

Edmonton's planners must find the solutions now to transportation and development problems and not wait for the 11th hour.

Addressing the Alberta Land Surveyors annual dinner, Commissioner G. C. Hamilton said, "We must take a bold approach to our problems."

He described the astronomical

Police Chief Convalesces After Heart Attack

Police chief M. F. E. Anthony left hospital Tuesday to begin convalescence at home following a mild heart attack.

The 61-year-old former RCMP assistant commissioner spent three weeks in University Hospital.

A family source said today the chief is expected to take a month's vacation before returning to work.

Hair Down to Here…

"… Mop-haired Edmonton youths are being barred from one of their favourite hangouts. Security guards at the entrance to the restaurant were told to bar anyone whom they considered shabby, mop-haired, noisy or smelly."

— Photo caption, Oct. 20, 1967

Sixties hair, the kind that was long, straight, shoulder-length and longer wasn't welcome by many Edmontonians.

Like many good things in the decade, long hair started with the Beatles, whose hair was more shocking than their music.

On Jan. 22, 1964, Victoria Composite high school student Dave Manning, wearing a neat sweater and tie, posed for *The Journal* in his trendy, new Beatle cut.

The newspaper's Pat Johnson took a bemused approach. "It started in England with the British musical team, the Beatles – four young lads who wear their hair combed straight down over their foreheads, almost covering their eyes.

"Now it's here."

Manning's school principal was not amused with the young man's daring. He scrawled, "Get a haircut" on Manning's report card.

"Will it last?" Johnson asked in her story.

"Who's to say? Or what's more the point perhaps when the Beatle gets long enough, who's to see?"

Within a month, however, some high school principals had had enough. Beatle cuts were banned at Vic and at St. Joseph's Composite high school. The latter also prohibited playing Beatle music at noon hour.

But for those students who lacked Manning's mettle, an Eaton's ad on Feb. 21, 1964, offered black-only Beatle wigs for sale at $1.98 each at the record bar in the downtown store.

By 1967, young people with long hair were being refused service in restaurants and were often booted out of public places.

On Oct. 5, 1967, *The Journal* quoted Mr. Justice W.H. Riley of the Alberta district court: "There are a couple of girls in this courtroom," he said when he spotted University of Alberta commerce student John Zwickstra, 18, and his 17-year-old friend, Ray Mercredi, in his courtroom.

"When you come in this courtroom, you come properly dressed, that is with haircuts and shirts and ties."

When court resumed that afternoon, Riley ordered the pair out.

"Mr. Justice Riley told the RCMP constable in the courtroom: 'Mr. Constable, I notice two girls in the court. Please remove them,' " *The Journal* reported.

The constable obeyed.

Edmonton commuters to find another way to get around.

***Sept. 3, 1969*:**
Karol Cardinal Wojtyla, 48, archbishop metropolitan of Krakow, Poland, visits Edmonton. He becomes Pope John Paul II.

***Sept. 13, 1969*:**
A *Journal* ad lists a lot sale in Broxton Park in Spruce Grove. Houses there sell for $17,000 – $1,500 down and $163 a month.

***Oct. 7, 1969*:**
The first self-serve liquor store in Alberta opens for business at Westmount and "it is just like your neighbourhood supermarket," says *The Journal*.

***Dec. 9, 1969*:**
Edmonton movie theatres will be open for business on Sundays, effective Dec. 14. The city announces its population as 410,000.

***Dec. 11, 1969*:**
The price of a seven-ounce glass of beer goes from 15 cents to 20 cents. "I won't pay it. I won't. I'll quit drinking beer, that's what I'll do," Haywood Conly tells *The Journal*. "I'll drink rubbing alcohol instead."

Topless gals in town...well barely

By KEITH ASHWELL
Of The Journal

Edmonton went topless Thursday night in a big bust-out that never was.

It happened at Zorba's, on 111th Street and 87th Avenue. Four young girls — the Hummingbirds — exposed their breasts, pasties and all, the city's morality watchdogs smiled and the show went on.

"As long as they don't go any further, don't gyrate excessively and don't tell any dirty jokes, it's all right," said two officers of the morality squad.

"They won't," Zorba's manager, Peter Matheos, assured them.

The show had been advertised to go on at 9:30 p.m. Most tables were filled; boys outnumbered girls by three to one.

At 9:44 out go the white lights. Someone shouts: "Come on with the filth."

Six minutes later the act appears by the refreshment counter. The girls look around and disappear.

9:56—back again, with instruments.

9:58 — on stage. Amplifying takes probably five minutes. Then suddenly the sound of three guitars and drums explodes on a quiet scene.

10:03 — one nonchalant couple begins a disinterested rock. It turns out to be a solo performance.

Mary, the lead guitar, tells the audience: "We're all-girl topless band." A brief riff and another shouts: "So let it all hang out."

10:06 — every light is out. Something's happening on stage. Off come the sequinned jackets, the lights are on again and we're looking at lots of flesh and plenty of strategic spangles.

The girls play another number but no one's dancing and no one's gawking.

"You're so quiet out there," complains Mary. "Maybe you've never seen boobies before?"

"Don't be shy," says Joanne. "We're not."

"How many out there have seen topless before?" A few laughs and the retort: "So that's the trouble."

At that two middle-aged teenagers walk out past the bandstand as if on a general salute.

It's now 10:20 and as the music crashes out, louder now, 10, 15 then 20 or more couples start dancing. They look like they are cautiously performing 5BX exercises and most girls have their backs to the players.

In a few more minutes the act is over and so's the excitement, more apparent than real.

The Hummingbirds — Mary, Jane, Joanne and Sandra — have made some sort of history for Alberta that is.

They've played topless in other provinces.

Sandra is a Winnipeg girl: the others are from San Francisco. They seem indifferent to the fuss that might have been.

Peter Matheos is happy. He'd publicised the topless part but hadn't informed the police. "Someone had to be first. What could I lose if I had been charged?"

The morality squad seems content. There was nothing really immoral about the show.

The customers? Whether indifferent, happy or just content, they didn't react. It could have been a let-down . . . literally.

WINNIPEG (CP) — John M. Hanson, manager of Winnipeg's playhouse theatre, said Thursday actors in Spring Thaw 70 will be restricted to an almost-nude scene.

Two men and a girl in the production appeared nude before Toronto audiences, but for the same scene here will be required to wear their underwear.

In an interview, Mr. Hanson said someone in the Winnipeg audience would be bound to complain of the nudity, forcing police to investigate and lay charges.

The Edmonton Journal

FORECAST: CLOUDY | EDMONTON, ALBERTA, FRIDAY, MAY 22, 1970 | 68 PAGES | 10¢

Year reprieve for Canadian TV content

By PATRICK O'CALLAGHAN
Southam News Services

OTTAWA—Private broadcasting today got a one-year reprieve from the Canadian Radio-Television Commission for the Canadianization of the air waves.

Full implementation of the regulations announced Feb. 12 has been set back to Oct. 1, 1972, for the private sector of broadcasting, though the CBC is still required to meet the objective by Oct. 1, 1970.

While the CRTC is not prepared to retreat from its stand of 60 per cent Canadian content for television and 70 per cent for radio, Chairman Peirre Juneau announced at a nationally-televised press conference here today that the commission is prepared to give a little ground in response to a host of views and comments.

It is also understood that the CRTC's rigid schedule had run into heavy weather at a recent Liberal caucus meeting and many regarded today's announcement as a compromise to appease these objectors.

Since the February announcement, the CRTC has received 111 briefs from broadcasters, writers, actors, advertisers, unions, students and members of the public. A public hearing in Ottawa April 14 - 22 heard views expressed by 51 groups and individuals.

The CRTC, saying it found these comments and expressions of great value in preparing the new regulations, then made the following concessions:

A three-step instead of a two-season progression for private TV station to meet the 60 per cent Canadian content ruling. All private broadcasters must meet this requirement in full by Oct. 1, 1972.

A maximum of five, rather than four, commercial interruptions in a one-hour TV program. However, 12 commercial minutes will still be the maximum allowed in the hour, though an extra 30 seconds an hour will be allowed for unpaid public service announcements.

- Calculation of the average of non-Canadian TV programs will be allowed over a calendar quarter rather than four weeks.
- AM Radio broadcasters can arrive at their 30 per cent average of Canadian musical compositions over the whole day rather than in four periods of four hours each.
- The amount of additional paper work required of AM radio broadcasters is reduced.
- After the first two years of AM radio Canadian music regulations, five per cent of musical compositions broadcast must be written or composed by Canadians.
- Date of the implementation

More CRTC Page 2

4 killed in plane, car crashes

A Sundre man was killed Thursday when his light plane crashed 75 yards from his front door.

Stanley Burrell, 42, was circling his ranch, about 75 miles northwest of Calgary, when the accident occurred shortly after takeoff.

Three other Albertans died in motor vehicle accidents.

A head-on collision between two cars near Lethbridge resulted in the death of both drivers, Florence Firby, 68, of Winnipeg, and William Humphrey, 50, of Nobleford, the only occupants of the vehicles.

One woman was killed and seven other injured after a two-car collision atop a hill five miles southeast of Airdrie. Three ambulances were required to take the injured to hospital.

Harvey Andrew McClure, 25, was killed when the light aircraft he was piloting crashed afer he overshot the sand bar runway at McKenzie Mountain Lodge, 90 miles southwest of Norman Wells in the Northwest Territories.

Stock market suffers reversal

NEW YORK (AP) — The stock market conceded all early gains and turned downward sharply in active trading today.

The Dow Jones average of 30 industrials had dropped 4.72 points to 660.53 by 12:30 p.m. after being ahead nearly five points shortly after the opening bell.

Sherwood Park without water for two days

Parts of Sherwood Park have been without water for two days and nobody seems to know why.

Bill Parker, president of the Sherwood Park Ratepayers' Association, said water amounts to no more than a dribble in many areas of the community.

There has been no water at all in Maple Grove, an area including up to 500 homes.

"If a fire broke out here this morning we'd be in trouble," Mr. Parker said.

Sherwood Park fire Chief Wayne Stanyer said the situation is serious but that if a fire

More WATER Page 2

Journal photo by Mike Vann

Orphan

Awkwardly struggling for survival, a motherless 12-day-old colt stretches to taste a special milk solution offered by Sherry Johnson, 8. Mr. and Mrs. Dave Johnson moved the colt to their basement on an acreage near Sherwood Park when its mother died shortly after giving birth. Mr. Johnson says its chances of survival are touch-and-go.

THEY GET WRONG MAN; HE GETS $1,000

By JOHN TOMPKINS
Of The Journal

A letter, sent to the employer of a city man, was found defamatory in Supreme Court this week, and has cost the Credit Bureau of Edmonton $1,000.

The letter was sent to Northern Alberta Railways indicating that one of their employees Larry Dwayne Sawatzky, of 13628 135th St., owed about $500 to one of the bureau's clients.

But the bureau had got the wrong Larry Sawatzky.

Other than stating Mr. Sawatzky's indebtedness the letter said that "despite numerous requests by letter and telephone the debtor (Mr. Sawatzky) has as yet shown no inclination to make satisfactory arrangements for payment."

The letter suggested "that possibly a word from you (Northern Alberta Railways) could impress on him the advantage of avoiding legal proceedings . . . and bring about amicable results."

Mr. Sawatzky, said he suffered considerable embarrassment because of the letter.

He claimed $10,000 for general, exemplary and punitive damages from the Credit Bureau.

In his judgment Chief Justice J. V. H. Milvain said the letter was a clear indication that Mr. Sawatzky was being branded as one who did not pay his bills.

"It's one of these sneak-up type of matters," he said.

"The choice of language is somehow or other insulting."

Chief Justice Milvain felt that in the hands of railway companies such correspondence was perhaps more of an insult and more damaging than with other employers.

"Railway companies are well known for taking a dim view of garnishees," he said.

Mr. Sawatzky had testified that one of his superiors at the company had, in fact, spoken quite severely to him about the matter. This occurence was in part the cause of the mental anguish he suffered through the affair.

"Railway companies, by and large, pay their employees an adequate salary from which decent people are expected to pay their way, so that again makes this, in my view, more eminently defamatory," said the chief justice.

He felt that the most elementary of checking with Mr. Sawatzky by the credit bureau brought the mistake to light.

The chief justice also felt that on discovery of the mistake the Credit Bureau should have written a letter of apology to Mr. Sawatzky.

But the fact that the bureau "just rested on its oars and didn't care much" demanded, in the chief justice's view some punitive damages.

He felt, however, that $10,000 was too high and settled on $1,000.

Committee to rule against omniplex vote

By PAUL BENNETT
Of The Journal

City council's aldermanic utilities committee is expected to recommend against a plebiscite being held on omniplex, a proposed multi-million dollar recreation and convention complex.

Ald. Neil Crawford, committee chairman, told The Journal in an interview Thursday night he believes a recommendation to this effect — and including the successful developer — will go to council June 8.

"Although a majority of aldermen apparently don't agree this course should be taken, I expect a majority recommendation from the committee in favor of going ahead without a plebiscite," he said. "The recommendation to council will be one that I think they should adopt," he said.

Ald. Crawford declined to name which proposal may be recommended or even which ones are on the committee's short list.

Observers speculate it will be the domed stadium of Marlboro Developments Ltd., perhaps the most exciting of the five proposals presented at the May 5 special meeting on the omniplex.

Ald. Crawford said council has three choices—to go ahead without a plebiscite, to hold a plebiscite, to reject an idea entirely.

"I know a majority (of aldermen) are in favor of holding a vote on whether the city should borrow the money and run it a a loss," he said, "but I expect the committee to go ahead with the recommendation anyway."

FINANCING

He rules out the possibility of financing by the Exhibition Association, which has offered to manage the sport, trade and convention facility planned north of the CN tracks between 96th and 97th streets on a 10.8-acre site.

Ald. Crawford said the Exhibition Association doesn't have the resourses to finance the facility—expected to cost up to $30,000,000 including land and parking—and it will be up to the developer or the city to provide money to build and pay it off.

In a letter to be considered by council Monday following the omniplex meeting, John Sydie, president of Marlboro Developments Ltd., said his development firm considered financing it privately in 1967.

But, he said, "we had to abandon any such idea as it very soon became apparent that to load the project with municipal and or federal corporation taxes would burden the operation with such heavy operational expenses that it would be impossible" to run at a profit.

Transplant patient dies

CAPE TOWN (Reuters)—The world's second longest-surviving heart transplant patient died today at Groote Schuur Hospital here.

Petrus Smith, 53, was South Africa's third heart transplant patient, receiving his new heart Sept. 7, 1968, in an operation performed by Dr. Christiaan Barnard. He apparently died from cancer.

Louis Russell, an Indianapolis teacher, still living, holds the longevity record.

2 arrested following clash at CLC meet

A man and woman were arrested after a scuffle involving about 12 persons outside the Canadian Labor Congress convention at the SportEx today.

About 50 delegates were involved in a shouting and pushing match described by some as a confrontation between Communist sympathizers and anti-Communist pickets.

Four carloads of policemen raced to the scene to quell the disturbance. One policeman is reported to have suffered a cut lip in the scuffle.

A half-dozen members of the Anti-Bolshevik Youth League of Edmonton carried signs at the entrance to the Canadian Labor Congress convention claiming victory over Communist attempts to seize control of the CLC.

The signs referred to two statements made Thursday by CLC president, Donald MacDonald saying Communist elements in the CLC had been thwarted in the attempts to "pervert this movement."

Geza Matrai, of the group, said four "Maoists" approached the demonstration, hurled insults, and tried to strike one of the pickets.

Sudbury, Ont. members of the United Steel Workers of America came to the aid of the pickets and more insults were exchanged.

The woman is charged with two counts of assaulting a police officer and one of causing a disturbance. The man is charged with causing a disturbance.

Picture on Page 2

Communist elements attacked

By NICK HILLS
Southam News Services

Canadian Labor Congress President Don MacDonald launched a bitter attack Thursday on Communist elements within the congress after the convention had defeated a bid by a British Columbia fishermen's union to return to the fold of organized labor.

Mr. MacDonald created a

More CLC Page 2

Magistrate competence before court

A large question looms over the judicial system today about what defines the level of competence of a practising magistrate.

The problem arises out of a case before the Supreme Court Thursday, in which a writ of prohibition against a magistrate without formal legal training was argued by lawyers.

In filing an application for the writ against Magistrate M. W. Hopkins of St. Paul, city lawyer Ronald Berger argued that his client, Henry Piche of Grande Centre, would be denied

More COURT Page 2

Where to find it

Art Evans	15	Music	56, 59
Ann Landers	18	News Digest	9
Barry Westgate	49	Sport	50-54
Births, Deaths, Marriages	24	Theatres, Entert'ment	64-67
Book Review	63	TV, Radio	60-62
Bridge	26	Youth News	21
Business, Stocks	11-13	Wayne Overland	50
Charles Lynch	5		
Classified ads	25-41		
Comics, Features	55		
Comment	4		
Crossword Puzzle	29		
Family Section	16-22		
Focus on People	23		
Health Column	10		
Horoscope	27		
Letters To The Journal	4, 6		

Weather

Cloudy with showers late this afternoon or evening. Clearing overnight. A little cooler Saturday. Winds west 20 and gusting this evening, northwest 15 Saturday. Low tonight 45, high Saturday 60. Details on Page 2.

EIGHT

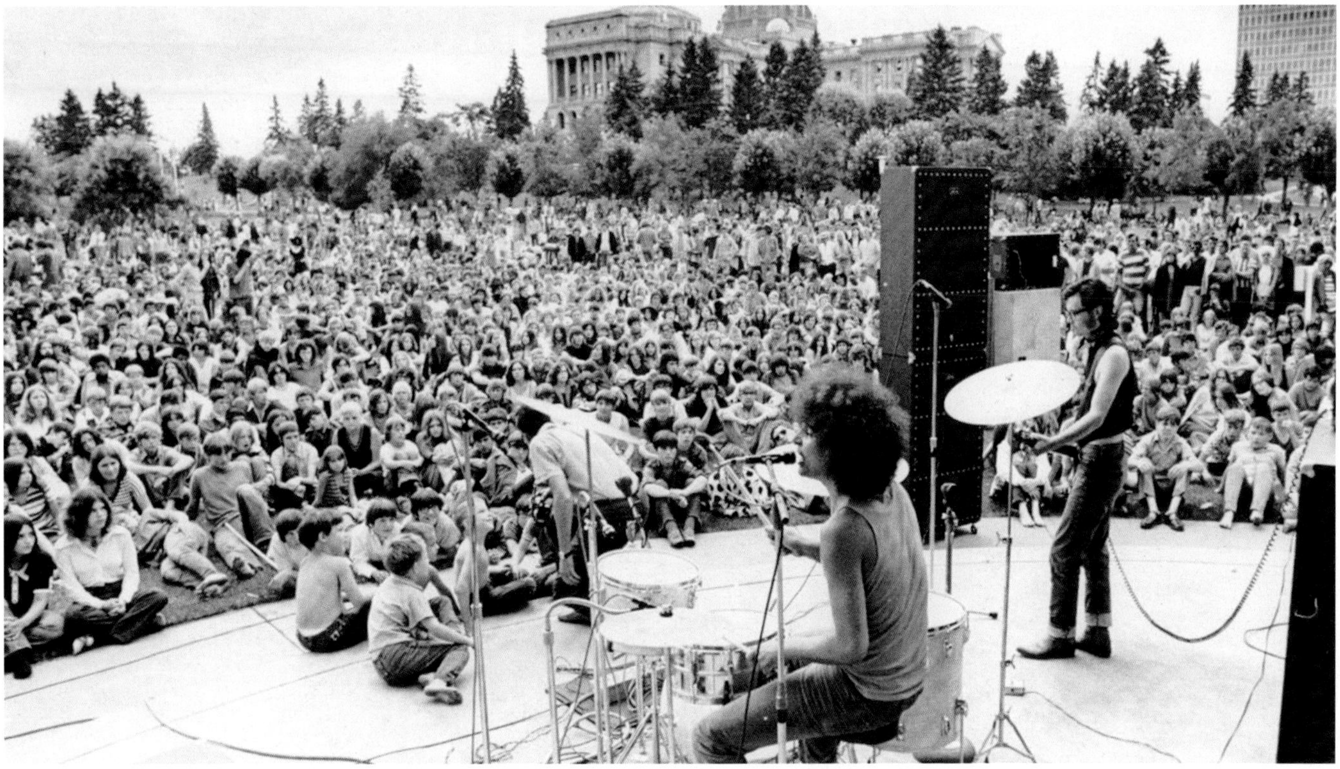
The Canadian Press

The outdoor rock festival craze hit Edmonton's legislative grounds in 1970, when 3,500 people gathered for a nine-hour concert featuring local bands.

Boundless Energy

1970 to 1979

"The downtown core isn't what it used to be. People – a lot of people – don't come here to buy groceries anymore. Too much traffic hassle when weighed against the handiness of suburban shopping centres."

— Assistant editor Stan Williams on the closing of Eaton's groceteria on May 26, 1977

Arena Mania / 299

A Gruesome Tale / 303

The Journal Bomber / 305

Going Metric / 307

Birth of Mill Woods / 309

Puffed with Pride / 311

"Unofficial Opposition" / 315

A single word defined Edmonton and Alberta in the 1970s: ENERGY.

Energy made oil rigs, pump jacks, gas wells and gas plants part of the rural landscape.

Energy meant everyone – politicians, reporters, editorial writers and voters – had to learn a new vocabulary that included terms like "wellhead prices," "tool pushes" and "stepout wells."

The learning curve in energy was often precipitously steep, but if you wanted to follow the political debate over energy, and the fortunes of the city and the province, it was a climb that had to be made.

After all, it was energy that gave Albertans the $10-$12 billion Heritage Savings and Trust Fund and the kind of collective self-assurance that came from having lots of money in the bank.

Energy, too, re-ignited the war between Alberta and Ottawa over resource rights, an issue that many thought was settled back in the late '20s in the days of Premier John Brownlee and Prime Minister Mackenzie King.

Edmonton Journal

FORECAST: RAIN | EDMONTON, ALBERTA, FRIDAY, JUNE 27, 1975 | PRICE 25c

Journal photos by Steve Makris

The Exorcist of Rock

Three cracked ribs cracked Alice Cooper's act in half before 16,000 at Edmonton's Coliseum Thursday night, but even with Cooper on the sidelines for much of the show, the majority of the crowd apparently found it a great night's entertainment. Cooper had to give up 40 minutes into his show, clutching ribs that were broken at an appearance in Vancouver Monday. But his band picked up the tempo and continued to entertain the packed-to-capacity Coliseum. Cooper somehow found an Oilers sweater backstage just before calling it quits, but in his condition it is unlikely Bill Hunter will expect him back in the fall for a team tryout. Story on Page 23 and review on Page 65.

FBI holds two for spying

WASHINGTON (AP) — FBI agents today arrested two men on charges of spying for the Soviet Union.

The FBI identified the two as Sarkis Paskalian, 36, who has been living in New York, and Sahag Dedeyan, 41, of Rockville, Md., a mathematician formerly employed by organizations doing secret defence work.

Both men are natives of Lebanon. Paskalian, who came to the United States in 1968, is a resident alien. Dedeyan is a U.S. citizen who held a top-secret clearance.

Paskalian was charged with conspiracy to gather classified defence information to aid a foreign country. The charge carries a maximum penalty of death.

Dedeyan was charged with not reporting the illegal photographing of national-defence information, a charge carrying a maximum penalty of 10 years in prison and a $10,000 fine.

Dedeyan worked for Operations Research Inc. of Silver Spring, Md., and was an associate mathematican at the Applied Physics Laboratory of Johns Hopkins University at Silver Spring from 1966 until September, 1973.

During that period, the FBI said, Paskalian approached Dedeyan, a distant relative.

While employed at Johns Hopkins, Dedeyan had prepared a secret study entitled "Vulnerability Analysis: U.S. Reinforcement of NATO."

The FBI alleged that Paskalian photographed the study in March, 1973, at Dedeyan's Rockville home. The FBI said the camera used by Paskalian was provided by Eduard Charchyan, an official of the Soviet mission to the United Nations.

The FBI said Paskalian received $1,500 from his Soviet contacts in May, 1974, and gave Dedeyan $1,000 "as a token of our appreciation."

The complaints filed against Paskalian and Dedeyan said that Paskalian was recruited as a spy in 1962 while he was in Soviet Armenia. He was sent to the United States in the summer of 1971.

Doctor's claims dismissed

CALGARY (CP) — The Canadian Medical Association (CMA) said Thursday it has found no evidence to indicate that convicted abortionist Dr. Henry Morgentaler was mistreated or denied medical treatment while at the Waterloo correctional centre near Montreal.

The CMA, in a statement released by its board of directors, said an investigation into Dr. Morgentaler's claims was conducted last Friday by Dr. Alex Scarlat, an executive member of the Quebec Medical Association.

The investigation "indicates Dr. Morgentaler is receiving the same treatment as other inmates."

Last week, Dr. Morgentaler, serving an 18-month sentence at Waterloo, charged that officials at the minimum security prison ignored his requests for medical attention. He now is being treated in hospital at Sherbrooke for symptoms of heart trouble.

Where to find it

Ann Landers ... 16
Art Evans ... 5
Barry Westgate ... 23
Births, Deaths, Marriages ... 24
Bridge ... 29
Business, Stocks ... 75-78
Charles Lynch ... 4
Classified ads ... 25-48
Comics, Features ... 67
Editorial ... 4
Crossword Puzzle ... 28
Entertainment ... 60-66
Family-Lifestyle ... 13-21
Focus on People ... 60
Horoscope ... 27
June Sheppard ... 17
Letters To The Journal ... 4
Patterns ... 33
Sport ... 69-74
Temperatures ... 2
Wayne Overland ... 69

Weather

About an inch of rain expected today; high near 16, low tonight near 10. 10. Intermittent light rain Saturday; high near 16. Details on Page 2.

Panarctic crash survivors say they won't testify now

By Brian Tucker
and Doug McConachie
Of The Journal

Two key witnesses involved in last October's fatal crash of a Panarctic Oil Ltd. aircraft in the Arctic, will not testify before the presently constituted coroner's inquest.

Co-pilot David Hatton and flight engineer Gary Weyman, aboard the Panarctic Lockheed Electra when it crashed near Rea Point on Melville Island, won't appear before Coroner Walter England or Crown attorney Ed Brogden, their solicitor stated Thursday.

A. M. Harradence of Calgary, who was only asked to represent the two Panarctic employees Wednesday, said however, "they are, and have always been ready to testify . . . and they will testify" before another inquest if such is established.

Mr. Hatton and Mr. Weyman appeared briefly at a Calgary news conference Thursday, and Mr. Harradence said "their whereabouts has never been concealed."

A spokesman for Mr. Harradence's office said the reason for Thursday's news conference was because Mr. Hatton and Mr. Weyman "wanted to set the record straight."

He said "their integrity was being questioned, and they came to us to get it straightened out."

The two were the only survivors of the crash Oct. 29 were killed 32 men, and Coroner Walter England of Yellowknife, and crown attorney Ed Brogden have expressed disappointment

More INQUEST Page 10

Civil servant suspended after beefs about Goyer

OTTAWA (CP) — A civil service union official has been suspended from his $25,000-a-year government job for speaking out publicly against his boss, Supply and Services Minister Jean-Pierre Goyer.

Arthur Stewart, president of the 8,000-member supply and services union of the Public Service Alliance of Canada (PSAC), was suspended for three months without pay earlier this week from his job as an engineering procurement officer in the department.

The PSAC, bargaining agent for most federal civil servants, immediately appealed the suspension claiming the action was a denial of Mr. Stewart's right to freedom of speech.

The suspension was ordered by J.M. DesRoches, deputy supply minister, who said an article written by Mr. Stewart in an Ottawa newspaper, The Citizen, June 12, conflicted with his duties as a department employee.

In the article, Mr. Stewart said that, as an executive member of the union, he could "no longer remain silent about the deplorable state of affairs" within Mr. Goyer's department.

The article accused Mr. Goyer of adding unnecessarily to the size of the department bureaucracy with an increase to 769 from 498 last year in the number of persons earning $20,000 to $30,000 a year.

"The blame for the current disillusionment and discontent within the department must be laid directly at

More CRITIC Page 11

2 FBI agents gunned down on reserve

PINE RIDGE, S.D. (AP) — "It looked like an execution. They were riddled with bullets." William Janklow, South Dakota attorney-general, said today after two Federal Bureau of Investigation (FBI) agents were shot to death on the Pine Ridge Indian Reservation.

Authorities said the agents were dragged out of their cars and killed Thursday when they tried to serve warrants on persons holed up in a house.

An Indian in the house was reported killed in an exchange of gunfire.

Federal agents pursued occupants of the house through the hills of the reservation Thursday night, but at 1:30 a.m. today, the FBI agent in charge of the operation said the gunfire had stopped, "as far as I know."

FBI special agent Joseph Trimbach said his men were continuing to patrol the reservation roads but no arrests had been made.

The house where agents Jack R. Coler and Ronald A. Williams were killed is about five miles southeast of the reservation community of Oglala, not far from the village of Wounded Knee which militant Indians occupied for 71 days in 1973.

Coler, 28, worked out of the Denver office of the FBI and was on special assignment to the reservation. Williams, also 28, worked out of the FBI office in Rapid City, S.D.

WRITER'S CRAMP

The Journal's intermittent "on the farm" correspondent Gladys Eldridge tells how she's forsaken hopes of living full-time off a writer's wages in The Journal Weekender Saturday.

But she declares firmly, she hasn't given up hopes yet of staying down on the farm.

Also in the Weekender, the Canadian Magazine explores the frustrations of fighting a strike-bound society.

Mrs. Gandhi silences opponents

Unshakeable convictions part of legacy

Indira Gandhi

By Joseph Lelyveld
N.Y. Times Service

Nearly four decades ago, the Indian independence movement was scandalized by an anonymous and defamatory portrait of its adored Jawaharlal Nehru that appeared in a Calcutta journal. Although Nehru called himself a democrat and a socialist, the article warned, he had "all the makings of a dictator in him," for he was too wilful and impatient to "brook for long the slow processes of democracy."

Only later was it revealed that the author of that portrait was Nehru himself. Indira Gandhi, his only child and political heir, has never displayed her father's literary flair or capacity for self-detachment, but she has inherited his impulses and an unshakeable conviction that her leadership is essential for India's unity and survival.

Now that she has chosen to silence her political opponents by sending hundreds to jail, including such leaders of the independence movement as the aging Jayaprakash Narayan and Morarji Desai, Mrs. Gandhi will inevitably be accused of destroying the liberal democracy that her father attempted to implant in a vast and seething country.

She will reply that she is attempting to make good on the unfulfilled promises of social justice that were another part of the Nehru legacy. But the issue that provoked Mrs. Gandhi into using the police powers that she has quietly amassed in recent years was clearly limited to her own survival in office. Wednesday night's arrests and declaration of a state of emergency followed by only two days a ruling of a Supreme Court justice that temporarily stripped her of her right to vote in Parliament as a result of her conviction by a lower court on two charges of corrupt electoral practices.

At first glance, Mrs. Gandhi, who is now 57, seems totally bereft of the dictatorial attributes that her father perceived in himself. Both as a public and private person, she is usually anything but magnetic. Remote and diffident in manner, her attention tends to wander in the middle of conversations and parliamentary debates. Only when she is on a rostrum in front of tens of thousands of massed Indian villagers does she display confidence in her ability to establish rapport with others, or a marked interest in doing so.

This misleading impression of faltering ineffectuality was partly responsible for her being chosen as Prime Minister in January 1966 when her father's immediate successor, Lal Bahadur Shastri, died suddenly of a heart attack. The political barons who then dominated the Congress Party imagined that Indira Gandhi would be easier to control than Desai, her main rival.

As they soon found out, that was one of the great political miscalculations of recent times. Within four years, she had recreated the Congress Party in her own image, forcing her would-be manipulators into impotent opposition. Since then, she has ruled as an unabashed strong woman.

Her withdrawn character and inner toughness are obvious by-products of a lonely and sometimes tormented childhood. Her earliest memories are steeped in politics.

"I have no recollection of games, children's parties or playing with other children," she said once. "My favorite occupation as a very small child was to deliver thunderous speeches to the servants, standing on a high table. All my games were political ones — I was like Joan of Arc, perpetually being burned at the stake."

Her father went to prison for the first time only a few weeks after her fourth birthday. Her mother, Kamala, was also periodically jailed by the colonial authorities. Still, she was a major presence in her daughter's life.

A shy and intense woman who is said to have been "dazzingly beautiful" when she married at 16, Kamala Nehru had little of the Western education or social ease on which her husband's family placed a high value. As a result, she was often slighted.

Her daughter never forgot or forgave those slights.

"I saw her being hurt and I was determined not to be hurt," she once told an interviewer who asked about her mother's influence.

Mother and daughter prayed together daily, and it is Kamala's influence that accounts for the fact that Mrs. Gandhi seems at home, as her father never was, in the religious culture of India.

More GANDHI Page 10

The '70s fight underlined, once again, the feelings of Western alienation sometimes threatened the fabric of Confederation itself.

And, suddenly, what Arab sheiks decided in meetings of an exclusive club called the Organization of Petroleum Exporting Countries became very important, because when they began using oil exports as a weapon during the Mideast war in October 1973, oil prices soared and the shock was felt throughout North America. With its oil production secure and safe, the province looked to profit.

Energy also led to a city building boom. A 1977 *Journal* construction survey of the Edmonton area listed 104 projects, either proposed or underway, totalling more than a billion dollars.

Included in that new and proposed construction were such projects as the new $50-million Canada Place at 98th Street and Jasper Avenue, a University Hospital expansion at $84 million, the $20-million Commonwealth Stadium, a $9-million Aquatic Centre at Kinsmen Park, the Phipps McKinnon Building on Rice Howard Way, Pacific Plaza at 109th Street and Jasper Avenue, the $110-million Edmonton Centre project that included a 28-storey Four Seasons Hotel and the 29-storey Oxford Tower.

"Nowadays, if a building in this city isn't worth $5 million, it's scarcely enough to raise an eyebrow," the story said. It also incorrectly predicted that Edmonton's population would easily top one million by the new millennium.

The energy in the air was reflected in the columns of *The Journal* and in the newspaper industry itself.

First, there were revolutionary technical changes shepherded through the paper by publisher Ross Munro, the quiet-spoken, pipe-smoking former war correspondent who oversaw the passing of the last linotype machine and the arrival of the first computer copy-editing terminals.

The Journal grew in physical size as well, and by the end of the decade often at 100-plus pages, it was bulkier than most newspapers in the country and the amount of space dedicated to news and features outstripped that of every other daily in Canada.

The newsroom staff, young and brash in the '60s, now had the seasoning that gave *Journal* stories the authority demanded by an increasingly sophisticated readership. Not all subscribers agreed with everything that was written, but few could protest that it was off-handed or shallow.

Legislature reporters such as Bob Bell and John Lindblad, and Olive Elliott at City Hall, gave political news and analysis the kind of heft that readers had not seen before. Other beats were equally well-served. Keith Ashwell provided his own unique brand of writing style in reporting on the arts, and Pete Brewster, *The Journal*'s business editor, offered balanced reporting in a hectic era.

Wayne Overland, Terry Jones, Don Fleming, Jim Matheson, Norm Cowley, Cam Cole and Ray Turchansky covered sports with thoroughness that was unmatched in *Journal* history. Their stories and criticism were leavened with wit, and always with a point of view that went beyond the confines of the rink or the stadium.

***In 1970*:**
A *Journal* cashier/clerk typist earns $70 a week, while a copy editor makes $205.

***Jan. 13, 1970*:**
"Every clinical study which I have seen indicates that approximately 96 per cent of all males and 88 per cent of all females have masturbated at some time during their lives. If masturbation caused blurring of sight, absent-mindedness and prostate trouble, there would be about 140 million blurry-eyed, absent-minded prostate sufferers wandering around."
– Ann Landers in a column saying it was OK for teenagers to masturbate.

***Jan. 26, 1970*:**
Grocery retailer Dominion Stores announces that it is closing its three stores in Edmonton and four in Calgary. It was the second major food chain that moved here from Eastern Canada and then was forced to withdraw in the face of stiff competition from Safeway.

***In August 1970*:**
The Lady Anne, a three-bedroom bungalow with 1½ baths and separate dining area in Leduc's Corinthia Park, costs $21,500.

PARENT LASHES OUT AT SCHOOL BOARD SESSION
. . . some school films were described as garbage

War on violent school films

By JEAN KOENIG
Of The Journal

About 60 angry parents clashed verbally with educators Wednesday over violence on the classroom screen.

The parents came to the board room of the Edmonton Public School Board office to view films they had heard were being shown in schools; the teachers came to explain the use of the films.

But irate parents and explaining teachers found no agreement in a heated session that lasted some two hours and ended when called off by audio-visual supervisor N.G. Spillios.

Wednesday's showing was the end result of a mother's complaint that her 13 and 14-year olds in Grade 8 had seen the films in school.

The Neighbors, The Lottery and a Discussion of The Lottery are the films involved.

The Neighbors, an Oscar-winning film from the early '50s, showed how two neighbors senselessly killed themselves and their families over a flower growing on the border between their property.

The Lottery dramatizes Shirley Jackson's story of persecution, blind following of tradition, and the failure of society to protest injustice. The "prize" in this lottery is death by stoning.

The third film is a 10-minute analysis of The Lottery.

Mr. Spillios said today the film The Lottery has been available for three to four months and has been shown in most of the high schools. The Neighbors has been available for about three years and has been shown in more of the schools.

This is the first time a complaint has been received. School systems in Eastern Canada have also been using the two films and have had no complaints.

Mr. Spillios said no decision has yet been made on whether to continue using the films in the schools. He said they have been purchased by the school board on the recommendation of teachers, but the films are available from other sources, including the National Film Board.

Dr. Rolland Jones, superintendent of schools, said that teachers lay the groundwork so that the films are viewed "within a certain framework. They are introduced carefully and are followed up by discussion."

Henry Dickie, head of the NFB office in Edmonton, said The Neighbors has been used in schools all over the world. About 10 or 12 years ago, there was a feeling that some of the scenes were too brutal and they were extracted.

"But the demand to have them put back in was so great that about three years ago, the original version came back into being," he said. "There has been a tremendous change in the general acceptance of films, especially those with a particular issue to cover."

An example, he said, is a film on teen-age pregnancy which was rejected by home and school groups and health education officials six or eight years ago, but now the NFB can't keep up with the demand for bookings.

One woman at the meeting contended that children, after seeing the lottery, had held a lottery of their own and had pelted a girl with snowballs.

The films were variously described by vocal, angry parents as junk, communist, fit only for the garbage and equal to putting stones into the hands of children.

Boos greeted suggestions that such films showing the senselessness of violence were needed to counteract violence.

One man declared that he would take his children out of school rather than have them see such films.

God and the Bible entered the discussion as a result of a biblical stoning depicted in the analysis film.

This prompted one man, who identified himself first as a minister and then as a teacher, to say that he was hearing "an awful lot of religious drivel, and what was the cross, for heaven's sake?"

The film and the short story on which it is based were designed to promote love, he declared, and asked if he could stand on the table

More VIOLENCE Page 6

The Edmonton Journal

FORECAST: SUNNY 46 PAGES EDMONTON, ALBERTA, THURSDAY, FEBRUARY 18, 1971 10c 15c with The Canadian and Color Comics

Snow dump

It almost looks as if some enterprising coal miners had found a rich seam below the Macdonald Hotel and are happily dumping the slag in the North Saskatchewan River. However, that's just the dirty snow that has been clogging city streets since October. And it will disappear with the spring thaw, but by a more direct route than if it had to wend its way through the city's storm sewer system. Despite its appearance, the snow apparently doesn't add to the pollution of the North Saskatchewan. J. P. Duncan, manager of the city's sanitation and drainage department, says the pollution content of the snow is so much less than the pollution level recorded in the river that it wouldn't make any appreciable difference.

Nixon commits U.S. air power to Indochina

WASHINGTON (AP) — President Nixon said Wednesday he will place no limitations on potential use of United States airpower anywhere in Indochina—except to bar use of tactical nuclear weapons.

Asked at a news conference about speculation that South Vietnam might send some of its forces across the demilitarized zone into North Vietnam, Nixon said he would decline to speculate on what the Saigon government might feel impelled to do to protect its own national security.

But he made it clear that, should the South Vietnamese army push northward, the operation would have to meet with his approval if American forces were involved in any way.

Asked whether he thought operations in Laos might prompt China to enter the conflict, the president said those operations were in no way intended to threaten China "and should not be interpreted by the Communist Chinese as a threat to them."

He added that he did not believe the Chinese would see the Laotian incursion as a threat.

What limits?

Nixon was questioned at the outset about the limits he would place on American involvement in Indochina. While restating that the United States would use neither ground forces nor advisers in Laos or Cambodia, he said: "I'm not going to place any limitation in our use of airpower."

Then he added that, of course, tactical nuclear weapons would be out of the question.

Most of the news conference session hinged on foreign policy matters. Some highlights:

—Nixon said U.S. troop withdrawals from South Vietnam will go forward on schedule and the Paris peace talks will be kept alive but, in that regard, he declared: "We're not going to make any more concessions" diplomatically.

Middle East

—The president described himself as encouraged by developments in the Middle East, declaring that he felt the United Arab Republic had been "more forthcoming" than expected and added Israel had taken a similar course. Saying the United States would not exert pressure on either side, he predicted that the Mideast ceasefire, when it expires, will be extended.

—Nixon said the United States is closely watching movements of a Soviet nuclear submarine in the Cuban area to determine whether it is being serviced there. Such servicing, he said, would be regarded as a violation of an understanding under which the Soviet Union has agreed to keep Cuba free of offensive weapons.

REDS WARN U.S.

PARIS (AP) — Communist delegates to the Vietnam peace talks charged today that President Nixon is preparing to attack North Vietnam and warned that such a move would threaten Communist China.

Xuan Thuy, head of the Hanoi delegation told reporters as he entered the 103rd session of the talks that Nixon's statements at his news conference Wednesday "prove he will not negotiate seriously but is hoping for a victory."

Ottawa spending aimed at expansion

By NICK HILLS
Southam News Services

OTTAWA — The government has unveiled "expansionary" spending estimates for 1971-72 totalling $14,352,200,000—an increase of more than one billion dollars over spending for the fiscal year ending March 31.

Treasury Board president C. M. Drury said the government intended to put more money into the economy than it takes out during the new fiscal year, and his would result in a budgetary deficit.

"These estimates will have an expansionary tendency," he said. "Public expenditures this year will be higher."

But he refused to predict how many new jobs the government's expansionary policies would create. The major part of this burden was on the private sector, he added.

The estimate of government spending for the year beginning April 1 is 11.2 per cent higher than the total of $12.9 billion originally estimated last February for the fiscal year 1970-71. That total for the 12 months, now ending, has risen to $13,348,000,000 with the addition of supplementary estimates through the year.

If supplementary spending

More SPENDING Page 6
Other spending stories on Page 45

French language spending up 500%

OTTAWA (CP) — Federal budget predictions for 1971-72 tabled in the Commons Wednesday showed a five-fold increase in the amount allotted for grants and contributions to world French-language organizations.

The total forecast was $1.1 million, compared with $218,500 budgeted in 1970-71 for Canada's participation in international French-language organizations.

In presenting the budget forecasts, Bud Drury, president of the treasury board, said Canada's contribution to the agency for cultural and technical co-operation between French-speaking countries will be increased to $615,000 from $110,000. An additional $85,000 would be spent on participation in certain activities of the agency.

Canada would provide $350,000 to the international conference of French-language states compared with $50,000 the previous year.

Where to find it

● TransCanada gets permission to start immediately on a major pipeline-building program, partly on grounds that it would provide winter jobs in northern Ontario. Story on Page 13.

Art Evans	13	Letters To The Journal	4
Ann Landers	16	News Digest	46
Barry Westgate	21	Patterns	34
Births, Deaths, Marriages	30	Sport	22-26
Bridge	32	Theatres, Entertainm't	18, 19
Business, Stocks	8, 9	TV, Radio	45
Charles Lynch	5	Wayne Overland	22
Classified Ads	31-42		
Comics, Features	27		
Comment	4		
Crossword Puzzle	35		
Family Section	14-17		
Focus on People	29		
Horoscope	33		
June Sheppard	14		

Weather

Mainly sunny with a high of 25-30. Winds southeast 15. Sunny and warmer Friday. High 30-35, low tonight near 15. Details on Page 2.

IT'S LARF-CENY

OLD HARLOW, England (AP) — A middle-aged bandit was laughed all the way out of the bank Wednesday.

Cashier Teresa Dellar took one look at the man with the gun and got an uncontrollable fit of the giggles.

"Put all the money you've got in this bag,'" he tried to snarl, handing her a plastic shopping bag and pointing a plastic toy pistol.

Teresa, 22, handed the bag back to him, empty, and kept on laughing.

"I'm not joking, you know,'" said the bandit.

His embarrassment then gave way to a total loss of nerve and he rushed out of the bank, hopped on his bike and pedalled away.

"I began giggling when I saw that silly plastic gun and I just couldn't stop," Teresa said. "He looked so pathetic."

FUDDLE
DUDDLE

FUDDLE-DUDDLE FAD
Trudeau's words immortalized on sweatshirt

HE SEES A BUNDLE IN FUDDLE-DUDDLE

TORONTO (CP) — Prime Minister Trudeau may or may not have mouthed it in the Commons, but Morris Hackman has it right on the button.

Says Mr. Hackman, a novelty store proprietor here:

"Fuddle-duddle buttons are just the beginning."

Mr. Hackman, also known as Morris the Button Man, is going along with Mr. Trudeau's suggestion that he may have mouthed the term "fuddle-duddle" in the Commons Tuesday rather than the frowned-upon four-letter expression some have attributed to him.

"It's fantastic," said Mr. Hackman, known for his varied stock of comic buttons. "It will be the greatest thing to hit North America in years.

"There's no telling how far this thing can go."

He may be right. Toronto shirtmaker Roy Silver already is planning to emblazon the phrase on sweatshirts.

Alberta Tories accused of jobless deceit

Municipal Affairs Minister Fred Colborne says the Progressive Conservative party in Alberta has distorted unemployment figures for political gain.

In a lengthy rebuttal to Opposition charges, Mr. Colborne said Wednesday an amendment reflecting non-confidence in the government is based on information that is false and misleading."

The Opposition amendment, submitted Monday by Dave Russell (PC—Calgary Victoria Park) "is a smokescreen designed to disguise the minority party's failure to recognize the soundness of government economic policy," he said.

Mr. Colborne was supported in debate by Ray Reierson, minister of labor and telephones, along with Keith Everett (St. Albert) and Charles Drain (Pincher Creek-Crowsnest).

The municipal affairs minister said Alberta's unemployment crisis will ease more quickly than in other provinces and insisted many times that Alberta's unemployment has been kept to a minimum.

He accused the Opposition of neglecting the "extent of public works projects being carried out which are providing employment in Alberta and . . . are responsible for the low rate of unemployment in Alberta."

Close examination of the record, said Mr. Colborne shows "the slowdown is not caused by a slowdown in government-financed construction projects; it is caused by a slowdown in construction projects by the private sector of our economy."

Mr. Reierson said the government has adopted a stringent policy of restricting overtime on construction and shiftwork

More COLBORNE Page 6

Alberta doctors received an average of $46,430 in first year of province's medicare program. Story on Page 21.

And Edmonton boosters found much to admire in City Hall columnist Frank Hutton – and often much to protest – as he kept a watchful eye on the city he loved so deeply.

It was a more activist newspaper as well. For example, feature writer Jim Davies was assigned to live on $204.27 for 30 days, and became the Pensioner-for-a-Month, one of the most successful series of the decade. Jan McMillan, another feature writer, went undercover as a patient in the mental health facility at Oliver, while 22-year-old Brian Tucker, who could pass for 15, hung out in the city's high schools for weeks, learning what teenagers were thinking and doing.

By the end of the decade, the newspaper offered its readers dozens of self-help columns on everything from gardening to dress patterns to car repair, and also inaugurated a Teen Page in the fall of 1978.

"We'll talk about drugs, sex, abortion, politics and all the other heavy duty things now and again," wrote Teen Page editor Ron Newton. "But we're also going to talk about music and entertainers. About parties, booze, dope, fathers, mothers, teachers, cars, clothes, jobs and junkies and a billion other things that makes the world happen."

The '70s may also have been the golden age of Letters to the Editor, as reader contributions often spilled over from the allocated page. Many writers were angry at perceived wrongs done to them at the hands of politicians, while others were critical of the newspaper itself.

Tuesday, Feb. 2, 1971, was a typical day for Letters to the Editor. They included a demand for increased ice time at indoor rinks for under-12 hockey players; a suggestion that cars be permitted to run red lights if there were no other vehicles in the area; a proposal that everyone rethink their stand on old-style Social Credit fiscal policies now that a new Depression was clearly at hand; a warning about the coming ice age, and finally a protest that car exhausts were the cause of pollution.

But a letter from March 11, 1972, was simply surreal.

"Dear Sir:

"My child, aged six months, eats your paper every day. Do you know anything in your printing ink that would be harmful to him or in other words would you advise me to stop feeding it to him?

"I love to give it to him. He enjoys it so much.

"Yours Sincerely,

....

"P.S.: I am very concerned and would appreciate it if you could help me."

To protect the innocent, the letter writer's name was withheld. Editor Andrew Snaddon, however, did publish a reply, advising the mother that a slim Monday edition would be a banquet for a child, but a heftier Wednesday newspaper might prove overwhelming.

The editorial page was another matter altogether, Snaddon said. "Unquestionably the Great Brain Food of The Journal daily diet, it is thought to be too heavy for some adults, let alone children," he told the troubled mother. "Again it is reasonably pointed out that it often proves indigestible, even to politicians who can stomach almost anything."

The arrival of publisher Pat O'Callaghan in 1976 also brought a

***Aug. 12, 1970*:** **Southgate Mall, the largest shopping centre west of Toronto, opens. "Southgate is magnificent. Southgate is lovely. I'm trying to find words to describe it," says Lt.-Gov. Grant MacEwan as he opens the $25-million complex. "It's like the opening of a world's fair or a city within a city."**

***Aug. 20, 1970*:** **"Who needs 'em – those long, draggy, frumpy outfits on the mannequins of every clothing store in town?... Certainly not the girls whose legs they are destined to cover. And most definitely not the males of Edmonton, presently enjoying the best leg-viewing in centuries...They're the ugliest dresses I've ever seen – they make girls of 18 look like old crones," said one man window-shopping with his mini-clad girlfriend at the fashion boutiques on Jasper Avenue. "I don't believe girls will really wear them," said another hemline watcher, a construction worker on a downtown street. "...married men don't seem any happier...'If my wife ever dares buy one of those things, I'd divorce her,' said one." – The midi, a mid-calf skirt, arrives in Edmonton.**

Town's caterpillar plague a squishy, popping mess

ALONSA, Man. (CP) — Forest tent caterpillars have blanketed this farming region 100 miles northwest of Winnipeg, destroying gardens, stripping poplar trees on thousands of acres and leaving many area residents feeling nauseous and near despair.

In the last two weeks, the caterpillars have hit the region in such hordes that it is impossible to take a step without hearing the sickening pop of a fat caterpillar bursting under foot.

This is the third consecutive year that the black pests have infested the area. Residents say each year's attack has been worse than the previous one.

"This is what we eat with, sleep with and live with," said Helen Oleschak, gesturing around her farm home. "The last thing you see before you shut your eyes at night are worms."

Her husband Bill said the well water has started to take on a foul smell that the caterpillars leave behind them, and the family has to boil the water before use.

Another local resident, Jean Dunn, said: "The kids can't go out to play. We have to go out to do chores, and you have to put a coat over your head in the barn and chicken house, or the worms drop down your neck.

"We have to keep both doors shut — they get under the screen door. There's no use cleaning the house."

The caterpillars, when squashed, leave a tar-like stain that local residents say is next to impossible to remove. The caterpillars lie still at night but when the morning sun warms them, they set off for the shade.

At another farm, the leaves of a poplar tree were gone and the caterpillars, having eaten tomato, cabbage and lettuce plants in the garden, were just starting on the beans.

"I shovel them into piles on the driveway," said Mrs. Edward Brown. "They seem to die when you pile them up. They're too wet to burn."

Storekeeper Arnold Weitzel, to seek help from the provincial government, said the government's student temporary employment program should be used to haul away the masses of dead caterpillars and to clean up in their wake.

To illustrate their case, Mr. Weitzel and Alonsa rancher Henry Oleschuk took a large bag full of caterpillars into the office of Sidney Green, minister of environmental management.

Mr. Green's first reaction was to order the bag out of his office. The subsequent talks were friendly and the visitors asked for government help after the caterpillars become dormant.

Mr. Green said he would consider clean-up aid "when the scourge passes." He was not optimistic, however, because there apparently is no way to prevent the infestations.

Mr. Weitzel said the caterpillars lie six inches deep around his Alonsa store. In trying to climb over a building, the worms pile up against it.

"We haul a half-ton truck load away every day," he said. He said people have tried dousing the caterpillars with salt, gasoline, lime and diesel fuel, all without success. "They seem to thrive on diesel," he said.

Picture on Page 2

Edmonton Journal

FORECAST CLOUDY | EDMONTON, ALBERTA, MONDAY, JUNE 24, 1974 | PRICE 15c

Crowd of thousands at opening of Ukrainian Cultural Heritage Village

Next war nuclear, Arabs say

By THE ASSOCIATED PRESS

The semi-official Egyptian newspaper Al Ahram warned today that the next Middle East war might be a nuclear confrontation. It said if Israel does not agree to a just and lasting peace in the area Tel Aviv will be responsible.

Meanwhile, the Palestinian Liberation organization (PLO) said disengagement of Israeli and Syrian forces was a step toward peace, but that it will continue to fight until the Palestinian problem is settled.

The Israeli-Syrian troop disengagement in the Golan Heights neared completion today, leaving only the ruins of the town of Kuneitra to be given up.

Israeli troops on the Golan Heights handed a one-mile strip of captured Syrian territory over to United Nations forces, and retreated to positions wes of he 1967 ceasefire line.

The strip of land was the last part of the 300-square-mile Syrian bulge captured during last October's Arab-Israeli war. The Israeli withdrawal from it was the third phase in the disengagement negotiated by United States State Secretary Henry Kissinger.

Spotters move

The disengagement is to be completed by Wednesday with the Israeli evacuation of Kuneitra, the war-ravaged Golan Heights town captured by Israel in the 1967 war.

Israel's semi-official state radio reported the withdrawal Syrian soldiers who acted as spotters for artillery batteries that attacked Israeli positions on Mount Hermon during and after the October war. Israel had said that the Syrian spotters disguised themselves as Palestinian guerrillas.

In Jerusalem, Premier Yitzhak Rabin said Israel's only chance for survival is to strengthen its defences while searching for peace. He told a group of Zionist leaders that Israel will continue to attack Arab guerrillas in Lebanon "in every place and at every time it deems necessary."

Ship in canal

Yosef Tekoah, Israel's ambassador to the United Nations, said that if the UN Security Council meets to discuss Israel's air attacks last week and Palestinian strongholds in Lebanon, he will call for sanctions against countries that allow terrorists to operate from their territory.

The U.S. Navy announced that a navy landing craft, the 522-foot LST Barnstable County, has moved halfway down the Suez canal and anchored off Ismailia to serve as a base for U.S. units helping to clear the waterway of wrecks and explosives.

Israelis leave village in ruins

KUNEITRA (CP) — High in the scarred Golan Heights, the overworked 150-man Canadian contingent is struggling to maintain supplies to the newest United Nations force while also keeping an uneasy eye on this ravaged town that might soon be a new threat to ultra-sensitive Israeli-Syrian relations.

In their last few days of occupation of the town proper, Israeli troops were busy wrecking its buildings. The town is within the new buffer zone, about 50 yards down the road from Canadian Camp Roofless, part of the United Nations Disengagement Observer Force (UNDOF) facilities.

Although the Israeli troops Sunday evacuated a mile-wide strip of Golan Heights land captured in the October war, they still were in possession of Kuneitra and some land around Rafid, both taken in 1967, and two positions at the peak of Mount Hermon seized in October.

When the Syrians finally start moving in at 5 p.m. local time Tuesday, after the Israelis withdraw in the fourth and final phase of the disengagement agreement, it seems likely that hardly a stone will be left on stone in Kuneitra.

The consensus here is that the Syrians have little idea what has been going on and are going to be dismayed and angry to inherit what one officer termed "a four-foot-high town."

Of the buildings still standing, most are daubed with a great white X—the sign they are marked for destruction. Local intelligence is that the only buildings left will be a couple of mosques, a Christian church and what is left of the hospital.

Israeli authorities openly

More VILLAGE Page 10

Gateway to Ukrainian past

By PAUL ROBERTON
Of The Journal

The Ukrainian Cultural Heritage Village was the doorway to the past for thousands Sunday afternoon.

The village is only two miles east of Elk Island Park but the distance is greater than just miles between the small village shops and Edmonton's mammoth stores and apartment blocks.

Looking down the village's main street — the Ukrainian Farmers Hall, the Cafe Sniatyn, Fedoruk's Photo Studio, Luzan Grocery and Wostok Hardware face the street — a project organizer said the village would grow as more buildings are found and transported to the site.

"It'll never be finished," said Dave Ruptash after the village was officially opened by Frank Lakusta, founder and president of the village. Working with a $270,000 Local Initiatives Program grant, organizers located and transported about 25 buildings that the Ukrainian pioneers used when settling in Alberta after the 1890s.

How are the buildings located? "This is our country, we live around here," Mr. Ruptash replied, adding the buildings weren't difficult to move.

The project started about 15 months ago when Mr. Lakusta donated the 23-acre site.

Why start it? "To preserve some of the past. So we can show the way our fathers built Western Canada. So the children can see what they did and how they lived and what they had to work with," Mr. Lakusta said.

And he has visions of even greater things. Why not have an old time railway between the village and North Cooking Lake, he asked the crowd sitting on the hills.

More than 3,000 people had swarmed to the village by mid-afternoon. The village is open daily from 10 a.m. to 6 p.m.

Crowds wandered through the hardware store, the blacksmith shop and the churches, the parents holding onto children and children onto soft drinks.

Once more the Cafe Sniatyn became a cafe with curious customers lining up to order pyrogy, holubtsi and kubassa. The food was the same as the pioneers ate in the old country. The prices were different, but still reasonable.

Adults laughed when they

More UKRAINIAN Page 10

RCMP Superintendent W. J. G. Perry and Mayor Ivor Dent opening police building

Forest crew stays on job until fire trail is cold

By JACK DANYLCHUK
Of The Journal

FOX CREEK — Dennis Halladay looked up from the laborious task of "cold trailing" the fire-blackened debris at the base of a lightning-splintered 80-foot balsam fir.

"Look, you might as well help me because we're not going home until I'm convinced this fire is out — and I'm not convinced.

The 23-year-old graduate of the Saskatoon Institute of Applied Arts and Sciences in his first year as an Alberta forestry officer was making a promise, not a threat to the eight-man crew.

Hot, tired and bothered to distraction by clouds of mosquitoes brought out by sun showers, the crew looked at the helicopter parked invitingly among grass and wild flowers, then at Mr. Halladay rooting bare handed through the charred moss and boughs.

Using pick-axes, shovels and water slogged uphill from a creek one-third of a mile away, the crew had battled the fire for an hour and a half and beaten it.

"Okay, get more water, and the rest of you start looking," ordered Mr. Halladay. A half-hour later, everyone had stowed the equipment and the helicopter was lifting off, taking the crew back to the Fox Creek base camp.

"Cold trailing is the only way to make certain that a fire like that is out," explained the forestry officer. He found a half-dozen hot spots in his search; still-glowing embers that could have brought the blaze to life during the night.

As a fire W1-15-74 was not impressive. It burned an area in a logged-out portion of the Whitecourt Forest about the size of a garden plot.

Forestry officer Halladay's report, which will be added to the statistical collection in the Edmonton forestry headquarters, said the eight-man crew arrived by helicopter at 1801 hours and had the fire under control by 1815 hours.

W1-15-74 was started by lightning on Crown land. Available fuels were grass and slash (logging debris). The fuel hazard was extreme, as was the potential for the fire to build and spread.

The small, local fire lacked

More FOREST Page 10

Where to find it

Ann Landers	16
Births, Deaths, Marriages	28
Bridge	32
Business, Stocks	63-65
Classified Ads	29-50
Comics, Features	17
Editorial	4
Crossword Puzzle	33
Entertainment	24, 25
Family Section	14-16
Frank Hutton	3
Focus on People	12
Horoscope	31
Letters To The Journal	4
News Digest	7
Patterns	38, 46
Sport	55-62
Temperatures	11
TV, Radio	19
Wayne Overland	55

Weather

Mosly cloudy this afternoon. Isolated thunderstorms this evening. Gusty west winds near the thunderstorms. Low near 50. Tomorrow sunny, high near 75.

WHALE OF PROTEST JUST BAG OF WIND

LONDON(AP) —An anti-whaling demonstration by a conservationist group was deflated today when its 30-foot plastic whale sank in the River Thames.

Friends of the Earth planned to moor the whale near Vauxhall Bridge to greet delegates arriving for the International Whaling Commission's annual meeting.

But as the whale was being inflated it sprang a leak in one of its seams. Repair efforts failed and the whale's floppy carcass was hauled aboard a police launch and taken away.

"It's a great pity. It was a splendid beast but it did not reach its full magnificence," said Richard Sandbrook, director of Friends of the Earth.

Nuclear admission leads to U.K. row

LONDON (AP) — Britain conducted a nuclear test a few weeks ago, Prime Minister Harold Wilson told the House of Commons today.

Wilson said the experiment took place within the framework of the partial test-ban treaty of 1963 and the non-proliferation treaty of 1968

Wilson was replying to questions from left-wing MPs of his own Labor party. They were angered by a weekend press report which said Britain was about to explode a nuclear device at the United States underground nuclear testing range in Nevada.

They claimed any nuclear testing by Britain goes against Labor party policy, as decided by its annual conference last year. A motion was passed then agreeing to scrap all nuclear bases in Britain, including the Polaris submarine bases in Scotland.

France and China set off nuclear explosions in the atmosphere a week ago, and India set off its first nuclear test under ground on May 18.

Wilson's announcement comes at a time when the U.S. and the Soviet Union appear to be moving toward an agreement on limiting underground nuclear testing.

It also coincides with agreements by the U.S. to supply Egypt and Israel with aid to develop nuclear power for peaceful purposes.

Ethiopian guerrillas offer apologies

Nurse shot because her shoe fell off

ADDIS ABABA (AP) — Ethiopian guerrillas killed a Dutch nurse they kidnapped because one of her shoes kept falling off and she couldn't keep up as they ran through the bush, said her companion.

Deborah Dortzbach, a pregnant, 24-year-old missionary nurse from Freehold, N.J., kidnapped May 27 with the Dutch nurse Anna Stickwerda, said the guerrillas of the Eritrean Liberation Front (E.L.F.) asked her to relay their apologies for the killing.

Mrs. Dortzbach, released unharmed Saturday, told her story to her associates in the Society of International Missions in Asmara, the capital of the northern province of Eritrea. She was reported in good health despite her ordeal but has been in seclusion with her husband Karl in the Asmara area since her release.

The guerrillas kidnapped Mrs. Dortzbach and Miss Stickwerda, 54, from an American Evangelical Mission hospital in an area partly controlled by the E.L.F. 25 miles from Asmara.

Mrs. Dortzbach's friends said she told this story:

After they were taken from the hospital at gunpoint, Miss Stickwerda and Mrs. Dortzbach were forced to run through the bush toward a hideout. But the Dutch nurse was unable to keep up.

One shoe fell off repeatedly, and the guerrillas told the woman she would have to hurry. She fell to the ground, gasping: "I can't go on. I can't go on."

A guerrilla bent down and shot her in the head.

There was speculation that the guerrilla might have been frightened into shooting by the appearance overhead of a helicopter. But the helicopter was piloted by Grant Wyatt, a Canadian, instead of by Ethiopian soldiers, and the guerrillas captured Wyatt when he landed nearby.

Wyatt, 30, of Calgary, had been hoping to meet E.L.F. leaders and rescue three Americans and two Canadians captured while prospecting for oil three months ago. Wyatt was later released, but the other five men are still held.

The guerrillas told Mrs. Dortzbach the shooting of the Dutch nurse was a "tactical mistake."

A spokesman for the Society of International Missions said the guerrillas released Mrs. Dortzbach unconditionally. He said she brought an apology from the E.L.F. for the shooting and assurances that the mission hospital will not be harassed again.

The Canadians and Americans still held by the E.L.F. are Don Wederfort, 27, of Calgary; Cliff James, 27, Walkerton, Ont.; Powers Cayce, 36, Plainview, Tex., Matte, 52, an American with landed-immigrant status in Canada; and U.S. citizen William Rogers.

Wederfort is president of CanWest Aviation Ltd. of Calgary and Wyatt is a company pilot. Wederfort and his party of four geologists were doing survey work for Tenneco Co. of Houston, Tex., when their helicopter was forced down by a storm and they were taken prisoner March 26.

different level of energy to the newspaper. The colourful, Irish-born O'Callaghan may never have actually looked for a fight, but he was never known to back down from one either.

Among other things, he fought city hall and won when aldermen gave up a pay raise they had secretly voted themselves. In order to notch that win, O'Callaghan and the newspaper engaged in a lengthy, and very public, court fight.

He then called on beer drinkers to boycott Molson products when that company – then the owners of the Montreal Canadiens – refused to support Edmonton's entry into the National Hockey League. He didn't win that one single-handedly, but certainly annoyed the brewery.

He also had confidence in the city and its future. In a front-page story from April 1, 1978, O'Callaghan announced the start of construction on a $35-million *Journal* production plant on a 7.5-acre site on the corner of 93rd Avenue and 49th Street. "We have grown with the city and intend be around for at least another 75 years."

There was energy, too, in the social changes felt by subscribers as they weighed the difference between multiculturalism and biculturalism and watched the beginnings of an environmental movement develop in the province.

There were also major strides made in the area of women's rights.

In fact, the decade had opened with the tabling of a 4,887-page report from the Royal Commission on the Status of Women that called for equality in every field in both public and private life.

The highlights of the recommendations included abortion on demand for women pregnant 12 weeks or less, a network of child-care centres, sterilization on demand for birth control reasons and 18 weeks of maternity leave with unemployment insurance.

The commission was chaired by "Mrs. John Bird, sometimes known as Anne Francis," *The Journal*'s page 1 story said. She was described as "the white-haired 62-year-old, who looks and talks like the principal of an English school for girls."

Editorially, the newspaper more or less supported the recommendations of the commission, although cautioned that progress might be slow.

"Any real advancement in the status of women depends on changes in public attitudes and in this area, women are as important as men. Perhaps they are more important since they play a bigger part – as mothers and teachers – in shaping the attitudes of the next generation. Basic changes in society – and this is what the question is all about – won't come overnight."

The RCMP proved the editorial writers correct. Three years after the commission recommended women recruits be accepted into the 100-year-old force, the necessary changes had not been made.

In a story from the spring of 1973, RCMP Commissioner W.L. Higgitt told the Justice and Legal Affairs Committee of the House of Commons that admitting women to the force presented some major obstacles.

"And would a girl want to go to Pond Inlet, N.W.T., where she might have to eat seal flippers for three years?" he asked.

***Oct. 14, 1970*:**
"Screaming and whooping, the beaded, feathered and war-painted Indians spurred their horses through the open gates of Fort Edmonton…Six Indians, five braves and a woman, reined their horses to a stop in the centre of the compound amid flashing photographers' bulbs and the applause of several hundred people…Fort Edmonton was officially open…." – First paragraphs of a story on the opening of Fort Edmonton.

***Nov. 7, 1970*:**
***The Journal* formally adopts the requirement of signed letters to the editor.**

***Nov. 12, 1970*:**
Albertans are allowed to buy drinks until midnight and have until 1 a.m. to finish them on weekdays. Previous regulations called for an 11:30 p.m. serving time closure with a 30-minute drink-up time.

***Nov. 28, 1970*:**
Ninety teenage girls, members of the Edmonton All-Girls Drum and Bugle Band, represent Edmonton in the annual Grey Cup parade in Toronto.

New Camaro.

We've never announced a car at this time before. But then nobody's ever announced a car like this before.

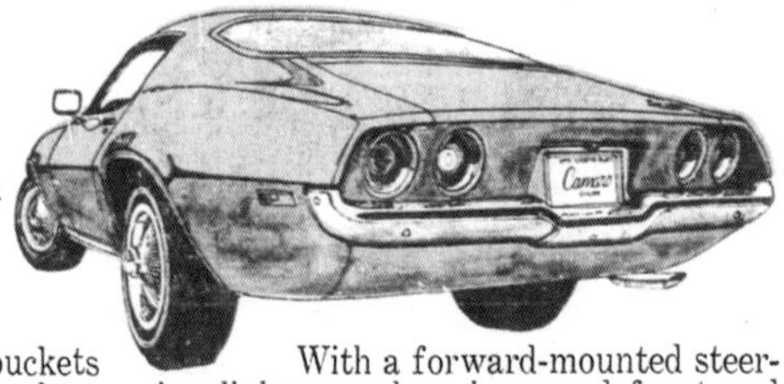

Super Hugger

If it were just an ordinary sportster, we might have introduced it at the ordinary time.

But we didn't.

And as you can see, time was on our side.

Because we didn't bother with the simulated air scoops. Or any other put-ons that might put you off.

Instead we took the time to build a whole new car from the ground up. In four distinctive versions: Standard, Rally Sport, Super Sport and Z28.

We started with a sleek new shape and a low road-hugging stance. So it hovers a few short inches from the pavement. Right down there with Corvette.

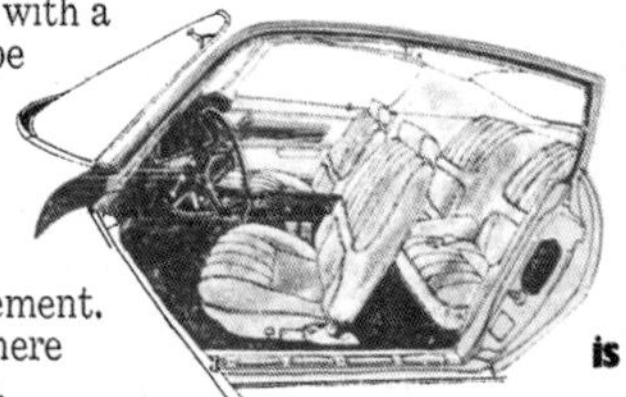

To that we added more hood. A faster fastback. More window area. And wider doors for easier entry.

On RS models, there's even a resilient bumper that surrounds the grille. To protect against nicks and knocks.

Compare the new Camaro with any competitive car in its field.

If you can find one.

Two extra buckets. No extra bucks.

Most sportsters give you two buckets in front. And a sofa in back. We've done them two better.

The back seat sofa is out. In are two rear bucket-styled cushions.

Up front the buckets are deeply contoured to put you firmly in place. And keep you there. Even in tight turns.

The instrument panel is just as functional. It's flat black and wraps around. With enough dials and instrumentation to make you think you're piloting a 747.

Only with this one you don't need a flight crew.

The special handling is built right in.

Camaro always had a tough reputation when it came to taking on tight turns. Now we've made it tougher.

With a forward-mounted steering linkage and an improved front and rear suspension that give the new Camaro a leech-like grip on the road.

It's something other cars will have a tough time coming to grips with.

What motivates all this?

Six power plants up to the 360-hp Turbo-Fire 350 you can order. And four transmissions.

Pick the combination that best suits your driving.

Then go pick on an open road.

Standard front disc brakes. You stop as well as you go.

It's only natural.

With all that go, you want an equal amount of stop. You've got it.

Front disc brakes are standard. For less heat buildup. And more resistance to fade.

New Camaro. The Super Hugger.

Other sportsters always feared it might come to this. And they were right.

Only their timing was wrong.

Putting you first, keeps us first.

CHEVROLET

See it. At your Chevrolet Sports Dept.

Camaro Sport Coupe with RS equipment.

GM

SEE YOUR LOCAL AUTHORIZED CHEVROLET DEALER

AUTHORIZED CAMARO DEALERS IN EDMONTON:

EDMONTON MOTORS LIMITED
115 STREET AND JASPER AVENUE
488-7211

DON WHEATON LTD.
10727 WHYTE (82) AVENUE
439-0071

STEDELBAUER CHEV. OLDS. LTD.
CORNER 97th STREET AND 132nd AVENUE
PHONE 476-6211

The Journal's fascination with the area of women's rights led to dozens of stories on women whose careers made them unique for their time, including a feature story on Maureen Trudel, the city's first female letter carrier in 1974. The newspaper pondered the issue of whether she should be called a "postgirl."

And in 1975 when the city had its first woman bus driver in Kathleen Andrews, *The Journal* conducted a survey of passengers to see how they reacted. Most seemed happy with the idea.

"I'm surprised how well she can handle the thing," said passenger Larry Madden. "Most men can't handle a bus as well."

City columnist Barry Westgate took a contrary view of women's equality. When a pro-choice group appeared before city council seeking funding, he told aldermen to ignore them. "Heck, they even kept their clothes on," he wrote. "Women's Lib gals should be prepared to punctuate the cause by baring all. Or at least some. In itself, that attracts attention, if the project never could.

"There have always been people around who live to parade, to parrot, to pander and pontificate about personal rights and social evils.

"Put 'em to work with a mop and pail. Not a shovel. Shovels are for men."

There was also another type of brute energy, the kind that meant construction cranes seemed a permanent part of the city's skyline as shiny new office towers thrust, storey after storey, into Edmonton's big blue sky.

Not everyone marvelled at the new construction, however. It was also a time when volunteers and businessmen used their energy to retain some of the city's past, and a start was made on turning Strathcona, on the city's south side, into a historic shopping and entertainment Mecca.

And *The Journal*'s William Thorsell, then an editorial writer who would become assistant editor in the '80s, noted the irony of a city that celebrated its connection with history by commemorating the Klondike gold rush each year, yet allowed its past to be torn up.

In a 1976 op-ed piece headlined "The city has lost its soul," Thorsell recalled watching a 1972 K-Days celebration in Sir Winston Churchill Square while "immediately across the street a giant crane swung a wrecking ball into the pillars of the old courthouse.

"Just as the Klondike girls launched into the recreation of dance-hall frivolity, the wrecking ball smashed through the cornice of the venerable building."

Meanwhile, on the other side of the square, the distinctive Victorian-style post office stood empty. It too, was destroyed, making way for the Westin Hotel.

"Both of these historic buildings were major urban landmarks in Edmonton, evidence of an age and of the values of an earlier time," Thorsell wrote. "Both provided priceless dimension and cultural continuity to our urban environment."

Other less-classic buildings and institutions went as well. Bargain stores such as the Met and Kresge's in the city's centre shut down, and the proud, classy King Edward Hotel on 101st Street burned to the ground. Downtown was going through fundamental changes, many of which were

***Dec. 19, 1970*:**
City council passes a bylaw establishing four north/south wards, each to elect three aldermen in the upcoming October 1971 election.

***April 1, 1971*:**
Eighteen-year-olds can now vote, run for city or town council and school boards, marry without parental consent and hold property. For many, however, that particular Fool's Day meant that they could also take their first legal drink in the province of Alberta.

***March 3, 1971*:**
City population is 435,504, up from 422,418 the year before. *Journal* circulation stands at 160,000.

***May 26, 1971*:**
Construction begins on the $22-million Londonderry Shopping Mall on 66th Street and 137th Avenue.

***Sept. 1, 1971*:**
Grant MacEwan Community College opens its doors for the first time. The college, part of which was located in an old Dominion store on 80th Street and 118th Avenue, "accepted any applicant who possesses the ability in any of its course offerings."

***Nov. 19, 1971*:**
***The Journal* devotes an entire**

Platforms are real big in these shoes

Two-toned shoe sample of what's ahead for men

Next winter's boots will have lot of sole

There's one thing you can say about the 1973 fall and winter boot fashions: They've got sole, sister.

In fact they're almost all sole.

If women follow fashion next winter they will be clumping along the street on thick soles and high heels, as stiff legged as a stilt walker.

Low heel boots are out and the trend is towards high platform boots with soles several inches high in leather, crepe or polyurethane, a light plastic.

These are the boots that were shown in Edmonton recently at the Winter Boot Show.

The bump or full toe has come in strong for next year but the single dominant feature is the sole treatment.

In the more conservative high fashion lines, the dominant boot is the plain shaft with a three-inch heel and a one-inch platform sole. But some of the funkier fashions have boots with towering 5½-inch heels and a 2½-inch platform sole.

Whether or not this type of boot will be harmful to the ankle is not known at this time. City orthopedic surgeons and podiatrists say they won't know until the boots are in and they have some experience with them.

They say they haven't had problems with platform soles so far but one orthopedic surgeon, Dr. John Gort, said he suspects women will "lose their balance and trip all over the place."

The trend is towards tall boots about 16 inches high but low boots are coming in. Some conservative styles are meant to be worn with pants while others are short sports boots and come in bright colors in soft suede. But again, many of these also have the platform sole.

For real comfort there are apres ski and snow boots both low and high made of suede, leather or fur.

There is considerably less interest in suede but leather and man-made materials are in. Women wanting a leather boot this year are really going to have to pay for it. The man-made materials are mostly vinyl-based. Many boots use a combination of man-made material and leather.

One retailer suggested the cost of leather boots could increase by five to 10 per cent. A boot that sold for $45 last fall could be $50 next fall. The reason, he explained, was that most high grade boots are made of goat skin which is supplied by Argentina, one of the world's largest suppliers of hides. Since early last year though the number of hides exported from that country has dropped and there is now a shortage of hides.

Simplicity in styling is the key word although some have non-functional lacing for decoration or a decorative trim.

The multi-color boot — so strong last year—is out now. There are some brown tone on tone boots as well as solid basic black and brown. Other colors include navy, green, red, purple, bone, the antique look. Tan is gaining in importance.

Boots were supplied by: Cristina Shoe Co. Ltd.; Rosita Shoe Co. and La Vallee Shoes.

The legs inside the boots are those of models Wendy Jewell and Sherri Tomlinson.

Two of the more conservative styles

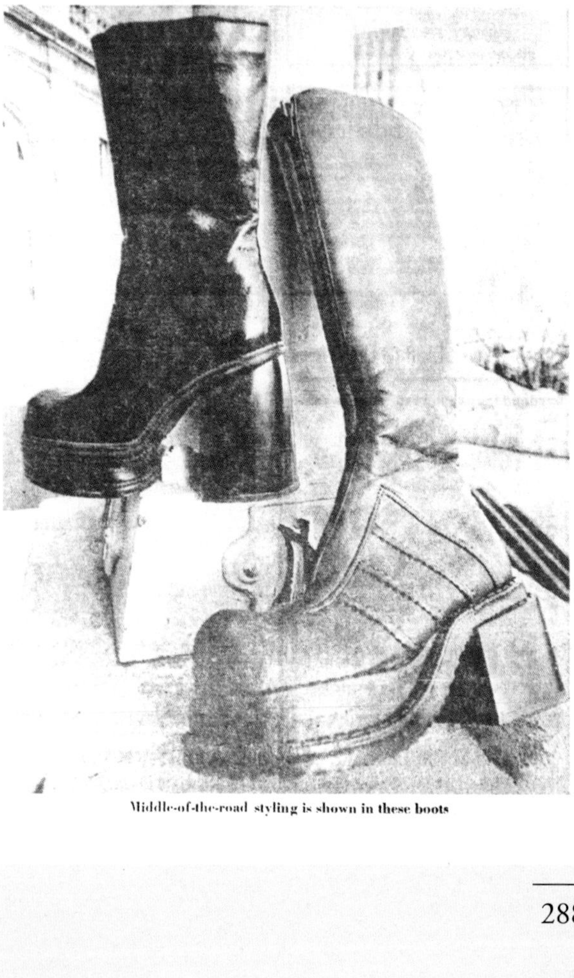

Middle-of-the-road styling is shown in these boots

Journal photos by Steve Makris
Text by Judy Gunion

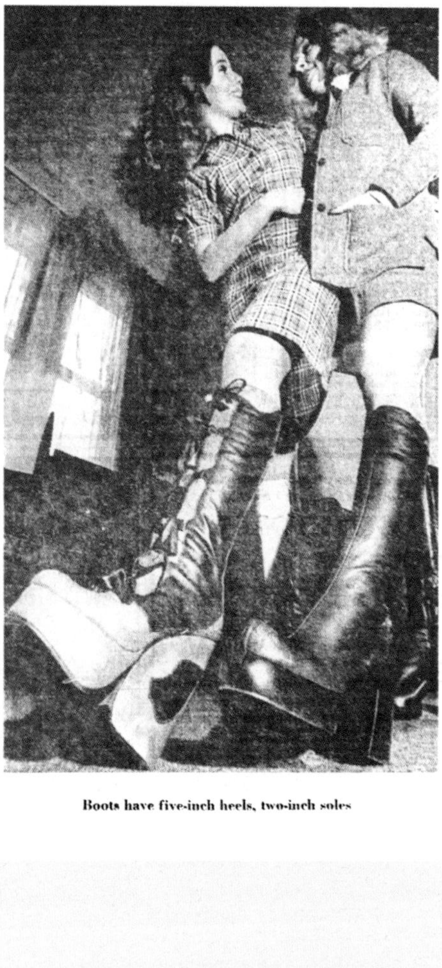

Boots have five-inch heels, two-inch soles

noted by assistant editor Stan Williams in a story published on the last day of operation for the food market at Eaton's city-centre store.

Williams was sorry to see the passing of the Eaton's groceteria, which in the mid-20s, had taken up 12,000 square-feet, as it closed forever on May 26, 1977, although he confessed he and his family no longer made the weekly shopping trip to the store.

"We stayed with the store until well into the '60s, but then we succumbed to a nearer shopping centre for the usual reason – coming downtown to shop took too much time.

"So long, old friend. Another case of sic transit gloria...."

But under those traffic-clogged downtown Edmonton streets, there was also the kind of energy that gave the city the muscle to build a rapid transit system that would be the envy of other cities in the West. When it opened there were 6.9 kilometres of track and five stations from downtown to Belvedere. Today there are 10 stations and almost 13 kilometres of track, five of which are underground.

"Edmonton has a winner," reporter Don Thomas wrote after LRT opening day on April 18, 1978. Fares then were set at 40 cents. Most of the people Thomas surveyed on that first day liked what they saw.

Nick Kuzma, however, took a different view. "The cars are uncomfortable," Kuzma grumped. "The seats are too small, and the cars are too hot."

He predicted a dire future for what he termed "the biggest, most expensive flop Edmonton ever had."

"There will be violence," he said, "and possibly suicides."

The newspaper also reflected the enthusiastic energy of thousands of volunteers, so convinced of Edmonton's place in the world that they didn't hesitate for a moment to work at hosting the Commonwealth Games in 1978. It was an event second only to the Summer Olympics when it came to the number of athletes and officials.

"We won't be mistaken for a dot on the map any longer," trumpeted Mayor Cec Purves when the Games opened. "We couldn't buy all the help it's given this city in a thousand years."

The city's sports teams brought their own special energy to the city, too. It was exemplified by the magic of a young hockey genius named Wayne Gretzky who performed miracles on the ice at the spanking new Coliseum, and in the boundless will to win of the late '70s Edmonton Eskimos playing out of the magnificent Commonwealth Stadium, still one of the finest outdoor stadiums on the continent.

In the arts, energy could be found in the self-confidence of Joe Shoctor and John Neville, respectively founder and artistic director of the Citadel Theatre. It was their combined drive that led to the building of a dazzling new theatre complex.

Their enthusiasm was matched by dozens of other directors, producers, writers and actors who spearheaded the development of other, vital theatre groups that turned Edmonton into Canada's premiere theatre city.

It was the energy of hustle and bustle, of being able to strut just a bit, of seeing no end to the opportunities presented in all areas of life.

There was energy, too, in a new Progressive Conservative

page to the Procul Harum-Edmonton Symphony Orchestra recorded concert at the Jubilee Auditorium. The album that results – *Live at Edmonton* – features the hit *Conquistador* which becomes a million-seller.

***January 1972*:**
Cost of a monthly ETS bus pass is $10.

***Jan. 6, 1972*:**
City transportation director Don MacDonald proposes to city council a light rapid transit system. It would cost $23 million. On Jan. 24, city council agrees to include rapid transit in the city's transportation bylaw.

***Jan. 10, 1972*:**
City council approves the first stage of a development that will become Castle Downs and provide housing for 100,000 Edmontonians.

***Feb. 9, 1972*:**
Merchants and residents of the Strathcona area form a committee to push for preservation of a block on Whyte Avenue as an historic village.

***March 9, 1972*:**
City council decides on an exact-change bus fare system to start in April 1972. The adult fare will

THE EDMONTON JOURNAL, Tuesday, June 3, 1971 9

shop at Chargex.®

Imagine taking a lot of the good things about department store shopping and stretching them out over a number of different shops. That's the thinking that made Chargex into the family shopping plan!

Chargex offers you a huge variety of goods and services—as big a selection as you'll find anywhere. And they're right in your neighbourhood stores—some small, some department stores themselves. So with Chargex you can take care of all your shopping needs right close to home.

You get the goods and, like a department store, you get lots more too. Because Chargex can match any other shopping plan when it comes to charge card convenience. We use a billing system that's as easy and efficient as four of Canada's leading banks knew how to make it.

Every month, all of your purchases are shown on a single statement and mailed to you. You simply send us one cheque. If you pay for these purchases within 25 days of your billing date, you avoid any service charges at all. But if you choose to spread your payments out, you can take advantage of terms and interest rates that are competitive with all the major retail shopping cards.

There you have it. We took some of the best ideas from the department stores and put those ideas to work in your neighbourhood.

Start shopping at Chargex by picking up an application form at your local bank or participating store.

CHARGEX

We've got a store near you.

SHOP

® Chargex is a registered trade mark

administration, elected in 1971. Led by Peter Lougheed, the young and exciting new premier, the Tories soundly defeated the 36-year-old moribund Social Credit government under Harry Strom, the ill-at-ease Southern Alberta farmer who had been chosen to replace the patrician Ernest Manning.

The Tory platform was a vigorous, action-oriented one, aimed at an electorate that was looking for change.

And the 43-year-old Lougheed seemed tireless. Political affairs reporter Bob Bell was with him through an exhausting Aug. 24, 1971, six days before the election. They had logged 1,600 miles in 20 gruelling hours, and using three different aircraft, three cars and a pickup truck in order to make it to community meetings in places as far apart as Pincher Creek in the south to Fort Chipewyan in the north.

Lougheed was an informal, shirtsleeve campaigner, meeting people on main streets and markets, community halls and farms.

In contrast, one of the many newspaper photographs taken during the election showed a dark-suited Strom, complete with white shirt and sensible necktie, looking uncomfortable at a Socred picnic.

And while Lougheed spoke off the cuff, Strom seemed to prefer standing at a lectern, consulting prepared notes. He was not light on his rhetorical feet.

Much of it came down to image, and it proved too much for Strom to overcome, although then-Senator Manning did his best to warn voters not to be seduced by slick campaigning.

"A 'Madison Avenue glamour boy' image has nothing whatsoever to do with a person's qualifications to govern the province wisely, Senator Ernest Manning said Wednesday," reported a story from an end-of-campaign rally at the city's Jubilee Auditorium.

The Socreds had given the province four decades of solid government and had earned the right to re-election, Manning told the crowd of 2,700. Voters should be wary, he said, of "an Ultra-Brite TV toothpaste smile and Avon Lady charm."

A week later, Lougheed was on the same stage. This time the auditorium was filled to overflowing with 4,000 cheering, placard-waving voters. "The short and slim PC leader, using a radio pocket mike that sometimes gave him trouble, appeared several times to be on the verge of heavy emotion as the partisan crowd roared him onward...."

The speech of the premier-to-be was interrupted again and again by chants of "NOW! NOW! NOW!" and "LOUGHEED! LOUGHEED! LOUGHEED!"

Former Social Credit cabinet minister Alf Hooke, who had been part of the 1935 Aberhart-led sweep, was button-holed by *The Journal* in the Jubilee Auditorium lobby after Lougheed's speech: "It looks ominous for the Stromites," Hooke told the paper.

Four days before the election, a *Journal* editorial came out in support of the Progressive Conservatives. "Premier Strom has predicted The Journal will oppose his re-election. Frankly, we do not presume the people are breathlessly awaiting our advice. However, he is right. We would not have much confidence in his administration if it were returned."

be 25 cents and the children's fare 15 cents.

***April 11, 1972*:**
The mayor's salary is raised to $25,000 a year, from $20,000 and councillor salaries go from $5,700 to $7,200. Only Mayor Ivor Dent and Ald. Ed Leger vote against the raises.

***April 22, 1972*:**
The Edmonton Exhibition Association announces plans to build a 16,000-seat, $9-million arena on its present grounds within two years.

***May 19, 1972*:**
Five Alberta daily newspapers, including the *Edmonton Journal*, establish the Alberta Press Council.

***June 20, 1972*:**
Bill Hunter, general manager of the Alberta Oilers of the World Hockey Association, signs Ray Kinasewich as the team's first coach.

***June 26, 1972*:**
Edmonton's new Law Courts Building opens. The new complex takes in two city blocks between 100th and 101st Streets and 102nd and 102A Avenues.

***Aug. 24, 1972*:**
The city learns it will host the 1978 Commonwealth Games.

Last American forces pull out of Vietnam

SAIGON (AP) — The last American forces pulled out of South Vietnam today after more than a decade of military intervention that cost 46,000 U.S. lives.

As the last 2,500 GIs flew home or to other bases in Southeast Asia, strong American air and naval forces remained on the perimeters of Indochina to keep up the war in Cambodia and to discourage a resumption of major fighting in South Vietnam and Laos.

The 7th Fleet was reported to have four carriers with 200 strike planes within range of Vietnam, and the Pentagon said there are 202 B-52 bombers at Guam and Thailand and more than 400 air force and marine fighter-bombers in Thailand.

Today's departures left a total of 1,034 uniformed American military men in Vietnam — 825 members of the U.S. delegation to the Joint Military Commission (JMC), 159 marine guards at the U.S. embassy and 50 military attaches at the embassy.

The JMC, made up of the United States, North and South Vietnam and the Viet Cong, was scheduled to be replaced today by a commission made up of South Vietnam and the Viet Cong. The 825 men of the U.S. delegation are scheduled to leave the country Friday and Saturday.

The U.S. failed in 11th-hour secret negotiations with Hanoi to keep alive the four-party Joint Military Commission (JMC) and prolong the American military presence, the North Vietnamese reported.

The U.S. sources said Washington had promised to press for an extension of the JMC set up to enforce the ceasefire agreement, in return for a guarantee that Canada would remain a member of the International Commission of Control and Supervision (ICCS). Only hours before the negotiations collapsed, Canada announced a decision to stay on the ICCS for an additional 60 days and urged "greater co-operation" among the four ICCS member nations —Indonesia, Hungary, Poland and Canada—to oversee the ceasefire.

The Canadians had coupled their willingness to serve on the ICCS force with a proviso that they would back out if fighting does not stop.

The last American troops left South Vietnam virtually around-the-clock in planes.

Some troops simply transferred to U.S. bases in Thailand, where the U.S. will continue to maintain a strong air arm to discourage any mass offensive in South Vietnam by the North Vietnamese.

The 825-man North Vietnamese and U.S. delegations to the JMC are to pull out Friday and Saturday.

Under terms of the agreement, the 60-day life of the commission expired at midnight Wednesday night, but it was extended another day to close out its business.

It now becomes a two-party Joint Military Commission made up of the two opposing South Vietnamese parties, the Saigon government and the Viet Cong.

Edmonton Journal

FORECAST: SUNNY — EDMONTON, ALBERTA, THURSDAY, MARCH 29, 1973 — 10c 15c with The Canadian and Color Comics

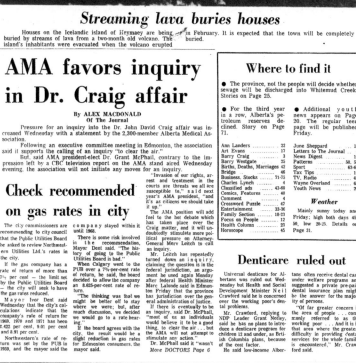

Streaming lava buries houses

Houses on the Icelandic island of Heymaey are being buried by streams of lava from a two-month old volcano. The island's inhabitants were evacuated when the volcano erupted in February. It is expected that the town will be completely buried.

Housewives ask national boycott of beef, pork

TORONTO (CP) — Some 600 Toronto housewives, organized to fight rising meat prices, are calling for a national boycott of beef and pork during the first week of April.

Women Against Soaring Prices (W.A.S.P.), plans to demonstrate against rising prices at a Toronto supermarket Saturday. Margaret Rouble, a spokesman for the group, hopes that "chain" phone calls and letters will result in a national boycott next week.

The women's call for a boycott followed similar action in the United States which has resulted in a sharp decline in the hog market. The U.S. National Farmers Organization has countered by telling its members to withhold hogs, cattle and lambs from the market.

Women in the group have been asked to call five friends to ask them to boycott "and they, in turn, have been asked to call others until this idea spreads right across the country," she said.

The response to calls made already has been "overwhelming."

But despite the response, city supermarket executives and food company executives say there is no indication of a consumer boycott coming.

Chester Wilcox, meat merchandising manager for Dominion Stores Ltd., said he didn't feel there was a boycott but added "... to some degree people have been switching from beef to pork and chicken."

Charles Gracey, manager of the Canadian Cattlemen's Association, said beef consumption is increasing with an "unprecedented consumer demand."

He said Canadians ate more than 86 pounds of beef per capita in 1971, 90 last year and will eat even more this year.

A boycott could hurt the consumer in the long run, he said. Cattle herds are increasing five times the rate of demand, and depressed beef prices could hurt this expansion and create shortages.

Hog markets in the Midwestern United States reported a second straight day of sharp price declines Wednesday as plans for next week's U.S.-wide meat boycott gained momentum.

Market officials called the falling prices unprecedented and said it appears farmers have panicked and are flooding the market.

There is no cause for alarm in the Alberta hog industry in the face of some price weak-

More PRICES Page 6

Ann Landers here

Mrs. Ross Munro (left) wife of Journal publisher Ross Munro, chats with Ann Landers at a Journal reception during the columnist's Edmonton visit Wednesday.

AMA favors inquiry in Dr. Craig affair

By ALEX MACDONALD
Of The Journal

Pressure for an inquiry into the Dr. John David Craig affair was increased Wednesday with a statement by the 2,300-member Alberta Medical Association.

Following an executive committee meeting in Edmonton, the association said it supports the calling of an inquiry "to clear the air."

But, said AMA president-elect Dr. Grant McPhail, contrary to the impression left by a CBC television report on the AMA stand aired Wednesday evening, the association will not initiate any moves for an inquiry.

"Invasion of our rights, arrest and treatment in the courts are threats we all are susceptible to," said next year's AMA president, "and it's as citizens we should take it up."

The AMA position will add fuel to the hot debate which has taken place over the Craig matter, and it will undoubtedly stimulate more political pressure on Attorney-General Merv Leitch to call an inquiry.

Mr. Leitch has repeatedly turned down an inquiry, claiming the question is in the federal jurisdiction, an argument he used again Monday after federal Health Minister Marc Lalonde said in Edmonton Friday that the province has jurisdiction over the general administration of justice.

If there is eventually to be an inquiry, said Dr. McPhail, "most of us as individuals would believe it to be a good thing, to clear the air ... but the AMA will not attempt to stimulate any action."

Dr. McPhail said it "wasn't

More DOCTORS Page 6

Check recommended on gas rates in city

The city commissioners are recommending to city council that the Public Utilities Board be asked to review Northwestern Utilities Ltd.'s rates in the city.

If the gas company has a rate of return of more than 7½ per cent — the limit set by the Public Utilities Board — the city will seek to have the gas rates reduced.

Mayor Ivor Dent said Wednesday that the city's calculations indicate that the company's rate of return for 1969, 1970 and 1971 has been 8.422 per cent, 9.01 per cent and 8.91 per cent.

Northwestern's rate of return was set by the PUB in 1959, and the mayor said the company stayed within it until 1968.

There is some risk involved in the recommendation, Mayor Dent said. "The history of going to the Public Utilities Board is bad."

When Calgary went to the PUB over a 7¾-per-cent rate of return, he said, the board decided to allow the company an 8.625-per-cent rate of return.

"The thinking was that we might be better off to stay where we were; but, after much discussion, we decided we would go to a rate hearing."

If the board agrees with the city, the result would be a slight reduction in gas rates for Edmonton consumers, the mayor said.

Where to find it

● The province, not the people will decide whether sewage will be discharged into Whitemud Creek. Stories on Page 25.

● For the third year in a row, Alberta's petroleum reserves declined. Story on Page 71.

● Additional youth news appears on Page 20. The regular teen page will be published Friday.

Ann Landers	22
Art Evans	17
Barry Craig	3
Barry Westgate	25
Births, Deaths, Marriages	42
Bridge	46
Business, Stocks	71-75
Charles Lynch	4
Classified ads	43-60
Comics, Features	40
Comment	4
Crossword Puzzle	47
Entertainment	33-36
Family Section	18-23
Focus on People	12
Health Column	23
Horoscope	45
June Sheppard	18
Letters to The Journal	4
News Digest	10
Patterns	50, 53
Sport	63-69
Tax Tips	14
TV, Radio	41
Wayne Overland	63
Youth News	20

Weather

Mainly sunny today and Friday; high both days 45-50, low 20-25. Details on Page 31.

Denticare ruled out

Universal denticare for Albertans was ruled out Wednesday but Health and Social Development Minister Neil Crawford said he is concerned over the working poor's dental problems.

Mr. Crawford, replying to NDP Leader Grant Notley, said he has no plans to introduce a denticare program for children 12 and under, as British Columbia plans, because of the cost factor.

He said low-income Albertans often receive dental care under welfare programs and suggested a private pre-paid dental insurance plan might be the answer for the majority of persons.

"Of far greater concern is the area of people ... commonly referred to as the working poor ... And it is in that area where the greatest difficulty in providing dental services for the whole family is encountered," Mr. Crawford said.

Dairy prices increase seen

OTTAWA (CP) — Consumers can expect to pay more for dairy products under dairy policy changes announced Thursday in the Commons by Agriculture Minister Eugene Whelan.

The Canadian dairy commission, federal regulator of butter, cheese and skim milk powder, has been authorized to increase its support, or guaranteed price for butter to 71 cents a pound from 68 cents, for skim milk powder to 35 cents a pound from 29 cents, and for cheddar cheese to 60 cents a pound from 54 cents.

All increases are effective April 1, the beginning of the new dairy year.

The government annually subsidizes the dairy industry by about $100 million.

Millions follow advice from Ann

By JAN McMILLAN
Of The Journal

Yes Virginia, there is an Ann Landers.

She's a real live person — kind, patient and basically much like any other mother of a grown-up daughter, interested in staying in touch with the youth scene and the world of people around her.

Mind you, Ann Landers is a pseudonym, the name given to an advice column that Mrs. Esther Lederer, wife of a Chicago businessman, took over in 1955 at the Chicago Sun-Times.

She pointed out in Edmonton Wednesday, "When I became Ann 18 years ago, I had never thought of a career."

On Banks' show

Miss Landers was in Edmonton to tape a Tommy Banks show which will appear on CBC May 4.

Years ago, in one of her columns, she outlined her qualifications for the job: "I had never written a line in for publication. I had never held a paying job in my life. I had never seen the inside of a newspaper plant. I had no degree, despite four years at Morningside College in Sioux City, where I majored in boys. I had not had a hard life. Worse yet, I didn't smoke or drink. I was a total square who believed in God and had been married to the same man for many years. Finally the Iowa hay was still apparent, not only in my hair but in the way I put words together. The only thing I had going for me was that I had a teen-age daughter. I could at least be described as 'a mother'."

Now she's a grandmother too but what a grandmother.

She looks younger than her 54 years, so much so that she's often wrongly accused of having had her dimpled face lifted.

She does admit, "It takes me longer to make myself up every day." Her trim figure reflects a daily 30-minute session of exercises.

Miss Landers easily captures a group's interest with her animated and positive comments on almost any subject, an ability that is displayed in her advice column.

Now some 54 million people read her advice daily, in more than 800 newspapers around the world from Edmonton to New York to Tokyo to San Juan, Puerto Rico.

Scorn from some

Some people take that advice as the final truth; others laugh or scorn or complain "who is she to tell people what to do with their lives?"

Miss Landers points out her advice is checked out and researched with all kinds of people in helping professions — lawyers, doctors, psychiatrists, social workers, the clergy, teachers.

And, she says, those are the same people she would go to if she had problems.

"I hope my advice does

More ANN Page 6

Union charges four as ouster bid fails

By JOHN TOMPKINS
Of The Journal

The first surge of Canadian nationalism in an Edmonton local has been temporarily contained by its international union.

Consequently, four men who led the drive to unseat Local 1007 of the International Brotherhood of Electrical Workers as bargaining agent for several hundred Edmonton Power workers have been charged under the international's constitution with anti-union activities.

City employees Walter Badowsky, George Tilroe, Dave Walker and Peter Bodnarchuk will face charges, under union procedural rules, connected with the attempt to certify the independent Edmonton Power Employees' Association in place of the IBEW as bargaining agent for city hall's electrical staff.

"We'll plead not guilty, though we are guilty," Dave Walker, secretary-treasurer of the EPEA told The Journal.

"We are going to get kicked out of the union. What difference does it make?"

Mr. Bodnarchuk, president of the EPEA, presented a similar indifference to the kind of plea he will offer, charging the local is about to try them "in a kangaroo court, anyway."

"What a farce. A Yankee union charging us with our legal right as Canadian citizens to appear before the board of industrial relations under the provisions of the Alberta Labor Act."

The punitive action by the IBEW follows a five-month conflict within Local 1007 which has seen Canadian nationalism grow among a sizable body of the men dissatisfied with the local's handling of contract talks preparations and general conduct.

The local, whose contract has expired, has had only one meeting with city hall's chief negotiator Harry Hill, prompting Mr. Hill to comment last week that internal difficulties in the local were likely to protract contract settlement, especially among the electrical workers.

Dave Jillings, business agent for the local, conceded the internal strife — and that it hinged on the efforts of the breakaway group.

He confirmed, however, that while "all the problems are not over", Local 1007's internal situation was now such that its negotiating teams were pressing ahead with the unprecedented concept of contracting separate agreements for the 500 telephones and 500 electrical workers.

The conflict within Local 1007 began late last fall with the formation of the independence-seeking Edmonton

More UNION Page 6

The headline on Aug. 31, 1971, said it all in huge letters: "NOW! IT'S LOUGHEED."

The Tories won 49 seats, the Socreds were reduced to 25 and the New Democrats were represented by a lone seat held by their leader, Grant Notley.

Lougheed's new 22-member cabinet reflected changes in the province. It had 13 members from ridings in Edmonton and Calgary, giving it a decidedly urban flavour, the newspaper noted. What's more, it was a younger group of ministers as well. The average age of Lougheed's cabinet team was 43. Strom's had been 10 years older.

One of the youngest was 38-year-old Don Getty in the newly minted portfolio of Inter-governmental Affairs. Only a week after his cabinet appointment, Getty sounded the alarm about relations with Ottawa; relations that grew increasingly sour over the coming years.

In an in-depth interview with *The Journal*, Getty indicated that there was a new game afoot. "There are just too many people in Ottawa who are creating programs and ideas that affect Canada and Alberta that we just never hear about until it's too late," he said.

He pointed to energy policies imposed by Ottawa and federal government programs designed for Prairie farmers but in which the Prairie provinces had no say.

No one could have foretold just how tough the fight would become between Alberta and Ottawa over oil and gas prices. The fight would result in increased feelings of Western alienation all across the prairies.

A page 1 *Journal* story from the spring of 1971 headlined "Izzy – fastest gun for the West" – underlined just how disaffected voters were in other provinces too.

Southam News reporter Nick Hills said Izzy Asper, the newly chosen leader of the Manitoba Liberals, had "developed into the most articulate voice of the western fact." Hills quoted Asper, who went on to found the Canwest group of companies that owns *The Journal*, as saying that if Louis Riel were "alive today he would win – and you'd be surprised at the number of people in the trenches with him."

It's likely that Lougheed, Getty and Co. agreed with Asper's final comment: "You must have ice water in your veins to negotiate with the prime minister."

And while Asper might have been the most effective Western voice at the beginning of the decade, that role was soon taken over by Lougheed.

Heading a government in a province that produced most of the country's oil and gas, Lougheed proved to be a doughty fighter for provincial rights. And, ever so briefly, it appeared in 1973 that Ottawa might finally be listening.

Prime Minister Pierre Trudeau and his Liberals had received the shock of their political lives in the election of 1972 when they had been very nearly defeated by Bob Stanfield's Progressive Conservatives.

With the help of the federal New Democrats, Trudeau cobbled together a minority government and began a brief, and some said insincere, courtship of the Prairies.

"It has taken more than four years and a stunning rebuff by voters but

***Aug. 26, 1972*:**
The 105-member Alberta All-Girls Drum and Bugle Band performs at a torch ceremony marking the opening of the Munich Olympics, during a three-week European tour.

***Nov. 8, 1972*:**
At their convention at the Macdonald Hotel, the Women of Unifarm call on the Lougheed government to reinstate the controversial Sterilization Act that had been first passed in 1928 but had been repealed by the new Lougheed government.

***In 1973*:**
A *Journal* pressman earns $6.25 an hour while a reporter makes $200 a week. And the weekly price of a home-delivered *Journal* rises to 75 cents. The price of a gallon of regular gasoline at the pump is 49.5 cents. That works out to about 11 cents a litre.

***Jan. 30, 1973*:**
New figures show that Edmonton's population declines by 9,111 while outlying communities such as Sherwood Park and St. Albert have grown by a similar amount.

***March 7, 1973*:**
Citadel Theatre president Max Ritchie and executive

Edmonton Journal

FORECAST: SUNNY EDMONTON, ALBERTA, TUESDAY, JUNE 10, 1975 PRICE 15c

15 hostages in B.C. jail drama

Mrs. Julie Paquette lowered by firemen

Winnipeg widow goes to the top in pension plea

WINNIPEG (CP) — A 60-year-old widow went to great heights Monday to protest proposed federal legislation and to advertise for a husband.

Julie Paquette climbed to the roof of the Information Canada building on Portage Avenue in downtown Winnipeg to attract prospective husbands and to focus attention on what she calls the discriminatory aspects in amendments to the Old Age Security Act.

She was eventually arrested and removed from the two-storey building on a stretcher by police and firemen. She is charged with causing a disturbance.

The amendment now before the House of Commons would extend pension benefits, subject to a means test, to any person between the age of 60 and 65 married to a pensioner. Mrs. Paquette, a mother of two, claims widows cannot benefit from the proposed legislation.

"It perpetuates the belief that because men are older than their spouses, women can accrue more benefits by setting their status by marriage," she said while atop the building.

Mrs. Paquette said the amendment contravenes a portion of the United Nations Human Rights Bill dealing with equality between married and unmarried women.

To dramatize her opinion, she carried a sign that read: "Spouse wanted. Woman, age 60, will share companionship. Any age if wealthy or will consider man of limited means if at least 65 years of age. Object matrimony."

NEW WESTMINSTER, B.C. (CP) — Fifteen hostages were on death row at the British Columbia Penitentiary today, held at knifepoint by three desperate prisoners.

The prisoners said they would kill the hostages, penitentiary employees, if their demands for safe passage from Canada were not met.

"Fifteen of them are on death row right now," one of the prisoners told an intermediary.

A cabinet committee met for 2½ hours today to discuss the demands, but Prime Minister Trudeau gave no indications that decisions had been reached.

"I think the less said about it the better," the prime minister told reporters as he emerged from the meeting. "We're concerned and we're trying to find a solution."

"I don't want to talk about it, really," Mr. Trudeau said. "We're in the process of trying to solve it (and) talking about it would create more difficulties."

Mr. Trudeau spoke to Solicitor-General Warren Allmand by phone in Toronto before he entered the cabinet committee meeting. But the prime minister declined to discuss the issue with reporters.

Told that many people are keenly interested in the government's reaction, the prime minister said he was "not concerned about what people think at this point—I am concerned with getting the problem solved."

In a Toronto interview, Mr. Allmand said "continuous negotiations" are taking place between federal officials and three prisoners.

Mr. Allmand said there has been no suggestion of a deadline and he could not say how long it might take to clear up the situation.

The solicitor-general declined to release any details of what were described as government proposals and counter-proposals because the situation was "too critical to negotiate in public."

The prisoners have asked for a *elicopter to carry them to Vancouver International Airport, from which they want to be flown to a foreign country.

Mr. Allmand said they have not specified the country.

Mr. Allmand was in Toronto for a conference preliminary to a United Nations-sponsored meeting there and said he and Prime Minister

More JAIL Page 11

Morgentaler acquitted; demands release

MONTREAL (CP) — Dr. Henry Morgentaler, acquitted for the second time Monday on a charge of having performed an illegal abortion, demanded that he be released from prison immediately.

"I have been acquitted by two juries on two separate charges of abortion and I demand that I be released from prison," he said from the prisoners' dock.

"The people of Canada have spoken."

Dr. Morgentaler was referring to his acquittal by a Quebec Superior Court jury in November, 1973 on a similar charge of having performed an illegal abortion.

The acquittal was reversed by the Quebec Court of Appeal and the reversal and an 18-month sentence imposed by the Appeal Court were upheld by the Supreme Court of Canada in February of this year.

Dr. Morgentaler was serving the first sentence when the latest trial opened May 28 before Mr. Justice Claude Bisson.

The seven men and five women of the jury deliberated less than an hour Monday before returning the "not guilty" verdict.

Dr. Morgentaler predicted it would have far-reaching consequences and called the verdict "the turning point in the fight to change the abortion laws in Canada."

"It is a verdict which will go to Ottawa and to Quebec (City)," said the 52-year-old doctor.

He appealed to Justice

More RELEASE Page 11

Where to find it

Don McGillivray, editor of the Financial Times of Canada, points out 16 reasons why Canadians should be optimistic about the Canadian and world economies. Page 48.

Ann Landers 20
Art Evans 5
Barry Westgate 57
Births, Deaths, Marriages 58
Business, Stocks 48-54
Charles Lynch 4
Classified ads 59-79
Comics, Features 39
Editorial 4
Crossword Puzzle 65
Entertainment 23, 24
Family-Lifestyle 17-22
Focus on People 15
Health Column 20
Horoscope 61
June Sheppard 19
Letters To The Journal 4
Patterns 76
Sport 41-47
Temperatures 2
TV, Radio 25
Wayne Overland 41

Weather

Mostly sunny with a high near 22; low tonight near 7. Mostly sunny Wednesday except for a few afternoon cloudy periods; high near 20. Details on Page 2.

No money or friends; just hope for new life

A whole new world for Vietnamese youngsters

Journal photo by Dave Reidie

New home for Vietnamese

By Vicki Barnett
Of The Journal

Khuu Tong Giang has nothing except five shirts, five pairs of pants, six-dollar running shoes—and lots of hope for the new life he starts today in Edmonton.

One of 18 Vietnamese refugees who arrived here Monday night from Camp Pendleton, Calif., the small man sat in the almost-empty International Airport lobby, waiting for other refugees to arrive on another flight. Never had he been out of his country before last month, he tells you.

He left Vietnam with no clothes, no shoes, "nothing."

He has no Canadian friends, no Canadian relatives and no money.

And he knows nothing about Canada except "it's very, very cold."

Today, with that as a basis, and the attitude "I can adjust to anything," the 33-year-old technical engineer begins looking for work — probably still wear ing his white running shoes because that's all he has.

"I sold my radio for $11, and spent six dollars on these shoes," he says. The remainder went for cigarettes.

Another refugee, 26, has fewer possessions and even less certainty about the future. He has a wife, 23, who is six months pregnant, and speaks no English.

"I have a lot of homesickness, and my wife cries every night. We cannot sleep very long," he says, adding, "Don't put my name in the paper. The Viet Cong could read it. I am safe now, but I am worried about my mother, father and 10 brothers still in Vietnam."

Some day he wants to return to his country. But at present, he—like the rest of the refugees—is anxious to be accepted, anxious to find a job, anxious to start a new life.

Of course, he brought nothing with him to start his life except some worthless South Vietnamese bills, he says. How could he when he didn't know he would be leaving the country until he was at sea?

"On the morning of April 29 (the day before Saigon unconditionally surrendered), I expected to go to work as usual, but my brother-in-law, a member of the South Vietnamese navy, picked me up because he knew the Communists were taking over. And I knew if I stayed in Saigon, they would kill me because I had a lot of U.S. books and things in my house."

A sergeant first class in the Vietnamese army, and a microwave repairman, he has worked in co-operation with the U.S. Federal Electrical Commission and International Telephone and Telegraph.

His story is typical of those told by Vietnamese coming to Edmonton.

"On the morning of April 30, we were at sea and heard the Viet Cong were in Saigon. I hadn't expected to leave my country.... I feel like I've been dreaming for the month since then."

Says Mr. Khuu: "It was very, very dangerous in the vessels. They might have sunk with so many people."

"And everytime we switched boats, the next one was more battered," adds the microwave repairman.

Eventually the refugees arrived at the Pacific Ocean island of Guam where they were interviewed by Canadians to determine their skills. The microwave repairman was told he might be given a job here.

But there wasn't room on a Canada-bound plane, so he and his wife flew to Camp Pendleton instead where they stayed about a week. There the Vietnamese encountered adverse reaction from Californians who felt they were a burden in an already overflowing job market.

Always, the first question the refugees in Edmonton ask is: "Will I be able to get a job?" And always the second question is: "What do you think of the Vietnamese coming here?"

However, they are generally careful not to complain. Sometimes there is a disappointed mention of the U.S., the fallen Saigon government, the boat ride. "But I have no complaints," says the microwave repairman.

"I know I"ll like it here; I'm sure you people are nice -better than in the U.S."

One member of the manpower greeting team at the airport says he expects there will be some barriers to be broken down with prospective employers. But the skilled people, such as the engineer, chauffeur-mechanic and airplane mechanic are expected to be employed within a couple of weeks, he says.

Wally Pickering, Edmonton manager of Canada Manpower in the department of manpower and immigration, says he doesn't know the refugees' job status, although he has heard they bring skills to Alberta that are needed here.

In fact, he doesn't know who they are, what they do or even whether or not they speak English. (Most do.) He was told Monday afternoon the Vietnamese would arrive via Vancouver Monday night.

So after spending the night in a local motel, their skills will be assessed and job-hunting will begin.

In addition, Mr. Pickering says he thinks more Vietnamese will arrive in Edmonton in the near future, "but I haven't a clue as to the numbers."

Mr. Pickering said the arrival of the Vietnamese was not a complete surprise since Canadian officials have known since May 1 that some immigrants would be arriving.

He said accommodation is likely to be a major problem for some of the new arrivals, particularly two families of seven each. He asks that anyone in Edmonton who can provide assistance in this area contact Canada Manpower officials.

For the time being, the Vietnamese are being put up by the Canadian government through a Canada Manpower adjustment program similar to that used for immigrating Ugandans and Chileans in recent times.

Mr. Pickering said the Vietnamese have not been "kicked out" by the U.S. and are in Canada largely through their own choice. For the time being, they are guests in our country, he said, until they can be placed in permanent jobs and homes.

Man's best friend may be a walking health hazard

By Don Sellar
Southam News Services

OTTAWA — Your Faithful dog, Fido, may not be man's best friend after all.

Indeed, Fido could be a walking public health hazard, warns an article in the Canadian Medical Association Journal.

The problem is not your pup's temperment but rather his excrement.

Those little calling cards he leaves on neighborhood lawns or pathways could contain tremendous numbers of wiggling worms—parasites—which can infect humans.

Dr. S. K. Seah, of Montreal, who investigated "the role of dogs as a reservoir of parasitic infections," says your pet could give you everything from diarrhea to blindness.

Tests he conducted on 239 dogs housed by the Society for the Prevention of Cruelty to Animals in Montreal turned up wormy parasites in 189, or 79 per cent, of the animals.

The dogs were strays which the SPACA normally destroys after four days if no owner claims them. But Dr. Seah's concern extends to the danger posed by all dogs, including house pets.

The health hazard seems greatest for children. A youngster at play isn't above tasting hunks of dirt which might be contaminated by dog excrement.

The researcher also points out that flies can carry parasite eggs from the same source and transmit infections to humans.

If the parasites penetrate an individual's digestive system, they can break through the intestine and reach the liver and other organs, Dr. Seah says.

This can cause a variety of health problems, including fever and enlarged liver. The parasites also can attack the eye or the brain, in their larva state.

Although no link has been established between intestinal parasites and bronchial asthma, Dr. Seah believes this medical problem may be traceable to dogs.

"Because of the close relations dogs have with humans, and as a result of our amazing tolerance of the dog's habit of depositing its feces in and around human habitation, we suspect dogs might be the source of these infections," he writes.

The absence of research on dogs and intestinal parasites in Canada is the main reason why Dr. Seah can't prove his contention that the health problem is worsening.

Noting that North America's pet population is growing by leaps and bounds, he makes a plea for doctors to alert governments and the general public about the parasite menace.

Dr. Seah laments the fact that dog owners and dog lovers are in a majority position now, and easily silence those who advocate control of dog "pollution" in streets and parks.

Dogs are considered worse offenders than cats, mainly because cat owners usually provide indoor bathroom facilities for their pets, which tend to bury their excrement anyway.

"Dogs, however, defecate outside the house and if these dogs harbour intestinal parasites, as the majority of them do, they are a hazard to humans and other dogs," he writes.

Among the control measures Dr. Seah advocates stricter enforcement of existing laws and bylaws concerning dogs, including municipal bylaws which forbid animals to enter markets or restaurants.

He is also worried about dogs which come into contact with children in playgrounds and parks, suggesting dogs should be barred from such places.

Another suggestion he makes is regular check-ups for dogs and cats, even though such treatments cost money, and mandatory examinations of pet shop and kennel animals before sale.

Dr. Seah's study was financed by a research grant from the Department of Veterans Affairs.

Prime Minister Trudeau at long last has discovered Western Canada, or so it seems," said a Jan. 5, 1973, editorial.

The optimism resulted from a proposed meeting between federal and provincial politicians that would attempt to hammer out agreement on such touchy issues as freight rates and their impact on economic development, regionally based banks and the all-important issue of energy prices.

While the editorial sounded a note of hope, there was also a hint of caution. "Of course, the meeting could turn out to be just another windy gathering of politicians."

It was windy, and nothing came of the meeting. Trudeau called another election for 1974 and the Liberals again assumed a majority, with 141 seats to the Tories' 95.

The Liberals didn't elect a single Albertan, and the stage was set for an energy fight that became bitter, personal, protracted and dangerous to the country itself.

By the time of the '74 election, the era of cheap oil had ended. In 1971, Libya and the OPEC states had shocked the world by raising the price of a barrel of oil to $2.81 – an increase of a buck – and a barrel of Alberta crude sold for $3.10.

And by the end of the decade the price of a barrel was almost $15. The federal government wanted cheap gas and oil from Alberta. Albertans wanted a fair price.

It was a time when a fringe political group in Calgary called the Western Canada First Association enjoyed a brief moment in the limelight when it produced bumper stickers that read, "Let the Eastern bastards freeze in the dark."

Some readers however weren't impressed with that slogan. "Let us hope that Eastern Canadians realize that a few ignorant louts, with their bumper stickers, are not expressing the views of most Westerners," wrote Mrs. F.D. Thompson of Barrhead.

"I am sure 99 per cent of Western people feel the same sense of disgust and shame that I do.

"If I had my way, no service station in the West would sell gas to anyone displaying one of the stickers – and let those bastards walk."

To the credit of Calgary Mayor Rod Sykes, he countered with a bumper sticker that said, "That Eastern bastard is my brother."

But any suggestion that the federal government should set the domestic and foreign price for Alberta oil or impose a per-barrel tax infringed on provincial rights, *The Journal* said.

Canada's oil needs come first, insisted Trudeau and his minister of energy, Donald Macdonald. There were sharply rising demands from the United States for Alberta's oil, and the federal government saw an opportunity to slap on a federal per-barrel surtax to act as both a curb and as a means of revenue.

"The significant point for Alberta is that we are now in a position to bargain hard for our rich energy reserves," said an editorial from January 1973.

"We are in a seller's market. And while we cannot yet compete with the

producer Joe Shoctor announce that John Neville will be their new artistic director.

***Sept. 8, 1973*:**
A quart of two-per-cent milk costs 36 cents.

***Nov. 1, 1973*:**
CheckStop, a program to control drinking and driving, goes into effect. According to a page 1 story the next day, not a single impaired driver was pulled over in Edmonton out of the 700 who were stopped.

***In 1973*:**
The United Community Fund becomes the United Way of Edmonton and Area. The campaign, under E.R.G. Burgess raises $2,089,293.

***In 1974*:**
A season ticket for the Edmonton Eskimos costs $47.50, while a *Journal* ad salesman earns $300 a week.

***Jan. 17, 1974*:**
The city's longest transit strike comes to an end after 50 days. At the end of the new 2½-year contract bus drivers will earn $6.12 an hour, up from $4.94 an hour.

***May 1, 1974*:**
Edmonton Centre officially opens.

***May 17, 1974*:**
Fort Edmonton officially opens.

Family allowances, pensions get mail delivery priority

By SHAWN WADDELL
Of The Journal

Edmonton post office union leaders were on their phones before dawn today, spreading the word:

"It's over. Get your boys back to work."

Family allowance and pension cheques were to get top priority. They were sorted out by supervisory staff during the strike. Other benefit cheques and first-class mail will be next in priority.

City postal workers returned at 6:30 a.m. and will likely be supplemented with casual employees to clear a backlog of six to seven million pieces of mail, an official said.

Toronto Local President Lou Murphy notified the post office that the Toronto membership would remain on strike until a meeting called for Sunday to vote on ratification of an agreement negotiated at Ottawa.

Vancouver workers also remained off the job. A meeting is set for later today to discuss the issue.

News of the mediated settlement of the nation-wide walkout reached Edmonton shortly after 3 a.m. in a curt 30-word telegram from Joe Davidson, acting president of the Canadian Union of Postal Workers recommending a return to work and promising further details.

By 5 a.m. word had passed down to local CUPW shop stewards and picket captains to relay to their 675 members and to officials of the Letter Carriers Union of Canada, whose 500 local members have honored inside workers' pickets throughout the dispute.

The morning shifts reported for duty by 7 a.m.

Judging from the few available details of the settlement, "it's looking pretty good," said local CUPW president John Pastor.

Establishment of a mediation committee headed by labor trouble-shooter Eric Taylor ensures that the government will sit down and discuss the automation issue, he said.

Full consultation on automation and technological change is provided for in the CUPW's current contract, but the government has nonetheless planned its automation programs without union input, he charged.

The settlement also includes a government guarantee not to impose penalties or reprisals on the men or union leaders, a condition that apparently stalled negotiations.

Union negotiators issued a statement Thursday night charging that the government representatives had refused compromise on this point and had failed to appear at mediation sessions for two days.

Several hundred copies of the statement for distribution to pickets this morning had been mimeographed when news of the settlement came in.

"It's nothing but scrap paper now,"

More POSTAL Page 10

Edmonton Journal

FORECAST: CLOUDY — EDMONTON, ALBERTA, FRIDAY, APRIL 26, 1974 — PRICE 15c

$30 million project for 9 miles of North Saskatchewan

Lake park plan for river valley

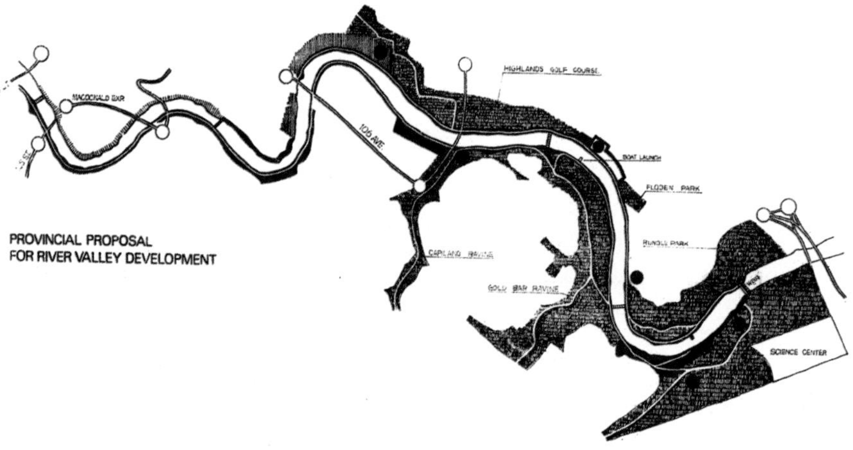
PROVINCIAL PROPOSAL
FOR RIVER VALLEY DEVELOPMENT
HIGHLANDS GOLF COURSE
106 AVE.
BOAT LAUNCH
RUNDLE PARK
CAPILANO RAVINE
GOLD BAR RAVINE
SCIENCE CENTER
WEIR

Proposed park for city with area in black part of a new lake

By BOB BELL
Of The Journal

A nine-mile section of the North Saskatchewan River valley—from Beverly bridge on the east to the legislative grounds downtown—will be developed into a huge urban park for Edmonton.

Premier Lougheed today unveiled the provincial government's concept for a $30 million to $35 million capital city recreation park that includes:

- A river flow control weir 2,000 feet upstream from the Beverly bridge that will back up the North Saskatchewan River to create a lake as far upstream as the legislative grounds.
- The river banks will be converted into a "water conservation area" running the full length of the lake stretching at least 150 feet from each shore.
- To protect the entire river valley in the metropolitan Edmonton region, the government will declare it a restricted development area, not only within the proposed park but also from Fort Saskatchewan on the northeast to Devon on the souhwest.
- More than 3,000 acres — about 4½ square miles — of green area will be developed in new provincial and city parks and recreation areas within the overall river valley park concept.

A breakdown of the approximate capital cost of the park is: $5 million for the weir; $1 million for each of four river crossings; $3 million to $4 million for property acquisition; between $500,000 and $3 million for upgrading water quality; and an average of $1 million a mile for landscaping and land stabilization totalling $18 million.

The provincial government, in co-operation with the city, hopes to complete the project within five years, and it may even be completed to tie in with the Commonwealth Games in Edmonton in 1978.

The park concept will give Edmonton a provincial urban recreation area to match Fish Creek Provincial Park announced for Calgary a year ago.

The park combines parts of various proposals previously examined by the lands and forests and environment departments—that of a provincial park at either the Hermitage site in northeast Edmonton, at Fulton Ravine in Gold Bar, or in the downtown Rossdale, Cloverdale, and Riverdale areas.

Premier Lougheed said the plan was endorsed by the provincial government even though it will cost more than the entire provincial parks construction budget for the past decade.

The premier called it "the most exciting and novel approach to assuring the quality of life for families in metropolitan centres as yet proposed for Canadian cities.

"We are prepared to commit such funds because we believe it is the concept that

More PARK Page 10

Mayor leads council's praise

With Mayor Ivor Dent leading the way and only Ald. Una Evans dissenting, City of Edmonton policy-makers appear pleased with the proposed river valley parks scheme.

Mayor Dent, on hand with the premier as the park plan was unveiled this morning, declared: "I think we're seeing the most magnificent and exciting thing any of us can imagine. Edmonton is moving towards being one of the most beautiful cities in the world."

Mayor Dent feels there has been no absence of consultation. He has had a series of meetings since last October with Premier Lougheed, Lands and Forests Minister Allan Warrack and Environment Minister Bill Yurko.

At the request of the province, he was unable to dis-

More REACTION Page 10

Where to find it

Ann Landers	18
Art Evans	13
Births, Deaths, Marriages	34
Bridge	40
Business, Stocks	84-86
Charles Lynch	4
Classified ads	35-63
Comics, Features	70
Editorial	4
Crossword Puzzle	39
Entertainment	26-30
Family Section	15-21
Focus on People	41
Horoscope	38
June Sheppard	15
Letters To The Journal	4
News Digest	31
Patterns	44, 47
Sport	77-81
Temperatures	23
TV, Radio	34

Weather

Cloudy periods: high 60-65, low near 35. Mainly sunny Saturday with a high of 55-60. Details on Page 23.

Existing parks will form part of project

By ARMIN HECHT
Of The Journal

A lake in the heart of the city, nine miles long and a quarter-mile wide, will be the core of a proposed provincial park in Edmonton.

The development has three objectives: To preserve open spaces and provide areas for recreation; to raise the North Saskatchewan water levels, enhancing the area's beauty and creating more opportunity for water-related recreation; and to stabilize riverbanks to reduce erosion.

A weir and related features are expected to cost between $4.16 million and $5.4 million.

The weir would incorporate a waterfall, "with a pedestrian and bicycle crossover to link park areas on both sides of the river."

It is also possible that a fish passage, boat portage and canoe run might be part of the weir.

Throughout the park there will be lay-bys adjacent to the man-made lake, to provide access for hiking and bicycle trails, and to link other parks and recreation facilities in the river valley.

Existing Edmonton parks will be incorporated in the over-all provincial park development. The most easterly part will be at Gold Bar, which will provide an athletic complex and sports field chiefly for use by people in the neighborhood. It is also intended to preserve that portion of Gold Bar ravine which remains in a relatively undistrubed state, and to provide a family recreation area.

Portions of the sports field are already developed at the south end of the ravine, the report says.

A master plan for a parcel of land south of the Ottewell Curling Club and bordering Highway 16A East calls for

More LAKE Page 10

Ravine would be winter sports paradise

The drawing, at left, depicts possible development at Gold Bar Ravine as part of the province's park plan for the city. Ski lodges, restaurants, a cable car terminal and a sports heritage centre with a viewing dome would be included in the area which would have facilities for tobogganing and ice boating in addition to skiing.

Firefighters back; all flights resuming by weekend

By The Canadian Press

Airport firefighters across Canada returned to work today with their contract dispute in the hands of a newly appointed federal mediator one praised for "his breery unpredictability."

Tom Stoyanoff, president of the Toronto firefighters' local, announced the men would return after the public service staff relation board said Thursday that Tom O'Connor of Toronto had been appointed to reopen contract negotiations between the men and the federal government.

An Air Canada spokesman in Montreal said the airline did not "expect any substantial change" today in the reduced operations that marked the firefighters' walkout.

He said the airline would recall personnel, including about 650 pilots, laid off during the firemen's walkout as normal operations resumed.

Airline spokesmen said full service would likely not be restored until Saturday, with only small aircraft using most airports today and transatlantic flights leaving from Ottawa.

It was announced Thursday in Ottawa that the firefighters, members of the Public Service Alliance of Canada, had rejected the latest government contract offer in a close vote. A spokesman said, however, the union had been waiting only for a mediator to be named before going back to work.

Mr. O'Connor, 48, is a labor relations specialist who has served as a middleman in more than 900 disputes since 1955. It was after his work in speeding up a settlement in the national postal dispute of August, 1970, that he was termed unpredictable by a member of the government negotiating team.

The government offer that the 1,430-member union rejected would have given the men an average annual wage increase of $3,000 over a 26-month contract. The firefighters currently earn an average of $9,100 a year but are seeking wage parity with municipal firemen who earn about $13,000 annually.

Vote figures were not released.

Most Canadian airports were restricted to handling planes no larger than the mid-size 737s and DC-9s during the walkout. Restrictions at Toronto International Airport were eased Thursday to permit the larger DC-8s to fly.

Flights out of Edmonton's International Airport are expected to return to normal by the weekend, following the return to work this morning of the airport's 35 federal firefighters.

Ron Lovett, shop steward for the firefighters at the International, said the men voted Thursday night to end their 11-day walkout and follow their counterparts at airports across the country back to work.

Middle East in terms of price, Canada's political stability and the assurance of a secure energy supply go a long way to tip the scales in our favour."

The scales may have been tipped, but that didn't mean everything was going to go Alberta's way.

There were lineups at U.S. gas pumps, and industry west of the Ottawa valley – east of the valley was served by imported oil, brought into eastern ports from Venezuela in huge tankers – wanted assurances that the flow from Alberta would continue.

Gas pricing was no easier. Alberta was determined to stand firm and not sell its resources below value to Ontario industry.

"If we did sell cheaply," Lougheed said in a mid-1973 front-page story, "we as a province which contributes equalization payments to have-not provinces would eventually become a have-not province ourselves."

Predictions on just where the price of oil might end up ranged from $6 a barrel to $20 a barrel.

Lougheed was sure that the price would settle in the $20 range, a number he felt was reasonable after he completed a 1977 tour of the Middle East.

The Journal accompanied the delegation and in an exclusive interview with Lougheed was told that oil prices would continue to soar. "After a series of meetings in Saudi Arabia and Iran, Premier Lougheed says it is 'highly probable' there will be a serious energy shortage in the early to mid-1980s. He sees the world price of oil rising to $20 US a barrel from the current price of $14.50 at the Persian Gulf ports by the early 1980s."

With rising prices, the Heritage Savings and Trust Fund grew by a billion dollars a year as the decade came to a close. The money was spent on earnest projects such as oilsands research, irrigation and new animal pastures.

None of it was "mad money" or "joy juice," wrote *The Journal*'s William Thorsell, and that rankled. He confessed he wanted to spend some of the money on, well, decadence. "Let's empower an utterly elitist group of Albertans, beyond direct government control, to spend part of the money on great and silly things that will really set Alberta aside.

"Let them buy some of the world's best sculpture from non-Canadians and fill our cities with it. Let them advertise for high-quality gigolos; pay incredibly provocative, creative people from elsewhere $50,000 a year (or more) to live in Edmonton, Calgary or Grande Prairie on condition they get to know a lot of people. Hire a mime to work Jasper Avenue.

"Choose a design for really distinctive street lighting standards to replace the soulless universal ones we have now. Buy out the Chateau Lacombe and tear it down. Show Alice in Wonderland...."

Thorsell's editorial may have been frivolous, but the issue wasn't.

What the country needed, the newspaper argued repeatedly throughout the decade, was a comprehensive national energy policy.

By not having one, Ottawa had simply been derelict in its duties. More than once, *The Journal* called for a "forward-looking policy."

When that policy came, it wasn't at all what the province, its leaders or the newspaper wanted. The National Energy Program of the '80s, in fact, attempted to roll back provincial advances in control of natural resources.

***June 23, 1974*:**
The Ukrainian Cultural Heritage Village opens two miles east of Elk Island Park.

***July 7, 1974*:**
The Alberta All-Girls Drum and Bugle Band, teenagers from Edmonton, perform before a world wide TV audience at the final game of the 1974 World Cup soccer championship in Munich.

***Aug. 2, 1974*:**
The Alberta government acquires controlling interest in Pacific Western Airlines. The $36-million deal, according to *The Journal*'s editorial page, means that the Tories "tossed a curve at socialists and conservatives alike." The editorial also ponders the possibility of keeping the PWA designation, but changing the official name of the airline to "People's Western Airline, for example, or Peter's Wonderful Asset, Peter's Weird Affectation or Profit Wacky Albertans...or maybe Peter's Way Ahead."

***Oct. 16, 1974*:**
Mayor Ivor Dent loses to former Mayor Bill Hawrelak in the civic election.

***Nov. 4, 1974*:**
The first Canadian Finals Rodeo, with

GRAND OPENING

BILL COMRIE'S FURNITURE WAREHOUSE
BILL COMRIE'S
FURNITURE WAREHOUSE LTD

"THAT BIG BRICK WAREHOUSE"
ON THE CORNER OF 101 ST. & 107 AVE.

BILL COMRIE HAS MOVED TO LARGER PREMISES
DON'T MISS THIS GRAND OPENING SPECIAL!

all new 1975 ZENITH® SOLID-STATE

CHROMACOLOR II®

20" DECORATOR COMPACT CONSOLES

SPACE SAVING CONSOLES AT A FABULOUS GRAND OPENING PRICE!

Ultramodern

THE AVANTE X F4082X
The Gloss-White Pedestal base gives this Ultramodern Styled console a smart, sophisticated profile.

Mediterranean

THE TITAN F4088
Classic Mediterranean styled console. Decorative end panels six simulated drawers and full base with concealed castors.

YOUR CHOICE
OF THESE FINE-FURNITURE STYLES

569.95

LIMITED TIME OFFER!
DON'T MISS OUT!

Early American

THE AUDUBON F4086M
Charming Early American styled space-saver console with decorative end panels, traditional bracket foot design and concealed castors.

Modern

THE LYMAN F4084P
Modern styled space saver console with Butcher-Black motif. Castors. Back of Cabinet completely finished in simulated woven cane.

Famous Zenith Quality and Performance Features
- Brilliant Chromacolor Picture Tube
- Solid-State Super Video Range Tuning System
- Synchromatic 70-Position UHF Channel Selector
- 100% Solid-State Chassis
- Patented Power Sentry Voltage Regulator
- Chromatic One-Button Tuning

ZENITH *The quality goes in before the name goes on*

FREE LAYAWAY PLAN!

BILL COMRIE'S FURNITURE WAREHOUSE

GUARANTEED LOWEST PRICES IN ALBERTA!

FREE DELIVERY ANYWHERE IN ALBERTA!

NOW AT **10705 - 101 ST.** OPEN DAILY 9 A.M. - 9 P.M. SATURDAYS 9 A.M. - 6 P.M. **429-1721**

FREE 90 DAY NO INTEREST PLAN!

Arena Mania

"This city has been talking about a convention centre for more than a decade. The talk is still going on. And on. And on. So far we haven't even selected a site."
— Editorial Feb. 7, 1974

In the beginning was the omniplex, a structure of glass and concrete in the very heart of Edmonton, or maybe by the municipal airport.

It featured a 30,000-seat football stadium (with expansion to 48,000), a 19,000-seat hockey arena and a convention centre. City hockey impresario Bill Hunter estimated the cost at $26.4 million (about $135 million in today's money).

Alas, 54 per cent of Edmonton voters rejected the package in an election plebiscite Nov. 25, 1970.

The next day, *The Journal*, which supported the complex, said that while 70 per cent of voters in the 1968 civic election supported the concept of an omniplex, when it came right down to paying for it, voters balked "because of the fear of cost. New approaches in this area are called for. The people have spoken, but it may not be their last word."

The "new approach" mentioned in the paper's editorial turned out to be hiving off the "omni" from the "plex" and building the facilities as stand-alone projects. First out of the gate was the Coliseum.

The Journal reported on June 20, 1972, "city council agreed to back the Edmonton Exhibition Association's $9-million arena plans and, according to Ald. Dave Ward, scuttled omniplex."

EXA (the '70s acronym for the exhibition association) proposed a $9 million, 16,000-seat hockey/convention complex and a $1.5 million race track expansion. It planned to put the financing together if the city came up with $3.7 million worth of land expenditures over 10 years. The city would hold title to the land.

Ward and Ald. Ed Leger stuck to their omniplex guns. Aldermen who did support the deal had various reasons for doing so. Ald. Una Evans, for instance, said: "I must confess that one of the reasons I am supporting this is because it will provide some influence over rapid transit."

The total package would be worth about $55 million today.

On Oct. 12, the paper reported the design for the building, created by a Vancouver and Edmonton corporate partnership had been approved.

Construction on the Edmonton Coliseum (it became Northlands Coliseum in 1978) began in June 1973, and the WHA Edmonton Oilers played the Cleveland Crusaders in their first game in the new facility Nov. 11, 1974, scoring three unanswered goals in the third period for a 4-1 win.

With hockey nailed down, the city had to turn to track and field and, ultimately, football.

On Aug. 24, 1972, Edmonton was chosen as the site for the 1978 Commonwealth Games.

Among other facilities, such as a shooting range and a bicycle-racing track called a velodrome, the city needed a new stadium. Forty-year-old,

prize money of about $25,000, is held in the Edmonton Gardens, along with the Farm Fair livestock show.

***Nov. 10, 1974*:**
The Edmonton Coliseum opens without all its seats installed. The Edmonton Oilers defeat the Cleveland Crusaders 4-1.

***June 4, 1975*:**
Bill Comrie's Big Brick Warehouse opens on the corner of 101st Street and 107th Avenue.

***June 17, 1975*:**
Goalie Glenn Hall is named to the Hockey Hall of Fame.

***July 1, 1975*:**
Alberta's minimum wage rises to $2.50 an hour, an increase of 25 cents.

***July 29, 1975*:**
More than 1,500 residents of Vegreville turn out for the dedication of the world's biggest Easter egg, a 5,000-pound aluminum pysanka.

***Sept. 27, 1975*:**
HMCS Nonsuch, the Edmonton naval reserve unit decommissioned in 1964, is recommissioned.

***Nov. 14, 1975*:**
Edmonton city council selects member Terry Cavanagh to complete the term

Edmonton Journal

FORECAST: CLOUDY 84 PAGES EDMONTON, ALBERTA, WEDNESDAY, SEPTEMBER 6, 1972 10c 15c with The Canadian and Color Comics

Olympics resume as Arab terror victims mourned

17 dead in Munich horror

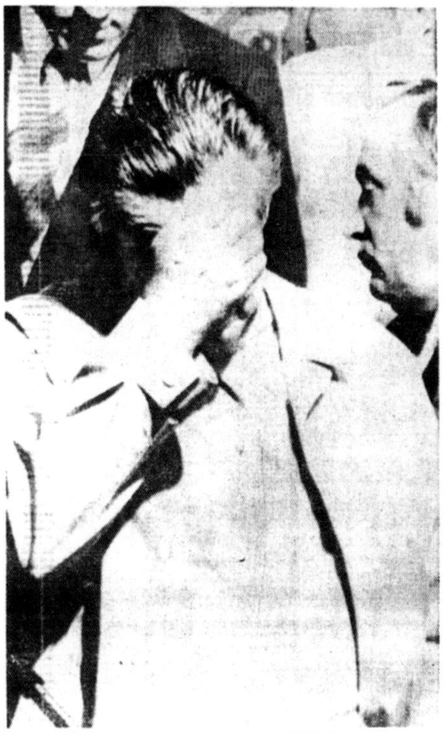

Saddened Olympics' chairman Willi Daume as he announced hostages' deaths

From AP-Reuter

MUNICH (CP) — The Olympic Games resumed today under the shadow of Arab terrorism and police action which together left 17 men dead.

An Arab raid on the Israeli athletes' quarters and a later shootout at the Munich military airport had killed 11 of the Israelis' Olympic team, five terrorists and a West German policeman.

German officials started an inquiry into all circumstances of the airport shooting, but said there was no alternative to the police action there.

The Olympics were suspended Tuesday after the Arabs shot their way into the Israeli quarters in Olympic Village. The announcement that the Games were resuming was made by Avery Brundage, president of the International Olympic Committee, in an address to 80,000 persons gathered for memorial services for the Israeli dead.

"We cannot allow a handful of terrorists to destroy this nucleus of international co-operation and good will that we have in the Olympic movement," Brundage said. "The games must go on."

Premier Golda Meir of Israel thanked the West German government for trying to free nine Israeli hostages who died at the airport. She endorsed the German decision to use force.

Interior Minister Hans-Dietrich Genscher told reporters that German authorities became convinced "a flight out of this country would have meant certain death for the athletes."

That led to the decision to use force.

Genscher said the police ambush at the airport, which backfired, was set up because "there was no chance" to storm the Olympic quarters where the Israelis had been held all day Tuesday. They and their captors were flown from Olympic Village to the airport in helicopters, ostensibly as the first stage of a flight to the Middle East.

Manfred Schreiber, chief of Munich police, said the order to police sharpshooters to open fire at the airport, "to kill or immobilize the terrorists," was a top-level decision.

Sharpshooters opened up, killed one of the Arabs and missed another out in the open. A second Arab then began firing at the hostages. All the hostages died in one of the helicopters, but just how was to be determined through official inquiries.

Two of the Israeli team members, a coach and a competitor, had been killed earlier in the Olympic Village when the Arabs first took over the hostages with a de-

More SLAYINGS Page 6

The developments

- A father for just three weeks, Moshe Weinberg, wrestling coach with the Israelis, was gunned down as he opened the door of the Israelis quarters by the Arab commandos. Page 70.
- Canadian athletes just missed meeting the commandos. They had been watching the Canadian-Russian hockey series. Page 71.
- A survivor of Bergen Belsen concentration camp, Dr. Shaul Ladany, was also lucky enough to escape the attack. He describes the morning events. Page 71.
- Spectators gathered in the warm afternoon sun to watch the drama, Southam News Services' Doug Gilbert reports. Page 71.

Meir demands nations expel terrorists

JERUSALEM (CP) — Israel demanded today that governments expel Arab terrorists from their terroritories.

It also warned that it will hold countries that assist Arab guerrillas responsible for the murder of 11 Israeli Olympians at Munich.

In a communique following an extraordinary session of the Israeli cabinet called by Premier Golda Meir, Israel said it has vowed to fight the guerrillas and "will not excuse those who aid them from responsibility."

The guerrillas constitute a danger not only to Israel but to the peace and well-being of all countries, the communique said in calling on world governments to take more effective action against the guerrillas.

The communique also expressed thanks to the West German government for its efforts to secure the release of the hostages. Mrs. Meir voiced support for the West

More MEIR Page 6

Olympic flag at half mast

Timetable to disaster

MUNICH (Reuter) — This is how the drama of the Palestine guerrilla attack on the Israeli Olympic team unfolded in Munich. All times local.

Tuesday

6 a.m.—Five commandos of the Black September guerrilla organization storm into the Israeli building at the Olympic Village, killing two Israeli members and holding nine as hostages. They demand the release of 200 Palestinian prisoners held in Israel and safe conduct out of West Germany.

7:30 a.m.—Police move in around the building and marksmen take up positions on the rooftops. The Munich police chief and Olympic village "mayor" Walter Troeger open negotiations with the Arabs. Interior Minister Hans-Dieter Genscher assumes over-all control.

11 a.m.—Commandos' first deadline expires uneventfully as negotiations continue.

1:20 p.m.—Lunch is brought to the guerrillas. A figure in a white floppy hat collects the food packages.

2 p.m.—Second deadline expires. West Germany's second television channel suspends programs so as to cut off guerrilla contact with outside world. A virtual news blackout is imposed.

2:15 p.m.—Munich Police Chief Manfred Schreiber tells his marksmen to shoot down the guerrillas if they get a chance.

2:25 p.m.—West German Chancellor Willy Brandt flies in to assess the situation.

2:35 p.m.—A mystery explosion echoes through the Olympic Village. Helicopter lands and takes off again without explanation.

3:35 p.m.—Olympic spokesman announces deadline put back to 5 p.m

6 p.m. — U.S. Olympic swimming hero Mark Spitz, who is Jewish, flies out secretly.

6:35 p.m. — Genscher, Troeger and Schreiber visit Israeli quarters for talks with guerrillas.

7:50 p.m. — Chancellor Brandt announces on television that leading West German politicians had offered themselves in exchange for the hostages, but that offer was rejected.

8 p.m.—Village sealed off, but order lifted after 45 minutes.

More TIMETABLE Page 12

Arabs defend guerrillas as deaths shock world

By THE ASSOCIATED PRESS

Arab newspapers came to the defence of the Palestinian guerrillas today as much of the world reacted with shock and outrage to the slaying of Israeli athletes at the Munich Olympics.

"The world may call these crimes," said the Egyptian Gazette, "but it must expect to continue until Palestinian rights are restored."

"As long as Israel refuses justice, it cannot expect the Arabs to leave it in peace."

The leftist Beirut paper Al Moharrer, which is close to the Palestinian commandos, commented that "public opinion has always been against the Arabs, never taking their side . . . into consideration."

"So public opinion needs a sharp blow to become impartial."

Beirut's Al Naha, apparently referring to peace feelers between Israel and Egypt, said the Munich assault had a political goal—to let certain Arab states know that any settlement with Israel will never be complete "because there will always be individuals, however few, who will continue to fight."

Government radio stations in Iraq and Syria and Arab nationalist newspapers in Lebanon accused the West Germans of treachery in opening fire on the guerrillas as they tried to leave with their Israeli hostages.

"Commandos at Munich victims of a trap," was the headline in the right-wing paper Safa.

In a telegram to the West German Olympic committee, Mayor Jean Drapeau of Montreal, where the 1976 Summer

More ARABS Page 6

Canadians-only rule for new police chiefs

Police chiefs appointed in Alberta cities or towns with populations over 5,000 will have to be Canadian citizens, the provincial cabinet has decided.

Regulations under the Police Act spelling out the qualifications for chiefs of police were contained in an order-in-council approved today.

In making the move, the cabinet agreed to a request from Calgary city council which asked that Canadian citizenship be required as a qualification for police chiefs, after the Charles Gain incident.

Attorney - General Merv Leitch said today there will be no conflict in the new amendment and the recently passed Alberta Bill of Rights. The only national qualification for a police chief will be Canadian citizenship and this will not violate the rights bill which outlaws discrimination because of origin, religion or race.

Mr. Leitch said if small towns wanted to hire non-Canadians, "that's their business."

The citizenship criterion for

More POLICE Page 2

Frost, snow put skids to summer

The first snow of autumn fell on Edmonton early today, three full weeks before its arrival last year.

The city also felt its first frost of the season, overnight temperatures hovering around 31 - 32 degrees. In 1971, the first frost struck Sept 17 when the temperature at the Industrial Airport plunged to 30 degrees.

The trace of snow which fell on the city, mixed with light rain, was part of the larger front which dumped snow on Alberta from the Peace River country to the south-central part of the province.

Snow fell on Edmonton for about two hours between 1 and 3 a.m., but disappeared almost immediately.

The mixed rain-snowfall dumped anything from a trace in most parts of the foothills to one inch at Banff and three inches around Pincher Creek in the extreme southern part of Alberta.

Pincher Creek's temperatures plunged from 77 Tuesday to an overnight low of 32.

Where to find it

Ann Landers	17
Art Evans	23
Barry Westgate	77
Births, Deaths, Marriages	48
Bridge	52
Business, Stocks	44-47
Charles Lynch	4
Classified Ads	49-64
Comics, Features	75
Comment	4
Crossword Puzzle	53
Entertainment	78, 79
Family Section	18 23
Focus on People	43
Health Column	21
Horoscope	51
June Sheppard	18
News Digest	31
Patterns	51
Sport	35-41
TV, Radio	68
Wayne Overland	35

Weather

Mainly cloudy; high 40-45, low 25-30. Cloudy periods Thursday with high near 45. Details on Page 2.

Kennedy

Socreds' Kennedy retires

The Social Credit League of Alberta this morning announced Orvis A. Kennedy, 65, executive director, has retired.

Eric Lingnau, 40, for the past three years executive assistant, has been appointed the new executive director.

William Johnson, president of the league, said Mr. Lingnau won't be going to "simply take over" but is expected to reshape the party organization for the next provincial election with the hope Socreds can win.

"Who knows, we might set a new 36 year record for Social Credit government," Mr. Johnson said.

Mr. Lingnau, a former in-

More Kenneay Page 2

Grim grain harvest seen

OTTAWA (CP) — Statistics Canada painted a bleak picture of the 1972 grain and oilseed crop Wednesday, predicting a drop in nearly all principal field crops in its first estimate of production. Wheat production, estimated at 307.5 million bushels, is four per cent lower than last year's 529.6 million bushels.

Ottawa proposes controls on quality of drugs

By PETER CALAMAI
Southam News Services

OTTAWA — New controls to safeguard the quality of prescription drugs sold in Canada have been proposed by the federal health department.

The tentative regulations, outlined in a letter received Tuesday by drug manufacturers and distributors, represent a major strengthening of the federal drug quality assurance program.

The quality assurance program provides the scientific underpinnings for legislation in six provinces allowing druggists to substitute cheaper "generic" drugs for more expensive brand-name varieties.

Under the new controls, likely to become effective early next year, drug manufacturers and distributors must have all raw pharmaceutical chemicals and finished drug products tested in Canada for identity, potency and purity.

The regulations also impose the printing of an expiration date on the labels of drugs which will deteriorate beyond certain potency and purity standards within three years after manufacture.

Under existing drug controls, manufacturers must supply information on identity, potency and purity to federal officials upon demand but need not carry out the required test in Canada.

"We think it makes good sense to have the drugs tested in the country where they're sold," said Dr. A. B. Morrison, head of the federal health protection branch.

The more stringent testing regulation is bound to have a major impact on the Canadian pharmaceutical industry, which is predominantly foreign-controlled and often merely imports raw materials from foreign parent companies and puts the chemicals into capsules or tablets here.

In 1969 for instance, the total cost of pharmaceutical material used in Canada was estimated at 57 million. Of this amount, 33 million was imported as raw, semi-processed or finished products.

But a drug industry spokesman welcomed the tougher quality regulations.

"We recognize that accepting pieces of paper from other countries is not adequate assurance that the product meets Canadian standards," said Don Harper of the Pharmaceutical Manufacturers Association of Canada. The VMAC represents 60 companies responsible for manufacturing 85 per cent of the prescription drugs sold in Canada.

In the past, the pharmaceutical association has charged that smaller generic drug houses import raw chemicals from suppliers in Italy, Poland and Hong Kong where quality controls may not be up to Canadian standards.

But Dr. Morrison rejected any suggestion that the tougher testing regulations were specifically aimed at the smaller manufacturers or generic drug houses.

The health protection branch chief also said the new expiration date labelling was designed to guard against a "potential hazard" of subpotency drugs.

"We know that potency deteriorates over a period of time for many drugs but our monitoring program doesn't indicate a potency problem among the 90 drugs most commonly prescribed." Dr. Morrison said.

26,500-seat Clarke Stadium was too old and small to use as the main venue for the Games.

The Edmonton Eskimos proposal for a $19.4-million, 45,220-seat domed facility to be used by the football team sparked an intense debate among *Journal* readers about "Cadillac" spending on "the elitist few."

In fact, *Journal* coverage of the debate leading up to sod turnings on the various Commonwealth Games venues was long and drawn out. Environmentalists didn't want the Kinsmen pool in thc river valley. Residents around the stadium site didn't want the stadium.

No one could figure out what we would do with a $900,000 velodrome once the Games were over.

The naysayers got up a petition and forced the issue to a plebiscite set for March 20, 1974.

"Some of these Edmontonians are deeply sincere and have the highest motives," fretted *The Journal's* March 19 editorial.

"And in a characteristically human way, they may feel that by voting 'no' they will be criticizing the things they resent and will be punishing the people they dislike."

But, points out the editorialist, reneging on the commitment to the Games would make the city look silly. "Vote yes and allow the games to proceed here. Then, if the conduct of the council is deserving of censure or punishment, the time to exercise the citizen's sanction is in the municipal elections later in the year."

No one needed to have worried; Edmontonians were overwhelmingly in favour of the Games. With federal, provincial and private contributions, Edmonton constructed $32.1 million worth of facilities.

Eventually, it all came together and the city did itself proud.

On July 18, 1978, the stadium opened and the paper called it "a triumph for all seasons." And it was.

The final item in the trilogy of major facilities building in the '70s was a convention centre, an item not as sexy as a stadium or arena. Once again there was controversy about the price tag and location.

Eventually, the Grierson Hill site was selected.

The tiered, built-into-the-hill centre was designed and a price tag, $32 million, was attached to the project.

When finally completed in 1983, the centre's price tag was $82 million, the largest cost overrun in the city's history.

And, once again, naysayers got a petition going to send the issue to plebiscite, and, once again, the people spoke in favour of development.

It was only a 25-per-cent turnout, but 86 per cent of them said borrow the money and build the thing.

The Journal was ecstatic. "There are many forces that would break down our faith in ourselves as a community," said the editorial on the 29th.

"(The plebiscite) did demonstrate that most Edmontonians are enthusiastic about their future. This is, after all, Alberta. If there is any place left in Canada where people should pursue the best with confidence, it is here."

No one mentioned that if Hunter was right about the cost, it would have been cheaper to build the omniplex in the first place.

of Mayor William Hawrelak, who died in office.

***Nov. 23, 1975*:**
The Edmonton Eskimos beat the Montreal Alouettes 9-8 for their first CFL title since 1956.

***Dec. 19, 1975*:**
Alberta's minimum wage increases by 25 cents an hour to $2.75 an hour, effective March 1976.

***Jan. 5, 1976*:**
J. Patrick O'Callaghan becomes publisher of *The Journal*, replacing Ross Munro who becomes publisher of the *Montreal Gazette*.

***March 3, 1976*:**
Kingsway Garden Mall shopping centre officially opens.

***June 11, 1976*:**
The Edmonton Oil Kings major junior hockey team moves to Portland, Oregon, where it's renamed the Winter Hawks.

***June 22, 1976*:**
The newspaper launches Junior Journal, including the Junior Press Club where members earned badges by submitting stories. They could move up the ranks from Junior Journal cub reporter to Junior Journal publisher.

***July 1, 1976*:**
The new Dog Control Bylaw

Farewell to those cold, soggy hospital meals

By ANDY IMLACH
Of The Journal

Soggy, tasteless vegetables and meat that was hot several hours ago, the traditional image of hospital food, is on the way out for Edmonton's two largest hospitals.

The Royal Alexandra and University hospitals announced Thursday a joint food production and distribution system which, beginning Jan. 1, 1976, will provide fresh, hot meals to patients at a reduced cost.

Harold Porter and Joseph Newhouse, finance directors of the Royal Alex and the University respectively, agreed it is almost impossible now to provide hot, undeteriorated food to all patients. The new system, similar to that employed by airlines, will give patients food that is "smoking hot."

Raw food will be purchased and cooked at the food pavilion at the Royal Alex, but the system will be independently run.

Instead of transporting cooked food around both hospitals on covered trays that allow the food to cool and become soggy, meals will be transported chilled or frozen and then heated at each nursing station.

The finance director explained that food will be cooked and then chilled or frozen at the central kitchen, transported to the hospitals and stored.

When it is required, the cold food will be placed on trays and transported to the wards, where the trays will be heated in ovens. Dishes which do not require heating would be insulated on the trays.

A total of 12,000 meals a day are to be served under the new system, which will provide 90 per cent of the meals for the two major hospitals, as well as for the Dr. W. W. Cross Cancer Institute, the Aberhart Pavilion and the Veterans' Home.

Some special diets, special-occasion dinners and food like milk, sandwiches and salads will still be prepared in the individual kitchens, as will other foods which don't freeze or chill well, such as scrambled eggs.

The hospitals hope other health-care institutions in the Edmonton area will join the system. The Misericordia Hospital and Alberta Hospital have shown interest.

As well as providing higher quality meals, the operation is supposed to be cheaper. A consultant's report predicts an eight-per-cent drop in food-purchasing costs through greater bulk buying. The hospitals pay about $1.5 million a year for food.

The main saving will stem from the reduced manpower necessary at each hospital to man the kitchens. A total of 99 jobs will be terminated, while 38 new ones will be created at the new centre. Overall cost saving is predicted to be $400,000 a year.

The finance director said staff turnover and absorption into other hospital jobs could take care of most of the displaced workers.

The system, which has been approved by the Alberta Hospital Services Commission, will require purchase of trucks to transport food to the University, $300,000 to $400,000 worth of renovations and extra equipment at the Royal Alex food pavilion, and ovens for the nursing stations.

Edmonton Journal

FORECAST: SUNNY PERIODS EDMONTON, ALBERTA, FRIDAY, MAY 31, 1974 PRICE 15c

Petrosar's argument rejected

By BOB BELL
Of The Journal

Petrosar failed to convince Premier Peter Lougheed Thursday to change his mind about Alberta's opposition to construction of its Sarnia-based petrochemical plant.

Mr. Lougheed said in an interview he wasn't satisfied with the reasons Petrosar gave why the plant had to be located in the existing petrochemical centre of Sarnia, or why its petrochemical needs couldn't be met through alternate methods—including development of part of the project in Alberta.

Top Petrosar officials, meeting with Mr. Lougheed and the Alberta cabinet energy committee Thursday, were asked if they would back up their plans with feasibility studies and figures.

Petrosar president I. C. Rush, in a frosty two-paragraph statement before TV cameras following the meeting, said the company will provide the premier with a recent evaluation made of a petrochemical process the company could develop in Alberta. He then flatly refused to answer reporters' questions.

The Petrosar submission to Mr. Lougheed indicated the Alberta-based idea was not suitable to Petrosar needs, and was discarded in favor of a plant located at Sarnia.

Mr. Rush hoped the meeting brought "a greater understanding and appreciation of each other's problems and aspirations," but the situation did not appear to budge from that of several weeks ago.

At that time Mr. Lougheed warned Petrosar it would be ill-advised to rely on Alberta as an assured source of crude oil feedstocks, and he cautioned again Thursday against building a plant that would require, over its life, 16 per cent of Alberta's current reserves.

Could jeopardize industry

The government objects to the Sarnia plant because it could jeopardize an Alberta petrochemical industry at a time when there is only the market for two plants.

Ottawa and Petrosar (it is 51-per-cent owned by the federal crown corporation Polysar) believe the market can support three world-scale plants by 1980.

The other proposals are the partially Alberta-based and partially Alberta-supported Dow Dome project, and the entirely Alberta-based and supported Alberta Gas Trunk Lines — Canadian Industries Ltd. (AGTL-CIL) plan.

The federal government has already hinted it could "force-feed" the Petrosar plant by diverting oil from that now going to export into the U.S., and the company expects to apply for Ontario zoning permission leading to construction June 6.

In the legislature, Mr. Lougheed told Social Credit House leader Bob Clark the government would be ready to talk with Petrosar again "when they provide us with a feasibility report that would show the various alternatives and identify the national public interest in terms of what would be desirable in regional economic development."

Examine more fully

He said Petrosar would "take under consideration to examine in a fuller way than in the past" the feasibility of modifying their project to bring some part of its development to Alberta, the appropriate use of energy resources, and alternate ways of meeting Ontario's requirements for petrochemical supplies.

While the Dow Dome and AGTL-CIL projects would use natural gas to process ethylene, the building block of the plastics industry, the Petrosar scheme uses crude oil.

While it doesn't yield as much ethylene, Petrosar wants to use the process because it does yield various other types of petrochemicals not available from natural gas to supply the needs of various eastern manufacturing plants.

To move the process to Alberta would mean the fuel-oil residue that also results from the operation would lose the ready Eastern market needed to absorb it.

To use a third process that produced the specialty petrochemicals but no fuel residues would result in a $55-million-a-year additional cost to get the products to Ontario.

"The cost of keeping the existing Canadian petrochemical industry supplied with feedstocks at competitive prices from such a facility has a prohibitive effect on its economics," the Petrosar statement to the premier said.

Cancelling the Petrosar project in Sarnia at this stage would result in loss of $25 million already spent in development costs.

Why Petrosar favors one oil complex — Analysis on Page 86.

Oops!

Oh, fuddle duddle! Tory Leader Bob Stanfield winces as he fumbles the football while taking a little time out from the federal campaign in North Bay, Ont. Thursday. Maybe the centreman, who snapped the ball, was a Grit . . . Stories on the election campaign on Page 17.

Bonds gamble fails

OTTAWA (CP) — The latest figures on the redemptions of Canada Savings Bonds indicates Finance Minister John Turner's plan to boost yields to account for inflation has fallen flat.

The Bank of Canada weekly report Thursday showed $57 million worth of bonds were cashed in during the week ended Wednesday.

More than $230 million worth of savings bonds have been cashed since Mr. Turner brought in his budget May 6, representing a substantial decline in value of government securities outstanding.

The only fiscal measure to survive the budget, on which the Liberal government was defeated May 8, was the move to provide a guaranteed yield of nine per cent for Canadian savings bonds.

Trust companies now are offering 10 per cent interest rates on five-year term deposits.

Savings bond yields are raised to nine per cent by paying a bonus at maturity or on Nov. 1, 1979.

Those who have to hold bonds until 1979 to get the bonus would be in the same position as those who now buy five-year term deposits, which also would mature in 1979.

But the 10-per-cent interest rate on term deposits when compounded provides a yield of more than 12 per cent.

The redemption total last week of $57 million compared with $56 million the previous week and $115 million during the week ended May 15. For the week to May 8, bonds

More BONDS Page 6

The will to live grows weaker each day

LONDON (AP) — Two sisters serving life sentences for their part in Irish Republican Army bombing in London are reported to have vowed to continue a six-month-old hunger strike despite their weakening condition.

Marian and Dolours Price are demanding permission to serve their terms in a jail in Northern Ireland. The militant Provisional wing to the Irish Republican Army has warned in Dublin that the consequences of their death would be "devastating."

A committee campaigning on behalf of the sisters said it received a letter from them, smuggled out of London's Brixton prison, in which they say they are "pretty worn out."

"Even to walk to the loo (toilet) drains us, and the least movement leaves my heart pounding like a big drum," one of the sisters wrote in the letter the committee said. "I get very listless, though, at night and every time I turn in bed I stab myself with my bones."

The reported letter continued: "Each day passes and we fade a little more, but no matter how the body may fade, our determination never will."

Marian, 20, and Dolours, 23, were fed until 10 days ago through tubes inserted into their throats. But the home office said this was stopped when they refused to co-operate with doctors.

Two English women prisoners began hunger strikes Thursday in sympathy with the Prices. They are Rose Dugdale, a self-styled revolutionary who is awaiting trial on charges connected with a $20-million art robbery in the Irish republic, and Pat Arrowsmith, a pacifist jailed for inciting British troops assigned to Northern Ireland to desert.

Alberta epidemic fear

Disease ravages cattle

By HEATHER MENZIES
Of The Journal

ST. PAUL — More than 400 cattle throughout Alberta have been slaughtered following an outbreak of brucellosis, a disease which causes abortions and sterility among the animals.

The proportions of the infestation have been compared to a situation in Saskatchewan last year, according to federal government agriculture department official.

Three herds have been destroyed in the St. Paul region where the heaviest outbreak has occurred, and a further seven herds are under quarantine while blood tests are analysed.

Four herds are under quarantine in the Vermilion area, two around Calgary, two at Wetaskiwin, one each at Drumheller, Fort Macleod and Wainwright, with another suspect herd at Camrose.

The health of animals division of the federal government department of agriculture is stepping up its testing programs in a desperate effort to stamp out the disease before it spreads further into the livestock industry.

Ordered destroyed

Already one case of infestation among hogs has been reported, with that farmer's herd ordered destroyed by federal veterinarians in the St. Paul region.

The disease is easily communicated from one affected animal to all the others in a herd and is also difficult to spot and thus to iolate, said Dr. George Eggink, federal veterinarion at St. Paul.

When in doubt, it is still better to order the whole herd destroyed, the government veterinarians have found. Even then, a farmer has to wait sometimes six months to a year before he can rid his feedlot, pastureland and sloughs of the last traces of bacterial infection.

Quarantine lift

Only then will the government lift its quarantine allowing the farmer to get back into the business for which he might be entirely dependent for his livelihood.

The animals present no danger when eaten, since the disease is confined to the animal's sexual organs. Thus farmers can recover the going market price for each animal when they are forced to slaughter their herds.

But included in the herds that have been destroyed so far is breeding stock worth thousands of dollars a head. The government compensation, which is paid when the quarantine is lifted, is $450 for an exotic or other recognized quality breeding animal.

Farmer kills pigs in price protest

By JIM DAVIES
and BRIAN BUTTERS
Of The Journal

WESTLOCK — For the past three days, farmer Maurice Letourneau has been shooting his 100-plus hogs, burning and burying them, or feeding them to the coyotes.

Mr. Letourneau says it's his personal protest against the low hog prices and high grain costs which he estimates are causing him to lose as much as $40 on every hog he produces.

"I guess I've shot 118 or 119 of them," Letourneau, 42, father of five, said this morning. "You lose track after you pile so many in a bucket (of an earth-moving machine).

"I've just buried most of them," he said. "But I saw there were four coyotes near the yard — one who's got some pups — so I figured I might as well feed them some cheap food."

The hog slaughter began Tuesday night, he said, "and we finished up late last (Thursday) night."

Mr. Letourneau, who has kept two sows for his family's use, says the hogs killed ranged from two-week-old piglets to 240-pounders.

He estimated that he lost only $1,000 by not selling the hogs, which he said represented an investment of up to $4,000 in feed costs alone.

He said he had tried to sell them recently but was told to keep them for awhile longer because the slaughtering houses were too busy.

"Then some guy offered me $7 for each 60- to 70-pound pig and I said I'd shoot them first. That's how it all started."

The dead hogs began piling up on the farm, so Mr. Letourneau buried 89 of them, fed a bunch to the coyotes,

More PIGS Page 6

Where to find it

Ann Landers	22	Legal & Auction Ads	77
Art Evans	17	Letters To The Journal	4
Barry Westgate	71	News Digest	2
Births, Deaths, Marriages	34	Patterns	45-52
Bridge	40	Sport	79-85
Business, Stocks	86-88	Temperatures	23
Charles Lynch	4	TV	22
Classified Ads	35-64	Radio	22
Comics, Features	30	Wayne Overland	79
Editorial	4		
Crossword Puzzle	39		
Entertainment	72-76		
Family Section	19-23		
Focus on People	78		
Horoscope	38		
June Sheppard	19		

Weather

Cloudy with sunny periods; high near 60, low near 40. Saturday: mainly sunny; high in the mid-60s. Details on Page 23.

Project was a hare-y disaster

By DON THOMAS
Of The Journal

The voracious appetite of the snowshoe hare forced the Alberta Forest Service (AFS) to scrap a major tree-plant-program aimed at providing a base for future pulp mills in northern Alberta.

AFS director F. W. McDougall says the program involved the planting of pine and spruce in areas where huge stands of poplar grew up after forest fires.

One huge block of land north of Lesser Slave Lake could conceivably support three pulp mills if it was stocked with pine and spruce instead of poplar.

Since the early 1960s "several thousand acres" of poplar forest were bulldozed and stocked with spruce and pine seedlings. Initially, things looked fine. Then the snowshoe hares went to work.

After AFS staff noticed rabbit damage, a team of biologists from the University of Wisconsin's Rochester Wildlife Research Centre, 60 miles north of Edmonton, was asked to survey the problem.

Their report in the fall of 1972, said basically there was no way that the AFS could keep more than a few hops ahead of the hares, and the program was halted.

Poplar forests and mixed spruce-pine forests are ideal habitat for the hares, which tremendously increase in population about every 10 years, building up to a density as high as 10 per acre.

When there are that many rabbis around, they soon eat themselves out of house and home and the population begins to nosedive.

Before it does, the hungry rabbits go for almost anything, including pine and spurce seedlings, which may be chewed right down to the ground.

Mr. McDougall notes that the hungry rabbits sometimes go after AFS signs and have even chewed on the shingles of an AFS ranger station.

The Rochester team's study notes that the hare population was at a low level through 1964 to 1966 and peaked from 1971-72. It is now going back to a low ebb and will peak again in 1979-81.

It suggested several measures which might discourage the rabbits from chewing the seedlings, but said studies could take several years.

In the long-run, it might make more sense to develop forestry technology to make use of poplar trees "rather than trying to fit the resources to existing technology," said the report.

A Gruesome Tale

"I am returning the front page of the March 1 Journal as I did not wish to contaminate our container with such garbage. This is the ultimate in crude reporting and I for one will have no part of it."
— Donald R. Kvill, letter to the editor, March 7, 1973

Thirty-one years ago, all of Canada came to know who Marten Hartwell was and what he did. Now, his historical designation is "wasn't he the guy who…?"

Yes, he was the guy who ate the nurse and that was the part of the story to which Mr. Kvill and a dozen more readers objected.

The story started Nov. 10, 1972. *The Journal's* northern affairs reporter, stationed in Yellowknife, was Steve Hume, but for some unspecified reason, Hume's wife, Susan Mayse, wrote the "Special to The Journal" story.

"An Eskimo woman about to give birth is one of the four persons missing after a mercy flight aircraft carrying the woman from Spence Bay to Yellowknife disappeared." The plane had been missing two days.

The pregnant woman was Neemee Nulliayok.

Also on the twin-engine Beechcraft were 14-year-old David Kootook and Spence Bay nurse Judy Hill.

Bush pilot Marten Hartwell, 48, had worked for Gateway Aviation since the previous May. He was, as the later stories indicated, a competent pilot but only qualified to fly in clear weather during daylight hours.

This was to be an 800-kilometre flight mostly at night. Hartwell was the only pilot available and the medical authorities judged Nulliayok's condition to be serious enough to preclude waiting for the scheduled PWA flight at midnight.

Planes were added to the search, but over the next four days there was little more to report and the stories moved from the front page to the inside pages. Then they dropped off *The Journal's* radar screen altogether.

The story was resurrected Monday, Dec. 11, when Hartwell, the lone survivor, was rescued after 32-days on an Arctic hillside some 320 kilometres off his flight path.

Many details about the ordeal came out that day. Hill and Nulliayok both died soon after the crash. Kootook held on for 24 days. Hartwell, whose ankles and kneecap were broken, credited the boy with saving his life, bringing lichen from trees to Hartwell to stave off starvation.

The bombshell dropped March 1, 1973, when Hume wrote from Yellowknife: "Martin Hartwell's personal agony, including the decision to eat human flesh, was revealed Wednesday evening before a coroner's jury and a packed public gallery." After Kootook died, Hartwell consumed part of nurse Hill's body to survive.

The same day an RCMP officer read Hartwell's statement to the Yellowknife jury, Hartwell was in Edmonton saying the same thing to reporter John Lindblad.

"There was no way out but to eat human flesh and this I did."

goes into effect. "It comes complete with pooper-scooper clauses, higher fines for offenders, and attempts to exclude dogs from parks and playgrounds."

***July 2, 1976*:**
Edmonton's population is 461,559, according to the civic census.

***July 24, 1976*:**
Edmonton swimmers Cheryl Gibson and Becky Smith win silver and bronze Olympic medals respectively in the same race, the 400-metre IM, at the Summer Games in Montreal. Edmonton swimmer Graham Smith wins a silver medal in the 4x100 medley relay at the Montreal Olympics.

***Aug. 3, 1976*:**
A story reports that 18,000 people attended the city's first Heritage Day festival in Hawrelak Park. There were 14 pavilions displaying various arts and crafts and selling ethnic foods. The next year, there were 50 pavilions.

***Sept. 1, 1976*:**
Peter Pocklington becomes 40-per-cent owner of the Edmonton Oilers.

***Sept. 3, 1976*:**
Edmonton's Muttart Conservatory is officially opened.

Mortgage rate hike fails to deter home buyers

By CLAIR BALFOUR
Financial Times Service

OTTAWA — At Central Mortgage and Housing Corp. a guessing game is what will happen if the open market interest rate for mortgages goes through 10 per cent. So far, with rates hovering between 9.75 and 10 per cent, "nobody's indicated that buyers are holding off in Toronto or anywhere else," says Arnold Wilson, executive director. "Market resistance is not there and has not shown in any statistics yet."

CMHC's concern about the public's reaction to rising interest rates is more than academic. The federal crown agency has two functions:

- To insure mortgage loans by banks, insurance and trust companies. This is done under the National Housing Act but such loans are a diminishing part of the agency's operations.
- To make direct mortgage loans from its funds to low income groups at interest rates well below prevailing rates from private lenders.

Early this week, CMHC came under attack from the Ontario Housing Corp. after raising the maximum rates under which it will insure NHA loans to 9.5 per cent from 8.75.

The NHA loans are still slightly lower than conventional loans but CMHC officials were piqued because they are already providing much cheaper mortgages to lower income borrowers.

The corporation has been concentrating its lending on the broad categories of housing for low income people, particularly since 1970. Of the total loans and capital commitments for housing, the proportion for low income earners rose to 89.9 per cent last year from 72.5 per cent in 1970. It was below 40 per cent as recently as 1968 but has climbed every year.

Last year, $484 million of $540 million in direct mortgages was devoted to low income housing. Officials say the promotion will be even higher this year.

This money is loaned, currently at 8 per cent, under a formula that bypasses the market and permits the corporation to lend money for almost the rate it obtains it. The formula is based on the government's own 20-year borrowing rate, plus a markup of less than one-quarter of one per cent to cover administrative cost.

The special rate is subject to quarterly adjustments.

The corporation anticipates housing will continue to boom this year. A record number of starts was made last month—$23,070, an 18 per cent gain compared with July, 1972. But mortgage money is expected to be harder to find. "We do certainly expect more competition for mortgage money from the rest of the market." says Mr. Wilson.

The corporation has consistently had budgets of about $1 billion for the last three years but not since 1970 has most of the budget been allocated and spent.

One official suggested that provincial governments, which participate in public housing have found trouble financing their share.

One official suggested "for provinces without the financial capability of Ontario, they can't afford it. It's certainly not somebody in Treasury Board saying (to CMHC) 'no, you can't have it'."

A colleague added, "We don't build this stuff. The provinces request it . . . we had more in the budget." A noteworthy exception is Manitoba, where a change in government to the New Democratic government in 1969 was followed by a jump in federal contribution to $72 million for public housing in 1970 from virtually nothing in the previous 18 years.

Amendments to the National Housing Act passed earlier this year are expected to result in a surge of lending under subsidy and assistance for home ownership to low income groups.

Edmonton Journal

FORECAST: THUNDERSHOWERS — EDMONTON, ALBERTA, THURSDAY, AUGUST 23, 1973 — PRICE 15c

Most rail workers return

TORONTO (CP) — Most of Canada's 56,000 non-operating railway workers were due back on the job today but two regional strikes — one of them unofficial — continued to paralyze much of the country's rail traffic.

Only in Quebec was a rotating strike, one of a series called by the Associated Non-Operating Rail Unions in a contract dispute with 11 railway companies, still in effect.

But workers in Hamilton and Windsor, due back on their jobs at the end of a 50-hour strike Wednesday, did not return.

A union official called their action "legal but not official."

The strike in Quebec was to have ended at 6 a.m. today, but was extended by the union for another 18 hours, to midnight tonight.

The non-ops ended a 48-hour strike in the Atlantic provinces at 6 a.m. today. Another walkout, encompassing Alberta, British Columbia and the Northwest Territories, ended at midnight Wednesday night.

The Atlantic strike left more than 500 loaded boxcars between Moncton and North Sydney, N.S., waiting for transfer to Newfoundland, isolated when the strike shut down ferries. There was a two-mile-long line of cars at North Sydney waiting for the Newfoundland ferries to go back into service.

Although no food shortages developed in insular Newfoundland, there were fears that remote communities in Labrador may not get their winter food and fuel supplies if the strikes continue.

In northwestern Ontario, an

More RAIL Page 6

Edmonton men back to work

Some 2,000 Edmonton non-operating railway employees returned to work at midnight Wednesday, ending western region's fourth cross-country rotating strike.

The Edmonton workers are among 8,000 in Alberta, British Columbia, the Yukon and Northwest Territories that took part in the 48-hour walkout.

Strike co-ordinator Dick Henham said he expected most of the men would return as scheduled, despite growing tension over the five-week-old strike.

"Naturally they're disappointed at this chap Munro (Labour Minister John Munro) not being able to settle it, and he's the government's top hand in this," he said.

John Munro "ran out of steam" in his unsuccessful attempt to settle the railway strike, according to a union official. Story Page 13.

THIS STATEMENT OR A BOMB

Following, by James Cameron, is the statement he demanded The Journal print or else he would blow up the plant.

MAN IS ROBBED OF TRUST IN HIS OWN POWER OF THOUGHT Dr. Albert Schweitzer writing in his book "Pilgrimage to Humanity" has this to say, I am completely, opposed to the spirit of this age, because it promotes the neglect of thought. Today there is not only a neglect of thought but an actual distrust or deprecation of it. The organized political, social, and religious groups of our time are bent on inducing the individual to take up uncritically ready-made beliefs rather than inviting him to work out for himself by thought his own convictions. A man who thinks for himself and therefore is free, is a troublesome and strange being. There is no assurance that he will fit comfortably into their organizations. All organized groups today find their strength, not so much in the spiritual values of their ideas, or of the people who are their members, but in achieving the highest possible degree of unity and exclusiveness. In this way find their strongest power and surest defence.

Throughout his life, modern man is the object of influences which are directed to the end of robbing him of trust in his own power of thought. The spirit of spiritual dependence, to which he is to surrender, is imbedded in everything he reads and hears. It is incarnate in the people he deals with. It lurks in the groups and associations of which he becomes a member. It threatens him in all the circumstances of his life. From all sides and in many ways, pressure is applied to convince him that the truths and trusts which he needs for life have already been manufactured by organizations which have rights over him. The spirit of the age never lets him become his own man. It strangles freedom. Again and again, beliefs are forced upon him in the same way in which commercial establishments which have sufficient money can put pressure on him through high powered advertising to buy their products.

The spirit of the age forces modern man to doubt his own capacity for thought in order to make him submit to authority. He cannot resist these insistent influences, because he is overworked, distraught and anxious. The many constraints within whose domain it is his lot to work conspire to make him believe that he is incapable of thinking for himself.

The continually increasing, huge mass of knowledge which he faces shatters his self-confidence. He can no longer assimilate all the new discoveries being proclaimed. Although he does not understand them, he must take them as matters of fact. Given this situation in the face of scientific truth he is confirmed in the feeling that in the matters of thought his judgment is not to be trusted. Thus the circumstances of modern life deliver man over as a victim to the authoritarian spirit of our time. The seed of scepticism has germinated. Modern man no longer possesses a spiritual self-confidence. Although he has tremendous abilities in material matters, he is intellectually stunted, because he does not use his capacity for individual free thinking. It is incomprehensible that our age, which has distinguished itself by its many achievements in knowledge and skills, could have descended to such spiritual depths that it abandoned thinking.

2 KNOW THE ROBBERS Ralph Waldo Trine, writing in his book "In Tune With the Infinite" has this to say, The true teacher is the one whose endeavor is to bring the one he teaches to a true knowledge of himself and hence to his own interior powers that he may become his own interpreter. For the man who would rob another of his free and unfettered search for truth, or who would stand as the interpreter of truth for another with the intent of remaining in this position, rather than leading him to the place where he can be his own interpreter is more to be shunned than a thief or a robber. The injury he works is far greater for he is doing direct and positive injury to the life of the one he thus holds, and to the extent he endeavors to hold men everywhere by such means, the greater injury he works toward all mankind.

3 BUILD THE INTEGRAL SOCIETY J. D. Hill and W. E. Stuermann, writing in their book "Philosophy and the American Heritage" have this to say, The integral person is one whose life does not betray devisiveness, unconquerable indecision, lack of controlling goals, or want of reflective foresight and resolution. The man of integrity (and a society with integrity also) has to some degree organized and related the various desires and impulses under the control of a single goal or loyalty. The idea of God or faith in God, properly framed or understood, can serve (perhaps must serve) as the high loyalty under which a man's life may be rendered integral. It would scarcely be philosophic or fitting to human finitude to insist, however, that any particular religious tradition has a monopoly on the divine concept or the religious faith which would be most useful for realizing the virtue.

Finally there is the long-suppressed righteous anger of the just man, says Dr. Solomon. This type of anger at the unfair treatment of minority groups, at political tyranny, at the world's hypocrisies—has been responsible for some of the most significant social and cultural advances.

"Through the ages when an achievement of this kind has been made you will find it has been initiated or carried through by one or a group of God's angry men," declares Dr. Solomon.

19

~~Don't print this but~~
Consider what is said
in reference to my case
print if you wish

~~Literary Gems
numbered 1 to 5~~
~~A and B are
my criticisms~~
Print all this
with corrections
re misled and
generally. 9c

Journal emptied in bomb threat

By MARC HORTON
Of The Journal

A man, demanding the publication of a "personal manifesto," entered The Journal building about 9:35 a.m. today and threatened to blow up the building.

The 400 Journal employees in the building at the time of the incident were evacuated at 9:40 a.m., although the pressmen were called back about 10:45 to permit the presses to roll. The pressmen are in an adjacent building.

Sgt. Jim Parks, of city police patrol, said they had been to his house "and there's not much doubt anymore that it's the real thing."

"The guy is an electronic genius."

He informed the composing room staff and the nearly-deserted newsroom that they could stay on a volunteer basis, "but you're a long time dead."

The man entered the library carrying a satchel and demanded to see the editor of the newspaper, Andrew Snaddon.

The library is located next to the newsroom on the third floor of the building.

A Journal librarian said the man came into the library, carrying a suitcase with his hand in a tin can, which he said contained the trigger for the explosive.

A Journal sub-editor, Jan Wenzel, in the library doing research when the man entered, was told to "shut up, and get the editor or the whole place is going to blow up."

By that time, however, Mr. Snaddon had already been informed of the incident and had ordered the building cleared.

Journal publisher Ross Munro met alone with the man in the library and was handed a document entitled "Special Request Printing of Five Literary Gems (from the scrapbook of James Cameron, 9515 87th Ave., Edmonton, Alberta)".

City police arrived, including two members of the bomb disposal unit, and joined Mr. Munro and the man in the library.

Along with the "personal manifesto," which quoted a number of philosophers and contained his own remarks, the man handed Mr. Munro a letter which also was to be run in today's newspaper.

Included in the leter was a statement saying he "is highly disturbed that the Edmonton Journal has not printed his letters to the editor over the last 25 years . . ."

In the letter, Mr. Cameron asked that his entire "manifesto" be printed without changes, and "that you call in reporters from the radio and television stations immediately that they may read a copy of literary items I want printed."

He also asked that everybody be kept away from the library "especially the police," and added that no one would be hurt and no property destroyed.

U.S. firefighters face new threat

BOISE, Idaho (AP)—Firefighters took a breather early today after reporting substantial progress in battling blazes on rangelands and forests in the western United States. But unfavorable weather predictions made the gains tenuous.

The Interagency Fire Centre here said late Wednesday that seven major blazes covering more than 50,000 acres remain out of control, with more than 6,000 men on the fire lines.

Only 24 hours earlier, the centre had listed 13 major fires on more than 100,000 acres as uncontrolled, with 12,000 men at work.

But the National Weather Service predicted extensive thunderstorms with lightning, high winds and little rain through Saturday for Idaho and Montana, with a chance of similar storms in eastern sections of Washington and Oregon.

Forestry officials have described this fire season as the worst in 20 years for the drought-plagued Northwest.

Dick Klade, information officer at the centre, said that in the last 10 days 50 major fires have destroyed 189,824 acres.

Firefighters said Wednesday that for the first time since the rash of fires began almost all the new blazes were caused by nature rather than by man. Klade said 151 fires were started by lightning, mostly in Idaho and Oregon, during a two-day period ending late Wednesday.

The centre gave this state-by-state breakdown on major fires still out of control early today:

Idaho—Pine Creek, 2,320 acres, 635 firefighters.

Oregon—Freezeout, 10,500 acres, about 1,000 firefighters.

Montana—Caribou Mountain, Goat Creek, Tri Creek, totalling 10,850 acres, about 2,000 firefighters.

California—Pilliken and Inskip Grade, totalling 30,000 acres, 2,478 firefighters.

The Pilliken fire, 25 miles east of Placerville, Calif., began running again Wednesday when high winds hit the area. Two thousand firefighters were hoping to contain the blaze sometime today.

POLICE TAKE NUDE HIKER FOR A RIDE

FORT LAUDERDALE, Fla. (AP) — Donald Albert Schott didn't have any luck when he tried to hitch a ride during rush-hour traffic in a business district here Wednesday, so, police said, he took off his clothes to attract attention.

Schott, 21, of Cincinnati, Ohio, strolled several blocks in the nude shouting "Somebody give me a ride," witnesses told police.

Officers arrived minutes later and offered Schott a ride. He was driven to jail where he was charged with "hitch-hiking and creating a diversion."

U.S. envoy to Israel

TEL AVIV (AP) — Kenneth B. Keating arrived here as the new United States ambassador to Israel. The post had been vacant for six months. Keating, 73, is a former Republican congressman and senator from New York and served as ambassador to India during the December, 1971, war between India and Pakistan.

South Africa economy up

PRETORIA (Reuter) — South Africa's economy is on an upward trend after two years of relatively slow growth, says the annual report of the South African Reserve Bank. With a healthy balance of payments and domestic production increasing, the most pressing problem is the high rate of price increases, the report says.

MOSQUITO INDEX

Rating: Extreme. Eight bites per minute.

Where to find it

Ann Landers	18
Barry Craig	3
Births, Deaths, Marriages	22
Bridge	26
Business, Stocks	62-67
Charles Lynch	4
Classified ads	23-42
Comics, Features	52
Comment	4
Crossword Puzzle	27
Eight Wheels	9
Entertainment	50-52
Family Section	15-19
Focus on People	11
Health Column	16
Horoscope	25
June Sheppard	15
Letters To The Journal	4
News Digest	10
Patterns	30, 31
Sport	55-61
TV, Radio	53
Wayne Overland	55

Today's weather

Isolated late afternoon and evening thundershowers today, lasting until midnight; high near 75, low 45-50. A few clouds Friday with afternoon and evening showers or thundershowers; high 70-75. Details on Page 8.

Pressure mounts for higher grain subsidy

By DON SELLAR
Southam News Services

OTTAWA — With Canada's poor forced to dig ever deeper into their wallets just to maintain humble macaroni-and-bread diets, Wheat Board Minister Otto Lang is examining ways of controlling sky-high grain prices.

But Mr. Lang is well aware of the fact that if he imposes a ceiling on Prairie grain prices without guaranteeing a decent minimum income for farmers, there will be new storms of protest from the anti-Liberal West.

The Trudeau government, however, is under increasing pressure from its political opponents and even from its own food prices review board to subidize basic foodstuffs, including grains, more heavily.

The food prices board last week predicted a 35-per-cent jump in bread prices and a 75-per-cent leap in macaroni and spaghetti prices this fall if current trends continue.

Amid the clamor for selective price controls on food staples of the poor, Mr. Lang is attempting to assemble a comprehensive grains policy, the bulk of which would require parliamentary approval.

According to government sources, the Lang plan may be ready for preliminary consideration by the cabinet in about three weeks, though it's by no means clear that the measures will be presented as a package.

Exactly what Mr. Lang will recommend to the cabinet as a solution to soaring grain prices isn't known, but a broad range of measures such as higher subsidies from the public treasury or even direct price controls are available to him.

The minister's recent public statements indicate that he doesn't believe the line can be held on the price of bread, for example, but action is possible to relieve the pressure somewhat.

In addition to some form of action to restrain grain price increases across the board, it is believed Mr. Trudeau is contemplating action to protect farm incomes, recognize rising production costs and create a workable grain storage system.

A vital component of this over-all grains policy which must meet the needs of consumers and farmers alike would be a resurrected and improved farm income stabilization plan to level out the wild fluctuations in farm incomes from year to year.

Late in 1971 the Trudeau government was forced to withdraw an earlier income insurance proposal amid widespread farmer complaints that it would ignore their rising production costs and simply freeze farm incomes at the poverty level.

But today—against a backdrop of international grain shortages, soaring world prices and Canadian farm cash receipts at mid-year running 21.7 per cent ahead of last year's pace—many farmers may be more receptive to a plan protecting them against future bad years.

Having learned his lesson from the political disaster which felled his previous income stabilization efforts, Mr. Lang is likely to propose to the cabinet a revamped plan which heeds farm production costs.

And, unlike the earlier version, this one would probably be voluntary rather than compulsory so that independent-minded farmers could continue to gamble on their annual incomes if they wished.

One of the big stumbling blocks to an effective income averaging scheme for farmers is the difficulty of determining with accuracy what the annual increase in production costs actually is.

The Journal Bomber

"A man who thinks for himself and therefore is free, is a troublesome and strange being."
— James Cameron, *The Journal*, Aug. 24, 1973

James Cameron, 65, was dying of leukemia. Maybe he wanted to leave a written legacy and thought the best way to do it was to get a "manifesto" published on the page 1 of *The Journal*.

Aug. 23 was a warmish summer day with a thunderstorm on the horizon when Cameron strolled into the third-floor *Journal* library about 9:30 a.m. to deliver his message. He had an orange-juice tin over his hand. A wire ran from the can to a suitcase.

Copy editor Jan Wenzel was in the library and was told to "shut up and get the editor or the whole place is going to blow up."

Publisher Ross Munro met alone with Cameron in the library and was handed a document titled "Special Request Printing of Five Literary Gems (from the scrapbook of James Cameron, 9515 87th Ave., Edmonton, Alberta)."

Munro didn't think Cameron, a retired electrician, was bluffing.

"It looked exactly like the stuff you see in all these bomb things."

Cameron demanded his words be published. He also wanted to talk to city Ald. Dave Ward and Fil Fraser, two CJCA open line radio hosts.

They weren't available, but Munro went outside where media had gathered to cover the unfolding drama and got CBC's Rossi Cameron (no relation) and Jerry Manegre of CJCA to come in.

Meanwhile, city police did a fast investigation. "Sgt. Jim Parks of city police patrol said they had been to his house 'and there's not much doubt anymore that it's the real thing,' " wrote Marc Horton in a story published in *The Journal* later that day. " 'The guy is an electronic genius.' "

In addition to his manifesto, Cameron also insisted Munro publish a letter to the editor that said he is "highly disturbed that the Edmonton Journal has not printed his letters to the editor over the past 25 years."

Following a futile effort by his wife to calm him and the discovery of a suicide note addressed to her, police advised Munro to print the document.

Volunteers in the composing room set up the page and 200 copies were run off (none of which reached the public) and Cameron was shown a stack of papers, and radio reporters Manegre and Rossi Cameron affirmed the paper had been distributed.

"The man then told (Rossi) Cameron: 'I'll take your word for it. I'm not so fussy that I can't trust anybody."

He then removed his hand from the can and declared "it's a hoax."

The can was just a can and the suitcase was full of books.

As he was being removed by police, Cameron shook Munro's hand and the drama was over.

Cameron was charged, but never made it to court.

He died Sept. 27 of leukemia at Alberta Hospital.

Its distinctive glass pyramids are a landmark in the river valley. It is the most northerly botanical conservatory in North America.

***Sept. 9, 1976*:**
***The Journal* adopts a new nameplate, a change in lettering from the Old English in use since 1912.**

***Oct. 12, 1976*:**
Mayfair Park in Edmonton's river valley is renamed in honour of former city mayor William Hawrelak, who died in 1975.

***Nov. 13, 1976*:**
The $6.3-million Citadel Theatre building in downtown Edmonton opens with a production of *Romeo and Juliet*.

***Nov. 29, 1976*:**
Ottawa announces the Canadian Forces' Airborne Regiment will be moving from Canadian Forces Base Edmonton to CFB Petawawa in Ontario.

***Dec. 5, 1976*:**
Edmonton's Eileen Gillese is one of four Canadian women named a Rhodes scholar, in the first year the prestigious Oxford scholarships are open to women.

***In 1977*:**
A copy editor at *The Journal* earns $376 a week.

Edmonton Journal

METRO 25c OTHER 30c SATURDAY JANUARY 29, 1977

Goodbye, big bottle!

A familiar Edmonton landmark came down from its perch Friday. The 50-foot-high milk bottle atop the now-demolished Silverwoods Dairies building, 109th Street and 102nd Ave. was dislodged by workmen. The eight-ton steel plate bottle, built in New York City, was brought to Edmonton 50 years ago. A private citizen is understood to have purchased it for $7,000 to erect it on the Exibition Grounds.

'There is a great danger'

Let's have the vote, PM tells Levesque

JOURNAL NEWS SERVICES

QUEBEC — Hold the separation referendum soon and live by the results, Prime Minister Trudeau told Quebec's Parti Quecois government on Friday.

In a hard-hitting speech, the prime minister said Quebecers had been dithering over the independence question for 20 years but the election of a separatist government had provided the opportunity to settle the issue for at least 15 years, if not forever.

It was Mr. Trudeau's first trip to Quebec city since that election, and his first lengthy comment on the Quebec situation since Mr. Levesque's policy speech Tuesday to financiers in New York.

"There is a crisis in Quebec and Canada, there is a great danger," the prime minister said. "But it is also an opportunity to assert ourselves as Quebecers and as Canadians too. We can be both, I think, though others may disagree."

In a direct challenge to Mr. Levesque, Mr. Trudeau said the referendum must be held soon to put an end to the climate of uncertainty which is hurting Quebec and Canada economically.

Evidence of the economic damage was offered even as Mr. Trudeau was speaking. In Dartmouth, Nova Scotia, city clerk Neil Colhoon announced that the city had shelved efforts to sell a $4.2 million bond issue in the U.S. because U.S. financial institutions were apprehensive over the current Canadian situation.

Mr. Levesque's speech on Tuesday "has had a dramatic effect on the reaction by American lending institutions regarding dealing with Canadian municipalities, especially in the Maritime provinces," Mr. Colhoon said.

While Mr. Levesque has made no public comment yet on the prime minister's challenge, an indication of his referendum plans was given Friday at a meeting with Quebec's largest employer association, the Conseil du Patronat du Quebec.

Association president Pierre Des Marais II said Mr. Levesque told the association the referendum would be held "as rapidly as possible, probably two years or a little longer."

Previously Mr. Levesque had said only that the referendum would be called within his five-year term of office.

More PM Page 3

How Trudeau grabbed and brandished the separatist flag. Page 8

Don't tear the tiles, civil servants told

By PAUL JACKSON

OTTAWA — Edmonton West MP Marcel Lambert refers to it as "Professor Lang's book of don'ts for dolts!"

Vegreville MP Don Mazankowski suggests the publication would make just as much sense if it was read inside out and upside down.

The MPs are talking about a lavish and stylish 24-page bilingual manual published by Transport Minister Otto Lang's department giving employees a few basic rules for work.

The booklet tells public servants to:

• Face the front of the elevator car so they can see when they have arrived at the floor they need;

• Not tear down tiles from the ceilings of government buildings;

• Not stand, walk or crawl on air-conditioning convertor covers;

• Adjust venetian blinds to a closed position on sunny days;

• Forget about removing one's hat when a woman enters an elevator or even to follow the old ladies-first tradition in letting a woman get on or off an elevator. Modern-day etiquette doesn't require such niceties;

• Remember that escalators are there to save people taking steps hence it isn't necessary to walk up them;

• Remember that alarm and emergency buttons in elevators should be used only in an emergency.

• Washroom walls are for privacy not poetry. Pencils should be left at a person's desk.

The rules go on page after page, after page.

"Most of the rules are basic common sense which no one needs to be reminded about. Some of the suggestions are idiotic, and the order not to be polite and proper to women is just plain bad manners," says Mr. Mazankowski.

The Vegreville MP is placing questions on the Commons order paper to find out how much the publication, called At Home With Transport, is costing the taxpayer.

Another night in mental hospital as wildlife man's case continues

Paul Cochlin spent another night locked up in the Alberta Hospital Friday, not knowing whether or not he is a free man.

Mr. Justice Cameron Steer of the Alberta Supreme Court was forced to adjourn the hearing into whether the 24-year-old provincial fish and wildlife officer "is a danger to himself or others".

Six witnesses, including two doctors, two RCMP constables, a fish and wildlife officer and an official of the provincial recreation, parks and wildlife department, gave testimony regarding Mr. Cochlin's behavior since the Manitoban became a wildlife officer in mid-1975.

But at 4.30 p.m. after more than five hours of testimony, Mr. Justice Steer ordered the adjournment.

And Mr. Cochlin, even though he knows he has been found to have been illegally incarcerated at the hospital since Jan. 19, had to return to the hospital under RCMP guard.

The question now facing Mr. Justice Steer is whether Mr. Cochlin is a threat to himself or others. If the judge should find this to be true, he has the power under Canadian law to order him to remain at the hospital for observation and treatment.

Friday's first witness, fish and wildlife officer Roger Gluckie of Cold Lake, said he found Mr. Cochlin a promising young government employee when he first met him in 1975, but in the late sumner and fall of 1976, there were often periods Mr. Cochlin was quite reserved and depressed.

Mr. Gluckie, who was Mr. Cochlin's immediate superior, said problems with Mr. Cochlin apparently started in the fall of 1976 when Mr. Cochlin asked for a transfer.

"I got the implication I had done something wrong and he wanted to leave Cold Lake," Mr. Gluckie told Ben Casson of the attorney-general's department.

Mr. Gluckie said he could not find out what was wrong with Mr. Cochlin and said the mood of the younger officer often changed from one of depression to one of joy.

Mr. Gluckie also said there were never any serious arguments or problems between him and Mr. Cochlin that he knew about.

He said he found a .303-calibre rifle belonging to Mr. Cochlin on the fish and wildlife floor on Jan. 9 with a full clip in the rifle.

Mr. Cochlin was not around and Mr. Gluckie said he removed the clip but that overnight the clip was replaced in the gun.

When he saw the gun the next morning the bolt was open and if it had been closed, Mr. Gluckie said a shell would have been placed in the magazine.

Mr. Gluckie said he had never seen Mr. Cochlin handle his gun in that manner before.

Mr. Gluckie also said he brought the matter of Mr. Cochlin's conduct and attitude to the attention of his superiors and that in early January

More HOSPITAL Page 3

Airborne study officer's exercise

Military authorities say they can't identify the author of a report choosing Edmonton as the best location for the Canadian Airborne Regiment.

But they do know the report was written in November, 1972 as an exercise by an officer or officers attending military staff college in Ontario.

A major or captain at the Canadian Land Forces and Command Staff College in Kingston or at Canadian Forces Staff College in Toronto was probably responsible, information officer Capt. Craig Mills says.

"We simply don't know who it was," said Capt. Mills. "And there's no way of even knowing what the sources of information are."

Friday, deputy defence minister Charles Nixon, touring CFB Edmonton, denied the report had any direct connection with the defence department.

"It certainly wasn't a departmental report," he said. "It's just one person's views."

A summary of the report was obtained by the Journal Thursday. Capt. Mills released a copy of the original 21-page document Friday but said he didn't know who located the report.

The report concludes CFB Petawawa, where the regiment is scheduled to transfer to this summer, isn't a suitable location due to an accommodation shortage, training limitations, aviation support and national policy on strategic locations.

Edmonton was selected over Petawawa and Rivers, Man. and Valcartier, Que., for its strong aviation support, suitability of drop zones, and social conditions including housing, sports facilities and bilingual schools.

The officer includes an estimate of the cost of upgrading the bases to regiment standards in his hand-written report, which Warrant Officer Jim Cochrane said "could well be very legitimate".

More EXERCISE Page 3

Inside the Weekender

Barry Westgate finds TV insights into the energy crisis well done but deeply disturbing. Page 18

Selling bagels to Israelis is even tougher than selling refrigerators to Eskimos but it can be done. People Page 25.

Play young Mark Howe as a defenceman and you might even make the fans forget about Bobby Orr, says Terry Jones. Page 55

District Page features Leduc's pioneer photographer Harry Bamber and his picture of the 1925 Calathumpian Parade. Page 16

Tourism is what makes the big money. Markets Page 61

IRA suspected as bombs rock downtown London. And there may be more to come. Page 18.

Eastern U.S. is up to its neck in snow and cold and there's no relief in sight: the 30-day outlook is for more of the same. On a warmer note, red tape has been cut to ship more Canadian natural gas to some beleaguered states. Page 2

Jimmy Carter's getting down to business and taking a hard look at nuclear curbs and disarmament. Page 18

Canadian Magazine

The makers and breakers of Canadian sport, to say nothing of Helen Gougeon tips on making great bread.

If man has a future, it will be found in space, writes Isaac Asimov. Page 21

Police and people co-operate to fight crime in Alberta. Page 13

The attorney-general is looking for change in Alberta's inflexible court system. Page 13

Ann Landers 24
Art Evans 25
Births, Deaths ....
Marriages 70
Bob Wyatt's SOS 24
Bridge 75
Business, Stocks 61-64
Charles Lynch 4
Classified Ads 71-104
Comics, Features 68
Crossword Puzzle 38,74
Editorials 4
Entertainment 40-45
Family-Lifestyle 21-24
Focus on People 25
Health Column 22
Horoscope 73
Leisure 37-54
Letters
to The Journal 5
Patterns 107
Religion 9-11
Sports 55-60
Travel 46-53
TV, Radio 20
Terry Jones 55

Weather

Mostly sunny today and Sunday. Overnight low minus 25 but milder Sunday with highs nears minus 10. Details Page 2

Going Metric

"Cheer up. The first five years will be the worst."
— Editorial on metric conversion, Dec. 30, 1974

The Journal had high hopes for the metric system. Canada, it reasoned, was a tiny island in the world sea still clinging to the outmoded, illogical, hard-to-use Imperial system of weights and measures.

The Canadian government had been talking "metrication" since the mid-1960s. Britain was heading in that direction and only retro-thinkers fought the move to decimal determinations.

That was the theory when the feds outlined its plan of action in January 1970. It was to take a decade. Maybe two.

"It won't be long before inches, feet, yards, fathoms, chains, miles, poles, gallons, pecks, stones, quarts, pints, ounces and drams are no longer with us," bubbled an editorial writer.

The first to go was Fahrenheit.

A series of articles prior to C (Celsius) Day, April 1, 1975, carefully explained the new temperature system.

For those who couldn't grasp whether –20 C (the temperature that day) was cold or not, all they had to do was multiply by nine, divide by five and add 32 to get the "real" temperature of –4 F.

The retro-thinkers were more numerous than expected. The metric system, said letters to the editor, was an affront to British tradition and would, ultimately, ruin the tourist trade from the United States.

In March 1976, food shoppers faced metric milk and other food products. Packaged food was converted, but fruits and vegetables were advertised in both units (and still are in some stores).

The Journal took a major step a year later on April 1, 1976, when it announced "permanent changes in *The Journal's* weather report."

Wind speed was now measured in kilometres an hour, atmospheric pressure in kilopascals and distances in kilometres.

"One kilopascal equals 10 millibars" the paper pointed out helpfully.

Not all writers embraced the new system. Southam sports columnist Jim Coleman wrote Jan. 18, 1978: "Those meddling bureaucrats in Ottawa are doing their best to louse up the noble sport of horse racing. Who the hell really NEEDS metric measurements in Canada?" The mindless bureaucrats were apparently trying to get the Ontario Jockey Club to change the Queen's Plate race "from the traditional mile and a quarter to the stupid and meaningless measurement of 2,012 metres."

While *The Journal* supported the switch to metric, the staff sometimes was a bit fuzzy. *Journal* ombudsman John Brown took note of the weaknesses on Oct. 26, 1979. "The change-over to the metric system hasn't been a painless one for the newspaper."

Brown mentioned several errant stories "someone was wielding a 177-centimetre-long kitchen knife and another said a rare dog was 5.5 metres tall. Another story said a youth was injured in an 80-kilometre fall at a rock concert."

***Jan. 1, 1977*:**
St. Albert gains city status.

***Jan. 26, 1977*:**
***Journal* photographer Mike Dean wins the Canadian Press feature picture of the year award for a photo of a grain elevator being moved down a highway.**

***March 1, 1977*:**
Adult fare on Edmonton Transit buses rises to 35¢.

***May 18, 1977*:**
The great horned owl is adopted as Alberta's official bird. Petrified wood is the official stone of Alberta.

***May 25, 1977*:**
Sales are brisk of Edmonton Oilers season tickets as a merger meeting is held between the World Hockey Association and the National Hockey League. A pair of tickets in the reds costs $640.

***June 9, 1977*:**
A sonic boom is heard in Edmonton when an American F-106 flying east of the city exceeds the speed of sound.

***Aug. 27, 1977*:**
Edmonton trap shooters Susan Nattrass and John Primrose are inducted into Canada's Sports Hall of Fame.

***Sept. 9, 1977*:**
The College universitaire Saint-

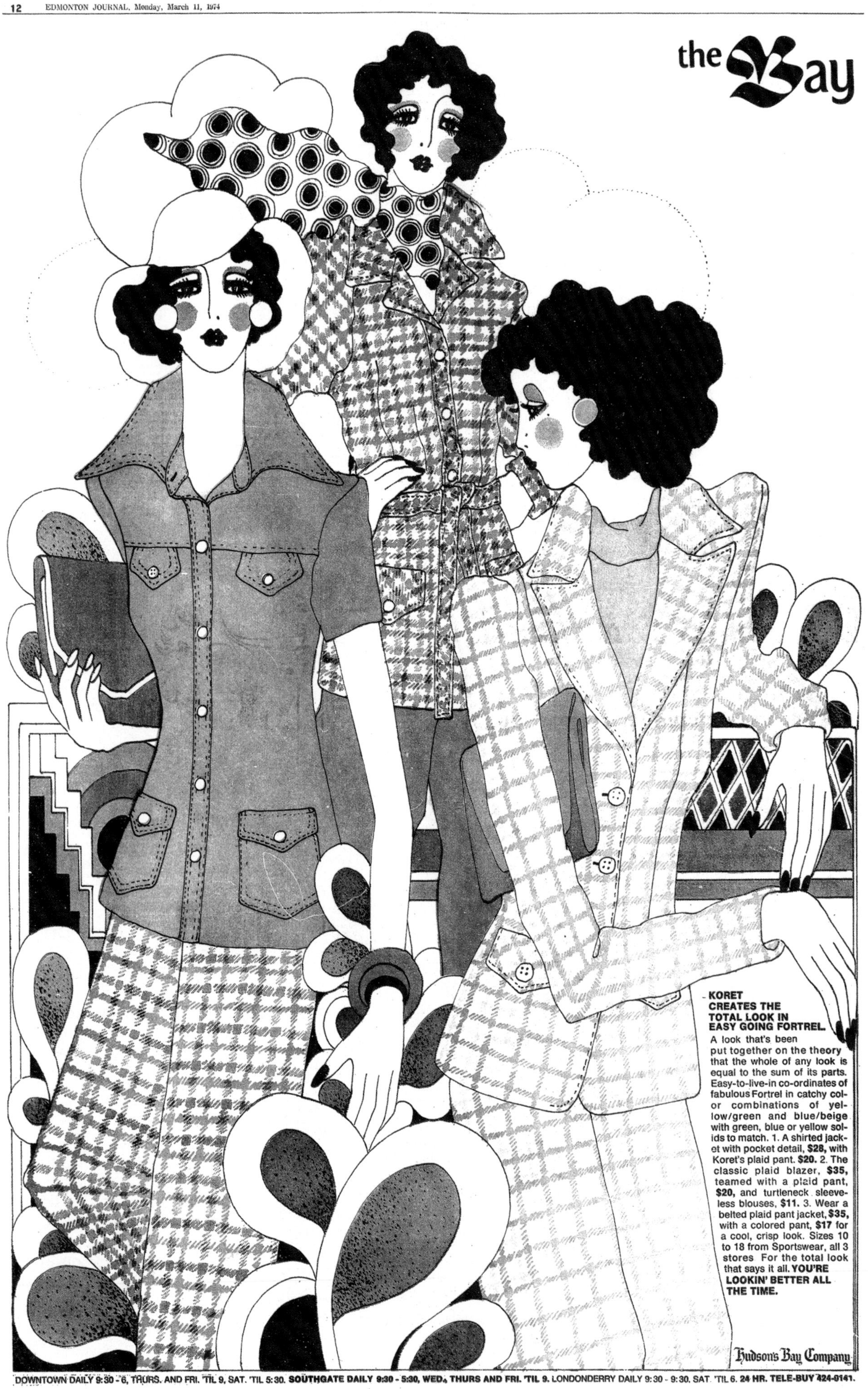

12 EDMONTON JOURNAL, Monday, March 11, 1974

the Bay

KORET CREATES THE TOTAL LOOK IN EASY GOING FORTREL.

A look that's been put together on the theory that the whole of any look is equal to the sum of its parts. Easy-to-live-in co-ordinates of fabulous Fortrel in catchy color combinations of yellow/green and blue/beige with green, blue or yellow solids to match. 1. A shirted jacket with pocket detail, **$28,** with Koret's plaid pant. **$20.** 2. The classic plaid blazer, **$35,** teamed with a plaid pant, **$20,** and turtleneck sleeveless blouses, **$11.** 3. Wear a belted plaid pant jacket, **$35,** with a colored pant, **$17** for a cool, crisp look. Sizes 10 to 18 from Sportswear, all 3 stores For the total look that says it all. **YOU'RE LOOKIN' BETTER ALL THE TIME.**

Hudson's Bay Company

DOWNTOWN DAILY 9:30 - 6, THURS. AND FRI. 'TIL 9, SAT. 'TIL 5:30. **SOUTHGATE DAILY 9:30 - 5:30, WED., THURS AND FRI. 'TIL 9.** LONDONDERRY DAILY 9:30 - 9:30. SAT. 'TIL 6. **24 HR. TELE-BUY 424-0141.**

Birth of Mill Woods

"It is a noble experiment. If it works, it might help Edmonton avoid some of the 'inner city' problems which plague older, larger cities elsewhere."

— Editorial on the creation of Mill Woods, May 12, 1971

Edmonton was out of land. More precisely, Edmonton was out of land not in the hands of a small cadre of speculators who bought up large tracts of low-cost property during the expansion years of the 1950s and '60s.

Lot prices at the start of the 1970s had soared to $7,000 from $2,700 and the provincial and city governments decided enough was enough.

Working through private agents who acquired the land for "unnamed buyers," the province picked up title to 5,085 acres southeast of Edmonton that it sold, over time, to the city for $600 to $3,200 an acre. The city serviced the land to sell it to individuals. In theory, profits would go toward more land banking, breaking the stranglehold speculators had on the housing market.

Mill Woods was not only the largest land assembly project on the continent, it would also become a social laboratory in a diverse choice of housing options as 120,000 people of all income levels tried to find ways to own homes when building costs and interest rates worked to confound their dreams.

But the road to Mill Woods, had there been one at the time, wasn't without bumps. In July 1971, Ald. Ed Leger raised some doubts about the project. *The Journal* was skeptical about Leger who had a reputation among reporters for crying "wolf" too often.

"Mayor (Ivor) Dent has known Ald. Leger long enough to realize Mr. Leger is up to his usual tactics of giving the impression he knows something when he's only embarking on a fishing expedition."

This time, however, there were apparently some fish to be caught.

The "secret" land assemblies provided an opportunity for even more secret wheeling and dealing. After a long, dry judicial inquiry in 1974, a former Alberta Housing Corporation director and a lawyer hired to buy land were convicted of being involved in a kickback scheme.

The lawyer returned $122,000 of the $305,000 he got in commissions to the director. Both got jail time. Despite the kickbacks, planning delays and shortages of ready cash to provide a steady stream of new lots, Mill Woods worked well enough to ease a critical situation.

The subdivision, laid out by city planners, was approved May 4, 1971. On April 28, 1973, *The Journal* reported: "the great Edmonton land rush" began as some 400 lots were sold, and over the course of the decade the community saw interesting innovations that allowed "ordinary" people a chance at home ownership. Communes were organized to share expense and work. To save land and make it less expensive, lots were cut in half and mostly covered with two-storey "smart houses" on "zero lot lines."

It was, an editorial said, a "noble experiment" and proof, perhaps, of the innovative spirit of the city.

Jean becomes a full-fledged faculty of the University of Alberta and officially becomes Faculte Saint-Jean.

***Oct. 19, 1977*:**
Cost of an easy-care 100-per-cent polyester pantsuit at Zellers is $15.97.

***Oct. 19, 1977*:**
Cec Purves wins Edmonton's mayoral election, defeating incumbent Terry Cavanagh.

***Nov. 15, 1977*:**
***The Journal* switches to numbering pages by section letter and page number, instead of continuous numbering throughout the paper.**

***Nov. 27, 1977*:**
The Montreal Alouettes win the Grey Cup, beating the Edmonton Eskimos 41-6.

***In 1978*:**
An ad taker at *The Journal* earns $156 a week.

***March 13, 1978*:**
***The Journal*'s annual slogan contest, based on city business slogans, appears for the 64th and final year.**

***April 1, 1978*:**
Edmonton Transit adult ticket price rises to 40¢; a monthly bus pass costs $15. *The Journal* announces plans to build a $35-million

Edmonton Journal

20 CENTS FINAL WEDNESDAY, AUGUST 2, 1978

XI Commonwealth Games Edmonton 1978

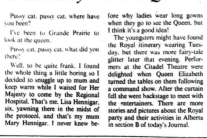

PHOTO BY KAREN SORNBERGER

A kid can yawn at a Queen!

Pussy cat, pussy cat, where have you been?

I've been to Grande Prairie to look at the queen.

Pussy cat, pussy cat, what did you there?

Well, to be quite frank, I found the whole thing a little boring so I decided to snuggle up to mum and keep warm while I waited for Her Majesty to come by the Regional Hospital. That's me, Lisa Hennigar, six, yawning there in the midst of the protocol, and that's my mum Mary Hennigar. I never knew before why ladies wear long gowns when they go to see the Queen, but I think it's a good idea!

The youngsters might have found the Royal itinerary wearing Tuesday, but there was more fairy-tale glitter later that evening. Performers at the Citadel Theatre were delighted when Queen Elizabeth turned the tables on them following a command show. After the curtain fell she went backstage to meet with the entertainers. There are more stories and pictures about the Royal party and their activities in Alberta in section B of today's Journal.

Queen backstage at Citadel Tuesday night

PHOTO BY JIM COCHRANE

PM promises to cut taxes, gov't spending

OTTAWA (CP) — Prime Minister Trudeau promised Tuesday to reduce federal taxes and curb government spending and employment to try to stimulate more economic activity.

And saying he is "fed up" with the Post Office, the prime minister also announced it will be made into a Crown corporation rather than run as a federal department.

Specific new proposals for the economy will be revealed in coming weeks, Trudeau said, adding that there will be no election "at this time". Some observers took this to mean there will not be a general election this fall because the government is working on its economic plans, but others said a fall election is still possible.

Trudeau refused to elaborate on his comment.

In his statement, Trudeau said the government will cut $2 billion from present and planned spending, but much of that "will be shifted to new economic priorities."

The prime minister's nationally televised address follows the economic summit of leading industrial nations two weeks ago in Bonn, West Germany. Trudeau, who returned to Canada last Sunday night after a Moroccan holiday, told the Bonn participants the government will try to get a five per cent real economic growth rate this year.

The prime minister announced several steps to lead up to the new economic measures coming in following weeks, and said several cabinet ministers have been recalled from holidays to start meetings next week.

Among the promises made by Trudeau are:

- No growth in the civil service and an actual reduction in the number of federal civil servants next year.
- A hard stand against public service unions in wage negotiations and a promise that their salary increases will follow, not lead, those paid by private employers.

More PM Page A3

More coverage on Trudeau's speech and reaction Page A13, A18, B6, B10 and C2

Arab slain as attacks against Iraqis growing

KARACHI (AP) — Two Arab youths opened fire on officials entering the Iraqi consulate-general in this Pakistani city today, wounding one official and a police guard. Police killed one of the attackers and arrested the other one.

It was the third attack on Iraqi officials or an Iraqi government office abroad in less than a week. Last Friday, a bomb blew up the automobile of the Iraqi ambassador in London, but he was not hurt.

On Monday a young Palestinian held nine persons hostage in the Iraqi embassy in Paris for more than eight hours demanding freedom for a woman arrested for the London attack.

Police said the two Arab youths arrived at the main gate of the Iraqi mission about 9:30 a.m. and fired at Consul-General Amer Naji Zain al-Din as he entered the building. He was not hurt.

Another consular official, Mohammad Ghaib, drove up soon after and was wounded seriously, the police said.

Police guards opened fire on the Arabs, killing one, and one policeman was wounded seriously. The second Arab was overpowered and was questioned at the consulate.

The rash of attacks on Iraqi foreign missions is blamed on the split among Palestinian guerrillas between radicals championed by Iraq's radical socialist government and more moderate faction led by Yasser Arafat.

Meanwhile, France will expel three Iraqi officials detained after a bloody gunbattle at the Iraqi embassy on Monday, Premier Raymond Barre's office said today.

A statement issued by the premier's press office said the three men's diplomatic immunity prevented French authorities from taking any legal action against them.

More ATTACKS Page A3

Inside The Journal

World — Section A

Thanks largely to his unofficial Israeli second, challenger Korchnoi snatched a draw from the jaws of defeat in the world chess championship's seventh game. Page A14.

Canada — Section A

Traffic at Montreal airports will be grounded Thursday during a union local's study session. Page A12.

Editorial — Section A

August in Edmonton will show the Commonwealth at its best and most varied, says Commonwealth Secretary-General Shridath Ramphal. Page A5. (Interview Page C1.)

Entertainment — Section E

Bash-bang-bop action and not much else. That's Hooper. Movie review Page E2.

Lifestyle — Section D

Consumer columnist Nancy Clegg Buck has been searching the city with souvenir-buying visitors in mind. Her three-part shopping guide starts today on Page D1.

Sport — Section H

Ottawa Rough Riders prove Edmonton Eskimos are human, halting their winning streak at three games with a narrow 24-23 win at Clarke Stadium. Page H1.

Specials

Junior Journal Page E20.
Herb Caen in China Page A8.
Canada Quiz Page E20.

Edmonton Journal
Souvenir Magazine
let the games begin!

Inside today's Journal, at no extra cost, is a super 64-page Games color souvenir magazine. The magazine is available separately, for $1, from Journal newsstand outlets. Extra copies can also be ordered with coupons available in the magazine itself and in forthcoming issues of The Journal.

City — Section C

CBC technicians have ratified their contract, so the Games will be televised. The federal nurses' dispute also looks closer to resolution. But there's trouble on the construction scene. Page C1.

Alex Mair	D1	Letters to The Journal	A5
Ann Landers	D2	Lifestyle	D1-D9
Barry Westgate	G15	Neighborhood	G16
Births, Deaths	E6	Patterns	E12
Marriages	E6	People	G15
Brian Swarbrick	C3	Real Estate	G1
Bridge	E11	Sports	H1-H12
Business, Stocks	F1-F4	TV	E5
Career ads	F5	Radio	E6
Charles Lynch	A4	Terry Jones	H1
Classified Ads	E7-E18	The Sawchuks	G15
Comics, Features	E19		
Crossword Puzzle	E10		
District	F7		
Editorials	A4		
Entertainment	E2-E4		
Frank Hutton	C1		
Horoscope	E9		
June Sheppard	G15		

Weather

Mostly sunny today; high 16 to 18, low tonight 4 to 6. Thursday, sunny; high near 25. Details on Page A2.

Puffed with Pride

"It has been said that a mind stretched by a new idea cannot return to its original dimensions. A city and its people stretched by this amazing experience can never return to its original size."

— Page 1 editorial after the closing of the Commonwealth Games, Aug. 12, 1978

The Commonwealth Games was the biggest event Edmonton had ever hosted, and the city had spent the past five years building world-class athletic facilities, and by the summer of 1978, it was time showtime.

Its new, $20-million, 49,000-seat stadium gleamed in the summer sun.

It had everything a state-of-the-art facility could have at the time, including a special "throne room," a washroom specifically designed for Queen Elizabeth.

The impressive Kinsman Aquatic Centre, a new shooting range and velodrome were in place and 7,000 volunteers in spiffy uniforms waited to shepherd dignitaries, athletes and visitors around the sites with the minimum of fuss.

The Journal was ready, too.

Every reporter, columnist and freelance writer had their designated duties, whether it was covering a specific sport or roaming around the venues looking for "people" features related to the event.

The entire front section had been dedicated to the Games. As the saying goes, the newspaper was to cover the 10-day event "like a blanket."

To set the scene, *The Journal* published a 62-page tabloid supplement that was inserted into the paper Aug. 2. Venues were described, bus routes were mapped out and restaurants were recommended.

Journal writer Gorde Sinclair dared to compare Edmonton's Commonwealth Games to Montreal's Olympic efforts in 1976.

"There are no pregnant men in Edmonton," he wrote, referring to Montreal Mayor Jean Drapeau's 1973 claim, "The Olympics can no more have a deficit than a man can have a baby."

Sinclair said "those strangely swollen profiles peculiar to the chief organizers of the Edmonton Games – those aren't tummies protruding, they're chests puffed out."

The Olympics came in $1 billion over its $310-million budget. Edmonton's deficit was a minuscule $30,000 on a $43.9-million budget.

One of the more interesting editorial decisions *The Journal* faced was to print a story outlining for visitors Alberta's convoluted liquor laws of the time.

"We are not prudes, neither are we wanton," wrote Brian Swarbrick. "Many provinces are tough on where you do your drinking. We are semi-tough."

He then proceeded to describe the antiquated laws that kept Albertans on that hard-to-define line between the straight and the narrow.

The Games were a huge success. Ray Turchansky covered the triumph of Edmonton's super-athlete, Diane Jones-Konihowski, on Aug. 7.

production plant in southeast Edmonton.

***April 13, 1978*:**
Aritha van Herk, an honours English student at the University of Alberta, wins the first Seal Book's First Novel Award. It's worth $50,000.

***April 22, 1978*:**
Edmonton's new Light Rail Transit (LRT) system officially opens.

***April 23, 1978*:**
The 72-year-old King Edward Hotel on 101st Street, north of Jasper Avenue, burns to the ground. Two guests die in the blaze.

***June 13, 1978*:**
City council passes a bylaw authorizing construction of the convention centre on Grierson Hill.

***May 22, 1978*:**
Food writer Mary Moore, who had been writing for *The Journal* for 50 years, dies.

***May 31, 1978*:**
The high-rise Four Seasons Hotel opens.

***July 9, 1978*:**
Capital City Recreation Park, a series of parks in Edmonton's river valley linked by trails, paths and bridges, opens.

Edmonton Journal

20 CENTS | FINAL | WEDNESDAY, JUNE 21, 1978

Judge orders council pay plebiscite

By JIM McNULTY

A judge today ordered city council to hold a public plebiscite on the controversial aldermanic salary issue.

In a decision released this morning, District Court Judge John Bracco granted The Journal's application for an order of mandamus, directing the city to submit the recent aldermanic salary increase to a vote.

He also approved the newspaper's application for a writ of certiorari, which claims city council improperly handled a 24,669-name, anti-pay-raise petition.

Although Judge Bracco granted The Journal's application for certiorari, quashing council's decision to receive the petition as information, he stated that he agreed with the submission by Bill Wilson, lawyer for the city, that once mandamus is granted it becomes unnecessary to proceed with the certiorari application.

Council decided Dec. 13, 1977, to raise aldermanic salaries by 60 per cent, and received the petition as information on Feb. 14.

Mayor Cec Purves was out of town attending his daughter's wedding and was not available for comment today.

Deputy Mayor William Chmiliar said the city would check with its solicitors to review the decision and find out if there were grounds for an appeal.

Should the plebiscite take place, he said, he was sure Edmontonians would approve the salary increase.

"If we go into a plebiscite I can assure you it's a waste of taxpayers' money. The plebiscite will support the increase in aldermen's remuneration."

He said it was absurd to spend $150,000 on a plebiscite when the salary increases amounted to $80,000 annually. If the salaries weren't increased, Mr. Chmiliar said, it would discourage potential candidates from lower-paying jobs from seeking office.

In his judgment, Judge Bracco said the document was in fact a petition within the terms of the Municipal Government Act, and that council was wrong in refusing to comply with the petition by holding a plebiscite.

"It is not disputed that the city council has jurisdiction to provide for payment of remuneration and expenses to members of the council," he said.

However, Judge Bracco went on to say, "The city council were wrong in refusing to comply with a petition properly presented to it."

In the judgment, Judge Bracco did not accept arguments put forth by Mr. Wilson against The Journal's action at a hearing April 21.

At the hearing, Mr. Wilson claimed Journal Publisher J. Patrick O'Callaghan did not have status to launch the action because he "did not have a clear legal right."

"As a taxpayer, he (Mr. O'Callaghan) certainly has status," said the judge. "In a matter as general as the remuneration paid to members of council, I find that any elector in the City of Edmonton has status to bring an application for mandamus."

The action was launched March 15 by Mr. O'Callaghan on behalf of the newspaper.

Mr. Wilson also argued the petition was not a legal document within the terms of the Municipal Government Act and was ambiguous because it offered council two choices.

The petition asked for council to "rescind its bylaw approving an increase in remuneration for members of council, or to submit the said bylaw for approval to a public referendum."

Judge Bracco said in his judgment: "I find no ambiguity in the petition, nor is there any lack of clarity or precision which would render any difficulty in the drafting of the bylaw to be submitted to a vote of the electors.

"I can find no merit in any of the other objections made regarding the validity of the petition."

Another argument put forth by Mr. Wilson, that council's decision to grant itself a salary raise was an administrative act and not legislative, was not accepted by Judge Bracco.

Section 126.2 of the Municipal Government Act states that a municipal council must act on a petition dealing with any matter within that council's legislative jurisdiction.

"I am satisfied that the resolution passed by council regarding an increase in remuneration and expenses to be paid to members of council was within its legislative jurisdiction," stated Judge Bracco.

A formal order setting out the judgment must be prepared and served on the City of Edmonton. This will likely be done within the next week.

Once the order has been served, the city is entitled to launch an appeal from the judgment.

Ald. Ed Leger welcomed the court's decision. He said it answers his question "if, in fact, citizens' views can force plebiscites on administrative matters."

He said the increase of 23 per cent in civic expenditures in the 1978 budget isn't acceptable.

Since most aldermen are "not knowledgeable enough or tough enough" to cut back civic spending, the public will have to do it.

Ald. Leger said he objected to the court action being taken by The Journal because it should not be creating news. He would have been happier if a citizen group had initiated the action, he said.

Statement by Journal publisher J. Patrick O'Callaghan is on Page A3

Reporter Lees unimpressed by $50,000 Games biffy

Reporter trumps the Royal Flush

By NICK LEES

It flushes as smoothly as a Rolls Royce runs.

But when $50,000 is at stake you surely go for a Royal Flush!

The Royal Retirement Room mechanism at the Commonwealth Games stadium is now fully operational.

Probably the most publicized edifice of its kind between the Alaska Highway and Hollywood, the room was built as an afterthought in the $20.9 million stadium.

Aldermen gave the thumbs-up sign for construction when it was noted that the Queen of Canada and England would have to hurry up 72 steps to the concourse-level washrooms if nature called.

The Queen will open the Games Aug. 3.

"Fifty thousand dollars for a biffy," declared veteran Ald. Ed Leger when council debated the cost.

"They have to be out of their bloody minds unless you can charge admission later to look at the folly of Edmonton."

Ald. Ron Hayter quipped: "What do you want, Johnny On The Spot?"

Tongue-in-cheek, Ald. Leger suggested jazzing up the eight-metre by five-metre room with gold braid and other finery after the games to enhance the tourist attraction.

More FLUSH Page A3

Lougheed cautious on proposed changes in constitution

By JOHN FORSYTHE

WHITECOURT — The provincial government will closely examine proposed federal constitutional reforms outlined Tuesday.

"We intend to examine even the first phase proposals as to whether technically there is something we can do on phase one," the premier told a news conference.

Asked whether this meant an appeal to the Supreme Court, Mr. Lougheed said: "It's too premature to say."

The premier reiterated his government's stand that provincial agreement should be secured even on Senate reform. The federal position is that such phase one proposals can be carried out without provincial consent.

"It is upsetting to myself that they, in a federation, are talking about changes in the constitution being carried out unilaterally. I think this is contrary to the spirit of Confederation, if not the law.

"The provinces originally came together to form Confederation and they should be involved in any change to it."

Mr. Lougheed also opposes the proposals because he says provincial powers, especially control over natural resources, would be threatened.

However, he said Tuesday he could not be more specific on the latter aspect until he has reviewed the constitutional change bill introduced in the Commons this week.

Trudeau in major gamble of career in new proposals: Journal view and comments, Pages A4, 5; More reaction, Pages A11, E15

Bare blonde thrills 'no frills'

The only way to fly?

MIAMI (UPI) — National Airlines Flight 51 was midway on its five-hour trip from Miami to Los Angeles when a naked blonde with a "beautiful body" came running out of first class into the "No Frills" section of the DC-10, holding a bottle of champagne, laughing and giggling.

Passengers gaped and stewardesses stared as the woman, in her mid 20s, climbed over the six middle seats of the wide cabin jet, whooping and waving the bottle.

"She had a beautiful body," a female passenger said. "Short blonde hair, a complete suntan all over.

"She perched on top of Row 27, guzzling champagne, and the passengers started laughing and clapping. She said she had just inherited $5 million and that's why she was doing it."

The chief flight attendant, carrying a blanket, chased the blonde up and down the aisles. The blonde, holding on to her bottle and cheered by the applauding passengers, was faster.

A stewardess finally subdued the unidentified woman, wrapped her in the blanket and took her beck to first class.

As crew members helped dress her, the blonde's traveling companion "just crawled under the seat," another passenger said. "He didn't even go after her or anything."

The woman "slept like a baby" until the flight got to Los Angeles.

"I never saw so many grins in my life," one woman said. "For the rest of the flight, we just sat there and smiled."

"It definitely did happen," a National spokesman, said of last Thursday's incident.

"It's just not part of our standard in-flight entertainment. We tend to stick to movies and stereo."

CHARGEX
VISA
master charge

Bay to accept bank charge cards

By GAIL GRAVELINES

The Hudson's Bay Company announced Tuesday that it will accept Master Charge and Chargex (Visa) cards in all its Canadian retail outlets by mid-summer.

The move marks the culmination of five years of bank attempts to enlist Canada's full-line department stores to their ever-growing league of merchants.

Speculation is that the entry of the bank-backed credit cards into Hudson's Bay will entice other department store majors — Eaton's, Woodward's, Simpsons-Sears — to follow suit.

However this morning both Eatons and Simpsons Ltd. said they are not following The Bay's lead in accepting Master Charge and Chargex (Visa) cards at their department stores.

"We're sort of funny and old-fashioned that way," said Ian Gibson, treasurer at Simpsons. "We think our customers should see their (itemized) bills."

Gibson said monthly statements from the banks that issue the cards tell customers only where and when goods were purchased and how much payment is due.

"We give our customers copies of the sales bills with their signature on them."

Morgan Payne, Eaton's vice-president of finance, said Eaton's "would not consider going to the bank credit cards for the present."

Morgan said the banks have been anxious to expand the use of their cards in retail stores but Eaton's has so far resisted.

"We would be increasing the costs of credit to our customers and our cash customers would suffer in the long run."

He said banks charge retailers a two-to five-per-cent fee for the use of their cards and this cost would inevitably be passed on to customers.

"I would view this as one step in the banks' continuing strategy to get all department stores to use their cards," said T.E. Reid, Eaton's general manager of credit and support services, in an earlier statement.

Under the bank-backed credit card scheme, the banks forward the payment of costs incurred by the individual card-holder to the merchant, and become the direct receiving agent of the card-holder's monthly payments.

More CARDS Page A3

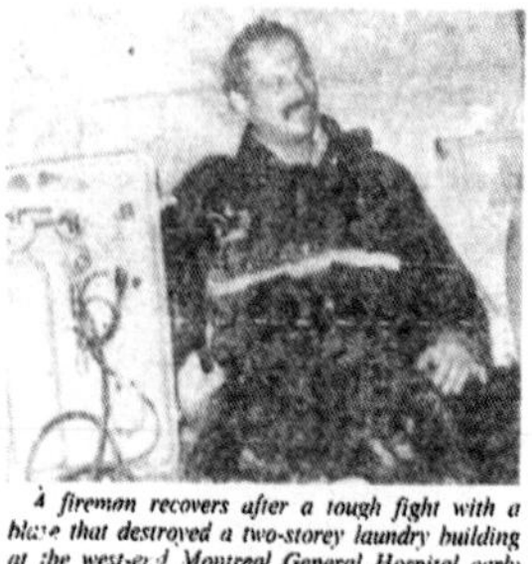

A fireman recovers after a tough fight with a blaze that destroyed a two-storey laundry building at the west-end Montreal General Hospital early today. About 30 firemen took almost three hours to get the fire under control. Story, Page A3.

World

Red Brigades claim responsiblility for the shooting of a former anti-terrorist squad leader on a crowded bus in Genoa. Page A13.

He won't lose his job despite reports that Israeli Defence Minister has accused Prime Minister Menachem Begin of leading the country to war. Page G5.

Canada — Section A

Travellers scrambling to change plans, while officials are confident the pilots' strike threatened next week may be avoided. Page A11

City — Section B

Games may not be on TV unless a srike by television technicians with the CBC can be avoided. Key decision to be made at talks in Ottawa next week. Page B1.

Best housewarming party ever expected at Commonwealth Stadium as Canadian track and field trials held. Page B1.

Editorial — Section A

What if Californians were right? Richard Gwynn looks at the implications of Proposition 13. Page A4.

Inside The Journal

Ann Landers C4
Art Evans A14
Barry Westgate A14
Births, Deaths D2
Marriages D2
Bridge D7
Business, Stocks ..H9-H12
Career ads H13
Charles Lynch A4
Classified Ads D3-E15
Comics, Features G10
Crossword Puzzle D6
District B11
Editorials A4
Entertainment F1-F5
Frank Hutton B1
Horoscope D5
June Sheppard A14
Junior Journal C10
Letters to The Journal A5
Lifestyle C1-C11
Neighborhood B10
Patterns D8
People A14
Real Estate E1
Sports H1-H8
TV, Radio F6
Terry Jones H1
The Sawchuks A14

Weather

Increasing cloudiness; showers this evening; high near 18, low tonight near 11. Thursday, cooler; periods of rain; high near 14. Details Page A2.

Business — Section H

Get off your assets federal Finance Minister Jean Chretien tells Canadian investment dealers at their Jasper convention. It is time for the business community to do its role to improve the economy, he says. Page H11.

Sport — Section H

Guaranteed money not for World Cup winners, who not only have to do their best on the playing field but also must go to the bargaining table for their rewards. Page H1

Specials

If you don't speak French you'd be at a loss in some Edmonton kindergartens these days. Page C1.

A crazy kids act five years ago confined him to a wheel chair, but today Jerry Schafer's plans are far-reaching. Page C1.

Junior Journal Page C10.

Canada Quiz Page C8.

"(She) completed a trade with Queen Elizabeth. On Thursday, Konihowski gave the Queen a baton containing the message to officially open the Commonwealth Games. Sunday, the Queen gave Konihowski a gold medal." Jones-Konihowski won the pentathlon with a record 4,768 points. Her medal, plus the six golds Edmonton swimmer Graham Smith took home, made the whole affair a pretty good outing for the home team.

With the Royals in town (Queen Elizabeth arrived with Prince Phillip and Princes Andrew and Edward) reporters were assigned to join the British press pack to follow their every move.

Reporter Damian Inwood covered the young princes' encounter with a cafeteria line at the University of Alberta's Lister Hall.

Prince Andrew had a hamburger. His brother selected baked chicken.

Prime Minister Pierre Trudeau was also in town for the Games.

Don Thomas followed PET around and came up with a more-entertaining story than baked chicken and hamburger.

Trudeau attended the kick-off party at the Athletes Village Aug. 3.

"He boogied nearly two hours in the Village disco called 'The Ship,' most of the time with middle-distance runner Diane Jones-Konihowski of Edmonton.

"When he toured the Village facilities, the smile on his face became positively radiant as he chatted with a bevy of buxom girls sunning themselves on the patio."

It's unlikely in today's *Journal* that the words, "bevy," "buxom" and "girls" would occur in the same sentence.

And as is often the case when they leave the 'comforts' of jolly old England, the British press found things not quite to their liking.

One London journalist complained about a minor glitch in some medal presentations, saying Albertans are more expert at "cattle round-ups and rodeos" than major athletic events.

The paper's Aug. 5 editorial dismissed the critics.

"As Alistair Cooke said of the Fleet Street press, it took American yellow journalism – and debased it."

The Journal's game plan of total coverage in the front section generally worked well – as long as there was no major crisis.

Unfortunately, Pope Paul died suddenly on Aug. 6, leaving editors with a decision of either breaking the rhythm of Games coverage by putting the pope on page 1 or putting the death in the "B" section.

They chose the latter, but did expand the front-page Games index to include a mug shot of the pope under the heading of "Other news."

"Pope Paul dies of heart attack— full details and tributes on Pages B1, B2, B6 and B7."

Not a perfect solution, but an adequate one and part of an amazing experience for the city and the paper.

***July 17, 1978*:**
"It's love at first sight for Commonwealth Stadium," writes reporter Gail Helgason on when 11,000 spectators attended the opening on a brilliant Sunday afternoon.

***Aug. 3, 1978*:**
In Edmonton, 42,400 spectators watch Queen Elizabeth II open the 11th Commonwealth Games.

***Aug. 9, 1978*:**
Edmonton swimmer Graham Smith sets a new Commonwealth Games record with his sixth gold medal in six events.

***Aug. 23, 1978*:**
The Edmonton Eskimos play their final CFL game in 40-year-old Clarke Stadium, beating the Winnipeg Blue Bombers 14-8.

***Sept. 15, 1978*:**
The $2.2-billion Syncrude oilsands plant at Mildred Lake, just north of Fort McMurray, opens.

***Oct. 15, 1979*:**
Kresge's, a downtown store on Jasper Avenue between 100th and 101A Streets with two popular lunch counters, closes after more than 40 years.

***Nov. 1, 1978*:**
Edmonton Oilers owner Peter Pocklington

Edmonton Journal

METRO 15c OTHER 20c FINAL MONDAY MAY 9, 1977

Gov't sources reveal Berger report recommendations

10-year pipeline delay urged

OTTAWA (CP) — The Berger Commission will recommend a 10-year delay on construction of a northern pipeline in a report to be tabled in the Commons later today, government sources said today.

Native groups have pressed Mr. Justice Thomas Berger of the British Columbia Supreme Court to put a moratorium on pipeline construction for 10 to 15 years after settlement of land claims to give them time to adjust.

But it is not clear if the judge will recommend a straight delay on the pipeline or a 10-year delay starting when the land claims are settled.

Sources said the judge also "buries the interior and coastal routes" proposed by Canadian Arctic Gas Pipeline Ltd. across northern Yukon and the Mackenzie River delta from Alaska.

Environmental groups hotly oppose any pipeline across the northern coastline, saying it could destroy the Porcupine caribou herd and disrupt important nesting areas for birds and the calving waters of the Beluga whale.

The judge leans towards a pipeline along the Alaska highway through the Yukon, with a route along the Dempster Highway to move the Mackenzie delta gas to market, the sources say.

But the report adds that those routes were not included in his terms of reference and need more study before any decision can be made.

Canadian Arctic Gas, which proposes a joint pipeline to move the Alaskan and delta gas to market, says it considered those routes early in its planning but rejected both.

Berger's recommendations will be considered by the federal government as it makes its decision on a northern pipeline. But they are not binding.

He was appointed to study the social, economic and environmental impact of a pipeline on the North and to make recommendations on conditions to be placed on any pipeline approval.

Any delay in the pipeline accepted by the federal government would hit hardest the Arctic Gas consortium since a major portion of the natural gas it hopes to move would come from Alaska.

If a Mackenzie Valley pipeline cannot go ahead immediately, the U.S. government is expected to choose instead a trans-Alaskan pipeline with tankers to move the supplies to the southern 48 mainland states. Foothills Pipe Lines Ltd., the second proponent of a northern pipeline from the delta, would not be so seriously affected.

The company says it does not feel additional gas will be needed domestically until the mid-1980s and doesn't plan to build a pipeline before then.

The federal government will decide on the pipeline later this summer after it receives another batch of recommendations, probably about July 1, from the National Energy Board.

The federal regulatory agency has been holding hearings parallel to the Berger inquiry but has concentrated on the financial and technical aspects of the project.

A bored Trudeau performs pirouette

LONDON (CP) — An apparently bored Prime Minister Trudeau did a pirouette behind the back of the Queen, U.S. President Carter and other western leaders as they were going to dinner Saturday night at Buckingham Palace.

The prime minister's surprise action was caught by a Canadian Press photographer, although it apparently escaped the notice of guests at the dinner.

The guests and the Queen were posing in the blue drawing room for pictures before they went to dinner. Trudeau was at the end of the line.

"He looked bored," CP photographer Doug Ball, a 1974 National Newspaper Award winner, said of Trudeau.

Job creation key economic goal for West

By DUART FARQUHARSON
Southam News Services

LONDON — The world's non-Communist leaders have expressed confidence that free society can survive a basic new challenge to the democratic way of life.

Seven presidents and prime ministers from North America, Europe and Japan were graphic about the perils ahead but vague on specific solutions in the campaign against an ill-defined enemy.

Japanese Prime Minister Takeo Fukuda told reporters at the end of the summit meeting Sunday current difficulties are greater than those which faced the Depression world of the 1930s.

"It is more than an economic concern," Prime Minister Trudeau told a press conference. "It is a concern for the survival of our industrial democracies, a realization that the problems are very deep, challenging the very nature of our society."

Trudeau said the Third World was watching "to see how we would be solving these problems and, therefore, ideological choices will be made that are of great importance to the survival of democracy."

The seven summiteers, all of whom except President Jimmy Carter are in political trouble at home, agreed in a communique their most urgent task was "to create more jobs while continuing to reduce inflation."

They expressed particular concern about youth unemployment but agreed only on "an exchange of experience and ideas on providing the young with job opportunities."

While the leaders of the more economically weak countries at the summit like Britain and Italy have argued in the past for more economic stimulus from West Germany, the U.S. and Japan, no new goals were set at the conference.

The Big Three simply promised to meet their "reasonably expansionist growth targets" for 1977.

"The governments of these countries will keep their policies under review, and commit themselves to adopt further policies, if needed, to achieve their stated target rates and to contribute to the adjustment of payments imbalances," an explanatory appendix said.

The communique promised "strong political leadership to expand opportunities for trade" and rejected protectionist policies which it said would increase unemployment and inflation.

More JOBS Page 3

Canada has the free world's best performing economy — Page 2

Violence in pubs — a mounting crisis

By HUBERT JOHNSON

Two men argue in a crowded pub and one pulls a gun. Without warning, he pumps bullets into his victim and disappears into the night before the stunned audience can react.

Outside another pub, a man shoots at a waiter because he had been ordered off the premises earlier in the evening. In another pub, two men vie for the affections of the same girl. One pulls a knife and plunges it between the other man's ribs.

At another pub, a man is struck with a beer bottle and requires 16 stitches to close the wound. In another pub, a man suspected of being high on drugs is asked to leave by an employee. The employee is stabbed in the ribs. Scenes from the Old West? No. Scenes from Edmonton — today.

City police say such pub violence is on the increase. Glass slashings, robbery with violence and assaults with fists and feet are considerably more common.

"It's an escalating problem, this pub violence, and I don't know where it will stop," said Superintendent George Mitchell, in charge of the city force's 540 patrol division officers, in an interview. It's patrol officers who usually are the first police on the scene of such incidents.

"But the situation hasn't always been this way, only in the last three or four years," Supt. Mitchell said.

People in the pub business generally agree with the police officer.

Supt. Mitchell said the force initiated a "pub patrol" program three years ago to try to curb violences. Initially, eight beat patrol officers included informal visits to pubs across the city as part of their regular duties.

"But we increased the number of officers about a year ago to provide better coverage across the city," Supt. Mitchell said.

The police officers simply visit pubs in their areas from time to time. They discuss with managers their rights under the Liquor Control Act and Criminal Code, how to deal with the public and rights of the public.

"Generally we tell the manager what to do if a patron doesn't do what he is told. And I must say it has been very well received."

Supt. Mitchell doubts whether police can do any more than they are doing to curb the pub violence.

"We can only carry on with our patrols and prosecute lawbreakers when we get the chance. I believe it will only be stopped if these people are dealt with severely by the

More VIOLENCE Page 3

After 59 years, words were not really necessary

By DICK SCHULER

Words weren't really necessary when Harry and Lavina flung themselves into each other's arms Saturday — after 59 years of separation.

They recognized each other immediately as brother and sister, and they just hugged each other silently.

Excited relatives were clicking the cameras and jumping for joy at Edmonton International Airport — and the fact that Harry couldn't say a word to them didn't really matter. That's because Harry is a deaf mute.

However, with the assistance of an airport staffer proficient in sign language, the initial lines of communication were quickly established.

Birth certificates were pulled out of handbags and compared. And it was confirmed that Harry and Lavina are brother and sister.

And, perhaps, they would have found each other sooner if only some clerk back in 1911 or 1912 had bothered to spell their names correctly.

Harry, 65, now of Lake Cowichan, B.C., was born as Aurel Nikiforuk — or Nikkiforeuk, or Nikiforiuk, depending on which document you consult — while his sister, now Mrs. Lavina Hodam, 66, of Forestburg, was registered as Profira Nikiforeuk.

They were separated in 1918, when their father was confined to the old Ponoka Mental Institute and their mother died soon after.

Harry was sent to a school for the deaf near Winnipeg

More REUNION Page 3

An injured fireman grimaces with pain as he is led away from a fire in downtown Toronto early Monday morning. The fire destroyed the annex building of the old Eaton complex and damaged several other builings close by. Picture, story Page 8.

Inside The Journal

City

Winston Churchill was better fitted for fighting the Second World War than for solving Britain's current economic problems, a former close associate says. Page 16.

Canada

A Halifax photographer who credits himself with teaching Margaret Trudeau "how to see artistically" is disappointed she chose photo-journalism. Page 12.

Entertainment

Keith Ashwell analyses a writer's acting performance in his own play and finds it beautifully refined. Page 32.

Barry Westgate says Robert Altman's wilfullness is detrimental to 3 Women, his latest offering. Page 32.

World

Investigators find $5 million in cash in fire-charred home of slain heiress. Page 8.

Sports

Team Canada salvages a measure of pride with an 8-2 verdict over Czechoslovakia. Page 43.

Monday Specials

Books — Christopher Young finds the late Grattan O'Leary an inconsistent but joyous autobiographer. Page 29.

Alex Mair — Harried fathers are undertaking that annual ritual: packing the car for summer vacation. Page 10.

This Canada — A violin appraiser kills an old man's dream. Other features from across the country on Page 19.

Lifestyle self-help section — Journal columnists offer advice on a wide range of topics. Pages 21 to 27.

Calendar — Your guide to what's happening. Page 30.

Ann Landers 24
Births, Deaths 58
Marriages 58
Bob Wyatt's SOS 25
Book Reviews 29
Bridge 62
Business, Stocks 50-53
Classified Ads 59-83
Comics, Features 28
Crossword Puzzle 65
Editorials 4
Entertainment 32,33
Family-Lifestyle 21-27
Focus on People 10
Horoscope 61
Jim Davies 15
Letters to The Journal 5
Neighborhood 18
Patterns 66,67
Sports 43-49
Television, Radio 20
Terry Jones 43

Weather

Mainly sunny this afternoon; high near 25, low tonight 8 to 10. Isolated thundershowers tonight. Tuesday, mostly cloudy with thundershowers; high 16 to 18. Details on Page 2.

"Unofficial Opposition"

"We do feel that where there is such an overwhelming majority and where there is such a totally dispirited opposition, that it is up to us to act out the assumed role, I suppose, of being a genuine opposition."

— From a CKUA interview with *Journal* publisher J. Patrick O'Callaghan, March 14, 1979

Premier Peter Lougheed had led his Progressive Conservative party to an overwhelming victory in the provincial election of March 1979, when the party captured 74 of the 79 seats in the legislature.

And suddenly, and without any explanation to *Journal* readers, the newspaper was labelled the self-proclaimed Unofficial Opposition.

Except publisher J. Patrick O'Callaghan never actually used the words "unofficial opposition" in the pages of his own newspaper until he wrote a farewell column four years later and listed it as being one of his accomplishments.

Prior to that, the first time "unofficial opposition" appeared in the pages of the newspaper was in a reprinted *Globe and Mail* editorial on March 20, 1979, six days after the election, when the Toronto newspaper lectured western journalists on what it perceived as a newspaper's duty.

"In this sort of situation, a special onus falls on the press to provide some counterbalance to the risks of one-way thinking. Loyal unofficial opposition of a reasoned sort is vastly preferable to comfortable unanimity of view with the government, and should be gladly accepted as an obligatory press role."

Nevertheless, The Canadian Press, Canada's national wire service, picked up O'Callaghan's CKUA interview and the CP story ran in both the *Calgary Albertan* and the *Calgary Herald.*

The story did not appear in *The Journal.*

Response was swift, and not altogether positive. William Gold, the editor of *The Herald*, puzzled over the decision. In a column that *The Journal* reprinted on March 26, Gold wondered how a newspaper could be both "unofficial opposition" and fairly cover the legislature at the same time.

"When all is said and done the primary responsibility of the press is still relatively simple and unromantic. It is to tell people what is going on within their government, and who is doing what with their money.

"That's a steady, grinding process of doing stories and analysis day in and day out so that people can get grip on things. It's hard work. It's not glamorous. But it is what newspapers are all about, big majorities or no big majorities."

Gold also issued a warning.

"We don't, however, feel ourselves to be part of the electoral process as such, and think it would be rather dangerous if we did."

Ian Seph, Premier Lougheed's former appointments secretary, also weighed into the fray, when in his letter to the editor he pointed out that he

announces he has acquired Wayne Gretzky from the Indianapolis Racers for $825,000.

***Nov. 26, 1978*:**
The Edmonton Eskimos win the first of five consecutive Grey Cups, beating the Montreal Alouettes 20-13 for the CFL title.

***Feb. 3, 1979*:**
Renaldo Nehemiah sets a world record in the 50-metre hurdles at the first Edmonton Journal International Indoor Games.

***March 2, 1979*:**
A propane pipeline explosion and fire forces 20,000 people to evacuate Edmonton's Mill Woods and Kaskitayo neighbourhoods.

***March 14, 1979*:**
Premier Peter Lougheed leads his Progressive Conservative party to a landslide victory in Alberta's provincial election, winning 74 of 79 seats. Grant Notley is the only NDP candidate elected.

***Sept. 15, 1979*:**
Edmonton's first man-made lake, Beaumaris Lake, opens.

***Sept. 27, 1979*:**
Martha Bielish is the first Alberta woman appointed to the Senate, by Prime Minister Joe Clark.

Edmonton Journal

XI Commonwealth Games Edmonton 1978

20 CENTS | FINAL | MONDAY, JUNE 12, 1978

Trudeau

Levesque scorns third attempt

PM pledges constitution by end of 1981

OTTAWA (CP) — Prime Minister Trudeau announced today that he is determined to give the country a new constitution by the end of 1981.

Releasing a set of constitutional reform proposals denounced in advance by Quebec Premier Rene Levesque as "profoundly insignificant," Trudeau said his government would move alone to change the 111-year-old legal underpinnings of the Senate, Supreme Court and federal executive.

It would also draw up a list of human rights that would be guaranteed by law.

Then it would attempt to get agreement with the 10 provinces for other changes in the country's underlying law — the 1867 British North America Act — that would be proclaimed two years later.

"The government has resolved to provide Canada with a new constitution by the end of 1981," Trudeau said in a 26-page document entitled A Time for Action, a set of proposals designed to chart smoother relations between the two levels of government and to reform an underlying law that has "generally served us well."

It is Trudeau's third major effort at constitutional reform during his 10 years in office. Others have foundered for lack of agreement between Ottawa and the provinces.

Trudeau indicated that the November, 1976, election of a separatist government is Quebec is behind his latest inititative, arguing that "a fundamental renewal of the federation is needed to resolve the crisis threatening the stability, unity and prosperity of the country."

In the past, Trudeau has attempted to get provincial agreement each time he moved to claim from Britain the BNA Act — a British law, that can only be amended at Westminster — with a formula for changing it at home.

This time, however, he has changed course, serving notice that the federal government will move without full

More CONSTITUTION Page A3

Inside The Journal

World — Section A

Diplomatic relations between the U.S. and China could be established. Page F3.

315 years in prison for David Berkowitz for six Son of Sam slayings and seven woundings. Page A7.

Canada

Vancouver may have egg on its face after a fight against a chicken-raising welfare mother. Page F3.

Moonlighters on Statistics Canada payrolls will be crimped by new rules forbidding emploiyees to sell agency information for personal gailn. Page A9.

City

$180 million yearly would be spent by a Tory government to get Prairie grain to the market, Joe Clark says. Page D1.

Editorial — Section A

Theme dominating contemporary Alberta politics is "Let us into Canada." says William Thorsell, Page A5.

Next year's babies will be 21 at the turn of the century, facing a world we can't imagine. Page A4.

Business — Section A

What's white, grows in the dark and is considered a delicacy by many? Page A10.

Alberta truckers gear for the day when they will be considered registered tradesmen. Page A11.

Sport — Section C

Sizzling 68 for a 15-year-old who had never broken 75 on his home course, gives him the early lead in the city junior golf championship. Page C5.

Some of the world's best swimmers were at the time trials this weekend, but where were the fans? Page C1.

Specials

Junior Journal Page B11.

Canada Quiz Page B8.

Crowd of 11,000 that flocked to the Coliseum to watch Boz Scaggs leaves reviewer Joe Sornberger wondering what causes such mass appeal. Page F4.

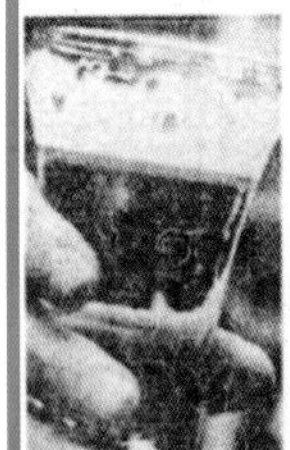

Drop of news

Despite the draught drought from the brewery strike, taverns can still offer bottled beer. Page B1.

Meanwhile, the two-case limit was embarrassing to a Saturday night drinker who parked his convertible to make a second stop at a liquor store. He emerged to find a thief making off with two cases he had earlier stashed on the back seat.

"Hey! There goes my beer!" he said, then blushed deeply as he realized he was already carrying his quota in his hands.

Ann Landers	B9	Patterns	D11
Brian Swarbrick	B3	People	A8
Births, Deaths	D2	Real Estate	E1
Marriages	D2	Sports	C1-C8
Bridge	D6	TV, Radio	F6
Business, Stocks	A10-A15	Terry Jones	C1
Career ads	A13	The Sawchuks	A8
Classified Ads	D3-F2		
Comics, Features	B10		
Crossword Puzzle	D7		
Editorials	A4		
Entertainment	F4-F6		
Horoscope	D12		
Junior Journal	B11		
Letters to The Journal	A5		
Lifestyle	B5-B9		
Neighborhood	B4		

Weather

Mostly sunny today; a chance of a shower this evening; high 18 to 20, low tonight 6 to 8. Tuesday, sunny, becoming cloudy, with showers in the afternoon; high 16 to 18. Details on Page A2.

Signing ends shaky WHA-NHL peace

By JIM MATHESON

The shaky ceasefire in the hockey wars ended Sunday night.

Indianapolis Racer owner Nelson Skalbania picked the night before the National Hockey League summer meetings to announce he'd signed underage junior star Wayne Gretzky.

The timing was a blockbuster.

"Personally, I think you've got to fight fire with fire," said Skalbania.

"I don't see why we (the World Hockey Association) have to sit back like nice guys and hope the NHL gives us a call concerning a merger or marriage. We got raped last year when he had to show them our books and make so many concessions like giving up TV revenue and draft choices."

Skalbania thinks the "mental giants" in the NHL are walking around with "blinkers on".

"A merger would solve all matters. Right now the WHA is costing each NHL team about $1 million more a year to operate because they've had to give kids huge signing bonuses and up player salaries to the moon.

More SIGNING Page A3

Another story, picture Page C1

PHOTO BY BRIAN GAVRILOFF

Invitation from princess

Princess Margriet of the Netherlands Sunday invited young people to Holland in 1980, the anniversary of the Canadian liberation of that country, The princess made the invitation while opening the 27th annual dominion convention of the Royal Canadian Legion in Edmonton this week. Stories, photos on pages B1, B2.

Gov't confirms Husky bid

CALGARY (CP) — Petro-Canada, the federal government's oil company, confirmed today it has placed a bid to acquire all the common shares of Husky Oil Ltd., a Calgary-based petroleum company with operations throughout Canada and the United States.

In a news release, Petro-Canada President W. H. Hopper said he has informed senior Husky officials of the national petroleum company's plans.

The deal would give Petro-Canada ownership of exploration, production, refining and marketing activities in both countries as well as exploration activities overseas.

Husky officials were to consider the offer at a meeting today.

Hopper's statement came after a meeting here Saturday between officials of both companies.

Hopper's statement said Petro-Canada expects to make a further announcement before the opening of the stock market Tuesday.

The Petro-Canada statement did not indicate how much it intends to offer for the 10.9 million outstanding Husky Common shares but stock market rumors last week suggested a price of about $50 per share was being considered by Petro-Canada.

Investment sources today said the $50 per share price — for a total of more than $500 million — would represent "a bargain" on Husky's involvement in conventional crude oil, natural gas and heavy oil assets.

The investment sources said the purchase of all Husky common shares would give Petro-Canada ownership of Husky Oil Ltd.'s two wholly-owned subsidiaries — Husky Oil Operations Ltd., which has activities in Canada, and Husky Oil Co., which operates in the U.S.

In addition, Husky Oil has two refineries in Canada — at Lloydminster and Prince George, B.C. It also has 379 service stations in Canada.

Motorists could be driving into their friendly government-operated service stations — Page A10

The joys and the sorrows of a school reunion

Oh, what the years have done!

You can go back, as long as you don't remember too much, look too searchingly or too long.

For those who remembered that at the King Edward Elementary, Junior High School reunion at the weekend, it was all whoops of recognition, embraces and firm handclasps.

As a participant, I found there were also lots of tentative smiles, attempts to read name cards from 15 feet with bespectacled and declining eyes and plenty of moments of embarrassment, well-covered, however, with understanding and goodwill.

Classmates of mine had left King Edward's halls about 35 years ago and some of us had not seen each other since that time, while others had maintained some contact over the years.

For those who had not, it was heart-warming to recognize and be recognized despite a bit of thickening of the body here and there, an extra wrinkle or fold elsewhere, glasses of various hues and hair changes the same.

It is disappointing, however, to know that you have passed in the halls and in the big barbecue and dance tent, others whom you would like to have said hello to — and hoped they would have liked to reciprocate — but the instant recognition which was needed was not forthcoming.

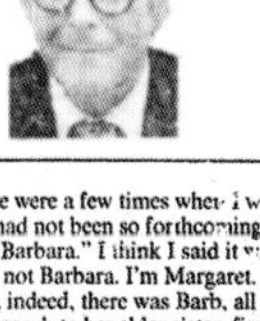

Report By Don Smith

There were a few times when I wished the instant recognition had not been so forthcoming. Such as:

"Hi, Barbara." I think I said it with a question mark.

"I'm not Barbara. I'm Margaret. That's Barb, there."

And, indeed, there was Barb, all smiles, sort of enjoying my approach to her elder sister, first. Oh-h-h-h, boy

Barb also made sure she included my wife in our conversation.

Once bitten, not twice shy. I managed to do it again, the following night, at the dance, suggesting it was Kay I knew. It was her younger sister, Margaret, who lighted my eyes way back then.

Kay did not know me. When I persisted by telling her where she lived, back then, she still refused to acknowledge.

Then, a nice-looking fellow steps forward.

"I'm Don, Kay's husband," he says and I am happy she married such a handsome chap but it isn't until a dance or two later that it dawns on me that it was not Kay I knew — well, I knew her but she didn't know me — but really her younger sister who would have, I hope, recognized me.

I'll be eternally grateful to Iona, Roberta, Robin and Mary who did know me in my mod-style body. There were cases when the placement in the proper time frame, the place on the real estate map of our piece of South Edmonton did not come until later. That's embarrassing.

There were guys there, too. Maybe Bob said it best, when he had a bit of trouble remembering.

"The guy I remember was slim, had a lot of black hair and didn't wear glasses."

He was describing me and himself and a lot of other guys there.

Anyway, his wife, Irene, knew me — instant recognition, or could she see my name card from 15 feet?

had read the story in the *Calgary Albertan*, and that O'Callaghan had stepped out of bounds.

"Mr. O'Callaghan has done a disservice to his profession, to the reputation of his newspaper and in particular to its readers by creating skepticism in the minds of the readers as to his paper's ability to provide impartial reporting of the Legislature," Seph wrote.

"The public is always entitled to comprehensive coverage of our provincial government. It will be interesting to see how Mr. O'Callaghan assumes the onerous responsibility of a 'genuine opposition' role for The Edmonton Journal and if it is capable of doing so without becoming vindictive."

O'Callaghan, for his part, was uncharacteristically silent.

At least until he left.

And even then in the list of accomplishments of which he felt most proud, declaring *The Journal* the unofficial opposition was well down on his list.

Ahead of it he put the construction of the $37-million plant at Eastgate that gave readers "more colour pictures daily than any other newspaper in the world" and the increased circulation that reached "the 200,000 monthly average circulation plateau."

Being the first newspaper in the Southam group to publish seven days a week was another source of pride.

Going to court to force a rollback in an "unjustified, secretly-agreed" 60-per-cent aldermanic pay raise also outranked the "official opposition" tag.

Nevertheless, O'Callaghan finally – and unapologetically – penned the two words that he himself had never before used in *The Journal*.

"It (The Journal) took on the overwhelming might of virtual one-party government in Alberta," O'Callaghan wrote in his farewell column, "by declaring itself the 'unofficial opposition' in order to ensure that democracy would not perish for want of another voice."

***Oct. 10, 1979*:**
The expansion Edmonton Oilers play their first NHL game, losing 4-2 on the road to Chicago.

***Oct. 14, 1979*:**
Susan Nattrass of Edmonton wins her fifth consecutive women's world trapshooting championship.

***Oct. 19, 1979*:**
The Edmonton Oilers defeat the Quebec Nordiques 6-3 for their first NHL win.

***Nov. 25, 1979*:**
The Edmonton Eskimos win the second of five consecutive Grey Cups, beating the Montreal Alouettes 17-9 before a sell-out crowd of over 65,000 in Montreal.

***Nov. 28, 1979*:**
In a plebiscite, Edmontonians vote 63 per cent in favour of building a $32-million convention centre.

Edmonton Journal

Your Journal Blooms Anew

NINE

Steve Makris, 1985
Peter Lougheed fought Ottawa over the NEP and won, by threatening to turn off the taps.

Rise, Fall & Recovery

1980 to 1989

The Hated NEP / 341

Diagnosis AIDS / 345

The Mall / 347

Sweet Victory / 349

Richler's Rant / 351

Labour Strife / 353

The Trade / 355

"We're going through a business cycle, and it's going to get worse. It's going to be at least 10 years, and maybe longer, before things finally begin to improve."
— Ian Strang, May 3, 1982

Ian Strang was a busy man in the spring of 1982, and he got a lot busier before the '90s arrived.

Strang was president of the Canadian Insolvency Association, a group often described as undertakers for dying businesses.

He was a "receiver," an accountant who specializes in administering the last rites to companies on their last legs. Even by 1982, Strang was familiar with the death rattle of expiring firms. It was a sound he would hear many more times before the decade was finished.

The companies in most trouble, Strang said, were the ones that started with little money and then borrowed to build their empires.

"It looked like they were building the country," Strang said, "but all they were were salesmen who took risks with borrowed money."

"It's not all that different from the '30s," Strang said.

In fact, it was probably closer to the decade between 1910 and 1919. Those years started with a boom based on soaring land values, and *Journal* stories of the day predicted Edmonton would overtake not only Toronto but would become the new Chicago. Then a pre-First World War bust hit and the city's population plummeted.

Our constitution

Our constitution and what it means

- Premier Peter Lougheed explains what it means for Alberta. Page B2
- A moment of elation for Pierre Trudeau. Page B2.
- For women struggling for equal rights, the new package is bewildering, writes Mary Trueman, Page B3.
- There will be no photos of Indians in tribal costume surrounding the Queen. Linda Goyette describes native anxiety and anger, Page B4.

Cover photo by Steve Makris

The '80s began with the same hopeful optimism that Edmontonians had felt in 1910. Instead of land values, however, this time dreams were fueled by predictions that oil would be selling for $100 a barrel by 1990 and that the good times would go on forever.

"The most serious economic problem facing the world today is the prospect of an international oil shortage," said Lou Hyndman, provincial treasurer in Peter Lougheed's Tory government.

That comment recounted in *The Journal* came in a 1980 speech when oil was selling at the unheard-of price of $32 a barrel, and OPEC, the Organization of Petroleum Exporting Countries, made up mostly of oil-rich Arab states, was planning price-boosting cutbacks.

And while an international oil shortage may have been a dark cloud on the world's economic horizon, it was clearly one that had a silver lining for Alberta.

The province sat on an underground lake of oil, and the Athabasca oilsands held billions more barrels locked in its heavy, black soil. With the promise of high prices, oilsands plants that could extract the higher-cost oil would become profitable money-spinners, returning billions of dollars in royalties to the provincial treasury.

The province was flush in 1980. Flush with money.

Flush with expectation for more. Flush with the certainty that Alberta was the leader in drawing economic power from central Canada.

"The beginnings of an economic shift away from central Canada, especially to the West, are now a reality," Hyndman said in that same speech.

Lougheed's dreams of building a western financial centre independent of Toronto were coming true, he said.

Explosive growth and lucrative energy revenue in Alberta while central Canada remained in growth slump meant that by 1980 workers were flocking to Edmonton, lured by jobless rates as low as three per cent, and per-capita incomes 10 per cent above the national average.

More people arriving to take part in the Alberta dream meant that the housing market was tight, and prices zoomed upwards. High prices also meant that many properties were mortgaged to the hilt, but those financial institutions about which Hyndman bragged were eager to lend the cash to prospective homeowners.

Borrowing was easy. Oil that would soon be selling at a sweet $100 a barrel made any deal attractive, and anything possible.

But on Oct. 26, 1980, two weeks after Hyndman's speech, the Trudeau Liberals unveiled the National Energy Program, designed to secure oil supplies and stabilize prices by having consumers pay significantly less for Alberta oil than the soaring world price.

Within less than a year, the world price for oil was $40 a barrel, while the Canadian price for Alberta oil was $18. Resource company head offices in Edmonton pulled up stakes and office towers started emptying. Oil rigs were loaded on flat-bed trucks for the U.S.

The energy fight was bitter, and often personal. In one news story, federal energy minister Marc Lalonde likened it to "Grade B movie."

"It has become a shootout between the good guys and the bad guys, a

***In 1980*:**
A compositor at *The Journal* earns $13.36 an hour, while a senior copy editor makes $558 a week.

***Feb. 26, 1980*:**
Edmonton city council approves a six-ward system for civic elections.

***March 13, 1980*:**
Edd Uluschak wins his second National Newspaper Award for cartooning, particularly for a cartoon of a Liberal party official re-inflating Pierre Trudeau.

***May 20, 1980*:**
***The Journal* publishes its first edition printed at its new $35-million Eastgate production plant.**

***Aug. 8, 1980*:**
The current version of the annual Edmonton Folk Music Festival opens, in the city's Gold Bar Park. A weekend pass is $20, in advance.

***Aug. 17, 1980*:**
Arnold Palmer wins the Labatt International Golf Classic at the Mayfair Club with a score of 271.

***Aug. 28, 1980*:**
Edmonton is hit by a record 24-hour rainfall of 83.5 mm, which causes flooding south of the city at Leduc.

***Sept. 1, 1980*:**
The Great Divide Waterfall on Edmonton's High

Sunday Journal

50 CENTS | EDMONTON, ALBERTA | SUNDAY, APRIL 18, 1982

IT'S OURS AT LAST!

PICTURES: CP

Queen inspects honor guard and, right, signs the Constitution Act as Trudeau watches

Constitution home with a stroke of pen

By JOHN FERGUSON and AILEEN McCABE
Southam News

OTTAWA — Choirs, cheers of ordinary citizens and a royal signature launched Canada into a new era Saturday, giving the country full control of its constitution for the first time in 115 years.

With a bold scrawl of "Elizabeth R," Queen Elizabeth II proclaimed the Constitution Act, 1982 at 9:35 a.m. MST in a ceremony filled with all of the military brass, pomp and color the state could muster.

With that stroke of the pen, Canada took full possession and control over its constitution, including the power to amend it, and imposed a sweeping charter of rights and freedoms.

"Today, at long last, Canada is acquiring full and complete national sovereignty," Prime Minister Trudeau told the crowd of about 40,000 that packed the lawns in front of the Parliament Buildings. "The constitution of Canada has come home."

But Saturday's joy was marred not only by a drenching downpour that started precisely as the Queen began her proclamation address, but by the absence of official representation from Quebec.

The Queen made a rare foray on to that treacherous political ground, regretting the absence of Premier Rene Levesque but asserting that the Quebec people should be proud of their role in helping to build a tolerant, bilingual and bicultural country.

"Although we regret the absence of the premier of Quebec it is right to associate the people of Quebec with this celebration because without them, Canada would not be what it is today," the Queen said in French in a speech largely written by her "Canadian advisers" — the Trudeau government.

But while tens of thousands of anti-constitution demonstrators assembled in an east-end Montreal park, Trudeau took more direct aim at Quebec's isolation. He contended the results of the May, 1980, referendum showed Quebec's "silent majority" remains strongly attached to Canada.

"By definition, the silent majority does not make a lot of noise," Trudeau said in French. "It is content to make history."

More PATRIATION on Page A3

1,000 Indians protest in Edmonton, Page B1

Rene Levesque

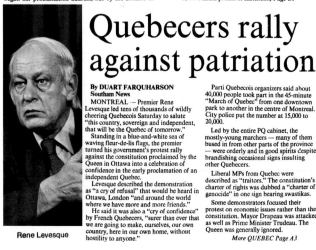

Quebecers rally against patriation

By DUART FARQUHARSON
Southam News

MONTREAL — Premier Rene Levesque led tens of thousands of wildly cheering Quebecois Saturday to salute "this country, sovereign and independent, that will be the Quebec of tomorrow."

Standing in a blue-and-white sea of waving fleur-de-lis flags, the premier turned his government's protest rally against the constitution proclaimed by the Queen in Ottawa into a celebration of confidence in the early proclamation of an independent Quebec.

Levesque described the demonstration as "a cry of refusal" that would be heard in Ottawa, London "and around the world where we have more and more friends."

He said it was also a "cry of confidence" by French Quebecers, "surer than ever that we are going to make, ourselves, our own country, here in our own home, without hostility to anyone."

Parti Quebecois organizers said about 40,000 people took part in the 45-minute "March of Quebec" from one downtown park to another in the centre of Montreal. City police put the number at 15,000 to 20,000.

Led by the entire PQ cabinet, the mostly-young marchers — many of them bused in from other parts of the province — were orderly and in good spirits despite brandishing occasional signs insulting other Quebecers.

Liberal MPs from Quebec were described as "traitors." The constitution's charter of rights was dubbed a "charter of genocide" in one sign bearing swastikas.

Some demonstrators focused their protest on economic issues rather than the constitution. Mayor Drapeau was attacked as well as Prime Minister Trudeau. The Queen was generally ignored.

More QUEBEC Page A3

Reflections of Danger. Nick Lees leaps before he looks, and it's tutu horrifying. — Sunday Brunch, Section C

Western separatism's best argument will vanish if Canada adopts an elected Senate that truly represents the provinces, says Journal columnist Don Braid.
— Page A4

Sexual comments such as "nice legs" were often noted on interview cards of job-seeking students in a federal student employment office, say former staff.
— Page A6

A sign of the times: 50 per cent more farmers have gone bankrupt this year, compared with last year, federal statistics show.
— Page A6

Weather

Mainly cloudy, chance of flurry, brisk northwesterly winds, high 3. Monday, mainly sunny. — Details on Classified Page E3.

Twenty dead, 45 wounded following battle between Moslem militias in Lebanon.
— Page A8

Moderate politician may lead El Salvador's new government coalition.
— Page A8

A black wreath marks Alberta Indians' celebration of Canada's constitution.
— Page B1

Purple in the face and elsewhere was a former mayoralty candidate on Saturday
— Page B1

St. Albert Saints' discipline pays off as they edge Prince Albert Raiders in the opening game of the Centennial Cup Western final.
— Page F1

Arm wrestlers test their strength in championships.
— Page B2

More ups and downs than a rollercoaster. That's the life of a jockey, says Rick Hedge.
— Pages F4-5

Scotland's finest comedian and the White Heather show's comfort of familiarity played on opposite sides of the street in Edmonton Saturday night.
— Page D5

Ann Landers ... C6
Births, marriages and deaths ... E2
Bridge ... E6
Bulletin board ... B4
Business ... A9-11
Canada Journal ... A6
Careers ... G12
Comics ... C12
Crossword Puzzle ... E6
Dineout directory ... C8
Do-it-yourself ... E6
Don Braid ... A4
Editorials ... A4
Entertainment ... D5-8
Flair ... H1-7
Horoscope ... E5
Justice column ... B8
Mini-Cross ... E4
Namedropper ... D2
Neighborhood ... B5
Nick Lees ... C1
Patterns ... E7
People Journal ... D1-4
Peter Birnie ... C11
Queen's English ... A4
Ron Collister ... A2
Science Journal ... C10
Scrambler contest ... D3
Seniors Journal ... B6
Sports ... F1-8
Sunday Alberta ... B7
Sunday Brunch ... C1-7
Sunday Forum ... A5
Terry Jones ... F1
TV listings ... C11
Wheels ... E9
World Journal ... A8

CLASSIFIED ADS

Index, order form ... E3
Employment ... E4-6
Vehicles ... E7-11
Real estate ... G1-11

Doris Retz won $1,250 in last week's exciting Scramblr' contest. Story, Page D2

Full contest details on Page D3

struggle between the forces of darkness and light, a battle between right and wrong," he said in a speech on March 1981.

What no one foresaw was that a worldwide recession would lower the demand for oil. All that oil that was supposed to have sold for $58 US a barrel was now selling for less than $10.

And while Edmonton's population inched slowly upwards by about 3,000 a year to reach 583,000 in 1989, foreclosures and visits to the food bank replaced home loans and holidays in Hawaii. The failure of banks and financial institutions robbed thousands of their life savings, and it was a desperate time for many.

As a decade-ending *Journal* survey reminded readers, the annual average jobless rate leapt from 3.8 per cent in 1981 to more than 11.1 per cent in 1985. In the winter months of 1986, the city's jobless rate in some trades often went above 18 per cent.

The survey also showed that a new Edmonton house bought for $137,000 in 1981, sold for $138,000 in May 1989 ($89,000 in 1981).

And inflation was driving up the price of everything else. According to *Journal* ads, a loaf of bread in 1980 cost 75 cents and $1.19 by 1989. Milk that sold for 66 cents a quart at the beginning of the decade was going for 90 cents a litre in 1989 – and a litre is smaller.

A 1980 case of beer sold for $4.25 and $12.40 in 1989. The price of a Toyota Tercel doubled to $9,449.

There was some good news, however. A microwave that cost $599 in 1980 sold for $289 in 1989.

Not all the tragedies of the '80s were economic, and new words were added to the language to describe fresh horrors.

AIDS was a regular topic of conversation, and a frequent subject of extensive newspaper coverage; a tornado tore through eastern Edmonton, killing 27; a horrifying train wreck killed 23 people and injured 71 others outside of Hinton; famine killed 20 million in Africa in the decade; Marc Lepine, armed with a semi-automatic rifle, murdered 14 women on the campus of the University of Montreal's Ecole Polytechnique; a drought in rural Alberta made the early years of the '80s even more precarious than usual for farmers … the list seemed endless.

But like everyone else at the beginning of the '80s, *The Journal* was in an expansive mood as papers weighing in at 150 pages were common. Circulation soared in 1980 and, by October, was at a high of 185,497.

The new $37-million production plant at Eastgate came online just in time to meet the increased demand. The Goss Metroliner offset presses put *The Journal* at the forefront of printing technology in North America.

While traditional black-and-white photographs were crisper on the Goss presses, it was their ability to run full-colour pictures that readers noticed the most.

On Saturday, May 17, 1980, the last *Journal* was printed on the old Hoe letterpresses at the downtown plant.

The 44 pressmen who worked in the noisy basement they called The Pit where the presses had rumbled and rolled for almost a quarter-century, had a three-day Victoria Day weekend to make the switchover from downtown.

Level Bridge flows for the first time, in celebration of Alberta's 75th anniversary as a province.

***Sept. 2, 1980*:**
***The Journal* begins publishing a morning edition.**

***Oct. 15, 1980*:**
Edmontonians re-elect Cec Purves as mayor.

***Nov. 23, 1980*:**
The Eskimos win the Grey Cup for the third of five consecutive years, beating Hamilton 48-10.

***Nov. 29, 1980*:**
The University of Alberta Golden Bears win the Canadian interuniversity football championship for the third time.

***Jan. 16, 1981*:**
Edmonton's food bank, the first in Canada, is incorporated.

***March 7, 1981*:**
The Edmonton Drillers beat the Chicago Sting to win the North American Indoor Soccer League title.

***April 1, 1981*:**
The Alberta government increases the minimum wage by 30 cents to $3.50 an hour.

***April 22, 1981*:**
The Edmonton Trappers, the AAA farm team for the Chicago White

Feedback D5
Wine Glass D6
SuperCook D8
Food Basket D11

Food

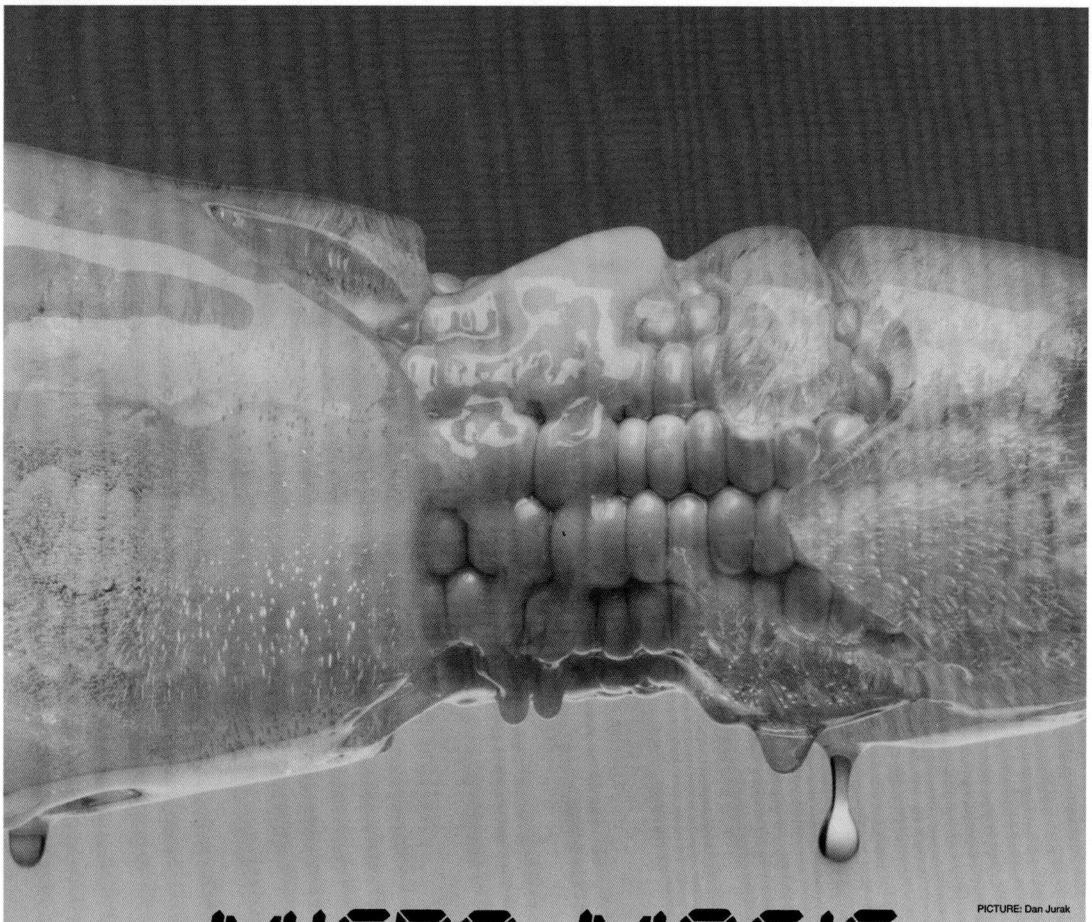

PICTURE: Dan Jurak

MICRO MAGIC

Stories by GORDON MORASH
Journal Staff Writer

When manufacturers began marketing the microwave oven to households in the early 1970s, they could have called it "the magic box" and just left it at that.

People believe in magic but they're frightened by science, and this may explain the microwave's haphazard acceptance by consumers over the past 15 years.

"It's still one of the most underutilized appliances in the market," says Russ Demchuk, microwave product manager for Inglis Ltd.

"People get one because the neighbor down the street has one, but they don't change their cooking habits."

You could hardly blame them. The microwave oven never had the chance of becoming a flash in the pan, simply because there was no flash to speak of.

And that's part of the image problem with a device that bends cooking time, but without showing us how or why.

You see no red element to indicate heat. Nor do you smell the tantalizing aroma of a roast that might show that cooking was actually happening.

All you get is a view *a la* time-lapse photography as you watch food cook. Quickly.

In fact, the microwave oven shares with the car engine and - microcomputer the opportunity for misunderstanding. It is perhaps the only time you should let a salesman get away with his sale-closure inducement line: "You don't have to understand the guts of the thing. Just use it."

The consumer has taken the advice to heart, particularly in Edmonton where microwave oven saturation is the highest in the country. Close to 30 per cent of the households here own microwaves, a higher penetration than for dishwashers, according to Demchuk.

He says that over the past five years, growth has been rapid and "phenomenal" and predicts that by 1990, national penetration will increase to 70 per cent.

The microwave's chief draws are price and amenities. What used to cost $700 for a basic two-power oven with a 45-minute timer, has dropped to $500 for a multi-power model with aroma sensors and a computer, "the electronic brain in these ovens that'll do wonderful things."

"The only things microwaves won't do is boil eggs or bake bread," says Linda Hunter, manager of the Micro Cooking Centre in Heritage Mall. "They're the cheapest appliance in your home. They're cheaper to run than your toaster."

Today's consumer has more of an idea what he's buying before he even steps into the shop, she adds.

"People are reading more — they know more about what the ovens will do for them. There are a lot of consumer reports, so people know there's no microwave leakage; the ovens go through three safety tests before they get to the stores."

Part of the education process comes from the dealers themselves. "We teach people what (microwaves) are about before they even buy," says Hunter, whose shop provides free cooking lessons with the purchase of an oven and a free 30-day home trial.

"There are so many manufacturers and kinds of ovens out on the market that it's nice to know that if it doesn't work out for you, then you can bring it back."

With the Edmonton market penetration being so high, Hunter sees the demand levelling out in 1986. At the moment, sales "are up slightly, though not the big boom we'd been used to."

Despite the levelling trend, the 50-store Micro Cooking Centre chain will open another 15 stores in Canada in 1986.

With the proliferation of brands on the market should come a slight price drop, she adds, and there is more interest being shown in microwave-convection oven combos, now that people know how they should be used.

"Over the last two years, microwave-convection ovens have dropped by more than $200 retail," says Demchuk. "They're more correctly priced now at under $800. They were overpriced before."

It is possible to buy a no-frills microwave oven for under $200, and Demchuk reports prices in the U.S. have dropped to under $100.

"We're at a level now where we won't see prices decrease that significantly. If anything, we'll be seeing more deluxe features for less money . . . The big coming thing is the sensor which sniffs the air or measures water vapor or the amount of infrared heat coming off the food that's cooking . . . You put your food in the oven, program the computer, and it'll cook perfectly every time."

With the magic box now having graduated to tool status, microwave shops report that it's not always the bells and whistles that sell a microwave, but whether the oven is perceived as a steady performer that is non-threatening and provides good value for the dollar.

"People now look on the kitchen as being fridge, stove and microwave," says Linda Hunt, with the trio routinely finding its way into newly-built homes.

With the dishwasher diminished in importance, who's going to do the washing up?

Converting conventional recipes for microwave can be tricky

Converting regular recipes for use in the microwave is often like comparing electronic apples and oranges.

Foods cook differently when microwaved and the oven itself introduces factors which demand a watchful eye when fine-tuning a recipe for conversion.

The major improvement of a converted recipe will be in cooking time. The microwave cuts conventional cooking time by a quarter to a half, but this is by no means uniform or applicable to all foods.

Eggs in the shell, for instance, will still explode when microwaved. Deep-fried foods cannot be microwaved because the fat will reach too high a temperature.

Limitations aside, it is possible to convert the majority of recipes with little difficulty, but it does mean knowing how the microwave oven cooks.

- Because no hot, dry air circulates in a microwave oven, there is little evaporation. The liquid proportions in many recipes must be altered.
- Food ingredients should be cut into approximately the same size to allow for equal microwave absorption. A whole potato, for instance, takes longer to cook than potato cubes.
- Food density can affect cooking times. Dense foods cook slower than liquids or soft foods with less-compact textures.
- Fat that prevents sticking during browning in conventional recipes can usually be omitted in conversions, since microwave cooking calls for no browning and hence there is no sticking.
- Delicate foods, such as cream or cheese, can handle cooking at medium power. At high power, cheese becomes stringy. However, this power setting can be used if cheese is to be stirred into a sauce.

In choosing a recipe for conversion, work first with something familiar whose flavor and texture you already know.

Next, with microwave cookbook in hand, try to find a recipe that resembles in method and perhaps ingredients, the one you wish to convert. Note how the ingredients are combined and the dish's cooking time.

Finally, alter your conventional recipe accordingly, with an eye to the differences in liquid proportions, cooking time and size of food pieces.

You're now ready to take the first experimental stab at cooking the dish the new way.

Be prepared for failure and act as your own guinea pig. You're the best judge of how it should turn out and there's no sense in disappointing the neighbors.

There are few books that address recipe conversion. Most microwave cookbooks devote a few pages to the subject, but **Recipe Conversion for Microwave** by Barbara Methven is a book every microwaver should have.

Recipes

MEATLOAF

1½ lb. ground beef
3 slices white bread, torn into pieces
1 cup milk
1 egg
¼ cup chopped onion
1 tbsp. Worcestershire sauce
1½ tsp. salt
¼ tsp. pepper

Preheat oven to 350 degrees F. Combine all ingredients. Spread in ungreased 9-by-5-inch loaf pan. Bake uncovered 1½ hours.

CONVERTED MEAT LOAF

1½ lb. ground beef
3 slices white bread, torn into pieces
¼ cup milk
2 eggs
¼ cup chopped onion
1 tbsp. Worcestershire sauce
1 tsp. salt
⅛ tsp. pepper

Combine all ingredients. Spread in ungreased 9-by-5-inch loaf dish. Microwave on high power 16 to 21 minutes, or until centre is firm and has lost its pink color (internal temperature 145 to 150 degrees F.), rotating dish after half the cooking time. Let stand 5 to 10 minutes. Approx. time: 25 mins.

A microwave renders more fat from hamburger, and there is no evaporation to carry off additional liquid.

To convert, alter the proportions of liquid by: increasing the dry filler (bread, cracker crumbs, quick rolled oats or crushed cereal) by ¼ cup for 1½ lb. of meat; decreasing the milk by half if filler is soft bread crumbs; or reducing the total liquid by half, substituting an extra egg as additional binder for ¼ cup of milk, as above.

MACARONI AND CHEESE

¼ cup dry bread crumbs
5 tbsp. butter, divided
¼ cup finely chopped onion
¼ cup flour
½ tsp. salt
⅛ tsp. pepper
2 cups milk
2 cups shredded cheddar cheese
1 7-oz. pkg. elbow macaroni, cooked and drained

Preheat oven to 350 degrees F. Combine bread crumbs and 1 tbsp. melted butter. Set aside. In saucepan, saute onion in 4 tbsp. butter over medium heat until tender. Blend in flour and seasonings. Slowly stir in milk. Cook until thick and bubbly, stirring constantly. Mix in cheese until melted. Add macaroni. Pour mixture into 1½-qt. casserole. Sprinkle with bread crumb mixture. Bake 30 to 35 minutes.

MICROWAVE CONVERTED MACARONI AND CHEESE

¼ cup dry bread crumbs
4 tbsp. butter, divided
¼ cup finely chopped onion
3tbsp. flour
½ tsp. salt
⅛ tsp. pepper
1½ cups milk
2 cups grated cheddar cheese
1 7-oz. pkg. elbow macaroni, cooked and drained

Combine bread crumbs and 1 tbsp. melted butter. Set aside. In 2-qt. casserole, combine onion and 3 tbsp. butter. Microwave on high 1½ to 2½ minutes or until onion is tender. Stir in flour and seasonings until smooth. Microwave 30 to 45 seconds or until bubbly. Blend in milk smoothly. Microwave 4½ to 6 minutes until thickened, stirring every minute. Stir in cheese until melted. Mix in macaroni. Sprinkle with bread crumb mixture. Microwave 4½ to 6 minutes, rotating dish after half the time.

Cheese sauce cooks rapidly in the microwave, so cook flour and butter briefly beforehand to avoid a raw flour flavor. Little evaporation will take place during a short microwaving period, so reduce liquid by a quarter.

The new presses also gave the newspaper the capability to publish two editions, and a new morning edition was launched on Sept. 1, 1980.

"The two editions will have the same number of pages, the same advertising but will be considerably different in news content," publisher Pat O'Callaghan promised.

The morning edition was available only in stores or from the 600 new paper boxes that sprung up on city streets.

The slogan was We're Ready When You Are! and promotional advertisements urged readers to pick up a copy of *The Journal* on their way to work, and then have the updated version, with all the latest news, delivered to their doorsteps at night.

The main story of the first Good Morning edition had a headline "Eau Edmonton!" which celebrated the successful inauguration of the Great Divide Waterfall, the dream of artist Peter Lewis who envisaged Edmonton's Niagara Falls where others only saw an iron railway bridge.

Part of the province's 75th anniversary party, the waterfall had been in the planning stages for a number of years.

"This is Edmonton Water's finest hour," gushed Mayor Cec Purves.

The Journal still published only six days a week, leaving Sunday to its relatively new rival, the *Edmonton Sun*.

That changed on Jan. 10, 1982, when the first Sunday edition of the *Edmonton Journal* came off the presses, making it the first Southam paper to publish seven days a week.

And that same month the last typewriter disappeared from the newsroom. There had been an evolution, of course, from clunky, indestructible manual Underwoods to equally clunky, not-so-solid IBM Selectrics.

The new technology combined with the morning edition helped the paper get news to readers more quickly and efficiently.

More importantly, however, it also meant that the paper brought tragedies, the unexpected and the inexplicable, to their readers with the kind of detail no other medium was able to provide.

The Journal's exhaustive coverage of the tornado that tore through the city on July 31, 1987, would have been impossible without the new technology.

The tornado, which killed 27 people, many from the Evergreen Mobile Home Park in northeast Edmonton, hit the city on a sultry Friday afternoon. The air was hanging heavily that day, and the humidity made it sticky. Most predicted a violent thunderstorm. No one, including the weather office, predicted tragedy.

"As news of the tornado came into the newsroom Friday, reporters and photographers scrambled to get out to areas being hit," recalled editor Linda Hughes in an Aug. 2 column.

"Every reporter, photographer and editor available pitched in to help and others came in from home as we responded to reports of devastation and tried to sort out what was happening."

Within minutes of the tornado touching down, 28 reporters and eight photographers followed the trail of death and destruction left as the tornado tore through the city from Millwoods to Claireview.

Sox, play their first home game in Renfrew Park against the Tacoma Tigers. The Trappers win 8-1 before 4,407 fans, almost a sellout.

***May 21, 1981*:**
The first legal beer is drunk at a sporting event in Alberta. More than 3,000 bottles are sold at Renfrew Park at an afternoon exhibition game between the Edmonton Trappers and their big-league affiliate, the Chicago White Sox.

***June 1, 1981*:**
Steve Hume becomes *The Journal's* editor-in-chief and William Thorsell is appointed assistant editor.

***Aug. 5, 1981*:**
Heritage Mall in southwest Edmonton is opened.

***Sept. 16, 1981*:**
West Edmonton Mall opens its doors for the first time. More than 180,000 shoppers flood the mall, looking for bargains in the 220 stores.

***Nov. 2, 1981*:**
Susan Nattrass of Edmonton wins a record sixth world women's trapshooting championship. She also wins the Lou Marsh Award as Canadian athlete of the year.

Carnage at Hinton

30-50 die in Alberta's worst rail accident

The Edmonton Journal
50 Cents (Metro only)
SUNDAY, FEBRUARY 9, 1986
Inside
Rescue workers continue the search for dead and injured inside the wreckage A2
Families gather in hopes of finding news of their relatives who were on the train A3
Survivors relate tales of tragedy and heroism as they arrive in Edmonton A3
Hinton clergymen unite to bring comfort to the survivors B5
Federal Transport Minister Don Mazankowski promises a full investigation B5

PICTURE: Jim Cochrane

Another 24 copy editors and support staff worked feverishly at the downtown office as intermittent power outages played havoc with their computers.

Power was also out at the Eastgate production plant, and by late evening it was clear that there was no possibility the plant could function.

"We abandoned the 86-page paper which was nearing completion and opted for a 12-page special section," wrote editor Linda Hughes, as she outlined the efforts needed to bring the paper to readers.

A Lear jet was chartered and six volunteer pressmen – Dave Kealy, Frank Holub, Chris Runnalls, Ted Payne, Larry Walker and Dennis Jakubec, along with news editor George Ward – flew to Calgary with the 12-page special.

They worked through the night at the *Calgary Herald's* plant to get the paper printed and on to the waiting trucks to be transported back to Edmonton.

"It was unthinkable that we wouldn't publish," Hughes wrote, "particularly when the community would desperately want news of the tragedy."

The community most certainly did. The special edition was distributed to as many subscribers' homes as possible, and sold out within minutes from convenience stores and vending boxes.

"Our problems were minor in comparison with the terror and tragedy of Friday's twister. But the paper struggled into print, in hopes that we could reflect the courage and spirit of the community in a desperate time," Hughes wrote.

In April 1985, the paper decided to abandon the concept of an all-day newspaper and join the industry-wide swing to a home-delivered morning edition. The change came in response to demands from *The Journal's* half-million-a-day readers, said publisher Bill Newbigging, who had replaced O'Callaghan in 1982.

"We met some of that demand in 1980 by launching a full morning edition, but readers are telling us in rapidly growing numbers that they want their paper delivered in the morning."

Besides, he added, it was part of a movement throughout Europe and North America. "It is not surprising that the trend should emerge in Edmonton before most other Canadian cities. As we have learned from the Commonwealth Games, Universiade and our dynamic business, industry, sport and fine arts communities, the audience here is both sophisticated and cosmopolitan compared to many other cities."

The size of the paper changed as well. A reworking of the presses meant that *The Journal* was about two inches narrower than it had been, all of which translated into a substantial cost saving in newsprint.

And instead of 150 pages, the newspaper was often less than 70. The amount of space devoted to news and features was cut back as well. Comic strips that had taken a full page were reduced in size and number to fit into a little more than half a page in the classified section.

Circulation fell slightly and, in 1988, readership surveys indicated *The Journal* was slipping in the market due partly to the fact the paper had doubled the single copy price from 25 cents to 50 cents the year before.

***Nov. 7, 1981*:**
***Journal* reporter Wendy Koenig wins the 1980 Michener Award for journalism for stories on abuses in Alberta's child welfare and foster care system.**

***Nov. 22, 1981*:**
A Dave Cutler field goal with three seconds left to play gives the Edmonton Eskimos their fourth straight Grey Cup, 26-23, this time over the Ottawa Rough Riders.

***Dec. 6, 1981*:**
A small plane crashes into the Royal Alexandra Hospital while trying to land at Edmonton's Municipal Airport, killing the pilot.

***Jan. 1, 1982*:**
Annexation increases the size of Edmonton by 84,000 acres and 9,000 people.

***March 7, 1982*:**
***The Journal* publishes a Sunday edition. It's the first Southam paper to appear seven days a week.**

***March 28, 1982*:**
Edmonton Transit union members vote in favour of a contract proposal, ending a strike that began 43 days earlier.

***April 18, 1982*:**
Edmonton's Youth Emergency Shelter opens.

The Edmonton Journal
C
Tuesday, April 29, 1986

Show Offs C4
Nicholas Lees C5
Shophound C6
Ann Landers C7

Flair

EDITOR: Vivienne Sosnowski, 429-5293

Splash

By VIVIENNE SOSNOWSKI

For oh, so many of us, April is a month of nightmares.

Yes, it's time to time to plunge into a local sportswear outlet and try on a bathing suit. And, yecch all the indescretions of the winter will now be bared to us in horrific detail.

Our bodies become frightening reminders of just how we've spent the winter months.

Too many dinners with friends, too many beers after the hockey games, too many glasses of champagne in hot bubble baths at the end of a sleety evening . . . oh, how it all adds up.

But while our silhouettes may not lift our spirits, the color of this year's swimwear is sure to humor our psyches. Summer '86 brings us vibrant tomes with a citrusy zest. Orange and lemon are the newest brights for the beach set.

Bold florals and abstract prints are important motifs, with stripes slowly making a figure-flattering comeback.

And best news of all, manufacturers have realized that not all of us boast sylph-like Size-8 torsos. Now they're producing bathing suits that do a little camouflage work on our behalf.

"They're realizing that the Canadian woman needs a little more extra detail to enhance her figure" says one local bathing suit retailer. Suits that come with belts to define a waist and help flatten a tummy, or with high-cut legs to add length to a torso, are all designed to make the most of what we've got.

Other details of the summer season?

Strings. "Millions of strings all over the place," is how one swimsuit buyer saw this new accent feature.

Bikinis are inching their way back into the arms of sun-worshippers who realize that when you're browning, the barer the better.

As well, many of the newest suits boast cut-outs

The Italians have provided the inspiration for body-baring suits that look like someone went wild with the scissors. Fendi took vast side scoops out of a basic black maillot. A Byblos suit bared almost the entire tummy. And Krizia's green-and-copper one-piece came without a huge triangular section across the ribcage.

"But do be careful with a cut-out," advises a sports retailer.

"We've found that there's a little problem with them. You can't wear them if you've got a figure that's even a little iffy. The slightest extra poundage will hang right out of a cut-out.

"They're definitely for the better body."

1. Belted suit with high-cut leg — flatters waist, tummy and legs

2. 1960s sun-duo — boyish-cut leg, hipster waist and bra top has a playful nostalgic look

3. Dramatic back detail makes this suit a definite head-turner on the beach

4. Strings galore — this suit features latest detail on front and back

5. Minimalism for the beach. Tiny bikini bottom is slung on black band

All suits from Le Soleil, Manulife Centre

Pix: Dan Jurak

There was also a feeling at the paper that throughout much of the '80s the paper had stagnated and needed to modernize, and a concrete decision was made to change the design, marketing and content of the paper.

The redesign was announced on Sept. 11, 1989, when *Journal* editor Hughes wrote: "We're making some dramatic changes in the design and content of The Journal. Today you have the first taste of those changes."

Physically, the paper changed radically.

The yellow name plate on the front of the paper was changed to blue.

There were better and more reader-friendly labels on pictures and special reports. Clean, easy-to-read typefaces were chosen.

"We've chosen a clean, modern design that combines the tradition Journal signature with a distinctive emphasis on Edmonton," said Hughes.

Beyond appearances, the paper also renewed its commitment to local coverage. Ten new reporters were hired to cover city news, bringing the metro staff up to 42.

Dozens more covered business, sports, entertainment and lifestyles.

A new emphasis was placed on the quality of writing instead of the quantity.

The new look was dramatically successful, 75 per cent of the readers who called in liked what they saw.

A week after relaunch, on Sept. 18, *Journal* ombudsman John Brown who usually took all the "bad news" phone calls from readers, wrote: "This is not the column I thought I'd be writing today.

"Previous experiences suggested not all readers are immediately delighted with changes in their newspaper. The introduction of the Sunday paper and the switch to morning publication brought howls of protest as well as bouquets.

"So it was highly likely there would be all sorts of complaints along the line of 'what have you done to my Journal?' Instead, the reaction from readers to the revamped paper has been overwhelmingly positive."

Circulation increases spiked as about 9,000 more daily papers sold.

No company, however, could be immune to the economic downturn that was having such a devastating impact on the lives of *Journal* readers.

Poor economic conditions also meant that a major redevelopment, in which the paper was involved on the south side of Jasper Avenue between 101st and 102nd streets, was cancelled in the mid-'80s.

Originally announced in 1981, the $250-million proposal called for three office towers of 40, 31 and 25 storeys to be built. Partners in the plan were *The Journal*, the Royal Bank and Princeton Developments Ltd.

A Delta Hotel would move into the first phase along with *The Journal*'s offices.

Then the recession hit, and the project was replaced by the new, and more modest, downtown *Journal* building that opened in the early '90s.

The newspaper still had some grand plans for downtown and Jasper Avenue in an editorial Feb. 11, 1982. "Edmonton is not a declining, mid-west American city. Jasper Avenue should reflect that fact."

The Journal contracted architect R.L. Wilkin to come up with a design for a refurbished main street.

"We are well aware that Edmontonians are highly suspicious of

***April 20, 1982*:**
Peter Pocklington is held hostage at his home for 11 hours after an attempt to kidnap the Edmonton Oilers owner and his wife Eva goes wrong.

***In June 1982*:**
Nobel Peace Prize winner Mother Teresa receives an honorary degree from the University of Alberta.

***Aug. 2, 1982*:**
William Newbigging replaces J. Patrick O'Callaghan as *Journal* publisher.

***Aug. 14, 1982*:**
Directed by Brian Paisley, Edmonton's first Fringe Theatre Festival opens in Old Strathcona.

***Aug. 15, 1982*:**
West Edmonton Mall has its first Sunday opening, in defiance of the 76-year-old Lord's Day Act.

***Oct. 15, 1982*:**
The Walter C. Mackenzie Health Sciences Centre opens.

***Nov. 28, 1982*:**
The Edmonton Eskimos defeat the Toronto Argonauts by a score of 32-16, winning their fifth Grey Cup in a row.

***In 1983*:**
A pressman at *The Journal* earns $17.30 an hour.

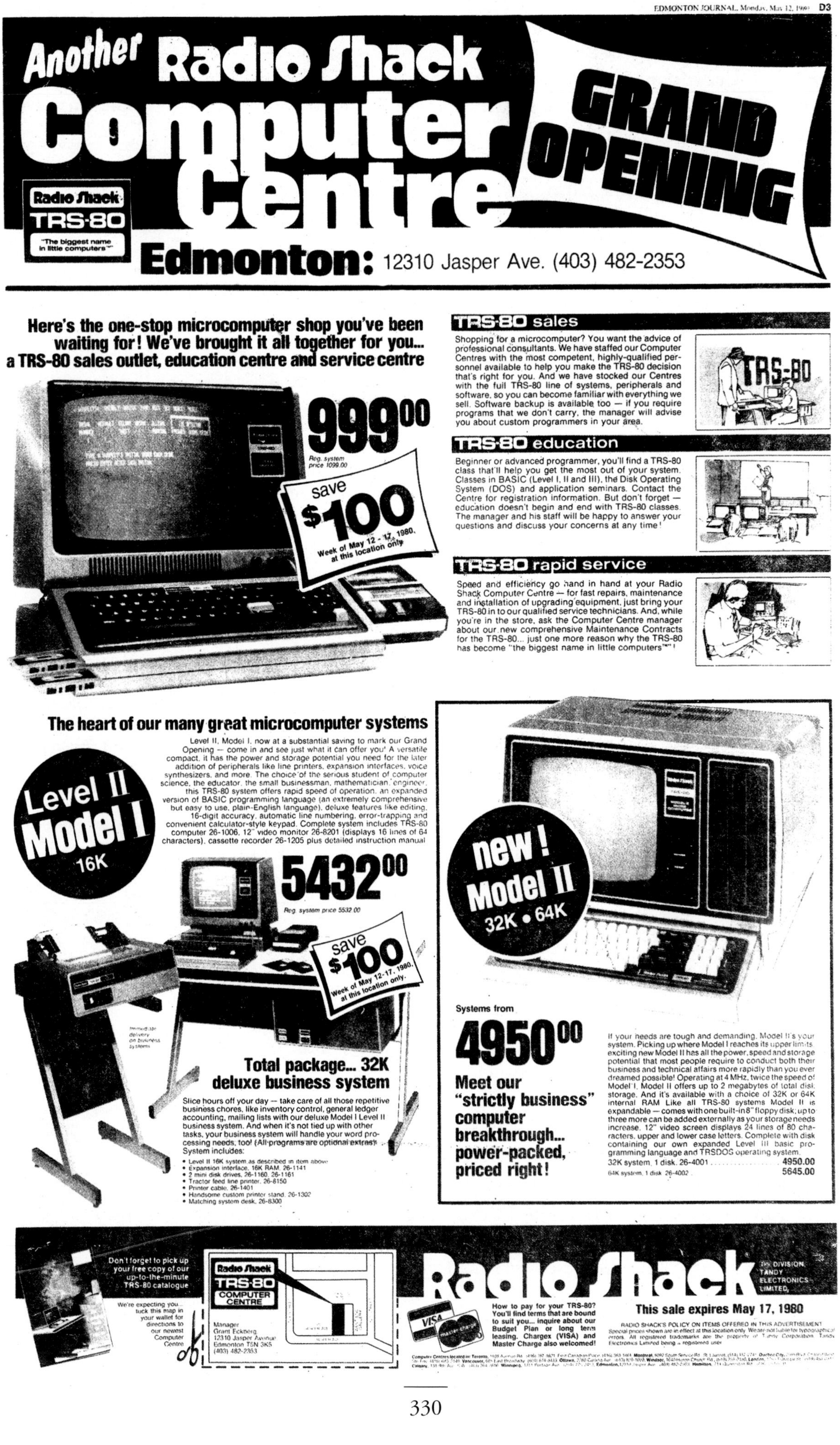

EDMONTON JOURNAL, Monday, May 12, 1980 D3

Another Radio Shack Computer Centre GRAND OPENING

Radio Shack TRS-80 "The biggest name in little computers™"

Edmonton: 12310 Jasper Ave. (403) 482-2353

Here's the one-stop microcomputer shop you've been waiting for! We've brought it all together for you... a TRS-80 sales outlet, education centre and service centre

999.00

Reg. system price 1099.00

save $100 Week of May 12 - 17, 1980, at this location only

TRS-80 sales

Shopping for a microcomputer? You want the advice of professional consultants. We have staffed our Computer Centres with the most competent, highly-qualified personnel available to help you make the TRS-80 decision that's right for you. And we have stocked our Centres with the full TRS-80 line of systems, peripherals and software, so you can become familiar with everything we sell. Software backup is available too — if you require programs that we don't carry, the manager will advise you about custom programmers in your area.

TRS-80 education

Beginner or advanced programmer, you'll find a TRS-80 class that'll help you get the most out of your system. Classes in BASIC (Level I, II and III), the Disk Operating System (DOS) and application seminars. Contact the Centre for registration information. But don't forget — education doesn't begin and end with TRS-80 classes. The manager and his staff will be happy to answer your questions and discuss your concerns at any time!

TRS-80 rapid service

Speed and efficiency go hand in hand at your Radio Shack Computer Centre — for fast repairs, maintenance and installation of upgrading equipment, just bring your TRS-80 in to our qualified service technicians. And, while you're in the store, ask the Computer Centre manager about our new comprehensive Maintenance Contracts for the TRS-80... just one more reason why the TRS-80 has become "the biggest name in little computers™"!

The heart of our many great microcomputer systems

Level II Model I 16K

Level II, Model I, now at a substantial saving to mark our Grand Opening — come in and see just what it can offer you! A versatile compact, it has the power and storage potential you need for the later addition of peripherals like line printers, expansion interfaces, voice synthesizers, and more. The choice of the serious student of computer science, the educator, the small businessman, mathematician, engineer, this TRS-80 system offers rapid speed of operation, an expanded version of BASIC programming language (an extremely comprehensive but easy to use, plain-English language), deluxe features like editing, 16-digit accuracy, automatic line numbering, error-trapping and convenient calculator-style keypad. Complete system includes TRS-80 computer 26-1006, 12" video monitor 26-8201 (displays 16 lines of 64 characters), cassette recorder 26-1205 plus detailed instruction manual

5432.00

Reg. system price 5532.00

save $100 Week of May 12-17, 1980, at this location only.

Total package... 32K deluxe business system

Slice hours off your day — take care of all those repetitive business chores, like inventory control, general ledger accounting, mailing lists with our deluxe Model I Level II business system. And when it's not tied up with other tasks, your business system will handle your word processing needs, too! (All programs are optional extras) System includes:

- Level II 16K system as described in item above
- Expansion interface, 16K RAM, 26-1141
- 2 mini disk drives, 26-1160, 26-1161
- Tractor feed line printer, 26-6150
- Printer cable, 26-1401
- Handsome custom printer stand, 26-1302
- Matching system desk, 26-8300

new! Model II 32K • 64K

Systems from

4950.00

Meet our "strictly business" computer breakthrough... power-packed, priced right!

If your needs are tough and demanding, Model II's your system. Picking up where Model I reaches its upper limits, exciting new Model II has all the power, speed and storage potential that most people require to conduct both their business and technical affairs more rapidly than you ever dreamed possible! Operating at 4 MHz, twice the speed of Model I, Model II offers up to 2 megabytes of total disk storage. And it's available with a choice of 32K or 64K internal RAM Like all TRS-80 systems Model II is expandable — comes with one built-in 8" floppy disk; up to three more can be added externally as your storage needs increase. 12" video screen displays 24 lines of 80 characters, upper and lower case letters. Complete with disk containing our own expanded Level III basic programming language and TRSDOS operating system.

32K system, 1 disk, 26-4001 .... 4950.00
64K system, 1 disk 26-4002 .... 5645.00

Don't forget to pick up your free copy of our up-to-the-minute TRS-80 catalogue

We're expecting you... tuck this map in your wallet for directions to our newest Computer Centre

Radio Shack TRS-80 COMPUTER CENTRE

Manager Grant Eckberg
12310 Jasper Avenue
Edmonton T5N 3K5
(403) 482-2353

Radio Shack

DIVISION, TANDY ELECTRONICS LIMITED

How to pay for your TRS-80? You'll find terms that are bound to suit you... inquire about our Budget Plan or long term leasing. Chargex (VISA) and Master Charge also welcomed!

This sale expires May 17, 1980

RADIO SHACK'S POLICY ON ITEMS OFFERED IN THIS ADVERTISEMENT
Special prices shown are in effect at this location only. We are not liable for typographical errors. All registered trademarks are the property of Tandy Corporation. Tandy Electronics Limited being a registered user

Computer Centres located in: Toronto, ... Montreal, ... Ottawa, ... Windsor, ... London, ... Vancouver, ... Calgary, ... Winnipeg, ... Edmonton, ... Hamilton, ...

grandiose plans these days, as well they should be. So this is not a grandiose plan. What it saves in dollars it makes up in common sense."

"We are not Detroit, battling valiantly against an awful legacy of decline. We are Edmonton, correcting a mistake on the way to greater heights. History has given us an opportunity to be city builders."

The Wilkin plan certainly looked impressive enough.

Associate editor William Thorsell declared himself a believer, in a page 1 story on Feb. 8, 1982. "The Journal's Wilkin proposal offers a grand series of colonnades, boulevards, canopies, open spaces and landmarks. At the same time, Jasper Avenue would be far more intimate and welcoming than it is now – a lively urban mishmash for shopping, strolling and grazing."

After all, he said, Jasper Avenue was one of Canada's "famous addresses," and the Wilkin plan reflected that fame.

No matter how grand, or how modest, Jasper Avenue revitalization plans were, the money to support them simply wasn't there.

Some development, of course, continued. The city granted $27 million in tax concessions to Triple Five Corporation, the developers of West Edmonton Mall, for their $600-million Eaton Centre development. That, and the Edmonton Centre development across 101st Street, drew energy and customers away from the shops along Jasper Avenue.

The quaint and handsome Tegler Building at 101st Street and 102nd Avenue came down, making way for a new Bank of Montreal building, and construction of the Manulife II building north of The Bay at 102nd Street and Jasper Avenue began in 1984.

"Although the province is still recovering from the recession, the future is bright for our energy, agriculture and tourism industries," the paper said when the development was announced. "It's ironic that a Toronto insurance company takes such a long view of our economy, while so many local firms remain blinkered."

Whyte Avenue was showing signs of life, too.

Greenwood's Bookshoppe opened, the venerable Princess Theatre became a movie house successfully specializing in art house and foreign cinema, and art galleries and eateries began moving into the area. The old Strathcona post office building on Whyte and 105th Street – vacant for more than a decade – reopened in 1986, housing restaurants and shops.

But Jasper Avenue continued to reflect the slumping economy. An Oct. 12, 1983, tag sale of more than 250,000 items at the Macdonald Hotel was symptomatic of what was happening. Table lamps sold for $60 each, while prints from the walls were priced at $15. The bar in the popular Can-Can Lounge sold for $1,850.

While renovations were slated to begin almost immediately, tight money meant that the stately hotel would remain empty and abandoned for the better part of a decade.

Merchants on Jasper blamed sagging business on everything from high taxes to the $5-million beautification project, which tore up the street to make way for the decorative dividers that remain today.

Isadore Burstyn, the owner of Vogue Shoes on 102nd Street and Jasper Avenue, pulled out because downtown had become a dead-end, he said.

***Feb. 28, 1983*:**
***The Journal* nameplate changes style (from green bars across the top of the front page to black type in a yellow box) and the width of the pages is reduced.**

***April 17, 1983*:**
***The Journal*'s Great Journal Gold Rush contest first appears. Readers study cartoon clues in the daily paper to determine the location of a $5,000 gold cache hidden somewhere in the city. The contest runs several times over the next few years.**

***June 22, 1983*:**
Edmonton's new convention centre officially opens.

***July, 1, 1983*:**
Prince Charles and Princess Di open the World University Games.

***Aug. 7, 1983*:**
David Bowie brings his stadium rock show to Commonwealth Stadium and 60,000 fans attend.

***Aug. 17, 1983*:**
West Edmonton Mall's Phase II expansion officially opens.

***Oct. 17, 1983*:**
Laurence Decore is elected mayor.

***Nov. 12, 1983*:**
Edmonton Wildcats beat the Ottawa Sooners 30-11 to win the Little Grey Cup.

Going or already gone were such long-standing Jasper Avenue merchants as Kline Jewellers, Val Berg's Men's Wear, Ben Moss Jewellers, the Book Warehouse and high-end women's wear outlets Burdine's and Harper's.

Many people blamed West Edmonton Mall for luring businesses from the once-vital Jasper Avenue and some merchants called on city council to halt the further expansion of the mall until downtown found the strength to fight back.

Developer Don Love, whose Oxford Developments was part owner of Edmonton Centre, agreed. "Downtown must be given time to revitalize," he insisted before a meeting of council in September 1983.

Not true, said Triple 5 spokesman Nader Ghermezian. Triple 5 was the company that built West Edmonton Mall.

"The people who shop at West Edmonton Mall aren't the ones who shop downtown," he told city council. "They're the ones who before would sit home watching television."

Aldermen sympathized with the downtown businessmen, but approved plans for Phase III anyway in the fall of 1983.

Regardless of the reasons, the deterioration of Jasper Avenue was only one symptom of bad times.

Flat wallets, unmet mortgage payments and hungry kids were overwhelming many *Journal* readers, as searching for a job became an exercise in futility.

Three out of four tradesmen in the province's once-busy construction industry were out of work in 1985, which translated to 30,000 workers unable to find even part-time employment.

It was a time of 21-per-cent home mortgage rates and 14-per-cent car loans.

Even millionaires couldn't run for cover. Consider Peter Pocklington, a high-flyer from the '70s whose slide downward began in the '80s, with the failure of his Fidelity Trust and the provincial takeover of the Gainer's meat-packing plant that had been plagued by one of the most acrimonious strikes in the province's history.

The end of Fidelity Trust meant that the Canada Deposit Insurance Corporation, a federal Crown corporation that protects individuals for up to $60,000 each, was forced to pay out $373 million.

And when Pocklington began to use his National Hockey League team, the Edmonton Oilers, as collateral, many Edmontonians thought things could get no worse for the team they loved so dearly.

Pocklington had been quoted repeatedly over the years that no one actually "owned" the Oilers.

Instead, he said, the team was held in "public trust."

For thousands of Edmontonians, that bond of trust was irrevocably broken on Aug. 9, 1988, when Pocklington called a press conference to announce that he had traded Wayne Gretzky, the world's greatest hockey player, to Bruce McNall, owner of the Los Angeles Kings.

The announcement confirmed *Journal* hockey writer Jim Matheson's story in that day's paper that Gretzky's days in Edmonton were numbered. "Sounds like the stuff of Hollywood dreams but hockey's Superman looks like he may be taking his cape to Los Angeles.

***March 19, 1984*:**
A bill to have the lodgepole pine as Alberta's official tree is introduced in the provincial legislature. It also defines the official provincial colours: blue and gold.

***April 14, 1984*:**
The AgriCom building officially opens on the Exhibition Grounds.

***May 19, 1984*:**
The Edmonton Oilers win their first Stanley Cup, beating four-time champion New York Islanders. A victory celebration on Jasper Avenue turns into a drunken near-riot.

***May 23, 1984*:**
City police arrest 65 as the Oilers Stanley Cup victory parade turns ugly.

***July 1, 1984*:**
Edmonton's Space Sciences Centre opens in Coronation Park. The centre includes a $1.3-million star projector.

***July 6, 1984*:**
Angry workers at Gainers, a meat-packing plant owned by entrepreneur Peter Pocklington, refuse overtime and are fired. Many of their fellow workers walk off the job.

***July 29, 1984*:**
Safeway opens Edmonton's first grocery mega-

The Edmonton Journal
C
Wednesday, March 19, 1986

Feedback C3
Food Basket C5
SuperCook C5
Wine Glass C8

Food

EDITOR: Judy Schultz, 429-5294

Tapping the sweetest Canadian

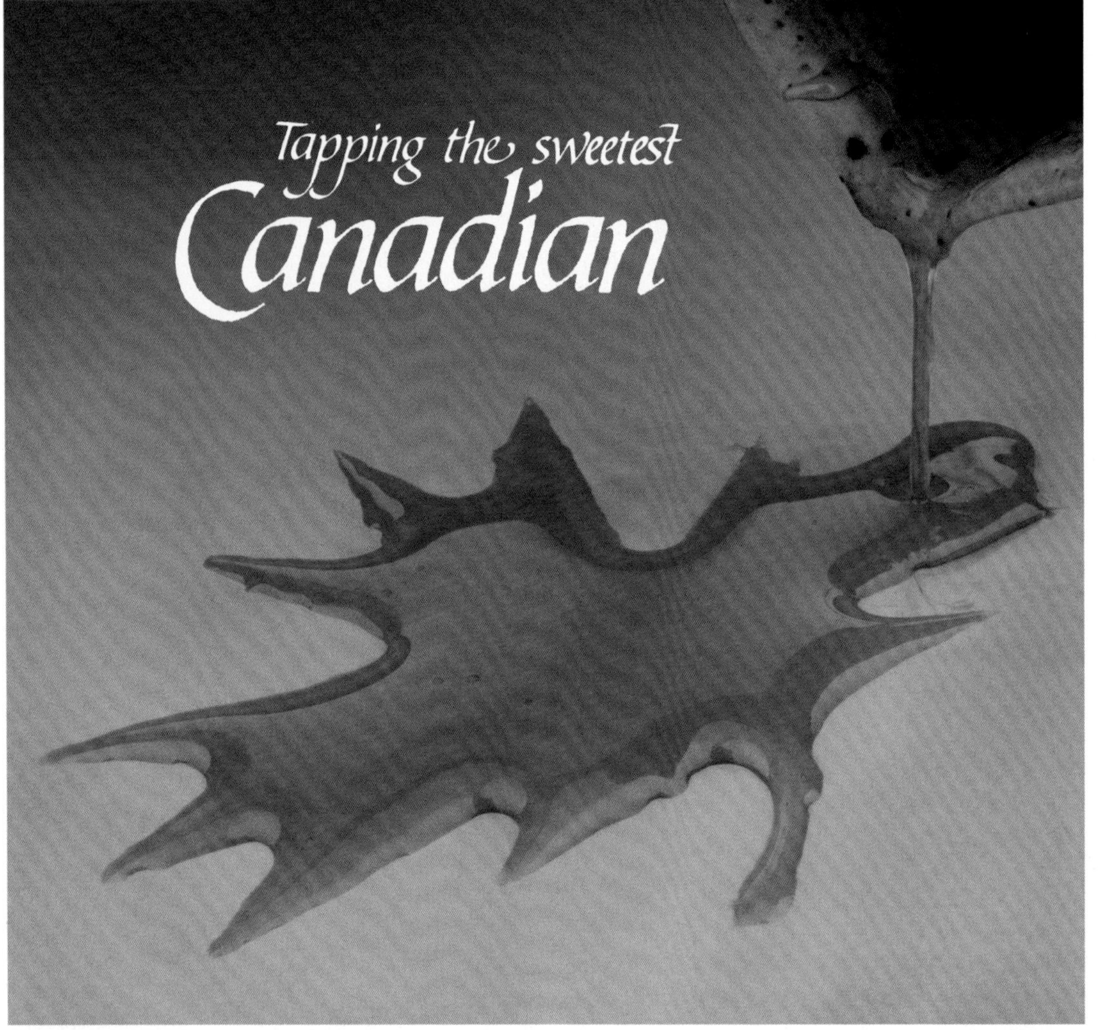

DESIGN: Rick Pape

PICTURE: Dan Jurak

Stories by GORDON MORASH
Journal Staff Writer

When you admit to loving sweets, you know you're an endangered species.

You're the pariah at parties where guests toe the federal government's Participaction line. Your dentist won't pay you the time of day — unless, of course, you're willing to pay him to fill the holes in your chompers, at which point you'll be his very best friend.

As you crawl into adulthood, however, you're supposed to outgrow sweets and exercise a little authority in your life when such temptations threaten. What bushwah! If that is indeed the case, why is chocolate such an all-time seller? And what is it that keeps the bakeries in business: love of the staff of life alone?

I'd be the last to claim that maple syrup is healthy, but it's a $75-million industry that's mostly ours. Seventy per cent of the world's maple syrup is produced in Eastern Canada (Ontario, Quebec, New Brunswick and Nova Scotia), with the rest coming from the northeastern United States.

Quebec provides up to 90 per cent of the syrup in Canada, the main reason why Quebec syrup is the only kind found in Edmonton.

Theoretically, maple sugar is simple enough to produce providing you have the trees (there are 10 varieties of maples in Canada, but only two — the sugar maple and the black maple — have sap sweet enough to produce syrup), spiles or taps for the tree trunks, pails to collect the sap, and an evaporator to drive off the water in the sap.

March is sugaring-off time in Quebec, during which the sap is collected and then boiled, with a fresh supply of syrup and sugar offered in April.

In Edmonton, maple products make their appearance mainly over the Christmas season, when producers find they can charge a premium for gift-givers if they package the syrup in glass or earthenware carafes, complete with a tiny combination cookbook and history of their sugarbush.

You'll also find maple sugar — though not in bulk amounts that will allow you to cook at moderate cost — in the form of candy, moulded maple bears and leaves being the most popular, all packaged in rustic wood containers. The price for all this folderol can be high; it is a luxury item, make no mistake, with the syrup ranging in price from 85 cents to $1.46 per 100 mL.

There are no preservatives in Canadian syrup — which is why it needs refrigeration after opening — though what it lacks in chemical additives, it more than makes up in the grading system.

Canada has three classes, with five color grades within those classes ranging from dark to extra light. The mild extra light is the most expensive and is rarely found in these parts.

A sweet irony exists with maple syrup. The longer the syrup is cooked to drive off the water, the thicker and darker it becomes, with an increased hardiness in flavor. With the more expensive lighter grades — the ones that have been cooked the least by producers — the maple flavor is not as pronounced, and personally, I can't see spending big bucks for something that doesn't taste of maple when that's the flavor you're buying.

The darkest grade is not found in Edmonton, either, except in some table syrups, a fortunate state of affairs as it has too strong a flavor on its own.

The syrup we buy here is the light or medium grade, and true syrup lovers can be found ferrying out 3-litre cans ($33.45 at Woodward's) of Camp's and then looking for a fridge big enough to store it. These same people will regale you with stories of the *cabanes a sucre* they've attended (Edmonton's was held at the beginning of March at Fort Edmonton), of their indulgence in miles of maple syrup snow taffy (simple enough: heat some syrup to 230 degrees F. on a candy thermometer, pour on snow — clean snow — and eat with a spoon — some easterners cut the sweet taste experience with a dill pickle), and of the tastings that have taken on almost oenological propensities. Your truly expert tasters will claim they can not only tell the difference between a light and an extra light grade, but also whether the syrup came from the Turkey Hill sugarbush in Brome, Que., or the Smokey Kettle Maple Company in Sunridge, Ont.

The recipes that follow barely scratch the surface of the maple syrup oeuvre, and include both sweet and savory, the latter being tough to track down as most cooks are intent on saving the maple for desserts or pancake breakfasts.

The result is that you find plenty of recipes for maple mousses and souffles, maple butters and maple syrup or sugar pies. Eggs cooked in boiling maple syrup. Maple syrup grated over fresh-from-the-oven biscuits. Maple syrup-sweetened yogurt, the tart facing off against the sweet. Pea soup with a sweet hit of maple syrup. And an impromptu late-night snack of inch-thick bread slices drenched in ice-cold cream, generously sprinkled with maple sugar and topped with fresh strawberries or raspberries.

Now I ask you: what could be more grown-up than all of this?

How sweet it is! Toothsome treats from the tree

LAYERED MAPLE

This is likely the most sinful indigenous dessert you'll ever make. Health-wise, it has absolutely nothing to recommend it. From a flavor point of view, however, you'll wonder where it's been all your life.

I've searched high and low to find other versions, but the only recipe I've found — and I'm assuming it's the definitive one — is from Sondra Gotlieb's gustatory cross-country gallop, **The Gourmet's Canada.** Published in 1972 by the now-defunct publisher new press (sic), the only place you're liable to find a copy is at a garage sale, second-hand bookstore, the library or in my kitchen.

Layered maple can be expensive to make if you don't have a source of block maple sugar, or are otherwise unwilling to make your own. Grating down the various moulded maple bears and leaves can run anywhere from $15 to $25, but then, the dessert should go a long way — no guest can be hungry enough at the end of a meal to munch through a pound of cream-drenched maple sugar and sour cream-laden pastry.

Sour cream dough:
2 cups flour sifted with 2 tsp. baking powder
¼ cup butter
½ to ⅔ cup sour cream
1 beaten egg

Maple filling:
1 lb. maple sugar
2 cups heavy cream, unwhipped

Cut butter into sifted flour and add the egg and sour cream. Divide the dough into two balls and roll out the first as thinly as possible so you get two oblong pieces from it. Each should cover the length of an ovenproof oblong dish. Prick the two pieces with a fork and lay one piece on the bottom of the dish.

Grate some maple sugar over the dough, and pour some unwhipped cream over the sugar. Place the other piece of dough on top of the cream and sugar.

Repeat the process with the other ball of dough — you should have 2 more oblong pieces, each pricked with a fork. In all, there should be 3 maple sugar-cream layers; keep the cream within those three layers and don't let it seep to the top. Cover the whole dish with the last piece of dough and seal well. Bake for 30 to 40 minutes in a 400 degree F. oven, without it browning too much. Let cool and slice. It should serve 12 people.

MAPLE APPLE PIE

½ cup melted butter
¼ tsp. salt
3 sliced Granny Smith apples
2⅔ tbsp. instant tapioca
1 egg, beaten
1 cup maple syrup
Unbaked pastry for a 9-inch pie

Mix together the melted butter, maple syrup, salt, tapioca and beaten egg and let sit for 15 minutes. Peel, core and slice the apples, placing the slices in a 9-inch pastry-lined pie plate. Bake for 10 minutes at 425 degrees F., and reduce temperature to 350 degrees F. and bake for a further 25 minutes. Serve hot or cold with whipped cream or ice cream.

BAKED MAPLE APPLES

4 tart apples
1 tbsp. cinnamon
¼ cup maple sugar
Butter
¾ cup boiling water
2 tbsp. sugar

Preheat oven to 375 degrees F. Wash the apples, removing the cores to within a ½ inch of the stem ends. Fill the hollowed apples with a mixture of the maple sugar and cinnamon. Dot the tops with butter. Bake in a covered pan with the boiling water and sugar 40 to 60 minutes until the apples are tender, not mushy. Remove from oven and baste with juices. Serve warm or chilled with cream.

BLACK BEAN SOUP WITH RUM AND MAPLE

Savory soups with an added sweetener are relatively rare. What you have here is not some cloyingly sweet confection like some cold fruit soups, but a sturdy, stick-to-the-ribs stock.

2 cups dried black beans
12 cups water
½ lb. ham
2 cloves garlic, minced
2 medium onions, chopped
¼ cup chopped celery
1 carrot, sliced
1 green pepper, chopped
2 tbsp. olive oil
2 large tomatoes, peeled and chopped
1 bay leaf
¼ tsp. dried ground chilli peppers
1 tsp. Spanish paprika
1 to 2 tsp. salt (depending on the saltiness of the ham)
2 tbsp. butter
2 tbsp. white flour
½ cup dark rum
½ cup maple syrup
3 hard-cooked eggs, sliced
6 slices lemon

Wash beans, and soak in water to cover overnight. Drain and rinse again. Cover with 12 cups water and the ham. Bring to a boil, cover and simmer over low heat for 3 hours.

Saute the onion, garlic, celery, carrot and green pepper in olive oil for 15 minutes, stirring frequently. Add to the beans, along with the tomato, bay leaf, chilli pepper, paprika and salt. Cover and cook over low heat for 1 hour. Puree in a blender or food processor, force through a sieve, or leave as is (but remove bay leaf).

Knead the butter and flour into a ball and add to the soup. Stir constantly over medium heat until the soup reaches the boiling point and begins to thicken. Taste and correct the seasoning. Add rum and maple syrup, and remove from heat. Garnish with egg and lemon.

"Wayne Gretzky might find himself King for a day – or a decade – later this week."

It was the bitterest day in Edmonton sports history, and the man who had brought the city the Trappers of baseball's Pacific Coast League and the Drillers of the North American Soccer League became Public Enemy No. 1.

The importance of the Oilers, and of Wayne Gretzky, to the city's self image was inestimable.

The team had brought the Stanley Cup to Edmonton in 1984, 1985, 1987 and 1988 – and they had given Edmontonians, buffeted by a terrible economy, a sense of pride. The city loved its team and its players. A month before the trade was announced, thousands had lined Jasper Avenue when Gretzky and his bride Janet Jones made their way to a fairy-tale wedding at St. Joseph's Basilica on 113th Street.

It would be the closest thing to a royal wedding – *The Journal* published an eight-page special supplement containing all the details.

No wonder, then, that the post-trade outpouring of hurt and anger on the pages of *The Journal* was unlike anything seen before in the history of the paper.

The deal involved other players, but it was the $15 million US that McNall put on the table to get Gretzky that counted.

Pocklington didn't endear himself any further with Oiler fans when he told *Journal* business columnist Rod Zeigler that the cash involved was important.

"It's probably enough to allow me to buy another company or two," he said. So much for holding the team in trust.

For a city on its knees, it was another blow to civic pride.

And then Donald Cormie, founder and major owner of the Principal group of companies, headquartered in Jasper Avenue's tallest office tower, watched as his empire cratered due to questionable financial practices.

That particular failure robbed thousands of their savings and did serious damage to the Progressive Conservative government of Don Getty after the Code Inquiry, established by the province to investigate Principal's collapse, determined that provincial watchdogs failed to do their duty.

The inquiry alone cost $24 million and left Alberta's taxpayers on the hook for $90 million owed to people who had put their savings in Principal's subsidiary companies, First Investors and Associated Investors.

Principal Savings and Trust itself cost a further $116.2 million as the Canada Deposit Insurance Corporation again paid off the claims of depositors.

At the height of the Principal debacle, *The Journal* sought a comment from Getty. Told by press secretary Geoff Davey that the premier was working out of the office that day, Getty was found and photographed on the seventh hole of the Derrick Golf and Country Club.

The Journal on Aug. 15, 1987, took him to task. "When the premier's staff tell reporters he is working out of the office and he's found golfing at the Derrick Club; when his staff claim he has evening meetings and he's spotted at Northland's racetrack; when he doesn't show up for work for three consecutive days following the failure of Principal, Albertans might well question his priorities.

store, Food for Less, on the south side.

***Sept. 9, 1984*:**
The Edmonton Trappers are the first Canadian team to win the Triple A level Pacific Coast League baseball championship.

***Sept. 16, 1984*:**
Pope John Paul II arrives in Edmonton; on the first day of his visit he leads an inter-faith service for 1,100 clergy at St. Joseph's Basilica.

***Sept. 17, 1984*:**
Pope John Paul II celebrates mass before 125,000 people at Namao during the second day of the papal visit to Edmonton. He then pays a surprise visit to Elk Island National Park.

***Sept. 17, 1984*:**
The Supreme Court of Canada rules that an April 19, 1982, raid on *The Journal*'s offices for federal combines investigators violated the constitutional guarantee against unreasonable search and seizure. The investigation was connected with newspaper closures that left *Journal* owner Southam Inc., with the only daily newspaper in Ottawa.

***Oct. 19, 1984*:**
Provincial NDP Leader Grant

Two hours of terror

The Edmonton
Journal
FRIDAY, AUGUST 7, 1987

PICTURE: Steve Simon

Fifteen of the 26 people who died as a result of Friday's tornado were residents of Evergreen Mobile Home Park in the city's northeast corner; others perished in a southeast industrial park

Tornado kills at least 26

By KIM McLEOD
Journal Staff Writer

Edmonton will remember July 31 as a day of carnage.

At 3:30 p.m., a killer tornado slammed into Mill Woods, ripping through the city's east end in an hour-long wrecking spree that claimed 26 lives and caused at least $150 million in property damage.

The twister chewed up houses, tossed huge trucks into the air like Tonka toys and buried its dead in makeshift graves, as buildings collapsed under the storm's fury.

Families were literally torn asunder by brute-force winds, which turned debris into flying spears that pierced and pummelled city residents without mercy.

One of the worst natural disasters in Canadian history, the tornado left a trail of death and destruction stretching about 30 kilometres.

Special Section

In response to many requests from Journal readers, we are reprinting this special edition on the tornado which hit Edmonton last Friday.

Included in this special supplement is updated information as well as original stories and pictures carried in The Journal in the days following the tragic storm.

PICTURE: Karen Sornberger

In the tornado's aftermath, Meda Merriam salvages what she can of her household goods amid the bleak wasteland of Evergreen Mobile Home Park

Survivors of a south-end machine shop thought hell had descended upon them, as winds screamed through the building with a sound like a jet engine.

"It seemed like the end of the world was here . . . we all thought we were going to die," said Ted Gartner, who was in the industrial park when the storm hit.

The tornado hit three areas with a vengeance — a Mill Woods neighborhood, an industrial park between Edmonton and Sherwood Park, and the Evergreen Mobile Home Park in the city's north-east corner.

Fifteen of the dead were found in the mobile home park, where the two-block-wide twister demolished 170 of the 700 trailers in the park.

Seventy-five homes outside the trailer park were destroyed, thousands of homes across Edmonton were damaged and from 50 to 100 businesses suffered serious damage.

Power lines snapped, plunging the south end of the city into darkness, turning major intersections into demolition derbies without functioning traffic lights.

At least 12 cars from a CN Rail freight train were blown off tracks in a yard near 17th Street and Yellowhead Highway.

An ashen-faced Mayor Laurence Decore declared the city in a state of emergency at 6:15 p.m. All off-duty firefighters and policemen were called in to man rescue services. Hundreds of volunteers bolstered this force, to search for the living amid heaps of rubble.

Residents who were away from the trailer park when the storm hit rushed there to find their homes and loved ones had disappeared. As Albert William searched for his two children, he shouted: "I don't know where the hell they are."

Brian Bowyer last saw his sister, Kelly Pancel, 18, pinned between two trailers before he was rushed to hospital. Pancel, the mother of a three-week-old baby girl, did not survive.

Rescue workers were forced to turn the Happy Pizza and Steak House into a temporary morgue, while medical staff in a nearby store frantically worked on injured people placed on desktops.

The Royal Alexandra Hospital's emergency department resembled a scene from M*A*S*H, said Dr. Don Nixon. Helicopters ferrying the wounded landed at a steady pace as more than 100 people flooded the hospital with injuries.

Endless generosity by city residents, coupled with the discovery of two infants who clung to life under piles of wreckage, emerged as the only bright spots during the day.

Premier Don Getty, along with provincial and federal cabinet ministers toured the mobile home park Saturday, promising to cut red tape to ensure tornado victims receive prompt disaster aid.

Some trailer park residents were left without a trace of loved ones after bulldozers were called in to plow through rubble in the search for the missing.

Edmontonians spared the fury of the storm opened their hearts to the survivors through the relief effort.

Residents donated 350 units of blood and jammed the city's emergency relief centre with enough food, clothing and supplies to fill more than five warehouses.

Mayor Decore also called for a review of the Alberta Weather Office's warning procedures, saying the forecasters should have issued an earlier warning of the approaching funnel clouds.

But weather office meteorologist Dave Burnett defended the work of the weather officials by saying the warning was issued at 3:07, shortly after funnel clouds touched down northeast of Leduc.

By Sunday, the indirect affects of the storm became apparent — more than 1,000 people would be out of work and Strathcona County stood to lose $1 million in tax revenue from the damaged area.

Insurance officials, who toured the disaster site, have assured residents that 90 per cent of the damage to their homes will be covered.

Many of those who lived through the storm sought counselling to help release the pain and suffering they carried around inside them.

Provincial mental health officials warned that some survivors, while coping now, may suffer emotional upheaval for months to come.

Scott Chrisp is one survivor who knows this is true.

Chrisp tells a story he heard a young boy who lived through the storm, who dreams night after night about being snatched away by treacherous winds.

"The minute he falls asleep, he wakes up with a start, screaming 'Mommy, Mommy, I'm falling.' "

"Alberta now, more than ever, needs a premier who's up to par. The back nine can wait."

But even if he had been at his desk rather than on the links, there was little he could have done. Financial institutions built on the easy money of the early '80s were failing and people were losing their houses as an oil glut eviscerated the petroleum industry.

Prior to the Principal collapse, both Edmonton-based Canadian Commercial Bank and the Northland Bank in Calgary had shut down in 1985. An unsuccessful government bailout cost taxpayers $1 billion.

In fact, the only bank that boomed was Edmonton's food bank. It had started in 1980 designed to help people over the rough spots when groceries and money ran out at the same time.

In January 1983, slightly more than 900 people used the food bank. By January 1986, that number was 17,000.

"One child in five is likely to be part of a family that has to be helped out from the food bank at some point in the year," Gerard Kennedy, the bank's executive director told the paper.

It was that year that *The Journal*, from time to time, inserted grocery bags in the newspaper, urging people to fill them with food and drop them off at fire halls and various other sites around the city.

The bust of the '80s was told in the pages of *The Journal* by bar graphs and charts, tables and grids, all buttressed by interviews with politicians and business leaders and annotated with statistics.

But statistics told half a story. It's an important half to be sure, but there were no bar graphs to measure the tears of a mom with hungry kids, or the trace the worry lines on the brow of an unemployed dad.

Getting to those desperate mothers and worried fathers was also *The Journal's* task as the mega-boom of the '70s and early '80s turned into mega-gloom.

The paper showed the human face of an economic downturn that, for much of the '80s, seemed bottomless.

Michael and Joyce Gunderman for example, invested their $60,000 life savings in Tower Mortgage in September 1988. In October, the company closed its doors.

"I just saw the ad in the paper saying they were paying 13.25 per cent interest on one-year term deposits. I put everything I had into Tower," Michael said. He was a retired barber, confined to a wheelchair and unable to work. With his $300-a-month pension, and the $600-a-month he had hoped to collect from Tower, Gunderman was certain he could have made ends meet.

"I'm an inexperienced investor," he confessed to readers. "I don't know anything. I glanced at the prospectus but didn't understand it. The salesman only tells you the good side."

Despite the sour economy, development, of course, didn't grind to a complete halt.

The University Games – the Universiade – in 1983 brought 3,000 athletes to Edmonton, adding a burst of energy to the city. The campus got the Butterdome and an upgraded track, and seats were added to Commonwealth Stadium.

Notley, 43, and five others die when their fog-bound Wapiti Aviation plane crashes in a lonely stretch of bush south of Lesser Slave Lake. "Grant Notley, in the prime of his manhood, has been swept away by the river of time," says a *Journal* editorial. "His death is a personal tragedy, but it is not a cause for despair – nor would he want it to be. He was a builder and a man who looked to the future in the cheerful belief that the future is where our possibilities as human beings lie."

***Nov. 18, 1984*:**
The Grey Cup is played in Edmonton for the first time. The Winnipeg Blue Bombers beat the Hamilton TigerCats 47-17.

***Dec. 12, 1984*:**
The federal government gives the go-ahead to the construction of Canada Place on Jasper Avenue and 97th Street. The project costs $200 million.

***Dec. 30, 1984*:**
Longtime columnist Art Evans writes his final *Journal* column; he began writing for the paper in 1948 (with a break 1953-62). "Oh, I'll miss being on the job and pecking away on the oldest typewriter in the West. There's no doubt about that.

Two hours of terror

Quick-thinking saved us—survivors

By ALLAN MAYER
Journal staff writer

"I can't believe we got out of there alive."

Darcy Elliot's two buddies agreed last night as they surveyed what was left of the Byer's Transport Building on 76th Avenue.

Cars were squashed like bugs. Huge trucks were pancake-flat. And their workplace was a jumble of shattered glass and twisted metal.

The three had crawled out of the wreckage just hours before, but returned to the scene to remind themselves of their good fortune and to take in the full horror of nature run amok.

Elliot and Shawn Hodgson saw the funnel cloud appear and had but a few moments to scramble for cover. They jumped into the cab of a truck in one of the loading docks as debris, including heavy carts, flew through the air around them.

Their quick thinking probably saved their lives. As the two huddled in the cab they could hear solid objects bounce off the truck. Two of the windows exploded and an overhead beam landed a few inches above the roof. The truck began to slide around.

"I figured we were finished. Beams were falling off the roof. The wind was explosive," said Hodgson.

In an nearby office, their friend Trevor Pacholoc dived under a desk.

It seemed like an eternity, but a few minutes later all three scrambled out of the building.

Vehicles weighing 3,000 to 4,000 pounds had been tossed around. "Before it hit I almost got sucked out the loading door. If we hadn't jumped in the truck, we would have been dead," Elliot said.

Late Friday, police and firemen continued to sift through the rubble at Byers although they were almost certain everyone had escaped.

One fireman said: "This looks more like Kansas then Edmonton."

What's left of Byer's Transport Building on 76th Avenue PICTURE: Ray Giguere

PICTURE: Karen Sornberger

Not a window was left intact in the upper storey of this building in the industrial area

Sherwood Park industrial area flattened, crushed

By MATTHEW McCLURE
and CATHY LORD
Journal Staff Writers

The Sherwood Park industrial area looked like a war zone, with debris from flattened buildings and crushed vehicles strewn everywhere.

From a vantage point on the Sherwood Park Expressway near 34th Street, there was destruction as far as the eye could see.

In a 20-block stretch on either side of the expressway, the tornado cut a path from the south which spared few buildings.

Amidst the chaos, people were lending police, firefighters and ambulance workers a hand in their search for survivors.

North of the congested expressway, Jim Werbicki and his fellow employees at the Canada Dry bottling plant carried two seriously-injured workers on a make-shift stretcher over 500 metres to where ambulances were hemmed in by downed power lines.

"We found them in the field," said Werbicki. "I don't know how they got there because the nearest building is quite a-ways away."

At Byers Transport on the south side of the freeway, dazed men stumbled through the wreckage of the loading dock and maintenance shop. They called, then listened for a reply from beneath the twisted wreckage.

Foreman Gary Cochrane was glad the twister didn't strike an hour later when afternoon shift workers would have been inside the truck terminal.

"We think we've got everyone accounted for, except that guy lying over there,' said Cochrane, pointing to a hastily-covered body lying next to the wrecked plant, "but it's still hard to know at this point."

Don Cariati, supervisor of the two-storey CN Rail Turnout Shop that was levelled by the tornado, said his staff of 45 men went home early at 3 p.m., a half-hour before the tornado struck.

"They asked me the night before if they could leave early (for the long weekend) — we're so lucky they did," said Cariati, who returned to the wreckage when he heard that the twister hit the area.

At Laidlaw Waste Systems building, a distraught woman waited for news of her aunt, seven months pregnant, and uncle — both employees in the building hit by the twister.

Dennis Bochon, who works at Atlas Crane, was also away from work when the twister hit. He returned to find out how his co-wokers fared, but no one was in the devastated building.

"I'm just sick,' he said. "I hope no one's lying in there because I've got real good friends in there."

Kurt Schiller was at work elsewhere in the industrial park at 3.30 p.m. when "the power cut and somebody said 'hey, there's a funnel cloud coming down,' so I went outside and watched it just miss our shop.

"Every time it hit something, all the debris would go flying — little did I know it was ripping buildings apart," said Schiller.

Brian Newmayer said it's the first time he's seen a twister and the last time he wants to.

"It's the most awesome thing I've ever seen — I was hoping it was a bad drug flashback."

Looking like the results of a giant god's meddling on a speedway, cars in the Sherwood Park area were flipped over and stacked atop each other

West Edmonton Mall continued to expand, and added a number of attractions, including the Fantasyland Hotel where guests could overnight in theme rooms ranging from Arabian Nights to the Alberta Truck Room, where the bed was in the back of a pickup.

Through it all, the paper became increasingly active in sponsoring events in the community.

The Edmonton Journal International Indoor Games continued into the '80s. The newspaper sponsored a number of world-class athletes to compete in top-level track events at the Coliseum.

It was a promotional tool for many newspapers throughout North America – Edmonton was one of the stops along the circuit – and the success of the Commonwealth Games in 1978 meant there was a base of support for track in Edmonton.

Canadians such as Angela Bailey and Angella Taylor, two Toronto track stars, were regular attendees, but the meet also attracted athletes such as New Zealand's John Walker, world-record holder for indoor 1,500 metres and Irishman Eamonn Coghlan, the indoor mile record holder.

The most popular events, despite the presence of the stars, involved Edmonton school kids taking part in relay events before thousands of fans.

The international circuit ended in the late '80s, the victim of dropping attendance and higher expenses, but the Indoor Games continued for schoolchildren and celebrated its 25th anniversary in 2003.

The newspaper also began to sponsor the arts festivals that became a hallmark of Edmonton summers. The Works, a major celebration of visual arts; Jazz City began in 1979 and was the first jazz festival in the country; the Edmonton Folk Music Festival, now an August fixture; and Heritage Days, a gathering of the ethnic groups that make up the city's cultural mosaic, all took solid root in the 1980s.

While Klondike Days continued to be the city's most popular fair, the '80s also brought The Fringe, a theatre festival unique to Canada. Over the years, The Fringe became the most important arts festival in Edmonton's summer and it was clear from the very first Fringe that it was something special.

Theatre critic Keith Ashwell enthusiastically, if not always positively, reviewed 40 shows over the course of that first nine-day festival in 1983.

"It must always be an opportunity for actors to do things that they desperately want to do, to do things that they would never otherwise have a chance to do and for the general public to say yes or no to their work at not much charge to themselves," Ashwell advised organizers of future Fringes when he wrote his wrap-up column that first year. For the most part, the festival has followed that advice and got better in the '90s.

In fact, so would everything else. Housing became more reasonable, oil prices climbed and stabilized, jobless rates and interest rates went down.

As the decade ended there was a sense of optimism in the city, wrote civic affairs reporter Mike Sadava. "The recession had hit hard; new office towers sat empty, and the focus of the city was shifting to West Edmonton Mall, which seemed to be opening a new attraction every six months.

"But today the old optimism was back, and downtown boosters are looking forward to a decade of renewed vitality."

But let us end on a light note and exit laughing."

***March 29, 1985*:**
Ten airmen are killed when two C-130 Hercules transport planes collide in mid-air and crash at Canadian Forces Base Edmonton.

***April 8, 1985*:**
***The Journal* becomes a morning-only paper, switching from afternoon home delivery. The paper also announces a *Journal*-sponsored team of three staff members – Allan Mayer, Ed Struzik and Brian Gavriloff – and a wilderness guide will attempt to become the first Canadian expedition to ski to the North Magnetic Pole in the High Arctic from Resolute Bay.**

***May 11, 1985*:**
The *Bub Slug* comic strip, drawn by Edmonton's Gerry Rasmussen and Gary Delainey, featuring city personalities and events, first appears in *The Journal*'s colour comics.

***May 30, 1985*:**
The Edmonton Oilers win their second straight Stanley Cup.

***July 17, 1985*:**
Queen Elizabeth, the Queen Mother, arrives in Edmonton for a two-day visit.

The Edmonton Journal

E

Tuesday, February 11, 1986

EDITOR: ROD ZIEGLER, 429 5325

Review & Forecast '86

...an Alberta profile

POISED FOR FLIGHT —

1985 was a turbulent year. We made it through the worst of the recession and saw the National Energy Program replaced by new oil and gas agreements that gave us hope — reason to plan for the future. We saw gentle, but steady recovery. Then, just as our hope turned to full-blown confidence, shaky world oil prices started to ruffle Alberta's economic tailfeathers. In our annual Review and Forecast, Journal reporters offer some answers to the question: will the Alberta economy fly?

THE ANSWERS:

E2: The Economy
E4: Energy
E8: The North
E9: Edmonton
E10: Communication
E11: Transportation
F1: Finance
F4: Labor
F5: Small Business
F5: Hi Tech
F7: Agriculture

PICTURE: Dan Jurak

The Hated NEP

"As the full dimensions of the Tuesday night massacre emerge, Ottawa's new National Energy Program comes through as a misdirected harpoon. Originally aimed at the energy industry's 'fat,' it has hit a vital area in a most unfair manner."

— Editorial six days after the NEP was announced, Oct. 28, 1980

Edmontonians should have seen the punch coming.

Prime Minister Pierre Trudeau mused about "made in Canada" energy prices and policies throughout the '70s. In the 1979 election he said there was no reason for Canadians to pay world prices for oil when they had oceans of the stuff under their own backyard.

Introduction of the National Energy Program (NEP) on Oct. 28, 1980, was simply the manifestation of the federal Liberal "what's yours is ours" resource philosophy.

"Today Alberta is selling its depleting oil reserves in Canada for $8 a barrel, $2.46 less than the comparable price charged by OPEC," said a *Journal* editorial Sept. 30, 1975.

Essentially, Alberta was subsidizing Eastern Canada.

By 1979, Alberta had lost $12 billion in foregone oil revenues and Trudeau was painting the Alberta government as the villain for demanding provincial control of resource development based on international prices predicted to hit $60 a barrel by 1990.

Claims that much-needed American risk capital would dry up if companies couldn't get full price for the product were dismissed by Trudeau who said if the private sector wouldn't do it, the public sector would through its new oil company, Petro Canada.

The socialist tinge to the philosophy didn't sit at all well in free-enterprise Alberta.

The National Energy Program was to secure oil supplies and ensure development of new supplies, especially in the North and off the east coast said federal Finance Minister Allan MacEacheran when he announced the program with the Tuesday, Oct. 28, 1980 budget.

By January 1981, there were almost daily predictions in *The Journal* of oil patch disaster as the results of the NEP.

Premier Peter Lougheed had responded to the NEP by threatening cutbacks in production and putting further oilsand development on the back burner, causing him and Alberta to be castigated by the Eastern press and politicians as the consummate blackmailer holding the country's future to ransom for its own gain.

But Alberta denied any villainy in the matter. If anything bad were going to happen, it would be the fault of the federal government.

Dissenting opinion in Alberta about the evils of the NEP was in short supply in the legislature, offices, bars and the newspaper.

But *Journal* editorial writer William Thorsell (somewhat courageously) gave it a try Feb. 17 just before federal provincial talks on the program were to begin.

***July 28, 1985*:**
Dr. Dennis Modry performs the first heart transplant operation in Western Canada, at Edmonton's University of Alberta Hospital.

***Aug. 1, 1985*:**
***The Journal* distributes special brown paper bags to raise donations for the Edmonton Food Bank during Heritage Days.**

***Aug. 4, 1985*:**
***The Journal*'s home delivery rate rises to $1.75 from $1.50 for seven days a week. A week's worth of single copies bought from street boxes or dealers costs $2.50.**

***Sept. 6, 1985*:**
Publisher Mel Hurtig launches the new *Canadian Encyclopedia* at a gala at the Citadel Theatre.

***Sept. 10, 1985*:**
Phase III with 300 more stores opens at West Edmonton Mall. The new phase costs an estimated $650 million.

***January 1986*:**
Edd Uluschak pens his last cartoon for *The Journal*.

***Feb. 8, 1986*:**
Twenty-six people are killed when a Via Rail passenger train and a Canadian National freight train collide head-on near Hinton, 265 kilometres west of

‘Mugger’ Uluschak wins big one again

Edmonton Journal cartoonist Edd Uluschak has done it again: he’s won the 1979 National Newspaper Award for cartooning.

Announcement was made today from the Toronto Press Club which judges the entries.

Judges particularly commended the cartoon of the re-inflated Trudeau (above).

Last time the 36-year-old cartoonist won the national award was in 1969, a year after he joined The Journal. Since then he has won at least a dozen national and international prizes, including The Basil Dean Memorial Award for Outstanding Contributions to Journalism, and prizes from Greece, Bulgaria, Germany and Japan.

Author Peter Desbarats in his history of Canadian cartooning, The Hecklers, described the Uluschak technique as “having all the subtlety of a mugging.”

Toronto produced winners in six of the nine categories in the 31st annual awards for excellence in journalism in 1979, one each going to Edmonton, Calgary, and Vancouver.

The other winners:

Enterprise reporting, Bill Dampier, Toronto Star.

Feature writing — Val Sears, Toronto Star.

Editorial writing — Oakland Ross, Toronto Globe and Mail.

Spot news reporting — the Toronto bureau of The Canadian Press.

More AWARDS Page A3

“Just one more time, Pierre.”

Lougheed was using much emotion and little fact in presenting the Alberta case, wrote Thorsell. "And we as Canadians living in Alberta, must reject simple melodrama as the diet of provincial politics.

"We are not at war in Canada. We have honest differences of opinion about some major national policies."

In February 1981, there was now a $22 a barrel difference between the "Canadian" oil price ($18 US) and the world price ($40 US). By April, 114 oil rigs were pulled out of Alberta and shipped to U.S. fields. Booming Alberta was flirting suddenly with recession.

Publisher J. Patrick O'Callaghan, in a May 4 essay, stirred the pot. "Pierre Trudeau is the arsonist of confederation. Not only has Mr. Trudeau supplied the matches for a conflagration of his own making, he has brought his torch to the future of Canada searing its unity for decades to come."

By September a federal-provincial deal was hammered out and reporter Duncan Thorne was in Ottawa for the occasion.

"Canadians and Albertans alike won under Tuesday's $212.8 billion energy deal, say Prime Minister Pierre Trudeau and Premier Peter Lougheed."

"You have to pay a fair price for peace," said federal energy minister Marc Lalonde.

While Alberta and Ottawa were having at each other, the world oil community had plans of its own.

Southam economic columnist Don McGillivray foreshadowed what was to come on Feb. 25, 1982.

"King Oil is falling off his throne. This recession is showing that energy is a commodity like any other, subject to the same forces of supply and demand."

By 1984, when the Canadian price for oil had reached about 95 per cent of world price, consumer fears about facing $70 barrel oil were abating. (McGillivray was right. Oil prices collapsed in 1986 to under $10 a barrel.)

On Sept. 17, 1984, Conservative leader Brian Mulroney became prime minister and Alberta finally had more of a philosophical soulmate in power.

Southam's Patrick Nagle followed Mulroney to New York on Dec. 11 to cover his speech to a gathering of top U.S. businessmen. He promised to at least "reshape" the NEP.

"Canada was not built by expropriating retroactively other peoples' property. This practice is odious and shall not be followed by the new government of Canada."

It took a year, but on Dec. 21, 1985, *The Journal* reported new federal legislation new offering tax incentives for oil exploration to replace the last of the disliked Liberal programs.

The final vestige of the NEP was erased from the books, but not from minds of Albertans.

Edmonton. More than 70 people are injured in the fiery wreck, which burns for several days.

***March 1986*:**
Malcolm Mayes' s first cartoon runs in *The Journal*.

***June 14, 1986*:**
Three people are killed when the Mindbender roller-coaster at West Edmonton Mall crashes. A lengthy inquiry into the accident puts the blame on design and manufacturing flaws, and criticizes safety and maintenance standards.

***June 27, 1986*:**
Edmonton's first The Works visual arts festival opens.

***July 13, 1986*:**
Gail Greenough of Edmonton wins the world show jumping championships riding Mr. T. She is the first woman to win the North American title.

***July 19, 1986*:**
Flood waters from the North Saskatchewan River sweep through parts of three Edmonton river valley communities, damaging hundreds of homes. The river peaks at 7.5 metres above its normal level.

***Sept. 16, 1986*:**
Work is completed on the Walter C. Mackenzie Health Sciences Centre

SEXUALLY TRANSMITTED DISEASE:

A JOURNAL SCIENCE SPECIAL

ILLUSTRATION: Rod Michalchuk

Loving someone to death

By RON CHALMERS
Journal Staff Writer

The spread of AIDS to over 100 countries since 1981 has dramatized the danger of sexually-transmitted diseases (STDs) — and the need to control them through responsible attitudes and behavior.

More than one million Americans — and five million Africans — may be infected with the AIDS virus.

In Alberta, only 51 cases of AIDS have been diagnosed. For every case, there could be up to 60 or 100 people carrying the virus. Most of them don't know they are infected and could still be spreading the virus.

Nobody knows how many of the infected people eventually will get AIDS. Estimates range from 10 per cent to 100 per cent. The disease leads to death, usually within three years.

In the United States, reported AIDS cases have about doubled every year, although the rate of increase may be falling. In Alberta, the rise is less dramatic, with 17 new cases in 1985 and 19 new cases in 1986.

"We're going to see more cases of AIDS," says Dr. Barbara Romanowski, director of the Edmonton Sexually Transmitted Disease Clinic. "But I don't think it will double every year."

AIDS is not the only important STD.

Alberta's most widespread STD is chlamydia. It has been less publicized than AIDS because it can be successfully treated.

But untreated chlamydia can be passed from mother to baby during birth, infecting the baby's eyes or lungs — or it can ruin a woman's reproductive organs.

During the last half of 1985, 3,932 chlamydia cases were reported. Romanowski believes the rate may have climbed during 1986.

In 1985, Albertans experienced 5,690 cases of gonorrhea — high, but only about half the epidemic level of 1980.

Most STDs are found among people under 30 years old.

They often have permissive attitudes toward sex — while lacking either the information or the social skills to avoid dangerous sexual behavior.

Reginald Bibby, a University of Lethbridge sociologist, surveyed 3,600 Canadian high school students in 1984 and found that 53 per cent endorsed sexual relations after a few dates.

"There are no signs of an ongoing sexual revolution," Bibby says. "They're simply mirroring the adults."

But they aren't talking to the adults. Bibby cites another study showing that 75 per cent of teenagers think their parents would disapprove of pre-marital sex. Many young people are unwilling to discuss, with parents, the facts of teen-age life. So they miss a chance to learn safe, responsible sexual attitudes.

Edward Herold, a sociologist at the University of Guelph, has found that people who become sexually active early often take the highest risks.

For instance, those who start sexual intercourse at an early age tend to have more sex partners before marriage — and more extramarital sex. The risk of acquiring or spreading STDs rises with the number of sex partners.

The failure to prevent unwanted pregnancy or disease reveals ignorance both of the risks — and of the means to avoid risks through abstinence or safe sex.

In Herold's research, 96 per cent of young women and 92 per cent of young men agreed that they or their partner should use contraception if they had premarital intercourse. Yet only one-third of young people actually use any kind of contraceptive during their first intercourse.

Sometimes, the failure to apply one's knowledge is caused by discomfort in discussing sex. Effective sex education must include the social skills needed to apply such knowledge.

Fortunately, information and counselling is increasingly available, both about the dangers and about the attitudes, behaviors and devices that can prevent the spread of sexually-transmitted diseases.

WARNING: Some material in this section is sexually explicit and may offend some readers

Diagnosis AIDS

"Four confirmed cases of the so-called gay plague that has killed at least 155 persons in the United States have surfaced so far in Canada."
— Story, July 21, 1982

That's the first mention of AIDS in the *Edmonton Journal.*

And it really was called "the gay plague."

The city's first reported suspected case of AIDS was Jan. 29, 1983.

A story by reporter Rick Pedersen said: "An Edmonton homosexual with symptoms linked to the so-called 'gay-plague' has gone to the United States for special tests."

Doctors dealing with the patient assured Pedersen the man, an American, "was celibate while he was here."

"No one knows what causes it or why most victims are promiscuous gays, Haitian immigrants, intravenous drug users or prisoners," wrote Pedersen. Whether the man actually had AIDS was never reported. Local health officials said they had lost track of him.

Alberta's first AIDS-related death was reported June 11, in Calgary. He was a bisexual American.

By February 1984, there were four confirmed cases of AIDS in Alberta, all in Calgary. But Jerry Katz, an Alberta doctor studying the disease, said in a Feb. 20 story he was keeping an eye on a dozen Edmonton men who were exhibiting some symptoms.

On March 4 researchers reported a chilling new development as the disease was spreading through Central Africa, through heterosexual contact.

The city's first confirmed AIDS case was reported July 17, 1984. Reporter Dene Creswell interviewed the victim Aug. 23. "Most people don't know I am the one," he said. "But sometimes I think people are being a little distant – maybe it's me – maybe I'm being paranoid."

Suddenly, in July 1985, AIDS had a very public face. Rock Hudson, a mainstay among Hollywood's stable of romantic lead actors, was reported to have AIDS. Details of his lifestyle began to emerge.

A *Journal* editorial Aug. 14 said, "The news that actor Rock Hudson has AIDS has focused public attention on the disease. Perhaps that will translate into pressure on governments to commit more resources to researching this deadly disease. For some victims, there is too little time."

Hudson, 59, died Oct. 3. Edmonton's first AIDS victim succumbed on Oct. 28, his identity never revealed.

By 1987, the story emphasis had evolved from hope of finding a cure to how to slow progress of the disease throughout society. "Condom" was no longer a word that wasn't printed in family newspapers.

The Journal put out a special section on sexually transmitted diseases March 19, 1987, with the warning: "Some material in this section is sexually explicit and may offend some readers."

That day's editorial explained the paper's reasoning: "The key to controlling the AIDS epidemic lies in education. Fear must be tempered by facts."

on campus. Construction on the $414-million project has taken almost a decade to finish.

***Oct. 20, 1986*:**
Laurence Decore is re-elected mayor of Edmonton.

***Nov. 5, 1986*:**
***The Journal* begins publishing *Neighbours*, a new weekly supplement to the paper containing news and information oriented to individual zones of the city.**

***Nov. 30, 1986*:**
The Hamilton TiCats demolish the Edmonton Eskimos 39-15 in the Grey Cup.

***Dec. 14, 1986*:**
Striking Edmonton Gainers meatpacking workers vote in favour of a new contract, ending a six-and-a-half month strike that is one of the most bitter and violent in Alberta history.

***In 1987*:**
A *Journal* copy editor makes $1,885 every 15 days.

***Jan. 13, 1987*:**
Treasurer Dick Johnston announces plans to lay off up to 2,000 civil servants.

***Jan. 15, 1987*:**
Wardair is bought by Canadian Airlines

THE EDMONTON JOURNAL, Friday, September 6, 1985 I-1

EXPLORE!
WEST EDMONTON MALL
GRAND OPENING
SEPTEMBER 11th

The Mall

"To suggest that people will now decide to come to this city because of West Edmonton Mall is, I say, a bit far fetched."
— Travel writer Guy Demarino, Aug. 27, 1983

A mall is a mall, or at least it was Aug. 28, 1980, when *The Journal* ran its first "construction is underway" story about West Edmonton Mall. The four-and-a-half inch piece was buried on page D11.

The Journal seemed a bit unsure about judging the size of the elephant. The first paragraph said, a bit awkwardly, West Edmonton Mall "is believed will become Canada's largest shopping centre." A bit farther on, the writer declared the 1.12-million-square-foot facility "is expected to be larger than any existing Edmonton shopping centre."

As it turned out, WEM became one of the city's defining characteristics. It became so much part of the local culture that someone going to The Mall was assumed to be going to West Edmonton Mall and nowhere else.

The Journal finally got the picture by Sept. 12, 1981, when Mayor Cec Purves cut the ribbon on Phase One.

Reporter Bob Gilmour wrote: "Everything about the mall is large: size, cost, landscaping, parking, interior, sculpture, opening budget."

Readers learned it was owned by the secretive Ghermezians, a family of Iranian immigrants who lived in west Edmonton, and *The Journal* dealt mostly with Nader Ghermezian, a tireless, black-moustached pitchman who promoted the family business as more of a social phenomenon than a mere shopping centre. The Ghermezians swam upstream to get to their goals. Every rezoning application, tax break and financing package was met with skepticism and opposition.

But they were also admired, sometimes even by *The Journal*'s questioning editorial writers, who commented on a controversial rezoning application by the Ghermezians May 29, 1983. "Where else in North America would an imaginative plan like West Edmonton Mall Phase Three receive so much opposition and face so many roadblocks? And where else would city politicians throw up condition after condition at a development that will give their constituents jobs and a brighter future in bleak economic times?"

Not all staffers were enthralled with the Ghermezian dream, especially editorial writer William Thorsell who wrote, "It's Middle America in drag," on Aug. 18, 1983, after the opening of Phase Two.

The Ghermezians also changed city working and shopping patterns forever when they ordered their tenants to stay open Sundays, defying the federal Lord's Day Act. The move sparked heated public debate and, ultimately, a Supreme Court of Canada decision that ruled the act invalid.

Along the way there was bad to go along with the good. The tragic Mindbender roller-coaster accident June 14, 1985, that killed three people, stunned the city and made headlines for weeks.

But bad or good, The Mall became a world-class tourist attraction.

International. A subdued but gracious Max Ward, the former bush pilot who founded the airline in 1961, tells a press conference that his airline had simply run out of money and couldn't hold out long enough to change from a charter to a scheduled airliner. The process would have taken about a year. Wardair had a staff of 4,500.

***March 12, 1987*: Linda Hughes, assistant managing editor, is appointed editor-in-chief, replacing Steve Hume who becomes general manager. George Oake becomes managing editor, replacing veteran Don Smith.**

***May 11, 1987*: Columnist Linda Goyette turns her guns on Premier Don Getty's push for a Triple-E Senate. "A premier with a one-track mind is infuriating at home, but not so intolerable at a distance...Don Getty's obsession with a Triple E senate is so boring it destroys brain cells. Albertans share a sincere desire for some sort of Senate reform, so we grudgingly put up with the mEEEowing of an inarticulate premier who won't explain what he's talking about... Getty is now under the mistaken impression that he is the brigadier-general in charge of that letter**

The Edmonton
Journal
25 Cents (Metro only)
MONDAY, JUNE 1, 1987
PICTURE: Mike Pinder

Sweet Victory

"Take away Gretzky and what are the Oilers? A team who can be wiped out by the Hartford Whalers."

— *Vancouver Sun* columnist James Lawton in *The Journal*, March 29, 1984

There was, in the spring of 1984, only faint hope the Edmonton Oilers could stop the New York Islanders "drive for five" Stanley Cups in a row. They'd crushed Oiler playoff hopes the year before. In fact, the Oilers hadn't beaten the Islanders in 10 meetings.

Still, with the likes of Wayne Gretzky, Jari Kurri, Paul Coffey and Grant Fuhr, the Oilers were good as they breezed past the Winnipeg Jets 4-0. After the Jets were eliminated, the Oilers' next challenge was the 10th-place Calgary Flames and they won the first game, April 13, 5-2.

"So much for those critics that suggest the Oilers have the defensive weaponry of Lichtenstein," quipped sports writer Jim Matheson.

The next day, however, the Flames beat the Oilers 6-5 in overtime on a goal by Carey Wilson, a player so obscure that he was described by Matheson as needing "an American Express card to identify himself."

With a flick of a wrist shot, the Oilers went from heroes to goats on April 15, in columnist Barry Westgate's playbook. "I'm sick and tired of the Oilers. Tap me when they decide to play."

By April 20, the series was tied 3-3 and the city held its breath, but not Westgate. "The Oilers are in very, very big trouble. When the going gets tough, too often they'll spit out the bit."

Westgate, of course, was wrong, but that didn't stop him from dumping on the party. "All I want to think of at the moment is that these lucksacks should have been out of this series as convincing winners long ago."

The Oilers dipped into their sack of luck and thumped the Minnesota North Stars in the Campbell Conference final series 4-0.

Now it was crunch time. The Islanders had punched their way past Montreal 4-2. Edmonton once again faced its nemesis.

The Oilers scratched out a 1-0 win in the first game, May 11 in Uniondale, and Westgate was beginning to come on side.

"Wasn't that just a hell of a hockey game? Wasn't that a breathtaking shutout by Grant Fuhr?"

Perhaps it wasn't so breathtaking two nights later when the Oilers were shelled 6-1. However, they roared back with a 7-2 win at home on May 15. "Billy Smith is human," wrote sports editor Marc Horton of the game. "He does not possess satanic powers when he stands in his goal crease."

Columnist Cam Cole, who had predicted an Oiler loss in the series, changed his mind.

"They have finally proven they're better than the best."

And they were, winning games four and five. Edmontonians went wild. From that first Stanley Cup through the end of the decade, the Oilers gave *Journal* readers bragging rights wherever they went.

between D and F. Somebody should tell Sesame Street. They might take him off our hands...."

***July 31, 1987*:**
One of the worst tornadoes in Canadian history kills 27 people and leaves hundreds more injured and homeless as it rips through eastern Edmonton.

***Aug. 1, 1987*:**
***The Journal* publishes a special 12-page edition reporting on yesterday's tornado, printed in Calgary after the storm leaves the Eastgate press plant without power and unable to publish.**

***Oct. 24, 1987*:**
The Chinatown Gate opens in Edmonton's oldest Chinese neighbourhood.

***Nov. 29, 1987*:**
The Edmonton Eskimos beat Toronto 38-36 for their sixth Grey Cup victory in 10 years.

***March 8, 1988*:**
***Journal* photographer Steve Simon wins The Canadian Press Picture of the Year for his 1987 shot of the killer tornado that swept through Edmonton.**

***May 5, 1988*:**
Edmonton's $114.5 million Grey Nuns Hospital in Mill Woods opens.

Sunny, high 18
Accu-weather/D14

IN COUNTRY: FACING UP TO VIETNAM
Entertainment/C8

BECKER SIZZLES IN U.S. OPEN
Sports/D5

HUNGARY FREES REFUGEES
World/A5

CASH IN ON CARS OF '60s
Money/D10

The Edmonton Journal

50 Cents Metro Only

MONDAY SEPTEMBER 11, 1989

New Ng murder evidence found

Edmonton Mounties uncover witness against accused mass killer

GREG OWENS and TOM BARRETT
Journal Staff Writers

Edmonton

Edmonton investigators have uncovered dramatic new evidence against alleged mass murderer Charles Ng that will bolster a weakening American case.

The new Canadian evidence is expected to lead to four new murder charges against Ng in the U.S. A new investigating task force is expected to be revealed later this week in Sacramento, Calif.

Ng is already charged with 13 murders in a bizarre string of killings in California in 1984-85. He is accused of running a sex slave camp in a bunker in California with partner Leonard Lake.

Lake committed suicide shortly after he was arrested in June 1985. Ng fled to Canada and has fought a high- profile battle against extradition to the U.S. for almost a year.

The Supreme Court of Canada refused on Aug. 31 to hear an appeal of Ng's extradition order. The decision on his extradition rests with federal Justice Minister Doug Lewis.

SPECIAL REPORT

The strongest evidence against Ng emerged after he was arrested in Calgary on July 6, 1985 and Edmonton police and RCMP were put on the case, sources have told The Journal.

Edmonton RCMP investigators uncovered a Canadian who will likely be a key witness in any U.S. murder trial against Ng.

While American authorities were separately investigating individual killings tied to Lake and Ng, Canadians dug up evidence showing a conspiracy to commit the killings.

The Canadian work on the conspiracy charges will become the cornerstone in the case against N[illegible] says Paul Cummin[illegible] trict Attorney for [illegible] Francisco and co-prosecutor for the Ng case.

In the past four years, the American case against Ng has been weakened. Two key witnesses died of natural causes and other witnesses have scattered across the U.S.

"Let's put it this way, it certainly isn't getting any stronger," said Cummins in a telephone interview from San Francisco.

The conspiracy case means any evidence of the killings associated with Lake can be brought into any trial Ng would face in the U.S. That evidence includes Lake's diary, which details a number of the murders.

The conspiracy evidence gathered by the RCMP has already produced a further charge that

Please see Charges/A10

Charles Ng

SIX GENERATIONS

Rick MacWilliam *The Journal*

A GREAT-GREAT-GREAT FAMILY— That's six generations of the Sisson family above, ranging from great-great-great grandmother Lydia Sisson, 92, to 3½-week-old Ashley Lazowski whose arrival caused a great deal of excitement in a family that loves babies. The generations are represented (from left) by great-great grandmother Hazel Reid, Lydia, Ashley, grandmother Beverley Bourassa, mother Stacey Bourassa, and great-grandmother Marlene Couturier. **Story B2**

Ukrainian group presses Soviets for independence

WARREN CARAGATA
The Canadian Press

Moscow

Ukrainians launched a movement seeking self-government and economic independence over the weekend.

The move was made by an organization called Ruk which claims 280,000 members.

The group apparently ignored a warning by Soviet President Mikhail Gorbachev against those who are trying to create a sense of anxiety and crisis.

"There's a tight knot of problems," Gorbachev said in a nationally televised address on Saturday night, referring to ethnic unrest and widespread shortages.

"One can discern voices that predict impending chaos, a coup, and even civil war," he said.

It is the second time Gorbachev has referred to a coup. Earlier this year, he denied that possibility in a speech to the Congress of People's Deputies.

But in Ukraine, radicals at the founding congress of a new mass movement called for economic independence for their region of more than 50 million people. It accounts for 25 per cent of the country's food output and even more of its industrial production.

There were also appeals for caution from other delegates who don't want to upset the Kremlin where leaders are anxious about spreading nationalist sentiment in areas such as the Baltic republics and Transcaucasia in the south.

Officially, the movement supports greater autonomy for the republic and a reassertion of the Ukrainian language, but does not call for political independence.

Speaking to reporters in Kiev on the final day of the founding congress of Ruk (Movement), which says it has 280,000 members, people on the organizing committee said their central aim is economic independence.

Members of the 1,700-strong audience stood up to clap and cheer frequent appeals for the removal of party leader Vladimir Shcherbitsky, an appointee of former Kremlin chief Leonid Brezhnev. Some speakers demanded he be put on trial for his handling of the 1986 Chernobyl nuclear disaster.

Gorbachev's speech marked his return to the public stage after his summer vacation. He said the government is putting together an emergency program to deal with the country's mounting political and economic problems.

"Some of the measures may prove unpopular. Some of their aspects may appear to be tough and painful."

Gorbachev said the time has come "like never before" for a consolidation of all progressive forces behind the party.

His words follow a concerted Soviet press campaign against national mass movements in Latvia, Lithuania and Estonia, the formerly independent Baltic republics.

At the same time, popular discontent has grown over the country's economic plight, which shows no sign of recovery more than three years after Gorbachev began his economic reform plan.

In his speech, Gorbachev did not directly mention any trouble spot. But he said that resort to job action to resolve problems holds "dangerous consequences."

Party arrogant, PCs find

Secret Tory memo calls for more concern and respect

BRIAN LAGHI
Journal Staff Writer

Edmonton

Grassroots Tories in the Edmonton area say their party is too arrogant and needs to show "more concern and respect", says an internal party document.

The confidential memo obtained by The Journal also shows Edmonton area PCs are calling for a new image for the party, new blood and a review of the party's leadership review and selection process.

The often-critical document was prepared by party organizers after Edmonton and area constituency executives met in late spring to review the March election campaign and Premier Don Getty's Stettler byelection win.

At that meeting, party organizers asked constituency executives for their views on three major issues: communication, policy development and organization.

According to the memo, Edmonton area Tories are concerned about the party's difficulties in communicating with voters and the media.

"Communication should be more professional in the legislature," the point-form memo says. "Less arrogance — show more concern and respect."

The memo also suggests the party practise honesty and that it treat the media with integrity.

" Don't fight them. . ." And it says a professional media communicator should be hired.

Several party members have blamed relations between Getty's office and the media as one reason for the party's drop in popularity.

The party entered the March campaign hoping to win back many of the 11 Edmonton ridings which went New Democrat in 1986. Instead, Getty's lost his Edmonton-Whitemud seat and cabinet veteran Les Young was also defeated.

The memo shows the constituencies want the party to review its "constitution, including leadership review and selection process."

The PC constitution currently calls for a leadership review only if the party is defeated.

The memo also highlights several other areas for the party to work on.

For example, rank-and-file members say they want popular Health Minister Nancy Betkowski more involved in party activities.

Asked how the party can improve policy development, one group of executives responded that the "party be consulted in major policy direction" and the government must "seek input of ALL Albertans on issues of concern."

PC executive director Bert Murray would not comment on the memo except to say it is an "in-family" document intended for internal use.

Jack Frost a little early for gardeners

Autumn doesn't officially arrive for another 10 days but Jack Frost is here already.

Below-zero temperatures were recorded Saturday everywhere in Alberta but Grande Prairie "and there may have been frost there as well," said Alberta weather centre meteorologist Randy Peterson.

Red Deer at -4 was the coldest spot in the province overnight Saturday. The temperature dropped to -3 at the municipal airport. A low of -2 was expected last night.

A cold blast from the eastern Arctic withered tomato vines and killed off annual flowers.

"The perennials are OK, but that's it for the geraniums," said Marilyn Bertsch of Golden Acre Garden Sentres.

Robert Wallish of Wallish Greenhouses said indoor crops "weren't touched at all by the frost but the potato tops are blackened."

Tourist boat sinks; 151 missing

The Associated Press

Vienna

A Romanian ship collided with a Bulgarian tugboat and sank in the Danube River on Sunday, leaving 151 people missing, Romania's official Agerpres news agency reported.

Apart from the 13 crew, most of the 169 passengers aboard the Romanian cruiser Mogoshoaja "were almost certainly western tourists," a London newspaper said.

Pleasure cruises on the Danube are a key source of foreign currency for Romania, the Independent said.

The collision occurred upstream of the port city of Galati, about 200 km northeast of the Romanian capital Bucharest.

A total of 169 passengers were aboard the Romanian ship. Only 18 of them and the ship's 13 crew members were rescued, Agerpres said.

The Bulgarian state BTA news agency said the Mogoshoaja collided with the Bulgarian ship Peter Karaminchev, which was tugging a convoy of loaded barges.

Inside

Alberta	A7	Patterns	B7
Ann Landers	C3	People	A2
Barry Westgate	B1	Sportsweek	D1
Bingos	D14	Television	C9
Births	B5	Weather	D14
Bob Remington	C9	World	A5
Bridge	C5	**CLASSIFIED ADS**	
Cam Cole	D1	Index	B5
Canada	A3	Order Form	B4
City	B1	Auctions	B14
Comics	C5	Employment	B5-9
Crossword	C5	Legals	B14
Deaths	B4	Mini Market	B8
Don Smith	C4	Real Estate	B10-12
Dr. Donohue	C3	Tenders	B14
Entertainment	C8	Vehicles	B12-13
Horoscope	C5	**The Journal**	
John Brown	A9	Information	B4
Life	C1	Phone numbers	B4
Opinion	A8		

0 558295 22

Published daily by the proprietor, Southam Inc., at The Journal Building, Edmonton, Alta., T5J 2S6. Second class mail registration number 0566

We've got news for you—a dramatic new look!

LINDA HUGHES
Journal Editor

Edmonton

Welcome to the new look of The Edmonton Journal.

We're making some dramatic changes in the design and content of The Journal. Today you have the first taste of those changes.

Throughout the week you'll see many new features in the paper, including much more city and community news, more entertainment and sports stories, more background and in-depth news and more people stories.

We're making these changes because readers are changing. You've told us you want more news and information, but you also have less time to read.

We've tried to design a paper that satisfies both those needs: a paper that tells you much more about the world and the community you live in and is also easier to read.

Newspapers are constantly changing. We change every day with each new edition. Newspaper designers here and around the world are always trying to improve the typography and adjust the make-up of newspaper pages to make them better for readers. We fine-tune the look of the paper every day, and every few years it's time for a major overhaul. The Journal has changed its typefaces at least six times since 1955. Each time, we changed because we found a new style that was easier to read. Our front page nameplate

> ***"We're changing because readers are changing."***
> *—Linda Hughes, editor*

has also evolved and been updated many times since we began as the Evening Journal in 1903.

We've always changed along with the community. The new nameplate gracing the top of our front page today maintains that tradition. We've chosen a clean, modern design that combines the traditional Journal signature with a distinctive emphasis on Edmonton. It's a lively, progressive design to reflect the dynamic community the Journal serves.

We brought together a large group of readers to look at prototypes of the new paper and they choose this nameplate over several others (it was our favorite as well). We liked blue for the nameplate and our readers also said they liked it better than any other color.

The new design encompasses dozens of other changes, large and small: from the way stories are placed on the page, to size of datelines, the style of index boxes and the spacing between letters. Every change was made with one purpose in mind: to make the paper more accessible, easier to handle, better organized and more enjoyable to read.

We began by choosing a new typeface, Corona, which is clean, attractive and easy to read.

Our new headline type, Helvetica,

Please see Design/A2

Linda Hughes

Richler's Rant

"Essentially, Richler is a rude little wimp who somehow thinks of himself as a superior, jock-macho type. He's stuffed full of his own concepts or moral rectitude without knowing a thing about decency, morality or simple good manners. He jealously guards his position in the U.S. by denigrating his fellow citizens."
— Edmonton publisher Mel Hurtig, in a letter, Oct. 9, 1985

It should have been so simple.

If only Mordecai Richler, the author of *The Apprenticeship of Duddy Kravitz* and arguably one of Canada's funniest and most acerbic writers, had been just a little nicer.

He was in Edmonton in March 1985 as the hockey season wound down, to write a freelance piece on Wayne Gretzky for the prestigious *New York Times Magazine.*

What he had to say about Gretzky – he called him "curiously bland" and "a whiner" and "incapable of genuine wit or irreverence" – incensed Oiler fans.

But what he had to say about the city was worse.

The Journal reprinted the offending article in its Oct. 6, 1985, Sunday Brunch section. "The capital of Alberta is a city you come from, not a place to visit, unless you happen to have relatives there or an interest in an oil well nearby. On first glance, and even on third, it seems not so much a city as a jumble of a used-building lot, where the spare office towers and box-shaped apartment buildings and cinder-block motels discarded in the construction of real cities have been abandoned to waste away in the cruel Prairie winter.

"If Canada were not a country, however, fragmented, but, instead, a house, Vancouver would be the solarium-cum-playroom, an afterthought of affluence; Toronto, the counting room, where money makes for the most glee; Montreal, the salon; and Edmonton, Edmonton the boiler room."

He didn't stop there. He kicked at a city that was down on its knees, struggling with a deteriorating downtown and a jobless rate that simply refused to go down.

"There is hardly a tree to be seen downtown, nothing to delight the eye on Jasper Avenue. On 30-below-zero nights, grim religious zealots loom on street corners, speaking in tongues, and intrepid streetwalkers in mini-skirts rap on the windows of cars that have stopped for traffic. There isn't a first-class restaurant in town…."

For his part, Gretzky took the personal attack in stride. "I'm used to being a little bit criticized – that part doesn't bother me that much. But he criticized the city, which is a little bit unfair."

Oiler owner Peter Pocklington defended the city, too.

"A lot of cities would lie down and die if they were devastated economically the way we've been, but not Edmonton."

***May 26, 1988*:**
The Edmonton Oilers win their fourth Stanley Cup championship in five seasons.

***June 13, 1988*:**
Edmonton pianist Angela Cheng is the first Canadian to win first prize in the Montreal International Music Competition.

***June 24, 1988*:**
***The Journal* begins printing with new inks based on canola oil instead of petroleum. It decreases smudging on readers' hands.**

***July 16, 1988*:**
Wayne Gretzky weds actress Janet Jones in a $1-million ceremony at St. Joseph's Basilica. *The Journal* publishes an eight-page special section the following day on the event.

***Aug. 9, 1988*:**
In a move that stuns the city, Edmonton Oilers superstar Wayne Gretzky is traded to the L.A. Kings.

***Oct. 9, 1988*:**
Laurence Decore is elected leader of the Alberta Liberals. Ald. Terry Cavanagh replaces him as mayor after an in-house council vote.

***Feb. 3, 1989*:**
***Journal* photographer Rick MacWilliam wins The Canadian**

SURVIVORS

Part 6: Moose, Deer — The Journal explores Alberta wildlife issues. Next: Woodland Caribou

Moose orphans run through a canola field near Olds to a tiny grove, where they can munch on tree shoots and succulent leaves; grains don't go down well. PICTURE: Rick Pape

Wild diet keeps harness off the moose

By DAVE COOPER
Journal Staff Writer

The moose riders of old Russia made life difficult for the cruel Cossacks led by Ivan the Terrible during the Middle Ages.

The czar was conquering new lands in Siberia, but his Cossacks on horseback were no match for the peasants atop trained moose, which easily escaped through the forests and muskeg.

Things got so bad that training moose to be ridden or used as pack animals was outlawed. Moose were shot on sight, and so were their riders.

Seeing a good thing, the king of Sweden tried to form a moose cavalry. On paper, the idea had merit. Moose are big — and grow bigger if castrated.

Raised by man, they can be friendly and trusting — like a gigantic dog.

And opposing cavalries were spooked. Horses are scared stiff of moose (which is why the gentle giants were banned from medieval towns).

What, then, could stop a moose cavalry? Their eating habits.

Moose like to roam and eat tender aspen, willow and aquatic plants. They dislike hay, or anything else cut and stored by man.

"That idea of large numbers of moose in a cavalry wouldn't work; you couldn't feed them. But it shows us the moose is quite an interesting animal," says Val Geist, University of Calgary wildlife expert.

He says a moose is so clever that, when led by its master, it will calmly walk by an idling aircraft engine and not flinch.

There are cases of pet moose noisily "asking" their masters to let them indoors, and one example of a moose that slept in a kitchen beside the stove.

But moose are really in their element out in the bush.

Gliding over obstacles by lifting their long legs, their movement is fluid — and makes it easy to escape wolves in dense bush and deep snow.

"They can carry packs extremely well, because their backs stay level when they go over logs or whatever. Just the legs move. They can put a pack horse to shame," says Geist.

Through the forests of much of Canada, moose are valued for meat and sport hunting.

In Alberta's prime moose-producing areas — the Grande Prairie, St. Paul and Edson regions — an average of two animals roam per square kilometre.

Further north, the habitat turns increasingly marginal, supporting as few as one moose over 10 sq. km.

More than 18,000 of the 118,000 estimated population are shot each year by licensed hunters and natives. Another 10,000 are likely killed by poachers.

Moose, like elk, prosper when foraging on the new growth of vegetation that follows forests fires. They grow rapidly when good browsing lands are available.

By quickly putting out forest fires, man has aggravated the long-term natural fluctuations in moose numbers. When the limit of the land is reached, moose can die in large numbers.

In the mid-1960s, biologists suspected a die-off disaster was looming in the lands north of Edmonton.

Ticked off
A weakened moose calf tries to rub off thousands of blood-sucking ticks on an outhouse wall during a dreadful infestation early in the 1980s. Many died. In trying to groom its coat and remove the ticks by rubbing against posts and trees, the animal often breaks off hairs of its coat, leaving bare patches. The outbreak has abated now. The last major infestation was during the late 1940s. PICTURE: Jim Cochrane

Moose populations in the region of Swan Hills and Grande Prairie had reached a peak after a decade of quick growth. Wolves had been dramatically reduced in an anti-rabies poisoning campaign, and forests were growing back after major fires.

But problems lay ahead. Forest fires had been kept in check, and the trees that had nourished the rising numbers of moose were maturing.

Aspen and balsam poplars had grown too tall for the moose to reach their succulent leaves and twigs.

The moose had to depend more heavily on willow, balsam, fir and dogwood. These bushes were severely overbrowsed and sometimes killed as the moose devoured two or even three years' growth and tore off twigs the diameter of a man's finger.

Large numbers of older animals dominated the herd, a condition government biologists say is not best for a healthy, viable population.

The average age of moose subjected to normal hunting pressure in Alberta is three to four years, but females averaged eight years in the Swan Hills, for example.

A healthy herd usually has up to 12 per cent calves. The Swan Hills moose averaged just over five per cent. It was an old herd producing few young.

"We all believed that this herd was in trouble," said Gerry Lynch, a Fish and Wildlife Division biologist responsible for moose.

"The yearlings and calves couldn't compete with the adults."

The response was to throw open the gates to moose hunters.

Limits were liberalized for Albertans. And non-Albertans — mostly American hunters — arrived in droves, up to 10,000 in 1967.

By 1972, a survey showed half the moose within three km of a road were killed during the hunting season. With an extensive network of roads through much of the area, it was clear that hunting was having an extensive impact.

But the intensive hunting did not result in more calf production.

In fact, Lynch said, the more liberalized hunting probably allowed too many moose to be shot.

"We were seeing many more young animals around; there was an imbalance."

So a more restricted hunting season was invoked, and the moose harvest was reduced. But many hard-to-reach areas of northern Alberta still have herds with many adults and few young.

Biologists worry most about the death of female animals in prime condition, and allow only a three-day female moose season in the popular northwestern zones.

Geist says the best way to protect moose from predators is to have a lot of older females.

While moose generally produce fewer calves later in life, Geist believes older females have the experience and size that translates into better protection for their calves from wolves and bears.

One way to encourage more older females has been to direct hunters to calves. Many European countries, and provinces such as Newfoundland and B.C., allow only hunting of six-month-old moose calves in many areas.

"I saw two orphans calves and one yearling moose when I was in the bush. Their mother had been shot, and they won't survive. Better to kill them and leave the mother to produce more calves next year," said Geist.

A hunter himself, Geist says too many are interested in shooting the largest animal they can.

Most wildlife biologists disdain trophy hunting.

Geist calls that breed of hunter "a Boone and Crocket fanatic," whose Bible is that record book.

"I don't have anything against listing the biggest animals taken, but do we have to list the 256th moose? Does anyone really care?"

Flawed strategy of mule deer breeds confused hybrid

By DAVE COOPER
Journal Staff Writer

Was that a mule deer, a white tail deer — or what?

In some parts of Alberta, the likely answer is a bit of both, offspring of a white tail buck and mule deer doe.

In areas with heavy hunting pressure, such as east of Calgary, hunters have killed so many mule deer bucks that white tails move in on the mule deer does at breeding time.

The result is a hybrid with a mixed-up sense of how to evade predators. The male hybrids are infertile, so there is no chance of a whole new sub-species developing.

Hybrids don't act like either of their parents, and biologists view them as undesirable — a sort of waste of effort since a good mule fawn could have been produced, instead, if a mule deer buck had been around.

The mule deer's failing is the way it evades man. Its defensive strategy is to bound across grasslands and open, rolling hillsides to escape predators, which heads for the bushes at the first sign of a predator or gun-toter.

The hybrids do a bit of each — usually unsuccessfully.

"They are not efficient at avoiding obstacles, or predators. They seem mixed up," says University of Calgary biologist Val Geist.

Research he supervised found that when faced with a maze, white tails ran through very quickly, very certain of their abilities.

Mule deer are great jumpers, and tend to clear obstacles rather than go through them.

"The first reaction of a hybrid, on reaching the obstacles, was to stop, then slowly pick its way through. In nature, that behavior translates into death.

"The hybrids are very pretty, and in captivity we find they are good mothers. But in nature, they and their offspring are coyote food," said Geist.

White tails are the oldest deer species in North America. Laboratory evidence shows Alberta's white tails are related to animals from the east. Mule deer likely came from white tails and black tails, a Pacific Coast sub- of these sub-species of deer produces animals that do not survive long in the wild.

Hybrids were first reported in the 1950s, says Bill Wishart, recently retired director of research for Alberta Fish and Wildlife.

"There are perhaps 35 good reports on file of hybrids. But there is also a lot of mis-identification. We get many reports from people who think they shot a hybrid," he said.

Mule deer are generally grey, trimmed with black. White tails are brownish, trimmed with white. But in a winter coat, they are grey with white trim.

With a wide variety in white tails and mule deer, the hybrids — looking a bit like each — are difficult to tell apart. But there is one foolproof way — the metatarsul gland on the outside of the back leg.

The lower part of the back leg — often mistaken for a shin bone but really it's the animals' extended bone from its heel to toe — contains the fur-covered scent gland. It's a sort of a silent communicator to deer, which leave a scent when they lie on the ground.

In the mule deer, the gland is about 12 cm long. On the white

PICTURE: Cam Hill

Young mule deer buck (left) and sterile hybrid buck meet in forest clearing.

situated almost midway between the knee and ankle.

Most of Alberta was mule deer country earlier this century, when the aspen parklands were largely open grasslands. White tails were uncommon in central areas, and the Edmonton area.

some grassy areas, going from 60,000 animals in the 1940s to about 118,000 today. They can thrive in agricultural areas, and enjoy eating farmers' forage crops in tough winters.

With a closing in of the landscape, the losers have been the mule deer. They numbered about

To protect more mule deer bucks, which improves their reproductive potential and lessens the hybrid problem, provincial game rules now allow hunters to shoot only mule deer bucks with at least three points on their antlers — animals at least two years old.

Mule deer can breed after 18 months of life, so they could have

Labour Strife

"It gave me a scare to see the undercarriage of a big truck but all I could do was grab onto the bumper – I was afraid it would tear my head off."

— Gainers striker Manfred Schmidt, Dec. 1, 1986

Miraculously, Schmidt walked away from the near-death experience on the picket line in front of the Gainers plant at Yellowhead Trail and 66th Street with only a few scrapes and bruises. A three-tonne truck carrying hogs into the plant had charged the line of strikers, and the 47-year-old Schmidt was grazed.

His story was among hundreds *The Journal* printed during one of the city's longest and most violent labour disputes.

Entrepreneur and Edmonton Oilers owner Peter Pocklington was at the top of his financial form when he bought the Gainers hog-packing plant in 1978, but by 1984 the market changed.

There was more competition and profits evaporated. Pocklington won a two-year wage freeze from members of the United Food and Commercial Workers Union.

But when the two years was up, Gainers sought a massive $4-$5 wage cut on maximum hourly rates of about $15.19 an hour. In contrast, the employees demanded a 52-cent-an-hour raise. On June 1, 1986, workers struck. The next day, Gainers shipped in busloads of $7-an-hour non-union replacements to keep the plant operating. Things got ugly.

"Rocks pelted plywood placed across bus windows as we inched towards the Gainers plant behind a police cruiser," wrote reporter Diana Coulter, who braved a bus ride with the replacement workers June 4.

That day, 115 strikers were arrested and *The Journal* ran graphic pictures of police dragging away defiant men and women from the site.

Pocklington threw gasoline on the fire on June 5 when he declared he was done with the union. He encouraged strikers to break ranks and sign on as non-union employees. "The jobs are going fast."

The Journal editorial that day pinned most of the blame for the violence on Alberta's labour law that allowed replacement workers. "There's no incentive to keep both parties there (at the bargaining table)."

Linda Goyette's debut political affairs column put a human face on the issue as it graphically described the dreary day of a worker on the killing floor at $12.47 an hour – "and what he refuses to do for less."

On Dec. 8, *The Journal* reported Premier Don Getty had asked both sides to take yet another stab at a settlement, and talks resumed Dec. 12 with a provincial mediator. Late in the day, an agreement was announced.

The membership approved the package by a slim 60.8 per cent Dec. 16. There was no wage rollback, but there was another two-year freeze.

But Pocklington, in financial trouble in 1989, lost the plant to the Alberta government. The government sold it to Burns Foods in 1993, which in turn sold it to Maple Leaf Foods in 1996.

The plant closed forever in 1997 during a strike for higher wages.

Press news picture of the year award for his shot of an Edmonton firefighter rescuing a four-year-old boy from his burning home. The shot also wins the National Newspaper Award spot news picture of the year prize in April.

***March 16, 1989*:**
Kurt Browning of Edmonton's Royal Glenora Club wins his first men's world figure skating title.

***April 9, 1989*:**
Pat Ryan's Edmonton rink of Randy Ferbey, Don Walchuk and Don McKenzie wins the Brier and the men's world curling titles.

***June 8, 1989*:**
The Supreme Court of Canada ruled unanimously that *Journal* reporter Marilyn Moysa cannot refuse to answer questions at a Labor Relations Board hearing. The case developed from a story Moysa wrote in 1985 about union organizing efforts at department stores in Edmonton and St. Albert.

***Aug. 31, 1989*:**
Grandin LRT station opens, extending the line from downtown to the legislature en route to the University of Alberta.

Oilers' new players
Sports H1

The Edmonton Journal

50 Cents (Metro Only) WEDNESDAY, AUGUST 10, 1988

Janet's expecting a baby
Sports H3

A city stumbles in shock
Sports H2

Oiler superstar now a King

Gretzky gone

By JIM MATHESON
Journal Staff Writer

Canada lost its Greatest One Tuesday.

After 10 dazzling years here, Wayne Gretzky was dealt to Los Angeles Kings in the most stunning hockey deal in history.

Gretzky flew here on a private jet in 1978 when former Indianapolis owner Nelson Skalbania sold him to Edmonton.

Tuesday he came to town in Kings' owner Bruce McNall's plane. But this time it was to say goodbye. It didn't look like he really wanted to.

Gretzky, who married actress Janet Jones last month and has been living in LA this summer, said he asked owner Peter Pocklington to trade him to the Kings.

Not wanting to be caught with an unhappy player — as with Paul Coffey last year — the Oilers regretfully accepted Gretzky's wishes in the early morning hours Tuesday and worked out a multi-player deal: Gretzky, defenceman Marty McSorley and centre Mike Krushelnyski for Kings' centre Jim Carson, disgruntled LA defenceman Craig Redmond, who quit the club last season, their No. 1 draft this June, Martin Gelinas, first-round picks in 1989, 1991 and 1993 and a bundle of cool money.

Reportedly it's between $10 million and $20 million; Oiler owner Peter Pocklington refused to say how much. "It should be enough to buy a couple of companies," said Pocklington.

"I appreciate Mr. Pocklington giving me the possibility to play for another club after 10 years in Edmonton. At this point in time I'm still young enough (27) and still capable enough to help a new franchise win the Stanley Cup," said a teary-eyed Gretzky, who broke down several times at a press conference at Molson House.

"I realize everyone likes to be somewhere where it's rosy and nice. The Oilers are the best team in the NHL. But my contract only lasted four more years. I'll be 31 then. That might be too old to test the free-agent market. If I was ever going to make a move, it had to be now if I want another shot at winning a Stanley Cup."

Gretzky said he talked to McNall, who's made his fortune in racehorses, movie companies and rare coins, and liked what he heard. "After spending some time with him I decided that for the benefit of myself, my new wife and our expected child in the New Year (apparently the first week in January), it would be beneficial for everyone involved to let me play for the Los Angeles Kings. I'm disappointed leaving Edmonton. I really admire all the fans and respect everyone over the years, but . . ." Then Gretzky broke down and couldn't continue with the formal part of the press gathering.

Gretzky, the second-leading point-producer in history behind his idol Gordie Howe, wouldn't say how long he'd been thinking of moving.

Pocklington said he didn't agree to the trade for the instant money fix, although he had been shopping him around. He'd talked to the Kings before and also Vancouver Canucks.

"Our owner (Frank Griffiths) was prepared to pay significant dollars for Gretzky but from a hockey standpoint I was hesitant to pay the type of price in draft choices," said Canucks' GM Pat Quinn. Still, it was the Oilers who balked. "I understand it (talks) broke down at their end."

Pocklington originally scoffed at the Kings' request for Gretzky. "I don't mind telling you that when Bruce McNall approached me and asked what it would take to get Wayne to Los Angeles I asked for the entire Kings' franchise and an option on Jerry Buss's (NBA) Lakers," said Pocklington.

"If people are upset about the trade, I understand. But I ask that you view it the same way Wayne asked me to view his request to be traded."

McNall was obviously ecstatic about his acquisition, although it cost him four first-round draft choices. "I want to see hockey become a major-league sport in California," said McNall.

Gretzky, who came here as an 18-year-old in November, 1978 and won eight straight Hart trophies until Mario Lemieux broke his stranglehold last season, was an institution here. But, nothing is forever.

"The future has to arrive some day. It arrived today in Los Angeles," said Calgary GM Cliff Fletcher.

PICTURE: Rob Galbraith

Fighting back the tears, Oilers' superstar Wayne Gretzky tells Tuesday's press conference he's going to play for the Kings

. . . 'I decided that for the benefit of myself, my new wife and our expected child . . . it would be beneficial to let me play for the Los Angeles Kings'

Wayne loses in trade

By CAM COLE
Journal Staff Writer

It is a good trade for the Los Angeles Kings, right now. It will be a good trade for the Edmonton Oilers, in three years.

It is a good trade for hockey in the United States, a good trade for parity in the National Hockey League, and for Jimmy Carson's profile and Martin Gelinas's development, a good trade for Peter Pocklington's cash-flow situation and a great trade for Janet Jones-Gretzky and her film career and the baby to be named later.

But where's the silver lining for Wayne Gretzky? Who is looking after what's best for him?

Cole column H1

That is the great mystery — and, potentially, the great tragedy — of Tuesday's hockey trade heard 'round the world.

The Great One picks up his skates, packs the best years of his life — and ours — into a trunk, and heads for Los Angeles, away from the people who live and breathe his existence . . . to what?

To millions of Angelenos who don't give a damn. To a town that doesn't love hockey or even hate it, but just doesn't pay any attention.

In Edmonton, before the deal was even announced Tuesday, outraged fans jammed all 21 incoming phone lines to the Oilers' offices, and when they couldn't get through to the hockey club to vent their spleen, they turned to the newspapers and the radio and TV stations, and even to city hall.

In Los Angeles, in that same period of time, the Kings' office received 12 calls from fans. Twelve. That is where Wayne Gretzky is going to play hockey. It will make you cry if you think about it.

It ought to make Wayne Gretzky cry. Maybe it already has.

Those didn't look much like tears of joy Gretzky was shedding Tuesday. They were miserable tears, the tears of a man who had given everything he had to a hockey team and a city — only to find that he was just, in the prophetic words of Alan Eagleson, "a depreciating asset."

At 27, he can bring Pocklington more money than he could at 28, or 29. That, and nothing else, is the reason the deal was consummated.

The rest — the stuff about wanting to be with his new family in L.A., wanting to carry hockey's message to the U.S. — it may have played a part. A small part, after the fact. But I'd prefer to believe Gretzky has a mind of his own, and the sense to want to play hockey where he can be successful.

And yet, Kings' owner Bruce McNall would not have paid the price he did, and Gretzky would not have approved the trade, in the end, had not both of them felt it was possible that No. 99 could bust through the L.A. apathy.

Do they have a chance?

Not much of one.

When all the hype has faded, the Kings must win to attract fans. And last year, they finished a distant fourth in the Smythe Division — with Carson and Luc Robitaille doing most of the scoring. Now, one of them is in Edmonton, and the team is expected to improve while operating without its first-round draft choices (Gelinas was this year's) in what amounts to four out of six years. It rarely works that way.

The Oilers, meanwhile, through the Gretzky and Paul Coffey trades, have already netted four players — Craig Simpson, Chris Joseph, Jimmy Carson and Martin Gelinas — who were in the top seven of their respective draft years.

And with three more No. 1 picks to come, plus their own five first-round selections through 1993, there is every reason to believe the Oilers have built a foundation that will keep them near the top for nearly a decade to come.

Gretzky knows exactly what he is leaving.

It's why he cried Tuesday.

Gretzky traded like a piece of meat, Coffey charges

By RAY TURCHANSKY
Journal Staff Writer

Paul Coffey says his best friend Wayne Gretzky was "just a piece of meat" traded for hard cash by Edmonton Oiler management.

Coffey spent seven record-laden seasons with the Oilers before his desire to renegotiate his contract resulted in a 20-game holdout at the beginning of the last National Hockey League season and his ultimate trade.

"I talked to Wayne three weeks ago," said Coffey, of first hearing about the trade. "But I am surprised at all the crap that's coming out."

Coffey insisted the trade was not Gretzky's idea.

"I think hockey was No. 1 to Wayne. There's no bloody way he wanted to go there. I don't think the people in Edmonton who know Wayne should believe that. He's a small-town guy, I don't care if he married the Queen of England.

"I kind of wished he hadn't broken up (at the media conference), and maybe he would have told us what really happened. But he doesn't do anything to rock the boat."

One source close to the Oilers said that Pocklington started testing the market to trade Gretzky during the summer. Gretzky found out and forced the issue so he could determine his own future, the source said.

Coffey, who openly feuded with general manager Glen Sather during his tenure here, said he'd talked to Gretzky at length at the time of the latter's wedding and that Gretzky was upset, saying "he (Pocklington) is going to trade me."

"So I called him a week ago just to say 'Gretz, relax.' But he said 'He's going to do this, I'll be traded in two weeks.'

"Outside of the fans, I don't think he was appreciated by management. The fans were good, they gave him his privacy. He would have played just about for nothing in Edmonton. But they (management) got afraid of his wanting to test the free-agency waters (in 1992). All you are is a piece of meat to them."

Regardless, the deed is done, and Coffey looked into the future.

"He'll play unbelievable. He's so competitive."

And the Oilers?

"I was just looking at our team picture at our first Stanley Cup. It's amazing, only Andy (Glenn Anderson), (Charlie) Huddy, Fuhrsie (Grant Fuhr), (Jari) Kurri and Mess (Mark Messier) are still there. And I think that's the greatest hockey team ever.

"Now it makes my situation look better. I'm glad I got out when I did."

Weather

Cloudy this afternoon, high 21, low 11. Thursday: mostly cloudy with scattered showers. High 21. Details F6

Published daily by the proprietor Southam Inc at The Journal Building Edmonton Alta. T5J 2S6 Second class mail registration number 0566

City
An escaped convict wanted for questioning in last week's brutal LRT slaying is captured in Vancouver. B1

Canada
Defence Minister Perrin Beatty says up to 500 Canadian soldiers may eventually join the UN force monitoring the Iran-Iraq ceasefire. A2

World
The Canada-U.S. free trade deal breezes through the House of Representatives in Washington. A3

Food
The taste of summer? A ripe, red tomato with a light sprinkling of salt and pepper. C1

Alberta	B2
Al Turner	B1
Ann Landers	C7
Bingos	B8
Births	F3
Bridge	F7
Business	E1
Cam Cole	H1
Canada	A2
Careers	E2
City	B1
Comics	G8
Crossword	G2
Deaths	F2
Don Smith	C7
Doonesbury	A4
Dr. Donohue	C7
Entertainment	B6
Feedback	C4
Food	C1
Horoscope	F5
Lifestyle	C7
Our Opinion	A6
Patterns	F5
People	A8
Sports	H1
Stocks	E4
Television	B6
Viewpoint	A7
Weather	F6
Wine	C5
World	A3
CLASSIFIED ADS	
Index	F3
Order form	F8
Auctions	G8
Employment	F3-8
Legals	G8,F2
Mini Market	F8
Real Estate	G1-5
Tenders	G8,F2
Vehicles	G5
The Journal	
Information	F2
Phone numbers	F2

HERMAN
BUS STOP
8/10

"I lost 10 pounds once. To be honest, I didn't notice any difference."

The Trade

"Our greatest champion is gone. The emptiness and anger consuming the city are not unlike the grief of a family that loses a loved one…."
— Editor Linda Hughes, Aug. 13, 1988

At first, the stories seemed impossible. Wild speculation at best. Who, in their right mind, would trade Wayne Gretzky, the greatest hockey player of all time leading the greatest hockey team of all time?

For a week in early August 1988, veteran *Journal* sports reporter Jim Matheson was on the trail of the hard-to-believe rumour that Gretzky was on the block.

Three weeks before, on July 16, The Great One had married Hollywood actress Janet Jones in a fairytale wedding at St. Joseph's Basilica.

"The Great One looked a little nervous. His beautiful bride clutched his hand and smiled at him reassuringly," said the story.

But what was going on in the brain behind the smile?

Jones, in Oilers fans' minds, became one of the key suspects in the drama that unfolded three weeks later.

"Is the Great One taking his act to Hollywood?" asked Matheson on Aug. 4. "Well, as far-fetched as it sounds, the hottest story is a Gretzky trade."

With a stop-the-press story on Aug. 9, Matheson had filled in a lot of blanks. "The hardest story line today has the Edmonton Oilers centre going to Los Angeles with one or two others (maybe Mike Krushelnyski) for either $10 million or $20 million…."

In that story Pocklington said the rumour was "pure speculation," however, a hastily called press conference later that day proved Matheson's "pure speculation" was pure chapter-and-verse.

"Gretzky gone" read the main headline.

It sent Edmontonians into shock as they tried to cope with the fact that The Kid who had made them so proud was gone.

Gretzky insisted the decision was his own, but many didn't buy it. Readers wrote in blaming his wife for applying pressure. She denied it, instead pointing the finger at Pocklington who had been deflecting growing criticism of himself by pointing fingers at Gretzky, saying he "stage managed" the tears he shed at his farewell press conference.

Journal sports writer Cam Cole addressed a column directly to Pocklington on Aug. 11.

"Maybe we're not any closer to knowing whether Gretzky wanted out or whether you wanted to sell him while his market value was high; whether the Temptress Janet lured him away to Hollywood or you merely used her as a convenient fall-girl. But at least we have seen again how easy it is to strip away that store-bought class and get down to the real Peter Puck."

Editor Linda Hughes put the turbulent week into perspective in a column Aug. 13. "This isn't a mortal blow for the city. We will always be Gretzky's adopted city and we'll remain a 'City of Champions.' "

***Sept. 11, 1989*:**
***The Journal* undergoes a major design change, including a new nameplate, coloured blue instead of yellow, and a new typeface.**

***Oct. 16, 1989*:**
Jan Reimer is elected Edmonton's first female mayor.

***Dec. 12, 1989*:**
Don Babick is appointed *Journal* publisher, replacing William Newbigging.

***Dec. 21, 1989*:**
The Supreme Court of Canada upholds *The Journal*'s constitutional challenge of a 1935 provincial press-gag law that restricted the right to publish information on divorce, separation and property-division cases before they go to trial.

Oilers board to meet about Sather-Ranger talks / *Sports D1*

Ultra-chic grocery debuts in Crestwood / ***Business H1***

EDMONTON JOURNAL

www.edmontonjournal.com | EDMONTON'S NEWSPAPER SINCE 1903 | THURSDAY, MAY 18, 2000

INSIDE TODAY

Edmonton weather

Mainly sunny. High 18. Low 6. Details / D8.

China moves to crush unrest

Chinese riot police, armed with automatic weapons and electric shock batons, have attacked up to 5,000 striking industrial workers in a northern city in an escalation of labour unrest. The demonstrators blocked streets in a demand for unpaid wages. They chanted: "It is not a crime to ask for our salaries." **Top Copy / A3**

Canadian makes it to Everest's summit

After a gruelling climb, a Canadian and a Pakistani climber stood for a few minutes at the top of Mount Everest on Wednesday before returning to camp for some rest. **World / A4**

Mulroney urged out of retirement

Tory Leader Joe Clark, who regularly seeks advice from Brian Mulroney, says he welcomes an upcoming Mulroney foray into the public arena. He's encouraging the former prime minister to play a role in the battle against the Canadian Alliance. **Canada / A5**

What has the gov't got on you?

Alberta's privacy commissioner says people upset about the federal government's knowledge of their lives should demand to see their files. "I think all Canadians … should be asking themselves: What information is being collected about me?" **Alberta / A6**

Catholics ponder who will be next

Pope John Paul II turns 80 today, and the question of his successor weighs on the minds of Church leaders. **Insight / A17**

Brewery workers locked out for good

The head of the beer distribution workers union says their fight with Brewers Distributor Ltd. is over. BDL is permanently closing its 50th Street warehouse. **City / B1**

Borrowing costs up, more hikes coming

Borrowing costs rose Wednesday in Canada as the central bank matched a U.S. increase, and analysts warned more rate hikes are on the way. **Business / H1**

INDEX

A/News, Opinion		Crossword	E8
B/City		Dr. Donohue	F4
C/Entertainment		Horoscope	E8
D/Sports		Lotteries	A2
E/Golf, Classified		Obituaries	B6
F/Living		Opinion	A18
G/Shopping.com		Puzzles	E8
H/Business		Television	C2
		Wonderword	E8
Ann Landers	F4		
Births	B6	THE JOURNAL	
Bridge	E8	Telephones	A2
Classified	F4	www.canada.com	
Comics	C7		

0 55829 00050 2

U of A team beats diabetes

Barking up the right tree

ED KAISER, THE JOURNAL

Some trees, like this one at Government House Park, just beg to be climbed. Taking the challenge Wednesday are (clockwise from left) Keyano Whiskeyjack, 8, Peter Thirwell, 6, at the top of the tree, and Lucy Thirwell, 8, on the ground. Hiding in the tree is six-year-old Serina Whiskeyjack.

Eight diabetics have not needed insulin shots since islet cell transplant

ANDY OGLE
Journal Staff Writer
EDMONTON

A University of Alberta research team has produced a diabetes breakthrough that has already freed eight people from their daily insulin injections for an average of 11 months.

The team, led by Dr. Ray Rajotte and including transplant surgeon James Shapiro, Dr. Jonathan Lakey and Dr. Greg Korbutt, injected insulin-producing cells from donor pancreases into the eight patients, aged 29 to 53.

Such a procedure has been tried before by doctors in other countries but this marks the first time patients have been completely freed from insulin injections.

Shapiro told a meeting of the American Society of Transplant Surgeons and the American Transplantation Society in Chicago this week that the patients have all done well since their islet-cell transplants. They continue to show no signs of damage from high blood sugar.

All the patients have had diabetes since childhood and were selected for the procedure because they had difficulty controlling their blood sugar with insulin injections. The needed up to 15 injections a day and lived under the constant threat of blackouts.

Shapiro said a new immune-suppression drug called Rapamune, which became available in the United States last year, was crucial to the new treatment.

It can be given in low doses and does not appear to have some of the side effects of most immune suppressants.

Joanne Langner of the Alberta Foundation for Diabetes Research, which has provided $1.8 million for the islet-cell transplant trial, said the results are amazing.

"This is extremely exciting for diabetics everywhere," Langner said. "There's a definite improvement in the quality of life for these individuals."

Langner said she's met most of the patients and all have told her the best thing is being able to live normal lives.

"Even being able to sleep in late is a novel experience for them," she said.

Neither Shapiro, who is still out of the country, nor his colleagues in Edmonton were available on Wednesday.

They have a paper ready to be published in the prestigious *New England Journal of Medicine*, which traditionally imposes a strict news blackout on anything it publishes until the day of publication.

But word of the talk in Chicago by Shapiro, who is originally from England, leaked out in the British press Wednesday.

See DIABETES / back of section

Federal surplus $11B higher than projected

ERIC BEAUCHESNE
Southam Newspapers
OTTAWA

The provisional federal surplus last year was $14.9 billion, $11 billion more than forecast in the February budget, thanks to a greater-than-projected tax grab from individuals and businesses.

It will allow the federal government to take a much bigger big whack off the $577-billion debt than it planned, a Finance Department official confirmed — possibly up to $10 billion more.

And it suggests that this year, the government will have more money for health care and even more debt reduction, Finance Minister Paul Martin said Wednesday after the department released preliminary figures for the fiscal year ended March 31.

The surplus is $5.4 billion more than last year's total. Revenues were up $8.5 billion or 5.5 per cent and program spending $3.3 billion or 3.1 per cent, while public debt charges were down $90 million, or 0.2 per cent.

Federal debt payments amounted to $41 billion last year, the largest single expenditure.

Of the $14.9 billion, $2.5 billion has already been spent on a one-time increase in transfers to the provinces for health care, education and social programs.

See SURPLUS / back of section

More money for health / A7

Day to woo Quebecers in a language they understand

No smear tactics in his drive to lead Canadian Alliance

NORM OVENDEN
Journal Ottawa Bureau
OTTAWA

Stockwell Day will repudiate Reform's anti-Quebec election ads in a major address designed to show he's the only Canadian Alliance leadership candidate capable of getting votes and winning seats in Quebec.

In distancing himself from the controversial attack ads in the 1997 campaign, Day makes a sharp distinction between his tolerant approach to national unity and the positions and strategies approved by former Reform leader Preston Manning, one of his main challengers for the Alliance top job.

CHRIS SCHWARZ, THE JOURNAL

Stockwell Day promises to be an effective fighter for Quebec.

The contrast is made in a comprehensive unity speech entitled "Canada's Renaissance Must Include Quebec," to be delivered tonight in Quebec City.

"During the next election campaign, be assured that if I lead the Canadian Alliance, our ads won't say that we need a prime minister from somewhere other than Quebec or focus on the speech difficulties of my adversaries," Day writes in a copy of the text obtained by *The Journal*.

The only Alliance leadership candidate who can get by in French, Day was also referring to a Conservative attack ad in the 1993 election which mocked the congenital speech defect of then Liberal leader Jean Chretien. The Tories quickly yanked those television commercials and admitted they had made a blunder.

But Manning has never apologized.

See DAY / back of section

Won't talk about abortion / B3

From fuel to firewater, the prices are rising

Journal Staff
EDMONTON

Edmonton motorists filled up with frustration Wednesday as the price of regular, self-serve gas went to 64.9 cents a litre from 61.9 cents earlier in the day.

But that's not all. On a day when Canadians found out interest rates were rising, Albertans were told it will get costlier to drown our sorrows about rising prices.

On June 30, the price of a bottle of liquor or wine jumps six cents. By then we might be accustomed to paying higher mortgage and loan rates, which were pushed up Wednesday when the Bank of Canada raised its trend-setting rate to six per cent from 5.5 per cent.

Experts say the increase was necessary to slow the economy, avoid inflation and protect the loonie, which dropped to 66.78 cents U.S. heading into the Victoria Day long weekend.

It was the long weekend that was on the minds of many motorists Wednesday.

"Consumers know they're getting the shaft but there's nothing they can do about it," said Calvin Brown, gassing up at the Esso on Whyte Avenue and 109th Street. "It'll be like this probably for most of the summer."

As for booze prices, they're going up because the Alberta government is dropping its recycling subsidy, Gaming Minister Murray Smith said Wednesday.

"The policy change is consistent with other beverage recycling practices," Smith said. "Recycling costs for liquor containers should not be subsidized with public funds."

The Alberta Gaming and Liquor Commission spends about $3.3 million a year to subsidize the cost of recycling liquor, wine, cider and wine cooler containers.

Under the change, the price of a 750-ml glass bottle will increase by six cents.

Beer prices will not be affected because there's no subsidy for the recycling.

TEN

Chris Schwarz photo

Gloom & Boom

1990 to 1999

"I'm the mayor of the capital of the greatest province of the best country in the world."
— Mayor Bill Smith to a group of Japanese business elite at a luncheon in Tokyo on Oct. 30, 1997

Mulroney's Mistake / 381
The People Speak / 383
VLT Menace / 385
Puck's Farewell / 387
Wiebo Ludwig / 389
Changing the Guard / 393

It was shortly before 1 a.m. on the morning of Oct. 17, 1995, that Bill Smith, the city's 59-year-old, newly elected mayor and former Edmonton Eskimos all-star defensive halfback, was hoisted on the shoulders of two burly campaign workers and carried to the podium in his election headquarters.

Jan Reimer, the city's two-term mayor, had just conceded victory to Smith after falling behind by 1,000 votes. It had been a nail-biter of a night as the lead in the mayoral election changed a dozen times in the four hours after the polls closed.

By midnight, however, the left-leaning Reimer found herself replaced by the right-leaning Smith, a retired tire store owner who was convinced he could sell Edmonton to the world.

Five of the 12 councillors on the fractious council over which Reimer had presided had also been voted out of office.

Civic affairs reporter Marta Gold called the election "an historic vote for change." Smith's victory, she said, was a stunning upset, and went against the predictions of even last-minute opinion polls.

Sunday *Images*

PHOTOGRAPHY EDITOR: Steve Makris, 429-5390

Vancouver Sun photographer Nick Didlick received permission to record a day in the life of Sue Rodriguez who is asking the courts to permit a physician-assisted suicide. The pictures were purposely shot in black and white.

John Hofsess of the Right to Die Society takes Rodriguez for a breath of fresh air. It was Hofsess who helped arrange the photographer's day with Rodriguez

Bear to **live** Dare to **die**

Sue Rodriguez spends most of the day in bed, but her life is anything but a holiday. Rodriguez has been given between three and 15 months to live. The Victoria woman suffers from terminal amyotrophic lateral sclerosis, commonly called Lou Gehrig's Disease. She is appealing to the courts to permit her to end her life with the help of a physician.

She's not ready to die yet, however. "As long as I experience joy and feel the love and support that I've been receiving, I am content with my life," she told the Vancouver Sun. Rodriguez needs assistance to complete the most common tasks: washing her face, getting a juice or eating an apple, answering the phone. She and her son share time after his school hours, watching TV or reading with him. "I've made the transition of accepting my body the way it is right now," she wrote recently. "That is not to say that all is well or that life is normal." She feels "grief and pain" for friends and relatives who watch her health ebb.

"These individuals have helped me to live a joyful life, have eased me through the painful transitions."

Simple tasks like eating require help

To sign a cheque, Rodriguez is aided by a writing device strapped to her hand

Washing and other essential needs are administered by home-maker Nadine Porter

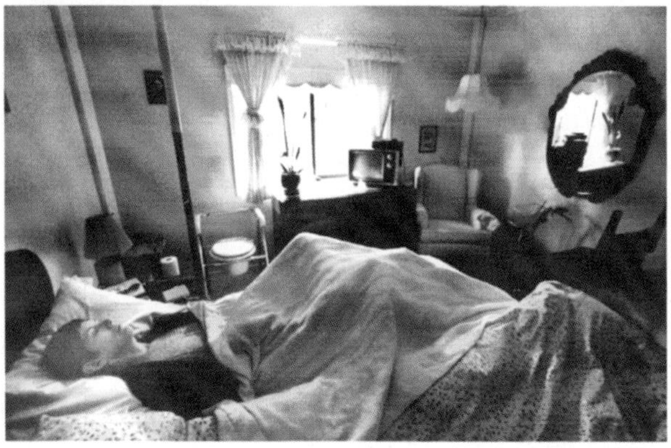

A nap from 12:30 to 3 p.m. every afternoon helps Rodriguez gather energy to spend some time with her son when he returns from school

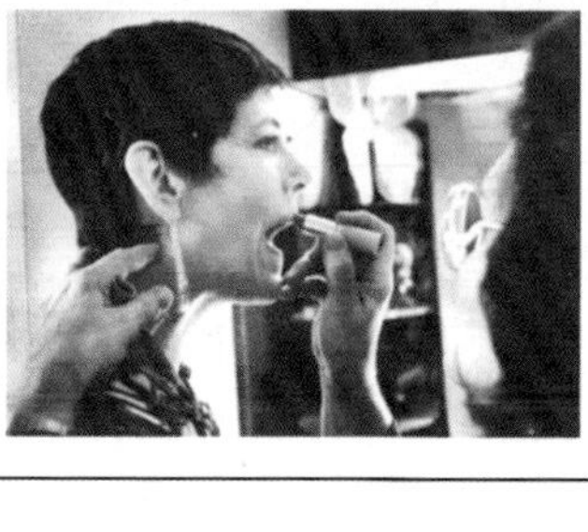

For his part, Smith vowed at his victory celebration that he would set the city on a new course.

While offering congratulations to Reimer for serving the city well for more than 15 years as both mayor and councillor, Smith also announced that starting immediately things would be different.

"Starting tomorrow morning," he told supporters, "this city is going to be open for business again.

"But I also want to pass on to Al Duerr (Calgary's mayor) to keep his head up because Edmonton is going to be the number one city in this province."

While the paper's editorial board supported Reimer, with the proviso that third-place finisher John Ramsay was also worth serious consideration from voters, its next-day editorial focused on the problems that confronted the new mayor. "Smith billed himself as the candidate who would sell Edmonton, the one who would be best able to return confidence and optimism to the city. With Smith, the city has turned over a new leaf.

"The next three years will be a make-or-break time for Edmonton: the era in which the city attempts a profound change from a government centre to a city of knowledge-based technology; a city that seeks new markets and opportunities in the global economy."

Smith, the paper said, brought "more confidence and dazzle to the job than the city has seen in many years."

To its new mayor, Edmonton was the "greatest city in the greatest province in the greatest country in the world," a mantra he would repeat countless times over the coming years.

In the mid-'90s, however, Edmonton was also a city that was in a funk. While there was activity in the suburbs as big-box stores crowded the new power centres on the city's perimeter, the downtown remained stagnant and for-lease signs were all too common on Jasper Avenue.

Head offices also continued their exodus from the city, and would do so for the rest of the decade. Major department stores such as Eaton's and Woodward's closed, and The Bay's block-long Jasper Avenue location remained virtually shuttered for most of the '90s.

The once-proud Edmonton Oilers of the National Hockey League, their glory days behind them, often played to fewer than 10,000 spectators in Northlands Coliseum. Owner Peter Pocklington, facing economic troubles of his own after more than 15 years of success, was threatening to sell the team.

Through a series of spending cuts in health, education and welfare, the government of Premier Ralph Klein had vowed to rid the province of its $30-billion debt. The cuts had cost many Edmontonians their jobs.

And the problem of having two airports, the Municipal and the International, remained unsolved. In a plebiscite held at the same time as Smith's election victory, voters by a majority of three-to-one had approved consolidating scheduled flights at the International.

But much work still needed to be done if new air links between Edmonton and the outside world were going to be forged. The issue of the two airports was far from over.

It had been a long-running debate throughout the city's recent political

***Jan. 1, 1990*:**
Don Babick officially succeeds William Newbigging as *Journal* publisher.

***Feb. 9, 1990*:**
Edmonton's Lisa Sargeant wins the Canadian women's figure skating championship.

***Feb. 11, 1990*:**
***The Journal* moves into the first half of its new building next door to its old site.**

***Feb. 19, 1990*:**
Alberta's provincial Family Day holiday is observed for the first time.

***April 11, 1990*:**
Alberta MPs David Kilgour and Alex Kindy are expelled from the Conservative caucus for voting against the government's GST bill.

***May 24, 1990*:**
The Edmonton Oilers win their fifth Stanley Cup in seven seasons, beating Boston in five games.

***June 25, 1990*:**
Veteran Edmonton police constable Ezio Faraone is shot and killed by a gunman hiding in the back seat of a car.

***July 15, 1990*:**
***The Journal*'s home-delivery rate rises to $2.25 a week from $2.**

EMBRACING THE EXECUTIONER

THE KITTYE & DEAN STORY

Sunday Insight

E1 December 13, 1992

An Edmonton Journal Special Report

How one man's obsession and one woman's fatal attraction turns to tragedy

DEAN CYR

January 14, 1965
—
November 3, 1992

SUICIDE

"I want to give my son everything I didn't get from my father."

KITTYE LOU SCHMIDT

October 6, 1965
—
November 3, 1992

MURDERED

"I hope my old heart can handle loving you forever."

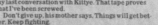

November 2, 1992, Monday

Dean Cyr is discussing his death.

Sitting at his mother's kitchen table, he drags deeply on a roll-your-own cigarette and names the songs he wants for his funeral service: Elvis' version of *(I did it) My Way* and, his favorite song, *Lonely Boy*.

Watching him, Dean's mother, Valerie, and sister, Gina, are thinking the same thing: *Here he goes again. Dean is always talking suicide.* Nothing new: he's been talking about killing himself for the last 15 years.

But Dean is being more specific tonight.

I want to be cremated, he says. Bury me with pictures of Tait — the two-year-old son he has never met.

Kittye's never going to let me see our boy, Dean says. The judge ruled against me. And that damn parole officer wouldn't listen, wouldn't even play that tape of my last conversation with Kittye. That tape proves that I've been screwed.

Don't give up, his mother says. Things will get better. Keep fighting.

No reason to live, he replies softly, twirling a beer bottle in his hands: "It's over. I'm tired."

Dean's black T-shirt sums up his attitude. It says FTW: "F—The World." A tattoo on one arm carries the same message.

It's 2 a.m. when he hugs his mother tightly, kisses her cheek and smiles.

"Mom, never cry for me."

A few hours later, he drives through the darkness, down the highway toward Fort Saskatchewan — the community where his ex-wife, Kittye, lives with her husband and two children.

A loaded sawed-off shotgun is at his side.

They meet: across a crowded room

November 10, 1989, Saturday

The place is packed. Kittye-Lou Schmidt and her friend Adrienne Fields can't find a place to sit, so they move through the crowd to a spot against the wall.

"I don't know about this," Adrienne says, talking over the '50s music blaring from the loudspeakers. "I'm not comfortable here."

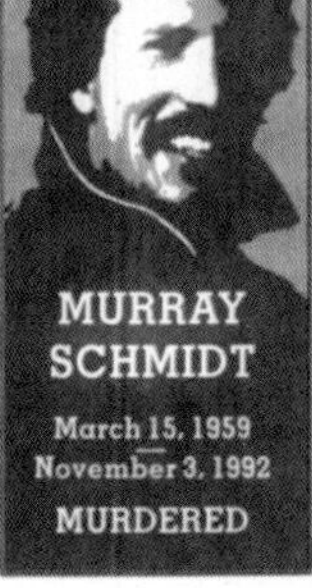

MURRAY SCHMIDT

March 15, 1959
—
November 3, 1992

MURDERED

This is the kind of place they've been cautioned about by Jehovah's Witness elders. They came for a bite to eat. But Sha-Na-Na and Platters Lounge is a night club. Loud, smoky, and dim except for the colored lights illuminating the bodies on the dance floor.

Within minutes a waitress arrives with two Paralyzers — a mix of vodka and Kahlua liqueur. Compliments of a secret admirer.

Kittye looks around the place. "Do you see that guy over there?" she asks Adrienne.

"You mean the one who's been eyeing you ever since we walked in?"

Guys are always looking at Kittye. She's slim, blonde, and dressed in the impeccable clothes she loves to tailor for herself.

This man seems alluring, with a chic black suit and hair slicked back. Elvis style. He's still looking at them when a flower salesman hands Kittye a single rose: "It's been paid for," the salesman says.

Sha-Na-Na
The Platters Lounge

Kittye is flattered when the handsome stranger walks up and asks for a dance. The attention feels good. And Kittye has been feeling down for more than a month, ever since she moved out on Murray, her husband of seven years.

She turns to Adrienne: "I'll just dance this one and then we'll leave."

Adrienne is worried. *What is Kittye doing? I want to get out of here*, she thinks. She marches out to the dance floor — fuming mad. She wants to leave. Right now.

"OK, Adrienne," says a surprised Kittye.

When Adrienne walks to the entrance to collect her coat, the bouncer stops her and issues a warning about the man Kittye was dancing with: "Your friend doesn't know who she's messing with. You should get her out of here.

"And, by the way, I sent you the drinks. I sent the rose."

Kittye leaves with Adrienne, walking into the chill November night without any idea that the chance meeting with a handsome stranger would change her life forever.

The man she met is Dean Rodney Cyr.

Continued on/E2

history, going back to the beginnings of the International airport itself in the early '60s. Even then, proponents of the one-airport system realized that Edmonton was too small to support two airports.

On the other hand, those who liked scheduled flights at the municipal airport – affectionately called the Muni by Edmontonians – pointed out that the downtown airport offered unbeatable convenience for travellers coming from the North to do business in the city.

Neither was the 1995 vote the first-ever on airport consolidation. Voters had rejected the idea in 1992, when 108,000 electors chose to keep the Muni open for another five years, compared with 84,000 who preferred consolidation. Three years later, 165,000 voters approved of consolidating flights at the International, compared with 50,000 who wanted the downtown airport to remain open to scheduled flights.

Debate had been furious leading up to the 1995 vote. On the "Yes" side stood the Edmonton Regional Airports Authority that had been formed in 1992 to take control of the International airport from Ottawa. The authority enjoyed the support of such business groups as the Edmonton Chamber of Commerce, Economic Development Edmonton (EDE), the Edmonton Visitor and Convention Association, Northlands, MacLab Enterprises and AMJ Campbell Van Lines.

The "Yes" side argued that splitting scheduled flights between the two airports meant poorer service overall for the city.

Having to make connections in Calgary for flights to other Canadian cities as well as many international destinations rankled Edmonton travellers. First, it was time-consuming and, one said, comparable to having to drive through Sherwood Park to get to St. Albert.

"We lose two flights a week to London and Calgary gains two," Rick LeLacheur, head of the EDE, said before the election.

"Who are they carrying from Calgary? Us!"

On the "No" side of the airport question were the Kingsway Business Association (KBA) and Air Services for Tomorrow, a 235-member group that had spearheaded the 1992 victory to keep the Muni open.

Proponents of the Muni, however, would not issue a list of public supporters. "Our support is fairly silent because they feel that they have nothing to gain by expressing their support," said Don Grimble of the KBA.

"A lot of them don't want to go public and be accused of being pro Calgary."

And if the Muni closed, Grimble warned that 900 people who worked there would lose their jobs.

Editorially, *The Journal* urged that consolidation take place. Two airports divided the market, the paper said, and benefited no one.

It also offered a solution to what it called "the much-exaggerated 'inconvenience'" of the International airport's location. A city centre check-in would help, and a ride-share service – three people sharing the same taxi – would make the cost of ground transportation irrelevant, the paper said.

"A Yes vote to consolidate traffic at the International is a vote of confidence in Edmonton."

In fact, Jim Shaw, founder of Shaw Communications in the early '70s

***Aug. 9, 1990*:**
Edmonton's population is 605,538, topping 600,000 for the first time.

***Aug. 31, 1990*:**
"Edmonton Oilers goalie Grant Fuhr has led the double life of a hockey star and cocaine user for about seven years...Fuhr said Thursday that he failed a private drug test and spent two weeks in a Florida drug treatment centre last August. He says he has not used an illegal substance since then." - Story by David Staples and Tom Barrett. Following a hearing by NHL officials, Fuhr was suspended for a year.

***Sept. 10, 1990*:**
Edmonton publisher Mel Hurtig launches the *Junior Encyclopedia of Canada*.

***Nov. 24, 1990*:**
The Winnipeg Blue Bombers beat the Edmonton Eskimos 50-11 to win the Grey Cup.

***Dec. 17, 1990*:**
Kurt Browning becomes the first figure skater ever to be named male athlete of the year by The Canadian Press and winner of the Lionel Conacher Award.

***Jan. 14, 1991*:**
The University of Alberta says it will withdraw financial support for the

Life

EDITOR : Barb Wilkinson, 429-5290

The Edmonton **Journal** Saturday, June 26, 1993

The last thing you'll notice about Jeff

DAVID STAPLES
Journal Staff Writer

Edmonton

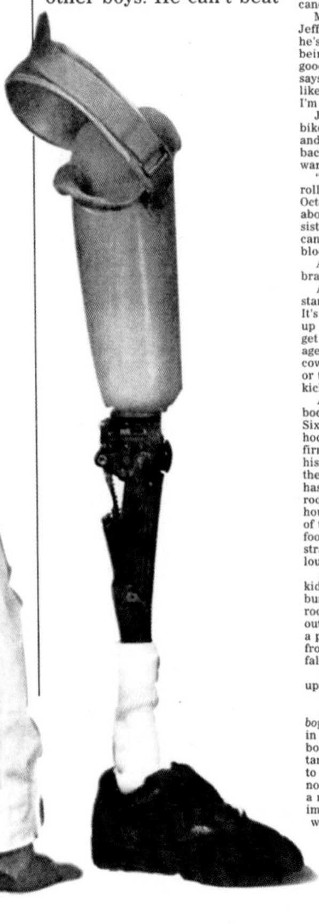

Larry Wong, *The* **Journal**

"One Leg!"

The school boys howl at recess. "Don't pass it to One Leg!"

The rhythm of Jeff Foss's gait is as mechanical as the heavy artificial leg wedged and strapped to his six-inch stump.

Step-hop-hop.

Jeff can't run, but he skips forward madly, stopping just inside the end zone of the football field.

He is open. He's always open, waiting for touchdown passes that will never come. No one bothers covering him. No one throws him the football.

Jeff hustles away from the field, herky-jerky. The intensity it takes to move the leg makes him hot. He loses his concentration, bangs the leg, trips, falls down.

Later, at home, he slams his glass on the table. When his dad asks him what's wrong, he cries.

Don't pass it to One Leg!

Jeff always moves quickly, much faster than other boys. He can't beat them on the field, but he passes them in the hallway at school.

Step-hop-hop. Stride with one leg, take two quick hops with the other. Step-hop-hop.

The way Jeff walks is etched in our hearts; it's the way our heroes have walked. But Jeff looks out-of-control when he moves, as if he's about to crash head over heels.

"I have to run to keep up with the other guys," he says. "It's not exactly easy for me to be a regular guy."

Don't pass it to One Leg!

In a nation where two one-legged men have been heroes, Jeff searches for what is heroic and good about it all.

If losing a leg to cancer is a curse, can it also be a blessing?

Terry Fox, dead hero. Steve Fonyo, fallen hero. Jeff Foss, 11 years old.

For an 11-year-old, one leg means you play goalie in soccer because you can't run or kick well enough to play in the field. It means you hit a baseball far, but get thrown out running the bases.

One leg means bullies taunt and push you. Little kids stare at you in shopping malls.

One leg also means some parents tell their children to stay away. The parents believe your disease is contagious or that you might die.

But having one leg means you beat cancer.

May 25 was the fifth anniversary of Jeff's amputation. In cancer patient lingo, he's a long term survivor. He's as close to being cured as he'll ever be. "I feel very good that I'm a long term survivor," he says, "although when I say that it sounds like I just got out of World War Two. But I'm just 11. I'm just a kid."

Jeff's life is Nintendo, his bike, minibike, rollerblades, skis and model cars and airplanes. His newest passion is his backyard trampoline. This summer, he wants to learn how to water ski.

"I had homework and I went rollerblading," he wrote in his diary last October. "Then I played Nintendo for about an hour. Then I pestered my older sister and her friends. It was really fun. I can push a 1991 Escort more than a block."

Another entry reads: "I saw a cow brain at the *Food For Less*."

At Jeff's age, kids want to fit in and stand out, but know how to do neither. It's an age to push for privileges, to stay up late, watch whatever you want on TV, get a bigger allowance. But it's also an age where a boy is still a boy, excited by cow brains, defined not by what he says or thinks, but by how he runs, throws kicks, and rolls.

At Lymburn Elementary School, the bodies of some of the girls in Jeff's Grade Six class have leapt into young womanhood, making everyone crazy. Jeff confirms one rumor that a boy and girl in his class were spotted necking behind the rink at recess. Jeff's cool about it. He has a poster of a sexy woman on his bedroom wall. He recently had a party at his house with both boys and girls. The drink of the night was ginger ale mixed with food coloring so it would look like a strange brew from the Ten Forward lounge on *Star Trek*.

At recess and in Lymburn's hallways, kids fly about, crashing into each other, bumping, yearning to touch. In the lunch room, the Grade Six boys make a game out of squashing a popular girl sitting on a picnic table bench. Two boys crush in from either side until she turns red and falls off.

"Oh no, she's going to start throwing up!"

"Don't let her back in!"

Across the table, Jeff plays his *Gameboy* video. He watches the action, joining in only to jump on top of a pile-up of bodies. The other kids respect his distance. Many of them are mature enough to see he is different, not strange. He's not the coolest boy in class, but he's not a nerd either. His classmates are impressed by his success on the ski hill where he is a champion disabled racer.

Continued on/B2

in Edmonton, had cited the airport issue when he announced in January 1995 that he was pulling up stakes and moving his head office to Calgary.

His advice was simple. "The recommendation to Edmonton is: Get one airport," he said.

His company wasn't the only one to move, but because it had started in Edmonton and expanded to become the second-largest cable provider in the country, the departure of Shaw stung. "This is a huge hit to us on a perception basis," said EDE's LeLacheur, "a solid corporate citizen moving its head office."

The Shaw decision wasn't the first example, nor would it be the last, of head offices moving from the city. The exodus throughout the '80s had seen such high-profile companies as Esso Resources, Alsands, Syncrude and Fluor pull up stakes, while others such as financial services companies Canadian Commercial Bank and the Principal Group collapsed.

It didn't help, either, that the city felt that it had borne the brunt of the Klein cuts in spending.

"Each time the Klein government announces cuts to the provincial payroll, the city reaches for the Band-Aids," said a story from Feb. 19, 1995.

"And now that the government town needs private sector growth, some companies are calling the moving vans."

Prominent firms such as IPL Energy, now Enbridge, left for Calgary after decades of running its pipeline business exclusively from Edmonton.

While Edmonton remained the operational headquarters for the company, its major decision makers had been relocated to the southern city in the spring of 1994. A *Journal* story said the company moved its corporate headquarters south so that it would be closer to its customers' crude oil producers and shippers.

Then in May, Nova Corporation transferred 55 workers out of Edmonton, a move that affected one out of every eight of the company's 430 employees. Fifty of those jobs went to Calgary.

It was another bruise on the city's tender psyche.

Another head-office departure came with the 1998 announcement that Telus, one of the last major corporate head offices in Edmonton, was moving to Burnaby, B.C.

Telus, one of the country's largest telecommunications companies, had grown out of AGT following the June 1990 decision of the Don Getty government to privatize the government-owned utility.

While privatization of government-owned business and agencies became a hallmark of the Klein government, the sale of AGT to the public was the first major privatization move seen in the province.

At the press conference announcing the sale of the $1-billion firm, Getty assured readers that the sell-off would not mean layoffs. Privatization, he said, "represents the logical, next step in AGT's evolution from a regional utility into a worldwide competitor." Two months later, AGT was renamed Telus Corporation.

Like corporations and governments throughout North America at the time, Telus almost immediately began downsizing, starting with 1,500 workers, the majority of them in Edmonton.

Golden Bears football program, saying the team cost $51,000 to operate but sold only $4,000 worth of tickets in 1990. The decision is later reversed.

***Jan. 31, 1991*: Edmonton Southeast MP David Kilgour becomes the first Liberal MP from Alberta in over a decade when the former Conservative joins the Liberal Party.**

***March 10, 1991*: Kevin Martin's Edmonton rink wins the Brier.**

***May 16, 1991*: After more than eight years of boarded-up abandonment, the Hotel Macdonald reopens with a gala party. "Today we regain a significant part of our past," says Mayor Jan Reimer.**

***June 25, 1991*: Bob Breen, better known as Klondike Mike, dies. He promoted Edmonton's Klondike festival for 25 years.**

***Aug. 14, 1991*: David Schindler of the University of Alberta is presented with the first Stockholm Water Prize for his research on Canadian lakes.**

***Sept. 3, 1991*: Publisher Don Babick officially opens *The Journal*'s $20-**

E

Fashion

Doing the crawl.
Life/E4

Express Yourself E2 / Spring Skin Care E3

The Edmonton **Journal** Tuesday, March 3, 1998

Bright & Beautiful BLACK

JEAN FRASER
JOURNAL STYLE WRITER

Edmonton

Not satisfied with winning the genetic lottery, fashion supermodels are sometimes suspected of dipping into the cosmetic surgery pool to even out what they perceive as flaws.

Who can blame them?

Elevated to iconic status, financially rewarded to a degree few women equal, they reign unrivalled in the public's perception of what it means to be beautiful.

That is slowly changing.

Fashion designers, magazine editors and influential advertisers, either bored with perfection or (less likely) responding to the complaint that such a standard is impossible for the majority of women to meet, recently began looking at alternatives.

Anyone who reads newspapers and magazines or watches runway fashion has picked up on this radical shift in the choice of models.

And nowhere is it more obvious that with the elevation of Alek Wek to favorite face-of-the-moment.

Arguably the first truly black model to hit the big time in the history of the industry, she is a leading player among the new crop of less-than-perfects peopling the style arena.

Skin tone, nose, lips, eye colour, hair and body type are totally her own.

She's got the requisite legs-for-days, of course, characteristic of all runway models, but they are topped with a refreshingly off-beat torso and a bone structure that presents a singular style of beauty completely unlike like that of her more famous black counterparts, Naomi Campbell, Tyra Banks and Iman.

That unconventional models are coming into their own is overdue.

That black women like Wek are showing up in the mix is even more welcome since they increasingly act as a source of inspiration for the design community.

Certainly, the most recent round of shows left no doubt that the black urban sense of how to wear colour is fueling the spring fashion engine.

And with the wealth of brights on tap for spring, we can all take a few tips from the ease with which black women carry it off.

Alek Wek photo: Gilles Bensimon, courtesy ELLE Magazine

From Club Monaco: Periwinkle blue polyester slip dress ($89), periwinkle blue v-neck sweater ($49). From Nine West: Floral-patterned espadrilles ($100), small blue shoulder bag ($35)

From Blu's Womenswear: Bright red Laurel pantsuit ($970). From Nine West: classic red pumps ($125)

From Cotton Ginny: Three-stripe colour block twin set ($46). From Holt Renfrew: black side-slit skirt ($145)

A BLACK *Beauty File*

HAIR

The news about hair is not so much about colour and curls as it is about texture. Black women typically have dry, thick hair that rarely requires volumizing products. That's why most women of colour take one of two routes when it comes to cut: short, short, short. Or big and full and lavish. And now that big hair is back, expect to see more of the latter.

The model on this page, for instance, had her hair chemically straightened so she can do more with it, a procedure that is quite common in the black community, says iTonica stylist Jeannette. New this season, she says, is the request to leave some curl in during the chemical process - "not so straight and smooth as has been the case in the past."

She recommends keeping the hair conditioned at all times to counteract the inherent dryness factor and any damage that results from the chemicals. "But be sure to use a moisturizing conditioner instead of a protein-based one," she says, "and leave it in all day. With strong hair like this model has, then it's just a question of maintenance and care."

"As for colouring, we typically do not recommend it, especially when the hair is chemically straightened. Colouring is very damaging to hair follicles and will dry it out even more."

MAKEUP

Faces at the spring shows presented different takes on healthy, natural skin and that works well for black women. The key to getting the look down is matching the makeup to skin tone. Which is a bit difficult to do, says makeup artist James Kershaw, "because the market is just gearing up for darker skin tones now."

"There is not a lot of product as yet in Edmonton, unfortunately. Bobbi Brown is perhaps the best choice at the moment because of the wide range of colours the line presents."

He says blacks need to be aware of the pigmentation levels of the makeup they choose; if they are not high enough, makeup can look washed out against the skin. Liquid foundation can present real problems.

"If there is too much pink in it, it adds an unwelcome grey tone to the skin. And nobody looks good like that."

The model on this page is wearing almond-coloured foundation brushed with a sand-coloured powder. On the cheeks: a light burgundy blush.

The same goes for lipstick choice, he says. Only this time, the culprit is an overabundance of white in the pigment. "If there is too much white, the lips will turn chalky and that is unattractive."

When making up black models, Kershaw likes to play up the eyes and lips.

With eyes, he says, as long as the undertone is correct - not too much white or opaque - anything goes.

"The rules about what is acceptable have all changed so you can even do baby blue now and get away with it."

On the model here, Kershaw used a combination of heather and wine on the eyes and a "true" black eyeshadow.

On the lips, a classic, true bright red.

"Because black models generally have fairly full lips that are often a different colour on the top lip than the bottom, I start with a light foundation or a lip balancer to even out the skin tone. Then I apply colour. I choose lipstick that is not overly glossy because, frankly, that can make the mouth look too big.

The lipstick doesn't have to have a matte finish, though. Satin finishes will work very well. And if there is no white in the lipstick pigment, blacks can wear virtually any colour."

In short, no matter what your skin tone, paying attention to makeup choice pays off in looks like the one featured here.

One that is chic, modern and absolutely right now.

From Fairweather's: Beecher's Brook side-slit skirt ($30). From Holt Renfrew: DKNY saturated violet shirt ($180). From Brown's Shoes: CK Calvin Klein espadrilles ($225)

Photography: Richard Siemens for *The* **Journal**
Hair: Jeannette from iTonica
Makeup: James Kershaw for Bobbi Brown Essentials
Stylist: Jean Fraser, *The* **Journal**
Page design: Rick Pape, *The* **Journal**

Then in 1994, Edmonton decided to privatize EdTel when nine of the 13 council members approved the sale of the city's 90-year-old utility to Telus. The price: $465 million, with the money to be put in the city's version of a Heritage Savings Trust Fund.

When the EdTel deal was completed, Telus took out a full-page ad on March 11, 1995, reassuring *Journal* readers that their commitment to the city was true.

The advertisement, signed by Telus CEO George Petty, was in the form of a letter to *Journal* readers. He promised that the head office of Telus would remain in Edmonton, and that his company was committed to playing an even bigger role in the city's future.

Three years later, Petty pulled the head office out of Edmonton – it was one of the last remaining major corporate head offices – and moved it to Burnaby, B.C., after Telus merged with BC Tel.

In a full-page advertisement in the paper on Oct. 27, 1998, again in the form of a letter to readers from Petty, no reference was made to his former promise. He did, however, commit himself and his company to "customer-driven quality of service."

Journal columnist Alan Kellogg was unimpressed when he wrote: "Remember Telus's lavish ad campaign? 'Hello World,' read the billboards and full-page spreads.

"What they didn't tell us was the 'Goodbye Edmonton' part."

It was not an easy privatization, most notably because of the problems with NovAtel, a company that was developing cell phone technology at plants in Lethbridge and Calgary. NovAtel was to have been part of the AGT privatization, but when it was revealed that the company's projected profit had turned into a $200-million loss, the province bought it back from the newly privatized Telus.

In the end, taxpayers took a $566.5-million bath on NovAtel. It turned out to be the most costly business collapse under Getty's watch.

Preceding the NovAtel loss there had been a $55-million write-off for a bailout of Gainers, $31 million on General Systems Research, a company specializing in laser beam cutting technology, and $115 million on a southern Alberta magnesium plant.

Job losses and the city's listless economy had ramifications everywhere as programs jointly funded by the city and the province were slashed.

"Certainly the province is in bad financial order," Mayor Reimer told the paper. "They are going to have to take steps to rectify it."

An auditor general's report on NovAtel agreed with Reimer.

"The NovAtel report does not name names," wrote political columnist Mark Lisac. "It gathers threads of failure which all turn out to come from the same spool – the Progressive Conservative style of government.

"It was the PC way. It was the weak side of an entire political culture – sloppiness, excessive trust, patronage, overconfidence, too much money, pride. The report is 200 pages of reading that can bring tears to your eyes."

Clearly, if you lived in Alberta in the '90s, you lived in Ralph's World, such was the large shadow the populist premier cast over the political life of the province.

Klein had shocked many observers by soundly trouncing Nancy

million downtown building, after the completion of Phase Two.

***Oct. 22, 1991*: Alberta's minimum wage is increased by 50 cents to $5 an hour.**

***In 1991*: United Way of Edmonton and Area becomes United Way of the Alberta Capital Region and, with Morley Handford as chair, raises $8,178,118.**

***Dec. 17, 1991*: Linda Hughes, who directed the successful 1989 redesign of *The Journal*, is appointed publisher, effective in the new year. She replaces Don Babick. In a story announcing her promotion, Hughes says that she saw herself as a populist running a populist newspaper. "I think that we can be the Voice of the West and we can be a tough watchdog for the public if we do what we do best, which is to serve our readers."**

***Jan. 9, 1992*: In a speech to the Rotary Club, Premier Don Getty calls for an end to bilingualism and multiculturalism.**

***Jan. 19, 1992*: Edmonton's Michael Slipchuk wins the Canadian men's figure skating title.**

Hunting
THE LONE WOLF

The Mounties believed their best hope to break the case was a respected veteran miner, Roger Warren. They hoped one day Warren would be the prosecution's star witness.

Part I

It took the RCMP's homicide task force thirteen months of unrelenting police work to track down the killer of nine men at Yellowknife's Giant mine. This two-part special report tells the inside story of how police zeroed in on the worst mass murderer in Canadian labor history. Part II appears in Sunday's Journal

BY DAVID STAPLES AND GREG OWENS
Journal Staff Writers

Yellowknife

RCMP Cpl. Dale McGowan had stepped into the middle of all kinds of drunken bar brawls, but they were nothing compared with the fighting he saw in Yellowknife on the day nine miners were massacred.

McGowan and a dozen other RCMP officers patrolled the streets through the night. They tried to get between miners from the striking union and their enemies, the replacement workers, miners who had crossed the picket line in the four-month-old strike at the Giant gold mine.

Anger boiled over in a second. At one point, McGowan jumped in to stop a furious miner who looked ready to kill his opponent right on the street in front of Yellowknife's famous Gold Range tavern.

"Calm down guy," McGowan told the man. "This is not the way to deal with it. Don't get yourself in trouble."

As soon as McGowan put a bear hug on the miner, the man went limp. He started to weep on McGowan's shoulder.

"I worked with those guys," the miner said. "I worked with them."

McGowan didn't know if the miner was a replacement worker or a striker, but he was a huge man, full of muscles used to hard manual labor. Now he was weeping. It was then McGowan understood what had happened that day, Sept. 18, 1992. All the threats, violence and rage of the picket line had created an open and throbbing wound.

The mass murder was the most evil and troubling crime in the history of the Canadian labor movement. McGowan found himself standing in the middle of it and here he would remain for thirteen of the most demanding, exhilarating and painful months a police officer could ever know. He is the officer who handled the file of mass murderer Roger Wallace Warren.

To start, McGowan had little experience as a homicide investigator.

He was used to policing in native settlements, dealing with small time thieves, drunks and bullies. He was a city boy from Edmonton who joined the force in 1978 and asked to be transferred to the Northwest Territories in 1985. He wanted the adventure of being a frontier law man.

Few of the Northern officers who assembled in Yellowknife after the explosion in Giant mine killed the nine men had ever worked in a complex homicide investigation. Few had ever taped interviews. They knew little about the special surveillance units needed to trail prime suspects. Few of them had worked with informants. There hadn't been a wiretap in Yellowknife in 12 years.

Sgt. Al McIntyre and half a dozen experienced murder investigators had to come up from Edmonton to lead the team. McIntyre was a veteran of more than 80 homicide investigations in Alberta.

The day after the blast, McGowan walked into the Yellowknife detachment to see Sgt. McIntyre already hard at it, surrounded by some of the 50 investigators already on the job. McGowan stood at the door, soaking up the feeling, the hum of knowledge and confidence. For a moment, he hesitated. He was a corporal, a senior rank for a street-level investigator in the force, but he was worried McIntyre would throw him in over his head.

"I'm Dale McGowan from Hay River," he told McIntyre at last. "I'm no great hot shot, but I'm a good worker. I'm just cannon fodder. You point me, you give me a job, and I'll go do it."

McIntyre laughed, then sent McGowan out to the Giant mine site. One of McGowan's tasks took him underground to the tunnel where the blast was set. To get where he needed to go, McGowan had to travel down the rail tracks and pass by the corpses of the nine miners.

McGowan stopped to take a look at the bodies, still stacked in a pile at the side of a tunnel. He was appalled, not by what he saw, but by what he didn't. It was hard to imagine the shapes had ever been human. All that remained was an anonymous pile of twisted limbs and parts of limbs, torsos, heads, shredded clothing, splintered wood, burned flesh, cracked helmets and remnants of mining equipment.

Many of the miners who saw the blast site were haunted by the carnage, especially if one of the anonymous corpses had once been a friend.

For McGowan, seeing the dead men was exactly what he needed. Suddenly, everything was clear. He could put aside any more questions about the convoluted issues of the strike, about the striking union, the mine owner and the townspeople. All of that was meaningless. Only this mattered.

This spot, the bomb crater beside the tracks, this blasted railcar, the nine dead men. *Who had come down here?* That was the only important question. *What makes a guy do this? Am I dealing with a total loony?*

One thing was obvious — the murderer had to have worked at Giant mine at some time. He needed detailed knowledge to make his way through the labyrinth of Giant's 160 kilometres of shafts and tunnels. No one else could find this choice spot on the railway tracks, then rig the bomb and escape.

With that in mind, the RCMP had about 400 good suspects. Half of them were the managers, linecrossers, replacement workers and Pinkerton guards working at Giant mine for Royal Oak Mining Inc. during the strike. The other half were the striking miners of the union, the Canadian Association of Smelter and Allied Workers, CASAW Local 4.

Even before the blast, many strikers were hostile towards the police. Through the strike, the union men had been sure they were in the right. After all, it was owner Peggy Witte of Royal Oak who had locked them out and brought in replacement workers. And the RCMP, well, obviously the police had been way too eager to take the company's side on the picket line.

After Sept. 18, however, the morality of the strike was turned upside down. Instead of challenging the company for bringing in replacement workers, the strikers found themselves answering questions about the murder of nine men.

The convulsion was so traumatic many of the strikers couldn't even accept that the blast was a homicide, let alone that one of their union brothers might be the culprit. The prevailing union theory was that the nine men were breaking mine rules by travelling in a railcar with explosives. When the car derailed, the explosives went off. After Royal Oak management discovered the accident, the strikers felt, Pinkerton security guards were sent to make it look like murder so the strikers would be blamed.

McGowan identified with many of the CASAW strikers, particularly the quiet ones who didn't say much, those who watched while the big mouths did the shouting. They were working men in a bad situation.

Still, if any striker refused to co-operate during questioning, or started spouting the union's denials about the blast, McGowan was all over them.

Deprogramming, he called it, peeling away the rhetoric of the strike. McGowan had to somehow get the strikers to realize why they were sitting with an RCMP officer. Did they understand that a man had gone into the mine and set up a murderous booby trap? Did they know anything about it? Were they involved?

McGowan often made progress with a striker only to suddenly have the man slip back into the union's denial.

"It was an accident," the striker would say.

"Hold it," McGowan shot back. He listed the evidence: the eyewitnesses who said no explosives were with the miners on the railcar; the fact that the blast came from beside the tracks, not from within the railcar; the fact it was all but impossible to ignite such explosives in a derailment, that they were far too stable.

If the striker continued his denial, perhaps saying the nine men would be alive if they hadn't crossed the picket line, McGowan got tougher:

"You say you're a man, but you sound like some kind of Nazi. You sound like one of those people who followed Adolf Hitler. But don't you think maybe today they look back and they think they did wrong? That's where I want you to put yourself. Get ahold of the big picture here. These men were human, not sub-human. They didn't deserve death."

The Mounties had a name for the least co-operative: knotheads. The strikers referred to the police as the Royal Oak Mounted Police.

A reward poster went up all over Yellowknife, the fund growing to $307,000. After the toughest of his interviews, McGowan always needed to look at it. He read the nine names: Joe Pandev, Vern Fullowka, Norm Hourie, Arnold Russell, Robert Rowsell, David Vodnoski, Shane Riggs, Malcolm Sawler, Chris Neill.

McGowan studied their faces. He couldn't stand the thought of how these men died. He thought about his own work, how it was dangerous enough that he could end up dead at some point, and his wife Sheila and three young kids would be in the same spot as the nine families of the dead miners. He hoped if that happened someone would work as hard to solve that crime as he was working now.

The goal of the RCMP investigation was to get an alibi for each of the hundreds of suspects, then put the men who still couldn't be eliminated as suspects on the polygraph machine, the lie detector.

Polygraph specialists Sgt. Pat Dauk of Winnipeg and Sgt. Gerry Keane of Edmonton worked full-time for several months doing more than 50 tests on strikers and union supporters, an unprecedented number of tests for an RCMP investigation.

The polygraph takes advantage of the primordial fight-or-flight syndrome.

When a person who is trying to hide something is asked a tough question, fight-or-flight immediately kicks in, giving the person a big jolt of adrenalin when he lies. The heart, blood pressure, breathing and perspiration monitors of the polygraph pick up the physiological reaction.

It was no use for a union man to be hostile and anti-police when he was hooked up to the FactFinder. The polygraph proved to be a powerful tonic on the strikers. The miners opened up to Dauk and Keane, talking about the agony caused by the strike and the murders. Miners who had called the dead men "scabs" on the line let go of their remorse and grief. The dead men had been their friends.

The test ended with two key questions: Did you set the blast at the 750-level at Giant mine on Sept. 18, 1992? Do you know for sure who set the blast?

Continued on H2

Photo: David Staples, *The* **Journal**

RCMP Cpl. Dale McGowan — "I'm no great hot shot, but I'm a good worker. I'm just cannon fodder. You point me, you give me a job, and I'll go do it."

The crime

Nine miners were killed when a railcar they were riding triggered a bomb in the 750-foot level of the Giant mine in Yellowknife Sept. 18, 1992. The dead miners were workers who crossed the picket line during a bitter labor dispute.

The verdict

A jury found miner Roger Wallace Warren, 49, guilty of second-degree murder Friday after the longest trial in Northwest Territories' history.

400 suspects

RCMP began the investigation with about 400 possible suspects, half of them the managers, linecrossers, replacement workers and guards at the mine, the other half the striking miners of the union, CASAW Local 4

Fight-or-flight

RCMP conducted an unprecedented number of tests on the lie detector, a device that relies on a person's primordial fight-or-flight syndrome. When a person is questioned about something he is trying to hide, the fight-or-flight instinct kicks in, generating a big jolt of adrenalin that can picked up on the machine's monitors.

SPECIAL REPORT

Staples

Owens

Journal reporters David Staples and Greg Owens have been following the story of the Yellowknife murders since the day the miners were killed.

EDITOR: BOB BELL
429-5209

DESIGN: RICK PAPE

Betkowski, the province's centrist health minister, in a province wide Conservative party ballot to select a leader to replace Premier Don Getty, who was retiring after serving for seven often-troubled years.

In fact, on Dec. 12, 1992, when Klein had been premier for only a week, Lisac wrote a column on what might lie ahead. "If Ralph Klein has enough time – you never know when someone's political number will come up – he may leave as deep an imprint on Alberta as Ronald Reagan left on the United States," Lisac wrote. "The thought of a Klein revolution may boggle the mind."

Lisac's column proved prophetic.

Klein's impact was felt in every area of government.

The Journal wrote hundreds of stories in the '90s showing how people were affected by the Klein drive to reduce government spending. Coverage included the protests in which demonstrators marched against cuts that they felt were too severe.

Two of the largest demonstrations focused on the closure of the Grey Nuns Hospital in Mill Woods, a state-of-the-art facility that had been built only a decade previously.

In April 1994, more than 15,000 protesters marched in the biggest such demonstration in the city's history, including the hunger marches of the Depression.

"Walking 15 abreast, it took an hour for the sea of protesters to inch the few blocks from the rally's starting point at Mill Woods town centre to the hospital," wrote reporter Adrienne Tanner of the first demonstration on April 7, 1994.

She talked to Bill Cisek, a father of three, who wanted the hospital to remain open as a full-service facility.

Despite carrying a darkly amusing placard that read, "If Ralph had his conscience taken out, it would be a minor operation," Cisek was truly in no laughing mood.

"We're sending a message to Ralph. He says he listens, he cares. Well, the people are here tonight to tell him," Cisek said.

While *The Journal* supported Klein's desire to reduce the heavy provincial debt load, the paper's editorial board questioned the government's methods at achieving its goals, and following the Grey Nuns demonstration in April the paper called for an end to the chaos that seemed to be governing hospital cutbacks.

Shirley McClellan, referred to as a "rural, southern Alberta health minister preoccupied with the campaign to cut $749 million over five years," was to blame, the editorial argued.

"Confusion and panic are running the show at the moment," the editorial said. "Hospital hysteria moves from one quadrant of the city to another…."

Another Grey Nuns protest took place on Sept. 9, 1994. Corky Meyer, the president of the Community Association for the Grey Nuns Hospital and the organizer of the rallies, put the crowd count as high as 25,000. One of the protesters was Mayor Jan Reimer.

"We must stand united to say this is wrong," she told the crowd. "We are here to fight."

Jan. 22, 1992:
Edmonton financier Donald Cormie pleads guilty to misleading investors and is fined $500,00 in connection with the 1987 collapse of the Principal Group financial services company.

Feb. 10, 1992:
Murdoch Davis, *The Journal*'s managing editor since May 1989, is appointed editor. Duart Farquharson, the paper's editorial page editor, is named associate editor. Michael Cooke replaces Davis as managing editor in August.

March 12, 1992:
Alberta Court of Appeal Justice Catherine Anne Fraser of Edmonton is the first woman named chief justice of Alberta.

March 31, 1992:
Alberta's minimum wage rises 50 cents, from $4.50 an hour to $5. Students under 18 years of age and attending school will get $4.50 an hour instead of $4.

April 4, 1992:
***The Journal*'s Linda Goyette, columnist and editorial writer, wins a National Newspaper Award for three individual columns, including one questioning Canada's involvement in the Gulf War. John Lucas, a freelance**

Reform will pay for breaking a promise on MP salaries.
Lorne Gunter /F8

Books F6

EDITOR: Bob Bell, 429-5209; insight@thejournal.southam.ca — *The Edmonton* **Journal** — Sunday, June 14, 1998

George Kraus with parents Gustav and Marie before the war: A comfortable life soon to be shattered

Czech-born George Kraus survived the death camps that claimed his parents. Now, the Edmonton man wants to settle three family insurance policies seized under the Nazis. The German insurance company in question, operating again in his native country, denies it's responsible. Kraus travelled to Prague recently on a one-man quest that echoes the hunt for Nazi gold

A Journey For Justice

SPECIAL REPORT

Six months ago, Journal reporter Allan Chambers got a tip that an Edmonton man, George Kraus, had an unresolved — and potentially precedent-setting — insurance claim dating back to the Holocaust. Chambers followed the tale and Kraus to Prague where he saw German insurance executives and Czech bureaucrats, dusty archives and a death camp Kraus survived.

Modern Prague: a sprawling city of ancient buildings, cobbled streets and budding capitalism

Who's who

SCHLOSSER KRAUS THIEMANN

GEORGE KRAUS: Edmonton resident and survivor of the Holocaust. He wants a German insurance company to honour three policies his father paid into until his death at Auschwitz.

GUSTAV AND MARIE KRAUS: Members of the Prague pre-war Jewish community, they were transported with their son George to the Nazi transit camp at Theresienstadt and then to Auschwitz. They died in the gas chambers.

VACLAV KRIVOHLAVEK: director general of the Czech department of insurance and pension funds. He is also a member of a working group set up by Czech president Vaclav Havel to look into who is responsible for honouring insurance policies confiscated by the Nazis.

MICHAL JIRKOVSKY: spokesperson for the Czech finance department.

VLASTIMIL UZEL: deputy general manager (retired) of the Czech national insurance company. He is also an expert on the nationalization of the Czech insurance industry after the war, and is a member of the working group created by Havel.

THOMAS THIEMANN: director of the Czech branch of the Victoria insurance company, which returned to the Czech Republic in 1994 — nearly 50 years after the Czechs nationalized the insurance industry.

GERT SCHLOSSER: a director of Victoria who is based in Dusseldorf, Germany, and has worked on Holocaust-era claims.

TOMAS KRAUS: executive director of the Federation of Jewish Communities in the Czech Republic. He also belongs to a group of scholars, known as Project Holocaust, which President Havel convened to examine issues of restitution growing out of the war.

Assets stolen from European Jews fuelled Hitler's war machine

INSIDE

❑ Maritza Berger has new hope in her fight for restitution/F3

Coming Monday

❑ The Canadian Jewish Congress wants the government to play a bigger role in restoring stolen Holocaust assets

MODERN PHOTOS: Allan Chambers, *The* **Journal**. DESIGN: Rick Pape, *The* **Journal**

Journey for Justice
Czech-born George Kraus survived the death camps that claimed his parents. Now, the Edmonton man wants to settle three family insurances policies seized under the Nazis. The insurance company denies it is responsible.

ALLAN CHAMBERS
JOURNAL STAFF WRITER

Prague

Just off Siroka Street, nestling against the Old Jewish Cemetery where the crows cry raucously, sits the ancient Pinkas Synagogue. By Prague standards it is a modest building, yellow-walled and capped with rust-coloured tiles. Inside, it has 77,297 names on its walls.

Inside, George Kraus is having a moment of panic. He can't find his parents' names — Gustav and Marie — in all the dense, black, claustrophobic script. "Kraus," he says. "I don't see Kraus."

The attendant comes over to help him look. She is from Chile, a retired Radio Prague announcer, trying to augment a small pension from Communist times by working part-time at the synagogue. She has grown accustomed to displays of emotion in this sorrowful place.

But now Kraus has found the names of his parents, their birthdates and the probable dates of their deaths. Oct. 28, 1942. Auschwitz. "And this is the only tombstone left," he says, gesturing towards the wall.

He has seen enough, and turns away. "Ah, what can you do?" he asks. "It's a depressing place. What can you do?"

Outside in the street, where tourists in horse-drawn buggies compete with speeding Skodas and Fiats and rusty Ladas for a share of the narrow, cobbled lanes, Kraus is in more combative, even high, spirits.

He has recently learned that a number of high-ranking insurance officials will meet with him over a claim he is pressing. It is a claim that, if accepted, would set a precedent for thousands of other Holocaust victims and their survivors. Thomas Thiemann, Gert Schlosser — they are company directors, not minions. One is even flying from Germany.

"Perhaps I will tell Mr. Thiemann he should take a list from his archives and come down to the Pinkas Synagogue and compare it to the names there," he says. "I think a few thousand names will match."

The 77,297 names on the walls of the synagogue are of Jews from Bohemia and Moravia — the present Czech Republic — who died in the Nazi death camps.

On the way to the Old Town Square, famous like all of Prague for its ancient buildings and laneways and towers, Kraus tells the story of how his family got its name.

It was in the 18th century during a program of Germanization undertaken by the Austro-Hungarian empress, Marie-Theresa. Jews, who commonly had only a first name and were referred to as "son of . . ." or "daughter of . . .", were required to take German names. His family was turned into Krauses.

"It means 'curly-headed,' " he says, running his hand over a mostly bald head. He is 72 years old, a compact and vigorous man with a strong will and an abiding, unsentimental sense of justice. He has survived some of the great crimes of the 20th century, Nazi and Communist. He is a survivor of Auschwitz, where his parents died, and of Buchenwald and the death marches.

As a 16-year-old, dispossessed of his family and the prosperous life they had led in pre-war Prague, he witnessed the execution of people he knew, and the deaths of many hundreds of others from hunger and suffering. Of the 1,866 people who travelled in Kraus' group to Auschwitz, only 28 survived the war.

He returned after the war to a country about to enter another long totalitarian period under Communism. Properties once confiscated by the Nazis now became the property of the state. People in central and eastern Europe were on their way to becoming, in a memorable phrase, "double victims" — first of the Nazis, then the Communists.

Now, during a warm May week 60 years after the Nazi occupation began, Kraus is back in Prague on some unfinished business.

WHO SHOULD PAY?

The business he wishes to do is among the most ordinary in the world. He wishes to settle three insurance policies taken out by his father many years ago — a mundane transaction. He has the documents, the policies, so pay up.

But it is not that simple. The policies, like the century itself, are drenched in blood and tied in bureaucratic rules. They amount to a few pages but, measured in guilt and responsibility, they weigh tons.

They — and Kraus — are an embarrassment to insurance officials and government bureaucrats alike. The documents are an accusation which, after so many years, cannot be escaped. Kraus himself is a walking indictment. He makes the officials and bureaucrats nervous. That much is apparent already in the correspondence he has struck up with them. It is a situation he doesn't mind at all.

The question, which Kraus will pursue in telephone calls and visits to ornate offices in the ancient heart of Prague, is a plain one. Who should pay? The German insurance company, which in all likelihood followed orders, pocketed some premiums and turned the policies over to the Nazis after the 1938 occupation? The German state, for the actions of the Nazis? The Czech Republic, for the nationalization of the insurance industry after the war? Who is responsible?

Kraus knows who he wants to bill — the insurance company. His father paid premiums to it for 16 years. He held three policies that offered both insurance and a savings plan. If he died, insurance would be paid to his

Fight or not, it was a battle the protesters would not win. Within two weeks of the September rally, surgery wards in the Grey Nuns were closed and the hospital was transformed into a much smaller community care centre. In the end, the Misericordia Hospital would share the same fate, the venerable Charles Camsell Hospital with its historic connections to the North would close completely, and the General Hospital, one of the first in the city, would be transformed into a long-term care facility.

However, by the end of the decade, spending levels had again increased so that both the Misericordia and the Grey Nuns were back in almost full operating mode.

Even if, by the decade's end, Edmonton's school and health systems were being hailed as among the nation's best, when the mid-'90s cuts were unleashed, hospitals and schools felt the pinch, and many citizens were outraged.

The Royal Alexandra Hospital and the University Hospital all tried to do more with less, and a number of *Journal* stories focused on people being given hallway health care or left to suffer in emergency wards.

"I think it's something like going to war," Dr. Richard Arnold, chief of radiology at the Royal Alexandra Hospital, told reporter Karen Sherlock shortly after the cuts began. "There's a lot of camaraderie."

But, he predicted, that feeling wouldn't last. "There's also starting to be tinges of cynicism and despair and desperation."

His department, he said, had been built to handle 25,000 patients a year. It was now faced with dealing with five times that number, with no real increase in staff numbers or equipment.

"At times, it's just a zoo. It's horrible. We've got kids, we've got drunks, we've got elderly people … It's sort of like stacking people in the hallways like cordwood," Arnold said.

The paper talked to patients and their families, too. The story of Bryan Kelly, age eight, was typical.

"A little boy with a mangled foot is wondering why so many Edmonton hospitals had no room for him when he needed them," wrote Richard Helm, a reporter covering the legislature.

Bryan had injured his foot in a mowing accident on his uncle's acreage on Edmonton's western outskirts. It had taken him 15 minutes to get to the Royal Alexandra Hospital and another six hours for him to be put in a pediatric bed and into surgery.

By then it was too late, Helm reported, and the mutilated toe on his right foot was amputated.

"He's asked me time and again, 'why didn't anyone want me?' " Bryan's mother told Helm. "We've told him time and again it's not that no one wanted you, it's just they didn't have any room."

Each government department had been directed to make 20-per-cent cuts in spending, and after health care, the impact on education seemed to attract the most attention from the newspaper and its readers. Education spending faced $369 million in cuts over five years and, again, there were protests from voters.

When Halvar Jonson, the Ponoka-area MLA who became Klein's first education minister, told teachers to keep the political fight over cuts out of

photographer, wins an award for a sequence of photos showing three children balancing and then jumping from a chain fence.

***May 20, 1992*:**
Over seven centimetres of snow falls on Edmonton, twice the May monthly average.

***June 9, 1992*:**
Jazz-blues singer and trombonist Clarence (Big) Miller, 69, a leading figure in Edmonton music circles, dies of heart failure.

***July 28, 1992*:**
Edmonton city council agrees to a $5.5-million deal with the Edmonton Trappers to build a new baseball stadium to replace Renfrew Park.

***Aug. 14, 1992*:**
Mayor Jan Reimer and Gov. Gen. Ray Hnatyshyn open City Hall's 61-metre-high Friendship Clock Tower, topped by 23 carillon bells. A public fundraising campaign raised more than $800,000 to finance the tower.

***Aug. 21, 1992*:**
Edmonton gets about one centimetre of snow in the earliest August snowfall ever recorded in the city.

C

Entertainment

Sir Paul has a message for the Millennium
Spotlight/C4

TV C2 / Comics C5 / Weather C6

SENIOR EDITOR: Wayne Moriarty, 429-5346; ent@thejournal.southam.ca *The Edmonton* **Journal** Thursday, September 2, 1999

Hum & Honk

A Symphony Under The Sky

D.T. Baker
Special to The Journal
Edmonton

Somewhere in between the conventional wisdom which says "If it ain't broke, don't fix it," and the demands of an age which constantly asks, "What have you done for us lately?", David Hoyt treads a careful middle ground.

With each new edition of the Edmonton Symphony Orchestra's Symphony Under the Sky festival, Hoyt (principal French horn with the orchestra, and also its resident guest conductor —and the man who puts together the festival) fills in a few more gaps, tries to find the right mix of new or unusual repertoire to mix in with the crowd-pleasers, and pretty much always hires guest artists who think like he does.

"The initial impetus for (the festival) was to provide performances of classical music of all sorts," Hoyt says. "And then, of course, Pub in the Park has become a little bit more important as well, and the idea of master classes ... if there's a strong response to that, we may go a little bit more in that direction."

This fifth annual edition of Symphony Under the Sky evolved from humble beginnings. In the years before it launched the festival, the ESO did a one-shot deal called Symphony in the Park in the Hawrelak Park amphitheatre.

Then successive weekend performances happened.

Then the Labour Day weekend was commandeered.

Now, Symphony Under the Sky spans five consecutive days, concluding on the Labour Day Monday afternoon. Attendance over the past few years has grown from 11,000 to 20,000.

Within that framework, other aspects have been added. The Pub in the Park Hoyt mentions is a post-concert beer tent featuring live, non-classical musical entertainment. Chamber music recitals, featuring festival guest artists and members of the ESO were added. This year, Hoyt is trying out workshops and "master classes."

"They're set up to be partly an entertainment, if you know what I mean," he explains. "We're not really expecting to become a pedagogical institute or anything like that. And since we're bringing in people from all over the world for this, why shouldn't we, as Edmontonians, have use of their knowledge and their expertise, rather than just appearing on the stage and disappearing?"

As it stands now, Symphony Under the Sky has enough, in Hoyt's words, "to keep a person really hopping." Particularly on Saturday and Sunday, events will unfold, one after another, all day long. "It is actually physically possible to go to everything," Hoyt estimates, "but I'm not sure everybody's going to do it."

And the weather, of course, could throw everything out of whack. "I feel a little bit like a farmer," Hoyt concedes. "I just do all the work that I can, then I just sit there and wait for divine providence. We've been very fortunate in the past. But you know, it could be a big financial bath if we have a week of really bad weather. And we're all aware of that. But no one's going to blame anyone for it — if it snows, it snows."

For the first year of workshops and master classes, Hoyt made sure that the guest artists he asked to participate would agree to the idea. "These are people that I know personally, and I don't choose people who are — what's the pop-psych term? — anally retentive," he laughs. "These are people who are flexible, who have a wide sort of personalities, and they just take it in stride. And I haven't had anybody say to me, 'No, I don't want to do it,' or, 'That's a lot of pressure.' They've just said, 'OK, great — if my talents are needed in that regard, let's use them.' "

Soprano Valdine Anderson, cellist Ani Aznavoorian, harpists Nora Bumanis and Julia Shaw, pianist Catherine Vickers, children's entertainer Al Simmons, clarinetist Charles Hudelson and violinist Martin Riseley will have feature parts to play at this year's Symphony Under the Sky (Bumanis, Hudelson and Riseley are all members of the ESO). As well, an instrument one does not ordinarily associate with orchestral music will be featured, when Shujaat Husain brings his sitar.

"I was down at Hertiage Days," Hoyt says. "It's unbelievable what is in this community. And there's really no reason why a major arts organization like our own should not be influenced by that. I mean, if Haydn could take a folk minuet and put it in a symphony, why can't we explore having the drummers from Ghana, or the dancers from Bali doing something with our orchestra? I think it's a normal thing for a living institution like a symphony orchestra to explore new ways of reaching their audience — and other audiences. I mean, there will be a whole bunch of people who are going to come down just to hear the sitar, and who knows? They might sit in and hear *Scheherazade* for the first time."

The way it is now, Symphony Under the Sky might be as full up as the five days it presently takes up will allow. And while has some thoughts on that he'd prefer to keep to himself about, he allows that the day may come when his workload on the festival might require him to surrender the baton once or twice to someone else. "That's certainly a possibility in the future," he grudgingly admits. "Although I've got to say I love working on it. It's one of the challenges I get a real kick out of."

But Hoyt is also willing to admit that each year, as the guns of the 20th Field Regiment of the Royal Canadian Artillery assist in the festival's grand finale (Tchaikovsky's *1812 Overture*), he looks forward to a little bit of a rest. "Just hearing 1812 makes me tired now," he laughs. "But usually, there's a week off there anyway before the season starts, so there's time for me to sort of come down and prepare to get started again on the season. But it's an exhausting process — but it's exhilarating too. It's that wonderful combination of very hard work and a lot of fun."

A few tips about Symphony Under the Sky

(Some notes from a 10-year veteran)

- If you're there for an all-day outing (like Saturday or Sunday), bring some extra clothes. Shorts for the day (we hope), and sweats for the evening. It gets cool once the sun's down, believe me.
- Sunscreen, bug spray (Duh).
- This year, ETS is doing a Park and Ride with Symphony Under the Sky. The ESO should be able to tell you more about it, but consider it. Especially on the Labour Day concert (with the cannons), Hawrelak Park's parking lot, and Groat Road, become pretty clogged.
- Bring food for the Food Bank. There are donation hampers on site.
- Birds will chirp, the odd plane will fly overhead. Heritage Amphitheatre isn't the Winspear Centre, acoustically speaking. But these are still concerts, and squealing kids, noisy sandwich bags and other needless noises are best left to before and after performances.

Festival Schedule

Thursday, Sept. 2
7 p.m. — "Summer Nights" (orchestral concert)
With: Valdine Anderson, soprano
Maya Rathnavulu, violin
9 p.m. — Fireworks (post-concert)
9 p.m. — Pub in the Park
With: Miguel Neri and His Compadres

Friday, Sept. 3
5 p.m. — Mainstage Recital
With: Catherine Vickers, piano
Martin Riseley, violin
7 p.m. — "Longings" (orchestral concert)
With: Ani Aznavoorian, cello
Mark van Manen, violin
9 p.m. — Pub in the Park
With: The Kit Kat Club

Saturday, Sept. 4
1 p.m. — Tent Workshop
With: Nora Bumanis & Julia Shaw, harps
2 p.m. — Mainstage Recital
With: Valdine Anderson, soprano
Charles Hudelson, clarinet
3 p.m. — Tent Workshop
With: Catherine Vickers, piano
4 p.m. — Mainstage Recital
With: Ani Aznavoorian, cello
Janet Scott-Hoyt, piano
5 p.m. — Vocal Masterclass
With: Valdine Anderson, soprano
7 p.m. — "The Exotic Muse" (orchestral concert)
With: Shujaat Husain, sitar
David Colwell, violin
9 p.m. — Pub in the Park
With: The Tommy Banks Big Band

Sunday, Sept. 5
12:30 p.m. — Teddy Bears' Picnic (free event)
2 p.m. — Mainstage Children's Concert
With: Al Simmons
3 p.m. — Tent Workshop
With: Shujaat Husain, sitar
4 p.m. — Mainstage Recital
With: Nora Bumanis & Julia Shaw, harps
5 p.m. — Cello Masterclass
With: Ani Aznavoorian, cello
7 p.m. — "Musical Stories" (orchestral concert)
With: Catherine Vickers, piano
Sheldon Person, violin
9 p.m. — Pub in the Park
With: Wild Colonial Boys

Monday, Sept. 6
2 p.m. — "War and Peace" (orchestral concert)
With: Julia Shaw & Nora Bumanis, harps
Maya Rathnavulu, violin
Kent Galie, narrator
20th Field Regiment, Royal Canadian Artillery

Summer '99: Bewitched by the Blair' Affair

John Anderson
Newsday

I don't know about you, but as this particular Summer Movie Season comes to a close, I feel like somebody who walked into the woods and was never seen again. Look for my long-lost footage to be released about this time next year.

What it will show is a movie-going populace without a clue and a movie industry in a state of apoplexy. *Star Wars: Episode One — The Phantom Menace*, just as a for-instance, has more or less fallen off everybody's radar screen; *The Blair Witch Project* — made for something smaller than a fraction of the cost of an *Episode One* — is still occupying theaters, having played havoc with everybody's summer-release schedule. (Anyone with a movie to sell was running away from it, hence the constantly shifting opening dates since *Blair Witch* hit the screens July 14.) More important, a lot of the big-budget movies — Wild Wild West being one glaring example — are being seen as failures, regardless of actual budget-to-box-office ratios, while the virtually no-budget *Blair Witch Project* has defined the summer of '99.

The scariest thing about *Blair Witch* is the rash of digital copycat crimes currently being committed that will be hitting screens some time in the spring.

The most reassuring thing about the *Blair Witch* phenomenon, though, seems to be how open people were for a new kind of movie.

Artisan Entertainment, the film's distributor, executed a masterpiece of marketing (it even had the directors remove their names from the opening of the film to make it seem more like a documentary). And the filmmakers may have been instinctively brilliant in showing how new media could be used to position old by erecting a Web site that gave not so much disinformation as no information.

But even if you didn't like *Blair Witch* when it was over — and there seem to be a lot of people who didn't — you knew going in that it wasn't your run-of-the-mill thriller. You may have even thought it was a documentary — I've overheard some pretty learned-sounding conversations about how "real" the story is. But either way, you knew you were in for something different. Just as with *The Haunting* and *Notting Hill* and *Mickey Blue Eyes* and *Big Daddy*, you knew you were in for the same old thing.

And the most predictable thing in an otherwise unpredictable summer? The critical worm-turning that has greeted *Blair Witch*'s success.

Think of the entire corpus of movie criticism as troops in a Sam Fuller film: There are infantrymen, and there are snipers; people who have to make a decision early on about whether a film is worthwhile and then take the flak, and those who come along after the smoke clears to pick off any stray losers who could have possibly endorsed such a film. When *Blair Witch* went to 1,000 more screens by the second week in August — having moved into an ever-increasing number in the preceding three weeks — the outcome was as predictable as a Jack Valenti speech on the ratings system. The film is hugely successful; ergo, it's bad.

It's fun to be contrarian. It's just tough to be contrarian when everyone else is trying to be. If *Blair Witch* had failed miserably, of course, it would be remembered as the definitive fin de sihcle vision that never got the adoration it deserved. As it is, the movie signifies the death of cinema and possibly Western civilization.

Consider just one particularly vitriolic screed. *Blair Witch*, this critic said, completely ignores film language — in other words, convention — and is thereby unclean. But isn't that the point? Oh, never mind. The real problem is the creeping connection between profits — real or potential — and the movies being assessed. This isn't just a problem limited to successful movies, either. I read a review recently of *Dick*, which pretty much panned the Nixon comedy because 16-year-olds wouldn't understand its historical references — which is like saying *Gone With the Wind* is a bad movie because you assume teenagers know even less about the Civil War.

Likewise, this particular critic, who I happen to know is in his 40s, though he claims not to have laughed any more than the unhappy teenagers he watched watching *Dick*, said *Election*, the satire about a race for student body president, was flawed because it was made not for people in high school, but for those who graduated at least 10 years ago.

Even if true, these allegations don't make *Election* or *Dick* bad movies. It makes them movies that might not work for teenagers. The qualities of a movie and its potential profits are mutually exclusive. But just as the public often is drawn to success, critics are repelled by it. And both sets of perception are flawed. We should keep this in mind, and look for all the analogies we can find, as long as *The Blair Witch Project* continues to turn expectations and assumptions upside down.

the classroom, an editorial took him to task. "To listen to the education minister, you'd think Alberta's teachers were happily volunteering for an extra five hours a week of Conservative bashing because they have nothing better to do with their time.

"When do they fit in this subversive activity, Mr. Jonson?

"After a full day's teaching, after substituting for the missing librarian, after coaching the basketball team, after counselling the pregnant teenager, after marking the math assignments? The reality is that few good teachers have time to go to the bathroom let alone indulge in off-hours protests.

"A teacher's first assignment is to defend the interests of the child. In a democratic society, that means speaking out when an education minister lacks the will to do so. You can call it cheap politics, Mr. Jonson. A lot of teachers would call it an act of conscience."

Students across the province demonstrated against the cuts. In a 2,000-word analysis written by education reporter Marilyn Moysa that ran on Nov. 6, 1993, readers heard from 17-year-old Naz Ismirli, a student at Edmonton's Austin O'Brien high school.

"I'm fed up," the Grade 12 student said. "Some people say you deserve the government you vote for. Well, we don't deserve these education cuts because we didn't even get to vote."

There had been six major education protests throughout the province in the preceding two weeks, Moysa reported, and not all of the demonstrators were students.

Jackie Manke, the mother of an 11-year-old daughter and a 13-month-old son, spoke with Moysa after hearing Jonson speak at a rally where he said every effort would be made to ensure that as much money as possible was directed to the classroom level.

"I'm scared for my kids," Manke said. "If the education system gets this bad now, what's going to happen by the time my son gets to school?"

Being part of Ralph's World also meant seeing government privatize everything from liquor stores to the motor vehicle registry to provincial parks management.

Steve West, the Klein minister responsible for the Alberta Liquor Control Board and one of cabinet's most aggressive privatizers and cost cutters, announced on Sept. 3, 1993, that all of the province's 204 liquor stores were to be sold.

"The free market will prevail," he said. "It's what built this country."

More than 1,500 jobs would be trimmed from the province's payroll, and the money saved – and generated from the sale of the stores – would all go to reduce the debt, he said.

It was at 10 p.m. on Jan. 8, 1994, that the Southgate Liquor Store, one of the largest run by the ALCB, closed its doors for the final time. *The Journal*'s Jim Farrell was there to watch. "Edmonton's Southgate liquor store offered its customers metre-upon-metre of empty shelf space, few deals, and a sense of gloom Saturday," he wrote.

While employees were forbidden under ALCB rules to talk to the press, many of them did. They were candid – and worried.

"This was a great store," said clerk Michael Barton. "Customers aren't going to find anything like this anywhere else – neither the prices nor the

***Aug. 23, 1992*:**
The first LRT train arrives at Edmonton's University station, crossing the river on a pedestrian, bicycle and rail bridge named for former city commissioner and alderman Dudley Menzies.

***Aug. 23, 1992*:**
Crowds line up to tour Edmonton's $48.9-million, pyramid-crowned City Hall, designed by architect (and former alderman) Gene Dub. It officially opens Aug. 28.

***Sept. 12, 1992*:**
Wetaskiwin's Reynolds-Alberta Museum opens.

***Sept. 24, 1992*:**
In Edmonton, AGT workers are told the telephone company plans to cut 1,500 jobs by the end of 1993.

***Oct. 19, 1992*:**
Jan Reimer is re-elected mayor. Voters also support the two-airport system, overturning a city council vote that would have moved all scheduled passenger flights to the International airport.

***Nov. 8, 1992*:**
Conrad Black becomes the largest single shareholder when he buys 23 per cent of Canada's biggest-circulation newspaper chain, Southam Inc., owner of *The Journal*.

E

GOODBYE England's Rose

The Edmonton Journal Sunday, September 7, 1997

Silence and sadness

Photos by The Associated Press

A hush fell over London Saturday as the funeral cortege of the Princess of Wales made its way to Westminster Abbey

Millions lined the hushed streets of London to say one last, tearful farewell to the Princess of Wales

R.W. APPLE JR.
New York Times

London

The silence — the awestruck, reverent, almost worshipful silence — was positively deafening.

Scarcely a sound rose from the millions who packed central London Friday night and Saturday morning for the funeral of Diana, Princess of Wales. It was a crowd unmatched at least since the end of the Second World War in this stately old city that has known so many moments of regal and imperial triumph and tragedy.

Yet for all the emotion, only the tread of the horses' hooves, the thwack-thwack-thwack of police helicopters, the tolling of church bells and the occasional wail of agony from a mourner pierced the stillness Saturday as the cortege wound its slow, sad way to Westminster Abbey.

More than a million bouquets by official count were stacked outside the royal palaces. People threw blossoms at the princess's casket as it rolled by on a gun carriage, draped in a royal standard with sprays of white roses, tulips and lilies atop it, one of them bearing the single word, "Mummy."

The crowds stood 10 and 15 deep along London's grand ceremonial boulevards. Necks were craned, and people rose onto tiptoes, but there was no pushing and shoving. As if venerating a saint, mourners in Hyde Park and outside Buckingham Palace lighted candles and improvised little shrines.

People of all classes seemed driven to make small gestures of devotion. Some made their first-ever trips to London. In the chic neighbourhood where Diana taught kindergarten as a 20-year-old, a basket filled with black ribbons had been set out, along with a sign urging people to "Take one and remember."

There was a surprising intensity to peoples' words and actions; a largely Protestant culture that epitomizes restraint and values privacy was galvanized by a need to display its powerful emotions publicly, if not noisily. Britain discovered feelings this week that it never knew it had.

Please see DIANA/E2

More inside:

THE FUNERAL
- A scathing eulogy/E3
- The procession of grief: Photographs/E6-7

THE PRINCES' FUTURE
- Growing up without their mum/E4

THE PRINCESS
- Diana's life in photographs/E5, E8
- Her final hours/E10

A GLOBAL GOODBYE
- Final journey brings tears around the world/E9

Prince Charles with his two sons Prince Harry, second from right, and Prince William, third from right, as well as Diana's brother Earl Spencer bow their heads as they watch the hearse bearing the coffin of the Princess of Wales leave Westminster Abbey

Millions of grief-stricken people, from all walks of life and from all over Britain, lined the streets to bid a final farewell to the Princess of Wales. With the death of Diana one week ago, Britain discovered emotions it never knew it had

Red-jacketed Welsh Guards carried away Diana's casket after the funeral service ended

selection." Barton, who held a master's degree in education, said he saw no future for himself in Alberta, and he had begun looking for an English teaching job abroad.

Jobs were clearly lost in the privatization of the liquor stores, but they were created as well. By the end of the decade, hundreds of private liquor stores, many of them offering specialty selections in everything from pricey Bordeaux wines to single-malt scotches, had opened in the province. By 2000, more than 900 private liquor stores were operating in the province.

The paper, however, did not always fully agree with the privatization measures taken by the province.

Editorials in February 1994 questioned Klein's "blind assumption, untested by fact or reality, that the government can do nothing well. Everything that was once in public hands, maintained as a public trust for the public interest, must be turned over to private hands.

"Much of what the government proposes has nothing to do with finances and everything to do with ideology, with power and control. Ideological positions are advanced in the name of deficit fighting. Deficit fears, even fiscal Armageddon as the treasurer puts it, are used to rebuff any questioning of the ideology."

Undeniably, the provincial government spending cuts had an impact on the city and its sense of self-esteem.

A 1995 story reported that the shrinking provincial government meant that more than 200,000 square feet of commercial office space downtown had become vacant in the preceding two years. It also pointed out that one million square feet of office space had been absorbed by corporate offices in the same period in Calgary.

The province, in fact, had never seen anything quite like Klein, a populist politician who insisted that everyone call him "Ralph." And while he would swear off drinking after a highly publicized confrontation with down-and-out men at a shelter in Edmonton in 2001, much of his early populism depended on his regular-guy image.

He could flash a finger at a protester as he did when he was Getty's environment minister and then suggest that maybe he ought not to have done it. "Maybe," he said, "I was just scratching my neck."

And his drinking bouts in the shabby tavern in Calgary's St. Louis Hotel took on the proportion of an urban myth.

A former smoker, he once said that he didn't agree with restaurants being designated 100-per-cent smoke-free. After all, he pointed out, the cigarette smoke in the St. Louis "sort of blends in with the grease from the chicken and chips, and it just sort of adds to the flavour."

Initially it was easy to peg him as just a good ol' boy. But opponents in the Tory leadership race, including front-runner Nancy Betkowski, underestimated his talents at their peril.

Opposition leaders learned the same hard lessons. He may have campaigned on the slogan of Ralph's Team, but it was the Ralph part of the equation that counted the most.

He seemed to possess an unerring sense of what would work in politics, an instinct that threatened to fail him only once.

On Jan. 25, 1996, the Court of Queen's Bench awarded 51-year-old

***Nov. 23, 1992*:**
Solicitor General Doug Lewis announces that Edmonton has been chosen as the site of a $10-million federal women's prison.

***Jan. 1, 1993*:**
The cost of a basic postage stamp rises one penny to 43 cents, plus GST.

***March 11, 1993*:**
Kurt Browning wins his fourth world figure skating title in five years.

***April 21, 1993*:**
***The Journal*'s David Staples and Greg Owens win the National Newspaper Award for spot news coverage for their stories on the September 1992 bomb explosion at the Giant Mine in Yellowknife that killed nine miners.**

***May 4, 1993*:**
***The Journal* wins the 1992 Michener Award for meritorious service in journalism for a series of articles by reporter Tom Barrett, examining the use of psychiatric testimony in Alberta courts.**

***July 24, 1993*:**
The Edmonton Centre Woodward's store is open for the last day. The 101-year-old department store first opened in downtown Edmonton in 1926.

We can promote universal values without kowtowing to western nations, says Susan Ruttan/G2

Religion G4

EDITOR: Bob Bell, 429-5209; insight@thejournal.southam.ca The Edmonton Journal Saturday, August 14, 1999

SIERRA LEONE

THE HEART OF DARKNESS

In a stark and haunted land, rebels have targeted civilians and their trademark is amputation. Murderous rampages ravage the country. In Kosovo, civilian abuses spurred the world's mightiest forces to spend billions on air strikes — and for reconstruction. But Sierra Leone's barbaric eight-year civil war has been largely ignored by the outside world. The stand has been branded 'democratic hypocrisy'

DRUSILLA MENAKER
DALLAS MORNING NEWS
Freetown, Sierra Leone

Eight-year-old Fatu Koroma just wanted to go to the bathroom. Now her right arm ends an inch below the elbow.

When she headed toward privacy in the bush that day in February, the rebel fighters who had descended on her village decided she was trying to escape. They made the little girl put her arm on a pounding stone and hacked it off with a machete.

"They just threw away her hand," said her grandmother, Fatmat Jalloh.

Now under a "peace at any cost" accord reached July 7 with the UN, the U.S. and Britain looking on, Fatu is being asked to forgive her attackers. They have all been granted amnesty and their leaders given positions in the government.

In Kosovo, gross human-rights abuses against civilians spurred the world's mightiest fighting forces to spend billions of dollars on battle, followed by similar sums for reconstruction. But Fatu's Sierra Leone stands in stark counterpoint.

Perhaps 50,000 of the West African nation's 4.5 million people have been killed and a million displaced in a barbarous eight-year civil war largely ignored by the outside world. With no powerful military alliance or Western outrage to rescue it, the democratically elected government has conceded to a peace that lets the rebels get away with butchery.

In the satellite TV age, the comparison with Kosovo is not missed by urban Sierra Leoneans such as James Kajue, a mourning father who lost six of his seven children and a grandson to a rebel executioner in January.

"It is the same old story, the international double standard ... democratic hypocrisy," said Kajue, an environmental engineer.

"It didn't really dawn on me until I saw the commitment the U.S. president was making in Kosovo — billions. Why did Kosovo get all the attention?"

The answer for Kajue and the handful of outsiders focused on Sierra Leone is clearly the priority that the world has given to European over African concerns.

SHORT-TERM EXPEDIENCE

Those involved in Sierra Leone question whether the negotiated peace is truly workable or just short-term expedience, and whether the UN lowered its standards by signing on to it.

"Is it for the international community to say forgive and forget?" asked Corinne Dufka, Human Rights Watch's expert in Sierra Leone.

"Who represents the people? They rely on the United Nations and the international community to represent the cause of justice and do the right thing."

Diamond-rich, South Carolina-sized Sierra Leone looks like a tropical paradise, but there are firebombed villages where the beach resorts should be and it ranks last on the UN's human development index.

Despite the years of fighting, the country did manage democratic elections in 1996. And an African regional peacekeeping force returned the government of President Ahmad Tejan Kabbah to power in 1998 after a coup. Those steps were both urged by the West.

But little foreign support came to help entrench stability or beat back the rebellion launched in 1991 by the Revolutionary United Front under Foday Sankoh.

The onetime commercial photographer and army corporal espouses a populist credo against corruption, but his policies are vague and a main goal of his group appears to be control of the nation's mineral resources.

For a slice of that, there has been some outside involvement, notably by Liberian warlord and now President Charles Taylor and mercenaries from the former Soviet Union.

The rebels have targeted civilians, and their terror trademark is amputation. When they cut off Fatu's hand and the limbs of thousands of others, the guerrillas told their victims, "Go to Pa Kabbah," eerily reminiscent of the Serbs' "Go to NATO" taunt to Albanians being forced from Kosovo.

NO NATO IN AFRICA

Of course, there is no NATO in Africa. The closest thing is the Economic Community of West African States Monitoring Group, a mainly Nigerian force known as ECOMOG. Its 1998 restoration of Kabbah's elected government was a first for the continent, an attempt at the "African solution for African problems" pressed for by the West. ECOMOG continues to prop the government now.

But in January, undermanned and overextended, ECOMOG was unable to keep the rebels from overrunning the capital, Freetown, in a murderous rampage. Even after regaining control by pushing the rebels back to positions in the bush, ECOMOG did not have the wherewithal to pursue a conclusive victory.

The United Nations sent in two dozen military observers, and President Kabbah came under pressure to negotiate a concessionary peace — from a new Nigerian government anxious to recall its troops and redirect resources toward its own democratic rebuilding, from Western powers scrambling to avert further humanitarian crisis and from the exhausted Sierra Leonean people.

Please see DARKNESS/G2

Drusilla Menaker, Dallas Morning News

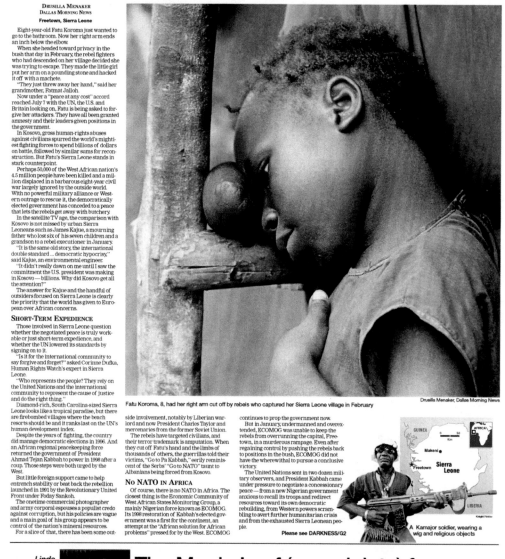

Fatu Koroma, 8, had her right arm cut off by rebels who captured her Sierra Leone village in February

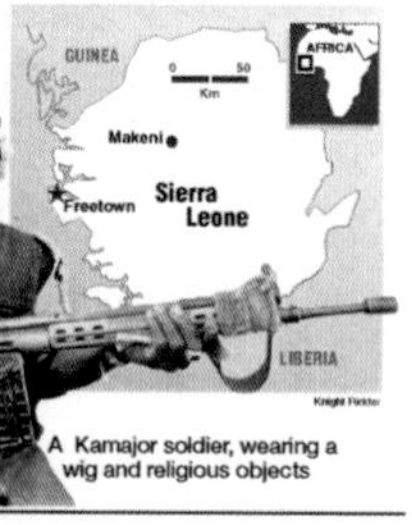
GUINEA
0 50
Km
AFRICA
Makeni
Freetown
Sierra Leone
LIBERIA
Knight Ridder

A Kamajor soldier, wearing a wig and religious objects

Linda Goyette

The Maple Leaf (complaints) forever

All right, all right, I repent. Down on my knees, I beg forgiveness. At least five million Canadians objected strenuously to a recent column in which I lampooned the Canuck tendency to wear Maple Leaf insignia when travelling outside the country.

All right, all right, that's exaggeration.

It couldn't have been more than three million people.

"Where were you coming from?" my sister asked on the phone with amazement in her voice. "You were kidding, right?" another friend asked. "You didn't mean it."

Oh, the angry letters, the irate phone calls, the hellfire and brimstone. Strangers stopped me to talk about Maple Leaf pins and badges they'd worn in other countries, with pride, and they'd do it again, and they didn't see anything wrong with it, and what on earth was I going on about anyway?

One woman wrote a stinging letter about my reference to Maple Leaf pins on heaving bosoms. Not all Canadian women have heaving bosoms, she said indignantly. I'll grant her that because my bosom couldn't heave if it tried.

Another offended patriot sent a religious tract with the suggestion I'd been duped by disciples of the anti-Christ.

"Repent sinner!" it said. I repent, sir. What should I do for penance? Stand on Jasper Avenue and sing a patriotic anthem at the top of my lungs? "The Maple Leaf, our emblem dear, the Maple Leaf forever!" Perhaps I could make my bosom heave. "God save our Queen, and heaven bless, the Maple Leaf forever!"

Newspaper readers deserve the last word on everything they read on these pages, but could we continue this noisy conversation just for a bit?

Serious objections tended to fall into two categories.

The first group of people contradicted my theory that Canadians wear this insignia to distinguish themselves from American travellers. They insisted they wore pins and badges purely out of national pride, with no ulterior motive, and I believe them.

The second group of people agreed with my hunch, but said Canadians need to distinguish themselves from Americans because we suffer great indignity if we're confused with our southern neighbours.

Some people even reported that American travellers have taken to wearing our Maple Leaf pins as a security measure because foreigners dislike them so much.

"I suggest they stop meddling, invading, bullying and bombing other countries whenever they feel their egos or their president's ratings need a boost," wrote one reader. "Then we wouldn't have to take precautions against mistaken identity."

Another reader suggested Americans were strident while Canadians enjoyed a global reputation for "cultural sensitivity and politeness."

Well, yes, we've all heard of the Ugly American. Let me tell you about a guy named Bill who fit the description so perfectly I've never forgotten him.

I had the misfortune to share a truck ride with the man all the way from Nairobi to Lusaka in 1983. Here's a notation from a travel journal:

"He came to Africa purely and simply to lose weight. Dropped from 240 to 180 while avoiding every encounter with Africans or African landscape. Camped within 500 metres of Victoria Falls but didn't bother to look at it.

"Bragged about same weight reduction schemes in trips to India and Middle East. Gourmet cook, and rhythm and blues devotee. Sexist, racist and entirely stupid. Boorish behaviour invited trouble."

Bill liked to toss bars of soap to Africans at the side of the road without looking at them. His other unforgettable habit? He told everyone he encountered he was from Toronto, Canada. To this day a few Africans can probably say the only Canadian they ever met regarded the entire continent as his personal dieting spa.

That's where I was coming from when I wrote about Maple Leaf insignia. I took the flag off my own backpack on that trip after I caught a few glimpses of American travellers, rolling their eyes, and turning away with exasperation.

They didn't bomb Cambodia. They didn't try to assassinate Fidel Castro. They didn't vote for Ronald Reagan. They were a lot more polite, and culturally sensitive, than that Ugly Canadian but like most Americans they paid the price of a stereotype.

Canadians are forever lamenting their national inferiority complex even though it disappeared into thin air three decades ago. The truth is many of us exhibit a superiority complex to Americans — not their government, not their foreign policy, but to Americans as individuals — that must sound so smug to them, so priggish and unpleasant.

Sometimes our generalizations march beyond national pride in the general direction of arrogance. We rarely insult those damn Yankees directly to their faces, but some of us indulge in passive-aggressive behaviour to let our neighbours know in no uncertain terms that we're a higher form of North American humanity.

Canadian journalist Geoffrey Stevens wrote in 1975 that the trouble with Canadians is that they suffer from an underdeveloped sense of the absurd. We don't laugh at ourselves enough. That's really what that guy from Illinois was trying to say when he ridiculed our omnipresent Maple Leaf insignia, and our determination to declare to the world that we're un-Americans, in his letter to *Maclean's*.

We can feel pride in Canada's achievements, and we can tell foreigners where we were born, without wrapping ourselves in flags.

We can declare our attitudes with our words, our actions, our curiosity, our ability to listen. We don't have to make scapegoats out of neighbours to declare our nationality.

John W. Dafoe, a great western Canadian who edited the *Winnipeg Free Press*, once said nationalism is simply a stop on the way to internationalism. That's the road we could travel: loving where we come from, but loving a larger place we call home even more.

Leilani Muir $750,000 for wrongful sterilization at the hands of the government, an event that had occurred when she was 14. Justice Joanne Veit, who decided the case, said that the money would "provide some succour for the pain she had suffered during these past decades."

The circumstances of Muir's sterilization were "so high-handed and so contemptuous and so little respected Ms. Muir's human dignity that the community's and the court's sense of decency is offended," said Veit in a *Journal* story.

Muir's sterilization had been one of 2,832 such operations performed in the province from 1929 to 1972, when the Lougheed government finally repealed the Sexual Sterilization Act.

However, the case didn't end with Muir, and on March 10, 1998, the Klein government presented legislation to limit the amount of damages paid to the remaining 700 victims of government-ordered sterilization.

The Tories hoped to invoke the "notwithstanding clause" of the federal Charter of Rights and Freedoms to prevent victims from going to court for more than the $150,000 the province was prepared to pay each of them.

It was page 1 news, and reader response was immediate and outraged.

An editorial the day after the legislation was introduced in the legislature reflected that anger. "It is big, bullying, paternalistic government at its worst, right here in Alberta, trampling on the rights of more than 700 of our more defenceless fellow citizens.

"How humiliating in the eyes of the world – and how frightening to realize there is nothing to prevent it happening to you."

When Klein's office received 250 calls on the day the news of the legislation broke, he reacted immediately. He withdrew the bill.

"My political sense probably didn't click into gear," he told reporters when he announced the bill would not be put before the legislature.

"It became abundantly clear," he said, "that to individuals in this country the Charter of Rights and Freedoms is something that should be used only in very, very rare circumstances."

In an editorial the next day, the paper paid tribute to the premier for his quick response to the outpouring of anger over the proposed legislation. "Admitting a mistake of this magnitude and backing down is something that too few governments do, too seldom. So Premier Ralph Klein and his government deserve credit for that.

"Now it can get on with settling these claims the right way."

In the fall of 1999, the government apologized to the sterilization victims and committed $80 million to settle almost 200 lawsuits.

Despite the perception that the city had borne much of the burden of the province's cuts, combined with a local economy that was often moribund, there were bright spots. Construction didn't completely stop, even in a downtown that one businessman in the early '90s compared to particularly down-and-out areas of New York's Bronx neighbourhood.

While it wouldn't be until the end of the decade that condominium and loft development brought new life in and around downtown, a certain lustre was added with the $49-million City Hall that opened on Aug. 23, 1992. More than 2,500 Edmontonians lined up on opening day for a peek at the glass pyramid roof and tinted windows.

***Sept. 2, 1993*:**
Alberta becomes the first province in Canada to fully privatize retail liquor sales, announcing 204 government stores will be closed or sold to private operators.

***Nov. 3, 1993*:**
A recount shows that Anne McLellan in Edmonton Northwest is the winner by 11 votes over Reform candidate Richard Kayler in one of the tightest races in the country. McLellan is appointed federal natural resources minister.

***Nov. 6, 1993*:**
Grant MacEwan Community College's $110-million city centre campus officially opens.

***Nov. 28, 1993*:**
The Edmonton Eskimos win the Grey Cup for the 11th time, defeating the Winnipeg Blue Bombers 33-23 in Calgary.

***Jan. 6, 1994*:**
Edmonton skier Edi Podivinsky wins his first World Cup race, a downhill event in Saalbach, Austria.

***Jan. 30, 1994*:**
Edmonton's Pierre Lueders wins the World Cup bobsled overall combined title. He and Dave MacEachern also win the two-man world title.

SECTION E

Farm Fair schedule / E14
The complete CFR stats package / F6-9

THE CANADIAN FINALS

RODEO

EDITOR: JOHN MacKINNON, 429-5303; sports@thejournal.southam.ca EDMONTON JOURNAL MONDAY, NOVEMBER 8, 1999

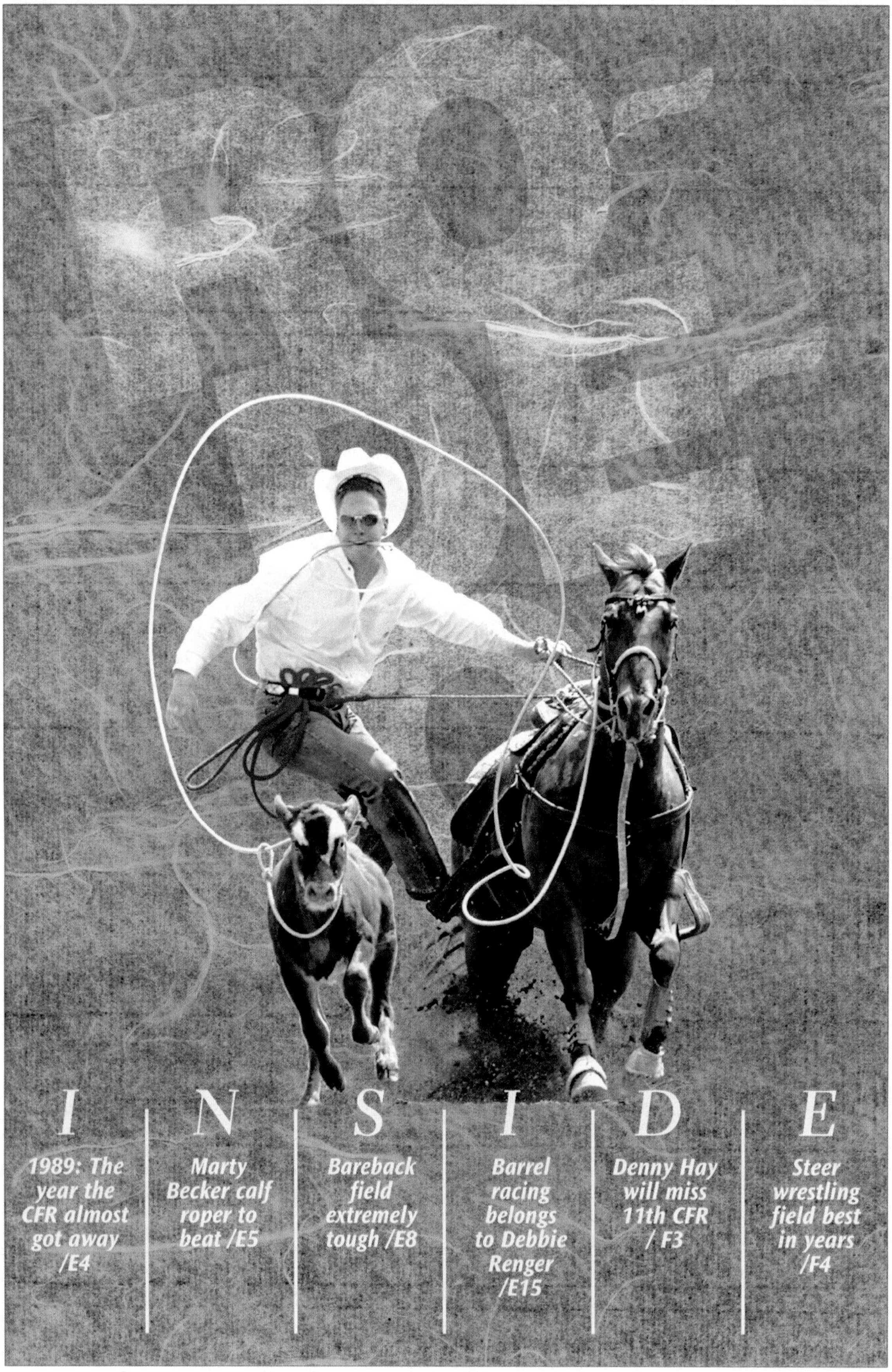

INSIDE

1989: The year the CFR almost got away /E4

Marty Becker calf roper to beat /E5

Bareback field extremely tough /E8

Barrel racing belongs to Debbie Renger /E15

Denny Hay will miss 11th CFR / F3

Steer wrestling field best in years /F4

Another boost for downtown occurred on Sept. 13, 1997, when the $45-million Winspear Centre for Music opened. The magnificent concert facility was another building block for a more vibrant downtown where arts facilities took up some of the slack created by commercial vacancies.

Furthermore, *The Journal* itself made a conscious decision to remain in the city's centre.

On Feb. 12, 1990, the first paper to be put together in the first phase of *The Journal's* new $20-million downtown offices hit the streets.

"After 69 years in its old, red brick home, *The Journal* is taking up residence in brand new headquarters right next door," the story on Feb. 10 told readers.

Phase Two of the completed downtown project opened Sept. 3, 1991.

If the paper felt a commitment to the city's core, it also displayed an understanding of one particular element that made Edmonton special.

For years, the Edmonton Oilers had been a struggling franchise, and owner Peter Pocklington kept threatening either to sell the team to an out-of-town buyer or to build his own rink on the outskirts of town so that he could make the kind of money he felt he needed to run the club.

Finally, he had enough.

Perhaps, too, the city had had enough of him as well.

"Edmonton is a great city," Pocklington told the newspaper, "but you can only be altruistic for so long."

By late 1997, the team was on the block, and it looked as if the Oilers would go the way of the Winnipeg Jets and the Quebec Nordiques – sold to American investors and moved to the U.S.

Indeed, Les Alexander, the owner of the Houston Rockets of the National Basketball Association, had been sniffing around. He liked what he saw and said that if he bought the team, and it managed to a show a profit within three years, he'd stick with Edmonton. Otherwise, he said, it would be gone.

When he found out that Pocklington had already committed to a deal with the city that would keep the Oilers here until 2004, an upset Alexander left town.

Finally, on Feb. 10, 1998, the Alberta Treasury Branches, which held an estimated $100 million in loans to Pocklington that were guaranteed by the hockey club, gave local investors 30 days to come up with an offer or they would start dealing with Alexander again, agreement or no agreement on staying in Edmonton.

A group of city businessmen hustled to put together a local bid to buy the Oilers and keep the team in the city. The paper ran day-by-day accounts as the clock ran down.

The local bidders prevailed, however, partly because *The Journal* committed $1 million to the cause seven days before the deadline.

Cal Nichols, spokesman for the bid group, said that the total raised as of March 6, 1998, was $48 million, not quite enough. But the group persevered, and two days before the deadline had raised enough money to put the fund over the $50-million mark.

When the announcement of the paper's commitment was made, *Journal* publisher Linda Hughes said the Oilers played a real role in the

***Feb. 12, 1994*:**
Figure skater Kurt Browning carries Canada's flag at the opening of the Winter Olympic Games at Lillehammer, Norway. It's the first time the Winter Games are not held the same year as the summer event.

***Feb. 13, 1994*:**
Edmonton skier Edi Podivinsky wins Canada's first medal at the Winter Olympics in Lillehammer, Norway, taking a bronze in the men's downhill.

***Feb. 18, 1994*:**
MPs approve a new, shortened Commons daily prayer that excludes reference to Christ, instead asking the blessing of "Almighty God."

***March 4, 1994*:**
***The Journal*'s Jim Cochrane wins The Canadian Press picture-of-the-year award for spot news for a shot of a city police officer shouting for help after an explosion.**

***April 16, 1994*:**
***The Journal* wins a National Newspaper Award in the special project category for its series of articles on the life stages of men and women, called "The Time of Your Life." The team consists of writer Lasha Morningstar, designers Rick Pape and Gail**

LIVING

EDITOR: BARB WILKINSON, 429-5374; living@thejournal.southam.ca EDMONTON JOURNAL SATURDAY, OCTOBER 30, 1999

HALLOWEEN APPLES

Inspiring news, tips and how-tos to make your Halloween the best ever

'Tis the night before

Halloween is just a day away, and the multitudes of last-minute types are peering into their closets, basements, garages and storage spaces wondering: What am I going to wear?

If you're one of those people, look no further. Wipe that cold sweat from your brow. You probably already own everything you need to get into the Halloween swing of things. If you don't own it all, guaranteed you'll be able to borrow it from your mother, brother, neighbour or friend.

Getiin' scarry

Last minute costume ideas for the party you weren't planning on going to:

1. Pin some socks and underwear to yourself and go as Static Cling.

2. Put on a trench coat and pin all your watches, and the watches of all your friends to the inside. If you don't have enough watches, use jewelry, stuffed animals or sunglasses. Now, you're a Brooklyn street vendor.

3. When you're really stuck, there's nothing wrong with that old standby - the white sheet with eyes cut out for an instant ghost costume.

4. Be a mummy. Rip up old sheets into strips. Wear your white long johns and pin the sheet strips to yourself. Wrap your head up too.

5. Dig out your old ripped jeans, top it off with a blazer, do your hair up with a portion of Hair Goo (see recipe on this page) and go as an '80s rock star of your choice. Don't forget to wear your sunglasses at night.

6. For women: be an instant Cleopatra. Adorn yourself with every scrap of jewelry you have. Drape a long necklace around your head, holding it into place with pins. Outline your eyes with black eyeliner. Wear a black body suit if you have one, otherwise just wear black. Then wrap yourself in some shiny fabric toga-style. A table cloth or curtain might work. If you end up at a party with someone who has a better Cleopatra outfit than you, say you're a gypsy.

7. For men: be an instant gigolo. Adorn yourself with every link of gold jewelry you have. Then borrow some more and put that on too. Wear an old T-shirt, white jacket and jeans, or better yet, a white tank top and dress pants.

8. Pumpkin: Get your hands on an orange garbage bag. Use a black marker to draw a jack-o'-lantern's eyes, nose and mouth on one side. Cut a hole for your head and two holes for your arms. Put the bag on, stuff the bag with crumpled newspaper (but hey, save this page out first). Tuck the ends of the garbage bag into your pants. It may be uncomfortable but at least it's cheap.

9. Go Greek: Wear your white long johns and a close fitting white T-shirt or tank top. Drape a white bedsheet about you in toga-style. If you're bald, carry a book and say you're Socrates. If you meet Cleopatra, say you're Julius Caesar. Romans wore togas too.

10. Skip ahead to Christmas and go as one of the Three Wise Men. Wear your housecoat, put a table cloth on your head, secure with a bandanna or scarf. Carry a jewelry box. Wear sandals if you can.

Hair Goo for Your 'Do

Recipe from a guy with 15 cm-high spiky blue hair at a downtown bus stop:

Dissolve one package of Knox gelatine in three tablespoons (50 mL) of boiling water and stir until dissolved. Allow to cool slightly, but don't let it set. When the gelatine is cool enough to handle, spread as much as you need in your hair. Twist your hair to new heights and allow it to set.

If you have any goo left and you'd like to use it later, put the stuff in the microwave for a few seconds and it's ready to use again.

Take care of your hair

Tips to make sure your Halloween hair doesn't come back to haunt you:

1. Do not use Kool-Aid to colour your hair for Halloween. "It will not come out," warns Rose Rimmer, a hair designer for film and theatre productions.

2. Before using coloured hair spray, mist your hair with leave-in conditioner. That will help prevent the temporary colour from adhering more permanently. This is especially important if you have light coloured, artificially coloured or recently permed hair.

SOUTHAM NEWSPAPERS, MONTREAL GAZETTE

Thierry Mugler's Witch Time look, a black, see-through, head-to-toe feathered chiffon is a great look for the up-scale party.

Low-cost party decorating

"Never underestimate the power of darkness with candles and pumpkins," says Linda Simmonds, owner of Shirley Potter's costume company. "Of course if you can get a candelabra, that's just like the best."

To get the abandoned haunted house feel, Simmonds suggests draping your furniture in old sheets. Faded or solid coloured sheets will work the best. Floral patterns aren't as great.

Put some organ music on the CD player and you're set.

LYNN LAU
Journal Staff Writer
EDMONTON

Halloween through the generations

Alex Mair, 73, local historian

"We would stand on the porch and shout 'Halloween apples' and we would always use an old pillowcase to carry the loot. We used to get a lot of apples, and we would get a handful of candies and a sucker or two. And we had a dentist in the neighbourhood who gave everyone a toothbrush, to our great distress. For costumes we would wear old clothes, usually our fathers', and instead of makeup we would take a burnt cork out of a wine bottle and rub it all over our faces."

Bob Lang, 69, magician and locksmith:

"I didn't know what Halloween was all about until I was about 11 years old. We were on a farm and we just never heard about it. Back in the '30s a lot of farms had housekeepers to help look after the kids. We had a housekeeper who was young ... she said, 'Come on, we're going to go Halloweening.' I didn't dress up at all but we had a mask that we put around our face. Of course it was dark and it was a lot of fun. I thought it was really neat. I had a wonderful time. What we got was mostly apples.

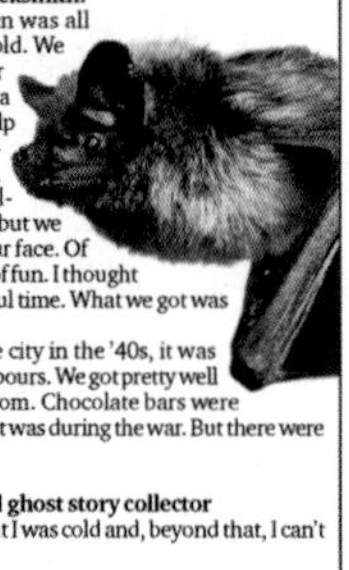

"Then when we moved into the city in the '40s, it was going around to some of the neighbours. We got pretty well apples and candy very, very seldom. Chocolate bars were totally out of the question because it was during the war. But there were always lots of apples."

Barbara Smith, 52, author and ghost story collector

"My most vivid recollection is that I was cold and, beyond that, I can't really remember anything else."

Carol Logan, 49, owner of Carol's Quality Sweets.

"We lived in Gold Bar at that time and we weren't allowed to eat anything before we got home, even in those days. But I remember us going to a park, and the moon shining above us, and I remember eating as much as we could before we got home. Candy was the favourite and little chocolate bars. I didn't like the sunflower seeds and the apples were kind of borning because you could have those at home."

Jane Dunbar, 49, teacher

"We lived in an area that was basically inner city, slummy, but we would always be out by ourselves. We actually used to go to places where we knew they would make something, like the popcorn balls and candied apples. One of the teachers in our neighbourhood would be one of the ones who gave candied apples. That was the biggest deal. We absolutely loved that."

Get a little gruesome

Cook up some blood and guts, right in your very own kitchen

The following recipes and suggestions are from Prudence Olenik, a film and television makeup artist. The stuff is all non-toxic and perfectly edible, if you are so inclined.

Face Goo

7 packets of Knox gelatine
1/2 cup (125 mL) of water
2 tablespoons (10 mL) glycerine
Face powder (loose or in a compact)
food colouring

Mix gelatine powder, water and glycerine in a small saucepan, and bring it to a slow boil, stirring over low heat. Allow the mixture to cool for about 45 minutes.

Transfer to a plastic container with a lid. At this point you can cover it and stick it in the fridge for later use (When you want to use it, microwave it a few seconds to make it liquid again). Or you can use it now.

To use: allow the gelatine to cool to the consistency of porridge. If it doesn't get thick enough add another packet of gelatine powder.

Blood: Add a few drops red food colouring with a half drop of green. (To get a half drop out of the bottle, put a drop of coloring on a plate. Then take a knife and touch it to the drop to stir into the gelatine). Mix well and smear it on.

Gory skin: Smear gelatine on your face or affected body part. Allow to set and dry, then powder the gelatine with face powder. You can then gash the gelatine skin gently with a butter knife to make a wound. Add blood-coloured face goo to the gash.

Slime: Add green food colouring and a drop of blue. Mix well and glop around.

To remove, simply peel off at the end of the night. Olenik says the food colouring in the gelatine will not stain your skin. But that doesn't mean you can paint your skin with plain food colouring — because that will never come out.

For more texture:

Use corn syrup to glue some cotton batting to your face. Then glob on your face goo. The blood-coloured stuff will make the cotton look like fleshy gore. With the green, it looks like globby slime.

For scabs: Burn some oatmeal under the grill. Allow it to cool. Then glue the flakes to the afflicted area using a bit of corn syrup.

For the diseased look: Crack an egg into a bowl, remove the yolk carefully. Whip the remaining egg white with a fork. Paint the egg white on your face, then stick some oatmeal to your face This egg white mask is guaranteed to be good for your pores. Rinse with water to remove.

Edible blood (used by dying characters on movie sets): Add a few drops of red food colouring to chocolate syrup (like Brown Cow). Apply as needed. Lick off after use.

Where ghosts roam

Five Reputedly Haunted Locales in Edmonton, according to Barbara Smith, author of *Ghost Stories of Alberta* and *More Ghost Stories of Alberta*

1. Edmonton Public Schools Archives and Museum, 10425 99th Ave.

Resident ghost, Peter, has been blamed for taking pictures off walls, turning on taps, turning on lights, and otherwise being a nuisance.

2. La Boheme Restaurant, 6427 112th Ave.

The ghost of a former laundry woman is believed to haunt this building, which used to house upscale apartments. The ghost just "makes people aware of her" and is otherwise benign.

3. Princess Theatre, 10337 82nd Ave.

This knocking phantom is heard on the stairway, knocking on walls and on the projection room window.

4. La Casa Ticino parking lot 8327 112th St.

Formerly a haunted restaurant by the University, the building has recently been torn down. "There's only a parking lot there now, but I'm kind of curious if there will be any ghostly occurences in that parking lot," says Smith.

5. Firkins house, now in Fort Edmonton Park

A former occupant still haunts this historic home. He has actually been seen and when the military was doing the renovations there, tools would get moved around and heavy objects would fall of their own accord.

alloween Fact File

Halloween originated as a religious Celtic festival about 2,000 years ago. On the night of Samain, as it was then called, spirits were believed to roam the earth with the living. To frighten the spirits off, Celts dressed as demons, hobgoblins and witches.

The date we currently celebrate as Halloween was picked in the 8th Century to honour Christian saints and martyrs. It was called All Hallows Eve or All Hallows E'en.

Pumpkins may make good lanterns, but the original jack-o-lanterns were made of turnip, says Hans Broedel, a medieval historian at Hamilton College in New York. "One of the nice things about jack-o-lanterns made from turnips is that you can actually use them as lanterns. Children suspend the carved root from string or a forked stick and carry it around when they go out at night."

More than 85 per cent of all Canadians buy Halloween candy, according to research from the International Mass Retail Association. On average consumers spend about $18 on sweets, and another $22 on costumes and decorations.

Source: Carlton Cards and Hamilton College

Inside Tips For Living

2 Have you heard this one?
3 What does Hollywood know about single motherhood?
4 Here's your chance to be truly horrific
5 A good time to pig out on pork

prosperity of the community and the paper benefited from that prosperity. "I think it is psychologically important for Edmonton to keep a hockey team," she said, although she emphasized that the newspaper would not take an active role in the affairs of the club.

"I don't want anyone to have any sense that this is going to change the way we cover them as a newspaper."

It didn't, although Cam Cole's next-day column on *The Journal's* involvement was a tongue-in-cheek classic.

It took the form of a letter to Oiler general manager Glen Sather.

In part, this is what he wrote:

"Dear Glen,

"First of all, let's clear this up: I want you to know you will not have to be especially nice to me, after I'm an owner of the Edmonton Oilers. In fact, for appearances' sake, it might be best if you continued to pretend you didn't particularly like me....

"As far as I'm concerned, *The Journal's* million bucks entitles me to no more than a simple 'Good morning, Mr. Cole, may I get you a coffee?' at practices. Our relationship will evolve from there as we both become more comfortable with our new roles....

"*The Journal* has no plans, at this time, to have any input into coaching decisions, although our staff obviously will monitor the Andre Kovalenko situation closely.

"In the area of cost-cutting, if it becomes necessary to trim the budget, I'm sure all would agree that a Mercedes sport utility vehicle is pretty much proof positive that some people have too much money, and we wouldn't want to be conspicuous in our high-end consumerism. So it might be best for all concerned, image-wise, etc., etc....

"Yours in ownership,

"R. Cameron Cole."

It had been a long road, however, to the final purchase and the saving of what had become the most important sports franchise in the city's history.

But the city never gave up the battle to save its beloved team, wrote Marta Gold and Jim Farrell in a two-page feature on the successful bid to keep the Oilers in Edmonton.

"The saga has been so prolonged, the dilemma so profound, the task so monumental, it would have driven most communities to despair."

Raising the necessary $50 million was the equivalent of piling $6,000 on every seat in the 17,000-seat Coliseum, they said.

Oilers season ticket holder Bob MacMillan understood how it happened.

"It just goes to show," he told the pair, "when you have quality people, good things happen to good people.

"Anything that Edmonton gets involved in gets a quality result, whether it's the Commonwealth Games, the Grey Cup or the Oilers. Our volunteers can come up with anything."

Echlin, editors, Barb Wilkinson, Wayne Moriarty and Vivienne Sosnowski.

***June 30, 1994*:**
The Edmonton Club, 10010 100th St., one of western Canada's oldest private clubs for the business elite, closes its doors. With only 400 members, there simply isn't enough revenue to keep the club open, according to Don Horner, past-president of the club. "I believe years ago the Edmonton Club literally represented the 'Who's Who' of the Edmonton business community...It's where you went and it's what you belonged to."

***July 26, 1994*:**
City council gives final approval to the Coliseum lease agreement reached by Edmonton Northlands and Oilers owner Peter Pocklington.

***Oct. 4, 1994*:**
The Rolling Stones perform the first of two sold-out shows at Commonwealth Stadium. "Who says you can't get no satisfaction?" writes rock critic David Howell.

***Nov. 15, 1994*:**
Edmonton novelist Rudy Wiebe wins his second Governor General's Award for literature, for *A*

Mess with a guy's car and you're asking for trouble.
Susan Ruttan/G2

Religion G4 / Life G6

EDITOR: Bob Bell, 429-5209; insight@thejournal.southam.ca The Edmonton Journal Saturday, August 1, 1998

Living With The Great Northern Diver

The loonie is plummeting. Angst, we're told, is abroad in the land and the government is doing nothing. Is this something we should be worried about?

SATYA DAS
FOREIGN AFFAIRS WRITER
Edmonton

On a gloriously sunny morning in Strathcona, the newspaper beside Gino Prete's steaming cup of coffee is spreading gloom.

"Canuck Buck Ducks Again" says the front page headline. And there's no shortage of experts to confirm the sky is falling. "Stick a fork in the Canadian dollar: it's done," says one of the money-market analysts about the so-called "limping loonie."

Prete can't quite understand what the fuss is all about. "The low dollar is good for the restaurant business, it's been great for us," he says.

In a couple of hours, he'll welcome the first guests of the day to Gino's Italian Kitchen. And if the pattern holds true for the end of the summer, "we'll get lots of folks I haven't seen in here before; most of them are from the States. They can't believe how cheap everything is."

> *Will you be paying more for coffee in the fall? Probably. But coffee always goes up in the fall.*
>
> — Bart Duguid of McBeans

Prete is a beneficiary of the brighter side of a lower dollar. The things we sell to non-Canadians are a lot cheaper.

But on the flip side, the things we import into Canada — especially those priced in U.S. dollars — are a lot more expensive.

Mazen Debaji knows all about it. "Our costs are definitely up," says Debaji, one of the brothers who runs Debaji's Fresh Market, a grocery specializing in top-of-the-line products. "I'm paying an extra $350 on every 50-case shipment of lettuce."

Romaine that cost 79 cents a bunch last summer is $1.29 a bunch this year. Yet it's more of an inconvenience, not the crisis many economic analysts make it out to be.

"People really take it in their stride," says Debaji. "They're very understanding."

Some items — like $3 eggplant — aren't moving at all, but overall, "our sales are still up."

In fact, despite price fluctuations, there's little indication that the lower dollar is fundamentally changing Albertans' lives.

"Will you be paying more for coffee in the fall? Probably. But coffee always goes up in the fall," says Bart Duguid, who runs the McBean's franchise in Commerce Place. The lower Canadian dollar means some types of beans have gone up in price. "But they had a bumper crop in Brazil, and that's really moderating prices."

Like many businesses, Duguid is looking for alternatives to products priced in U.S. dollars.

But on balance, there's ample evidence the falling loonie is helping to keep Alberta's economy robust.

Premier Ralph Klein says the exchange rate is "an economic boon" for the province. With an "economy based on extracting resources and adding value to them," exports are Alberta's lifeblood. And with the bulk of Alberta's exports — such as oil and natural gas — heading to the United States the low dollar means more windfall revenues for the Alberta treasury.

Klein cautions there might be reason to worry if the dollar goes into free fall, but he doesn't see "that it can go much lower."

For now, says the premier, a 65-cent dollar is more help than hindrance. Small wonder. Without it, Alberta might be taking a big hit on oil revenues. At roughly $14 U.S. the world price of oil is significantly below the Alberta budget forecast of $17.50 U.S. a barrel. In normal circumstances that would mean a $500 million loss to the Alberta treasury.

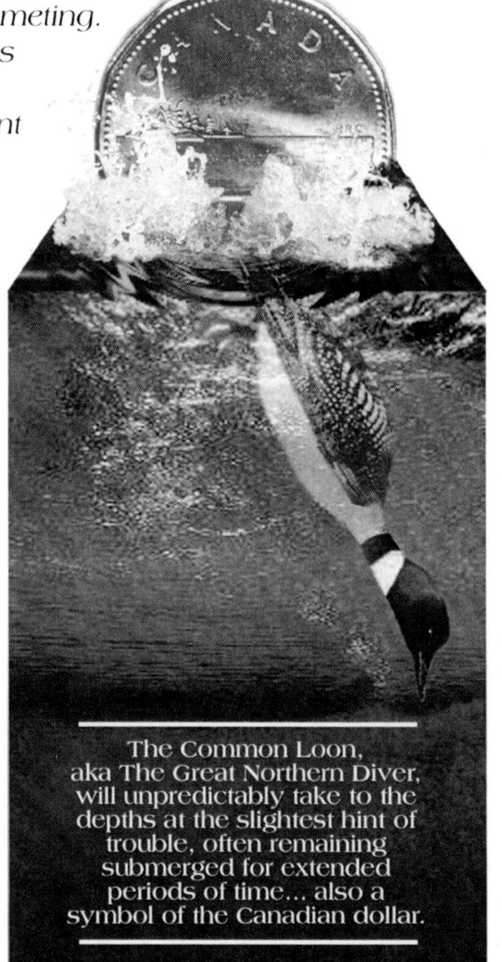
CANADA

The Common Loon, aka The Great Northern Diver, will unpredictably take to the depths at the slightest hint of trouble, often remaining submerged for extended periods of time... also a symbol of the Canadian dollar.

Illustration; Rick Pape, *The Journal*

But the collapse in oil price is more than offset by the exchange rate advantage, and the low dollar means Alberta's riches keep rolling in. This year's provincial budget expected a barrel of oil to fetch the equivalent of $20.36 Canadian; this week, the benchmark price for a barrel of oil was $20.67 Canadian.

And despite the doomsaying by some experts, the lower dollar doesn't seem to be having much effect on people's lives.

Imports from the U.S. are most expensive — but that doesn't mean consumers will necessarily suffer. That's because the Canadian dollar is doing well against other currencies, and businesses are diversifying their supplies.

Debaji's is a good example. "We're getting more specialty product like vinegars and oils from Europe now," says Mazen Debaji.

And with more produce from Mexico, Debaji is picking up bargains where he can find them. "Mangoes have never been cheaper," he says.

Gino Prete says the low dollar doesn't add to his costs, "because 90 per cent of the things we use and sell are Canadian."

But people are being forced to give up some things — like holidays in the U.S. and some parts of Europe.

Leisure travel is taking a big hit — bookings to London are way down because of the strong pound — but that's more than offset by an increase in business travel, says Firoz Moorji, manager of the American Express travel agency in downtown Edmonton.

"We're seeing a lot more European travellers come through Edmonton," but travel in the other direction is scant. Moorji notes fares to Britain are rock bottom — a summer return trip can be had for less than $600 — but there are few takers because of "how much it costs just to sleep once you get there."

The other big drop is in cruises. "The bookings are down at least 20 per cent. When it hit $1.50 for every U.S. dollar, we started getting lots of cancellations."

Until the loonie's slide, many cruises offered the Canadian dollar at par with the U.S. No longer. Suddenly, that $3,000 cruise costs $4,500 and people are backing off.

> *I don't think too many peoples' lives are going to change if the dollar is down.*
>
> — restaurateur Gino Prete

"But you know, the high-priced cruises (costing $10,000 or more for longer voyages to exotic destinations) are still selling quite well."

On the face of it, there's no economic reason the Canadian dollar should be heading toward 65 cents U.S. The last time the dollar was below 70 cents — in 1985 and 1986 — Canada had a $38 billion budget deficit, virtually every province ran a deficit, inflation was much higher and jobs were scarcer.

Right now, in the second quarter of the current fiscal year, Ottawa is running a $18 billion surplus, inflation is firmly controlled, there's steady job growth and the economy is chugging along faster than most of the developed world.

So why is the dollar low? It's a matter of context. It's low against the U.S. dollar and the surging British pound. But it's virtually unchanged against the French franc, the German mark and the Italian lira.

And despite the "limping loonie" label, it's substantially higher against the crisis-beset Asian currencies. The dollar has gained enough against the Japanese yen, for instance, that a good hotel room can be had in Tokyo for $200 Canadian a night. Less than three years ago, the same room would have cost about $350.

Please see DOLLAR/G2

Linda Goyette

Bedtime stories: sex scandals all our own

Canada is a little kid sitting on the stairs at midnight, spying through the bannister at the wild American party down below.

Our eyes get wider by the minute. We sit up here on the top step of North America, agog at the shenanigans down in the living room. Will Monica Lewinsky blab about her sexual escapades with President Bill Clinton? We lean forward to eavesdrop but we can barely make sense of the dull buzz of grown-up conversation.

Squinting at the female guests, we struggle to remember their names. Is that Gennifer Flowers or Kathleen Willey or Paula Jones? Is that Monica Lewinsky talking to Linda Tripp? Which one is Dolly Kyle Browning?

Not everyone up here is transfixed. The sex scandal in the United States leaves many Canadians cold, our usual temperature come to think of it.

"I am Lewinskied right out," a colleague admitted yesterday. She isn't the only Canadian bored to exhaustion with the repetition of sleazy details.

The CBC carries Clinton's denial so often most of us can recite it backwards in an Arkansas accent: "Ah did not have a sexual relationship with that wuhmunn, Monica Lewinsky. Ah did not tell ennuh-one to lah."

Yawning and sleepy, some of us kids are ready to toddle off to bed. We do try to look on the bright side of American difficulties.

"U.S. sex scandal lifts loonie," the *Globe's* Report on Business chirped the other day. "Dollar rises to 66.3 cents on fears Lewinsky case will breed deep political turmoil."

That theory sounds a bit optimistic to me. If American sex scandals were all it took to boost the value of our currency, our poor old loonie would be worth $3.42 US by now.

Even so, to stay on the safe side, maybe all 30 million Canadians should beg Lewinsky to spill the beans to independent counsel Kenneth Starr for the benefit of her friendly, northern neighbours. Perhaps she'd consider candid testimony about loony behaviour in the White House to boost the value of our loonie.

The bare-naked suggestion of presidential sexual hijinks in Washington is enough to put the Canadian superiority complex into overdrive.

Many people feel obliged to mention the comparative sainthood of Jean and Aline Chretien in any conversation about the Clintons. This attitude reminds me of my retort to a girl in Grade 4 when she explained the precise acrobatics of sex: "Your parents might do that, Darlene Vienneau," I sniffed. "But mine never would."

At times Canada can be the world capital of smug. The truth is this country is not exactly as pure as its driven snow in the sex scandal department.

We seem to have collective amnesia this summer about Margaret Trudeau dancing with a male companion at a Manhattan disco, sans underwear, as a prime minister seethed. Cabinet minister Francis Fox resigned over his signature for a married friend's abortion. Gerda Munsinger, sexpot and possible spy, seduced a cabinet minister and turned Ottawa upside down. Premier John Brownlee of Alberta was humiliated in a courtroom melodrama after his affair in the 1930s.

These are just our well-known sex scandals. Beyond them, Canada has had its fair share of Monica Lewinskys. We barely know their names, partly because of Canada's obsession with its deadly and sexless constitutional history, and partly because the Bill Clintons in our past had a habit of hiding their extramarital lady friends.

For a peek behind Ottawa's lace curtains, pick up a copy of Heather Robertson's intriguing social history, *More than a Rose: Prime Ministers, Wives and Other Women.*

You'll read about Charles Tupper, nicknamed "the ram of Cumberland County" for good reason. In Washington with a trade delegation, the senior Tory black sheep regularly visited a secretary, Josephine Bailey, who filed a lawsuit in 1891 saying she had become pregnant and was advised by him to have an abortion.

She later came to Ottawa and asked Tupper for a civil service job. He turned her down, but wild rumours in town didn't hurt him. He became prime minister five years later.

Then there's Wilfrid Laurier. "Proud I am of your friendship, nay of your affections," a married Laurier wrote to his married friend Emilie Lavergne in 1891, "and could I yell it on the top of the houses, prouder yet would I be. Goodbye to you, friend, so every day dearer. I must close and still my heart clings to this paper."

When Laurier became prime minister, rumours flew that the influential society woman at his side had borne his illegitimate son. Ottawa had a different *Frank* magazine back then. Amaryllis, gossip columnist for *Saturday Night*, described Lavergne in 1897 as "the Canadian Lady Chesterfield." This was political code for mistress. In Britain, Lady Chesterfield was considered the Monica Lewinsky of former prime minister, Benjamin Disraeli.

Is the name Joan Patteson familiar? Probably not. Mackenzie King met the married woman in 1918, and their intimate partnership would continue through all his years as prime minister. He even supplied Patteson and her husband with a cottage beside his summer home at Kingsmere.

"Joan and I pledged our lives to united effort and service today," King wrote in his diary. "God grant we may be given strength to endure." Was it a sexual relationship? Does it matter? After decades in his regular company, she was at his deathbed in 1950.

"Historians who cross the Styx into the murky world of King's diary were so spooked to find Mrs. Patteson," writes Robertson, "that they expurgated her relationship with King from the original transcript. When not referred to as "Mrs. Patteson" she appears only as "J" or "..."

How many "..." stories punctuate the sexual history of Canadian politics? The kids at the top of the stairs will never know.

Mulroney's Mistake

From now until the end of the Mulroney government's term of office – and perhaps thereafter – we'll pay a seven-per-cent government tax on most things we buy or consume.
— Editorial, Dec. 31, 1990

If Canadians were ever of one mind about anything it was their dislike for the Goods and Services Tax (GST) imposed by Brian Mulroney's Tory government.

The Journal agreed with Canadians in that New Year's Eve editorial. "The GST is a cash cow for the government, because it takes a bite out of most transactions in the economy. The government finally admits that the GST will not be 'revenue neutral' as promised during the last election."

The GST was implemented Jan. 1, 1991.

Almost a year later, on Dec. 28, *The Journal* examined the impact of the tax in a series of stories. "Almost 12 months after its implementation, the tax remains highly unpopular."

Merchants had been using GST hostility in sales gimmicks. One car dealership said it would sell lemons for $3,000 each and throw in a car for free. Lemons aren't subject to GST.

An "underground" tax-dodging economy was rapidly developing. Some tradesmen and retailers let customers avoid the GST if they paid cash, didn't want a receipt and didn't ask questions.

In September, there had already been reports about Canadians avoiding the tax by cross-border shopping in the United States.

"The tax is a sort of straw that broke the taxpayer's back. Canadians might once have felt more loyalty to their hometown businesses and communities, but no more," said a Sept. 20 editorial.

The GST was a focal point of the Oct. 25, 1993, federal election. In their policy "Red Book," the Liberals promised to replace the GST with something more fair.

On Oct. 18, Norm Ovenden, *The Journal*'s Ottawa correspondent, reported Sheila Copps's vow to resign her seat if a Liberal government didn't dump the reviled tax.

The Tories won two seats. The Liberals, with 177, formed the government, but by 1996 there were still no signs the Liberals were going to dump the tax.

Deputy Prime Minister Sheila Copps, somewhat reluctantly, fulfilled her election vow to quit when her government didn't axe the tax. She resigned May 1, 1996, only to run again for her Hamilton East seat in a hastily called byelection. By June, she was safely back in cabinet.

Chretien had steadfastly maintained he hadn't promised to dump the GST.

But on Dec. 18, 1996, this odd apology from Chretien appeared in the paper: "If I and others left the impression with anyone that we would be able to do away with the (GST) tax without a replacement, I want to tell them that I was sorry."

Discovery of Strangers.

***Nov. 18, 1994*:**
Edmonton city council decides to sell the city-owned Edmonton Telephones to Telus Corp. for $465 million. (On the same day in 1904, Edmonton aldermen agreed to purchase the Edmonton District Telephone system from owner Alex Taylor; his price was $17,000.)

***Dec. 9, 1994*:**
Edmonton flyweight boxer Scott (Bulldog) Olson wins the IBO world title in a 12-round decision.

***March 19, 1995*:**
The University of Alberta Golden Bears win the national intercollegiate basketball title for the second year in a row.

***March 31, 1995*:**
CFB Edmonton's base at Namao officially changes hands from the air force to the army and the newly named Edmonton Garrison becomes Western Canada's "superbase" in a reorganization of Canada's military. A massive building program begins as regiments are transferred to the city from Calgary, Manitoba and B.C.

***April 11, 1995*:**
Mayor Jan Reimer announces that the High Level Bridge will be closed for seven

DRESSING TO WIN

Shawinigan's Street Fighter

Now that talk of politics is on the menu at smart dinner parties, why is it that politicians themselves look anything but smart? If they dressed a little better, more people might pay more attention to what they have to say.

Dear Abby may have already covered this, but since I have yet to read about it in a style manual, here is Dressing To Win, a lighthearted take on what a little political image polishing might do to raise the fashion bar.

Over the next few days, fashion experts, interested onlookers and industry forecasters will cast their (slightly jaded) eyes over the five front-runners, sharing their opinions, comic, serious and in-between. A fashion astrologer shares advice from the stars. And tips, hints and how-tos flow in from our hot-shot design team.

First up to the (fashion) plate: Prime Minister Jean Chretien, who, like the Rolling Stones' Mick Jagger, occasionally taps into a street fighter stance.

Hint to Liberal spin-doctors: trade up to the look when you trade off on the image.

Jean Fraser
Fashion

ASTRO STYLE

By Greg Polkosnik, astrological fashion forecaster and author of *Cosmically Chic*.

Jean Chretien: born January 11, 1934.
Astrological Sun sign: Capricorn.
Astrological Symbol: Goat.
Chinese Calendar Symbol: Monkey

"The Prime Minister displays many of the traditional characteristics of the Goat: businesslike, reserved, competent and a bit too aloof for his own good. As for fashion, boring is the rule when Capricorn politicians get dressed. Fellow goat Richard Nixon? Always in a dark suit. Mao Tse Tsung? Invented the Chairman Mao outfit. Enough said.

Capricorn men are often too conservative to use fashion in a creative or expressive manner. Chretien would be wise to reinvent himself by looking for inspiration from Jean Paul Gaultier. With one of the French designer's slinky silver suits clinging to his body like chain mail, the PM could show Stockwell Day that he's ready for more than just a battle of words. And this typically French look should not only endear him to his Quebecois constituents, it should also appeal to the multi-pierced and tattooed voters too hip to cast their votes for the ultra-unhip Canadian Alliance.

CAMPAIGN SONG

The Rolling Stones' *Street Fightin' Man*.

Next up for Dressing To Win

- Stockwell Day
- Joe Clark
- Alexa McDonough
- Gilles Duceppe

BUSINESS CLASS

By Fred Singer of HENRY SINGER MENS WEAR

"Clothing is a reflection of personality. If yours is rigid and boring, then that is the way you dress."

The first thing he should do is wear something different from the blue suit/white shirt/ print tie he always wears that is so boring. Show a little style. For a more youthful image, try a charcoal suit, blue shirt and gold tie. Jazz it up further with a pair of brown shoes for a continental look. He is in pretty good shape for his age. He could carry off a 3-button suit and a flat-front trouser. He should always wear Canadian, like Warren K. Cook or Coppley.

And get a new haircut.

Chretien looks bad in casual. In a sweater, he just looks like he took his suit jacket off. Trudeau was one politician who knew how to dress but there are very few guys like him.

'Cause where I live the game to play is compromise solution —Rolling Stones, *Street Fightin' Man*.

The PM riding into battle.
At right: a confident Custer strikes a pose.

SEPARATED AT BIRTH?

Jean Chretien and Gen. George Custer. Last Stand Gunslingers?

POWER DRESSING

By Bill Kissel, fashion writer, *L.A Times* and *Dallas Morning News*. Fashion editor, *The Robb Report*

"President Clinton and Prime Minister Chretien are men who wield enormous power. They don't want anything to detract from that."

Politicians are so controlled by the people around them, you don't get to see much personal style. Most of them dress in the same uniform: blue suit, white dress shirt and a repeat stripe or jacquard print tie. They do that because they don't want to offend anyone. They don't want to look as if they spend any time on their clothes. That might make them seem frivolous. And when you're the leader of your country, anything is better than frivolous. They prefer bland, which doesn't take away from their message.

But this can be a problem with the young voter, the Generation Ys, who are hugely influential in the States. In California, they are constantly being urged on the Internet and at political rallies to get out and vote. These people have an increasingly large say in the political process and they are very much into personal style. That's a problem for spin-doctors. Politicians have to dress in a way that will not offend people who have voted for years and give money to campaigns. Then there is the young vote connect a guy with conviction with a sense of style. A smart politician would realize he has to look the part if he wants this vote. Start thinking custom clothes. Because of their input, I think we will see changes in the style of suit dressing soon. But not right now. Right now the money comes from the Old Guard and that is who these politicians dress for. As for women, they want to see a man in a good suit and good shoes. That's the bottom line.

PET ACCESSORY

An English pug. Homely but loveable. Pugnacious. Tenacious. Temperamental. A wiry little fighter

BLAND VS. BRAND NAMES

By Jean Fraser

Irony has ruined any chance of having an earnest conversation about anything other than gossip, so the resurgence of politics as a topic of cocktail conversation has been all the more difficult to navigate. But one thing stays constant. No matter what women think of President Clinton, they give him top marks for looking good.

Clinton is a babe.

Part of it's the hair. Boomer women value hair the way rockers love tattoos. It's a carryover from the heyday of the hippie, when hair was as meaningful as music.

Jean Chretien has bad hair. He is not a babe.

It could be the comb-over.

Despite astonishing popularity with middle aged men who live in Quebec, the look is brutal. The only message it sends is, "I'm pretending I have more hair than I do."

And he could use a stylist. Someone who understands fashion, appreciates a good suit, gets the "Regis factor." The sixtysomething host of *Who Wants To Be a Millionaire* knows how to wear clothes, looks believable on television and makes men half his age look dull. Not conventionally handsome nor fashionably fit, Regis has a look anyone can copy. A well-cut suit, a solid-coloured shirt, tone-on-tone tie and a great pair of shoes. What could be simpler than that?

C2 EDMONTON JOURNAL

CELEBRITY

SUNDAY, OCTOBER 10, 1999

GOSSIP

Survival of the politically fittest

After leading Canada, could the PM star in some kind of martial arts show on TV? Why not!

Paul Mather
Celebrity Comment

It used to be that washed-up film stars did TV and washed-up TV stars did dinner theatre. Now, it seems, washed-up entertainers of all kinds have a new profession to fall back on: politics.

Gopher from — *The Love Boat* — pioneered it. He was a congressman for four terms. Sonny Bono was a congressman too. Former wrestler Jesse "The Body" Ventura is a governor — probably the only governor in U.S. history to be nicknamed "The Body." And now a new generation of celebrity politicians is coming into its own: Warren Beatty might run for president. Cybill Shepherd too. And why not? Her sitcom tanked, and Candice Bergen's hogging all the good phone commercials.

Even Arnold Schwarzenegger says he hasn't ruled out one day running for governor of California. It would be cool if he got the job — that way, if California and Minnesota ever had a war, they could settle it by putting Schwarzenegger and Jesse Ventura into a pit somewhere and having them fight it out.

Come to think of it, all governors should probably be musclemen. That way, if they're about to execute someone, they don't need to worry about one of those special phones connected to the governor's mansion. If a pardon is needed, the governor can just come bursting through a wall at the last minute and rip the electric chair out of the ground with his bare hands. Then he can say something cool, like, "I declare clemency … with a vengeance!"

So far, Canadian politics has been almost totally celebrity-free — except for Governor General Adrienne Clarkson, who used to have a TV show on CBC. Actually, come to think of it, being Governor General doesn't really make you a politician. Heck, having a TV show on CBC doesn't really make you a celebrity. So forget I mentioned her.

American trends do tend to find their way north, so I feel confident that someday we'll find ourselves voting Canadian celebrities into office. I mean, who better to lead a united right-wing party than that mountie guy who used to be on *The Beachcombers*? He's so likeable … and he's got a dimple on his chin! Besides, who else you gonna vote for?

Relic? He steals logs!

Somebody like Al Waxman would do well as a politician. He's got the common touch, and besides, he's already halfway there: when he walks down the street, he smiles at everyone. Now he just needs to shake hands and pass out buttons with his own picture on them and he'll already be campaigning.

Of course, when Canadian performers take over politics it'll leave our present generation of politicians without a job. What are people like Chretien, Bouchard, Clark, McDonough and Manning going to do when they've lost their jobs to people like Pierre Berton, David Suzuki, John Byner, Mr. Dressup and The Littlest Hobo?

They'll do what they have to do. The only thing they can do. Get Canadian TV shows. And Canadian politicians might actually improve Canadian TV. Bouchard and Manning could do a wicked French/English version of *The Odd Couple*. Alexa McDonough could be a MuchMusic VJ. Joe Clark could do a cooking show — "Today we will be preparing plain boiled potatoes." And Chretien could star in some kind of martial arts show where he attacks various kinds of protesters.

Canadian entertainers almost certainly couldn't do a worse job of politics, and Canadian politicians just might do a better job of entertainment, so what the heck! Bring it on, I say. Besides, what've we got to lose?

Most of us will be watching American TV anyway.

Journal designer Rick Pape used a little photoshop magic to turn our PM into a kick-boxing superstar.

CONVERSATIONS

"When I was in elementary school during the whole disco craze, I used to dance, but so many people made fun of me — even in my own family — that I can't get up and dance anymore."
Nicolas Cage

"Somehow my daughter got taken to see *There's Something About Mary* and I was furious! But when I asked her about it, she hadn't really taken in the grody parts. She thought it was funny, but didn't know why."
Courtney Love on why she needs a new baby-sitter for her six-year-old daughter Frances Bean

"The whole string-of-failed-relationships thing is really annoying. I dated one actor — well, two, but who's counting? — and it didn't work out. But because it was publicized, I was branded 'The Woman Who Can't Make Relationships Work.' That really bugs me."
Starlet Minnie Driver, now virtually engaged to James Brolin's son Josh

"I liked them all. I like to learn new things. That's what makes us human."
Starlet Keri Russell on her favourite subjects in school

"For me, God is an energy that bonds all life … you're meant to be your own Buddha and your own Jesus."
Singer Paula Cole

THE CANADIAN PRESS

Melanie C., the solo-performing version of the Spice Girl's Sporty Spice, dropped into Toronto recently. The well-toned, newly cropped Sporty Spice now dabbles in tough (by Spice Girls standards, anyway), distorted, Garbage-style electro-rock in a few spots on her forthcoming solo debut, *Northern Star*. Oh, how positively frightening!

THE ASSOCIATED PRESS

Welsh film star Catherine Zeta Jones and Hollywood star Michael Douglas recently celebrated their birthdays (her 30th and his 55th) with 150 of their closest friends at New York's trendy nightclub One51. Although friends say the two make an adorable couple, the wedding bells aren't ringing just yet — there's still the little matter of Douglas' 22-year marriage to Diandra. Michael and Diandra separated in 1995, but their divorce has yet to be finalized. As Diandra told The Times of London, "Before Michael can marry, he has to divorce me — or become a Muslim so he can have two wives."

DRESSING TO WIN

A Cat With Attitude

Fashion deserves its reputation as a cynical industry.

But pitting Stockwell Day against Jean Chretien is something even we would think twice about.

Let's face it: Day has the edge in the fitness department. No one who looks that good in a wetsuit could fake it, as any fashionista worth her weight in personal trainers could tell you.

And skin-tight, elasticized rubber is merciless.

Day has also mastered the photo-op. He knows an ocean backdrop or a kick-boxing gym always looks good. And he photographs well. He's working the smooth-but-tough angle. And he's handsome: not quite babe material but easy on the eyes.

With such a pronounced *Vogue* factor at play, then, why is it that he doesn't show well in a suit?

He can't wear rubber clothes to work. He's not a candidate for velvet, Austin-Powers style. Sassy frilled shirts, beloved by Westerners at weddings, are frowned upon in the East.

But he could wear Boss, as in Hugo Boss. Or a suit from Kenneth Cole, a label that fits a form as feline as his.

He'd look like such a guy's guy. Which would leave no doubt he's in the running as leader of the pack.

Yeah, baby, yeah!

Jean Fraser
Fashion

ASTRO STYLE

By Greg Polkosnik, astrological forecaster, author of *Cosmically Chic*.

Stockwell Day: born August 16, 1950.
Astrological Sun Sign: Leo.
Astrological Symbol: Lion
Chinese Calendar Symbol: Tiger

Leos demand attention from the people around them. They can be gracious. They can be generous leaders. But they are some of the astrology world's worst control freaks, even though they prefer to rule with a velvet glove rather than an iron fist. They like to have the last word.

Day exhibits many of the characteristics typical of his sun sign, but his personal style is far too reserved for astrology's golden boy. It's time to re-invent his squeaky clean image and start dressing like a Leo.

Coming up with an updated image should be easy since Leos are inherently creative. Take a few tips from Whitney Houston, a diva, public figure and a fellow Leo.

Despite a ton of bad publicity, the high-powered songbird has been able to contrive an entirely new public persona by virtue of an image makeover. She recorded an album aimed at younger listeners, refuses to refute those nasty rumours swirling about her and dresses in drop-dead fabulous clothes. And she's got a little bit of bad-girl about her that makes make her more popular than ever.

Maybe Day should learn to cultivate some bad-boy style. If he does, Dolce & Gabbana is a design team he might try. Treading the line between good and bad taste, they appeal to the ultra-hip, the young and the idealistic. And to gay men and jet-set women, two of Day's least supportive constituencies.

D&G's sexy, beefcake clothes guarantee he'd capture the attention of the nation, no matter what kind of political trenching he's engaged in. Stumping for votes. Lounging, *apres* swim. Or walking the hand-shake gauntlet with his wife.

And a man like him needs a relaxed pant with a wider bottom. But no pleats. And a very modern shoe, one with a square toe like all the Prada knockoffs we're seeing now.

Shirts? Tone-on-tone in dark greys and burgundies. But nothing like Regis is wearing. The real urban cool cat has moved way past that.

Things Leos should avoid: cuffed pants and ill-fitting suits. And watch out for Dolce & Gabbana because their look can be way too extravagant.

Had the guts, got the glory
Went the distance
Now I'm not gonna stop. — *Eye of the Tiger*, Theme from Sylvester Stallone's Rocky, right.

Stock Day goes the distance, right.

PET ACCESSORY

The Siamese Cat. Sleek. Reliable. Steadfast. Smooth operator.

CAMPAIGN SONG

Survivor's *Eye of the Tiger*, famous as the theme song from the movie *Rocky*.

SEPARATED AT BIRTH

Beefcake movie star Sly Stallone and Stockwell Day. Campaign Motto: More beef, less cake.

GIVE ME SVELTER

By Kevin Knaus Atlanta-based creative director of Fairchild Publications' and Urban Exhibitions' Material World.

That image of Day on the SeaDoo is similar in effect to the one of Al Gore on the cover of *Rolling Stone*. And it looks like he's got a the same kind of smart, sexy relationship with his wife that Gore has.

But I don't know if either of us wants the guy running our country showing up pictured like that. That kind of photo op is clearly directed to the youth vote. It's a blatant attempt to capture the interest of the powerful Generation Y.

In the U.S., every rap star, television personality and fashion leader is out there urging Gen Ys to vote.

But the thing is, the blue/brown suit uniform just doesn't cut it with that demographic. They are seriously into stylin'. Smart politicians get that. When you've got Clinton answering the "boxers or briefs?" question on MTV (he wears boxers), you can see what Day is getting at by focusing on his physique.

But there is a problem staking your image on a finess angle. The navy blue suit, white shirt and conservative tie is the uniform of power, the uniform of leadership. Would the respect level still be there among foreign dignitaries if the leader of your country showed up in Hugo Boss and a turtleneck? There is a whole credibility thing tied into the blue-suit uniform that has to do with the comfort level of everyone involved. And it's not likely to change overnight, no matter how much influence the young voter wields.

HIP DUDE OR FAT CAT?

By Duane Pasieka, owner URBAN MEN

"The man would look killer in colour. Colour is actually his strongest suit. He should pop it in whenever he can. Orange or red or whatever.

What looks modern now is a turtleneck, something orange from DKNY, for instance. And he's so fit, he can do T-shirts well, as well. A colourful look like that has that '60s thing going on, but it's really retro, very chic, anything but Austin Powers flash. Getting him into a leather jacket from, say, RudSak, is an option, as long as the shape is clean, minimalist and uniquely urban.

When he's wearing a suit, try something from a designer like Kenneth Cole. Either a three- or four-button jacket would work because it would give him the right silhouette: clean, simple and close to the body.

"Oh Behave!" — Mini Me's advice.

Stockwell Day — International Man of Mystery.

DIGITAL ILLUSTRATIONS: RICK PAPE, THE JOURNAL

The People Speak

"How sweet it is that just for once, the secrecy, manipulation and total disregard for democracy that seems to prevail in Canadian politics have failed."

— Lyn Brockelsby, letter to the editor, June 28, 1990

"Meech Lake is dead and it didn't die well," said the editorial obituary for the failed constitutional accord, June 23, 1990.

Two years in the making, the behind-closed-doors proposal to get Quebec to sign the Canadian Constitution needed the assent of all 10 provinces by a June 22 deadline. Newfoundland and Manitoba didn't get on board.

But no one mourned the loss, especially *Journal* columnist Linda Goyette, who saw no merit in such deals being made without public input. "A club of 11 privileged, middle-aged, white men tried to patch together Canada's Constitution in secret, excluding the people who elected them," she scolded June 24.

Canadians had been on a fast learning curve of constitutional law since the debate really got going in 1978. Quebec refused to sign on in 1981 when the country patriated its own constitution from Britain.

Meech was designed to bring Quebec into the constitutional fold by guaranteeing, among other things, its status as a "distinct society." It also carried the seeds of possible Senate reform, which Alberta wanted.

But what it pointedly ignored was any provision for public debate and any inclusion of aboriginal concerns.

Prime Minister Brian Mulroney and the premiers started a new round of constitutional talks in P.E.I. in the summer of 1992. This time, the proposal, called the Charlottetown Accord, was put to the people in the form of a national referendum Oct. 26, 1992.

Polls, however, said voters would reject the accord, not so much for its contents but because Canadians were not in the mood to believe the assurances of their political establishment that it was a good deal.

All the premiers were for it. The prime minister was for it. *The Journal* came out for it on Oct. 1.

"There is nothing in the reform package itself that unduly favours Quebec. In accepting genuine Senate reform, compromised for the sake of Albertans, we should be prepared to do no less."

Still the polls showed skeptical Canadians were going to vote "no."

Tory Deputy Prime Minister Don Mazankowski told *Journal* reporter Norm Ovenden on Oct. 23: "I'm aware of the mistrust, the deep division, the misunderstanding, the suspicion and particularly the esteem in which politicians are held these days."

But he urged people angry with the GST, free trade or the government in general not to use the referendum to settle old scores.

Apparently, the lust for revenge was too much. Canadians dumped the accord 54 per cent to 46.

Sixty per cent of Albertans voted against it.

months for much-needed repairs. She suggests that motorists caught in the upcoming traffic snarls get a little light reading. Her suggestion: *War and Peace*. *Journal* columnist Alan Kellogg does a quick survey of readers to determine what colour the bridge should be painted once it's reopened. Former mayor Ivor Dent suggests green, auto dealer Pat Healy opts for taupe, art gallery director Alf Bogusky chooses sky blue, fashion designer Deidre Hackman wants pink and Dale Cameron, guitar master craftsman and Whyte Avenue businessman, suggests black with flames on the side like a '51 Merc.

***April 29, 1995*:**
Linda Goyette wins her second National Newspaper Award for editorial writing.

***May 1995*:**
Sheila Pratt becomes *The Journal*'s managing editor, replacing Michael Cooke.

***May 23, 1995*:**
After a sensational Edmonton trial. Marilyn Tan is acquitted of injecting ex-lover Con Boland with the AIDS virus, though she's convicted on a lesser charge related to the scandal.

Search your subject on the Web

David Zgodzinski
For Southam Newspapers

Montreal

What's your favourite subject in school? What's your least favourite subject? Kids will head to the Web when they're keen about a topic and they want to find out more, or when they have problems with a certain subject and they're looking for another way to learn. Either way, there's plenty out there. We'll take a couple of examples — Canadian History and Math, and see what we can find.

There's a lot that can be learned on the Web about Canadian History, with plenty of helpful information, images, essays, and archives. The Canadian Museum of Civilization has done a fine job of transposing their historical exhibit called Canada Hall to the Web. The site is an overview of the range of Canada's past, useful for kids in primary school, or high-school kids who want to go over the basics.

The site is indexed according to historical period — pre-colonization days, early settlers, expansion west. Each major time frame has a few subheadings. These subheadings, such as Early Acadia, or the Fur Trade, are paths to exhibits at the museum, represented with their own pages on the site.

A concise history of the period or lifestyle accompanies images from the museum's exhibits. You see reconstructions of life as it was hundreds of years ago when Europeans first settled here, and how their lives evolved.

To accompany the museum's exhibits, the concise text descriptions of the topic contain many links from key words in the text to other historical Web sites.

Personal accounts bring history to life. Some of the images that stay with kids about Canadian history are the early adventures of the Jesuit missionaries in New France. The Jesuits were meticulous in their records, and a work called the Jesuit Relations and Allied Documents is a chronicle of life in the 1600s and early 1700s.

A joint effort of the Le Moyne College in Syracuse, and the Jesuit College of Central New York has produced a Web site with an English translation of these works. The texts are indexed by time frame. You can read the accounts of dedicated Jesuit priests, their stories and their descriptions of the country and the Indians they encountered.

Another great journal that can be read online is that of Samuel Hearne, who related the stories of his explorations. Chipewyan Indians had brought copper nuggets to Fort Prince of Wales on Hudson's Bay. The 24-year-old Hearne was dispatched to find the source of the copper, and/or the Northwest passage. The story of his voyages in Canada's north from the years 1769-1772 are all here in Hearne's own words.

Reference sources for Canadian History on the Web are plentiful. Early Canadiana Online is a library of books, documents and letters from early European contact with the New World, on through the late 19th century. The site is an effort of Universite Laval, University of Toronto, and the National Library of Canada. Books and documents have been scanned, and optical character recognition used to compile the texts in some cases.

You can do a keyword search, or search by author, and find a collection of books. The images of the pages were scanned and stored on the site, so you can still read books that are now possibly crumbling.

The Canpix Gallery calls itself the Great Canadian Image Base. This is a collection of 3,500 images of people, places and events. Images are indexed according to time periods. Choose the era and the category (people, place, event) and you get a list of descriptions of images, and then click to see the graphic.

There are nicely reproduced paintings and photographs, of major events and smaller dramas, important historical figures, and everyday folk.

There are so many good Canadian History sites, that a few links sites have popped up to keep track of them all. One of the best is Canadian History on the Web, maintained by Susan Neylan, an enthusiastic Webmistress, and history lecturer at the University of British Columbia.

Whether you are a nerd who needs a constant stream of mathematical problems and puzzles to solve for fun, or you are terrified of equations and geometry, the Web has some great math Web sites to suit you.

A+Math is a site for elementary school pupils to work on their math skills. There are flashcard quizzes that help kids practice the basic multiplication, division and square root skills.

The site also has a games section with a bunch of interesting math based games. A+Math gets kids to solve math puzzles and learn in a playful way.

Math Central is another site for K-12 math education. It's produced by faculty and students of the Department of Mathematics at the University of Regina.

The site has a question and answer forum, a section called Quandaries and Queries. You can submit elementary or high school level mathematical questions, and someone from the site will reply. The questions and answers are posted to the site.

Math Central has mathematical glossaries with a host of definitions of terms. Do you remember what a coefficient is? If not, this is the place to look.

The Math Forum site has similar functions. The Ask Dr. Math function allows you to ask a math question. There's a data base of previous questions and answers. There are elementary, middle and high school level questions. Read the subject headings and you can search through previous questions on that topic.

The Math Forum also has a thorough "Question of the Week" section. There are Geometry, Algebra, Trigonometry and Calculus sections as well. You can submit your answer to the problem. Here too you can search back through old questions and learn the elegant solutions that were submitted.

Math Forum also has a good math Web links section classified by subject.

Mathmania is for the more advanced students. It's another Canadian site, product of the University of Victoria.

Mathmania is divided into principal sections - a section on graphs, a section on sorting networks, and another on knots. Each section has a story that's kind of a math myth, telling a story that works with the essence of the math concept. There are also exercises and tutorials on each topic. Finally there's a glossary for the topic. This is a high level site that looks at sophisticated mathematical concepts in a playful and original way.

Curious and Useful Math is a site that brings out the quirkier side of numbers. The site has a number of tricks, classified by type, like multiplication tricks or squaring tricks.

It's time to start hunting around for some of the sites that will help you with the school subjects you hate and those you like. You may get lucky and find a site that has just what you need to help you understand your schoolwork a little better.

Photo illustration: Rick Pape, *The Journal*

> *"Virginia was then ruled by a ferocious Englishman, who was extremely hostile to the French name and to our Society. When he heard that Jesuits had arrived, he exclaimed that such extremely wicked men, the sepulchers of piety and religion, ought to be destroyed. Argall strove against him, and declared that, while he lived, no annoyance or injury should be offered to the Fathers, for he had given them this assurance; and he produced the royal commission, by authority of which the French colony was brought to New France. Incensed by this commission, the man declared in a rage that the French must be driven from New France. In this decision the English councilors agreed. Argall was ordered. to retrace his path; to expel those of the French who remained; to destroy their buildings, and level them with the ground. He returned, burned the forts built upon the Canadian coast, destroyed everything, and seized two ships which he found at Port Royal."*
>
> — From the Jesuit's Lemoyne Web site

- Museum Of Civilization — Canada Hall: **www.cmcc.muse.digital.ca/cmc/cmceng/canp1eng.html**
- Jesuit Relations and Allied Documents: **http://vc.lemoyne.edu/relations/**
- Arctic Dawn — the Journeys of Samuel Hearne: **http://web.idirect.com/~hland/sh/title2.html**
- Early Canadian Online: **www.canadiana.org/cgi-bin/ECO/mtq**
- CanPix Gallery: **www.nelson.com/nelson/school/discovery/images/ncdimag.htm**
- Canadian History on the Web: **www.interchange.ubc.ca/sneylan/cdnhist.htm**
- funA+Math: **www.aplusmath.com**
- Math Central: **http://MathCentral.uregina.ca/index.html**
- The Math Forum: **http://forum.swarthmore.edu/**
- Mathmania: **http://csr.uvic.ca/7/8mmania/graphs/menu.htm**
- Curious and Useful Math: **http://personal.cfw.com/~clayford/**

Internet took its first baby steps 30 years ago

David Plotnikoff
Knight Ridder Newspapers

Thirty years have not dimmed our collective memory of Neil Armstrong's walk on the moon. How is it that the other giant leap of 1969 — the birth of the Internet — could be so obscured by the passage of time?

For decades, none of the researchers who built and tested that first Net connection have been able to recall the exact date of the transmission. Although the Net has been the subject of innumerable articles, books and documentaries in recent years, none has been able to establish a birthdate for the mother of all networks.

Ultimately, it was the death of one of the Net's founding fathers that brought the date to light. Based on that recently re-discovered documentation and new recollections by individuals on both ends of that first communication, I'm pleased to say that for the first time the Internet has a real birthday — Oct. 29, 1969.

Actually, it has two birthdays — one that's passed and the one next month.

And therein lies a bit of a political problem. Given the propensity for endless debate among historians and Net-geeks of longstanding, it's quite possible scholars could be slugging it out over the date right up until the Net turns 40.

There is a plausible explanation for how such a key milestone could be effectively forgotten for so long: In the race to get the network up and running, that one communication simply wasn't considered terribly important.

"The truth is nobody paid much attention to it," said Doug Engelbart, the computer visionary who oversaw one end of the early network back in '69. "It was more like, 'Well, OK, they brought in the motor so we can get our vehicle running.'

"It was just part of getting the plumbing to work."

The basic outline of the Net's Genesis story is clear: The first node of the Pentagon-funded Advanced Research Projects Agency network (ARPAnet) was installed in the lab of a UCLA computer-science professor, Leonard Kleinrock, on Labor Day weekend of 1969.

Please see TECHNICAL/G6

WHAT'S HOT

Cool cubes

Forget megawatts and subwoofers. The colours on Pioneer's new musiQube Micro Systems are loud enough.

With the "rainbow rave" option, the CD/radio unit and the two speakers each come in its own hue. If this day-glo approach is too peppy, try the more sedate French bleu or the office-acceptable white mist.

MusiQube was designed to catch the fancy of teens and young adults, which would explain its SoundScape buttons. They let the listener mix music from a CD or the radio with audio from a connected MiniDisc player, available as a separate option. The Happy Tune MiniDisc supplied with the test unit held the sounds of crashing waves, UFOs and other ethereal material. The effect ranged from annoying to oddly relaxing.

A nimble musiQube operator could use the MiniDisc to mix tracks in conjunction with the CD player for, say, a small dorm dance party. But don't bet on big decibels because the musiQube is untamed in the high frequencies. Crashing cymbals or electric guitars will send listeners diving for the treble control, only to find an equalization button that offers such puzzling options as Natural, Happy, Refresh and Deep.

SoundScape and a frisky look are the musiQube's best attributes. If sonic quality is a high priority and MiniDisc isn't, other shelf systems, including Pioneer's, sound much better at a comparable price. The musiQube's suggested price is $270 US, and the MiniDisc player option adds $330 US. Info: **www.pioneerelectronics.com** or call 213-746-6337 to learn more.

John Hanan, The Dallas Morning News

Text Storage to go

Iomega's Zip drives are popular, and for good reason. Their disks hold lots of big files. Their disks are portable. And because Zip is practically an industry standard, the disks transfer easily from one computer to another.

Now Iomega is introducing a removable disk drive especially for notebook computers called Clik. It's an ingenious little device bound to impress your friends.

The Windows-compatible Clik drive, about the size of a couple of stacked credit cards, fits into a notebook's standard PC card slot. Its disks are smaller than a Zip drive disk and store less data: 40 megabytes, the equivalent of more than 25 standard floppies. The latest Zip disks hold 250MB. There's also no guarantee that Cliks will become as ubiquitous as Zips, meaning that sharing the disks with other users may be difficult.

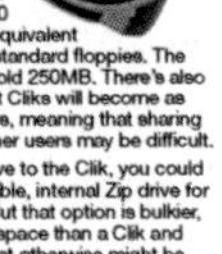
clik!
40

As an alternative to the Clik, you could choose a removable, internal Zip drive for your notebook. But that option is bulkier, occupying more space than a Clik and claiming a bay that otherwise might be used for an extra battery, CD or floppy drive. Personally, I'd prefer the Clik.

The Clik PC Card, which comes with one disk, costs $199.95 US. Additional disks are $9.99 US each when purchased in a 10-pack.

Info: On the Web at **www.iomega.com** or call 1-888-446-6342.

Alan Goldstein, The Dallas Morning News

Importing video the USB way

Personal computers can play videos and display still images, but it takes a special device — such as the USB VideoBus from Belkin Components to transfer those images from a camcorder or VCR.

The USB VideoBus makes importing video to a PC easier than ever. Its composite video jack connects to virtually any camcorder or VCR, and the USB connector goes directly to a PC's USB port. A separate cable is included for simultaneous audio capture using your sound card.

The USB VideoBus complies with Video For Windows standards and is compatible with most video and imaging applications for Windows 98. Belkin provides two of them — MGI PhotoSuite SE and VideoWave SE Plus — to handle all your editing needs.

Using these capable titles, you could easily freeze still images in 24-bit colour or capture full-motion video at up to 30 frames per second, although using this maximum frame rate requires displaying the image in a smaller window.

Laptop users with limited expansion capability and those who don't want to crack open their computer cases to install a capture board can benefit greatly from the USB VideoBus. It sells for about $80 US. Visit **usb.belkin.com** or phone 1-800-223-5546.

Jim Buu, The Dallas Morning News

www.Hot Web Sites

LOOK HERE, SAPPHIRE

www.americansapphire.com

This item actually came to me as former business editor, but it's more fun in the Technology pages. American Gem Corp., celebrates September — sapphire month — with a win your weight in sapphires contest (ok, up to 200 pounds). You can enter on the Web site to win a trip for two to their Gem Mountain, Montana mine to dig for sapphires and tour picturesque countryside around Philipsburg or "dig" through different links on the Web site each day in hopes of finding a sapphire that will be yours at the click of a mouse.

Peter Collum

A FAT LADY REMEMBERED

www.foodtv.com/fn/recipes/reclist/rladies.htm

Food Network star Jennifer Paterson of the *Two Fat Ladies* fame died recently, but her favourite recipes remain online. Visitors can also send a message to the surviving Lady, Clarissa Dickson Wright, from this Web site.

LUCKY MEALS

irishmall.ie/breakfast/irbkrec.htm

Have a hankering for an authentic Irish meal? Visit the Irish Recipes site and get the lowdown on making Pasta with Irish Bacon and Broccoli, Sausage and Mushroom Pie, Traditional Irish Breakfast, and other lucky dishes.

ANGLING FOR ASPARAGUS

www.asparagus.org/consume.htm

Members of the loyal (if not small) asparagus club will appreciate the Michigan Asparagus Advisory Board's recipes for Asparagus Guacamole, Asparagus and Brown Rice Stir-Fry, Asparagus Pizza, Turkey Asparagus Quiche and many other healthful dishes.

Food sites from James Romenesko, KRT

STREAMING VIDEO!

www.video-link.com

Larry at video-link thought you might like to view the company's portfolio. They're streaming video online in Hi-Low Bandwidth selections for Realplayer, NetShow and QuickTime 4. You supposedly can watch some of the summer festivals, they covered most of them since Canada day. You should enjoy the latest addition — "Banff" — it's nine minutes of Real Rockies.

BOORS ONLY NEED APPLY

net.indra.com/~karma/formletter.html

Are you cursed with a tendency toward moronic behavior in your relationships and an inability to explain yourself out of predicaments? A site called Mark's Apology Note Generator is a kind of do-it yourself doghouse-extraction letter-creator geared toward idiotic men.

Using multiple-choice phrases on pull-down menus, the site creates an apology letter that can be e-mailed to a wife or girlfriend for free. (Warning: Skip the link to the women's site. The language is offensive, and content is meager in comparison.)

The site is included in the September issue of *Yahoo Internet Life* magazine's roundup of Incredibly Useful Sites.

Mark Clothier, Cox News Service

VLT Menace

"Perhaps the machines should carry warning labels, as cigarettes do. This is what the labels might say: 'This shiny gambling machine with the nifty video doodads is here to collect taxes. You don't have to pay these taxes, but we're betting (ha ha) that you will, otherwise this machine wouldn't be here.' "

— Editorial, July 6, 1991

The Journal had video lottery terminals pegged for what they are almost from day one when the provincial government installed them at the Klondike Days casino in the summer of 1991 as an "experiment."

Reporter Helen Metella was assigned to the story and concluded on July 26: "They're computer-driven, high-tech gizmos, but the video-lottery terminals at the Klondike Days fairgrounds rake in profits on a principle as old as the shell game."

The technology was new, but the bottom line was known by every casino shill in history – people won't walk away with their winnings. They'll gamble until it's all gone.

The machines were about to become part of the landscape in most bars in Alberta. "More Albertans will be able to try their luck while dousing their thirst when Alberta Lotteries begins installing 3,000 video gambling machines in provincial bars," wrote Florence Loyie on June 19, 1992.

The 3,000 were the first instalment of 8,600 VLTs planned for Alberta watering holes over the next three years. (Actually, public pressure forced the Klein government to cap the number of VLTs at 6,500 in 1995.)

Government lotteries minister Ken Kowalski had said the VLT take would be used to enhance lottery-supported community programs.

An editorial Feb. 2, 1994, said the budget numbers didn't support the minister. "Kowalski speaks about provincial gambling revenue as if almost all of it went to Alberta's charitable and community organizations. Yet of the $1.2 billion collected last year, community groups kept $100 million in earnings from bingos, casinos, raffles and pull-tickets."

When activists started talking about the use of plebiscites to rid their community of the money-sucking machines, *The Journal* hopped on the bandwagon.

Rocky Mountain House was the first, Sylvan Lake the second in a 1996 vote. The VLTs were removed from the towns in 1997.

Thirty-six towns, cities and counties, including Edmonton, held plebiscites in conjunction with the 1998 municipal elections.

Nine voted to ban the machines: Canmore, Coaldale, County of Lethbridge, High Level, Lacombe, M.D. of Opportunity, Rocky Mountain House, Stony Plain and Wood Buffalo.

Bar owners in the communities took the issue to court.

It took more than five years, but in April 2003 the bar owners gave up their challenge and the machines were removed from their towns.

As the May 1, 2003, editorial observed: "In the end, the people won."

***Aug. 21, 1995*:**
***The Journal* trims one inch off the width of the paper.**

***Oct. 16 1995*:**
By a margin of three to one, Edmontonians vote in a plebiscite to close the Municipal Airport to scheduled flights, moving them to an enlarged and renovated Edmonton International Airport.

***Oct. 24, 1995*:**
Steve Ramsankar, principal of Alex Taylor school, wins the prestigious Global Citizens Award from the United Nations. Asked why his principal should be so honoured, Andrew Truong, Grade 3, had the answer: "He's a polite man. He's a very kind man."

***Oct. 24, 1995*:**
Bill Smith is sworn in as mayor of Edmonton after narrowly defeating incumbent Jan Reimer in the recent election. The city's new council members opt to drop the traditional title of alderman for councillor.

***Nov. 3, 1995*:**
Const. Robinder Gill becomes the first Sikh officer of the Edmonton police force to wear the service's official turban.

***Nov. 30, 1995*:**
Edmonton finishes the month with

EDITOR: Bob Remington, 429-5303; golf@thejournal.southam.ca *The Edmonton* **Journal** Thursday, July 8, 1999

Think; Loosen up; Cross your hands; Check alignment: And if that doesn't work try holding your tongue Juussst Ssooo!

10 GOLF TIPS FOR DUFFERS FROM THE PROS

CURTIS STOCK
JOURNAL SPORTS WRITER
Edmonton

TAKE YOUR TIME AND THINK

Tip from Jim Rutledge. Winner of six Canadian Tour victories. Member of two World Cup and two Dunhill Cup teams. Holds Canadian Tour record for most consecutive cuts made —44.

"Too many amateurs get frustrated. They don't think about what they are trying to do. Think about the basics of the golf swing. Whether it's their grip, stance, posture. And take your time getting into that rhythm every time you take a shot.

"A lot of people get up there and just whack it. They're not thinking about what they want to do.

"Do it on the driving range. The golf course isn't the time to practice. On the driving range, get your basic stance of your golf swing and think about them every time you hit the ball on the course."

Tip: Think about a target line. Instead of trying to pick a target 200 yards away, pick a spot a foot in front of your ball where you want the ball to start off on its target line.

Jim Rutledge

Ken Duke

CAN'T PUTT? TRY CROSS-HANDED

Tip from Tyler Rumpel, assistant head pro at Highlands. Won the 1998 Northern Alberta Assistants Tour.

"Cross-handed keeps your hands — especially your left hand — out of the putting stroke a little more than a conventional grip. With a conventional grip they'll get a little too much wrist action going. Especially with their lower hand. Then, the putter cannot stay on line. The face will go all over the place — opening or closing.

"What we tell people to do with cross-handed putting is to lead with your left hand — if you're a right handed golfer — and lead it out to the hole. That will keep the putter on line better than with a conventional grip."

Tyler Rumpel

How to do it: Hold your hands conventionally, taking your normal grip. Now, take your left hand off the putter. Slide your right hand up to the top of the putter and put your left hand low.

You can interlock your fingers. Or overlap your fingers. Or just have a normal 10-finger grip.

"But whatever you do. The key is to keep the left hand going out to the hole at all times. For somebody struggling with the putter or isn't a good putter to begin with, it might help you. I know it really helped me."

A SIMPLE TIP ON HOW TO STOP SLICING

Tip from Rich Massey. Named New Jersey's golfer of the decade: 1980-1990.

"Instead of having the logo (on the ball) running parallel to the target, turn it about 45 degrees toward you. Angle the logo so that your right eye is looking right at it and the number on the ball.

"Now try and hit the logo. The only way you can do it is by coming from the inside of the ball. It will stop you from coming over the top of it.

"Focus on hitting the inside part of the ball. Feel like you are hitting the ball to right field. And that will be the end of your slice.

"My old pro gave it to me as a kid in New Jersey. I don't slice obviously. But sometimes I pull it. This stops me from pulling it."

LOOSEN UP

Tip from Jason Bohn. Won $1 million in a hole-in-one contest.

"What I see in a lot of players is way too much grip pressure on their putter. You can see the veins on their forearms popping out.

"The biggest key to a good putting stroke is really light grip pressure. Barely holding onto the golf club and letting the shoulders and the arms work the club back and forth. A lot of guys get up over those three-foot putts for their pars or their bogeys and they get so tight with their putter that they can't make a good stroke.

"If there is too much pressure you'll pull it or you'll push it. But you won't be able to make a good, smooth stroke at the golf ball.

"It even happens with the pros. Coming down the stretch, they get a little pressure and they really start to grip the putter."

How to do it:

Squeeze the putter three times as hard as you can. On the third time when you release the tension, that's the time to go. Then you know you'll have a loose grip pressure.

"That will help a lot of golfers make those little three footers. From three feet, all it takes is a small, little simple move. Real smooth. Real relaxed."

HOW TO LOWER YOUR HANDICAP BY SIX

Tip from Phil Jonas. Winner of the 1996 and 1997 Peru Open. Winner of the 1990 Goodyear Classic on the South African Tour. Second in three Canadian Tour events.

"The whole key to reducing your handicap is in the short game.

"If you went to a pro and told him you wanted to reduce your handicap by six shots and he took you to a driving range, you're going to the wrong spot. You need to work on your short game.

"If you took an average 8-handicap golfer, paired them up with a pro and then had the pro hit their balls from 50 yards in, that golfer would probably be a four handicap.

"With a 20-handicap golfer, the difference will even be greater. Most 20-handicap golfers can improve their score six shots just by working on their short game.

Jason Bohn

Phil Jonas

"A lot of the problem is in the pace of their swing with their chip shots. It's their stroke that causes their problems. It's either too slow or too fast. They don't chip like a pendulum.

"When you putt, the putter is supposed to go back and through the same distance. In fact, it's the same in all golf shots.

"But a high handicap golfer will take his wedge way back and try to manipulate the speed of the shot on the downward motion."

One way to do it:

Think about throwing a baseball 10 feet. You wouldn't bring your arm back slowly and then suddenly accelerate. And, you wouldn't take your arm back real quick and then try and slow it down just before you released the ball either.

KEEP YOUR HEAD STILL

Tip from Ken Duke, winner of the Payless Classic, second in the Telus Henry Singer, third in the BC Tel; fifth in the Telus Calgary Open.

"The thing I see from a lot of amateur players is they want to see where the ball goes. Keep your head still. With all your shots: driving; mid-irons; short irons and especially putting.

"Even us, if we move our heads when we're putting, it's off-line.

"It doesn't matter where your head is. As long as you keep it still. That's my motto. If I keep my head still, I know I'm going to hit a good shot."

Quick tip: See your divot. Watching the divot on the ground will make sure you keep your head still.

ALIGNMENT CHECK

Tip from Stuart Hendley. Three Canadian Tour wins, also the winner of the 1994 Bermuda Open.

"When I'm playing with my amateur friends, or in Pro Ams, most people are not set up to the ball properly. Their alignment is all off and their set up is all off.

Stuart Hendley

"We all shot 120 when we started. I still remember the day I shot 120. But you can improve and it can start with your set up.

"Setting up properly it's much easier to hit shots consistently. If you set up to the ball properly and you hit a bad shot, it's closer to your target. But, if your alignment is off and you hit a bad shot, it's off in the trees somewhere.

"If you set up to the ball properly, with proper alignment, you will be able to swing the club more naturally."

Quick tip: Put a couple of clubs down on the ground. One aiming at the target. The other aligned with the way your feet are pointing. Are they going in the same direction?

THE REVERSE C

Tip from Perry Parker. Winner of five Canadian Tour events — two last year: the MTS Classic and the Eagle Creek Classic.

"The most common thing I see in amateur golfers is the reverse pivot. They don't know how to shift their weight. On the back swing, the golfer should shift their weight to the right side and on the follow through, the weight should shift to the left side. You want to finish your swing on balance on your left side.

Perry Parker

"A lot of amateurs get their weight on their heels and they shift their weight the opposite direction. They keep it on the left side and they fall back on the right because they can't shift. They're stuck. That causes a blade shot, a chunk shot or a slice."

Quick tip: When you set up and get your balance position, put the weight on the balls of your feet. That's going to allow you to shift your weight onto your right side.

GETTING IT OUT OF THE SAND

Tip from Ray Freeman.

"Take as weak a grip as possible with your left hand. Make sure you hit behind the ball two or three inches. Make your normal swing.

"You want your left hand weak — turning your left thumb pointing left of centre — so you won't have a tendency to close the clubface down and where the club will dig into the sand.

Ray Freeman

"You want to be able to use the bounce of the club. The more the clubface stays open the more bounce you have. You don't want to hit the ball with the clubface out of the sand. You actually want to hit it with the back end of the flange."

THE FEWER MOVING PARTS THE BETTER

Tip from Matthew Lane. Winner of the 1999 New Zealand Open.

"What I see from a lot of Pro Ams is amateurs over rotating their hips on the backswing.

"The club gets way inside and that's why the majority of amateurs hit fades.

"My advice is to try and resist moving your lower body — trying to keep your lower body more stable.

"With less moving parts, you'll be able to get the club more in front.

"Amateurs turn everything. There's far too much movement. It's almost like they start their swing by turning their hips. And when they turn their hips the club goes inside. Then they make a loop and they come over the top.

"With pros the lower body is more stable.

Quick tip: Keep your left heel on the ground.

Puck's Farewell

"I have no idea where the hatred came from. But, boy, it was sure there."
— Peter Pocklington interview, Oct. 20, 2002

Before the bad times, there were good times.

Twenty-nine-year-old Peter Pocklington roared into Edmonton from Ontario in August 1971. He was a car salesman with a "you get the beer and I'll buy the Cadillac" kind of expansiveness that separated the players from the pretenders.

The Journal became interested in him in 1976 when he became co-owner of the Edmonton Oilers.

He raced jet boats, gave money to charity, tipped 15 per cent for good service and had a passion for buying sports teams. He also owned the Trappers baseball club and brought professional soccer to town.

Edmonton liked Pocklington, and Pocklington returned the affection.

"Edmonton is a city of winners," he said Oct. 4, 1979. "The people who come here are winners, they're here because there's always a new challenge or new deal."

But the marriage began to sour in the '80s.

The 1983 collapse of Fidelity Trust, the financial institution he had taken over several years earlier, left Alberta taxpayers holding a $359-million bill. His handling of employees at his Gainers meat plant was viewed unkindly. A long, violent strike there in 1986 didn't help his image.

Selling Oiler superstar Wayne Gretzky to Los Angeles infuriated the city. Pocklington began making incessant demands for concessions for the team, threatening to move it or build his own arena.

By the '90s, his financial empire started to unravel and *The Journal* was there to cover the fall, as it had been there to cover the rise.

In January 1997, he started the process of selling the Oilers to cover some of his debt. A group of local business people scraped up $50 million to ensure the team would stay in Edmonton.

In July 1998, he said he'd had it with Edmonton and was leaving for "greener pastures."

Public reaction was fairly reflected in a Linda Goyette column July 4. "Let him make wine from his sour grapes, and let him drink every last drop of that plonk in any old entrepreneur's paradise he can find. He has called Edmonton's bluff for the last time."

In an interview from his home in Indian Wells, Calif., on Oct. 20, 2002, two years after he left Edmonton, he seemed genuinely in the dark about all the animosity that followed him out of town.

He told sport writer Curtis Stock: "In life, the more good you do the more crap is heaped upon you by the politics of envy.

"No good deed goes unpunished. And all I tried to do was make Edmonton a better community."

55.5 cm of snow, more than three times the average snowfall of 16.3 cm.

***In 1996*:**
Edmonton hosts the World Figure Skating Championships, the World Firefighter Games and the LPGA du Maurier Classic.

***Feb. 27, 1996*:**
All 200 schools in the Edmonton Public School system are hooked up to the Internet. "It's easier to find information on the Internet," said Sarah Cowman, a Grade 5 student.

***March 25, 1996*:**
Edmonton LRT worker Salim Kara is sentenced to four years in prison for theft of $2.3 million from LRT fare boxes.

***Aug. 16, 1996*:**
Canadian Forces ship HMCS Edmonton is launched in Halifax.

***Sept. 5, 1996*:**
AGT Ltd. announces it is changing its name to Telus Communications; Ed Tel, formerly Edmonton Telephones, will become Telus Communications (Edmonton).

***Nov. 12, 1996*:**
Edmonton writer E.D. (Ted) Blodgett wins the Governor General's Award for Poetry in English.

INSIGHT

EDITOR: PETER COLLUM, 429-5340; pcollum@thejournal.southam.ca EDMONTON JOURNAL SATURDAY, DECEMBER 11, 1999

OF FAITH AND FURY, PART ONE / *Wiebo Ludwig's strong religious beliefs led to clashes with his family, his seminary professors, his congregations, the oil industry and his neighbours*

A harsh shepherd

SPECIAL REPORT

In a special two-day report — Of Faith and Fury — *The Journal's* David Staples looks at of one of Alberta's most controversial figures — Wiebo Ludwig, from his boyhood in Central Alberta to his stormy years as an ordained minister.

PART TWO IN SUNDAY READER

Trouble in Trickle Creek: Seeking a sanctuary, Ludwig and his followers instead find conflict and tragedy in the Peace Country.

TRICKLE CREEK

Three years ago, Wiebo Ludwig visited his mother, Mem, at her home in Red Deer. Ludwig hoped to discuss with Mem his view of her supposed failings as a Christian wife and mother.

His main criticism was that Mem and his father Harry had not provided an adequate Christian upbringing for him and his siblings. His parents, Ludwig believed, had been caught up and overwhelmed trying to fit into materialistic, secular Canadian society.

Mem also hadn't properly submitted to Harry's spiritual authority, Ludwig thought, which had caused stress in the family.

The Red Deer meeting was attended by two elders from Mem's church.

Though Mem was 90 years old, she was self-confident and as sharp as ever.

Her own faith in Christ had carried her through the Second World War, the Nazi occupation of Holland, post-war privation and immigration, all the while raising eight children.

Her son's criticisms didn't shake her.

At the end of his visit, Ludwig was left believing Mem didn't want true discussion and repentance, only compromise. He put on his shoes to leave.

The two church elders tried to smooth things over one final time. They asked Ludwig if he would at least give his mom a hug.

At that point, Ludwig recalls, he shook his head. "You know, I would sooner hug a prostitute," he told them. "I think you need to hear that. We're not in agreement. I have some serious things, and you want me to hug you. That makes me feel sick and ucky."

This past summer, in an effort to make amends, Ludwig explained to Mem his outrageous comment wasn't meant to be personal. He ended up kissing her on the forehead.

Mem says she loves her son dearly. "Wiebo is outspoken, that is his personality, but he is honest and has a good heart."

That's how Mem Ludwig loves.

Wiebo Ludwig's love is a much different matter. It's love like a hurricane, fierce and overwhelming.

Ludwig is rude, gutsy, harsh, intolerant of disobedience, emphatic and demanding an emphatic response.

His way of dealing with people has led his own family and followers to dearly love him, to see him not only as a decent and loving father, but as a prophet.

They see him as their leader in a heroic battle against money-loving, secular forces, forces such as powerful oil and gas companies which the Ludwigs believe are poisoning them with pollution.

His followers revere him, the rest of the world doesn't

Ludwig's way, however, has pushed away much of the rest of the world.

Early on, his views led many of his religion professors to oppose his ordination as minister.

"When Wiebo Ludwig was in a leadership role, he would assert his own will, and would allow for no differences of opinion and questions of his authority," says Rev. Mel Hugen, who taught Ludwig at Calvin Theological Seminary in Grand Rapids, Michigan, from 1970-'75.

"It was a pattern we recognized would get him in great trouble in the ministry."

From 1976-1985, Ludwig engaged in bitter conflicts with two congregations, first in Thunder Bay, then Goderich, a small town of 7,500 on Lake Huron.

Many church members could not accept his insistence on obedience to both the husband in marriage and to the male elders in the Christian Reformed Church.

In 1982, Ludwig had a falling out with organized religion, then started to have conflicts with his wife and remaining followers, disciplining them by having their heads shaved and by banishing them at times from their home and families.

At one point, Ludwig and two zealous supporters, Richard Boonstra and Bill Schilthuis, belt-spanked Bill's wife Stephanie, the same woman with whom Ludwig, in admitted weakness, had had an affair.

In 1985, Ludwig moved to a remote farm in northwestern Alberta.

He continued to battle his family and his relatives, then later fought with the oil and gas industry, his neighbours, the RCMP, the court system and the government.

This latest ongoing fight has seen death threats, bombs, criminal charges, a boycott of the Ludwigs' doing business in the Grande Prairie area, and the death of a 16-year-old girl, Karman Willis.

ROB GANZEVELD, FOR THE JOURNAL

Wiebo Ludwig, with his Bible at his home on Trickle Creek Farm, near Hythe.

"The little kids, like myself, spent too much time alone, and a child left to himself, says the Scripture, will bring grief to his mother."

Ludwig, on his childhood

LUDWIG FAMILY PHOTO

Mem Ludwig and Wiebo's eldest brother, John

This past June, Willis was shot while driving with a bunch of friends in two trucks late at night on Ludwig's Trickle Creek property.

The shooting hangs over Trickle Creek and the surrounding towns, haunting people, poisoning their efforts to find peace

"I was just taken up in it. I was very lonely, but during the storm, with the power of the waves, I felt a sense of the power of God, and 'Oh, I'm not so lonely.' "

Ludwig, explaining how he found some meaning to his life

Ludwig, 57 years old now, is unapologetic about his beliefs and methods, his way of firmly putting his hands on people so he can lead them towards his perception of God's love.

This isn't just his little trip, he says.

It's the Bible.

Much of the time, he's tender and patient in his love, he says, but not always.

"You know, the Scripture says, 'He who loves, reproves boldly.' "

"Christianity is not something that puts its arms around everybody and says, 'I love everybody, it's OK, it doesn't matter what you believe.' God judges those who do not believe in him severely. Those who play a pretending game, he judges even more severely."

In the end, his views will be proven right, he believes, because he feels he's led his family to a happy and profoundly Christian way of living.

"Wiebo's not afraid to deal with the brokenness in life," says his wife Mamie.

"A lot of people just like to say, 'Let's love each other and let's have birthday parties and let's have Christmas together and let's forget about our troubles and move on.' But Wiebo isn't that way. He gets into the nitty gritty of life, and a lot of people can't handle that. He wants us to be real."

Storm at sea brought Ludwig a sense of God

When considering Wiebo Ludwig, it's helpful to picture him as he often pictures himself: eighteen years old, struggling to find meaning in life, serving in the Canadian Navy on board HMCS Iroquois in the Caribbean.

A hurricane-force storm blew up one day, he recalls. All the life boats were knocked loose. The ship itself was knocked over several times, only to be righted by the next wave. Most of the men were below deck, but not Ludwig.

He says he braved the storm from the deck.

"Half the crew was puking its guts out and others were scared witless. I didn't think about it myself. I just thought, 'What a wonderful powerful thing.'

"I was just taken up in it. I was very lonely, but during the storm, with the power of the waves, I felt a sense of the power of God, and 'Oh, I'm not so lonely.' "

That was Ludwig: more gutsy and aggressive than other men, but more isolated, hungry for something to fill that hole, so closed off to others that he needed a hurricane to touch him.

He grew up an immigrant kid in Sylvan Lake and Red Deer, not wanting to buy into his new Canadian culture, no longer rooted in his old.

He was the youngest boy of eight children. His family came to Canada in 1952 from Holland, when he was 10. He was gregarious by nature, but shy in front of crowds, which would haunt him into his early years as a minister.

His Grade 3 teacher Canadianized his name to "Bill" and it stuck for decades. Little Bill Ludwig was teased for his Dutch dress and foreign manners at school.

The older Ludwig children went to work to help establish the family. Ludwig's father worked constantly, too, in his tailor shop. Ludwig says he never had much to do with his father, who had been a war hero, a leader in the Dutch resistance.

"The little kids, like myself, spent too much time alone, and a child left to himself, says the Scripture, will bring grief to his mother," Ludwig says.

Has he done that?

"I certainly have, to both my parents. Especially during those years."

His family, Ludwig started to believe, was like so many Dutch immigrant families, dominated by the spirit of materialism.

He was revulsed by that, and by what he saw as his community's nit-picky morals. If one didn't wear a tie and go to church twice on Sunday, that was the thing that was clucked about in the group.

"All this superficial crap!" Ludwig scoffs. "They were throwing their kids to the dogs, not attending to their needs, spending their time making money and trying to have equal status among

Continued on H2

Wiebo Ludwig

"About 200 residents attended the closed-door meeting, shouting bitter epithets at reporters as they came and went from the community hall. 'They're ready to go to the front door right now and do what needs to be done,' said one woman, referring to Wiebo Ludwig's farming commune outside of Hythe."
— Story, June 22, 1999

Reporters weren't popular in the small communities in the Hythe-Beaverlodge area, some 85 kilometres east of Grande Prairie.

Edmonton Journal staff had been looking into the area since February 1997, trying to get to the bottom of an eco-terror campaign seemingly aimed at Calgary-based AEC West that operated a string of sour gas wells near Hythe. Many residents lived in the area simply to enjoy a quiet, somewhat challenging lifestyle. Publicity and notoriety stemming from vandals attacking gas wells was the last thing they wanted.

But on June 21, 1999, the story changed from an investigation of well and equipment damage to one involving the tragic death of 16-year-old Karman Willis.

She had been partying with a group of friends in the bush and wound up joyriding in Wiebo Ludwig's family compound at 4:30 a.m. Shots rang out and Willis was dead, her friend Shaun Westwater wounded.

The mood of the citizens, who were suspicious and fearful of the activist Ludwig clan, was ugly. Intrusive press coverage of the town's grief was certainly not wanted. One television reporter was punched. Others were cursed at on the streets.

How the media and the residents got to this point began Feb. 15, 1997, when *Journal* reporter Adrienne Tanner went to Hythe do a story on vandalism of eight AEC wells in the area. It was the paper's first encounter with Ludwig, patriarch of a religious commune at a farm at Trickle Creek.

Ludwig and his family had a fairly long history of protesting sour gas well activity in the area, claiming pollutants had caused two women to miscarry and farm animals to be born deformed.

"Rev. Wiebo Ludwig simply shrugs and smiles when asked if he or any other of his 27 family members had anything to do with vandalizing the wells that ring his homestead about eight km from Hythe," wrote Tanner.

On April 3, Ludwig was convicted of mischief for spilling malodorous crude oil on a government office floor in Grande Prairie on Jan. 2, 1997.

He was given a conditional discharge as well as some publicity for his protest that sour gas wells in the area were unsafe.

At this point, the story was one of those David and Goliath affairs. Ludwig was defending his family, fighting the polluting oilpatch giant that was backstopped by government and laws that favoured resource developers over landowners.

Feature writer Ric Dolphin wrote a story on the situation Dec. 17, 1998.

"He (Ludwig) compares the situation to 'two men sleeping with the

***Nov. 24, 1996*:**
The Edmonton Eskimos lose the Grey Cup to the Toronto Argonauts, 43-37.

***Feb. 3, 1997*:**
Edmonton's Phoenix Theatre lays off its entire staff and suspends operations as a result of a cash crunch.

***June 14, 1997*:**
The Irish rock band U2 plays before 60,000 fans at Commonwealth Stadium. Rock critic Shawn Ohler is impressed. He calls U2 the best band in the world "unafraid to stir up its own fans and go after new ones with challenging, forward-looking music."

***Sept. 11, 1997*:**
The Edmonton Trappers win a second consecutive Pacific Coast League championship.

***Sept. 13, 1997*:**
The $45-million Francis Winspear Centre for Music officially opens in downtown Edmonton. It's named for the city business leader and philanthropist whose $6-million donation was key to the hall's fundraising drive.

***Sept. 18, 1997*:**
Edmonton's newest TV station, A-Channel, goes on the air from its location in the vacated historic Hudson's Bay

Heaven's Domes

In the last in a three-part series of country drives, we take you to Eastern Rite churches northeast of Edmonton, over some of the prettiest backroads in Alberta. Along the way, smell the wild roses on Eagle Tail Hill, see the coyote cross the road near Cucumber Lake and eat fresh, homemade french fries with Big Bob Herrick at his Maple Tree Grill.

†††

Photographs: Larry Wong, *The Journal*

Nativity of the Virgin Mary Church at Leeshore in Lamont county, above. The copper domes, top left, of the Ukrainian Orthodox Church in Smoky Lake

Judy Schultz
Travel

When I was a kid growing up on the prairies, most villages had two buildings that were architecturally astonishing: the grain elevator and the church with the onion-shaped domes.

Children don't distinguish among denominations until an adult intervenes, so whether the churches were Ukrainian Orthodox, Ukrainian Catholic or Greek Catholic was immaterial to us. The important thing was their strangely beautiful, east-facing, sun-glinting Byzantine domes.

There was something exotic about these churches. They could have come straight from the pages of *The Arabian Nights*, with touches of the Taj Mahal.

Inside, they were even better. There were stars painted in sky-blue ceilings and the choirs sang *a capella*, sweet sad notes in a minor key floating down from the loft built over the back of the nave while the smell of incense and candle wax filled the air.

Today, if not for the faithful few who mow the grass, polish the icons and keep the keys, the churches would smell of dust.

The priests — never enough to go around, even in the days when competing churches were sometimes built side-by-side — are in short supply, and many of the more than 100 Eastern Rite churches are seldom used in the tourist area northeast of Edmonton known as Kalyna Country.

In the village of Chipman, the St. Mary Ukrainian Catholic Church, with its wealth of religious art painted by the famous church artist Peter Lipinski, stands empty most of the time.

"You have to die to get a service in this church now," a woman tells me.

Around the turn of the century, as Ukrainian settlers arrived, the churches were dotted all over northeastern Alberta, from Andrew to nearby Zawale, to Elk Point and Innisfree, Cossack and Ispas, Luzan, Radway, Smoky Lake and Waskatenau. Sometimes three to a village. Sometimes two to a field. The churches often became ideological battlegrounds for different factions, and more than one has gone up in flames, consumed by the unholy wrath of an arsonist.

Assumption of the Blessed Virgin Mary Ukrainian Catholic Church at Star-Peno

Some of the battles reached soap-opera proportions. At Easter in 1899, the Russo-Orthodox Church of the Transfiguration at Edna-Star found both a Catholic and an Orthodox priest on its doorstep, each intent on saying mass. They were soon joined by a sheriff, who arrived to padlock the door. The scrap escalated and finally went all the way to the Privy Council in London, with the result that the Ukrainian Catholic Church of the Asumption of the Blessed Virgin Mary was built just down the road at Star-Peno.

Today, the church at Star-Peno is alive and well, with 58 families in the parish. The plain exterior belies the jewel-box interior, with faux-marble and stone on the lower walls, a beautiful Lipinski icon wall, traditional stencilling around the ceiling and the usual magnificent chandelier suspended above the nave.

St. Mary Ukrainian Orthodox Church at Szypenitz

A number of country churches still hold services on patron saints' days and maybe an Easter mass, and they play host to weddings and funerals.

Those that are open a few Sundays a year, like the beautiful old St. Mary Ukrainian Orthodox Church at Szypenitz, near Two Hills, are lovingly maintained by a handful of parishioners, usually senior citizens.

But the day comes when there's nobody left to look after such treasures. Sadly, the multi-domed Ukrainian Catholic church in Hilliard, long abandoned, had to be taken down three weeks ago to save it from the ravages of repeated vandalism.

A hand-painted icon

The future of these wonderful buildings and of the wealth of liturgical art they contain is uncertain. More than 40 have *iconostasis* painted by the famous religious artist, Peter Lipinski, with his trademark *faux* marble walls and star-studded domes. Others were painted by Wadym Dobrolige, another well-known artist.

While we have them, they're worth a leisurely trip along the backroads.

The days when country churches could be left unlocked are long gone, but there's invariably a citizen in the village who holds the keys.

†††

In Chipman, Helen Sharun stands before the altar of St. Mary Ukrainian Catholic Church, admiring the beautiful *iconostasis*, the wall separating the nave of the church from the sanctuary. She remembers another summer morning 61 years ago, when she stood here for hours, on her wedding day.

CAA
St Demtro
Uk.C.Church
Krakow
R.C.Church
FOR SALE

"No pews then. We stood for the whole service," she remembers. "Hours! And we were wearing new shoes!"

Please see DOMES/K2

same woman' the landholder being the faithful husband; the oil company being the rogue who has his way with her, then turns her back, tarnished, to the husband."

There was little doubt in the minds of local RCMP that Ludwig and his group were responsible for vandalizing wells, but charges against them had been dismissed for lack of evidence.

So the Mounties set up a sting called Operation Kabriole to try to harden their case.

An informant, K4029 (neighbour Robert Wraight) was hired to win the trust of Ludwig and his followers, presumably to elicit confessions.

When mere verbal persuasion failed, the Mounties blew up an AEC shed themselves to help him out.

Ludwig and follower Richard Boonstra were arrested Jan. 15, 1999, for possessing explosives and conspiracy to bomb gas wells.

It took more than a year for the case to wind through court – feelings were so high in Grande Prairie, a judge ordered a change of venue to Edmonton.

The pair was found guilty April 19, 2000, and sentenced April 26. Ludwig got 28 months, Boonstra six.

The editorial about the verdict on April 20 was hopeful.

Some Beaverlodge-area residents were on hand to hear the outcome.

"Those people, many of them wearing buttons that read 'Remember Karman,' were probably less interested in oilpatch vandalism than in the shooting of Karman Willis, the teenager killed last June at Ludwig's farm. No charges have been laid in her death.

"Hopefully, the end of this trial will bring them some relief, and their community some peace. Maybe now they can return to their homes secure in the knowledge that justice has been done."

Police have still not identified the killer of Karman Willis.

store on Jasper Avenue.

***Nov. 17, 1997*:**
Glen Sather is inducted into the Hockey Hall of Fame.

***Nov. 26, 1997*:**
Thelma Chalifoux of Morinville, a 68-year-old Metis educator and activist, is the first aboriginal woman appointed to Canada's Senate.

***Feb. 15, 1998*:**
Edmonton's Pierre Lueders steers Canada's two-man bobsled team to a tie for the gold medal at the Winter Olympics in Nagano, Japan.

***March 5, 1998*:**
***The Journal* announces it has joined a consortium to buy the Edmonton Oilers, committing $1 million for a share. The 37 local investors take over the team from Peter Pocklington and keep it from being moved.**

***Oct. 19, 1998*:**
Bill Smith is re-elected mayor of Edmonton.

***Oct. 19, 1998*:**
Telus and BC Tel merge, with the head office of the new company to be in Burnaby, B.C.

***Jan. 19, 1999*:**
Hollinger takes control of all of Southam Inc., which owns *The Journal*.

EDITOR: Keri Sweetman, 429-5290; travel@thejournal.southam.ca The Edmonton Journal Saturday, May 15, 1999

The Non-stop Weekend

JUDY SCHULTZ
JOURNAL FEATURE WRITER
Edmonton

Every now and then, everybody needs a lost weekend.

That's the one where your significant other calls at noon on Friday, tells you to fling a few things in an overnight bag, and meet him/her at the airport after work.

Your ticket to paradise is a non-stop flight — and that makes all the difference.

No four-hour waits over airport coffee. No pulse-thumping dashes along endless corridors to catch a connecting flight (which could be overbooked, cancelled or already airborne). It happens.

People sometimes complain that they feel isolated in Edmonton, with relatively few direct flights out of the city — compared to, say, Toronto, Vancouver or even Calgary.

So where can you go from Edmonton International, non-stop?

We have a choice of four cross-border destinations and eight Canadian non-stops offering good weekend potential.

Airline fares change faster than the weather. They vary from hour to hour, day to day. If you can stay over a Saturday night, you'll usually save a few bucks on the fare. To avoid confusion, no fares are listed here. Simply ask your airline or travel agent for best available fare. Remember, the canny traveller watches for seat sales and considers charters.

Photo Illustrations: Rick Pape, *The Journal*

KELOWNA

Airline: One-hour flight on WestJet. Leave Friday 4:30 p.m., return Sunday 7:10 p.m.

Best Bets: The beach, the water sports, the arts colony, golf courses, the vineyards for winery tours in the surrounding hills are all good possibilities. Hiking, mountain biking on Knox Mountain and Mission Creek Regional Park. In town, Calona Wines has a good tour with tasting. Lots of sidewalk cafés, coffee houses, summer events. Call the Chamber of Commerce at 1-800-663-4345 for more information. Web site **www.kelownachamber.org**

Splurge Sleeps: Grand Okanagan Resort, 1310 Water Street, tops the list for its downtown lakefront location. The Lake Okanagan Resort, 2751 Westside, is also a luxury choice.

Cheap Sleeps: The Chinook Motel, 1864 Gordon Drive, is a good value at under $100. Or try Le Mission Motor Inn, 579 Trusswell Rd.

Splurge Eats: Le Papillon, 375 Leon Ave.

Cheap Eats: Lena's Pancake and Omelet House, at 533 Bernard Ave.

SEA

SEATTLE

Airline: Horizon Air has two flights daily. Under two hours.

Best Bets: Seattle has the Space Needle, a good zoo, a wonderful aquarium, parks and more parks, the splendid Pacific Science Centre, the original Starbuck's, the Washington Park Arboretum and Japanese Gardens, and a terrific area for strolling and eating — Pike's Place Market, along the waterfront. Yes, the fish-throwing guy is still there. Gray Line of Seattle runs a number of tours. Call Visitor Information at (206)461-5840. Web site **www.seeseattle.org**

Splurge Sleeps: The Alexis Hotel, First Avenue and Madison Street, is elegant, with lots of luxurious touches in the premier suites. The Inn at the Market is also a fine hotel with prices to match. It overlooks Pike's Place.

Cheap Sleeps: The Econo Lodge, 325 Aurora Ave. North. Small, clean, good value. Nothing fancy.

Splurge Eats: Ray's Boathouse, 6049 Seaview Ave. N.W. Great seafood, great view.

Cheap Eats: Salmon Bay Café, 5109 Shishole Ave. N.W. A working man's café with good food at good prices.

MONTREAL

Airlines: Air Canada, under five hours.

Best Bets: The Paris of North America is great fun for a fast visit. A weekend would never be long enough, but the city breathes romance. For a weekend, Old Montreal offers great restaurants, clubs, sidewalk cafés, galleries, plus Notre Dame de Bonsecours, a wonderful church on Rue St. Paul. More clubs and bistros along Rue St. Denis, between Sherbrooke and Maisonneuve. There are four wonderful markets for foodies — Jean Talon, Atwater, Marché de Maisonneuve and the Old Montreal farmers' market. Call 1-800-363-7777 for tourist information. Web site **www.tourisme.gouv.qc.ca**

Splurge Sleeps: Le Chateau Champlain. Historic, charming, European-style.

Cheap Sleeps: Motel Sunrise, just west of Decarie Boulevard at 6120 Rue Saint Jacques Ouest; rooms under $70.

Splurge Eats: Montreal is a city with so many great restaurants that you needn't spend a bundle, but if you have extra cash, these places are definite splurges. In Old Montreal, try Chez La Mere Michel, 1209 Rue Guy; or Chez Queux, 158 Rue Saint-Paul. Downtown there's Le Latini, for an excellent wine list and superb Italian food, at 1130 Rue Jeanne Mance. The Beaver Club, in the Queen Elizabeth Hotel, is old, reliable and expensive.

Cheap Eats: Cage aux Sports, 395 Rue Lemoyne; or Dunn's, 892 Rue Sainte Catherine Ouest. Great smoked meat sandwiches. For more of the similar, there's Ben's, at 900 Maisonneuve West, or Schwartz, at 3895 at Blvd. St. Laurent, right on The Main.

VICTORIA

Airline: WestJet offers morning and evening flights Monday to Friday, 1 hour and 35 minutes.

Best Bets: Take your walking shoes. This city has a tiny, perfect Chinatown. Walk through the Gate of Harmonious Interest and amble along the south side of Fisgard to Fan Tan Alley. Go back to the Empress Hotel, walk down to the harbour and take the harbour ferry to Fisherman's Wharf for lunch.

Do not miss the wonderful Royal British Columbia Museum, at 675 Belleville St. If you have time, the Art Gallery of Greater Victoria, 1040 Moss St., has a clutch of Emily Carr's best work and a small Japanese Garden. Beacon Hill Park is lovely.

Call 1-800-663-6000. Web site **www.travel.bc.ca**

Splurge Sleeps: The Empress, on Government Street. If you can afford the rates here, ask for a room on the front, overlooking the harbour. Otherwise, try the Ocean Pointe Resort, 45 Songhese Rd. If you'd rather stay in a bit of Olde England, check out the Oak Bay Beach Hotel, 1175 Beach Drive. View rooms over Oak Bay, a good pub, afternoon tea.

Cheap Sleeps: The Crystal Court Motel, at 701 Bellville St., is worn but cosy. All the amenities, including kitchenettes, for a small dollar, and it's walking distance to everything.

Splurge Eats: Rent a car and take the 20-minute drive north, to the Aerie, at 600 Ebedora Lane, Malahat. Or drive east about 45 minutes, to Sooke Harbor House, at 1528 Whiffen Spit Road. Frederica and Sinclair Philip are charming hosts and the food is the freshest and most imaginative cuisine you'll find anywhere. Great wine list. Either spot will be memorable. Take LOTS of money.

Cheap Eats: Barb's Fish 'n Chips, on Fisherman's Wharf. Park yourself on the wharf with the fishermen and construction workers, and eat up.

YELLOWKNIFE

Airline: Canadian North and First Air. Six flights daily except Sundays. Flight time is about 1½ hours.

Best Best: Franklin Avenue runs the length of Old Town, Downtown and Frame Lake South. Put on your walking shoes and, as one distinguished guidebook says, "get your behind over to Ragged Ass Road." See Latham Island, The Rock, Peace River Flats and Willow Flats. Frame Lake Trail and Niven Lake Trail are also good bets. For more on tours and celebrations, call Tourist Information at (867) 873-4262. Web site **www.northernfrontier.com**

YZF

ORD

Splurge Sleep: Try the Explorer or the Yellowknife Inn. Both are big, comfortable hotels with lots of amenities.

Cheap Sleep: Bed-and-breakfasts are popping up all over, with about 20 listed. Ask Visitor Information for a list of B&Bs. value at around $65; (867) 873-4786.

Splurge Eats: The Wildcat Café (June 1 to end of August) for caribou bourgignon. For fresh fish and chips, Bullock's Bistro, which has moved from its spot beside the float plane base to Wiley Road. Our Place is also recommended for drinks and dinner. For traditional native dishes, don't miss the Smokehouse Cafe, in Ndilo, just at the end of Latham Island.

Cheap Eats: The Diner, beside the Gold Range Hotel, is the place for big, cheap breakfasts. Very smoky. The Picnic Nook, in the Panda II Mall, is great for homemade soup, sandwiches and take-out.

CALGARY

Airline: Many flights a day, Air Canada, Canadian, WestJet.

Best Bets: The Glenbow Museum and Art Gallery; Heritage Park; the Chinese Cultural Centre; Prince's Island Park, the Eau Claire Market, the Calgary Zoo. For more information, call 1-800-661-1678. Web site **www.tourismcalgary.com**

Splurge Sleeps: The Palliser, a historic hotel right downtown.

Cheap Sleeps: The Savory Lodge, on the Banff Trail.

Splurge Eats: The River Café on Prince's Island. The location is superb. So is the chef.

Cheap Eats: The Stephen Avenue Mall offers more than a dozen food kiosks serving snack-type international fare. More kiosks and cheap eats in the Eau Claire Market.

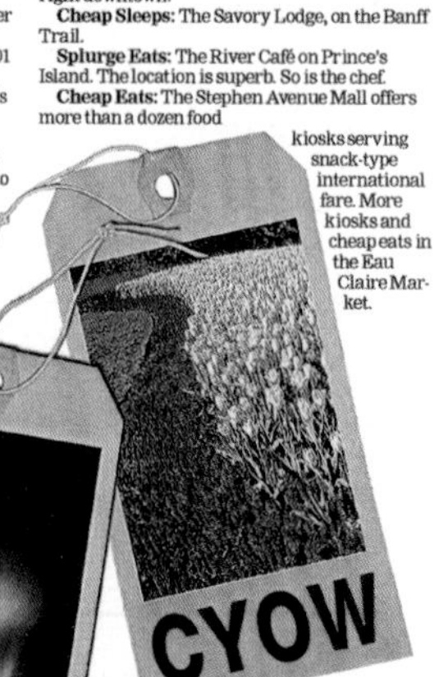
CYOW

MINNEAPOLIS/ST. PAUL

Airlines: Northwest Airlines flies to Minnesota's twin cities. The airport is actually in Bloomington, near the Mall of America, which is a must-see. About a four-hour trip.

Best Bets: Twins they may be, but the two cities have different personalities. Though they share equal access to nearly 1,000 lakes in their vicinity, they are essentially river towns, linked by the winding Mississippi. You think Edmonton and Calgary are rivals? The Twin Cities have been called the Cain and Abel of the Mississippi.

Apart from the obvious charms of lakes and river, St. Paul is the capital city. Both have interesting markets and breweries. Don't miss The Mall. Call the Minnesota Office of Tourism, (651) 296-5029. Web site **www.exploreminnesota.com**

Splurge Sleeps: The St. Paul Hotel in St. Paul; the Hyatt Whitney in Minneapolis.

Cheap Sleeps: Try any Super A — there are several in the Twin Cities area.

Splurge Eats: Kincaid's or D'Amico Cucina. Murray's for steak and romantic atmosphere.

Cheap Eats: Fuddruckers — they're everywhere.

CHICAGO

Airline: Canadian Airlines. The flight departs at 7:50 a.m. and has you on the ground at 12:25 p.m., which gives you the shank of the day in Chicago. Return flight leaves at 3 p.m. and arrives here at a respectable 6 p.m.

Best Bets: The best way to see Chicago is on foot. Get a map at your hotel and start walking or book a walking tour. This city is stuffed with things to see and do. The Sears Tower. Galleries. Museums. Jazz clubs. Do not miss the Art Institute of Chicago, even if you only have a couple of hours to devote to its fantastic collections. The Taste of Chicago is a mammoth street food fair that attracts 3.5 million foodies for 10 days before the glorious Fourth.

Call Chicago Convention and Tourism at (312) 567-8500. Web site is **www.chicago.digitalcity.com/**

Splurge Sleeps: The Fairmont, 200 N Columbus, is opulent with prices to match. Regular rates are a stratospheric $325 US for a double, but a weekend special drops to as low as $129 US. Ask for the special weekend rate. Even ritzier, in the Gold Coast area, the Four Seasons is arguably Chicago's top hostelerie. At $415 US for a double, it should be.

Cheap Sleeps: The Ohio House Motel, at 600 N LaSalle at Ohio. By all reports, it's basic. Period. Rooms start at $75 US for a double.

Splurge Eats: Charlie Trotter's, 816 W Armitage. This place will set you back about $125 US a person for impeccable food, impeccably served. He has 40,000 bottles in his wine cellar. There's a vegetarian tasting menu. Book ahead, hopefully weeks.

Cheap Eats: Pizzeria Uno is where Chicago-style pizza was born. There are several outlets, but go to the original, at 29 E Ohio at Wabash. Or try the Pita Pavilion, 8th floor, Chicago Place., 700 North Michigan. It's mall food with a view.

OTTAWA

Airlines: Air Canada. About four hours.

Best Bets: Parliament Hill, a free tour of the Parliament Buildings, the National Gallery, the museums, the Byward Market area — Ottawa is a small city, easy for walking. If you have a car, visit the beautiful Gatineau Park across the river near Hull. For information, call 1-800-363-4465 for the tourist office. Web site **www.tourottawa.org**

Splurge Sleeps: The Chateau Laurier has character, fine service and good location. The Westin, right next to the Rideau Centre downtown, is also a good bet.

Cheap Sleeps: Call Ottawa B&B, (613) 563-0161 for a list of possibilities. Or there's Days Inn, starting at $65.

Splurge Eats: Chez Jean Pierre, 210 Somerset St. West.

Cheap Eats: Zak's Diner at 14 Byward, near the Market.

Please see WEEKEND/K2

Changing the Guard

"It will take working together across the country, not from the top down, to create a multimedia company that works in practice. Journalists will have more to say and more platforms from which to say it."

— CanWest president and CEO Leonard Asper, Sept. 7, 2000

The Journal newsroom was buzzing when reporters got to work Monday, Nov. 9, 1992.

After 80 years of ownership by the Southam family, corporate giant Conrad Black had acquired effective control of the company and along with it, the careers of thousands of employees.

"In a sudden strike that took his target by surprise, media mogul Conrad Black has acquired 23 per cent of Southam Inc., Canada's largest newspaper chain," said the front-page story.

The Southam family and Torstar Inc. (owners of the Toronto Star) each held about 23 per cent of Southam stock. Black, through his holding company Hollinger Inc., had bought out Torstar's share for $259 million.

Despite the change, *Journal* staff and readers noticed little change in content or policies.

At the corporate level however, things were changing. In a complex deal announced March 20, 1993, $180 million worth of new stock was issued to Power Corp. of Canada, a cash-rich Montreal holding company run by Paul Demarais. Demarais and Black were allies and together controlled 37 per cent of Southam.

Hollinger, on May 24, 1996, bought out Power Corp's interest for $294 million. Black's company now owned 41 per cent of Southam's stock. In August, in a bid to increase his ownership to more than 50 per cent, Black made an offer to all shareholders to buy their stock for $18.75 a share.

By January 1999, Hollinger owned 71 per cent of the company. Black still wanted complete ownership and on Jan. 6 he sweetened the deal to $25.25.

On Jan 20, his quest for the whole pie finally succeeded. Hollinger announced it now owned 94 per cent of the stock – it could force the six per cent of holdouts to sell. Black's empire now included 60 of 105 daily newspapers in Canada and 43 per cent of national circulation. He started the *National Post* in 1997 to compete with the *Globe and Mail.*

The stock chase was over, but not the story. Twenty months later, Black and Hollinger disappeared from the Canadian media landscape almost overnight as once again Southam and *The Journal* changed hands.

Black sold nearly all of his media holdings to CanWest Global Communications, owned by Winnipeg's Asper family, for $3.2 billion. CanWest, until then known primarily for its ownership of the Global television network, became Canada's largest media company and the dominant newspaper publisher.

The deal was announced Aug. 5, 2000, and finalized Nov. 5.

***Jan. 25, 1999*:**
Edmonton and northern Alberta switch to new area code, from 403 to 780.

***Feb. 16: 1999*:**
Edmonton Eskimos football team buys the Edmonton Trappers from Peter Pocklington.

***May 8, 1999*:**
***Journal* editor Murdoch Davis wins a National Newspaper Award for editorial writing.**

***Sept. 29, 1999*:**
***The Journal* gets a design makeover, adopting a new nameplate, new typefaces and new content and features.**

***Nov. 22, 1999*:**
Wayne Gretzky is inducted into the Hockey Hall of Fame (without the usual waiting period after retirement).

***Dec. 2, 1999*:**
Edmonton's first Mormon temple opens for public tours before it is dedicated Dec. 11 and 12, making it the second in Alberta since the historic Cardston temple in southern Alberta was built in 1923.

EDMONTON JOURNAL

SPECIAL EDITION:
ATTACK ON AMERICA

www.edmontonjournal.com | EDMONTON'S NEWSPAPER SINCE 1903 | TUESDAY, SEPTEMBER 11, 2001

TERRORISTS CRASH SECOND HIJACKED JETLINER INTO NEW YORK'S WORLD TRADE CENTRE

Terrorism hammers America: 12 pages of Special Coverage

FIFTY CENTS

NEW YORKERS FLEE

Associated Press, Suzanne Plunkett
People run from the collapse of World Trade Centre Tower on Tuesday in New York.
2

PENTAGON STRUCK

Associated Press, Will Morris
Flames and smoke pour from a building at the Pentagon in Washington, D.C., after a direct, devastating hit from an aircraft.
8

AIRPORTS CLOSE

John Lucas, Edmonton Journal
Passengers exit from an Air France flight diverted to Edmonton after all the U.S. airports were closed.
11

ELEVEN

Chris Schwarz photo

Sarah Hauck was one of hundreds of Edmontonians who signed a petition on the steps of the legislature, protesting violent retribution for the Sept. 11 terrorist attacks in the United States.

Millennium Madness

2000 to 2003

"Canadians, who share with the United States this once-safe continent, know that those jetliners could have come down in Toronto, Edmonton or Vancouver. The closure of our airports and the U.S. border were chilling reminders that we are also under threat. No one can feel as safe today as they did before this happened."
— Editorial, Sept. 12, 2001

A dozen *Journal* reporters, columnists and editors watched the bank of newsroom televisions in shock shortly after 8 a.m. on Tuesday, Sept. 11, 2001. They were seeing their world change.

***Feb. 10, 2000*:**
Lois Hole is installed at the legislature as Alberta's 15th lieutenant-governor.

***March 4, 2000*:**
The University of Alberta Pandas win a record-tying sixth straight

ed
the magazine
COVER STORY
YOUNG GUYS TAKE A CHANCE / 6-7
jennifer
local mogul star
catches some air – 3
mari
on twindom and
turning 30 – 5,11

Photo of Connor Wollis at Baccarat Casino by Ian Jackson

Most had already learned of the terrorist attack on New York's World Trade Center from early radio reports. From the scant details available they knew that a hijacked American Airlines Boeing 767 had been rammed into the 110-storey North Tower at 6:45 MDT.

An updated report 18 minutes later reported hijackers had crashed a United Airlines Boeing 767 into the South Tower of the Trade Center.

The news quickly got worse. Three-quarters of an hour after the South Tower was in flames, another American Airlines jetliner, this time a Boeing 757, slammed into the Pentagon in Washington, D.C., setting it afire, too.

Twenty-five minutes later, a United Airlines Boeing 757 plunged into a farmer's field in rural Pennsylvania, killing all on board.

Shortly after 8 a.m., the reporters and editors watched the South Tower collapse, followed 20 minutes later by the North Tower.

While the newsroom is often a raucous, occasionally even profane place, it was deathly quiet that morning. Watchers were stunned into silence by the images on television.

Among them was publisher Linda Hughes, who made the decision to publish *The Journal*'s first extra edition in decades. She knew, that while readers might be glued to their television sets all day, the reality of the horror would come only when readers could hold a newspaper in their hands and ponder what had happened.

Deadlines were shifted for feature sections to make way for the mid-afternoon special edition even as the next day's paper was being put together. Editors began choosing the best from the hundreds of stories and photographs pouring in from wire services.

As local reporters started to work on stories on the impact the assaults were having on Edmonton, wire stories pointed to a shadowy terrorist organization known as al-Qaeda, led by the enigmatic, Saudi-born Osama bin Laden, as responsible for the co-ordinated hijackings.

Unspeakably tragic as the attacks were on Sept. 11, 2001, it was the kind of day that brings out the best in journalists. It brought with it the drama of earth-shattering events, pressing deadlines and the necessity of providing quick, accurate coverage for readers.

Calls began to flood into the newsroom. Former *Journal* technology writer Andy Walker, on his way to a conference in Manhattan, was at La Guardia airport on Long Island when he telephoned.

"You could smell the city burning," he told reporter David Staples.

Entertainment writer Todd Babiak managed to contact a friend who was scheduled to take a course in an office building near the Trade Center.

"I'm in a state of disbelief," Babiak's friend said. "All I know is that sitting in Calgary or Edmonton you see these things happening in other places. Now I'm in New York. I'm in that other place."

Reporters that morning also went to the International airport to interview passengers from U.S. and international flights that had been ordered out of North American skies. The grounded passengers crowded the city's hotels as they waited two days for the flight ban to be lifted.

Journal writer Jeff Holubitsky quizzed schoolteachers on how they would calm the fears of their students and explain the attacks. Most schools maintained regular schedules, although all set aside time to address

Canadian university volleyball championship.

***March 26, 2000*:**
University of Alberta Golden Bears win the CIAU hockey championship.

***April 2, 2000*:**
It's the last day traffic runs through the 109th Street Rathole. The underpass was built in 1927.

***May 12, 2000*:**
***Journal* photographer Chris Schwarz wins the 1999 National Newspaper Award for feature photograph.**

***May 18, 2000*:**
University of Alberta researchers announce the success of the Edmonton Protocol an experimental treatment for diabetes involving transplanting insulin-producing islet cells into severe diabetics.

***July 22, 2000*:**
Raymond Lemieux, an award-winning chemist considered the grandfather of Alberta's biotechnology industry, dies at age 80.

***July 31, 2000*:**
Conrad Black (Hollinger Inc.) sells almost his entire stock of Canadian

SECTION F

The new Garden Sensations salads recently introduced at Wendy's are truly a meal in a bowl. The mandarin chicken salad, $5.99, is a big mixed green salad with lots of variety, plus cubes of marinated chicken and mandarin oranges. Comes with packages of sliced almonds, crisp rice noodles and a delicious sesame seed dressing. The BLT chicken salad ($5.99) and the taco supremo salad ($4.99) are also good bets. At all Wendy's in Edmonton.
— Judy Schultz

Dishing

JOURNAL **BISTRO**

Valentine's Day
February 14th
Order today!
DEBAJ'S
7115-109 Street 496-9559

EDITOR: BARB WILKINSON, 429-5374; living@thejournal.southam.ca

WEDNESDAY, FEBRUARY 13, 2002

Lewd Food

FOOD express

Popovers for breakfast?

Try French's Yorkshire Pudding mix. Add an egg and a bit of oil, beat the batter, pour it into six large muffin tins and fling it in a hot oven. Twenty minutes later — voila! Six popovers, crunchy outside, soft within. The flavour and texture are just as good as the scratch version.

A 45 g pouch for around $1.25 at IGA and other supermarkets.

PHOTOS BY BRUCE EDWARDS, THE JOURNAL

Getting the scoop

Melon ballers are handy for lots of things, including sample-sized servings of ice cream. Try three flavours in the same dish, drizzled with chocolate sauce. Available from Le Gnome in West Edmonton Mall in many sizes and themes, including one with a melon for a handle. From $2.95 to around $15.

Fresh and fizzy

Bottle Green brand, slightly sweetened, this is spring-water flavoured with lemongrass and ginger. Serve over ice with a lemon slice. Around $4 at supermarkets that carry it.
— *Judy Schultz*

LINDEMANS
HUNTER VALLEY
SHIRAZ
BIN 9003

BRUCE EDWARDS, THE JOURNAL

WINE PICKS

■ FABIANO VERONESE BIANCO GRAN SOLE, VENETO, ITALY, NO VINTAGE SPECIFIED, $8.95.

Sorrentino restaurants are featuring the cuisine and wine from Veneto this month and selected this wine. But it will be on the market everywhere in March. It's a zesty blend of trebbiano and garganega grapes and great with lighter dishes, such as salads, unadorned fish dishes and pasta with olive oil.

■ MONDAVI COASTAL PINOT NOIR, CALIFORNIA, 1999, $18.95.

A medium-bodied wine with vibrant black cherry and blackberry fruit that's perfect with a wide range of food, from salmon to steak. It's on many local restaurant wine lists and Mondavi is donating 50 cents from every Coastal, Woodbridge Napa red wine sold this month in participating restaurants to the Heart & Stroke Foundation.

■ LINDEMAN'S HUNTER VALLEY SHIRAZ, AUSTRALIA, 1995, $22.95.

Here's a drink-now complex drop of shiraz from one of Australia's hotter regions. The plums and spice on the nose are continued on the palate. Some may find it a tad austere for an Aussie shiraz, but it's a good choice with steaks, roasts and game. Lindeman's is an official Canadian team sponsor at the Winter Olympics.

— Nick Lees, Journal wine writer

CHEF COOKS AT HOME

Chef Thomas Hennig, TASTY TOM'S

JASON SCOTT, THE JOURNAL

No two days are alike at Tasty Tom's. Owner and chef Thomas Hennig says the best way to keep his customers from getting bored with the menu is to keep himself from getting bored with it, too.

"I don't want to just serve one thing all the time," says Hennig. The special could be a German dish one day, Thai the next. "I'm also eating here, too, don't forget. And when people come in they expect different stuff."

Hennig gives his patrons a lot of say in what is served. "They rule. They are the ones who run my business." He says customer response keeps him "pumped" about cooking and keeps his menu varied. Most of the people who dine at Tasty Tom's are regulars who know what they want.

Hennig says experimenting with new foods and tastes is what he loves most about cooking for people.

But his approach is entirely different when he cooks for himself.

"I don't cook at home anymore," says Hennig. He works such long hours that by the time he gets home, making an elaborate meal is the last thing on his mind. "I look for the simplest thing. If I'm hungry I think, 'What can I eat really quick?'"

Hennig keeps jars of homemade pastes in his fridge for making quick meals. A yellow curry paste is a feisty favourite in his home. He often adds it to rice or stir fry for extra spicy flavour.

See CURRY PASTE / F2

Judy Schultz
Food

Ever since Adam and Eve had their little tryst in the garden, human beings have been on the lookout for the ultimate aphrodisiac.

Too bad that every time they thought they'd found it, some miserable killjoy jumped up and tried to stop the fun.

Irene Cabanas, a marketing representative for the California Avocado Information Bureau, says her favourite fruit was once forbidden fruit.

"The Aztecs considered avocados to be a powerful sexual stimulant," she says.

They locked up their daughters while avocados were being harvested, though we're not sure whose virtue was being protected here, the guys or the girls. And did you actually have to eat it, or did just handling it count?

PHOTOS SUBMITTED

The Aztecs thought avocados were a powerful sexual stimulant, and they would lock up their daughters while avocados were being harvested.

The early Christian missionaries didn't help the situation. They took one look at the avocado's sensuous contours and smooth, buttery flesh and declared it to be lewd food. Banned. Off-limits, because of those "erotic undertones."

And the result? Guacamole is everybody's favourite dip.

Especially for lovers and wannabes, try our French Kiss Guacamole, laced with a dash of dry vermouth. No vermouth in the pantry? Use gin. Both are made with aromatic spices that punch up their erotic rating.

Sexy Popcorn

Popcorn fans, take note: Your favourite snack has made the list of aphrodisiacs that are most fun to eat.

That's right, movie lovers. Along with oysters, avocados, eggs, caviar and chocolate, popcorn is now sexy.

It's a rare vegetable source of the amino acid L-arginine, referred to as a "sexy nutrient" by Ian Marber, co-author of *In Bed with the Food Doctor.*

Marber calls L-arginine the "natural Viagra."

"It works by increasing the body's levels of a chemical called nitric oxide, which acts as a nerve transmitter, increasing blood flow to the penis," says Marber.

He doesn't say how many buckets of Orville Redenbacher it would take to give the libido a good zap.

But he does give us a food shopping list, starting with a dozen oysters and a bottle of champagne, for a sexy weekend.

Recipes on F2

MORE LIBIDINOUS TREATS

Along with bee pollen, royal jelly, evening primrose, blue-green algae, dong quai, and the oddly-named chaste berry, the following are named by Ian Marber and Vicki Edgson as natural aphrodisiacs.

- SIBERIAN GINSENG: This energy booster increases honey production in bees, milk secretion in cows and sperm count in bulls.
- YERBE MATE: An herbal tea made from tree bark, rich in minerals that boost short-term energy and efficient blood flow.
- YOHIMBE: More tree bark tea. Increases blood flow to the genitals, improves strength and enhances overall sensitivity.
- SARSAPARILLA: Contains hormone-like compounds that form the basis of some synthetic hormones, including testosterone.
- SAW PALMETTO: Another tree, this one from the West Indies. Contains substances regulating hormonal stimulation of the prostate gland.

concerns that students might have. Fearing an anti-Arab backlash, the private Edmonton Islamic School kept students indoors during both recess and noon hour.

While the terrorist attacks forced stock markets to close, energy writer Dave Finlayson reported on the beefed-up security in local refineries and along the all-important oil and gas pipeline system.

Indeed, one executive compared the oilpatch alert to the precautions taken in the face of the millennium bug, a predicted international computer meltdown that was to have occurred at midnight on Dec. 31, 1999.

That had been a dud; 9-11 was all too real.

And it was the defining event of the still-young decade.

The newspaper's editorial position was clear the day after the attacks. "The response to this monstrous act must be commensurate with the magnitude of the attack. The hunt for those responsible should be relentless and uncompromising."

By mid-November, the U.S. response to the attacks was outlined by President George W. Bush, who put the focus on Afghanistan as the first target in his declared all-out war on terrorism.

Canada immediately volunteered 2,000 troops to help ferret out bin Laden and his al-Qaeda cohorts and rout the Islamic fundamentalist government that was hiding them.

"Virtually from the moment the dust began to settle Sept. 11, it was clear the nature of government in countries nurturing terrorists was as important in the long run as capturing the current crop of killers," said an editorial.

"Edmontonians should be proud our own Princess Patricia's Canadian Light Infantry will form the core of our initial effort."

Once again, the city was sending servicemen and women who called Edmonton home to a dangerous and deadly hot spot on another continent, and in the following months there were dozens of stories, photos and maps that brought home to the readers the hardship and bravery of the Canadian armed forces. The most tragic story, however, appeared on April 18, 2002.

The day before, an American F-16 jet mistakenly dropped a 500-pound, laser-guided bomb on a unit of soldiers from the PPCLI engaged in night exercises.

Edmonton had to say goodbye to the four young soldiers killed: Sgt. Marc Leger, 29, Pte. Richard Green, 22, Pte. Nathan Smith, 27, and Cpl. Ainsworth Dyer, 25. Six others were wounded in the friendly fire incident.

More than 16,000 Edmontonians joined national and provincial leaders at Skyreach Centre for a nationally broadcast memorial service on April 28.

Columnist Paula Simons put the country's grief into perspective. "We sent these men to Afghanistan to fight our battles for us. To keep us safe. We sent them, too, to uphold our battered sense of national pride and honour.

"Now, their blood is on our hands.

"And, yes, we were naïve. I think we are so cozy, so many generations removed from the reality of the battlefield, that we had honestly forgotten the first truth of war – that young men die."

newspapers, including *The Journal*, to Winnipeg-based CanWest Global Communications for $3.5-billion, one of the biggest deals in Canada's media history.

***Aug. 15, 2000*:**
Murdoch Davis leaves his post as editor-in-chief of *The Journal* after eight years. He is replaced by Giles Gherson, editor-in-chief of Southam News and political editor of the *National Post*.

***Sept. 13, 2000*:**
Edmontonian Bob Steadward is elected to the International Olympic Committee.

***Nov. 13, 2000*:**
***Journal* sports writer Jim Matheson, who has written about pro hockey in Edmonton since the Oilers were founded in 1973, is inducted into the Hockey Hall of Fame in the media category.**

***March 21, 2001*:**
Canadians Jamie Sale and David Pelletier, who live and train in Edmonton, win a gold medal at the World Figure Skating Championships.

***July 1, 2001*:**
Canada Day riot on Whyte Avenue results in numerous arrests by city police.

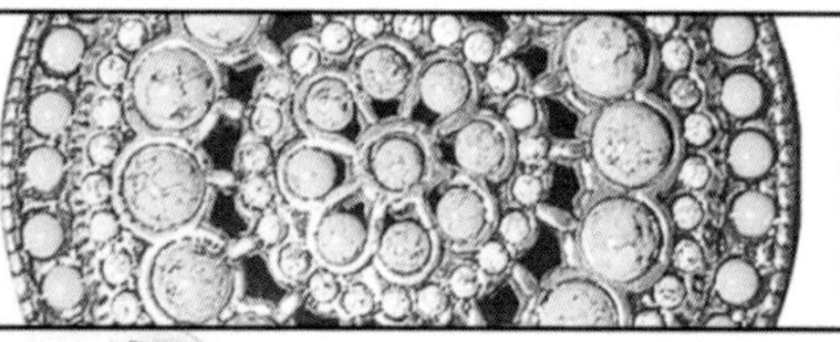

shopping tip

The cerulean casts of turquoise have been a part of Native American tradition for thousands of years but have struggled to become a fixture in mainstream fashion. Until recently, that is.

It's time to revisit the old high school jewelry case because your favourite turquoise accessories are enjoying a healthy comeback. Over the past two years, stars such as Cameron Diaz — who insisted on wearing a $1,200 Lena Wald turquoise ring from her private collection for *The Sweetest Thing* — have been flaunting the primordial stone of the Southwest.

When shopping for turquoise, understanding its unique hues is paramount. The blue in turquoise is enhanced when there is lots of copper present, making it a popular, earthy choice. If the mining site contains more aluminum, the turquoise will shade to green, a hue favoured by many natives of Santa Fe. When zinc is present, the deposits are a yellow-green colour, a rare combination found only in select areas, such as the Carico Lake and Orville Jack mines in Nevada.

— Misty Harris

SECTION E

JOURNAL LOOK

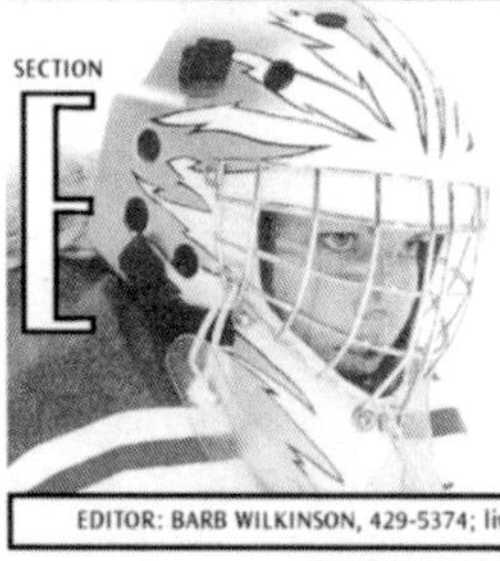

Woman of Vision: Shannon Szabados / E3

EDITOR: BARB WILKINSON, 429-5374; living@thejournal.southam.ca EDMONTON JOURNAL TUESDAY, NOVEMBER 5, 2002

GEAR

STEVE MAKRIS
Journal Technology Writer
EDMONTON

The new Java-based BlackBerry 6710 from Rogers AT&T, starting at $749, will happily replace your cellphone, personal organizer, messenging and Web browsing devices.
The wireless, dual-band-frequency, handheld device works in GSM/GPRS networks in North America, Europe and Asia Pacific and combines your phone calls and e-mails allowing you to keep in touch with other cellphone or landphone users and e-mail from Internet-connected computers. The integrated speaker/microphone, which also works without headphones, and removable battery can keep you on the road and in touch for weeks at a time. Includes the BlackBerry Web Client, which allows you to access multiple existing e-mail accounts, including ISP (Internet Service Provider) accounts. Features bright screen and keyboard backlight and a plug-in SIM card for multiple accounts. Monthly rates for the data (e-mail) service start at $40, in addition to the cellphone service, which starts at $20. For more info go to: www.rogers.com

RODE-HAUTE

HOW THE WEST WILL BE WORN

Denim skirt, $68, Stretch cord jacket, $78 both from The Gap

Plaid shirt, $13, denim jacket, $78, bootcut jean, $49.50, all from The Gap; western boots, $195, from Holt Renfrew; cowboy hat, $90, from Lammle's

MISTY HARRIS
Journal Staff Writer
EDMONTON

Legendary cowboy Billy the Kid would likely fire off a few rounds to salute this season's rebellious fusion of outlaw appeal with giddy-up glamour. Possessed by an insatiable wanderlust for the great southwest, designs with a western flair are sweeping the country in a prairie storm of vintage denim, embroidery and opulent Indian prints.

Just in time to cash in on country chic, Canadian Finals Rodeo kicks off Wednesday in Edmonton and runs until Nov. 10. The event will marry urban cowgirls with honky tonk cowboys in a spectacular showing of Wrangler jeans and cowhide leather coats, prairie skirts and tall barrelled boots.

"Western is now a lifestyle, it's fashion, it's something that's tasteful," says Doug Lammle, president of Lammle's Western Wear. He breathes a sigh of relief that the days of the retro-cowboy with coloured boots, fringe and satin are dead.

See RODEO / E2

Shot on location at Longriders, 11733 78th St. Styling by James Kershaw

HOUSE & HOME

Huckleberry and Chin

Antique-store addicts who have grown accustomed to the musty odour of overcrowded shelves brimming with old wood, freshly oiled metals and dusty heirlooms may be surprised when they get a whiff of Huckleberry and Chin. Although the successful chain of stores deals in antiques, its look — and smell — is far from antiquated.

Huckleberry and Chin could be the lovechild that resulted from a romantic affair between a florist and an antiques dealer. The stunning store combines the Gaussian appeal of myriad flower arrangements with the nostalgia of knick-knacks from days past, costume jewelry and vintage home decor.

LARRY WONG, THE JOURNAL
Elf doll,$263.99, at Huckleberry and Chin, in The Bay, City Centre

"I've been to antique stores with my mom and they can be so dirty and grungy and you don't want to move because you're afraid something is going to collapse," says Michele Aylwin, owner of the store. "We add in a lot of giftware and flowers and it gives it more of a comfort look."

Back in 1993, Huckleberry and Chin had its humble beginning in a 500-square-foot store across from Turtle Creek Cafe. Not six months after opening its doors, H & C outgrew the space and uprooted to a larger location.

Word about the little-store-that-could spread like wildfire and Aylwin was eventually contracted to do some display work for the Bay at Southgate. When customers started making offers to buy the stunning centrepieces she designed, Aylwin's services were enlisted on a more permanent basis by the retail empire.

"We started off small in Southgate and it did really well, so we opened up a full store downtown," she says. "I still like the small business idea, so I'm not into franchising. But I do want (stores in) all of Alberta."

Huckleberry and Chin currently has outlets in the Bay at Edmonton Centre and downtown Calgary in addition to a stand-alone store on Whyte Avenue. The prices are competitive, ranging from $10 to $10,000, depending on the rarity and quality of the antique.

"We started off just selling little things," Aylwin says fondly. "And now, well, we're not an empire but our business has quadrupled."

— *Misty Harris, Journal Staff Writer*

LOOKING GOOD

LARRY WONG, THE JOURNAL

SAMANTHA KING, 17, IS A HOMETOWN GIRL WHOSE DEBUT COUNTRY-WESTERN CD HITS STORES THIS WEEK. SHE WILL BE PERFORMING AT FARM FAIR AND CANADIAN FINALS RODEO.

★ HOW DOES COUNTRY MUSIC INFLUENCE THE WAY YOU DRESS? Definitely the cowboy hat has to be there. I think the whole Wranger-wearing, neutral coloured, cowboy hat thing goes together so well and that's what makes country music so cool.

★ HOW CAN YOU RECOGNIZE A COUNTRY GIRL IN EDMONTON BY STYLE ALONE? Just by the way she'll wear jeans with a really cool top and warm colours. It's very classic and you can add so much to it with leather and jean.

★ WHAT FASHION LOOKS ARE YOU INTO RIGHT NOW? I'm into the more fun thing, the flashy look. I'll wear a hat with Wranglers, but I'll add a really cool blouse, colourful vest or jacket to dress it up. Today, my whole outfit is from Lammle's but I also mixed in this shirt from Le Chateau.

★ WHAT IS YOUR FAVOURITE THING TO WEAR TO FEEL CONFIDENT? I have to wear things that I'm comfortable in, like jeans and a T-shirt. It makes you feel confident that you can do anything you want, from shopping to school to going out and having fun.

★ COUNTRY DRESSING HAS A REPUTATION FOR BEING OVER-THE-TOP. WHAT DO YOU THINK? Country has always had a different touch about it. But I think it's becoming more modern and they're taking away the decals and going for something a little more mainstream.

★ WHAT SHOULD A TRUE COUNTRY GIRL NEVER BE WITHOUT? She can't be without her cowboy hat and Wranglers. I'm one for long earrings that will stand out with my outfit. If I'm going to a rodeo, I have to have dangling earrings on.

★ WHAT DO YOU THINK OF THE OSBOURNES' FAMILY STYLE? I don't know if I'd ever go for the black capes, but he's got some cool music and he'll always be there for me as a singer.

★ WHO ON THE COUNTRY MUSIC SCENE HAS THE HOTTEST LOOK RIGHT NOW? Shania Twain has a pretty cool touch. Her style is in between pop and country, which makes it attractive to most people.

Misty Harris, Journal Staff Writer

The threat of death continued. Canadian peacekeepers patrolled an unsettled Afghanistan. Bin Laden had not been caught and Taliban and al-Qaeda elements continued to attack peacekeeping forces.

After Afghanistan, the Americans turned their attention to Iraq, launching an attack on that country on March 19, 2003.

Canada chose not to participate in the war as one of President Bush's "coalition of the willing."

The Journal disagreed with Prime Minister Jean Chretien's decision to support the United Nations' stand that nothing should be done until further inspections for weapons of mass destruction were conducted.

"He has said the war is at best preventable and at worst premature, although he has also said he 'respects' the U.S. action. Many Canadians, and Albertans, support the Prime Minister," said the March 20 editorial.

"We believe he made the easier, cautious choice but not, on balance, the right one – The (U.S.) will draw its own conclusions about Canada's steadfastness as an ally, and treat us accordingly. Given our overwhelming economic and security reliance on the U.S., our core national interests are dangerously exposed. And for what?"

It was hard to believe on that terrible day in September 2001, when the world seemed to change forever, that, only a month before, the newspaper had been devoting pages daily to an event that proved once again Edmonton deserved its reputation as a city that could get things done. With the success of the Commonwealth Games in 1978 and the Universiade in 1983, the city, not surprisingly, embraced the 2001 World Track and Field Championships that took place in August.

"Our community fell on some hard times in the '80s and early '90s," said WTFC organizer Jack Agrios in a year-end look-back story that ran Dec. 26, 2001.

"This event helped restore our pride. Not only are we good, we know we're good, and we've demonstrated to the world that we're good."

The 10-day event had all drama, triumph and controversy of an Olympics. And when aging Canadian Olympic gold medallist and 100-metre sprinter Donovan Bailey finished a poor sixth in the semi-final on Aug. 6, the crowd and the other athletes on the track still acted as if they knew they were in the presence of greatness.

"When Donovan Bailey walked around the Commonwealth Stadium track for one final lap, the youngsters stopped their strutting around and gave Bailey his final moment on the world stage," wrote sports columnist Mark Spector.

The city seemed to shake off some of the gloom of 9-11 with the approach of Christmas.

Lights went up on houses and commercial buildings, and Edmontonians seemed determined to find some peace on Earth in the holiday season.

There was, however, a tempest on Dec. 14, when *The Journal* broke the story that an apparently intoxicated Premier Ralph Klein had made a midnight visit to the city's downtown Herb Jamieson Centre and argued with the homeless men in the centre's lobby.

***July 22, 2001*:**
Edmonton hosts the World Triathlon Championship, with the swim portion taking place in the pond in Hawrelak Park

***Aug. 3, 2001*:**
World athletics championships open in Edmonton.

***Sept. 11, 2001*:**
***The Journal* publishes a special 12-page afternoon edition on the terrorist attack on the United States.**

***Oct. 15, 2001*:**
Bill Smith is the first mayor to win a third three-year term (earlier multi-term mayors elected to one- or two-year terms); Ron Hayter wins record ninth-council term.

***Dec. 17, 2001*:**
Alberta Premier Ralph Klein vows to "control and curb" his drinking after confronting residents of an Edmonton men's shelter during a late-night visit.

***Jan. 7, 2002*:**
The 750 Edmonton-based soldiers are sent to Afghanistan, heading into the nation's first combat assignment since the Korean War.

***March 3, 2002*:**
The University of Alberta Pandas win the Canadian Interuniversity women's hockey championship.

RELAYS

The grande finale of the World's, the relays, can lift spectators out of their seats and forge countrymen in the record books — the one event that features simultaneous races between individuals and teams.

Even Marion Jones has become a fan.

"I have fallen in love with the 1,600 relay," America's golden girl said of the 4 x 400 relay.

Jones said months ago she wasn't going to compete in the long jump in Edmonton but would run with the relay team. She'll also compete in the 100- and 200-metre sprints and will no doubt anchor the 4 x 100 relay entry.

The 4 x 100 calls for the utmost precision because the baton must be handed off at top speeds in a limited zone. For the men, that could be less than two seconds. Any changes made outside the box will result in disqualification while bungled exchanges will slow down the fastest of teams.

In the 4 x 400, tactics are more important than changeovers.

IN THE BLOCKS

Saturday, Aug. 11, 2:35 p.m. — First round, women's 4 x 100
3:10 p.m. — First round, men's 4 x 100
4:15 p.m. — First round, women's 4 x 400
4:40 p.m. — First round, men's 4 x 400
5:40 p.m. — Final, women's 4 x 100
Sunday, Aug. 12, 3:15 p.m. — Semifinal, men's 4 x 100
4:20 p.m. — Final, men's 4 x 400
4:40 p.m. — Final, women's 4 x 400
5:10 p.m. — Final, men's 4 x 100

MEN's 4 x 100 WORLD RECORD, 37.40
USA, 1992 — Michael Marsh, Leroy Burrell, Dennis Mitchell, Carl Lewis
USA, 1993 — Jon Drummond, Andre Cason, Dennis Michell, Leroy Burrell

WOMEN's 4 X 100 WORLD RECORD, 41.37
GDR, 1985 — Silke Gladisch, Sabine Rieger, Ingrid Auerswald, Marlies Gohr

MEN's 4 x 400 WORLD RECORD, 2:54.20
USA, 1998 — Jerome Young, Antonio Pettigrew, Tyree Washington, Michael Johnson

WOMEN's 4 X 400 WORLD RECORD, 3:15.17
USSR, 1988 — Tatyana Ledovskaya, Olga Nazarova, Maria Pinigina, Olga Bryzgina

CANADA
Atlanta
CAN

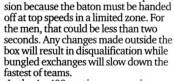

THE CANADIAN PRESS, FILE
Canadian sprinter Bruny Surin hands off the baton to teammate Donovan Bailey during preliminary heats of the men's 4x100-metre relay race at the 1996 Olympic Games in Atlanta, Georgia.

ON THE PODIUM

Men's 4 x 100
1. USA — Tim Montgomery, Bernard Williams, Dennis Mitchell, Maurice Greene
The world title is already theirs.
They won't drop the ball, er, baton here.
2. Brazil
3. Jamaica

4 x 400
1. USA — Antonio Pettigrew, Leonard Byrd, Jerome Young, Angelo Taylor
No Michael Johnson? No problem.
2. Jamaica
3. Bahamas

Women's 4 x 100
1. Bahamas — Sevatheda Fynes, Chandra Sturrup, Pauline Davis-Thompson, Debbie Ferguson
Defending Olympic champs. Defending world champions.
Any argument?
2. USA
3. Jamaica

4 x 400
1. USA — Monique Hennagan, Michelle Collins, LaTasha Richardson, Marion Jones
With golden girl running anchor,
Americans snap up another gold medal.
2. Russia
3. Jamaica

Klein later apologized to the residents of the centre and, in a tearful press conference, promised to give up alcohol. *Journal* writers Chris Purdy and Graham Thomson won a National Newspaper Award for the story.

In many ways, it was a remarkable Christmas season as the city defied national and world fallout from 9-11. In a post-holiday wrap-up on Jan. 30, 2002, business writer Ray Turchansky wrote: "While the world swirls in a global recession, insiders say Edmonton's retail trade will be relatively unharmed in the eye of the storm."

And so it was. One indicator of economic buoyancy was found in housing starts. A story in early 2003 reported that a record-setting 4,412 single-family home building permits had been issued in 2002, breaking a two-decade-old record set in 1979.

It was also a hectic year in the commercial and industrial sectors as massive new investment in oilsands development in Fort McMurray and oil refinery expansion in the Edmonton area sparked a new boom for the city.

Overall construction surpassed the $1-billion mark for the first time since 1980.

So interesting was the trend, *The Journal* put it down on paper in an in-depth, five-part Economic Outlook series on Edmonton and the four surrounding counties that make up the capital region. The series appeared in the winter and spring of 2002 with a wrap-up special produced by *The Journal* for a Canada-wide audience in the *National Post.* The stories provided evidence about why the city was apparently ducking the worst effects of the recession that had dampened other world markets.

Wrote Roy Cook: "Edmonton is the major service and supply centre for a $60-billion wave of economic activity sweeping across Northern Alberta – the largest concentration of economic activity anywhere in the world."

Resource development in northern oilsands, forests, gas fields and diamond mines meant the city remained the chief supplier of goods, skilled labour and know-how needed to get the job done.

As the city evolved, so did *The Journal.*

Feature pages changed. The ever-growing presence of exotic restaurants and specialized food stores, reflecting the multicultural nature of the city, showed the city to be more than a meat-and-potatoes town. The recipe-heavy Food section was replaced in November 2001 with the more urbane Bistro, aimed at people with less time to cook but who still wanted great food. Women-oriented Fashion was changed to Look in February 2002 with a broader focus on local design that included clothes as well as everything from architecture to furniture to teakettles.

A major attempt to reach 18-to-34-year-old readers was made in December 2001 with the launch of Saturday's *ed,* a feisty, tabloid-size magazine featuring opinions and stories about young up-and-coming Edmontonians not found in the mainstream sections of the newspaper.

And to provide readers more detailed coverage and perspective of the day's issues and hard news, pages 2 and 3 in the A section were cleared for what was dubbed Top Copy. This allowed *Journal* editors to package a larger range of in-depth stories about major local, provincial, national and international events.

***April 17, 2002*:**
Four Canadian soldiers from Edmonton-based Princess Patricia's Canadian Light Infantry are killed when a U.S. fighter jet mistakenly bombs them during a training exercise near Kandahar, Afghanistan.

***April 26, 2002*:**
***The Journal* wins National Newspaper Awards: reporter Chris Purdy and political editor Graham Thomson win the spot news reporting category and Ed Struzik takes top honours in the business reporting category.**

***June 17, 2002*:**
The Citadel nabs an unprecedented nine Sterling Awards for its production of *Cabaret*, starring Pamela Gordon and John Ullyatt.

***July 28, 2002*:**
First wave of Canadian troops returns from Afghanistan.

***Sept. 1, 2002*:**
A crowd of 47,784 watches the final of the FIFA under-19 women's world championship. Canada loses to the U.S., 1-0 in extra time.

***Nov. 24, 2002*:**
Edmonton hosts the Grey Cup, but the Eskimos are beaten 25-16 by the Montreal Alouettes.

EDMONTON JOURNAL
FRIDAY, JULY 26, 2002

SECTION E

WHAT'S ON

EDITOR: RICHARD HELM
…46; ent@thejournal…

CATCHING UP WITH MIKE MYERS

Yeah baby, the international man of mystery returns for a 3rd outing of the spy spoof series

IVOR DAVIS
Special to The Journal

Comic actor Mike Myers has become a very rich man thanks to his alter ego — the strutting, hip-twisting, sex-crazed British spy known as Austin Powers, a spoof of all those hyper-suave James Bond films. Now he's back as Powers for the third and (we are told) final time.

The Toronto-reared comic who this time out is a travelling spy in *Austin Powers: Goldmember* is, in person, a million miles from the over the top wildman he plays onscreen.

Before Austin came into his sights, he'd honed his comedy in Chicago's Second City and on *Saturday Night Live*. He successfully brought his *SNL* character Wayne Campbell to the big screen in *Wayne's World* and its sequel. After roles in such films as *So I Married an Axe Murderer* and *54*, he struck the moviegoer's funnybone again with *Austin Powers*. In this third film, the zany, bed-hopping Powers is joined again by the nasty Dr. Evil, the bagpipe-playing, kilted Scotsman Fat Bastard and a new character, Johann van der Smut, better known as the infamous Goldmember.

Onscreen, Myers is a fellow with a raging libido surrounded by scantily clad beauties. In person, he's a perfect gentleman sitting in a suite in the Four Seasons Hotel in Los Angeles in a drab, short-sleeved striped shirt over blue jeans and tennis shoes, sipping an iced Cola, warming to his favourite subject, his beloved Toronto Maple Leafs.

And unlike his screen alter ego, Myers is resolutely monogamous. He's been married for more than 10 years to New York actress Robin Ruzan. He tries to keep his off-screen life private but lately it's been a losing battle.

(**Editor's Note:** Myers did surprisingly little publicity for this latest *Austin Powers* outing. He's coming off a year where he was sued by Ron Howard for pulling out of *Dieter*, a movie based on one of his popular *SNL* characters. Countersuits and bizarre allegations followed, including a complaint from Myers' old improv buddy, Edmonton's Dana Andersen, who helped create Dieter.)

How did you ever come up with a weirdo like Goldmember?

I was watching HBO's show *Real Sex* about an exclusive sex club outside Amsterdam. I am fixated on European swingers — those guys at the beach who wear banana hammocks and have lotion bags and are the first to take off their swim trunks and dare uptight North Americans like me to show ourselves. The guy on *Real Sex* looked like a puppet. He was so funny — and so he became the genesis for Goldmember.

How is this Austin different from the first two?

Now he's at his pinnacle, knighted by the Queen but his father Nigel (Michael Caine) still doesn't give him any respect. Austin has spent his whole life seeking his father's approval. He eventually finds out how his father thinks of him — and he has to cope as all his childhood pain comes flooding back.

Surely there must be a little of Austin Powers in Mike Myers?

On screen I'm surrounded by these gorgeous ladies and if you knew me well you'd find it very funny because I'm a real nerd. Look at me. I've got no chin, I've got acne scarring and I'm five foot nothing. And you think that's a recipe for sexual dynamism. I look like those fellows in those old World War II newsreel footage — showing white bodied British Army types taking a shower. Oh yeah, — I'm a real sex machine.

Who is the passion of your life then?

I'm in love with my wife. She's my secret weapon and she grounds me. She's very blunt. I'm Canadian Protestant, she's New York Jewish — and we're the ying to each other's yang.

Myers's wife of 10 years Robin Ruzan

Where did you meet?

One night after I caught a puck at an ice hockey game in Chicago I met Robin at a bar across from the place. I didn't think she liked me and I didn't hook up with her until two days later. I showed her my puck and was tempted to say, "Come up to my place and see my puck — and my etchings."

What's the key to Austin Powers?

My mother, who was a trained actress, used to say that Austin is a happy survivor in the way that Bugs Bunny and James Bond were. The character has the ability to create his own fun.

Are people surprised to find you so normal?

I'm a very shy person and I think it's ultimately because I'm Canadian, growing up in a British-Canadian house. We're an observer nation. Canadians don't cry a lot. We tend to shake hands, not hug. In Canada there isn't much noise and not much stress. When was the last time you went out for Canadian food? We're not America and we're not England and we're not the country your parents came from. We're not a melting pot — we're a salad bowl. And we're the country of ice hockey.

How can this be when your humour is so — out there?

People might be shocked to know that left to my own devices I'm actually introverted. I think it's in proportion to how shy you are and how actually repressed you are as to how silly you'll allow yourself to go. It's all a fantasy to be able to play Powers, who is so extroverted; Dr. Evil, who is so worldly; and Fat Bastard, who is so gross.

Where did the idea of Austin Powers come from?

My late father Eric, who had emigrated to Canada from Liverpool, introduced me and my brothers to British zany comics like *The Goon Show* and *Monty Python* and comic talents like Peter Sellers, Peter Cooke and Dudley Moore. One day I'm driving to hockey practice and I hear this song, *The Look of Love*, and I say, "I wanna be in a movie with that song and everything it implies." It reminded me of Swinging England and *Casino Royale* and my Dad, the Peter Sellers fan. At that time people were unabashedly horny, always on the prowl, which no one is anymore. And I thought that was hilarious.

So where did it go from there?

I called this studio guy I knew and said, "I've got this story about a spy who is frozen in ice and then thawed out in the swinging sixties." And the same day he gave me the green light.

How has the concept progressed?

In our first movie we were learning how to make it. The second time around all we had to do was show up and have fun. We decided to do a third one to honour the fact that people followed us through one and two. We wrote it from a backwards approach and explained the origins of the worlds of Austin and Dr. Evil. It was screenwriting meets Mad Libs. It went like a party.

How do you mean party?

The film is in a long tradition of naughty British seaside postcard humour — where they take any opportunity to get naked or in a dress. There's a long tradition of British cross-dressing and partial male nudity. And who am I to buck that tradition?

Kingsley lost in Love
Flicks /E3

Whistling Dixie
Ten Best /E5

No fiddling with Natalie's faith
Music /E8

Countdown to Fringe
On Stage /E7

It's no longer Miller time
Television /E12

It was on those pages that *Journal* readers learned the full details of such events as the drought that crippled the province's agricultural industry in the summer of 2002.

Ontario and Quebec farmers helped out by organizing the Hay West program to provide desperately needed feed for the stock owned by their Western cousins. "The Hay West campaign can't solve the feed problems for all farmers," the paper said, "but it will help many. And it delivers a good measure of hope and good-heartedness at a bleak time for many on the land."

In-depth stories in Top Copy were also used to explore the outbreak of sudden acute respiratory syndrome (SARS), centred in Toronto in the spring of 2003. SARS devastated that city's billion-dollar tourist industry.

But it was an announcement of bovine spongiform encephalopathy – mad cow disease – that called on the newspaper's resources to provide full and complete coverage to its readers after one mad cow had been traced to a northern Alberta ranch in the spring of 2003. The result was almost a total shutdown of the beef industry.

"Alberta beef is rightly renowned – and promoted – in Canada and around the world as the gold standard," a May 21 editorial said. "It's a reputation that is worth billions. But now, in a stroke, the discovery of a case of mad cow disease has put that sterling reputation on the line."

Restrictions on shipping beef and cattle south to the U.S. meant massive losses for the province's cattlemen, but as the summer drew to a close some processed beef was allowed across the border, and there were indications that approval on exporting young, live cattle might be near.

Issues that had crowded the pages of *The Journal* over the years continued. The question of the municipal airport remained at least partly unsettled, government funding for health and education was, as always, under scrutiny, and crime and the problem of the homeless nagged as well.

Of course, it wasn't all gloom, as in August 2002 the city welcomed the FIFA under-19 women's World Cup of soccer. Fans embraced the sport, and more than 47,000 packed Commonwealth Stadium to watch Canada drop a 1-0 overtime heartbreaker to the U.S. In November, the city hosted a wildly successful Grey Cup, and while the Eskimos lost 25-16 to the Montreal Alouettes, Edmonton proved again that it was a city that knew how to party.

And the downtown, a constant, recurring concern for the city and the newspaper for the past two decades, was showing real signs of revival. A clutch of downtown buildings were transformed into loft apartments and new, toney restaurants moved into the downtown area. On the retail side, the City Centre complex was given a major facelift.

Entertainment and cultural venues got a boost with the massive new pipe organ at the world-class Winspear Centre and an impressive new theatre complex in the revamped bus barns of Old Strathcona to serve The Fringe, the city's annual summer theatre extravaganza.

As Edmonton approached its own centennial, it remained an exciting, vibrant place to live, work and play.

And, as it has for the last 100 years, *The Journal* continued to be the voice of the city.

May 20, 2003:
Officials report a northern Alberta cow slaughtered in January was infected with BSE, or mad cow disease, leading to the closure of export markets to Canadian beef and devastating the meat-packing and ranching industries.

***May 24, 2003*:**
***Journal* senior writer Ed Struzik and photographer Chris Schwarz win awards from the Canadian Association of Journalists for outstanding investigative journalism in 2002.**

***June 19, 2003*:**
The University of Alberta announces that publisher Linda Hughes will receive an honorary doctorate of laws degree on Nov. 19, 2003.

***July 1, 2003*:**
Changes to Edmonton's smoking bylaw ban smoking in all restaurants and attached patios, as well as in private clubs.

***Oct.7, 2003*:**
Israel (Izzy) Asper, founder and chair of the CanWest Global media empire which owns *The Journal*, dies in Winnipeg at age 71.

***Nov 16, 2003*:**
Edmonton Eskimos beat the Montreal Alouettes 34-22 to win the Grey Cup.

EDMONTON JOURNAL

TRIATHLON

Sydney 2000

ENDURANCE INSURANCE NEEDED

Some sports have been knocking on the Olympic door for decades and are never allowed entry. The triathlon, around for only 27 years, has busted the door off its hinges and will makes its debut in Sydney. In fact, the women's triathlon is the opening event of the Games and the men follow the next day. Now that's the way to make an entrance.

The Competition

- The triathlon begins with a mass start and continues non-stop through 1,500 metres of swimming, 40 kilometres of cycling and 10 km of running.
- The top men finish in about one hour and 50 minutes (20 minutes for the swim leg, 60 minutes for the cycling and 30 minutes for the run), while the top women take about 12 minutes longer.
- Each race has a maximum of 50 competitors.

Phase 1: Swimming

- Swimmers follow a triangular course marked by buoys and ropes, and face penalties if they cut any corners. Although the swimmers are allowed to use the stroke of their choice, virtually all choose freestyle.

Phase 2: Cycling

- Once out of the water, the triathletes collect their bicycles and begin cycling.
- During the cycling, all movement along the course must be by bicycle. If an athlete gets a flat tire, he or she is permitted to run with the bike to a tire-change station.
- Cyclists are free to ride in each other's draft (riding close behind a cyclist), but an unwritten rule among triathletes obliges each rider in a bunch to take a turn in the lead.

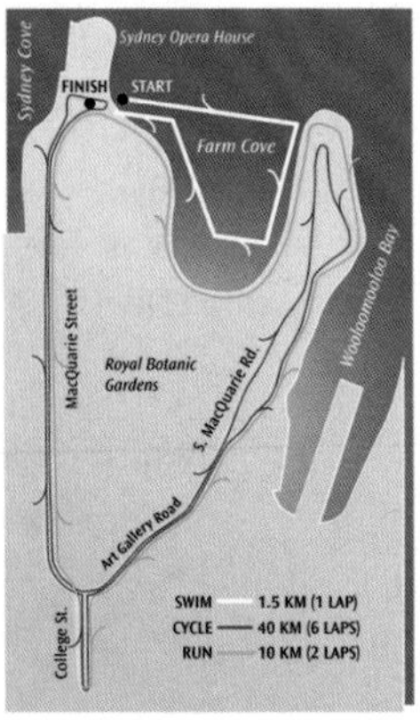
Sydney Cove
Sydney Opera House
FINISH
START
Farm Cove
Woolloomooloo Bay
MacQuarie Street
Royal Botanic Gardens
S. MacQuarie Rd.
Art Gallery Road
College St.
SWIM 1.5 KM (1 LAP)
CYCLE 40 KM (6 LAPS)
RUN 10 KM (2 LAPS)

Phase 3: Running

- Transitions can be tough on the body. Although the first transition from swimming to cycling is bearable, rubber legs and lead feet are common between cycling and running.
- Competitors cannot interfere with another competitor's equipment in the transition area.
- It is against the rules in Sydney to crawl across the finish line. Athletes must complete the course on foot.

Penalties

- Athletes cannot race in a dangerous or erratic manner. Offenders are required to stop for 30 seconds at the end of the swim before continuing. During the cycling and running legs, a race official may issue a warning with a yellow card. The athlete must stop and await the official's word to continue. For more dangerous or repeat offences, an athlete can be disqualified with a red card. Two yellow cards during a race results in a red card and automatic disqualification.

Venue

- Sydney Harbour and the Sydney Opera House provide a magnificent setting for the triathlon. Competitors swim around Farm Cove in Sydney Harbour, then cycle through the Royal Botanic Gardens, Hyde Park, MacQuarie Street and past the Opera House, before finishing with the run.
- Olympic competition dates: Sept. 16-17, 2000.

Sources: The Sports Rules Book, Triathlon: The Skills of the Game, National Federation for the Sport of Triathlon and Duathlon in Canada, Sydney Organizing Committee for the Olympic Games.

DUM DUM. DUM DUM DUM DUM

Olympic organizers will deploy a team of divers in Sydney Harbour to scare off sharks during the swimming leg of the triathlon — even though they insist sharks will not pose a threat to competitors.

Esther Wolsey turned to the triathlon after getting bored silly running marathons.
After taking a couple of lessons to learn how to swim, Esther's finish in her first triathlon was fourth. OK. She's determined. In a typical week of training Esther will run 150 kilometres, swim about the width of Lake Ontario and cycle the width of Saskatchewan.
Watch for Esther on the world-level circuit this year.

ON CBC-TV

TRIATHLON
Friday, Sept. 15 at 7 p.m. EDT: Women's final.
Saturday, Sept. 16 at 7 p.m. EDT: Men's final

COMPILED BY GEOFFERY VANDERBURG / DESIGN: RICK PAPE: THE JOURNAL

CHRIS SCHWARZ, THE JOURNAL

Epilogue

Poring over 100 years of the *Edmonton Journal*, following the threads of history through a million or so newspaper pages, reveals a city that's vital, resilient, hard-working and playful. *The Journal* archives depict a place where good things happen because its citizens have learned to pull together. It's a city where volunteers build things that endure.

That tradition has made Edmonton home to the Eskimos, a team that is the class of the Canadian Football League. It has built a professional theatre community with facilities such as the Citadel. A string of hugely successful festivals such as Jazz City, the Folk Festival and The Works add to the city's vitality.

It means that community initiatives work, whether it's the Fringe Theatre Festival, the food bank, the Christmas Bureau or the annual United Way drive. Those initiatives are also the power behind successful international events such as the Commonwealth Games in 1978, the 1983 World University Games and the 2001 World Track and Field Championships.

It's a thread of tradition that has made for a generous city, too.

Follow that thread and you come to John Michaels, the open-handed expatriate New Yorker who began Mike's News in the early years of the century. He started the Edmonton Newsboys' Band, hosted – and paid for – an annual Christmas dinner for war veterans who found themselves down-and-out, and served on dozens of committees designed to make the city a better place to live.

The thread is a long, strong one. It brings us to men like Joe Shoctor, whose belief in both theatre and football helped bring Edmonton the Citadel Theatre and the Edmonton Eskimos; Henry Singer, who had an abiding interest in promoting football, the game he loved, and jazz, his music of choice; Walter Sprague, who was another Eskimo founder and a tireless volunteer; Bob Stollery, who ran one of Edmonton's most successful companies and gave back to the community in spades, challenging others to do the same; Bob Westbury, generous and seemingly inexhaustible in dozens of areas; Jack Agrios, whose boundless belief in the city brought it the World Track and Field Championships; Bob Steadward, whose work with disabled athletes around the world brought honour to his city; Gordie Russell, whose quiet work with inner city kids saved hundreds from lives of despair; Elizabeth Sterling Haynes, whose Depression-era work with community theatre throughout the province is recalled each year by the Edmonton's prestigious Sterling Awards, prizes given to the best in live theatre; Zoie Gardner, who won an Order of Canada medal for being a foster mother to more than 100 youngsters over six decades; Cal Nichols, who knew the city needed the Oilers and then set about to make sure the team stayed here.

Another bright thread is the remarkable leadership this city has spawned. This includes the ground-breaking women, who early in the century led the nation and the British Empire in smashing the gender barrier in politics, law and the fight for equality – women such as Nellie McClung, Emily Murphy and Louise McKinney. Or men like pilot and air entrepreneur Max Ward and First World War flying ace Wop May. Or Percy Page, who coached the Grads to international renown. The list of names of those who have committed millions of hours to improving the city is endless.

There are other, more tangible, threads that weave their way through the pages of the newspaper.

It is fitting, for example, that Edmonton today is famous as the home of the world's largest shopping mall. To most Edmontonians, it's simply The Mall, a place that's earned an upper-case designation by virtue of its inescapable and commanding presence. Love it or loathe it, West Edmonton Mall reflects a city that, since its early days as a trading post huddled behind the palisades on the banks of the North Saskatchewan River, has always been a place where people came to buy and sell. Retail is in Edmonton's DNA.

It started when traders bartered with the trappers who hauled their catch to old Fort Edmonton and returned home laden with the treasures of civilization.

The 20th century brought farmers, eager to carve a new life from a new land. Edmonton merchants sold them what they needed: implements to clear the land and plant their crops, tools and lumber to build their houses, schools and churches in dozens of new towns.

Oilmen followed. And the city became a hub, selling everything from steel-toed boots to the massive earth-moving equipment used to extract the oil locked in the Athabasca oilsands. Oil company head offices may have migrated to Calgary, but service companies – the ones that keep the rigs working and the oil and gas flowing – are located in Edmonton.

City merchants also took to heart the city's Gateway to the North slogan. It meant they could sell anything and everything to towns and villages from Peace River to the Arctic Coast.

And just as it cuts a deep swath through the city itself, the North Saskatchewan River valley is yet another thread running through Edmonton's history.

When the first *Journal* editions came off the press in 1903, the river was a link to the outside world. John Walter's ferry ran people and goods back and forth to the town of Strathcona and the terminus of the CPR. Paddlewheel steamers took fans and athletes to sporting events at Fort Saskatchewan. Freighters brought supplies to settlers to the east and west. Its riverbanks gave early Edmontonians coal for heating and clay for the bricks to build homes and businesses.

The paper favoured the conservation of the valley. In 1906, it called it "one of the picturesque spots in Canada." And a succession of city councils, whether by design or because of the river's tendency to surpass previous flood levels, turned it into the largest stretch of urban parkland in North America. But it's been a headache as well. It snarls traffic, demands bridges and tempts developers and road builders.

Aviation has been important to the city, too. From the first flight in 1909, when a rickety biplane flew over the exhibition grounds, and in 1926 when it became the first Canadian city to have a municipal airport, Edmonton has been closely linked with airplanes. Early pilots who serviced the north were local heroes, and the newspaper regularly reported their exploits on page 1.

Aviation, of course, also led to the long-running battle that continues to this day over whether the downtown airport is good for the city.

And despite the city's great strengths, hindsight shows us Edmonton has always been a little uncertain of itself when guests come to call. It is a city that wants to be liked. Reporters usually rounded out a story by asking visitors, kings or commoners, exactly what they thought about us.

For example, the paper was puffed with pride when soprano and movie star Jeanette MacDonald, after a concert here in the 1940s, kindly observed that she liked the place. She was gracious even when it came to performing in the Edmonton Gardens, saying that she understood why young cities often preferred investing in sports rather than the arts.

Finally, reading 100 years of the paper transforms pessimists into optimists. It's not that the news columns are crowded with sunny stories. In fact, the opposite is over true.

Like newspapers around the world, *The Journal*'s pages are often dominated by stories of war, drought, economic depression, tragedy and crime. Editorial writers, columnists and letter writers are more likely to focus on problems and more willing to predict doom and gloom.

The truth is that newspapers chronicle change, and change is never easy. The path of progress is seldom smooth, and the 20th century has provided more challenges and more opportunities than any other century in the history of humanity.

The pages of *The Journal* are also filled with stories about meeting those challenges and capitalizing on those opportunities.

They tell of a strong community doing good work to build a city on the banks of the North Saskatchewan River that would astound and impress our founders.

And there is clear evidence in a century of stories that the city's future is bright as we face our second century.

Index

Bold page numbers refer to reprints from *The Edmonton Journal*

A

A-Channel TV station, 391
Abdulla Yusuf Ali, 163
Aberhart, William, 139, 141, 151, 153, **160**, 161, 177, 179
Aberhart Memorial Hospital, 193, 213
abortion, 267, 285
Accurate News and Information Act, 141, 157, 159, 161
AEC West, 393
AgriCom, 333
Agrios, Jack, 401, 407
AGT Tower, 271
A&GW Railway, 39, 41, 43, 109
A.H. Esch and Co., 97
AID/HIV, 323, **344**, 345, 385
Ainlay, Harry, 181, 185, 189, 191
Air Services for Tomorrow, 361
air shows, 49, 81, 131, 133, 135, 145
airline service, 83, **100**, 157, 159, 189, 215, 249, **252**, 259, 297, 345, 347
airmail delivery, 79, **80**, 81, **82**, 83, 157
airplane crashes, 145, 159, 205, 263, 265, 303, 327, 337, 339
airplanes, 83, **92**, 159
airports, two-airports issue, 215, **218**, 359, 361, 363, 371, 405
al-Qaeda, 395, 397, 399
Al Rashid Mosque, 161, 163
Alaska Highway, 173, 175
Alberta, official emblems, 131, 307, 333
Alberta, population, 89, 135
Alberta All-Girls Drum and Bugle Band, 293, 297
Alberta and Great Waterways Railway (A&GW Railway), 39, 41, 43, 109
Alberta Autonomy Bill, 13, 37
Alberta Ballet Company, 209
Alberta Beach, 79
Alberta College, 5, 23, **36**
19th Alberta Dragoons, **46**, 167
Alberta government, early history, 15, 19, **21**, 23, 27, **34**, 35
Alberta Government Telephones (AGT), **74**, 363, 371, 387
Alberta Hotel, 7, 11
Alberta Legislature building and grounds, 27, 279
Alberta Liquor Control Board, 371
Alberta Lotteries, 385
Alberta Moral and Temperance Association, 85
Alberta Press Council, 291
Alberta Provincial Police, 75, **101**, 107, 139
Alberta Referendum Act, 85, 121
Alberta Slot Machine Act, 217
Alberta Teachers' Association, 219
Alberta Treasury Branch, 161, 377
Alberta Wheat Pool, 111, 149
alcohol. *See* liquor; Prohibition
Alex Taylor School, 381
Alexander, Les, 377
Alice Cooper, **280**
alienation in Alberta, 37, 113, 279, 281, 295, 297, 343
All-American Girl's Baseball League, 191
All Saints Anglican Cathedral, 229, 253
Allan Cup (amateur hockey), 193
Allen, Harry, 231
Allendale, 65
Alsands, 363
ambulance services, 57
AMJ Campbell Van Lines, 361
Andreieff, Feodor, 121
Andrew, Prince, 313
animal hospitals, 191
Anton, Ron, 251
Arabian Moslem Association, 163
Arcade, 133
area codes, 393
Arlington apartment building, 133
Armistice Day, 133
Armstrong, George, 55, 57, **80**
Army and Navy, 133, 143
Arnold, Richard, 369
Arthur, Prince. Duke of Connaught, 19
Ashwell, Keith, 281, 339
Asper, Israel (Izzy), 293, 405
Asper, Leonard, 393
asphalt, 59
Associated Press, 57, 69, 245
Athabasca oil sands, 255, 321
automobiles
speed limits, 23, 179, 189
  (1903–1920), 2, **4**, **7**, 11, **49**, 55, **60**, **78**
  (1921–1940), 87, 95, 101, **102**, 125, 129, 133, **138**, 147
  (1940–1979), 175, 177, **226**, **286**
Avison, D.J., 207
Avro Avian, **92**
Awrey, Don, 273, 275

B

Babiak, Todd, 397
Babick, Don, 355, 359, 363, 365
Bailey, Donovan, 401, **402**
Baldwin, Matt, 221, 231, 235
Banff Centre, 143
Bank of Montreal building, 15, 331
Banting, Frederick, 109
Barber, Butch, 275
barber shops, 155
Barclay, Helen, 91
Barnes, S.A.G., 137
Barnhouse, Frank, 143
Barrett, Garry R., 29
Barrett, Tom, 373
Barton, Michael, 373
baseball, 19, 23, 51, 53, 143, 191
  See also Edmonton Eskimos (baseball); Edmonton Trappers (baseball)
49th Battalion, 67, 73, 77, 79, 81
51st Battalion, **52**
Bay. *See* Hudson's Bay store
BC Tel, 391
Bears. *See* Golden Bears, U of A
Beatles, **276**, 277
Beauchamp, Olive Marie Poncella, 149
Beaumaris Lake, 315
Beaverlodge, 389
beef industry, 403, 405
Beevers, Frank, 79
Bel-Air apartments, 211, 221
Bell, Bob, 281, 291
Bell, Jimmy, 145
Bellamy, Mayor, 19
Belmont, 59
Ben Moss Jewellers, 333
Bennett, R.B., 15, 39, 129, 133
Bernhardt, Sarah, 59, **76**, 77, 99
Berry, Matt, 145
Best, Charles, 111
Betkowski, Nancy, 365, 367
Beverly, 91, 175, 217, 219, 229, 239, 253
bicycles, **82**
Bielish, Martha, 315
big box stores, 359, 407
Big Chief Wahoo (comic strip), **146**
Bijou Theatre, **8**, 23, 41
bilingualism and biculturalism, 24, 243, 245, 261, 263, **356**, 365
bin Laden, Osama, 395, 397, 399
Birks, 129
birth control, 255, 257, 267
Bishop, Charles, 117
Bishop, E.T., 13
Bisset, Robert, 163
Black, Conrad, 371, 393, 397
black Canadians, 55, **56**, 57, **364**
Black Tuesday, 117
Blair, Sidney, 211
Blanchard, E.M. (Joe), 249
Blatchford, Ken, 103, 117
Blatchford Field. See Edmonton Municipal Airport
Blodgett, E.D. (Ted), 389
bobsledding, 375, 391
Bogusky, Alf, 381
Boland, Con, 385
bomb threat at *Edmonton Journal*, **304**, 305
Bombardier, J. Armand, 157
Bonnie Doon, 247
Bonnie Doon Composite High School, 213, 237
Book Warehouse, 333
bookstores, 97, 331, 333
Boonstra, Richard, 391
Borden, Robert, 51, **51**, 63, 65, 71
Bourassa, Christine and Robert, 179, 181
Bourbonnais, Roger, 275
Bow, M.R., 92, 137
Bowen, John C., 159, 161, 169
Bowen, Ruth, 273
Bowlen, J.J., 223
Bowlen, P.D., 207
boxing, 19, **56**, 63, 383
Boxing Day, 151
Boyle, J.R., 23, 41
Boys' Own Journal, **96**
Brayshaw, Buster, 275
breathalyzer, 231
Breen, Bob, 363
Brewster, Pete, 281
The Brick, **298**, 299
Brier (curling), 141, 155, 221, 231, 235, 251, 353, 363
Bringing Up Father (comic strip), **94**
British North America Act of 1867, 111
Brockelsby, Lyn, 383
Brooke, Jim, 235
Brown, Alf, 93
Brown, John, 307, 329
Brown, Roy, 81
Brown, Thomas G., 119, 121
Browning, Kurt, 353, 361, 373
Brownlee, John Edward
  (1920–1929), **103**, 103, **104**, 109, 113, 119, 123, 125
  (1930–1939), 129, 131, 135, 137, 145, 147, **150**, 151, **152**, 165
BSE (mad cow disease), 403, 405
Bub Slug (comic strip), 339
buffalo coats, **90**
The Bulletin. See The Edmonton Bulletin
Bulyea, George, 35
Bunner, Paul, vii
Burdine's, 333
Burgess, E.R.G., 295
Burgett, A.E., 145
Burns, Pat, 133
Burns, Tommy, 63
Burns Foods, 353
Burstyn, Isadore, 331
Bury, Ambrose, **92**
Bush, George W., 399
Buster Brown and His Dog Tige (comic strip), **12**
Byer's Transport (tornado), **338**
Byfield, Ted, vii

C

Calder area, 39, 75, 201
Calgary-Edmonton rivalry, **10**, 13, 15, **26**, 65, 235, 359
The Calgary Herald, 13, 101
Calgary Tank Regiment, **184**, 185
Cameron, Dale, 381
Cameron, James, 305
Cameron, Rossi, 305
Campbell, Charles, 195
Campbell, Clarence, 183
Campbell, Horace, 117
Camrose, 225, 239
Canada
  Charter of Rights and Freedoms, 375
  Constitution, **320**, **322**
  income tax, **70**, 71
  population, 89
  provincial status of Alberta, 15

See also names of individual prime ministers; National Energy Program (NEP)
Canada Place, 281, 337
Canadian Airlines International, 159, 345, 347
Canadian Commercial Bank, 337, 363
Canadian Expeditionary Force, 69
Canadian Finals Rodeo, 297, 299, **376**
Canadian Forces Airborne Regiment, 305
Canadian Forces Base Edmonton, 339, 383
Canadian Insolvency Association, 319
Canadian National Institute for the Blind, 201
Canadian National Railway, 43, 65, 105, 109, 123, 133, 143, 161, **326**, 341, 343
Canadian Newspapers Ltd., 49, 57
Canadian Northern Railway, 15, 17, 37, **38**, **40**, 42, 43, 65, 69, 77, 79, 85, 155
Canadian Pacific Railway, 17, 37, 39, 43, 65, 109, 123, **138**
Canadian Press news service, 57
Canadian Press Picture of the Year, 307, 349, 353, 377
Canmore, 385
CanWest Global Communications, 393, 399
Capital Hill, **42**
Capitol Motors, 101
Capitol Theatre, 95, 97, **124**, 125, 143, 207, 215
Capt. Hawks' Time Ray (comic strip), **134**
Carlyle, S.G., 137
Carruthers, James, 83
Carse, Ruth, 209
cartoons, 275, 321, 341, **342**, 343
Cashman, Tony, vii
Casselman, Cora T., 171
Castle Downs, 289
cats, 145
cattle industry, 405
Cavanagh, Terry, 299, 301, 309, 351
CBC-TV, 215, 247, 271
CBX (CBC) Edmonton (radio), 195
CBXT-TV (CBC) Edmonton (television), 253
CCF (Co-operative Commonwealth Federation), 141, **222**, 255
Cecil Hotel, 33
Celanese Corporation, 211
census, 199
Centennial celebrations (1967), 247
Centennial Library, 107, 247, 273
CFAC (CHCQ) Edmonton (radio), 99
CFCN Calgary (radio), **160**
CFRN (CBC) Edmonton (radio), 143, 147
CFRN (CBC) Edmonton (television), 223
CFRN Edmonton (television), **238**, 239, 247, 271
Chalifoux, Thelma, 391
Chargex, **290**, **312**
Charles, Prince of Wales, **274**, 331
Charles Camsell Hospital, 369
Chateau Lacombe, 273
Checkstop program, 295
CHED Edmonton (radio), 221
Cheng, Angela, 351
CHFA Edmonton (radio), 201
Chinatown Gate, 349
Chippewa, 223
Chisholm Block, 63
Chrétien, Jean, 381
Christiansen, Jim, 231
Christie Grants department store, 131
circuses, **9**
Cisek, Bill, 367
Citadel Theatre, 269, 271, 289, 293, 295, 305, 403
City Centre Airport, 83
City of Edmonton (steamer), **10**, **11**
CJCA Edmonton (radio), **86**, **87**, 91, 93, 99, 113, 143, 239, 257, 305
CJCJ Calgary (radio), 143
CJCQ Calgary (radio), 99
CKCK Regina (radio), 105
CKJL Red Deer (radio), 143
CKUA Edmonton (radio), 137, 145, 315
Clancy, Frank (King), 105
Clark, Joseph Prime Minister, 255
Clark, W.H., 55
Clarke, Ed, 225
Clarke, J.A., 137
Clarke, Joseph, 81, 83, 85, 151, 153, 159
Clarke, T.R., 257
Clarke Park, **26**
Clarke Stadium, 159, 161, 301, 313
Clements, Lillian, 71
Clover Bar, 193, 219
CN Tower, **246**, 271
Co-operative Commonwealth Federation (CCF), 141, **222**, 255
coal mines, 7, **18**, 31, 91, 115, 177, 191, **198**
Coaldale, 385
Coar, John F., 165
Cochrane, Jim, 377
Code Inquiry, 335
Cody, Buffalo Bill, 61
Coffey, Paul, 349, **354**
Cole, Cam, 281, 349, 355, 379
Coleman, Jim, 307
Collip, J.B., 111
coloured margarine ban, 197
Colville, Dave, 245
comic books, 239
comic strips
  during polio epidemic, 143
  Big Chief Wahoo, **146**
  Bringing Up Father, **94**
  Bub Slug, 339
  Buster Brown, **12**
  Capt. Hawks' Time Ray (comic strip), **134**
  Dinglehoofer and His Dog, **140**
  Katzenjammer Kids, **140**
  Les Canadiens, 261
  Mutt and Jeff, **112**
  Snapshot Bill, **54**
Commerce Drug Co., Ltd., 129
Commonwealth Games (1978), 291, 293, 299, 301, 311, 313, 339
Commonwealth Stadium, **26**, 281, 289, 331, 337, 379, 393
Communists and Communist Party, 97, **98**, 127, 133, 135, 173, 187, 217, 219
Community Association for the Grey Nuns Hospital, 367
computers, 235, **330**, **384**
Comrie, Bill, **298**, 299
Concordia College, 95
condominiums, 261
Congreve, George, 217
Conly, Haywood, 277
Connaught Armoury, 167
Connolly and McKinley, 55
contraception, 255, 267
convenience foods, 219
Cook, Constable, **101**
Cook, Fred, 63
Cook, Roy, 399, 403
Cooke, Michael, 367, 381
Cooper, George B., 33
Copps, Sheila, 381
Cormie, Donald, 335, 367
Corona Hotel, 65, 139, 249
Coronation Park, 333
Coultis, S.G., 207
Coutts, James, 255
Cove, Lynne, 229
Cowley, Norm, 281
Cowman, Sarah, 387
Craig, John Dixon, 47
Crash of 1929, 117
Crawley, Rev. David, 253
Cream, **268**
credit cards, **290**, **312**
Cree, **10**
Creswell, Dene, 345
Crisp, Terry, 273, 275
Cristall, Abe, 43
Cross, Wally, 273
Cummings, A.C., 165
Cunningham, J.W., 5, 13, 23, 35
curling, **5**, 19, 155, 353, 363
Cutler, Dave, 327
Cyr, Dean, **360**

D

Dahl, Al, 273
Daily Capital, 37
Dantzer, Vincent, 229, 271
Darling, Marsh, 231
Davey, Geoff, 335
Davie, Rob, 231
Davies, Arthur, 53
Davies, Jack, 231
Davies, Jim, 283
Davis, Murdoch, 367, 393, 399
Dawe, Billy, 231
Dawson Bridge, 61
Day, Billy, **6**
De La Pole, Mr., 199
de Wind, Edmund, 77
Deakin, Jack, 223
Dean, Basil, 145, 245, 247, 253, 257
Dean, Bob, 235
Dean, Mike, 307
Decore, Laurence, 331, 345, 351
Decoteau, Alex, **47**
Delainey, Gary, 339
Delaney, Wilbert, 231
Delta Hotels, 329
Demarais, Paul, 393
Demarino, Guy, 347
demonstrations, 133, 135, 141
Dent, Ivor, 261, 291, 297, 309, 381
Detwiler Plan, 205, 209, 211
deVleiger, Dan, 255
Devon, 201
Dewar, Max, 213
diabetes, **356**, 397
Diana, Princess of Wales, 331, **372**
Dieppe, Battle of, **184**, 185, **186**, 187
Dinglehoofer and His Dog (comic strip), **140**
Dingwall, Robert, 167, 169
dinosaur fossils, 163
Dionne Quints, **148**
diphtheria, 93, 95
Dobson, Hugh, 123
Dog Control Bylaw, 303
Dollar Cleaners, 133
Dolphin, Ric, 389
Dominion Motors Ltd., 125, **226**
Dominion Police, 89
Dominion Stores, 281
Dornhoefer, Gary, 273, 275
Douglas, Clifford Hugh, 139
Douglas, James, 119, 125, 133, 135
Doyle, Sir Arthur Conan, 61
Dreamland Theatre, **124**, 125
driver's licences, 123, 129, 219
drunk drivers, 233
Dub, Gene, 371
Ducey, Brant, vii
Ducey Park, 143
Duff, Lyman, 153
Duggan, David Milwyn, 89, 93, 99, 103
Duggan, Eric, 217
Dunn, Dr., 13
Dwyer, Joseph, 183
Dyer, Ainsworth, 399

E

Eastgate production plant (EJ), 321, 323, 327, 349
Eastglen Composite High School, 213, 221
Eaton Centre, 331
Eaton's, 119, 129, 179, 233, 279, 289, 331, 359
Economic Development Edmonton (EDE), 361
Ecuador kidnapping, 393
Edmonton
  early history as Alberta's capital, 13, 15, 19, **34**
  Calgary rivalry, **10**, 13, 15, **26**, 65, 235, 359
  elections, 111, 133, 173, 191, 255, 265, 287, 321, 385
  flower, 265
  fluoridation of water, 213, 239
  immigration, 55, 57, 65
  as new city, 1, 11
  parking meters, 193, 197
  relief efforts, 23, 131
  slogan, 203
  streets, 29, 65, 119, 217, 233
Edmonton, population
  (1903–1919), 1, 13, 53, 63, 65, 67, 69
  (1920–1939), 91, 115, 129, 157, 163
  (1940–1949), 169, 175, 181, 183, 189, 197
  (1950–1959), 205, 209, 215, 229, 231, 233, 239
  (1960–1969), 245, 253, 261, 265, 271, 277
  (1970–2003), 281, 287, 293, 303, 323, 327, 361
Edmonton, Yukon and Pacific railroad, 223
Edmonton All-Girls Drum and Bugle Band, 285
Edmonton and Fort McMurray Oil and Asphalt Co., Ltd., 59
Edmonton Arena, 115

Edmonton Art Gallery, 115
Edmonton Athletic Club (junior hockey), 163
Edmonton Board of Health, 75
The Edmonton Bulletin, 3, 11, 13, 15, 137, 151, 153, **194**, 195, **196**, 207
Edmonton Centre, 281, 331
Edmonton Chamber of Commerce, 111, 361
Edmonton Chinese Benevolent Association, 157
Edmonton City Hall, 213, 231, 369, 371, 375
Edmonton Club, 33, 261, 377, 379
Edmonton Coliseum, **254**, 289, 299, 379
Edmonton Commercial Graduates ("Grads") basketball team, 67, 93, 99, 107, **114**, 115, 125, 129, **142**, 143, 161, 169, 183
Edmonton Convention Centre, 301, 311, 317, 331
Edmonton District Telephone Service, 11
Edmonton Drillers (soccer), 323, 335
Edmonton Eskimos (baseball), 235
Edmonton Eskimos (football)
 (1920–1929), 97, 99, 103, 105
 (1930–1959), 161, 199, 215, 225, 227, 231, **234**, 235, 237
 (1960–1979), 257, 295, 301, 309, 313, 315, 317
 (1980–1989), 323, 327, 329, **332**, 345, 349, 351
 (1990–2003), 361, 375, 389, 393, 403, 405
Edmonton Eskimos (hockey), **30**, 31, 33, 39, 143, 235
Edmonton Exhibition, **50**, 63, 123, 221, 291, 299
Edmonton Federation of Community Leagues, 95
Edmonton Fire Department, 243
Edmonton Flyers (hockey), 193, 231, 235
Edmonton Folk Music Festival, 261, 321, 339
Edmonton Food Bank, 323, 337, 341
Edmonton Gardens, 65, 93, 221, 261, 273, 408
Edmonton Garrison, 183, 383
Edmonton Huskies (football), 255, 263
Edmonton Industrial Association, 67, 69
Edmonton International Airport, 215, **218**, 249, 263, 359, 361, 371, 385, 397
Edmonton Interurban Railway, 63
Edmonton Islamic School, 397
The Edmonton Journal
 founding and early history, **iv**, 1–7, 11, 17–23
 bomb threat, **304**, 305
 Bulletin and, **194**, 195, **196**, 207
 circulation, 7, 13, 39, 55, 65, 85, 91, 207, 215, 287, 317, 323, 327, 329
 CJCA ownership, **86**, 87, 89, 91, 99
 contests, 5, 61, 99, 101, 134, 149, 309, 331
 delivery and sales, **32**, **49**, 69, **80**, 105, 359
 International Indoor Games, 315, 339
 labour disputes, 183, 195
 layout and design, recent changes, 281, 305, 309, 327, 329, 331, **350**, **352**, 355, 385, 393
 Oilers part-ownership, 377, 379
 photography, 145, 147, 245, 317, 323
 purchase and sale, 13, 35, 49, 55, 57
 special promotions, 51, **58**, 69, **82**, 341
 subscriptions, 3, 83, **174**, **203**, 235, 341, 359
 as "unofficial opposition," 315, 317
 wire services, 3, 7, 33, 47, 57, 69, 97, 99, 169, 245
 See also Southam Newspapers
The Edmonton Journal, awards and honours
 CP Picture of the Year, 307, 349, 353, 377
 Hockey Hall of Fame (media), 399
 Michener Award, 327, 373
 National Newspaper Award, 263, 265, 321, 353, 367, 373, 377, 383, 393, 397, 399
 National Press Club, 209
 Pulitzer, 141, 159, 161
The Edmonton Journal, features, sections and special editions
 automobiles, 53, 55, **60**, **100**, 129
 children and youth, 53, **96**, 283, 301
 comic strips, **12**, **54**, **94**, **112**, **134**, **140**, **146**, 255, 339
 Dissent page, 245, **250**, 259
 economy, 399
 ed the magazine, **396**, 403
 entertainment, 91, **370**, **404**
 fashion and style, **16**, 283, **288**, **308**, **328**, **364**, **382**, **400**, 403
 food and bistro, 25, **324**, **334**, **398**
 insight, **360**, **366**, **368**, **374**, **380**, **388**
 letters to the editor, 3, 17, 283, 285
 life and living, 345, **362**, **378**
 oil industry, **119**
 rodeos, **376**
 sexually transmitted diseases, **344**, 345
 sports, 19, **114**, 143, 191, 227, **386**, **402**, **406**
 technology, **384**
 terrorist attacks, **394**, 397, 401
 top copy, 403
 tornado, 325, 327, 349
 travel, **390**, **392**
 women's page, 7, 17, 53, 57, **110**, 111, **112**
The Edmonton Journal, site
 early history, **3**, 13, 15, 25, 41
 buildings and plants, **48**, 85, 91, 95, **108**, 205, 229, 285, 309, 321, 359, 365, 377
 presses and inks, 65, 149, 205, 215, 323, 351
Edmonton Motors, 143
Edmonton Municipal Airport (Blatchford Field), 83, 95, 117, 119, 131, 133, 145, 159, 169, 177, 185, **218**, 359, 361, 385
Edmonton Newsboys Band, 67, 93, 103, 407
Edmonton Oil Kings (hockey), 217, 231, 235, **244**, **256**, 257, **272**, 273, 275, 301
Edmonton Oilers (hockey), 299, 307, 317, 333, 339, 349, 351, 359
 sale of Gretzky, **354**, 355
 sale by Pocklington, 377, 379, 391
Edmonton Opera, 263, 267
Edmonton Opera House, **8**, **9**, 33
Edmonton Parks and Recreation, **254**, 261
Edmonton Penitentiary, **26**, 29, 89, 91
Edmonton Petroleum Club, 207
Edmonton Police Department, 47, 61, **61**, 65, **78**, 85, 243, 385
The Edmonton Post, 5, 11
Edmonton Public Library, 61, 107, 155, 171, 247, 261, 273
Edmonton Public Schools, 71, 211, 213, 221, 227, 237, 243, 245, 253, 387
Edmonton Radial Railway, 7
Edmonton Regional Airports Authority, 361
Edmonton Rotary Club, 73
Edmonton Stock Exchange, 217
Edmonton Symphony, 143, 205, 207, 215, 237, 239, 245, 269, 289, **370**
Edmonton Telephones (EdTel), 243, 365, 383
Edmonton Transit System, 165, **258**, 275, 277, 289, 295, 327
Edmonton Trappers (baseball), 323, 325, 335, 369, 387, 389, 393
Edmonton Typographical Union, 157
Edmonton Visitor and Convention Association, 361
Edmonton Weekly News, 37
Edmonton Yacht Club, 143
Edson, **38**
education, 47, 369, 371, 393, 405
Edward, Prince, 313
Edward VII, 41
Edward VIII. Duke of Windsor, 85, 145, **154**, 155
Edwards, Charles, 191
Edwards, Henrietta Muir, 107, 111
electrical power, early, 15, 71
Eleniak, Wasyl, 187
elevators, 15, 17
Elizabeth, Queen Mother, 145, **154**, 155, 157, 163, 339
Elizabeth II, Queen of England, **202**, **274**, **312**, 313, **322**, 339
Elk Island National park, 61
Elliott, Olive, 241, 261, 281
Emms, Hap, 273
Empire Building, 15, 17, **45**, **80**
Empire Theatre, 61, **76**, 77, 91, 97, **124**, 125, 221
Empress of Canada, **208**
Empress Theatre, 97, 143, 187, 189
Enbridge, 363
encephalitis epidemic, 171
Energy Resources Conservation Board, 217
Ensor, R.W., 65
Erickson, Dwayne, 275
Esso Resources, 363
eugenics, 113, 375
Evans, Art, 181, 197, 243, **246**, **256**, 259, **260**, **264**, 337, 339
Evans, Harry M.E., 13, 77
Evans, Una, 299
The Evening Journal, **iv**, **viii**, 1–7
Evergreen Mobile Home Park (tornado), 325, **336**, 349
Exhibition Grounds, 333

F

Faculté Saint-Jean, 177, 309
Falkenberg, Bob, 275
Family Day, 359
Famous Five (Persons Case), 73, 107, 111, 123
Fantasyland Hotel, 339
Faraone, Ezio, 359
Farm Fair, 299
Farm Weekly, 105
Farmer Smith's Rainbow Children's Page, 53
Farquharson, Duart, 367
Farrell, Jim, 379
Federal Building, 211, 235
Fehr family, **130**
Ferbey, Randy, 353
ferry, John Walter's, **21**
Fidelity Trust, 333, 387
FIFA (soccer) championships, 403, 405
figure skating, 353, 359, 361, 365, 373, 387, 399
Findlay, J.W., 135
Finlay, Cam, 275
Finlayson, Dave, 397
Fire Hall, 243
First Nations, 25, 27, 37, 47, 59, 157, 223, 391
firsts
 aboriginal woman appointed to Senate, 391
 AIDS-related death, 345
 air commercial flight, 83
 air show, 49, 81, 131, 135
 airfield in a municipality in Canada, 117
 airmail delivery, 79, **80**, 81, **82**, 83
 airplane city-to-city flight, 81
 airplane crash at city airport, 145
 airport in a Canadian city, 408
 animal hospital for small animals, 191
 auto ambulance for Edmonton, 55, 57
 auto in Edmonton, 7
 auto show, 133
 auto to drive from Fort McMurray to Edmonton, 231
 auto traffic jam, 147
 charitable trust in Alberta, 95
 computer at University of Alberta, 235
 curling rink to win Brier, 141
 divided highway in Alberta, 221
 drive-in hotel, 225
 drive-in movie theatre, 197
 Edmonton Gardens hockey game, 65
 elevator, 15, 17
 Family Day observance, 359
 food bank in Canada, 323
 Fringe Theatre Festival, 329, 339
 graduating class at University of Alberta, 59, 63
 Great Divide waterfall, 321, 323, 325
 Grey Cup game televised by CBC, 215
 Grey Cup played in Edmonton, 337
 Grey Cup western team, 99
 heart transplant in Western Canada, 341
 Heritage Days, 303
 horse show, 49
 legislature session, 51
 liquor (beer sales) at a sporting event, 325
 liquor sales, privatization, 375
 liquor sales, self-serve, 277
 liquor store owned by government, 123
 MLA of Ukrainian descent, 63
 Montreal International Music Competition winner from Canada, 351
 Mormon temple, 393
 mosque in Canada, 161
 municipal planetarium in Canada, 247
 Oilers game in Coliseum, 299
 opera, 11, 263
 popcorn machine in a theatre, 189
 premier of Alberta, 15
 provincial election in which women could vote, 75
 provincial political scandal, 17, 39, 41, 43
 public swimming pool, 101
 radio broadcast, 87, 89, 91
 radio broadcast of a live sporting event, 93
 railway car to arrive in Edmonton, **38**
 reigning British monarch to visit Edmonton, 163
 royal visitor to Edmonton, 19
 Sikh police officer to wear service's official turban, 385
 singing telegram delivered in Edmonton, 169
 skyscraper, 95

Social Credit party convention, **149**
talking movies, 125
911 telephone system, 275
television broadcast of live surgery, 233
touch-tone telephone, 271
traffic signals, 147
train across High Level Bridge, 63
train robbery, 33
treaty Indian police officer, 47
UFA MLA elected, 55
underground parking garage in Canada, 225
United Way campaign, **173**
woman airplane passenger to fly from Edmonton to Calgary, 83
woman bus driver, 287
woman chief justice of Alberta, 367
woman elected to city council, 99
woman elected to public office in Edmonton, 55
woman from Alberta appointed to Senate, 315
woman lawyer in Alberta, 71, 91
woman Liberal in parliament, 171
woman mayor of Edmonton, 355
woman police magistrate, 73
woman police officer in Edmonton, 61
woman to hold municipal office, 57
woman to win world show jumping championships, 343
women elected to a legislature in Canada, 75
women's world basketball title (Grads), 107
The Works Festival, 343
firsts for *The Edmonton Journal*
airmail delivery, 81, **82**, 83
classified ad, 3
contest, 5
correction, 5
edition in red ink, 11
issue of *The Evening Journal* (1903), viii, 1, 3
letter to the editor, 3
serialized novel, 3
seven-page edition, 325, 327
six-page edition, 11
sports story, 19
systems crash, 7
flags, Canadian, 69, 247, 249
Fleming, Don, 181, 251, 257, 281
floods, 67, **68**, 69, 71, 343
Flores, Ralph, 263, 265
Fluor, 363
fluoridation of water, 213, 239
Food for Less, 335
Fort Edmonton, 7, 29, **62**, 71, 161, 163, 285
Fort McMurray, 39, 131, 231, 265, 313, 399, 401
Fort Vermilion mercy flight, **92**, 93, 95, 121
Fortune, W.G.W. and Mark, 69, 85
Foulds, A.D., 207
Four Seasons Hotel, 281
Fox, Doug, 275
Francophones, **40**, 177, 201
Fraser, Catherine Anne, 367
Fraser, Colin and Harry, 59
Fraser, D.R., **10**
Fraser, Fil, 305
free trade issues, 53
Friendship Clock Tower, 369
The Fringe Theatre Festival, 329, 339, 405
Fry, John, 159, 163, 169, 171, 185
Fuhr, Grant, 349, 361
funeral service industry, **60**
funny money (scrip), **127**, 139, 153
fur trade, 59, 71

G

Gagne, Art, 143
Gainers Meat Packing Plant, 31, 333, 345, 353, 365, 387
Galicians, 27
gambling, 63, 217, 385, **396**
Gardner, George, 273
Gardner, Zoie, 407
Gatty, Harold, 133
Gauf, Don, 231
Gavriloff, Brian, 339
General Hospital, 169, 211, 369
General Systems Research, 365
George VI, King of England, 145, **154**, 155, 157, 163
Gerrie, Fraser M., 49
Gervais, Hec, 251
Getty, Don, 293, 335, 337, 347, 353, 365
Ghermezian, Nader, 333, 347
Gherson, Giles, 399
Giant Mine, Yellowknife, 373
Gibson, Cheryl, 303
Giffen, Perry J., 119
Gilbert, J.A., 237
Gilbert, Walter, 159
Gill, Robinder, 385
Gillese, Eileen, 305
Gilmour, Bob, 345, 347
Giovanni Caboto Park, 101, 105
Girls' Own Journal, **96**
Glashen, Bill, 273
Glenn, Robert, 269
Glenrose Provincial General Hospital, 263
Global network, 393
Globe and Mail, 393
Glover, Ron, 275
Goertz Studios, 245
Gold, Marta, 357, 379
Gold, William, 315
Gold Bar Park, 321
gold panning, 131
Golden Bears (basketball), U of A, 383
Golden Bears (football), U of A, 323, 363
Golden Pandas (hockey), U of A, 401, 403
Golden Pandas (volleyball), U of A, 395, 397
Goldstick, Cecil "Tiger" and Hazel, 259
Goldsworthy, Bill, 273, 275
golf, 143, **386**, 387
Gordon, Pamela, 403
Gorman, George, **82**, 83
Government House, 43, 63
Government Liquor Control Act, 113
Governor General's Awards, 227, 229, 381, 389
Goyette, Linda, 347, 353, 367, **374**, 383, 387
"Grads" basketball team. See Edmonton Commercial Graduates ("Grads")
Graham, Jim, 231
Grand Theatre, 37
Grand Trunk Pacific Hotel (Macdonald Hotel), **64**, 65, 69
Grand Trunk Pacific Railway, 37, **38**, 43, 69, 105
Grant MacEwan Community College, 287, 375
Great Depression, 117, 119, 127–137
Great Divide Waterfall, 321, 325
Great Journal Gold Rush, 331
Green, Richard, 399
Greenfield, Herbert, **109**
Greenough, Gail, 343
Greenwood's Bookshoppe, 331
Gretzky, Wayne, 289, 315, 333, 335, **348**, 349, 351, **354**, 355, 387, 393
Grey, Earl, **34**, 35
Grey Cup
(1920–1959), 97, 99, 103, 215, 225, 227, 231, **234**, 235, **236**, 237
(1970–2003), 309, 315, 317, 323, 327, 329, 337, 345, 349, 351, 375, 389, 403, 405
Grey Nuns Hospital, 349, 367, 369
Greyhound Bus, 193
Griesbach, William A., 13, **18**, 35, 63, 97, 145
Griesbach Barracks, 235
Grimble, Don, 361
Groat, Malcolm, 59
Groat Bridge, 227
Grotto, 133
GST (Goods and Services Tax), 359, 381, 383
Gunderman, Michael and Joyce, 337
Guttman, Irving, 267

H

Hackman, Deidre, 381
Hagmann farm, 117, 159
Hall, Bryan, 257
Hall, Glenn, 229, 299
Hamilton, Chuck, 263
Hamman, Dr., 93
Handford, Morley, 365
hangings, 25, 27, 29, 107, **132**
Hardisty, 221
Harland, Marion, 25
Harmer, Gary, 273
Harper's, 333
Harris, W.S., 13, 17, 35
Hartwell, Marten, 303
Hawrelak, William, 215, 219, **224**, 225, 227, 229, 233, 265, 297, 301, 305
Hawrelak Park, 253, 305, 401
Hawryluk, Nick, **97**
Hay West program, 403
Hayter, Ron, 401
Hayward, Edward, 25, 27
H.B. Kline jeweller, 131
head office exodus, 359, 363
Healy, Pat, 381
Helgason, Gail, 313
Helm, Richard, 369
Henry Singer Ltd., 205, **214**
Hepner, Lee, 207, 215
Herb Jamieson Centre, 401
Hergott, Ron, 273
Heritage Days, 303, 339, 341
Heritage Mall, 325
Heritage Savings Trust Fund, 279, 297
Hiebert, C., 13
Higgitt, W.L., 285
High Level, 385
High Level Bridge, **62**, 63, 131, 149, 321, 323, 379
highways, 189, 221, 223
Higinbotham, E.N., 121, 123
Hill, Bob, 263, 265
Hill, Judy, 303
Hills, Nick, 293
Hinman, E.W., 255
Hinton train wreck, **326**, 341, 343
hippies, 251, 253, 255, **276**, 277
Hiroshima, **200**, 201
Hitler, Adolf, 99, 147, 149, **164**, 165, **166**, **192**
HMCS Edmonton (ship), 387
HMCS Nonsuch naval reserve, 299
Hnatyshyn, Ray, 369
Hodgins, Fred, 145
Hole, Lois, 395
Hollinger Inc., 393, 397
Hollingsworth, Pat, 181
Hollingworth, Frank, **89**
Hollingworth, Sybil, 155
Hollinshead, J.F., 251
Holocaust, 193
Holtz, J., 61
Holub, Frank, 327
Holubitsky, Jeff, 397
homelessness, 69, 129, 131
homesteading, **21**, 55
homework controversy, 47
Hook Signs Ltd., 155
Hooke, Alf, 291
Hooper, S.G., 253
Horner, Don, 377, 379
Horner, Vic, **92**, 93, 95, 121
horse meat sales, 213
horse races, 63
horse shows, 49
Hortie, Paul, 407
Horton, Marc, 349
housing shortages, 181
Howard, Mrs. Wesley, 85
Howell, David, 379
Howitt, Eaton, 243
Hub Hotel, 7
Hudson Bay Reserve land, 59, **66–67**, 67, 135, 157
Hudson's Bay store, 3, 13, 129, 133, 157, 177, 179, 219, 233, 253, **266**, **308**, 359, 391
Hughes, Howard, **146**
Hughes, Linda, 325, 327, 329, 347, 355, 365, 377, 395, 405
Hulburt, John, 269
Hume, Steve, 229, 303, 325
Hunter, Bill, 291, 299
Hurtig, Mel, 229, 341, 361
Hutton, Frank, 283
Hyndman, J.D., 13, 55
Hyndman, Lou, 321
Hythe, 389

I

ice hockey, 19, 65, 183
Idylwylde, Edmonton Public Library, 247
immigration, 55, 57, 65
Imperial Bank building, **22**
Imperial Oil Co., 189, 191, 193, 195, **198**, 199, 201, 205
Imrie, John M., 95, 161
Incline Railway, **10**, 31
income tax, **70**, 71, 101

incomes and salaries
average per capita incomes, 119, 131
bus drivers, 295
city aldermen, 71
construction worker, 27
mayor, 291
minimum wage, 199, 273, 299, 301, 323, 365, 367
old age pensions, 189
stenographer, 173
teachers, 243
tradesmen, 91
incomes and salaries at *The Edmonton Journal*
ad sales, 173, 179, 205, 227, 263, 267, 273, 309
addressograph operator, 197, 275
annual payroll (1909), 39
clerks, 71, 175, 225, 267, 281
collections agent, 105, 171, 219
compositor, 77, 205, 321
copy chaser, 161, 253
copy editor, 275, 305, 321
editors, 53, 91, 345
first owners, 5
mailer, 243
mailroom worker, 225
printers and pressmen, 51, 293, 329
proofreaders, 231, 271
reporters, 151, 215, 257, 293
stenographers, 81, 119, 237, 273
telephone operator, 121, 197
Indian Association of Alberta, 223
Indians. *See* First Nations
infant mortality rate, 267
influenza epidemics, 69, **72**, 73, **74**, 75, 81, 101
Ingram, Wesley, 25
internet, **384**, 387
Interprovincial Pipelines, 221
Inuit, **78**, 79, 219, 223
Inwood, Damian, 313
IPL Energy, 363
Iraq War (2003), 399
Islamic community, 163
Ismirli, Naz, 371
ITU World Triathlon Championships, **406**
Ives, W.C., 137, **152**, 153

J

Jackson, Annie, **61**
Jakubec, Dennis, 327
Jamieson, Dr., 13
Jasper Avenue, **1**, **2**, **6**, 19, **22**, 29, **45**, **52**, 65, **241**, 249, 255, **260**, 331, 333, 359
Jasper House Hotel, 7
Jasper National Park, 43
Jasper Park Lodge, 215
Jasper Place, 175, 207, 217, 229, 237, 239, 265
Jasper Place Composite High School, 253
Jazz City, 339
J.D. McArthur Company, 43
Jennings, Carolyn, 83
Jennings, M.R., 35, 57, **82**, 83
John Ducey Park, 143
John Paul II, 277, 335
Johns, John, 75
Johnson, Albert ("Mad Trapper"), 137, 139
Johnson, Eddie, 217
Johnson, "Jack," **56**
Johnson, Pat, 277
Johnston, Dick, 345
Jones, Janet, 335, 351, 355
Jones, Terry, 281
Jones, Yardley, 273
Jones-Konihowski, Diane, 311, 313
Jonson, Halvar, 369, 371
The Journal Company Limited, 13, 49, 57
Joyal, Dave, 217
Jubilee Auditorium, 211, 221, 231, 247
Junior Journal, 301

K

Kara, Salim, 387
Kaskitayo, 315
Katz, Jerry, 345
The Katzenjammer Kids (comic strip), **140**
Kayler, Richard, 375
Kealy, Dave, 327
Keats, "Duke," **30**, 143
Kellogg, Alan, 365, 379, 381
Kelly, Bryan, 369
Kennedale, 61
Kennedy, Gerard, 337
Kennedy, John F., **240**, 259
Kennedy, Robert., **264**, **274**
Kerr, John Chipman, 73, 75, 79
Keys, Eagle, 237
Kilburn, Jim, 231
Kilgour, David, 359, 363
Killips, Archie, **97**
Kinaswewich, Ray, 291
Kindy, Alex, 359
King, Charles, 25, 27
King Edward Hotel, 17, 33, 131, 287, 311
Kingsway Avenue, 147, 157
Kingsway Business Association (KBA), 361
Kingsway Garden Mall, 301
Kiniski, Julia, 253
Kinross, Cecil, 77
Kinsmen Sports Centre, 219, 281, 301, 311
Kitchen, Karl, 165
Klaben, Helen, 263, 265
Klein, Ralph, 365, 367, 369, 371, 373, 375, 401
Klein government cuts, 345, 359, 363, 365, 367, 369, 371, 373
Kline Jewellers, 333
Klondike Days, 247, 251, 255, 287, 339, 385
Klondike Mike (Bob Breen), 363
Knott, Dan, 103, 135
Koe, C.D.C., 137
Koenig, Wendy, 327
Kootook, David, 303
Kowalski, Ken, 385
Kresge, Stanley, 233
Kresge's, 287
Krol, Joe, 185
Krushelnyski, Mike, 355
Ku Klux Klan, **112**, 117, 157
Kurri, Jari, 349
Kuzma, Nick, 289
Kvill, Donald R., 303

L

La Fleche Brothers, 113, 133
La Guardia, Fiorello, 175
La Ronde Restaurant, 273
Labor Relations Board, 353
labour disputes, 27, 115, 183, 191, **258**, 295, 327, 345, 353
Lacombe, 157, 385
Lamb, George, **18**, 31
Lamb, William, 171
Lamont, 249
Land Titles Office, **21**
LaNeuze, Denny, **78**
LaRiviere, Annette, 149
Lassandro, Florence, 107
Laubman, Don, 175
Laughy, H.W., 83
Laundy, Dave, 271
Laurie, John, 223
Laurier, Sir Wilfred, 15, 35, **35**, **36**, 53, 65
Law Courts Building, 291
Law Society of Alberta, 71, 91
Le Roux, Father, 79
Leacock, Stephen, 155
Learn-to-Swim, 141
Led Zeppelin, **268**
Leduc, 189, 281
Leduc Hotel explosion, 211
Leduc No. 1 oil well, 167, 169, **17**8, 185, 189, **198**, 199
Lees, Nick, **322**
Leger, Ed, 225, 227, 291, 299, 309
Leger, Marc, 399
Legislature Building, 7, 27, 51, **62**, 63
LeLacheur, Rick, 363
Lemarchand, Rene, **40**
Lemieux, Raymond, 397
Les Canadiens (comic strip), 261
Lessard, P.E., 133
Lethbridge County, 385
Levesque, Rene, **322**
Lewis, Doug, 373
Lewis, Peter, 325
Liberal Party (Alberta), 11, 17, 95, 97, 107, 129, 139, **248**, 255
Liberal Party (Canada), 15, 37, 197, 251, 295, 341, 363, 381
light rail transit system (LRT), 289, 311, 353, 371, 387
Lindblad, John, 281, 303
Lindsay, Bert, 33
liquor laws and liquor use, 181, 219, 235, 237, 255, 277, 285, 287, 325
liquor privatization, 371, 373, 375
Lisac, Mark, 365, 367
Little, G.M., 155
Little Grey Cup (football), 255, 331
Little Red River, 93, 95
Londonderry Shopping Mall, 287
Lord's Day Act, **40**, **42**, 329, 347
lotteries, 217
Lougheed, Peter, 113, 243, **248**, 291, 293, 297, 315, **319**, 321, 341, 343, 375
Love, Don, 333
Low Level Bridge, 17, **21**, **42**, 69, 197
Loyal Edmonton Regiment, 67, 75, 165, 171, 173, 175, 177, 181, 189
Loyie, Florence, 385
LPGA du Maurier classic, 387
LRT (light rail transit system), 289, 311, 353, 371, 387
LSD, 253
Lucas, John, 369
Lucchini, Lee, 231
Ludwig, Wiebo, **388**, 389, 391
Lueders, Pierre, 375, 391
lumber mills, 41
Lunde, Len, 217
Lynch, Charles, 269
Lyon, Bob, 183

M

MacAdams, Roberta, 75, 77
Macauley, Doug, 231
MacBurney, Margaret, 115
Maccagno, Mike, **248**
Macdonald, Donald, **258**, 289
MacDonald, Ian, 199
MacDonald, Noel, 115, 161
Macdonald, Ollie, 257
MacDonald, W.A., 171
Macdonald Hotel, **64**, 65, 69, 73, 147, 157, 159, 167, 183, 233, 255, 331, 363
MacEwan, Grant, 283
MacGregor, J.G., vii
MacKay, A.G., 73
Mackenzie, K.W., 35
Mackenzie Air Services, 145
MacKinnon, James A., 31
Mackintosh, George, 51, 169, 181
MacLab Enterprises, 361
MacLean, Robinson, 147, 149
Macleod, J.J.R., 109
MacMillan, Allen D., 137, 145, 147, 151
MacMillan, Bob, 379
MacMillan, Vivian, 135, 137, 145, 147, 151, 165
Macpherson, John, 1, 3, **5**, 5, 7, 11, 13, 23, 35
MacWilliam, Rick, 353
mad cow disease (BSE), 403, 405
Madden, Larry, 287
Magee Building, 91
Manahan, Cliff, 141, 155
Manegre, Jerry, 305
Manke, Jackie, 371
Manning, Dave, 277
Manning, Ernest Charles, 139, 141, 169, 179, 183, 193, **210**, 211, 243, **248**, 269, **270**, 291
Manning, Ernest Preston, 243
Manson, Jack, 231
Manuel, John, 81
Manulife, 331
Maple Leaf Foods, 353
marijuana, 253
Market Square riot, 127, 129, 133, 135, 141
Martell, Henry, 185
Martin, Kevin, 363
Masonic Temple, 167
Mastinsek, Max, 275
Matheson, Jim, 281, 333, 349, 355, 399
Maxner, Wayne, 273
May, Wilfred (Wop,) 81, **92**, **93**, 93, 95, 113, 121, 139, 158, **159**, 407
Mayer, Allan, 339
Mayes, Malcolm, 343

Mayfair Golf and Country Club, 101, 251, 321
Mayfair Hotel, 225
Mayse, Susan, 303
Mazankowski, Don, 383
McAuley, Mille Warwick, 191
McCarthy, Joseph, 217, 219
McCauley, Matt, 131
McCauley Plaza, 33
McClellan, Shirley, 367
McClung, Nellie, 57, 97, 107, 109, **110**, 111, 113, 407
McCombs, Elsie, 155
McConachie, Grant, 157
McConnell, John P., 13, 35
McDonald, J.W., 129
McDougall and Secord store, **1**, 15, 59
McDougall Commercial High School, 115
McDougall Hill, **2**
McDougall United Church, 217, 221
McGillivray, Don, 343
McKay Avenue School, 23
McKean, George, 79
McKenzie, Colin, 99, 101
McKenzie, Don, 353
McKernan, 191
McKinley, J.H., 55
McKinney, Louise, 57, 59, **59**, 75, 77, 107, 111, 407
McLaren, John, 35
McLaurin, C.C., 229
McLellan, Anne, 375
McLeod, Doreen, 231
McLeod Building, 163
McLuhan, Marshall, 49
McMillan, Jan, 283
McMullen, J.F., 111
McNamara, W.J., 67, 69
McNeill, Jock, 83
medicare, **254**, **256**
Meech Lake, 383
Melody Lane, 255
Memorial Cup (junior hockey), 163, **244**, 257
mental health facilities, 283
Menzies, Dudley, 371
Mercredi, Ray, 277
Merrill, Anne, 57, 89
Metella, Helen, 385
Métis, 161, 391
metric system, 307
Mewburn Pavilion, 179
Meyer, Corky, 367
Michaels, John, **80**, 103, 407
Michener Award, 327, 373
microwave ovens, 323, **324**
Middle Earth, 253
Mike's News, **80**, 103, 407
Mill Woods, 309, 315
Millen, Edgar, 137
millennium, 395
Miller, Clarence (Big), 369
Mills, Edith, 213
Milner, Stanley, 227
Mindbender roller coaster, 343, 347
Miner, Bill, **31**, 33
minimum wage, 199, 273, 299, 301, 323, 365, 367
Misericordia Hospital, 211, 369
Modry, Dennis, 341
Molson, 285
Moore, Arthur, 5, **5**, 17, 23
Moore, Mary, 311
Moostoos, Chief, 25, 27
Morin, Rich, 273
Mormon Temple, 393
The Morning Journal, 27, **56**
Morris, Joseph H., 7, **7**, 11
Morrison, C.R., 47
mosque, Al Rashid Mosque, 161, 163
Motor Sales, Ltd., **102**
Motordrome Limited, 101
Mountbatten, Earl (of Burma), 269
Moysa, Marilyn, 353, 371
Muir, Leilani, 113, 375
Mulcahy, Sean, 271
Mulroney, Brian, 381, 383
Municipal Aerodrome, 131
Munro, Ross, 185, **186**, 187, 273, 281, 301, 305
Munro, Scotty, 175
Murphy, Emily, 19, 57, **57**, 73, 107, 111, 133, 135, 407
Mutt and Jeff (comic strip), **112**
Muttart Conservatory, 303, 305

N

Nagasaki, **200**, 201
Nagle, Patrick, 343
Naismith, James, 115
Namao, 169, 239, 335, 339, 383
National Energy Program (NEP), 297, 319, 321, 323, **340**, 341, 343
National Newspaper Award, 263, 265, 321, 353, 367, 373, 377, 383, 393, 397, 399, 401, 403
National Post, 393
National Press Club awards, 209
Nattrass, Susan, 307, 317, 325
Nazi Party (Germany), 147, 149
Neal, Ronald Charles, 53
Neville, John, 289, 295
New Democratic Party (Alberta), 141, **248**, 293, 315, 337
The New Edmonton Opera House, 27
New Year's Day levee, 169
New York City terrorist attacks, **394**, 395, 397
Newbigging, William, 327, 329, 359
Newsome, Ab, 231
Newton, Robert, 179
Newton, Ron, 283
Nicholls, Thomas, **25**
Nicholls, Boogie H., 55, 57, **58**
Nichols, Cal, 377, 407
Nichols, L.H., 137
Nicol, Helen, 191
Nisku, 189, 215
Nixon, William, 83
No. 1 Fire Hall, 243
North Edmonton, 43, 59
North Saskatchewan River, 17, **18**, **20**, 41, 67, 69, 131, **296**, 408
North Saskatchewan River, floods, 67, **68**, 69, 71, 343
Northern Alberta Institute of Technology (NAIT), 259
Northern Alberta Railways (N.A.R.), 43, 123
Northland Bank, 337
Northlands Coliseum, 299
Northrup Motor Service Co., **60**
Northwest Airlines, 215
Northwestern Utilities, 111, **216**
Norwood School, **22**
Notley, Grant, 293, 315, 335, 337
Nova Corporation, 363
NovAtel, 365
Nulliayok, Neemee, 303

O

O'Callaghan, J. Patrick, 283, 285, 301, 315, 317, 325, 327, 329, 343
O'Connor, Gerald, 171
Ohler, Shawn, 389
Oil and Gas Conservation Board, 225
oil and gas industry
  early, **52**, 59, **118**, **119**
  Leduc No. 1 oil well, 169, **178**, 185, 189, **198**
  after Leduc No. 1 well, 191, 195, 197, 199, 201, 205, 211, **212**, 215, **216**, 217, 221, 225
  1970s and 1980s, 279, 281, 295, 297, **314**, 321
  National Energy Program, 297, 319, 321, 323, **340**, 341, 343
  oilsands, 131, 211, 217, 255, 265, 313, 401
  resources rights issues (pre-1970s), 15, 37, 103, **104**, 105, 109, 125, 131
  resources rights issues (1970s–1980s), 279, 297, 319, **340**, 341
  Wiebo Ludwig, **388**, 389, 391
Oilers. *See* Edmonton Oilers
old-age pensions (Alberta), 105
O'Leary, Henry J., 93, 115
Oliver, Alberta, 91
Oliver, Frank, 11, 13, 33, 63, 109
Olson, Scott (Bulldog), 383
Olympic Games, 115, 213, 231, 293, **300**, 303, 377, 387, 391, 399
Omar, Sydney, 261
omniplex, 261, **278**, 299
Opportunity, M.D. of, 385
Order of Canada, 229
Orpheum Theatre, **8**, 33, **76**
Ortona, Battle of, **188**, 189
Osama bin Laden, 395, 397
Ostlund, May, 75
Ottewell, 211
Ottewell, A.E., 37
Ovenden, Norm, 381
Overland, Wayne, 247, 281
Owens, Greg, 373
ox carts, **2**
Oxford Developments, 333
Oxford Tower, 281

P

Pacific Plaza, 281
Pacific Western Airlines, **252**, 259, 297
Page, Percy, 67, 115, 183, 407
Paisley, Brian, 329
Pankhurst, Emmeline, **110**
Pantages, Alexander, 59, 61
Pantages Theatre, 61, 63, 97, **124**, 125
Paramount Theatre, 205, 215
Parker, Jackie, 235, 257
Parker, Pete, 105
parking meters, 193, 197
Parks, Jim, 305
Parlby, Irene, 57, 105, 107, 111, **113**, 149
Parlee, S.S., 233
Passchendaele, 77
Patricia Gyro Playground, 101
Patrick, Lester, 31, 33
Paul, Butch, 275
Pawson, Hal, 181, 235, 237, 273, 275
Paylitz, Clarence, 211, 233
Payne, Ted, 327
Peace River, 201
Peacock Room, 133
Pearson, Lester B., 249, 251, 267
Pedersen, Rick, 345
Pelletier, David, 399
Pembina, 221
Pembina Hall, University of Alberta, 81
Pendleton, Joan, 261
Pentagon terrorist attacks, **394**, 395, 397
Persons Case (1928), 73, 107, 111, 123
Peterson, Oscar, 185
Pete's oil scam, 57, 59
Petrie, Didier, 33
Petty, George, 365
Phillip, Prince, 313
Phillips, Bruce, 257
Phipps McKinnon Building, 281
Phoenix Theatre, 389
Picard, J.H., **2**, **18**
Picariello, Emilio, 105
Pilling, Greg, 273, 275
pipelines, 189, 209, **314**
Planetarium, Queen Elizabeth, 247
Pocklington, Peter and Eva, 303, 315, 329, 333, 335, 351, 353, 355, 359, 377, 379, 387, 391
Podivinsky, Edi, 375, 377
polio epidemics, 47, 101, 141, 143, 171, **180**, **206**
Portage Avenue, 147, 157
Porter, Marshall, 227
Post, Wiley, 133
postal service, 31
Power Corp. of Canada, 393
Pratt, Sheila, 381
Praystow, John, 199
Press Act, 157
prices
  air fares, 189
  automobiles, **4**, 55, **60**, 101, 125, 129, 133, 139, 175, 323
  Beatle wigs, 277
  beef, 177, 213, 223
  bread, 75, 93, 177, 181, 207, 323
  bus fares, 185, 193, 197, 289, 291, 307, 309
  Canadian flag, 69
  cigarettes, 91, 177, 211
  coats, 169, 177
  concerts, 183
  dinners, 131, 133
  driver's licence, 123
  dry cleaning, 133
  Edmonton Folk Festival, 321
  Edmonton Journal early issues, 1, 3, 5
  Edmonton Journal subscriptions, 3, 83, 203, 235, 293, 341, 359
  fried chicken, 219

gas ranges, 133
gasoline, 293
gum, 91
haircuts, 83, 133, 155
hot dogs and wieners, 177
jam, 133
Jasper Park Lodge, 143
liquor, 277, 323
LRT fares, 289
men's suits, 113, 177, 179
microwave, 323
milk, 295, 323
pants, 131
pantsuits, 309
phonographs and records, 81, 221
postage stamp, 373
radios, 91
real estate, **14**, 37, **42**, 281
rents, 133, 177
shave, 155
shirts, 205
shoes and socks, 169, 177
snowmobiles, 157
sports events, 19, 295
swimsuits, 177
telephone service, 247
televisions, 221, 257, **298**
toilet paper, 133
train fares, 17, **42**, 51, 77, 79, 85, 117, 133, 143, 161
tuition at U of A, 267
turkeys, 201
TV trays, 257
wheat, **116**

Priestly, Norman, 137
Primrose, John, 307
Prince of Wales Armouries, 183
Princess Patricia's Canadian Light Infantry, 235, 399, 403
Princess Theatre, 69, 143, 331
Princeton Developments Ltd., 329
Principal Group, 335
prisons, **26**, 29, 89, 91, 373
privatization, 363, 365, 371, 373, 375
Privilege, **268**
Progressive Conservative (Canada), 381
Progressive Conservatives (Alberta), 11, 13, 15, 39, 139, **248**, 255, 289, 291, 293, 315, 365, 367
See also names of premiers
Prohibition
events (1916–1924), 61, 63, 73, **84**, 85, 93, 105, 121
repeal (1924), 107, 111, **120**, 121, **122**, 123
Prosperity Certificates, **127**, 139, 151
protests and protest marches, **241**, 253, 261
Provincial Museum, 247
Pulitzer awards, 141, 159, 161
Purdy, Chris, 401, 403
Purves, Cec, 229, 289, 309, 323, 325, 347
Purvis, Al, 231

Q

Queen Elizabeth Planetarium, 247
Queen Elizabeth Pool, 101
Quinn, Pat, 273, 275

R

race relations, 55, 57, 59, 79, 223
Radcliffe, the executioner, 29
Radio Shack, **330**
radios and radio stations, **86**, 87, **88**, 89, 91, 93, 99, 105, 143, 145, 147, **160**, **162**, 221
rain (record amounts), 219, 321
Ramage, Homer, 145
Ramsankar, Steve, 381
Ramsay, Bob, 253
Ramsay, John, 359
Rasmussen, Gerry, 339
Rathole, 397
real estate
(pre-1950s), 17, 33, 37, 43, 65, **66–67**, 183
(1950–1969), **204**, 205, 211, 217, 245, **246**, 261, 277
(1970–2003), 281, 289, 309, 319, 323, 329, 373, 399, 401
Red Cross Society, **167**
Red Deer, 129, 163
Redwater, 195, 201
Refinery Row, 219
101st Regiment, 67
Reid, Richard Gavin, 137, 139, 147
Reimer, Jan, 355, 357, 359, 363, 365, 367, 369, 371, 379, 385
Remembrance Day, 133
Renfrew Park, 141, 143, 209, 325, 369
Repka, Lionel, 217
retail, 40, 359, 407, 408
Reuters news service, 57, 69
Revillon Freres, 17, **40–41**
Reynolds-Alberta Museum, 371
Rialto Theatre, 143, **162**
Rice, Dick, 89, 147, **238**, 239
Richfield Oil Corporation, 217
Richler, Mordecai, 351
Riddell, J.H., 23
Riley, W.H., 277
Ringwood, Mrs. I., 137
Ritchie, Max, 293
river valley development, **296**
Riverside Pool, 101
Roberts, Lorne, 175
Robertson, A.J., 13
Robertson Hall, 11
Robinson, Hugh Armstrong, 49
rock and roll shows, 221, 255, **268**, **279**, **280**, 331, 379, 389
Rocky Mountain House, 385
rodeo, **376**
Rodriguez, Sue, **358**
roller coaster accident (WEM), 343, 347
Rolling Stones, 379
Roper, Elmer, 239, 253
Ross, Izena, 99
Ross, Lucella McLean, 191
Ross Hall, 15
Ross Sheppard High School, 213, 239
Rossdale, **10**
Rothman's Tobacco "I am a Canadian," 247
Rotter, Pete, 27
Rouviere, Father, 79
Royal Alexandra Hospital, 43, 211, 257, 263, 369
Royal Bank, 329
Royal Canadian Mounted Police (RCMP), 75, 89, 139, 167, 223, 285
Royal Commission on the Status of Women, 285
Royal George Hotel, 43
Royal Glenora Club, 251
Royal North-West Mounted Police (RNWMP), 25, 89, 139
Runnalls, Chris, 327
Rural North West, 53
Russell, Gordie, 407
Rutherford, Alexander Cameron, 15, 17, 23, 37, **39**, 39, 41, 43, 63
Ryan, Pat, 353

S

Sadava, Mike, 339
Safeway, **228**, 333
Sale, Jamie, 399
Sales Pavilion, 221
Salvation Army, 177
Sargeant, Lisa, 359
SARS (sudden acute respiratory syndrome), 403
Sather, Glen, 275, 379, 391
Schindler, David, 363
Schmidt, Kittyelou, **360**
Schmidt, Manfred, 353
Schmidt, Murray, **360**
School for the Deaf, 227
Schultz, Judy, **390**, **398**
Schwarz, Chris, 397, 405
scrip (funny money), **127**, 139, 153
sculpture (metal geese), 213, 215
Secord, Richard, 11, 13
Selkirk Hotel, 7, 177, 257, **260**
Seph, Ian, 315
September 11, 2001, terrorist attacks, **394**, 395, 397
sexual orientation, 257, 345
sexual standards, 151, 255, 265, 267, **278**, 281, **344**
Sexual Sterilization Act, 113, 293, 375
sexually transmitted diseases, 323, **344**, 345, 385
Seymour, Lynn, 163
Shamrock Fruit Store, 1, **3**, 5
Shandro, Andrew, 63
Shanksville, Pa., terrorist attacks, **394**, 395, 397
Shasta Cafe, 133, 143
Shaw, Jim, 361
Shaw Communications, 361, 363
Sherlock, Karen, 369
Sherwood Park, 217, 293, **338**
Shoctor, Joseph, 269, 271, 289, 295, 407
Short, William, 7
Sifton, Arthur, 39, 63, **65**, 85
Sikhs, 385
Silverwoods Dairies, **306**
Simon, Steve, 349
Simons, Paula, 399
Simpson, Joe, **30**
Sinclair, Gordon, 311
Singer, Henry, 205, **214**, 407
Sinnisiak, **78**, 79
skiing, 375, 377
Skyreach Centre, 399
Slipchuk, Michael, 365
Small, Charles M., 197
Smith, Becky, 303
Smith, Bill, 357, 359, 385, 391, 401
Smith, Billy, 349
Smith, Don, 273
Smith, Graham, 303, 313
Smith, Harry R., 13
Smith, Nathan, 399
smoking laws, **28**, **32**, 405
Snaddon, Andrew, 247, 273, 283
Snapshot Bill (comic strip), **54**
snow (record amounts), 173, 175, **282**, 369, 385, 387
soccer, 143, 323, 335
Social Credit Party, 127, **136**, 139, 141, 147, 149, 151, 153, 157, 159, 161, 177, 179, **210**, 211, 221, 243, **248**, 255, 291, 293
Somme, Battle of, 75
sonic booms, 307
sour gas wells, 389
Southam, William, 57
Southam, Wilson, 13
Southam Newspapers, 13, 55, 57, **194**, 195, 209, 317, 325, 327, 335, 371, 393, 399
Southgate Mall, 283
space exploration, **242**, 257, **262**, **274**
space exploration (fantasy), 123
Space Sciences Centre, 333
Spanish flu. See influenza epidemics
speed limits, 23, 179, 189
speed skating, 231
Sprague, Walter, 407
Spruce Grove, 225, 277
Srigley, Evalyn, 155
S.S. Titanic disaster, **68**, 69
St. Albert, 217, 245, 293, 307
St. Albert Protestant Separate School Board, 251
St. Joseph's Basilica, 115, 251, 335, 351
St. Joseph's High School, 213
stagecoach (Edmonton to Calgary), **20**
Stanley, Don, 231
Stanley A. Milner Library, 133
Stanley Cup, 31, 33, 35, 39, 333, 335, 339, **348**, 351, 359
Staples, David, 373
Stark, W.J., **80**
Starlite Drive-in Theatre, 197
Steadward, Bob, 399, 407
Stedman, Richard H., **28**, **29**
Steele, Bill, 257
sterilization, 113, 375
Sterling Awards, 403
Stevens, G.R., vii
Stewart, Charles, 97, 107
Stinson, Katherine, 79, **80**, 81
Stock, Curtis, 387
Stollery, Bob, 407
Stony Plain, 385
store and theatre hours, 223, 277, 329, 347
store hours, **22**, 139
Straight, H.L., 207
Strand Theatre, 143
Strang, Ian, 319
Strathcona, **18**, 51, 53, 55, 63, 69, 221, 275, 289, 331
Strathcona Composite High School, 227
Strathcona Library, 61
105th Street Bridge, 63

street paving, 29, 217, 233
streetcar system, 7, 17, **42**, 179, 191
Streit, Marlene Stewart, 143
Strom, Harry, 245, 291
Struzik, Ed, 339, 403, 405
Stuart, A.M., 33
Sucker Creek Reserve, 25, 27
sudden acute respiratory syndrome (SARS), 403
suffrage movement, **64**
Summers, Jaron, 251
Sunshine Society, **130**
Sunwapta Broadcasting, 147
Swarbrick, Brian, 311
Sweeny, Edward, 257
Sykes, Rod, 295
Sylvan Lake, 385
synchronized swimming, 387
Syncrude Canada, 265, 313, 363

T

Tait, C.M., 3
Tan, Marilyn, 385
Tanner, Adrienne, 367, 389
tar sands, 59
Taylor, A. Williamson, 13
Taylor, Alex, 11, 71, 383
Taylor and Pearson Ltd., 91
Taylor-Musson Auto Company, 55
technology, **384**
Tegler, Robert, 95
Tegler Building, 95, 163, 331
Teha, D.M., 163
telephone system, 11, 71, 193, 247, 271, 275, 365, 387, 391
television, 221, 233, **238**, 239, 271, **298**
Telus Corp., 363, 365, 383, 387, 391
Telus Field, 35
Telus Tower, 261, 271
temperance movement, 85
temperatures (record), 115, 135, 157, 275
tent homes, **6**
terrorist attacks, **394**, 395, 397
theatre companies, 125, 269, 271
theatres and movie houses, **8**, **9**, **18**, 23, 27, 33, 59, 69, 73, 77, 97, **124**, 125, 143, **162**, 205, **218**
Thistle Rink, 19, 35
Thomas, Don, 289
Thomas, Lionel, 213
Thompson, Annabelle, 191
Thomson, Graham, 403
Thorhild, 125
Thorsell, William, 297, 325, 331, 341, 343, 347
tipping issue, 53
tobacco, **132**, 373
Tomyn, William, 219
Tookey, Ron, 217
Toonerville Trolley, 191
tornado (1987), 325, 327, **336**, **338**, 349
Torstar Inc., 393
Tower Mortgage, 337
traffic signals, 137, 147, 191
Trans-Canada Air Lines, 249, 251
trapshooting, 307, 317, 325
Tretheway, W.G., 7
triathlon, 401, **406**
Trickle Creek, 389
Triple-E Senate, 347
Triple Five Corporation, 331, 333
Trocadero Ballroom, 183, 187
Trocadero Club, 221
Trudeau, Pierre Elliott, 251, 257, 267, **270**, **282**, 293, 295, **314**, **316**, **322**, 341, **342**, 343
Trudel Fur Mfg. Co., **90**
Truong, Alex, 381
tuberculosis, 193, 213
Tucker, Brian, 283
Turchansky, Ray, 281, 311, 401

U

Ukrainian Heritage Village, **284**, 297
Ukrainians, 63, 187, 219
Ullyatt, John, 403
Uluksuk, **78**, 79
Uluschak, Edd, 275, 321, 341, **342**
unemployment, 67, 109, 117, 119, 127–139, 141, 323, 333, 337, 365
Union Bank Building, 43
Union Buses, 143
United Farm Women of Alberta (UFWA), 105, 107, 113
United Farmers of Alberta (UFA), 55, 85, 95, 97, 105, 107, 109, 113, 129, 131, 139, 147, 151, 161
United Food and Commercial Workers Union, 353
United States terrorist attacks, **394**, 395, 397
United Way, 173, 249, 295, 365
University Games, 337
University Hospital, 179, 213, 233, 281, 369
University of Alberta
convocation, 155, 169, 193, 207, **220**
faculties, 143, 197, 235, 267
honourary degrees, 85, 103, 117, 141, 149, 193, 329, 405
Mackenzie Health Centre, 329, 343, 356
protests, 253, 255
Rutherford Library, 195, 213
site, 17, **18**, 29, 75, 81, 213
sports, 247, 323, 361, 363, 383, 395, 397, 401
students and alumni, 37, 59, 63, **106**, 179, 252, 267, 311
University of Alberta Hospital, 341
University of Calgary, 247
Ursuliak, Wally, 251
U2 Irish rock band, 389

V

Vair, Charlie, 33
Val Berg's Men's Wear, 333
Valley Zoo, 239
van Herk, Aritha, vii, 311
Varscona theatre, 171
Vegreville, 177, 299
Veit, Joanne, 113, 375
Victoria Composite High School, 211, 213, 221
Victoria Cross heroes, 75, 77, 79, 157
Vietnam war, 259, **292**
Vietnamese Canadians, **294**
Viking #2 oil well, **52**
Vimy Ridge, 49, 51, 53
VLTs (video lottery terminals), 385
Vogue Shoes, 331
volleyball, 395, 397
volunteerism, 407

W

Wagner, W.P., 245
Wainwright, 165
Walchuk, Don, 353
Walker, Andy, 395
Walker, Byron E., 3
Walker, Larry, 327
Wall, O.W., 207
Wallace, Clifford S., 121
Walter, John, ferry, **21**
Walter S. Mackenzie Health Centre, 329, 343, 345
Walterdale Bridge, **21**
Wapiti Aviation, 337
"War of the Worlds" radio broadcast, **162**
War Stamp tax, 71
Ward, Dave, 299, 305
Ward, George, 327
Ward, Max, 347, 407
Wardair, 345, 347
Warnock, Gladys, 155
Waterloo Mercurys (hockey), 181, 207, 213, **230**, 231
Watson, Wilfred, 227
Watt, Arthur Balmer, 37, 39, 161, 179
Watt, Bob, 231
Watt, Laura, 155
Welch, Paul, 103
Wenzel, Jan, 305
Werner, Ray, 251
West, Steve, 371
West Edmonton Mall, 325, 329, 331, 333, 339, 341, 343, **346**, 397, 407
Westbury, Bob, 407
Western Airlines, 215
Western alienation, 37, 113, 279, 281, 295, 297, 343
Western Canada First Association, 295
Western Canada Hockey League, 105
Western Canada Professional Hockey League, 143
Westgate, Barry, 247, 269, 287, 349
Westmount, 221
Westmount Shopping Centre, 211, 225, 233
Westwater, Shaun, 389
Wetaskiwin air drop, **82**, 83
wheat, **116**, 117, **128**, 129, 131, 135, 149
Whitcroft, Fred, 31
White, Deacon, 51, 53, 235
Whitemud, 209
The Who, **268**
Whyte Avenue, **18**, 289, 331, 399
Wiebe, Rudy, 229, 381
Wilkin, R.L., 329, 331
Wilkins, F.A., 175
Williams, Ethel, 85
Williams, Stan, 247, 279, 289
Willis, Charles W., 239
Willis, Karman, 389, 391
Wilson, J.L., 207
wind (record speeds), 201
Windsor Hotel, 7
Winspear, Francis, 389
Winspear Centre for Music, 377, 389, 405
wire services for *Edmonton Journal*, 3, 7, 33, 47, 57, 69, 97, 99, 169, 245
Women of Unifarm, 293
Women's Christian Temperance Union, 85
women's movements, 179, 267, 285, 287
women's suffrage, 17, 19, 57, **64**, 71, 75, 79, 109
Wood, Henry Wise, 105, 109
Wood, Kerry, 227
Wood Buffalo, 103, 385
Woods, J.H., 13
Woodward, W.C., 233
Woodward's, 177, **232**, 233, 359, 373
Wop May Airplanes, Ltd., 83
The Works, 339, 343
World Figure Skating Championships, 387
World Firefighter Games, 387
World Track and Field Championships, 401, **402**, 407
World Trade Center, New York City, **394**, 395, 397
World University Games, 331
World War I, 47–83
19th Alberta Dragoons, **46**
49th Battalion, 67, 73, 77, 79
51st Battalion, **52**
101st Regiment, 67
beginning, 67
Armistice Day, 53, 75, 133
battles, 49, 75, 77, 79
casualties, 47, 49, 83
conscription, 51
dairymen enlistees, **74**
EJ essay contests, 99
Loyal Edmonton Regiment, 67, 75
monuments in Edmonton, 91, 153
number of Albertans in military service, 83
trench at Exhibition Grounds, **50**
Victoria Cross heroes, 99, 157
World War II, 163–201
beginning, 163–169
bonds, **168**, 177, **182**
casualty lists, 187
conscription, 177
death camps, 193
Dieppe, 184, 185, 186, 187
Hiroshima and Nagasaki, 200, 201
home front conditions, 170, 172, 175, 177, 179, 181, 191
Loyal Edmonton Regiment, 165, 171, 173, 175, 177, 181, 189
Ortona, 188, 189
Wraight, Robert, 391
Wright, G.S.D., 215
Wright, Peter, 231

Y

Yockney, Arthur, 75
Young, Harrison, 231
Youth Emergency Shelter, 327
Ypres, Battle of, 49

Z

Zeigler, Rod, 335
Zellers, 165, 309
Zwickstra, John, 277